# THE COMPLETE ENCYCLOPEDIA OF

# THE COMPLETE ENCYCLOPEDIA OF

# Arms & Weapons

THE MOST COMPREHENSIVE REFERENCE WORK EVER PUBLISHED ON ARMS AND ARMOR FROM PREHISTORIC TIMES TO THE PRESENT—WITH OVER 1,250 ILLUSTRATIONS

Edited by Leonid Tarassuk
and Claude Blair

SIMON AND SCHUSTER
NEW YORK

*The publishers would like to thank Nolfo di Carpegna for his invaluable assistance.*
*Translated from the Italian by Sylvia Mulcahy, Simon Pleasance and Hugh Young.*

Claude Blair

Curator of the Department of Metalwork at the Victoria and Albert Museum, London, and formerly honorary editor of the *Journal of the Arms and Armour Society*. He is the author of numerous publications on arms, armor, and metalwork and a contributor to the *Archaeological Journal*, *The Connoisseur*, *Waffen- und Kostümkunde*, and other specialist publications.

Leonid Tarassuk

Research associate at the Department of Arms and Armor, Metropolitan Museum of Art, New York; formerly Keeper of European and American Arms and Armor, The Hermitage, Leningrad; author of several monographs and contributor to various specialist periodicals on arms and armor.

Clement Bosson

Supervisor of the Arms and Armor Room at the Musée d'Art et d'Histoire, Geneva, and the delegate for Switzerland to conferences on arms and military history. He has published over a hundred studies, chiefly on ancient arms and Swiss armor.

Carlo de Vita

Responsible for the cataloging of the ancient arms kept at the Museo Storico Vaticano (the Vatican's new Historical Museum), and honorary inspector of ancient arms at the Soprintendenza per i Beni Artistici e Storici delle Marche. He is a frequent contributor to scholarly books and periodicals.

Irena Grabowska

Curator of the Department of Arms and Armor at the National Museum in Kraków, and a specialist in metalwork, she has published several articles on the decoration of European arms and armor.

Marco Morin

Expert on arms at the Soprintendenze ai Beni Artistici e Storici del Veneto e di Venezia (Association for the History and Art of Venice and the Veneto Region), for whom he is compiling an index of the Armory of the Council of Ten. He is the author of many publications on the history of armor and a frequent contributor to specialist periodicals.

Anthony Richard Eustace North

Research assistant in the Department of Metalwork, Victoria and Albert Museum, London, and a member of the Museums Association of Great Britain. He has contributed to international publications on arms and armor.

Francesco Rossi

Curator of the Musei Civici (Civic Museums), Brescia, attached to the Museo L. Marzoli of ancient arms, and director of the Art Gallery of the Accademia Carrara, Bergamo. He is author of numerous publications dealing with history, art, and ancient armament.

Zdzislaw Zygulski Jr.

Curator of the National Museum in Kraków, and past president of the International Association of Museums of Arms and Military History (IAMAM). A well-known Orientalist, he has contributed to numerous international specialist periodicals.

PUBLISHED BY SIMON AND SCHUSTER
A DIVISION OF GULF & WESTERN CORPORATION
SIMON & SCHUSTER BUILDING
ROCKEFELLER CENTER
1230 AVENUE OF THE AMERICAS
NEW YORK, NEW YORK 10020
SIMON AND SCHUSTER AND COLOPHON ARE TRADEMARKS
OF SIMON & SCHUSTER
PRINTED AND BOUND IN ITALY BY OFFICINE GRAFICHE DI
ARNOLDO MONDADORI EDITORE, VERONA
ORIGINALLY PUBLISHED IN ITALY UNDER THE TITLE
*ENCICLOPEDIA RAGIONATA DELLE ARMI*
BY ARNOLDO MONDADORI EDITORE, S.P.A., MILANO
BLACK-AND-WHITE ILLUSTRATIONS BY CARLO GIORDANA
CREATED BY ERVIN SRL ROME
UNDER THE DIRECTION OF ADRIANO ZANNINO
EDITORIAL DIRECTOR: SETTIMIO PAOLO CAVALLI

10 9 8 7 6 5 4 3 2 1

LIBRARY OF CONGRESS CATALOGING IN PUBLICATION DATA

BLAIR, CLAUDE.
THE COMPLETE ENCYCLOPEDIA OF ARMS AND WEAPONS.

BIBLIOGRAPHY: P.
1. ARMS AND ARMOR—DICTIONARIES. I. TITLE.
U815.B55 623.4′03 80-5922

ISBN 0-671-42257-X

# Preface

The guiding principle behind this encyclopedia has been to provide extensive information on offensive and defensive weapons and armor over a wide period of history and a vast range of countries. Great interest has been shown in arms and armor ever since the 18th century when enthusiasm for collecting first became fashionable. Perhaps it was the idea of possessing objects that might have belonged to an emperor, a king, or a prince that was so attractive. Whatever the reason, the warlike significance and economics of weaponry in general were—and still are—lost to view and the items became appreciated for their distinctive qualities, workmanship, and history alone.

The encyclopedia concentrates, therefore, on individual weapons and styles of armor, with particular emphasis on their component parts. Under the main headings—which are integrated into the book in alphabetical order—the principal developments in both arms and armor are traced from their origins through to the present day. As far as possible, the various gadgets, machines, and attachments that had to be imposed upon the original conception later, enabling the object to continue to fulfill its original warlike purpose, have been excluded.

The Publisher

# Foreword

The study of arms and armor as a modern antiquarian subject can be said to have started with the publication of Francis Grose's *Treatise on Ancient Armour and Weapons* in 1786, though Père Daniel in his *Histoire de la milice françoise* of 1721 had paved the way. Grose's book, like J. B. L. Carré's *Panoplie*, published in 1797 (though actually completed in 1783), was a combination of learning and absurdity, in the manner of many other antiquarian studies of the period. Both works brought together much interesting documentary material, but neither author had any real knowledge of the physical evolution of arms and armor, and readily accepted the wildly erroneous dates and attributions attached to pieces in the collections they consulted. In doing so they made their books into invaluable primary sources of information about 18th-century arms collections in Britain and France, but their uncritical approach made them worse than useless as sources of information about what forms of arms and armor were current at any given period.

The work that really marked the beginning of the serious historical study of arms and armor was by Dr. (later Sir) Samuel Rush Meyrick and appeared in 1824 under the appropriate (in view of what had gone before) title *A Critical Inquiry into Ancient Armour*; a second edition was published in 1842. Here, for the first time, was a book which provided a chronological survey of the development of arms and armor based on a study of iconographic sources and, to a lesser degree, actual specimens, as well as of documents. The importance of Meyrick's book and his subsequent writings—in particular his *Engraved Illustrations of Ancient Armour* with illustrations by Joseph Skelton (1830)—cannot be exaggerated, and every later writer on arms and armor has owed him a great debt. The *Critical Inquiry* remained the *only* worthwhile general account of its subject in any language until 1855, when the first volume of John Hewitt's *Ancient Armour and Weapons* appeared. Hardly surprisingly, therefore, Meyrick's work was enormously influential, and not merely on the study of arms and armor itself: his opinions were widely disseminated through a whole range of publications—from encyclopedias to specialized works on other antiquarian subjects—whose authors, for one reason or another, wished to include information about arms and armor and, since no other source was available, naturally obtained it from the *Critical Inquiry*. The result was that Meyrick's influence so permeated the whole subject that his successors have found it difficult to suppress all his misconceptions and errors—which were many—especially those stemming from the technical terminology he devised. Even now, over a century and a half after the appearance of his great work, they still turn up occasionally in new publications.

Hewitt's *Ancient Armour and Weapons*, published in three volumes between 1855 and 1860, is very much in the Meyrick manner, with more attention given to iconographic and documentary sources than to actual specimens of arms and armor, but as a work of scholarship it is superior to Meyrick's book in every way, and is still very useful. After Hewitt a number of distinguished scholars entered the field, stimulated, no doubt, by the great interest in collecting arms and armor that developed in the second half of the 19th century. This, of course, had started earlier, and was part and parcel of the general 19th-century interest in the Middle Ages, but it undoubtedly owed a great deal to the influence of such distinguished arms collectors as Tsar Nicholas I, King Carlo Alberto of Savoy, and Emperor Napoleon III. The researches of these scholars, in many countries, brought about enormous advances in knowledge of the history of arms and armor. It would be pointless to list all their names here, but the members of one small group call for special mention because they laid the foundations for modern methods of study

Meyrick's followers were much more concerned with studying historical evolution from iconographic and documentary sources than with examining surviving pieces critically (Hewitt, for example, includes only twenty-one actual examples of arms and armor in the 237 illustrations in his three volumes). Furthermore, since they paid almost no attention to basic details of construction and form, they were prone to assume that all contemporary illustrations were equally accurate, and were easily taken in by fakers like Samuel Pratt of London (even Hewitt illustrated a helmet by him). The first scholar to turn his attention seriously to such matters was the brilliant French architect and medievalist Eugène Emmanuel Viollet-le-Duc, in the second, fifth, and sixth volumes of his great *Dictionnaire raisonné du mobilier français*, published in 1874. In this work the emphasis is still in the direction of documentary and iconographic sources (especially manuscript illuminations), although it contains many carefully drawn engravings of actual specimens with details of their construction. It differs, however, from everything that had gone before in that the author attempts to give practical reconstructions of the arms and armor shown in the contemporary illustrations he reproduces, and where possible, to relate them to surviving pieces. He often allows his imagination to carry him further than the evidence warrants, but the fundamental rightness of his approach gave his book an importance that is no longer appreciated fully.

Viollet-le-Duc's methods were taken further by C. A. de Cosson and William Burges in their catalogue of the exhibition Ancient Helmets and Examples of Mail, held in London by the Royal Archaeological Institute in June 1880. Burges was another brilliant architect, and his aims and interests were similar to those of Viollet-le-Duc, with whose work he was familiar; he was also an arms collector. The exhibition appears to have been the first one dealing with arms or armor to be organized in the manner that is now normal for all art exhibitions, and also the first one to be accompanied by a catalogue raisonné of modern type. The introduction to the section on European helmets, written by de Cosson, contains a passage laying down methods for the study of armor that are a complete reversal of those used by Meyrick and his followers, and are still valid today:

For the study of ancient armour to be successfully pursued, it is of primary importance that a careful examination should be made of every existing specimen within our reach. This alone will enable us to derive full profit from our researches into ancient authors and our examination of ancient monuments. Every hole and rivet in a piece must be studied and its use and object thought out. The reasons for the varied forms, thicknesses and structure of the different parts of armour must have special attention. The methods of work by which the pieces were produced, and the nature, quality, hardness, and colour of the metal should all be the subject of close investigation.

The methods of study outlined by de Cosson were followed by the outstanding arms and armor scholar of the late 19th century, Wendelin Boeheim, an Austrian, who in 1878 was made curator of the Imperial Armory in Vienna. There is no reason to think that he was directly influenced by Viollet-le-Duc or de Cosson and Burges. His early career was a military one, but his personal interests were in history and art history, and he applied the disciplines learned in those fields to the study of arms and armor. He had a tremendous advantage in having at his disposal an armory that was not only the greatest in the world, but was also one for which much original documentation lay hidden in the imperial archives. He made full use of this advantage and in a series of brilliant and learned articles, most of them published in the *Jahrbuch der Kunsthistorischen Sammlungen in Wien* between 1884 and just before his death in 1900, he produced documented dates and identifications for pieces at Vienna and identified for the first time the major European schools of armor-making, as well as the work and marks of many of the major armorers. In 1890 he published a textbook, *Handbuch der Waffenkunde*, which despite rather poor illustrations was to remain the best one on the subject until after the Second World War. Boeheim was one of the people responsible for the founding in 1897 of the Verein für Historische Waffenkunde, whose periodical, now called *Waffen- und Kostümkunde*, has ever since been one of the most important vehicles for the publication of original research material.

Modern arms and armor scholarship is based almost entirely on the foundations laid by Boeheim, but this is not to say that he was exclusively responsible for the new direction that studies began to take from the late 19th century onward. Scholars who were his contemporaries, or near contemporaries, such as Angelo Angelucci in Italy, Charles Buttin in France, the Conde de Valencia de Don Juan in Spain, Lord Dillon in England, and Bashford Dean in the United States, all played their part in bringing about the change. The work that probably did more than any other to make the new concepts and discoveries widely known, especially outside the German-speaking areas, was not published until more than twenty years after Boeheim's death. This was Sir Guy Laking's *Record of European Armour and*

*Arms*, which appeared in five volumes in 1920 and 1921.

Laking was a collector and art connoisseur in the late Victorian manner, still much under the influence of Meyrick in some areas and with no pretensions to scholarship, and his *Record* is full of statements that are based on nothing stronger than his personal opinions. He was, however, a protégé of de Cosson, and therefore had the same views about the way in which its subject should be treated, while he also made extensive use of the publications of the scholars whose names are mentioned in the preceding paragraph. The most lavishly illustrated book on arms and armor ever produced, the *Record* was almost as influential in its day as Meyrick's *Critical Inquiry* had been in the previous century, despite the fact that its scholarship left so much to be desired.

Laking's influence was to be much shorter-lived than Meyrick's, however, and before the end of the decade during which Laking's *Record* was published a new group of young scholars had begun to make their influence felt. They were few in number, because the First World War had brought about a decline in interest in arms and armor, as in so many things, but they had more exacting standards of scholarship than had hitherto prevailed in the field, coupled with a much more critical approach to their subject and to the work of their predecessors. They were also much more aware, since a number of them had been trained as art historians, of the need to relate arms and armor to the general cultural, social, and artistic background of their time as well as to their more obvious background of warfare and tournaments. Discoveries in Swiss and German castles, at Swedish Migration Period sites, and above all, on the site of the battle of Wisby (1361) in Gotland, also brought medieval arms and armor into the ambit of the field archeologist to a much greater extent than ever before.

The work of the scholars who had begun to make their names in the 1920s was, of course, interrupted by the Second World War. Within a few years after the war, it began to become clear that, for some reason that has still to be explained, an unprecedented growth in the study and collecting of arms and armor was taking place. The result has been that during the last thirty years more has been published on the subject in almost every European country as well as in America than in the previous 150 years. Though many of the publications are of little merit, they also include original scholarly work, and our knowledge of the whole field is both greater than ever before and more diversified.

Before the war, writers, with a few exceptions, tended to concentrate on European arms and armor produced before the middle of the 17th century, while only a handful of books about the development of firearms or Oriental arms was available. Since the war, interest in arms of all periods has increased enormously, and especially—to an extent that would have been inconceivable forty years ago—interest in firearms. Whereas in 1939 there were probably not more than a couple of dozen books dealing with the history of firearms available in all languages, there must now be several hundred. There has been a corresponding, but much smaller, growth in publications on European and American arms of other kinds, but, apart from Japanese swords, Oriental arms and armor have been given less attention.

The fluctuations in the number of books on any given aspect of arms and armor are directly linked to what is available to collectors in the auction houses and antique shops, and they are the people to whom credit should be given (though it rarely is) for much of the publishing activity I have been describing. Without their devotion to their collections very few such books would appear, since there would not be enough people to buy them, while many of the journals of arms and armor societies would lapse for want of members. Most collectors have a need for a comprehensive reference work, preferably with a large number of illustrations, to give them general guidance to the whole of their subject, however narrow the section is in which they are particularly interested. The ideal form for a work of this kind is a dictionary or encyclopedia, but, so far as I am aware, only one serious and substantial dictionary of arms and armor claiming to be fully comprehensive has ever appeared. This is George Cameron Stone's *Glossary of the Construction, Decoration and Use of Arms and Armor in All Countries and in All Times*, first published in the United States in 1934 and reprinted many times since. This is a remarkable work, but it suffers from the fact that the author's knowledge was not comprehensive (he was a specialist in Eastern arms and armor) and, even judged by the standards of its time, it is uneven in coverage, incomplete, and, not infrequently, inaccurate, especially in the European sections. The author also apparently concluded that "All Times" ended in the first half of the 19th century!

An up-to-date publication on similar lines to Stone's is clearly long overdue, but with the vast increase in knowledge and range of interests of students and collectors of arms and armor since his day, the task of doing so has become formidable, especially for one author. The present book makes the attempt, but, for the reasons just given, it is the work of several authors, each of whom writes on subjects within his own specialized field, and covers a wider period than did Stone. Inevitably, because of its range, much information has had to be omitted. What the book seeks to do is to make general information about the whole field of arms and armor readily accessible, and for the reader who wishes to pursue a specific topic, there is an extensive Bibliography arranged by subject. It is hoped, in short, that it will perform the same useful and indispensable basic reference function of any fine dictionary or encyclopedia.

*Claude Blair*

# A

**abumi** A Japanese stirrup. The stirrup is an Asian invention, but its early stages are little known. Some early Japanese stirrups from before the 4th century A.D., made of iron, had hooded toes and long loops for the leather straps. In some hooded stirrups the footplates were perforated to let out water picked up when crossing rivers; these were named *suiba abumi.* The later abumi, used till the end of the Tokugawa (Edo) period (1603–1867), have no hood but large footplates for the entire foot to rest on. They have a peculiar swanlike shape, curved up and backward at the front so as to bring the loop for the leather over the instep and achieve a correct balance. Occasionally, in early examples, there is an iron rod from the loop to the footplate near the heel to prevent the foot from slipping out. Cheap sorts of abumi were made of wood framed by a metal bar in the shape described above, but they were perishable. Most of the surviving specimens are constructed entirely of iron inlaid with silver and covered with lacquer. There are also abumi with holes in the front forming sockets for a lance or banner.

*Japanese abumi, 19th century. Museo Stibbert, Florence.*

**acconzius** (Greek *akóntion*) Generic term for various types of JAVELIN, often associated with the PILUM, a heavy throwing spear with a long steel head used by the Roman infantry, and the VERUTUM, a lightweight javelin.

**achico** A South American missile consisting of three balls connected by a strong cord which is thrown to bring down an enemy's horse (or a hunted animal) by becoming entangled around its legs. *See also* BOLAS.

**acinaces** (Greek *akinakēs*) Latin transliteration of Greek term meaning a large, straight, double-edged dagger, 35–45 cm. (14–18 in.) in length. The acinaces was encased in a sheath of peculiar shape, having an extension so that it could be suspended from a wide belt on the wearer's right side. It was mainly used in the first millennium B.C. in the eastern Mediterranean, especially by the Scythians and Persians, who introduced it to the Greeks.

The ancient Romans believed that this weapon had originated with the Medes. Q. Curtius Rufus, who wrote a history of Alexander the Great early in the 1st century A.D., recounted that the military equipment belonging to Cyrus the Younger, king of the Achaemenid Empire in the 6th century B.C. (whose tomb had been violated two centuries later on Alexander's orders), included an acinaces which had been placed alongside his sword and two double-curved Scythian bows.

**aclys** (Greek *agkulis*) Latin name for a small JAVELIN, about 2 m. (79 in.) long, thrown with the aid of a strap or AMENTUM; every soldier was issued at least two. The name was also applied to a short, stout mace equipped with a number of spikes. This was attached to one arm of the antagonist by a strap of adjustable length to enable the weapon to be brought back after it had been hurled at the adversary. Its use probably goes back to the Oscan tribe (6th century A.D.) in southeastern Italy.

**adarga** Moorish shield, its name deriving from the Arabic *el-daraqa* or *daraq*, noted in many medieval and later sources. For a long time an important center of manufacture of the adarga was Fez, in Morocco. The typical adarga was made from the skin of the antelope called by the Arabs *lamt* (probably being the species defined as *Oryx tao*). Leather made from this animal's hide was very resistant to cuts from sword, lance, and arrow, but other kinds of leather were used as well.

Originally the adarga was round or oval, then heart-shaped, and finally, from the end of the 14th century, it took the form of two ellipses with the longer sides overlapping, being about 69–80 cm. (27–32 in.) in the long axis. Two layers of leather were glued and sewn together, so that the adarga was rigid and elastic at the same time, this adding to its protective ability. Incised and gilt ornaments, often with Moorish inscriptions, and sometimes metal appliqués and borders adorned the adarga. Inside, in the center, it had two rigid leather handles and a small cushion beneath. Usually both handles were held by the hand to enable free movement of the shield in any direction for parrying the enemy's weapon. European shields were always much less maneuverable, with the exception of small bucklers.

The adarga was the only defense of the Moorish light-horseman, while a long lance was his principal offensive weapon. Soon, probably throughout the 14th and 15th centuries, the adarga was adopted by Christian soldiers in Spain, and some troops of light cavalry ("á la jineta") were created after the Moorish patterns. The adarga shields were used till the 16th century, but progress in firearms sounded their death knell. Some exquisite examples of the adarga are preserved in the Real Armería in Madrid, with occasional specimens found in Paris and a few other places. A unique example of an adarga made of a large tortoise shell, taken at the battle of Vienna in 1683 from Turkish hands, is preserved in the armory of the Mons Clara Monastery at Częstochowa, Poland.

**agkúle** The Greek word for a strap or thong by which a weapon was attached to a soldier's arm; it was also used by Roman soldiers, by whom it was known as an AMENTUM.

**agkulis** The Greek word for a short javelin, known to Roman soldiers as an ACLYS.

**Ahlspiess** (German, "awl-spear") A staff weapon of German origin having a long spike, in most cases quadrangular in section. A rondel guard was usually fixed at the joint of the spike with the staff to protect the forward hand. Its length was generally about 125 cm. (50 in.). In the 15th and early 16th centuries, it was occasionally used by foot soldiers and was very popular for the knightly combats on foot in the lists.

**aikuchi** (or **haikuchi**) A Japanese dagger, whose name implies "a pleasant companion" and may also be interpreted as "flush mouth" as there is no guard between hilt and blade. It is also called by its old name, *kusungobu*, which is a measure equal to .95 of a Japanese foot (about 29 cm.), the original length of its blade. This was a knife used by various classes of people; it was a simple weapon, made with a wooden hilt and horn fittings, and it was not until the late Tokugawa (Edo) period (1603–1867) that it became accepted by men of rank, by which time it had become much more richly decorated, following the style of the TANTO dagger. Among older men and those who lived in religious semi-retirement, it was accepted as a symbol; not wishing to appear unarmed, they wore it as a purely social gesture.

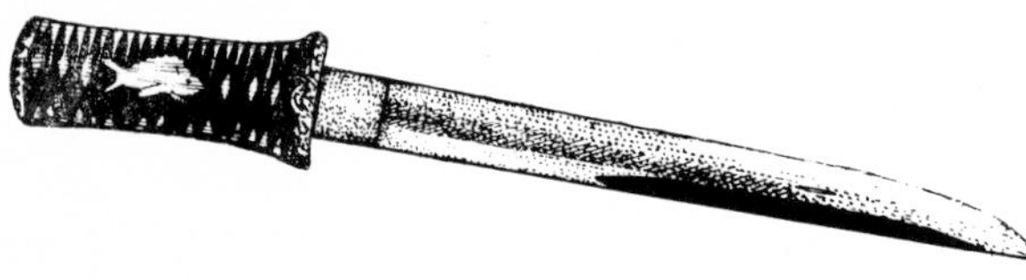

*Aikuchi, 19th-century Japanese dagger. Museo Orientale, Ca' Pesaro, Venice.*

The aikuchi was also used for ritual suicide, seppuku (so-called hara-kiri), but for this purpose it was furnished with an old-fashioned hilt of white wood and a wooden sheath. It also had the prescribed length of kusungobu.

A typical Tokugawa aikuchi has a single-edged blade, slightly curved or almost straight, not longer than 20–24 cm. (8–10 in.), with a hilt covered in fine lacquer or fishskin; it is frequently bound with cord and decorated with MENUKI ornaments. The scabbard, similarly decorated with lacquer, is equipped with both KOZUKA and KŌGAI, with mountings of gold, silver, copper, or SHIBUICHI and SHAKUDO alloys.

**air guns** There is a large group of weapons that use air to provide propulsive energy, whether precompressed in cylinders or compressed at the moment of firing by the rapid extension of one or more springs of the mechanism.

The first guns to work efficiently by means of compressed air probably date back to the 16th century and can be divided into two categories. In one category, bellows—housed in the butt—functioned by means of a spring; when the trigger was pulled, the release mechanism freed the spring, which immediately closed the bellows, causing a rush of air to the barrel and expelling the projectile, the energy transmitted to it being in proportion to the force of the bellows-spring combination. In the other category, a spring—usually spiral—extends with some force, propelling a piston which, in turn, compresses the air in a cylinder. The compressed air then rushes out of a small hole which is in direct contact with the barrel. This is the fundamental principle of all modern weapons using compressed air.

The first gun with an air reservoir, with air precompressed by a pump, was probably one made by the famous inventor Marin le Bourgeoys of Lisieux for Henry IV of France, sometime before 1608, and described in detail in *Les Eléments de l'artillerie*, by R. de Flurance (1607).

Toward the middle of the 17th century, Georg Fehr of Dresden made a great many air guns, the air reservoir being situated between the barrel and a brass sleeve fitted coaxially and enclosing it. In the case of a gun, this was equipped with a piston-operated pump housed in the butt, or in the case of a pistol, fitted independently. When sufficient pressure had built up, pressing the trigger caused a valve to open, allowing some of the compressed air to rush into the breech. At this point the projectile—which would already have been loaded through the muzzle—was ejected violently from the barrel.

In the following century, a new system was introduced whereby the air reservoir (or cylinder) was housed in the butt (or, in the case of a pistol, in the handle), though it was sometimes screwed on under the battery in the form of a round container. Most gunmakers made air guns outwardly resembling ordinary wheel-lock or flintlock guns. Considerable progress was made when, in 1780, the

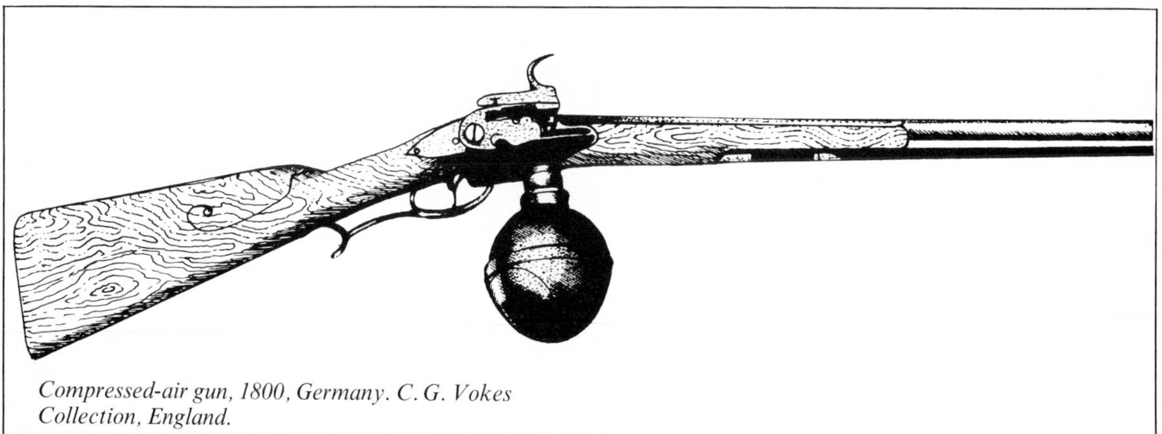

*Compressed-air gun, 1800, Germany. C. G. Vokes Collection, England.*

Austrian Army adopted the repeating air gun invented by Bartolomeo Girandoni of Cortina. In this unusual gun, the air reservoir consisted of a sturdy iron container in the form of a truncated cone, which also served as a butt. Due to the transversal movement of the breechblock (obturator), the ammunition—consisting of twenty pellets or balls contained in a tubular holder fixed parallel to the barrel—was always carried in the firing position. By cocking the lock, a lever was compressed which, when the trigger was pulled, would be released and rebound against the valve of the air reservoir, allowing just the right amount of compressed air to escape. The first repeating gun to have been taken up by an army—the Repetier-Windbüchse model 1780—was really too delicate and complicated to be entirely satisfactory. It remained in service for a long period, however, and many fine sporting guns were produced on the same principle by a number of gunsmiths.

From the middle of the 19th century, the production of air guns was almost entirely concentrated on the spring-and-piston system. In most instances, the spring is compressed as the gun is "broken"—i.e., barrel and stock are angled on a hinge for breechloading—and the barrel also acts as a lever, though many other systems were also used. The modern development of guns and pistols of this type was considerably influenced by the 19th-century fashion for gallery shooting in the United States. The key figure in this development was Henry Marcus Quackenbush of Herkimer, New York, who patented an air pistol and gun in 1871 and 1876 respectively and manufactured them by mass-production methods.

The production of some of the best weapons of this type, which are extremely accurate when fired at relatively short ranges, is concentrated in Germany, among the best-known companies in the gunmaking industry being Anschütz, Feinwerkbau Westinger & Altenburger, and Carl Walther.

Beginning with Leonardo da Vinci, a number of inventors have tried to use the power of steam as a propellant for guns. None has been successful.

**aketon** (also **acton**, from Spanish *alcotón* derived from Arabic *al-qutum*, "cotton") A plain quilted sleeveless garment worn under armor from at least the 12th to the early 15th century. It ensured a better fit of protective pieces and also served as a shock absorber. Quite often it was worn as the sole body protection, mostly by warriors of inferior rank. Occasionally, aketons worn as an outer garment were decorated with appliquéd ornaments. From the early 15th century, the function of the aketon as under-armor equipment was replaced by the ARMING DOUBLET.

**akinakēs** *See* ACINACES.

**akóntion** *See* ACCONZIUS.

**Almain collar** *See* GORGET.

**amentum** (Greek *agkúle*, *amma*, *enamma*) A thong attached to the shaft of a javelin to increase the propulsion of the throw. It is generally accepted by the experts that its derivation is Greco-Etruscan and that it was in use in Rome during the end of the republic and first two centuries of the empire.

The amentum, into which the first two fingers were placed, was positioned in different ways: in the middle of the weapon, at its central point of gravity, or sometimes much closer to the heel of the shaft. It is plausible, after looking at pictorial representations, that the amentum was used both to increase the length of the throw and to cause the javelin to spin in flight.

In the middle of the last century, some of the inhabitants of New Caledonia were using this system, having discovered that the thong made it possible to hit targets at remarkably long distances.

**amma** Greek word for AMENTUM.

**ammentum** Alternative spelling of AMENTUM.

**ammunition** A general term for anything needed to load firearms: powder, cartridge, shot, bomb, shell, fuze, etc.

**amusette** A French term for a heavy musket, like a wall gun but mounted on a light man-driven carriage with two wheels. It was about 160 cm. (63 in.) in length, with a caliber of about 40 mm. ($1\frac{3}{4}$ in.). The amusette is believed to have been the brainchild of Maurice, comte de Saxe (1696–1750), who became marshal of France. With a range of more than 2000 m. (2187 yds.), it fired projectiles of 250–300 g. (8–9 oz.). It was designed as an infantry support weapon but never came into general use.

**angon** An ancient Germanic (Frankish) type of javelin, whose use spread over all of western Europe. Similar in many ways to, and probably derived from, the Roman

*Greek warrior wielding javelin with amentum. From an Ionian-Attic goblet.*

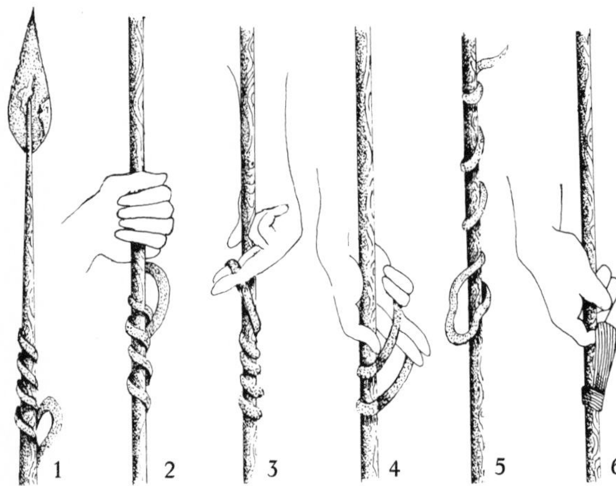


*Various ways of attaching the amentum (from ancient Greek vase paintings): 1, 2, 3, 5 to achieve a rotary movement; 4, 6 for a straight throw.*

PILUM, it was equipped with an iron fusiform barbed head forged at the top of a long slender haft provided with a socket for the wooden staff.

**anime** A type of laminated cuirass introduced in the second quarter of the 16th century and probably first designed in Italy. It was built up of horizontal overlapping lames connected by sliding rivets and leather straps. This form went out of fashion in western Europe at the end of the 16th century but remained in wide use throughout the next century in eastern European countries, particularly Hungary and Poland, where it was part of the heavy-cavalry armor (Hussar armor).

**ankus** The Indian elephant goad in the form of a spike and a hook mounted on a handle, resembling a boat hook. There are three variants of ankus, two of them for practical use: one with a handle of about 35–50 cm. (14–20 in.) to help the rider drive the elephant, the other with a staff about 150 cm. (5 ft.) long and a small hook for the man walking beside the elephant. The third variety has a strictly ceremonial character, with a short handle decorated with gold, enamel, or precious stones. In the first two types, the head is of steel, sometimes carved or inlaid with silver, and the handle of wood or ivory; occasionally the ankus is made entirely of steel.

**anlace** (or **anelace**) A form of the medieval French *alenas* which has the same root as the modern French *alène* (an awl) and refers to a medieval DAGGER with a stiff narrow pointed blade.

**"antennae" dagger** *See* DAGGER.

**aor** Poetic Greek term referring mainly to the *xíphos*, the straight (usually double-edged) sword of classical Greece. The sword belt or baldric on which it was worn was thus known as an aorter.

**aori** Side pieces or flanchards in Japanese equestrian equipment introduced during the Tokugawa (Edo) period (1603–1867). Aori consisted of large oval leather plates attached to rings on the saddle, richly tooled and decorated in gold lacquer and adorned with colored silk braids and tassels; they averaged in size 50 by 65 cm. (20 by 26 in.).

**aorter** Greek word for a sword belt or BALDRIC. *See also* AOR; BALTEUS.

**arame** A style of fastening on Japanese armor. *See also* ODOSHI.

**archer's thumb ring** A sturdy ring worn to protect the top joint of an archer's thumb when drawing the bowstring, especially when using the method of Asian origin known as the Mongolian release. Thumb rings, which were widely used throughout the Orient, eastern Mediterranean, Africa, and southern Europe, are known to have been employed by the Assyrians in the 7th century B.C., and they remained in use in Asia up to the 18th century. Two basic forms of the thumb ring are known. The Chinese rings, usually made of jade, were either cylindrical or D-shaped. In other regions, the thumb rings were truncated-conical in profile, with a projecting lip at the side that held the bowstring in place. These rings were made of a variety of materials, including horn, ivory, bronze, silver, and gold.

In drawing the bowstring, it was first hitched behind the pointed lip of the ring with the nock of the arrow resting close against it, fitting into the angle formed by the bowstring when fully drawn. The forefinger would now be pressing tightly against the sloping surface of the thumb ring. As the bow was bent, the forefinger moved toward the lip, and when the pressure of the forefinger on the ring was removed by separating forefinger and thumb, the bowstring immediately slipped off the lip with a sharply audible click.

One of the most interesting examples of an archer's ring belonged to the Donati family of Venice; it dates from the 15th century and is in the British Museum. On it is engraved, in addition to the family's crest, a verse from St. Luke's Gospel. This ring, Oriental in pattern but

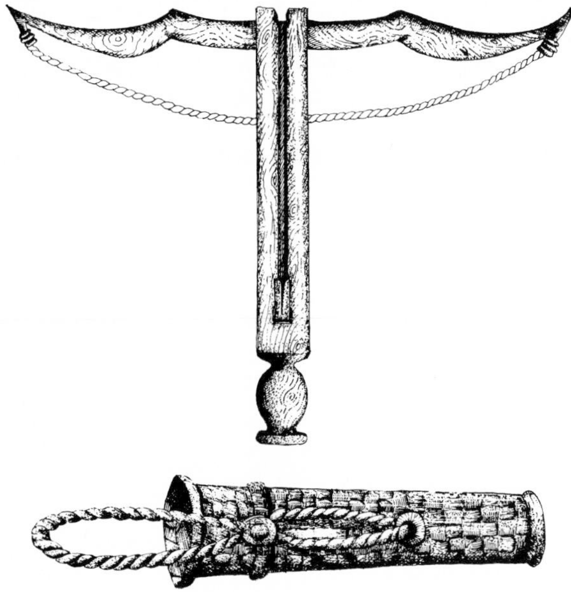

*Hand ballista (crossbow) for the chase and quiver. From a bas-relief dating from the time of imperial Rome, found at Solignac-sur-Loire, France.*

decorated in Venice, is to be regarded as an extreme rarity whose presence in Venice can be explained by the highly developed contacts of the Republic with the Orient.

**arcuballista** Also called ballista, an ancient missile thrower based on the same principle as the crossbow, of which it was the forerunner. The first known reference to this weapon appears in *Epitoma rei militaris* by Vegetius (4th–5th century A.D.), from which it would appear to have been in use since the time of the emperor Diocletian (284–305), together with other projectile-launching devices such as the bow, scorpion, fustibale (Chaucer's "fel staf" sling) or staff sling, and catapult. Again according to Vegetius, the weapons which in his day were called "hand ballistae" had been referred to as "scorpions" several centuries before and, in fact, this is borne out by Livy (59 B.C.–A.D. 17) and Polybius (c. 205–120 B.C.). Polybius divided them into two main categories: large, to include the great war machines which were used in the vanguard of an assault, especially when laying siege to a city; and small, to include the other missile-throwing weapons used by individual combatants. The hand ballista was also used in the chase, evidence for which can be seen on a fine funeral pillar from the time of imperial Rome and now preserved in the Crozatier Museum at Le Puy-en-Velay, France.

**arm of the hilt** Part of the sword hilt extending on each side from the cross guard (or quillons) toward the blade and having the form of a small arc. The arms of the hilt are known to have been in use from the 15th century but they had probably made their appearance in the 14th, protecting the forefinger when it gripped the ricasso. They represented an important step in the development of the guard. In the swords of the 16th and 17th centuries the arms of the hilt served as a support for loops and rings of the guard, as well as for bars of the counterguard. The arms of the hilt have survived in the Italian-type hilt of fencing foils up to the present time.

**armet** A type of helmet which completely enclosed the head, used during the 15th and 16th centuries. It consisted of a SKULL, full VISOR (or upper BEVOR), and CHEEKPIECES. Early forms of the armet appeared about 1420 as an alternative to the BASNET and SALLET with bevor. The skull was generally ogival or rounded, with a keel but no comb and with small holes pierced around the neck and brow edges for attaching the lining. The full visor, with eye slit, was detachable and fastened to the sides of the skull by two pivoted hinges. The two cheekpieces, hinged to the skull by their upper edges, closed together at the chin with a turning pin. The lower edges of both skull and cheekpieces terminated at the same level with a mail throat guard (fringe) laced to them.

Toward the middle of the 15th century the armet had developed into a shape called the "sparrow's beak" because of the blunt point of the visor. The contour of the skull had changed too, having become rounded with a hole at the top for a crest holder. The neck guard was contoured to the nape, where there was also a RONDEL, which served to protect the joint of the cheekpieces at a vulnerable point and to support a strap of reinforcing bevor. The front of the skull often had an additional plate, the BROW REINFORCE, which was riveted to the skull.

This style was to remain in use, with such modifications as a gradual increase in the size of the brow reinforce and the development of a small comb, until the end of the century. The one-piece visor, however, survived into the 16th century and was applied to the CLOSE HELMET. The

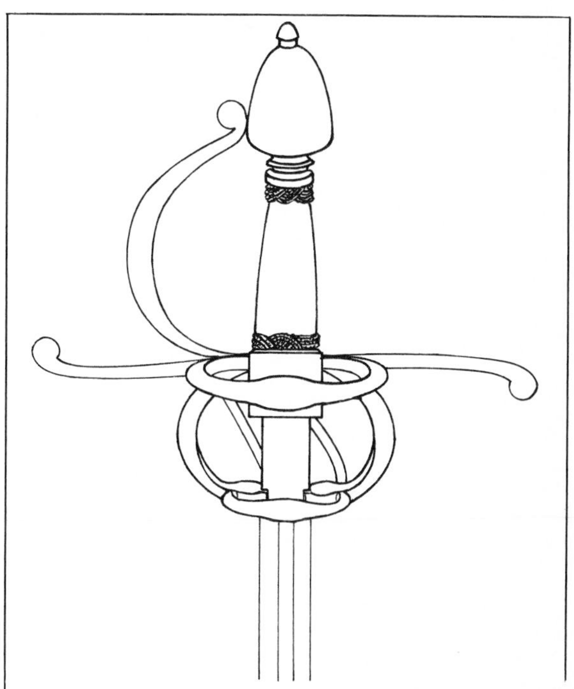

*Arms of the hilt.*

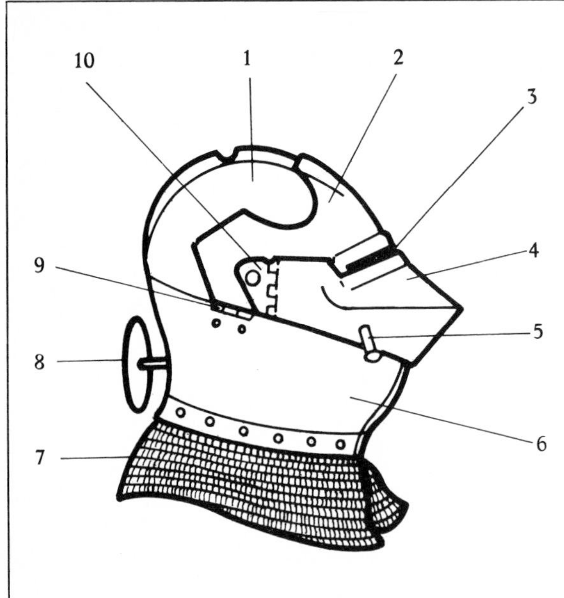


Armet*: 1. skull; 2. brow reinforce; 3. sight; 4. visor; 5. Lifting peg; 6. cheek piece; 7. mail fringe; 8. rondel; 9. cheek piece hinge; 10. visor hinge and pivot. From the* Glossarium Armorum.

most remarkable variations took place in the German-style armets in which the skull tended to jut backward, the cheekpieces were hinged by their rear edges, and the lower edge of the skull and cheekpieces formed a hollow rim to rotate on the armor's gorget. This type of armet was favored in Austria and Germany up to the 1520s for field and tilt. By 1530 the visor of both the armet and the close helmet had been divided into two parts, visor and ventail (or upper bevor), but no further changes were brought to the structure of the armet, which was finally abandoned in the early 17th century.

**arming cap** The Arming cap was worn under medieval helmets, either under or over a mail coif. It consisted of a close-fitting cloth skullcap with a padded circlet and ear lappets terminating in laces to be tied under the chin. It served to keep the head defense away from the head to prevent chafing and to act as an intermediary buffer against the impact of an opponent's blows. From the 13th century it was supplanted in some helmets by the padded LINING, but was still being worn into the 16th century with heavy helmets—as, for example, in conjunction with the jousting helm.

**arming doublet** A quilted garment with sleeves, armpits, and skirt covered with mail, worn in the 14th and 15th centuries under armor to give protection where plates or lames did not provide an adequate defense.

**arming points** Cords or laces on a garment worn under armor for attaching parts of the armor, which had special holes or leather loops for arming points.

**arming sword** A general term for swords carried by the mounted knight attached to his sword belt. *See also* SWORD.

**Armor**

The general development of Western armor and the main types of European armor are dealt with under this heading from prehistoric times onward. For more details about particular forms of armor, see CUIRASS; HELMET; LORICA. For Chinese armor, see the final section of this entry. For Japanese armor, see DŌ-MARU; GUSOKU; HARA-ATE; HARAMAKI; KEIKŌ; TANKŌ; YOROI. For Middle Eastern, see CHAR-AINA; KAZAGHAND; KORAZIN. For eastern European, see BEKHTER; JACK; YUSHMAN. In addition, see the appropriate section of the Bibliography.

**armor** Any equipment designed to protect the body in combat. During the earliest periods of civilization it was made of wood, hide, horn, bone, textiles; later, metals were preferred, and in modern times plastics have been used for this purpose. Hide was among the earliest materials employed to protect the body. Six or seven layers of rhinoceros skin were sewn together for making Chinese cuirasses in the 11th century, and other kinds of hide, leather, and *cuir-bouilli*—leather hardened by boiling in wax—were used for various parts of armor up to the early 20th century (for example, in some types of European helmets). Although textiles are rarely preserved well enough to be found in archeological sites, it is known that multilayer linen armor for the trunk was already used by Egyptians some five thousand years ago, by Mycenaeans in the 16th century B.C., by Greek foot warriors in the first millennium B.C., and by Assyrian troops of the Persian king Xerxes in the 5th century B.C. Strong fabrics with padding or metal reinforcement were employed in Europe throughout the Middle Ages and later.

An early form of body protection was simply a large belt to cover the abdomen. At first this was made from tree bark, leather, or similar materials, but as the world entered the Bronze Age, metal or reinforced cloth was used. These defenses were known in both East and West from prehistoric to historical times.

The first example of personal defensive wear to cover more than the combatant's torso seems to have been an enlarged form of the primitive body belt. It appeared in Egypt toward the third millennium B.C. and was supplied with a strap passing over the right shoulder to protect it and to hold the garment in position. Later, during the XVIII Dynasty in Egypt (c. 1570–1318 B.C.), a still more extensive protection was introduced which covered the soldier's body from about armpit level to halfway down his thighs and was supported by broad shoulder straps which crossed over his chest. Subsequently the Egyptians also adopted a cloth tunic reinforced with ribbed bands.

In Mesopotamia, discoveries in the royal tombs of Ur and, in particular, the famous standard of Ur (first half of the third millennium B.C.), have produced iconographic evidence that the Sumerians used long cloaks, probably reinforced with metal discs, as body defense.

Another of the basic types of ancient armor was the scale coat, which consisted of a short-sleeved tunic reaching to the knees upon which were sewn overlapping

*Abdomen plate. Museum of Herakleion, Crete.*

bronze scales. There is evidence of this type of protection in the Middle East from the second millennium B.C. A direct descendant of the scale coat was the lamellar armor, which was made up of horizontal rows of small, narrow metal lames laced together and slightly overlapping each other, without the need for any backing material. Evidence of the earliest use of lamellar armor can be seen in Assyrian iconographic works dating from the 8th century B.C. Reliefs in the palaces of Nineveh, Assur, and Nimrud depict Assyrian infantry as well as cavalry troops wearing this type of defense. The use of both scale and lamellar protection spread rapidly east and west from the Middle East and remained in use for many centuries. Even in the early 19th century, lamellar armor was still being made in China and Japan.

MAIL was another type of basic material from which ancient armor was constructed. This was created by interlinking metal rings—each ring usually having four others linked through it—or by interweaving loops of wire. Mail was probably of Celtic origin, having begun to develop about the 6th or 5th century B.C., although the earliest coat of mail of which evidence exists today dates from the 2nd century B.C. A frieze on a pagan altar (c. 160–155 B.C.) from the ancient site of Pergamum, now housed in Berlin, depicts Galatian weapons among which a coat of mail is clearly recognizable. From the 1st Century B.C. there is a steady increase of evidence to the rapid and widespread use of this type of body defense in Europe and the eastern Mediterranean countries.

Up to the 13th century mail shirts remained the principal means of body protection for European heavy cavalry and those warriors on foot who could afford, or capture, mail armor. Called byrnie and HAUBERK, these mail shirts were of various length. Foot soldiers often wore a short hauberk (later known as the haubergeon) covering the torso down to hips or mid-thighs so as not to impede fast movements in combat. Mounted warriors preferred a long shirt of mail extending down to the knees; it also protected the lower legs, its skirt being slitted for riding. To reduce impacts from blows, a quilted garment, the AKETON, was worn under mail, and a similar battle dress, well stuffed with cotton or wool, was often the main protection for less wealthy men on foot. The head was covered by a mail hood, the COIF, and by a helmet, usually conical or flat-topped, with a strong nose guard or, more rarely, a steel face guard with eye slits and ventilation holes. Sleeves of the hauberk initially covered the arms only down to the elbows, but by the late 12th century, extended to the fingertips, forming mail gloves. In the 11th century quilted hose were reinforced with strips of mail covering the front and laced behind the legs, but in the next century full mail hose were often used. A long almond-shaped shield (usually termed "kite-shaped"), completed the protection of the warrior on horseback. Men on foot often used much smaller round shields.

Since mail could not adequately defend the warrior against thrusts of a spear or blows of a war hammer, attempts were made to design stiffer forms of armor. Hauberks covered with overlapping iron scales appeared in the 11th century, and leather cuirasses reinforced with steel bands shaped to the torso, the COAT OF PLATES, were introduced around 1200. During the next century LEGHARNESSES were developed, protecting the knees with appropriately shaped steel caps, called POLEYNS, and the shins with gutter-shaped steel GREAVES, both being attached with buckled straps passing behind the leg. Similar caps, called COWTERS, were designed for the elbows, while small steel discs, laced to the hauberk, acted as shoulder guards. The outer arms were covered with VAMBRACES, shaped and attached like the greaves. With the progressive improvement of legharnesses, it became possible to reduce the size of the long heavy shield to a much smaller triangular form (the "heater-shaped" shield), which was used by knights from the late 13th century up to the early 15th. The conical, round- and flat-

*Warriors wearing protective cloaks, detail from the standard of Ur, British Museum, London.*

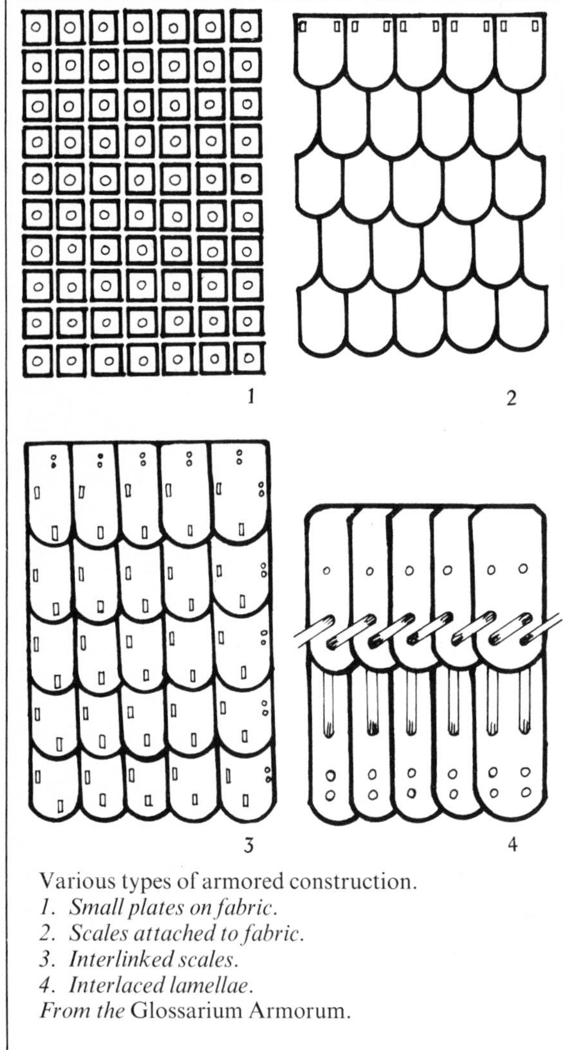

Various types of armored construction.
*1. Small plates on fabric.*
*2. Scales attached to fabric.*
*3. Interlinked scales.*
*4. Interlaced lamellae.*
*From the* Glossarium Armorum.

topped helmets of the earlier period underwent gradual modifications in size and construction of their face and neck guards, the result being a deep, heavy, barrel-shaped HELM which completely covered the knight's head. It was used during the 13th and 14th centuries and was worn later, again in somewhat modified forms, as part of jousting armor.

By about 1330 the fully armored knight would wear a hauberk over an aketon, and a coat of plates over the hauberk. A knee-long sleeveless gown covered his armor. A well-padded ARMING CAP, a coif, and a helmet protected his head. His legs were defended by mail CHAUSSES reinforced with plates. By this time GAUNTLETS made of steel plates and scales had also been developed, and toward the end of the century full legharnesses had developed consisting of SABATONS, greaves, poleyns, and CUISSES.

Further important changes occurred in the 14th century leading to the formation of complete plate armor, which by 1425 had replaced the coat of plates. For better protection of the front, the coat of plates had often been reinforced with an over-plate (placate), covering, initially, only the abdomen. It was also worn as an independent defense, which, gradually growing in size, developed in 1350–1400 into a BREASTPLATE shaped to the torso and convex in the center. At first attached with straps crossed on the wearer's back, it was later supplemented by a BACKPLATE, both parts of this "pair of cuirasses" being connected by shoulder straps on the top and by hinges and buckles with straps on the sides. To the lower edges of the cuirass was attached a horizontally laminated SKIRT protecting the abdomen, hips, and loins. The upper edges of each plate were hammered into the turns—rounded flanges at the neck and armpits, designed to deflect bladed weapons. Rigid and strong, the cuirass made it possible to develop an important accessory, the REST, attached at the right armpit on the breastplate to couch the lance when attacking and to prevent it from being knocked backward on the impact of a hit.

By about 1420 armor was virtually as complete as it could be, in most essential details. Articulation and joints had been perfected to a point where there were few "dead spots," which had to be protected by mail. Development continued, however, with modifications and refinements being made throughout the century. These technical improvements were largely the work of Italian armorers of Milan and their German counterparts in Nuremberg, Landshut, Innsbruck, and above all, Augsburg.

The protection of the head was still entrusted to the BASNET, although this was gradually being replaced by various types of SALLET combined with the BEVOR attached to the breastplate or, more rarely, to the helmet. Breast- and backplates were supplemented on the top with a collar, or GORGET, and with shoulder guards, the PAULDRONS. To improve shoulder protection, the pauldrons began to be made of articulated plates, the lower being linked to the tubular upper-arm guards, the vambraces. The gauntlets had become larger and no longer had separated fingers, thus becoming mitten gauntlets, with attached thumb scales.

By 1450 the front of the skirt and its rear part, the rump guard, were fastened on the sides to form one circular laminated defense; in front, to its lower lame, were attached the TASSETS. The cuisses were reinforced with hinged side plates to protect the outside of the legs. The poleyns consisted of three articulated plates, the main one shaped to the knee and widened on the outer side to form an oval side wing—a screen to protect the joint. The poleyns overlapped the top of the greaves, to which they were attached either by a rivet or a turning pin; the greaves, comprising two pieces, were shaped to enclose the lower leg completely and were hinged, with straps and slots to fasten. In some instances they ended at the ankles but in most cases reached to the ground, arching over the instep to overlap the upper back lames of the long, pointed sabatons.

The second half of the 15th century saw no great changes in the structural development of armor, although a great deal was done to improve articulation. The basnet had by now become obsolete, although the BARBUT—a deep helmet with a T-shaped opening for sight and ventilation—was still in use, as was the sallet with its neck guard and a movable bevor. An important innovation, first introduced in Italy in the early 15th century, was the ARMET, a closed helmet with a pointed visor and a bevor shaped in front in the "sparrow's beak." By 1450 the first examples of separate gorgets, worn either under or over the breastplate, had appeared. Breast- and backplates of the cuirass took on a more compact appearance, with increased mobility, sometimes achieved by the use of several jointed plates on each part of the cuirass. The lower breastplate of a two-piece breast, used on many cuirasses, now came up so much higher that it formed a double layer of iron where it overlapped the upper breastplate. At the same time, the skirt was becoming smaller and the tassets—often ribbed and sometimes consisting of several lames—were increasing in importance. The vambraces and greaves, however, remained much the same, although the side wings on the cowters and poleyns were noticeably more inward-curving. Armor made in Germany, mainly for export, began to be imitated in other European countries, one of the features that was particularly copied being the SPAUDLERS—gutter-shaped laminated protection for the upper arms—with small circular shields as armpit defense, called BESAGEWS, attached to them.

By the end of the 14th century the first examples of decoration applied directly onto plates of an armor were seen. This generally took the form of pointillé (engraving with dots and strokes), and was restricted to a few parts of the helmet and breastplate, consisting mainly of rather formal foliate designs and "wolf's teeth" patterns. Etched decoration also appeared in the late 15th century.

The two main "schools" that had the greatest influence on all European armorers were the Northern Italian and the German. The former was characterized by its smooth finish and rounded surfaces, while the latter was renowned for its Gothic stylization which showed particularly in elaborate curves ending in cusps, rippling, fluting, etc., and, when it reached its peak toward the end of the 15th century, in an elegant slenderness of line. Around the beginning of the 16th century there was a certain tendency for the two styles to blend, the typically rounded lines of Italian armor being adopted in Germany while the German system of fluting the plates was sometimes used in Italy.

From about 1510–30 the so-called Maximilian style of armor came into use, although it was not to get this name until some 19th-century collectors decided that the style must have been introduced by the emperor Maximilian. Its characteristic features were large rounded shapes and radiating flutings on all surfaces except the leg armor. The later examples had quite narrow flutes, set close together. This style was widely used, especially in Germany, although fluted armor never superseded smooth-surfaced armor, which always remained more popular in the rest of Europe.

During the 16th century armor was to become more and more specialized. Three main categories emerged: for specific purposes of war; for various types of jousts and tourneys; and for ceremonial displays, parades, etc. Many

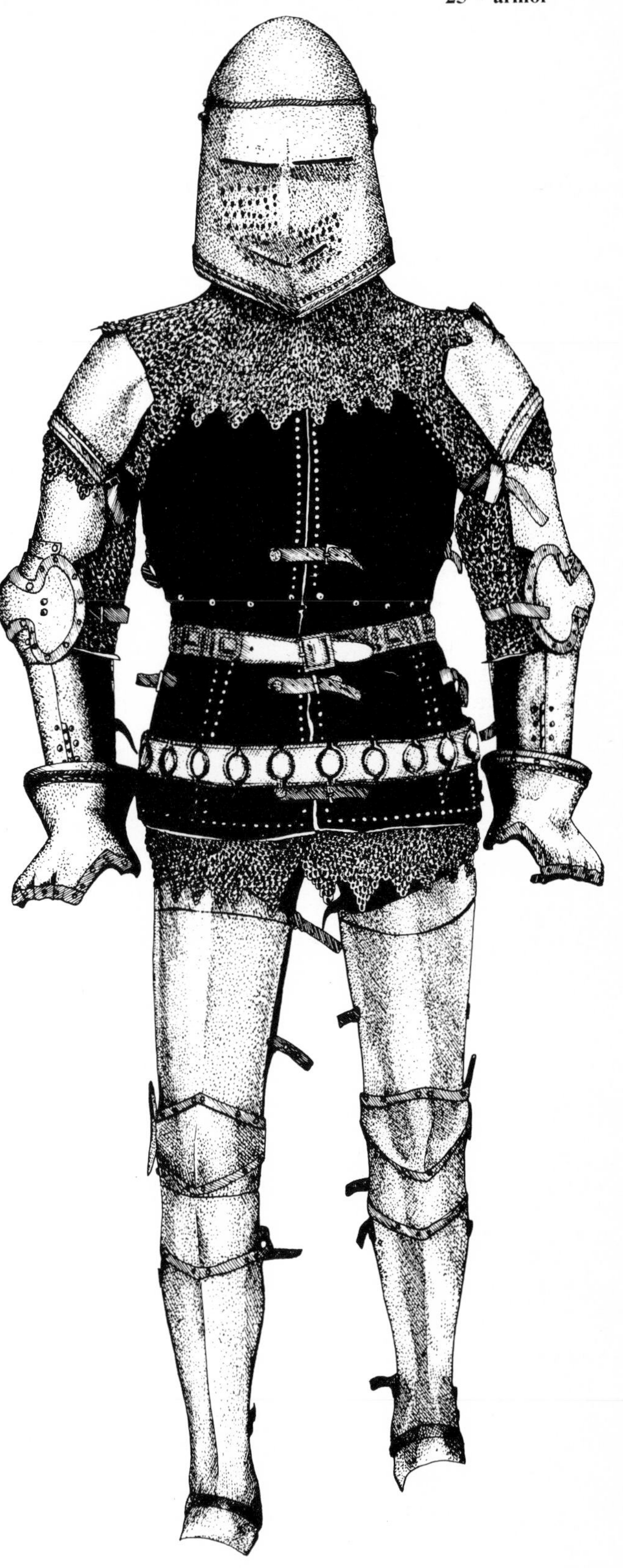

*Composite armor (plate and mail), N. Italy, c. 1400–1415. Metropolitan Museum, New York.*

*Armor of Ulrich IX, Castellan of Matsch, made by Pier Innocenzo da Faerno, Antonio Missaglia, and Giovanni Negroli, Milan, c. 1445–50. Churburg Armory, Sluderno.*

*Armor of Roberto da San Severino, Count of Caiazzo, made by Bernardo and Giovan Pietro da Carnago and Antonio Missaglia, N. Italy, c. 1480. Waffensammlung, Vienna.*

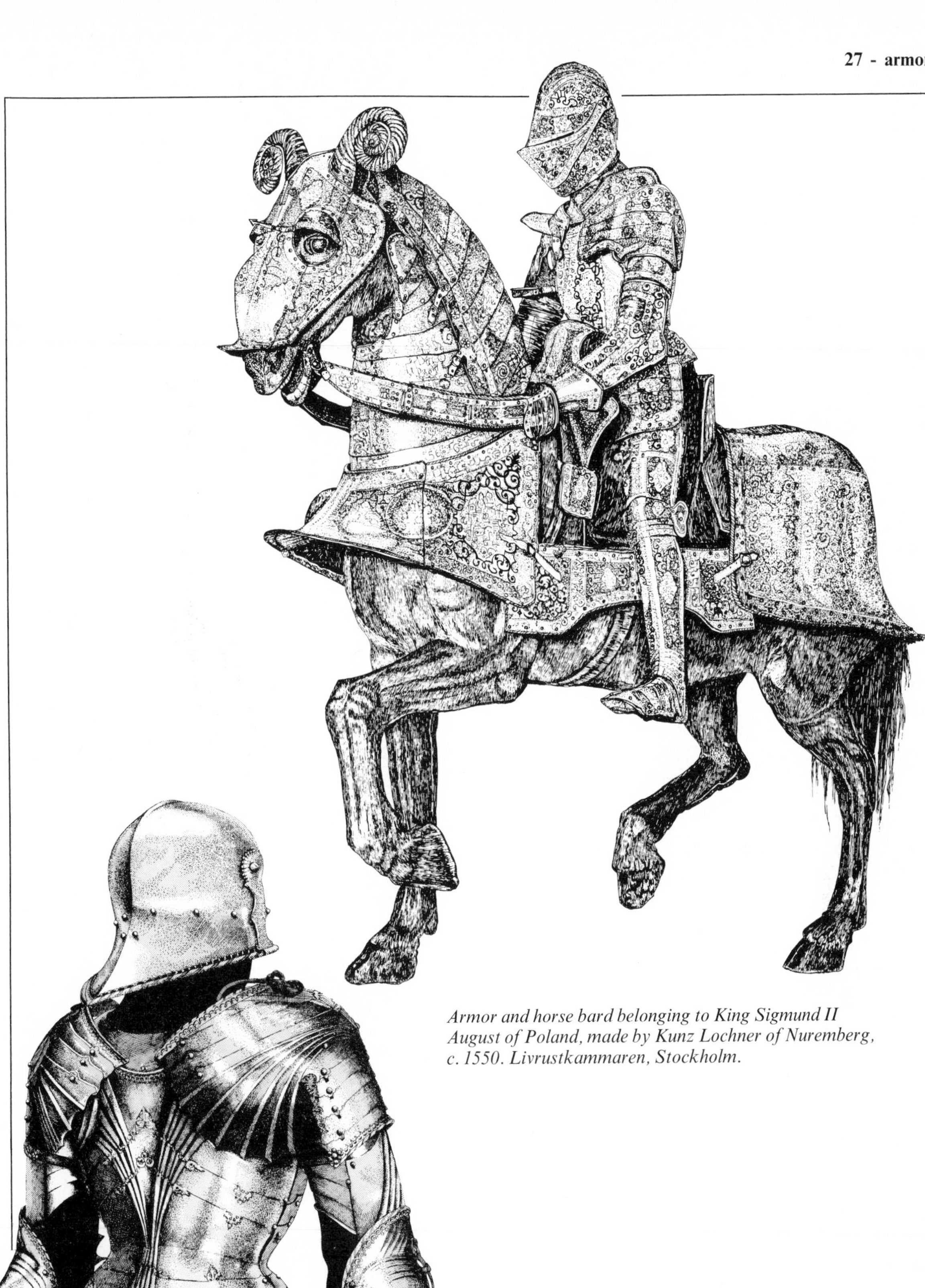

*Armor and horse bard belonging to King Sigmund II August of Poland, made by Kunz Lochner of Nuremberg, c. 1550. Livrustkammaren, Stockholm.*

*Rear view of the field armor belonging to Sigmund of Tirol, made by Lorenz Helmschmid of Augsburg, c. 1485. Waffensammlung, Vienna.*

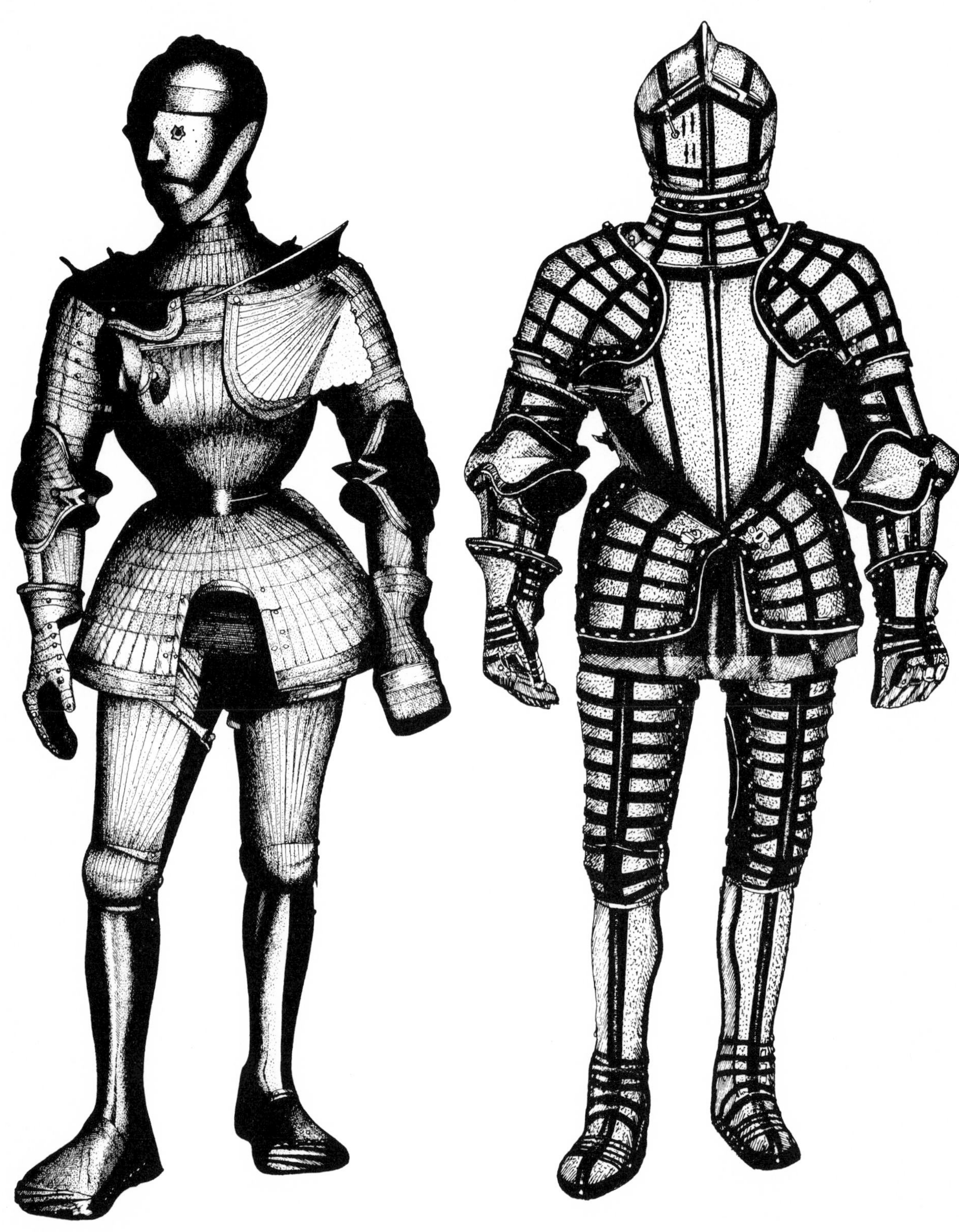

*Field armor belonging to Duke Ulrich of Württemberg, made by Wilhelm von Worms the Elder of Nuremberg, c. 1525. Waffensammlung, Vienna.*

*Armor belonging to Sir James Scudamore, made in Greenwich, England, c. 1580–85. Metropolitan Museum, New York.*

armors had interchangeable parts to enable the basic form to be used for different purposes. These composite armors frequently consisted of a great many pieces for exchange or reinforcement and are known as GARNITURES.

During the first half of the century mounted troops were still equipped in the style of the men-at-arms of the previous century. The helmet was of the armet type or of the form known as the CLOSE HELMET; the pauldrons were asymmetrical due to the deep cutout at the right armpit for the lance; the side wings of the cowters almost completely covered the elbow joint; the sabatons were shaped in either the "duck's bill" or "bear's paw" style; the gauntlets were either in the form of mittens or had articulated fingers.

A specially modified form of armor was introduced for the infantry as an alternative to the BRIGANDINE. This consisted of an open helmet, the BURGONET, MORION, or KETTLE HAT; the trunk was protected by a light cuirass without a rest for the lance, and there was a skirt to which the tassets were attached; the shoulders and upper arms were covered by spaudlers, but no plate defense was provided for the rest of the arms or for the legs. Most frequently used by light cavalry and heavy infantry were light forms of armor that are usually called "half armor" since they do not include legharnesses. This consisted basically of a light helmet, such as a burgonet or morion, a gorget, pauldrons, and a cuirass with long, broad tassets.

By the middle of the 16th century mounted troops had begun to be equipped with special medium armor, now often termed "three-quarter armor" since it covers the body to the knees only. In England these troops were known as lances or demi-lances, their light lance being used without the rest. This type of armor included a close helmet or a burgonet, with a detachable bevor (*see* BUFFE); pauldrons with full vambraces; a gorget and a cuirass with long tassets ending with poleyns; and high boots, replacing the greaves.

A common type of armor throughout the 16th century was munition armor for foot soldiers, which was used not only by heavy infantry but also by guardsmen, sentries, patrol troops, etc. It was usually consistent in its component parts, being made up of a light helmet (burgonet, kettle hat, or morion), a SKULL; a collar, which kept the pauldrons or spaudlers in position; a cuirass with laminated tassets that were strapped to the skirt plates and could be easily detached to make the armor still lighter. The arms were protected either by vambraces or by mail sleeves (if the armor was provided with spaudlers). While this was initially rather a cheap kind of armor for the common soldier, it was ultimately to be adopted by the Papal Guard (see separate subheading below).

The production of specialized armor for the joust and tourney continued into the second half of the 16th century, with a number of variations according to the type of contest, on horseback or on foot. Some of the garnitures were also intended for ceremonial occasions, and thus were richly decorated. The Milanese armorers were in the forefront of this kind of work, probably the greatest being the Negroli family. Lucio Piccinino also made a name for himself as an armorer-embosser, as did Bartolomeo Campi of Pesaro and Giorgio Ghisi of Mantua. In Germany, some of the finest embossed armor was produced by the goldsmith Jörg Sigman of Augsburg.

By the beginning of the 17th century firearms had greatly improved in efficiency and were being used more and more widely. The result was a noticeable decline in the importance of armor. However, the cuirassier armor was to remain in use by heavy cavalry for several more decades. It was composed of a closed helmet—a burgonet with a bevor or a "Savoyard" (*Todenkopf*) close helmet; a ZISCHÄGGE (added in mid-century); a gorget; and a heavy cuirass with very long tassets, known as "lobster tails," which included poleyns. Usually russeted or painted black with heavily engraved decoration and gilding, the general appearance was rather stocky and inelegant. From the middle of the 17th century the cuirassier armor was worn by a few regiments—mostly in Germany. A BUFF COAT and a heavy cuirass with a flat breastplate joined to a backplate were preferred by a new generation of heavy cavalry.

In the course of millennia, armor was constantly developed and perfected to confront improvements in offensive weapons. In the end, armor lost this competition to firearms, which had attained such force and rate of fire as to impose on armor the contradictory requirements of ensuring greater resistance by use of heavier plates while preserving the wearer's mobility in combat. However, body armor has never disappeared from battlefields, since it remains as good a protection as it has always been against a saber, lance, or bayonet. A "siege armor," consisting of a helmet with a reinforcing skull plate and a breastplate with an over-plate, was still used by sappers and advance troopers under enemy fire well into the 18th century. An "arquebus armor" of steel, including a burgonet, gorget and spaudlers, a cuirass, and a long left-hand gauntlet ("bridle gauntlet"), was used in the second half of the 17th century, and in Germany and Poland some carabineer and cuirassier units continued to wear much the same armor, including laminated spaudlers, up to the mid-18th century. A lighter form of armor, consisting of a steel helmet and cuirass, was used by cuirassier regiments well into the second half of the 19th century, and French cuirassiers still carried this armor in the field during the First World War. For ceremonial occasions, special helmets and cuirasses, made of a light alloy and sometimes silvered or gilded, have been used by Britain's Household Cavalry since the last century up to the present time.

Some parts of armor have survived in modified forms. The gorget, a crescent-shaped plate with an emblem or a royal coat of arms displayed at the neck, was worn by officers from the 18th century well into the 19th; special German units wore the gorget as part of their uniform during the Second World War, and in some armies it is still displayed by officers in full dress. In the last century, many cavalry regiments were issued epaulettes with a steel plate inside or metal scales on the upper surface to protect the shoulders against saber strikes. Since the early 1900s, revived interest in helmets, breastplates, and cuirasses capable of effective protection against firearms has led to many experiments with steel and plastics, resulting in helmets and bulletproof vests which are, in fact, not so distant descendants of medieval armor.

The following survey gives a classification of some basic types of armor used during the late 15th to the 17th century. All forms of armor fall into three main groups: battle armor, parade armor, and armor for sporting contests. The latter included tournaments, on horseback or on foot, involving two opposing groups of participants; jousts, in which two men fought on horseback; and foot combat, involving two opponents.

*Field armor* A type of armor used by heavy cavalry in the 15th and 16th centuries. It was a complete suit of armor, matched by a horse armor (*see* BARD), with a steel-plated saddlebow giving additional protection to the horseman. Head protection consisted of a sallet with a separate bevor, an armet, or a close helmet; in the second half of the 16th century, a lighter helmet, the burgonet, with or without a bevor, was often preferred. From the 16th century, the gorget, worn in most cases under the cuirass, was covered by gorget plates of a helmet, thus doubling the protection of the neck. The cuirass had a skirt with tassets and was equipped with a rest for the lance on the right side. The pauldrons with "wings" extending almost to the center of the breast were, until the late 16th century, asymmetrical since the right one had a cutout for the butt of the lance. A HAUTE-PIECE on each pauldron gave additional protection to the neck and head, but from the mid-16th century it fell into disuse and the pauldrons themselves became lighter, often with besagews instead of the "wings." The vambraces completely encircled the arms, with bracelet-like cowters to protect the elbow joints and tendons. In about 1500–1530 the gauntlets were usually without separate fingers (mitten gauntlets), but before and later were mostly made with articulated fingers. The legs were entirely protected by legharnesses, which consisted of articulated cuisses, poleyns, full closed greaves encircling the calf, and articulated lamellar sabatons. A lighter form of greaves was quite often used in the 16th century, with a gutter-shaped plate covering only the outside of the leg and with mail sabatons ending in a steel toe cap. Later in the century, laminated tassets and cuisses were often made to lock together, forming, in fact, long tassets.

The suit was generally worn over an ARMING DOUBLET reinforced with mail where joints were not sufficiently protected by plates of the armor. This type of armor lent itself very well to various exchange pieces and to the addition of reinforcing pieces for jousting and tournament. Field armor was thus the main component of a garniture used to form different types of armor for corresponding military uses and sporting contests.

*Cuirassier armor* A type of armor for heavy cavalry in use during the first half of the 17th century, the successor to the full field armor. In fact, already in the 16th century a lighter form of field armor ("three-quarter armor"), without greaves and sabatons, was worn, composed very much like the cuirassier armor but different stylistically. In the cuirassier armor the head was protected by a close helmet or a burgonet with a visor and bevor, but from about 1640 a heavy Zischägge was often preferred. The breastplate of the cuirass was fairly flat and sturdy, with a flange for attachment of a laminated defense combining a short skirt with long lobster-tailed tassets ending with poleyns. Greaves had by now been replaced by high leather boots. The lance being no longer in use, the pauldrons were symmetrical. The full vambraces were completed by gauntlets with separated fingers.

Cuirassier armors were mostly either blued or russeted or else varnished in black. Rivet heads were often brass-plated to serve as a decoration.

*Arquebus armor* A type of armor which from the second half of the 16th century was worn by light cavalry armed with pistols and short arquebuses (as well as with swords). Basically it consisted of a cuirass, made up of a heavy breast- and backplate, and a gorget, sometimes with light pauldrons; a buff coat was worn underneath. The cuirasses often show signs of having been tested—"proved"—against pistol, caliver, or musket, as was also done with cuirasses for cuirassier armors. In some cases, rather crude straight tassets and a rump guard were worn with the cuirass, but these parts were generally discarded from the late 1500s. A burgonet was most often used to protect the head, but from mid-17th century a light Zischägge was carried instead or a steel skullcap, the secrète, was sometimes worn inside an ordinary felt hat. The upper arms were protected by spaudlers, and only one long left-hand gauntlet (bridle gauntlet) was used.

Similar types of armor were still in service with some carabineer and cuirassier guard units in Germany up to the mid-18th century.

*Half armor for infantry and cavalry* A light armor worn throughout the 16th and 17th centuries by soldiers of heavy infantry and light cavalry. The head was protected by either a morion or a burgonet, the latter being often worn with various types of buffes—detachable bevors. The gorget supported the cuirass and the pauldrons, which were equipped with either large "wings" or besagews. The arms were protected by full vambraces and gauntlets. The breastplate had a short skirt, its two or three lames supporting the tassets. When used on horseback, the short tassets could be easily unbuckled and replaced with long tassets provided with poleyns.

Another type of half armor, called the corslet (also, probably, "Almain rivet" in England), was worn from the early 1500s, especially by heavily armed men on foot, including the landsknechts. It had long, large laminated tassets up to above the knees, most often with a detachable lower half.

A still lighter type of half armor was in use by light cavalry during the second half of the 16th century and the beginning of the 17th. It generally consisted of a burgonet supplemented with a detachable bevor (usually of the type called "falling buffe" because its lames could be lowered to open the face). The gorget incorporated short pauldrons protecting only the top of the shoulders, the arms being covered with mail and gauntlets. The breastplate had a low straight neck reinforced with a strong turn. The lower edges of the cuirass held a short laminated skirt extended in front into wide tassets. No rest for the lance was provided since light cavalry used javelins or short light spears.

A very similar light half armor was worn by infantry soldiers, instead of a heavier form like the landsknecht

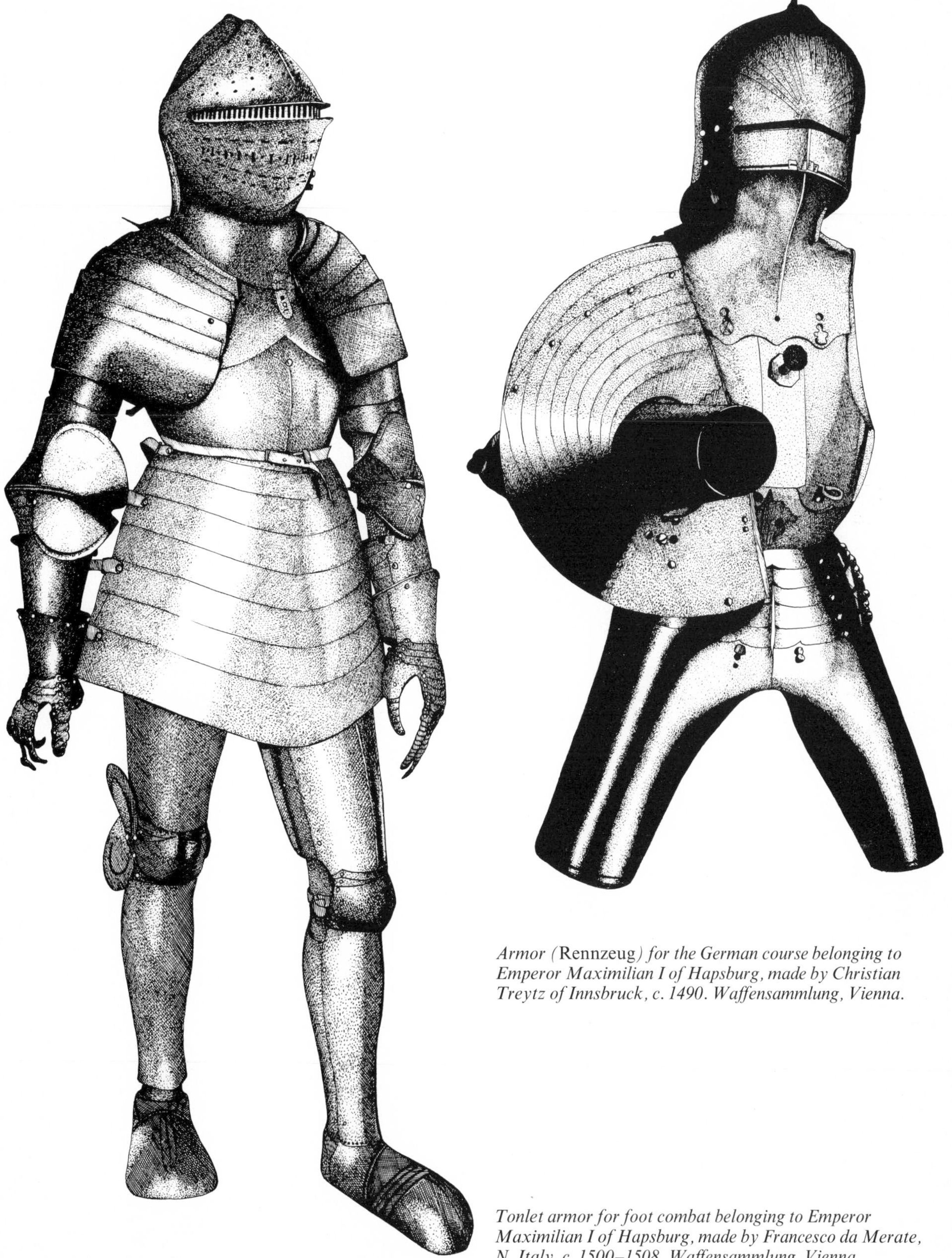

*Armor (*Rennzeug*) for the German course belonging to Emperor Maximilian I of Hapsburg, made by Christian Treytz of Innsbruck, c. 1490. Waffensammlung, Vienna.*

*Tonlet armor for foot combat belonging to Emperor Maximilian I of Hapsburg, made by Francesco da Merate, N. Italy, c. 1500–1508. Waffensammlung, Vienna.*

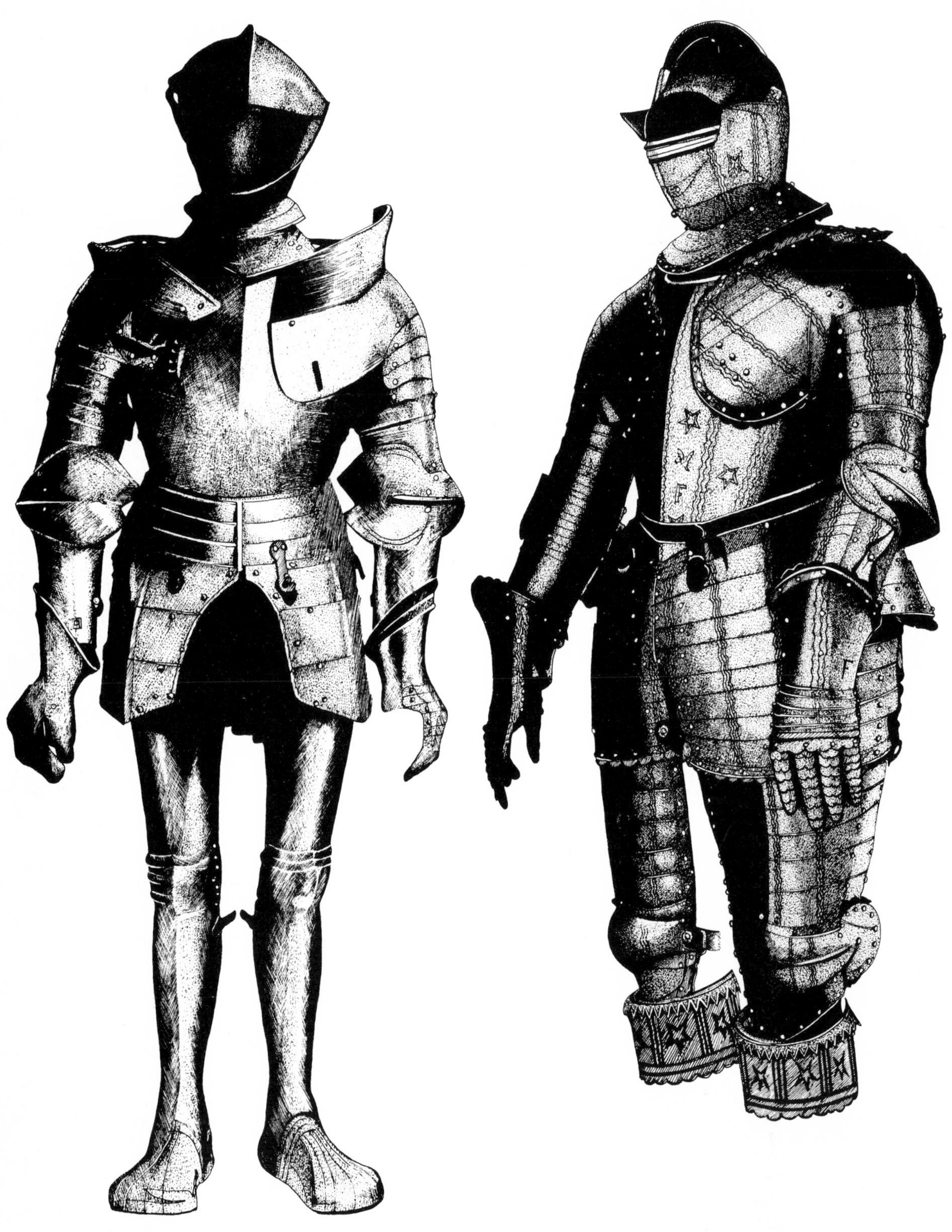

*Field armor for a horseman, made by Niccolò Silva, Italy, c. 1510. Musée de l'Armée, Paris.*

*Cuirassier armor ("three-quarter armor") of Don Diego Felipe de Guzman, Marquis of Leganés, N. Italy, c. 1627. Armeria Reale, Turin.*

# Early weapons and armor

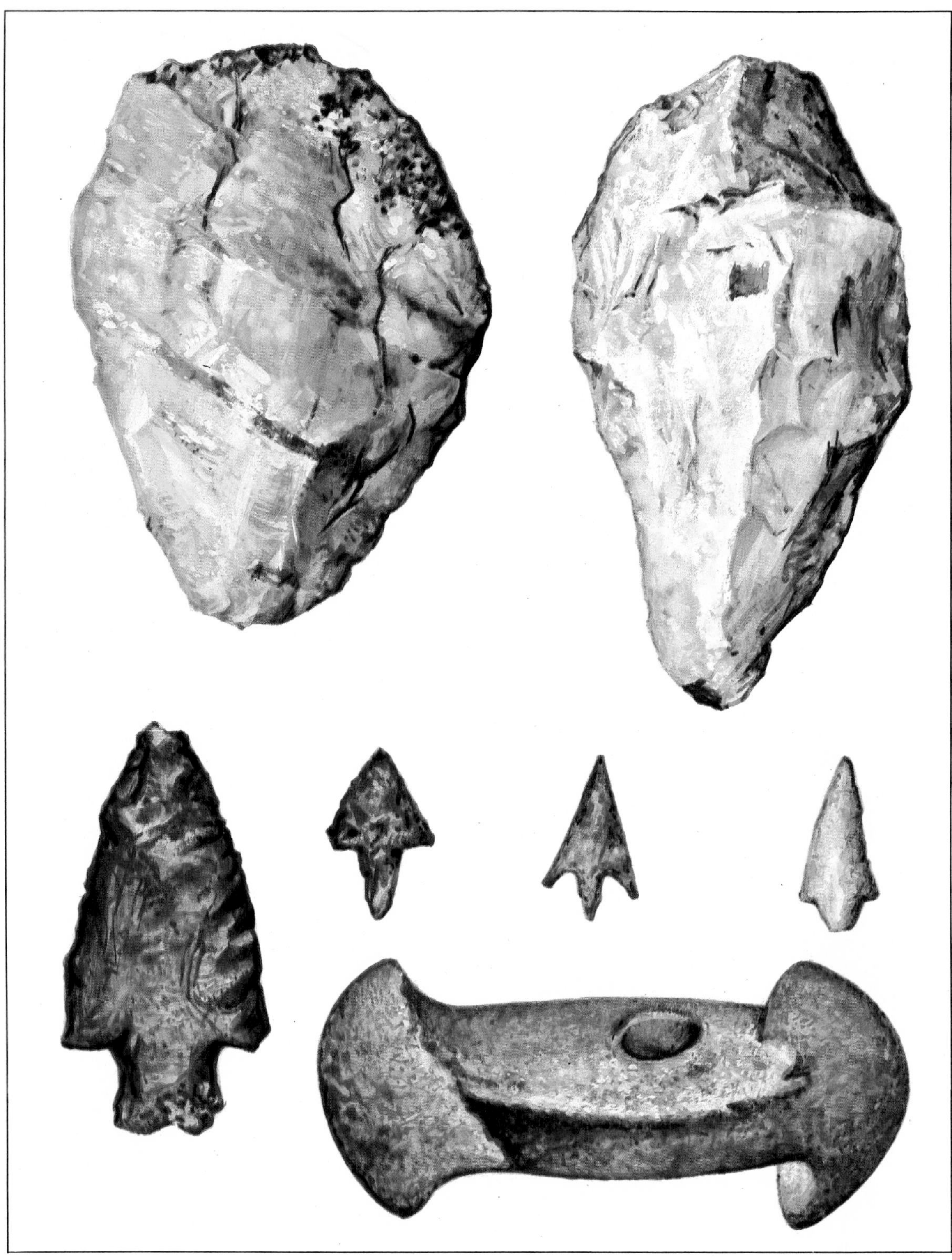

**Plate 1 Weapons of primitive man** (top) *Paleolithic bifacial chipped-flint hand axes. Dept. of Paleontology, Milan University.* (middle) *Various types of Paleolithic chipped-flint arrowheads. Aroldi Collection, Milan.* (bottom) *Neolithic polished-flint double-edged hatchet. Museo Civico, Bologna.*

**Plate 2 The conquest of metals** (top) *Bronze helmet, 7th–6th century* B.C. *Museo Archeologico, Florence.* (left) *Bronze Age sword, c. 9th century* B.C. *Dept. of Paleontology, Milan University.* (middle) *"Antenna"-type sword hilt, late Bronze Age. Aroldi Collection, Milan.* (right) *Anthropomorphic sword hilt of iron, Iron Age, La Tène I. Civico Museo Archeologico, Bergamo.*

**Plate 3 Weapons of the Creto-Mycenaean culture** (top) *Dagger with gold-decorated handle and damascened bronze blade depicting a leopard hunt, from a tomb near Pylos, c. 1500* B.C. (middle) *Detail of a damascened bronze dagger depicting a lion hunt, from a tomb in the Acropolis of Mycenae, c. 1570–50* B.C. (lower left) *Part of the gold furniture of a bronze sword depicting an acrobat, Palace of Mállia, Middle Minoan period, c. 1600* B.C. (lower right) *Bronze helmet with cheekpieces, from a tomb near Knossus, Late Minoan period.*

**Plate 4 Helmets of pre-Roman Italy** (top) *Greek-type Etruscan helmet with cheekpieces, 6th century* B.C. *Museo di Villa Giulia, Rome.* (bottom) *Crested Etruscan helmet from Veio, 8th–7th century* B.C. *Museo di Villa Giulia, Rome.*

**Plate 5 Gladiatorial helmets of classical Rome** (top) *Bronze helmet. Museo Nazionale, Naples.* (middle) *Bronze helmet decorated with episodes from the Trojan War. Museo Nazionale, Naples.* (bottom) *Bronze helmet. Museo Nazionale, Naples.*

**Plate 6 Roman armor** (top) *So-called jockey-cap iron helmet with movable cheekpieces (bucculae), third quarter of the 1st century* B.C. *National Museum of Wales, Cardiff.* (right) *Lorica segmentata, 1st century* B.C., *reconstruction by H. R. Robinson.* (lower left) *Parade helmet with mask visor, end of the 1st century* B.C., *reconstruction by H. R. Robinson.*

*Composite armor for a foot soldier, Nuremberg, c. 1550–60. Museo Stibbert, Florence.*

corslet of the first half of the 16th century. In the infantry version, the half armor usually had longer tassets buckled to a short skirt, thus easily detachable. An open burgonet without a buffe, a morion, or other light helmet was worn. The gauntlets were replaced by gloves. This type of armor was a direct precursor of the pikeman's corslet used throughout the 17th century, which was even more simplified since it consisted only of an open helmet, a gorget, and a cuirass with large tassets.

Although mass-produced soldier's armor had been known since the early 1500s, munition half armor, generally of poor quality and simple finish, was made on a larger scale from the middle of the century. There were many variations of munition armor, with most of them including a light helmet, e.g., an open burgonet or a morion; a gorget, with or without spaudlers; and a cuirass with tassets. Stored during peacetime in a local armory, these armors were often marked with the community's name, being issued to local militia when necessary. Matching parts of each half armor were sometimes stamped with the same number, an arrangement of dots, or other symbol.

*Armor "alla romana"* A special type of armor made around the middle of the 16th century purely for ceremonial parades and entertainments. A few very rare examples have survived to our day, a particularly fine one, made in 1546 by Bartolomeo Campi of Pesaro for Emperor Charles V, being in the Real Armería, Madrid. It was, in fact, an imitation of the ancient Roman officer's armor, with a so-called muscled cuirass and laminated vertical strips forming the skirt and the pauldrons. There were no legharnesses but, instead, special boots modeled after the Roman soldier's *caligae*. The helmet was a type of burgonet in the so-called antique style, whose design was rather freely adapted from the Roman helmet, the GALEA. Its outstanding feature was its superb decoration executed in a skillful combination of embossing, casting, chiseling, and encrusting with silver and gold.

*Papal Guard armor* A type of half armor worn from the second half of the 16th century to the late 18th, reintroduced in the 19th and still in use by members of the Papal Guard. Basically, it consists of a morion or a light burgonet and a cuirass without tassets. Officer's half armor can include a gorget, symmetrical pauldrons with complete vambraces, and tassets buckled to the cuirass. Parts of the armor are russeted, gilded, engraved, and occasionally embossed.

*Tournament armor* A type of armor used mainly during the first half of the 16th century in mock cavalry combat in the open field with rebated (blunted) weapons. Basically, it was a field armor to which were added a number of reinforcing pieces. There were no precise specifications for these, but the armor had to be suitably adapted to withstand the weapons to be used in a particular tournament. The most common reinforcing pieces were the following. For the head, protected by an armet or a close helmet: a GUPFE to reinforce the skull, and WRAPPER to cover the bevor and the front of the gorget (the wrapper was made either as one piece or in two parts: the lower, with gorget plates, and the upper, to cover the face guard of the helmet). For the trunk: a reinforcing breastplate, the placate, screwed onto the cuirass. For the left arm: a reinforcing pauldron with a haute-piece, a reinforcing cowter plate, the pasguard, and a special stiff, one-piece reinforcing gauntlet, the MANIFER. For the right hand: a locking gauntlet to prevent the weapon from being knocked out. Tournament armor could also include a steel round shield, the TARGE, when this was allowed by rules of the contest.

Tournaments fought in the 15th century in Germany

with rebated swords or wooden clubs (*Kolbenturnier*) required a special helmet, the great basnet, which had a large face guard made up of vertical bars to give necessary protection while providing good ventilation. The skull of such helmets was often made of hardened leather mounted on a steel framework.

*Armor for the barriers* A type of armor used in the 16th century for a tournament on foot fought over a wooden fence. Since the fence protected the lower part of the body, no legharnesses were worn in this form of contest. It was basically an ordinary field half armor, strong enough to withstand attack from such weapons as a poleax or spear and sometimes a mace or sword. This half armor consisted of a close helmet with gorget plates covering the gorget (alternatively a close helmet locked and rotating on the gorget, with a one-piece visor, was used); a sturdy cuirass with a stomach lame and tassets; symmetrical pauldrons, since the rest for the lance was not needed (though some contestants preferred to wear a spaudler on the right shoulder, instead of a large pauldron, to have more freedom of movement); and full vambraces and gauntlets.

*Armor for the German joust* (*Gestech*) A special armor required for each of two mounted contestants who would approach each other at full gallop, trying to score a hit with a heavy lance, which had a blunt head with prongs, the CORONEL. The basic parts of this armor included a heavy frog-mouthed helm with an eye slit placed high between the face guard and the skull; the wearer could see and aim his lance when his body was leaning forward during the charge, but he had to straighten himself up just before the impact to protect his eyes with the upper edge of the face guard. The helm was attached with screws or hasps to the breast and the back of the cuirass. The latter was flattened on the right side to fix the rest and the queue to couch the lance (this device being sometimes referred to in England as a "rest of advantage"). A central over-plate with laminated skirt and tassets was riveted to the lower edge of the breastplate to protect the abdomen and thighs. The shoulders were covered by spaudlers and besagews, and the lower arms by special full vambraces. On the left hand there was a POLDERMITTON, a stiff gauntlet with a shell protecting the elbow joint. A similar shell was riveted to the lower CANNON on the right arm, but no gauntlet was provided for the hand since it was covered by the round shield on the lance, the VAMPLATE. A small leather-covered wooden shield, shaped to protect the left side of the body and the hand with the bridle, was suspended from the cuirass. A well-padded large bumper, the *Stechsack*, was carried around the neck of the horse to protect its chest and the rider's legs; his groin was shielded by a wide steel-plated saddlebow. The backplate of the cuirass was relatively light and consisted of two riveted pieces with a strong bracket for the helm and various leather straps for the breastplate and other parts of the outfit.

An important feature of the equipment was the special wooden saddle covered with pigskin or leather. It was made so as to allow the rider to fall backward if he was hit by a powerful blow. In earlier models, there was no seat proper and the rider had to stand upright, being supported in this position by two curved side pieces extending from a very large saddlebow and protecting the rider from feet to waist.

*Armor for the German course with sharp lances* (*Scharfrennen*) A special type of armor (*Rennzeug*) used particularly during the late 15th and the first half of the 16th century in this form of jousting, both in the lists and in the open field. The style was largely based upon German field armor of the end of the 15th century, but the extremely dangerous nature of this contest, with no barrier between the opponents, made the use of a wide variety of reinforcing pieces essential.

The basic elements of the armor included a large sallet with a BROW REINFORCE and a bevor, the latter being screwed down to the cuirass. The cuirass was similar in construction to that of armor for the German joust (*Gestech*) and had much the same "rest of advantage" for the lance. Here, too, the lower part of the breastplate was covered by an over-plate from which hung a skirt and tassets; on the inside these parts were reinforced by a plate shaped below to the curve of the saddle seat. The

*Carabineer armor ("arquebus armor"), made by Lorenzo Saiano, N. Italy, c. 1680–90. Musée de l'Armée, Paris.*

backplate, made of two pieces, took the form of a body belt provided with leather straps for attachment of the breastplate and thigh defenses. The right arm was covered by a large semicircular vamplate reinforced by a riveted over-plate below the shaft of the lance. The left arm was protected by a special steel targe shaped so as to cover also the whole bevor and the left side of the breastplate down to the waist. The targe was screwed onto the bevor and the breast, thus reinforcing the armor on the left side, which in all forms of jousting was aimed at by the opponent. No vambrace was required in this type of armor. To defend thighs and knees, special heavy plates, properly shaped (*Dilgen*; called in English "tilting sockets"), were hung below the saddle. The saddle did not have a cantle, thus enabling the contestant to fall backward or from the horse, should he receive a powerful blow from his opponent.
*Tilt armor* A type of armor used during the 16th and early part of the 17th century for a joust in which the contestants were separated by a wooden barrier, or tilt, erected along the center line of the lists. Like the other

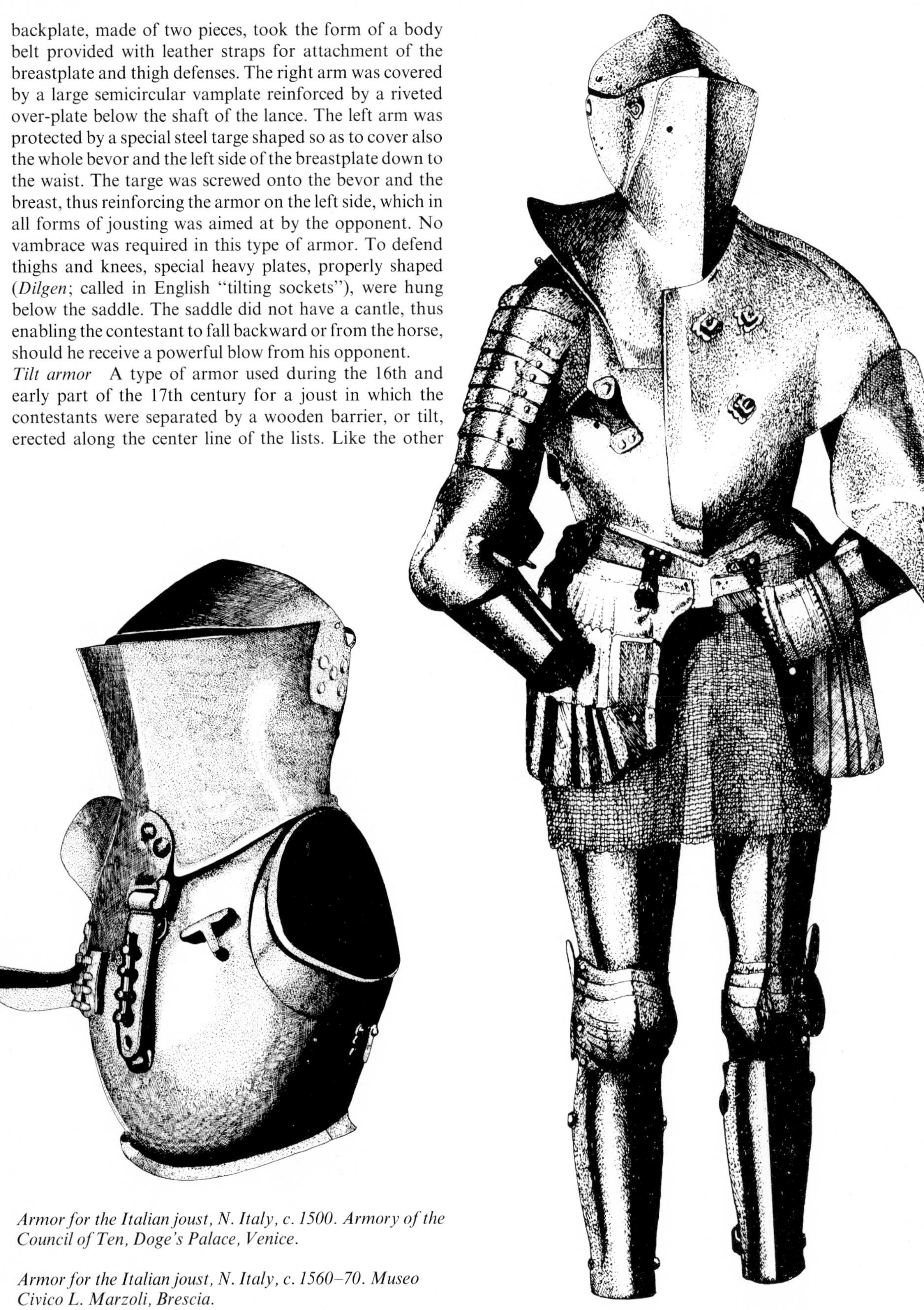

*Armor for the Italian joust, N. Italy, c. 1500. Armory of the Council of Ten, Doge's Palace, Venice.*

*Armor for the Italian joust, N. Italy, c. 1560–70. Museo Civico L. Marzoli, Brescia.*

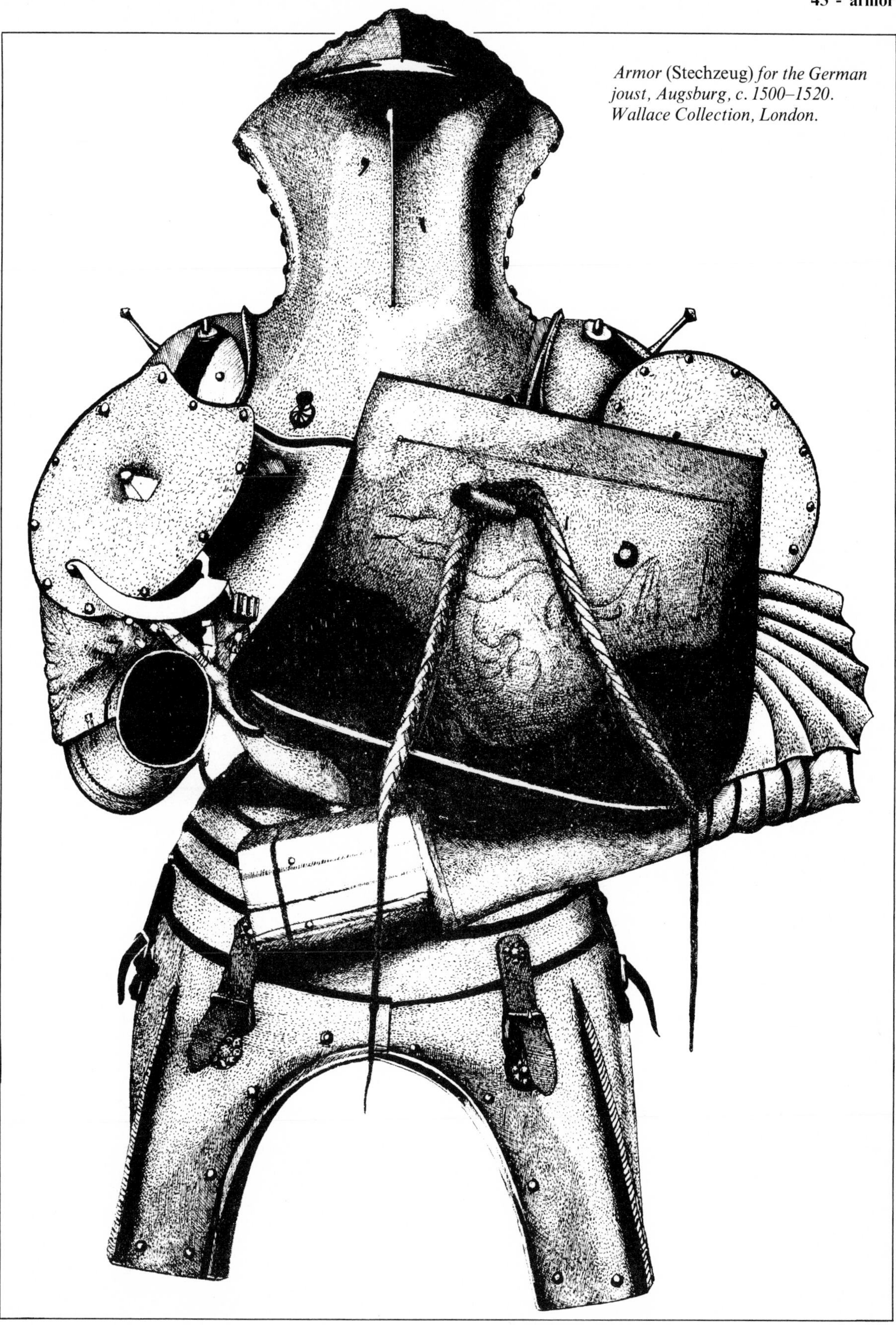

*Armor* (Stechzeug) *for the German joust, Augsburg, c. 1500–1520. Wallace Collection, London.*

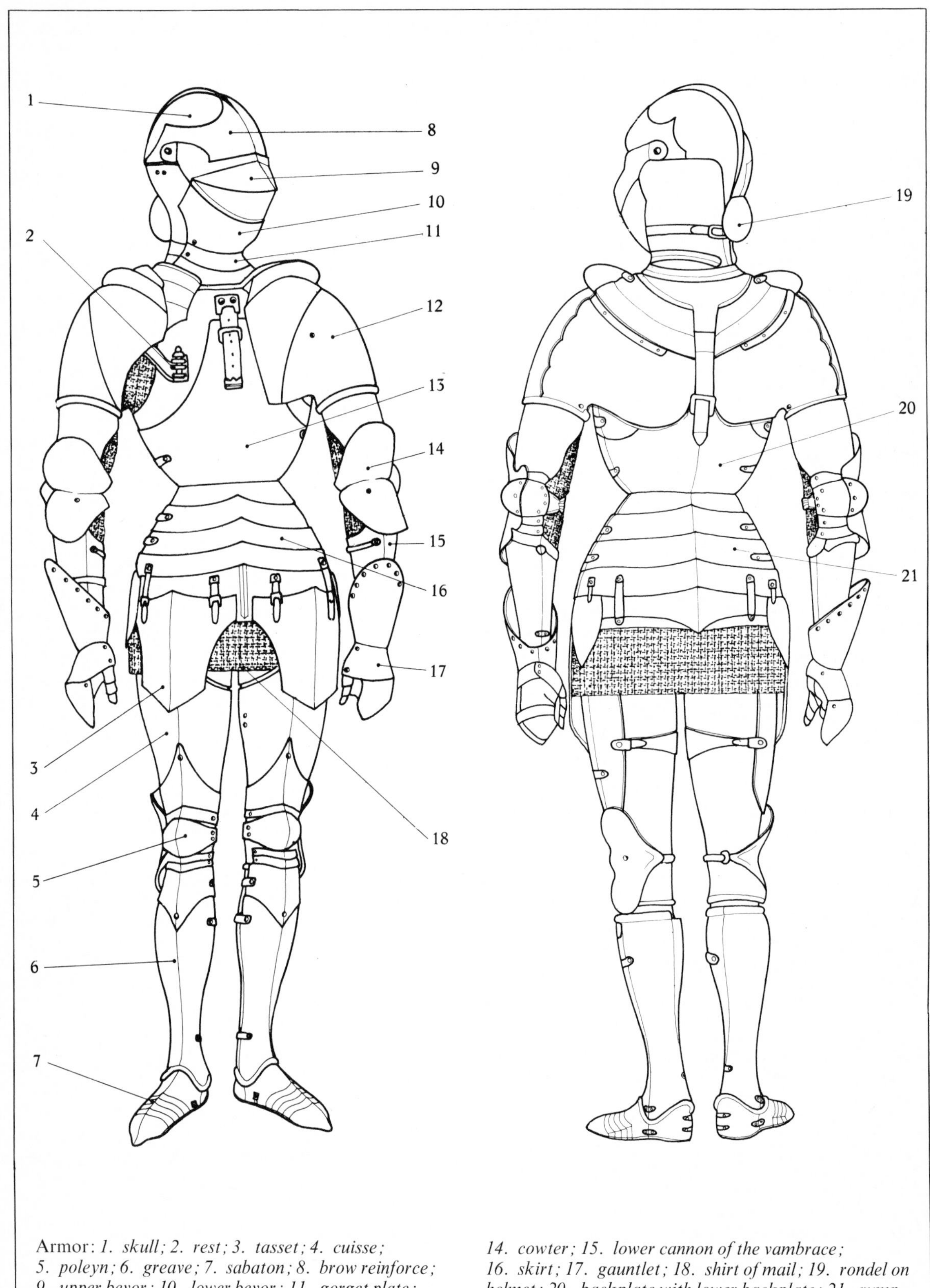


Armor: *1. skull; 2. rest; 3. tasset; 4. cuisse; 5. poleyn; 6. greave; 7. sabaton; 8. brow reinforce; 9. upper bevor; 10. lower bevor; 11. gorget plate; 12. pauldron; 13. breastplate with lower breastplate; 14. cowter; 15. lower cannon of the vambrace; 16. skirt; 17. gauntlet; 18. shirt of mail; 19. rondel on helmet; 20. backplate with lower backplate; 21. rump guard.*

forms of jousting, tilting necessitated special protection for the left side of the body, which was the target area of the opposing lance. Jousting across the tilt was introduced in Italy in the 1420s and spread to other countries of western Europe, being called in Germany *Welschgestech über die Planke* ("Italian joust over the tilt").

Tilt armor was built up like a full field armor, with many of its basic parts made exceptionally strong, and was provided with a number of reinforcing pieces. The head was protected by a close helmet locked and turning on the gorget; its skull had a brow reinforce, and its one-piece visor had a trapdoor on the right side for ventilation between bouts. An alternative form of helmet, used in the Italian version of tilt armor, was a modified basnet constructed like the close helmet just described but with bevor and skull extended downward into massive plates, which were screwed onto the cuirass. The breastplate had a flange shielding the right shoulder, a rigid rest for the lance, and a number of threaded holes for attaching the GRANDGUARD. This important reinforcing piece, made in one or two parts, covered the lower left side of the helmet, the gorget, the left shoulder, and the left side of the breast.

To increase freedom of movement, spaudlers were used instead of winged pauldrons to protect the shoulders, but the left one was well covered by the grandguard or a steel targe (described below), while the right spaudler had a special reinforcing over-plate. Full vambraces with sturdy mitten gauntlets also had some additional pieces. The right cowter was reinforced with an elbow guard—a shaped plate screwed onto the front of the cowter; the hand and forearm were well defended by the vamplate. A similar but much larger elbow guard, the pasguard, covered all the left cowter and a good part of the arm. Full legharnesses completed the tilt armor.

The Italian version of this suit used a very large grandguard made usually, but not always, in one piece and supplemented with a kind of over-vambrace, or grand pasguard, covering not only the left cowter but also substantial parts of both cannons of the vambrace. Alternative defense of the left side was provided by a concave steel targe, instead of a grandguard, screwed onto the breast and overlapping the shoulder. The targe was either forged or covered with trelliswork to prevent a hitting lance head from slipping off. When the targe was used, a smaller pasguard was attached to the left cowter. Another reinforcement for an Italian-style tilt armor was a stomach lame with an over-tasset, screwed onto the left side of the breastplate. In English-style tilt armor, among reinforcing pieces were a grandguard, in one or two pieces, a large pasguard, and a manifer entirely overlapping the left gauntlet.

*Foot-combat armor* A special suit of armor worn by each of two contestants fighting in the lists with poleaxes, spears, maces, swords, and daggers. Foot combat practiced in the 15th and 16th centuries historically derived from knightly duels often fought to the death. It was the most dangerous form of all competitions and required an armor giving top-to-toe protection to the wearer. In the 15th century a field armor was used for foot combat, but instead of a field helmet (an armet or a sallet) a great basnet was worn, equipped with a globular face guard pierced with many holes for ventilation. The great basnet continued in use until the mid-16th century, being provided with a more rigid visor, often of the "bellows" form. In the early 1500s German armorers developed a foot-combat armor which had large symmetrical pauldrons with haute-pieces, full closed vambraces with laminated joint defense opposite the cowters, and full legharnesses with closed cuisses and laminated defense opposite the poleyns. As an additional protection, the TONLET—a long circular laminated skirt flaring toward its lower edge like a bell—covered the body from waist to knees. Instead of the tonlet, steel breeches were occasionally made for foot-combat armor in the first half of the 16th century. They consisted of a laminated defense shaped to the hips and rump; the upper lames were attached to the cuirass while the lower were locked with turning pins to the top of the cuisses. A steel CODPIECE protected the groin.

As an alternative to the basnet, a close helmet with a reinforcing bevor was used with foot-combat armor, and the pauldrons were sometimes doubled by the addition of over-plates. The locking gauntlet for the right hand prevented the weapon from being knocked out. In the later part of the 16th century, traditional forms of armor for foot combat were gradually replaced by a sturdy field armor with long tassets, worn with high boots ("three-quarter armor"). Understandably, large symmetrical pauldrons and full vambraces with laminated joints were preserved for this contest, and special gauntlets with flanged cuffs were worn to prevent a blade from slipping into the gauntlet when the arm was raised for an attack or a parry.

*Chinese armor* Throughout history some form of body protection has been employed in China, as is evidenced by specimens of bronze helmets from the Shang Dynasty (second millennium B.C.). The first regulations governing the work of court armorers date from the Chou Dynasty, which ended in the 3rd century B.C. In those early times, two kinds of hide armor predominated. One was *kia*, a sleeveless coat, and the other was *kiai*, a tunic made up of small scales. To make a kia cuirass, a tailor's dummy was first constructed; pieces of rhinoceros hide were cut and

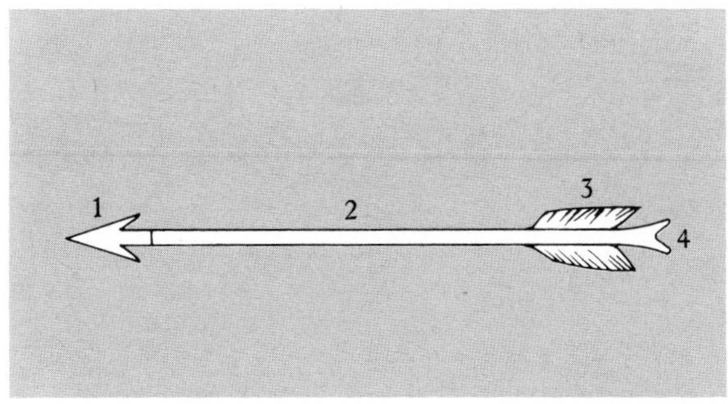


Arrow. *1. head or pile; 2. shaft or stele; 3. feathers or fletchings; 4. nock.*

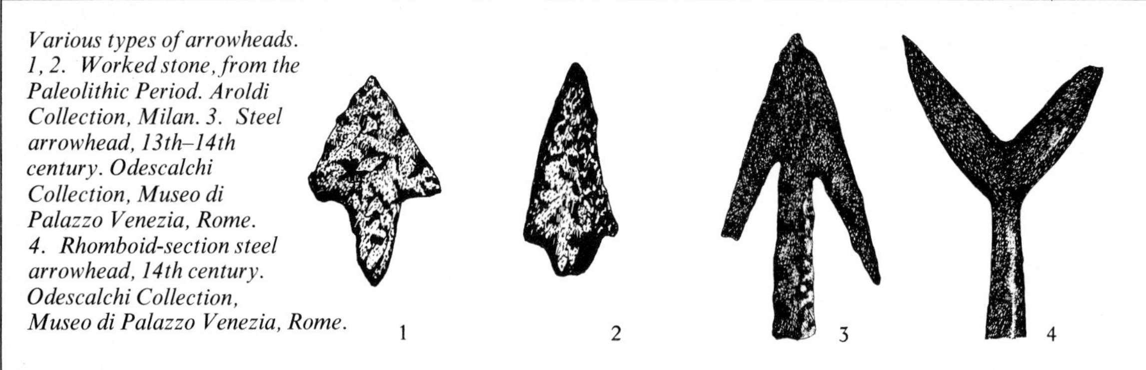


*Various types of arrowheads. 1, 2. Worked stone, from the Paleolithic Period. Aroldi Collection, Milan. 3. Steel arrowhead, 13th–14th century. Odescalchi Collection, Museo di Palazzo Venezia, Rome. 4. Rhomboid-section steel arrowhead, 14th century. Odescalchi Collection, Museo di Palazzo Venezia, Rome.*

fitted to the dummy, in several layers, which were then sewn around the edges. The finished cuirass reached to the knees, the lower part forming a skirt. The Chinese continued to use rhinoceros skin until it became scarce, around the time of the collapse of the T'ang Dynasty (A.D. 618–907), when buffalo or oxhide, sometimes lacquered, was used instead.

Kiai was made from small leather scales, rounded at the lower edge, which overlapped each other like tiles and were fastened to a fabric or soft leather. From the period of the Han Dynasty (206 B.C.–A.D. 220), kiai armor was made of copper, bronze, or iron scales. Mail armor—which had been brought from Persia through Central Asia—found only limited use in China.

Lamellar armor—known as *t'ie cha*—was also used in China; examples were among the archeological finds from the Han Dynasty. This consisted of small iron or leather lames laced together with thongs, such construction having reached China from the Middle East via the nomads of Central Asia.

The emperor Wu (140–87 B.C.) reorganized the Chinese cavalry and ordered the introduction of scale and lamellar armor, although leather helmets continued to be used for a long time. From clay figurines we know that even horses were covered with scaled defenses, and fully armed horsemen looked very much like Roman cataphracts.

The Mongol invasions, from the 12th century, had a powerful influence upon the development of Chinese arms and armor. Quite common were armors in which leather, scales, lames, fabric, and fur were combined. Loose clothes were often worn over armor, in which the lamellar construction predominated over a long period. It was probably around the 12th or 13th century that a kind of banded armor, *t'ao*, was introduced into China. Judging from the rare descriptions and a few paintings, t'ao armor consisted of horizontal iron bands resembling the "segmented" Roman LORICA.

A type of defense that was unique to China was the paper armor invented during the T'ang period. This was officially recognized as an efficient defense during the Sung Dynasty (960–1279) and, later still, in southern China during the Ming Dynasty (1368–1644). To make this seemingly frail armor, ten to fifteen sheets of paper were glued together, then cut and sewn into a sleeveless coat which would probably have withstood a musket ball.

More sumptuous was a kind of brigandine, the *ting kia*, meaning "armor with nails." This was usually worn by generals and other high-ranking officers and court officials of the Ming period. Some splendid examples of ting kia, taken from Peking's Summer Palace by the French in 1861, are now in the Musée de l'Armée in Paris. Helmets with tall, conical bowls of silvered copper with mounts of pierced and engraved copper gilt, topped with crests of red hair and stiff tails of sable-like rushes, feathers, and fine netting, were part of the accoutrements for this armor. The ting kia itself was a textile garment underlain with square, medium-sized plates of iron, copper, or leather attached with rivets, whose rounded and usually gilded heads were visible on the outside. Sometimes the plates were lined with a fabric. This brigandine normally consisted of a short jacket, with or without sleeves, with a large collar and semicircular shoulder pieces, and there was also an ankle-length skirt, like a divided apron. Reinforcing pieces were frequently used, such as a rectangular plate over the genitals. This type of armor had close counterparts in the Indian and Persian brigandines known as "coats of a thousand nails." The ting kia marked the final phase in the long history of Chinese armor.

**arms** A broad generic term to indicate any artifact used as a means of defense or offense. Defensive arms would include mainly protective items such as all forms of armor and shields. Offensive arms cover a very wide field and can be divided into groups such as: edged weapons—knives, swords, dirks, daggers, and bayonets; staff weapons—spears, halberds, lances, clubs, maces, axes; firearms—guns of all kinds including ordnance, artillery, machine guns, pistols, etc.

**arquebus** (or **harquebus**) Its name deriving originally from the German *Hakenbüchse*, "gun with a hook," the arquebus was a type of 14th–15th century gun with a hooklike projection on the underside of the barrel. However, the word is usually used to describe a light gun which could be fired without the use of a rest. References to "arcubusariis" are found in Latin documents as early as 1417. Later, "arquebus" was used to describe various kinds of light guns, as opposed to the heavier musket, introduced in the mid-16th century; and it is sometimes found in 16th-century documents to indicate a wheel-lock rather than a matchlock gun. The English Council of War Order issued in 1630 states that the dimensions of an arquebus should be: a barrel of 75 cm. (2½ ft.), a bore of 17, and an overall length of 90 cm. (3 ft.).

The arquebus declined in popularity during the first quarter of the 17th century and was superseded by the carbine before the middle of the century. The name "harquebusier" continued to be used during the English Civil War (1642–46), however, to denote a type of mounted troops who were armed with carbines.

**arrest** *See* REST.

**arrow** A missile weapon consisting, in its original form, of a pointed wooden shaft which was shot from a bow. Before long it underwent certain fundamental alterations which turned it from a simple projectile into a more complex weapon, made up of the various elements which constitute its present typology.

As far back as the Neolithic Age, the shaft was fitted with a head made of a harder material—bone or splintered stone (flint, obsidian)—which was almond- or ogive-shaped, or rhomboid. This type in turn gave rise to triangular heads, with straight or hooked barbs; these heads usually had a short tang which was inserted inside the end of the arrow shaft, then fixed with glues and bindings. The arrival of bronze did not cause any formal alterations and stone heads continued to be used for some time, not least because of the staggered spread of the use of this metal. The greater possibilities of working bronze led to increased variety and specialization of the heads, depending on the use of the arrow—for battle or for hunting. A different method of attaching the head to the shaft was also devised: the head was made with a socket, and the arrow shaft was fitted inside it. The iron arrowheads, of which there is evidence in the Mediterranean basin dating back to about the 6th century B.C., initially copied the bronze designs but gradually developed their own style, based principally on the greater malleability of iron.

It is probably correct to attribute the appearance of highly specialized heads, depending on the use of the arrow and the type of bow, to the advances made in the blacksmith's art in the 13th to 15th centuries. From this period we find simple cone-shaped heads, rhomboid heads, hooked heads (resembling fishhooks), heads with variously curved barbs, heads in the shape of willow leaves, triangular and flat bladed heads, crescent-shaped heads, and, more rarely, petal-shaped and battering heads.

The shaft (or stele) of the arrow, which was initially made with a straight stick or reed, was later fashioned from a wooden block, usually of ash because of that wood's strength and elasticity, and sometimes, depending on the period, turned on a lathe. The shaft might also be made of metal, forming a single piece with the arrowhead, especially when it was shot from particular bows; at the rear end it had a notch—known as a nock—in which the bowstring was fitted, this part often being made of a different material (bone or horn) to stand up better to the stress involved. In European arrows the nock was U-shaped, loosely fitting the bowstring. In the Middle East, nocks with a narrower opening than the bowstring itself were preferred; slight pressure had to be applied to the bowstring to fit it into the nock. This made it possible to

*Bronze aspis, Cyprus, 7th century* B.C.

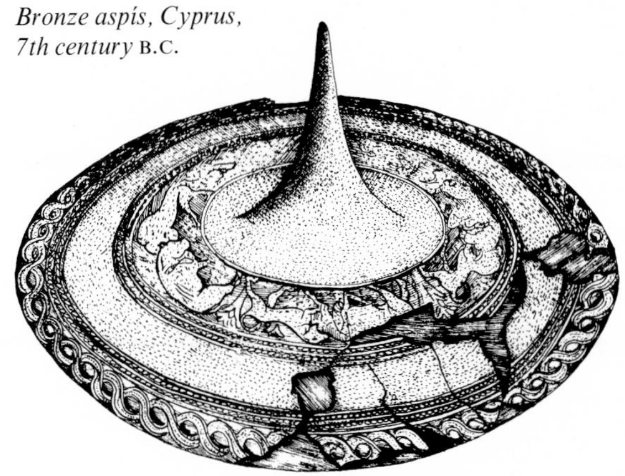

get the bow ready with the arrow already nocked, and held in one hand, while the other controlled the horse, for example; the reins were lain on the horse's neck just for a few seconds to pull, aim, and shoot.

It is thought that as far back as in the days of Homer the arrow was fitted with feathers or vanes; these were an important feature, both for maintaining the direction of the arrow and for its range. Two or more feathers set coaxially to the shaft create an effect of aerodynamic lift as the arrow flies; if the feathers are set slightly diagonally to the axis of the shaft they give the arrow a rotating movement, which has the effect of stabilizing it in flight. The feathers used were usually taken from a goose's wing. For a brief period parrot feathers were used, as were pressed paper and leather. Arrows or darts shot with a blowpipe or blowgun have a wad of cotton in place of the vanes; this wad wedges against the bore of the pipe (like a packing ring in a piston), thus reducing the dispersion of the air blown through it.

Apart from the large darts shot by war machines, and sometimes by hand as well, the size of arrows varies a great deal, but is determined essentially by the type of bow: they are slender and long, 70–100 cm. (27–40 in.) for the English type of longbow which was used in northern Europe; 50–70 cm. (20–27 in.) for the continental bow; and shorter and stronger for the crossbow (see BOLT). In addition to the ordinary arrow described above there were also arrows designed to produce special effects; particularly important were the incendiary arrows and bolts (see MALLEOLUS), used in earliest times, then abandoned in the West, and revived from the time of the Crusades onward. The fire was produced by soaking a wad of tow in a bituminous substance; this was fixed just beneath the head, and lit before the arrow was shot. As a weapon of war the arrow was superseded by firearms, although it coexisted with them for some time. It was still being used early in the 19th century by auxiliary Asian units in the Russian army.

The bow and arrow have come back into use for hunting and sporting purposes, although they have undergone certain modifications in materials and forms. In a modern arrow the shaft may be made of fiberglass, light metal alloys, or wood; the shape of the head varies depending on the use, and the usual length is 80–100 cm. (31–40 in.).

**arsons** The upward-arching parts of a saddle designed to keep the rider from being unhorsed when in action and to give him some protection from the blows and thrusts in combat. The front bow, or saddlebow, which was considerably higher than the hind bow, or cantle, curved inward to follow the shape of the horse's shoulders. The upper part—which was usually rounded but was sometimes squared—was raised to protect the horseman's abdomen and chest; it was here that a pommel might be fitted, for the rider to steady himself, or a ring to take the reins. The semicircular hind bow, also curved to accommodate the horse's crupper, was shaped to the seated position of the man; it was usually rather low but padded and occasionally had side cushions. Usually constructed on a wooden framework, the arson was covered in leather or some decorative fabric such as velvet or damask. A particularly lavish version might be decorated with worked metals and precious or semiprecious stones. Arsons of war saddles were covered with iron plates on the outside, which were frequently etched or chased, as a fitting accompaniment to the rider's other accoutrements.

**Artillery**

In this section the history of artillery is examined in detail. It contains full technical descriptions of modern artillery, especially in regard to locking and obturation systems in breechloading artillery. Details of individual pieces can be found under the headings CANNON; CARRONADE; CULVERIN; GUN MOUNTINGS; MORTAR; RIBAULD. In addition, see the section on artillery in the Bibliography.

**artillery** A collective name given to all heavy guns and those military units that use them.

*History*

The most ancient of all artillery, virtually corresponding to the oldest known firearms, were iron pots from which heavy arrows—often incendiary—were hurled.

In the 14th century, artillery—although rather small—was being cast in bronze or made by means of a trapezoidal construction of iron rods which were packed around a temporary core like the staves of a barrel and encircled with iron hoops. A few interesting details as to weight and costs of such artillery have been found in some English documents dated about 1350. The smaller guns (*gunnae parvae*) weighed between 15 and 25 lbs. (6–12 kg.), exclusive of the mounting; the medium-sized (*gunnae de pondere medio*) weighed between 25 and 50 lbs. (12–24 kg.); the next size between 50 and 100 lbs. (24–48 kg.); and the heaviest of all (*gunnae maximae*) between 100 and 300 lbs. (48–140 kg.). The majority of these appear to have been made from a copper alloy generally referred to as cuprum, although some were probably made of brass (*latten*) or bronze (*aresme*), and the average price was about 3 pence per pound.

During the siege of Calais, Edward III employed at least twenty pieces of artillery. These were mainly used to block access to the port and thus cut off supplies to the city, which was forced to surrender on August 3, 1347, because the people were starving. Some bombardment did take place, however, in which a total of 3 quintals (about 6 cwt. or 329 kg.) of saltpeter and 1.5 quintals (about 3 cwt. or 164 kg.) of sulfur were consumed, at the enormous cost of 325 pounds sterling.

Toward the end of the century, heavy bombards (or bombardes)—the first cannon—had come into use and were extensively employed in siege operations with great success. During the war between the Genoese and Venetians that was fought at Chioggia in 1379, the Venetians brought two bombards into action, the larger of which fired stone cannonballs weighing 88.5 kg. (195 lbs.) and had a caliber of about 34 cm. (14 in.).

The first makers of artillery in bronze were bell founders, since it was they who had the greatest knowledge of casting at that period. But this meant production had to be limited to fairly small cannon. Iron could only be used as a wrought (forged) metal, because its high point of fusion made it impossible for uniform results to be achieved in casting—and uniformity of thickness throughout the length of the barrel was absolutely essential since it would be subjected to considerable internal pressure. The system of construction with wrought-iron rods, however, presented a big problem in that the barrel remained open at both ends because of the

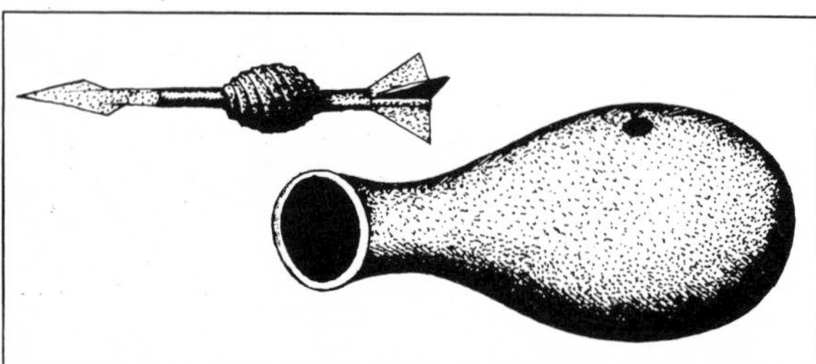

*Small bronze handgun from about the 14th century, found at Loshult, Sweden.*

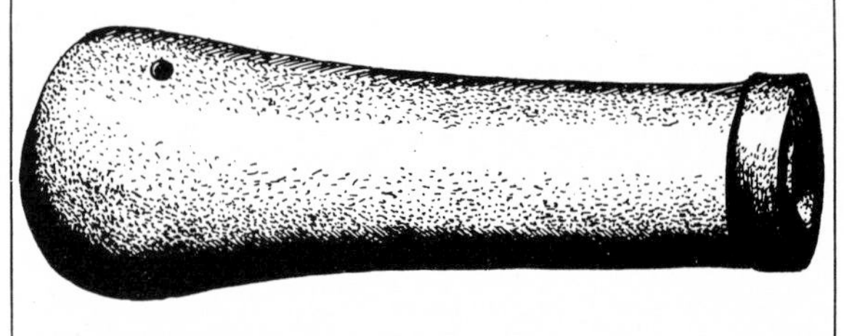

*One of the oldest known pieces of artillery is this iron cannon, illustrated in a manuscript of 1327 by W. Milemete, at Christ Church, Oxford.*

*Fourteenth-century Italian cannon with wooden carriage and rudimentary elevating gear.*

mandrel or core around which the blacksmith had to clamp the rods with the red-hot hoops. In consequence, bombards were made in two pieces—the "tube," or barrel, and the "cannon," or powder chamber. The powder chamber was plugged into the breech and either wedged or screwed into position. Thus evolved the first breech loading cannon.

Throughout the 15th century, the bulky pieces of artillery that had been devised were of little practical use except to a besieging army. They might be dragged into position before a gate or similar weak point in a city wall or fortress that was to be attacked, but every change of siting and laying (i.e., training the gun in the right direction for firing) was always a lengthy and complicated operation. The small cannon or mortars were of doubtful efficacy and the large ones so clumsy to handle that it was to be a long time before they could be employed on the battlefield—at most, they were sometimes moved to an emplacement from which they could defend troops in entrenched positions.

Toward the middle of the century, ribaulds, or "death organs," made their appearance. These consisted of a number of barrels—possibly twenty or more—mounted on a trail or gun carriage. This multibarreled weapon could either be fired from all barrels simultaneously or in quick succession. A major weakness, however, was the length of time required to reload it. Although ribaulds are known to have been used occasionally, they were never very highly regarded.

Advances in weaponry came but slowly, and bombards were the most important pieces of artillery being developed. This meant that while the military forces were relatively well equipped with siege artillery, they were not always as successful in defensive operations. Even at the beginning of the 15th century, well-defended cities with stout walls were able to withstand a siege for several months, two examples of this being Rouen, which was finally starved into submission in 1419, and Meaux, besieged in 1421–22. The projectiles fired from the bombards were roughly hewn spherical masses of limestone or marble, which meant that the difference in diameter between barrel and projectile might be considerable. Small artillery, on the other hand, fired round missiles of lead, wrought iron, or other metal.

The propellant being used was known as black powder—or gunpowder, as it came to be called. It consisted of saltpeter (niter), sulfur, and charcoal, which were simply mixed together in rather uncertain proportions. When the powder was being carried by troops on the move, the jolting caused the ingredients to stratify, and it always had to be well mixed again before it could be used effectively. It is fairly certain that a high proportion of charcoal was used in order to produce rather slow ignition. From examination of such artillery of this period as has survived, it is not difficult to understand why even gunpowder of the 4–1–1 type (see chart, p. 52) would have been far too powerful for early guns with their weak construction.

*Cannon probably dating from the 15th century, mounted on a primitive form of carriage (reconstruction).*

It was, of course, necessary to have some kind of base for these cannon, and long-barreled bombards were mounted on wooden blocks or "boxes" and secured, in the early days, with ropes, which were later replaced by iron hoops. The blocks stood directly on the ground, and elevation of the gun was achieved either by pushing wooden wedges under the breech or by building up the ground. A short-barreled bombard would have been positioned on a strong wooden plank that was sometimes fitted with two wheels, which, apart from making it easier to trail the gun, facilitated elevation. A great many such gun carriages were fitted with "mantlets"—wooden partitions which could be slued around to protect the gunner from the enemy's arrows or bolts.

Artillery was to make considerable progress during the 15th century, especially toward the end. It was now universally accepted and was regarded as indispensable for besieging purposes. It was also playing an increasingly important part in pitched battles. The bombard continued to hold pride of place until the end of the century, but alongside it was a range of weapons with a smaller bore that were considerably more manageable: curtals, falcons, sakers, culverins, and cannon were just some of the names given to this extensive group of weapons, which were inclined to be given local names according to the area in which they found themselves.

By now even very large bronze pieces were no longer beyond the skills of metal founders, although this was not the reason for the fall-off in the use of wrought iron. In 1409–11, Pasquier den Kick—*Donderbusmeester* ("Master of the Thunderbox") to Antoine de Brabant—cast a bombard weighing 35 tons, while the famous Dulle Griet, which was used by the inhabitants of Ghent in 1452 during the siege of Audenarde—and which can still be admired today in the Flemish capital—weighed over 16 tons.

During the siege of Constantinople in 1453, Sultan Mohammed II employed sixty-two heavy pieces, mostly of bronze, which were able to fire cannonballs weighing up to 91 kg. (200 lbs.). Within six weeks the renowned triple wall of the city had been demolished at several points, and Christian Europe was stunned to learn of the capure and bestial sacking that followed.

When it came to employing artillery in the field, the French troops of Charles VII (1422–61) were well in advance of other countries, and it was owing to this superior ability that they were able to turn the final important battles of the Hundred Years War to their advantage. Among the creators of the powerful French artillery—apart from the king himself—were Artur de Richemont and the famous Bureau brothers. Jean Bureau is credited with having standardized gun calibers to take projectiles of 2, 4, 8, 16, 32, and 64 lbs., thus eliminating the utter confusion that had previously existed. In the French army, the greater part of the artillery was deployed on the following basis: (a) heavy ordnance was formed into an artillery park and remained apart from the troops, until it was to be brought into action for besieging operations; and (b) light artillery was divided between the various units, supporting both infantry and cavalry in all their engagements on the battlefield.

Charles the Bold, Duke of Burgundy (1467–77), also did a great deal to improve his own artillery and to make the most of the latest developments. But he was ill-advised to employ his heavy guns in terrain for which they were totally unsuited and against a formidable enemy, the Swiss infantry. The results were disastrous, as his three last major battles were all complete failures. These were the battles of Grandson, Morat, and the one that was to prove fatal to the duke, Nancy. These defeats did not, however, stem the increasing use of this relatively new means of making war.

When the French king Charles VIII led his troops on an expedition into Italy in 1494, it was not the number or quality of his heavy guns but their method of transportation that most amazed all onlookers. Paolo Giovio, in his *Historiae sui temporis* ("History of Our Times"), includes this description in his account of the French army's entry into Rome: "But above all everyone marveled at the thirty-six artillery guns on carriages pulled by horses at an incredible speed over flat and uneven surfaces alike. Most of them were eight feet long and the bronze of which they were made weighed six thousand pounds. They were called cannon and could fire cannonballs as big as a man's head. Then there were the

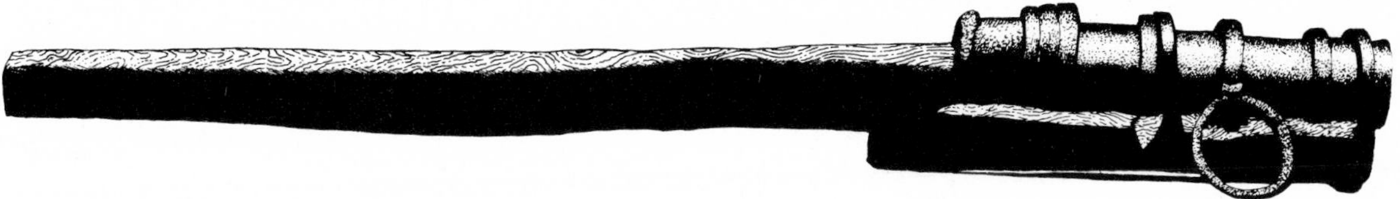

*Fifteenth-century hand cannon, found in the Tiber in Rome.*

*Fifteenth-century French breechloading cannon (carriage reconstructed).*

culverins, which were half as long again but had narrower barrels and could fire rather smaller balls. After these came the falcons of various sizes, the smallest of which was capable of firing cannonballs the size of an orange. Each of these pieces [of ordnance] was mounted between two great axles [trunnions], with the clasps on top, being suspended by their grips in such a way that, in taking aim to fire, the cannon would swivel on its pivot. The carriages of the small guns ran on two wheels, while the heavy ones had four, of which the two at the rear could be raised or lowered [to the ground] in order to increase or reduce speed."

The innovation of gun carriages was of great advantage both from the strategic and tactical point of view as well as in financial terms. The Venetians, for instance, who had been involved in some military campaigns in Romagna in 1499, frequently dismantled the cannon and curtals in order to transport them at less expense.

One of the most important technical improvements in large guns was undoubtedly the introduction of trunnions in the latter 15th century. These large pivots made it possible not only to mount the gun onto the carriage comparatively simply but also facilitated vertical pointing. Before the invention of trunnions, mobile gun carriages consisted of a solid wooden beam whose front end was mounted on a wooden axle fitted with two wheels and whose other end rested on the ground. The beam was shaped in such a way that when the rear was laid down, the front returned to a horizontal position, and it was on this frontal part that the gun was fixed with strong iron hoops. Although transportation and pointing had now been made easier than ever before, change of elevation meant either raising the rear part of the beam (to be known later as the "trail") or lowering it into a depression dug in the ground.

When cannon came to be equipped with trunnions, however, they were mounted and transported on gun carriages on which the single beam was replaced by two parallel ones. These were positioned sufficiently far apart to be able to support the gun between them, which was held in place by transoms and crossbeams. Toward the front of each of these two beams was an ironclad groove into which the trunnions were slotted. Thus all that was needed to adjust the angle of fire were a few wedges, which could be inserted or withdrawn as required, between the breech and one of the transoms.

As Giovio observed, toward the end of the 15th century the French medium artillery were using cast-iron cannonballs, and the advantages offered by this new type of projectile were considerable. Production was speeded up and, in time, was to prove more economical. The effect of cast-iron cannonballs on an enemy's fortifications was

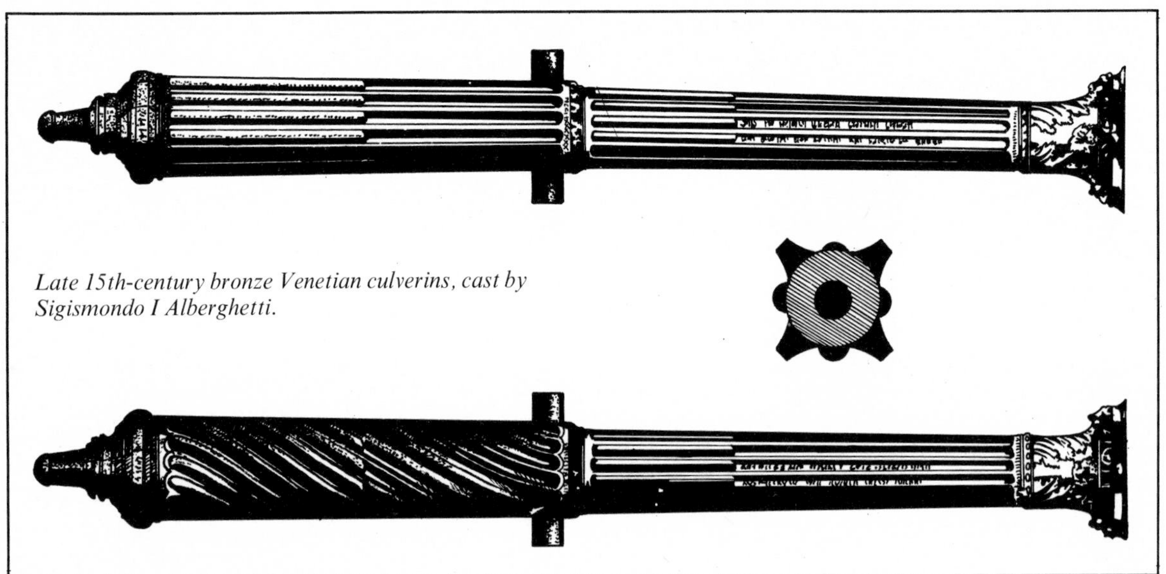

*Late 15th-century bronze Venetian culverins, cast by Sigismondo I Alberghetti.*

vastly superior to that of stone missiles. And gunpowder, too, was slowly being improved as the proportions of the three ingredients became stabilized into various formulae appropriate to the different classes of guns. Francesco di Giorgio Martini, in his treatise on civil and military architecture (late 16th century), cites the following proportions:

| | Saltpeter | Sulfur | Charcoal |
|---|---|---|---|
| For heavy bombards | $\frac{2}{3}$ | $\frac{1}{3}$ | 1 |
| For medium bombards, curtals, cannon, springals, etc. | 4 | 2 | 1 |
| For culverins, basilisks, etc. | 4 | $1\frac{1}{2}$ | 1 |
| For hand firearms | 7 | $1\frac{1}{2}$ | 1 |

The last of these formulae contains a little too much saltpeter in relation to what would, in theory, be necessary, while the others contain too little. In each case, the proportions have been calculated on the basis of the quantity of saltpeter, which determines the combustibility of the powder, the amount of saltpeter in turn being controlled by the caliber of the gun—the smaller the bore, the greater the proportion. It must be remembered, however, that these mixtures were of a relatively low strength since they were intended for guns fashioned by craftsmen whose technological knowledge was still fairly limited.

### *The 16th Century*

By the 16th century, the artillery had become the third indispensable element in the fighting forces, alongside the

*Wrought-iron breechloading cannon, one of the guns aboard the* Mary Rose *when she sank in 1545.*

cavalry and infantry. The period of exorbitantly costly experiments—such as the two-piece heavy bombards—had ended and ordnance pieces had reached a form which, by the end of the Italian Wars (1494–1559), was to remain substantially unchanged for three and a half centuries. Of course, the heavy bombards did not disappear immediately, and in 1509, during the siege of Padua, two pieces were brought into use again by Emperor Maximilian I, the *Gnad dir Gott* ("May God have mercy on you") and *Die shöne Käthl* ("the beautiful Kathy"), which fired granite balls 46 cm. (18 in.) in diameter. Generally speaking, though, the difficulty of making long barrels of large caliber was fully recognized, and it was considered preferable to sacrifice size for precision, manageability, and above all, power. In several of the more important battles fought during the War of the League of Cambrai, the artillery played an outstanding part—such as in the battle of Ravenna (1512) when the French fire drove the Spanish cavalry out of their fortified positions and forced them to attack.

A general picture of the guns in use during the first half of the century can be gained from a treatise on powder and guns by Vannoccio Biringuccio entitled *De la pirotechnia* (Venice, 1540), from which the following modern translation has been extracted:

The people of today are more ingenious and able to understand what they are about and so they develop new ideas because they have the experiences of others to guide them. They have moderated the unnecessary and strengthened the weaknesses. In place of the ungainly and unwieldy bombards, which required a great deal of gunpowder and skilled labor to fire their huge stone balls, as well as pioneers and large numbers of draft animals, they now make long cannon which, because of their light weight, are far easier to handle and maneuver. They fire iron balls which, although smaller than those fired by bombards, do more damage than the bombards ever did because they can fire more often and with such hard material. They also require fewer wooden structures and other defenses to create emplacements when engaged in assaults. There are three kinds of these: double cannon, cannon, and demi-cannon. It is usual for the cannon to measure five and a half to six arm's lengths [about 4 m. or 13 ft.], this being equal to approximately 22 calibers of the cannon [thus, caliber was 7 in. or 18 cm.]. The weight of the iron ball that it fires is from 50 to 60 lbs. [Italian; i.e., 17–20 kg.] and the weight of the bronze [cannon] from 6000 to 7000 lbs. [2000–2400 kg.], while those heaviest [can weigh] up to 8000 or 9000 lbs. [2700–3000 kg.] and even more, according to the decision of the master gun founder or of the person for whom it is being made. The demi-cannon fires balls from 25 to 30 lbs. [8.5–10 kg.]. The double, 120 lbs. [40 kg.]. And their weights are proportionate to their qualities. They are all of one piece and the bronze thickness where the powder is put [i.e., the chamber] is three-quarters the diameter of the ball, and at the mouth, excluding the strengthening band, one-third. ...

... Besides this group, lighter cannon are also made with a greater firing range, from which iron is not fired but stone. These are not good against walls but serve only for firing at infantry or cavalry and at warships. In all these types of artillery, which have the appearance of cannon, it is usual to make combustion chambers, and there is a great difference in the making of them from one master gun founder to another because each wants to demonstrate his own particular skill and secret methods, so that some make them wider than the bore and some narrower, etc. ...

In place of basilisks—which, to make them longer, were made in two or three pieces screwed together, just as was done at one time with the tailpieces of bombards and also of passevolants—culverins and middle culverins are made today, which, although they have not changed in name since olden times, have improved considerably in effectiveness because they are made in one piece, are quick firing and easy to load. They are easy to transport to wherever they are needed and, instead of stone, [culverins] fire iron balls which generally weigh 30 lbs. [about 10 kg.], while those fired by middle culverins weigh about 15 lbs. They are built more heavily and sturdily in bronze than the old ones, and each piece usually measures eight or nine arm's lengths [5.6–6.3 m.]; the thickness of the barrel walls at the breech is of the diameter of the ball or more, and at the mouth, excluding the molding, one-half the diameter in some and one-third in others. And these are approximately the standards maintained for culverins according to what I have done myself and what I have seen done.

... In place of springalds, cerbottanas, "chasing rooks" and similar, sakers, falcons, and falconets are made, which all fire iron. The saker fires 12 lbs. [4 kg.] and many people call it a quarter-cannon, the falcon fires 6 lbs., and the falconet 3–4 lbs. [1–1.7 kg.], and it can be seen that the bronze thickness at the breech is the same diameter as the ball and a little more, and half that of the mouth. The length is at the discretion of the master [gun founder] or his employer. In a similar way falconets and muskets are being made, weapons well able to fire speedily; they need little powder and can be managed by almost every man, for which reason the captains of infantry are quite willing to take them on their campaigns not only as offensive weapons but also as defensive weapons, for which purpose they are very suitable. They fire iron balls and lead balls from 1 to 2 lbs. [340–680 g.]. Similar to these are the wall arquebus, arquebus with rest, and the hand-held arquebus, and these, like the other artillery, are regularly being cast in bronze. Today, because they are lighter and because they are also safer for the user, the workshops are producing them in iron, like other hardware, which—when made by a good master craftsman and both welded and soldered equally well, and then well copied—are extremely good and are an important feature of the defenses.

It is true to say, however, that the classification of artillery pieces varied considerably in different countries, which does not emerge from Biringuccio's survey. In Spain, pieces of ordnance were generally divided into three categories, each with a well-defined function, and these were classified by Luys Collado in his *Plática manual de*

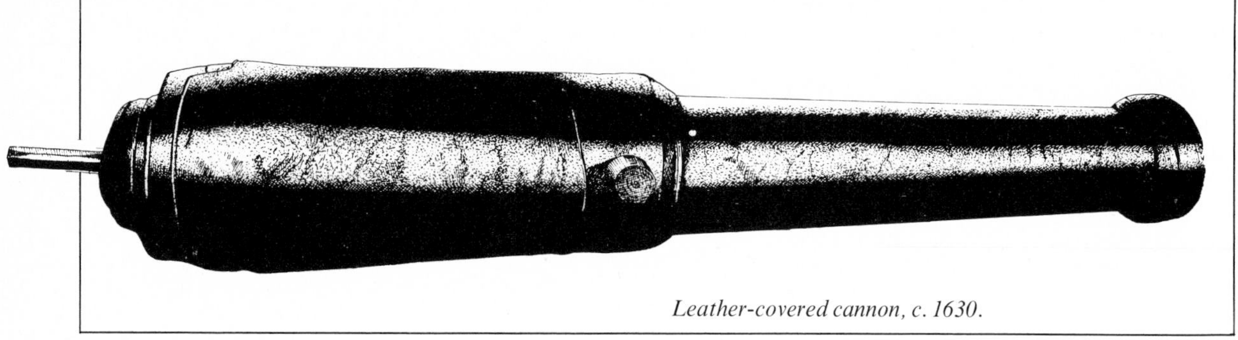

*Leather-covered cannon, c. 1630.*

*artillería* (Milan, 1592) as follows:

*First category:* long-barreled pieces suitable for attack from as great a distance as possible. These include the arquebus, musket, ribauldequin, hawk, falconet, demi-saker, zebratanas, "medium," saker, aspic, bastard culverin, middle culverin, and culverin.

*Second category:* cannon, such as the serpentine and basilisk, for demolishing fortifications.

*Third category:* stone-throwing cannon (*pedrero*) suitable for destroying and sinking ships in naval operations.

Although these divisions are quite clear-cut, other Spanish writers of the period such as Diego Ufano and Diego de Alaba y Viamont were inclined to use different names for the guns, and it would therefore seem advisable to treat them with considerable reserve.

The Republic of Venice—the most powerful of the Italian states during this period—categorized its artillery as follows (the Venetian pound being 1.05 U.S. pound):

*Muzzleloading Guns*

Wall gun (heavy musket on a swivel), projectile 1 lb. with a caliber of approx. 1¾ in. (45 mm.) and 60 in. (150 cm.) in length

Falconet, projectile 3 lbs. with a caliber of approx. 2⅛ in. (52 mm.) and 55–63 in. (140–160 cm.) in length

Falcon, projectile 6 lbs. with a caliber of approx. 2½ in. (62 mm.) and 60–67 in. (150–170 cm.) in length

Aspic, projectile 12 lbs. with a caliber of approx. 3¾–4 in. (95–100 mm.) and 67–71 in. (170–180 cm.) in length

Saker, projectile 12 lbs. with a caliber of approx. 3¾–4 in. (95–100 mm.) and 79–83 in. (200–210 cm.) in length

Then there were the various types of culverins, projectiles 14, 20, 30, 40, 50, 60, 90, 100, and 120 lbs., and cannon, projectiles 16, 20, 30, 40, 50, 60, 90, 100, and 120 lbs. The culverins were of equal caliber to the cannon but were respectively one-third longer and heavier.

Pieces of ordnance were categorized according to projectile weights and, down to 12 lbs., these were designated on the actual weight of the lead ball fired when the gun was tested. A saker, however, was subjected to a test with lead balls weighing 12 lbs., although, in normal use, it would have fired cast-iron balls of the same diameter but—due to the difference in the specific weight of the two metals—weighing only 9 lbs. For higher-caliber pieces of artillery, the tests were carried out with the same type of iron balls as were normally used in them.

Examples of the more important breechloading pieces include: the swivel gun, a pounder (1 lb.), with a caliber of approx. 1¾ in. (45 mm.) and approx. 39 in. (100 cm.) barrel; the 6-pounder stone-thrower (*pedrero*) with movable chamber, having a caliber of 2¾ in. (70 mm.) and a 39-in. (100 cm.) barrel; and the 12-pounder pedrero with movable chamber, having a caliber of 3¾ in. (95 mm.) and a 53-in. (135 cm.) barrel.

The manufacture of gunpowder improved considerably during the 16th century. The proportions used for artillery propellant were 4–1–1, that is to say, four parts saltpeter mixed with one part sulfur and one part charcoal. These ingredients were first ground separately, then moistened and mixed together into a kind of coarse paste and allowed to dry. The resulting "cake" was then reduced to granules of the required size by means of a "granulator." This granulated form was found to have great advantages over the old-type powder, particularly when troops were on the move, as there was no risk of the ingredients stratifying. Ignition was more rapid and uniform, and the buildup of pressures considerably better. This advance inevitably influenced the construction of gun barrels, which became bulkier and heavier. The thickness of the barrel walls of a culverin or long cannon, for instance, was greater at the breech than the actual caliber of the gun, while at the trunnions the thickness equaled the caliber and at the muzzle it was reduced to half the caliber.

Bronze, the material most in use during the 16th century in the manufacture of artillery pieces, was obtained by fusing 80 to 100 lbs. (36–45 kg.) of tin with every 1000 lbs. (455 kg.) of copper. To obviate the tendency of the resulting alloy to be brittle—for the copper was often debased with lead—it was customary for 100 lbs. of brass to be added to every 1000 lbs. of alloy when the metals were half smelted. The liquid bronze was then poured into a mold placed in a pit alongside the furnace, with the muzzle pointing upward so that the metal tended to run back toward the breech and build up there while the dross collected around the mouth of the muzzle.

Cannon and culverins were thrice tried out with a powder charge of the same weight as the cannonball, although in normal use a charge of two-thirds the weight of the ball was used in a cannon and four-fifths in a culverin. It is still a moot point exactly what the effective ranges of 16th-century artillery pieces really were, as the achievements described by contemporary writers would appear to be grossly exaggerated. The following table shows some results of point-blank firing included by Alessandro Capobianco in his book *Corona e palma militare di artiglieria* ("Some Military Highlights of Artillery, Venice, 1598):

| | Paces | Meters |
|---|---|---|
| Swivel gun musket—pounder (1 lb.) | 120 | 208 |
| Falconet—3-pounder | 150 | 260 |
| Falcon—6-pounder | 220 | 382 |
| Passevolant—9-pounder | 260 | 452 |
| Saker—12-pounder | 250 | 435 |
| Aspic—12-pounder | 180 | 313 |
| Culverin—14-pounder | 290 | 505 |
| Culverin—40-pounder | 330 | 573 |
| Culverin—60-pounder | 370 | 643 |
| Culverin—120-pounder | 450 | 782 |
| Cannon—16-pounder | 200 | 347 |
| Cannon—40-pounder | 270 | 470 |
| Cannon—60-pounder | 300 | 521 |
| Cannon—120-pounder | 380 | 660 |
| Stone-throwing cannon (pedrero)—200-pounder | 180 | 312 |
| Breechloading pedrero—12-pounder | 80 | 140 |
| Breechloading swivel gun (musket)—pounder (1 lb.) | 60 | 105 |

In order to clarify what is meant by "firing at point-blank range," some explanation is necessary. For 16th-century artillery—and in all successive centuries, too—the "natural line of sight" ordinarily taken was the line of vision that skimmed the highest points of the reinforcing hoops or moldings encircling the breech and the muzzle of the gun. Because of the differing radii of these two hoops, this line of sight was never parallel to the gun's axis and thus, by utilizing this discrepancy, it was possible to calculate any particular elevation of the muzzle—a calculation which varied from gun to gun. The "blank" point is where the trajectory meets the natural line of sight, and the "point-blank distance" means the corresponding range.

Angles of elevation were plotted by means of an instrument known as a gunner's quadrant, which consisted of two wooden arms, one longer than the other, joined at right angles. Spanning the two arms was a metal arc marked off in degrees—generally of 12 "points"—with a plumb line hanging from the top of the quadrant. The angle of aim was found by inserting the longer arm of the instrument into the bore and reading off the point on the arc indicated by the plumb line. According to Capobianco, with the quadrant divided into 12 degrees, the following ranges could be assumed at the various "points": at 1 point, 5 times the distance of point blank; at 2 points, $8\frac{1}{2}$ times; at 3 points, $10\frac{3}{5}$ times; at 4 points, $11\frac{2}{5}$ times; at 5 points, $11\frac{4}{5}$ times; at 6 points, 12 times.

We do, in fact, have some data on the actual range of the various pieces of ordnance as the result of official tests carried out in Venice in September 1544. These results, which may be regarded as reliable, show that it was possible for mid-16th-century guns to have a range of over

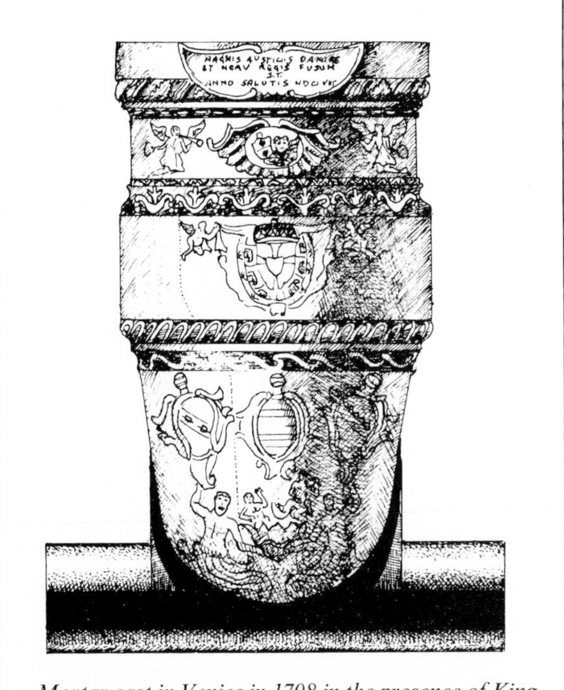

*Mortar cast in Venice in 1708 in the presence of King Frederick IV of Denmark.*

*Eighteenth-century Venetian howitzers, with trunnions.*

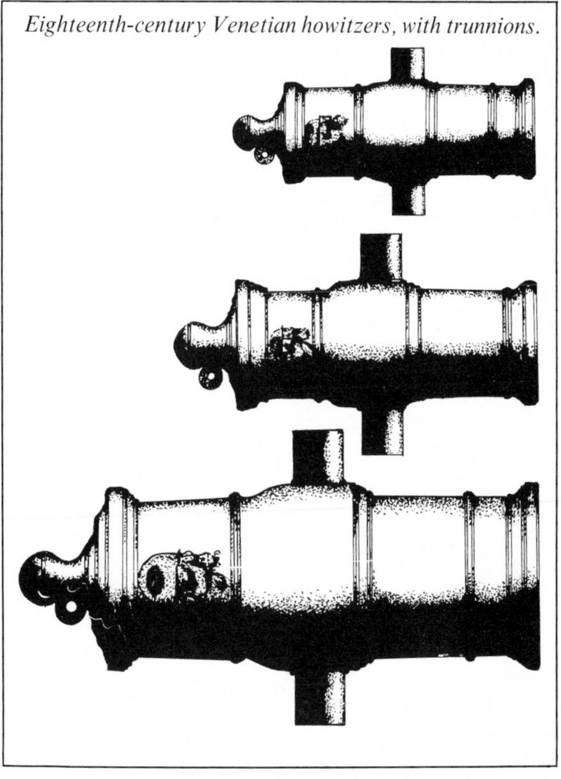

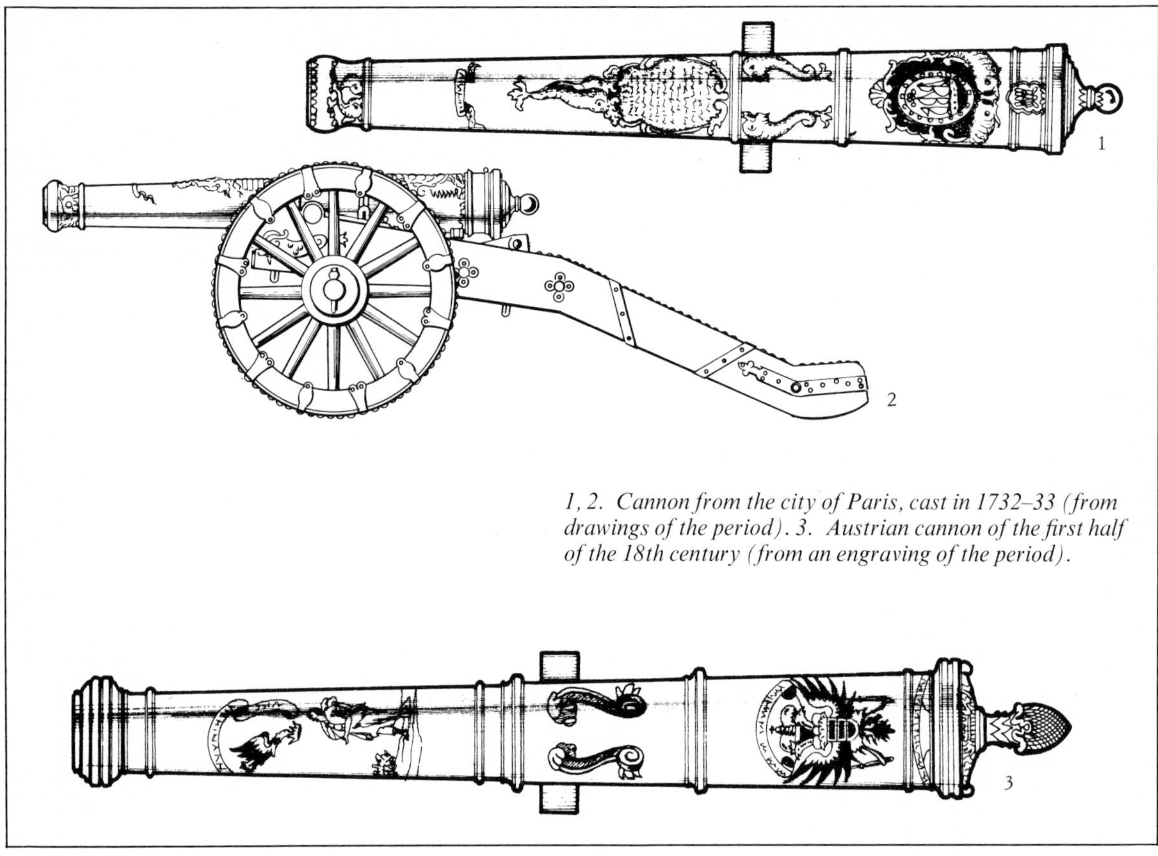

*1, 2. Cannon from the city of Paris, cast in 1732–33 (from drawings of the period). 3. Austrian cannon of the first half of the 18th century (from an engraving of the period).*

4500 m. (4921 yds.)—quite an impressive performance.

Iron guns, too, were developing during the 16th century. Despite the superiority of cast bronze over forged iron, the demand for it fell away, particularly for small guns in the arming of merchant ships, since these vessels—while necessarily having to maintain defensive armament on board—did not keep their guns in constant use, and the high price of bronze artillery pieces was thus not justified. In countries such as England that were particularly rich in iron-ore deposits, methods were soon being sought for casting cannon in iron. In the early years of Henry VIII's reign (1509–47) this type of production had already been established in Sussex, although with rather unsatisfactory results at first.

A Venetian chronicler named Sanudo told of a letter sent from Palermo, Sicily, in March 1515 describing a confrontation between a galley and an English three-masted bark which "had on board an iron bombarde; it fired a shot and caused much damage to all those in the galley; on firing again, the bombarde itself broke into pieces"—an eloquent example of the quality of a cast-iron gun. In 1543, however, under the efficient direction of the Reverend William Levett, the Royal Foundry at Newbridge in Sussex started to produce some really fine cast-iron artillery pieces of a quality which enabled them to compete at almost any level with similar guns in bronze, while costing less than a third. This was the beginning of an important industry which was to exert considerable influence on the future of Britain's political and commercial fortunes.

## *The 17th Century*

Artillery was not so different in the first half of the 17th century from that of the previous fifty years. In the 1614 German edition of Ufano's treatise on artillery, we find the "dragon," or double culverin of 40 lbs., among the legitimate pieces, and the "basilisk," or bastard double culverin of 48 lbs., the "serpentine," or bastard culverin of 24 lbs., and the "pelican," or quarter-culverin of 6 lbs., among the "bastard" pieces. In France and Spain, however, legislation was soon passed to standardize the four pieces that seemed to be most practical, though the plethora of pieces of intermediate sizes could not be completely eliminated. Gustavus Adolphus of Sweden implemented reforms of great significance when he equipped each battalion with two (and later with three) 3-pounder guns to form the first real field artillery. When this powerful king landed at Peenemünde with his army on July 6, 1630, to intervene in the Thirty Years War, he brought with him 81 3-pounders and a siege artillery park of 24 cannon of 25 lbs. and 25 mortars. During this war the Swedes also used their famous "leather guns," weighing only 90 lbs. (40 kg.) and mounted on two-wheel carriages. Examination of the only remaining example by X rays has recently revealed that it was only the outside jacket that was made of leather; the rest of the cannon barrel consisted of lightweight copper tubes at the center, bound with metal wire and rope.

Mortars played an even more important role. By the second half of the century they were able to throw explosive balls as big (but not as heavy) as solid balls of a thousand pounds or more. During the wars in Flanders a new type of gun was introduced, longer than the mortar but, like the mortar, intended to fire big explosive projectiles in a high, curved trajectory; it inherited the name of a short type of gun used in the Hussite wars in the 15th century, the "howitzer" (from the Bohemian word *houfnice*). It was about five calibers long, so that it was reasonably easy to charge and load the "bomb" by hand onto the hemispherical section forming the chamber. In central and southern Europe artillery was nearly all cast in bronze; iron pieces, of which numbers were produced in England and Sweden, were mostly preferred for naval use. As more ships were built with several decks, the cost of bronze guns became extremely burdensome even to the richest countries, which accounts for the fact that in 1661 alone Sweden was able to export no fewer than 2440 iron guns. The Republic of Venice, after trying unsuccessfully to have iron guns cast in the provinces of Brescia and Bergamo, sent the gun founder Sigismondo III Alberghetti to England in 1683 to purchase two hundred such guns and to learn the technique of producing them. After visiting foundries in Germany, France, and Flanders and looking at some Swedish guns in Amsterdam, Alberghetti went on to England, where in the course of a year's stay he was able to watch the casting of a number of the pieces ordered for Venice. In 1685 he went home and was at once sent to the province of Brescia to have furnaces of the English type built and teach the local craftsmen all he had learned. From then on the Venetian republic had a supply of good cast-iron artillery pieces produced at Sarazzo (Brescia) and at Clanezzo (Bergamo).

Ever since the previous century there had been a growing tendency to use faster types of gunpowder; the formulae were fixed at 5-1-1 and 6-1-1, the latter used in "reinforced" guns. Important advances were made in the production of a perfect mixture, and it was laid down that the three ingredients of the powder must be pounded in a mortar for at least twenty-four hours—a requirement that had the unfortunate effect of substantially increasing the number of accidental explosions. The tried and trusted ladle used to measure the powder in charging the pieces gave way more and more to "cartouches," paper bags already filled with the right quantity of powder, which had been introduced in naval gunnery in the previous century. For naval use too, round or cylindrical stone projectiles came back into favor, since they did more serious damage to the planking than iron projectiles.

### *The 18th Century*

In the 18th century, as in the 17th, the progress made in artillery from a purely technical point of view was fairly limited. Very large guns disappeared almost entirely, at any rate from the most important armies, and the number of calibers used was further reduced. Field artillery fell into a decline, from which it was only rescued by the genius of Napoleon, due to a change in infantry tactics. The infantry units, now all armed with flintlock muskets fitted with bayonets, were drawn up in battle formations of two or three parallel ranks. In battle, therefore, the gun crews found themselves firing at long, thin infantry lines—not a very substantial target; spaced out along the front, with their crews vulnerable to fire from muskets and rifles, the guns lost a good deal of the dominance they had gained earlier.

But if technical progress was slight, remarkable progress in organization was made in many countries. In France, the "five calibers" system suggested by Vallière was

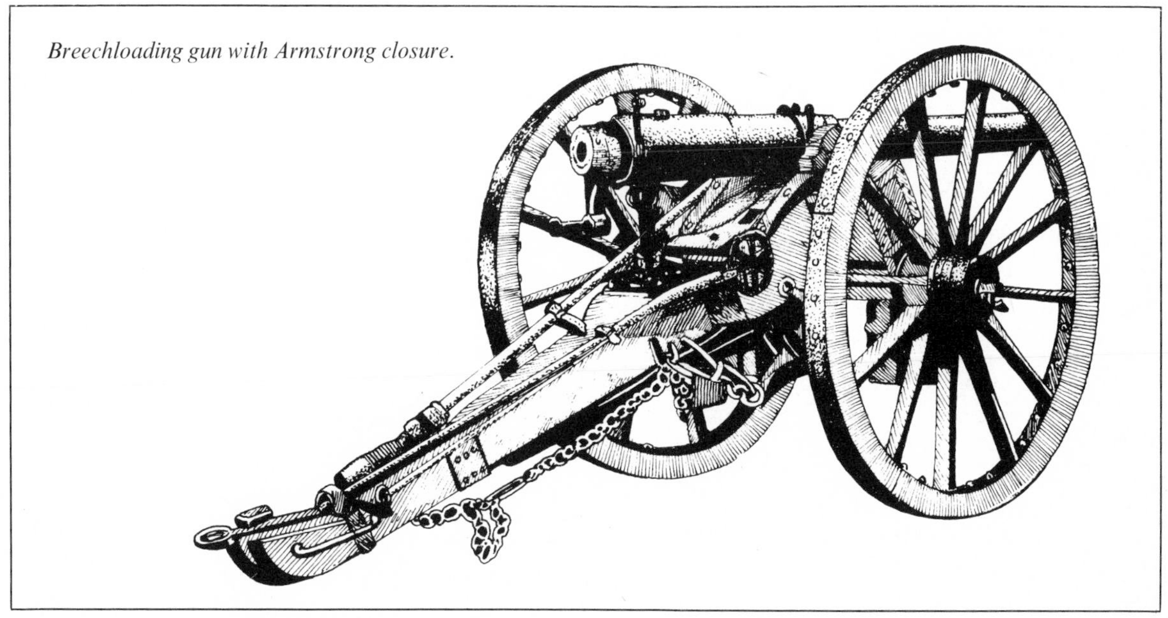
*Breechloading gun with Armstrong closure.*

adopted in 1732, with the 24-pounder siege cannon, the 16-pounder demi-cannon, the 12-pounder, the "bastard" of 8 lbs., and the "medium" (*moyane*) of 4 lbs. Other light 4-pounder guns in service, called "Swedish guns," were designated to accompany the infantry. A "Swedish" piece was 4½ ft. (about 145 cm.) long and weighed 600–625 lbs. (an average of 375 kg.), while the moyane of the same caliber measured 7 ft. 3 in. (about 230 cm.) and weighed 1150 lbs (about 540 kg.). By a decree of January 20, 1757, every battalion of infantry had to have one Swedish piece, hauled by three horses and served by a sergeant and sixteen soldiers. For operations in mountainous country, small pieces, also 4-pounders, were in service, which could be carried by pack animals and were in fact known as "mule-back" guns. Frederick II of Prussia, one of the greatest of military commanders, distinguished clearly between siege artillery and field artillery, and was the first to form the unit called a "battery," in those days consisting of ten to fifteen guns. Having adopted a system of lighter, more mobile guns, of calibers of 3, 6, 12, and 24 lbs., he formed the first regular horse artillery, whose mobility gave him a remarkable tactical superiority. But the most important and rational reform was undoubtedly that carried out in France between 1765 and 1774 by General Gribeauval, based on the principle that each special branch of the artillery (field, siege, garrison, and coastal) should be given the equipment best suited to its task. Three cannon were adopted for the field artillery, of 4, 8, and 12 lbs. (actual calibers 85 mm., 106 mm., and 117 mm.), all 18 calibers long, with an 8¼-in. howitzer.

Siege artillery, in contrast, was equipped with cannon of 24 lbs. and 16 lbs., with a barrel length of about 23 calibers, and with two mortars of calibers of 12 in. and 8.3 in. The cannon were used for both ground and coastal defense, but were mounted on different, specially designed carriages for the different tasks. The external outline of the guns was of three slightly tapering cylinders, with raised rings at the steps where they joined and a "swell" at the muzzle; ornamentation was limited to the royal cipher and the designation of the piece. An important innovation was the introduction of trunnion "bases": the normal size of the trunnions was equal to one caliber both in length and diameter, and the cylindrical bases, of about double the diameter, enabled the gun to lie better in the trunnion plates (bearings) and at the same time strengthened the attachment of the trunnions to the piece. The charge used now was only a third of the weight of the ball, but with reduced windage, the muzzle velocity was as great as that obtained with more powder in the old pieces.

Gribeauval also introduced important new features in gun carriages, which he standardized and provided with interchangeable parts. Besides the elevating screw, he brought in the iron axletree, the trail box, head and tail shackles, road trunnion bearings so that the piece was better balanced when transported, and limbers with wheels of almost the same diameter as those of the gun carriage.

Another important innovation was the adoption of Gribeauval's backsight. The sight consisted of a straight post sliding vertically in guides on a clamp on the breech, which could be fixed in various positions by a setscrew with a wing nut. A linear scale was cut on the post in twelfths and twenty-fourths of an inch, from 0 to 18. The reading on this scale was lined up with a crosspiece on the clamp, the zero mark giving the natural line of sight. Range tables for different muzzle velocities gave the sight settings for distances above point blank.

The manufacture of gunpowder reached a very high standard during the 18th century; it was rigorously tested before being accepted by the military. In France, it had since 1686 been subject to test firing in a special powder-testing mortar. Three ounces of powder, precisely weighed, when ignited in this instrument—a small mortar at a fixed elevation of 45 degrees—had to fire a 60-lb. (about 28 kg.) ball a distance of more than 60 yds. (about 55 m.).

### *The 19th Century*

Artillery made enormous progress in the 19th century, not so rapid in the first fifty years but remarkably swift after that, especially in the last three decades. One of the first steps in this progress was the adoption in 1803–4 of case shot, or shrapnel, invented in 1784 by British Lieutenant (later General) Henry Shrapnel and still extensively used. Another very important invention was the friction tube, introduced in France by 1830, which quickly replaced all other systems of ignition (the fuze tube, slow match, etc.). The device consisted of a thin brass or copper tube about 2 in. (5 cm.) long which fitted into the vent of the gun. One end was closed with wax and pitch, on top of which came a quantity of highly compressed gunpowder, ignited by a detonator using a mixture of saltpeter and antimony. This mixture was contained in a smaller copper tube inserted into the tube with the powder. A thin copper wire, flattened and saw-edged at one end, was fitted into the detonating mixture; when pulled hard, it created violent friction and ignited the powder.

Toward the middle of the century, a radical innovation effected the replacement of round shot by hollow elongated projectiles. The chief reason for this change lay in the fact that, since it was practically impossible to make shot whose center of gravity coincided with their geometric center, a rotary couple formed by the two centers changed the direction of flight from moment to moment, producing what is known in ballistics as "deviation." Since this eccentricity, the reason for the deviation, was different for every shot, it followed that the deviation was different for every shot fired and was quite unpredictable. Elongated projectiles gave the trajectory the greatest possible precision; the deviation was no longer unpredictable but could be calculated in advance as a result of the rapid rotation of the projectile around its own axis. The hardest problem was how to give the rotary motion to the projectile. Brilliant results had been obtained with small arms with lead bullets that forced themselves into spiral grooves in the barrel, but that system could not be applied to guns that fired iron projectiles. In muzzleloading guns, for which windage had to be retained to allow the shot to be loaded from the

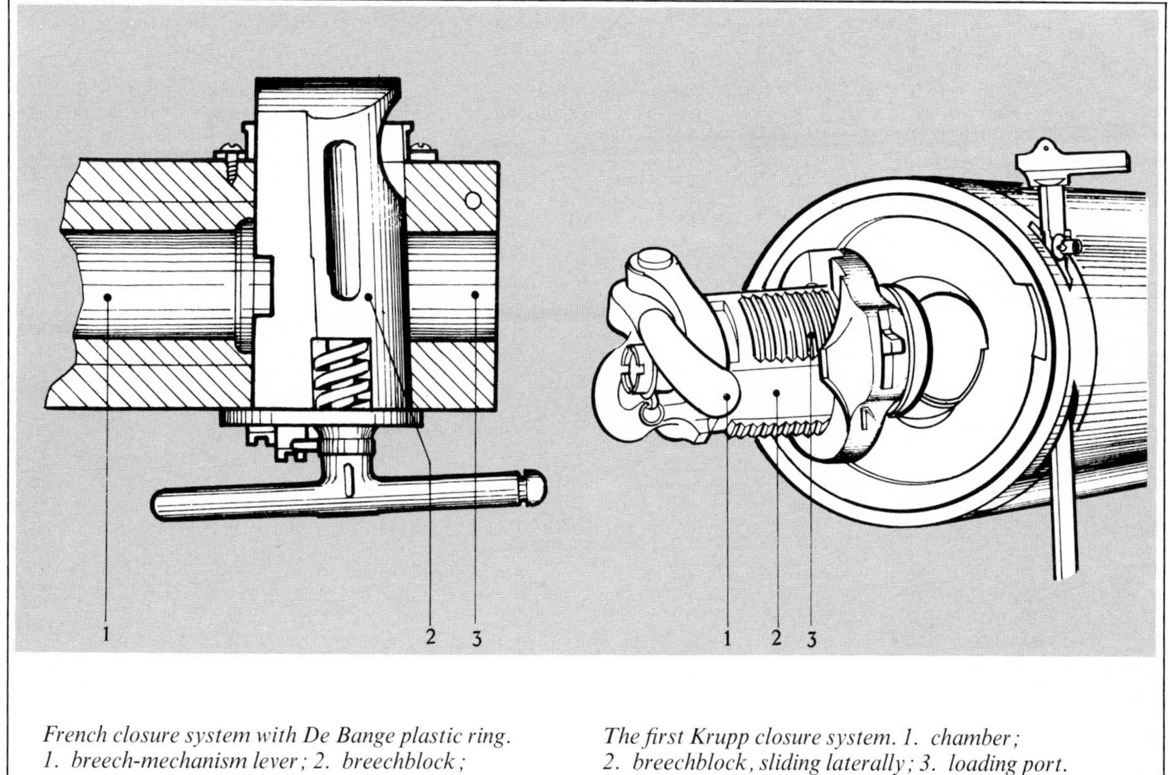


*French closure system with De Bange plastic ring. 1. breech-mechanism lever; 2. breechblock; 3. interrupted screw.*

*The first Krupp closure system. 1. chamber; 2. breechblock, sliding laterally; 3. loading port.*

muzzle, big studs or a belt were cast with bullets, engaging in corresponding grooves in the bore.

Among the first to study these problems was the Italian general Ettore Cavalli, who in 1846 designed a breechloading cannon with a rifled bore with two grooves opposite each other. It was a simple system, but it had serious faults and soon gave way to the French system with six grooves. In Cavalli's design, two studs were made by casting them with the iron body of the projectile, but the French preferred an elastic metal, less hard than bronze. They got their best results with zinc, and the projectiles were given two circles of six studs each, one at the base of the cylindrical section and the other just below the beginning of the ogive. The French system was followed by a number of other systems, all using deep grooves and projectiles with large studs; there was Sir William Armstrong's "diversion" system, the French Navy system, the English Woolwich system and the Whitworth system. But it was not until the general introduction of breechloading with reliable obturation that complete advantage could actually be taken of spiral rifling while at the same time eliminating the harmful effects of windage.

*Closure Systems*

Before discussing the various breech-closure systems that were tested and adopted, we should look for a moment at the problem of obtaining a hermetic seal at the breech on firing. It will be remembered that the many breechloading pieces constructed in early times were never properly sealed, and consequently were never developed further. On the assumption that whatever form of obturator was used it would still be impossible to seal the breech hermetically, inventors were compelled to fit some additional device that would ensure the closure through the action of the propellant gases. They used pads of expanding and not highly combustible materials such as leather or hemp board, which made an adequate circular lip that was forced against the bore on firing. For the biggest guns these pads were sometimes made of metal, or metal rings were used instead of pads with some success, attached to the bore or to the obturator. One interesting device was the steel Broadwell ring, designed by the American inventor Lewis W. Broadwell, the special shape of which prevented the escape of gas.

The Wahrendorff system, or "piston system," got the latter name from the form of the obturator, which looked like a piston with a cylindrical head and flat rod. The head fitted exactly into the breech; the rod had a round hole bored across it for the locking bolt. This bolt fitted into a housing across the breech; to load the gun, the shell was inserted from the breech first, then the charge. The obturator was then closed and locked in the breech by the bolt. This simple system, developed in 1846, had its Achilles heel in the locking device, which had to be

*German 17 cm. coast defense gun.*

constantly cleaned and oiled; it was adopted in Austria, but scrapped after 1866.

The Armstrong system, designed by 1854 and adopted for some years in Britain, consisted of a breechblock of parallelepiped shape inserted into or withdrawn from a slot at the top of the breech. A large hollow breech screw with one or two strong handles fitted into a cylindrical extension of the breech. With the breechblock raised the gun was loaded through this screw, and when the block was lowered the screw tightly pressed it against the breech.

The French Navy system, or Treuille de Beaulieu system, designed as early as 1842 by Captain (later Admiral) Treuille de Beaulieu, had an obturator that moved along the axis of the barrel and was screwed into the breech by a screw interrupted in three sections. In front of the breech were two slightly tapered sections which fitted the sealing base of the obturator. The obturator thus consisted of three main parts: the screw or "plug," a steel cylinder with an interrupted thread engaging with that in the breech; the head, with a shaft running through the cylindrical screw; and the base or "closure plate," made of tungsten steel, on the front of the head. When the gun was fired, the gases tried to expand the edges of the base and adhered to the walls of the chamber, sealing it completely. To close the breech, the obturator was inserted into it and rotated through one-sixth of a turn so that the threaded sections engaged with each other.

The Broadwell system was a "wedge" system, with a breechblock that slid horizontally in a slot cut in the breech at right angles. Sealing was by the soft-metal ring, designed by the same inventor, while the breechblock was driven home by a large steel screw hinged on the left side of the block itself and turned by a double handle. The thread of the screw was interrupted to engage a corresponding thread within the breech. The Krupp system also used a sliding wedge as a breechblock, which was provided with the soft-metal "Broadwell rings" for sealing the breech.

The Kreiner system had a breechblock made of two cast-steel wedges in contact along their sloping faces. The opening made in the gun for this block was of parallelepiped form, with the top and the bottom grooved to guide the two wedges. Locking of the breechblock was effected by holding the front wedge against the breech and sliding the rear wedge to the right by means of a screw of very long pitch. There was a strong crank with a handle on the outside end of the screw, to move its threaded part in the rear wedge.

An important advance in hermetic closure was made with the plastic obturator designed by the French colonel C. Ragon de Bange and widely adopted in the 1880s. This consisted of a canvas bag filled with fat and asbestos, with two tinfoil washers pressed onto the outside so as to cover all the bag except for a small periphery on the outside and the inside. Two copper rings were fitted to make the obturator's shape cylindrical and to anchor the tinfoil washers. To hold the plastic obturator against its head and also to transmit the gas pressure uniformly, a short mushroom valve was fitted in the obturator head. On firing, the gas pressure on the valve head drove it back and the squeezed plastic bag expanded outward to press hard against the walls of the breech, making a gas-tight seal. The De Bange system, used with Treuille de Beaulieu's interrupted-screw breechblock, worked so well that a century later it was still used in big-caliber guns using bagged charges.

The construction of the artillery pieces was greatly improved during the 19th century in step with growing

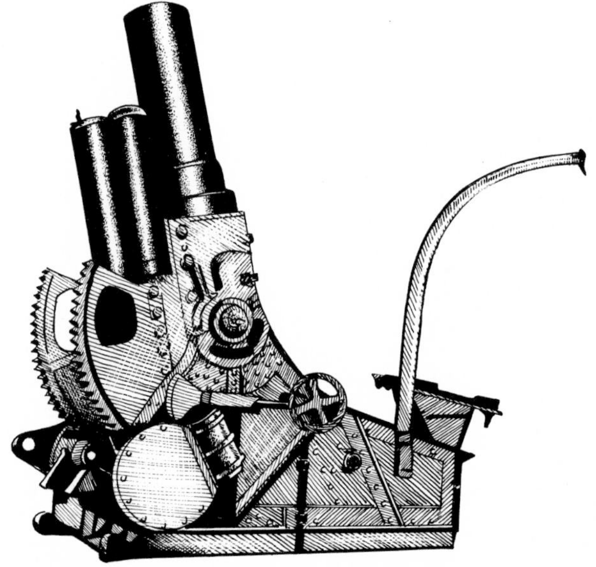

*Italian 305/10 mortar.*

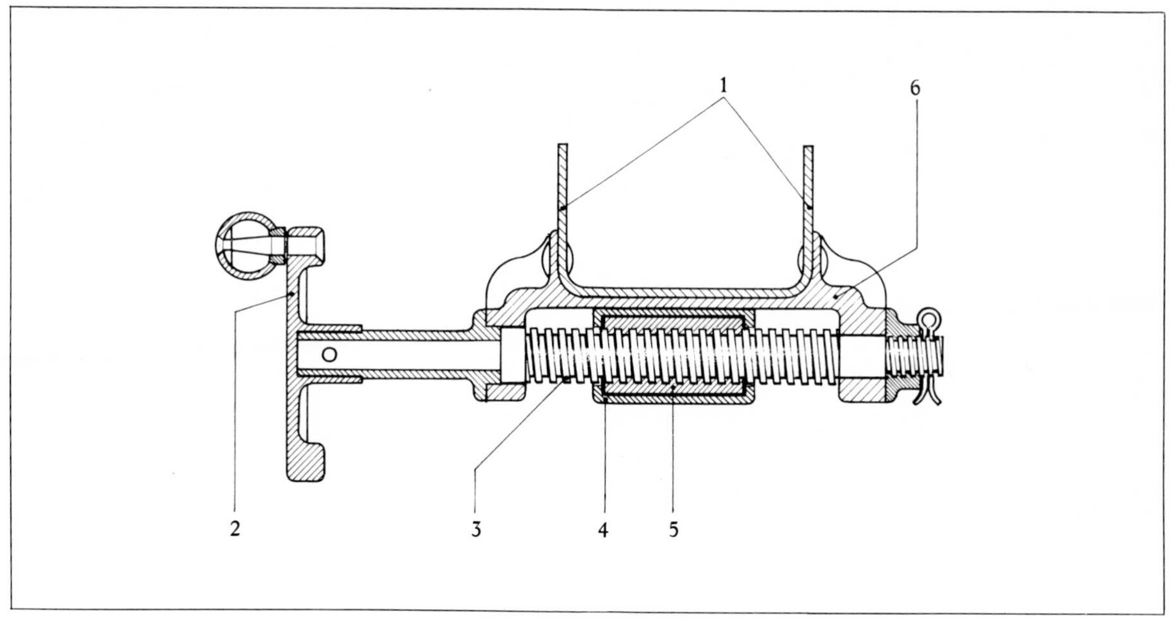


*Cross section of the traversing gear of an Italian 75/27 mm. Model 906 gun. 1. cradle; 2. handwheel; 3. traversing screw; 4. cradle housing; 5. nut; 6. bracket.*

industrialization and technological progress. Bronze was still used for a long time on account of its outstanding durability, but it began to give way to steel, which soon came to be the preferred material. A great number of guns, especially those of large caliber, were made of cast iron, which was relatively cheap; to counter the poor elasticity of the metal, the breech was reinforced with external hoops of wrought iron. A clear improvement in cast-iron pieces came with the adoption of the casting technique devised by Captain (later General) Thomas J. Rodman, an American, by which the guns were cast already bored (previously they had been bored out after casting) and cooled from the inside by a current of cold water or air. Bronze guns were no longer cast in refractory molds as they had been in the past, but in cast-iron molds which could be reused at least forty times. The pieces were then bored to a little less than the designated caliber, and finished off by a mechanical widening process: a series of steel pins was passed down the bore, driven by the shaft of a powerful hydraulic piston. Using this method, devised by the Austrian general Franz Uchatius, the barrel was subjected to very high tensions and so was less liable to distortion during firing. The reinforcing hoops mentioned earlier did not allow full use to be made of the resistance of the metals used for barrels, and improved systems of construction were introduced by which a number of concentric tubes were shrunk onto each other. The best-known methods were the Armstrong, Armstrong-Fraser, and Whitworth. With the adoption of efficient breechloading systems, it was possible to give up the quite impractical shells with studs, and by fitting shrunk-on copper driving bands to the shells, to eliminate windage, with consequent improvement in the accuracy of shooting. Rifling was given more and shallower grooves, and propellant charges were by now between one-ninth and one-fourteenth the weight of the projectile.

Gun carriages also benefitted from technological progress and, from the second half of the century, were most often made from sheet steel or, for the heaviest pieces, from cast iron. There was also a notable improvement in sighting systems, and recoil buffers were introduced for the biggest guns toward the end of the century, first mechanical, then hydraulic. Improvements were made to the backsight, which now consisted of a post calibrated to indicate elevation and a crossbar with a backsight notch calibrated for laying off. To adjust the sights, the post could slide in the walls of the piece and be fixed at the required height with a setscrew or spring; the crossbar could be moved horizontally at the top of the post. In some sights the crossbar was made in the form of a cursor which could slide in two directions, both sideways and up and down the post. And the 19th century saw one more important innovation, the introduction for smaller-caliber guns of fixed ammunition, with a brass case and percussion cap.

## *The 20th Century*

A foremost problem facing military technicians at the beginning of the 20th century was that of field gun carriages. In order to offer a more difficult target to enemy artillery fire, infantry in the field had to take up more and more extended positions, and if the guns were not to lose their recently gained superiority they had to be capable of an extremely high rate of fire. But this was impossible with the rigid carriages used up to that time; the gun had to be relaid after every shot, which took a great deal of time. The problem was solved with the adoption of full-recoil

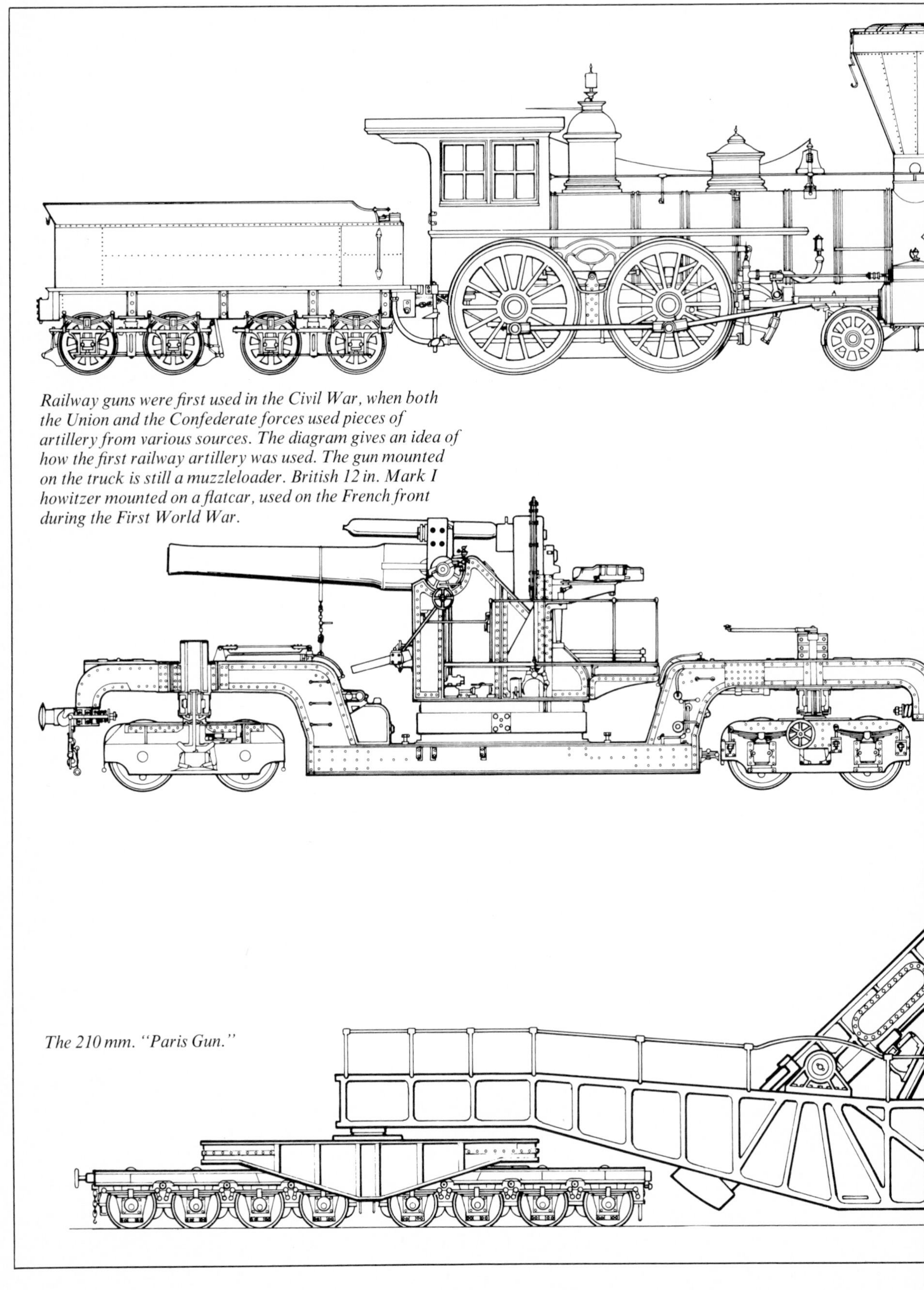

*Railway guns were first used in the Civil War, when both the Union and the Confederate forces used pieces of artillery from various sources. The diagram gives an idea of how the first railway artillery was used. The gun mounted on the truck is still a muzzleloader. British 12 in. Mark I howitzer mounted on a flatcar, used on the French front during the First World War.*

*The 210 mm. "Paris Gun."*

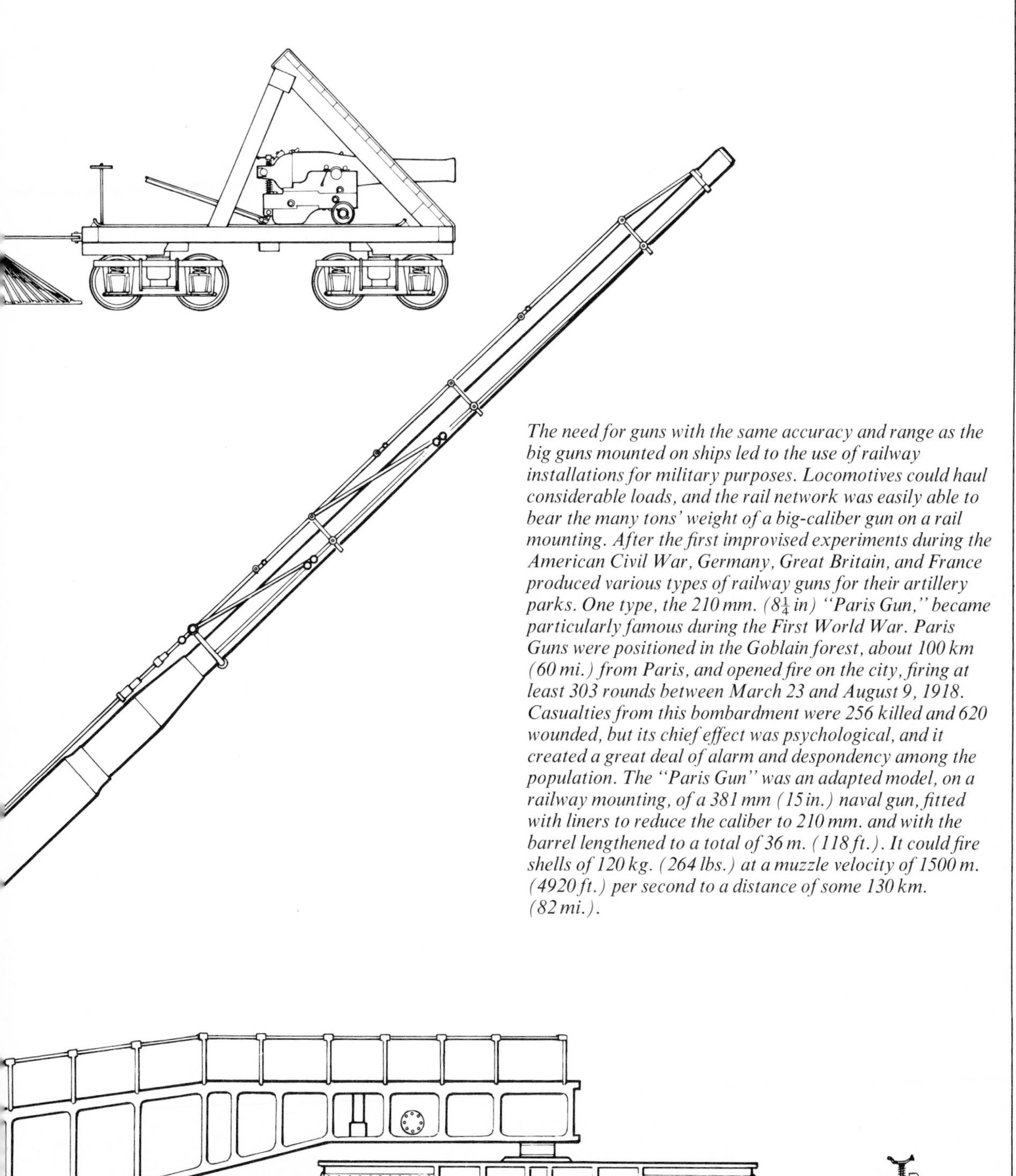

*The need for guns with the same accuracy and range as the big guns mounted on ships led to the use of railway installations for military purposes. Locomotives could haul considerable loads, and the rail network was easily able to bear the many tons' weight of a big-caliber gun on a rail mounting. After the first improvised experiments during the American Civil War, Germany, Great Britain, and France produced various types of railway guns for their artillery parks. One type, the 210 mm. ($8\frac{1}{4}$ in) "Paris Gun," became particularly famous during the First World War. Paris Guns were positioned in the Goblain forest, about 100 km (60 mi.) from Paris, and opened fire on the city, firing at least 303 rounds between March 23 and August 9, 1918. Casualties from this bombardment were 256 killed and 620 wounded, but its chief effect was psychological, and it created a great deal of alarm and despondency among the population. The "Paris Gun" was an adapted model, on a railway mounting, of a 381 mm (15 in.) naval gun, fitted with liners to reduce the caliber to 210 mm. and with the barrel lengthened to a total of 36 m. (118 ft.). It could fire shells of 120 kg. (264 lbs.) at a muzzle velocity of 1500 m. (4920 ft.) per second to a distance of some 130 km. (82 mi.).*

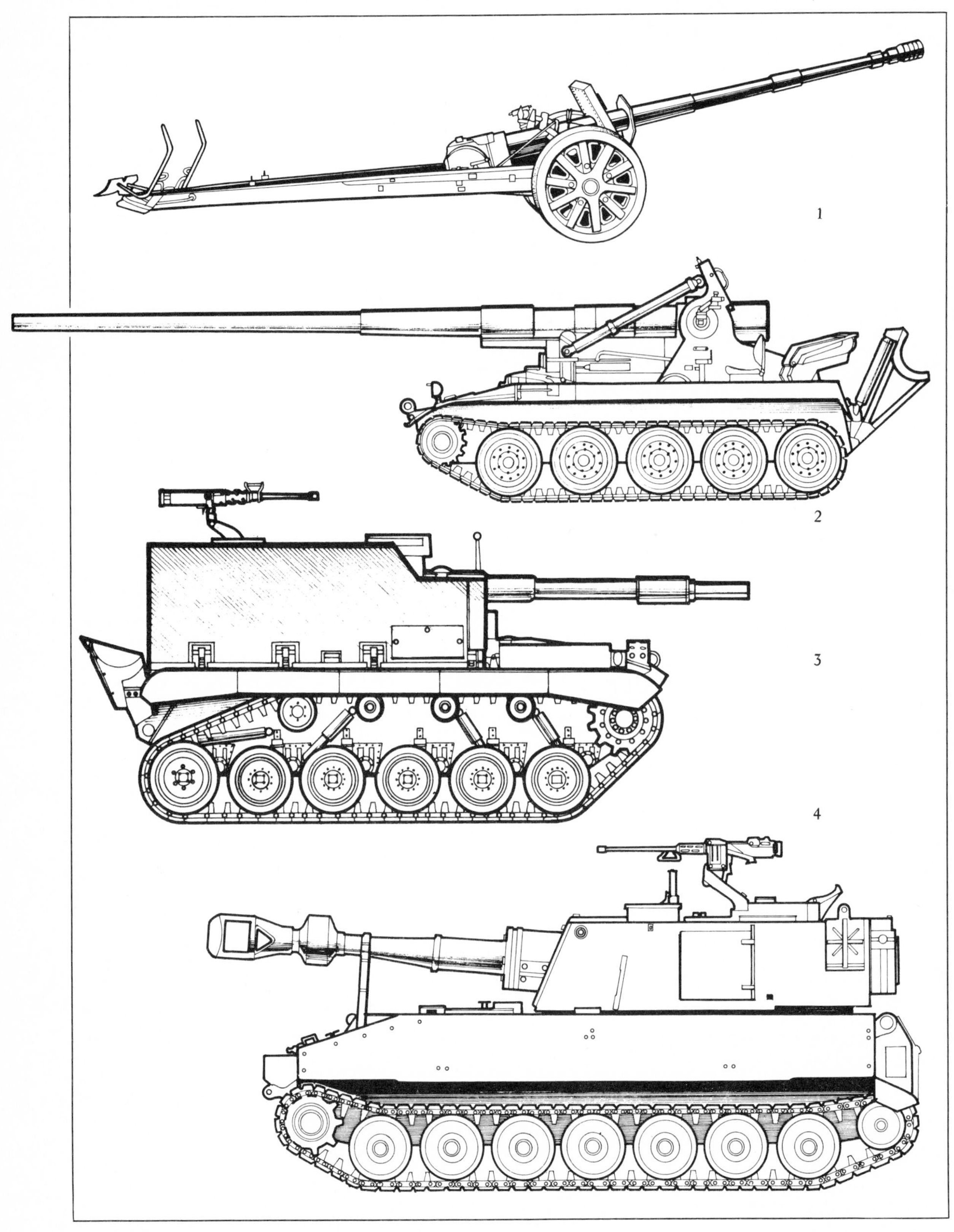


*1. German 75 mm. PAK-41. Self-propelled guns: 2. U.S. M-107 armed with 175 mm. cannon; 3. U.S. M-44, 150 mm. howitzer; 4. U.S. M-109 armed with 155 mm. gun.*

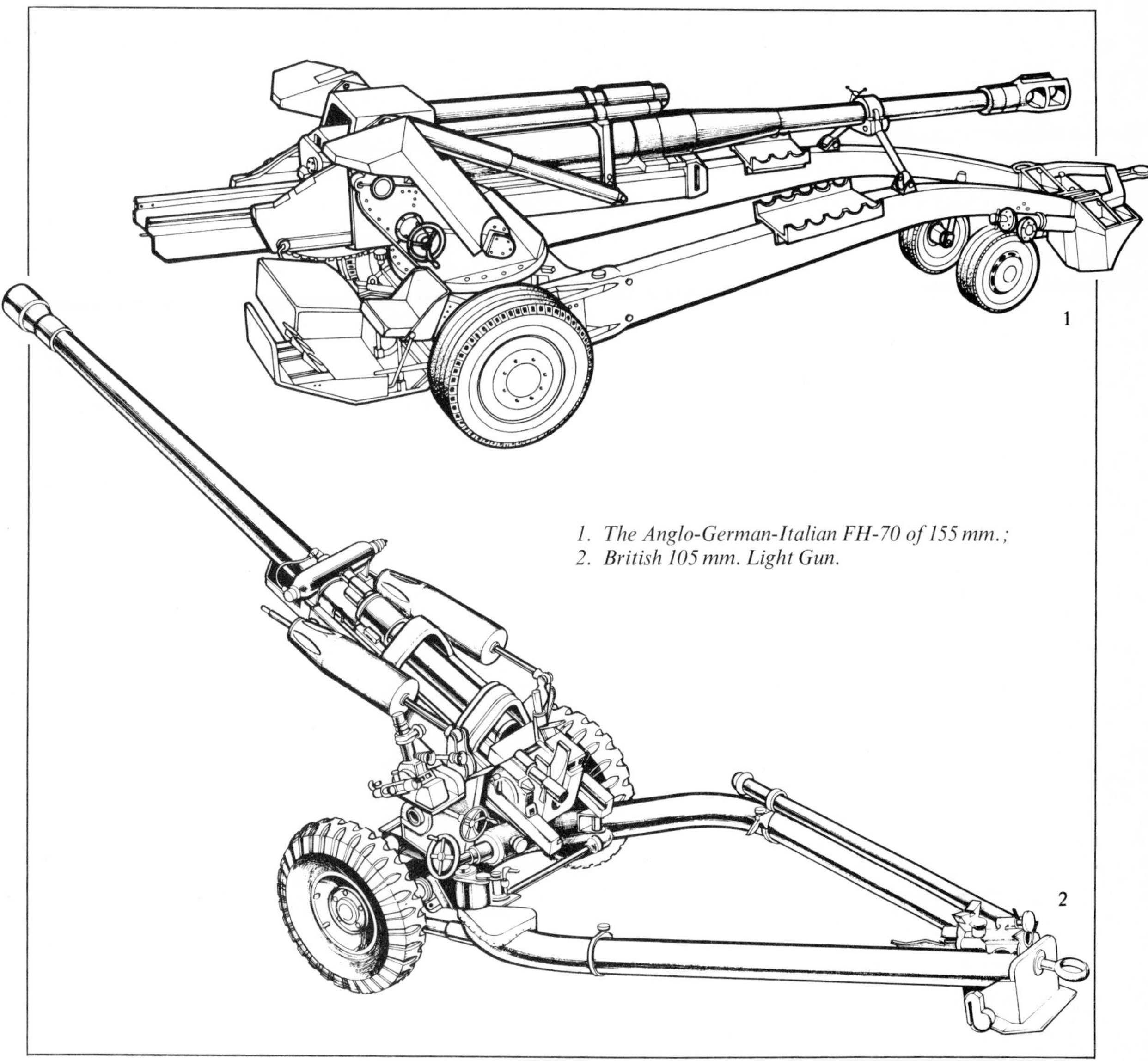

1. The Anglo-German-Italian FH-70 of 155 mm.; 2. British 105 mm. Light Gun.

carriages, on which could be fitted shields, to protect the crew, and optical sights, which had been too delicate for use on carriages that had to take the shock of recoil. Another development made it possible to obtain resistance to very high pressures in steel guns with single barrel tubes without making them excessively thick. This was a process of radial expansion ("auto-frettage"), very similar in concept to the Uchatius process for bronze pieces, by which the piece during construction was subjected to interior hydraulic pressures far greater than those reached in firing (4–5 atmospheres). This altered the molecular structure of the metal (a permanent deformation in the inner layers and an elastic deformation in the outer), so that the outer layers played a greater part in resistance to stresses. Notable progress was made in "tubing" the piece; a relatively thin steel tube (about a quarter of the caliber) was fitted inside the barrel for the whole length of the bore, and rifled, which not only gave the barrel greater durability but made it possible to change one of the parts most subject to rapid deterioration.

Obturation systems in use could be divided into three categories: screw, wedge, and block systems. Screw systems, based on the French Navy system, consisted of a powerful cylindrical or tapered screw fitting into the breech. The commonest types were: (1) The interrupted or segmented breech screw, in which the screw was divided into smooth and threaded segments of equal width so that the obturator could be inserted in the breech and locked by a quarter-turn. This allowed the breech to be closed very quickly, but required a rather long obturator to give adequate support. (2) The eccentric breech screw, patented by Nordenfelt, which could be used with a shorter obturator and was quick in operation. It consisted of a screw with uninterrupted thread rotating round an axis parallel with but eccentric to the axis of the barrel. A loading aperture corresponded with the breech when the screw was rotated through 180 degrees. The breech had to be asymmetrical with the axis of the barrel, so that the system was only suitable for small-caliber guns. (3) The breech screw with stepped threads, the most modern form of screw obturation, with the advantages over other cylindrical screw obturators of more rapid operation and a much greater support surface. The obturator was most commonly divided into four 90-degree sections, each subdivided into three 30-degree areas, of different diameters, one smooth and two threaded. These areas were arranged in the same order and had, respectively, the same diameters in each section. The breech aperture had a corresponding structure, but its steps were arranged in reverse order. When the obturator was closed, its threaded areas were engaged with those of the breech, while the smooth areas were opposite each other. With this arrangement the obturator when closed was supported for two-thirds of its circumference, as against only half the circumference with the ordinary interrupted breech screw. If the stepped areas were increased to four or five, the support increased to three-quarters or four-fifths of the circumference.

Wedge obturators consisted of steel blocks of prismatic or cylindro-prismatic form sliding, generally horizontally, in a slot in the breech. The rear face of this slot, called the mortise, provided support for the obturator on firing. The front face of the wedge was at right angles to the bore, the rear face at an angle to the front called the "wedge angle," which made sliding easier but had to be calculated as to prevent the system from opening spontaneously on firing. In order that the wedge need not be extracted completely on opening, and also to make it lighter, a cutout was made in one end to allow loading.

Block obturators consisted of blocks of steel, of a variety of shapes, which could be rotated around an axis parallel with that of the barrel, sometimes with a sliding or other movement first. They worked quickly and were sometimes used in small-caliber guns.

Until the end of the First World War almost every country gave preference to a plastic ring system for sealing the breech, using the De Bange ring or an expanding steel ring, for medium and large calibers, while for small calibers the metal cartridge case reigned supreme for obturation. After the war some countries, particularly Britain and Germany, generally turned to metal cases even for large and very large calibers, though for these last the cases were separate from the projectiles to facilitate handling. Great improvements were made in the design of gun carriages; rigid carriages disappeared from the major armed forces, while recoil carriages were improved by the fitting of efficient brakes and hydropneumatic recuperators. During the Second World War self-propelled equipment began for the first time to be employed on a large scale, especially by Germany and the United States, with guns mounted on tracked vehicles, sometimes on tank chassis. Among the German guns were the 7.5 cm. gun mounted on the PzKpfw III chassis, the 10.5 cm. assault howitzer on the same chassis, and the Sturmpanzer 43 (a 15 cm. howitzer on the PzKpfw IV). American equipment included the 105 mm. M-7 Self-Propelled Gun armed with the 105/24 M-2A1 howitzer, the 155 mm. M-12 Self-Propelled Gun with the 155 mm. M-1917A1 gun, and the 155 mm. M-40 Self-Propelled Gun with the 155/45 M-2 gun ("Long Tom"). The outstanding features of these guns, and the tactical advantages they gave, were fully appreciated, and after the war development of them was continued. Nowadays the greater part of all field, medium, and heavy artillery is self-propelled. Among guns adopted by the Atlantic Treaty countries are three French howitzers, the 155 mm. AMX-155 and 105 mm. AMX-105A and B; the U.S. 155 mm. M-44 and M-108 howitzers and 203 mm. M-55 heavy howitzer, the U.S. 175 mm. M-107 gun; and the British 105 mm. howitzer F.V. 433 ("Abbot"). A very interesting gun is the Swedish VK-155 self-propelled gun with a 155/50 automatic cannon that can fire three rounds per second. Built by the famous Bofors company, it has a feed system consisting of a caisson holding fourteen shells and an articulated structure with a balance lever to carry the shells from the magazine to the loading position. The breech mechanism is a vertically sliding wedge with a loading cutout at the bottom; the firing mechanism requires ammunition with electric ignition. With the most powerful charge (16.5 kg. of powder), the muzzle velocity of the shell is 865 m. (2837 ft.) per second; the maximum range is 26 km. (16 mi.). In battle order this exceptional self-propelled gun weighs over 51 tons. The self-propelled M-107, adopted in the United States, West Germany, Great Britain, the Netherlands, Israel, and Italy, weighs 28 tons and mounts the 175/60 M-113 gun. Its 420 HP diesel engine gives it a maximum speed of over 55 km. per hour (35 mph) with a range of 725 km. (450 mi.). The gun, 10.5 m. (35 ft.) long, fires separate ammunition and has a Welin screw obturator with plastic ring seal. Maximum range with the 66.5-kg. (147 lb.) HE shell is 32,700 m. (35,760 yds.). Since, like all pieces of a caliber over 150 mm., it can also fire tactical nuclear projectiles, it is easy to understand that such mobility and range make this an extremely versatile weapon.

A modern example of light artillery on a wheel carriage is the British 105 mm. Light Gun. It uses the same separate ammunition (projectile, metal case with percussion cap, charges) as the self-propelled Abbot Mark II, though its barrel can be replaced in two hours by another that enables it to fire U.S. M-1 ammunition. The shells include HE, phosphorus, smoke, HESH (High Explosive Squash Head), training HESH, illuminating shell, and target marker. The charges—six at present—are the same as those for the Abbot except that the 5 High Angle is replaced by the No. 4½ (for distances between 7000 and 13,250 m.—7650 and 14,500 yds.). A seventh, "supercharge," is planned which will increase the range to 17,400 m. (19,000 yds.). The vertically sliding wedge breechblock is worked by a lever fitted high up on the gun to allow it to be used easily at different elevations. The electromagnetic firing device, designed for use with the Cap Conducting Composition primers of the Abbot ammunition, is fitted to the breech. The double sights have internal illumination by Trilux nuclear light, so that no accumulators or batteries are needed. Both the sights and the armament are 100 percent compatible with the various automation systems for sighting and firing, even the most sophisticated such as the FACE (Field Artillery Computer Equipment), which enables targets to be picked up with a speed and precision unimaginable in the past. The use of special material (with Firth Vickers steel the barrel has an average life of 3250 rounds with full charge) and the application of the most modern technology put the 105 mm. Light Gun well to the fore in its class. Three important technical innovations effected during the past forty years have had considerable influence on the development of artillery. First, the taper-bore armor-piercing shell for use against tanks by guns with tapered bores. It consists of a pointed cylindrical core of tungsten carbide (the hardest known material after diamond) with either an aluminum jacket or a big driving band at the back and soft support lugs at the center. Invented in Germany, these shells were used during the Second World War in the 2.8 cm. heavy antitank gun Panzerbüchse 41, the 4.2 cm. PAK-41, and the 7.5 cm. PAK-41, the caliber of which was reduced from 75 mm. to 55 mm. After the charge was ignited, the surface of the relatively soft base was gradually reduced as the shell moved up the barrel, whose caliber continuously decreased from breech to muzzle, and the pressure of the gases correspondingly increased. The muzzle velocity achieved by this means was more than 1000 m. (3300 ft.) per second. Only lack of tungsten prevented the Germans from making the most of this design; it might well have given them an enormous superiority over any tanks of that period. Steel would have been of no use in such shells: with the velocity so greatly increased, they would have shattered on impact.

The second notable innovation, also during the Second World War, was the so-called recoilless gun. The principle on which it worked was extremely simple; given the basic recoil equation $Pv = pV$, in which $P$ is the weight of the weapon and $v$ the recoil velocity, $p$ the weight of the projectile and $V$ its velocity, it was thought that the value of $v$ might be considerably increased and $P$ reduced in proportion. Since it was obviously out of the question to reduce considerably the weight of normal weapons or to increase their recoil velocity, recourse was made to the idea of leaving the chamber open at the back, allowing the gases to escape through one or more Venturi tubes. When the propellant charge is ignited, the gases act on the projectile to the front and issue from the rear of the gun at an extremely high velocity that compensates for their very low mass. The equation quoted above is satisfied, and the gun remains stationary. Since some of the gas of the charge escapes from the chamber before the projectile has left the barrel, the force exerted on the projectile, and consequently the range of the weapon, are less than those of a conventional gun of the same caliber. The advantages, however, especially in weight and size, are so substantial that the system is being used extensively; among models in service are the U.S. Davy Crockett M-28 and M-29 versions, which can throw a nuclear warhead as powerful as 40 tons of TNT for, respectively, 2500 and 5000 m. (2730 and 5460 yds.).

The third great advance came when efforts to increase the range of traditional artillery during the Second World War led to the adoption of various types of RAP (Rocket Assisted Projectiles)—projectiles semi-self-propelled by rockets. This principle now makes possible an increase of 30–35 percent in useful range with no noticeable loss of accuracy.

**aspís** A general term used to describe the typical round shield—Doric in origin—of classical Greece. In Homer's writings, however, the word is used in reference to the great two-lobed or oval shield carried by the warriors of the Trojan War. This succeeded the *sàkos*, to which Homer also refers.

The aspís was generally made of layers of cowhide which were sewn together and then secured firmly with special metal nails called *omphalói*, the heads of which formed a decorative pattern on the outside. It was carried on a baldric or belt slung over one shoulder and across the body and, when in use, was held in the left hand by means of one or more handles fitted on the inside. According to Homer, the shields of the heroes he extolled were huge and frequently laminated on the outside with richly embossed metal. Apart from reinforcement, this decoration served as a talisman to ward off bad luck and to instill terror in the foe.

A little later appeared the true aspís, which was smaller than the classical version but still round and made of layers of cowhide. It was particularly manageable and efficient in combat as it was fitted on the inside with an armlet, set diagonally, with a handle near the edge. Although the aspís gave protection to most of the body, it can sometimes be seen in vase paintings equipped with a sort of apron, of leather or fabric of some kind, attached to the lower part of the shield as a leg defense.

The decoration of the field (*episemon*) of the aspís was an important feature; battle and hunting scenes, mythological episodes, Gorgon's heads, and geometrical designs were frequently depicted. It is not unusual, too, to find the owner's armorial bearing or motto and, on the ordinary soldiers' combat shields, the symbols and coat of arms of their polis.

**assagai** (or **assegai**; also **zaghaya**) A term of Arabic origin for a light spear, about $1\frac{1}{4}$ m. (4 ft.) long, used by the Zulus and related South African tribes, mainly as a missile weapon. Its head was often lancet-shaped or barbed, with a long tang inserted into a slender wooden shaft, which was reinforced at the joint with a cord. Similar spears used since the early 19th century for close combat were equipped with wider leaf-shaped heads on sturdy staffs. The term may have been borrowed to form the word LANCEGAY (*lance + assegai*), denoting a European light spear, also used as a missile.

**assault rifle** An automatic firearm developed from the SUBMACHINE GUN during the Second World War for use with intermediate cartridges, i.e., having the size and power between those of pistol and rifle cartridges. Like submachine guns, assault rifles are capable of both automatic and semiautomatic fire. Some assault rifles—as, for instance, the Soviet AK-47 and its modifications—are provided with bayonets. *See also* GUN: semiautomatic and automatic rifles.

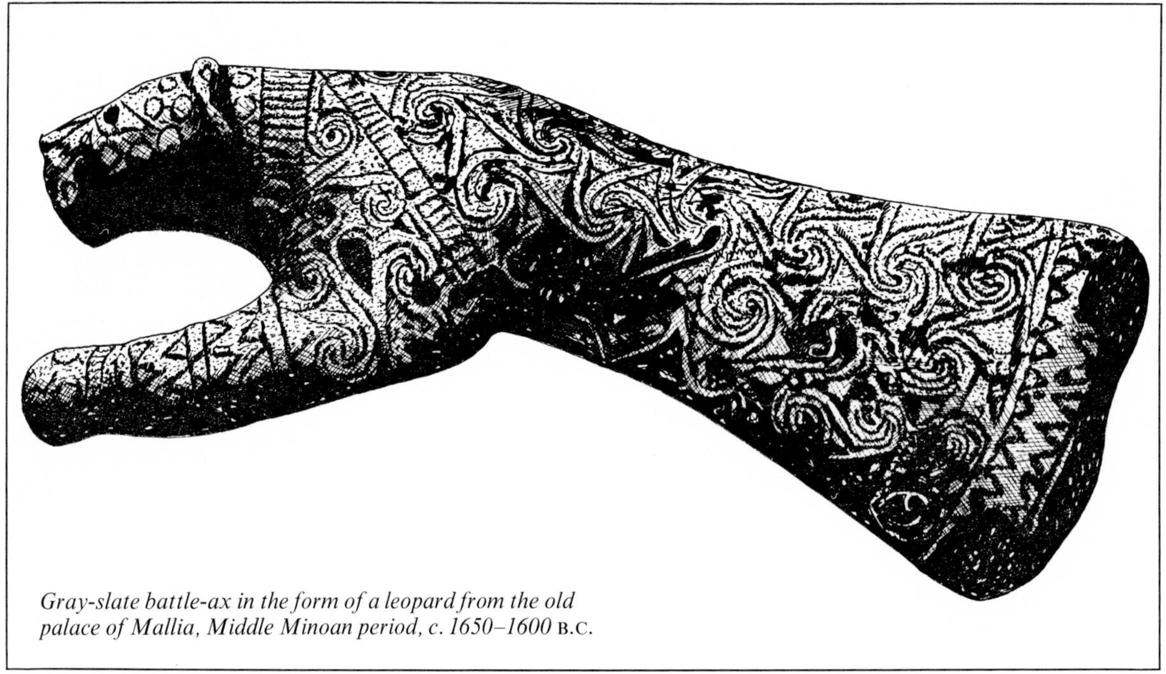

*Gray-slate battle-ax in the form of a leopard from the old palace of Mallia, Middle Minoan period, c. 1650–1600* B.C.

**atomic bomb** *See* BOMB.

**automatic weapons** Category of firearms in which, after initial manual or mechanical loading, the process of firing, extraction, ejection, and reloading is actuated by the harnessing of some of the energy released by the combustion of the cartridges and continues as long as the trigger is pressed, until the gun runs out of ammunition. In semiautomatic weapons the processes are repeated in the same way, but the trigger must be pressed each time a shot is fired; an automatic gives continuous rapid fire, a semiautomatic fires single shots. The functioning of automatic and semiautomatic guns may be one of three basic types: by short or long recoil; by tapping gas from the barrel, at the muzzle, or at the primer; or by expulsion of the cartridge case or the primer by the gases.

In the short-recoil system, the mobile barrel and breechblock are locked together for enough time to allow the bullet to leave the barrel and the internal pressure to fall to the surrounding level. The recoiling barrel is then arrested and some device unlocks the breechblock. The breechblock has by now acquired a certain momentum and continues to move backward to complete the cycle, extracting the spent case, compressing the return spring, and cocking the gun. At the end of its backward movement the breechblock is driven forward again by the spring, chambering a new cartridge and relocking into the barrel. The barrel and breechblock then complete their forward movement together until they reach the position at which the cartridge can be struck by the striker and fired. Weapons using this system include almost all large-caliber pistols (Browning system: the Colt 1911 model, the 1935 model HP, the Random; Walther system: the P-38, the Beretta 51, etc.; the Luger, the 1911 Steyr, etc.), the Johnson Model 41 semiautomatic rifle, the German Mg-42 machine gun.

In the long-recoil system, the barrel and breechblock recoil together for a distance at least equal to the length of a cartridge. At the end of this distance, when the spent case has been ejected, a device unlocks the barrel and a return spring drives it forward again, while the breechblock remains locked at the rear. Meanwhile the feed system positions a new cartridge, and the breechblock, released by another device, is driven forward by its separate return spring. This system, not used very much, has been employed successfully in rifled weapons of calibers over 20 mm. and in a number of smooth-bore sporting guns.

In gas-operated weapons, one or more gas ports are bored at some point in the barrel leading into a cylinder, generally mounted below or at the side of the barrel. The cylinder contains a piston which is connected to the breechblock or bolt. When, on firing, the bullet passes the gas port, a small part of the propellant gases expands into the cylinder and acts on the piston, which is forced back and actuates the breechblock, unlocking it and driving it to the rear. The return spring now drives the piston forward again, and with it the breechblock, which pushes a new round into the chamber. The gun is then ready to repeat the cycle; the final movement of the piston locks the breechblock, and the firing pin strikes the cartridge. Guns that use this system include the Hotchkiss and Lewis machine guns, the Cei-Rigotti rifles, the Clair pistol, the Chatellerault, CZ, Bren, and Breda 57 machine guns, the Garand rifle, the FN assault rifle, the Beretta 70/.223 assault rifle, and many others. In some other gas-operated weapons there is no piston, and the gases are channeled directly onto the breechblock (Armalite AR-10 and AR-15).

The system in which the gases are trapped at the muzzle is a variation of the foregoing; the gases are trapped by a cone fitted to the muzzle and drive a piston which works through a rod to unlock the bolt and open the breech. Typical examples were the Browning experimental rifles of 1889 and 1890 and the German semiautomatic rifles Gewehr 41M and 41W.

One of the few known examples of a "primer-recoil" weapon was that devised by the Austrian designer G. Roth in the 1890s. It required the use of special cartridge cases with a long housing for the primer cap. On firing, the cap recoiled in its housing and drove back the striker to unlock the bolt. The system in which the cartridge case is expelled to act on an unlocked breechblock—the "blowback" system with unstable obturation—relies on the direct use of gas pressure on the breechblock via the base of the spent case, driving it back, extracting and ejecting the case, compressing the return spring, and cocking the gun. The only resistance to the opening of the breech comes from the friction between the case and the chamber wall and from the inertia of the breechblock. This is the system used in almost all semiautomatic pistols of medium and small power and in virtually all submachine guns.

In a "delayed blowback" system with semi-stable obturation, the mechanism is again actuated by the expulsion of the case, but in addition to the resistance described in the previous type there is also a system of mechanical braking, by a system of levers (as in the Schwarzlose machine gun) or by friction (as in the 1921 model Thompson submachine gun).

A blowback system with stable obturation can be defined as a system in which the breechblock remains firmly locked to the barrel until the gas pressure falls to a sufficiently low level. The breechblock is then unlocked by some form of mechanism and the residual pressure drives it back, acting via the base of the cartridge case with enough force to carry out the complete cycle. The unlocking of the breechblock may in practice be partly gas-operated, as in the Scotti Model X rifle, or by short recoil, as in the Revelli Fiat 14 machine gun.

For historical and technical notes on different types of automatic weapons, see GUN; MACHINE GUN; SUBMACHINE GUN; PISTOL.

**aventail** A form of mail tippet worn with medieval armor to protect the shoulders, neck, and part of the face. The aventail, which was very thick and sometimes used double, was attached to the BASNET by means of staples (*vervelles*) riveted along the lower edge of the helmet and the sides of the face opening. A leather band pierced with holes was fitted over the vervelles, and the aventail attached by eyelet rings along its upper edge; a cord, wire, or thong was then passed through the vervelles and secured at each end. The lower edge of the aventail spread over the neck and shoulders. The size varied according to the shape of the helmet, and was sometimes reduced to little more than a mail collar. Known as a pizaine or standard (standing collar), this type of mail throat guard was sometimes attached to the haubergeon or worn separately. The aventail disappeared around the beginning of the 16th century, when it was replaced by the GORGET and neck guards.

**ax** One of the oldest tools and weapons of man, the ax dates back to the Old Stone (Paleolithic) Age. The earliest axes, made out of a single piece of stone, were almond-shaped (amygdaloid), 20–25 cm. (8–10 in.) long, with both faces curved by flaking to form the cutting edge. Such axes (or hatchets) were produced from about 500,000 to 50,000 years ago by the Early Paleolithic cultures of Abbeville and St. Acheul in Europe, by cultures of the Chellean-Acheulean period in Africa, and corresponding periods in Asia. They were made preferably from flint or obsidian, but also from whatever stone was at hand.

*Battle-ax.* During the Upper Paleolithic Period, about 35,000 years ago, a great invention revolutionized tools and weapons, making them much more efficient. This was the haft, or wooden handle. Bent wood, horn sockets, gum, and lashing were used to attach the haft to the ax head. Other technological advances occurred some 9000 to 8000 years ago, during the New Stone (Neolithic) Age, when civilizations of the Mediterranean, India, and China first developed methods of grinding, polishing, and drilling the stone, techniques which later spread over other regions. Often fitted to their handles using an "eye," i.e., a circular hole in the center or near the back of the ax head, Neolithic axes were powerful and reliable combat weapons, provided with a convex cutting edge; some had a symmetrical double head with an "eye" in the center. During the Bronze Age (about 8000 to 3000 years ago, depending on the region), at first copper and later a copper-and-tin alloy were used for cast battle-axes and other weapons and tools. In Egypt, crescentic axes having one or two ends of the blade lashed to the shaft were strikingly similar to European medieval staff weapons known as the GISARME and the BERDYSH. The socket for the haft, cast as part of the blade, was also developed at this period. From northern Europe spread a peculiar type of ax, the CELT, which had a socket with a dead end facing toward the cutting edge. The celt was greatly improved in cast-bronze battle-axes by hammering and sharpening, techniques inherited by the smiths of the Iron Age beginning about 3000 years ago.

The battle-ax was widely distributed throughout the pre-classical period, although it was never used as a weapon by either the Greek or Roman world, where it was seen as a "barbarian" weapon. It was in fact these "barbarian" peoples (Franks, Merovingians, Celts, Lombards, Vikings) who used the battle-ax consistently in combat from the earliest Christian period onward. It retained very similar forms throughout Central Europe, where it was typified by the FRANCISCA, whereas farther to the north we find axes of the Danish type with a fairly broad, crescent-shaped blade and flat back. Such were the battle-axes of foot soldiers and mounted men depicted on the Bayeux Tapestry (1066–77), which celebrates the victory of William the Conqueror at the Battle of Hastings; both the Normans and the English were armed with the same Danish type of battle-ax, the horsemen's version having a short handle. An earlier variation of the Danish ax was the so-called Viking form, in which the "bearded" blade had a deep circular cutout at the lower edge. Battle-axes of the Danish type, having developed various specialized forms, continued in use up till the late

16th century, sometimes being called the sparth in English texts.

With the addition of the fluke and the spike, in the 13th century, the battle-ax acquired more versatility in its combat functions and later became a favorite knightly weapon for foot combat (see POLEAX). Another development led to a Swiss form, the *Mordaxt*, in which the curved blade was forged with a spiked top, the back being provided with a massive long fluke. Smaller and lighter variations of the battle-ax, with short, often all-metal handles, were used by western European mounted warriors until the late 16th century and somewhat longer in eastern Europe. As boarding weapons, axes were still issued to naval crews until recent times. Some forms of the battle-ax have survived to the present day as national ceremonial weapons as well as convenient implements. Such is the case of the Hungarian *fokos* (Polish and Russian *topor*), an ax with a small down-curved head, often made of bronze, and a long handle usually decorated with engraved stag's horn or carving. Popular in the Carpathian region, the fokos is still used as a walking stick, its head being sometimes made of a hard wood embellished like the handle.

*Throwing ax.* A missile weapon shaped as a cruciform hatchet, made of steel. Its blade was forged into a sharp tip and balanced by a pointed fluke; the short handle was similarly pointed at the bottom and often extended into a spike on the top. Analogous in use to the WAR HAMMER, throwing axes were quite popular in central Europe between the 14th and 16th centuries.

*Sapper's ax, agricultural ax.* This was an ax-shaped tool-cum-weapon with a large blade offset by a strong fluke. With the reorganization that took place in the various European armies in the late 18th century, it was issued to pioneers and other units of the engineer corps in the form of a large Roman-type ax, inspired by the upsurge of classical studies and neoclassical art. Although military regulations recommended the choice of tall, strong soldiers for the engineer corps, the weight and relative nonfunctional nature of this implement suggest that the figure of the pioneer with his large ax over his shoulder had more to do with military pageantry than with actual fieldwork. The sapper's ax disappeared from the equipment of the European armies during the 19th century.

*Executioner's ax.* A large, heavy ax for use with both hands. It was used in central and northern Europe until fairly recently for beheadings.

*Saxon miner's ax.* The miner's ax is neither an arm nor a tool. Its head and, in particular, the way in which the head is attached to the shaft, makes it too fragile for anything other than ceremonial use. The ax head was usually made of iron, though sometimes of zinc or brass, and was flat and light. The cutting edge, continuing upward in a slight curve to form a spike, often ended in a copper or brass ball. There were openings in the center of the head, usually in the shape of a clover, a heart or, sometimes, a cross, and groups of three and five circles, always in the same two places. The handles, with their unsophisticated but varied designs, are the most interesting part of the axes. They can be divided into four main types: (1) handles made entirely from engraved stag's horn; (2) wooden handles inlaid with gold or engraved stag's horn; (3) wooden handles with only the lower part covered with engraved stag's horn; (4) wooden handles decorated with pokerwork.

This ax originated in the 16th century from the ax used as a tool by the miners of the Dresden region, an area rich in forests and mines, whose center was the town of Freiberg, 50 km. (30 mi.) to the southwest of Dresden. The town's museum and its Königliche Bergakademie contain both examples and illustrations of miner's axes. At the end of the last century, there was still an altar in the Freiberg cathedral known as the "miners' throne"; this was decorated with statuettes, one of which showed a miner in festive dress, with his ax over his right shoulder and a piece of ore in his left hand. He held a shield, dated 1546, bearing the emblems of his profession, a hammer and pickax. The dates found on the axes cover the period 1622–1730, although they continued to be carried in festival processions by miners' guilds for a long time afterward. There still were such processions in Saxony in the late 19th century.

The decorations found on these axes include scenes from mining life, miners in festive dress, Christ on the cross and other religious motifs, important personages of the time, and landscapes. This was the work of elderly and disabled miners, which explains their naïve quality and simplicity of technique.

**ayda katti** A typical knife used in the Coorg region of India. Its blade is broad and heavy, curved and single-edged, widening toward the point and sharp on the concave side. Its wooden hilt—often painted red and decorated with silver rosettes—has no guard but a large, flat, kite-shaped pommel. Ivory hilts are also frequently seen. About 40–50 cm. (16–20 in.) long, the ayda katti is carried without a scabbard on the wearer's back, where it passes through a flattened brass ring, a *todunga*, which is fastened to his belt.

# B

**back edge** *See* FALSE EDGE.
**backpiece** The metal part of the hilt of edged weapons which closes off the grip at the top and the back. In European military sabers, it appeared as early as the 18th century.
**backplate** An important piece of armor to protect the back of the trunk, the counterpart of the BREASTPLATE, to which it was fastened by various means: a strap and buckle over each shoulder; a waist belt; hinges on one side and straps and buckles on the other; studs and slots at the sides.

In the first half of the 14th century there was really no backplate, the trunk being protected by a HAUBERK and a COAT OF PLATES over the back of which passed the crossed straps and belt that held the reinforcing breastplate in position. Toward the middle of the century, body defense was improved by the introduction of two back lames which clipped into the breastplate at each side and were buckled together to form the CUIRASS. This divided backplate remained in use until well into the 16th century, its survival being due to its convenience in the joust, where complete back protection was not required.

*Backplate of an armor belonging to Duke Francesco I de' Medici, made in central Italy, C. 1574. Museo Nazionale del Bargello, Florence.*

The more developed forms of the backplate appeared towards the middle of the 1400s, at first consisting of several wide lames riveted together, which formed the upper backplate, and a large plate below, the so-called lower backplate. This type had a high neck flange between the shoulder straps, the underarm gussets were widely cut on the slant, it was slightly convex in contour and hardly shaped at all to the shoulder blades. The lower backplate was fastened at the sides to the lower breastplate—which it resembled—and supported from the center of the upper backplate by a buckle and strap fixed to its center point. The backplate made of one piece of steel was also introduced around 1400. A few modifications which took place in the course of time included the reinforcement of the neck flange and the addition to the bottom edge of the lower backplate of overlapping rear lames of the skirt, the last of which, called the hind TASSET, formed the loin guard. These changes were inseparable from the devlopments that took place in the design of the breastplate toward the end of the 15th century.

Two basic types of 16th-century backplates are easily distinguishable and also correspond to the evolution of the breastplate. The commonest type was the "Italian" style, with its high neck flange between the shoulder straps, the slightly rounded, slanting underarm gussets, and the tendency to narrow at the waist. This corresponded to the so-called bag-form breastplate of the second half of the 16th century, and it terminated with a riveted waist lame or with a raised lower edge of the plate, its main purpose being to prevent the waist belt from slipping down. During the first half of the 16th century, the "German"-style backplate had a low, straight neckline, without shoulder prongs, and was slightly globular in contour towards the waist. Common to both types, however, was the pronounced shaping over the shoulder blades and a median depression along the spine.

In the 17th-century cuirass, the backplate took the form of a shaped plate with the neck flange and underarm gussets barely apparent, in an almost mirror reflection of the breastplate. Because of its secondary importance in combat, whether in battle or the courses, the backplate was not usually equipped to take reinforcing pieces. However, a typical feature was the hole—or group of holes—especially in some 16th-century examples, just below the neck flange to fix a support for the jousting helm.

**backsight** *See* SIGHTS.

**backsword** A general term for heavy military swords which had a straight single-edged blade and a well-developed closed guard—usually a basket hilt or a shell guard. The blade, sometimes grooved and ridged on both faces, had a more or less thick back to give the blade the necessary rigidity. A short section of the back near the point often had a sharpened edge to carry out cutting strikes without changing the position of the sword. The point itself was sometimes rather ogivally contoured since the backsword was essentially a cutting weapon; however, some military models had blades gradually narrowing into a sharp point designed for thrusts. The backsword was widely used by European heavy cavalry from the 17th century, and a most popular variety was the PALLASCH.

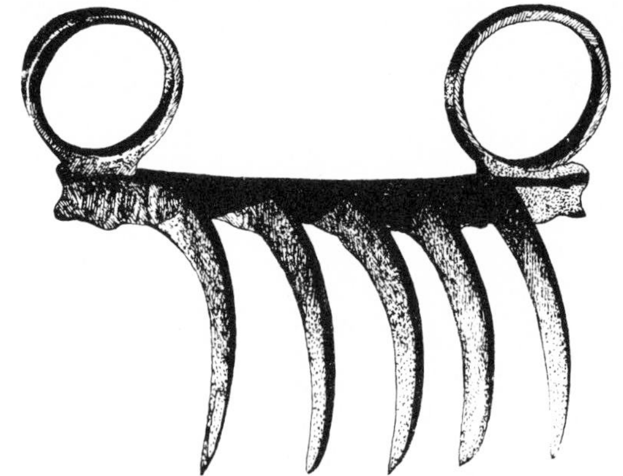

*Five-clawed Indian bagh-nakh.*

**baculus** A Latin term for a heavy hardwood club or staff with protruding knots, and in some cases sheathed with metal, to be used as a mace. In civilian life the term was also used to describe the wayfarer's staff and the ordinary walking stick.

**badan** The Arabic term for BAIDANA.

**bade-bade** *See* BATTIG.

**bagh-nakh** (or **wagh-nakh, wahar-nuk, nahar-nakh**) An Indian weapon, not unlike the European knuckle-duster. Its name means "tiger's claws," which was particularly apt since it consisted of four or five steel claws riveted to a flat bar fitted with two rings to slip over the aggressor's fingers. Sometimes there was also a spike at the side. The bagh-nakh was never regarded as a prestigious weapon and was used mostly by thieves and murderers.

**baidana** (or **badan**) A type of the coat of mail, used mainly in Russia and Middle Eastern countries. The word is of Arab origin, meaning a shirt made of large interlinked iron rings, up to 2.5 cm. (1 in.) in diameter. The flat surface of the rings was often decorated with stamped ornaments and such inscriptions as "God is with us, none shall touch us." A typical 16th-century Russian baidana consisted of about 10,000 rings, weighed about 6 kg. (13 lbs.) and was roughly 80 cm. (31 in.) long. The edges of a baidana were sometimes decorated with gilded copper rings and the breast with medallions of the same material. It was usually worn over a regular coat of mail made of small rings, thus doubling the protection.

The best examples of baidana armor—including that of the tsar Boris Godunov—are preserved in the Kremlin State Armory in Moscow.

**bakhterets** *See* BEKHTER.

**baldric** A shoulder belt of leather or cloth generally worn over the right shoulder and across the body to the left hip for carrying a sword, bayonet, or saber and sometimes a drum or flag. The baldric, an updated version of the ancient Roman BALTEUS, was in use mainly from the Middle Ages up to the 19th century. It is still part of the standard accoutrements of certain regiments and is frequently worn with full-dress uniform, for displaying the regimental badge.

**ball powder** Nitrocellulose powder in spherical granules. *See also* SMOKELESS POWDERS.

**ballista** *See* ARCUBALLISTA.

**ballistic cap** A hollow cap fitted over the PENETRATING CAP of an armor-piercing shell to preserve its aerodynamic form.

**ballistite** Colloidal powder combining nitroglycerin and nitrocellulose. *See also* SMOKELESS POWDERS.

**balteus** (or **balteum**; Greek *telamon* or *aorter*) Latin word for the baldric or belt which passed over one shoulder across the body to the opposite hip; a sword, shield, or quiver could be hung from it. During the Middle Ages it was synonymous with CINGULUM.

The balteus was generally worn by Romans from the right shoulder, over the armor. While for the ordinary soldier it was a plain belt of leather or some kind of fabric, for high-ranking personages, it was bedecked with ornamental plaques or decorations. From Homer, we learn that the balteus of Agamemnon's shield was made of silver with sky-blue figures and embellished with a three-headed dragon.

It sometimes happened that, if a balteus were rather large and thick, it also had a defensive value. A fine example of this is recounted by Homer when describing how Ajax was saved from Hector's javelin because it struck him at the spot where his two baltei crossed.

**banduk** An Indian word meaning "gun" which derives from the Arabic *bunduk*. Guns were brought into India in the early 16th century through the Portuguese colonies on the west coast of the subcontinent. The first handguns to reach India were primitively constructed matchlocks, and this style of gun continued to be used for a long time. Turkish and French flintlocks were introduced during the 18th century, and it is possible that the term "banduk" referred to flintlock guns while TORADAR was reserved for the old matchlocks.

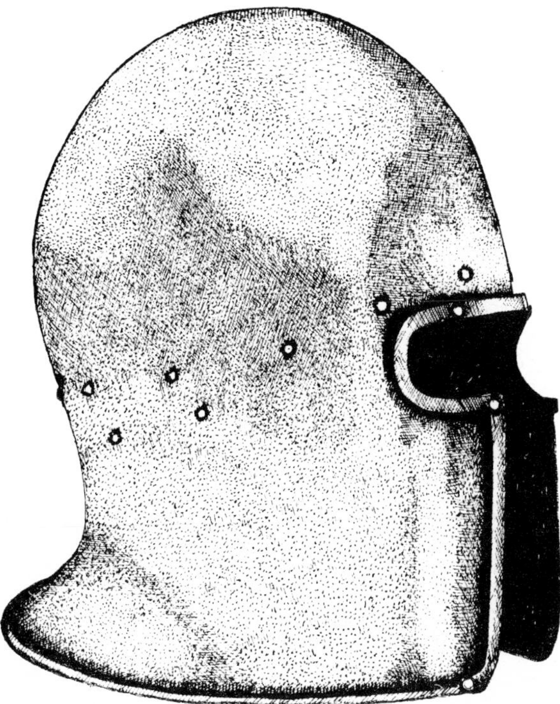

*Barbut, Milan, c. 1470. Museo Civico L. Marzoli, Brescia.*

**barbut** A type of helmet used from the second half of the 14th century to the late 15th. The barbut was generally forged in one piece. In its earliest form the skull was ogival—that is, shaped rather like a Gothic arch—with a pronounced apex. Towards the end of 14th and throughout the 15th century, however, the skull became much more rounded with a central reinforcing keel at the top of which a slot was pierced for the crest. At first, the lower part of the helmet was almost vertical with only a slight outward curve at the nape, but toward the end of the century it became rather more splayed out.

The part protecting the face evolved into a form which caused this type of helmet to be called the "Corinthian" barbut because of its strong similarity to classical Greek helmets. The skull extended down to cover the whole face, with a vertical slit almost closing in front and two wide arched eye openings separated by the fixed nasal bar. In other barbuts, this opening was T-shaped, often with a small cusp instead of a nasal. A series of small holes was punched—usually along the neck edge of the skull—to which the helmet lining was attached. In some helmets a leather band was riveted inside the skull, to which a lining was stitched. Made from tempered steel, the barbut was nearly always quite plain and probably polished, although it was sometimes russeted. Decoration was restricted to studs or rivet heads along the edges.

There were a few rare versions of the barbut. One, which was fitted with a pivoted visor, is documented only for the latter part of the 14th century, while another had hinged cheekpieces.

**bard** All the pieces that made up the complete protective armor for a war-horse up to the end of the 16th century. In the Middle Ages, the bard consisted of a TRAPPER made of mail or quilted cloth. It was sometimes in more than one piece and covered the horse to its knees, with a gap at the sides to allow for the stirrups. The trapper was extended over the horse's head, covering it completely rather like a cowl, with openings for the mouth and bit, eyes and ears.

By the 15th century, complete plate bards had been introduced—legend has it, by a condottiere commander, Alberico da Barciano—and these remained in use up to the mid-16th century with only minor modifications. Full bards, however, were fairly rare largely because they were extremely heavy, and lighter horse armor was increasingly in favor since it gave greater freedom of movement. Basically, bards consisted of a combination of protective plates with an armored harness. The head protection, called a SHAFFRON (or chanfron), was made up of articulated plates connected with the CRINET, or neck guard. The forelegs were afforded some protection by a large plate, the PEYTRAL, the lower edge of which jutted forward and was sometimes shaped into two raised curves to allow the horse to move more freely.

The horse's flanks were protected by FLANCHARDS hanging from the war saddle, to which were attached armored reins and stirrup leathers. The flanchards were themselves linked together by thongs and were placed over

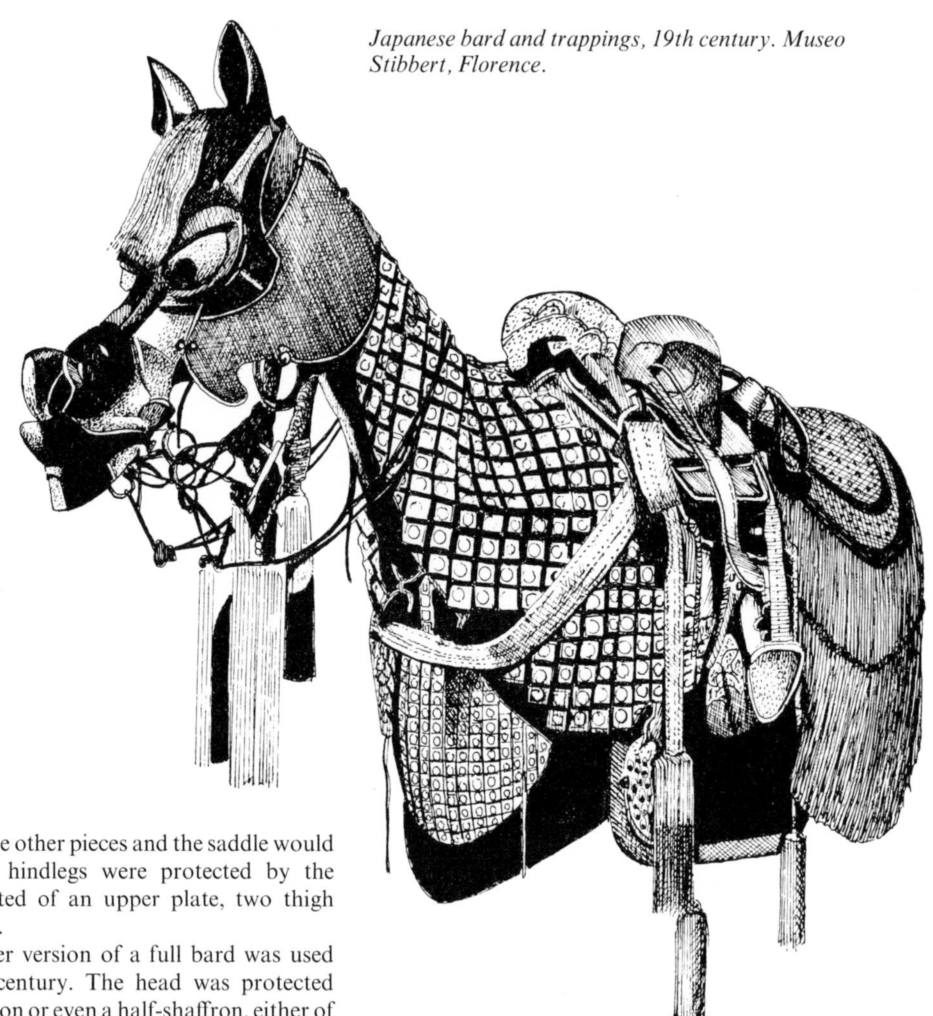

*Japanese bard and trappings, 19th century. Museo Stibbert, Florence.*

the horse first so that the other pieces and the saddle would hold them firm. The hindlegs were protected by the crupper, which consisted of an upper plate, two thigh pieces, and a tail guard.

A lighter and simpler version of a full bard was used throughout the 16th century. The head was protected solely by an open shaffron or even a half-shaffron, either of which would have been fitted with a neck lame. The curb rein would have been laminated, but the second rein was seldom present. The half crinet, strapped around the neck, was frequently plated and constituted the only protection for the back of the neck. The peytral was replaced by a breast band which was generally armored. Flanchards were not used, but the war saddle was often reinforced with metal. The place of the heavy crupper was taken by much lighter leather straps covered with metal scales.

There was no clear distinction between light horse armors and armored caparison or trappings, since there was no consistency in the use of armored pieces which were really characteristic of light horse armor as distinct from the leather harness with metal trappings.

From a decorative point of view, bards kept very much in line with the evolution of armor mainly because, during the 16th century in particular, they formed an integral part of a fighting man's garniture. Although they were inclined to be undecorated in the 15th century, by the following century they were being embellished with engraving and embossing in the usual designs found on armor. The techniques of making horse armor differed little from those of making armor for men, but there were no famous armorers who made it their specialty. One of the earliest, however, is known to have been Pier Innocenzo da Faerno, active in the mid-15th century, who produced a complete set of bards which is preserved in Vienna.

Japanese horse armor was introduced in Japan in Tokugawa (Edo) period (1603–1867), probably as a result of European influence. However, as Japan was at peace, the bards took on the character of parade trappings and were never actually needed for battle. The shaffron was shaped like the head of a fabulous monster or dragon and was made of papier-mâché or leather decorated with gilded lacquer; it was rarely made of iron but, when it was, the plate was so thin that its protective value would have been negligible. The body coverings consisted of a crinet or mane guard, crupper, tail guard, and flanchards, which all weighed very little since everything was made of small squares of molded leather that were lacquered and gilded with heraldic devices and sewn onto cloth. Heavy cords of red silk, ending in long tassels, were used to keep the pieces in place, rather than straps.

**bardiche** Usual, but incorrect, spelling of BERDYSH.

**barong** A term of the same common origin as PARANG for a knife used mostly by the Moro tribes in Borneo, Sulu,

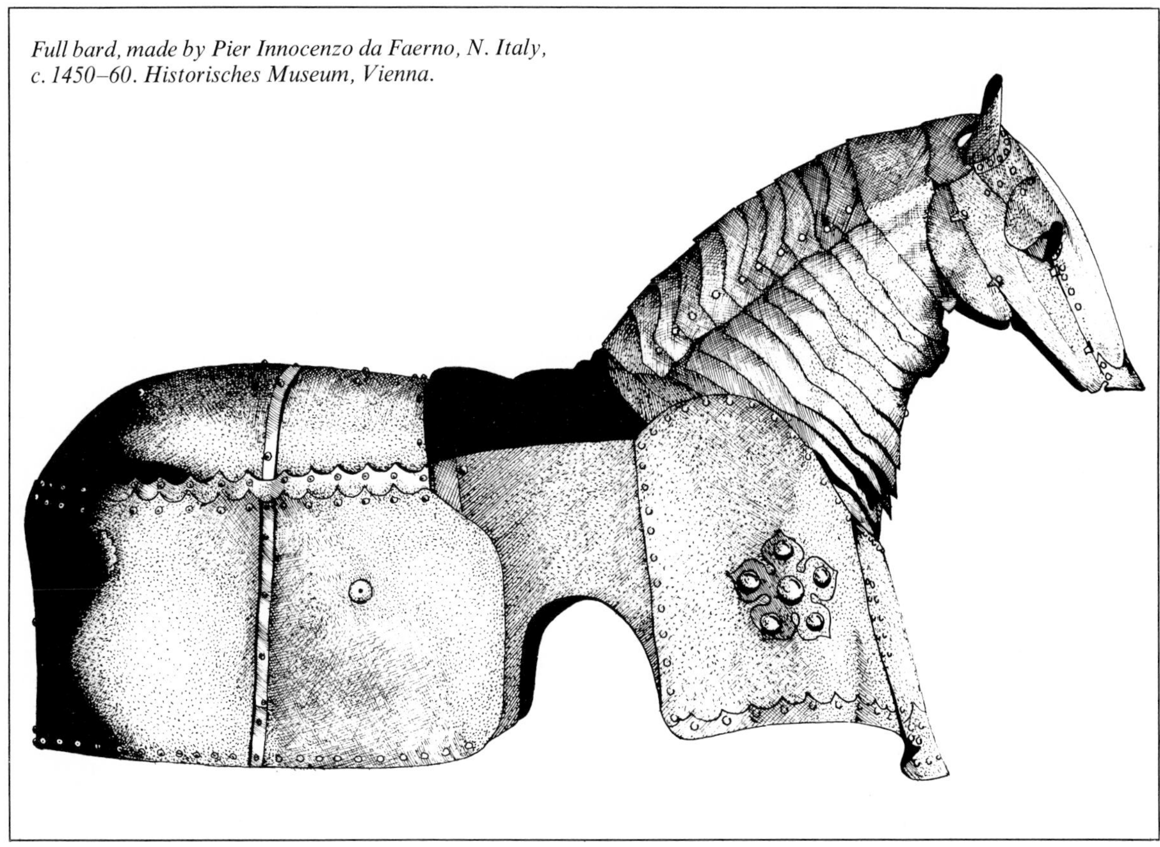

*Full bard, made by Pier Innocenzo da Faerno, N. Italy, c. 1450–60. Historisches Museum, Vienna.*

and Mindanao. Its heavy, spatulate blade is usually single-edged, but there are examples of barongs that are double-edged for about half of their 40 cm. (16 in.) blades. This well-balanced knife has no guard, and the hilt may be of wood, horn, or silver, often worked with ivory. The hilt of a war barong, however, is made of black horn and kept severely simple.

One of the main characteristics of a barong is its pommel, which is formed into two lateral extensions resembling the head of an exotic bird or animal. Invariably the flat, wooden scabbard is elaborately carved.

**barrel** In firearms, a metal tube to hold the cartridge (or the projectile and the propellant charge) and, utilizing the explosive force of the charge, to act as a path for the projectile, giving it a very high velocity. The oldest barrels for muzzleloading guns were made of cast bronze. Bronze gave way to iron, which was more resistant; a block of the metal was first beaten with a hammer to make a long rectangular plate, which was then wrapped around a cylinder of hardened iron by heating and hammering, and finally made to form a tube by overlapping the edges and forging them together. The thick tube thus obtained was then bored out, smoothed, ground, and fitted with a breechblock to make the finished barrel. This was the method most widely used from the end of the 15th century until the 19th. Externally, barrels were given a slightly tapered form, narrowing toward the muzzle and wider at the breech, where the metal was to withstand maximum pressure. The outside surface might be round or squared (actually octagonal) and marked off by raised bands at one or more points.

The barrel of a modern breechloader comprises the breech, the rear end, in which the cartridge is inserted and which is sealed by the breechblock; the barrel proper, in front of the breech; the mouth of the breech, being the rear face of the breech; the muzzle, the front face of the barrel; the bore, the inside of the tube, which is divided into two parts, (a) the chamber, the rear section of the barrel, of which the front part houses the projectile and guides it through the tapered "lead" into the bore, while the back part contains the cartridge or shell case, and (b) the bore itself, along which the projectile passes, acquiring a rotary motion due to the rifling, the system of grooves and "lands" cut in a spiral pattern along the surface of the bore.

**bars** Parts of the HILT of edged weapons, having a protective function. Made in various forms, the bars join the knuckle guard to other parts of the hilt: loops, rings, and arms of the hilt. Bars appeared toward the mid-16th century, increasing the protection to the hand in a type of swordplay that concentrated mainly on the thrust. They were still in use in the late 17th century, when other types of guard—the shell, cup, and dish—made them obsolete.

**bascinet** *See* BASNET.

**baselard** (or **basilard**) A DAGGER or a short sword used in the 13th to 15th centuries having an I-shaped hilt formed by the guard, grip, and the crosspiece of the pommel. Their form varied greatly. In Italy the guard and the pommel were usually straight and of the same length, whereas in other European countries the upper crosspiece was usually markedly upward-curving and the guard straight. Another popular shape had both crosspieces curving slightly toward each other. The blade was double-edged, pointed, and reinforced by central ribbing.

The term "baselard" was contemporary with the appearance of the weapon itself. For many years it was thought to derive from the town of Basel, as indicated by certain features in the hilt which, at a later stage, were to become specialized in the Swiss dagger, wherein guard and pommel curved toward each other. The hilt was thus better adapted to firm, secure holding. The form of the baselard blade, in which the forte or upper section had straight and parallel edges which ended in an ogive-shaped tip, also bore some resemblance to the Swiss dagger. A theory has recently been put forward that the baselard came originally from Solingen, although the clear association with the name Basel and the existence of certain documents seem to indicate that the Swiss town was indeed the place of manufacture and that it was from there that this weapon was distributed throughout Europe. While the name was contemporary with the weapon itself, it cannot be maintained with certainty that it actually applied to this short sword, or dagger, rather than to a larger weapon of the *storta* (curved sword) type or to the weapon represented in a fresco dating back to the mid-14th century and preserved in Fiesole. This weapon also had an I-shaped hilt, but its blade was shaped with a straight back, single edge, and point.

**bases** A flared, pleated textile skirt worn over the skirt and tassets of an armor during the first quarter of the 16th century. The term also applied to a contemporary steel imitation of this textile skirt, which was attached to the cuirass instead of normal skirt and tassets. Steel bases comprised two main parts joined together by straps; in front and rear the bases had a deep arched cutout to enable the wearer to ride on horseback.

**basilisk** According to Diego Ufano, the famous Spanish gunner and writer on the subject, who lived at the turn of the 16th and 17th centuries, the basilisk was the biggest of the bastard pieces of ARTILLERY, thus corresponding to the double bastard CULVERIN. It was 26 calibers (15 ft.) in length, weighed more than 5525 kg. (12,000 lbs.), and fired 22-kg. (48-lb.) iron balls. These measurements refer to Spanish artillery.

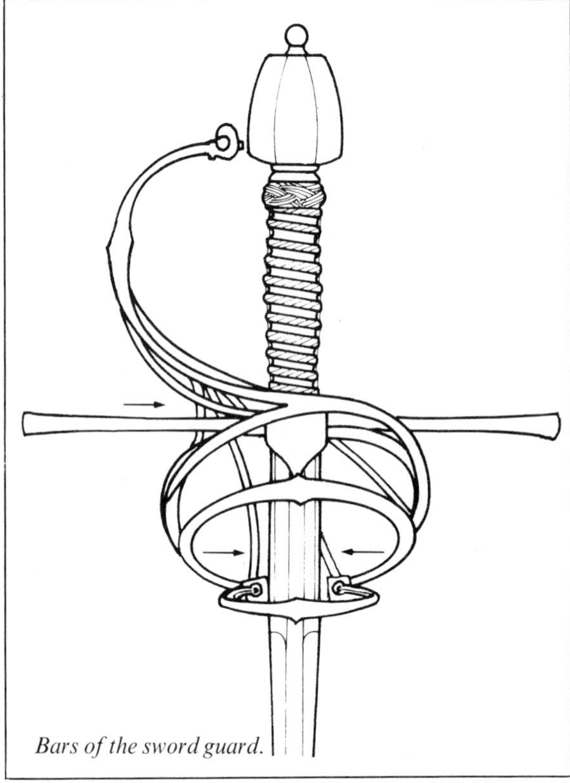
*Bars of the sword guard.*

**basnet** (also **basinet**, **bascinet**) A type of helmet used from the early 13th century to the 15th. Its earliest forms (then called CERVELLIÈRE) consisted solely of a simple skullcap (hence its name, diminutive of "basin") but were often worn with a coif or an AVENTAIL, which was attached to the helmet to protect the lower part of the face, the neck, and shoulders. The visor, introduced by c. 1300, was always made in one piece and fixed to the skull at the temples with hinge-and-pin pivots. Another visor type and method of attachment was widely favored in Germany and is known by the German name *Klappvisier*, in which the visor was hinged at the center of its upper edge to a curved, vertical bar attached by two studs to the brow of the basinet.

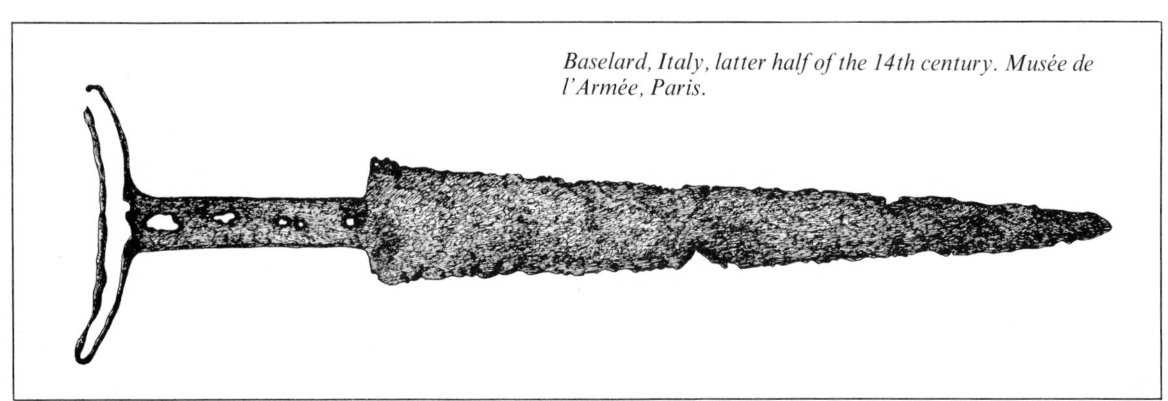
*Baselard, Italy, latter half of the 14th century. Musée de l'Armée, Paris.*

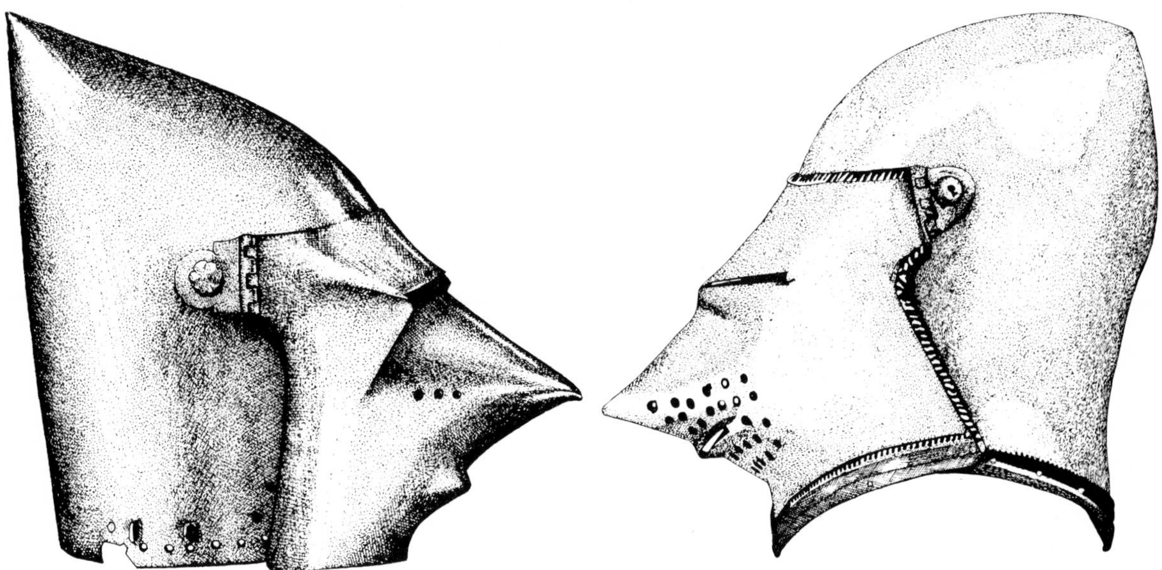

*Basnets.* (left) *N. Italy, c. 1400. Odescalchi Collection, Museo di Palazzo Venezia, Rome.* (right) *N. Italy, c. 1400–1420 (the visor is a modern reconstruction). Metropolitan Museum, New York.*

Pointed visors were known as "houndskull" and "pig-face" by 19th-century collectors. The sights were sometimes merely two horizontal slits or a series of vertical piercings at eye level. The conical snout became very pronounced by the late 14th century, the purpose of this being to add more protection for the face, since a hitting lance would be deflected by the very shape of the visor. A series of piercings in the visor provided ventilation. It was always worn with an aventail and sometimes reinforced with circular ear guards. This type of helmet was in use during the 14th century and first half of the 15th.

A special type of basnet, called the great basnet, was worn from the late 14th century to the early 16th. It was a large helmet with a neck guard, reinforced with a wide bevor in such a way that its weight was taken on the shoulders and not on the head. Its skull was generally more rounded, and the neck guard was lengthened into a crescent-shaped plate which dipped down over the top of the backplate. Its visor was either shaped into the characteristic "pig-face" or rounded; there was an eye slit, and the whole visor was hinged to each side of the skull. Its lower edge was overlapped by a heavy bevor (also called gorget plate), which was riveted to the skull.

Toward the end of the 15th century the great basnet developed into a particularly heavy type of helmet, extending down to the shoulders, with full visor—which was usually of the "bellows" type—and its large bevor reaching down to the breastplate, to which it was fastened. This type was used in the tourneys and for fighting in the lists.

A peculiar form of basnet had an ogival skull with a neck guard all forged from one plate.

**bastard** Adjective used between the 16th and 18th centuries to indicate artillery pieces whose dimensions differed from the normal or usual.

**bastard string** A device used with the crossbow to help fitting or replacing of the bowstring to the weapon. It was a

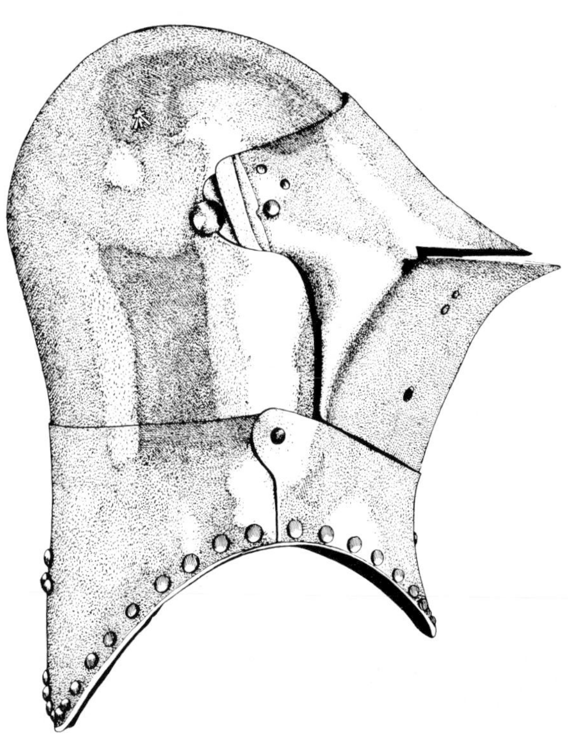

*Great basnet, N. Italy, c. 1455–50. Churburg Armory, Sluderno.*

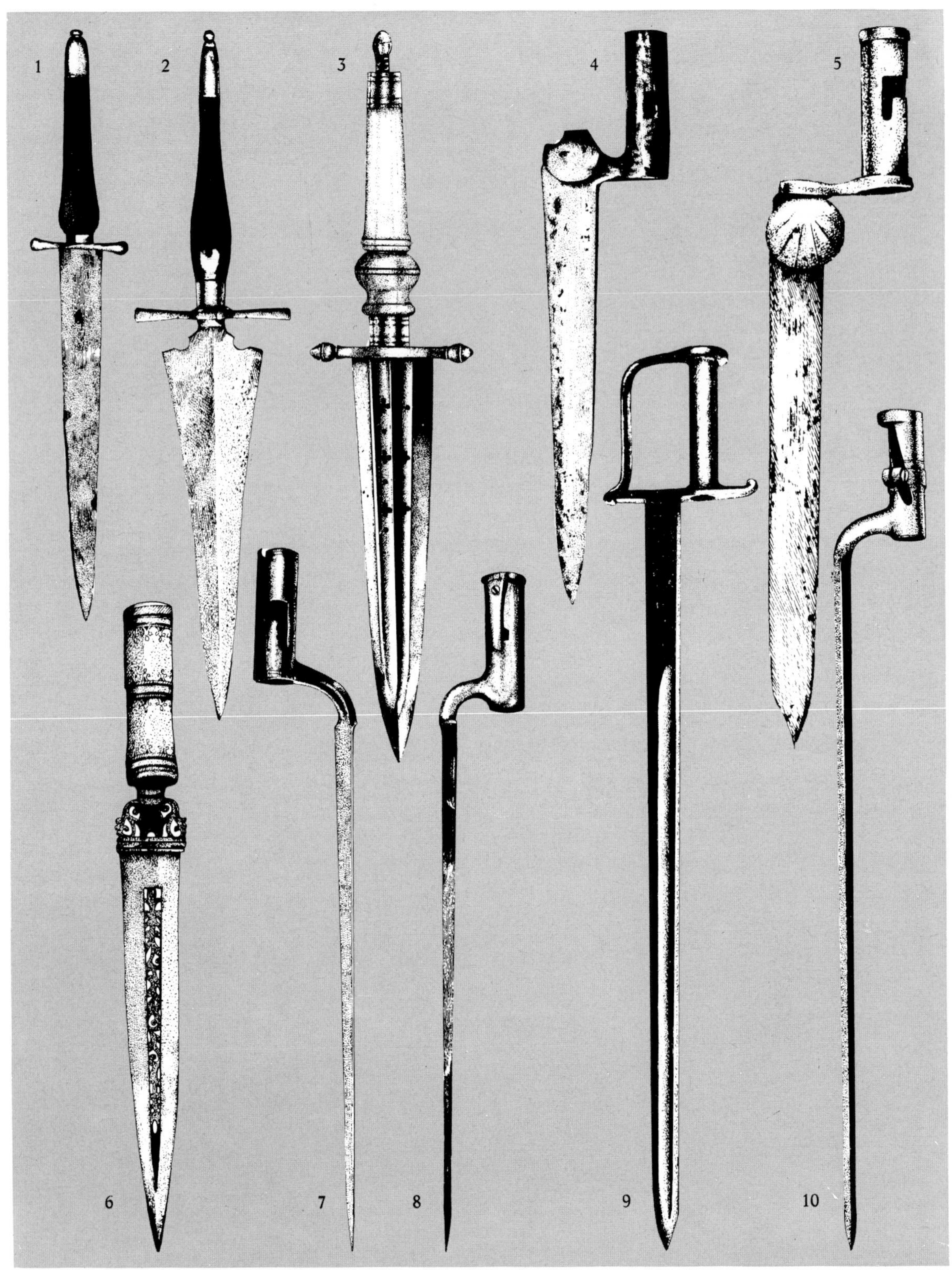


*1. Plug bayonet, Germany, 17th century. 2. Plug bayonet, Europe, late 17th century. 3. Plug bayonet, Spain, c. 1850. 4. Socket bayonet, Great Britain or France, late 17th century. 5. Socket bayonet, Europe, early 18th century. 6. Socket bayonet, S. Italy, late 18th century. 7. Socket bayonet, Great Britain, c. 1800. 9. Sword bayonet, Great Britain, c. 1800. 10. Socket bayonet for Lorenz musket, Austria, c. 1856.*

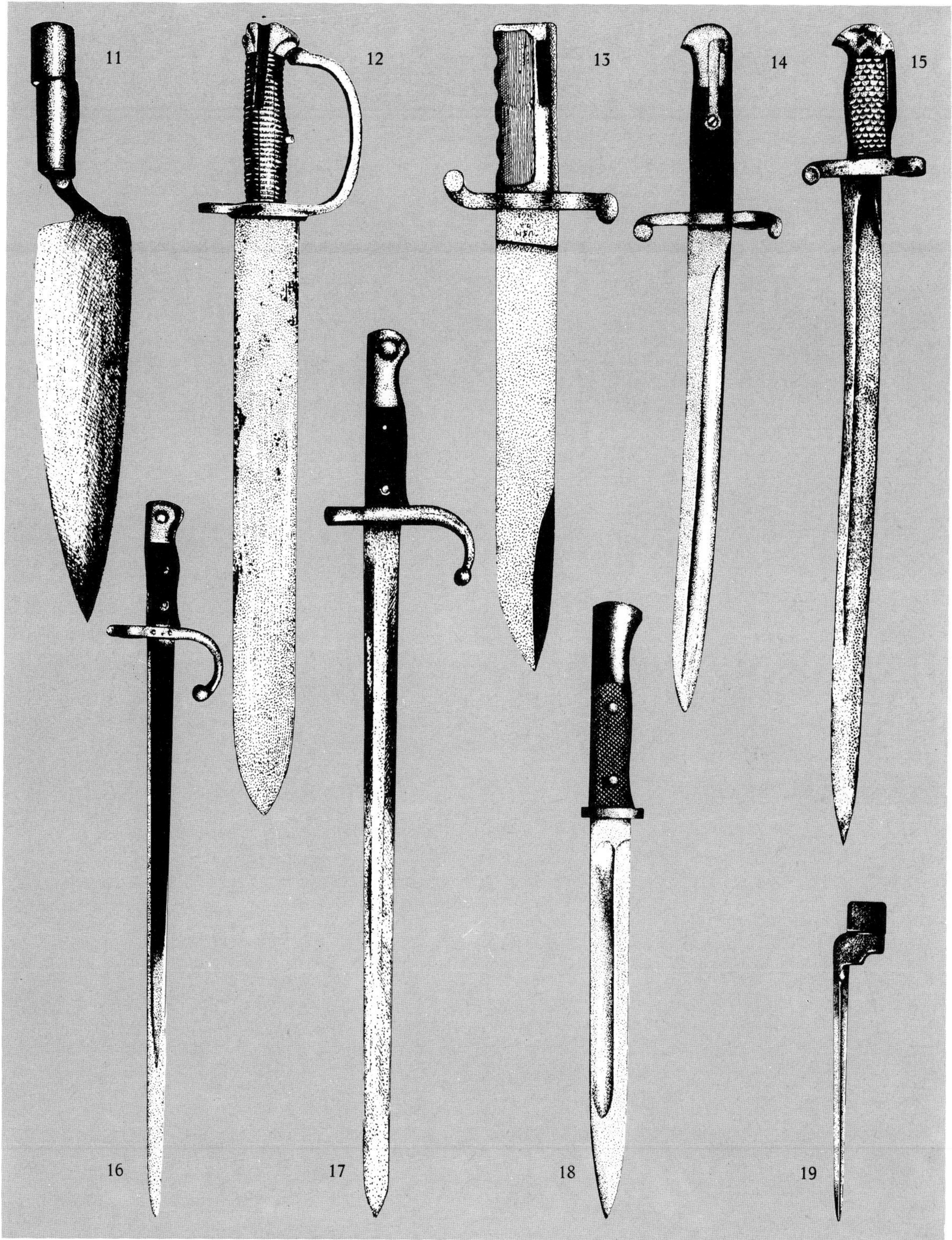


*11. Trowel bayonet for Springfield rifle, United States, c. 1873. 12. Sword Bayonet, Great Britain, c. 1820. 13. Knife bayonet for 1861 (naval) rifle, United States. 14. Knife bayonet for Martini-Enfield 1888 rifle, Great Britain. 15. "Yatagan" bayonet for Remington 1870 (naval) rifle, United States. 16. Sword bayonet for Gras 1874 rifle, France. 17. Sword bayonet for Mauser rifle, Germany, c. 1887. 18. Knife bayonet for 1898 rifle, Germany. 19. Poniard bayonet, United States, Second World War.*

cord with two clamps, which were screwed onto both ends of the bow before the notches. The cord was then pulled with a spanner, bending the bow, and the bowstring properly fitted. Finally, the bastard string was removed by releasing the spanner and unscrewing the clamps.

**bastard sword** A term used in the 15th and 16th centuries for a large sword with a broad double-edged blade and a long grip, which, when necessary, could accommodate both hands to wield it. It was also known as a "hand-and-a-half sword" inasmuch as its size, 115–140 cm. (45–55 in.), placed it halfway between the usual sword and the two handed sword. This type appeared from the second half of the 13th century and was particularly favored in Germany and Switzerland, where it was produced up to the mid-17th century.

The hilts of German bastard swords before the middle of the 16th century were basically cruciform, with long straight or curved quillons, ring guards, and one or two arms of the hilt. In some later types a more developed guard included two knuckle bows connected by a loop, all looking not unlike a basket hilt.

From the early 16th century, the hilts of the Swiss bastard swords were provided with knuckle guards, as well as with recurved quillons and ring guards. It was also the time which saw a new and lasting form of the Swiss bastard sword, which had a slightly curved blade and an asymmetrical pommel often shaped like a bird's or animal's head.

**battig** Also called bade-bade or *raentjan*, the battig is a typical single-edged knife of the Malay Archipelago with a narrow, incurving blade of brass or iron, about 15–25 cm. (6–10 in.) long and sharp on the concave side. The hilt, which has no guard, may be of hardwood, horn, or ivory and is more or less curved; it is sometimes forked at the pommel or fitted with a grip of a shape related to the kris. The wooden sheath has a characteristic protrusion at the neck, like the scabbards for krises, and is often ringed with silver bands. The chape is occasionally of carved horn, and it is not unusual to see a sheath that has been plated in embossed gold or silver.

**battle-ax** *See* AX.

**bayonet** A steel stabbing weapon, generally short, used in warfare and, to a lesser extent in hunting, as a complement to the firearm to which it is attached. The word *bayonnette* was originally used for a large dagger made in the city of Bayonne, in southwest France; it does not seem to have been associated with firearms until the second quarter of the 17th century.

A knife or dagger in the form of what was later called a "plug bayonet" may possibly have been used from the late 1500s; the name was applied to a narrow blade with a handle that could be inserted in the muzzle of the gun to make a weapon with a long shaft. It was used increasingly in warfare in the 17th century; the first to have it issued as standard equipment were the French fusiliers of the Royal Regiment, soon followed by other corps and other European armies. The advantage of having a long-shafted military combination weapon, however, brought with it the corresponding disadvantage that when the bayonet was fitted the musket could not be used as a firearm; another method of fixing the weapons together had to be sought which would enable them to be used at the same time, or alternatively, without the necessity of detaching them. The problem was solved in 1688 by a French field marshal, Sébastien Le Prestre de Vauban, who designed a bayonet with a socket that would slide onto the barrel of the musket like a sleeve; a curved tang raised the blade above the muzzle and far enough from the axis of the barrel to allow the weapon to be loaded with the bayonet fixed. This bayonet soon led to the disappearance of pikemen from European armies, though the plug bayonet was still used, at least until the mid-19th century, for sporting guns.

Along with continued use of socket bayonets, from the middle of the 19th century another system was developed, in which a stud on the barrel of the gun fitted into a groove of corresponding size in the handle of the bayonet, provided with a spring catch. Still earlier were introduced folding bayonets with a spring catch mounted directly on the barrels of pistols and guns. The spring catch locked the bayonet in two positions, under the barrel or ready for attack. They have since been used on both civil and military weapons.

The manufacture of bayonets was normally entrusted to contractors, and to ensure they were turned out exactly to specification a steel tool called the "bayonet pattern" was used. The 19th century was the period that saw the greatest variation in the shape of the blade. Studies of external ballistics in the second half of the century led to a reduction in the length of the bayonet blade and the moving of the bayonet lug from the barrel of the rifle to the stock; often, to ensure that it was firmly fixed, the bayonet was given a ring at the hilt which went around the muzzle. Studies during the present century, especially between the two world wars, taking into account the increased volume and firepower of modern firearms, have led to a considerable shortening of the blade.

There have been numerous examples of bayonets that could be used as swords and daggers when detached from the rifle, from the mid-19th century to the present time. These bayonets might be carried (a) in a scabbard hanging from the belt or bandolier; (b) in a scabbard fitted beside the hanger scabbard; (c) turned back to the barrel or forestock of the firearm, for bayonets fixed to the muzzle; (d) or in a slot inside the forestock of the firearm.

**bayonet boss** On some 19th-century guns, a short lug on the front of the barrel fitting into a longitudinal groove in the handle of the bayonet to hold it firm.

**bazooka** A slang name generally used for the American 2.36 in. (60.2 mm.) Anti-Tank Rocket Launcher. The bazooka consisted of a light metal tube (steel in the M-9 and M-9A1 versions, aluminum in the M-18) from which an electrically activated hollow-charge rocket (Rocket High Explosive Anti-Tank 2.30 in the M-6A3) was fired. Later the name "bazooka" was applied to the 3.3 in the Anti-Tank Rocket Launcher M-20 and its variants, the M-20B1, M-20A1, and M-20A1B1. The M-20A1B1 was made of two cast-aluminum tubes joined together and was fitted with a periscopic sight and a magnetic generator in the pistol grip, having maximum range of 900 m. (980 yds.).

**bazuband** The forearm guard and gauntlet in various types of armor used in Asia, particularly in Persia—where the word originated—Turkey, and India. A similar defense was also known in several eastern European countries such as Russia and Poland (it was known in Poland as the *karwasz*). We know from archeological findings and iconographic sources—such as the figure of a warrior on the golden jug of Nagy Szent Miklós (c. 9th century), preserved in the Kunsthistorisches Museum of Vienna—that the bazuband was known from the early Middle Ages. It was an important piece of defense for the fighting arm and hand. It was usually part of mail armor but was also found in combination with other types of Oriental armor (*see* BAIDANA; BEKHTER; CHAR-AINA; KORAZIN).

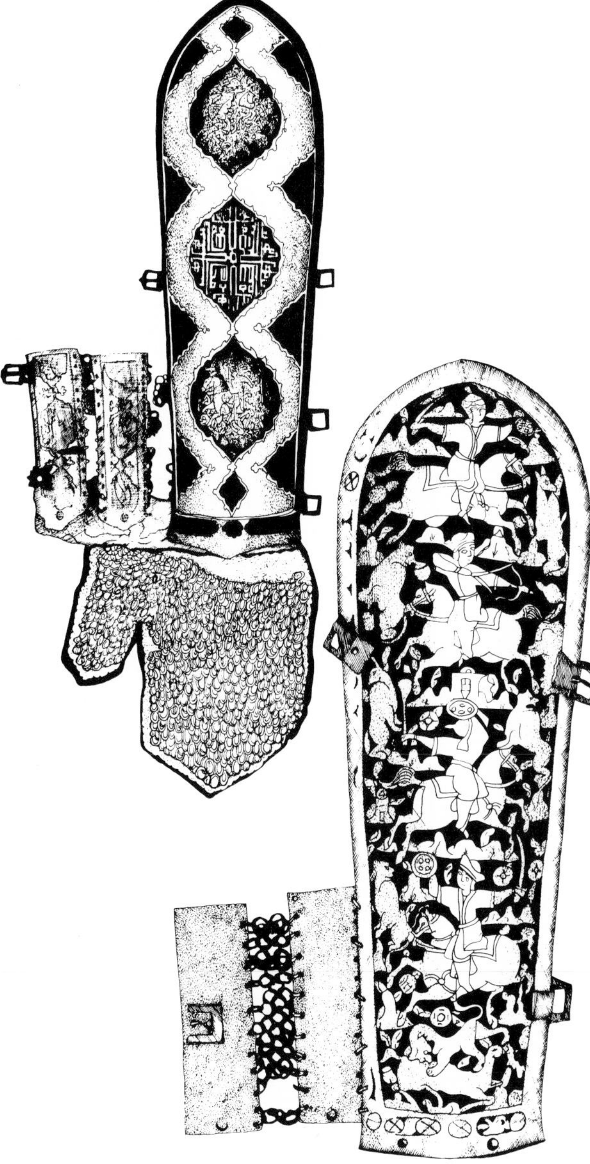

*Bazubands from 19th-century Persian armors. Rijksmuseum voor Volkenkunde, Leiden, Netherlands.*

The widespread use of the bazuband resulted in many types evolving over the centuries. Basically, it consisted of an elongated convex plate covering the outer side of the arm from elbow to wrist, where smaller wrist plates, either single or double, encircled the whole wrist. In some cases, these were joined to the main plate with an insertion of mail, and in others, with a hinge on one side and straps and buckles on the other. When a gauntlet was incorporated, it was made either of mail or scales, lined with cloth and attached to the main plate. This was really a covering for the back of the hand only, since there were no fingers or mitten.

In Persia, the bazuband was usually made of Damascus steel and consisted of a long, convex main plate, rounded at the elbow end, with two narrow plates at the wrist and a mail gauntlet. As the Persian style of fighting involved the use of a large, round shield, the bazuband was worn only on the arm holding an offensive weapon.

The Turkish-style bazuband was also rounded at the top, but the plate was shorter and flatter than the Persian. Decoration generally took the form of simple engraved motifs overlaid with gold. Occasionally small gems and inscriptions were used to ornament the plate. The two small wrist plates were linked to each other and to the main plate by strips of mail, while the gauntlet, when this was present, was usually made of mail-covered leather and lined with cloth. Mameluke pieces were often decorated with inscriptions in silver in bold, calligraphic letters.

In India, the elbow end of the arm plate was pointed, although, in the south, it frequently curved outward to the point which was finished off with a knob or an acorn. There was only one wrist plate, hinged to the main plate. The Indian gauntlet was sometimes of mail or overlapping scales but, more usually, was made of padded cloth decorated with gilt studs.

In Poland, the karwasz was used in cavalry armor. It consisted of a main plate and double wrist plates inlaid with brass. With the hussar plate armor, the karwasz had no gauntlets; with the mail armor, gauntlets were fitted to the karwosz; and with the korazin, scale gauntlets supplemented the karwasz.

In Russia, the long forearm guard was sometimes grooved and richly decorated. No gauntlet was incorporated in this style, and it was used with mail and other types of armor.

**bebut** A Caucasian dagger similar to the KAMA but with a curved blade. The bebut was less popular and usually less decorated than the kama. During the First World War it was issued as a regulation weapon to machine-gun companies and some artillery units of the Russian Imperial Army.

**bec-de-faucon** or **bec-de-corbin** Meaning "falcon's beak" and "crow's beak," respectively, these old French terms, were sometimes used by English writers to indicate the particular shape of the PEEN of the WAR HAMMER and battle-ax. The names were also applied, from time to time, to the whole weapon if it had a massive curved peen resembling a bird's beak.

**beidana** An Italian peasant's sword, with a single-edged blade, narrow at the heel and broader toward the end, which was truncated. The size varied from 50 to 75 cm. (20–30 in.), with the handle accounting for some 10 cm. (4 in.). The cutting edge ran up only part of the blade, which was often set off from the grip by a decorative baluster. The cutting part was asymmetrical, with one side flat and the other slightly convex. This asymmetry clearly indicated that it was derived from the similar tool for chopping wood.

The top of the back edge was almost invariably fitted with a spiral or volute-shaped piece bent backward. At the end of the grip, usually made of horn and fixed with rivets on the tang, a curved hook protected the hand and enabled the weapon to be carried at the belt, like billhooks used by peasants.

The beidana always remained somewhat of a dual-purpose object, and it is for this reason that most of the examples of it are well worn. It was used in the area of the central Alps in the 17th and 18th centuries since it was well suited to the guerrillas operating in mountainous regions. The term "beidana" is a fairly recent one, suggested because it is specific to the Val Pellice, where this tool-weapon was widely used. It was also described by the terms *mannarino* or *mannarese* (pruning hook), *mannaieta* (chopper), *falcetto* (billhook), and *storta contadina* (peasant sword).

**bekhter** (or, diminutively, **bekhterets**) A sleeveless body protection in small metal plates connected by mail. Since the 15th century—and probably even earlier—it was especially well known in Russia and was also used in Turkey, Mameluke Egypt, Mogul India, Hungary, and Poland. The oldest specimens remaining today are from the 16th century and are preserved in Poland and Turkey, while some especially fine 17th-century Muscovite examples are in Moscow's State Armory in the Kremlin.

The word "bekhter" is of Mongol origin, and this type of armor would almost certainly have been worn by the Tartars. It was an intricately worked defensive garment: sometimes as many as 1200 small convex lames, arranged in 12–21 vertical rows, were used in the manufacture of one bekhter. These plates overlapped from top to bottom or vice versa, the rows being ingeniously interlinked with rings. Thus each lame was reinforced by two of its neighboring plates, tripling its protective power. The plates were usually decorated with designs and inscriptions in gold damascening, and even the rings were sometimes inscribed and dated.

The back and front of the bekhter were joined by straps over the shoulders and clasps on the left side. Having no arm defenses, it was worn over a coat of mail as an outer armor, like the BAIDANA. An average bekhter was about 70 cm. ($27\frac{1}{2}$ in.) long and 12 kg. ($26\frac{1}{2}$ lbs.) in weight.

In the National Museum of Kraków there is a bekhter made in Poznan in 1580 which resembles a Renaissance doublet, but it is of inferior technical quality to the Muscovite bekhters. Also in Poland, in the National Museum of Warsaw, there is an interesting painting—*The Battle of Orsha* (sometime after 1514)—in which most of the Muscovites are depicted in bekhters worn over quilted caftans. This probably expresses a certain amount of artistic license, however, as it was an expensive armor and would only have been worn by the wealthier warriors and military leaders.

**bender** *See* GAFFE.

**bendo** *See* GOLOK.

**berdysh** Russian term for an ax with a long, narrow, curved head about 60–80 cm. (24–32 in.) long. The elongated upper end of the blade could be used for thrusting, while the lower end was forged into a langet, which was nailed to the shaft (and sometimes also bound with a leather lace), thus reinforcing the main attachment at the ax's socket. It was mostly used by foot soldiers, especially the *streltsy* ("shooters"), Muscovy's infantry in the 16th and 17th centuries. When used by foot soldiers, the berdysh served also as a gun rest, its shaft having a piked ferrule (shoe) to fix the weapon on the ground. Smaller berdyshes were used by mounted streltsy, this variation having a much shorter shaft, with two rings for attaching it to a shoulder strap. For ceremonial occasions, elite foot soldiers were given so-called ambassadorial berdyshes, with the heads of monstrous size (about 150 cm. 60 in. long) decorated with incised ornamentation and pierced holes (which occur on many regular weapons as well). To a much lesser extent this weapon was also used in Scandinavia and eastern Europe. Typologically, it may have developed from medieval crescentic axes.

**besagew** An accessory of the PAULDRON during the 15th century and first half of the 16th, particularly in the Germanic countries. It consisted of a small iron disc, sometimes slightly shaped to the body, positioned between breast and upper arm to protect the armpit. The large pauldrons virtually supplanted the besagew, which was mainly worn in association with monnions or SPAUDLERS. In Italy besagews were only used to complete the asymmetrical right spaudler-fronted pauldron. Particularly large besagews were part of the armor for the German joust.

**bevor** A part of armor protecting the lower part of the face and the front of the neck. It appeared as an essential piece of complete harness in the 14th century but did not become common until the 15th. Initially it was a gorget plate worn with the BASNET and was usually riveted to this helmet or to the breastplate. From the second quarter of the 15th century it was worn with a helmet called the SALLET. This form of bevor usually consisted of two or three plates shaped to the face and joined by pivoting rivets. The lower plate was shaped to the chin and extended to an elongated V-shaped part which was attached to the breastplate with a lock or with a strap and buckle. In a similar way the bevor was worn up to c. 1500 with a helmet of Spanish origin, whose later and lighter form was called the SPANISH MORION.

In the ARMET, the face was protected, instead of by a bevor, by very wide cheekpieces hinged on the skull. As a distinctive part the bevor was incorporated into the new defensive covering, the CLOSE HELMET, developed in the early 16th century. The bevor of the close helmet was pivoted along with the VISOR on both sides of the skull. The earliest form was made of a single plate shaped to the chin and extending below to cover the neck; the upper edge of the bevor was overlapped by the visor. In close helmets after c. 1525 the bevor consisted of two main parts: the upper bevor, replacing the lower part of the full visor, covered the face from eye level down to the chin, where it overlapped the lower bevor, which protected the chin and the neck. The upper bevor often had small slots and holes for ventilation, hence the alternative name "ventail" applied to it. At its upper-right edge there also was a cutout for the lifting peg of the visor.

In close helmets used for tilts and foot combat in the lists, the lower border of the bevor was formed into a hollow rim joining that of the skull, to lock onto the gorget of the armor; the whole of the bevor could be reinforced with the GRANDGUARD attached to the bevor with a screw and nut. The close helmets for the field had their own gorget plates riveted to the skull and the lower bevor. This construction was still used in the 17th century, as can be seen, for instance, in the so-called Savoyard BURGONET, which was actually a variant of the close helmet.

Detachable bevors were often used as reinforcing pieces with the tournament armor (*see* WRAPPER), and they sometimes were worn with the burgonet either as an integral pivoted part of the helmet or as a supplement attached to its skull with a strap and buckle (*see* BUFFE).

The bevor was usually locked to the skull with a spring catch or a small hook passing through a pin riveted to the skull. The same devices were used to lock together the upper and the lower bevor in the two-piece construction.

**bevor, reinforcing** *See* WRAPPER.

**bevor support** *See* VISOR SUPPORT.

**bhuj** (or **kutti**) A characteristic dagger from the state of Sind in northern India, the bhuj is also called an "elephant knife" because of the representation of an elephant's head which is usually part of the decoration, either chased on metal at the heel or modeled in brass between haft and blade. The blade is single-edged, with a short back edge at the point, between 18 and 26 cm. (7–10 in.) long. It is rather

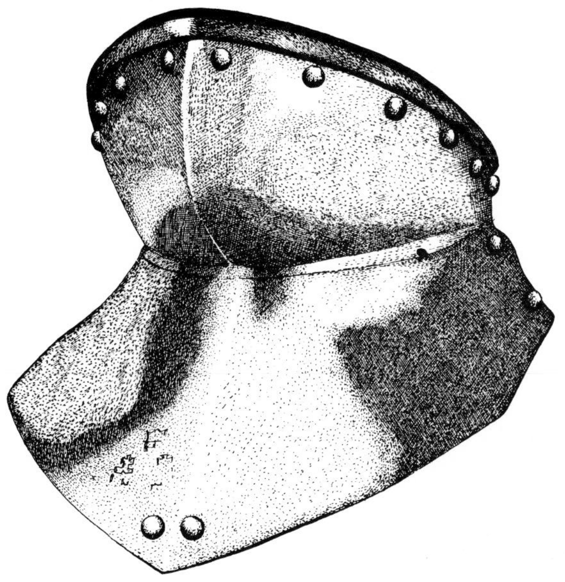

*Bevor for a sallet, Italy, c. 1450. Armeria Reale, Turin.*

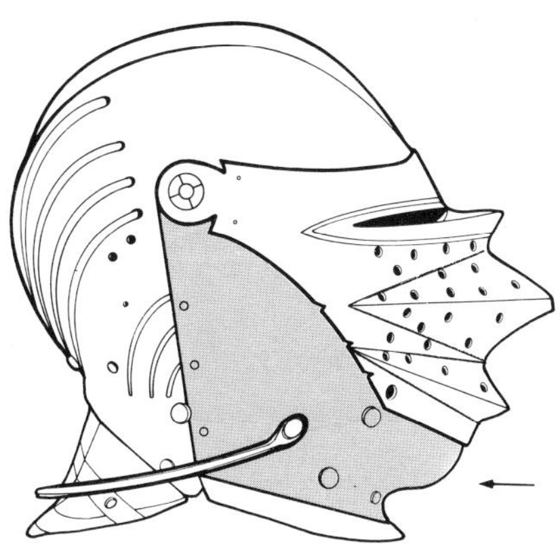

*Bevor of a close helmet, early 15th century.*

broad and heavy, slightly curved, often with an engraved or gilded silver mount. The haft consists of a metal rod, also usually engraved or inlaid with silver, and finished off with a decorative knob which is, in fact, frequently the pommel of a screw-in dagger contained in the hollow haft. An embossed copper sheath usually completes the weapon, which may measure 41–61 cm. (16–24 in.) overall.

**bichwa** Although *bichwa* means "the sting of a scorpion," the shape of this Indian dagger is based on the curve of a buffalo's horns, and the blades were, in fact, made of horn in the earliest examples. The more modern metal blade has retained the original double curve and is sometimes forked, often fluted, always double-edged, and about 25 cm. (10 in.) long. The steel hilt is looped to form a grip and knuckle guard, and may carry silver embellishments with bosses on guard and pommel.

The bichwa is sometimes used in conjunction with a BAGH-NAKH, the bar joining the claws being attached to the grip. This combination makes a very nasty weapon indeed and has a reputation for having been the weapon used in treacherous assassinations.

**bickford** A type of slow-burning FUSE, also called safety fuse, invented by the British engineer William Bickford in 1831.

**bill** A staff weapon deriving from an agricultural tool, billhook. Its head was made in various sizes, but was invariably fitted with a sturdy hook whose inside and outside curves were cutting edges. The bill is documented from the 13th to 17th centuries and referred to as the weapon of the combatants on foot. In the earliest forms we find a compact blade with a slightly convex cutting edge topped by a spike. Subsequently the head became longer, the center of its edge more pointed, and the fluke more salient, and the faces were sometimes finished with faceting or fullers. At the base of the head, there were two sharp lugs serving as a guard. The socket was mainly truncated-pyramidal in shape, with a rectangular base with rounded corners, often with brass fittings inlaid; the langets, which were important for a combat weapon, formed extensions of the socket.

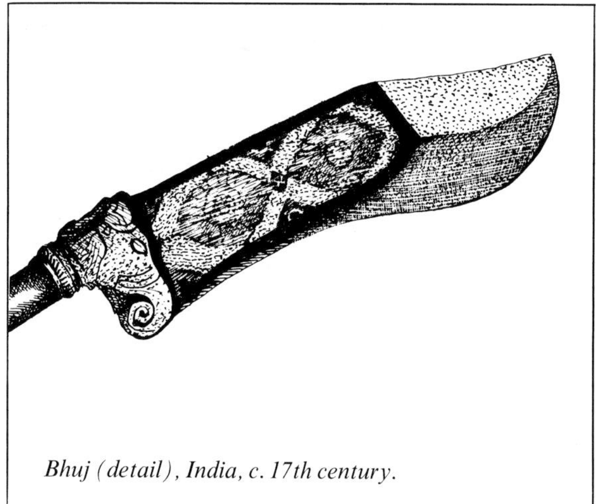

*Bhuj (detail), India, c. 17th century.*

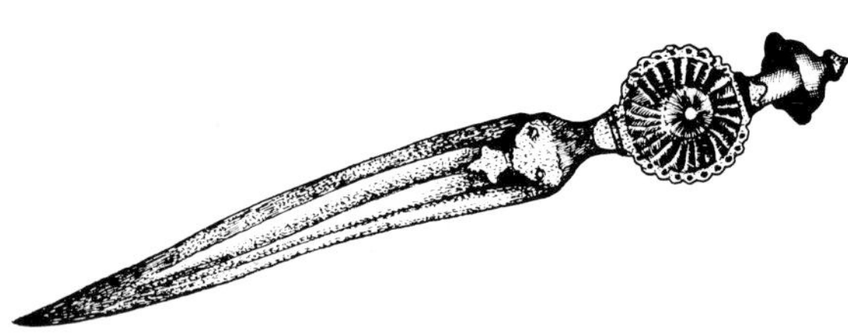

*Bichwa, India, 19th century.*

Use of the bill by foot soldiers did not continue beyond the mid-16th century. In later times we often find it as a ceremonial weapon; despite this its original form remained basically unchanged. Both faces of the parade bills were often richly decorated and bore the insignia and coat of arms of the rulers whose guards were armed with these weapons.

**bipennis** (Latin; Greek *pelekus, distomos, boiplex*) An ax with two blades, used mainly in the preclassical period, both as a weapon and as a tool. As a weapon it appears in particular as part of the attire of the "barbarians" (i.e., non-Romans), the Scythians, and the Amazons, and in connection with foreign religious cults. It was used in the worship of Bacchus and Vulcan and was therefore at once a weapon and a sacrificial instrument: it was used to slaughter the bull or other animal victim which replaced the human victim in primitive sacrificial ceremonies. Via the Etruscan civilization, it changed from being a symbol of divine power to one of political power in Rome: the fasces with the double-edged ax were the insignia of the Roman Empire.

**birding piece** An old term for a shotgun. *See also* GUN: sporting.

**"bishop's mantle"** A type of CAPE OF MAIL.

**bit** A metal device attached to the cheek straps of a bridle and inserted into the horse's mouth to enable the rider to control and guide the animal by means of the reins fastened to the bit. It consists basically of the mouthpiece,

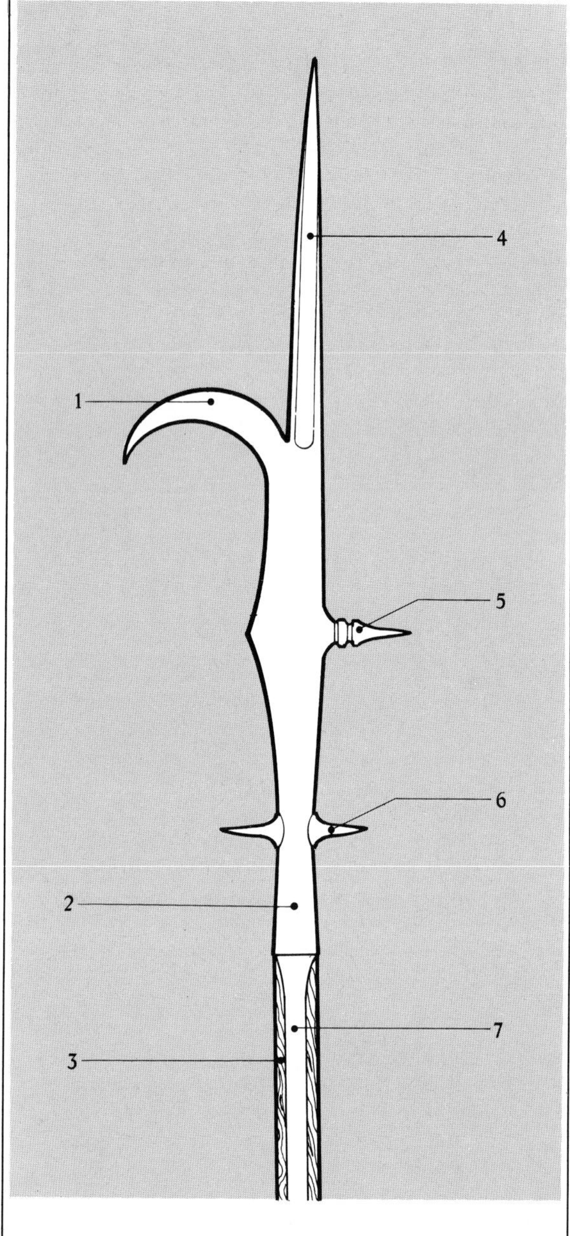


*Bill. 1. Fluke; 2. socket; 3. shaft; 4. spike; 5. peen; 6. lugs (cross guard); 7. langet.*

which rests in the horse's mouth between the front and back teeth.

The Roman bit was generally one solid, straight piece, but from the 9th century onward it was commonly made in two jointed pieces, often with a tongue plate or port in the center. Metal BRANCHES or cheeks (not to be confused with the leather cheek straps of the bridle) retained the bit in position. The upper part of each branch had a loop for attaching to the cheek strap and an open hook to take the

CURB CHAIN, while the lower part had a ring attached to take the reins. To this point, the bit of a horse in full bard or light armor was much the same as today, in principle. However, the branches of medieval bits were often quite long and massive (30 cm. [12 in.] or more in length), the proportions between their upper and lower parts determining the amount of action given the bit. The curb chain, which was sometimes attached quite far down the branches (in some cases, two chains were used), had a lever effect, inducing the horse to open (flex) its lower jaw and bend its head from the poll, provided the horse had been trained to it and its conformation allowed it.

Medieval bits were usually jointed or "ported" in the middle (i.e., the mouthpiece was made with an arch or three-sided square in the middle); these two kinds are known, respectively, as snaffles and curbs. Sometimes the bit was fitted with small plates with which the horse's tongue could "play," perhaps helping to keep the saliva flowing and thus reducing friction from the bit.

Although the bit was a strictly functional fitting, it was often regarded as a prominent part of the bard, particularly in the 17th and 18th centuries, and great care was lavished on its ornamentation. The most usual form of decoration was gilding and chiseling.

**black powder** *See* GUNPOWDER.

**blade** The cutting and/or thrusting part of edged weapons, excluding the hilt. The blade has consistently demonstrated the degree of technical evolution of the weapon as a whole.

The prehistoric stone implement is defined as a blade when its length is more than twice its breadth; blades with a back and two cutting edges date from that early period.

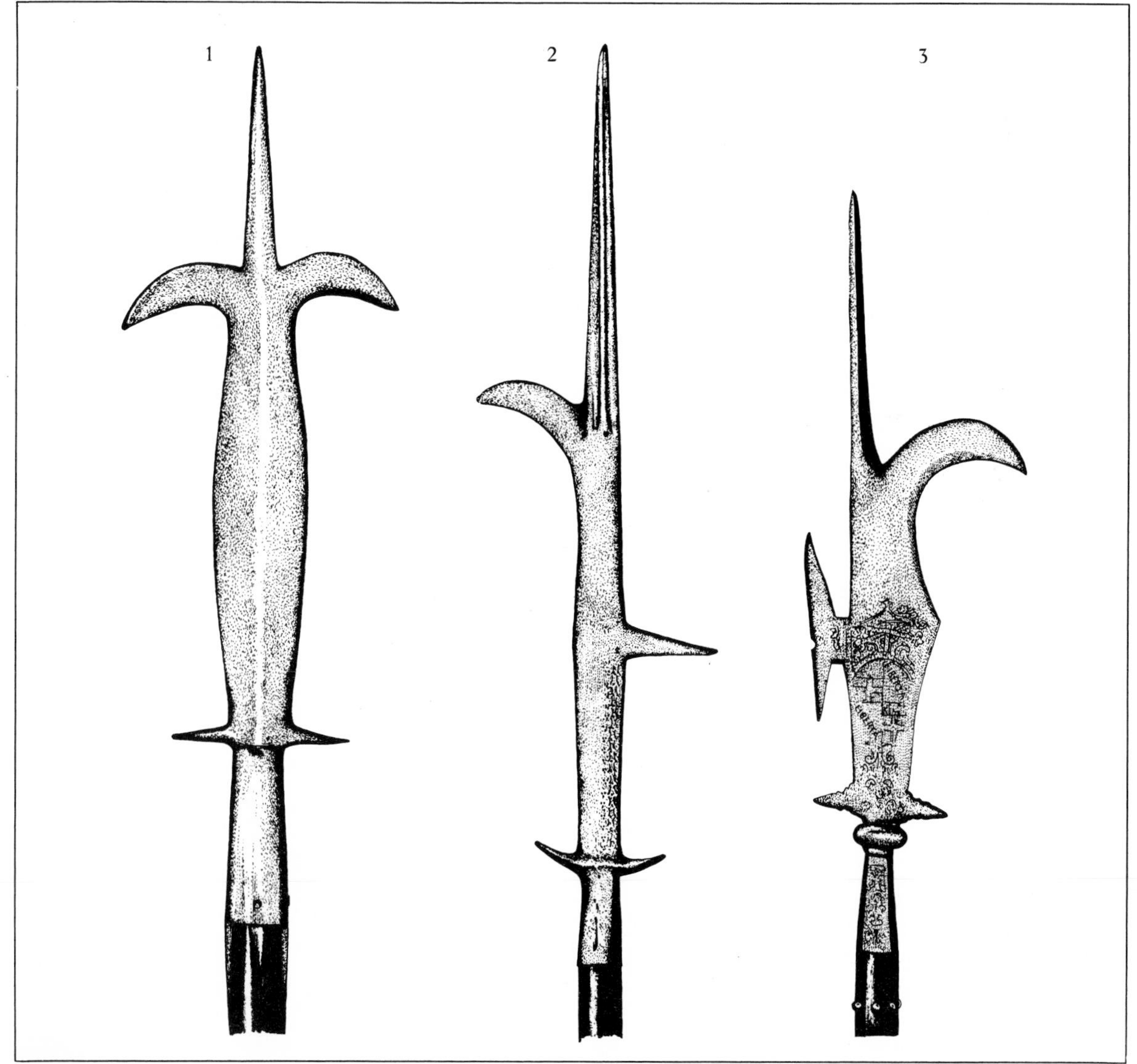


*1. Double bill, N. Italy (Veneto), c. 1480. Museo Civico Correr, Venice. 2. Bill, N. Italy, c. 1500. Poldi Pezzoli Museum, Milan. 3. Bill, N. Italy (Bologna), c. 1580–1600, Museo Civico, Bologna.*

But the blade really started to evolve with the discovery of metals. In the beginning, very short metal blades were made, copying the Stone Age models; these were designed essentially for thrusting, and in this respect there was a formal similarity between spear and dagger blades. As early as during the period of transition from the Copper to the Bronze Age, blades designed for cutting were being made. The Mycenaean type of sword (c. 1500 B.C.) represents the last stage of the thrusting weapon, which was subsequently shortened and rendered suitable for cutting.

Between the end of the Bronze Age and the beginning of the Iron Age swords were designed for both thrusting and cutting. But this new method of delivering blows gave rise to certain technical problems to do with achieving a stronger join between the blade and the grip of the weapon; this led to the entire sword being cast in one piece, but the result was a somewhat heavy and bulky weapon.

In the early stages of the Iron Age blades made from the new metal were based on the previous bronze models, and the two coexisted for some time; it was only in the subsequent period of the Iron Age—the La Tène culture—that the sword became a weapon which was easy to handle and thus an excellent instrument of war.

After the 7th century B.C. the blades of swords were made consistently of iron or steel; however, in the Middle East (Anatolia) archeological excavations have brought to light swords made of steel dating back to the second millennium B.C. Bronze continued to be used for blades of ritual weapons, or was relegated to form part of the grip and scabbard.

Metallurgical progress made it possible—in the transition from the Hallstatt to the La Tène culture—to meet the requirement, for combat purposes, of a weapon with a larger blade; the blade increased in length to about

*Bits* (top) *Bronze, Villanovian culture. Museo Poldi Pezzoli, Milan.* (middle) *Bronze gilt, latter 15th century.* (bottom) *Iron, Great Britain, 17th–18th century.*

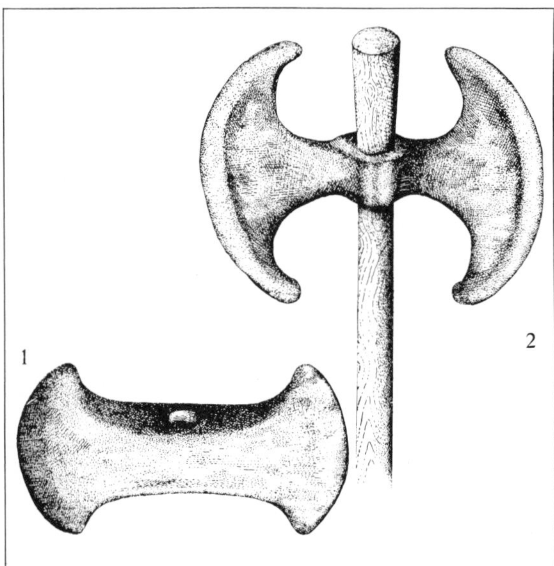


*1. Stone double-edged ax found in Britain. 2. Double-edged ax from a Roman mosaic of the imperial period.*

80–90 cm. (31–35 in.). The peoples in the Teutonic world, incidentally, already had a weapon with a blade designed exclusively for cutting (it had a rounded point), the length of which ranged from 75 to 95 cm. (30–37 in.); this remained virtually unchanged until the time of the "barbarian" migrations. In this period we find the emergence of the constructional technique known as pattern welding, which involved twisting and hammer-welding steel and iron bars joined together. This procedure gave rise to a blade which was at once strong and elastic and had, as an additional feature, an attractive watered pattern on its surface. This technique remained in use in Europe until the 11th or 12th century; a variation of the process was used for making the blades of the Malayan KRIS, and it was brought to a high degree of perfection by the famous Japanese swordsmiths.

The weapons used by the Merovingians and Carolingians in the 6th to 9th centuries had very similar features. These warriors were armed with a broad-bladed sword with a rounded point, often with a shallow central groove running almost its entire length. In the Romanesque period which followed, the characteristics of the blade remained virtually unaltered; there was simply a tendency to lengthen the blade, and this trend persisted in the 12th and 13th centuries as well.

It was above all with the Gothic period that the various typological differentiations started to appear, which were closely linked to the purpose and use of the weapon. The blades of swords were forged either mainly for thrusting or mainly for cutting blows, or alternatively with characteristics enabling them to be used for delivering both types of blows. There was no uniform preference in the European region, the choice of weapon being influenced at different times and in different areas by specific customs and the development of body armor. Thus in the 14th century we find the appearance of blades in the shape of very pointed isosceles triangles, with a flattened rhomboid section, very appropriate for thrusts but capable also of cutting blows.

In the case of bastard swords and two-handed swords, for use as weapons of war, blades of varied shapes were made, designed for cutting and thrusting; or, alternatively, for one or the other type of blow, depending on personal fighting technique. Special blades were also manufactured with the forte devoid of a cutting edge, so that the sword could be used with both hands: one hand held the grip, the other the blunt section of the blade. The blades made for two-handed swords sometimes also had an extended ricasso running some way below the hilt; this section was covered with leather, which enabled the user to wear the weapon on his shoulder without damaging the costume and, in battle, to grip the sword firmly with both hands. The forward end of the ricasso was protected by two pointed lugs.

North of the Alps, in the 16th century, special thrusting swords for hunting were manufactured which had long blades consisting of a willow-leaf-shaped point and a long and slender but strong blade; a crosspiece, set perpendicular to the point and in some cases movable, prevented the sword from penetrating the prey too deeply.

The production and specialization of weapons received considerable momentum as a result of developments in the art of warfare. Up to the end of the 15th century, swords had been made for the knight or mounted soldier; but the new role taken by men on foot and professional armies in the service of princes meant that swords suitable for foot soldiers had to be made. These swords had strong but somewhat compact blades, while their width and the design of their section depended on local preferences and the type of combat technique.

After the 17th century the sword went into a period of progressive decline, and was gradually replaced by a smaller, lighter weapon known as the SMALL SWORD, which had blades designed exclusively for thrusting. An anomaly among sword blades was the COLICHEMARDE, whose blade was broad at the forte with two cutting edges, and then narrowed abruptly into a long, quadrangular section.

*Dagger blades* were among the first metal edged weapons; in the intermediate period between the Copper Age and the early Bronze Age, fairly compact blades were produced suitable for fitting with a handle, for use as daggers, or for mounting on shafts and used as spears. In Europe during the Bronze Age, there was a dagger which had a blade in

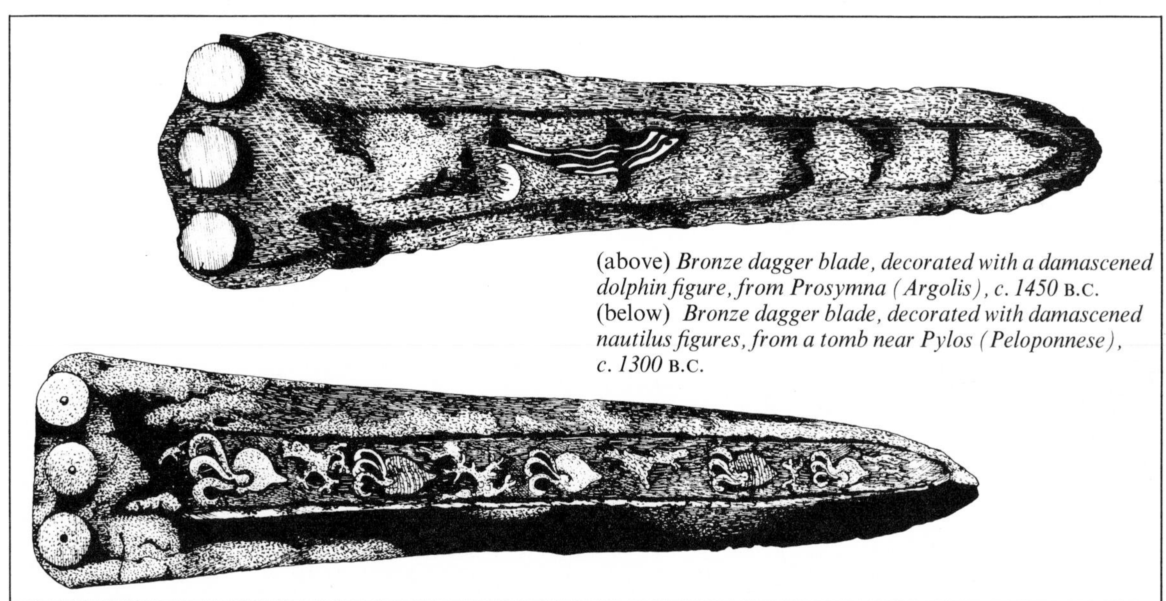

(above) *Bronze dagger blade, decorated with a damascened dolphin figure, from Prosymna (Argolis), c. 1450* B.C.
(below) *Bronze dagger blade, decorated with damascened nautilus figures, from a tomb near Pylos (Peloponnese), c. 1300* B.C.

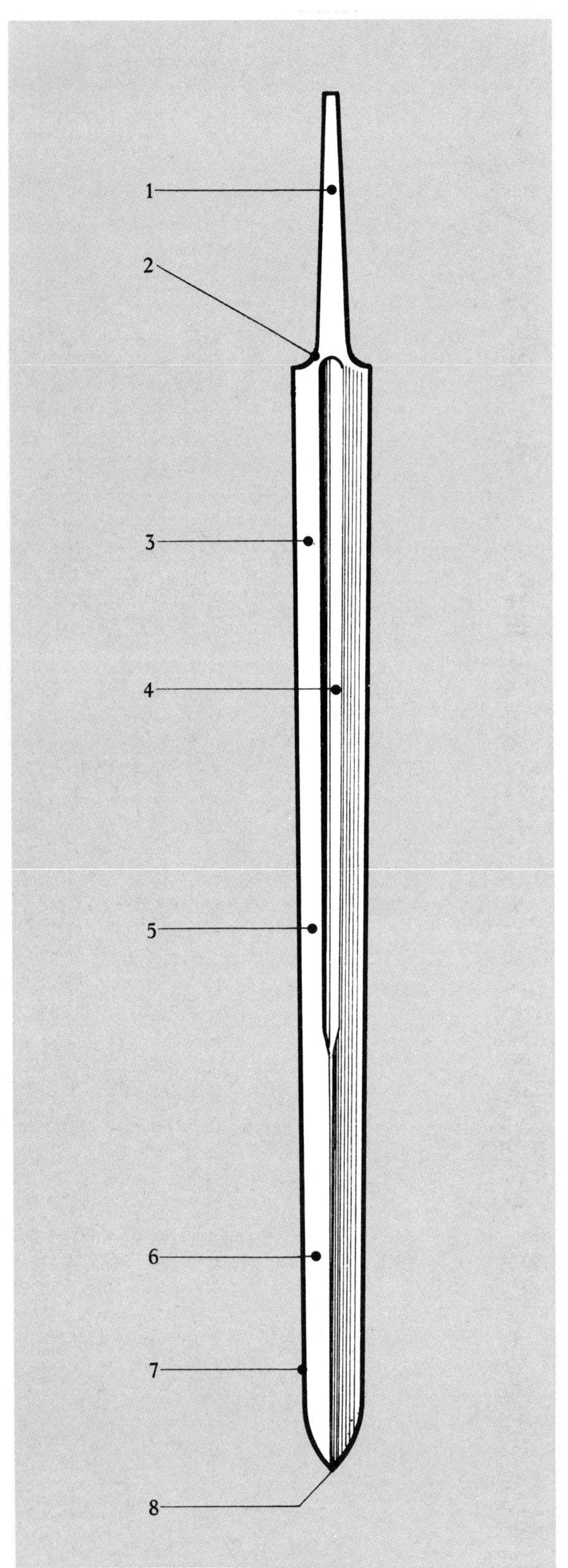


*Blade. 1. tang; 2. shoulder; 3. forte; 4. fuller; 5. middle section; 6. foible; 7. cutting edge; 8. point.*

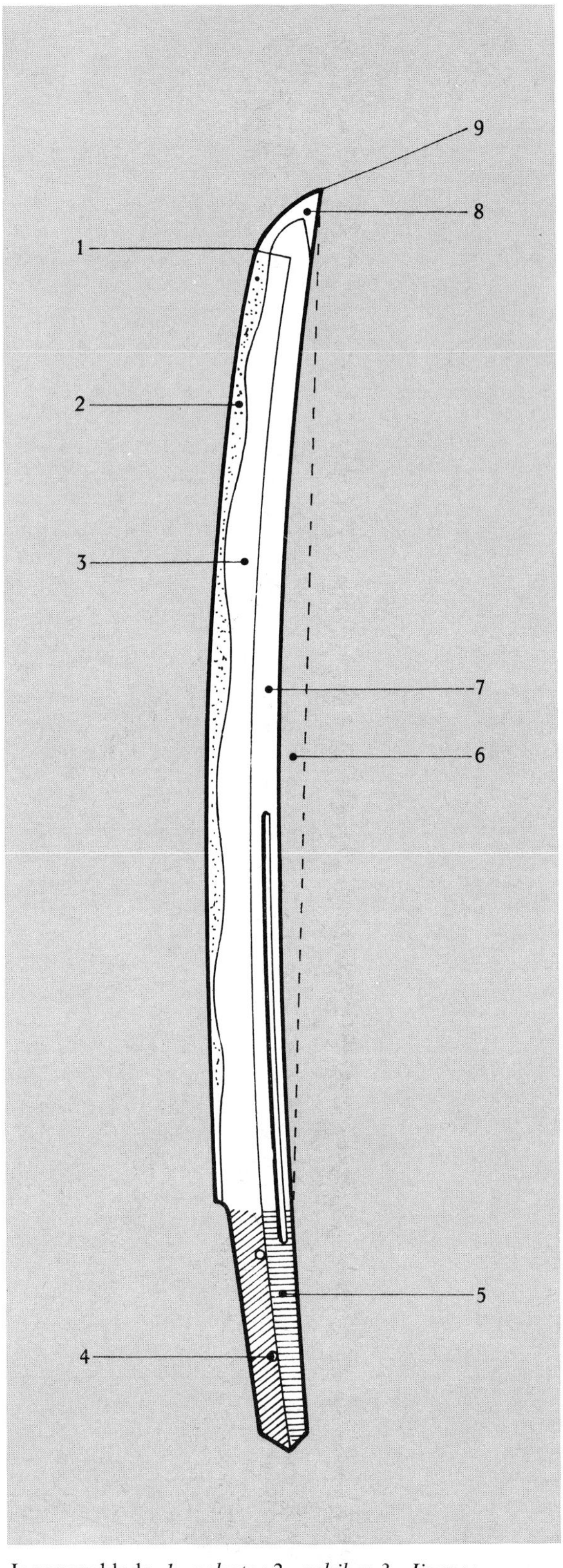

Japanese blade. *1. yokote; 2. yakiba; 3. Jigane; 4. Mekugi; 5. nakago; 6. Sori; 7. shinogi; 8. bōshi; 9. kisaki.*

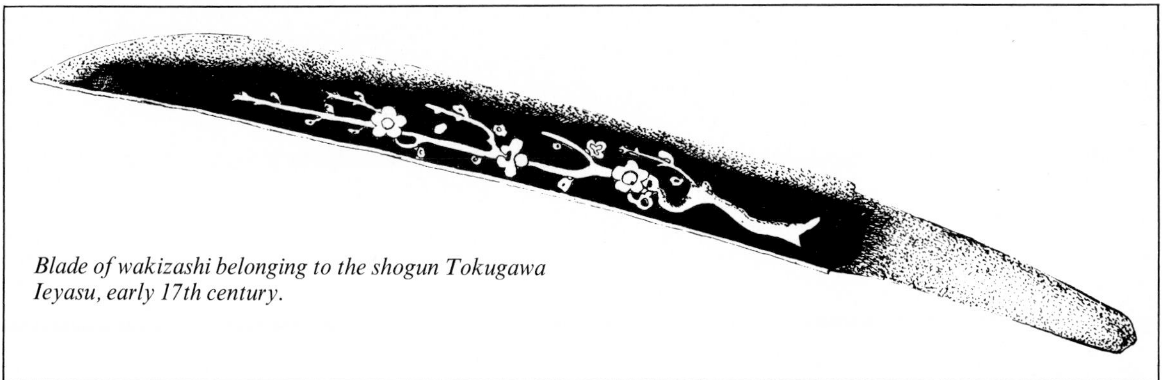
*Blade of wakizashi belonging to the shogun Tokugawa Ieyasu, early 17th century.*

the shape of an isosceles triangle. This type of blade lasted up until the Hallstatt period, when the blade started to become narrower and lighter; in fact, the new metal, iron, made it possible to reduce the thickness and at the same time provide the blade with considerable strength. It was in this period that single-edged blades started to appear with a straight back and a slightly curved cutting edge.

In the Roman period the allies of Rome used mainly their own weapons; from the Etruscans the Romans borrowed a type of dagger with a curved blade used primarily for religious ceremonies. Broadly speaking, the medieval daggers had a single- or double-edged blade which was short and sturdy, with a sharp point, indicating that it was designed essentially for thrusting. Local forms or specialized uses evolved independently.

The Renaissance developed various types and styles of the dagger, turning it into a magnificent object. By now each weapon had its own particular task. The variations in the forms of blades can only be kept track of by following local typology. The spread of the Italian and Spanish schools of fencing led to the introduction of a PARRYING DAGGER as an auxiliary weapon in swordplay; its blade was quite long and sturdy, sometimes with sophisticated guards. The concept of standardization started to be applied to military weaponry, including the edged weapons, but those carried by princes and other dignitaries remained outside this development.

The replacement of staff weapons by the BAYONET made a new weapon available to the military and to hunters; it was also used as a dagger. The blade of the bayonet copied that of the various daggers, but later underwent its own specific development. While the sword emerged as a long weapon designed mainly for the mounted soldier, foot soldiers were gradually armed with shorter single-edged weapons, some being influenced by Middle Eastern types and designed for delivering cutting blows. In Europe these weapons were introduced in two waves; during the Celtic and Teutonic invasions from the north, and from contacts with the eastern Mediterranean world from the south. In the Middle Ages this gave rise to the FALCHION, a sword with a curved single-edged blade, which broadened out toward the point.

For hunting, special single-edged swords were manufactured, such as the HANGER and hunting sword. Among other blades with a single cutting edge we should mention the KNIFE, both those designed for domestic use and those transformed from implements into weapons of war. These ranged from the Teutonic war knife or SAX to the large hunting and war knives carried by the rank and file and used for finishing off wounded foes, to the blades inspired by the YATAGAN, to the various daggers made in the 19th century.

### *Japanese blades*

The Japanese have a great tradition of employing complicated metallurgical processes in the making of blades, which has given them many fine qualities. This Japanese science has created a large vocabulary of terms to distinguish the various parts of the blade and all its marks and attributes, and it is difficult for outsiders to identify and appreciate their many subtleties. Some of the most important parts are: *jigane*, the main surface of the blade between hardened edge and ridge; *shinogi*, the ridge along the blade; *yakiba*, the hardened edge; *boshi*, the pointed end; *yokote*, the short transverse ridge near the point; *kisaki*, the point plane; and *nakago*, the tang. The curvature of the blade, *sori*, is measured by the greatest distance from the back of the blade to a straight line drawn from the point up to the hilt.

All Japanese blades were produced by the same methods, the steel being made from impure magnetite smelted in small blast furnaces, the mass of steel varying from very hard to very soft. It was then broken into pieces, selected for the specific purposes, and welded into bars. It was the fusing of soft and hard steel into a bar that was the important stage of the process. Various methods of welding, doubling, laminating, and forging were applied, each resulting product having a particular name. The basic operation was to weld a flat strip of soft metal to a hard one, producing a bar that was hard on one side and soft on the other, called *kataha*. The kataha, doubled on itself and welded, with the operation repeated fifteen times, gave a practically homogeneous bar of about 32,000 layers. In other methods the layers in such a bar could reach 4 million or more. From this bar the blade was roughly forged and worked out with a kind of drawing knife. The initial curvature was so calculated that it reached its desired proportion only in the next processes of heating. There were various kinds of blade cross-sections, but all were wedge-shaped. The back could be rounded or pointed, and the body flat or with one fuller or, more rarely, two; the section was occasionally almost rhomboid. At this stage the metalsmith shaped the tang and filed it in a special way. These file marks, called *yasuri*, were dots, irregular cuts, or scratched parallel lines going in various directions. An expert can easily tell from the yasuri in which smith's workshop, and the approximate date, a blade was made. A small hole in the tang enabled the handle to be attached with a bamboo plug.

In preparing a high-quality blade, cementation was sometimes needed, i.e., increasing the carbon at the edge to make it possible to harden it. This was done by packing the rough blade in charcoal and heating it to a defined temperature. The watering of the blade surface was produced through special forging processes, to give visible lines and cloudy patches. Then came the moment of hardening the edge to produce the yakiba. The blade was first covered with a thin layer of clay diluted in water; this was carefully dried, then partly removed from the edge, heated, and quenched in warm water. This operation required great skill, as the blade was hardened and

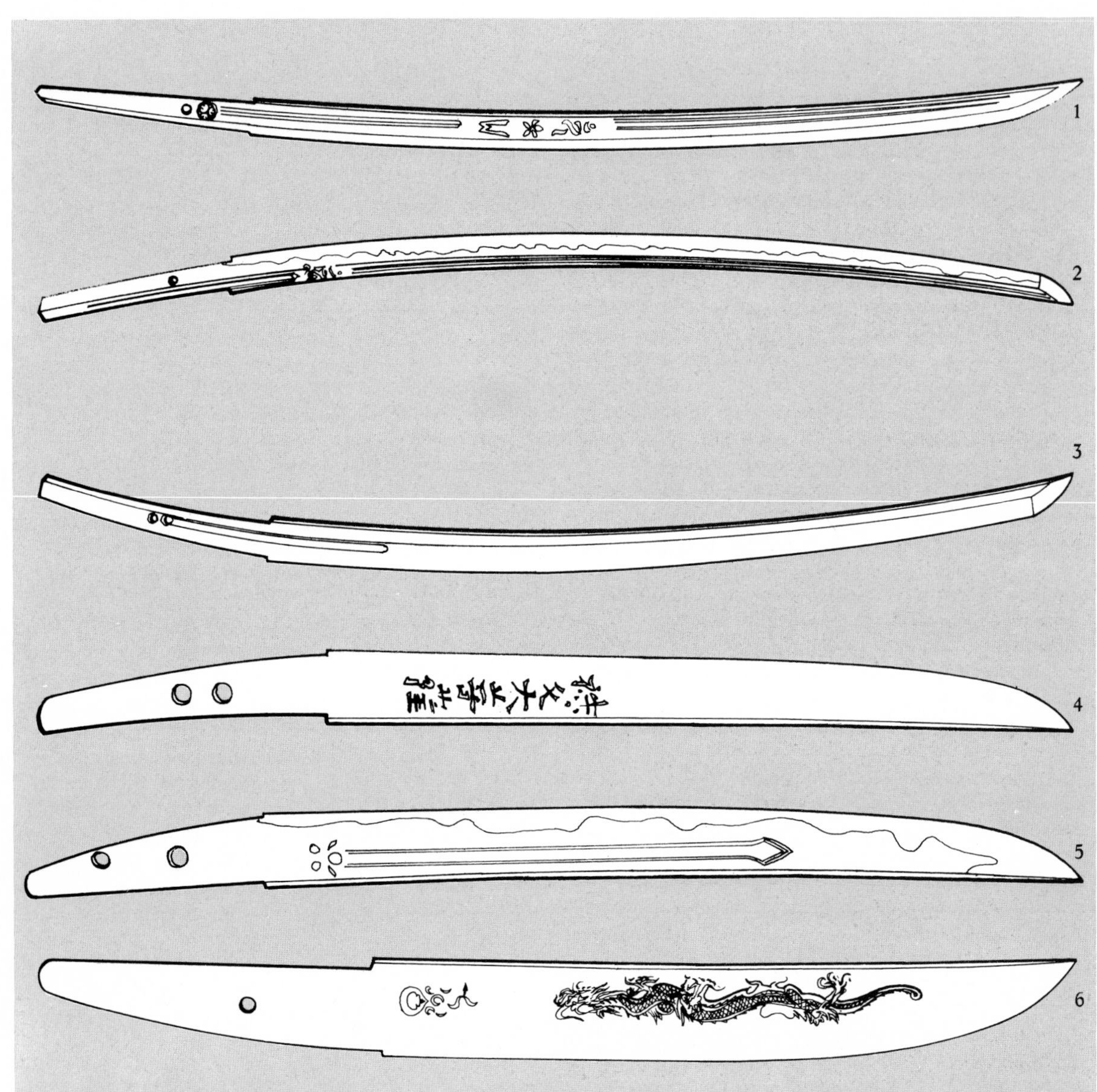


Japanese blades *1. Katana by Yasutsugu. Taguchi Collection, Osaka. 2. Katana attributed to Sadamune. Aoyama Collection, Tokyo. 3. Tachi by Mitsuyo. Maida Ikutoku-kai Foundation, Tokyo. 4. Tantō by Kagemitsu. Okano Collection, Okayama. 5. Tantō by Akihiro. Naga Collection, Osaka. 6. Tantō by Umetada Myujo. Furukawa Collection, Tokyo.*

tempered at the same time. If done well, the edge was made extremely hard without being brittle, while the body was left soft and tough.

The next step was the grinding and polishing of the blade, in which a series of fixed stones and oil were used. If the blade was to be decorated with engraving, this was done now, the parts to be engraved having been given an extra coating of clay before hardening so that they would remain soft. Sometimes engraving was done to eliminate minor defects that would detract from the value of the blade. Motifs from the ancient sword known as KEN or a dragon motif were often the subjects of decoration, although occasionally the branch of a flowering plant or *bonji* (Sanskrit) characters were depicted. Finally, the blade was signed on the tang and, in some cases, additional information was inscribed. Sometimes, however, blades of the highest quality remained unsigned, this being indicative of the maker's pride: a masterpiece speaks for itself.

The two traditional tests of a fine blade were that it should be able to cut a common blade in two without having its edge nicked, and that, if it were held in running water with the edge upstream and a lotus plant allowed to float against it, the stem would be cut. There were, however, more robust practical tests, and these are sometimes recorded, alongside the smith's signature, on the tang. Since a fighting sword should be capable of cutting a man's head off at a single stroke, blades were sometimes tried either on corpses or on criminals condemned to death, various recognized cuts being employed.

When not in use the blades were fitted with plain wooden grips and kept in plain wooden scabbards, the only furniture being the HABAKI, and even this was often made of wood. Basically, Japanese sword blades are divided into the *koto*, old (prior to the 17th century), and the *shinto*, new (made after 1603).

Japanese blade-makers were people of importance and esteem, their work having a semireligious character in which several rituals were observed. Their blades were undoubtedly the finest that have ever been produced. The most renowned of all the blade-makers of old Japan were Masamune (c. 1290) and Muramasa (c. 1340). *See also* YAKIBA.

**blowback operation** *See* AUTOMATIC WEAPONS.

**blowgun** A long, hollow wooden or metal tube or pipe through which small arrows or pellets are shot, propelled by the user's lungs. The blowgun was used in earliest times, but mainly for hunting: a clay pellet could stun small birds, an arrow—which had a wad of cotton in place of the flights in order to build up pressure from the user's breath—could catch larger wildfowl and other small prey. It disappeared in Europe with the advent of firearms, but it probably influenced this development by demonstrating how, as a launching tube, it was necessary to close off one end in order to convey the whole force of the explosion in the desired direction. It is still used by certain tribes of the Amazon forest who are considered to be at the evolutionary stage of the Stone Age.

**bludgeon** *See* CLUB.

**blunderbuss** A short, large-bore gun with a widely flared muzzle. The word "blunderbuss" almost certainly derives from the German word *Donnerbüchse*, meaning "thunder-gun," because of the terrible noise it made when discharged. This type of gun was evidently first developed in Europe, probably during the 16th century, as guns with blunderbuss-type muzzles are depicted in engravings illustrating the entry of Emperor Charles V into Bologna in 1530. The short barrel, of either iron or brass, was charged with shot, the theory being that the flared muzzle would spread it over a wide area. In fact, this theory proved incorrect.

Blunderbusses were used to a limited extent by armies, but more commonly on board ship, during the 17th century, where their use in fighting at close quarters was particularly effective. During the 18th century, blunderbusses were often carried by the guards of stagecoaches as protection against highwaymen. As late as 1840 it is recorded that flintlock blunderbusses were being specially made for the Royal Mail coach guards, who were advised to load them with ten or twelve large pellets rather than the customary small shot. Toward the end of the 1700s, some blunderbusses were fitted with a short bayonet hinged at the muzzle and secured by a spring, thus providing an alternative means of defense.

**boarding pike** A staff weapon with a stout shaft, half the size of a PIKE, in use aboard warships from the 16th to 19th centuries. A similar weapon used by infantry officers was called a HALF-PIKE.

**boar spear** *See* SPEAR.

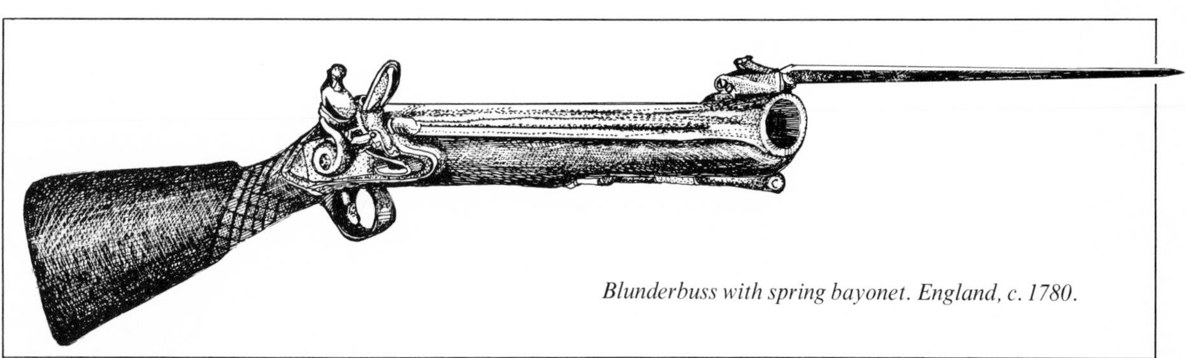

*Blunderbuss with spring bayonet. England, c. 1780.*

**boat hook** A pole with a spike on the top and a hook jutting out to one side; or it may be blunt with a hook and spike jutting out on each side. The boat hook is an essential piece of equipment for a number of maneuvers at sea, especially in a small boat, such as going alongside a ship, making fast to a jetty and casting off, holding ropes, etc. In times past, it was not unknown for boat hooks to be used in combat, where they proved to be formidable weapons.

**bolas** A missile weapon of prehistoric Asian origin. It is widely used by the Eskimos and by the Indians of the South American plains.

The Eskimo bolas, which is employed mostly for hunting wildfowl, consists of four, six, or ten weights—made of walrus ivory or bone—which may be egg-shaped, spherical, or even carved to represent animals. These weights, which are about 2.5–5 cm. (1–2 in.) in diameter, are each fastened to a cord about 70 cm. (28 in.) long, the opposite ends being joined to form a short handle. When the hunter goes into action, he grasps the handle in one hand, the balls in the other and, with a quick jerk, straightens out the strings; as soon as he spies a flock of birds he lets the balls go, whirls them around his head, and releases the handle. This weapon is effective up to 30–40 m. (33–44 yds.).

The South American bolas is almost twice as big, consisting of a cord or thong with a leather-covered stone ball fastened to each end. Sometimes the leather covering is not used, and a groove is cut around each ball with the cord tied into the groove. A second cord, with a smaller ball, is usually attached to the middle of the first cord, and it is this third ball that is held in the horseman's hand as he rides after his prey, whirling the other two around his head until they have attained sufficient velocity. The weapon is then released so as to strike or entangle the legs of the enemy or of an animal or large bird such as an emu. A two-balled bolas is known as a *somai* and a triple-balled one as an *achico*.

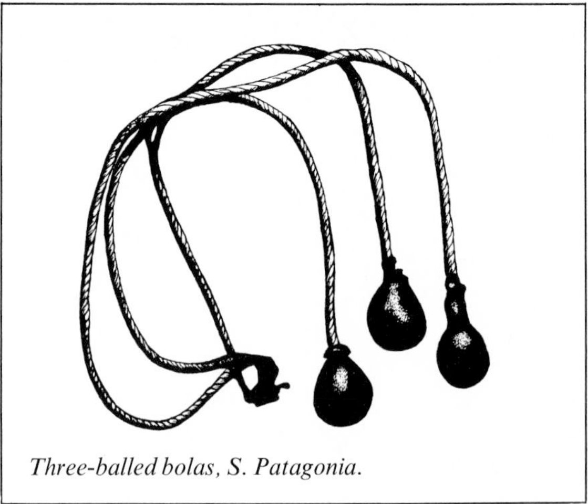

*Three-balled bolas, S. Patagonia.*

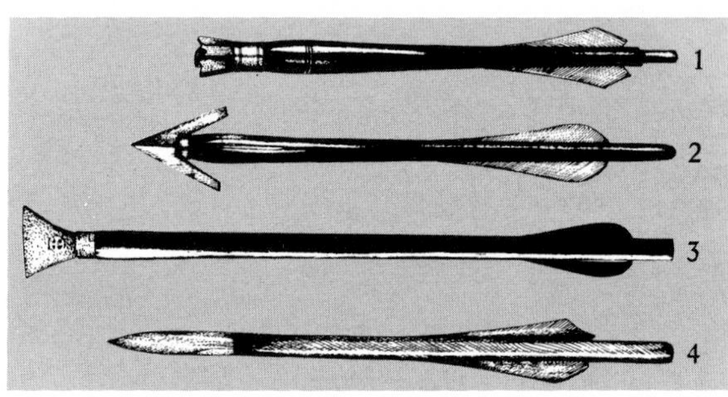


*1. Hunting bolt with battering head, late 16th century. 2. Hunting bolt with barbed head, late 16th century. 3. Hunting bolt with trapezoid cutting tip, 16th–17th century. 4. War bolt, with pyramidal head, 16th century. Odescalchi Collection, Museo di Palazzo Venezia, Rome.*

**bolt** (also **quarrel**) A missile consisting of a small wooden shaft which carries a head (or pile), designed to inflict wounds, fitted with feathers or vanes (also fletches) to hold the bolt's direction; it is, in other words, an ARROW, but more massive and compact, which was shot from a crossbow. Depending on the use required of it, the heads were of different shapes. For use in battle, bolts with conical or pyramidal iron heads were mainly used, but for hunting purposes the typology was more varied: there were, for example, heads with parted, V-shaped barbs with cutting edges along the inside, trapezoid in shape, with the long side foremost, which were recommended by hunting manuals for wildfowl; ordinary barbed heads for medium-sized animals, or when the hunter did not want the bolt to be easy to dislodge; and battering cylindrical heads for smaller animals, so as not to damage the fur. To stabilize the flight of the missile and thus make the hits more accurate, successful attempts were made to impart rotation to the flying bolt by setting the vanes at an angle to its longer axis. This principle of rotation was later applied to the missiles in rifled firearms.

**bolt** A term commonly used for the breechblock of bolt-action rifles, semiautomatic and automatic rifles, machine guns and submachine guns with blowback action. It generally consists of a metal block with a depression on the front face, fitting over the base of the cartridge on firing. The firing pin, fixed or moving, comes out of a hole at the center of this depression, and the extractor is fitted at one side. There is a small notch in the underside into which the sear fits, and the rear end of the block is in contact with the return spring. The bolt is generally fitted with a handle or cocking piece, which runs in a slot in the receiver and allows the bolt to be drawn back or, if necessary, to be let forward slowly.

The main functions of the breechblock are: (1) as it moves rapidly forward, to detach the first cartridge projecting from the magazine and drive it forward into the chamber; (2) as the cartridge is chambered (or an instant before, in systems with "advanced primer ignition"), to fire it; (3) to prevent premature opening of the breech through the substantial inertia of the bolt or through a locking device; and (4) to extract the spent case and draw it back until it reaches the ejector.

**bomb** Generally a hollow projectile filled with an explosive (or with poison gas, biological poison, incendiary substance, etc.) and fitted with a detonating device. Drawings in manuscripts by J. Mariano, known as Il Taccola (the Jackdaw), tell us that incendiary bombs were being used as long ago as the mid-15th century (*see* MORTAR), but the first explosive bombs were probably not used until the following century. Generally fired from guns with a short barrel and high, curved trajectory, they were made of wrought or cast iron and activated by a wooden fuze filled with a mixture of black powder plus saltpeter and sulfur.

Present-day bombs can be classified according to the way they are employed:

*Aerial bombs.* Bombs for aerial bombardment, used sporadically in the First World War, grew in importance as military aviation developed. They can be divided into categories according to the nature of the target,

(1) Bombs for general purposes and for demolition. Bombs of this kind can meet the requirements of the great majority of situations and are used for demolition, against personnel, and as land mines. They have a relatively light steel case—either forged in a single piece, or in several sections stamped out and welded together—forming the nose cone, the cylindrical body, and the tapering tail to which the fins are attached. Filled with TNT, amatol, or other suitable explosive, they may be fuzed either at the nose or at the tail, or quite often in both places.

(2) Armor-piercing or semi-armor-piercing bombs, used against heavily armored targets. The case is always in one piece and so made that it will not fragment as it penetrates the armor but will burst only after penetration. The fuze is always in the tail. Armor-piercing bombs are filled with explosives which, while highly destructive, are as little sensitive as possible to shock and to friction. Semi-armor-piercing bombs are similar to general-purpose bombs, but with a heavier case.

(3) Anti-personnel bombs, with delayed fragmentation. These work by discharging splinters or pellets, and are used against personnel or unprotected targets. They generally consist of a thin-walled tubular steel case with either a series of rings around it cut from a solid steel tube, or a spiral of drawn steel. They have a bursting charge of TNT, with a fuze at the tail timed to explode either in the air or immediately on impact with the ground. Among the bombs of this type, one of particular interest for its special features is the American 4-lb. M-83 "Destructor," or so-called butterfly bomb. The outside of the case is made of four sections hinged together around a central pivot at the top, and when the bomb is dropped the air current forces these open. The bomb thus has a "retarder"—a kind of fan rotating around the central pivot, with its blades giving enough lift to ensure a soft landing.

(4) Incendiary bombs, which can be subdivided into two classes, one with very light cases filled with incendiary substances in a liquid or jellied state, the other with thick cases made of a magnesium alloy and a solid incendiary filling. All incendiaries have fuzes that act instantaneously, to prevent the bomb from burying itself before it spreads its incendiary charge. Among liquid incendiary fillings used are IM (isobutyl methacrylate), a very thick substance obtained by dissolving polymerized sodium methacrylate, mixed with a calcium soap, in gasoline; and napalm, obtained by mixing aluminum salts of naphthenic and palmitic acids in gasoline. Napalm is a very thick liquid that can spread over the ground very quickly without evaporating, burning with an intense heat. Solid incendiary substances include magnesium, thermite (aluminum powder and iron oxide), flakes of metallic aluminum mixed with barium nitrate and sulfur, and Pyrogel P.T., made by mixing polymerized sodium methacrylate with asphalt and magnesium powder.

(5) Gas bombs. The case consists of a thin steel tube with a hemispherical head. Fuzed in the nose cone, gas bombs have the bursting charge contained in a cylinder passing down the center of the case. British and American gas bombs are painted blue or blue-gray, with one or two differently colored stripes in the center to show whether or not the gas is persistent. The color of the stripes also indicates the effects of the bomb: green for blistering gases, red for tear gas, yellow for smoke, purple for incendiary. In most cases initials are also marked on the case to indicate the filling: HS = yperite (mustard gas), AC = prussic acid, CG = phosgene, MI = lewisite, ED = ethyldichloroarsine, PS = chloropicrin, DP = diphosgene, DA = diphenylchloroarsine, CA = bromobenzylcyanidrine, CN = chloroacetophenone, FS = sulfur dioxide, WP = white phosphorus, TH = thermite, FM = titanium tetrachloride, DM = adamsite (diphenylaminechloroarsine), CL = chlorine.

*Depth charges.* Large cylindrical containers with relatively thin walls (3–4 mm.) filled with a very large explosive charge—generally of an underwater type—that may make up more than 70 percent of the total weight. The fuze may be at both the nose and the tail, or only at the tail, and may be actuated by water pressure, by mechanical means on impact, or magnetically. Depth charges are used against submarines, underwater installations, and the underwater part of unarmored hulls; they are fired by ships having the appropriate equipment (destroyers, etc.) and sometimes by aircraft.

*Nuclear bombs.* Bombs in which the explosive force is of nuclear origin. Nuclear bombs are commonly, if not with strict accuracy, divided into two classes: atomic bombs, in which the energy is produced by fission of the nucleus, and thermo nuclear bombs (hydrogen bombs or H-bombs), in which it is produced by fusion.

Atomic bombs make use of the energy released in a fission chain reaction; a nucleus of high atomic number (Z  90), when bombarded by a neutron (or also by such charged particles as protons, deuterons, etc.), absorbs it, and at the same time splits into two fragments with atomic numbers about half that of the initial nucleus, plus a certain number of free neutrons. The energy released in this reaction is some 180–200 MV (1 MV [megavolt] = 1 million volts) for each atom, contained in the kinetic energy of the liberated neutrons, the energy of the electrons emitted (the beta particles of the fission products), the energy of the neutrinos that accompany the particles, and lastly, the energy of the gamma rays emitted.

If there is more than one atom of the fissionable substance present (the substances most commonly used are uranium 235, plutonium 239, or uranium 233, or a mixture of all three), other nuclei may be struck by the neutrons as they are released, and the fission reaction will extend rapidly so as to affect the entire mass, setting off a chain reaction.

In the typical fission reaction of U-235, the most probable fission fragments are strontium and xenon, with the atomic numbers 38 and 54; both will be radioactive, since the heavier stable isotope of strontium is Sr-88 and that of xenon, Xe-138. In an uncontrolled fission chain reaction, 85 percent of the energy developed is present initially in the form of kinetic energy. Of this, only 50 percent accounts for the formation of the shock wave, the wave that causes the purely mechanical destructive effects like those caused by conventional explosions. The other 35 percent takes the form of heat, light, and ultraviolet radiation. This is due to the very high temperatures (of the order of millions of degrees centigrade), as against only about 5000°C. in conventional explosions. The remaining 15 percent of the energy produced is released in the form of various nuclear radiations which are extremely dangerous on account of the biological destruction they may cause. About a third of these radiations appear at the time of the explosion; the other two-thirds, which last a comparatively long time, appear when dust with a high content of nuclear radiation falls to earth as fallout. Fallout may be local, appearing a few hours after the explosion; tropospherical, appearing after a few months; or stratospherical, remaining active over a period of several years.

One kilogram of U-235 or Pu-239, which makes a mass about the size of a golf ball and has an explosive power equivalent to 17,000 kg. (17 tons) of TNT, will not explode by itself. The reason is that, if one of its nuclei is subjected to the process of fission, the neutrons produced generally escape from the mass without causing a second fission, so that there is no chain reaction. But when the quantity of fissionable material reaches a certain level, about 15 kg. for plutonium 239 and 50 kg. for uranium 235, at least one of the neutrons produced is certain to cause a second fission, starting off a chain reaction, and the energy released within the material causes an explosion equal to that of several hundred tons of high explosive. The mass of plutonium or uranium that produces this effect is called the "critical mass." The "criticality" of a given fissionable material depends also on the type and quantity of the substance in which the material is enclosed. A jacket of U-235 that is 25 mm. (1 in.) thick around a central mass of plutonium reduces its critical mass from 15 kg. to 10 kg.

The fissionable material in atomic bombs is kept in subcritical conditions until the instant of explosion and then brought into critical conditions by one of two different means. In the first, the fissionable substance is divided into two or more masses, each itself subcritical, and at the required moment a small amount of conventional explosive drives these masses together at very high velocity (less than one microsecond), so that the critical mass is reached, and immediately after it, the "supercritical mass," with the consequent setting off of the chain reaction and the resultant explosion. In the second system, the fissionable material is kept in subcritical conditions by being prepared in a spongy form, and made to reach criticality, followed by supercriticality, by a sudden reduction of its volume; conventional explosive charges set symmetrically in a sphere around the fissile mass compress it uniformly so as to cause an implosion.

Thermonuclear bombs (hydrogen bombs) depend on the enormous energy released in nuclear fusion reactions. In direct contrast to nuclear fission, nuclear fusion is the process of combining two nuclei; the resultant mass is less than the sum of the two individual masses, and the difference is converted into energy according to Einstein's famous equation: $E = mc^2$. To bring about the collision between two nuclei and the subsequent rearrangement of the nucleons into a single configuration, it is necessary to find means of overcoming the electrostatic repulsion between the two similarly charged nuclei. Since that repulsion becomes greater with the greater atomic numbers, nuclear fusion reactions are more easily effected with light elements than with heavy. Fusion reactions, discovered early in the 1930s, are highly exoergic; while the energy produced is generally less than that in fission reactions, the latter can only take place with heavy elements, which are relatively rare, whereas fusion reactions call for light elements, particularly hydrogen, which occurs very abundantly in nature, and its isotopes deuterium and tritium. The energy needed to initiate a fusion reaction, to overcome the electrostatic repulsion between the nuclei, may be obtained by raising the interacting particles to extremely high temperatures such as can only be reached by a nuclear fission explosion. In practice, therefore, a thermonuclear bomb includes an ignition system consisting of a fission explosive device—an atomic bomb—and a given quantity of a substance—hydrogen, deuterium, or tritium—which actually provides the material for the fusion reaction.

**bombard** A large piece of ARTILLERY in use between the end of the 14th and the beginning of the 16th century. It fired stone balls and might be made of wrought iron or cast bronze. Many bombards were made in two pieces, the chamber being screwed onto the barrel at the breech. The term was used again by the Italians in the First World War to apply to a large, pneumatically operated mortar, and a "spigot mortar" used by the British in the Second World War was christened the Blacker Bombard after its inventor.

**boomerang** A missile weapon of the Australian aborigines (the word originates from a tribe in New South Wales) and of other peoples in India, Africa, and the Americas. It was also known to the ancient Egyptians and probably to the Romans of classical times as well.

Sickle-shaped, the boomerang is usually made of hardwood, although horn, ivory, and metal ones are not uncommon. Its average length is about 40–70 cm. (16–28 in.) and its width 5–7 cm. (2–3 in.). It has sharp edges and is slightly more convex on one side than the other. There are two main types: the return boomerang and the nonreturn or war boomerang.

The return boomerang is more of a plaything, although it can be used for killing birds and is often as dangerous to

*"Mons Meg," mid-15th-century bombard, built in Flanders. Edinburgh Castle.*

the thrower as to the target. In Australia, the two arms are always curved at an angle of at least 90 degrees; in other areas, this may vary between 70 and 120 degrees. The special quality of the boomerang's flight is made possible by the slight skew at which the arms are set, which consists of a 2- or 3-degree variation from the coplanar. A special technique is required, too, in the throwing, but when this is done correctly the boomerang will travel straight for some 30 m. (100 ft.) or more, with nearly vertical rotation; it then inclines to the left, lies over on its flat side, and rises into the air, returning to the thrower when it has described a circle about 50 m. (165 ft.) in diameter. Some highly skilled Australian aborigines can achieve throws of 100 m. (330 ft.) before the leftward curve begins. It is even claimed that a boomerang has been seen to return to its thrower after having hit its target.

The war boomerang is altogether bigger and heavier, and may be 100 cm. (40 in.) or more in length. It is a deadly weapon in the hands of an expert.

There are various boomerang-type weapons, especially in India, each one having it own local name.

**bore** The interior of the barrel of a gun, having a constant diameter, the CALIBER, down which the projectile passes. In modern rifled firearms it is grooved—or rifled—helicoidally (spirally).

**bōshi** Shape of the tip of a Japanese blade. *See also* BLADE: Japanese.

**bourdonass** A hollow lance used from the late 15th century to the 17th for jousts and various equestrian exercises like the running at the ring and the carousel. Appearing big and heavy, it was in fact quite light and could be easily broken on impact.

**bow** A stringed projectile weapon designed to throw arrows. It consists of a long, slender, flexible stave with a length of cord (the bowstring) fastened to it at each end (the tips) under a certain tension. By drawing the string and the arrow back with one hand and holding the stave firmly with the other, the stave is forced to bend. As soon as the traction ceases and the string is released, the string immediately springs forward, impelling the arrow.

The bow, used in both hunting and war, has been known to man since the Mesolithic period (about 10,000–6000 B.C.), and its advent represented an important stepping-stone in mankind's evolutionary process. Different environmental conditions produced variety both in materials and construction technique. In attempting to produce a bow that would give sufficient impetus to an arrow, two methods were tried. One was to lengthen the stave, within the limits of locally available materials, and the other was to increase its flexibility while leaving the length unchanged.

Even in places far apart from each other and culturally totally dissimilar (as, for example, the British Isles and Japan), and where the materials were different—yew wood and bamboo, respectively—the tendency was to lengthen the bow. This trend was also conditioned by the fact that the archer, whether a warrior or a hunter, would have been on foot. In areas where there was a shortage of materials suitable for making bows from which arrows could be shot equally well from horseback or from a war chariot, the composite bow was developed. Sometimes, however, the two trends existed side by side within the same cultural environment. The simple (or self) bow, in the normal range of sizes and made usually of wood, would have been used by ordinary people and soldiers, whereas the composite bow would have been reserved for use by the upper strata of society.

Graffiti and rock paintings, as well as some remarkable discoveries of arrowheads, offer evidence that the bow of the Mesolithic period was merely a long, slender rod with a cord of vegetable fiber or animal tendon.

Historical records show that the bow was extensively used by the armies of ancient Egypt, where even the Pharaoh himself went hunting or to war armed with a bow.

It was held in equally high regard by other civilizations including the Babylonian, Assyrian, Hyksos, Hittite, Syrian, Jewish and, generally speaking, by all the peoples who inhabited the central part of the eastern Mediterranean basin. The typical bow of this region had a very compact form, making it suitable for a wide variety of purposes, both in hunting and in war. Iconography of the period allows us to see the Assyrians as they shot their arrows from war chariots, on horseback, and on foot.

Bow-and-arrow shooting contests were very popular with the pre-Hellenic people of the Aegean, and they had been a favorite sport in Crete since the Minoan period. With the Dorian invasion, which occurred toward the middle of the second millenium B.C., the bow became relegated purely to hunting purposes. It saw use again, however, in the Peloponnesian War (431–404 B.C.) and in the Greek areas of Pontus, where, being in perpetual conflict with the Scythians and Thracians, who were formidable bowmen, the troops had to be equipped with equivalent arms. In Italy and the western Mediterranean, the Greek troops met with the same situation when they found themselves confronting the bowmen of Umbria, Etruria, Lucania, Sardinia, and Carthage. A historic instance of archers being held in particularly high regard was when, in the 4th century B.C., the Athenians entrusted the policing of their city to Scythian archers known as Speusinios, who were, in fact, public slaves.

In the world of classical Rome, too, the bow was relegated to hunting activities. However, a permanent nucleus of auxiliary troops was established, made up of Syrians, Cretans, and Parthians—nations that excelled in bowmanship—as a war reserve (but which, in fact, was only called upon to fight in the Second Punic War [218–201 B.C.]). This fitted in perfectly with the Romans' conception of military organization. Their system was to entrust the center of a formation to national troops, arming each man with a javelin, shield, and sword. The flanking forces consisted of auxiliaries from among the allies, who were all men chosen for their specialized skills—Parthian and Numidian horsemen, Balearic slingsmen, and Scythian bowmen, for example.

*Bows depicted in an Upper Paleolithic rock painting, Alpera, Spain.*

*A Sassanian king hunting with a bow. From a silver cup dating from the 6th or 5th century* B.C. *Private Collection.*

Of all the invading nations that swarmed over Italy from the north during the first centuries A.D. in search of plunder, only the Huns were feared for their great skill with the bow as a fighting weapon. All the others, including the Franks, were by now using the bow almost exclusively for the chase, despite its proven value in defense. The bow was used, however, against the invading Saracens from the East, who found themselves confronted by a united people, many of whom had themselves arrived as invaders but had long since settled down with the indigenous population.

The emperor Charlemagne (768–814), who made a great many changes in military organization, ordered that the bow be made a regulation weapon for certain troops. He also decreed that the yew tree be cultivated to ensure a plentiful supply of this wood so suitable for bow staves. Many centuries later, in the first half of the 15th century, another king of France, Charles VII, was to issue a similar order, stipulating that yew trees be grown in every Normandy churchyard.

The largest consumers of yew in Europe were the British, whose use of the bow was on a much wider scale than on the Continent, where—after about the year 1000—the CROSSBOW rapidly overtook it, both for hunting and for war. In Britain, the bow developed along quite particular lines until it achieved that characteristic form known as the longbow. The best wood for this weapon was considered to be Italian yew and, in order to procure it, a trade agreement was entered into whereby the British agreed to import Italian wine with the proviso that every barrel be accompanied by the trunk of a yew tree from which a longbow could be made. Bow staves were also imported into Britain from Austria and Spain.

The Normans imposed the use of the bow on other regions of northern Europe during their migrations and conquests. Theirs was a simple weapon, quite small, being only about $1\frac{1}{2}$ m. (5 ft.) in length, but it was with this bow

*Archer, detail from a 7th-century silk tapestry. Cathedral of St. Servatius, Maastricht, Netherlands.*

that the Norman army, led by William the Conqueror, overthrew Harold's forces at Hastings in 1066 by attacking them, as they stood to leeward of their defenses, with a down-curving hail of arrows.

The British learned a great deal from this lesson and, over the centuries that followed, considerably improved the ordinary bow until it became the famous longbow whose height corresponded to that of the archer. (There is also a tradition, however, that says the English bow was introduced from Wales in the latter part of the 13th century.)

There were many famous occasions when the British demonstrated their skill in using their longbow as an offensive weapon. At Crécy in 1346, English archers—led by Edward III against Philip VI of France—completely routed the Genoese crossbowmen who were fighting under Riniero de' Grimaldi, although they may have been helped somewhat by weather conditions favorable to them. Ten years later, English archers played an important part in defeating the French at Poitiers. In 1415 they demonstrated at Agincourt, yet again, that—with accurate aiming, the exceptional shooting range of the longbow, and above all, the superior number of arrows that could be projected at one time—a barrier could be put up which was quite impenetrable and against which neither foot soldiers nor mounted troops could survive for long. Nor should the distracting effect of the arrows on the enemy be underestimated; the visible approach of these missiles would undoubtedly have made the soldier look up from time to time in order to see whether he should be taking evasive action against an arrow, and his concentration would have been lost.

The core of many of the medieval armies and mercenary bands was formed of bowmen and crossbowmen. Particularly good examples of this existed in Italy, where many cities had their own militia—drawn mainly from among laborers and peasants—and they often gave an excellent account of themselves, as, for example, at the famous battle of Legnano against Frederick Barbarossa in 1176.

Instruction in the use of the bow was particularly widespread in Piedmont and, in 1206, Thomas I of Savoy founded the Compagnia dell' Arco (Company of Archers) in order to encourage people to use it. Heads of the principalities would often choose archers as bodyguards—as did Thomas I—and Prince Emanuel Philibert recruited his supporters from among the Savoyards.

Neither the bow nor the crossbow ever had a clear lead over the other, so far as effectiveness was concerned, although the crossbow may have seemed to have had some advantages at times. Two exceptions were the Papal States (to a certain extent) and almost all the territories belonging to the Republic of Venice, where the devlopment of the bow was strongly influenced from the East. In fact, it was mainly from Venice—where the Turkish bow had been completely adopted—that this weapon spread throughout the Italian peninsula and to the rest of Europe, with the exception of the northern islands, where longbows dominated and were replaced only by firearms.

In many countries, archers retained their military importance until recent times. At the battle of Friedland in January 1807, some Kalmuck mounted archers, irregulars in the Russian army, succeeded in harassing the Napoleonic troops several times. And in the Second World War, a few detachments of American archers were deployed in several specialized actions in the Asian sector.

*English archers at the battle of Crécy in 1346, from the 15th-century Chronicles of Froissart.*

During the earlier part of the 20th century, plain bows made of steel were in vogue for competitions and for shooting game. The former military importance of archery is commemorated by the Royal Company of Archers who form the Queen's Scottish Bodyguard.

*Technical Characteristics*

The structure of the bow can be divided into two main categories: the plain, or self, bow and the composite, or built-up, bow. The archaic bow used by Neolithic man belonged to the first group: the stave was made in one piece, thickening toward the middle and tapering at the ends. The plain bow—which was made in many different lengths—developed, as we have seen, from the short European bow into the British longbow.

The bow has not completely disappeared in the so-called underdeveloped parts of the world. In Africa it may still be found in use, here and there, by the Pygmies; theirs is a simple, very short bow with a rounded stave. The bow still exists, too, among the indigenous people of the Amazon. This is usually made from iron-bark wood (a species of eucalyptus tree) and shaped by means of such primitive tools as flints and the jaws of piranha fish; it is then polished, using river sand as an abrasive. Although belonging to the plain-bow category, the bow used in Melanesia is somewhat unique because of the elliptical form of its transverse section. The bows of the mountain people of the Andes are shaped to a rectangular cross-section, while in the Congo and New Guinea they are semicircular.

A bow is described as "composite" when the stave is composed of two or more materials which are not necessarily of different types. The earliest bows were undoubtedly plain, and the transition to a composite structure almost certainly took place in Asia. The core of the stave was generally of wood, and materials with contrasting characteristics were used to cover almost its entire length. On the back of the stave—that is, the side facing the target—eanimal tendons or sinews would generally have been applied, offering strong resistance to the traction to which the bow had to be subjected. The belly (inner face) was covered with a material that offered strong resistance to compression, such as thin strips of horn or metal. These components were then glued together, wound around tightly with tendons, and lacquered or painted.

When a composite bow is not under traction or is unstrung, it may have a single or double reflex curve, according to its composition. The Japanese longbow (*yumi*) had a single curve and consisted solely of strips of bamboo (*Bambusa mitis*) at various stages of seasoning to produce different characteristics; for the back (outer face)—the part subjected to the greatest tension—a strip cut from the living plant at the end of autumn (that is, at the end of the annual vegetative cycle) would have been used; for the belly, a rather dry strip of bamboo was employed that had been cut a year before, at the end of summer, before the autumn rains. These were made fast with vegetable glues, tied with vegetable fibers, and then

*Archers armed with longbows at the siege of Mortagne-sur-Sèvre in 1377. From a contemporary miniature.*

lacquered. Chinese bows were similar but rather smaller (see section on the Chinese bow, below).

An intermediate type of bow, coming between the plain and the composite, was the reinforced bow, of which there were two versions. It had a rather flat wooden stave and was reinforced on the back with a tendon which increased and distributed the tension of the curve under traction. Sometimes it was merely bound tightly to the stave (so-called free version), or molded, damp, onto the stave so as to become almost a part of it ("close" version).

The Turkish bow curved in two directions, depending upon whether it was strung or unstrung. In fact, it had the double characteristic of being a composite bow (structurally) and a reflex bow: when unstrung, it had such a strong reflex curve that the bow tips were nearly touching; when strung or in use, the curve was reversed. Constructed of horn, tendons, and cherrywood, the first part to be made was the "core" of the stave; this was formed from three pieces—two arms and a handgrip—jointed together and then glued. By now, the curve of the stave was already taking shape. On the inside of this curve—which was to be the back of the bow—a tendon was laid, then glued and clamped to ensure perfect bonding. Two strips of horn were then placed on the outside and allowed to take up their naturally curved shape before being glued into position. The whole bow was then covered with skin or fine leather, which was stretched and glued into place. Lastly, the bow was lacquered in bright colors, and gold ornamentation frequently gave it

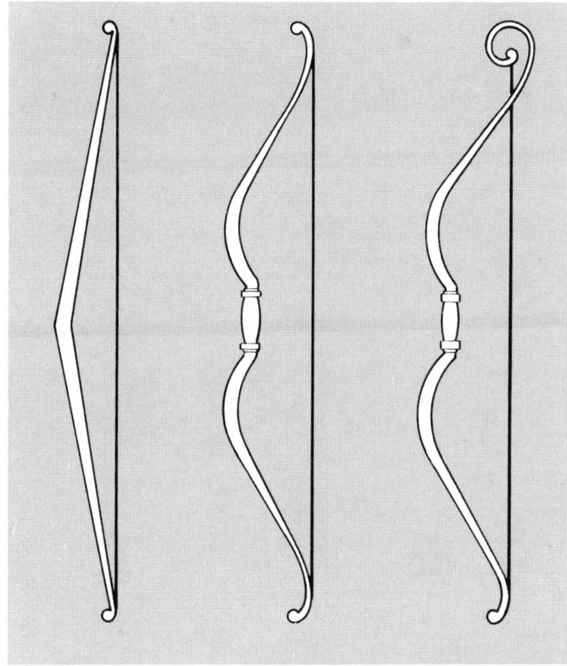

(left to right) *Assyrian angled bow; Hellenistic double-curved composite bow; Hellenistic composite "serpent's tail" bow.*

the final touch of elegance. The date when it was made was usually imprinted on one horn and the maker's name on the other.

At both tips of the bow a nock (notch) was made for insertion of the bowstring. The nock was usually made on the back of the bow, but sometimes on the sides as well. Given that the thickness of the bow gradually increases from the tips toward the grip, no nock was made in some instances, since the loop at the end of the bowstring, slipped around the tip of the bow, was held fast unaided. The shape of the tip depended on the type of fastening; a direct fastening almost invariably required notching at the base of the tip.

The flat bow could have the bowstring attached in two different ways: if the ends of the bow were brought closer, a normal bowstring with loops could be fitted; if the bow was finished with an all-around nock a few centimeters from the tip and with another notch set crosswise, these were used to fit a bowstring with frontal tension (this type is used mainly in central Africa for the short Pygmy bows). The bowstring was fitted to the nock around one end, passed over the tip along the back to the other tip by applying necessary tension, then passed over this tip to its nock. Modern bows have very pronounced tips, shaped in accordance with the requirements based on studies of the vibrations and aerodynamic properties of the bow.

As well as arrows, other projectiles could be shot, such as small clay balls (shot) or round pebbles. For this purpose, the bow was equipped with two strings separated by spacers and fitted in the center with a small leather or cloth pouch to hold the missile. When the string was drawn and released, the pouch with missile had to be turned around and twisted so that the projectile would not hit the stave. The stone-shooting bow is recorded in China from the second millennium B.C. and was widely used throughout the East—even until quite recent times in some areas. In Europe, however, records exist of it as having been employed only from the 14th to 18th centuries, when it was certainly being used to bring down wild fowl on the lagoons of Venice.

### *Archery as a Sport*

It is not easy to determine exactly when archery began to be regarded as a sport. However, enthusiasm for training to perfect the skills necessary in its use as a weapon has, for a very long time, run parallel with the pleasure of exercising such skills purely for their own sake.

The world of ancient Greece, the poems of Homer, the historical works of Herodotus and Xenophon, and even the vase paintings of classical times have all handed down a wealth of evidence to us of the esteem in which the art of bowmanship was held.

By the 12th century the whole of Europe seemed to be forming itself into archery and crossbow societies. Their main purpose, however, was always to ensure that a certain number of people were well trained for the local militia. Archery as a social skill was greatly encouraged and cultivated in France but on a rather elite level. *Gildes*

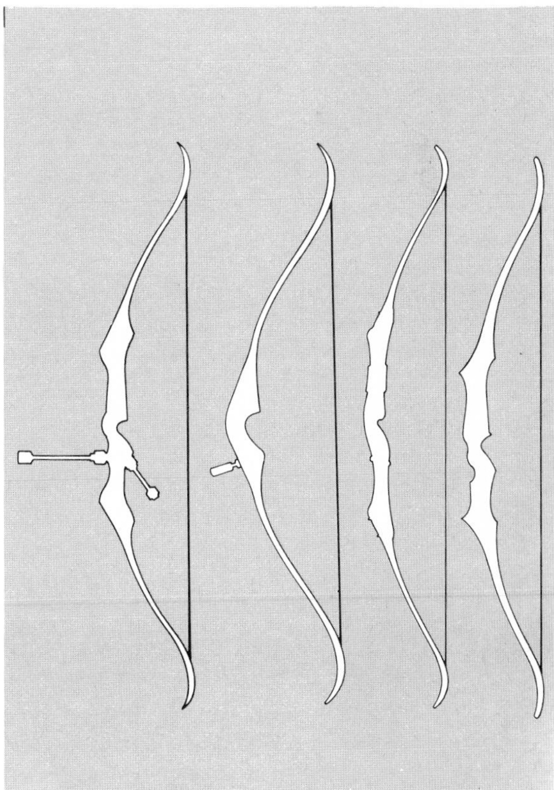

*Various types of modern bows.*

and *serments* thrived and prospered until the turmoil created by the Revolution of 1789 made such activities impossible. Archery returned to fashion in Britain in the 18th century but it was not until the latter part of the 19th century that archery really became simply a question of sportsmanship throughout Europe. Even then, the observance of certain ancient traditions was still upheld with fervid enthusiasm. The sport is currently so widespread that national and international competitions take place regularly.

Modern sporting bows are of the composite type, made from various kinds of wood and laminated plastics bonded together with modern adhesives. Unfortunately, the addition of sights, counterweights, etc., has spoiled their natural elegance of line.

*Chinese Bow*

Archery in China has a very old tradition going back to prehistoric times, having been involved in various aspects of hunting, war, and sport. In fact, throughout Chinese history the bow was always respected as an effective fighting instrument, and its manufacture achieved a high level of perfection. Chinese bows, of various sorts, all belong to the great range of Asian composite bows. Elaborate techniques were employed in their creation, requiring great skill and experience on the part of the craftsmen, who kept some of the processes secret, to be passed on only within their own families.

Chinese bows were, on the average, larger than in any other Asian country. They were made in four sizes for the army—70, 80, 90, and 100 pounds pull—which were practicable for any battle task and could be operated by bowmen according to their individual strength. Some larger sizes, up to 150 or 200 pounds pull, were also produced, but these were intended only for parades and ceremonial occasions—as an ostentatious display of power. Arrows were made according to the bow sizes, usually about 100 cm. (39 in.) or more in length.

The construction of a Chinese bow was very complicated. The frame was of bamboo with pieces of a deciduous wood glued onto the handgrip and at the sharp bends near the ends. Pieces of horn were glued onto the belly, and sinews were similarly applied to the back. The handgrip and ends were bound with leather or fishskin. Parts of the back were covered with a thin layer of birch bark which was frequently decorated with zigzag or swastika motifs, or a plum tree, lotus flower, or other symbolic design. Narrow blocks were glued and doweled onto the belly of the bow about 20–25 cm. (8–10 in.) from each end, and it was on these that the string bore when the bow was not in use. Many handgrips were covered with cork. The Chinese also made sectional bows that could be folded for convenience in carrying.

A particular method of holding the bow, widely used in China, was called the Mongolian release. This necessitated the use of cylindrical thumbrings, which were often made of jade.

**bowie knife** A hunting knife having a long blade with a cutting edge and a false cutting edge, a short hilt with the

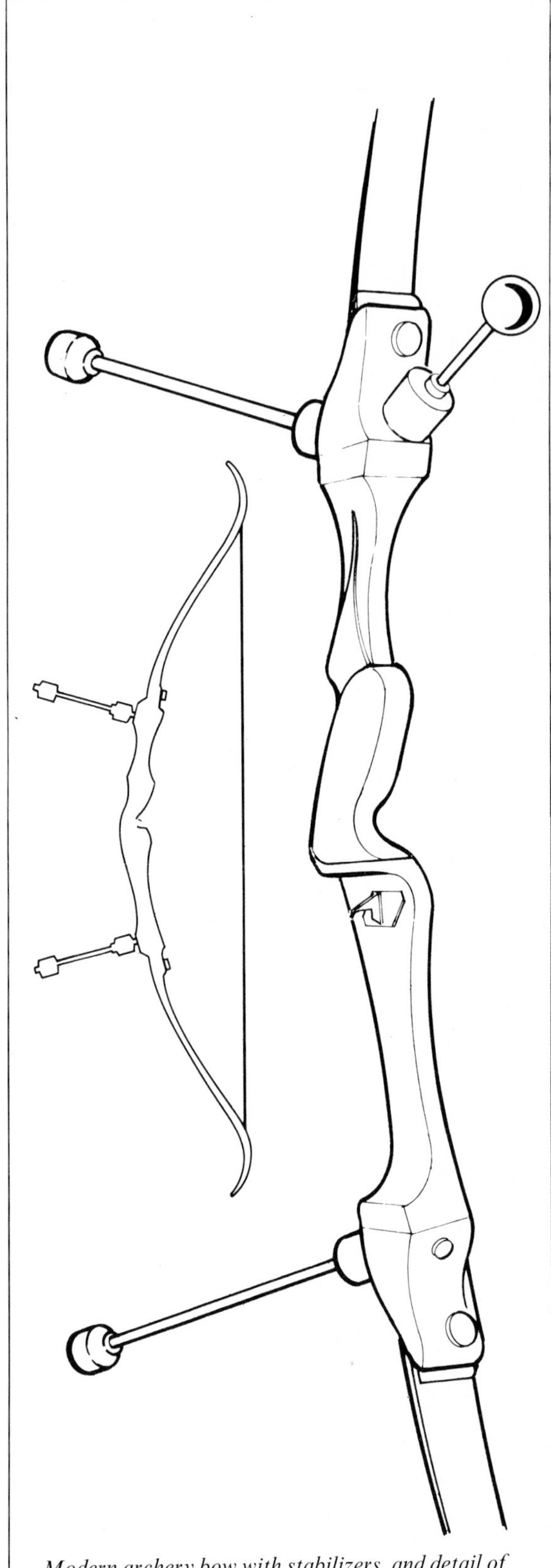

*Modern archery bow with stabilizers, and detail of central section.*

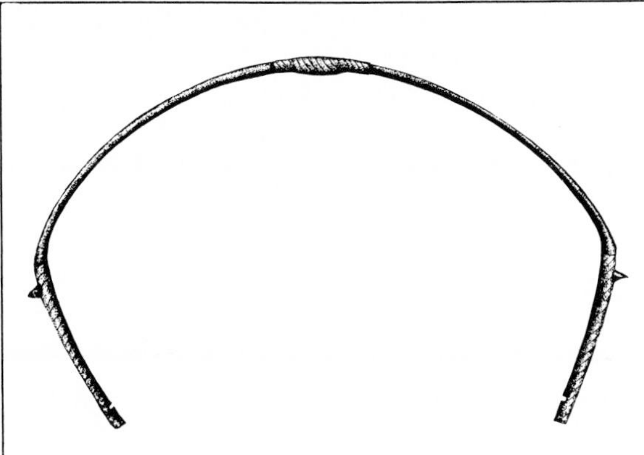

*Chinese bow with handgrip and ends bound with fishskin and a thin layer of bark on the back.*

arms often ending in knobs, and a grip with wooden or horn sidepieces. The name is associated with James Bowie, an American frontiersman who ended his turbulent days during the siege of Fort Alamo in Texas in 1836. It is said that the knife that bears his name was designed by his brother, Rezin P. Bowie, who gave it to James in 1827. It is also thought that Rezin Bowie produced a more advanced model of this knife in about 1830, with the help of a blacksmith from Arkansas by the name of James Black.

**bowstring** The string which, when drawn, spans or bends the bow and thus provides the arrow (or bolt) with the necessary thrust.

In early bows, the string was a tough cord made of either gut or sinew, according to the particular requirements of the bow, with knots at both ends. For the longbow the sciatic nerve of an ox was used, or a thin strip of hide, or a length of twine made of horsehair or vegetable fiber. In order to make a bowstring for a crossbow it was necessary to measure the distance between the tips of the bow, bearing in mind that, even when the bow was not drawn, the string had to keep the bow slightly bent. Then two cylindrical lugs were fixed into a board at the determined distance, and around them several dozen windings were made. Next, this bundle of sinew was covered with a tight binding which protected the central section of the bowstring from rubbing against the tiller and the nut. The same was done with the loops at the ends.

*Bowie knife, mid-19th century.*

The bowstring of the longbow was considerably lighter than the string required to shoot bolts with a heavy crossbow having a composite bow or metal bow, but the two types were made in the same manner. The double bowstring for the stone-shooting was made in virtually the same way. In order to fit the bowstring to a longbow, one tip of the bow was placed in one of the loops of the bowstring; then the knotted tip was held fast by the archer's foot, forcing the bow to bend over the thigh of the other leg until the other end of the bowstring could be slipped over it.

A different procedure was followed for the heavy crossbow. A special cord called the "bastard string" was used; this was a tough crossbow cord with two clamps at the ends. These were screwed onto the bow, which was then bent with the spanning device of the crossbow. By drawing the tips of the bow toward each other, it was then possible to hook the loops of the bowstring over them. When the bastard string was released and removed, the bowstring was in its correct position.

**box lock** A type of lock construction in which the cock is placed on top in the center of the lock and is mounted between two plates, with the steel and pan set above the breech. This method of lock construction became standard for small pocket pistols in the 18th century, having the obvious advantage of a less obtrusive external mechanism to catch in clothes or pockets. Probably the earliest pistols recorded that show this construction are a pair of silver mounted pistols by Lewis Barber in the Duke of Buccleuch's Collection dating from about 1710; unlike the later examples which are enclosed in a metal frame, the locks are set into the wooden stock. The box-lock construction became more common after 1750 and was widely used in England until the latter half of the 19th century.

**braces** *See* ENARMES.

**branches** Part of a horse's BIT, which served to link it to the headstall and reins. Basically, branches (also called cheeks) consisted of metal bars attached by toggle loops at each end of the mouthpiece, with more of the branch extending below the mouthpiece than above it. The upper part was straight and had a loop to which the leather cheek strap of the bridle was attached and which also took the CURB CHAIN, although there was sometimes a separate attachment for the chain. The lower part was usually longer and curved, ending in a curlicue and a ring to take the reins. The reins pivoted the mouthpiece in the horse's mouth, moving the top of the branches with the curb chain forward. Medieval branches were 30 cm. (12 in.) or more in length, which would have made the control very severe indeed.

**brandestoc** *See* BRANDISTOCK.

**brandistock** (from Italian *brandistocco*) An edged weapon, a kind of TUCK, concealed within a stout hollow stick. In order to release the thrusting blade it was necessary to "brandish" the stick in a forward direction;

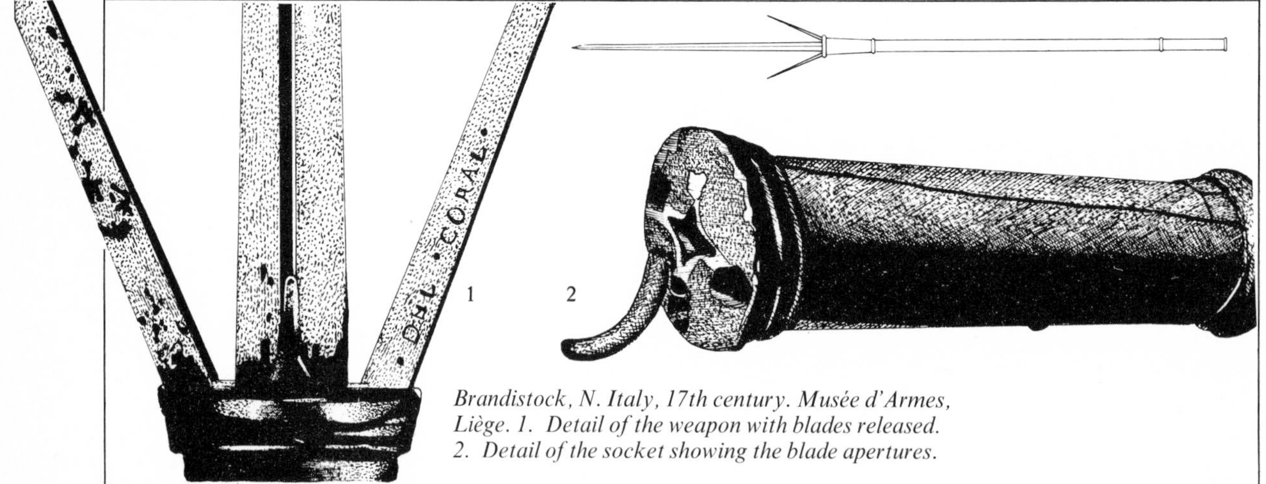


*Brandistock, N. Italy, 17th century. Musée d'Armes, Liège. 1. Detail of the weapon with blades released. 2. Detail of the socket showing the blade apertures.*

by so doing, the blade could slide outward from the stick to the right position, where it was locked by a catch with a spring release. The compact size of this weapon made it eminently portable and ideal for footmen and coachmen, and possibly also for pilgrims (*see* PILGRIM'S STAFF). The staff used by the wayfarer on his long journeys must have seemed harmless enough, but when required, it could be turned into a fearsome weapon. In addition to this type, with one blade, which can to some extent be considered the forerunner of the SWORD STICK, there was another type with fairly consistent features which was designed for military use. It had three blades: the central one, some 70 cm. (27 in.) long, and a much shorter blade sticking outward on either side of it; these were housed in a metal tube which normally was closed at the top with a hinged cap.

The names for weapons of this type indicate that they came from towns in Lombardy, probably as early as the 14th century. They were produced in northern Italy in the 16th to 19th centuries, but were also quite widely used throughout Europe. Some of the brandistocks had the metal tube open at the bottom end to fit it to a shaft, which turned it into a proper staff weapon. These must have been the numerous weapons described in 17th-century Italian inventories as staved swordsticks (*brandistocchi inastati*).

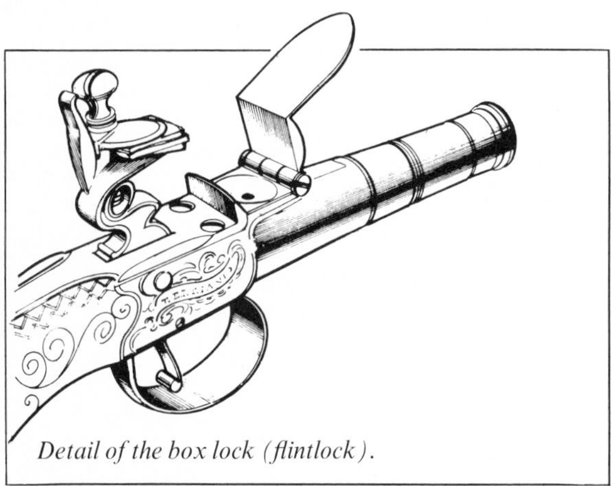

*Detail of the box lock (flintlock).*

**breast band** *See* PECTORAL.

**breastplate** One of the most important parts of plate ARMOR, protecting the front of the torso. It came into use during the 14th century, initially as a reinforcing piece attached with straps and buckles over a COAT OF PLATES. It was probably also worn occasionally as an independent protection and as such had been developed by the last quarter of the century. The earliest breastplates were rounded in shape, sometimes with a median ridge or shallow grooves (fluting) to increase the rigidity of the piece. Some contemporary works of art show these breastplates worn without backplates and attached to the body with straps passing over the shoulders and crossed on the back (a method still used in the 18th century and revived in the 20th in modern body armor). A matching piece of armor, the BACKPLATE, appeared around 1400 to join the breastplate, thus forming a defense termed "a pair of cuirasses" by contemporary texts. At the neck and armpits, properly contoured edges of the breastplate were forged into the turns, or low flanges, which both reinforced the edges and deterred an opponent's bladed weapons. A V-shaped stop rib riveted below the neck edge served as an additional deterrent. The lower edge of the breastplate was connected at the waist with the laminated SKIRT.

Early in the 15th century Italian armorers developed a distinctive style of armor, in which the breastplate was composed of two pieces: a rounded upper part cut straight at the waist, where it was overlapped by the so-called lower breastplate protecting the abdomen. The upper edge of the lower breastplate was fashioned as a long symmetric cusp provided with three buckles for attaching to the upper breastplate, where corresponding leather straps were riveted; the lower edge joined a laminated skirt. At the right armpit, the upper breastplate was fitted with staples for attaching the REST to couch the lance. This basic structure of the breastplate was matched by plate defenses forming the backplate of a CUIRASS. With various modifications in shape and size, this style of breastplate prevailed during the 15th century in Italy and, to a large extent, in Germany. By c. 1450 the lower breastplate had

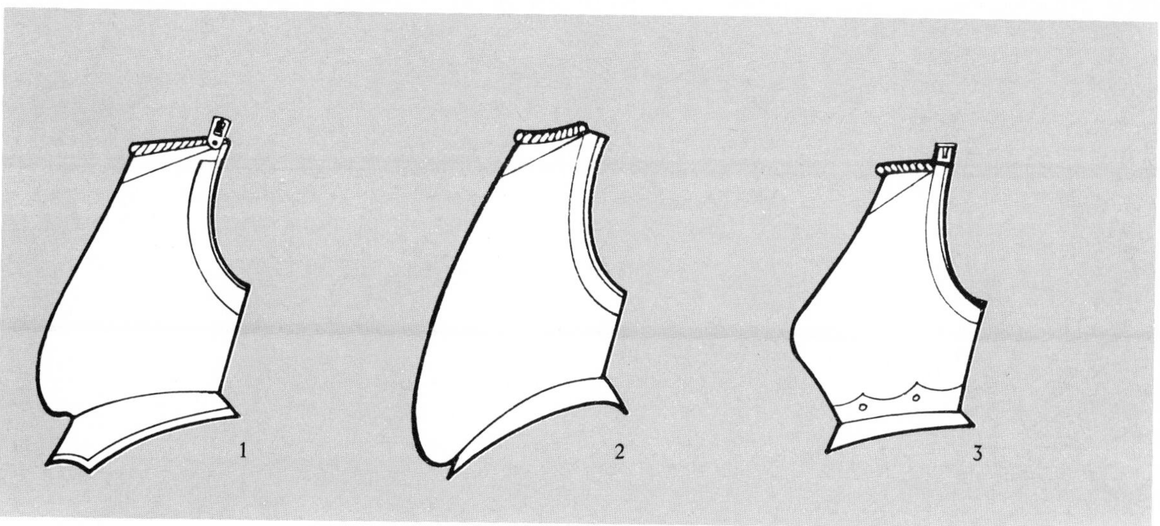


Breastplates. *1. Bag form. 2. Peascod. 3. With pointed median ridge.*

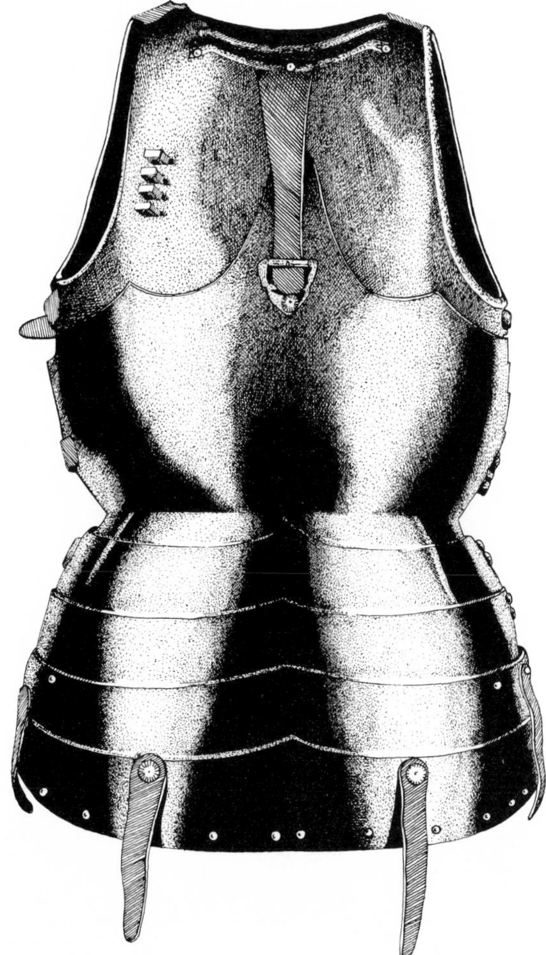

*Breastplate, with lower breastplate and skirt, of an Italian armor, mid-15th century. Santuario della Madonna delle Grazie, Curtatone, near Mantua, Italy.*

become much higher, its median cusp protruding upward well beyond the center of the breast, sometimes almost to the neck edge, being attached here with a strap and buckle to the upper breastplate. The front and back of a cuirass were connected, at the early period, by the shoulder straps and either side hinges and studs or straps and buckles, these side fastenings later being replaced by a waist belt.

In some cuirasses of the late 15th century the lower breastplate reached such size that it completely covered the upper piece, forming, in fact, the second breastplate usually classified as the PLACATE. This double breast protection was later fairly widely used on heavy cuirassier armor, due to the increased effectiveness of firearms, and it remained a reinforcing piece for armor used in tourneys. By the end of the century, the armorers returned to the one-piece construction of the breastplate, and the lower breastplate, very strong but small in size, remained in later use only in armor for German jousts (*Stechzeug* and *Rennzeug*).

Development of the breastplate in Germany was marked by some specific features, one of them being the so-called *Kastenbrust* ("box-shaped breast"), in use during the period 1420–60. It had a flat, sometimes fluted, surface sloping slightly forward from top to bottom, where it formed an angle with a slope to the waist. The abdomen was protected by several articulated lames, which were replaced, by the middle of the century, by one piece attached to the breastplate with sliding rivets. The rest for the lance was permanently attached to the *Kastenbrust* with strong rivets. After 1450, German breastplates were made, like Italian ones, in two pieces, but there were many differences between the two styles. The shape of the German breastplate was generally very graceful, with a slender waist and multiple fine fluting ("rippling"). The lower and the upper breastplates were joined by sliding rivets (instead of a strap and buckle), the cusp of the lower breastplate being used for a staple engaging a spring catch of the BEVOR. The upper edges developed strong turnovers as an efficient deterrent against edged weapons. By the late 15th century the breastplate was fitted with GUSSETS on sliding rivets and a pronounced flange on the lower edge for the skirt. The later feature was duplicated on the backplate, and this construction remained in use as long as the cuirass itself. The one-piece breastplate returned in favor in Germany, as it had in Italy, by the early 16th century.

The rounded breastplate, with a narrow waist plate holding the skirt, prevailed in the period 1500–40. In Italy, and often in Austria, its surface was usually made smooth, while in Germany curved or straight fluting added to the elegance of the so-called Maximilian armor. In the second quarter of the century, however, fluted and ridged surfaces were supplanted by smooth polished plates, more likely to cause a bullet to ricochet. Some new forms of breastplate developed in western Europe after 1530. One of them, particularly favored in Germanic lands, looked quite short due to a high waistline and a low straight neck edge with a massive turn (also present at the armpit edges). It had a marked median ridge with a cusp protruding initially in the center but later, around 1550, forged closer to the waist. Another form of breastplate, in use from the 1530s to the end of the century, was tall, oblong, and almost flat in appearance, with a low upcurved waistline. During the last third of the century, the form of a fashionable civilian peascod doublet was reflected in a similarly shaped breastplate. In c. 1600–50 the breastplate was rather a short piece, often with a median ridge and a small flange both at the cusped waistline and at the neck.

After c. 1650 the breastplate remained one of the only few pieces of a light armor used by pikemen, until their gradual disappearance before 1700, and by heavy cavalry, which continued, however, to use the steel cuirass or the breastplate alone throughout the 18th and part of the 19th century. The breastplate of steel, attached to the torso in archaic manner with straps crossed on the back, has returned to military life since the First World War, being occasionally issued to special assault infantry units.

**breech** The rear end of the BARREL of a firearm, within which is the chamber. Since the breech has to stand up to the greatest pressure on firing, it is considerably thicker than the rest of the barrel.

**breechblock** *See* ARTILLERY; BOLT; GUN: breechloading.

**breech box** In artillery of the 15th and 16th centuries, a big iron "receiver" used in breechloading cannon to connect the reloadable powder chamber with the barrel. It was attached rigidly to the barrel by bosses fitting into two brackets on the sides of the breech box. It was generally extended backward in a kind of long tail, used for aiming the gun. After inserting the powder chamber into the breech box, closure was ensured by driving a piece of iron, the "wedge," between the base of the chamber and the rear of the breech box.

**breeches of steel** Part of certain special armors for foot combat in the lists, very few of which are extant—three in Paris, one in London (belonging to Henry VIII), and one in Vienna. In place of a tonlet or a skirt with tassets and rump guard, the wearer was protected by two sections of laminated plates shaped, like breeches, to the lower part of the body and fastened at the sides with turning pins. These steel breeches were fitted with a codpiece, also attached with turning pins, and locked over the tops of the full cuisses, which completely enclosed the thighs.

**breeching** Part of a HORSE HARNESS and of light horse armor (half bards). It consists of a broad strap around the hindquarters of the horse about 30–35 cm (12–14 in.) below the root of the tail (dock). In light horse armor it is supported by the crupper straps, while in horse harness it is attached to the loin straps, which are held in place by the back strap.

**breechloader** A firearm loaded from the breech, that is, the rear end of the barrel. *See also* GUN: breechloading; PISTOL.

**breke of mail** A piece of mail attached to the center of the lower edge of a shirt of mail to protect the genitals. In plate armor, it was a small appendage of mail hung at the fork of the skirt. *See also* CODPIECE.

**bridle** The leather equipment fitted over a horse's head and supplemented by the REINS to enable the rider to exercise control over the animal. The basic elements were much the same as those incorporated in a bridle today, comprising the brow band, CHEEK STRAPS, THROAT LATCH (pronounced "lash"), and the BIT or mouthpiece, kept in place by the NOSEBAND. The reins are attached to each side of the bit.

The leather of which these various pieces were generally made (apart, of course, from the metal bit) was sometimes colored or tooled and often ornamented with rivets, rosette washers, studs, etc., or elaborated with fittings of iron, brass, and even silver and other precious metals. *See also* BRANCHES; BRIDOON; CURB CHAIN; SHAFFRON; SNAFFLE.

**bridoon** A simplified BIT, without cheeks. It consists of a jointed mouthpiece, that is, divided into two parts linked by small rings in the middle. The ends of the bit are provided with rings for the reins. This is one of the oldest types of bits and still widely used today.

**brigandine** A medieval term of Italian origin for a type of armored sleeveless jacket weighing about 9 kg. (20 lbs.)

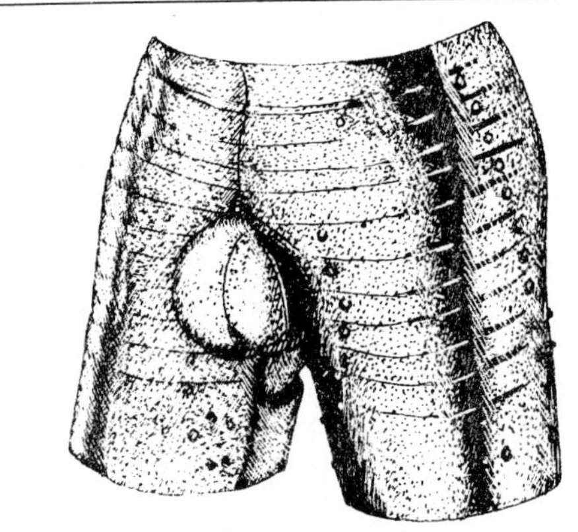

*Laminated steel breeches, part of an armor made for Henry VIII in the Royal Workshops at Greenwich, c. 1520. Tower of London Armouries.*

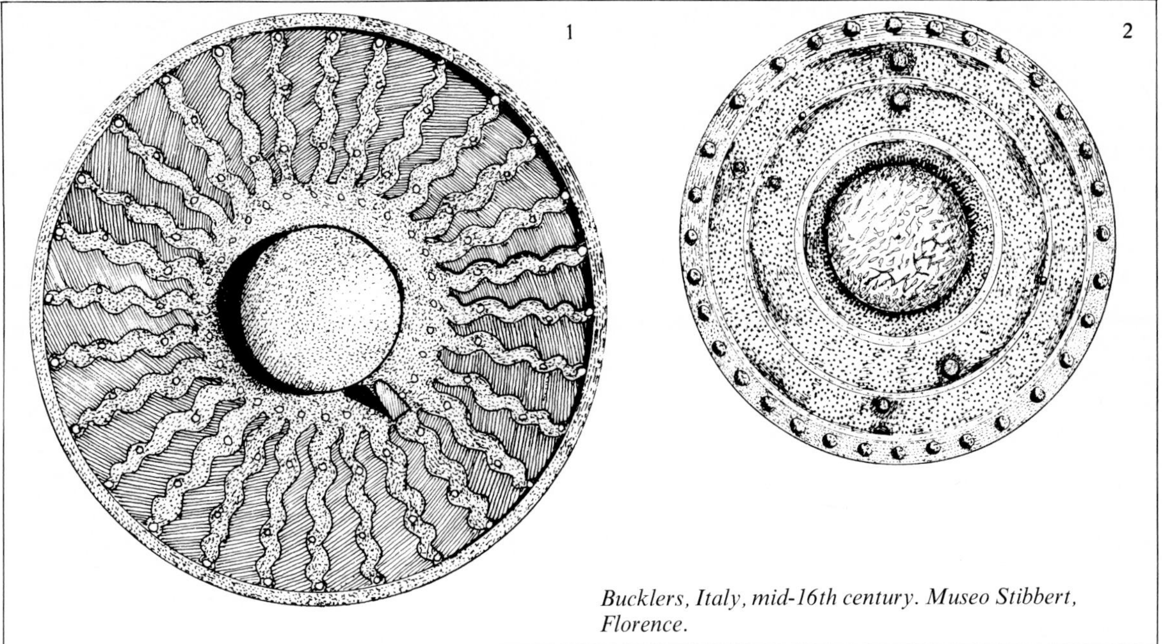


*Bucklers, Italy, mid-16th century. Museo Stibbert, Florence.*

and used by the infantry from the mid-14th century to the beginning of the 17th. In its simplest form, it included breast (sometimes complete with skirt) and back protection, but there are also examples extant fitted with a collar and side defenses. The structure consisted of small rectangular lames arranged in vertical strips, overlapping like roof tiles, then mounted on a supporting cloth or hide in parallel rows, the attachment being made with rivets whose heads were visible outside. This defensive construction was sewn to a quilted jacket which gave the garment its final shape. In fact, it was a light version of the COAT OF PLATES. Being light and flexible, the brigandine gained widespread popularity, especially among foot soldiers during the 15th and 16th centuries.

Almost the only examples that can be seen today are those made as town wear or parade dress for wealthy owners. These spectacular models were built up on a foundation of velvet, attached with gilded rivet heads, and their cut followed the line of contemporary fashion.

**broadsword** A general term applied from the 17th century to heavy military swords with a large double-edged blade, designed mainly for cutting, and either a basket hilt or a well-developed shell guard. Particularly favored by European heavy cavalry up to the early 19th century, the broadswords can be divided into many groups and types classified mainly by various hilt forms. Late (basket-hilted) schavoni, Scottish basket-hilted broadswords, Walloon swords, and some types of eastern European Pallasches and western European cavalry swords are among the broadswords.

**brow reinforce** A plate of a helmet that gave additional protection to the forehead, curving down over the skull to the line of the eyebrows. It first appeared before the middle of the 15th century in the SALLET and in various forms of the ARMET. A form which was to remain in use through the first decades of the 16th century consisted of a heavy contoured plate, often cusped on the upper edge; it fitted close and was riveted to the skull.

A detachable brow reinforce was introduced in the late 15th century for the sallets used in a German course, the *Rennen*. It consisted of two symmetrical plates, each pivoted on the respective side of the skull and usually joined and retained in this position by a spring catch on the front of the skull. If hit by a lance, both parts of the brow reinforce fell apart and detached themselves from the helmet. A similar arrangement was used in other types of jousting helmets up to the mid-16th century.

In some forms of visored sallets of the 15th century, the visor plate extended far upwards, thus serving the purpose of a brow reinforce.

**browning** *See* RUSSETING; DECORATIVE TECHNIQUES.

**buckler** A small shield used mainly in the 13th to 17th centuries, designed to protect the contenders in foot combat. Its basic structure consisted of a strong iron plate—round, square, or occasionally trapezoidal—fitted on the inside with a hand strap, the ENARME. Its border was reinforced with a strip of metal riveted all around it, while a hook or spike sometimes projected from the center to break or jam the opponent's blade. This device is frequently referred to as a SWORD-BREAKER. The spike or hook was often fixed in the middle of a group of metal strips attached to the main surface with a slight clearance; these served the same purpose of catching the blade and were arranged in various ways, such as concentric circles, trellisworks, etc.

Some bucklers were equipped with a long steel spike which was fixed on a hinge and could be folded when not needed. In close combat, the buckler with a spike could also well serve as an offensive weapon. A small hook on the upper part of the buckler was used to suspend a lantern to

*Buckler, Italy, c. 1550–60. Museo Stibbert, Florence.*

light the bearer's way at night. Other bucklers had a small built-in lantern with a hinged door to hide the light when necessary. Some bucklers of the mid-16th century were combined with a wheel-lock or matchlock pistol. A remarkable group of such gun shields produced by Giovanbattista da Ravenna is preserved in the Tower of London.

**buff coat** A sleeveless jacket made of buffalo leather, worn in the 16th and 17th centuries under a cuirass or alone as a protection against edged weapons.

**buffe** A BEVOR often worn with the BURGONET from the early 16th century. In most cases it was a detachable piece joined to the helmet by hasps at the sides and with a buckled strap around the neck guard. In some closed burgonets the buffe and the fall were pivoted at the sides of the skull, like the visor and the bevor in a close helmet. *See also* FALLING BUFFE.

**buffer** Part of the recoil system of a piece of artillery which in full-recoil carriages allows the piece to recoil independently of the carriage. The buffers generally used are hydraulic; from a hydrodynamic point of view they may have constant-flow apertures or variable-flow apertures and constant resistance. From a mechanical point of view a buffer consists of a cylinder filled with liquid (glycerin and water or mineral oil), with a piston traveling in it with apertures in the head. The cylinder is attached to the carriage and the piston to the piece (or vice versa); as the gun recoils, the piston travels along the cylinder and the liquid passing through the apertures in the piston head creates a resistance that absorbs part of the energy due to the recoil. The buffer is also a part of hydropneumatic recoil systems, in which it is combined with the RECUPERATOR.

**bulawa** A mace with a globular or pear-shaped head, known for centuries in many Oriental and eastern European countries such as India, Persia, Turkey, Russia, Hungary, and Poland (where the word "bulawa" originated). It also made sporadic appearances in western Europe.

In ancient Egypt and Mesopotamia, the mace of similar forms was regarded as a symbol of rank in the hands of the Pharaohs and kings. It was also used as a votive offering, when it would have had a simple stone or clay head. Although it was used as a war club, it remained chiefly a token of military rank or sovereignty and would have been given, for example, to the Transylvanian princes or Walachian hospodars. In Poland, Russia, and the Ukraine it denoted the office of hetman or commander-in-chief of the army.

The Turkish war bulawa (*topus*) was usually made of steel. A symbolic one, however, was made with a decorative head of some precious metal or of rock crystal, horn, or ivory and, according to the material used, chased, gilded, nielloed, or encrusted with gems. The wooden handle was covered with decorated metal and sometimes concealed a stylus.

**bullet** A projectile fired from small arms, spherical, cylindro-ogival, cylindro-conoidal, or bi-ogival (streamlined or boat-tailed) in shape. It consists of a lead core, sometimes hardened by the addition of antimony, with an envelope of steel, copper, brass, cupronickel, etc., to avoid lead fouling of the barrel and prevent deformation or stripping of the bullet. This envelope, fitted over the lead core under pressure, is thus made of a

*Falling buffe for a burgonet, Italy, c. 1570. Odescalchi Collection, Museo di Palazzo Venezia, Rome.*

*Closed burgonet with barred visor and falling buffe, Italy, c. 1640. Museo Stibbert, Florence.*

metal much lighter than lead; it is made no thicker than is necessary to avoid its becoming bent or torn (0.45–0.55 mm.). The diameter of the bullet is generally 0.2–0.3 mm. greater than the diameter of the barrel measured to the bottom of the grooves, so that there is an initial "shrinkage"; the core and envelope together must therefore have a certain measure of plasticity, which can be obtained by the use of not more than 3 percent of antimony in the alloy.

**bullet mold** Usually a metal form into which molten lead was poured to manufacture bullets. Among the earliest references to molds for casting balls are those in the English Wardrobe Accounts for about 1375, in which latten molds and iron ladles are mentioned, the ladles being used to pour the lead into the molds. During the 16th century it was apparently usual for each type of firearm to have its own bullet mold. An inventory of the armory of the Gonzaga family of Mantua, dating from about 1550, refers to 1550 molds for musketoons and 1750 molds for arquebuses. The earliest surviving bullet molds seem to date from the latter part of the 16th century. In one private collection there is a French mold which consists of a series of bars hinged together—rather like a carpenter's rule—the faces of each bar being hollowed out so that a number of balls could be cast at one time.

During the 17th century, the scissor type of mold was developed, each face of the scissor arm containing a cavity which, when the arms were brought together, formed a hollow spherical chamber into which the lead could be poured. Molds of this type were often fitted with a cutting device so that the excess lead or "sprue" could be trimmed off.

During the 18th century, greater attention was paid to the finish of the bullet. The molds accompanying cased pairs of dueling pistols were most carefully manufactured. The casting of the ball for a duel became an elaborate ritual, each stage of which was supervised by the seconds. Some bullet molds were designed to produce as many as twenty balls of different calibers. Eighteenth-century molds were often hinged at the top—like a nutcracker—with the opposite ends fitting into wooden handles.

The technical improvements of the 19th century led to a demand for more sophisticated bullet molds. The mold for the bullet of the Minié rifle, for example, was fitted with a movable plug to cast the special Minié bullet with its hollow base. Bullet molds were usually made of brass or steel, although occasionally soapstone was used, particularly in America. As the 19th century advanced, standardization of firearms—and particularly the adoption of the metal self-contained cartridge—led to the obsolescence of the bullet mold.

**bunduk** *See* BANDUK.

**burgonet** A type of light helmet, worn by infantry and light cavalry in Europe from about 1520 to the end of the 16th century. An open helmet with a pointed peak, called the FALL, and a neck guard, the burgonet was fitted with hinged cheekpieces. The skull was generally made in two interlocking halves which were then riveted and hammered together along the comb. In better-quality helmets, the skull was made of one plate. The basic shape of the skull was hemispherical, broken only by the comb,

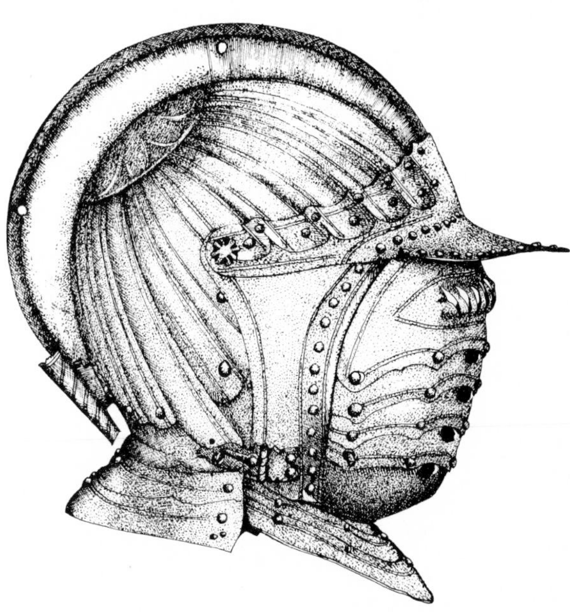

*Burgonet with falling buffe, France, c. 1625–35. Odescalchi Collection, Museo di Palazzo Venezia, Rome.*

*Closed burgonet with "Savoyard"-style visor, N. Italy, c. 1630. Museo Stibbert, Florence.*

which tended to assume more and more exaggerated proportions during the third quarter of the century but then diminished. There were, however, some examples of ogival skulls, with or without a pointed "spur" on the apex. The fall projected from the skull over the face, and the neck guard projected over the nape, both being reinforced by a rim along their edges. The cheekpieces consisted of contoured plates, often shaped in the center to accommodate the ears, and pierced with ventilation holes. The cheekpieces, too, had border rims and could be closed under the chin with buckled straps.

The closed type of burgonet often included a detachable BEVOR, or buffe. In another style, the cheekpieces were enlarged to cover the face, thus forming the bevor. Two parts of the bevor were kept in closed position by a strap around the neck or by hasps and pierced lugs. The FALLING BUFFE, sometimes termed "Hungarian bevor," had two pivoted collapsible lames protecting the face; they could fall to open the face when retaining spring studs were pressed. A rare variation of the burgonet had a skull with a central comb flanked by a lower one on each side; it was nicknamed the "three-combed burgonet."

During the first half of the 17th century, two types of burgonet resembled in appearance and construction the CLOSE HELMET with gorget plates. Both types had the bevor and one-piece visor pivoted on the sides of the skull (like early close helmets), but they were also provided with a burgonet peak (fall) attached to the same side pivots. One of these types is often termed the "Savoyard" burgonet, its name deriving from the fact that it was standard issue to the men of the Duke of Savoy's army. The skull was generally hemispherical and sometimes made with a comb. The pivoted brow extended into a short peak, which followed the arched contours of the eye sockets and together with the full visor represented a grotesque human face. The bevor was fitted with a neck guard and was attached to the skull with a hook or with a buckle and strap passing in front of the neckpiece. The Savoyard burgonet was nearly always russeted or painted black, and it was this, together with its "human" appearance, that caused it to be also known as a *Todenkopf* ("death's head").

Another burgonet resembling close helmets was also used with cuirassier armor. Its hemispherical skull as made with a short comb and tail lames, while the brow was pivoted onto the skull and extended forward into a short peak. The bevor with gorget was of ordinary construction, the distinctive feature of this helmet being its large visor with several vertical bars providing both good ventilation and protection against sword cuts.

**burgonet-morion** A type of light helmet worn by the infantry and light horse in the second half of the 16th century. It was really a variation of both the MORION and the BURGONET. The lower curved edge of the hemispherical combed skull was shaped into a pointed tail and FALL, thus emphasizing the burgonet's influence. A small laminated cheekpiece consisting of a broad leather chin strap covered with riveted plates was sometimes fitted at each side of the brim, to be tied with a thong under the chin.

**burgundian dagger** *See* DAGGER.

*Burgonet (so-called casquetel), German style, for a foot soldier, N. Italy (probably Milanese), c. 1505–10. Wallace Collection, London.*

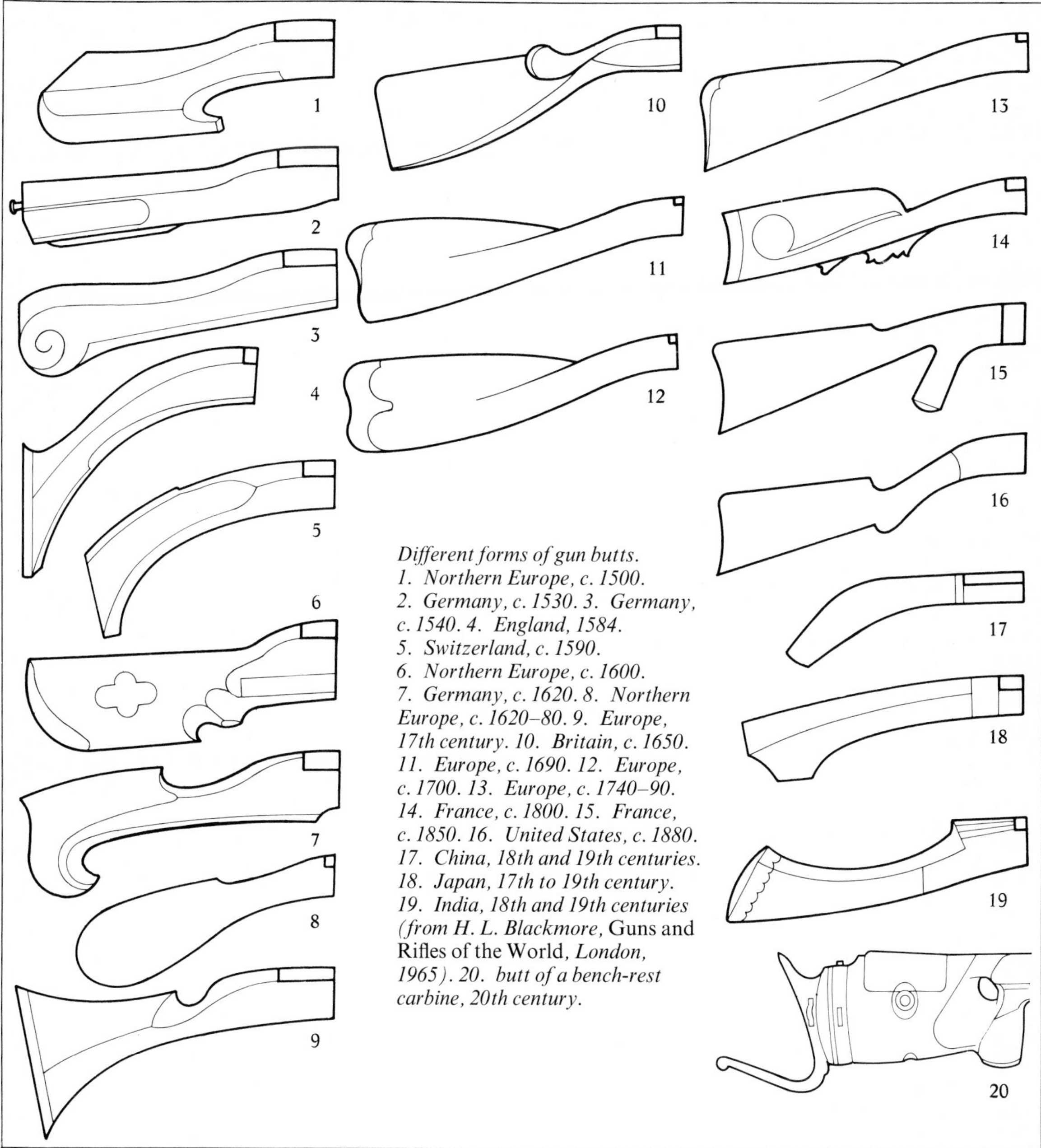


*Different forms of gun butts.*
*1. Northern Europe, c. 1500.*
*2. Germany, c. 1530. 3. Germany, c. 1540. 4. England, 1584.*
*5. Switzerland, c. 1590.*
*6. Northern Europe, c. 1600.*
*7. Germany, c. 1620. 8. Northern Europe, c. 1620–80. 9. Europe, 17th century. 10. Britain, c. 1650. 11. Europe, c. 1690. 12. Europe, c. 1700. 13. Europe, c. 1740–90. 14. France, c. 1800. 15. France, c. 1850. 16. United States, c. 1880. 17. China, 18th and 19th centuries. 18. Japan, 17th to 19th century. 19. India, 18th and 19th centuries (from H. L. Blackmore,* Guns and Rifles of the World, *London, 1965). 20. butt of a bench-rest carbine, 20th century.*

**burnishing** A finishing technique used on metal—particularly on the barrels of portable firearms—consisting of lengthy rubbing with appropriate steel tools (burnishers) or hard stone. The effect was not only to improve the appearance of the weapon but also to make it more resistant to oxidization (rusting). Burnished metal becomes a deep blue-gray color or even black.

**butt** The rear part of the stock of a gun, and by extension, the grip of a pistol. The shape, cross-section, and size of butts have changed over the years with usage and fashion, with the aim of making personal firearms more efficient and more comfortable to hold. Thus there are butts that are practically in line with the stock, or very slightly inclined, with the angle of the butt approaching zero; butts at a considerable angle, or with fanciful shapes and decorations; rifle butts with the heel specially shaped for support against the shoulder or the side.

Both in its shape and in the material from which it is made—generally wood—the butt has always provided an ideal field for the imagination and skill of artisans. While for the rank and file they were generally left smooth, the butts of princes' and rich men's guns were not only made from valuable materials—walnut, even ivory or solid silver—but were engraved, inlaid, covered with enamel or precious stones; there was hardly any decorative technique that was not applied to them.

There are solid and hollow butts, butts that contain the mechanism of the magazine (notably, of course, the butts of modern pistols, which are made of an outer metal frame with two removable sidepieces of wood or plastic), fixed butts and folding or detachable butts (found typically in machine pistols), and even anatomical butts for target rifles, specially shaped to fit the hand or shoulder of the individual marksman.

Sporting guns are often fitted with a rubber butt plate to reduce the shock of recoil and sometimes also to improve the length of the butt.

**butt cap** In pistols, a metal cap on the end of the butt.

**button** A raised piece on the pommel of swords, daggers, and knives, to which the tip of the tang of the blade was riveted. It usually formed part of the pommel, but could also be a separate piece; it was sometimes made of a different material. Since the 19th century the button on military weapons has had a threaded hole inside to be screwed onto the threaded end of the tang.

**butt plate** A metal plate on guns which strengthens the base of the butt and protects it from possible splintering when it strikes the ground. Butt plates may have hinged and sprung openings to allow such accessories as the oil can and cleaning tools to be lodged in the butt. In sporting guns or target rifles the butt plate may be made of plastic or, to reduce the recoil shock, of rubber.

**buturlik** A type of leg defense in Oriental armor, used particularly in Turkey and Russia, and equivalent to the European greaves. It was probably also used in Mongol armor, since the word "buturlik" is of Turkic origin. In museums it is often seen erroneously displayed as a forearm defense, as it closely resembles the bazuband.

Turkish buturliks consisted of a long plate modeled to the curve of the calf, and two narrower plates were usually joined to the main plate with mail strips, the whole unit being fastened to the leg with straps and buckles. Sometimes the buturlik was part of a full leg defense for heavy cavalry.

In Russia, buturliks consisted of double plates entirely covering the lower part of the leg, often being grooved and decorated in keeping with the zertsalo armor (*see* CHARAINA) and bazubands.

Buturliks of Mameluke Egypt were often inscribed with large silver letters.

**buzdygan** (or **buzdykhan**) Turkic term for a mace with a head of six, seven, eight, or more radiating flanges and a short straight handle. Probably of Oriental origin, it is difficult to date but it was adopted by the Western world during the great migrations from the north. Archeological excavations have confirmed its presence in Europe during the early Middle Ages, and there is visual evidence of it in contemporary works such as the Bayeux Tapestry (about 1077). Variants of the buzdygan are to be found in many countries, including China, India, Persia, Turkey, Arabia, Hungary, Russia, and Poland (where the word was transformed to *buzogany*).

War maces, of which a number of examples exist, were either made entirely of iron or with a metal head and wooden handle. Ornamental ones were often symbols of military rank or of *salvus conductus*—a guarantee of safe conduct through a foreign country.

In India a buzdygan frequently had a guarded hilt, like a KHANDA, and in Poland a slim dagger was sometimes concealed in the handle which could be screwed up to the end of it and used for thrusts.

**byrnie** Medieval term for a shirt of mail. *See also* HAUBERK.

# C

**cabasset** An alternative term for the SPANISH MORION.

**caliber** In a rifled gun, the diameter of the bore measured between the lands; in smooth-bore guns, the diameter of the bore. In Europe, the caliber is generally expressed in millimeters (e.g., 7.65 mm.; 381 mm.); in Commonwealth countries and the United States, usually in hundredths or tenths of an inch for personal weapons (e.g., .223, .38) and in inches for artillery (e.g., 5′ 5″, 18″). Recently the United States and Britain have adopted the metric system for artillery calibers.

Approximate Conversion Table for Some Calibers in Metric and Decimal Measurements

| 1/100 inch | Millimeters |
|---|---|
| 22 | 5.59 |
| 25 | 6.35 |
| 30 | 7.62 |
| 38 | 9.65 |
| 45 | 11.43 |

For ancient weapons, the "nominal caliber" which indicated the number of lead balls to a pound, was generally used and has been continued for modern shotguns.

**caliber gauge** A gauge, consisting of a plate pierced with holes corresponding to the diameters of various bullets, used to measure the weight of a bullet. An early example in the Tøjhusmuseum in Copenhagen, dated 1740, shows a number of brass leaves pinned together. One leaf, specially tapered to fit a barrel, has been marked with a scale giving the number of bullets to a pound; the other leaves are pierced with holes corresponding to the various sizes of bullets.

**caliver** A term used in England to describe a type of long gun used without a rest principally for military purposes. An English account dating from the late 16th century recorded that the term had been derived from the French word *calibre* and was first used in about 1555, when a governor of Piedmont caused his troops to be armed with "arquebuses of the same caliber." Military writers of the late 16th and early 17th centuries gave contradictory accounts of the dimensions of a caliver. It appears to have been larger than an arquebus but smaller than a musket. In 1630 the dimensions of English firearms were established in an order issued by the Council of War. A caliver was described as having a barrel length of 100 cm., (39 in.), an overall length of 137 cm. ($4\frac{1}{2}$ ft.), and a bore of 17. Calivers appear not to have been used in England after the Civil War.

**caltrop** *See* TRIBULUS.

**campilan** An alternative spelling of KAMPILAN.

**cane gun** A pistol or a gun concealed in a walking stick. In the case of a pistol, the weapon was hidden in the handle, which had to be detached from the stick before the pistol could be fired. In the gun version, the metal stick, covered with leather or painted to imitate wood, was the actual barrel, whose muzzle was usually closed by a spring plug or a screw-on cap. The handle, straight or bent, contained a percussion mechanism that was cocked by pulling a button or a ring; the same act exposed a folding trigger. Such guns, made in the 19th and early 20th centuries were used for self-defense as well as by naturalists and poachers. Some cane guns were breechloaders designed for center-fire cartridges.

Beginning early in the 17th century the AIR GUN, whose handle contained an air reservoir, was made in the form of a walking stick. The air reservoir had to be pumped by hand. A pump was usually kept separately but could be incorporated in the cane. Some air guns were still in use in the early 20th century.

**canister shot** Also called case shot, a quantity of shot or fragments and splinters of iron packed in a sheet-metal cylindrical container, used by artillery from the beginning of the 18th century for close-range fire against personnel. The fragments (then called "langridge") used in earlier smooth-bore guns were put into wooden or wicker baskets, inserted above the charge, and separated from the charge by wooden discs or "bottoms." True canister or case shot accompanied the introduction of rifled artillery;

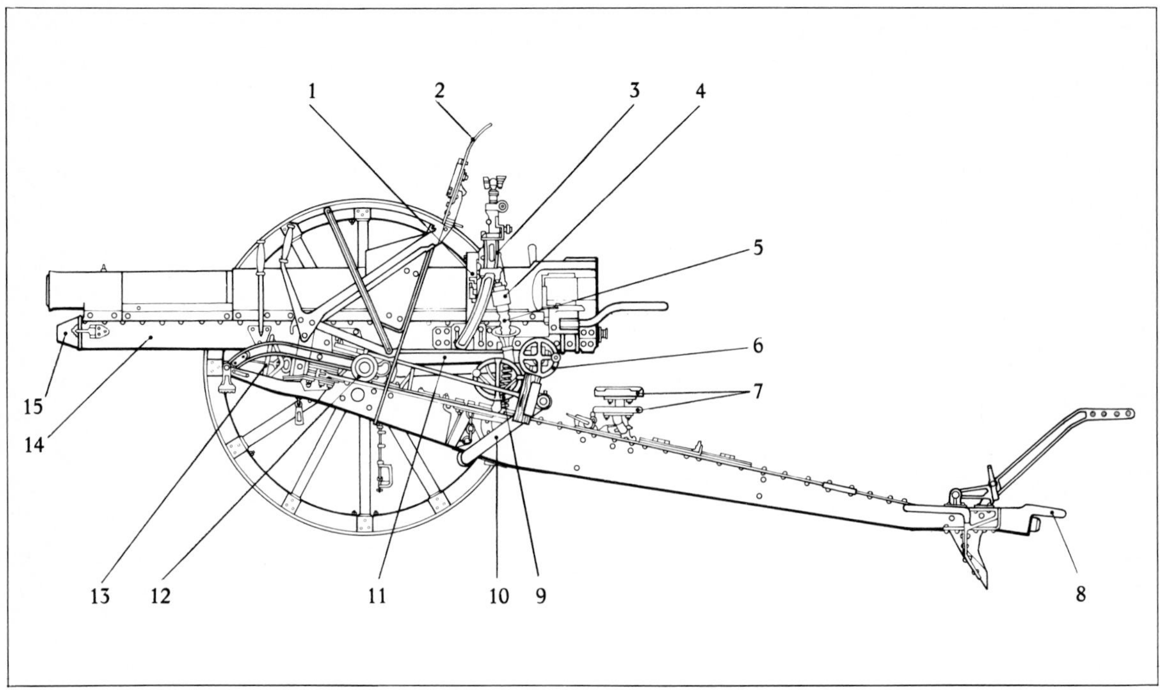


*Italian 75/27 cannon, Model 906, with carriage: 1. sight bracket; 2. shield; 3. sight carrier; 4. quick release; 5. universal joint; 6. traversing handwheel; 7. seats; 8. towing eye; 9. elevating handwheel; 10. brake lever; 11. cradle carrier; 12. axle; 13. road brake handwheel; 14. cradle; 15. front cap.*

a canister was made of a tube of sheet zinc reinforced with riveted metal straps so that it would not break up before leaving the barrel.

**cannon** In ARTILLERY, a word applied in a general sense to nonportable firearms with a caliber of more than 20 mm. (0.8 in.) and a long barrel, usually more than 20 calibers. In the muzzleloading form in use between the end of the 15th century and the end of the 18th, the features of the exterior of a cannon, from muzzle to breech, included, at the front, the swell of the muzzle, a thick molding designed to strengthen the piece at a particularly sensitive place, and behind the swell, the muzzle astragal and fillets, that is, a raised band around the barrel and narrower bands on either side. From the swell back to the so-called second reinforce was the chase, a smooth, externally tapered section of the barrel, and near the back of the chase, the chase astragal and fillets. Then came the second reinforce, the thicker part of the barrel that gave it extra strength. The trunnions, which supported the piece on the carriage, were near the front of the second reinforce. Behind the second reinforce was the first reinforce, the thickest part of the barrel body; the vent astragal and fillets; the vent itself; at the rear of the barrel, the base ring and ogee, that is, the thickest molded band around the barrel, and between that and the vent, the breech. The breech was closed at the rear by the cascabel, which had moldings tapering sharply down to a round knob called the button.

Modern cannon are guns with bores between 25 and 100 calibers long, high muzzle velocity, and very long ranges capable of firing in the upper register. Virtually all are built of modern high-strength steel whose elasticity enables them to withstand the enormous pressures generated by firing without suffering permanent distortion. The piece can be bored from a solid forging or built up from a number of tubes superimposed on one another. The first tube is called "monobloc," the second "composite." Composite guns are constructed by shrinking steel tubes around the barrel, by winding the barrel with steel wire, or by pressing concentric tubes into one another. The most modern are of monobloc type and provided with liners that can be removed and changed when worn out.

On the exterior, starting at the muzzle, are the muzzle swell; the slides, if the piece is on a cradle mounting, or the cylinders, if it is on a platform mounting; the barrel jacket, a thicker section that begins on a level with the chamber; and the breech ring, fixed firmly over the breech, with two attachments for the recuperators and the recoil system, designed to take, according to the design of the gun, the slides for the breechblock (carriage with cradle) or the breech screw, which holds the lever breech mechanism (carriage with platform). *See also* ARTILLERY; GUN MOUNTINGS.

**cannons** (or **canons**) Parts of the VAMBRACE, consisting of upper cannons to protect the upper arms and lower cannons for the forearms, linked by COWTERS at the elbow. During the first half of the 14th century they consisted of two gutter-shaped plates strapped over the sleeve of the hauberk; thereafter they encircled the entire arm.

**cap** A small soft-metal capsule made of copper or brass,

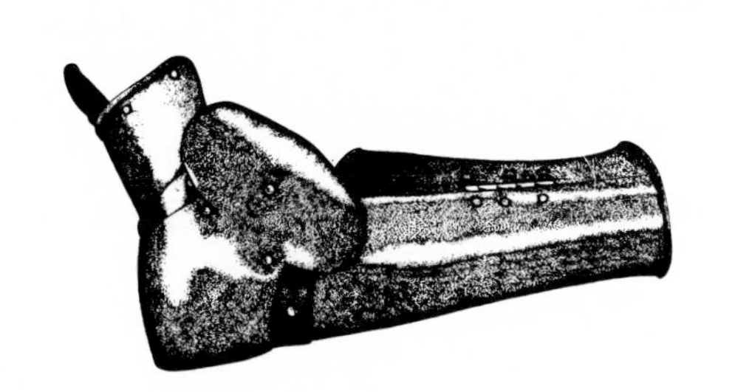

*Vambrace with cannons for the upper- and forearm. From an Italian armor, c. 1390–1400. Churburg Armory, Sluderno.*

containing the PRIMER used to ignite powder in the barrel or the cartridge; also called percussion cap.

**capacete** *See* SPANISH MORION.

**cape of mail** A protective piece of mail, worn from the 14th to 16th centuries to cover the shoulders, the upper parts of the trunk, and, sometimes, the head. It consisted of a kind of brief cape or cowl made of particularly sturdy riveted mail. Infantry and light-horse troops wore it under or over their armor. Although there was no standard type, the cape usually took the form of a large triangular piece of mail placed over the shoulders and fastened down the front with one or more buckles. Some capes were circular pieces of mail; the separate collars were fastened with a buckle and strap. Other types included capes with sleeves, capes with a high collar, and capes with a cowl to cover the head.

The so-called bishop's mantle, was a large cape, usually with a standing collar, worn over armor by German landsknechts during the 16th century.

**cappellina** An Italian term denoting a light infantry or cavalry helmet used during the first half of the 16th century. In Italy, where the cappellina was adapted from German light-cavalry helmets, it was usually associated with foot soldiers. Its shallow, spherical skull had a short laminated tail and a peak (the FALL), which was usually pivoted but could be fixed in a stationary position. Some were fitted with small laminated cheekpieces attached to leather and riveted or hinged to the skull at each side of the fall. This type of helmet, known to have been part of several suits of "alla romana" armor characteristic of the workmanship of the Negroli family of Milan, featured curls worked into the skull decoration and cheekpieces following the contours of the face.

The cappellina disappeared toward the middle of the 16th century, when it was replaced by the BURGONET.

**carbine** A term used to describe a short, light gun originally designed to be used by a combatant on horseback. According to some authorities, the word "carbine" derives from *Carabins*, light-cavalry troops raised in France in the late 16th century who were apparently armed with pistols and short, light guns. English references in the 17th century describe the carbine as being "about a yard or more long in the barrel." According to an order issued by the Council of War in England in 1630, the carbine had a barrel of 76 cm. (30 in.) in length, with a bore of 24 balls to the pound. The overall length of a carbine was given as 114 cm. (44 in.).

During the 16th and 17th centuries the carbine was usually fitted with a wheel-lock or a snap-lock and had a sliding ring affixed to a bar so that it could be carried on a shoulder sling. During the 18th century flintlock carbines were used by cavalry and infantry. In 18th-century England there was some variation in the barrel length. For example, the carbine designed in 1756 for the Light Dragoons had a 91.5 cm (3 ft.) barrel whereas that designed in 1780 by Elliott was some 15 cm. (6 in.) shorter. Seventeen years later Henry Nock, an English gunmaker, produced, at the request of the Board of Ordnance, a series of carbines fitted with his patented screwless lock. The carbine was also popular in the 19th century.

In the United States Christian Sharps and his partner William Hankins made the .52 rimfire Sharps and Hankins carbine, which was used by the Union troops in the Civil War. The most celebrated Sharps carbine was the model produced in 1859 and simplified in 1863. This carbine was used extensively in the Civil War. In 1860 Christopher Spencer patented a carbine with a rifled barrel 99 cm (39 in.) in length; it had a tubular magazine holding seven cartridges. When the trigger guard was moved downwards, the breechlock dropped, extracted the fired cartridge case, and moved a fresh cartridge into the breech. The Spencer, perhaps the most successful carbine produced in the 19th century, was capable of sustained and rapid fire.

Well-known carbines of the 20th century include the Russian SKS-46, produced after 1945 and chambered for the 7.62 mm. short cartridge, and the U.S. Army carbine 30 M.1, originally a semiautomatic that was later

*Spencer carbine, United States, 19th century.*

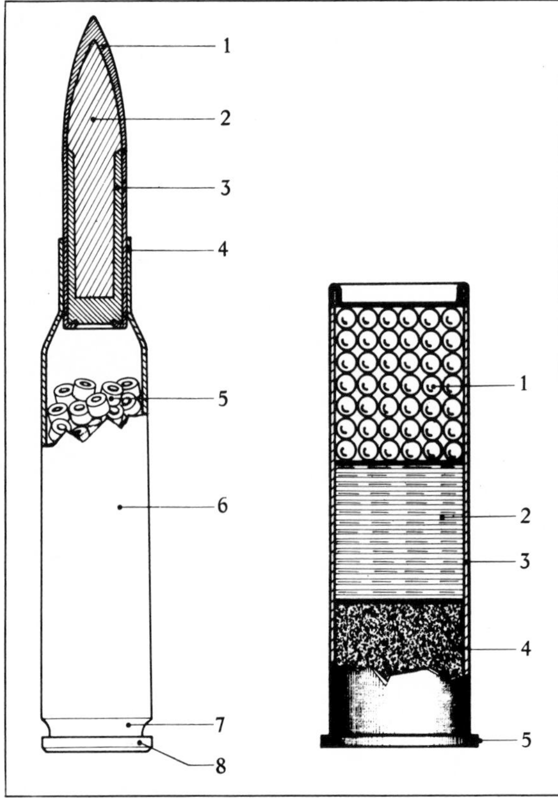


*Cartridge with solid bullet: 1. nickel-silver jacket; 2. steel core; 3. lead base; 4. collar; 5. propellant charge; 6. case; 7. extraction groove; 8. base. Sporting cartridge: 1. pellets; 2. wad; 3. cardboard case; 4. charge; 5. base.*

converted to fully automatic. The modern equivalent of the carbine is the self-loading assault rifle such as the Armalite.

**carronade** An iron piece of artillery, shorter and lighter than ordinary cannon of the same caliber, used almost exclusively on ships as a complement to standard armament. Designed by Captain (later Lieutenant General) Robert Melville in collaboration with Charles Gascoigne between 1751 and 1755, the carronade got its name from the firm that built it, the Scottish Carron Company of Carron, near Falkirk. It usually lacked a muzzle swell, a cup, shackles, and sometimes trunnions; instead, it was fitted with a solid iron block under the barrel, which was bored transversely for a pivot. It was aimed by moving an elevating screw at the rear, which enabled the sling cable to go through an eye at the top of the button. On ships the carronade was mounted on a carriage with two platforms; the upper platform, with the elevating screw, slid along grooves in the lower and had two shoes to which the block under the barrel was clamped. The lower platform was pivoted at the front and had rollers at the back so that it could be swiveled around to place the piece in a horizontal position.

Similar to carronades but cast in bronze, were the Venetian *obusieri*, which were adopted in 1789 to arm the quarterdeck and forecastle of ships. These guns were adopted after it was observed that in naval engagements between ships in line, the firepower of the usual broadside at close range was largely wasted. However, not all cannon could be replaced by carronades because when they were mounted between decks, the strong flash from the short barrels often set fire to the gun ports.

**cartridge** The ammunition of modern personal firearms. As can be inferred from the word, the term was used in the past for the cylindrical rolls of paper (Italian *carta*, French *cartouche*) enclosing a measured quantity of propellant powder and the ball, introduced to simplify loading procedure for muzzleloaders. As early as the second half of the 16th century, the powder, rolled up in paper, was carried in measured charges ready for use; after 1650 it became commonplace to insert the projectile in this prepared charge in order to make a primitive form of cartridge.

Credit for the invention of the cartridge containing its own primer is generally given to Samuel Johannes Pauly (1766–1820), a Swiss, who in 1812 obtained a patent in Paris for a breechloading mechanism using a paper cartridge with a reusable metal base that had a cavity in the center for detonating powder; a striker worked by a spring caused the ignition. In its essential features, Pauly's mechanism was the direct ancestor of the modern breechloading system with central fire, and although Pauly was never able to enjoy the success that his revolutionary invention should have bestowed on him, his ideas were taken up by others who derived advantages from them.

The cartridge used in present-day weapons consists of the case, the percussion cap or primer, the propellant charge, and the projectile or bullet. The case serves several functions, the most important being (a) to join the various components of the cartridge; (b) to preserve the charge and the cap; (c) to ensure the sealing of the breech on firing as the case expands elastically; (d) to locate the cartridge in the chamber precisely and uniformly. The metal preferred for making cartridge cases is brass, although the Germans used steel successfully in the Second World War. The case of a rifle cartridge is generally bottlenecked; the back section, called the *body*, is slightly tapered (which is helpful in the process of extraction), leading to a narrower, shorter, cylindrical section called the *neck*; the bottom of the case is closed by a circular base. The charge is loaded inside the body; the neck holds the bullet and seals the breech when the neck expands as the shot is fired. In cartridges that are not bottlenecked, the front face of the case, where the bullet is fitted, holds the cartridge in place in the chamber so that the base of the nose of the bullet comes up against the start of the rifling and the cap is the right distance from the bolt head. The percussion cap or primer is fitted in a cavity at the center of the base. In a Flobert cartridge, which is much less powerful, it is fitted along the rim. The base of the case has a grip for the extractor—either a projecting rim or a circular groove just above the base. A rimmed case offers the advantage of positioning the cartridge precisely in the chamber, with the rim resting against the rear face of the breech or against a circular groove cut around the mouth of the chamber.

Cartridge cases are generally drawn fron rectangular brass blanks between 3 and 4 cm. (1–1½ in.) thick by a system of tube-drawing machines and presses. The cartridge for smooth-bore shotguns is cylindrical, with a steel or brass base and a stiff paper case; inside there is a layer of powder, pressed down by a cylindrical wad of felt or some similar substance, that on firing works like a piston to expel the shot held in position above it by a cardboard closure.

In hand-firearms ammunition with metal cases, one of the first forms of primer used was that called "rimfire"; the detonating compound (based on mercury fulminate or potassium chlorate) was located in the rim of the cartridge base so that on firing it was crushed between the striker and the face of the breech. This system is still widely used (.22 Rim Fire and Flobert cartridges). In other systems used in the 19th century, the primer was located inside the cartridge case, in the space for the propellant charge, or even in the base of the bullet (as in the cartridge for the needle gun patented by J. N. von Dreyse in 1831).

Many kinds of cartridges were made on the pinfire principle; a pin projecting from the case near the base (such were the cartridges patented by C. Lefaucheux in 1835 and W. Greener in 1864). The inside end of the pin was in direct contact with the detonating compound, and a blow on the outside end caused detonation. Nowadays only Boxer and Berdan types of primers are used in small-arms ammunition. The first of these, invented by an Englishman, Colonel E. M. Boxer, by 1866, consists of a brass cap containing the detonating compound and a plate called the anvil, against which the fulminate is crushed on impact. The cap is pressed into a hollow at the center of the base of the cartridge case, where a small aperture leads to the interior of the case. In the Berdan type of primer, there is a small dome at the center of the base on the inside, which acts as an anvil, with a brass cap containing the fulminate pressed against it. This system, invented by U.S. Colonel Hiram Berdan and patented in 1866, is simpler and cheaper than the Boxer, but the Boxer system is easier to recharge after firing.

Today the majority of primers for cartridges use nonmercuric, noncorrosive detonating compounds, mostly based on lead styphnate.

**case shot** *See* CANISTER SHOT.

**casquetel** A 19th-century term for CAPPELLINA.

**cateia** A throwing weapon consisting of a pointed head fixed to a flexible pole, more than 1 m. (3 ft.) long, with nails; at the center of the pole there was a loop, which was used for throwing the cateia and picking it up. The earliest literary reference to it appeared in Virgil (70–19 B.C.), who referred to its use by the people of Campania, although he attributed its origin to the Germanic or Celtic people. Aulus Gellius (2nd century A.D.) mentioned it as a throwing weapon and included it among the *tela* and the *jacula*.

**celt** (from Latin *celtis*, "chisel") A stone or cast-bronze ax (derived from stone prototypes) developed at the early stage of the northern European Bronze Age (about 3500 years ago). First inserted in a split wooden handle and then lashed, the bronze celt was later made with a socket going from the back toward the blade. It included a handle bent at right angles on the top end, which was inserted into the socket.

**cervellière** (French, "head cover") A steel skullcap widely used from about 1220 to the first half of the 15th century. This small, hemispherical helmet was worn over or under the mail coif. Sometimes the part of the cervillière around the ears was cut away, and holes were pierced along the edge to enable a pad to be attached. If the cervellière was not worn with a coif, an aventail was attached to it by means of eyelet holes pierced along the edges. The cervellière was no longer worn by the early 15th century; in the 17th century, a skullcap similar in form to the cervellière was worn under an ordinary felt hat. It was usually made in the form of riveted strips of steel. This form of head defense is often called the STEEL SKULL or secrète.

**cestrosphendone** Derived from the Greek words for "dart" and "slings," the cestrosphendone was a sling operated mechanically, in an engine, or by hand, which threw special darts. The dart was about 38 cm. (15 in.) long and consisted of a wooden pole fitted with a strong, pointed iron head, either many-sided or leaf-shaped, immediately behind which were fixed two or three vanes made of wood. In the hand-operated sling, two straps were affixed at the tip and behind the vanes. By spinning the cestrosphendone at ever-increasing speed, a hurler lent tremendous impetus to his weapon, which could hit targets some distance away. Described by both Livy (59 B.C.–A.D. 17) and Polybius (c. 205–120 B.C.), the weapon seems to have been especially popular with the Athenians between the 2nd century B.C. and the 1st century A.D.

**chakram** (or **chacka**) A quoit weapon used mainly by Sikhs, and unknown outside India. It consisted of a flat steel ring, from 12–30 cm. (4¾–12 in.) in diameter and 2–4 cm. (¾–1½ in.) in width, with a very sharp outer edge and a rounded inner edge, which was used to whirl the weapon around the forefinger before throwing. Another method of whirling consisted of holding the chakram between the thumb and the first finger and throwing it to coincide with the full swing of the body, like a discus. Its effective range was 40–50 m. (42–54 yds.).

The surface of a chakram was usually quite plain, but some examples of these weapons show elaborately inlaid or line-engraved surfaces.

**chamber** In medieval breechloading cannon, this term was applied to a hollow cylinder loaded with powder. Having a vent, it was used as the reloadable chamber in which the charge was ignited. It was often fitted with a handle and looked like a pot; its mouth could be plugged with a removable disc to prevent the powder from spilling in transportation and handling. The chamber was secured to the breech opening by a packing of twine and by wedges driven between the rear of the chamber and the base of the breech.

In firearms, the chamber is the section at the barrel breech or a compartment in the cylinder of a revolver, bored out to hold the charge or the cartridge. Some types of breechloading firearms had detachable, reloadable chambers as early as the 15th century. Modern firearms using rimmed cartridges have a circular groove around the mouth of the chamber to take the rim; for rimless ammunition a small cutout section admits the head of the extractor, enabling it to grip the base of the cartridge.

**chandelier** An ironic nickname for the PLANÇON-À-PICOT.

**chanfron** *See* SHAFFRON.

**chape** A metal mounting at the end of the scabbard or the sheath of edged weapons; it was often fitted with a small button or a piece called the "shoe," which was designed to prevent the sheath from striking the ground.

In the case of staff weapons, the chape was either a blunt metal tip attached to the butt, which protected the haft when resting on the ground, or a socket with a nail like projection.

**char-aina** (Persian, "four mirrors") A type of Oriental armor widely used between the 15th and 18th centuries in Persia, India, Turkey, and Russia, where it was known as *zertsalo* ("mirror").

An outer defense worn over a quilted caftan or a mail tunic, it consisted of four plates, usually but not always rectangular, hung from the shoulders on straps and connected to one another by straps and buckles. These plates, which were not very big and often left exposed as much of the wearer's protective underclothing as they covered, were slightly convex to fit the body and were cut away near the armpits to allow for freedom of movement. Plates that were long enough to reach the throat were also cut away at the neckline.

In Persia standard plates were made of heavily watered Damascus steel, whereas those worn by dignitaries were chased, that is, inlaid with gold or silver and decorated with floral motifs and inscriptions. During the Safavid period in Persia, char-aina armor was usually made of large hinged plates; the two pieces of the breastplate were joined by slotting a long pin through the hinges. The backplate worn during this period was usually larger than the breastplate.

Turkish char-aina was sometimes covered in velvet.

Nepalese char-aina—probably the most ancient type—

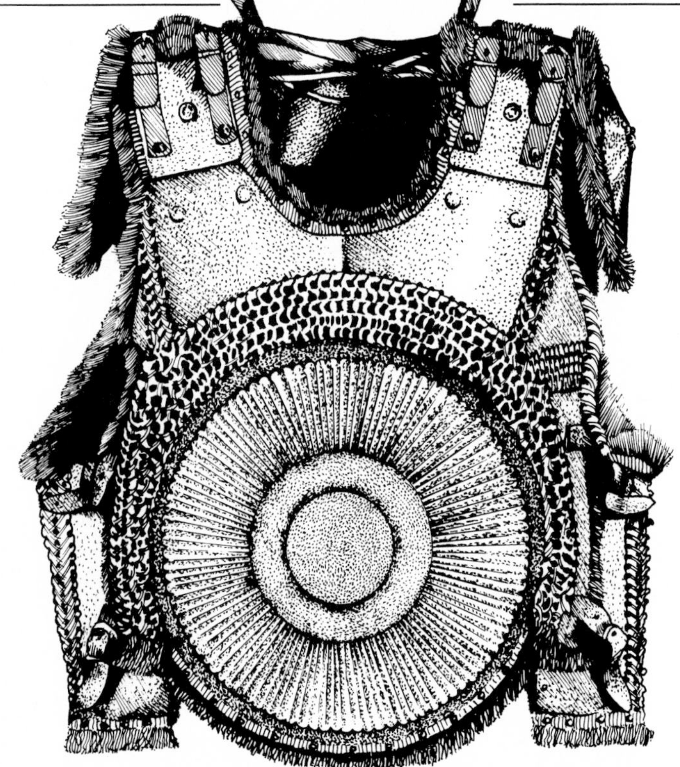

*Char-aina, Turkey, 16th century. Museo Stibbert, Florence. The same style of armor, called* zertsalo, *was used widely in Russia.*

was a kind of pectoral armor. It consisted of four round plates of equal size.

In old Russia, *zertsalo* evolved from the Turkish pattern. This kind of armor consisted of a large round plate worn in the center of the breast and flanked by several rectangular or triangular plates. The back was constructed in the same way. The plates were usually fluted, gilded, and decorated. Many char-aina were lined, probably for warmth as well as for added protection.

**charge** In modern ammunition, the substance contained in the cartridge case and ignited by the primer to create the sudden increase of pressure inside the barrel that provides the force required to propel the projectile. It consists of a certain proportion of GUNPOWDER or SMOKELESS POWDER. It is of paramount importance to work out the proper charge, which must often satisfy contradictory criteria: great ballistic power with little destructive force, great amounts of heat without excessively high temperatures, and so on.

A satisfactory charge for personal firearms is characterized by (1) the form and the density of the grains; (2) progressive action—the aim being to keep down the maximum pressure while increasing the average pressure in order to get progressive combustion, which gives an outstanding, almost continuous generation of gases; (3) its erosive power, which depends on the temperature and the pressure developed—developments that in turn affect the life of the gun; (4) the pressure developed—in military rifles with nitroglycerin powder, pressures of 3000–3500 atmospheres; with nitrocellulose powders, pressures reach levels of between 2000 and 3000 atmospheres.

**charger** A metal bracket containing cartridges that can be pressed into the magazine of a firearm with the thumb, as developed by Mannlicher. (Chargers are often incorrectly called "clips," the distinction being that a clip with cartridges passes into the magazine and is ejected when empty, whereas a charger holds the rounds in readiness for filling the magazine; it is discarded or used again.) Special chargers, sometimes called "speed loaders," are used for revolvers; they are cylindrical, corresponding to the cylinder of a revolver.

**chasing** *See* DECORATIVE TECHNIQUES.

**chausse** Also called hose of mail, a leg defense worn from at least the 11th century until the introduction of full

*Char-aina, Persian, 18th century. Wallace Collection, London.*

*Drawing showing the char-aina of four plates linked together by buckles and straps.*

GREAVES in the 14th century. There were two forms of the chausse. One, a strip of mail that protected the front of the leg, was laced at the back of the leg and under the sole. The more developed form was shaped like stockings or hose; it was laced around the leg and secured under the knee with a cord threaded through mail rings. From about the middle of the 13th century, chausses coexisted with schynbalds, plate defenses that protected the shins.

**chauve-souris** *See* CORSESCA.

**cheekpieces** Side plates on many types of helmets that protected the cheeks and sometimes the ears or the chin. In helmets such as the barbut, cheekpieces were extensions of the skull that covered the sides and the lower part of the face, but it has become customary to apply the term only to the movable appendages attached to each side of the skull of light forms of helmets such as morions, burgonets, and Zischägge.

Cheekpieces were of various types. In armets, they consisted of two heavy plates closing at the chin to form a BEVOR; cheekpieces were attached to the skull either with horizontal hinges that opened upward (Italian style) or with vertical hinges that opened sideways (in the later German form, the so-called Maximilian armet). By the 16th century cheekpieces had become part of the bevor.

In the burgonet and various types of Zischägge, cheekpieces were contoured, sometimes providing embossed shaping for the ears and pierced ventilation holes. The lower part of the plates in the burgonet was curved and tapered backward into the tail; the plates fastened to the skull with horizontal hinges, closed with a buckle and strap under the chin. In the closed burgonet, cheekpieces closed on the face like a bevor and were held in place by a buckle and strap fastened around the neck. Morions and English pots were equipped with triangular or trapezoidal laminated or rigid cheekpieces riveted to leather strips; they were fastened under the chin in the style of the burgonet.

**cheeks** (parts of the bit) *See* BRANCHES.

**cheek straps** Two leather straps that were (and still are) part of the BRIDLE. They were attached to the sides of the brow band and passed over the jowls; two buckles on the lower ends of the straps were attached to the rings of the bit or to the branches of the curb bit. In some cases, cheek straps were connected by a noseband designed to support a muzzle.

**chekan** *See* WAR HAMMER.

**chikiri odoshi** A type of lacing used in Japanese armor. *See also* ODOSHI.

**chikuto** A Japanese fencing sword made of bamboo. It has a straight blade consisting of four slightly separated strips of bamboo that make a tremendous clatter when a hit is scored. The long, straight hilt has a round, leather-covered guard. The overall length of a chikuto sword is about 110 cm. (43 in.).

**Chinese firearms (early)** *See* TUKHOTSIAN.

**chisa katana** *See* KATANA.

**chiseling** *See* DECORATIVE TECHNIQUES.

**chiza katana** A medium-sized Japanese sword, between the long KATANA and the shorter WAKIZASHI, averaging about 45 cm. ($17\frac{3}{4}$ in.) overall. Its blade, hilt, and scabbard did not differ from those of the shorter and longer swords.

The chiza katana was mainly a dress sword worn with court attire, particularly by those who attended the shogun, a hereditary commander-in-chief and the virtual ruler of Japan until 1868.

**choke** A narrowing of the bore of the barrel toward the muzzle, which is found in varying degrees in shotguns. The choke causes a concentration of the pellets, enabling them to travel close together for a greater distance which gives a closer pattern.

**cinctorium** (Greek *zone*) A large leather girdle worn by Roman officers to designate rank. It was used in the 6th century by the Etruscans and later by the Italic peoples; the differences between the Italic and the Roman type centered on the shape of the girdle, the buckling system, and the shape of the front pendant, which was triangular or semicircular.

The cinctorium—a military emblem *par excellence*—served the practical purpose of protecting the stomach. It was adopted toward the 1st century A.D. and was closely associated with a Germanic outfit of the period. A cinctorium consisted of a girdle that ended with four metal-decorated strips, one of which was inserted in the buckle or clasp; the others fell freely in front. A second type of cinctorium, developed after the one described above, consisted of a large girdle with four strips attached to its upper border in the centre to protect the stomach. A variation had a metal plate below the belt, to which strips were attached. The *parazonium* or some other type of dagger or short sword was usually worn on this type of girdle.

**cingulum** (Greek *zoster*) A leather girdle with metal decorations worn by a Roman soldier; it formed an essential part of his military outfit and designated membership in the army or the militia. In most cases a dagger or a short sword was hung from the cingulum, whereas the longer sword was attached to the balteus or to some other type of belt. The cingulum was of Etruscan origin; it came into use with the end of the monarchy (6th century B.C.). For a description of its defensive function. *See* CINCTORIUM.

**cinquedea** A term found in 16th- and 17th-century Italian writings (and in contemporary French documents as *sang de dez*). It referred to a particular type of large dagger or short sword, suggesting Venetian origin. Writers of the day described it as a dagger with blade "five fingers" wide. Since the 19th century the term has been applied to an Italian dagger in use in the 15th and early 16th centuries.

This dagger had a long, triangular blade of the specified width at the base; its tip was often ogive-shaped. The guard, which had two short quillons that curved forward, was pointed at the center. The handle was often plated on the flats with ivory and decorated with *à jour* rosettes on each side. The wider parts of the blade were decorated with etching, engravings and gilding, bearing mottoes or quotations from the Gospels. The sheath was made of dark hardened leather (*cuir-bouilli*) and was finely decorated with embossed designs. Based on the number of flutings on the blade, these weapons can be divided into

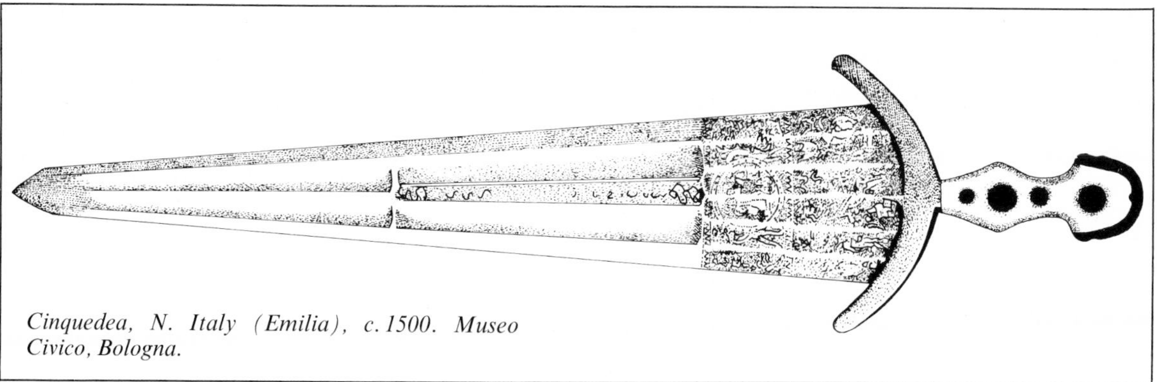

*Cinquedea, N. Italy (Emilia), c.1500. Museo Civico, Bologna.*

two groups: those with a four-three-two arrangement and the later types with only two flutes, one on each side of the blade.

The cinquedea was a typically Italian weapon. It was developed in an area centered in Emilia and Veneto in the 15th century, a period of creative fervor (which coincided with the development of the Swiss dagger north of the Alps) in which efforts were made to redesign weapons as well as armor. The cinquedea survived only until the early part of the 16th century.

In addition to bold fluting, the decoration on the blade of the cinquedea reflected the influences of the Tuscan and Bolognese schools of painting associated with great masters such as Mantegna, Cosmé Tura, Ercole de' Roberti, and artists of the Ferrara school. Decorative themes, borrowed from both classical iconography and the Christian tradition, were often combined on the same blade. The dominant motif of all the decorations was the human figure, nude or attired in the classical manner, sometimes depicted in an architectural setting. The heroic quality of the figure was reinforced by mottoes exhorting the owners of the weapons to pursue high standards of conduct and life.

In the Casa Caetani in Rome there is a long sword resembling a cinquedea form that was made for Cesare Borgia, probably in about 1498. Although the blade is decorated with typical engravings, it is unique because the decoration contains the signature HOPVS HERC (Opus Herculis), the same signature that appears on a cinquedea sheath of tooled leather in the Musée de l'Armée in Paris. The identity of this Hercules is still uncertain, though some authors identify him as Ercole de' Fideli, a goldsmith known to have worked at the ducal court of Ferrara between 1478 and 1518.

**clasp knife** A knife with a blade that folds into the handle, which also houses a strong spring with a catch to fix the blade in either the open or the closed position. It is also called a jackknife.

**claw** A device for drawing the CROSSBOW used in the 13th to 15th centuries. There were two types. The simpler, which derived its force from the archer's strength, consisted of a claw with one or two hooks attached to a strong belt. In order to keep the crossbow steady as it was drawn, the crossbowman had to place his foot in the stirrup of the crossbow; then, stooping down, he hooked the string with the claw. When he stood up, he drew the bow by pulling the string back to the notch on the nut.

To reduce the effort required, in the second type a pulley was combined with the hook. A cord of a specific length fixed to the belt was attached at the butt of the tiller; a small pulley with a claw ran over it. To draw the bow, the bowman had to hold fast to the crossbow and hook the claw to the bowstring by bending forward. When he stood up, he pulled back both the cord and the pulley, setting the bowstring in the nut.

**claymore** A term derived from the Gaelic *claidheamoh-mor*, meaning "great sword." It was first used to describe the large cross-hilted broadsword used in the Scottish Highlands and by Scottish mercenaries in Ireland from the late 15th to the early 17th century. In its classic form, the claymore consisted of a straight, broad, double-edged blade, long, diamond-section quillons angling toward the blade and terminating in quatrefoils, a quillon block extending to form a long spur on each side, and a tubular section leather-covered grip with a wheel-shaped pommel. The blade was generally shorter than blades of Continental two-handed swords of the same period.

The claymore almost certainly developed from a late medieval cross-hilted sword that can be seen on some effigies and tomb slabs in the West Highlands and the Isles.

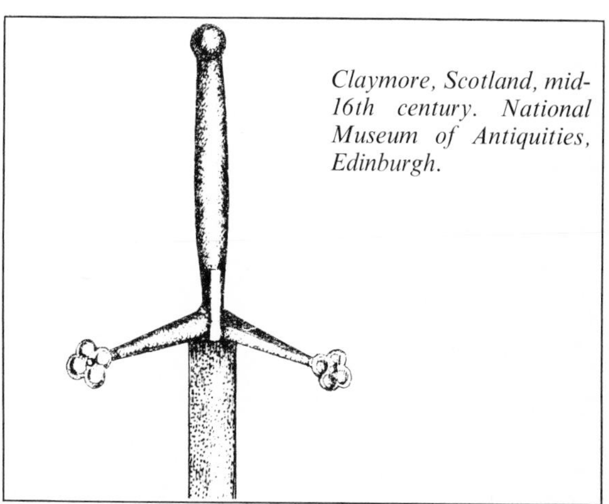

*Claymore, Scotland, mid-16th century. National Museum of Antiquities, Edinburgh.*

This sword exhibited two of the characteristics found on the claymore, namely, the long, downward-angled quillons and the central part of the quillon block extending in a long spur. The dating of claymores is complex and imprecise, although there is a claymore of classic form depicted on a grave slab from Oronsay dated 1539. In the latter part of the 16th century, although retaining the characteristic form of quillon and blade, claymores sometimes had large spherical pommels.

A sword related to the claymore is known as the "Lowland" form because of the fact that several examples came from southern Scotland. Lowland swords had angular, round-section quillons, the terminals arranged as turned knobs set at right angles; some have open rings affixed to the center of the quillons on each side. They retained the feature of the quillon block extending to a spur on each side but, unlike the claymore's, this spur was small and pointed. The pommels of these swords were large and spherical, the long tubular-section grips being of wood covered with leather. One form of the Lowland sword had quillons in the form of an arched cross, and in the center a solid oval plate bent down as an extra guard for the hands. Although Lowland swords have been dated to the second half of the 16th century and those with arched quillons and plates have been dated to the early 17th, little evidence is at present available that would lead to more precise dating.

Most of the blades of both the Highland and the Lowland claymores appear to be of German origin, whereas the hilts were made by Scottish craftsmen.

Several Scottish literary references indicate that the term "claymore" was applied by Gaelic speakers in the Highlands to both the old-fashioned, two-handed sword and the characteristic Scottish basket-hilted sword of the early 18th century.

**cleaning rod** *See* RAMROD.

**clip** A cartridge holder inserted in the magazine of an automatic or, more rarely, a repeating firearm. It usually contains a spring with a follower that delivers the rounds into the receiver of the weapon. *See also* CHARGER.

**clipeum** *See* CLIPEUS.

**clipeus** (or **clipeum**) A circular or, sometimes, oval bronze shield used by Roman heavy infantry. There is documentation of its existence in Rome and Latium (Lazio) from the end of the 8th century B.C. It seems to have derived from the typical round shield of classical Greece, the ASPIS. The clipeus, made entirely of bronze and having a diameter of about 90–100 cm. (36–40 in.), must have been particularly heavy and costly; consequently, a lighter type of clipeus was made, using one or two layers of leather covered by plates or by a thin sheet of bronze. Inside the clipeus was a strong metal handle; the outside was often decorated in motifs arranged concentrically.

The clipeus was no longer part of the Roman soldier's equipment after the period of Camillus (4th century B.C.), having been replaced by the more elongated SCUTUM.

**close gauntlet** *See* GAUNTLET.

**close helmet** A modern term for helmets of a particular construction widely used from the 16th to the mid-17th century. The close helmet originated in the early 1500s

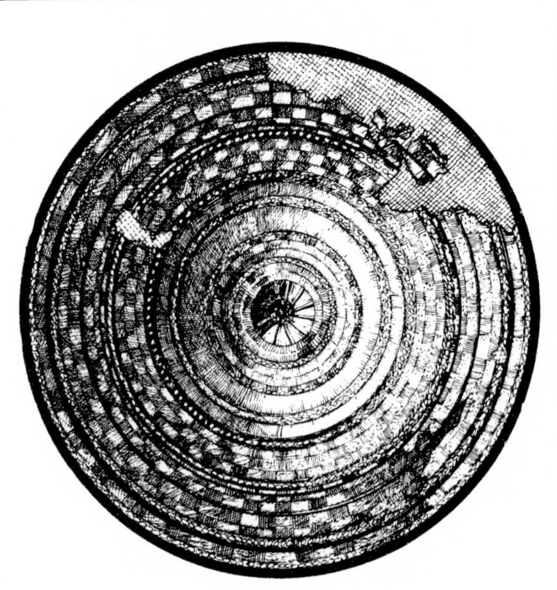

*Clipeus from an archaeological site at Cerveteri, Vatican Museums, Rome.*

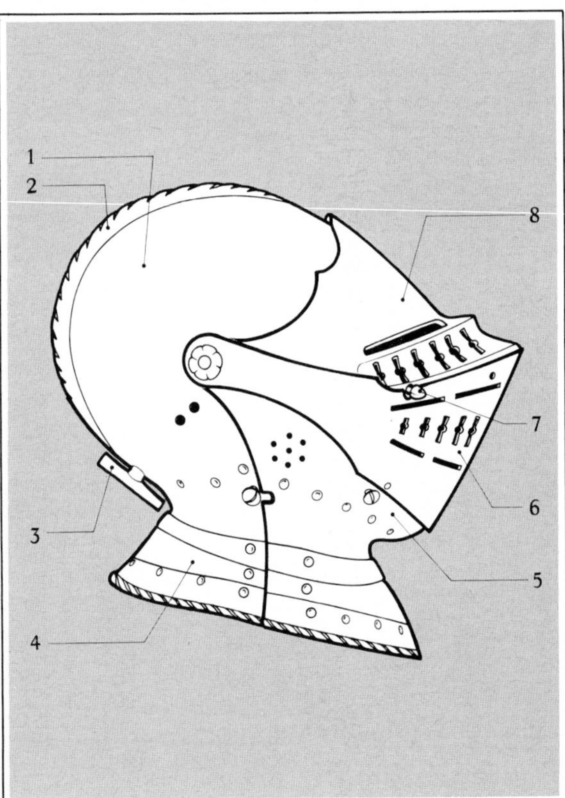


*Close helmet. 1. skull; 2. comb; 3. plume holder; 4. gorget plates; 5. bevor; 6. upper bevor; 7. lifting peg; 8. visor.*

# Weapons and armor from the 9th to the 15th century

**Plate 7 Viking weapons** (top) *Battle-ax head with silver-damascened ribbon patterns and stylized animal designs, from Mammen (Jütland), late 10th century. Nationalmuseet, Copenhagen.* (left) *Sword with silver furniture, with decoration in English style, from the Skåne region of southern Sweden, 10th–11th century. Nationalmuseet, Copenhagen.* (right) *Sword with furniture with silver and bronze damascening, from Broa (Gotland), 9th–10th century. Statens Sjöhistoriska Museum, Stockholm.*

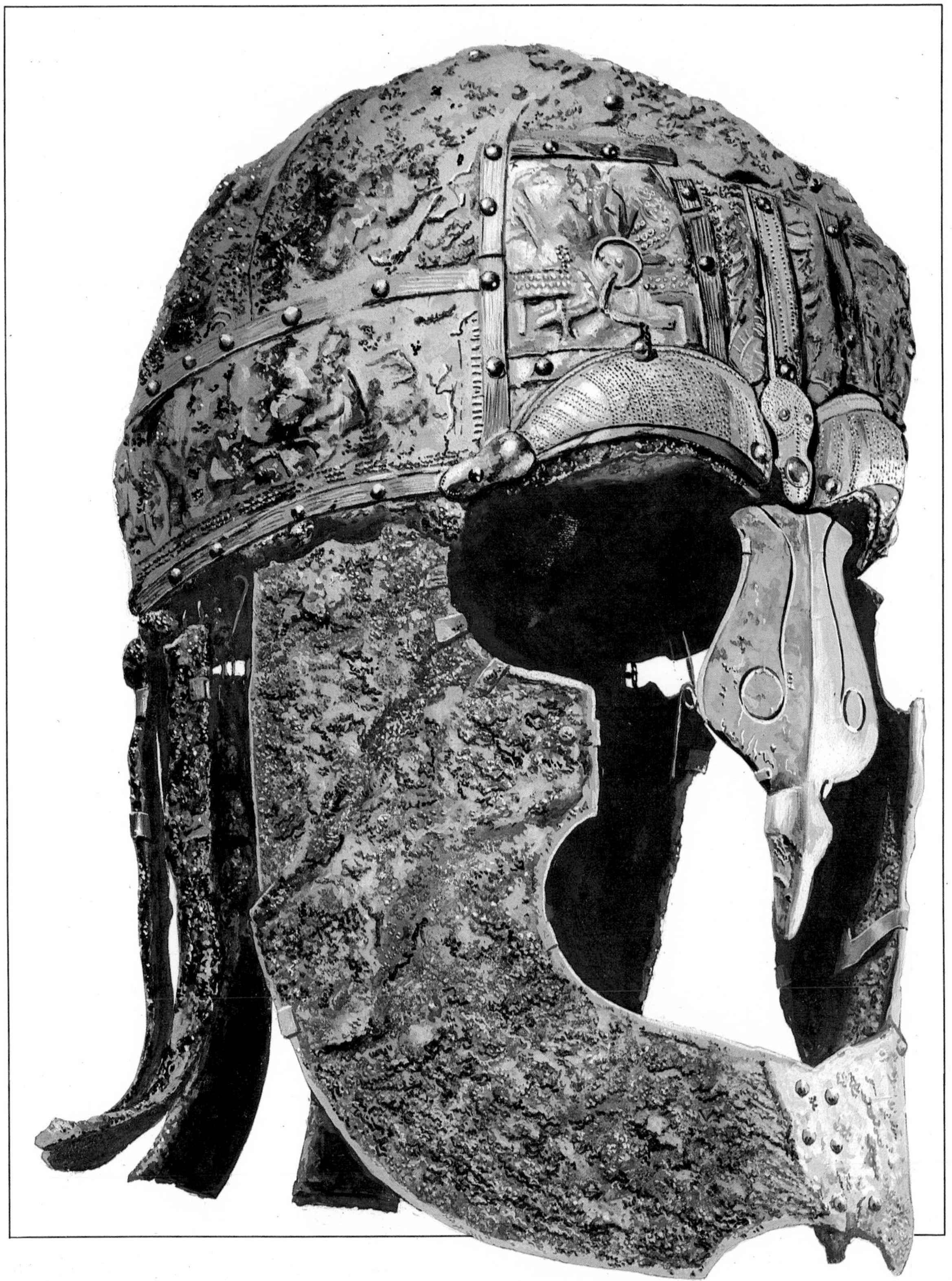

**Plate 8 Helmet** *Iron helmet overlaid with engraved bronze, 7th century, discovered at Uppland, Sweden. Statens Sjöhistoriska Museum, Stockholm.*

**Plate 9 Swords of the Romanesque period** (left) *Sword with furniture decorated with precious stones, enamel, and gold filigree; scabbard covered with embossed gold plate with spiral designs, 11th century. Cathedral, Essen.* (right) *The sword claimed to be Charlemagne's "Joyeuse", with gold furniture, used as the coronation sword of the kings of France, 12th century. Galerie d'Apollon, Louvre, Paris.*

**Plate 10 14th-century great helms** (left) *Helm belonging to Sir Richard Pembridge (d. 1375), at one time on his tomb in Hereford Cathedral. Royal Scottish Museum, Edinburgh.* (right) *Crested funeral helmet of Albert von Prankh, Austria, c. 1350. Waffensammlung, Vienna.*

**Plate 11 14th-century armor** (left) *Basnet with "pig-faced" visor and aventail, N. Italy, c. 1380–1400, from the Churburg Armory, Sluderno. Tower of London Armouries.* (right) *Composite armor belonging to a Vogt von Matsch, made by the master armorers "P," "IO," and others, N. Italy, c. 1380–90. Churburg Armory, Sluderno.*

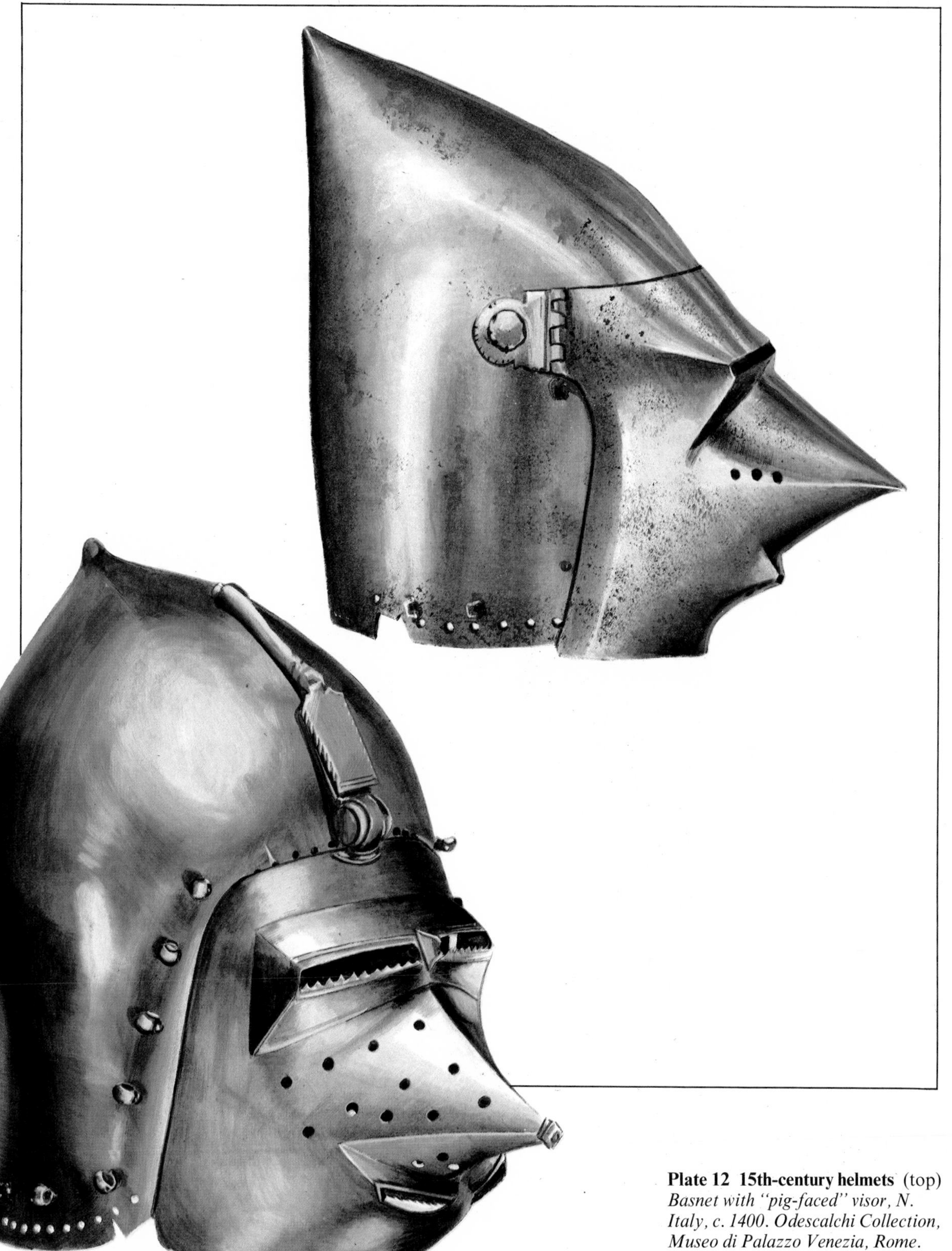

**Plate 12 15th-century helmets** (top) *Basnet with "pig-faced" visor, N. Italy, c. 1400. Odescalchi Collection, Museo di Palazzo Venezia, Rome.* (bottom) *"Houndskull" basnet with hinged visor* (klappvisier), *Germany, c. 1400–1410. Kunstsammlung der Veste, Coburg, West Germany.*

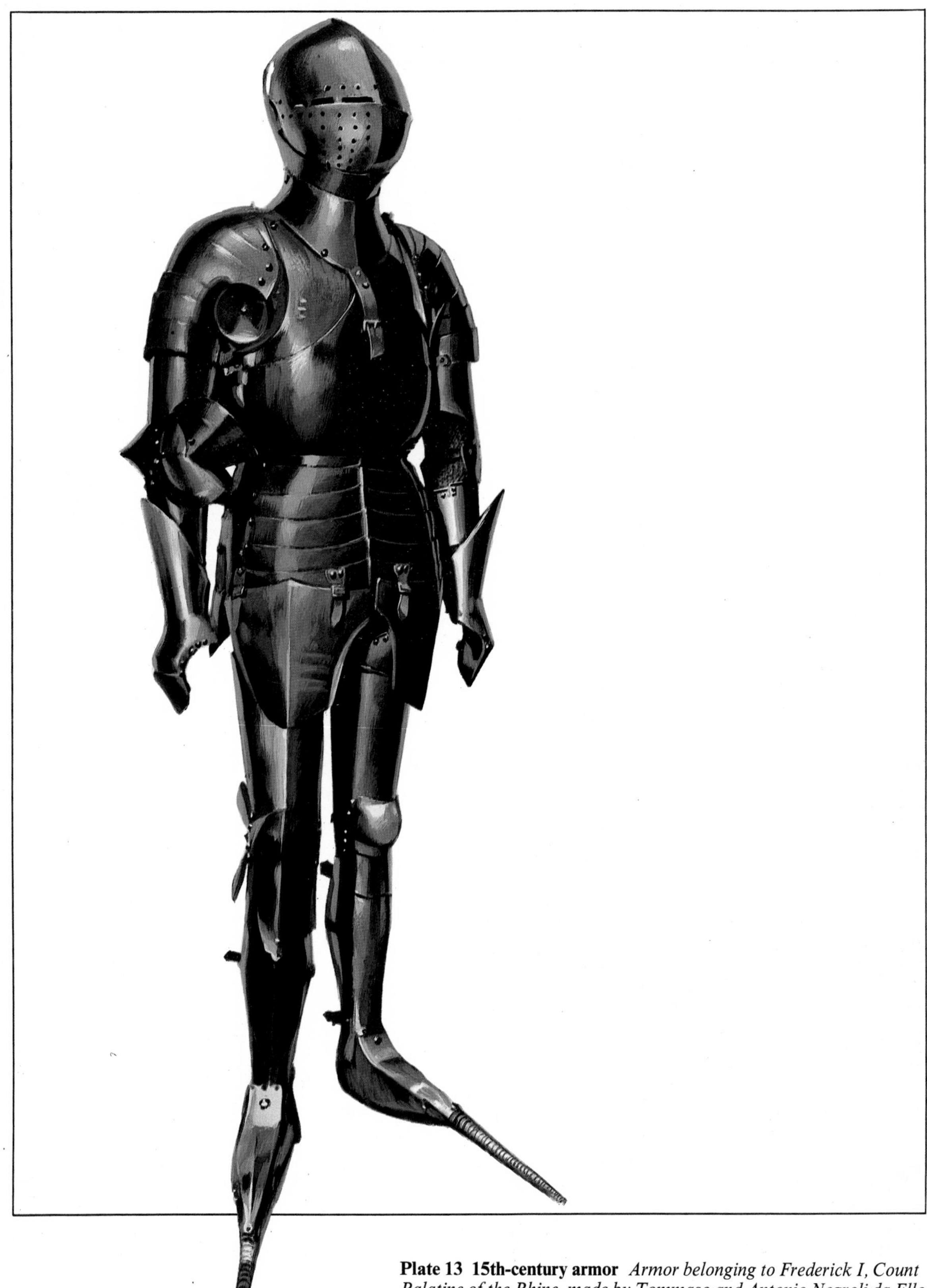

**Plate 13 15th-century armor** *Armor belonging to Frederick I, Count Palatine of the Rhine, made by Tommaso and Antonio Negroli da Ello (jointly known as Missaglia), Pier Innocenzo da Faerno, and Antonio Seroni, Milan, c. 1450. Waffensammlung, Vienna.*

**Plate 14 15th-century armor** (right) *Composite armor with a gardbrace on the left pauldron, N. Italy, c. 1450–60. Santuario della Madonna delle Grazie, Mantua.* (left) *Helmet of the above armor.*

**Plate 15 15th-century armor** *Late Gothic field armor belonging to Archduke Sigismund of the Tyrol, made by Lorenz Helmschmied, Augsburg, c. 1485. Waffensammlung, Vienna.*

**Plate 16 15th-century swords** (left) *The hand-and-a-half sword of Duke Christopher of Bavaria, with furniture and scabbard of gilded silver, S. Germany, c. 1480. Schatzkammer, Munich.* (right) *The hunting sword of Emperor Maximilian I, with two small knives and a bodkin in the scabbard, made by Hanns Sumersperger, Hall, Tyrol, 1496. Waffensammlung, Vienna.*

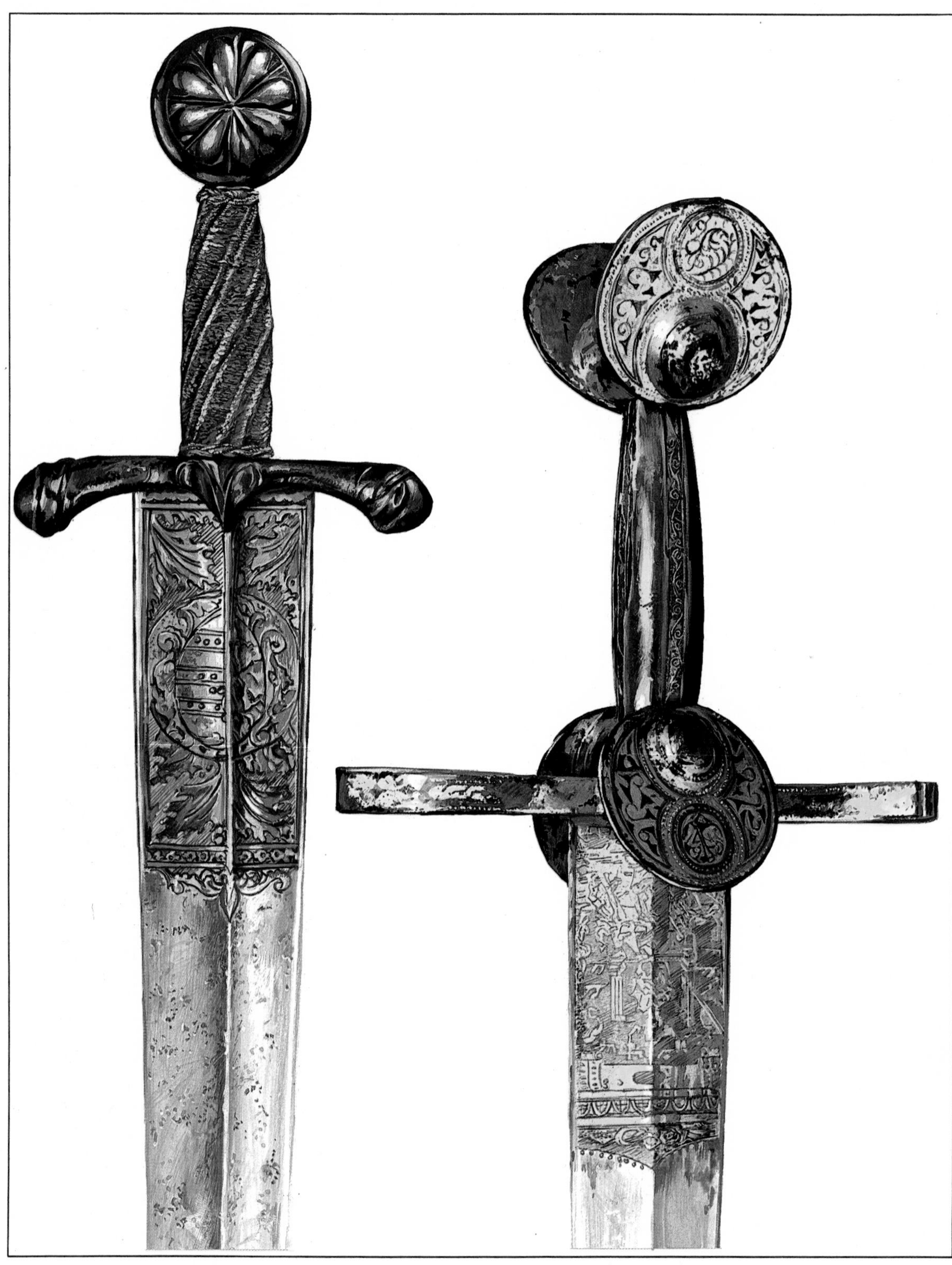

**Plate 17 15th-century swords** (right) *Sword, N. Italy (Veneto), late 15th century. Museo Nazionale del Bargello, Florence.* (left) *Sword, N. Italy, second half of the 15th century. Museo Civico L. Marzoli, Brescia.*

**Plate 18 15th-century swords of honor** (left) *The ceremonial sword of Emperor Sigismund I, king of Hungary, with ivory grip; the quillons represent the symbol of the Order of the Dragon, founded by Sigismund in 1408, N. Italy, c. 1433. Waffensammlung, Vienna.* (right) *Papal sword with furniture of gilded bronze, sent by Pope Nicholas V to Giovanni Bentivoglio, seigneur of Bologna, Rome, 1454. Museo Civico, Bologna.*

**Plate 19 15th-century artillery** (top) *Late 14th- or early 15th-century cannon, reconstruction based on a drawing dated 1390–1400. Bernisches Historisches Museum, Bern.* (middle) *Breechloading cannon, c. 1460–70 (carriage reconstructed). Bernisches Historisches Museum, Bern.* (bottom) *Breechloading cannon, 15th century. British Museum, London.*

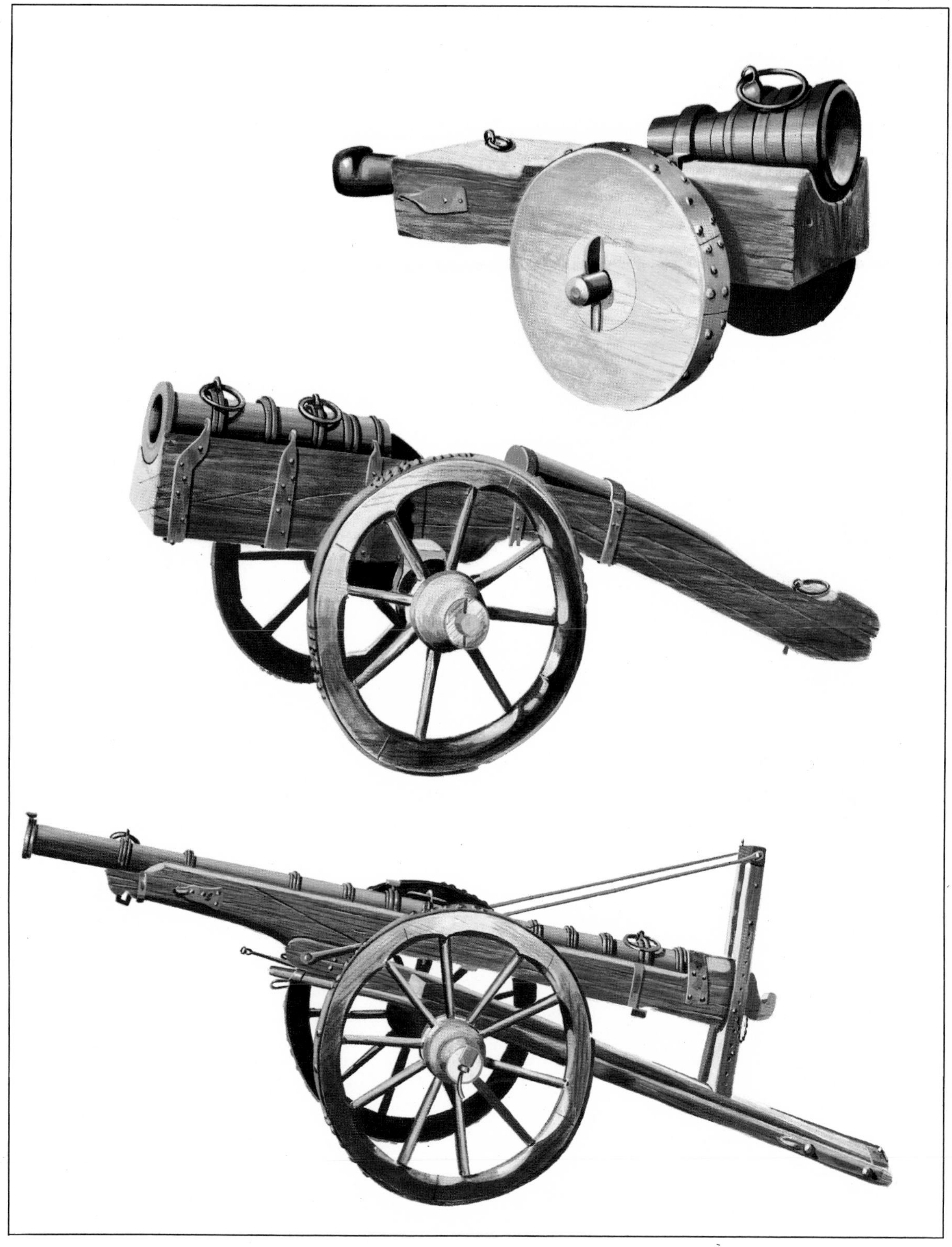

**Plate 20 15th-century artillery** (top) *Iron mortar, 15th century (reconstruction). Bernisches Historisches Museum, Bern.* (middle) *Iron culverin, Burgundy, c. 1450 (reconstruction). City of Morat Museum (Switzerland).* (bottom) *Iron culverin, Burgundy, c. 1460 (reconstruction). City of Neuveville Museum (Switzerland).*

from those forms of the SALLET that had both a visor and a bevor pivoted on the sides of the skull. Early close helmets strongly resembled such sallets since, in addition to this arrangement, they also had a short-tailed, laminated neck guard. However, at an early date close helmets developed a feature that distinguished them from sallets, that is, a bevor shaped to the chin and joined with a front neck guard that overlapped its counterpart on the skull, thus forming a gorget.

From the second quarter of the 16th century, the face guard of the close helmet (and of the armet) usually consisted of a visor with eye slits, protecting the upper portion of the face; it was shaped to the front of the comb and could be slid up onto the brow of the skull. The lower edge of the visor was contoured to a prominent point and was fitted into the upper bevor (or ventail). The upper bevor, with piercings for ventilation or to serve as another eye slit, enabling the wearer to see downward, also projected to a point. The one-piece lower bevor was shaped to the chin and was fastened to the skull at the sides, usually either with a pierced stud and hook or a stud and keyhole slot. The two parts of the bevor were locked together with a locking catch or a pivoted hook. The lower bevor, the upper bevor, and the visor were movable; they were attached to the skull by the same pair of washered pivots at the temples. The neck guard was of two types: laminated gorget plates on the helmet itself, and a gorget of the armor. In the latter form, the lower edges of the skull and bevor had a hollow rim that locked over and rotated on the turn of the collar.

Certain types of the closed BURGONET were so similar in construction and appearance to the close helmet that they could be classified as such were it not for their characteristic peaks.

**club** (Greek *ropalon, corune*) A stout hardwood stick, narrower where held and broader at the tip, used as a weapon since earliest times. This club, or bludgeon, was a weapon wielded by many mythical heroes such as Hercules, Theseus, and the Centaurs.

Before long, in order to increase its offensive capability, the club was fitted with spikes and subsequently with a metal head (*see* MACE). In the ancient Greco–Roman world, it was considered a "barbarian" weapon and thus issued only to auxiliary troops. The *clavateres* depicted on Trajan's Column (A.D. 112–113) were Teutonic auxiliaries, and their national weapon, clearly displayed, was the club.

*Clava lignea* "wooden club" was the term given to the instrument used for sword drill.

**cludon** A term used by the Latin author Apuleius (2nd century A.D.) to describe a particular type of dagger. It was considered more of a theatrical instrument than a weapon because it was made in such a way that when the blade struck something, it retracted into the handle, thus feigning the thrust.

**clunaculum** A term used by the Latin author Festus (2nd–3rd centuries A.D.) to describe a dagger hanging from the CINGULUM (belt) at the back, probably in the same way as that depicted on Trajan's Column, which shows a soldier building a fortification. The term also seems to have referred to a sacrificial knife.

**coat armor** Also called surcoat or jupon, a textile garment worn over armor from about the middle of the 12th century, if not earlier, to the first quarter of the 15th. During this period its forms and styles varied greatly according to fashion and the type of armor worn. In the 12th century, coat armor was a long, loosely fitting gown, with or without sleeves; its skirt was split for riding. Sleeveless coat armor prevailed from the early 1200s to the early 1300s and again from about 1350 to about 1425. It is known that in c. 1250–1350 coat armor was occasionally reinforced on the inside with riveted, vertically set rectangular plates; in this form it served as body armor (*see* COAT OF PLATES). After the mid-14th century, coat armor was made in the form of a short, sleeveless garment with a small skirt that reached to just below the hips, tightly fitting the cuirass. When worn without armor, coat armor made of padded and quilted fabrics, with full sleeves and a skirt, could serve as protective equipment. Coat armor used with armor had openings laced on the back or the sides, whereas independently worn surcoats were sometimes buttoned from top to bottom in the front, and embroidered with ornaments and coats of arms.

**coat of mail and plate** *See* BEKHTER; YUSHMAN.

**coat of plates** Armor for the trunk introduced toward the end of the 12th century, at an early stage in the development of plate armor, it was also called "pair of plates." Although coats of plates were made in many versions, the basic form consisted of rectangular, overlapping plates set vertically or horizontally and riveted to a strong fabric or leather cover; sometimes the insides of the plates were lined with fabric. In many instances different plate settings were combined in one armor; for example, short upper breastplates and side plates were fixed vertically, whereas the main part of the breast was protected by large horizontal plates concave to the body. The base to which the plates were riveted was cut in various styles. A poncho-like coat was widely used, as can be seen from numerous examples excavated at the site of the battle of Wisby (1361); the front and the back were made separately, or the coat opened on one side. Parts of the coat were joined with laces or straps and buckles.

Toward the middle of the 14th century, small upper breastplates were replaced by one large plate, which in a few decades extended down to the line of the hips. From the 1370s this breastplate had a predominantly rounded shape and was often riveted between a rich fabric cover and a canvas lining. A downward extension of these textiles served to rivet in between iron hoops, forming the overlapping lames of the skirt. The coat of plates was gradually replaced by more developed forms of plate armor beginning in the early 15th century, but its lighter version (*see* BRIGANDINE) remained in use until the beginning of the 17th century.

**cock** A hammer in the lock or action of a firearm, pivoting on a strong hinge that enables it to turn in both directions—backward, set by the firer either manually or by some mechanism, and forward, with violence, to strike the steel in a flintlock or the cap on the nipple of a percussion firearm (*see* IGNITION) or to drive the striker forward. The motive power for this forward movement

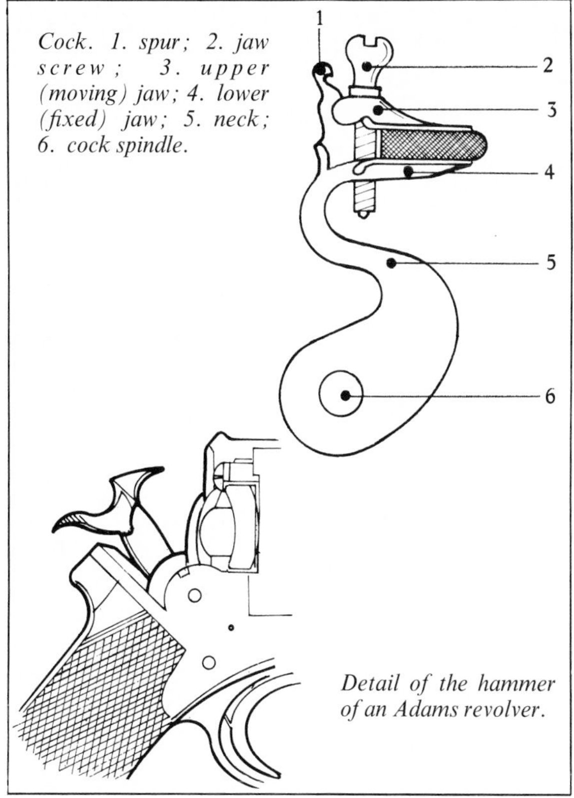


*Cock. 1. spur; 2. jaw screw; 3. upper (moving) jaw; 4. lower (fixed) jaw; 5. neck; 6. cock spindle.*

*Detail of the hammer of an Adams revolver.*

comes from a strong spring that is compressed when the cock is moved backwards.

In most old ignition systems, the cock consisted of a movable iron bar fixed to the lock mechanism by a hinge, with two jaws at the top to hold the pyrite or flint. In modern weapons, the cock is called the hammer, but a gun ready for firing is still said to be "cocked."

In some weapons, especially in the majority of revolvers, the striker is rigidly attached to the hammer so that when the hammer springs forward, it comes into direct contact with the percussion cap to fire the cartridge. In modern weapons, in which the striker is not directly attached to the hammer, the hammer is normally fitted inside the body and is cocked by the backward movement of the action.

**codpiece** An accessory of armor that protected the genitals. In its simplest form, the codpiece consisted of a rigid, cuplike bag made of leather or hide, sometimes covered in scales or lames. It was attached under the skirt at the crotch. Metal-plate codpieces were also quite frequently worn in the 16th century; they were attached to the lower lame of the skirt with turning pins. Whichever type was used, codpieces were thickly padded on the inside. *See also* BREKE OF MAIL.

**coif** Medieval protective armor for the head used mainly from the 11th century to the beginning of the 14th. It consisted of a close-fitting mail hood, either joined to the hauberk or an integral part of it. There was also a flap, the ventail, that was drawn across the chin; it was secured by a strap and buckle or a lacing thong at the side of the head. Ordinary soldiers appear to have worn a conical helmet, with a nasal bar, over the coif, whereas the knightly classes wore a basnet over the coif with a great helm extending down to the chest.

**colichemarde** A French term, used internationally, denoting light thrusting swords with blades of a particular form. Wide at the forte, the blade narrowed abruptly to a slender part ending in a sharp point. Blades of this shape were either triangular or flat hexagonal in section at the forte, which was used to beat and parry the opponent's sword; the slender part served for attacking actions.

The popularity of the colichemarde from the mid-17th century seems to have been closely related to the progress of the French school of fencing, which employed the one sword for all actions, unlike the Italian and Spanish schools, which used swords in both hands. The French system required a light yet strong thrusting sword, and the colichemarde satisfied this criterion. This form of blade was superseded by an equally light and rigid blade, gradually narrowing and triangular in section over the whole of its length. Although this blade had been used for three centuries, it became a standard feature in dueling swords and practice épées only in the mid-18th century.

The strange word *colichemarde* is thought to have originated as a corruption of Königsmark, the family name of several German noblemen who distinguished themselves in the military service of Sweden, the Netherlands, and France. The colichemarde might have been nicknamed after one of them Count Otto Wilhelm von Königsmark (1639–88), who served with distinction under Turenne and was promoted to *marechal de camp* by Louis XIV. His nephew Karl Johann (d. 1688) was reputed to have been a skillful swordsman and swashbuckler.

**collar** *See* GORGET.

**comb** A raised ridge running along the central line of the skull of a helmet from the brow to the nape. It was already defined on many late 15th-century helmets, and in the following century it became a salient characteristic. Although it was upstanding on the comb morion and the burgonet, its proportions were modest on other types of helmets. The comb was invariably roped or finished off with parallel, slanting incisions to give the effect of roping; either method served to mask the hammered join of two halves of the skull and at the same time to decorate the top edge. The best examples of these combs, however, were those skillfully forged with the skull from one piece of metal, despite the sometimes considerable height of the comb.

One rather rare version of the comb, found on a few morions and burgonets, was the triple comb, in which the central ridge was flanked by two smaller, less prominent ones running parallel.

**comb morion** *See* MORION.

**combination weapons** A generic term for weapons that are hidden or appear to be innocent articles of everyday use, such as a SWORD STICK, the FAKIR'S CRUTCH, and the Japanese TANTŌ, a dagger whose sheath was sometimes made to look like a fan. The term also includes any weapon that combines different kinds of arms and fulfills various functions.

As firearms were developed, gunsmiths exercised great

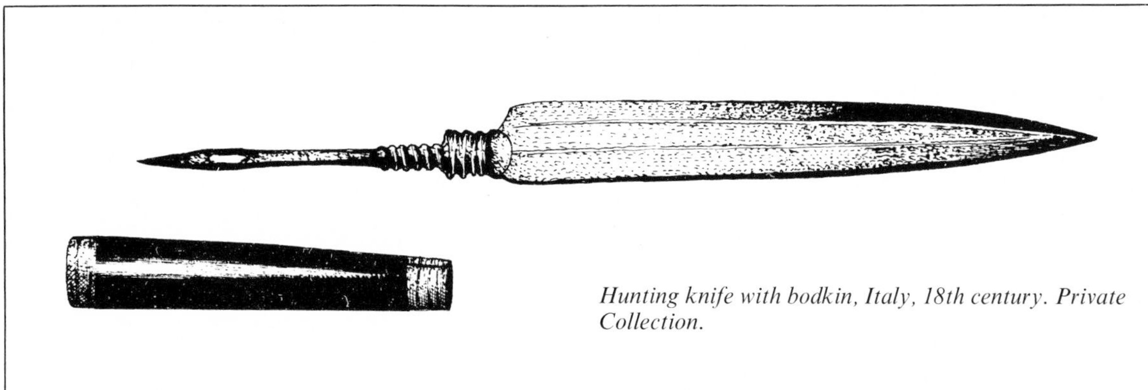

*Hunting knife with bodkin, Italy, 18th century. Private Collection.*

*Combined dagger and flintlock pistol, N. Italy, c. 1650. Museo Civico L. Marzoli, Brescia.*

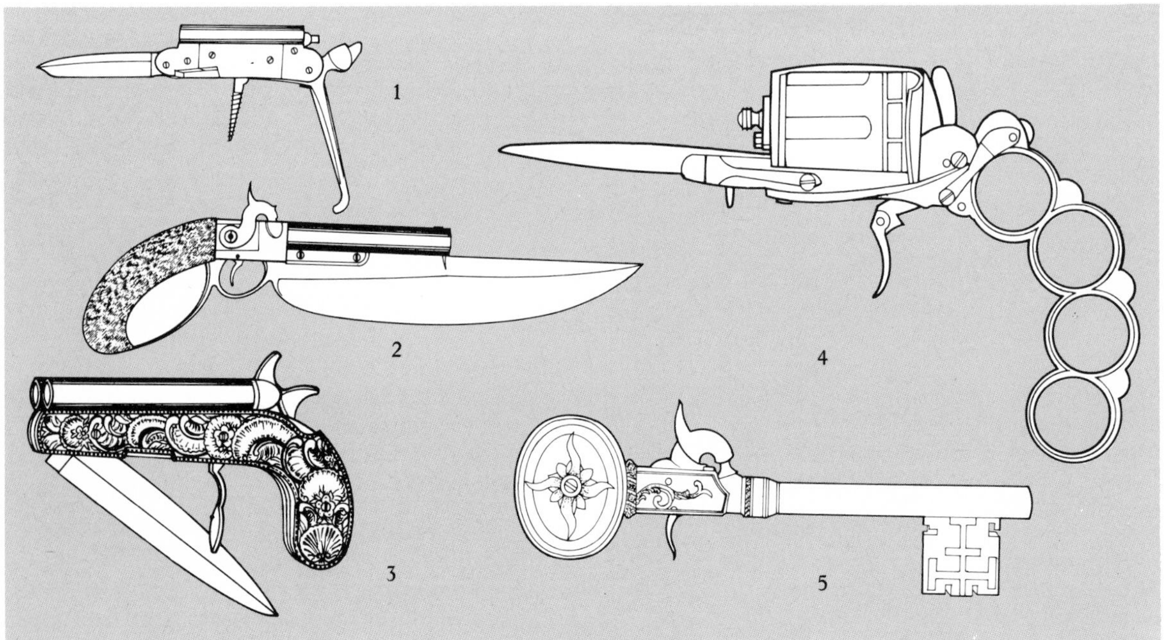


*Different types of combination weapons. 1. Knife–percussion pistol, Belgium, second half of the 19th century. 2. Knife–percussion pistol, U.S. Navy, 1837. 3. Knife–percussion pistol, Belgium, third quarter of the 19th century. 4. French "Apache" revolver with knife and knuckle-duster, Belgium, second half of the 19th century. 5. Key pistol, c. 1850.*

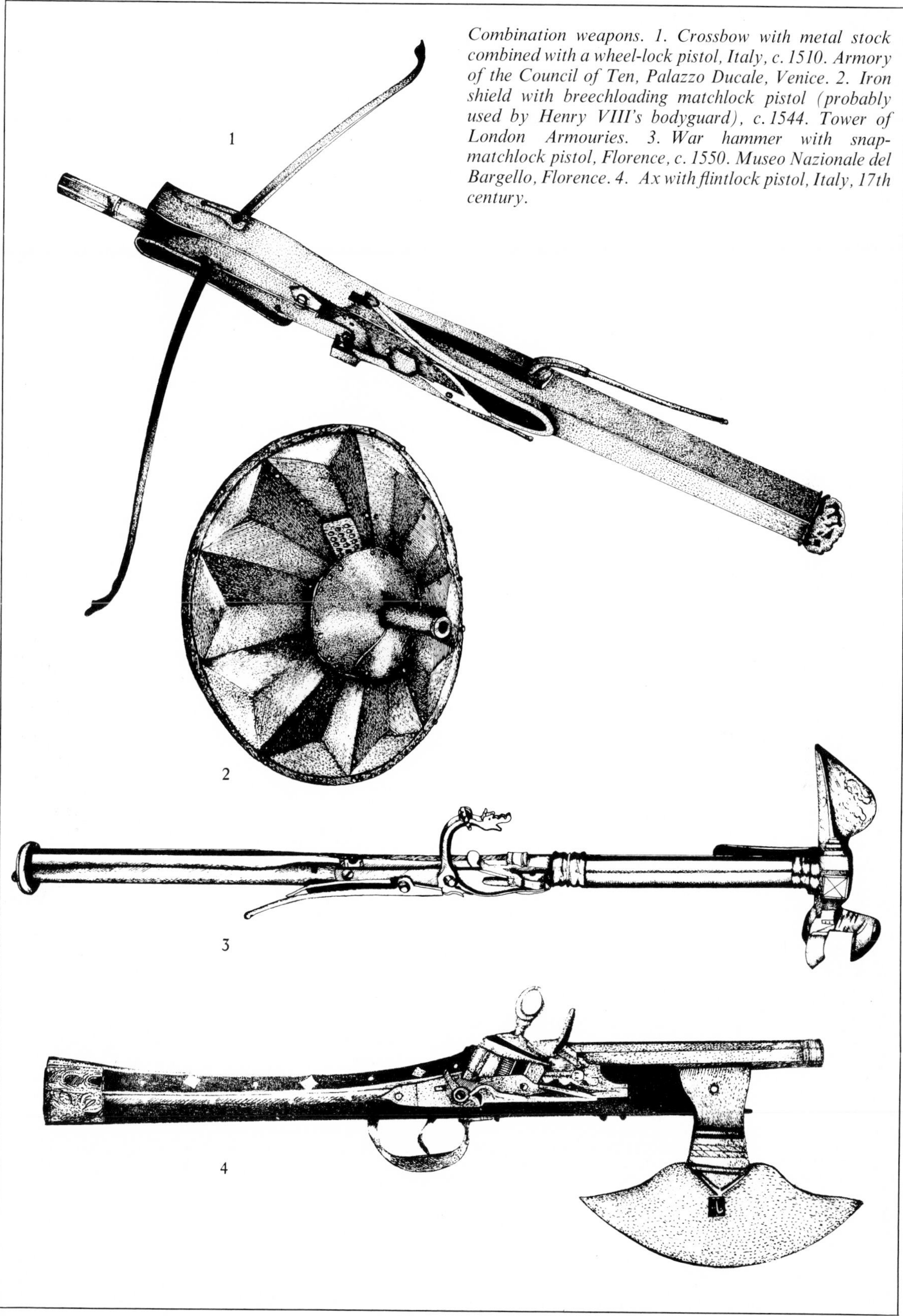


*Combination weapons. 1. Crossbow with metal stock combined with a wheel-lock pistol, Italy, c. 1510. Armory of the Council of Ten, Palazzo Ducale, Venice. 2. Iron shield with breechloading matchlock pistol (probably used by Henry VIII's bodyguard), c. 1544. Tower of London Armouries. 3. War hammer with snap-matchlock pistol, Florence, c. 1550. Museo Nazionale del Bargello, Florence. 4. Ax with flintlock pistol, Italy, 17th century.*

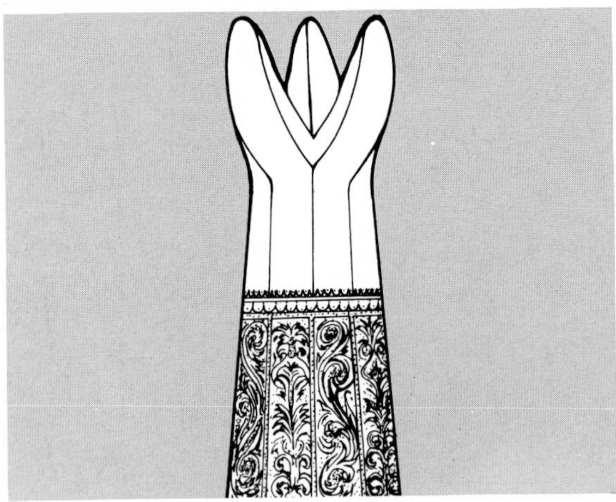

*Coronel of a tilting lance, Italy, c. 1500. Armería Real, Madrid.*

ingenuity in producing combination weapons. A number of shields associated with Henry VIII combined breechloading matchlock pistols with round iron shields, perhaps supplied by Giovanbattista of Ravenna in 1544. Also associated with this English king is the famous "holy water sprinkler," which is preserved in the Tower of London and was known in the 17th century as "King Henry Ye 8th's walking staff." This weapon, probably made in the early 16th century, is in the form of a mace, with a spiked head containing three barrels and fitted with a swivel cover to keep out the rain. A number of daggers, also dating from the first half of the 16th century, were fitted with wheel-lock mechanisms near the hilt; the barrel was adjacent to the blade. Many combination weapons of this period were finely decorated, and it is possible that they were made as curiosities rather than for actual use.

One of the most important early examples of the wheel-lock mechanism was combined with a crossbow; it is preserved in the Doge's Palace in Venice. Beginning in about 1510, the steel crossbow stock was made to conceal a short gun barrel, the lock mechanism being attached to the side of the stock. In the 16th century firearms were combined with axes, maces, and war hammers. It has been suggested that lack of faith in the reliability of firearms necessitated the introduction of a second line of defense, although some of the mechanisms were so delicate that it is difficult to imagine that they could have been effective.

Of a more functional nature was the musket rest of the 17th century; one prong of its fork support extended to form a blade. The comparatively rare musket rest was a variation of "Swedish feathers"—spiked palisades carried by dragoons in the 17th century as a defense against cavalry. A number of hunting hangers, dating from the 18th century, have a flintlock pistol attached to the blade; the trigger was hinged so that it would not catch in the scabbard. It has been suggested that this weapon was used to give the *coup de grâce* to a wounded animal.

Even small items such as cutlery were combined with pistols. A set consisting of a knife, fork, and spoon—probably made in Germany in the early 18th century—had small flintlock mechanisms and handles that concealed small barrels. Some English carbines and blunderbusses made in 1780–90 had folding bayonets held by spring clips along the top or underneath the barrels. A more spectacular example of a firearm combined with a blade was the percussion pistol–sword patented by George Elgin of the United States in 1837. Attached to the underside of the barrel of this single-shot percussion pistol was a large bowie knife. In 1823 an English provincial gunmaker, John Day of Barnstaple, patented an all-metal pistol-truncheon as well as a percussion pistol–cane, examples of which have been preserved. During the 19th century, pistols combined with walking sticks became very popular, and, it has been suggested, were the favourite weapons of poachers. Pistols were also made to fit other objects of everyday use, such as purses. In the National Museum of Antiquities in Edinburgh there is an 18th-century sporran containing four pistols that fired when the sporran was opened. Preserved in the Institute de Don Juan, Madrid, is a mid-17th-century key with a miquelet lock and a push-button trigger. As recently as the early part of the 20th century, six-shot pinfire PEPPERBOX pistols with a folding trigger were built into the handlebars of some bicycles manufactured in Belgium and France, although they seem not to have been made in large quantities.

**composition B** A type of explosive based on TRINITROTOLUENE.

**compound** A projectile with a jacket of softer metal around a harder core.

**contus** (Greek *kontos*) A Roman term for a long pole with a metal tip used for taking soundings, pushing a boat, and other maritime operations. Synonymous with the words meaning "spear" and "javelin," the contus was used by the Roman cavalry in the days of Vespasian (A.D. 9–79); the word also lent itself to the mounted soldiers thus armed—*contarii*—who formed the wings of battle formations. Its features and functions were similar to those of the later BOARDING PIKE and BOAT HOOK.

**cordite** A compound of nitroglycerin, nitrocellulose, and mineral jelly forming a SMOKELESS POWDER.

**coronel** (from Latin *corona*, "crown") The head of a jousting lance, consisting of a socket, either round or with rounded corners, from which flared prongs extended upward. The coronel was the courtly weapon used to demonstrate a jouster's skills.

**corsesca** (French *corseque*; also *couseque*) A staff weapon used from the 15th to the early 17th centuries, mostly in Italy and France. It derived from the earlier winged spear and had a three-pronged head with a central triangular double-edged blade and two sharp upturned wings.

A well-developed form of this weapon, with large, cusped side blades, was sometimes called *chauve-souris* (French for "bat"). The side blades served several functions: as a guard when a thrust was delivered with the central blade, thus protecting the warrior's forward hand; as a stopping device, preventing a deep penetration of the thrusting central blade; as a hook for unseating a mounted

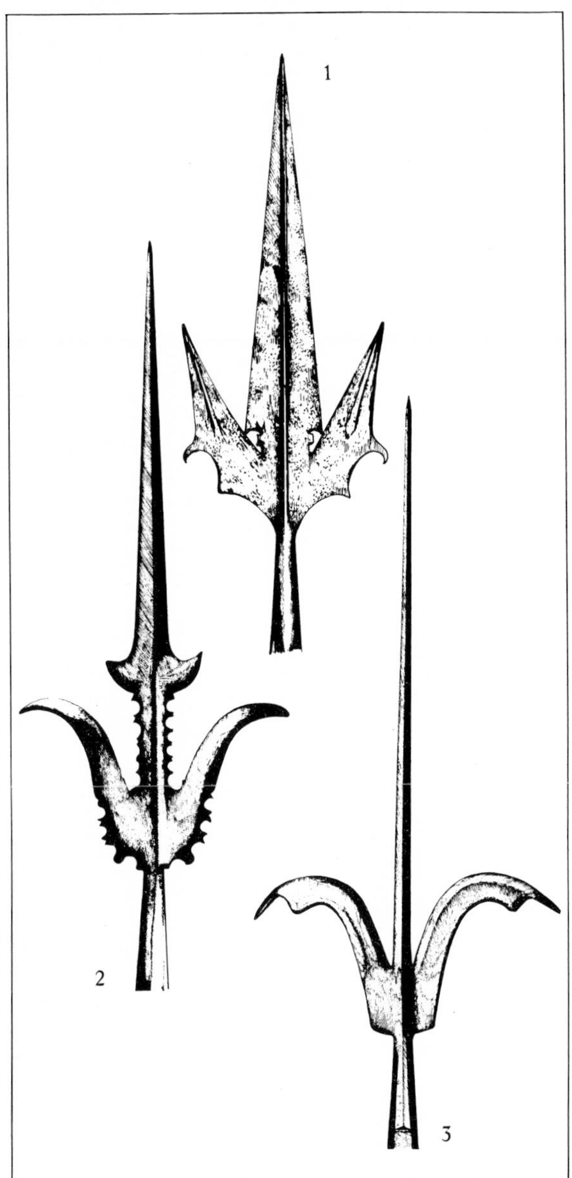


*Corsesca. 1. The type called* chauve-souris, *N. Italy, c. 1530. Museo Civico L. Marzoli, Brescia. 2. The so-called Friuli spear, N. Italy, c. 1600–1620. Museo Bardini, Florence. 3. The so-called Friuli spear, N. Italy, c. 1600–1620. Museo Civico, Bologna.*

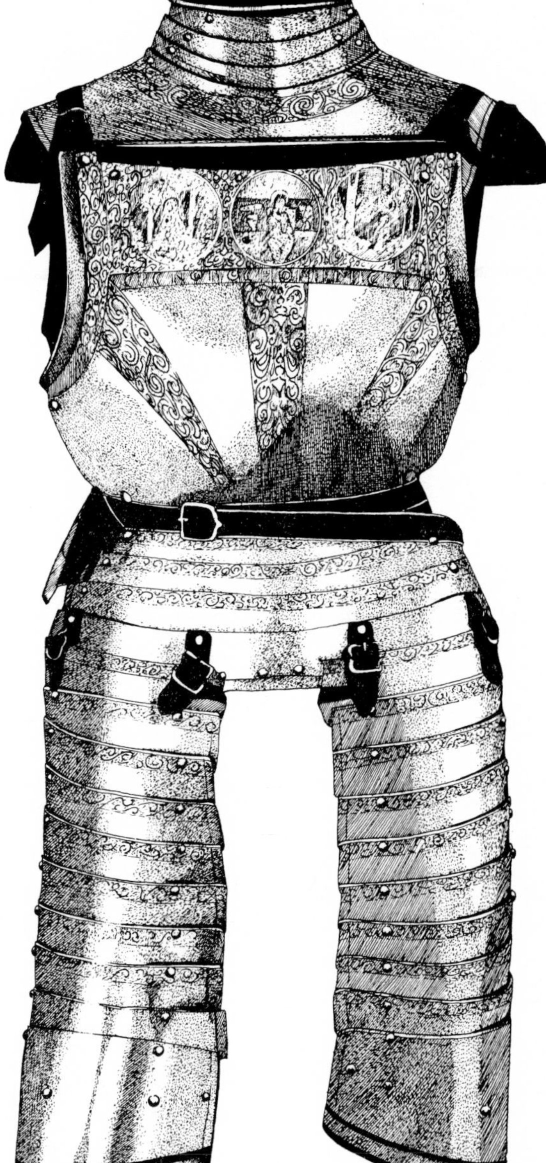

*Corselet, half armor for infantry and light cavalry, Italy, c. 1510–15. Churburg Armory, Sluderno.*

opponent and tripping his horse.

A variation of the weapon, with a long, narrow spike and two upcurving side blades, served as a boarding weapon in naval warfare. Apparently, it was widely used by troops and by naval forces aboard warships in Venice and in Friuli. (Trieste, the most important city in Friuli, has chosen this weapon as its coat of arms.) This form of the consesca is sometimes called the "Friuli spear."

**corslet** A light half armor worn by heavy infantry from the early 1500s to the mid-17th century, usually comprised of a collar, breastplate, backplate, tassets, vambraces, gauntlets, and an open helmet but no legharness; in the 17th century, arm defenses were usually not included. *See also* ARMOR.

**corune** A Greek term for CLUB.

**counterguard** Also called *inner guard*, a system of rings, loops, and bars in a sword guard which was developed in c. 1500 to protect the inner side of the hand and body (for a right-hander, to the left of the sword; vice versa for a left-hander). Bars or branches of the counterguard usually

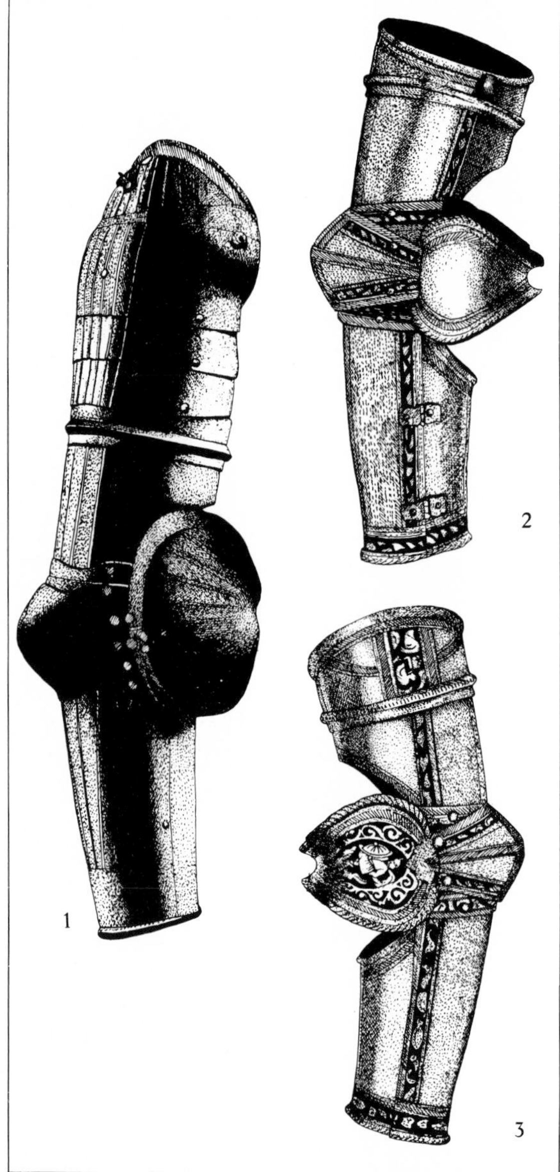


*Vambraces with cowter. 1. In a German-style horseman's armor, Italy, c. 1515. Santuario della Madonna delle Grazie, Mantua. 2, 3. In a composite infantry armor for an officer in the Medicean Guard, c. 1570–75. Museo Nazionale del Bargello, Florence.*

joined the knuckle guard and the arms of the hilt.

**Couse** *See* GLAIVE.

**cowter** A piece of armor to protect the elbow joint, riveted between the upper and lower cannons of the right and left VAMBRACES. Having been introduced during the 15th century, it was used until about the middle of the 17th, during which period it underwent little change. The basic structure of the cowter consisted of a series of mobile lames held in place with loose rivets on the inside. The main lame on each cowter (in the 15th century it was usually the second one, the third in the next century) was cuplike in shape and was positioned over the other lames; on the inside it carried a side wing—a plate to guard the joint.

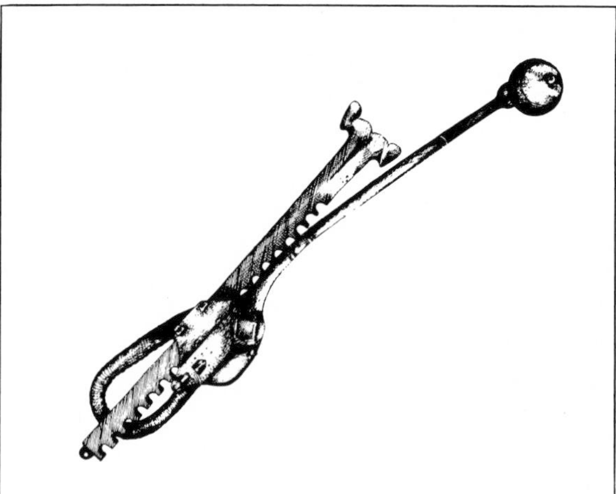

*Cranequin for a crossbow, Germany, first half of the 16th century. Odescalchi Collection, Museo di Palazzo Venezia, Rome.*

In the 15th century cowters, with wings of various shapes, were "open," and were fastened around the arms with a buckle and strap. Toward the latter part of the century, the wings were made to follow the contour of the arms in order to give greater protection to the tendons. The definitive form of the cowter was developed toward the middle of the 16th century; it was made in five lames, the middle, cup-shaped one being placed over the other four, and the side wing completely encircled the arm, thus forming the "full" or "bracelet" cowter. Roping was nearly always worked on the edges. The open form was retained only with the laminated vambrace, with small wings that were often detachable.

The German 16th-century cowter was of the bracelet style but was made in one piece, with pronounced fluting. it was strapped directly onto the arm instead of being riveted to the cannons.

For the joust or tilt, cowters were generally reinforced with special pieces, such as the PASSGUARD.

**cradle** In modern pieces of artillery, that part of the GUN MOUNTING on which the piece recoils on firing. The piece is hinged to guides by trunnions and trunnion bearings, and these slide on the ribs of the cradle. With this layout, the recoil does not directly affect the carriage; the recoil moves in the direction in which the gun is laid.

**cranequin** Also called the rack, the cranequin was a spanning mechanism for the crossbow, consisting of a series of cogwheels in a housing. A small handle controlled the first cog, which usually had only three or four teeth. This handle engaged the teeth in a cog with a larger diameter (40–45 teeth), which turned very slowly but with greater force and transmitted the rotation to another gear of small diameter, which in turn moved the rack, which

*Crests. Detail from a painting by Paolo Uccello,* Niccolò da Tolentino at the Battle of San Romano, *Italy, 15th century. National Gallery, London.*

was provided with a grapple for the bowstring. At the other end the rack had a belt hook. Beneath the gearbox was an eyelet for attaching a strong loop made of sinew and leather. To span the crossbow it was necessary to fit the tiller in the loop, pushing it as far as the lugs on both sides of the tiller would permit. The handle was then turned, first moving the rack forward until the grapple caught the bowstring; when the direction was reversed, the grapple pulled the bowstring into the nock on the nut. When the direction was reversed once more, the grapple was released from the bowstring, and the stock was removed from the loop of the cranequin.

This mechanism was used in Germany, Switzerland, France, and England in the 15th to 17th centuries, particularly for drawing or spanning heavy hunting crossbows with a composite or metal bow.

**crest** An attachment to a helmet which remained in use from antiquity until well into the 16th century. Because it was designed only for identification and decoration, the crest was often made from perishable materials. Thus only a few examples have survived.

The crest was kept in place by various devices, including screws and nuts in later examples. Some crests made of fabric might have been useful in protecting the wearer's head from the heat of the sun. From the Middle Ages, decorative devices and heraldic symbols were combined in various fantastic figures, such as dragons, lions, eagles, and other animals, that represented the armorial bearings of the wearer or of his overlord. Sometimes, however, there was no particular significance in such things as antlers, the horns of a bull, brightly colored feathers, etc., except to make the wearers more impressive and to instill fear in their adversaries.

The crest was usually screwed into the crest holder on the skull. But in some early examples a figure made of molded and painted leather (*cuir-bouilli*) was mounted on a leather cap and attached to the helm by laces. The lower part of the crest frequently ended in a flowing cloth called mantling.

During the 14th century much lighter crests, made of feathers, cloth, and so on, were introduced. The only record that we have of them today is in works of art. Such crests were mainly used in various courses and tournaments. In the 15th century most crests were very high and complex. They were kept upright by a kind of flagpole that was inserted in the top of the helm and was either fastened with screws or with a spring-loaded catch.

In the early 16th century, crests were worn only in tournaments and processions. They were soon relegated to heraldic usage, superseded by plumes that were colorful as well as elegant.

**crinet** An important component of full BARD, light horse armor, and armored caparison protecting the horse's neck. In the full bard, it was comprised of two combinations of lames that were articulated on loose rivets, one covering the crest and the mane and the other covering the neck below, connecting to the PEYTRAL. Hinged together on one side, they were closed on the other with either pierced studs and hooks or with turning pins and keyhole slots. The crinet was fixed to the neck lame at the top of the SHAFFRON, usually by means of a stud and slot.

In light horse armor, only the upper lames of the crinet were used, covering the crest and mane. The crinet was held in place by two or three laminated straps fastened around the neck. A similar form of neck guard was used in armoured caparisons, except that overlapping leather pieces reinforced with metal were substituted for full metal lames.

**crossbow** A stringed projectile weapon consisting of a bow mounted crosswise by means of a system of cord or gut bindings or by a metal bridle at the end of a wooden shaft called the tiller. On the tiller, at the correct distance from the bow, a shaped disc called the nut was mounted with its axis across the stock. The nut was usually made of bone and was grooved on the upper surface to hold the string and to serve as a runner for the bolt. Another notch, on the lower face of the disc, in which the tooth of the sear or the release lever was placed, either stopped the nut from turning or allowed it to turn. In many types of crossbows,

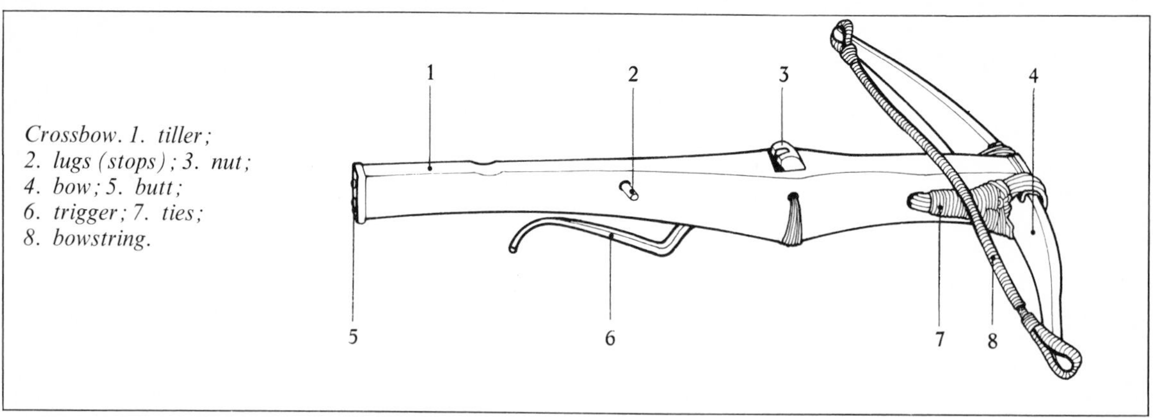


*Crossbow. 1. tiller; 2. lugs (stops); 3. nut; 4. bow; 5. butt; 6. trigger; 7. ties; 8. bowstring.*

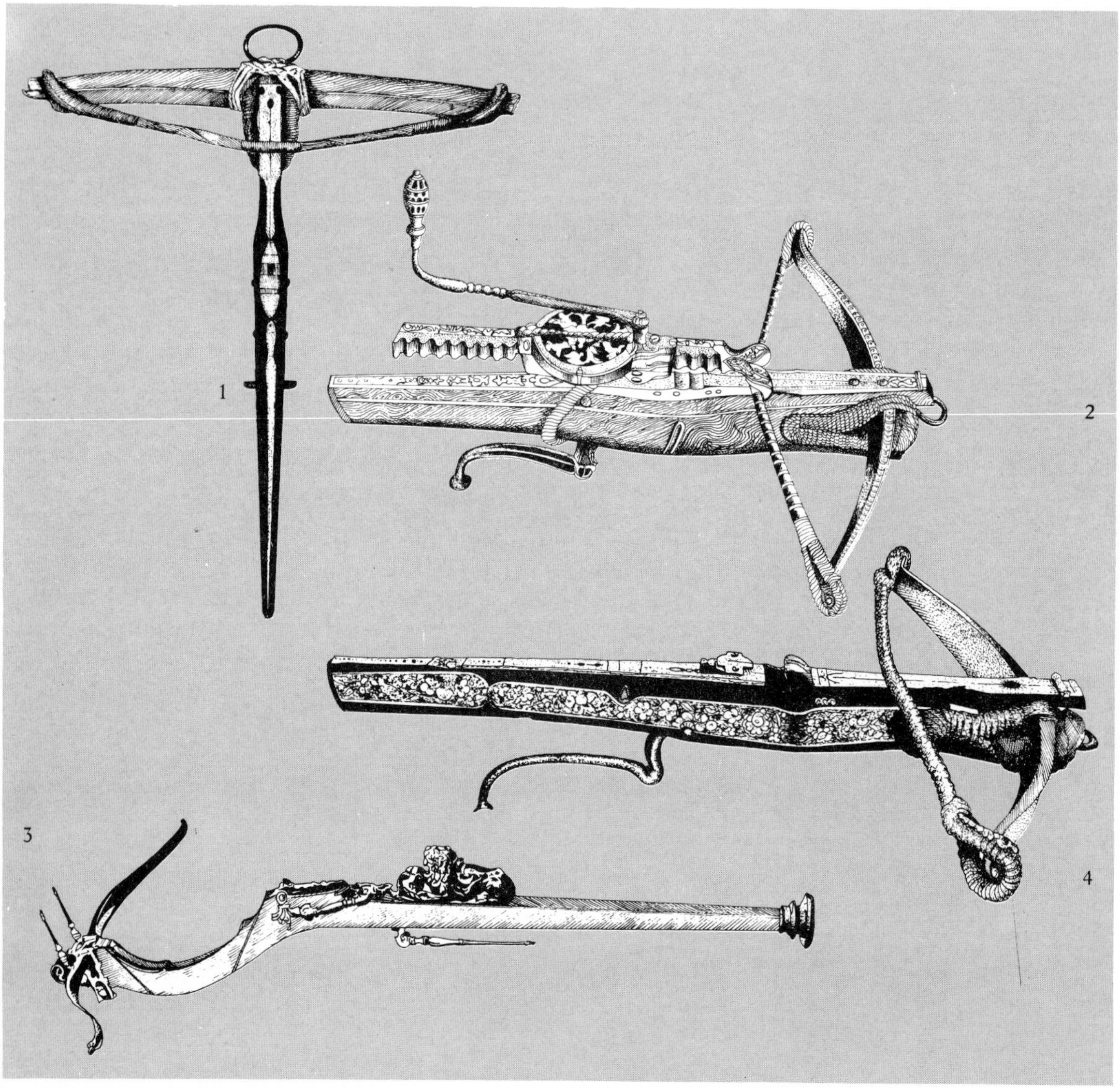

*1. Lever crossbow, Europe, second half of the 15th century. Odescalchi Collection, Museo di Palazzo Venezia, Rome.*
*2. Crossbow with cranequin, half-cocked, Germany, 16th century. 3. Pellet crossbow, central Italy (Florence), c. 1600.*
*4. Cranequin crossbow, Germany, 17th century.* ***Museo Stibbert, Florence.***

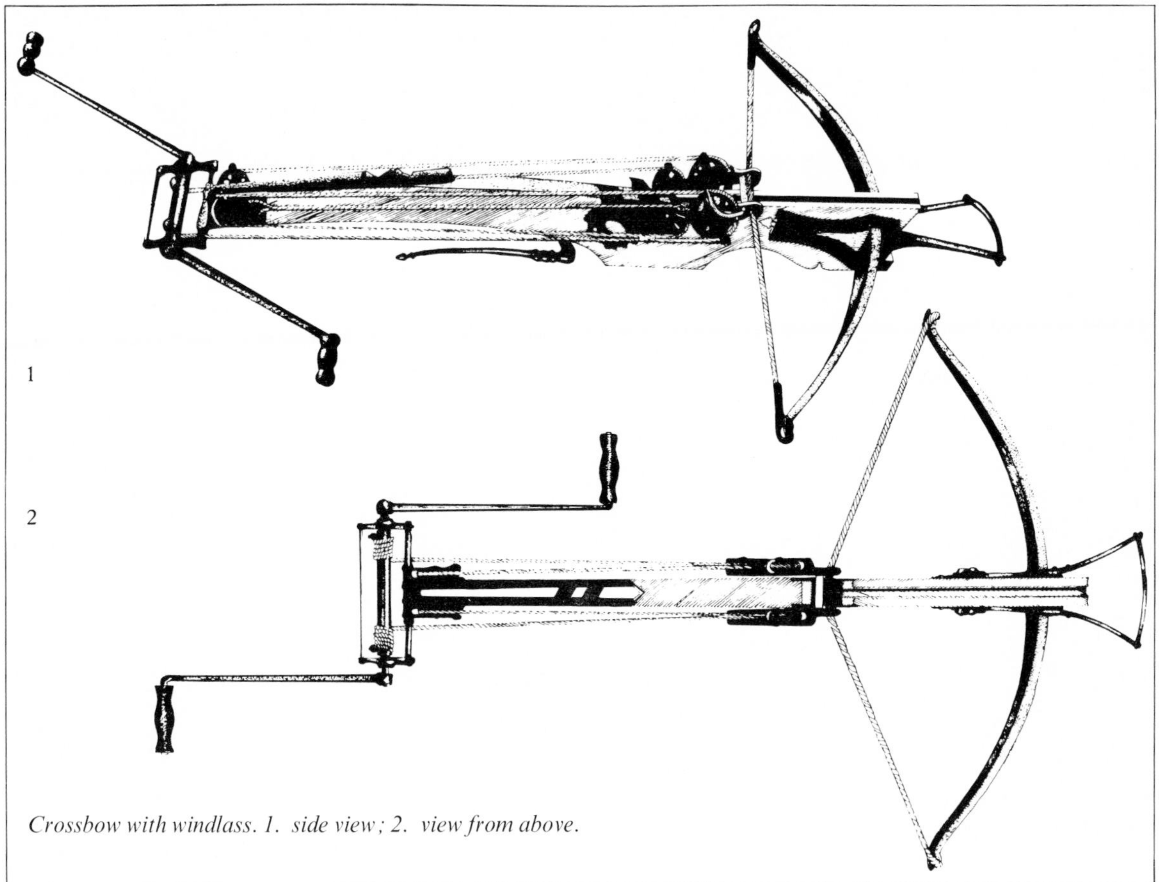


*Crossbow with windlass. 1. side view; 2. view from above.*

there were two transverse lugs behind the nut, protruding from both sides of the stock. They served as catches for the spanning mechanism of the lever or CRANEQUIN.

The crossbow was commonly used for hunting as early as the 4th century A.D., and there is evidence of its use in war in Europe before the year 1000. In the 11th century there is evidence of its use in England, probably introduced by the Normans, but it appeared considerably later (14th–15th centuries) in Scotland and Ireland.

Until the 16th century, units of mercenary crossbowmen (the Gascons and the Genoese were at the top of the league), were hired from time to time by princes and rulers. Although the crossbow continued to be used in European wars until almost the end of the 15th century, the longbow gained in popularity in England, and longbowmen acquitted themselves well at the battles of Crécy (1346) and Agincourt (1415). Whereas the crossbow was more powerful and its arrow (bolt) was heavier, and could be used in cramped positions, the longbow acted faster and could shoot a larger number of arrows, thus producing a more pernicious psychological impact on the enemy. Nevertheless the use of the crossbow by English foot soldiers and mounted soldiers was not discontinued altogether during the 14th and 15th centuries.

In every army in Europe crossbowmen were considered an elite corps, and as such they occupied the central position in battle formations. Membership in this corps was regarded so highly that in Spain the crossbowman was ranked on a par with the cavalryman; the rank of the commanding officer of a crossbowman corps was one of the loftiest positions in the military.

The use of the crossbow in war often provoked much heated debate, particularly in the 12th century, as can be seen from the prohibition of its use except against infidels, a proscription ratified by the Second Lateran Council of 1139. The church's decision led to the banning of the crossbow in Germany.

In the first half of the 16th century, the wartime use of the crossbow waned and was eventually discontinued throughout Europe; but it remained in use, at least until the first half of the 17th century, in Italy, France, and Spain for hunting large or dangerous animals such as wolves, bears, and stags; in this same period stone and bullet crossbows were used to hunt small animals and wildfowl; later on, this type of crossbow was used for poaching and sporting purposes, particularly in northern Germany, Belgium, England, and Switzerland.

*Technical Data*

The bow of the earliest crossbows was made from a block of hard wood, usually ash or yew. The string was pulled to the nut with no more than the bowman's strength: his feet, placed on either side of the stock, held the bow pressed to the ground while his hands drew the bow and pulled the string. To protect the bindings of the bow, which otherwise would have been in contact with the ground, the front end of the crossbow was usually fitted with a stirrup (a foot strap), originally made of wood and later of metal, large enough to take one or both feet, which held the crossbow in place and enabled the bowman to draw it. In many 13th- and 14th-century military writings, a distinction in terminology was made between the one-foot and the two-foot crossbow. The terminology indicated the dimensions of the crossbow: two-foot crossbows used two-foot bolts.

In their battles against the Saracens, beginning in the 12th century, the Crusaders became acquainted with the composite-bow crossbow and before long made this model popular on the Continent. (After a certain amount of use, the hardwood bow became deformed, fragile, and more important, inferior to the bow of Islamic origin.) This type of bow was made with layers of different materials—wood, horn, and sinew glued and tightly bound with animal tendons (preferably the neck nerve of an ox or a horse), then covered with leather or parchment. Despite its size, this crossbow was quite light, flexible, and powerful, and turned out to be the most efficient individual missile weapon until the development of the longbow or the metal-bow crossbow. The term "horn bow" referred to the material that made up the composite bow. The term was used to distinguish the composite bow from models with wooden and steel bows. (The steel bow was used from the early 14th century onwards; it eventually replaced the less costly but no less powerful composite bow.)

The problems involved in mounting the bowstring of the crossbow were the same as those encountered with the bow, but the crossbow required much greater efforts in order to mount a string on a bow with a smaller radius. The back and sides of wooden and composite bows had a nock on the tips, and with the appearance of the steel bow in the 14th century, it became possible to make two small, forward-turned tips at the ends of the bow to which the string could be attached.

A man's strength was sufficient to bend and draw the wooden bow; but when the much more powerful composite and steel bows were adopted, drawing mechanisms had to be developed. Many designs were created and tested. The various crossbows that were developed were called after their respective spanning devices: for example, claw and belt, goat's-foot lever, cranequin, windlass. The claw was a metal forked hook attached to a strong belt. The archer held the crossbow in place on the ground by placing his foot in the foot strap: by kneeling down, he placed the claw over the string, then he drew the bow by standing upright. To reduce the effort, a hook with a pully was used: one end of a cord was placed in the archer's belt; the other end was placed on the tiller; the claw was fixed to the pulley; by standing up the archer expended only half the usual force required to trigger the loading operation. The hook system was also used on horseback by archers who positioned the hook on their chest.

The lever-drawing system offered the greatest number of variations. The earliest lever might have been the push type: a wooden rod, fitted with a pivoted flat piece, was mounted on the front of the tiller, and the ends of the hinged pusher were positioned on the string; by pressing the rod, the pusher drove the string into the nut. In pull-type levers, a pivoted arm with a claw slid and pulled the string with the help of a long lever with curved prongs fixed over the rests in the tiller behind the nut. In less common types, the lever could be adapted for use on foot or on horseback. Instead of the handle, a large, flat knob was placed against the chest, or a curved, hollow base was placed against the leg; in these types, the stock of the crossbow was used as a lever.

More common north of the Alps, particularly in Switzerland, Austria, and Germany, was the cranequin (rack), which was well suited to the shape of the stock of the hunting crossbow used in the region. The mechanism contained reduction cogs controlled by a long crank and moving a toothed rod (rack) with a double hook; the housing had an eye with a strong loop. The tiller was fitted into this loop, which was stopped by two rests protruding from the sides of the stock; turning the crank moved the rack forward until the hooks caught the string. Drawing was done by reversing the direction of the crank.

The windlass mechanism consisted of a box in which the butt of the tiller was placed and on which was mounted a winding drum with a pair of pulleys controlled by two opposing cranks with handles. Another pair of pulleys with a double hook was connected to the drum by a system of cords. Turning the handles unwound the cords from the drum until the hook caught the bowstring; drawing required reversing the direction of the drum rotation.

*Light crossbow.* A small crossbow often made with a steel tiller. Because it could be easily concealed, the light crossbow was considered an underhanded weapon and was banned from time to time during the latter half of the 16th century. In the 17th and 18th centuries, similar prohibitions were applied to the arquebus and other portable firearms. These light crossbows were designed for shooting small bolts; many of them had a reloading mechanism in the tiller. Inside was a bar with screw threading ending at the front with the nut and trigger mechanism. This bar emerged from the butt, where there was a wing nut. Turning the wing nut moved the bar forward until the bowstring was caught in the nut; reversing the turns of the wing nut moved the bar backward, thus drawing the weapon.

*Stone and bullet crossbow.* A small crossbow designed in Italy in the first half of the 16th century for hunting wildfowl; it had a steel bow with a double string at the center of which was a pouch in which the projectile—usually a pebble, a bullet, or a pellet of baked clay—was placed. Because this model had a light bow, it could easily be spanned with the archer's hands, but a lever was often used. These crossbows were usually identified at first glance because of their features: the particular shape of the tiller, which curved downward between the nut and the bow; a sighting fork in the middle of the bow, and a knob at the butt. This knob was placed against the chest in order

*Various methods of drawing the crossbow. 1. From Manuscript 2813 in the Bibliothèque Nationale, Paris, c. 1370. 2. From Viollet-Le-Duc,* Dictionnaire raisonné du mobilier français *(Paris, 1875). 3. From a painting by Antonio del Pollaiolo, c. 1475. 4. From a painting by Hans Holbein the Elder, c. 1515.*

to load the crossbow by hand. In Germany this type of crossbow was popular in the 17th century, and a type of crossbow combining a metal tiller and a short wooden butt was subsequently developed. Each of these crossbows usually incorporated a goat's-foot-lever drawing mechanism. The form of the butt was greatly influenced by the shape of contemporary firearms and often reflected their lines. The stone crossbow lacked a discoidal nut; to hold the spanning ring in the bowstring a simple hook, originally controlled by a handle and subsequently by a trigger, was used. Bullet crossbows were used in England, especially in the northern counties, for target shooting until the 19th century.

**cross guard** A part of the furniture of edged weapons, positioned crosswise to the blade and the grip. As the simplest form of guard, it has been known since antiquity. In some swords of the 16th to 18th centuries, cross guards were extended forward and backward to form the fore and rear QUILLONS. Cross guards can also be seen on some staff weapons, on which they served the same purpose of protecting the hand.

**crupper** A part of the leather harness for a horse's hindquarters, it consisted of a combination of straps used in conjunction with the back strap and the BREECHING.

The same name was applied to the part of the BARD designed to protect a horse's hindquarters and, to a certain extent, its hind legs. In its complete form, the crupper was comprised of three heavy, oblong plates: one was keeled and shaped to the top of the horse's rump, ending in the TAIL GUARD; the other two plates were riveted to the top plate and hung down on each side to form a kind of "flounce" all around the hindquarters. In light horse armor, armored caparison, and harness, the crupper consisted of several harness straps, often armored, which usually included the crupper or back strap, which ran along the spine to the tail guard; the breeching, which hung horizontally below the root of the tail and linked the two sides of the crupper; and the loin straps, which linked the crupper strap to the breeching on each side.

**cuff** The part of the GAUNTLET that protected the wrist and, indirectly, part of the forearm. The only closed plate on the whole gauntlet, it was riveted under the upper lames and was fitted over the front end of the lower cannon of the VAMBRACE.

In its oldest recorded form, dating to the early part of the 14th century, the cuff flared out like a motorcyclist's cuff of today. In the gauntlet of around 1350, however, the cuff was considerably shorter and was almost bell-shaped. By the beginning of the next century, the cuff, although retaining its bell-like form, had become longer and its top edge had been cut away at a sharp angle to form a point. Several variations of this pointed upper edge were adopted during the first half of the 15th century, and from the beginning of the 16th century, wrist shaping became more pronounced. A typical feature of this period was roped edges, with or without a double sunken border.

In addition to those mentioned, there were several specific variations of the cuff to suit specialized types of gauntlets, and in the second half of the 16th century, the elbow-length cuff was introduced. It was secured to the COWTER by a turning pin and replaced the lower cannon. When worn with a buff coat, it was attached to a button on the sleeve. A special reinforcing cuff was worn on the right hand with the armor for the German course (*Rennen*).

**cuirass** The part of ARMOR, or sometimes an independent defense, that protected the torso. The term derived from Latin *corius*, meaning "hide" or "leather," and was first recorded in 12th-century texts as *cuirie* (French *cuir*), indicating the kind of material widely used in the past for this protective equipment. Cuirasses made of hide or of several layers of rhinoceros skin were worn in China from at least the 11th century B.C., and hide and hardened leather (*cuir-bouilli*) were used for making cuirasses well into the medieval period in both the East and West.

The earliest protection for the trunk was made of many layers of linen sewn together. Such cuirasses were worn, for example, by Mycenaean warriors in the 16th century B.C. and by Persian soldiers in the 5th century B.C. Another style of cuirass was comprised of cloth or leather covered with sewn or riveted scales of horn, hide, metal, or other resistant material. Scale cuirasses were used in Egypt in the 17th century B.C. and later in ancient Greece and Rome. A variation of this construction had scales inside layers of cloth; it was known in China in the 8th century B.C. and was used in Europe until the 17th century in the body defense known as the BRIGANDINE.

The full metal cuirass was known to Mycenaean soldiers from about the middle of the second millennium B.C., as bronze pieces found during excavations at Dendra, near Tírins, have shown. These pieces must have formed part of a metal cuirass, complete with BREASTPLATES and BACKPLATES, PAULDRONS, and a kind of skirt made of metal hoops to protect the abdomen. The warrior's defense might have been completed by a helmet and short GREAVES. The archaic Greek cuirass was known as "bell shaped" because of the contour of its lower edge. It was formed from two pieces of bronze, slightly flared toward the lower edge and fastened at the sides and the shoulders by hooks, leather straps, and buckles or hinges. From about the 7th century B.C., the front and the back pieces began to be shaped to the contours of the trunk muscles. This *thórax stàdios*—the "muscled cuirass" of classical Greece—became a type of "Roman" armor borrowed from the Etruscans. The *thórax* is known to us today almost exclusively through sculptures and vase paintings. It was sometimes decorated with incised or inlaid work of stylized polychromatic designs and emphasized anatomical features.

In addition to the metal thórax stàdios, another type of cuirass, the *thórax pholidotós*, which consisted of leather breastplates and backplates often reinforced with overlapping metal scales, was used in Greece. A kind of leather apron was frequently suspended from the bottom of the thorax to protect the abdomen. However, this apron impeded movement to such an extent that it was soon replaced by a short skirt made of leather strips (Greek *ptéryges*) sometimes reinforced with metal discs.

In pre-Roman Italy, various types of protection for the trunk were used. One of the most common was the *kardiophylox*, a roughly triangular pectoral made up of three discs. The pectoral was joined to a similar type of back defense by means of shoulder straps and side-protecting laminations. This cuirass was probably worn over a leather or cloth garment. In addition to this type, which was used extensively in southern Italy, square, trapezoidal, and rectangular pectorals were in use throughout the italic regions.

The Etruscans adopted both the leather and metal types of Greek "anatomical" cuirass. They also used scaled and laminated cuirasses, probably beginning in the first half of the 4th century B.C. A particularly interesting representation of a cuirass from that period can be seen in Todi, about 25 miles south of Perugia, in the famous bronze sculpture of a warrior—generally known as Mars—dating from about 380–370 B.C. His cuirass consists of overlapping horizontal bands formed of metal lames placed side by side and probably sewn onto a leather support. The design of this cuirass made provision for large pauldrons to be buttoned onto the breast.

In the early centuries of imperial Roman history, the design of armor was strongly influenced by the Italic-Etruscans. The legionnaire's "segmented" cuirass was of cylindrical form and was comprised of seven horizontal hoops of steel, with openings in the front and back where the two halves of the cuirass were laced together. The cuirass was completed by a system of overlapping lames protecting the upper part of the body and the shoulders. The Roman and, later, Byzantine officers' cuirass was made of bronze or steel embossed to conform to torso muscles like its prototype, the greek thorax. A lighter and more flexible type of officer's cuirass was made of mail covered with bronze scales linked to mail rings.

Beginning in the late 12th century, leather cuirasses were often reinforced with overlapping metal plates that greatly increased the protective properties of the cuirass without impeding mobility. This type of trunk defense, usually called the COAT OF PLATES, was used throughout the next two centuries, but gradual modifications in its design, which began in about the mid-1300s, constituted important stages in the development of full armor composed of large steel plates. One such plate, which was enlarged as time passed, replaced the multiplate construction of the cuirass breast. This piece—the breastplate—was soon supplemented by the backplate. A laminated skirt, composed of steel hoops, was attached to the lower edges of both parts of the cuirass.

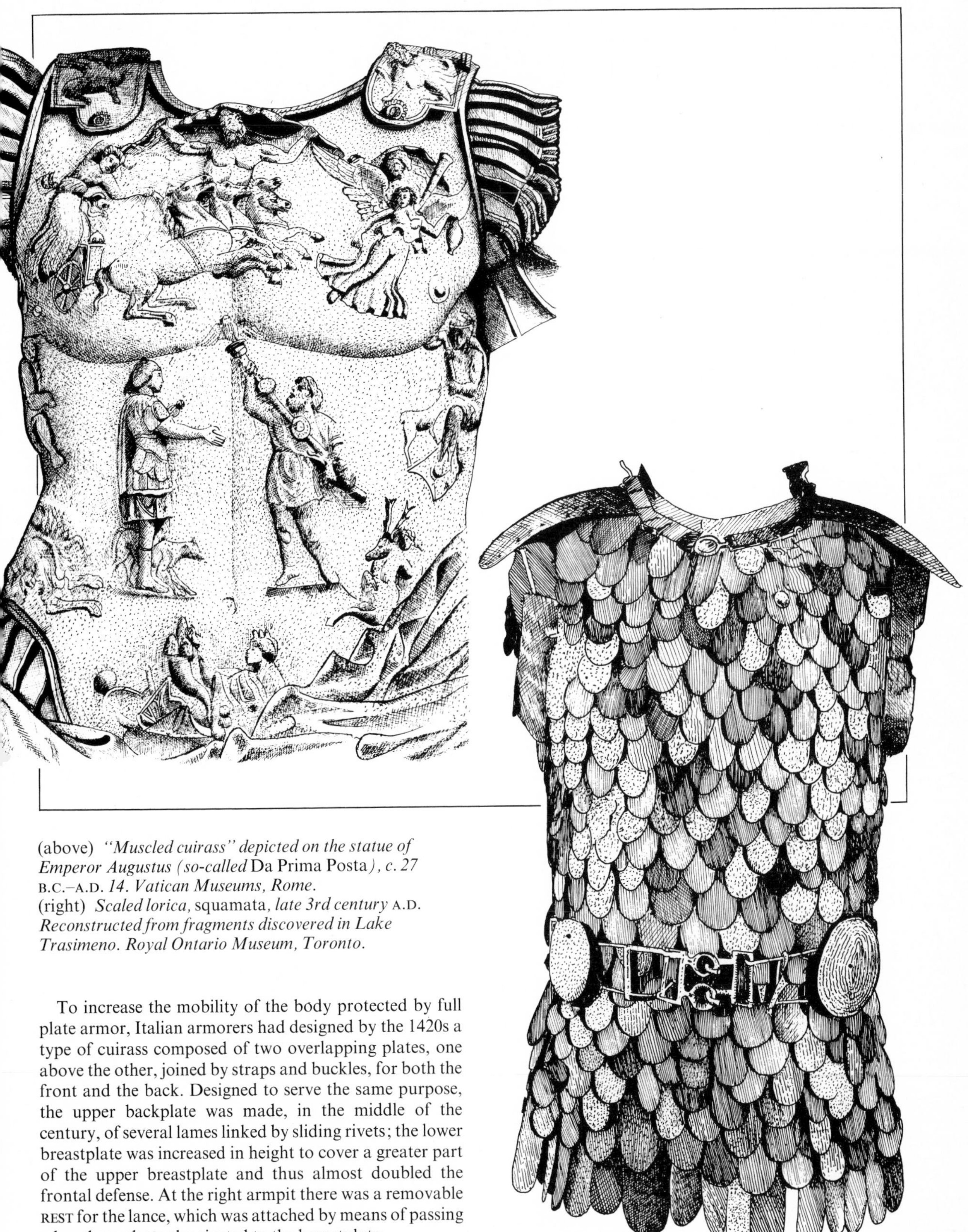

(above) *"Muscled cuirass" depicted on the statue of Emperor Augustus (so-called* Da Prima Posta*), c. 27* B.C.–A.D. *14. Vatican Museums, Rome.*
(right) *Scaled lorica,* squamata, *late 3rd century* A.D. *Reconstructed from fragments discovered in Lake Trasimeno. Royal Ontario Museum, Toronto.*

To increase the mobility of the body protected by full plate armor, Italian armorers had designed by the 1420s a type of cuirass composed of two overlapping plates, one above the other, joined by straps and buckles, for both the front and the back. Designed to serve the same purpose, the upper backplate was made, in the middle of the century, of several lames linked by sliding rivets; the lower breastplate was increased in height to cover a greater part of the upper breastplate and thus almost doubled the frontal defense. At the right armpit there was a removable REST for the lance, which was attached by means of passing a bar through staples riveted to the breastplate.

A peculiar form of cuirass was used between 1420 and

1460 in some German armor. Called the *Kastenbrust* ("box breast"), this cuirass, unlike the rounded Italian form, had angular contours. Its flat front formed an edge with a slope toward the waist. The lance rest on this and later types of German cuirasses was permanently riveted to the breastplate but was usually hinged so that it could be folded when not in use. In the second half of the 15th century, most cuirasses in Italy and in Germany were made with a two-piece breastplate, and the backplate was comprised of several large lames joined by hinges and sliding rivets. The front and the back of a cuirass were usually connected on the top and the sides with leather straps and buckles, but from the late 15th century the side fastenings were gradually replaced by a strong waist belt buckled in front after the edges of the backplate were inserted in those of the breastplate. There was a marked stylistic difference between the Italian and German cuirasses and consequently between the respective suits of armor. The Italian cuirass had a smooth globular breastplate, whereas the German cuirass was shaped to the natural contours of the body, with a slender waistline, and on the surfaces of its front and back were sprays of curved grooves that enhanced the gracefulness of the armor. The turns on the neck edge and at the armpits, capable of deterring edged weapons, were features of all cuirasses.

In the early 16th century, the one-piece construction for the breast and the back of a cuirass was reintroduced by most European armorers. Whereas Italian cuirasses preserved an even surface, sometimes decorated with bands of etched ornament, German cuirasses as well as other parts of armor had multiple fluting, the grooves being spread uniformly or grouped in radiating strips. By 1540 the rounded breastplate was replaced by a different shape, with a median ridge forming a pronounced apex about halfway between the low, straight neck edge and the waist lame. In about 1560 this cusp was forged closer to the waist, and by the last quarter of the century it had evolved into a boss over the waist. This fashionable form of the cuirass followed the somewhat grotesque shape of the civilian peascod doublet, which served a practical purpose when adapted to the cuirass: the "cod" contributed to the rigidity of the breastplate and held the waist belt in position. A variation of the peascod form was the so-called waistcoat cuirass, which consisted of two halves hinged to the median strip at the back and fastened at the front with pierced studs locked by hooks; to enhance the imitation, the frontal joint was usually decorated with false buttons. Another form of cuirass that had been developing since the 1530s had an oblong breastplate with an almost flat front surface.

Beginning in 1500, the cuirass started to play an increasingly independent role, often being worn by foot soldiers and officers as the main defensive piece, supplemented only by long tassets, a mail cap, and a helmet. In the latter part of the century, infantry and light cavalry wore light cuirasses with tassets and an assortment of other pieces, which always included a gorget and a light helmet. In the next century, as it became the most essential part of the heavy cavalry's defensive equipment, the cuirass gave its name to that branch of the cavalry, which came to be called the cuirassiers. After c. 1600 the form of the cuirass changed again. It was shortened to accommodate the high waistline, which curved symmetrically downward to form a cusp in the center,

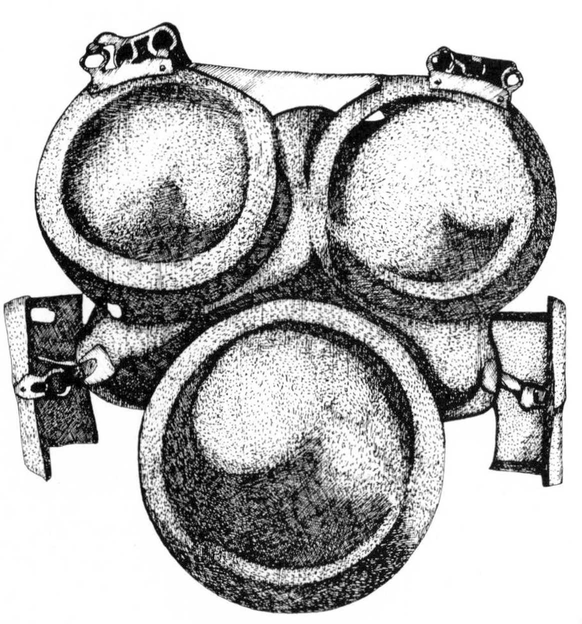

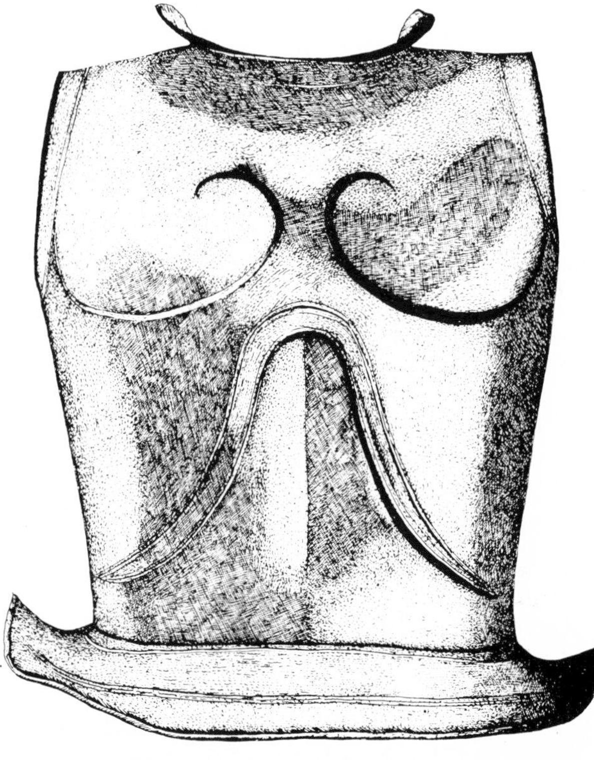

(left) *Samnite cuirass. Museo Preistorico Etnografico L. Pigorini, Rome.* (right) *Greek bronze cuirass, first half of the 6th century* B.C.

where it met the median ridge of the breastplate. The lower edge of the cuirass was forged into a flange for attaching waist lames with tassets and a large laminated rump guard.

To counter the growing power of firearms, attempts were made to reinforce the cuirass by using thicker steel plates and by attaching a second heavy plate, the PLACATE, over the breastplate. Such bulletproof cuirasses usually had a depression in the front resulting from the firing of either a pistol or a musket in experiments conducted to test the effectiveness of the plates. By the end of the 17th century, pikemen and their armor no longer played a part in military life; the cuirass remained in use only in so-called siege armor (worn mostly by sappers and commanders in dangerous locations) and as protective equipment worn by cuirassiers. Although sometimes they wore only a breastplate in the 18th century, many European armies retained the full steel cuirass well into the 19th century because it provided an effective defense against the sword and the lance and offered some protection against the bullet. As part of full-dress and combat uniforms, the cuirass was worn by some heavy-cavalry regiments until the First World War, but for ceremonial occasions it was usually made of a light alloy (e.g., tombac), sometimes enhanced by silvering or gilding. Certain elite military units—for instance, the Life Guards and the Royal Horse Guards in Britain—still wear cuirasses on formal occasions. The two world wars revived interest in helmets and cuirasses that could protect the wearer against modern firearms. As a result of numerous experiments with modern steels and plastics, bulletproof breastplates and vests, descendants of plate armor, are now in use.

**cuisse** The upper part of the LEGHARNESS worn by mounted troops and men-at-arms as a thigh defense, usually riveted to the POLEYN. Plate cuisses were introduced during the 14th century, replacing the CHAUSSES or mail hose and the quilted thigh defenses with attached poleyns that had been worn over them. The cuisse was sometimes ribbed and protected only the front of the thigh (open or half cuisse). The top edge, which was either straight or slightly concave, was reinforced with a turn of the edge and pierced with holes for lacing to the coat of mail. The main lame was fitted with two buckles and straps fastened around the leg, and the lower edge was overlapped by the top of the poleyn. In the early 15th century Italian armorers developed cuisses of a more sophisticated design. Cuisses were finished at the top with a riveted extension lame whose upper, convex edge went under the mail shirt. Toward the middle of the century, this lame had a crescent-shaped form; its upper edge being bordered by a turn. Sometimes this terminal lame was fastened around the leg with a buckle and strap, but this method of attachment was soon replaced by a suspension tab—a strip of leather riveted to the upper lame, to which a lace was attached and then fastened to the girdle.

The main lame was reinforced by a central ridge. By the early 15th century, an extension plate had been hinged to the outside edge of the cuisse to give protection to the side of the thigh. Toward the middle of the century, two or three more lames were added to each cuisse for the same purpose. Generally asymmetrical and trapezoidal, the side plates tended to close the back of the leg, anticipating the closed cuisse that was to follow. There was little change in this style during the first half of the 16th century except that the system of fastening varied from time to time.

In the second half of the 15th century, the side plates were extended around the thigh and were joined at the back. This development led to the evolution of the full cuisse in the beginning of the 16th century. This form consisted of two curved lames that were almost symmetrical. The lames were hinged at one side and were closed with a projecting rivet and a slot on the other, thus encircling the entire thigh. The full cuisse never superseded the open cuisse, however, both were used concurrently.

During the 16th century, more lames were used in the construction of the cuisse in order to make it more flexible. Although all lames were articulated on loose rivets, the lower lame was positioned over the others and under the first lame of the poleyn. A relatively rare variation, which had been developed by the beginning of the century, consisted of an arrangement of several small articulated slats, which replaced the back lame of the full cuisse and covered the flexor muscle of the leg; it was similar to the construction of the later closed form of the VAMBRACE. This variant seems to have been particularly favored in armor for foot combat.

In the 17th century, cuirass armor still included leg defenses, but it had been reduced to a lobster-tail cuisses, which consisted of a system of articulated lames curving around the leg. This type of cuisse was an alternative to and served the same purpose as long lobster-tail TASSETS.

**culet** *See* RUMP GUARD.

**culverin** (from Latin *coluter*, "snake") A term used in the 15th to 17th centuries for pieces of ARTILLERY that had the

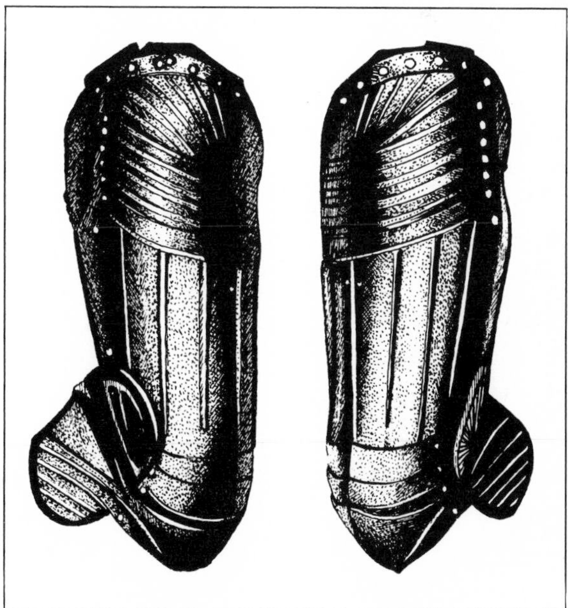

*Cuisses with poleyns, Italy, c. 1500–1510. Wallace Collection, London.*

same caliber and fired the same shot as cannon, but were one-quarter to one-third longer.

**cup guard** A hemispherical guard developed by the middle of the 17th century from large shell guards. An excellent protection for the hand, it was widely used, particularly in Italian and Spanish swords, as late as the 19th century. The cup guard was then adapted to the dueling sword and its sporting version, the ÉPÉE, which is still used today.

**curb chain** (or **curb strap**) One of the pieces of a BRIDLE, the curb chain was (and is today) attached by open hooks to the upper part of the BRANCHES on each side of the mouthpiece in order to rest in the chin groove of the horse's lower jaw. This control piece sometimes consisted of a light strap instead of a chain.

In some cases, especially when armored reins were used, the branches were 30 cm. (12 in.) or more in length; there were two curb chains and a lip strap. The pull of the reins on the lower end of the branches pivoted the mouthpiece and moved forward the upper part of the branches with the curb chain. The resultant pressure on the chin groove caused the horse to flex its lower jaw and to arch its head.

**cutting edge** The tapered cutting part of the blade of edged sidearms and of the head of staff weapons. The contour of this edge varied according to the use for which the weapon was designed.

**cutto** (from French *couteau-de-chasse*, "hunting knife") Another name for a hunting hanger or a short sword in use from the 17th to 19th centuries.

**cylinder** A steel rotating cylinder in which the charges or cartridges are loaded in a REVOLVER.

**czákan** *See* WAR HAMMER.

# D

**Dagger**

This heading describes the general typology of the short-bladed weapon and its historical development, particularly in the West, and some specific kinds of daggers. For other types, *see* BASELARD; BAYONET; BLADE; CINQUEDEA; DIRK; HILT; JAMBIYA; KNIFE; KRIS; KUKRI; PARRYING DAGGER; PONIARD; SAX; STYLET.

**dagger** A general term, used at least from the period of Middle English (c. 1050–1450), for edged weapons with a short, pointed blade and a handle. Similar names, all deriving from postclassical Latin *dagua*, were used in some other European languages. Such weapons probably originated as a result of using handheld spearheads as early as the Neolithic period. From those remote days we also have daggers made of reindeer bone, with a long, sharpened "blade" and the grip fashioned in the form of a leaping reindeer. Later the fragile bone was replaced by a tougher material, stone, even though this was harder to work. Of all the different types of rock available, flint was chosen because of its hardness and because it could be worked with softer tools. The pressure exercised on the block by a chisel made of bone or hardwood made it possible to chip or flake small splinters and slivers of desired shape. Flint points worked in this way were fitted into a short wooden handle, some of which had a broader end: the dagger was then ready. However, the weak spot in this weapon was the way in which parts were joined together: hence the need to make the whole weapon from a single block of stone. The stone daggers had a blade in the shape of a broad leaf and were usually very thick in the central section. The grip consisted of a straight extension, or a section that broadened out toward the end; when covered with a strip of hide it guaranteed a firm hold. Some stone daggers measured 30 cm. (12 in.) or so in length.

After copper and then bronze had been mastered, the dagger was still modeled on the stone forms already in existence. A plate of copper was fitted by means of a short heel into a slot cut in the grip; two or three copper rivets then secured the join. Another technique was to extend the blade at the base into a long tang which passed through the entire length of the grip and could be bent back at its top end. Just as the Stone Age produced daggers made in a single piece of stone, so in the Bronze Age similarly shaped weapons were also cast in a mold as one piece. This metal served to lengthen the blade: from blades measuring 10–20 cm. (4–8 in.), which was the normal length of a stone dagger, there was a fairly rapid increase to blades measuring 30 or 40 cm. (12–16 in.) and even longer. The

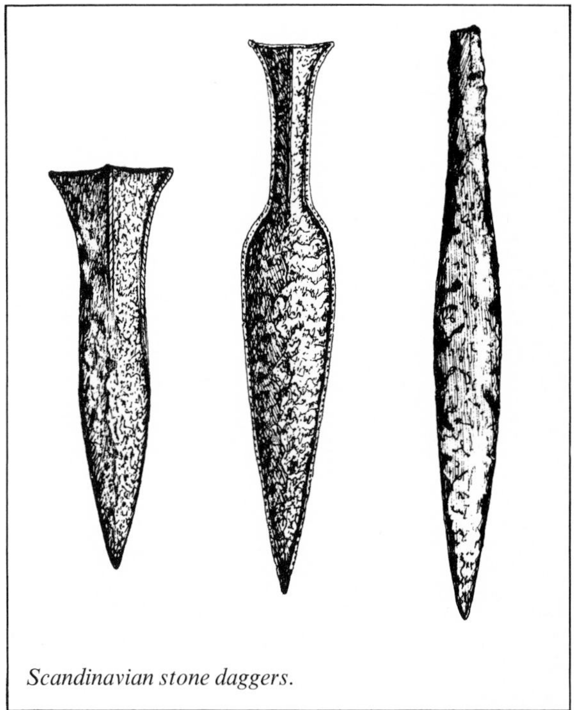

*Scandinavian stone daggers.*

length of the blade continued to increase, but when it exceeded 60 cm. (24 in.), a new type of weapon was created: this was not so much a long dagger but rather a short sword. And it was this weapon which caught the interest both of the craftsman who made and decorated it, and of the combatant who actually used it. The dagger, which had contributed so vitally to the inception of the sword, subsequently waned as a primary weapon and became a simple backup arm to the longer form.

The size of the dagger then decreased to around 30 cm. (12 in.); it remained in use as a weapon for hand-to-hand combat. Because it was often a delicate and elaborate object, it was protected by a special sheath made of leather, wood, or bronze. In many examples the more fragile parts of the dagger and sheath were further protected by bronze mounts.

In Roman times the dagger was not directly included in the weaponry of the foot soldier, who was armed with the short GLADIUS. Daggers, however, were used by the Teutonic peoples; they were armed with long, single-edged swords, and in combat at close quarters they found a short-bladed weapon particularly useful. During the period when the Western world came under the sway of the newly arrived "barbarians"—a development which gave birth to new national entities—it was the weapons of the conquerors which formed the basis from which the weaponry developed. The dagger used with the sword by the man-at-arms in the Carolingian period was a direct derivation of the Teutonic SAX, and was in turn the prototype of a varied typology of medieval daggers which were expressions of specific local cultures, particularly in the form of the grip and in the decorative techniques and designs used. For a long period, which overlaps the early part of the modern age, it was not so much the grip as the blade which constituted a common denominator in Europe (because the blade now had clearly defined special functions). And so it happened that daggers with blades fulfilling the same function were called by equivalent names in the various countries.

In order to pierce mail and protective leather pieces, it was necessary to have a solid blade with a strong point. North of the Alps the blade was mounted on a grip with discs or rondels; in the north of Europe the grip with a guard formed by two lobes was the commonest form; in Spain the "eared" hilt was the most popular. In the 16th century the various forms became standardized, while structural details of the blade, such as the form and proportion of the heel, the presence of ribbing and fullers, and the forms of the blade section, which were determined by local tradition, characterized the production of the various countries. The furniture also became more standardized: quillons of varying length, either straight or curved toward the blade; spindle-shaped grips and roundish pommels coming in various shapes—elongated, flattened, faceted—often matching the forms of the sword which the dagger went with. To a certain extent the proportions and the working and decorative techniques make it easier to single out the area of manufacture. This applies to weapons made for princes and noblemen, who were aware of changing fashions and ordered their

*Dagger with sheath from the Hallstatt period, 6th century* B.C. *Naturhistorisches Museum, Vienna.*

weapons from the swordmaker in accordance with the most up-to-date style. The attribution becomes more difficult with weapons made in places which, being subject to local traditions, produced and decorated arms on the basis of designs and methods developed in remote centers.

In the case of weapons of war, the movement of armies over the length and breadth of Europe spread the most commonplace forms and types of weapons. It was not until the formation of national armies, which laid down the bases of general regulations for armaments, that we find

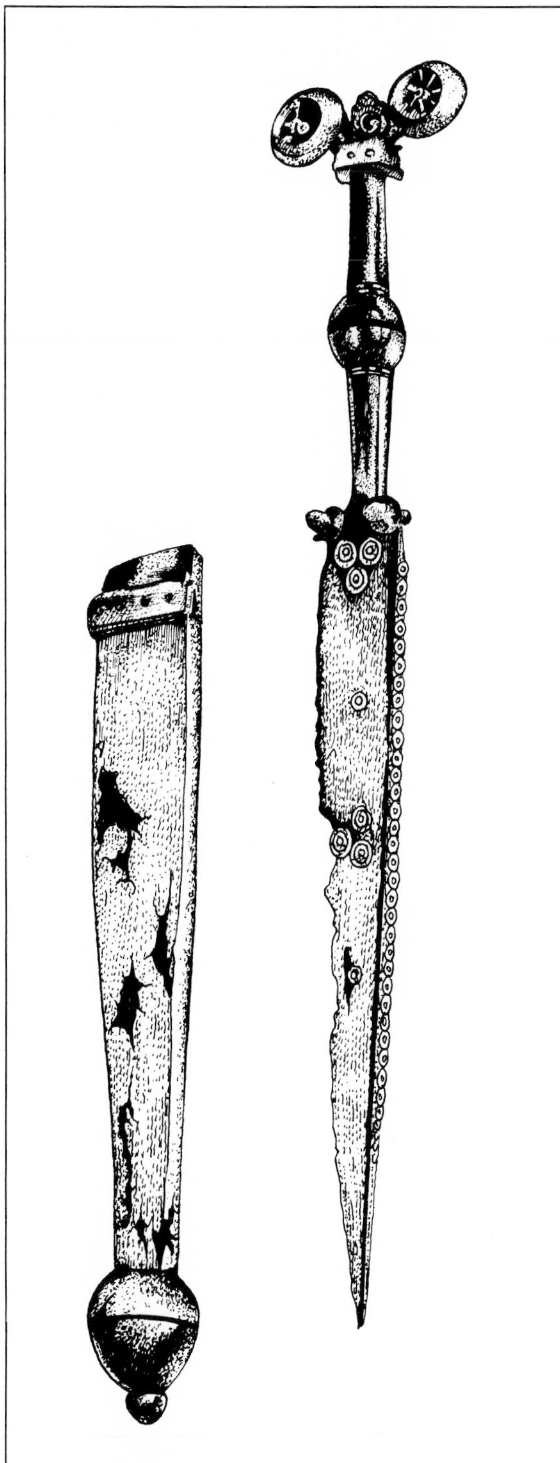

*Rondel dagger with sheath, Italy, c. 1500. Victoria and Albert Museum, London.*

fairly constant forms within the context of the same cultural group. In the 16th century, with the establishment of schools of fencing, which brought into use the dagger and sword combined, there was a new wave of forms for the dagger as complementary weapon. But before long the huge spread of firearms, the development of the sword, and the appearance of the bayonet caused the dagger's use to dwindle and then fade away from the battlefield and dueling ground.

The dagger remained part of military equipment only in certain specialized forms, such as the GUNNER'S STILETTO, but as a civilian weapon it gradually disappeared. It has remained, however, as an auxiliary weapon for hunting purposes, and as such it still exists. In present-day armies it is used sometimes as a form of the detachable bayonet, and in some cases the dagger is merely part of military uniform.

Some specific forms of daggers are described below.

*Roundel daggers.* These had the grip enclosed at either end by two identical, horizontal discs, fixed at right angles to the grip. In vogue as early as the 14th century, they remained in use until the early 16th century. The grip, a variant of the sword hilt, had a flat pommel set horizontally; this characteristic had already been used in bronze weapons. The earliest grips were cylindrical in shape; later, they became gradually broader in the uppermost section where they met the upper disc, while the lower disc serving as a guard was reduced in size. The blade was originally single-edged and later also had a reinforced tip: from the functional point of view this type of dagger would be more accurately described as a "mail breaker."

A later type, which was fairly common in Germany and appeared in various versions, had a triangular-sectioned, almost isosceles-shaped blade. This dagger, which was used throughout Europe, did not show any structural variations from place to place; the decorations and the type of blade help in situating it both historically and geographically.

*"Antennae" daggers.* This distinctive group of daggers had the upper end of the grip, the pommel, shaped either like antennae or like a ring (*anulus* in Latin, hence association with medieval term "anlace"). These daggers had a flat tang with the side pieces attached to it by rivets and short quillons which, when straight, were combined with a single-edged blade; the blade was double-edged if the quillons were slightly curved toward the blade. The "antennae" daggers appear in figurative depictions from the mid-13th century onward, and by the 14th century they were in common use throughout western Europe. The "ring" daggers, which were probably a final development of the antennae type, did not appear before the mid-14th century and were already going out of vogue by the end of that century. The presence of the ring is usually attributed to the securing of the dagger to the costume by means of a loop or strap, so as not to lose the weapon. Forerunners of these ring daggers go back to earliest times and crop up in far-flung parts of the world: knives with grips ending in a ring were a feature of the La Tène culture; swords with ringed pommels were in use in China in the second millennium B.C. Iconographic documentation, especially from the 14th century, shows warriors securing weapons to their armors with special chains, so as not to lose them in battle.

*Burgundian dagger.* Of particular interest to the collector,

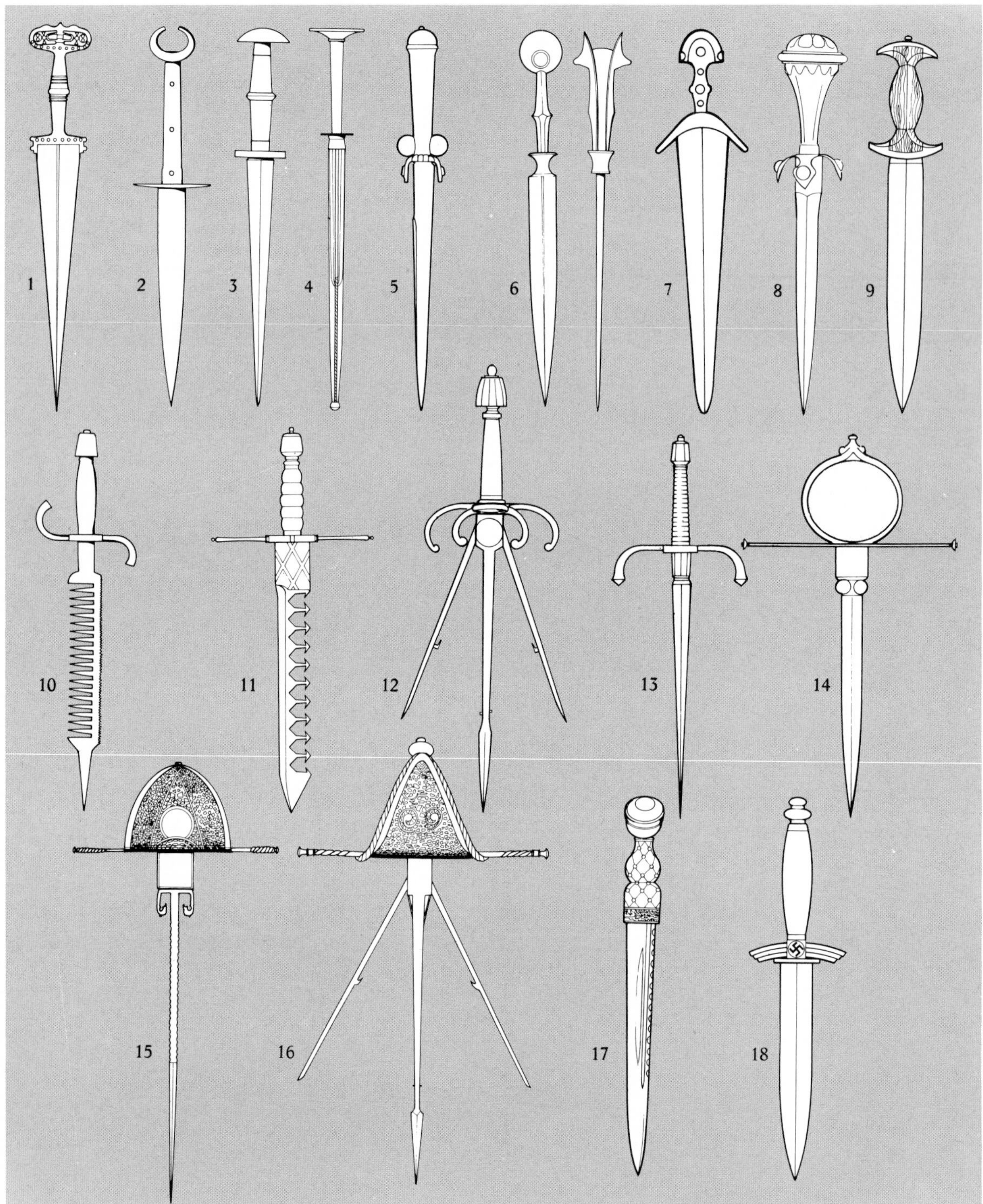


*Daggers. 1. Hallstatt culture, c. 6th century* B.C. *2. "Antennae" dagger, Europe, c. 1350–1400. 3. Roundel dagger, France, 15th century. 4. Roundel dagger, Germany, 16th century. 5. Ballock knife, second half of the 15th century. 6. "Eared" dagger, second half of the 15th century. 7. So-called cinquedea, Italy, late 15th–early 16th century. 8. Landsknecht dagger, Germany, second half of the 16th century. 9. Swiss dagger, second half of the 16th century. 10. Parrying dagger "sword-breaker", Germany, early 17th century. 11. Parrying dagger "sword-breaker", Italy, early 17th century. 12. Parrying dagger with triple blade, Europe, early 17th century. 13. Parrying dagger, Europe, early 17th century. 14. Parrying dagger, Spain, second half of the 17th century. 15. Parrying dagger, second half of the 17th century. 16. Parrying dagger with triple blade, Spain, mid-17th century. 17. Dirk, Scotland, late 19th century. 18. Nazi Luftwaffe dagger, Germany, 20th century.*

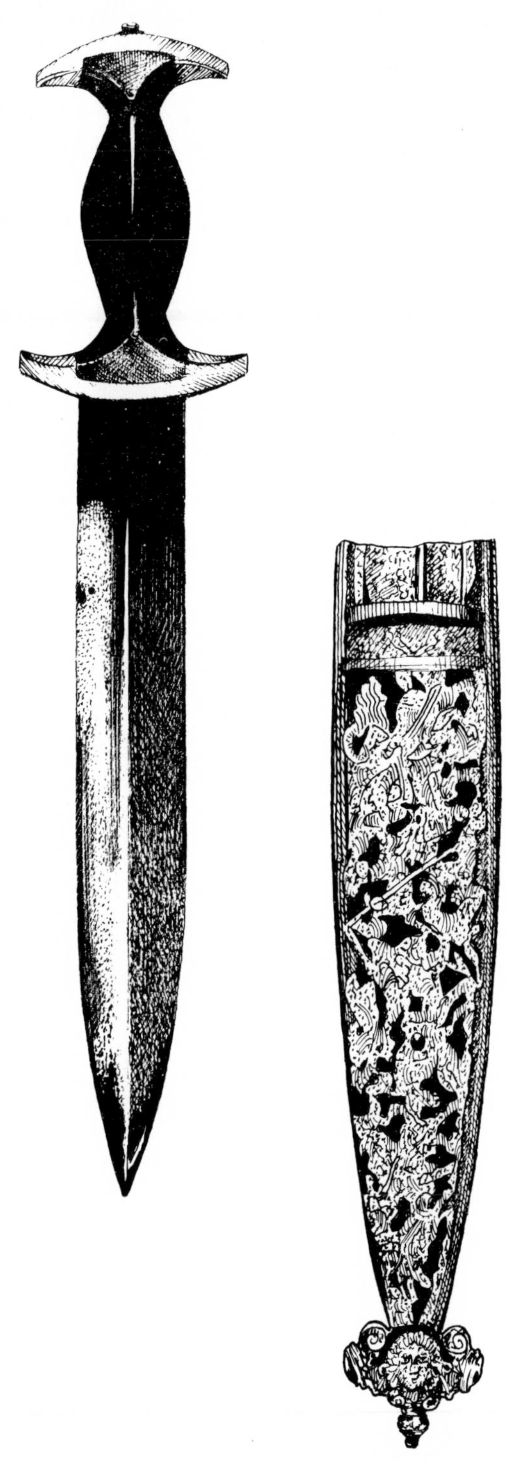

*Swiss dagger with sheath, Germany, c. 1555. Odescalchi Collection, Museo di Palazzo Venezia, Rome.*

this has a fairly large pommel, either four-sided, polygonal, or star-shaped, with rounded edges, and bear a raised emblem with heraldic designs. They usually have squared quillons curving slightly toward the blade, which is single-edged. In use during the first half of the 14th century, they seem to have been restricted to the Burgundian area. The working and decoration, together with the heraldic references, indicate that these daggers were carried solely by members of the aristocracy.

"Landsknecht" *dagger*. This weapon was carried by the rank and file. In the 16th century this type had a strong double-edged blade and a spiraled grip which flared toward the top, where it was surmounted by a button or large cap; the guard had a shell or side ring and two quillons, either straight or curving toward the blade; the sheath, usually made of metal, ended with a conspicuous chape and was often heavily ringed.

*Ballock knife* (*or kidney dagger*). This is the medieval term describing a dagger which has a grip bearing a considerable resemblance to a phallic symbol. From the 19th century it has been also called "kidney dagger." At the base of the grip there are two roundish, symmetrical globes, with the grip itself emerging upward between them and flaring slightly toward the top, sometimes surmounted by a cap. The narrow, strong blade was usually single-edged and often spurred or reinforced at the tip. It is depicted iconographically from the early 14th century onward as a weapon used by knights and soldiers but later also by citizens and country folk. It remained in vogue until the 17th century; in England and in the Netherlands it remained in use until the early 19th century, and it probably was a prototype of the Scottish DIRK.

*Eared dagger*. This term is commonly applied to a dagger with a grip which is usually slender and has, at the top, two parted, salient "ears"; at the bottom of the grip it had a small disc guard with a deep groove all around it. The stout, double-edged blade was asymmetrical at the heel, which was almost invariably longer on one side than on the other; its shape indicates that it was a thrusting weapon, and it may have been used as a mail-piercing weapon.

Of clearly Eastern origin, it reached Europe as a result of contacts with the Islamic world via Spain and Italy, where it was in vogue in the 14th and 15th centuries.

*Swiss dagger*. There existed in Switzerland as early as the 13th century a type of sword and dagger hilt with a pommel and guard which opened out into a crescent shape, thus enclosing the hand around the wooden grip. This type of guard does not seem to have been imitated in other countries.

In the 15th century and early part of the 16th, the Swiss-dagger sheath was of a conventional type—that is, the blade was held between two slats of wood covered with leather or hide. One of the rare daggers illustrated in the chronicle of Benedikt Tschachtlan (1470) is depicted like this. Fifteen years later, when Diebold Schilling's *Spiezerchronik* was compiled, several of the characters illustrated in it carried long daggers, in a simple type of sheath, with the hilts of the typical form firmly associated later with Swiss daggers.

The dagger of this specific type came to be particularly associated with Switzerland, and this national status was confirmed by the fact that two Swiss men who combined their artistic talents with soldiery, Urs Graf (c. 1485–1527/8) and Niklaus Manuel Deutsch (1484–1530), were in the habit of portraying a small dagger as an identification mark on their respective works along with initials. Up until the early 16th century, contemporary drawings show that daggers were carried in plain leather sheaths and always had the same type of mount. Soon after 1510, however, the first decorative designs for sheaths began to appear, some of the most notable having been created around 1520 by Urs Graf (these are now in the Kunstmuseum in Basel). A famous artist whose designs can often be seen on ornate Swiss-dagger sheaths was Hans Holbein. He adapted them himself from his book *The Dance of Death*, first published in Lyons in 1523–24.

Many scenes from classical mythology, Roman and Swiss history, the Old Testament, etc., are depicted on the sheaths of long daggers produced in Switzerland from about 1550 and, despite the wide variety of subjects covered, they all belong to the same category. There is evidence to show that they were still in use nearly two centuries later, well into the first quarter of the 17th century. The sheath of the Swiss dagger always had two small pockets for a knife and a bodkin.

While the sheaths that have survived to this day were certainly the work of metal decorators, the blades of Swiss daggers were always very plain and forged with care to produce effective weapons. Even the most elegant daggers, whose fittings displayed the highest skills of the goldsmith's craft, always had a plain, solid blade.

The Swiss dagger served as a model for some regulation daggers in Germany under the Nazis (worn with uniform by members of S.S., S.A., and N.S.K.K. formations).

**dai-shō** A term, meaning "large and small," usually referring to the classical set of Japanese weapons consisting of the long, slightly curved fighting sword, the KATANA, and its smaller, similarly shaped companion sword, the WAKIZASHI. The latter was a supplementary weapon and was sometimes also used for ceremonial suicide, seppuku (so-called hara-kiri).

A katana blade was about 50–70 cm. (20–28 in.) long, and that of the wakizashi 35–45 cm. (14–18 in.) long. The two swords were made and decorated *en suite*, and even the guards and mounts—TSUBA and MENUKI—as well as the scabbards were produced in proportionally sized pairs, also known as dai-shō.

It was customary for a visitor on entering a house to leave his katana in the entrance hall but to take his wakizashi in with him, placing it on the mat at his right side. When he wished to show even greater respect for his host, he left both swords outside.

**damascening** The ornamentation of iron or steel by inlaying or overlaying with another metal, usually gold or silver. It is also used to describe the watered effect achieved by welding iron and steel together, such as is seen on a "Damascus"-bladed sword. *See also* DECORATIVE TECHNIQUES.

**daraq** An Arab word for a Moorish shield from which the term ADARGA derives.

**dart** A light missile weapon similar to the JAVELIN. It was known from the late Paleolithic period, when its wooden shaft was equipped with a head, or tip, made of stone or bone. During antiquity and the Middle Ages, the darts had leaf- or arrow-shaped heads, often with stabilizers, or vanes, on the butt end of their shafts, like the arrows and quarrels. Darts were used in Europe and the Middle East during the 15th to 17th centuries for sporting games, hunting, and land and naval warfare.

**date** The crest of a Japanese helmet, usually made of a lightweight material such as wood, leather, horn, or whalebone, but occasionally of metal. It was often very prominent and painted in bright colors or gilded. When the crest was in its customary position on the front of the helmet, it was known as a MAIDATE; when it was on the top, it was called a *kashira-date*; at the side, a *waki-date*; and at the back, a *ushiro-date*.

**Decorative Techniques**

Under this heading are discussed the main decorative techniques and their development in western Europe: chiseling, coloring (including gilding and silvering), damascening, embossing and chasing, enameling, engraving, etching, nielloing, painting, and applied decorations. For Oriental techniques, see individual weapons, armors, and pieces of armor; BLADE: Japanese; and TSUBA.

**decorative techniques** Throughout the centuries, until arms began to be mass-produced in factories, the relationship between the fine arts and martial implements was very close. Since early history, decoration of weapons played an important role as a manifestation of the culture of the society which created them. Arms became symbols of authority, power, and justice, thus conveying ideas which far surpassed their original function. These two aspects—the utilitarian and the representative—were the decisive characteristics in the past history of arms and armor.

The ideological significance was demonstrated by the widely adopted practice of treating arms decoratively. Every effort was made to lend them an aesthetic value directly related to the social status and artistic taste of the owner. The ornamentation of arms always reflected the general development of style in the decorative art of the period, and any changes in it were eagerly noted. Almost every decorative technique found its way into the manufacture of arms: they were embossed and chiseled in relief as well as painted, engraved, damascened, and etched, these techniques often being combined.

Surviving examples of finely decorated arms show a large range of motifs. In the early stages, abstract designs, conventionalized foliate patterns, and animal themes prevailed; in later periods, heraldry, the Bible, mythology, classical history, the court, and military life supplied

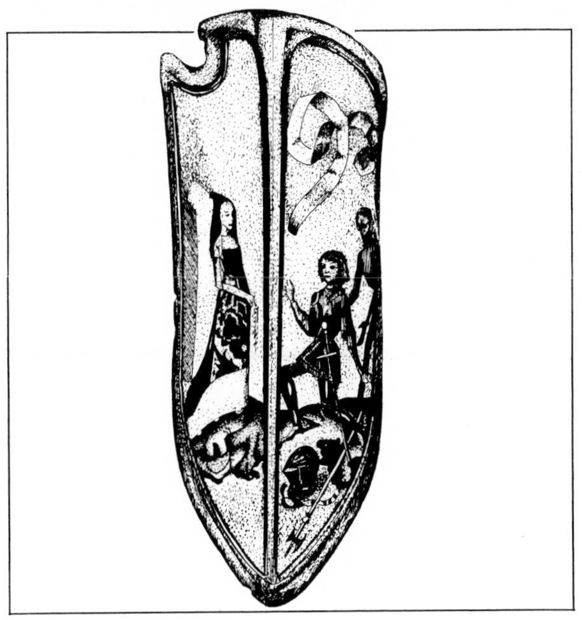

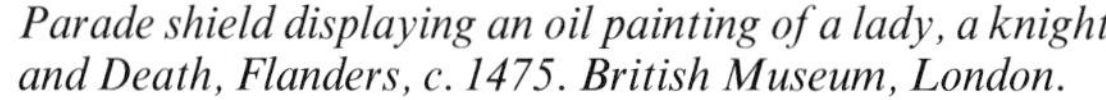

*Parade shield displaying an oil painting of a lady, a knight, and Death, Flanders, c. 1475. British Museum, London.*

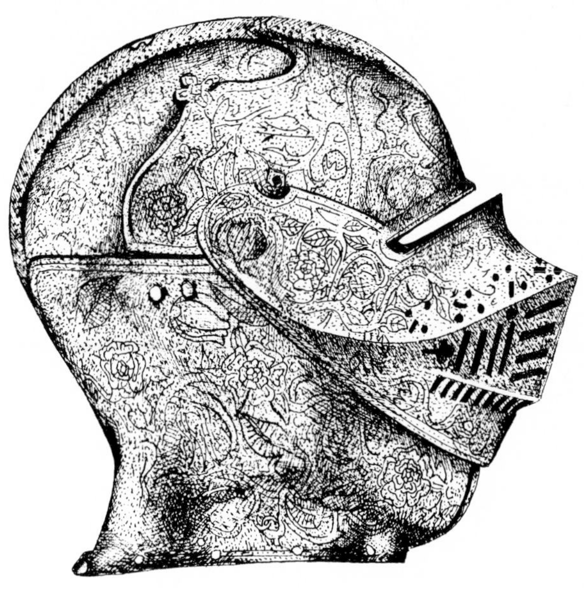

*Engraved and silvered armet, part of an armor belonging to Henry VIII, probably made and decorated by Italian and Flemish masters at the Royal Workshops in Greenwich, c. 1515. Tower of London Armouries.*

subject material. In many cases the decorations contained symbolic and apotropaic (intended to ward off evil) conceptions such as endless knots, the Gorgon's head, the evil eye, signs of contempt and good luck, symbols of strength and courage, as well as allegories with subtle and complex meanings. From the beginning of the 16th century onward, many—perhaps most—of these motifs were derived from contemporary prints, especially from pattern books published for the use of goldsmiths. These pattern books supplied the fashionable ornamentations from which the decorators of arms (and other objects) evolved ideas for their own compositions. There is no doubt that, from the early Bronze Age until the end of the 18th century, and even later, metal craftsmen and goldsmiths played an important part in the decoration of arms. The trend to extravagant richness and the use of costly materials, however, often resulted in armors and arms being determined by aesthetic and ideological rather than practical considerations. Sometimes their function was lost sight of altogether, which happened when a knightly class was being transformed into courtiers.

The diversity of forms and styles in decoration is worthy of a detailed study not only from an aesthetic point of view but also because it often enables an approximate date and place of manufacture to be established. Furthermore, an examination of the decoration of arms enables us to appreciate the ancient crafts before they had been replaced by modern methods. In this short survey it has only been possible to discuss the decorative techniques briefly and to exemplify them by citing some outstanding pieces.

*Painting.* A decorative technique used from the earliest times. Weapons with well-preserved painted decorations are comparatively rare and late in date. Iconographical sources confirm that painting was already applied to shields in distant and classical antiquity. Among the earliest surviving shields there is one covered with a painted canvas that dates back to the end of the 12th century (Schweizerisches Museum, Zurich). Inscriptions, the arms of cities, and heraldic emblems, as well as fairly simple ornamental patterns, were also usually painted on 14th- and 15th-century shields and pavises. More ambitious subjects appeared on jousting shields, such as a South German shield of about 1480–90 on which a lady is depicted sitting between two blossoming plants (Waffensammlung, Vienna). The well-balanced composition and flowing design, as well as the fact that the shield belonged to Emperor Maximilian I, suggest that the decoration was entrusted to a professional painter.

Painted bands and squares adorned early 15th-century basnets. An example of a more advanced decoration is provided by a German basnet from the mid-15th century, which is constructed of *cuir-bouilli* (hardened leather) and embellished with painted spiky leaves (Metropolitan Museum, New York). A coat of paint was also often used on battle armors as a rust preventive. In the second half of the 16th century numerous German armors were given a simple but effective decoration of blackened surfaces alternating with polished sunken backgrounds. As a rule, however, painting as a decorative and protective technique appeared on cheaper pieces produced for soldiers of lower rank, but this rule did not apply to those armors which had a blued surface decorated with designs painted with a kind of gold lacquer, an example of which—made by Hieronymus Ringler in 1622 in Augsburg for Elector

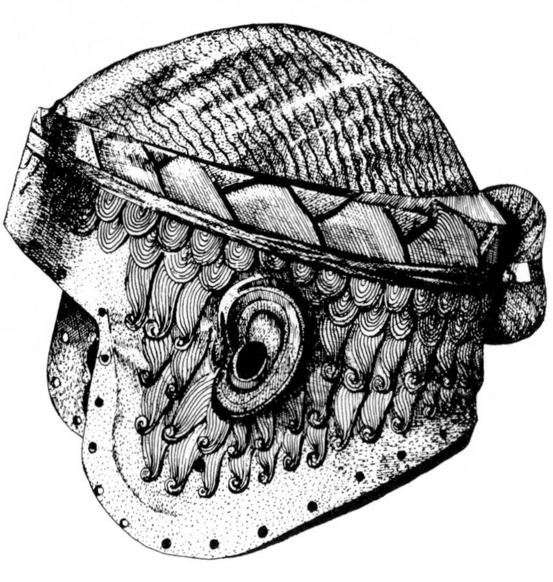

*Embossed gold helmet belonging to Prince Mes-Kalamdug, from the Royal Cemetery of Ur (tomb no. 755), Mesopotamia, third millennium* B.C. *Iraqi Museum, Baghdad.*

*Enamelled powder flask, Germany, c. 1640. Victoria and Albert Museum, London.*

Johann Georg I of Saxony and his horse—may be seen in the Historisches Museum, Dresden.

*Engraving.* An incised pattern made by a pointed tool was the earliest method of decoration for bronze swords, spears, and axes. The difficulty of engraving on wrought iron, however, considerably limited the use of this technique. When it did appear on armor, it was generally confined to the latten borders of the plates as, for instance, in a Milanese armor of a Vogt (bailiff) of Match dated about 1390 (Churburg Castle, Sluderno). To produce incised designs on the main surfaces, burins or chisels were used. This method was used by Paul van Vrelant of Brussels on Henry VIII's silvered armor, dating from 1514–19. Its entire surface is covered with entwined roses framing the representations of St. George and St. Barbara (Tower of London Armouries). The engraved decoration of two silvered jousting half armors, made in 1591 for the Saxon court, reveals the flamboyant style of the Baroque (Historisches Museum, Dresden). Even more gradiose is Louis XIV's silvered armor of 1668. The profuse ornamental composition engraved by Francesco da Garbagnate includes views of cities commemorating the king's victories (Musée de l'Armée, Paris).

Engraving also often appeared on the metal parts of fine-quality firearms and was frequently applied to bone, stag's horn, or mother-of-pearl inlays on stocks. Here the artist-craftsmen found ample opportunity to display their skill and imaginative power. For greater contrast the lines were sometimes filled in with black ink and parts of the inlays stained. Most of the engraved bone designs, though picturesque and vivid, were clumsy and overloaded with details, but there were also pieces of remarkable artistic merit. To this class belongs the decoration of the stock of a gun made in 1570 by Hans Paumgarten (Waffensammlung, Vienna) and of a musket, carbine, and powder flasks decorated by three outstanding masters working in the first decade of the 16th century in Munich: a chiseler, Emanuel Sadeler; a stocker, Adam Vischer; and a talented graphic artist who was responsible for the extremely fine engraving of bone inlays. Although it is not known for certain who this artist was, from the complexity and delicacy of the engraving he was obviously in the first rank, probably Johann Sadeler, a cousin of Emanuel (Armeria Reale, Turin; Museo Civico, Trieste).

*Etching.* Decidedly the most popular technique in the decoration of arms, the exact date when etching was first used is not known, An etched inscription on a sword of Sancho IV, king of Castille and León (?–1295), however, is evidence that this technique was already practiced at the end of the 13th century. A 14th-century manuscript recommends a solution of saltpeter and Roman vitriol "for writing in steel." Prescriptions from the 15th century introduced solutions of grilled salt and charcoal in sour wine or of sal ammoniac, sulfuric acid, and vinegar. The steel plate had to be covered with a protective coat of oil paint or hardened wax in which ornamental designs or inscriptions were scratched before the plate was dipped in acid. After the coat had been removed, etched lines resembling the effect of engraving remained. The second method, in which the protective coat was used for painting designs while the ground was etched away, gave almost sculptural results.

Etching was technically far easier than engraving or chiseling on steel and enabled corrections to be made while preparing the surface for the chemical process. However, the most important advantage was that it did not diminish the practical function of the decorated object. For these reasons, from the end of the 15th century onward this technique was employed in almost every arms-producing center. At that time, Italians adopted the method of linear etching against a hatched ground. In most cases workmanship was fairly indifferent, but the haute-piece of one of the armors made by Nicolò Silva of Milan was etched with a splendidly composed battle scene (Bargello, Florence). Etching also appeared on blades of swords and cinquedeas. The decorations of some cinquedeas are attributed to "Master Ercole," a court goldsmith to the Duke d'Este. He also worked for Cesare Borgia, for whom he decorated a sword in 1498 (Collection of the Duke di Sermoneta, Rome). The practice of gilding the etched lines enhanced the effect of these decorations.

Etching was employed almost contemporaneously in Germany. At first, the Italian method of a hatched ground was imitated, but very soon German etchers evolved their own style, which was characterized by a rich ornamentation and a number of technical innovations. Motifs left in relief were preferred, the effect being emphasized by gilded ornaments and an etched blackened ground. The first specimen embellished in this way was a shield made in 1495 in Innsbruck for Emperor Maximilian I, its decoration displaying a bizarre agglomeration of different motifs, the picturesqueness of which made up for the crowded composition and lack of proportion (Waffensammlung, Vienna). Further development led to the habit of enlivening the blackened ground with tiny dots in relief. The foremost representative of the German school was Daniel Hopfer (c. 1470–1536), who worked as an etcher and graphic artist in Augsburg. His signature can be seen on the decoration of a jousting targe, dated 1536, that belonged to Emperor Charles V (Armería Real, Madrid), and on a sword blade (Germanisches Museum, Nuremberg). Several other objects may also be attributable to Hopfer, in which his typically vigorous style, a mingling of vivid imagination with realism, seems to reveal itself. Another Augsburg master was Jörg Sorg, a painter by profession, whose work is well documented in an album of drawings representing forty-five suits of armor which he etched in the period from 1548 until 1563. His precisely drawn arabesques and neatly designed birds and animals show the transition from the florid but somewhat sketchy style of Hopfer. In Munich, Ambrosius Gemlich etched armors and incised calendars on the blades of swords and hunting knives (Waffensammlung, Vienna; Metropolitan Museum, New York). Lively narration, often with a moralizing sense and a touch of humor, characterized etched decorations stemming from Saxony and Brunswick.

Etching was commonly used in France and England. An armor for man and horse, known as Gaillot de Genouilhac's armor, made in Greenwich in 1527, is particularly effective because its entire surface is ornamentally etched and gilded (Metropolitan Museum, New York). In later English armor, the choice of motifs was rather restricted, the effect of richness being attained

1

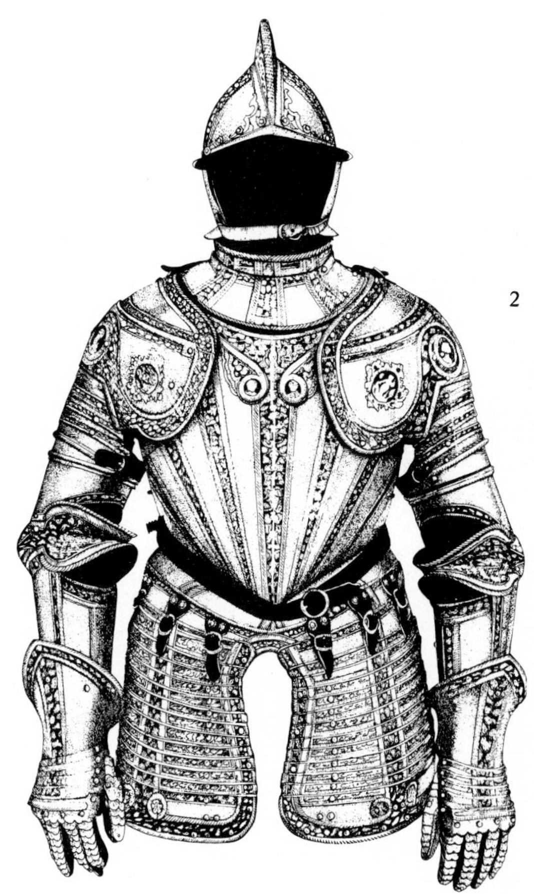

2

*1. Detail from etching on a breastplate, in the style of Daniel Hopfer of Augsburg, c. 1510. Metropolitan Museum, New York. 2. Etching on infantry half armor, N. Italy, c. 1571. Metropolitan Museum, New York.*

by contrasting gilded ornamentation with the blued or russeted coloring of the steel background, features which can clearly be seen in a suit of armor by George Clifford, dating from the end of the 16th century (Metropolitan Museum, New York).

Etching was also widely used in the decoration of barrels, locks, mounts, and steel-stocked firearms, for example, a Brunswick wheel-lock gun, c. 1580 (National Museum, Kraków).

Another method of etching was already used from the end of the 15th century. This was the so-called blue etching, which was applied onto fire-blued steel. Designs and parts of the ground which were meant to remain blue were covered with a protective coat, while the blue hue was removed from other parts with warm vinegar. This method was employed in 1477 in the decoration of a horse bard of Frederic III (Waffensammlung, Vienna).

*Embossing and chasing*. The first step in embossed work required the preparation of a full-size design which was transferred onto the back of a metal plate. The plate was then pressed, face down, onto a pliable anvil of pitch or soft wood or a sand-filled cushion. The next step was to hammer out those parts of the decoration which should be in relief on the face. Then the plate was reversed and the sunken parts of the front were further wrought out. Work in soft metals presented no great difficulties, but the embossing of a thick steel plate called for special care to avoid splitting and delamination. In the final phase, the right side was chased, also on a cushion, the raised outlines brought into sharper relief with gravers and chisels, and the ground usually ornamentally punched, etched, or gilded. The gold helmet of Prince Mes-Kalam-dug of the 24th century B.C., excavated in Ur, bears witness to the fact that embossing was known in the remote past (Iraqi Museum, Baghdad). Embossed bronze helmets, thórax armors, and greaves were also popular in Greek and Roman antiquity, and centuries later, in the early Middle Ages, the technique was still being applied to gold overlays on the hilts and scabbards of ceremonial swords, of which many beautiful examples have survived.

The 15th century developed the fashion of armors embossed with skillfully arranged ripples and flutes. The first recorded figural embossing dates back to 1477 and is represented in the bard belonging to Frederic III, already mentioned, the peytral of which was adorned with a demifigure of an angel and the crupper with two imperial eagles. A bard of Charles V, from about 1525, shows considerable progress in technique. Scenes representing the labors of Hercules were raised up in much bolder relief, with vivid, expressive movements, the background ornamentally pierced, and borders enriched with etched patterns (Armería Real, Madrid).

When the element of pomp became an increasingly important factor in arms production, the way was open to lavishly embossed decorations. In this, the skill of the Negroli family of Milan was unsurpassed. They worked for only the most prominent patrons, and the best remembered member of the family is Filippo, who worked in 1519–61. A striking, though somewhat sinister, example of his early work is an armor made about 1529 for Guidobaldo II, Duke of Urbino. The russeted breastplate of this armor is embossed with two dragon's wings and apotropaic eyes (Bargello, Florence), while the helmet is shaped in the form of a monster's head with fangs, horns, and pointed ears (The Hermitage, Leningrad). In later decorations his work approaches sculpture, apparent in his burgonets with superbly modeled figures projected in such high relief that they give the impression of being carved in the round. His compositions are always well balanced and finished with extraordinary crispness. Interest in classical antiquity led to the imitation of ancient thórax armor. Two armors "alla romana" were copied in 1546 from a Roman statue representing Lucius Verus. The first was embossed by Filippo Negroli (Bargello, Florence); the second, by Bartolomeo Campi of Pesaro (Armerí Real, Madrid). Another Milanese master of whom mention should be made is Lucio Piccinino (c. 1531–93) and, judging by the number of attributed pieces, his skill must have been highly appreciated. Also an expert damascener, he enriched embossed decorations with inlaid gold and silver. Piccinino's compositions were lively and natural in movement, although sometimes the artist was unable to prevent the surface from being overcrowded, as in an armor for Alessandro Farnese, about 1578 (Waffensammlung, Vienna).

Embossed decoration of a very distinctive style appeared in France in the mid-16th century. Superbly executed examples have survived in several pieces. They show the influence of ornamental designs by Etienne Delaune, a court goldsmith and die-cutter to Henry II of France. In the use of strap work, with rolled-over borders and elongated figures, he was closely related to the Mannerist school at Fontainebleau, although, at the same time, his designs are more classical, finer and lighter. These traits can be clearly seen in two exquisitely embossed shields and a shaffron of Henry II (Musée de l'Armée, Paris; Metropolitan Museum, New York), as well as a shield and morion of Charles IX (Louvre, Paris).

The French Mannerist style is also recognizable in armors and shields embossed by the goldsmith Eliseus Libaerts of Antwerp, whose talent equaled that of the Italian masters. One of his most distinguished works, the Hercules armor, dates from 1562–64. In spite of the prolificacy and the diversity of embossed, chiseled, and etched motifs, which were typical of the aesthetic climate of the period, Libearts kept an exquisite sense of proportion (Historisches Museum, Dresden).

Many armors, burgonets, and shields were embossed in Augsburg, where the most renowned artist was Jörg Sigman. Besides other richly decorated weapons, he embossed and damascened an armor for Prince Philip, later Philip II of Spain (Armería Real, Madrid).

The technique was also used to decorate firearms. Embossed silver and bronze pommels often took the form of grotesque masks and human or animal heads, while foliage, classical deities, allegories of virtues, or battle scenes rendered in low relief appeared on many mounts.

*Chiseling*. This work was similar to that of a medalist, the result being a sculpture on a miniature scale. Carried out with burins and chisels on such a hard material as steel,

*Burgonet of blue steel, covered with chiseled appliqué decorations of gilded silver. Made for Grand Duke Cosimo II of Tuscany by Gasparo Mola, c. 1608–09. Museo Nazionale del Bargello, Florence.*

chiseling was a laborious process. Its use was restricted to smaller objects such as the hilts of swords, daggers, and metal parts of firearms. The sculptural effect was often enhanced by gilding. In the more sumptuous examples, the ground was plated with gold, which was sometimes matted with a very small punch to provide a more striking contrast to the brightly polished relief.

Gothic swords with chiseled hilts and scabbards have survived in great numbers. Among them is a splendidly decorated 15th-century sword of Duke Christopher of Bavaria. The quillons and scabbard are chiseled with vine scrolls inhabited by human and animal subjects, and the hilt is sculptured in high relief with the figures of two naked girls and two young men in court dress (Schatzkammer, Munich).

During the 16th century some distinct local features evolved. Franz of Torgau, Ullrich Jahn, and Othmar Wetter worked in the second half of the century in Dresden. Their chiseled decorations of rapier hilts, done in low relief with the utmost care, consisted of foliage interspersed with medallions containing allegorical figures, classical deities, battle scenes, and biblical subjects. Wetter, who was a native of Munich but for several years worked in Dresden, placed chiseled ornaments against a gilded or blackened ground (Bayerisches Nationalmuseum, Munich; Historisches Museum, Dresden). In the field of superbly chiseled weapons, Munich took first place. A workshop was established there at the end of the 16th century by Emanuel Sadeler of Antwerp, who was employed as chiseler to the court of the Wittelsbachs. After his death in 1610, he was succeeded by his younger brother, Daniel, who had, for a time, been working in Prague for Emperor Rudolph II. Their elegantly modeled figures, grotesques, draperies, and clusters of fruit were greatly influenced by the French Mannerist style. Whereas it had previously been the custom for the relief work to be gilded, the Sadelers preferred a different system; the weapons decorated by them have blued chiseled ornamentation against a gilded or gold-plated ground. Some details are additionally encrusted with gold studs. Both brothers collaborated with gunmakers and swordmakers who were in the service of the Bavarian court. The elder Sadeler was responsible for the decoration of barrels and wheel-locks for a carbine and musket with its fork, which were made about 1610 for Duke Maximilian of Bavaria. Painstakingly chiseled ornaments and cocks of the locks were carved in the form of coiling monsters and bear witness to the technical virtuosity and artistic taste of the maker. From the time this set was made, it was regarded as a work of art rather than an object of practical use and was immediately placed in the duke's art gallery (now in Armeria Reale, Turin, and Waffensammlung, Vienna). Surviving firearms and rapier hilts ornamented by Daniel Sadeler are more numerous. The decoration of a wheel-lock gun for Rudolph II, made in 1610 in Prague, shows that the style of the two brothers was almost indistinguishable (Waffensammlung, Vienna). From 1632 until 1655, the workshop was under the management of Caspar Spät, who continued to produce work in the style and technique of the Sadelers; it did not compare with theirs in quality, however, since his relief was flatter and less crisp.

In Spain and Italy precision of design kept pace with technical perfection, which was almost on a par with the goldsmith's art. The Italian masters of Bargi, Brescia, and Naples excelled in the decoration of metal parts of firearms and hilts of rapiers and parrying daggers. Chiseled and pierced ornaments were executed so delicately as to give the impression of lace. The main element was an intricate tracery of arabesques and floral scrolls containing putti, birds, animals, and monsters. They are executed in minute scale with such care that they can really only be fully appreciated if viewed through a magnifying glass. Particularly gifted was Matteo Acquafresca of Bargi, a gunsmith and iron chiseler. In spite of design derivations from French pattern books, he was able to create an individual artistic conception, engraving lock plates with delicate foliage and giving sculptural treatment to the cock, battery, and pan. Such features can be seen on the lock plates of his snaphance pistols, made in 1689 (Bayerisches Nationalmuseum, Munich). Another master was Piero Anchini of Reggio Emilia, who was entrusted with the decoration of swords, smallswords, and gun locks for the Dukes d'Este; his preference for softly modeled figural subjects and fleshy scrolls certainly indicates the hand of a professional sculptor (Bargello, Florence; Musée de l'Armée, Paris; Odescalchi Collection, Rome).

Some hilts produced in the late 16th century in France demonstrate an original feature in that the decoration is enriched with soldered chains and plaques of chased silver (Kunstsammlungen, Veste Koburg; Victoria and Albert Museum, London; Musée de l'Armée, Paris).

*Damascening and encrustation.* This technique of inlaying a metal with ornamental designs in another, softer metal dates back to prehistoric times, when two methods were employed. In the first, the outlines of a required design were traced with deep grooves which were undercut at the bottom to provide a better hold for the wire. After it had been hammered in, the plate was polished until the surface of the inlay was flush with that of the ground. Silver or gold wire was generally used, but on less sumptuous objects brass or copper was also employed. In the second method, sometimes referred to as "counterfeit damascening," a surface was roughened with files and then wire or foil was sunk by means of a copper burnisher into the hatches. Both methods gave an almost identical effect, but the latter, though less durable, was easier and produced more pliable designs. Sometimes the inlaid decoration was given an additional treatment by engraving or chiseling.

The earliest damascened decoration, on a Mycenaean dagger blade of the 16th century B.C., represented a faultlessly designed hunting scene, the high standard of which reflects the artistic culture of the period (National Museum, Athens). Over the centuries patterns became coarser until finally, by the Middle Ages, damascening was limited to inscriptions and signs on blades. At the end of the 15th century, under the influence of Islamic art, the technique began to regain its former splendor, and during the first decades of the 16th century it spread to all European countries. Although true damascening was practiced, counterfeit damascening—because of its technical advantages—enjoyed a far greater popularity. It was employed by a Spaniard, Diego de Çaias, a journeyman artist, who stayed for some time in France, then in England, and also possibly in Antwerp. His florid style must have been well formed before he appeared in France in 1535 because it displays a combination of current European patterns with Oriental motifs. One of his most talented followers, probably a pupil, was Damianus de Nerve (Nerven), believed to be of Flemish origin. Together they left a considerable number of damascened hilts, maces, barrels, and wheel-locks. Apart from the picturesque quality of their work, a particular feature of the workshop was the damascened designs which stood in relief above the surface of the steel.

Decorators of armor often combined embossing with damascening, but a small number of armors have survived on which the entire decoration consisted of damascening. A blued parade armor made between 1537 and 1547 for the dauphin of France, later Henry II, belongs to this category. It is ornamented with bands of silver scrolls, curling tendrils, bows, and quivers, to which Henry's monogram is added (Musée de l'Armée, Paris). An expert damascener was Lucio Piccinino. In the decoration of parade shields he managed to create a remarkably successful combination of embossing in low relief and damascening with gold wire and foil, resulting in shields that have the quality of embossed pictures (Historisches Museum, Dresden).

The damascened patterns on hilts, barrels, and locks originating from the second half of the 16th century strove for a greater lucidity, giving pride of place to pliable and graceful arabesques. As with chiseled decoration, the dark blue color of the steel background emphasized the effect of gold and silver ornamentation. Unfortunately, very little is known of the masters who produced damascened decoration in Spain, Italy, France, England, and Germany.

A method similar to damascening was adopted on the stocks of firearms. They were adorned with scrolls of silver, gilt-brass, or pewter wire, which were hammered into lines cut in the wood. A more laborious process was the cutting of intaglio designs and filling them with bone, stag's horn, mother-of-pearl, or metal inlays, which were often engraved. The stock of a double-barreled gun made by Le Conte before 1673 was decorated in this way by Jean Bérain, an artist whose, activity in the domain of applied arts was of considerable importance. The silver inlays of the stock belong to the late Baroque style, in which, however, the diversity of motifs was subordinated to the dictates of good taste (Livrustkammaren, Stockholm).

*Enameling.* This method of decoration provided the much sought-after polychrome effects. These were attained by applying onto a gold, silver, or copper ground a paste of distilled water, powdered quartz, carbonates of sodium and magnesium, chalk, and lead oxide. The paste was tinted with oxides of other metals and, when dry, fired until the glaze was molten. In the course of many centuries different methods of fixing enamel to a ground were developed, examples of which can be seen on many specimens of weapons and other objects.

In the cloisonné enamel, cells made of narrow strips of gold or copper were soldered onto the ground and filled with opaque enamel, which contained a small quantity of tin oxide or charred bone. After firing and polishing, the cells outlined every detail of the design. This method was popular in the decoration of many hilts and scabbards of ceremonial swords, such as the scabbard of the so-called Sword of St. Maurice, dating from the 11th century (Weltliche Schatzkammer, Vienna). An alternative to this method developed during the 14th century in Hungary when twisted wire was introduced to form a pattern; this system was employed in the decoration of the scabbard for a sword owned by Elector Frederic of Saxony (Historisches Museum, Dresden).

From the 12th century onward champleve enamel became popular. Preparation for this required cutting grooves or recesses for enamel in a metal ground; such a method was used in the decoration of a gold hilt of a rapier made in Munich in about 1560. The enameling on this is remarkable for its brilliance and transparency of color, as well as for the clarity of the design, which consists of coiling snakes biting into clusters of fruit (Historisches Museum, Dresden). The same technique was applied to the magnificent wheel-lock gun and powder flask of Emperor Rudolph II. As has been mentioned, the chiseling of the barrel and lock plate was executed by Daniel Sadeler, while David Altenstetter, a goldsmith of Augsburg, decorated silver panels set in the stock with champlevé-enameled trophies of war, candelabra patterns, and floral scrollwork. The outstanding standard of chiseling, precision of enameling, and artistic merit of the designs place this set among the masterpieces of art of the period.

Several rapier hilts, dating from the third quarter of the 16th century, are attributed to Pery Juan Pockh, a goldsmith of Barcelona, who must have been a master of high repute because he was called in to work for the imperial court. These hilts are exquisitely fashioned of pure gold, pierced and chiseled in high relief with a net of interlacing strap work enclosing masks, serpents, and clusters of fruit. Besides the superb chiseling, the most attractive feature of these hilts is the discreet use of polychrome enamels (Historisches Museum, Dresden; Louvre, Paris; Kassel Museum, Germany).

Enameled work of very fine quality was also produced in Germany, an example of which is a gold rapier hilt decorated with wrought and cast ornaments, enriched by polychrome enamel. Made in 1571, the hilt bears the initials *HR*, which are probably those of the Munich goldsmith Hans Reimer. The use of figural motifs, which constitute the most important element of this hilt and which do not often appear in contemporary Spanish work, suggests that the attribution to a German master is valid (Schatzkammer, Munich).

In France, one of the chief masters of enameled decoration was a Parisian goldsmith, Pierre Redon, who was entrusted, in about 1570, with the enameling of an embossed morion and shield for Charles IX. The way in which he used relief together with the lavish application of gold and translucent and opaque enamels resulted in the brilliant and rich effect that can still be seen today on these pieces in the Louvre, Paris.

Only two suits of armor with enameled decoration have survived, which, it must be stressed, was not a fired enamel but a kind of lacquer. These armors were made in the mid-16th century in the Nuremberg workshop of Kunz Lochner the Younger for his Polish clients, King Sigismund II August and Prince Nicolas IV Radziwill. The identical decorative scheme of the armors consists of straps which are partly etched and gilded and partly enameled. The colors of the king's armor are white, gold, and black (Livrustkammaren, Stockholm), while red is added to Nicolas's armor (Waffensammlung, Vienna; Musée de l'Armée, Paris; Metropolitan Museum, New York).

*Nielloing*. This process produced the best results when applied to a silver or gold ground, in which shallow grooves or recesses were cut to be filled with a powder composed of silver, copper, and lead sulfides. During the process of heating the powder became molten, leaving black, lustrous designs. The technique, probably devised in Mycenae, was widely practiced in ancient Rome and in the Byzantine Empire. During the Middle Ages it spread to other parts of Europe and became one of the favorite methods of decoration in Poland and Russia. The hilt of the Polish coronation sword, the "Dented Sword," which dates from the second quarter of the 13th century, is an exceptionally beautiful example of niello applied to gilded silver. The decoration gives the impression of grandeur and solemnity; it consists of the nielloed symbols of the four Evangelists, their names, the tetragrammaton (a symbol of God with the letters alpha and omega), and of a delicately drawn running pattern of leaves set against a nielloed ground (State Art Collections of Wawel Castle, Kraków).

Niello remained in fashion up to the 18th century in the

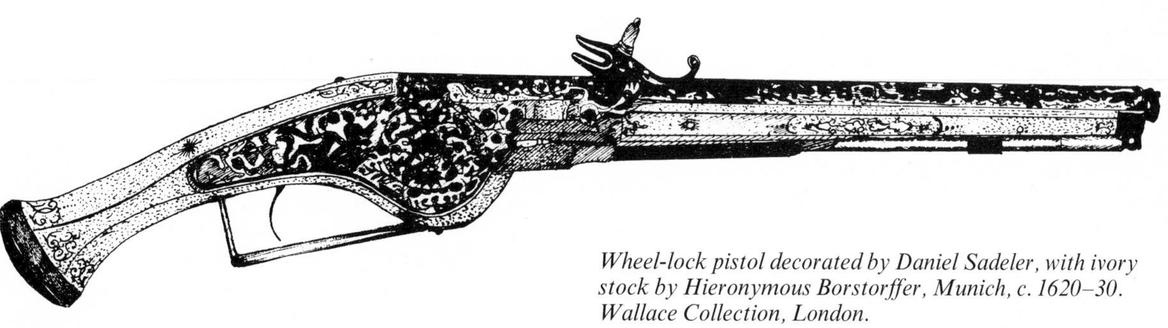

*Wheel-lock pistol decorated by Daniel Sadeler, with ivory stock by Hieronymous Borstorffer, Munich, c. 1620–30. Wallace Collection, London.*

*Sword hilt with damascening by Damianus de Nerve, c. 1555. Waffensammlung, Vienna.*

decoration of hilts and scabbard mounts of Polish sabers, of winged maces, and of cartridge boxes, which were adorned with a harmonious mixture of European and Eastern decorative motifs. Niello in the form of floral scrolls and arabesques was also frequently used on sabers, daggers, barrels, and the mounts of firearms produced in the Caucasus region.

*Applied decoration.* From the "barbarian" migrations until the end of the 12th century, helmets of high-ranking persons were distinguished by bands or plaques of precious metals. These were engraved, punched, or embossed in low relief with fairly simple patterns, and sometimes colored paste in high collets was added to simulate the effect of precious stones (National Museum, Budapest). As is known from iconographical sources, medieval basnets were adorned with applied ornamental bands or coronets. From the second quarter of the 14th century, applied ornaments began to appear on plate armor, too. These took the form of latten plaques, like those seen on a breastplate (c. 1361) found on the site of the battle of Visby, or were confined to the narrow latten borders of the plates, as can be seen on a Milanese armor and basnet (c. 1390) in Churburg Castle, Sluderno. The effect of polished steel and latten must have been well received, because this practice survived well into the late 15th century and even much later in Polish hussar armor. A more elaborate example is a tonlet armor made between 1512 and 1514 for young Charles, later Emperor Charles V, which is decorated with strips of gilded silver and chased and pierced with the emblems of the Order of the Golden Fleece (Waffensammlung, Vienna).

Applied decoration again became fashionable during the Baroque period, when armor, burgonets, and shields began to be adorned with riveted or soldered ornaments. This kind of decoration was used in 1608 by a goldsmith, Gasparo Mola, on a shield and burgonet for Grand Duke Cosimo II of Tuscany, the gilded tracery of cast ornaments, chased silver medallions, and a blued ground creating an exceptionally attractive play of colors (Bargello, Florence). Another notable example is a blued armor of Emperor Maximilian II, made in 1557 in Augsburg and adorned with riveted gilded bands of cast auricular ornamental motifs (Waffensammlung, Vienna).

Precious stones, rock crystals, pearls, and corals contributed a great deal to the sumptuous appearance of arms. These costly materials appeared on medieval state swords, Renaissance and Baroque rapiers, smallswords, and hunting knives. There is no doubt that artistic taste was sometimes sacrificed on the altar of opulence, as in the case of a rapier hilt heavily inlaid with diamonds and rubies in the Historisches Museum, Dresden. Some of the 17th-century firearms produced for carousel riding—a festive occasion that always gave a good excuse for indulging in the passion for display—were decorated with valuable stones or with foiled rock crystals (a pair of holster flintlock pistols by Le Grange, Rosenborg Castle, Copenhagen).

Shell cameos were also employed in the decoration of the hilts of hunting knives and gunstocks, although their brittleness rendered these pieces useful only for demonstrating the wealth of their owner and the technical skill of their maker. The same spirit of pomp characterized pageant cuirasses, helmets, and shields made of thin copper sheet and embossed in high relief, frequently being set with imitations of precious stones (C. O. von Kienbusch Bequest, Philadelphia Museum of Art).

Ivory was one of the favorite materials used during the Mannerist and Baroque periods, and the decorators of arms did not fail to take advantage of this exotic material, from which they carved the hilts of hunting knives, powder flasks, and overlays of stocks for firearms. Ivory panels, magnificently carved in high relief with figural themes, were a constant feature of gunstocks produced in the second half of the 16th century by Johann Michael Maucher of Swabia. In the 17th century, a workshop in Maastricht specialized in the making of pistol stocks of solid ivory with pommels sculptured in the form of warriors' or heroes' heads.

*Coloring.* This was imparted to steel by gilding, silvering, blueing or russeting. The favorite technique was gilding, which was effected either by burnishing sheets of gold foil onto a roughened surface or by applying an amalgam of gold and mercury onto a coppered ground. In the latter method, during the process of heating the mercury evaporated, to leave a coat of pure gold. For better results the process was repeated until the layer of gold achieved the desired thickness. The final stage consisted of polishing the plated metal with a bloodstone or agate moistened in vinegar. A variation of this method was *Goldschmelz*,

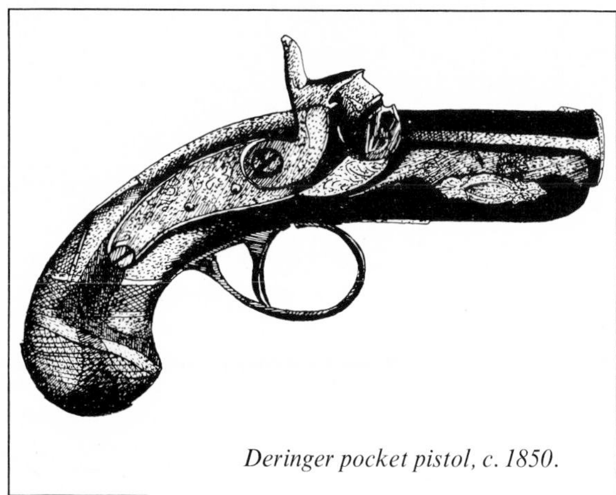

*Deringer pocket pistol, c. 1850.*

introduced and widely used by German decorators. It required preparation, in accordance with ornamental design, of recesses or grooves etched in steel, which were then coppered and filled with an amalgam of gold and mercury, the latter being burned off in the process of firing. Exceptionally handsome decoration of this kind was achieved by Hans Sumersperger, a Tyrolese, who at the end of the 15th century adorned three sword blades and one blade of a hunting knife; he worked gold etchings of the Madonna and saints in a frame of entwined foliage against a brilliant blue ground. The reputation of this master artist-craftsman was evidently great, for three of these blades were ordered by the German emperor.

This technique was revived in the 17th and 18th centuries for decoration of blades and gun barrels, particularly those produced by German and Russian masters working in Tula. Because of its durability, the method of gilding by fire was by far the most popular. The gilding by rubbing a solution of gold dissolved in aqua regia into the plate, although more economical, was used only occasionally.

*Silvering.* This was done by burnishing silver foil onto a hatched ground. Examples having a well-preserved silvered surface are rare, the best one being Henry VIII's silvered armor, which has already been discussed.

It was discovered in the 15th century that an attractive blue color could be imparted to steel by heating the plate to the point of glowing, then quenching it, and, finally, treating it with warmed linseed oil. The range of color from purple to dark blue depended on temperature and time of quenching. The highly appreciated dark blue was achieved at temperatures above 608° F. (320° C.). Apart from the lustrous surface constituting an excellent background for chiseled, embossed, or damascened decorations, blueing also served the practical purpose of protecting steel against rust. Russet patination or browning of some armors and barrels was produced by a chemical process of treating the steel surface with a mild corrosive medium.

**demi-lance** A term of French origin denoting, during the 16th century, a light spear of the half-armored horsemen who formed the so-called medium cavalry and were themselves called demi-lances. This weapon, unlike the lance of the heavy cavalry, had no vamplate or graper.

**deringer** American single-shot, muzzleloading percussion pistol of small size which took its name from its maker, J. H. Deringer of Philadelphia (1786–1868). It was very popular from the 1840s as a pocket pistol. Later the term came to be used for any similar pocket pistol, and spelled "derringer."

**detonator** Part of a projectile case which contains the priming explosive charge; by extension, this explosive is also called a detonator. Normally the fuze acts as the detonator.

**dha** The national sword of Burma, used also in some neighboring countries. Its single-edged blade varies in length from about 30 to 100 cm. (12–40 in.) and is slightly curved; the point is usually long, apart from a few specimens which are square-ended. Some blades are plain but others are grooved and decorated with scrolls, figures, and inscriptions inlaid in copper or silver. Its hilt is long, rather like Japanese sword hilts, and the hardwood, horn, silver, or ivory of which it is made is often beautifully carved or engraved. Sharkskin is sometimes used to cover it.

The wooden dha scabbards have brass or silver fittings with bands of cane, silver, or even gold. A cord is often wound around the scabbard and secured with a knot and a long loop to enable the weapon to be slung round the neck.

**dirk** A Scottish dagger-knife, carried by the Highlanders. When required, it was used as a weapon, but its main use was as a knife, which was carried permanently at the side, ready for a wide range of activities. It was in fact a version of the ballock knife (*see* DAGGER) and was documented as such from the third quarter of the 17th century. It echoed the appearance of the ballock knife in the particular form of the grip, which, though made from different materials (leather, ivy root, ivory), retained a consistent and typical shape and was often decorated with intricate designs typical of the Celtic culture. The round, flat pommel and the guard were usually covered with brass or, more rarely and on earlier models, silver; there are also examples having the grip made entirely of brass. From the end of the 18th century, following the revival of the Highlander's traditional costume, the dirk was often richly mounted in silver (and sometimes even gold) with semiprecious quartz (cairngorm). The dirk blade was often made from a large fragment of a sword blade; it was usually single-edged with a back edge near the point, grooved, and with a decorative notch at the base of the back. There are, however, examples with double-edged blades. The dirk had a distinctive scabbard made of hide or leather with two small holders on the front, one below the other, for containing a small knife and fork; these were furnished in the same way as the dirk itself. As well as being a civilian weapon, a military version, faithful to the original form of the dirk, was produced when Scottish men were incorporated in the regular army of the United Kingdom.

**distomos** Greek term for BIPENNIS.

**djerid** *See* JARID.

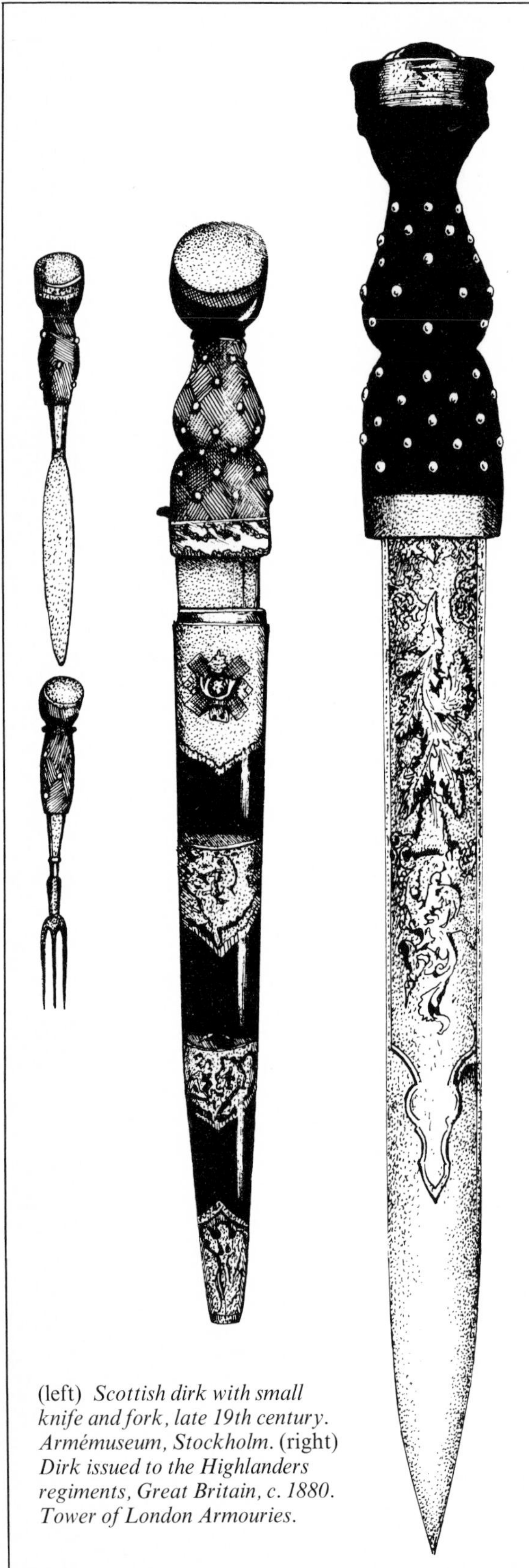

(left) *Scottish dirk with small knife and fork, late 19th century. Armémuseum, Stockholm.* (right) *Dirk issued to the Highlanders regiments, Great Britain, c. 1880. Tower of London Armouries.*

**do** The cuirass of Japanese light armor. Its main developments have occurred since the 14th century, several additions having been made. As a result, two main types have emerged: the DŌ-MARU, opening at the side, and the HAKAMAKI, opening at the back. Both were made in the classical way from small lacquered lamellae of metal, leather, or whalebone. These were laced together with silk cords, and it was on the closeness of this lacing that the quality of the armor depended.

Laced laminated armor was quite elastic and cool in summer, but if the cords became wet they were very heavy. They also chafed badly and wore out quickly. It is not surprising, therefore, that rigid, full-plate cuirasses were introduced with single plates for breast and back, in various styles. Their metal surfaces were either embossed or overlaid with cloth, leather, fishskin, or tortoiseshell.

**dokyu** The Japanese repeating crossbow, copied from the Chinese *chu-ko-nu* but inferior to it. Its horn bow is usually about 70–80 cm. (27–32 in.) long and fixed to a wooden stock. The bolts are contained in a box which slides along the top of the stock and is moved by a lever pivoted to both. When the lever is thrown forward and back, the bow is spanned, a bolt placed in the weapon and discharged. This is a very practical weapon.

**dolabra** (or **dolabella**) A cutting weapon and agricultural tool (mattock) of the Roman period. It was an AX with the head having, on one side, a blade parallel to the handle and, on the other, a slightly upcurved fluke. As a weapon it was used in battle and in ceremonial sacrifices, although less frequently than the battle-ax. It is one of the few weapons of which there exists clear evidence—in the form of a detailed depiction on an epitaph of the imperial period found in the vicinity of Aquileia.

**dolo** (Greek *dolon*) A term used by Virgil (70–19 B.C.) and Suetonius (A.D. c. 69–c. 140) to describe a weapon with a blade concealed in a stick or cane; in effect this was the forerunner of the SWORD STICK.

**dō-maru** A type of Japanese light armor, opening under the right arm. The standard dō-maru consisted of a corslet made of small pieces of lacquered metal (scales or lamellae) laced together with colored silk cords. Another kind was the *tatami-dō*, which was made up of several fairly large lames, with breast- and back-plates in two parts and with hinged side plates which overlapped each other.

There were also dō-maru armors with European-style cuirasses made of large single plates for breast and back called *hatomune-dō*. Somewhat macabre was the *hotoke-dō*, which was modeled to the form of the naked torso with grotesque human faces superimposed on it.

Sometimes attempts were made to adapt real European armor, but it was too stiff, uncomfortable, and quite unsuited to traditional Japanese usage.

**double action** A particular arrangement of the firing system, used especially in revolvers. In a double-action system the hammer can either be cocked by hand and then released by light pressure on the trigger (single action) or cocked and then released entirely by pressing the trigger. With single action the weapon is held more firmly so that shooting can be more accurate; double action enables the

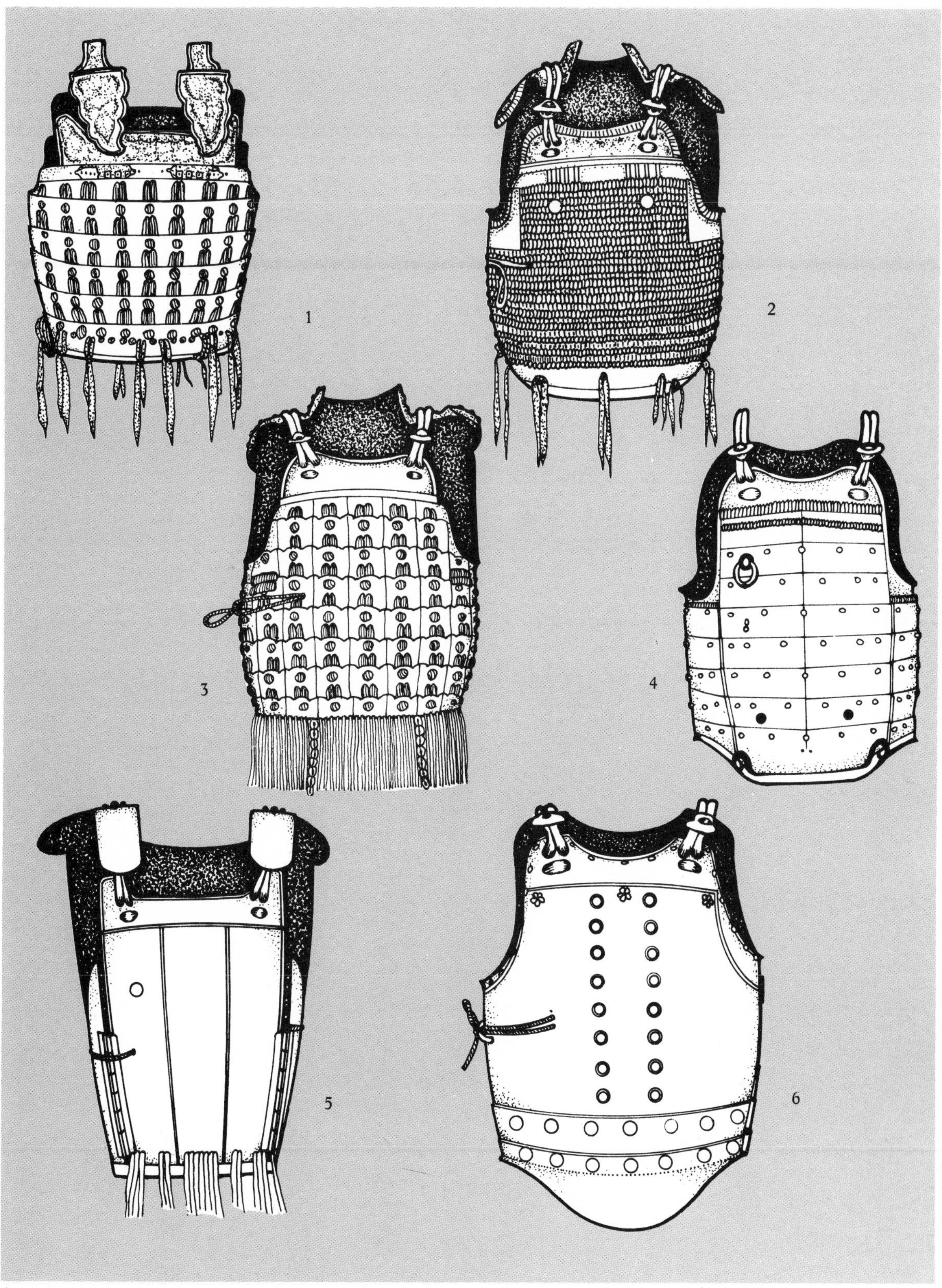


*Various types of dō. 1. Mogami-dō laced in sugake style. 2. Tachi-dō laced in kebiki style. 3. Nuinobe-dō. 4. Yokohagi-dō. 5. Sendai-dō. 6. Hotoko-dō. Anderson Collection, London.*

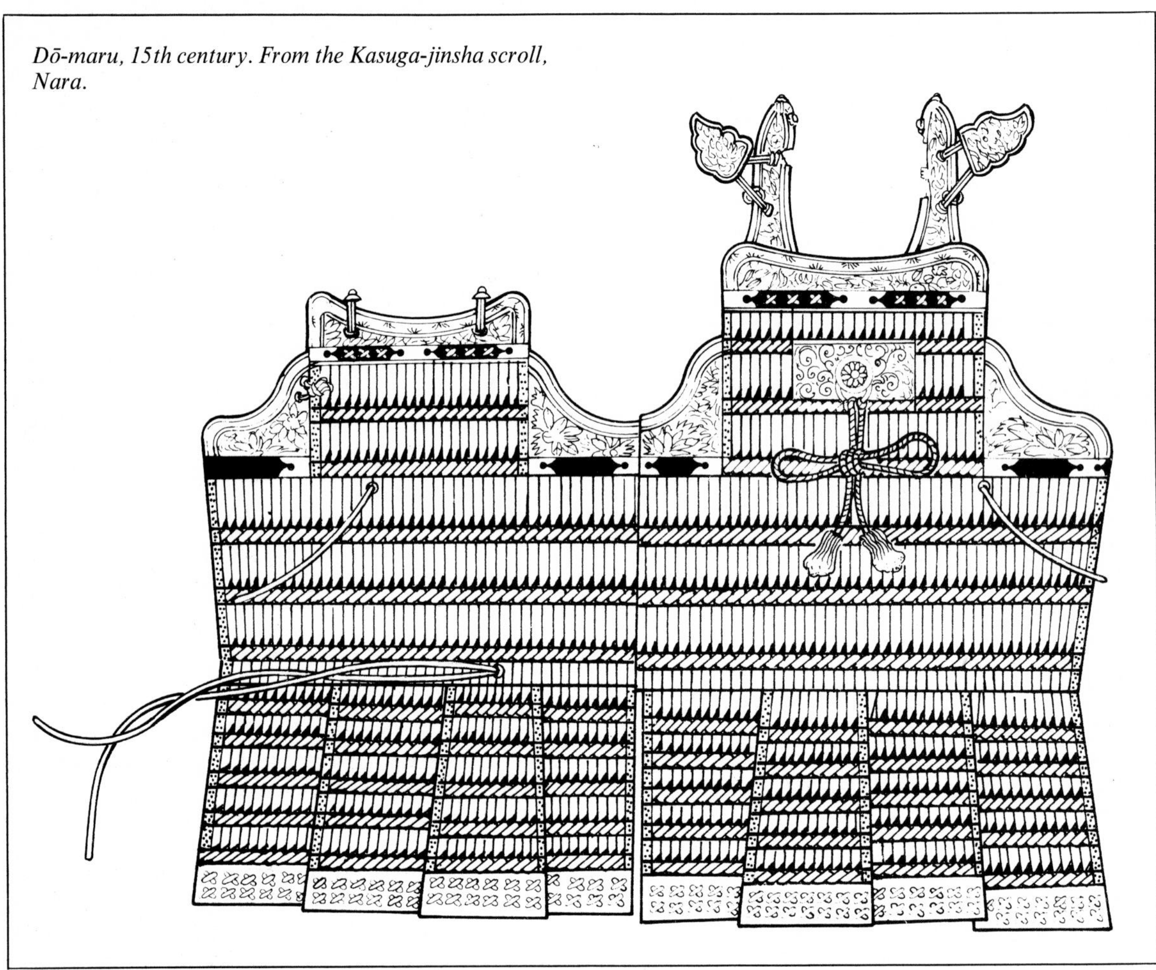
*Dō-maru, 15th century. From the Kasuga-jinsha scroll, Nara.*

firer to shoot more quickly. As applied to modern semiautomatic pistols, double action allows the weapon to be carried safely with a round in the chamber, ready for immediate use.

**double-barreled gun** A type of sporting gun with two barrels side by side or over and under. The hammers may be external or, in so-called hammerless guns, internal; the ammunition used is normally shot, but special cartridges with bullets (Brenneke, etc.) are used on rare occasions. In double-barreled guns, the barrels are attached to the breech-action frame by a hinge and fitted with ejectors that work automatically when the gun is broken. The side-by-side double-barreled shotgun is undoubtedly the commonest sporting gun of the present day. *See also* GUN: sporting.

**double pieces** *See* PIECES OF EXCHANGE.

**dress sword** A regulation light sword worn by officers with dress or full-dress uniforms from the 18th century on.

**driving band** A band fitted around an artillery shell, since the second half of the 19th century, to give it the rotary motion imparted by the rifling and to prevent any escape of gas past the shell or through the breech. It is generally made of copper and firmly fitted into a circular groove in the cylindrical part of the projectile. When the shell is fired, the driving band is forced into the grooves so that their spiral twist gives the projectile a rotary motion as it passes down the barrel. There is usually only one driving band, fitted near the base of the shell. Two driving bands are only found on ammunition for very big or very powerful guns in order to give the guiding areas more strength. In the past, steadying bands were fitted to hold the shell straight; smaller in diameter than the driving bands, they fitted about halfway up the projectile. In the present day a wider section of the shell casing itself is preferred for that purpose.

**duck gun** *See* GUN: sporting.

**ducksfoot pistol** A pistol made with several splayed-out barrels discharged simultaneously. *See also* VOLLEY GUN.

**dueling pistols** A pair of pistols, with smooth-bore or rifled barrels, often having a HAIR TRIGGER, made expressly for formal personal combat (but used also for practice shooting) after duels with pistols became fashionable in the later part of the 18th century. Dueling pistols, always single-shot weapons, were rather modestly decorated but usually had technical qualities much above the average. Always included with the pistols was a lined wooden case

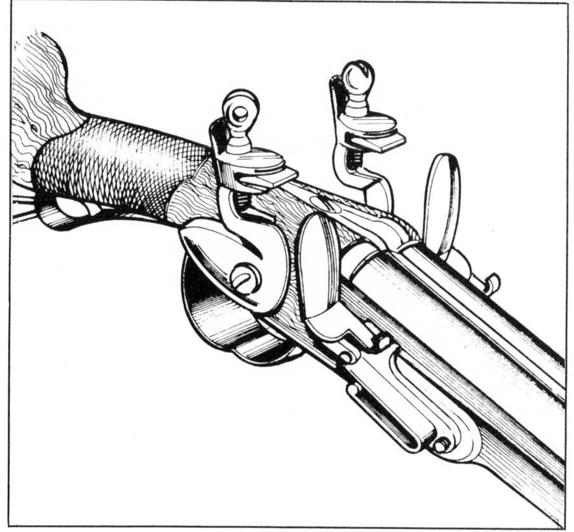

*English side-by-side double-barreled flintlock shotgun, late 18th century.*

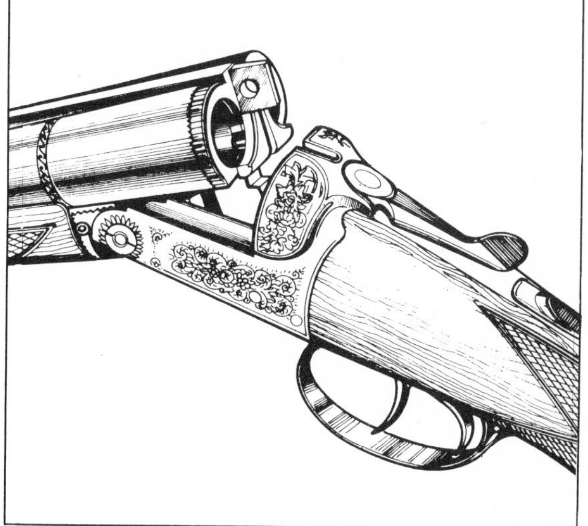

*Italian hammerless double-barreled shotgun with side-by-side barrels.*

containing the accessories for maintenance and loading.

**du'l-fikar** *See* ZULFIKAR.

**dum-dum** The general name for soft-nosed expanding bullets. The word comes from the town of that name in western Bengal, some 10 km. (6 mi.) from Calcutta; the first dum-dum bullets, used later by British troops, were made in the ammunition factory there. The military use of dum-dum bullets was forbidden by the 1899 Hague Convention.

**dung** A traditional Tibetan spear, about 220–360 cm. (7–12 ft.) in length with a long, narrow, double-edged head and a socket for the shaft. The shaft, which was frequently wound around with a reinforcing spiral band of iron, was also fitted with a heavy iron ferrule on the butt end. Apart from its more obvious uses, the dung spear was also used sometimes by the Tibetans as a kind of vaulting pole when mounting a saddle.

**Dusägge** (or **Düssägge**, **Düsack**) A German short saber used in the 16th century for fencing practice. It soon developed into an infantry hanger, a prototype of the weapon used up to the second half of the 19th century. Most types had a short and fairly large curved blade and a hilt with a knuckle guard and short rear quillon. The Dusägge itself had probably derived from the Bohemian saber called *tésak*, consisting of a short, wide blade with a slot at one end, forming both the grip and the knuckle guard.

**dynamite** An explosive obtained by mixing nitroglycerin with various substances. *See also* EXPLOSIVE.

# E

**eared dagger** *See* DAGGER.
**ear lappets** The two flaps attached to the sides of an ARMING CAP which covered the ears and tied under the chin with laces.
**ear pieces** Tubular defenses—from about the middle of the 14th century—which were built into the sides of the SHAFFRON to protect the horse's ears.
**ebira** A type of Japanese quiver which was hung from the left shoulder. It usually consisted of an open box fitted with bars to steady the arrowheads and an open metal or whalebone frame, rising from the back of the box, with cords to hold the shafts. The box, often made of bamboo, was finely lacquered and decorated with a monogram or family crest. Gold lacquer or a powdered gold ground was frequently used. A small drawer in the lower part of the box was often arranged to contain an extra bowstring, an ink slab, or other small accessory.
**eboshi cap** A special samurai cap worn under the EBOSHI-KABUTO. Picture rolls dating from as early as the 11th century show that the cap was tall and made of black felt. It resembled the Phrygian cap, but it was worn the other way around, with the pendant top at the back. To keep the cap in place, a kind of towel was bound over the forehead and knotted at the back of the head.
**eboshi-kabuto** A Japanese samurai helmet shaped in the same way as the EBOSHI CAP but having an iron skull and downward-sloping front peak, with a crest and laced neck guard, the SHIKORO, at the back. During the Tokugawa (Edo) period (1603–1867), the eboshi-kabuto sometimes had an exaggeratedly tall skull.
**écusson** *See* QUILLON BLOCK.
**ejector** A part, or set of parts, of a firearm that acts on the cartridge case as it is extracted and ejects it from the gun. The ejector may be attached to the RECEIVER or may be fitted at the front of the bolt. In some smooth-bore shotguns the EXTRACTORS are fitted with springs so that they themselves act as ejectors. In certain semi-automatic weapons the function of this indispensable component is performed either by the striker or by the point of the next cartridge in the magazine.

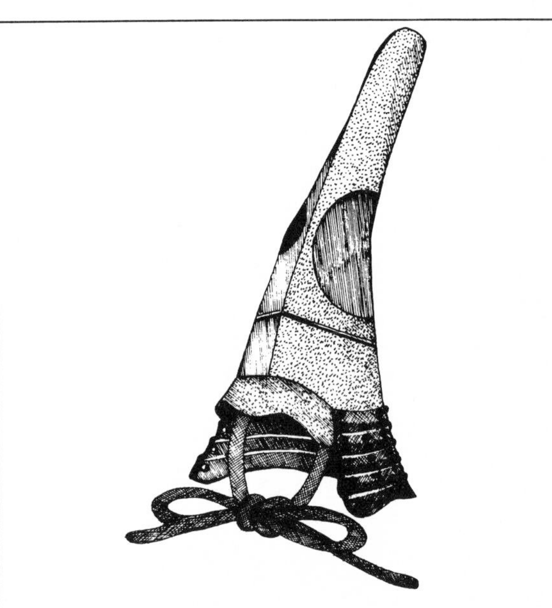

*Eboshi-kabuto, ceremonial Japanese helmet, 16th–17th century. Tokugawa Art Museum, Nagoya.*

**elbow guard** A reinforcing plate for the right COWTER in a tilt armor. It consisted of a heavy, shaped plate screwed over the cowter.
**elephant dagger** Popular name for the BHUJ.
**elephant's trunk** The projection on a KRIS.
**embossing** *See* DECORATIVE TECHNIQUES.
**enameling** *See* DECORATIVE TECHNIQUES.
**enamma** Greek term for AMENTUM.
**enarmes** Also called braces, the handles by which the shield is held. In their most common form, there are two loops, the first of which is fixed—and held with the left hand—and the second, in which the left arm is placed, is movable and can be adjusted by means of a buckle. Usually made of leather, or more rarely of wood, they are

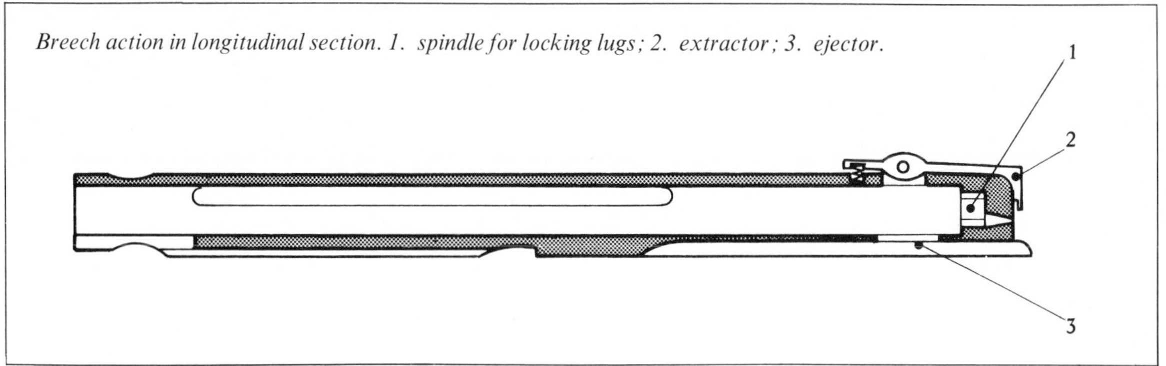

*Breech action in longitudinal section. 1. spindle for locking lugs; 2. extractor; 3. ejector.*

attached to the inside of the shield with rivets.

**English lock** This lock incorporated elements of both the snaphance and the "French" flintlock. The lock consisted of a STEEL and a PAN COVER made as one element and a laterally operating sear working through an aperture in the lock plate. This sear was fitted with a wedge-shaped projection which caught in a recess in the tumbler at half cock. On some of the later examples—dating from just before the middle of the 17th century—the sear caught in a recess in the tumbler at full cock. It has been suggested that the English lock provided an intermediate stage between the snaphance and the French flintlock. However, the lack of precisely datable English locks that can be shown definitely to predate the French flintlock makes the relationship between the two locks uncertain.

**English pot** (also nicknamed **lobster-tailed pot**) A type of helmet for heavy cavalry, similar to the 17th-century German ZISCHÄGGE, which derived from the Islamic SHISHAK. This type was introduced into eastern Europe toward the end of the 16th century and was soon being used widely throughout western Europe. The English form appeared about 1630.

Structurally, it consisted of a hemispherical SKULL with a low comb, usually worn with an iron skullcap to double the protection of the head. The laminated tail, riveted to the skull and articulated on sliding rivets, was partially shaped to the neck and then projected backward, while CHEEKPIECES were hinged from each side of the skull and fastened under the chin with a buckle and strap.

The characteristic English pot had a pivoted FALL with a face guard formed of three vertical bars which joined below the chin, replacing the usual form of nasal bar.

Pot helmets were usually padded with linen canvas, held in place on the inside by rows of rivets arranged in such a way as to form a decorative motif of studs outside. Roping along the edges also produced an ornamental effect, and it was not uncommon for the skull to be engraved with small designs. These helmets were also frequently russeted.

**engraving** One of the DECORATIVE TECHNIQUES used on weapons and armor.

**épée** (French, "sword") An international term for a modern dueling sword and its sporting version. It was designed in France before the last quarter of the 19th century when duels with swords regained their past vogue. The épée combines the sword elements in use centuries earlier. Its gradually narrowing thrusting blade, unlike that of the FLEURET, is quite rigid, being three-edged and deeply grooved almost its whole length; in fact, it is a type of blade widely used in the smallswords from the late 17th century on. The guard of the épée had as a prototype the large cup guard of the 17th- and 18th-century swords and rapiers made in Spanish style (less the rimmed edge of the guard and the long quillons, both forbidden in the épée). The grip is surmounted by a heavy pommel to counterbalance the blade.

Since the épée and its use in a duel are markedly different from the fleuret and a fencing lesson, a training and contest version of the combat épée was devised to recreate actual dueling conditions. At first, the point was simply blunted; then it was hammered into a solid flat button. By the late 19th century, fencing with épées became a sporting discipline of its own, and the weapon used in practice and contests was slightly modified by displacing the blade up to 3.5 cm. (1⅜ in.) from the center of the guard to give a better cover to the hand. To improve the catch on the opponent's protective dress, the button was almost always provided with a four-prong *pointe-d'arrêt*, a miniature copy of the

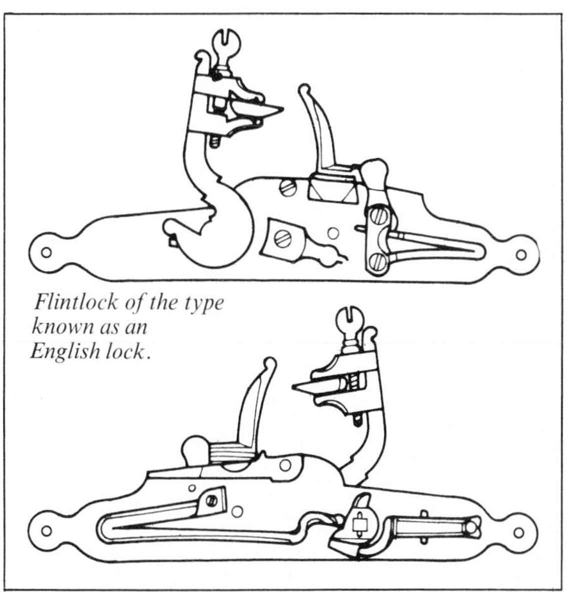
*Flintlock of the type known as an English lock.*

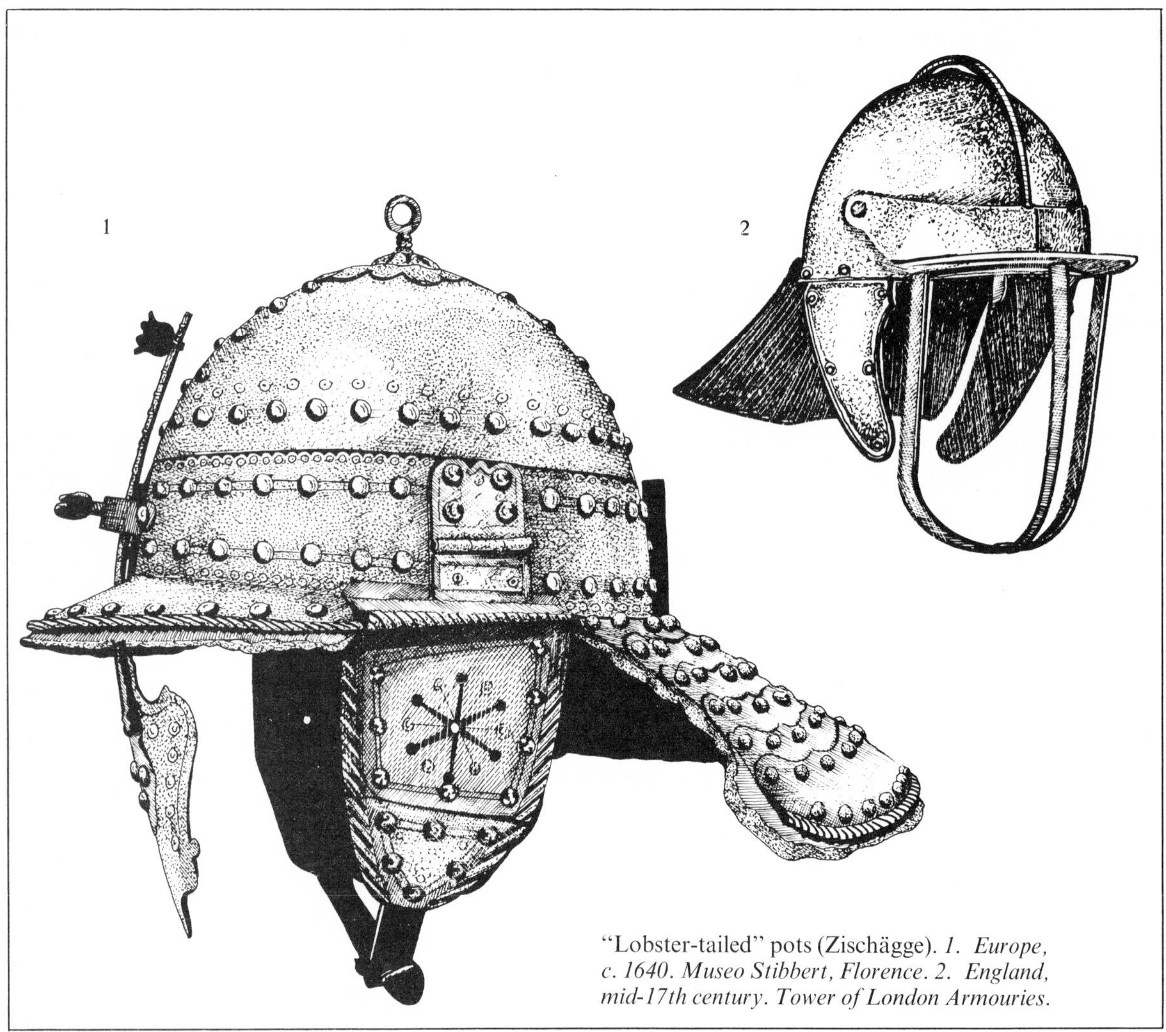


"Lobster-tailed" pots (Zischägge). *1. Europe, c. 1640. Museo Stibbert, Florence. 2. England, mid-17th century. Tower of London Armouries.*

medieval CORONEL used on jousting lances. From the 1930s the button has been made as a movable spring-loaded contact device acting on pressure to score the hits by a system of electrical signals.

The sporting épée, considerably heavier than the fleuret, must weigh between 500 and 770 g. (18–28 oz.). The length of the blade may vary from 88 to 90 cm ($34\frac{1}{2}$–$35\frac{1}{2}$ in.), the total maximum length of the weapon being 110 cm. (43 in.). The maximum authorized diameter of the guard is 13.5 cm. ($5\frac{1}{4}$ in.). The handle can be either of French type—that is, straight and slightly shaped to the holding palm—or of the so-called anatomical or orthopedical form (also called "pistol grip"), which allows a very strong hold but no freedom in the *doigté*, or finger control of the weapon.

**eriva** *See* NODOWA.

**espadas á la jineta** *See* HISPANO-MORESQUE SWORDS.

**espontoon** *See* SPONTOON.

**estock** *See* TUCK.

**etching** A style of DECORATIVE TECHNIQUE in which nitric acid is used to eat away areas of metal not protected by wax or resin to form a design.

**explosive** A substance—generally in the solid state, sometimes liquid—which can be made by some external means suddenly to develop a large amount of gas at a high temperature. In conventional explosives this rapid development of gas is started by a combustion that causes the explosive's chemical to combine with the production of gaseous products at very high temperatures. The combustion is generally the result of a reaction between oxygen, an element that stimulates combustion, and one or more combustible substances in the explosive mixture. The oxygen, which combines with the combustible element or elements, comes from an oxygen compound that decomposes at the moment of explosion. The explosion thus actually consists of two chemical reactions: one, the decomposition of the oxygen compound, and the other, the oxidation of the combustible substances. In order to produce the explosion it is thus necessary to initiate the decomposition of the compound containing oxygen to produce the heat sufficient to cause the decomposition of the whole explosive mass. The speed at which this decomposition takes place depends on the degree of chemical stability of the oxygen compound. The oldest explosive used by man was black powder or GUNPOWDER. Gunpowder was the only explosive known until after the middle of the 19th century.

The history of modern explosives can be said to begin with the discovery of nitroglycerin and nitrocellulose. Nitroglycerin was produced for the first time in 1846 by the Italian chemist Ascanio Sobrero (1812–1888) and recorded in a letter published in *L'Institut* on February 15, 1847. In the same month Sobrero presented a thesis at the Turin Royal Academy ("On Some New Detonating Compounds Obtained by the Action of Nitric Acid on Vegetable Organic Substances"), in which he described nitroglycerin, nitromannite, and nitrolactose. He discovered that a violent reaction accompanied by red fumes occurs when concentrated nitric acid is added to glycerin. However, if glycerin was poured into a mixture of two volumes of sulfuric acid (density 1.84) and one of nitric acid (density 1.50), stirring them and keeping the temperature below 0°C., the results were different; the glycerin dissolved and the solution, when poured into water, gave an oily precipitate of nitroglycerin.

About the same time, Schönbein at Basel and Böttger at Frankfurt, working independently, nitrated cotton; recognizing the potentialities of the product, they were soon working together to develop their work for artillery. The fact that Pelouze had already nitrated paper makes it even harder to know where to give credit for the invention of nitrocellulose. The industrial production of this compound began at once for use as a propellant in cannon, especially in Austria through the work of Marshal von Lenk. A few years later, however, following a series of accidents caused by the instability of the compound, the manufacture of nitrocellulose was stopped. In 1865, however, a chemist in the British Royal Navy, F. Abel (1827–1902), patented a process for the manufacture of completely stable guncotton suitable for use as a charge in shells.

In 1863 the Swedish chemist Alfred Nobel (1833–1896) found an ingenious solution to the problem of using nitroglycerin: absorbing it in kieselguhr (a spongy earth, an unconsolidated form of diatomite), thus producing dynamite, which to this day, though differently composed, is the most commonly used explosive in mining. Another of Nobel's applications of practical value is the production of detonators from fulminate of mercury (1867), an explosive produced first by J. K. von Löwenstern (1630–1703), fully described in 1800 by E. Howard, and used later in metal caps by the American Joshua Shaw for ignition in small arms. In 1875 it was again Nobel who discovered explosive gelatin and the gelignites.

Between 1885 and 1888 there were three great discoveries in the technique of explosives. In 1885 the French expert F. E. Turpin (1849–1927) suggested the use of picric acid (discovered by Woulff in 1771) as a charge in projectiles. In the same year Vieille, a pupil of Berthelot, discovered SMOKELESS POWDER B, obtained by partial gelatinization in a mixture of alcohol and ether of a mixture of guncotton and nitrocotton. In 1888 Nobel, mixing nitroglycerin with nitrocotton, prepared ballistite.

*Properties and Classification of Explosives*

The speed of explosive decomposition, great as it is, is by no means equally rapid in all explosives. Basically there are two kinds of explosion: combustion and detonation. Explosives that decompose in the first of these two ways are called *deflagrating explosives*, or *propellants*, since they are used to propel the projectiles from guns. Those that detonate are known as *detonating explosives* and may be divided into high or bursting explosives, blasting explosives, and priming explosives, according to whether they are used as bursting charges in shells or bombs, for breaking down or loosening minerals, rocks or other obstructions, or, in small quantities, in fuzes to procure the explosion of much larger quantities of other explosives. With regard to their chemical composition, explosives may be divided into two main categories: explosive mixtures and explosive chemical compounds, commonly called chemical explosives.

Explosive mixtures consist of an intimate mixture of two or more different substances which, generally, are not themselves explosive but contain oxygen or some other combustible element that gives rise to the reaction. The essential combustible element in explosive mixtures is carbon, while the oxygen is usually obtained from a nitrate, a characteristic component of explosives. A typical example of an explosive mixture is black powder, in which the oxygen is obtained from potassium nitrate (saltpeter), for many centuries the only substance used for this purpose.

The great majority of chemical explosives used at present depend on the reaction of nitric acid on some organic substance; the aliphatic and aromatic series of hydrocarbons, together with the carbohydrates, have provided a great number of substances which become explosive as a result of nitration. Also included among the chemical explosives are a certain number of substances not obtained by nitration of organic substances: the fulminates, the perchlorates, the chlorates, and others, some of which form the basis of mixtures which are too violent for use as charges but are used to detonate other explosives. Among the main chemical explosives are:

*Nitric ethers*. These are obtained by the action of a mixture of nitric and sulfuric acids on base substances, the sulfuric acid having only the function of absorbing the water produced during the reaction, which would otherwise dilute the nitric acid and progressively slow down the reaction. Nitric ethers in the pure state are either colorless liquids or white solids, odorless and not oxidized on exposure to the air; they are more sensitive to heat than the nitro derivatives.

(a) *Nitroglycerin*: an oily liquid, colorless if pure; being highly sensitive to shock, it is never used by itself but always mixed with other substances. It is a component of some smokeless powders and of dynamites, which may have an inert base (examples are kieselguhr, used for Nobel dynamite, and dynamites using aluminum, randanite, powdered brick, tripoli, magnesium carbonate, ashes, kaolin, powdered mica, etc.,) an active base (some simple combustible such as charcoal, sulfur, sawdust, starch, etc.); a nitrate base (gunpowder, potassium nitrate and charcoal, barium nitrate and resin, sodium nitrate and charcoal, etc.), or nitrocellular base (guncotton, with or without potassium nitrate; nitrated paper of wood; nitrocotton, etc.); an independent explosive base (ammonium nitrate, potassium chlorate); or a mixed base (Nobel dynamites with kieselguhr, sodium or potassium nitrate, charcoal, etc.). The most powerful dynamites are of course those with an active base. Among these are blasting gelatin, the explosive most commonly used for blasting, which consists of 92 parts of nitroglycerin and 8 of nitrocotton; and gelatinous dynamites, for example, Nobel's extra dynamite (48% nitroglycerin, 1.6% nitrocellulose, 34.5% ammonium nitrate, 5% charcoal, 9% rye flour, 1% soda, and 0.5% ocher), and gelatin dynamite No. 1 (71% nitroglycerin, 4% nitrocotton, 18% sodium nitrate, and 7% absorbent powder).

(b) *Pentaerythritol tetranitrate*, known also as Pentrite and (in the United States) as PETN, discovered by Tollens in 1891. It is obtained by nitration of pentaerythritol and, being extremely sensitive to shock, is used as a secondary detonator or as an explosive in torpedoes and mines, mixed with pentaerythritol tetracetate (for example, PA 35, which contains 65% pentrite and 35% tetracetate) or other substances.

(c) *Dinitrocellulose*, also known as nitrocotton, prepared by Schönbein in 1846 by the nitration of cellulose. On account of its low explosive properties it is hardly ever used by itself, but it is a component of almost all smokeless powders and of all blasting gelatins and gelatin dynamites. For practical purposes it is "pulped," or broken down into very small fibers.

(d) *Trinitrocellulose*, better known as guncotton, also discovered by Schönbein in 1846. Manufacture is identical to that of nitrocotton except that a higher proportion of nitric acid to sulfuric acid is required in the mixture. Formerly used as a charge for shells and torpedoes (with 20% humidity) and for fuzes and for blasting in its dry state, it is no longer used by itself because of its instability; however, it is still contained in some smokeless powders.

*Nitro derivatives*. Nitroamines. One of the most important is trimethylenetrinitroamine, known under a number of names—Exogene, $T_4$, Cyclonite, RDX (Research Department formula X). Discovered by Kenning in 1899, it is prepared by treating hexamethylenetetramine with nitric acid. It is very sensitive; it is used pure as a secondary detonator and 5% phlegmatized with paraffin as a charge for shells and bombs. Phlegmatized with TNT it gives Composition B, which is used in the United States instead of TNT as a standard explosive for hand grenades and artillery shells. Phlegmatized with petroleum jelly, it is called plastic $T_4$, and has a consistency like putty, so that it can be fitted around the objects that are to be destroyed. It is currently one of the most commonly used explosives for military demolitions. Fluid mixtures based on $T_4$ have been used, and some are still in use. Tritolite is composed of $T_4$ (40–60%) incorporated in molten TNT (60–40%). Tritolital generally consists of TNT (60%), $T_4$ (20%), and powdered aluminum (20%). The aluminum has the effect of reducing the amount of gas generated by the explosion, forming alumina; at the same time it greatly increases the temperature of the explosion, thus also increasing its power. The reaction of the aluminum does not begin until the temperature has reached a certain level. It is used essentially for charges in underwater weapons (torpedoes and mines).

*Aromatic derivatives*. Dinitrotoluene is obtained by nitration of toluene. It has very low explosive properties and is never used by itself. It is used as an antifreeze in nitroglycerin and to gelatinize dilute ballistite C.G.13. Trinitrotoluene (1 methyl 2–4 trinitrotoluene), better known as TNT and also as trotyl, tolite and so on, was prepared by Wilbrand in 1863 by nitration of toluene with a mixture of nitric and sulfuric acids. Later it was prepared by Khulberg and Beilstein by nitration of ortho- and paramononitrotoluene and by Tiemann by nitration of 2–4 binitrotoluene.

On account of its remarkable destructive power and rapidity of detonation, of its slight sensitivity to shock and of the fact that it does not corrode metals, TNT is widely used for bursting charges in shells, hand grenades, aerial bombs, torpedoes, mines, and so on, usually in cast form in view of its low melting point, 76–78° for low-grade and 80–81.5° for high-grade. It can be turned, milled, sawn, or drilled without danger. Raw low-grade TNT consists of dark yellow crystals; the crystals are lighter in pure, high-grade TNT. The surface turns brown in the light, especially in intense light. Insoluble in water, it is highly soluble in alcohol, ether, acetone, benzene, and so on. Large masses of it in the cast state need a secondary detonator of compressed TNT, which is more sensitive. The technical exploitation of it began in 1891, when C. Häussermann, with the Griesheim Chemical Works, made practical use of Wilbrand's discovery. In the course of his work Häussermann described the explosive properties of TNT; but practical research on this substance when mixed with potassium nitrate had already been carried out in Germany toward the end of the 1880s.

The preparation of TNT became more practical after the manufacture of fuming sulfuric acid by the contact process, in which highly concentrated acid mixtures were used. In industry TNT is normally prepared by the nitration of toluene in two phases; a first nitration of toluene produces mononitrotoluene (a mixture of the three isomers ortho-, para-, and meta-) or dinitrotoluene (a mixture of the two isomers 1–2–4 and 1–2–6, with a preponderance of the former); the second nitration, using either mononitrotoluene or dinitrotoluene, gives trinitrotoluene.

Trinitrophenol, or picric acid, is also known in Britain as lyddite, in France as mélinite, in Italy as pertite, in Germany as Granatfullung 88, in Japan as shimose, and in Austria as ecrasite. It is mainly used as a base for many other explosive mixtures, including English lyddite (87% trinitrophenol, 10% binitrobenzene, 3% petroleum jelly). Picric acid was first prepared by Woulff in 1771 by the action of nitric acid on indigo. Haumann isolated the pure acid in 1778, and in 1788 he published a detailed study of it in which he drew attention to its bitter smell. In 1799

*Explosive Mixtures*

| *With Ammonium Nitrate Base* | | *With Sodium or Potassium Base* | |
|---|---|---|---|
| Schneiderite | ammonium nitrate 87.4%—dinitronaphthalene 12.6% | Cheddite I.S. | potassium chlorate 90%—paraffin 7%—petroleum jelly 3%—traces of carbon black |
| Siperite | ammonium nitrate 72.84%—dinitronaphthalene 10.5%—trinitrotoluene 16.66% | Cheddite O.S. | sodium chlorate 90%—paraffin 7%—petroleum jelly 3%—traces of carbon black |
| Amatol | ammonium nitrate 60–80%—trinitrotoluene 40–20% | Cheddite O extra | sodium chlorate 79%—dinitrotoluene 16%—castor oil 5% |
| Ammonal | ammonium nitrate, powdered aluminum, potassium or barium nitrate, powdered carbon | Cheddite gelatin | sodium chlorate 75%—nitro derivatives of toluene 23.2%—nitrocotton 1.8% |

Welter obtained picric acid by the action of nitric acid on silk; the result of his reaction was called "Welter's bitter."

It is prepared industrially by the action of sulfuric acid and nitric acid on phenol. Picric acid crystallizes out of water or alcohol to form light yellow plates, which melt at 122.5°. It is not very soluble in cold water, slightly more in boiling water, but readily soluble in alcohol, ether, acetone, and so on. It forms salts (picrates) with several metals, especially in the presence of humidity; lead and cadmium are attacked most readily, iron a little less, nickel and aluminum very little.

It is a good explosive, although it has some disadvantages: the formation of picrates, high melting point, considerable sensitivity to shock. Consequently its use as a bursting charge, once very common (it was loaded in the melted state), has now almost entirely disappeared. It was widely used in the following compounds: M.A.T. (60% picric acid, 40% TNT), M.B.T. (60% picric acid, 40% dinitrophenol), M.A.B.T. ( a mixture of these two).

Tetranitromethylaniline, also known as tetryl, tetralite, or pyronite, was obtained by Michler and Meyer in 1879 by nitration of methylaniline. It is a light yellow crystalline powder, insoluble in water, slightly soluble in hot alcohol, highly soluble in benzene, acetone, and toluene. It melts at 129°, is fairly sensitive to shock, and not very stable. It is used, especially in Britain and the United States, in shell detonators and percussion caps. In the First World War some of the belligerents used it mixed with TNT as a bursting charge for shells.

*Explosives obtained by nitration of metals.* Mercury fulminate, discovered by Löwenstern (1630–1703) and investigated in depth by Howard in 1799, is prepared by dissolving mercury in nitric acid and pouring the resulting nitrate into ethyl alcohol. The product forms minute trapezoidal crystals of a color varying from light yellow to white. It is extremely sensitive to shock, although this sensitivity is reduced with humidity. It explodes at 170°–180° and can be detonated by an electric spark. On account of its great sensitivity to shock, it is always used in very small quantities. It must be protected from damp and from contact with many metals, with which it reacts to form fulminates. It is most often used in mixtures, usually with potassium chlorate, to obtain oxidation and make the most of its explosive potential. Until the advent of smokeless powders, mercury fulminate was the main component of cartridge primers.

Lead azide, obtained by treating sodium azide with lead nitrate, separates on filtration into white crystals. It is preferred to mercury fulminate for its lower sensitivity to shock, greater detonating power, and greater compressibility. Another chemical explosive widely used today as a primer is lead styphnate, combined in some U.S. compounds (PA 100, PA 101, 793, NOL 60, etc.) with limited quantities of tetrazene or guanylnitrosoamine, barium nitrate, and antimony sulphide.

In the past certain liquid explosives, in particular those using liquid air and the panclastites, were of some importance. The liquid air explosives are essentially mixtures consisting of a combustible impregnated with liquid air or liquid oxygen. Linde, basing his experiment on the fact that nitrogen is the first to evaporate from liquid air, thus increasing the concentration of oxygen, made a new explosive by causing liquid air to evaporate until it contained some 56 percent of oxygen and then mixing it with powdered charcoal. Later he modified the formula and prepared oxyliquite, consisting of the liquid air mixture (with the higher oxygen content obtained by evaporation of nitrogen) into which he inserted cartridges of sugar carbon (which is highly absorbent) and petrol just before use.

Penclastite, invented by Turpin, is completely liquid. It is a homogeneous mixture of hydrogen peroxide and carbon sulfide, with nitric derivatives of the hydrocarbons, or with the hydrocarbons themselves. The mixtures are very powerful, with great speed of detonation.

**Express** A large-caliber rifle with two barrels side by side, similar externally to the ordinary side-by-side double-barreled shotgun. The term "Express Train,"

*Express rifle, Belgium. Fabrique Nationale Herstal.*

shortened to "Express," was first used by the famous English gunmaker Purdey in 1856, referring to guns having a long point-blank range and very flat trajectory. The Express is still the favorite gun for shooting dangerous or big game. Among calibers used in these powerful rifles today are the .500/.465 Nitro-Express, the .475 Nitro-Express, the .500 Nitro-Express (3 in.), and the .577 Nitro-Express (3 in.). Obsolete calibers include the .600 Nitro-Express, which had cartridges that were for many decades the most powerful in the trade.

**extractor** A mechanism in a firearm which extracts the cartridge case from the chamber. Generally a form of claw, it is attached to the bolt and clips over the rim or groove at the base of the cartridge; the slight play needed to allow it to seize the case is given either by a spring in the bolt or by the extractor itself, which is elastic longitudinally. In some semiautomatic weapons having a blowback action there is no extractor; on firing, the spent case is expelled by the gases, and it is actually the base of the cartridge that drives the bolt or breechblock back.

# F

**face** In striking weapons, this is the extremity used for striking. It may be of various shapes: flat, rounded, or with raised teeth; it is opposite the PEEN.

**fakir's crutch** A rather rare form of Indian mace or pick used, as the name implies, mostly by religious mendicants forbidden by law to carry arms. Usually made from a solid piece of steel, it has a short handle on one side of which is a head shaped like a hand holding an antelope's horn and, on the other, a serpent with a tiger's head. This "crutch" is placed under the arm when the fakir is seated and, should the need arise, can be a very efficient weapon.

**fakir's horns** A rare form of Indian weapon used by some fakirs, who as holy mendicants have never been allowed to carry ordinary weapons. It consists of a pair of black buck horns fastened together with their points going in opposite directions. The tips of the horns are sometimes furnished with steel spikes.

**falarica** Also called "saguntine spear," a heavy missile weapon used by the Romans. Pliny the Elder (A.D. 23–79) gives a fairly exhaustive depiction of it, describing it as a javelin with a long head and a round shaft, except for the part where it meets the head, which is four-sided as in the PILUM. The head was about 1 m. (39 in.) in length, with a triangular-section point. In order to increase the impact of the weapon, the joint where the head met the shaft was fitted with a round lead piece. This is possibly why it was said that it took a mighty arm to hurl the Saguntine spear, whether in battle or on the hunt.

The incendiary missile spear was a specific version of the above: the head was fitted with a large wad or ball of tow soaked in pitch or some other inflammable substance; this was lit before the spear was hurled; the flames were kindled by the spear's flight; and the device would reach its target fully ablaze. This type of missile was thrown either by hand or with a torsion-powered or a spring-powered machine (like the ARCUBALLISTA).

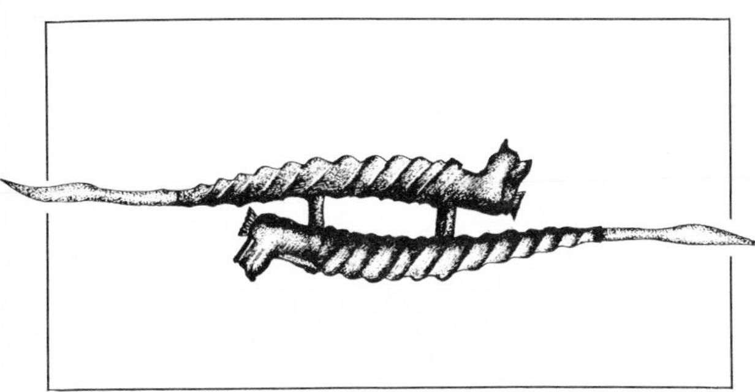

*Fakir's horns, India, 17th century.*

**falchion** A sword with a heavy single-edged blade, whose back was either straight or slightly concave, while the edge had a pronounced convex curve. The blade also broadened considerably toward the point where the back formed a long cut-off sharpened section (back edge). It was in use in northern Europe from at least as early as the 13th century and throughout the 14th and 15th centuries. Its origins cannot be accurately pinpointed, even though there is much backing for the theory that it derived from the SAX of northern Europe, with which it had many features in common, particularly the broadening of the blade toward the point. It is also thought that the later development of the falchion may have been the result of Eastern influences. However, its hilt always reflected forms of other European swords in use at that time.

**falcon** An ancient piece of light artillery which fired shots weighing from 1 to 6 lbs. A typical Venetian falcon of the second half of the 16th century, for instance, was (in local measures) 32 calibers (229 cm./6½ ft.) long, with a caliber of 72/75 mm. (2½ in.), fired lead balls weighing 1.8 kg. (4 lbs.), and weighed 482 kg. (1060 lbs.). The value of a single piece was about 151 ducats; complete with carriage it cost 160 ducats. An English falcon of the same period (1574) had a caliber of 63.5 mm. (2½ in.), weighed 363 kg. (800 lbs.), and fired 1135 g. (2½ lb.) shot.

**falconet** An ancient piece of light artillery which fired shots of 1 to 3 lbs. Smaller than the FALCON, in the 16th century in Venice it was generally 36 calibers long, with a caliber of 60/63 mm. ($2\frac{1}{2}$ in.), and so measured 6 feet; it weighed about 162 kg. (357 lbs.) and fired lead balls weighing 900 g. (2 lbs.). The gun cost 90 ducats; complete with carriage it cost 97 ducats. (Nonmetric measures given here are those used in Venice.) A contemporary (1574) English falconet weighed about 230 kg. (500 lbs.), had a caliber of 51 mm. (2 in.), and fired 908 g. (2 lb.) shots.

**fall** A projecting peak on many types of 16th- and 17th-century helmets of BURGONET type, which served to protect the eyes both from blows from above and from the sun. It consisted of a horizontal lame positioned above eye level and projecting for about the width of three fingers. The fall lame had a rounded contour and was either riveted to the skull or attached by two hinged side fastenings, which enabled it to be raised and even detached. The fall on the burgonet was made in one piece with the skull.

**falling buffe** A type of bevor for a BURGONET to protect the face; it is also called the "Hungarian visor." In its classic form, this buffe consisted of two or three lames, articulated on sliding rivets, each lame being held closed by spring-operated studs projecting through the lame below. The lames could be lowered by depressing the studs to give more ventilation, hence the term "falling" buffe. The lames were also provided with ventilation holes. The upper lame ended at eye level, just below the peak of the helmet. Often three lames were attached to the lower edge of the buffe to form gorget plates joining those on the skull.

In many German armors, buffes are attached to the top of the breastplate by means of catches or staples and pins in a similar way to the bevor for a sallet. Methods of attaching the buffe to the burgonet varied, but because it was usually a separate piece, it was held in place by a strap around the neck and hasps at the sides. In the case of Greenwich burgonets, there were hasps and two lugs on the cheekpieces engaging in slots on the buffe.

**false edge** In single-edged weapons, a sharpened portion of the back near the point; it is also called the back edge. It served both for better thrusting penetration and for cutting strikes carried out from the same position of the sword (without turning the hand).

**falx supina** (Latin, "recurving sickle") A particular type of war knife of Oriental origin, with a curved blade and concave cutting edge, used in Roman times by Thracian gladiators. It was so named because of its shape close resembled that of a sickle. A similar weapon was developed in the western Mediterranean area, where it was considered as a sacrificial instrument and associated with various mythical figures, including Zeus striving with Typhon and Hercules fighting the Hydra of Lerna. *See also* HARPÉ.

**farangi** *See* FIRANGI.

**fauchard** (from French *faus,*, *faux*, "scythe") A term occurring in French and English texts of the 12th to 14th centuries for a staff weapon which probably had a large pointed head with curved edge and a fluke. It belongs to the type of pole arm classified as the GLAIVE.

**fauld** A medieval term for the skirt of the shirt of mail (*see* HAUBERK). It has also been applied by association to the SKIRT of plate armor, which replaced mail as the main body defense.

**feathers** (or **fletching**) A part of the BOLT and ARROW, consisting of two or more vanes situated at the rear of the shaft to maintain its direction in flight. The need to add vanes became evident as soon as the shaft was fitted with a head, which shifted the center of gravity of the arrow too far forward. Down through the ages the vanes have been made of a wide variety of materials, but it was not long before birds' feathers became the principal material—

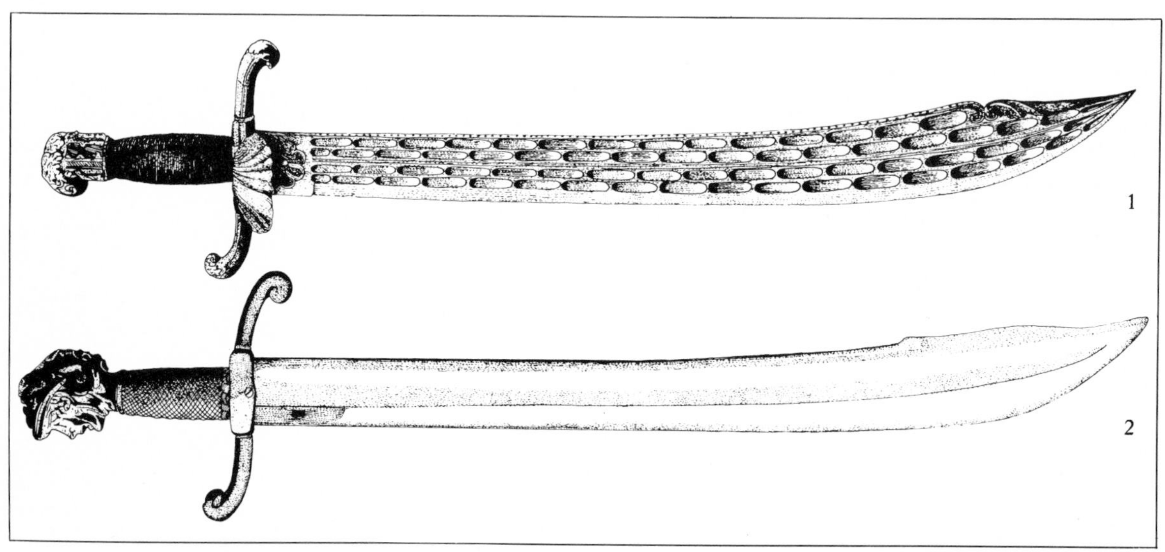


*1. Falchion which belonged to Don Juan of Austria, N. Italy, c. 1565–70. Armería Real, Madrid. 2. Falchion, N. Italy, c. 1550. Museo Nazionale del Bargello, Florence.*

hence the name. The feathers most preferred because of their strength were the wing quills of the goose. But fashion and other whims also dictated the use of other types of plumage, although not for long—even parrot feathers having been used. On crossbow bolts stronger vanes were preferred, and as a result they were made of parchment, *cuir-bouilli* (hardened leather), thin slivers of wood, and so on. Plastic vanes are used in this century.

The feathers or vanes were made in different ways, depending on whether a longer range or greater accuracy was required. In the first instance the vanes were set parallel to the axis of the arrow, which produced an effect of aerodynamic lift in the arrow's trajectory; for greater accuracy they were placed on a slant with the axis, which gave the arrow a rotating notion in the air, and this had a stabilizing effect.

There are several methods of attaching the vanes to the shaft. Both ends of the feather may be fixed by thin windings around the arrow shaft, or the entire feather may be fixed by a broad, spiral fastening to the shaft. In yet another method, the quill of the feather is inserted in the shaft at the nock and the tip is attached by the winding.

**feather staff** *See* LEADING STAFF.

**feeding, systems of** Feeding a modern firearm is based on the mechanical principle, static and/or kinematic, which provides a rapid and continuous flow of cartridges to the point from which they will be impelled into the (explosion) chamber.

The organization and structure of such systems vary widely, ranging from the angled and vertical feed hoppers of the first Gatlings to such highly sophisticated devices as those found on the Cleereman or Bertran & Lesnick. Feed systems for ordinary repeating weapons, both semiautomatic and automatic, may—in their simplest form—consist of a single magazine, such as is found on the Lee. Repeating guns with a tubular magazine also used to have a lifting "spoon," with all its relative mechanism. Light and ordinary machine guns contain a complicated structure, too, whose job it is to convey the cartridges from the magazine (or belt) to a position in the receiver opposite the chamber.

Today, feeding by means of detachable, vertical magazines is the most favored method for army rifles, submachine guns, assault rifles, and several types of light machine guns. In the case of medium and heavy machine guns, belts made of disintegrating or nondisintegrating metal links, rather like chain mail, are now being used. *See also* GUN; MACHINE GUN; SUBMACHINE GUN.

**feikho** A primitive Chinese firearm. *See also* TUKHOTSIAN.

**ferrule** A ring or cap reinforcing the grip of an edged weapon or the shaft of a pole arm. The term also is sometimes applied to scabbard bands.

**feruzue** An unusual Japanese weapon consisting of a hollow stave about 1 m. (39 in.) long, which contains a chain to which is attached an iron ball. When the stave is brandished, the ball flies out with sufficient force to kill a man. Its invention is traditionally attributed to the priest of Nara Hozoin Inei (1521–1607).

**firangi** (also **phirangi, farangi**; from *feringi*, "Frank") An Indian word denoting "a foreign thing," in this case referring to a sword with a closed hilt and a straight, cut-and-thrust imported blade. These were mainly brought to India by the Portuguese, but local swordsmiths also imitated the European style. Some of the blades were fairly long, up to about 100 cm. (39 in.), and broadsword blades with shallow grooves were quite common.

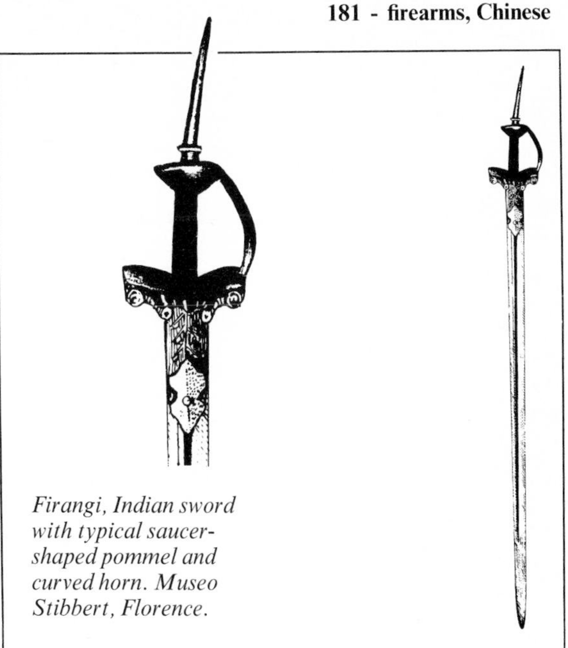

*Firangi, Indian sword with typical saucer-shaped pommel and curved horn. Museo Stibbert, Florence.*

Used mostly in the Mahratta empire, firangi blades were mounted in local style, the hilt being of steel with a round grip and a discoidal pommel topped by a slightly curved short spike. The long tang to which the blade was riveted ran out at the root of the blade into two upturned flange like quillons.

A firangi sword was sometimes fitted with a Hindu basket-type hilt, the grip being bound with velvet and the guards padded with the same material; it had large seatings and quillons, while the pommel was saucer-shaped with a curved spike projecting from its center.

The same type of sword but with a locally manufactured blade is called *sukhela* and *dhup*.

**firearms, Chinese** Gunpowder was probably invented in China in the 7th century as a result of the advances made in the natural sciences and the general economic development during the T'ang Dynasty. In 682 Sun-Sy-miao, in his work entitled *The Canon on the Philosopher's Stone*, stated that the mixture of sulfur, saltpeter, and charcoal had explosive properties; this is the oldest known recipe for gunpowder. It was not, however, used by the Chinese for war purposes before the 10th century. First, they constructed primitive petards, consisting of a paper bag with a burning match fired from a bow with a special arrow; this weapon was called the *feikho* and was mentioned in 904 in the treatise of Siui Tung. A special type of grenade thrown with a catapult was known as a *khopao*. The charges were made of bamboo segments filled with sulfur, saltpeter, charcoal, colophony, wax, red lead, hemp, and paper. As might be expected, a terrible noise and toxic smoke accompanied the explosion.

From the 11th century the production of gunpowder was controlled by the state and, in the next century, flamethrowers similar to Byzantine syphons for the so-called Greek fire were in use. During the Sung Dynasty the first genuine firearms with bullets were mentioned in documents dated 1259, under the term *tukhotsian*. These early guns were made of bamboo tubes reinforced on the inside with clay and iron bands and bound on the outside with cord. Such a barrel could stand the pressure of gunpowder gases up to 40 kg. (88 lbs.) per square inch, and the stone balls reached a distance of about 100 m (109 yds.). Bamboo barrels were next replaced by ones made of copper or iron but still in the shape of bamboo segments, enlarged at the breech and at the muzzle. These metal guns were called *khotun*, and they fired stone and metal balls. The Chinese were still pursuing the development of firearms quite independently, and in the 16th century tried to pass from heavy guns to small calibers by making smaller barrels and setting them in wooden stocks, although with little success. Ignition was accomplished by hand, with a match, because no lock mechanism was then available.

In the following periods foreign influences and inventions were adopted, especially in the construction of small arms. In the 17th and 18th centuries matchlock handguns produced in China were being modeled mainly on Indian patterns, but from the technical point of view they were among the roughest and poorest ever made. The surviving examples vary in length from 110–160 cm. (43–63 in.) and are furnished either with the Indian matchlock or with an even more primitive lock, in which the serpentine is pivoted in front of the pan and is connected to the trigger by a piece of string. When the string was pulled, this dragged the serpentine over and tipped the match into the pan. Usually there is no sight on the barrels, which are secured on the stock by means of brass rings. The stocks, often painted red, have characteristic pistol butts. The grip was held with the right

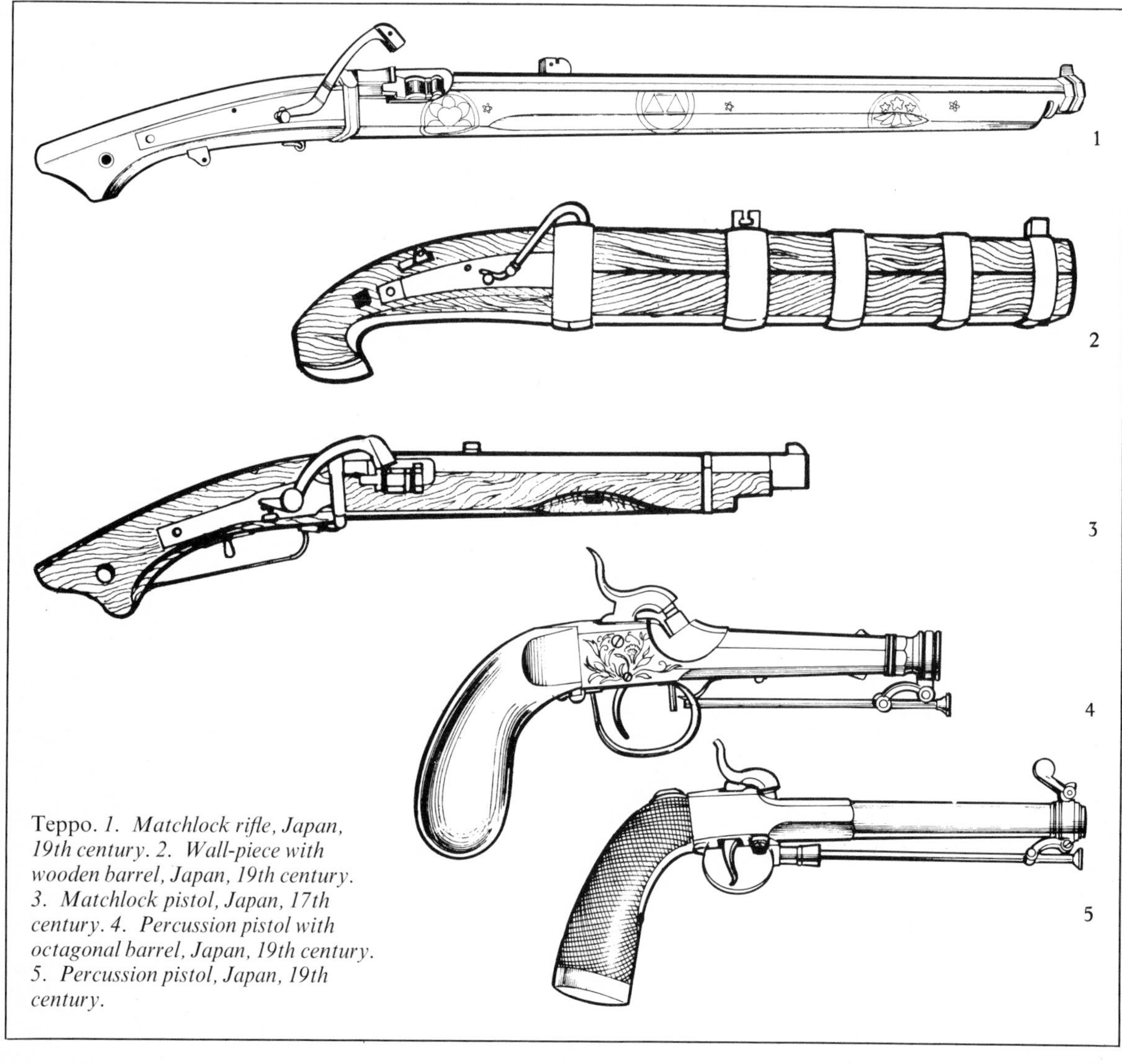


Teppo. *1. Matchlock rifle, Japan, 19th century. 2. Wall-piece with wooden barrel, Japan, 19th century. 3. Matchlock pistol, Japan, 17th century. 4. Percussion pistol with octagonal barrel, Japan, 19th century. 5. Percussion pistol, Japan, 19th century.*

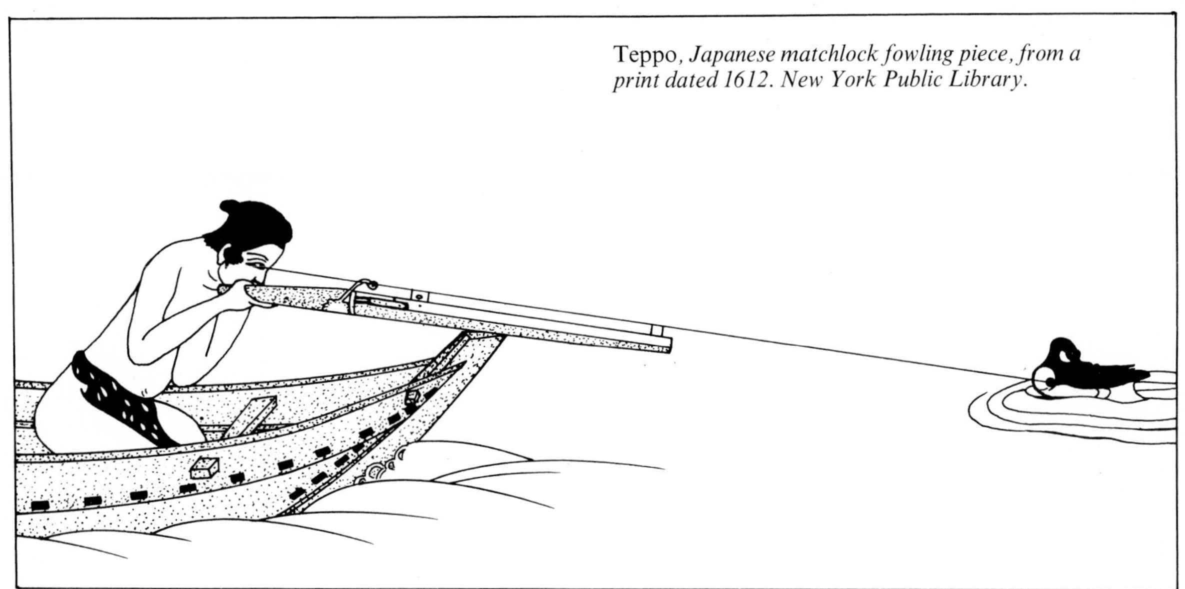

Teppo, *Japanese matchlock fowling piece, from a print dated 1612. New York Public Library.*

hand, while the left hand supported the stock. In some cases, the guns were fired from the hip. Also used in China were guns with long Indian stocks like the TORADAR, and, occasionally, those with curved Afghan butts like the JEZAIL.

**firearms, Japanese** *Teppo*, the general Japanese term for firearms, were introduced into Japan by the Portuguese in 1543. Never very popular in warfare, firearms were indeed inconsistent with the samurai code, although small arms were used for sport and hunting. The matchlock was used with guns and pistols up to the middle of the 19th century, after which the percussion and pinfire systems were adopted without the intermediary of other ignition devices. The primitive matchlock, however, was brought as near to mechanical perfection as possible in the hands of the Japanese gunsmiths, who made it of brass, with an iron pan and a wooden stock. The serpentine was held cocked by a sear and sent downward by a coiled spring or a U-spring when the trigger was pulled. The barrels, although generally rather heavy, were of very good quality and demonstrated the remarkably high standard of Japanese metallurgy.

Ornamentation frequently consisted of silver damascening or incrustation of other metals, and many of these guns bear the signature of the maker. The barrel, usually octagonal or round, was regarded as a continuous decorative field on which individual motifs were placed at intervals over its whole length instead of being covered by a rambling foliate or scroll design, as seen on some European barrels.

Most of these guns had two sights and some three, although the size and shape of the stocks often rendered them useless. Their hardwood stock had a very short butt, which served as a grip. Intended for firing from the hip, it was usually mounted with chased brass or silver. The guns, to which a ramrod was fastened on a swivel, varied in length from about 90–140 cm. (35–55 in.).

Very heavy guns of the same pattern were used as wall-pieces, that is, on the ramparts. Some of these had about a 3 cm. bore and weighed 25 kg. (55 lbs.). It is interesting to note that Japanese pistols were built rather like miniature guns. Three-barreled revolvers were also produced. Surviving Japanese bronze cannon and mortars are of excellent quality but comparatively small—barely over 1 m. (39 in.) in length. If we can rely upon contemporary illustrations, larger pieces were, in fact, occasionally used against castles and fortresses.

**firelock** A 16th-century term first used in some German documents (*Feuerschloss*) to designate mechanical devices for automatic IGNITION in firearms. The word may well have been applied both to wheel-locks and to any early flintlocks, like the snaphance.

**firing pin** A part of the firing mechanism which, propelled either by its own spring or by the action of the hammer, strikes the percussion cap or primer to cause ignition. For the various types, see also ARTILLERY; AUTOMATIC WEAPONS; GUN; MACHINE GUN; PISTOL.

**flail** A weapon consisting of a stout handle at the end of which was fitted, by means of a link or hinge, another short iron-shod bar or a wooden rod with iron spikes. Among the weapons with which the humble followers of Peter the Hermit armed themselves for the Crusades during the 11th and 12th centuries we find the flail, which was originally used for threshing grain; they had turned the head into a short rod with spikes. This weapon in turn gave rise to a more specialized weapon which, instead of having a single head, had two or more iron-shod balls. During the 13th and 14th centuries, this was used both in the larger versions by foot warriors, especially from the peasantry, and in the smaller versions by mounted men. Flails were still used by Polish peasants against Soviet troops in 1920.

**flamberge** A French word (meaning "flamboyant") which originally was a nickname given by the legendary knight Renaut de Montauban (8th century) to his sword.

Later it came to denote knightly swords in general, but in the 17th and 18th centuries the name was sometimes applied to special dueling swords. In modern times "flamberge" has been often erroneously applied to swords having wavy blades, which were actually called flambards or flammards, these terms being recorded since the 13th century.

**flamethrower** A portable or transportable apparatus able to discharge long jets of flaming liquid—the modern equivalent of Greek fire. In their simplest form flamethrowers consist of metal tanks containing liquids subjected to pressure by cylinders of compressed air (about 150 atmospheres); the cylinders are connected to the tanks by a system of tubes and taps. Compressed air from the cylinders enters the tank through a pipe, exerting great pressure on the surface of the liquid and ejecting it violently through a launching tube. Among portable flamethrowers used in the First World War were the intermittent-jet Italian model with automatic ignition; the DFL, also Italian; the Schilt No. 3 continuous jet; and the Schilt No. 3A with intermittent jet. Heavy flamethrowers included the Schilt No. 2 medium, the Schilt No. 2 large, and the H-T (Hersent-Thirion), mounted on a carriage. Automatic ignition was effected by a platinum sponge rendered incandescent by a jet of hydrogen from a cylinder at the end of the launching tube. The jet could be turned on and off by a valve on the launch tube, controlled by a lever.

The inflammable liquid was generally a mixture of five parts of light creosote oil from which the phenols had been extracted and one part of gasoline or benzene; a 5 percent solution of carbon disulfide was added to increase its inflammability and calorific power. Flamethrowers used during the Second World War included among others: by the Germans, Flammenwerfer models 35, 40, 41, and 42; by the Italians, models 35, 40, and 41; by the British, the Ack Pack; and by the Americans, the Flamethrower M-2A2.

**flanchards** A modern term for the part of a BARD which protects the horse's flanks. They consisted of a pair of heavy plates which were hung on each side from under the saddle, their lower edges reaching to just below the line of the underbelly. The two flanchards were generally placed under the PEYTRAL and the CRUPPER, with an opening at the center of each plate for the STIRRUPS and the SPURS. Only some sets of full bard were furnished with flanchards, and they did not figure at all in light horse armor or in various other protective harnesses.

**flange** A metal plate embedded at the head of a MACE. The first reinforcements of this type at the head of maces appeared in the 14th century; their shape was then gradually modified through the centuries. In the beginning, the edge of the flange was straight and almost parallel to the handle, but in the 15th century the edges became conspicuously shaped with central points, often fitted with a transverse reinforcement. North of the Alps, particularly in Flanders and southern Germany, these shaped flanges were worked to a considerable degree, possibly influenced by decorations in the Gothic style; in Italy they were much simpler. In eastern Europe the edge of the flanges was always much more rounded, influenced by Turkish models. Flanges were used almost to the end of the 17th century.

**flat** The side of a bladed weapon, as opposed to the CUTTING EDGE, the FALSE EDGE, or the RIB. It refers to the fairly flat surface of the blade which might have fullers, grooves, and decoration.

**fletching** *See* FEATHERS.

**fleuret** A French term, adopted also in English usage, for a light thrusting sword, or foil, used for teaching the art of fencing. The term first appeared in the 1630s, applied to the practice weapon whose hilt, formed only by a pommeled handle and two symmetrical petal-like ring or shell guards (fashioned after contemporary predecessors of smallswords), resembled a flower (*fleur* in French). Practice swords had been known at least from the 16th century, but these were rather crude, unfinished versions of the ordinary swords, provided with blunt blades or edged rods bent at the tip to form a bulbous button.

The fleuret has a slender, flexible blade, rectangular in section, with a flat button, often bound with a small leather pouch, instead of a point. Until the mid-19th century, the hilt of the French type preserved its original form of a "flower," the two symmetrical ring guards being often reinforced by thick leather shields. Later, however, the predominant form of the guard was a metal cup whose diameter must not exceed 12 cm. ($4\frac{3}{4}$ in.). The hilt of Italian type preserves the construction used in the 17th-century rapiers; it has, inside the cup guard, small arms of the hilt and a short crossbar, the remnant of the long quillons. While the hold of such a weapon is very strong, making the disarming quite difficult, it does not allow as fine a finger control of the fleuret as is possible with the hilt of the French form. The so-called *orthopedical* or *pistol grip* is also used when a strong hold is preferred.

The total length of the fleuret does not exceed 110 cm. (43 in.), while the blade may vary between 88 and 90 cm.

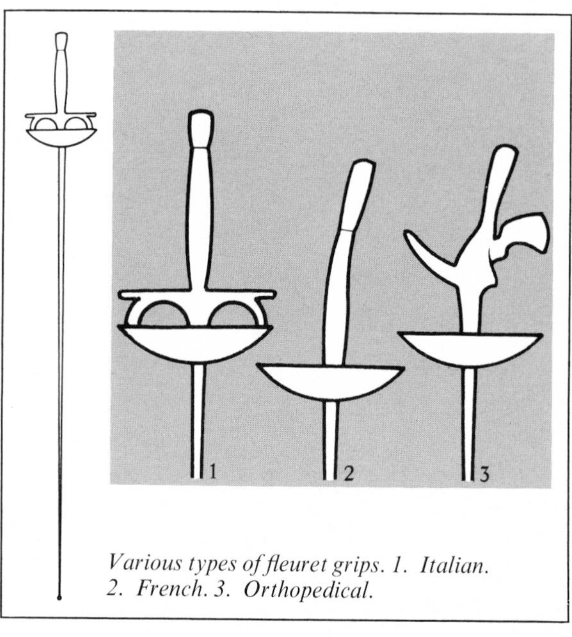


*Various types of fleuret grips. 1. Italian. 2. French. 3. Orthopedical.*

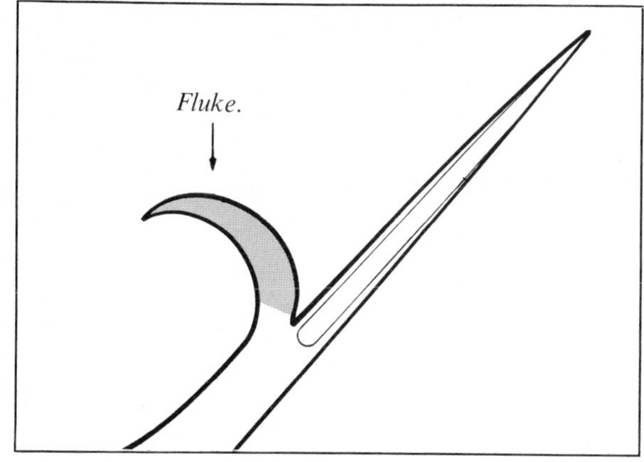


(34½–35½ in.). The weapon can weigh as little as 275 g. (10 oz.) but no more than 500 g. (18 oz.). Since the 1930s, when electrical scoring apparatus was introduced to signal the hits, the button of the "electrified" fleuret was made as a spring-loaded device contacting on pressure.

**flissa** (or **flyssa**) An Algerian sword related to the YATAGAN and resembling the SHASHKA, it probably developed in the early 19th century. However, its history was considerably older as similar weapons had been made in Kabyle villages for generations, especially by the Iflisen tribe, from whom the name derived. Emir Abd-el-Kader (1807–1883) possessed several examples in his armory, and in 1827 King Ferdinand VII of Spain, through his envoy in Algeria, was presented with a flissa.

This sword has a single-edged blade, quite straight on the back, with a long point. The cutting edge has a double curve, like a yatagan, the widest part of the blade being at about the central point of percussion, roughly at one-third of its length from the point, narrowing above and then widening nearly to its maximum again at the hilt. The average blade is almost 100 cm. (39 in.) long, frequently engraved and inlaid with brass in simple geometrical designs of triangles, semicircles, and scrolls. The hilt is small with a one-sided pommel, without guards, and formed in the shape of a bird's head. The lower part of the hilt is made of steel, together with the blade and tang, but its upper part—around the tang—is of wood and covered with ornamented brass or copper. The cross section of the grip is octagonal, and the pommel is fixed by a transverse rivet, the ends of which look like bird's eyes. A conical knob on the top is engraved in crescent-shaped designs.

The scabbard, made in two halves from carved wood, is joined together by several rings of copper or iron—usually six, seven, or eight—with a chape at the end. Sometimes these rings are of plaited thongs or tendons instead of metal. The surface is carved in geometric motifs, and there are two sling hoops on the outside of its upper part which are carved in one with the scabbard.

The entire decoration of the flissa resembles the designs of Kabyle rugs and Berber ceramics and jewelry, which are probably symbols of clans and tribes. The signs worked into the blade are of special interest because these conceal disguised symbolic meanings.

Flissas of smaller size can also be found, with a blade about 30 cm. (12 in.) long. The blade of this weapon, which actually is a dagger, curves slightly at the point, and the hilt—usually covered with brass or copper—is simpler than on the sword, while the pommel always retains the bird shape.

**fluke** A hook on the head of staff weapons, made in various forms, depending on the use for which it was designed. This device is found, for example, on the CORSESCA and the BOAT HOOK, where it served mainly for grappling. In the case of the RUNCA, the cutting edge was on the inside of the fluke, and in the BILL, which was more specialized for use in battle, both edges of the fluke, inner and outer, were cutting.

**flyssa** *See* FLISSA.

**foible** (or **faible**) The upper third of the blade, ending in the point. The division of the blade into three zones (forte, terzo, and foible) is attributed to the classical Italian school of fencing.

**foil** *See* FLEURET.

**fokos** *See* AX.

**folding gun** A type of 17th-century Italian firearm—usually a wheel-lock or a flintlock—with a folding stock which was hinged at the bottom of the small of the butt and held by a spring-loaded stud. When this stud was pressed, the butt could be folded down to the forestock for ease of transportation or concealment.

**follower** The platform in the magazine of a rifle or pistol that lifts the cartridges into place so that they can be pushed into the chamber, generally by the bolt. In weapons with fixed magazines, the lifter is an integral part of the rifle, actuated by the movement of the bolt (as in the Kropatchek system) or by a spring (as in the Mannlicher and Mauser systems). In rifles with detachable magazines, the lifter is contained within the magazine and has its own spring. In magazines containing two rows of cartridges, the top surface of the lifter is shaped so as to select the appropriate cartridge and prevent jamming.

**foresight** The front element, generally fixed at the front of the barrel, of the SIGHTS of a gun. It first appeared by c. 1450 in the form of a metal bead. In small arms the shape of the foresight blade can vary; it is commonly triangular or tapering in section, the height decreasing toward the muzzle, the rear face flat and at right angles to the axis of the barrel. The height and width of the foresight in military repeating rifles are about four times those of the backsight notch.

**fork (military)** A hafted weapon arm consisting of a head with two straight, parallel or slightly flared spikes of various shapes and sizes, often fitted with hooks at the socket. Basically, it was one of the agricultural tools adapted and transformed for use in combat. Such weapons appeared in large numbers during the Crusades, but they were also used in later periods during the peasant uprisings and revolts from the 15th to the 19th centuries. For military use, the prongs, which were curved in the agricultural version (e.g., the pitchfork), were straightened and sometimes fitted with spurs, which gave the weapon a dual function; it could either deliver a thrust or be used for pulling, to unseat a mounted enemy. Military forks were

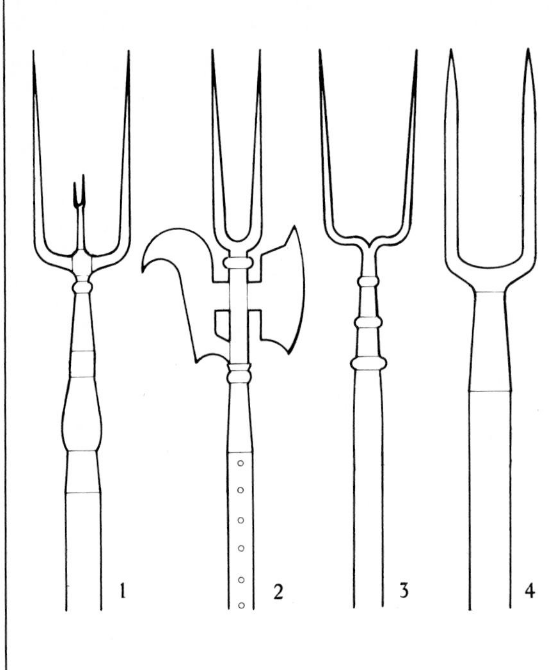


*Military forks. 1. France, latter half of the 16th century. 2. Savoy, c. 1580. 3. Europe, second half of the 17th century. 4. Switzerland, late 17th century.*

also used for scaling ramparts and other fortifications, for hoisting up baskets and faggots, and for setting up ladders.

At the end of the 17th century, forks were part of the service weaponry in Italy, France, and Germany. Many different versions were made, with prongs emerging from a broad curved base, flattened in section, and with cutting edges; or with prongs set like a *V* and a socket with a fluke and an ax. In the late 16th century, Duke Emmanuel Philibert of Savoy equipped his palace guard with a fork combined with an ax and a bill. In France, in memory of an act of valor dating back to the late 17th century, the sergeants of the Régiment Dauphin had their halberds replaced with a military fork, which remained in use until 1816.

The shape of the fork head was also well suited to housing, in the hollow shaft, a long additional spike; a barrel could also be fitted to it, as in the case of a combined weapon made by Bergamin in the first half of the 17th century (now in the Armory of the Council of Ten in Venice). This was a military fork-halberd with a wheel-lock pistol.

As a peasant's weapon, the fork was used during popular uprisings up to the 20th century; in 1920 Polish peasants armed with forks, flails, and scythes helped the army to defeat Soviet invaders besieging Warsaw.

**forte** The upper third of the blade of a sword, nearest the hilt, where the center of impact is situated. The division of the blade into forte, terzo, and foible is attributed to the Italian school of fencing, which enjoyed a fine reputation in the 16th and 17th centuries.

**fowling piece** An old term for a smooth-bore sporting gun, now commonly called the shotgun. *See also* GUN: sporting.

**frame** In modern pistols, the lower part of the weapon that holds the barrel and contains the firing system and in which the breechblock slides. The butt forms the back end of the frame. In shotguns and automatic and semiautomatic rifles, the frame is the metal body that connects or contains all the other components.

**francisca** (also **francisc**, **francisque**, **francesque**) An elegantly shaped battle-ax used by the Franks. Its arched head widened toward the cutting edge, which ended in a prominent point at the top corner and was often pointed at the lower one, too. The handle was fairly short, curving slightly toward the cutting edge of the blade and weighing about 600 g (21 oz.). It was, in fact, merely a rather unusually shaped hatchet which the Franks used as a missile, with an efficient throwing range of about 15 m. (50 ft.). It was already a characteristic national weapon of the Franks at the time of the Merovingians (c. 500–750) and is known to have been used during the reign of Charlemagne (768–814), as well as by the Germans, Burgundians, Lombards, and Goths. The Scandinavian battle-ax, and possibly that of the Vikings, probably derived from this ancient weapon.

**Frankish spear** A German form of the JAVELIN; the term is used by Tacitus in his *Germania*, which was published in A.D. 98.

**fringe** A collar of mail attached to a helmet to protect the neck, a version of the AVENTAIL. A mail fringe was mostly worn with the 15th-century helmets that had a visor and/or cheekpieces to protect the face, such as the armet. It was attached to the bottom edge of the helmet by means of pierced studs or rivets.

**Friuli spear** *See* CORSESCA.

**frizzen** The steel of the lock in a snaphance or flintlock firearm.

**fuchi** The ornamental metal collar which went around the hilt of a Japanese sword or dagger next to the guard. The word means "border" or "margin." The fuchi was

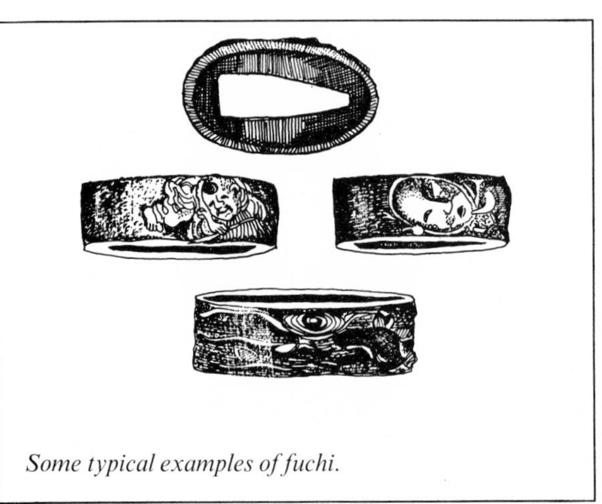

*Some typical examples of fuchi.*

very often made *en suite* with the KASHIRA—the pommel cap (which was sometimes made of plain horn). At the bottom of the fuchi there was a plate, generally made of a different metal, called the *tenjo kane*, or "ceiling," because, while the sword is being used in combat, it is above the head of the fighter.

Both the fuchi and the kashira were usually made *en suite* with the other mountings in iron, in shakudo, shibuichi, or sentoku alloy, or in silver. These materials were engraved, embossed, inlaid or overlaid with other metals, gold being the most widely used. Small figures of people—sometimes in landscapes—animals, birds, fishes, and plants were depicted very realistically; fantastic creatures like dragons or the ho-o bird (the Japanese phoenix) were also motifs.

The fuchi and kashira were the products of a specialized craft, sold separately and then mounted on the weapon, and are often signed and dated by the makers. The same craftsmen were usually responsible for the other sword mounts.

**fukidake** A Japanese blowpipe used rather for hunting birds than for any other purpose. In the primitive form, the fukidake was made of two grooved pieces of wood fastened together and wound around with several layers of a heavy paper, called *minogame*, to make it airtight. It was very light, though about 280 cm. (9 ft.) long with a bore of about 6 mm., and fitted with a small mouthpiece, the arrows being of bamboo with paper feathers. The later, more developed kind of fukidake is a tube of cane about 150 cm. (5 ft.) long, with a small trumpet-shaped mouthpiece projecting from the side at some distance from the end. The opening at the rear is closed by a wooden plug on the end of a crook handle. This plug is pulled out, and the dart is inserted and then pushed forward by the plug until it is beyond the opening of the mouthpiece; in this position the fukidake is held by the handle, the mouth applied to the mouthpiece, and the dart—which has an average length of about 25 cm. (10 in.)—can be blown out.

**fukigayeshi** The side guards on a Japanese helmet, whose basic function was to prevent the neck-guard lames, which were laced together by cords, from being cut off. There were several ways of constructing fukigayeshi but, in effect, they always formed convex wings at the sides of the helmet's peak. The first system was to lengthen the neck-guard lames and turn them back. Because there were usually five lames, made of scales, they were sometimes all turned back, although it was occasionally only done with one or two of the upper ones. On some helmets the fukigayeshi were made of separate pieces of iron, while on others they were formed by extending the ends of the helmet's peak and turning them upwards. Sometimes they were absent altogether. The fukigayeshi were often overlaid with leather, lacquered, and ornamented with metal emblems.

**fuller** The groove running along some of the length of the blade of an edged weapon, designed to both lighten it and make it more elastic. Compared with the various other structural modifications made to blades, the fuller appeared relatively late and only after considerable technological advances had been made in metalworking. In the Bronze Age there were opposite forms, with various angling and ribbing methods designed to reinforce the blade. During the "barbarian" migrations, we find swords with blades having a wide, shallow groove running down both faces. At a later stage the first signatures or marks of the craftsman appeared in these grooves. Through the centuries the fuller became an even more integral part of the blade until, in the 16th and 17th centuries, it also became a demonstration of the craftsman's skill and a display of his prowess. In some daggers the blade has six or eight fullers on each side and the grooves were pierced *à jour*.

**fulminate of mercury** A compound of metallic salts of mercury used as an EXPLOSIVE.

**funda** (Greek *sfendone*) A Roman term for a sling, consisting of a strap made of flax, leather, or horsehair, in the middle of which there was a pocket or pouch which held the missile. As a rule three slings of different lengths were carried for hurling the missile different distances—the maximum being some 150 m. (500 ft.). The idea of replacing the hand and arm with a weapon which offered far greater range came into being at a very early stage in virtually all primitive peoples and, apart from the well-documented use of it described in the Bible, there is evidence of it at Mycenae and throughout the Mediterranean basin. In Italy it was used by the Etruscans and by the Italic peoples under the sway of Rome, together with other allies who were used as auxiliary troops and placed on the flanks of battle formations, along with the archers. It was still in use in the time of Vegetius, in the 4th–5th centuries, who had words of praise for its usefulness, especially during naval battles and sieges. It was also used for hunting large wildfowl—waterfowl in particular. As a military weapon, slings were used in Europe until the 14th century and occasionally later.

**furnishings** A generic word used to describe all attachments, fittings, and accessories on large guns such as

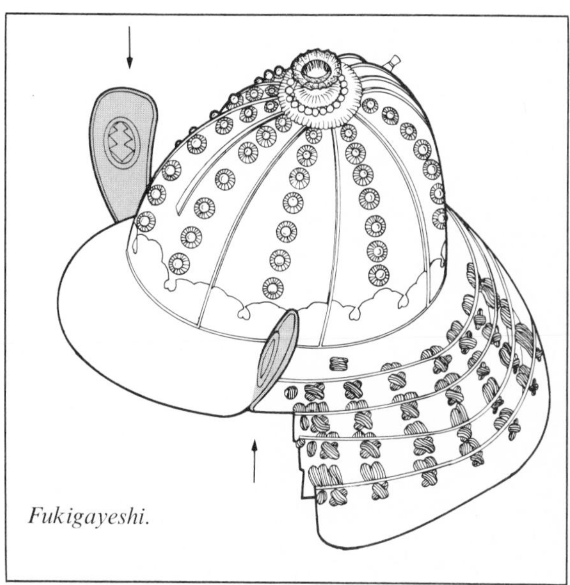

*Fukigayeshi.*

cannon. It is also used sometimes when referring to horse armor, particularly the more decorative types of trappings and caparisons.

**furniture** A generic word used to describe the accessories and fittings on various types of weapons. It refers, in particular, to everything built onto the tang of any cut-and-thrust weapon to facilitate its use and any decorative mounts on the handle, blade, or scabbard. It is also used, in a general sense, when referring to attachments, fittings, and accessories or armor and horse armor. In relation to small arms, all the pieces that link one part of a gun to another and ensure its smooth operation are known as furniture.

**fuses** Also called slow match. Mine fuses were widely used during the 19th century, especially the slow-burning or "safety" fuses (Bickford type), which measured 5 mm. ($\frac{1}{4}$ in.) in diameter. These were hollow and filled with black powder and then covered with a paste made from chalk and talc.

**fustibalus** (or **fustibal**) A staff sling, that is, a throwing weapon, consisting of a sling attached to the end of a rod about 1 m. (39 in.) in length. With this weapon, which was used with both hands, it was possible to hurl pebbles, glans, or stone or metal pellets more than 170 m. (550 ft.). It became obsolete in the latter part of the ancient period, but there is evidence of its use in the late Middle Ages. In his *Codex Atlanticus*, which deals with various war machines and throwing techniques, Leonardo da Vinci studied and proposed various staff slings.

**futomata-yari** Another word for SASUMATA.

**fuze** A device that ignites the charge of a projectile or bomb at the required moment. The earliest fuzes, used in mortar bombs, were simple wooden tubes turned on a lathe and filled with fine, compressed gunpowder. The tube was then forced into a hole in the casing of the bomb. The earliest forms were lit with the linstock just before it was applied to the vent to fire the mortar, but later it was found that, with the bomb inserted in the right way, the fuze was ignited by the flash from the charge. Credit for inventing the time fuze, with units of time marked on the outside of the tube, belongs to the Belgian General Bormann, while Colonel Breithaupt was the first to produce a metal time fuze that had a rotating cap. The Bormann and Breithaupt fuzes were followed by those, each showing some improvement, of Richter, Lancelle, Bazzichelli, Cavalli, Damarest, Baranzow, Romberg, Henriette and Budin, Gressly, Kreutz, and Pettman. But some basic features are common to them all: the explosive capacity must always be commensurate with the quantity and sensitivity of the explosive, and all rely on percussion to ignite the bursting charge of projectiles, with some form of striker detonating a capsule containing a small quantity of highly sensitive explosive. If the shell has to act on impact, the capsule is struck as the shell hits the target; if it is a time fuze, the capsule is struck as a shell begins to move and ignites a tube of precisely calculated length, which burns just long enough to ignite the bursting charge at the required moment.

The fuzes in use at the start of the Second World War were percussion, time, and double-action.

*Percussion fuzes* may work either by direct impact or concussion. Those that work on impact generally have the striker fixed to a fairly long rod projecting from the fuze; on impact, the rod is driven back against the capsule and causes the explosion. Such a projectile functions instantaneously; by adapting the length of the rod, it can be made to explode before its body hits the target. Concussion fuzes function by using the inertia of heavy masses. Single-concussion fuzes require only one concussion; when the projectile hits the target, a heavy mass carrying either the striker or the capsule continues to move under its own momentum and hits the capsule or striker, as the case may be, to cause the explosion. Double-concussion fuzes use two concussions, the first releasing a safety device and the second causing the explosion. Double-concussion fuzes are the most commonly used, with the fuze fitted at the point or in the base.

*Time fuzes* work by means of a quick match, a train of gunpowder whose length can be adjusted to control the time taken for combustion. The train is ignited as the projectile is fired by the flash produced by a detonator actuated by the inertia of a concussion-ignition device. The train may be enclosed or open, coiled around the fuze, or compressed in channels made in the rings that fit into the ogival section of the fuze. These rings (two or three, one fixed, the others movable) are arranged above one another and connected by ports; by adjusting the relative positions of the moving rings and the ports, the length of the powder train can be varied. Since the powder burns at a known speed, the fuze can thus be set to take a predetermined time.

*Double-action fuzes* are like time fuzes, but they also contain a percussion device. They can work by percussion alone or by time and percussion; in the latter case, if the projectile does not explode in the air it explodes on hitting the target.

A great advance in the effectiveness of fuzes was made during the Second World War with the introduction into service of optical fuzes and proximity fuzes. Optical fuzes contained a photoelectric-cell device that signaled a variation in luminosity as it approached the target. Proximity fuzes contained a radio transmitter and receiver; when near the target, part of the radio waves transmitted were reflected and received by the receiver, which activated the detonator. An important step forward since the war has been the introduction of fully transistorized proximity fuzes, which are more reliable in operation and able to be used on land as well as against aircraft.

# G

**gaesum** (Greek *gaidos*) A javelin carried by the Roman light infantry—the velites—which was probably fitted with an AMENTUM. It was made entirely of iron, and came in various forms: with a wavy-edged head as long as a sword, or with a conical or a leaf-shaped head. From the 4th century B.C. it was issued instead of the VERUTUM. Classical sources claim it is of Celtic derivation. It must have been a highly thought of weapon if, as we are told by Polybius (c. 205–120 B.C.), a soldier who had slain an enemy was given a gaesum as a reward.

**gaffe** Also called "bender" or "goat's-foot lever," the gaffe was a device used for spanning the crossbow, designed to reduce the effort necessary to charge the crossbow. The oldest type, often made of wood, consisted of a lever to which a shorter piece was attached by a pivot. In order to span the crossbow it was necessary to form a pivot with the lever, hooking it on two prongs of the tiller or on a ring at the front of the tiller. The hinged piece was then placed against the bowstring so as to form an obtuse angle; by pushing the lever toward the tiller, the angle increased and the hinged rod pushed the bowstring into the nut.

*"Goat's foot" lever, Europe, late 16th century. Odescalchi Collection, Museo di Palazzo Venezia, Rome.*

Before long, this type of lever was being made of steel: a metal arm, bifurcated about halfway down, having curved tips and pivoted hooks for catching the bowstring. The crossbow was adapted to this type of lever by fitting it with two steel prongs serving as pivots set across the tiller just behind the nut. Once the hooks were set in place on the bowstring and the curved tips of the lever were placed on the pivots, by pushing the metal lever the hooks moved along and pulled the string to the nock on the nut. This system could also be made to work in the other direction: instead of holding the crossbow steady and moving the lever, the lever was held firm against the thigh or chest (it was sometimes fitted with special pieces for this purpose) and in order to span the crossbow, pressure was applied to the tiller, which formed a longer lever requiring less effort. These levers were also known as leg or chest levers.

The gaffes could be used either on foot or on horseback and were most popular in southern Europe for both combat and hunting crossbows. Their use spread in the 17th century in Germany, Belgium, Switzerland, and Austria, mainly for sporting or light hunting crossbows. This led to the adoption of a metal tiller with a lever mechanism incorporated in it; instead of having the "goat's foot," the lever ended in a rounded pommel. It was this lever which moved forward and caught the bowstring; by pushing on the lever the crossbow was then spanned.

**gaidos** Greek term for GAESUM.

**gaku-no-ita** Japanese armor for the upper arm, part of the KOTE.

**galea** A Latin word referring to the leather HELMET worn by Roman soldiers, as distinct from the metal helmet, or *cassis*. The term "galea" was later to become the generic word for any type of helmet (and it has, in fact, been absorbed into contemporary English in botanical and zoological parlance to indicate any helmet-like structure).

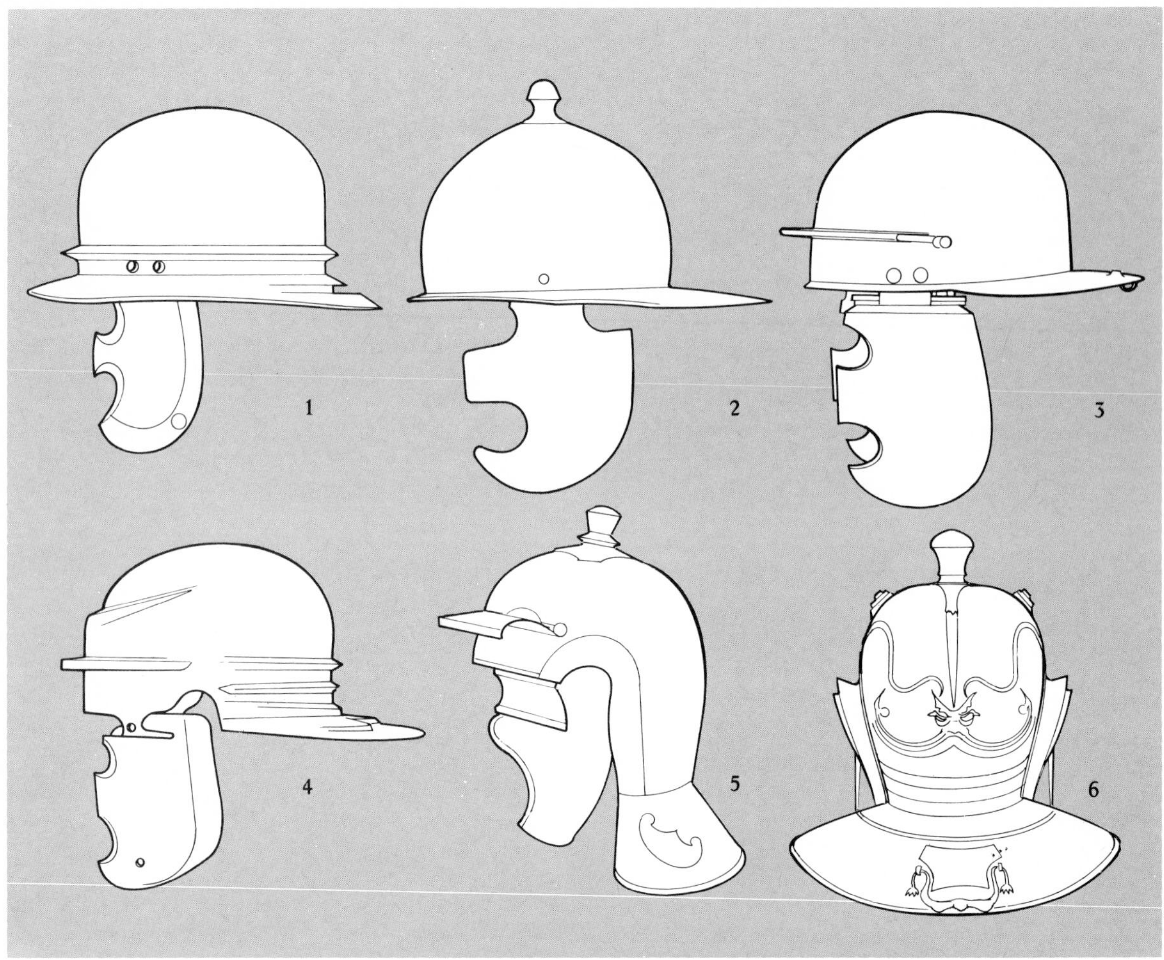


*1. Iron galea, Agen/Port type, 1st century* B.C. *2. Bronze galea, Montefortino type, 1st century* A.D. *3. Bronze galea, Coolus type, 1st century* B.C.*–1st century* A.D. *4. Iron galea, Imperial-Gallic type, 1st century* B.C.*–1st century* A.D. *5, 6. Iron galea of the auxiliary cavalry, 2nd–3rd centuries* A.D. *(side and rear views).*

There is evidence to show that from the earliest centuries of Roman history leather and bronze helmets of Graeco-Etruscan derivation were being used along with purely Italic ones. The historian Polybius (c. 205–120 B.C.), maintained that the leather casque disappeared from Roman armor at the time of Camillus (c. 396 B.C.), when it was replaced by the bronze or iron casque. It was around the 4th century B.C. that the casque that was to become known under the modern term "jockey cap" began to appear in Italy. This was a style of helmet extensively worn by the invading Gauls, who had many bitter encounters with the Romans.

One of the results of this contact with foreigners was that the Roman armies themselves started to adopt the "jockey cap" casque, probably from about the 2nd or 1st century B.C., at the same time gradually modifying its shape to make it more functional. There were, therefore, numerous variations of this type of helmet, due to the changes made to it over a long period in different areas. In order to clarify them, they are usually categorized under geographical headings based on the places where most examples of particular types have been discovered. Although there are many smaller groups, the two main ones are: the Montefortino type, named after a burial ground of the Senonese Gauls in the Marches region of central Italy; and the Coolus type, from the name of a district in the Marne department of France. Even these groups can be subdivided, as there were many variations within them.

The basic structure of the Roman "jockey cap" casque consisted of a more or less hemispherical skull with a peak (FALL) and a tail, the lengths of which varied according to type, while on the top there was a button to which a crest was sometimes fixed. Two broad, shaped cheekpieces (*bucculae*) were hinged to the sides of the skull and tied under the chin with a strap.

In imperial Rome, galeae belonging to officers or being used for parades were frequently adorned with small, shaped medallions in gilded bronze or brass, or engraved with impressive figures of eagles, deities, winged Victory, legion badges, or amuletic symbols. Sometimes there was a ring or loop on the tail or skull of the galea for a strap, to enable it to be slung over the shoulder while on the march.

Some cavalry units were issued with a distinctive type of helmet for parades and warlike sports which incorporated a mask made to resemble human features and covering part or all of the face except, of course, the eyes. Probably of Greco-Hellenistic origin, these masked helmets were adopted by the Romans in about the 2nd or 3rd century A.D. They were also heavily decorated, often being plated in silver or gold. The mask and skull were embossed and engraved to represent the anatomical details of the head—hair, beard, nose, eyes, etc.—in a very realistic way.

In complete contrast to the military styles were the gladiatorial helmets. These took various forms, according to the type of contest in which they were to be used. They were made of bronze or iron and usually had an extensive fall which extended around to the back of the neck to form a tail, and there was generally a high comb. A gladiator's helmet was also equipped with a mask to protect the face, with two circular holes for the eyes which were often shielded with a fine metal grille. These helmets were frequently embossed and engraved with scenes of heroic fights and mythological episodes.

**Galway sparth** Irish term for the Danish AX.

**gambeson** A quilted garment used in the 12th to 14th centuries. Made of plain fabrics, it was worn under an armor and was, in fact, functionally identical with the AKETON. The gambeson might also be made of rich materials decorated with embroidered ornaments and coats of arms, in which instance it served either as a surcoat put on over an armor (*see* COAT ARMOR) or as an independent protective dress.

**ganja** The upper section of the blade of the KRIS.

**gardbraces** A reinforcing plate for the PAULDRON. Although the gardbraces were sometimes riveted in position, usually they were attached by pierced pegs and split pins—especially in the 15th-century examples—or by two turning pins with a catch. These reinforcing shoulder plates, which were widely used by mounted troops, made their appearance in Italy at the beginning of the 15th century in the form of a large plate on the left side covering the entire pauldron. From about 1470 both gardbraces tended to become thinner, extending lower and leaving the upper lames of the pauldrons free. Their upper edges often had a stop rib embossed diagonally across them and, after the turn of the century, outward curving flanges called HAUTE-PIECES. The right and left gardbraces can be distinguished because the former, following the shape of the right pauldron, has a deep cutout for the lance.

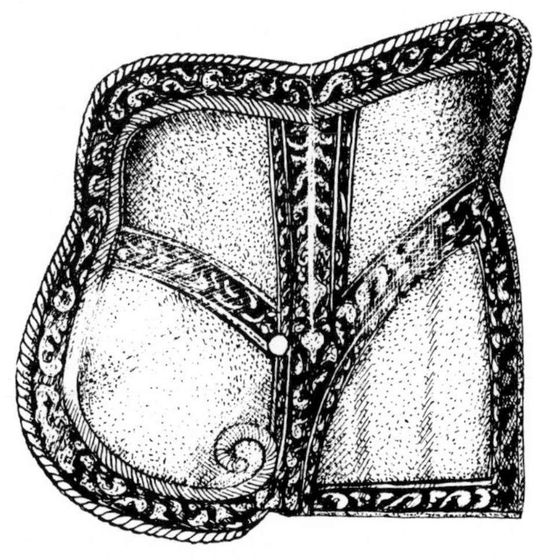

*Gardbrace for left pauldron, with a haute-piece, Italy, c. 1560–70. Museo Stibbert, Florence.*

In the 16th century, the gardbrace was used almost exclusively for the joust and tournament. One or both gardbraces were included in tournament and tilting armors.

**garniture** A set consisting of a suit of armor and reinforcing and alternative pieces which could either be integrated with or substituted for usual pieces in the basic suit (sometimes referred to as the "hosting" armor), thus converting it into various forms for use in the field or in the joust or tournament. As far as is now known, the first such set appeared in Germany in the late 15th century. Each garniture was invariably made for an important person according to a precise design for specific types of events. Every piece, therefore, was strictly functional with a purpose of its own, but the whole garniture would have been designed, both structurally and decoratively, to harmonize. Completely preserved garnitures are rare, but great hereditary armories in Vienna, Dresden, and Madrid contain examples. These garnitures have been made with great technical skill and elaborate decoration *en suite* on all parts of each set.

There were no strict rules on which the composition of a garniture was based, apart from established forms of armor and the owner's preferences. For the sake of convenience garnitures have become loosely categorized into two groups, "small" and "great." A small garniture would, generally, have comprised a full field armor with exchange pieces to form a foot soldier's half armor, a horseman's three-quarter armor, and an armor for the carriers (i.e., a tournament on foot). A great garniture would additionally have included reinforcing pieces for full armor to form suits for field, tourney course, tilt, and foot combat, with a full bard instead of light horse armor.

The term "double armor" is sometimes used to refer to a garniture which consisted of a full field armor with reinforcing pieces only for the tourney and the tilt. (For individual components of a garniture, *see* ARMOR.

The term "garniture" is also applied to a set of firearms comprising one or more guns and a pair of pistols (more rarely, two pairs of pistols). Such sets had first appeared by the middle of the 17th century and were quite often produced in the 18th for noblemen and wealthy persons. It goes without saying that all objects in a garniture were decorated *en suite*.

**gas guns** Rifles and pistols using chemically produced gas as a propellant. The first known use of gas in this way

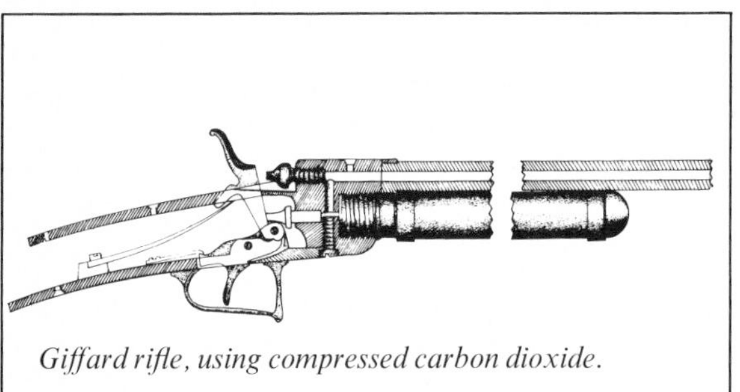
*Giffard rifle, using compressed carbon dioxide.*

goes back to the Dane Peder Rasmussen, who experimented with something of the sort in 1834, though details have not survived. The earliest gun to be actually manufactured was invented by the Frenchman Paul Giffard, who in 1872 patented an air gun used with an "air cartridge" containing compressed air. In the following year he took out an American patent for a similar gun using a steel container of carbon dioxide (like the modern refillable soda siphon), which had a much greater expanding force than air. Using a system of valves, and operated by a striker (usually with an outside hammer), the gas was made to flow in the appropriate quantity from the container into the breech. The gun was manufactured in St. Etienne and also, in 1890–94, in London. Production seems to have ceased by about 1900, but the system has been revived several times since.

Carbon dioxide is still used in some U.S. weapons, such as the Benjamin and the Crosman, but these are very little used in other countries because of the difficulty of getting charges for them and also because of their modest performance, which is never as good as that of ordinary air guns. Of some interest is the German Barakuda system, which makes use of an air-ether mixer fitted to fairly powerful air guns. When, on firing, the piston compresses the mixture in the cylinder, the mixture rapidly heats up and explodes (the Diesel effect), adding its power to that of the compressor.

**gas operation** One of the methods of operating AUTOMATIC WEAPONS.

**gauntlet** Part of a complete armor to protect the hand and wrist. A gauntlet normally comprised a CUFF covering the wrist, a back or metacarpal plate (or lames), and fingers, either joined or separated from each other. It was always worn with a leather glove, except for the dueling gauntlet, which was doubled by a mail glove. In fact, the oldest type of plate gauntlet on record, dating to the early 14th century, replaced the mail glove and was similar to the wide-cuffed leather gauntlet worn today by motorcyclists. It, too, was made of leather but covered with small riveted lames.

This type was followed by the so-called hourglass gauntlet which was used from the middle of the 14th century to the early decades of the 15th. The cuff, short and flared, was at first open on the inside of the wrist, but it was soon to be joined up into an encircling bracelet. The back consisted of a single plate which also covered the sides of the hand; its front was embossed to the shape of the knuckles and to the base of the thumb. The fingers were sometimes separate and protected by small scales riveted to leather strips, which in turn were riveted by their ends to the main plate. An ordinary leather glove would have been

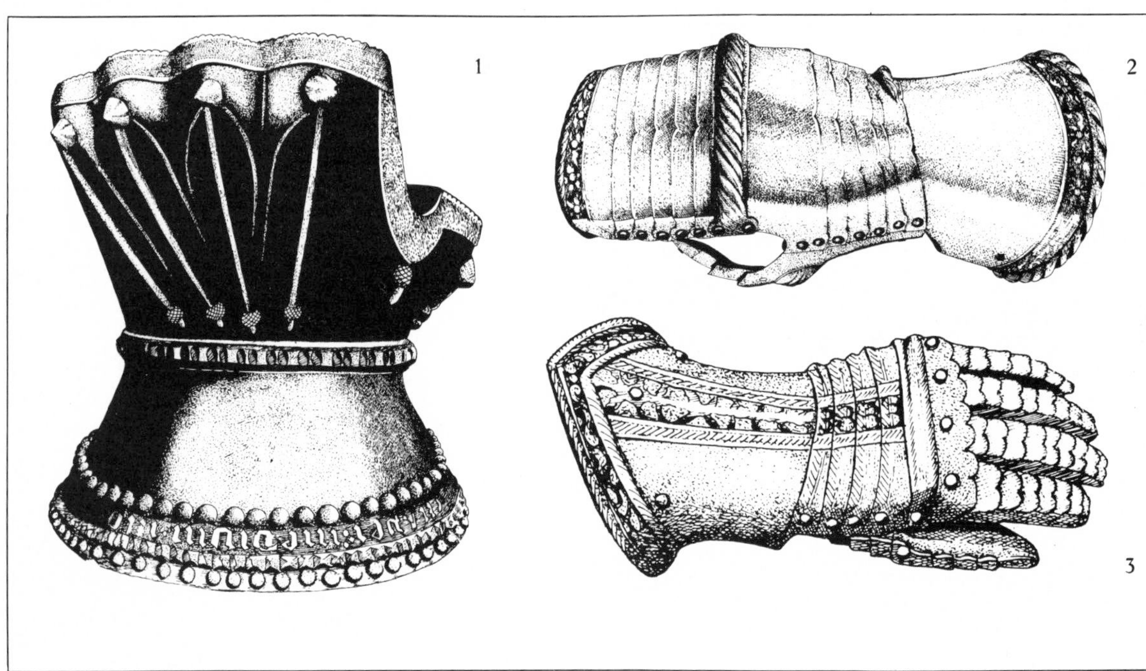

*Gauntlets. 1. "Hourglass' style, N. Italy, c. 1380–90. 2. Mitten gauntlet, Augsburg, c. 1520. Museo Stibbert, Florence. 3. With articulated fingers, Italy, c. 1570. Metropolitan Museum, New York.*

sewn inside to hold the gauntlet to the hand, while the outside was often covered with cloth.

By the beginning of the 15th century, the "mitten gauntlet" had become popular and was to remain so for the rest of the century and into the first half of the 16th, especially in the German-dominated areas of Europe. This consisted of a longer, narrow conical cuff tapering to the wrist and cut on the top to form a point; the back, composed of a plate or a few articulated lames, the last of which was shaped to the knuckles; and the fingers, comprising a varying number of articulated scales. An important variation to emerge during the third quarter of the 15th century was the gauntlet with a particularly long, pointed cuff. A few other types evolved for special purposes, which are dealt with under the subheadings below.

With the start of the 16th century, gauntlets with articulated fingers became increasingly popular and were a feature of many armors produced until about the middle of the following century. The cuff had become shorter but was still flared, while its top was cusped, usually with a rounded and roped edge. The articulated back was formed of several lames, with embossed shaping over the knuckles. The separate fingers—with scales riveted to leather strips (or sometimes onto the glove)—were themselves riveted onto the knuckle lame.

*Close or locking gauntlet.* A specialized type of gauntlet for the right hand, used in the 16th century for foot combat and the tourney course. This was a variation of the mitten gauntlet in which the lames on the fingers were articulated only in line with the knuckles, the last lame being extended so that, when the hand was closed, it could be fastened to the cuff by a turning pin or some other form of catch. The wearer's grip on his weapon—sword, mace, poleax, etc.—was thus rendered almost unbreakable. Such a gauntlet was never used with a lance.

*Tilt gauntlet.* A specialized type of gauntlet for the left hand, used in the 16th century for the Italian and German joust. It was a variation of the mitten gauntlet in which the metacarpal and finger lames were each made in one embossed plate rounded so as to cover entirely, together with the thumb scales, the inside of the hand when the gauntlet was closed.

*Elbow or bridle gauntlet.* A specialized type of gauntlet used—particularly in German regions—in the 16th century. Also known as the "long gauntlet," it was basically the mitten gauntlet (although there were also examples with separate articulated fingers), except that the cuff encircled almost all forearm up to the elbow. The top edge was often roped and cut at an angle to form a point. The elbow gauntlet was a characteristic feature of foot soldiers' armor and was worn in association with a spaudler over a mail sleeve. In the earlier part of the 17th century it was still being worn by light cavalry as part of the so-called arquebus armor, but only on the left hand; it was shaped to the curve of the arm for greater freedom on horseback, since this was the bridle arm, and worn over a buff coat or mail shirt. *See also* GLOVES, MAIL; GUANTI DI PRESA; MANIFER; MITTENS.

**giornea** An Italian overgarment consisting of two straight pieces of cloth joined at the shoulders and falling to about halfway down the thighs, worn either belted or caught in at the sides with buckles and straps. It was worn from the 14th to the early part of the 16th century, and was sometimes reinforced with iron lames.

**girdle** A term used from the middle of the 16th century for a waist belt to which both the sword hanger and the dagger scabbard were attached.

**gisarme** (also **giserne, guisarme**) A term occurring from the 12th to the 17th century describing a type of crescentic AX attached to a long staff with the socket and either both ends or, more often, only the lower end of the blade. The socket was forged into a fluke, and a thrusting spike was fixed on the top of the shaft. This form may have contributed to the development of the HALBERD and BERDYSH.

**giserne** *See* GISARME.

**giyo-yo-ita** Leaf-shaped plates worn as armpit guards with the later Japanese armor. The name comes from a Chinese word meaning "leaf of the icho tree." The plates are made of iron scales covered with lacquer or of mail decorated in the middle with medallions of gold lacquer, lined with fabric, and secured on the shoulders with straps.

**gladius** A general term that refers to the short double-edged, pointed Roman sword with an almost nonexistent guard, which was carried by the infantry. As it evolved it followed both metallurgical progress and changing combat techniques. In the 4th and 3rd centuries B.C. the Roman sword was pointed and designed principally for thrusting; from the 2nd century B.C. it changed into a weapon that had two edges and a strong point, which was made to carry out both cuts and thrusts. As such it consisted, from the classical period onward, of a large sphere-shaped or bilenticular pommel mounted on an "anatomical" grip formed by a cylindrical piece with four depressions for the fingers; a guard that was rectangular and not very salient; and a blade about 50–55 cm. (20–22 in.) in length. The length would increase in later centuries, until it reached 75–85 cm. (30–33 in.) in the 2nd and 3rd centuries A.D.

The gladius was carried on the right-hand side in a sheath slung from a baldric. Both methods of attaching the sheath to the baldric are documented: that of Gallic-Teutonic origin (which involved a loop on the back of the sheath) and that of Eastern origin (with two rings on the sides of the sheath).

**glaive** (from Latin *gladius*, "sword") A term with various connotations used from the 13th century for weapons which had a large head shaped like a knife or sword. During the early period, it denoted the lances, probably equipped with a long head having cutting edges. It is believed that *falcione* for foot soldiers, mentioned in the records of Italian armories since the early 13th century, referred to such types of pole arms. From the 15th century, the term "glaive" denoted swords and large daggers and, by association, the pole arms, whose head resembled these edged weapons.

In its simplest form, the glaive probably had a knifelike head, which later increased in size and became typical for spectacular parade weapons decorated with coats of arms.

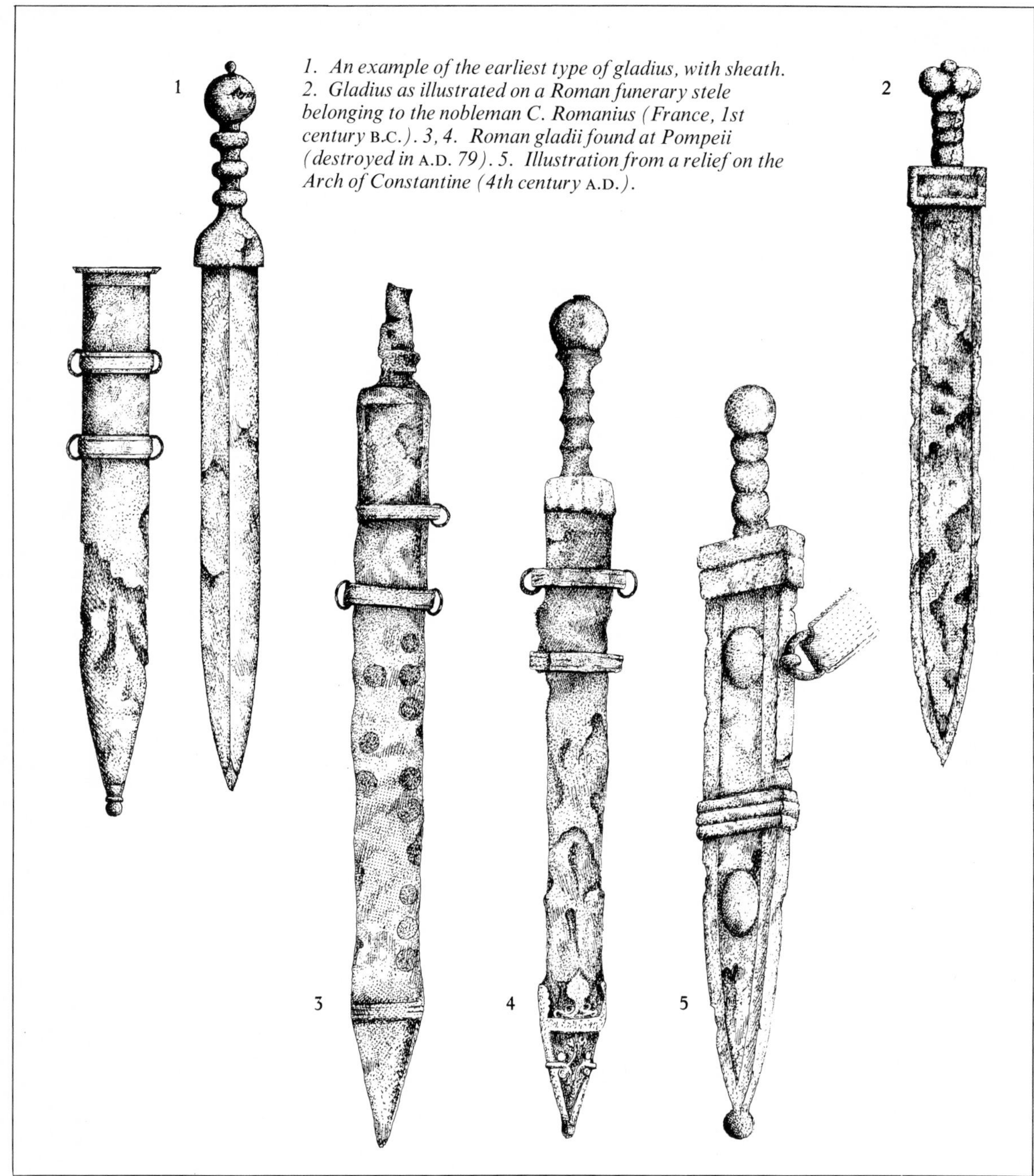


*1. An example of the earliest type of gladius, with sheath. 2. Gladius as illustrated on a Roman funerary stele belonging to the nobleman C. Romanius (France, 1st century* B.C.*). 3, 4. Roman gladii found at Pompeii (destroyed in* A.D. *79). 5. Illustration from a relief on the Arch of Constantine (4th century* A.D.*).*

It was particularly popular as a palace-guard and processional weapon in Germany, where it was supposedly called *Couse* (or *Kuse*). Another developed form of the glaive, while preserving a large knife-shaped head with curved edge and short back edge, had flukes of various shapes and, very often, two prongs as a guard at the socket. In the 16th and 17th centuries, it also became popular, especially in Italy, as a palace-guard weapon.

The large faces of the head made this weapon well suited for bearing the coat of arms of the seigneur and other elaborate decoration. Its use as a ceremonial weapon meant that for a long time the forms remained unchanged, and in many cases it is the decorative designs or the insignia depicted that make it possible to date these weapons with accuracy.

The Italian glaive had a broad, flat head, curved on the cutting edge, with an almost straight back from which a lug protruded where the back edge ended, and a fluke lower down; where the head met the socket there were two shaped prongs. Some ceremonial glaives had heads curved backward at the point and large, purely ornamental flukes.

**glans** (Latin, "mast," "nut") A Roman term for a missile

*1. Glaive carried by the personal guard of Guglielmo Gonzaga, Mantova, c. 1575. Metropolitan Museum, New York. 2. Glaive carried by palace guards, N. Italy, c. 1590–1600. Museo Civico Correr, Venice. 3. Glaive carried by the guard of Cardinal Scipione Borghese, c. 1600–20. Odescalchi Collection, Museo di Palazzo Venezia, Rome.*

used in a sling. Initially the most common missiles were pebbles about the size of a man's fist. In order to hit the target with greater accuracy and force, and at a greater distance, these natural missiles were subsequently replaced by artificial types, the size, shape, and weight of which offered the maximum offensive potential required, depending on the use (in hunting or war). It was the Carthaginians who invented the small terracotta pellets for hunting wild fowl and larger globe-shaped missiles filled with an inflammable liquid, designed to set fire to enemy installations. With the use of lead, from the 4th century B.C. onward, which was cast in flattened ovoid shapes or in the form of two flattish rhomboid pyramids joined at the base and sometimes fitted with iron spikes protruding from the corners, particularly harmful missiles were produced. Their measurements ranged from 40 to 60 mm. (1.5–2.5 in.) in length and 14 to 30 mm. (0.5–1.25 in.) in width; the weight varied from 23 to 135 g. (0.8–5 oz.) but averaged 30–60 g. (1–2 oz.). In the Middle Ages the glans was used mainly for hunting, although chronicles and depictions show that it was also used in war.

*Processional glaive, Veneto, c. 1700–1730. Musée de l'Armée, Paris.*

The *glandes plumbei* ("leaden glans"), on which one often finds inscriptions or depictions referring to the state waging war or the army's leader, invocations to the gods, insults addressed to the foe, and exhortations to the missile to strike true, became a popular item among forgers in the 19th century.

**gloves, dueling** *See* GUANTI DI PRESA.

**gloves, mail** Used with medieval armor until the end of the 14th century, these were made of fine mail and consisted of a compartment for the four fingers and a separate stall for the thumb. They were worn over gloves. Frequently they were merely an extension of the hauberk's sleeves, and the hand could be disengaged by slipping it through a slit in the leather or fabric palm when the wearer was not actually involved in fighting. A thong or cord was often threaded through the links around the wrist, presumably to ensure a firm fit and to prevent the sleeve from dragging on the hand. After about 1250, mail gloves were sometimes made with separate fingers.

**goat's-foot lever** *See* GAFFE.

**godendag** (Flemish, "good day") Ironical nickname for a staff weapon used in Flanders and, to a lesser extent, in France, from the late 13th up to the 15th century. Its steel head, with a spiked tip and a fluke on the back, was used for slashing and thrusting. It was probably a predecessor of the HALBERD.

**golang** *See* GOLOK.

**golok** (also **golang**, **bendo**) A typical Malay jungle knife or chopper, also used in war. Deriving possibly from the KUKRI of Nepal, it has a heavy, single-edged blade with a straight back and a pronounced convex cutting edge, varying from 15 cm. (6 in.) to about 70 cm. ($27\frac{1}{2}$ in.) long.

Golok hilts usually have a small disc guard or no guard at all, and a grip like a curved knife handle. Some are of carved horn, ivory, or wood and set in cast brass or silver; they are frequently studded with semiprecious stones. The carved wooden scabbards, painted red, are overlaid with metal or tortoiseshell. Some scabbards are made entirely of metal.

**gomai-kabuto** A type of Japanese helmet used mainly between the 11th and 13th centuries with the YOROI armor. Its hemispherical skull, the *hachi*, consisted of several

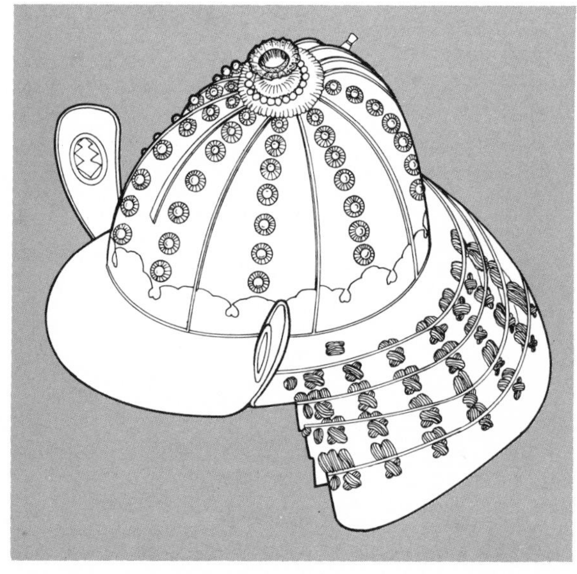

*Gomai-kabuto, Japanese helmet with five-plate shikoro.*

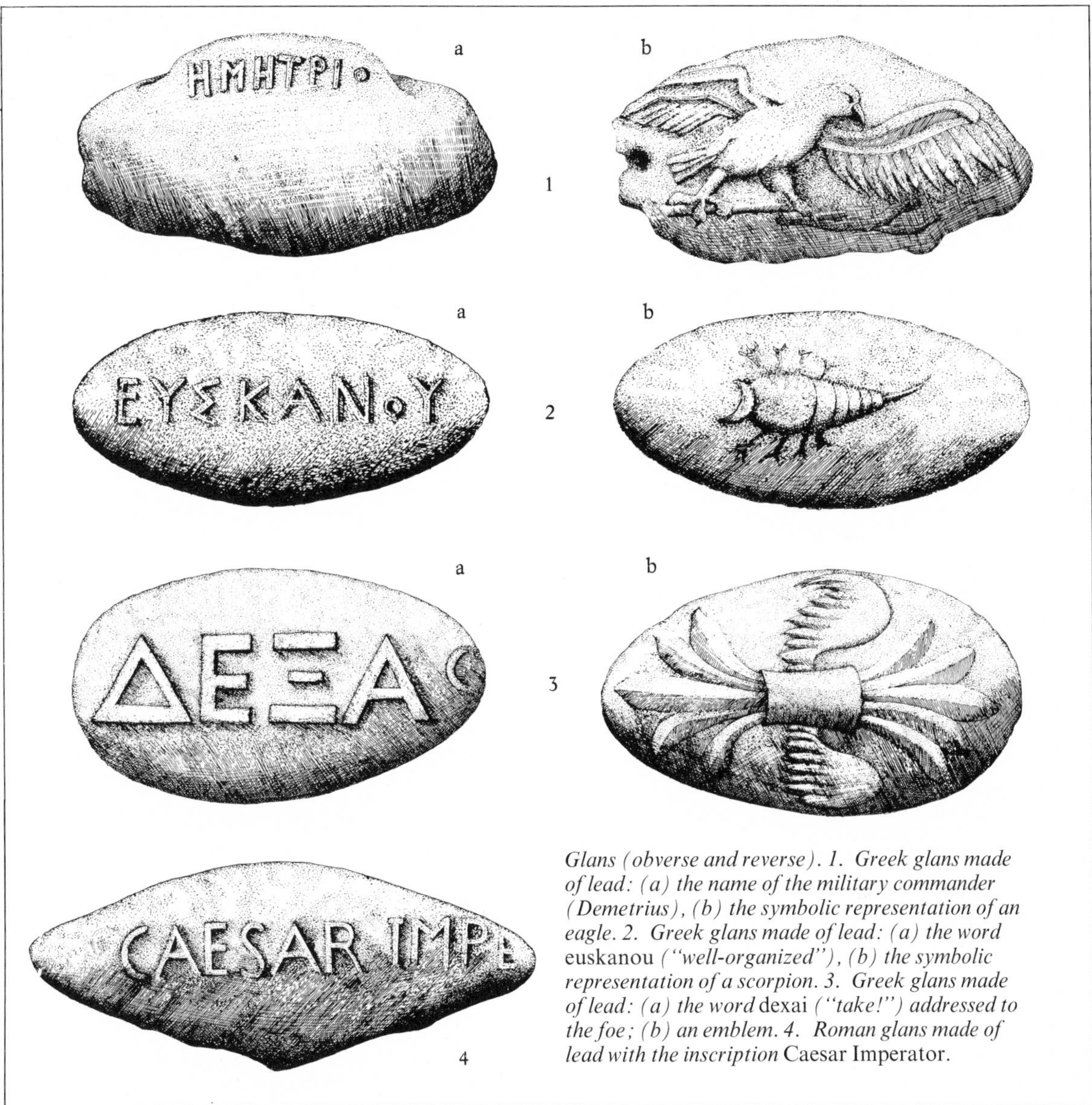


*Glans (obverse and reverse). 1. Greek glans made of lead: (a) the name of the military commander (Demetrius), (b) the symbolic representation of an eagle. 2. Greek glans made of lead: (a) the word* euskanou *("well-organized"), (b) the symbolic representation of a scorpion. 3. Greek glans made of lead: (a) the word* dexai *("take!") addressed to the foe; (b) an emblem. 4. Roman glans made of lead with the inscription* Caesar Imperator.

riveted lames with a reinforcing plate or visor, the *mabezashi*, at the front, and a hole, the TEHEN, in the top. There was a ring, the *kasa-jirushi no kwan*, fixed in the back of the skull for attaching a small cloth badge. Its neck guard, the SHIKORO, consisted of five rows of laced lamellae (scales)—hence the term "gomai," meaning "five plates"—while the winglike FUKIGAYESHI protected the neck guards on each side of the brow. A cord was attached to the inside of the helmet to hold it firmly on the head.

**gorget** A piece of armor protecting the neck, found in nearly every style of armor from the late 13th century. Structurally it consisted either of a single lame or of two main plates, one at the front and one at the rear, enclosing the neck and extending down over the top of the chest and back. On the upper edges of most gorgets two or three narrow lames encircled the neck; the two halves were hinged together on one side, and the other side was fastened by a peg engaging in a keyhole slot.

The gorget as an early form of the BEVOR for a heavy helmet, the BASNET, appeared toward the end of the 14th century and comprised a single, rather shallow lame which just covered the throat and whose lower edge barely covered the top of the cuirass. As a defense separate from the helmet and worn either over or under the cuirass, the gorget developed from the 1430s, but it was not until the early 16th century that it took on its definitive form, which evolved in field armor, and was to remain almost unchanged for the rest of the century. It is usually possible to distinguish between the three- or four-lame gorget that was worn with the field helmet and that worn with the close helmet, which rotated on the gorget. The gorget for the latter was generally slightly higher and its top bordered

*Front and back views of the gorget of an armor belonging to Francesco I de' Medici, Grand Duke of Tuscany, made in Italy, c. 1574. Museo Nazionale del Bargello, Florence.*

with a rim engaging in the groove of the helmet, which allowed it a rotary movement. There were also some exceptionally shallow gorgets, made of only one or two lames, which were probably part of a foot soldier's armor.

A fairly common type of gorget was the Almain collar, which covered the top of the shoulders and, designed to be worn with mail sleeves, was usually provided with SPAUDLERS or very small PAULDRONS. This style originated in Germany in the 1530s (hence the term, a debased form of *Allemagne*, French for "Germany") for light-cavalry and infantry officers and was worn with a straight breasted cuirass (with lowered upper edge).

For some time the gorget was worn separately, often with a buff coat, but it disappeared around the middle of the 17th century, since cuirassier armor did not require one. A single-lame decorated gorget was worn on the breast without armor in the late 16th and 17th centuries purely for display, often with clothes designed for grand occasions. Later this last remnant of armor became a distinctive insignia of officers and as such is still used with full dress in some countries.

**gorget plate** Part of some types of CLOSE HELMET and closed BURGONET, protecting the neck. It consisted of a combination of two or three articulated lames riveted at the front to the BEVOR and at the rear to the SKULL. Gorget plates also formed the lower part of the BUFFE for a burgonet.

The term "gorget plate" is also applied to an early form of bevor worn with the BASNET, or great basnet, from the late 14th century.

**grain d'orge** (French, "barley grain") A medieval term of uncertain connotation used to denote a type of mail. It may refer to the form of the small boss produced by riveting the ends of each ring.

**grandguard** A reinforcing piece for Italian and German jousting armors to give added protection to the breast, neck, and face against blows from an opponent's lance. It consisted of a heavy plate, shaped to cover the left side and center of the breastplate (sometimes with a wing on the gusset to protect the arm pit), the gorget, the bevor, and the whole of the left pauldron. It was held in place with screws on the breast and pauldron—or, occasionally, with staples and pegs—and its top edge butted against the lower edge of the helmet's bevor. In many cases, the upper part of the grandguard, reinforcing the bevor and the collar, was made separately from the lower part, which reinforced the breast and the pauldron; this type of protection is generally referred to as a "two-piece grandguard."

The grandguard, which was introduced in the 15th century, remained in use until about the end of the following century, with only minor modifications.

**granulation** Also called "corning"; the final process in the manufacture of GUNPOWDER.

**graper** (or **grate**) A wide ring or a thick strap of leather nailed around the butt of the lance behind the grip. From the early 14th century, at latest, this device was used to protect the armpit by braking the backward jerk of the weapon on impact. From the late 14th century, the REST was added to the breastplate of the armor and the graper engaged against this steel bracket when the lance was couched (in attacking position).

**grappling iron** An iron head with four or more hooks, attached to a length of hemp or a chain, which was used for catching hold of bulkheads or rigging on enemy vessels and pulling them into closer quarters. They came in various sizes, the smaller ones being used for throwing by hand by upper yardmen, the larger ones situated at the ends of the yards or bowsprit; once the enemy ship was alongside, the grappling irons were quickly hauled in and the ship was held fast by them.

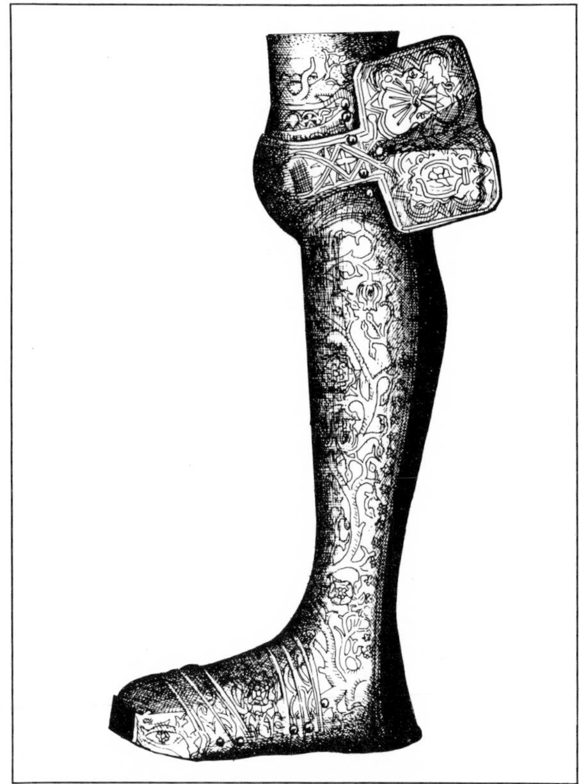

*Greave with sabaton and poleyn for a tonlet armor belonging to Henry VIII, probably made in Greenwich and decorated by Italian and Flemish masters, c. 1515. Tower of London Armouries.*

**grate** *See* GRAPER.

**great basnet** *See* BASNET.

**great helm** *See* HELM.

**greave** Part of armor constituting the lower section of the legharness, and worn from the 14th century to the end of the 16th to protect the calf and shin. The earliest form of which there is evidence dates back to the middle of the 13th century and seems to have been open and cut off at the ankle. These were known as "schynbalds" or "demi-greaves" and consisted of a pair of gutter-like tubes made of metal or hide, which protected only the shins and terminated just above the anklebones. They were fixed to the POLEYNS with rivets or turning pins and had two buckles and straps at the side to fasten around the calf; a few small holes pierced along the lower edge allowed for the lacing-on of the mail SABATONS.

Before the middle of the 14th century, closed greaves had been introduced. These consisted of two vertical hinged lames, either with straps that buckled into slots on the rear part or with pin catches. This construction remained almost unaltered to the end of the 16th century, the only variations being in the introduction of pronounced ridging on the front lame and shaping the greave to the contour of the leg by making it swell out over the calf and embossing it to accommodate the anklebone. Full greaves extended down to the ground at the back and each side of the heel, arching over the instep.

Mail sabatons were attached with rings to the greaves, while sabatons made of lames were loosely riveted to the greaves. Among a few innovations of the 16th-century greaves were articulated lames at the bottom end of the greave where the sabaton linked up with it, to give the ankle maximum flexibility. Greaves ceased to be used toward the end of the 16th century, when they were gradually replaced by top boots.

**Greek fire** An incendiary, and almost certainly liquid, mixture, the exact composition of which is unknown to this day. One of the first historical accounts concerning Greek fire (also known as wild fire) was written by the Byzantine chronicler Theophanes, in his description of the victory scored against the Saracens in A.D. 673 by the emperor Constantine IV: "Then it was that Callinicus, the architect of Heliopolis in Syria, who had invented a marine fire, set light to the vessels of the Arabs and burnt them utterly, together with their crews." There has been much discussion about the nature of the "fire" in question, but no certain conclusion has yet been reached.

In his treatise "Les Compositions incendiares dans l'Antiquité et au Moyen Age" (in *Revue des Deux Mondes*, vol. 106, 1891, p. 787 ff.), Marcelin Berthelot concludes with the words: "Greek fire was based on the discovery of a new principle, which was the association of a fuel, saltpeter, with combustible substances." Gabriel Lippmann ("Zur Geschichte des Schiesspulvers," in *Abhandl. und Vorträge zur Gesch. der Naturwiss.*, Leipzig, 1906) states that Greek fire was simply a mixture of inflammable derivates distilled from naphtha and quicklime. When the lime came into contact with water, it reacted and caused enough heat to set the distillates alight. This thesis loses all credence, however, if one considers that the evidence refers to a fire directly on board the ships; a fire such as the one proposed by Lippmann could only be effective if spread over water. (The Byzantines did use quicklime in their naval battles, independently of Greek fire.) A tempting hypothesis has been put forward by C. Zenghelis ("Le Feu grégeois et les armes à feu des Byzantins," in *Byzantion. Revue Internationale des Etudes Byzantines*, vol. VII, Brussels, 1932). He believed in the existence of two fires: one solid, and not unlike gunpowder, which was used as a propellant for Greek fire proper, which could be made up, not only of saltpeter, but also of naphtha, resin, sulfur, colophony, etc.

Greek fire gave the Byzantines an overwhelming superiority which enabled them to resist the expansionist pressures of the Asian peoples for many centuries. But in time the Muslims also managed to unravel the secret, and from the Fifth Crusade (1219–21) onward they used Greek fire with disastrous effect against the Christian fleets. With the arrival and improvement of the firearm, Greek fire gradually disappeared altogether from the battlefield.

**grenade** In the 17th and 18th centuries this term was used both for explosive balls fired from artillery pieces and for those thrown by hand (*see* HAND GRENADE). They were hollow balls filled with explosives, the interior of which was generally a sphere concentric with the outside and of a radius such as to give the walls of the grenade a thickness sufficient to resist the action of the propellant charge and the battering it received as it passed down the barrel, and not to break when striking the ground or penetrating earthworks. Long experience showed that the best thickness was between a third and a quarter of the radius. With walls of that thickness, spherical grenades were not usually able to penetrate masonry and broke on striking it; that explains why, in the days of smooth-bore artillery (in practice, up to the second half of the 19th century), breaching fire was a task always given to cannon firing solid balls. A hole was bored in the wall of the grenade to take the fuze; it was of a different form according to the fuze to be inserted in it.

In the 19th century the term "grenade" was also applied to the big explosive projectiles for mortars and howitzers, which were previously called bombs. A distinction was made not only on the ground of its large size but also as to whether or not the projectile had lugs with holes to take the hooks required to lift it.

**grenade launcher** A special gun or rifle, or a detachable accessory fitted to the muzzle of a rifle, for the firing of special anti-tank or anti-personnel grenades. The first grenade launchers (sometimes called hand mortars) appeared in the late 16th century. They often had bronze barrels and either a pistol grip or a gunstock. Detachable discharge caps for grenades launched by firing muskets have been known from the early 18th century.

**grenade, rifle and gun** A small explosive projectile thrown by means of a hand firearm with a special barrel or discharge cup. They were used at least from the last quarter of the 16th century. One of the oldest systems, invented by the Englishman John Tinker in 1681, used a hollow metal butt that worked as a launcher; other launchers were detachable and could be fitted to the barrel of the gun. The grenades fired were the ordinary hand grenades of the period. A considerable advance was made during the First World War, when the British introduced the Hale grenade, fitted with a long steel rod that was inserted in the rifle barrel; a special blank cartridge fired the grenade quite a long distance, but with no great accuracy. Better results were obtained with mortars, which, in greatly improved form, are still extensively used. Among many different types are the U.S. M-7A1, M-7A2, and M-7A3, which can be used to fire M-31 HEAT (High Explosive Anti-Tank) grenades or normal hand grenades mounted on M-1A2 supports. Among the most widely used rifle grenades are the Belgian MECAR and ENERGA, which can be used in the assault rifle on specially fitted barrels.

**grip** The part of edged weapons which is gripped by the hand. In the Stone Age it was made by rounding off and smoothing the part held, then binding it with leather or fabric. In the Bronze Age, because of the greater

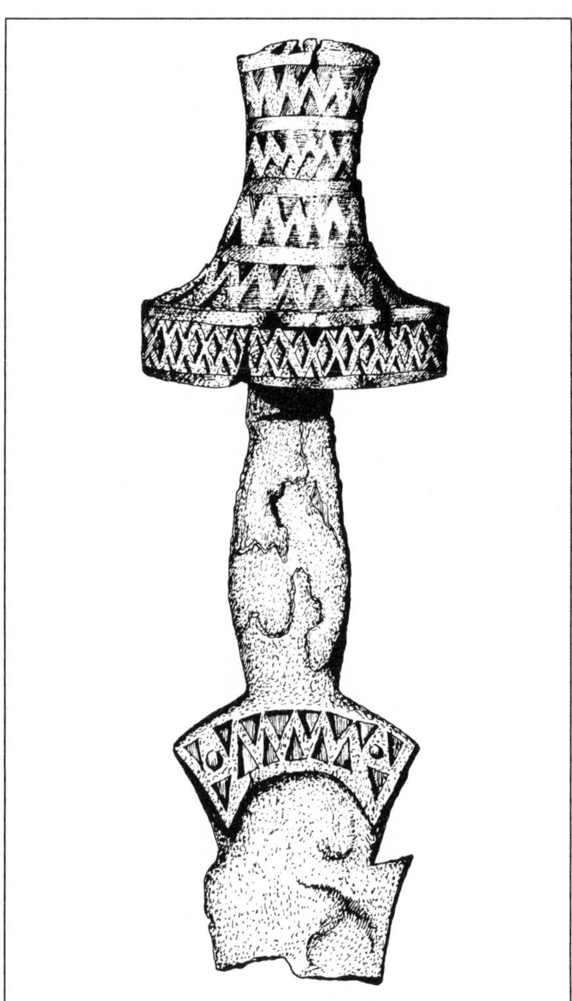

*The hilt of an iron sword found in Hallstatt tomb No. 573, c. 800–600* B.C. *Naturhistorisches Museum, Vienna.*

# Jousting, parade and field armor from the 14th to the 16th century

**Plate 21 Jousts and tournaments** (top) *From a miniature depicting Sir Geoffrey Luttrel of Irnham, Lincolnshire, preparing for a combat, Luttrel Psalter, England, 1340.* (bottom) *From a miniature depicting a joust over the tilt,* Le Roman des Aventures de Jean de Saintré, *15th century, France.*

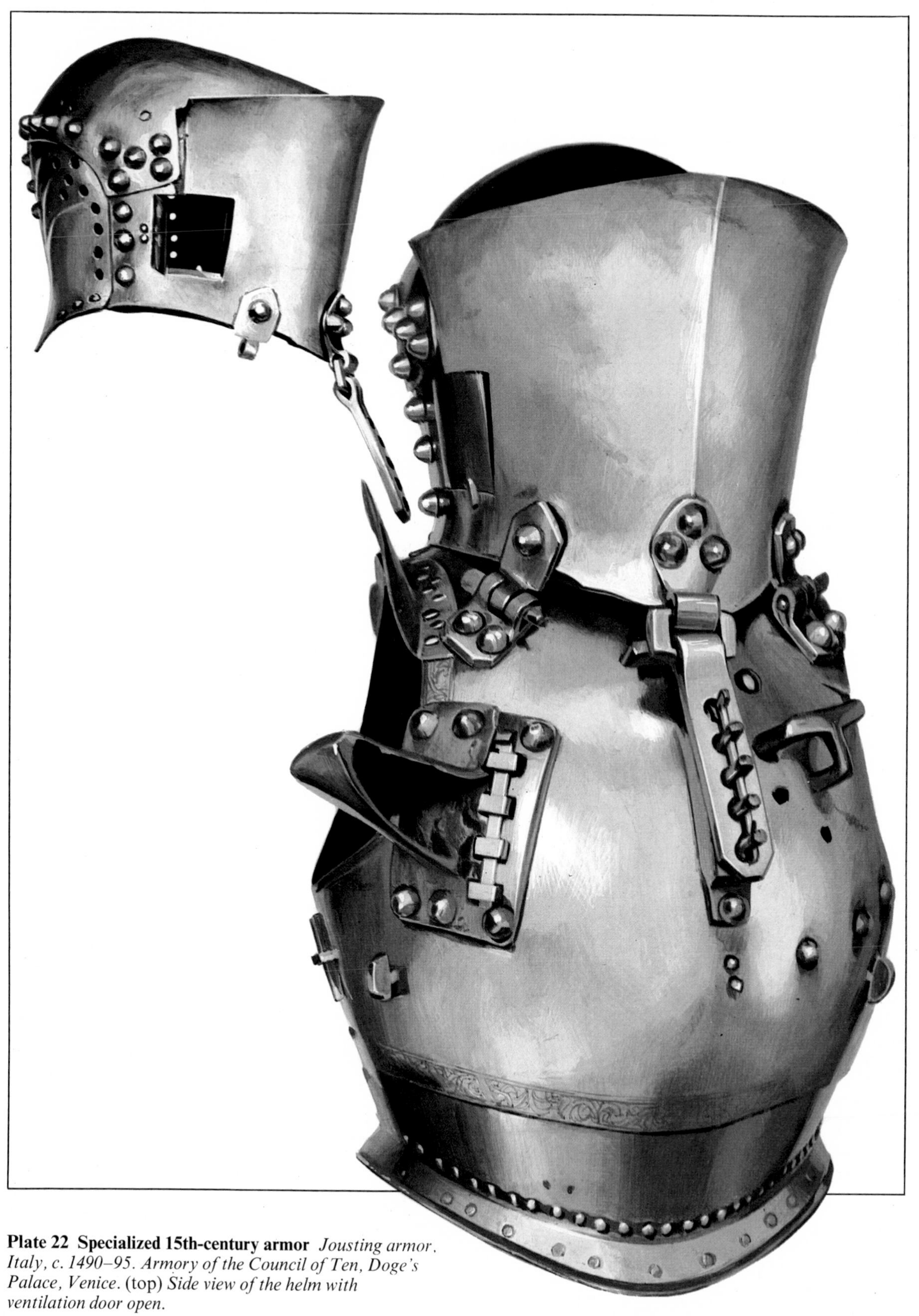

**Plate 22 Specialized 15th-century armor** *Jousting armor. Italy, c. 1490–95. Armory of the Council of Ten, Doge's Palace, Venice.* (top) *Side view of the helm with ventilation door open.*

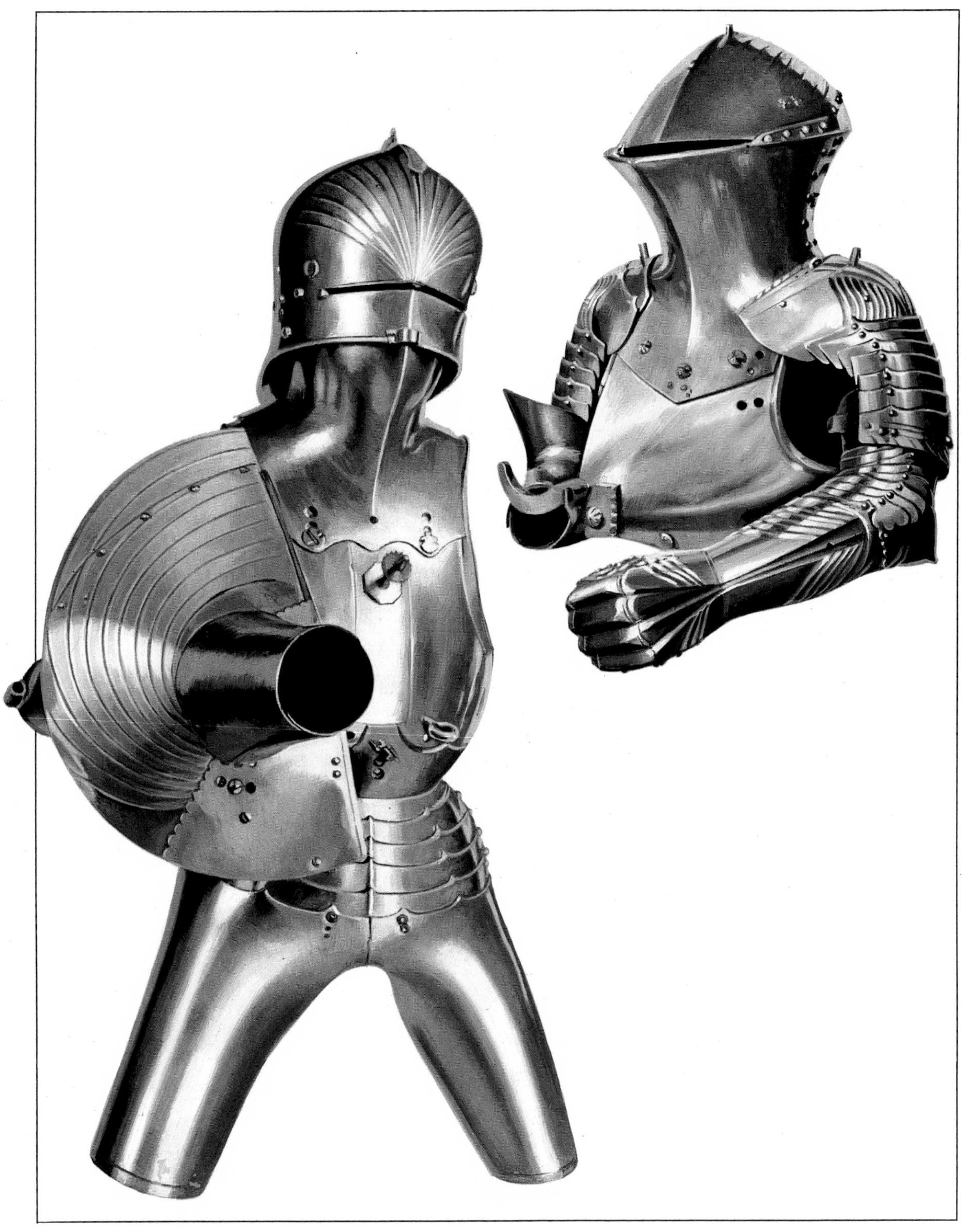

**Plate 23 Specialized 15th-century armor** (left) *Armor for the German course* (Scharfrennen) *belonging to Emperor Maximilian I of Hapsburg, made by Christian Treytz, Innsbruck, c. 1490. Waffensammlung, Vienna.* (right) *Armor for the German joust* (Gestech) *belonging to Emperor Maximilian I of Hapsburg, made by Jörg Helmschmied the Younger, Augsburg, 1494–97. Waffensammlung, Vienna.*

**Plate 24 16th-century parade armor** *Breastplate of an armor in the classical "alla romana" style, belonging to Cosimo I de' Medici, made by Filippo Negroli, Milan, c. 1546. Museo Nazionale del Bargello, Florence.*

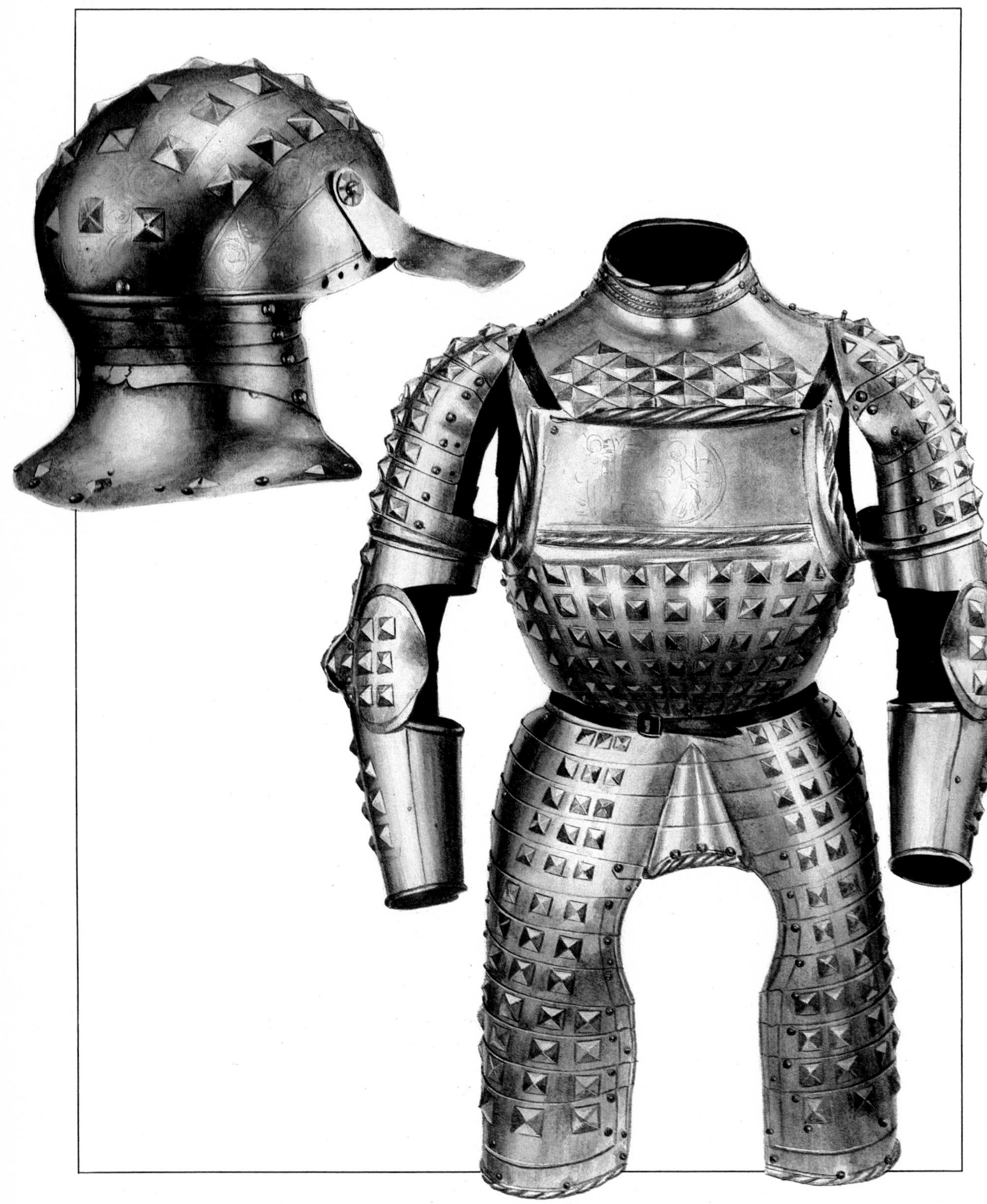

**Plate 25 16th-century armor** *Burgonet and corslet attributed to Francesco Maria I della Rovere, Duke of Urbino, made in Italy, c. 1515. Museo Nazionale del Bargello, Florence.*

**Plate 26 16th-century armor** *Brigandine belonging to Francesco Maria I della Rovere, Duke of Urbino, made by Filippo Negroli, Milan, c. 1532 (the parade burgonet, although contemporary, is not part of this armor). Waffensammlung, Vienna.*

**Plate 27 16th-century parade armor** *Targe and burgonet belonging to Prince Alessandro Farnese of Parma, made in Italy, c. 1563–65. Museo di Capodimonte, Naples.*

**Plate 28 16th-century parade armor** *Half armor from a "small garniture" belonging to Duke Alessandro Farnese of Parma, made by Lucio Piccinino, Milan, c. 1578–79. Waffensammlung, Vienna.*

**Plate 29 16th-century mounted knight** *Field armor for man and horse, Italy, c. 1550–1600. Armeria Reale, Turin.*

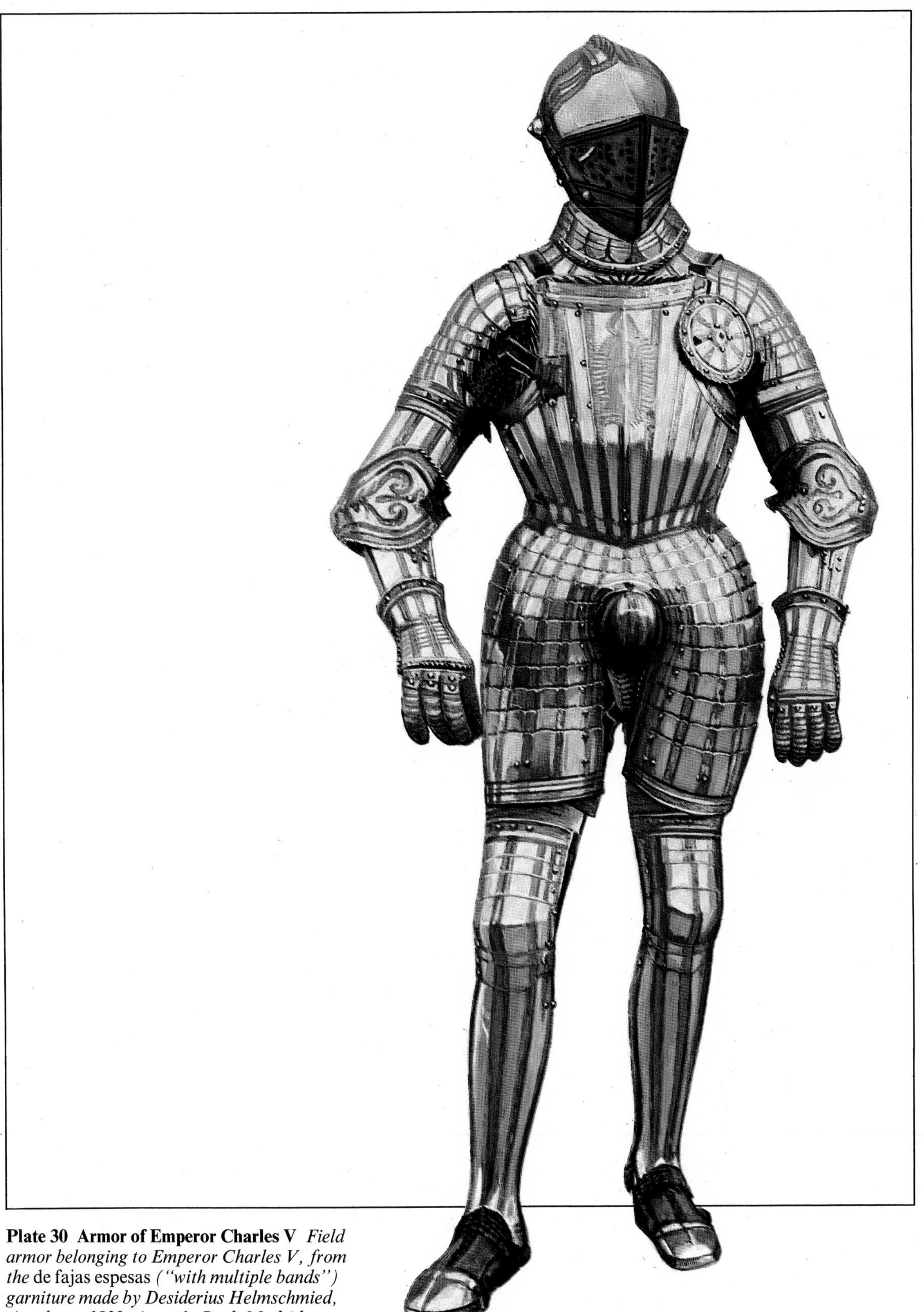

**Plate 30 Armor of Emperor Charles V** *Field armor belonging to Emperor Charles V, from the* de fajas espesas *("with multiple bands") garniture made by Desiderius Helmschmied, Augsburg, 1538. Armería Real, Madrid.*

**Plate 31 Armor of Prince Nicholas IV Radziwill** *Half armor from a garniture belonging to Prince Nicholas IV Radziwill ("The Black"), Marshal of Lithuania, made by Kunz Lochner, Nuremberg, c. 1555. Waffensammlung, Vienna.*

**Plate 32 Armor of Emperor Rudolph II** *Jousting armor, part of the "interwoven bands" garniture belonging to Emperor Rudolph II of Hapsburg, made in Augsburg, 1571. Waffensammlung, Vienna.*

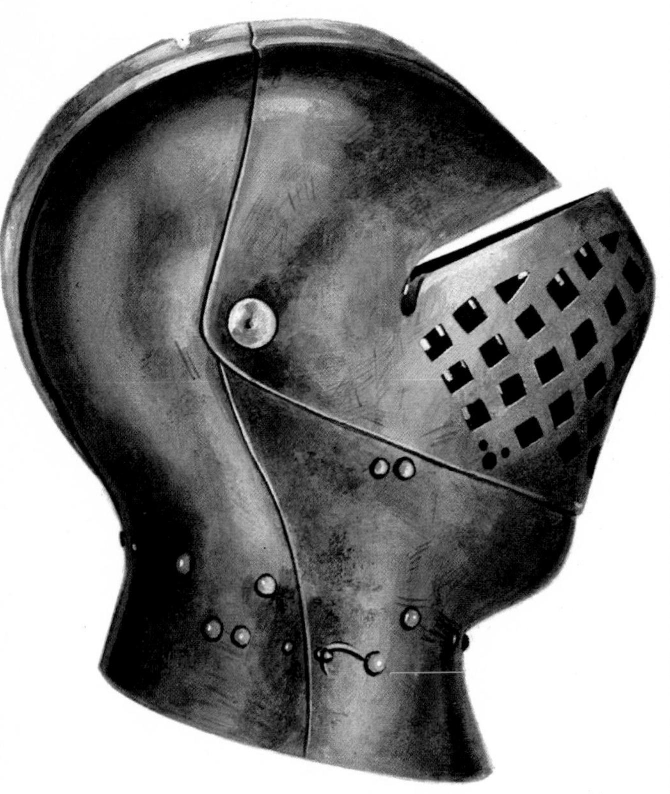

*Helmet for the foot combat belonging to Henry VIII, made in the Royal Workshops, Greenwich, c. 1520. Tower of London Armouries.*

**Plates 33–34 King Henry VIII's armor** *Garniture belonging to Henry VIII, made in the Royal Workshops, Greenwich, 1540.* On this page: *reinforcing pieces for the tilt and a locked gauntlet.* Opposite page: *armor for the foot combat, from the garniture.*

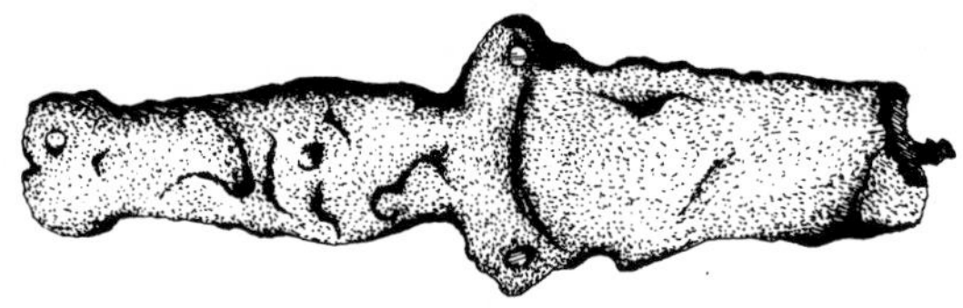

*Hilt of a sword from the Hallstatt period. Kunsthistorisches Museum, Vienna.*

possibilities offered by this metal, the grip became markedly different from the rest of the weapon and added some sort of protection for the hand, as in the swords of the Hallstatt culture. In the Roman GLADIUS we find the first anatomical grip: three depressions corresponding to the spaces between the fingers. The form of the grip and the protective elements of the hilt were conditioned by the manner of holding and handling the weapon. It was made of a wide variety of materials, depending on the importance and use of the weapon. From the late Middle Ages, the wooden shaft was predominantly used, covered with colored fabrics, sheets of decorated precious metal, polished leather, or twisted and braided wire. In order to provide a firm hold, the grip almost invariably had a spindle-like form, was fairly rounded, and trimmed and grooved.

In pistols the grip is the same as the butt; in guns it is that part of the stock which is held by the hand behind the trigger. In semiautomatic pistols and in some machine pistols it is also used to house the magazine. Its outer sides are usually covered with wooden, plastic, or metal plaques.

**guanti di presa** (Italian, "grasping gloves") Dueling gauntlets or long gloves used mainly in Italy in the 16th and 17th centuries. Made of leather and tough canvas covered in mail and scales, they had narrow, tubular cuffs which sometimes extended almost to the elbow, with finger scales overlapping toward the wrist. Even the palm of one glove was overlaid with mail so that it could be used to parry an opponent's thrust or to seize his blade and twist it out of his hand, thus taking the place of a parrying weapon. The glove for the hand holding the sword usually had no mail covering—certainly not on the palm—as this would have hampered the duelist in the handling of his weapon. Sometimes dueling gauntlets were made of steel scales and lames overlapping toward the forearm.

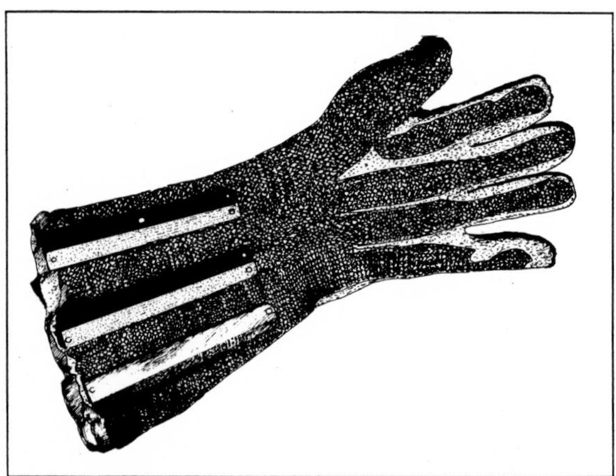

Guanto di presa, *Italian dueling glove, c. 1550–60. Museo Bardini, Florence.*

**guard** In edged weapons, a device or a part designed to protect the user's hand. In armor, a special piece defending a part of the body.

**guard chains** Attachments to enable a soldier—usually mounted—to retain his weapon should it be knocked from his hand in combat. These were at first fastened to the girdle of the surcoat but, after about 1300, they were more inclined to be fastened to the breastplate or the coat of plates by rivets or staples. Two long chains, holding the sword and dagger, hung from a ring positioned high on the right side or at the center. Sometimes there were also one or two shorter chains, each with a toggle on the end, fitted to the left side of the breast or to the central ring. These served as anchors for the helm, which, when not needed on the head, could be hung behind on the wearer's back; if there was only one chain, the helm was slung over one shoulder.

**guidon** *See* PENNONSEL.

**guige** A long, buckled strap fitted at the inside top of a TARGE to suspend the shield from the shoulder or, in the case of a horseman, from the bard while on the move. It was also used to hang the shield around the neck while the lance was couched. Most 15th-century shields had a notch, called the bouche, cut into the top right-hand corner to support the couched lance.

**guisarme** *See* GISARME.

**gun**

Under this term are grouped hand firearms fired from the shoulder, together with an account of the historical development of the muzzleloader and a detailed examination of the breechloading guns, including repeating, semiautomatic, and automatic rifles; finally, information is given on sporting guns. For further material on the subject, see the entries: AIR GUNS; ARQUEBUS; BAYONET; BLUNDERBUSS; CALIVER; CARBINE; CARTRIDGE; GAS GUNS; IGNITION; MUSKET; PETRONEL; VOLLEY GUN. For Oriental guns, *see* FIREARMS, CHINESE; FIREARMS, JAPANESE. See also the relevant section of the Bibliography.

**gun** A portable, individual firearm consisting basically of an iron, steel, bronze, or brass barrel built lengthwise into a wooden stock. In the early stages of such weapons, it is difficult to distinguish any particular type of gun from the generic group known as "firearms." The first real division of types came with the introduction of large guns mounted on a permanent emplacement and guns which were difficult to transport, requiring a team of men to operate them, i.e., artillery, while handguns—which were both easily portable and operable by one man—continued to develop along independent lines.

The first information we have regarding firearms dates

*Bronze hand gun, found at Mörkö (Sweden), end of the 14th century. National Historical Museum, Stockholm.*

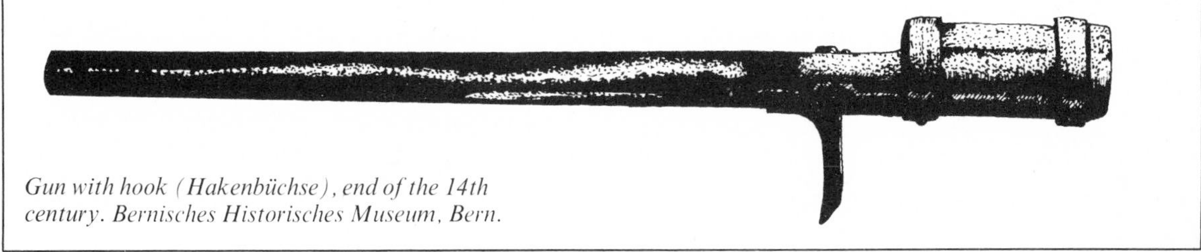

*Gun with hook (Hakenbüchse), end of the 14th century. Bernisches Historisches Museum, Bern.*

from the early 14th century. In the year 1326 the Council of Florence appointed two officials to manufacture what were described as *pilas seu pallectas ferreas et canones de metallo* ("missiles or iron bullets and metal cannon"); this Florentine decree is the earliest definitely datable reference to guns. The earliest illustration of a gun, however, appears in an English manuscript in Christ Church College Library, Oxford, also dated 1326. Entitled *De nobilitatibus sapientis et prudentiis regum*, it was written for the English king Edward III by Walter de Milemete. The illustrations depict a variety of siege engines and included among these is a picture of a gun shaped like a vase placed on a flat board supported by trestles. An arrow or bolt appears to be emerging from its muzzle. The gun has a touchhole on top to which a soldier in mail is applying what appears to be a rod, at the end of which is a piece of glowing tinder. Although few illustrations of guns were made until the last few years of the 14th century, nevertheless there were many references to them in documents throughout the century. A French document in the Bibliothèque Nationale in Paris, dated 1338, describes *un pot de fer a traire garros a feu quarante huit garros ferres et emporte en deux casses une livre de souffre vif pour faire poudre pour traire les dis garros* ("an iron pot to fire iron

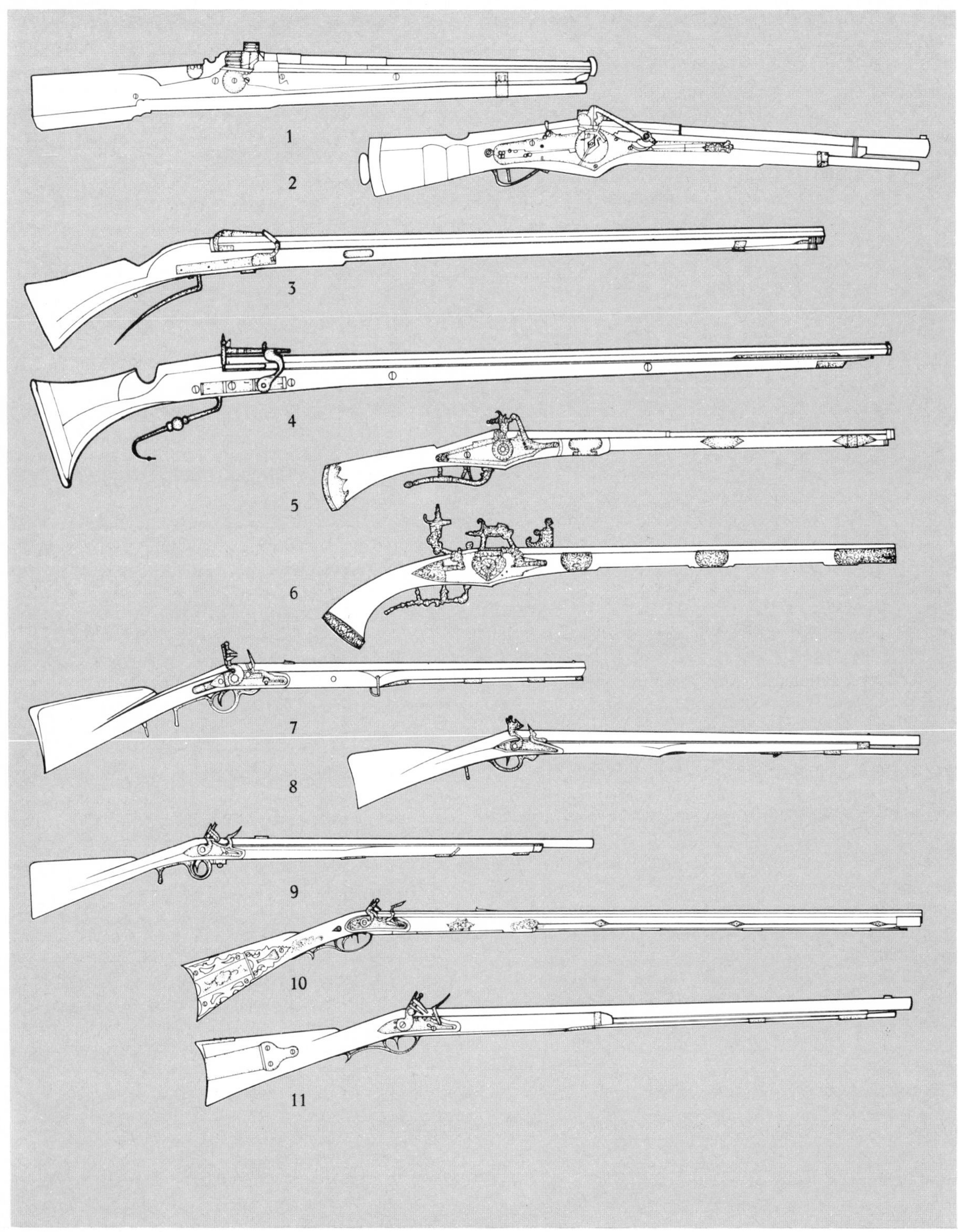


*Various types of guns. 1. Snap-matchlock, Germany, c. 1500. 2. Wheel-lock, Germany, 1530. 3. Sear matchlock, Germany, end of the 16th century. 4. Sear matchlock, Netherlands, end of the 16th century. 5. Wheel-lock, Italy, c. 1630. 6. Wheel-lock with two cocks, Naples, c. 1660. 7. Cavalry breechloading rifle (carbine), Great Britain, 1776. 8. Ferguson breechloading rifle, Great Britain, 1776. 9. Flintlock breechloading rifle, Great Britain, c. 1795. 10. Kentucky rifle, United States, 1825–40. 11. Harper's Ferry flintlock rifle, United States, 1815.*

arrows, forty-eight iron arrows in two chests, a pound of sulfur with which to make powder to fire the said arrows"). The English Privy Wardrobe Accounts of 1345 describe the repair of "guns firing arrows and bullets." In 1346 reference is made to what are described as "guns with tillers," which almost certainly means handguns, as "tiller" is the term used to describe the stock of a crossbow. In 1388 the term "handgun" is used for the first time in these accounts when *iii canones parvos vocatos handgunnes* ("three small cannons called handguns") are mentioned.

The earliest surviving example of a gun is accepted by most authorities as being the small bronze vase-shaped gun excavated in 1861 at Loshult in Sweden. This gun is preserved in the National Historical Museum, Stockholm, and closely resembles the vase-shaped gun depicted in the Milemete manuscript. It is just under 30 cm. (1 ft.) in length, made from a single piece of bronze with a raised molding at the muzzle. The gun swells considerably at the breech—like the Milemete gun—and is pierced with a large touchhole at the top. There are no flanges or lugs by which the gun could be attached to a stock; similar guns of somewhat later date, however, were simply slotted into a short wooden stock, and it seems likely that this method of seating was also used with the Loshult gun. This gun has been dated to the first half of the 14th century on the basis of its similarity to the one in the Milemete manuscript. Its shortness would seem to indicate that it was designed as a handgun rather than a piece of artillery, although this is by no means certain.

Also in the National Historical Museum, Stockholm, is a gun which was found in the sea off Mörkö, Sweden. The Mörkö gun is also quite small, about 19 cm. ($7\frac{1}{2}$ in.) long, and is of particular interest because it is decorated. The polygonal barrel, in two sections, is crosshatched and bears the inscriptions MARIA PLEA and HIELP. GOT. HELP. UNS. in Gothic script. The touchhole is surrounded by a raised square molding, behind which is the bust of a bearded man. Directly under the cannon at this point is a large hooklike projection which corresponds with the numerous references in 15th-century manuscripts to *Hakenbüchse*, "guns with hooks." The book was presumably placed against a wall or edge of a support to reduce the recoil. The Mörkö gun has been dated, on the basis of the style of the figure, to the last quarter of the 14th century.

Similar to the Mörkö gun—but without its decoration—is a bronze gun in the Germanisches Museum, Nuremberg. This comes from a datable context, for it was excavated from Schloss Tannenberg in Hesse, which is known to have been destroyed in 1399. The Tannenberg gun shows a considerable technical sophistication in its manufacture, for the inside of the barrel has a substantial ring near the powder chamber on which the ball might sit and which, it has been suggested, would also concentrate the force of the explosion.

### *Muzzleloading Guns*

All the guns discussed above are presumed to have been used with a wooden stock, although a group of early guns have survived which extend at the breech end to form a long iron pole as a handle. In the Tøjhusmuseet in Copenhagen there is an iron gun of the Hakenbüchse type, the hook being part of a ring which is fitted over the barrel. The polygonal barrel extends to form a long iron rod with a knob at the end. This gun was excavated from Vedelspang Castle, Schleswig, Germany, which is known to have been destroyed in 1426. Some early handguns can be seen in the Bern Historical Museum, together with their original wooden stocks. These are crudely shaped wooden poles to which the gun is held by iron bands or by hoops over the barrel which are nailed to the sides of the stock. One of the Bern guns is butted up against a stepped stock—presumably to reduce recoil. This particular gun, instead of being made in one piece, is made of an iron tube onto which substantial iron rings have been fitted. The Bern guns have been dated to the early 1400s.

Manuscripts illustrate how guns in the 15th century were held, some being held under the arm or resting on the shoulder, the other hand being needed to apply the match to the powder in the touchhole. It is not clear from the manuscript illustrations what was used to ignite the gunpowder. At least one 15th-century illustration shows a coil of lighted match being used, while others depict a rod or stick, the end of which appears to be glowing, and it seems probable that there was some means by which a piece of match could be held in place at one end of the rod. But since it was awkward to hold the weapon firmly in one hand while trying to ignite the powder in the touchhole with the other, ignition by means of the serpentine, that is, a match holder, was devised, examples of which going back to 1411 are found in a Vienna manuscript. During the last quarter of the 15th century other technical improvements to the matchlock were introduced, the spring, the sear, and the trigger, or rather, sear lever. These led to other improvements in the weapon, notably in the shape of the stock. The old wooden stocks had been made to be held with one hand; now that it was possible to hold the weapon with both hands the stock was given a flat, oblong shape which could fit into the shoulder or be held against the cheek.

Other important features were introduced in the 15th century. The snap-matchlock and trigger lock were fixed to a plate screwed to the side of the stock, and the pan for the powder was fitted with a lid which could be turned sideways, to ensure that the powder in the pan was kept dry before firing. Toward the end of the century improvements were made to the barrel; instead of being constructed in a single piece it was now made like a tube, with one end closed by a threaded breech plug. The attachment of the barrel to the stock was also improved. Instead of using rings and loops, small flanges with a hole were fixed under the barrel to take pins which passed through the sides of the stock. By the end of the century the basic shape of the gun and the position of the lock were already more or less fixed.

At the beginning of the 16th century the wheel-lock was invented. Its complicated and delicate mechanism attracted rich noblemen to interest themselves in firearms, mainly for hunting. As a result a demand grew up for guns

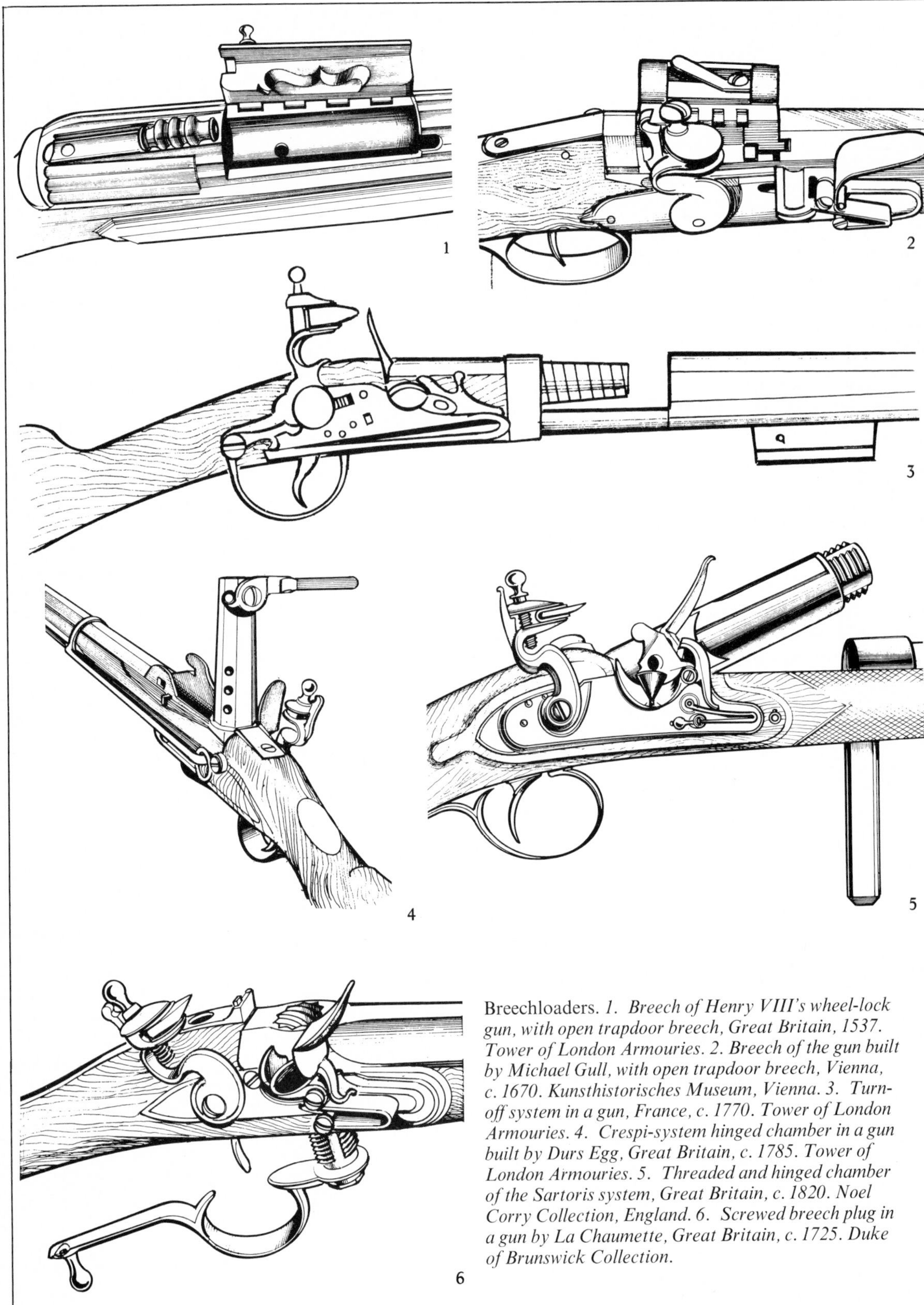


Breechloaders. *1. Breech of Henry VIII's wheel-lock gun, with open trapdoor breech, Great Britain, 1537. Tower of London Armouries. 2. Breech of the gun built by Michael Gull, with open trapdoor breech, Vienna, c. 1670. Kunsthistorisches Museum, Vienna. 3. Turn-off system in a gun, France, c. 1770. Tower of London Armouries. 4. Crespi-system hinged chamber in a gun built by Durs Egg, Great Britain, c. 1785. Tower of London Armouries. 5. Threaded and hinged chamber of the Sartoris system, Great Britain, c. 1820. Noel Corry Collection, England. 6. Screwed breech plug in a gun by La Chaumette, Great Britain, c. 1725. Duke of Brunswick Collection.*

which were not merely functional but also decorative. Sporting guns very soon became luxury articles on which the makers lavished all sorts of embellishments, from the chiseling, engraving, and gilding of the metal parts to the use of rare woods like ebony for the stock, with decorative inlays of horn and ivory. In addition to the improvement of mechanisms for ignition, another important development occurred at about the same time, the "rifling" of the barrel to give the projectile a rotary motion to improve accuracy and range. The oldest known example of a gun with a rifled barrel seems to be one made around 1500 for Emperor Maximilian I. Another rifle is in the Tøjhusmuseet in Copenhagen; it is also a German wheel-lock gun, dated 1542. However, the use of rifling was spreading gradually, and it did not come into general use until the later part of the 16th and the 17th century.

After 1530 many guns had a short trigger which acted on the end of the sear lever and was attached by a pin under the stock; to prevent its being accidentally struck, the trigger was surrounded by a metal trigger guard. During the 16th century some changes were made in the shape of the stock. From about 1520 the butt was made with a slight angle on one side so that it could be held more conveniently against the cheek. By the end of the century the butt also had an angular step just behind the breech for a better grip. At a certain point in the last quarter of the century another type of butt was introduced which strongly sloped down at an angle and was designed to be held with the butt plate against the chest. At the end of the century the flat base of the butt was sometimes carved into a fishtail shape. The 16th century saw a proliferation of many different kinds of guns (arquebus, caliver, petronel, etc.), the most important of which for military purposes was the musket, a long, heavy weapon which had to be fired from a support (musket rest). Brought into use in the second half of the century, by the end of the century it had been adopted by the majority of European armies.

The 17th century is notable for the introduction of the flintlock, an ignition system that remained dominant until the advent of the percussion lock at the beginning of the 19th century, and for the influence of the French on the manufacture of firearms, as can be seen from the almost general adoption of the French-type stock with a butt having a projection or hump on the top of the butt plate.

The metal parts of firearms, especially in France, were often decorated with chiseling and engraving; indeed, the flat lock plates of the period around the middle of the century offered an ideal surface for engravers. Fortunately, collections of designs have survived which contain not only motifs for engravings suitable for firearms, but in some cases actual proofs taken from such engravings. One of the outstanding collections of this kind (*Plusieurs Pièces d'arquebuserie recueillées et inventées par François Marcou Maistre arquebusier à Paris*) was published in 1657; the plates, engravings by the Frenchman C. Jacquinet, illustrate among other things wheel-lock guns with sculptured stocks and finely chiseled and engraved lock plates. Jacquinet was also responsible for some designs published about 1660 for two of the most famous French gunmakers, who boasted the title *arquebusier ordinaire* to the king of France; these drawings are designs for the decoration of the trigger guard, trigger, and cock and also of certain parts of the stock. At the end of the 17th and early 18th century a profound influence on European gunmakers was exercised by two collections of plates published in Paris, *Diverses Pièces d'arquebuserie*, with engravings by Nicolas Guérard, and *Nouveaux Dessins d'arquebuserie*, with engravings by Lacollombe. Rather curiously, Lacollombe's work, in the Louis XIV style already growing old-fashioned, was republished in 1730 in a single volume with the work of another engraver, De Marteau, which was fully up to date with the rising Rococo tradition.

The dominance of France in the technical and artistic development of firearms construction in the 17th century is to a great extent attributable to the influence of Louis XIII (1610–43). While still a child the king had become interested in firearms and before he was ten years old he had an impressive collection. In the course of his life he amassed a very fine collection of firearms and other weapons, chosen not only for their artistic value but also for the interesting technical features of the different parts. Catalogs of this collection were compiled in 1673 and in 1729, so that it has been possible to trace a number of items from it even though many of them were scattered after the French Revolution and the Napoleonic Wars.

From the last quarter of the 17th century the length of guns began to be reduced, and the butt was shaped so that its lower edge followed on from the trigger guard in a gradual downward slope; in the course of the 18th century the heel of the butt was reduced in size. By far the most important development of the end of the century, however, was the wider use of rifling, which, as we saw, had been invented a long time earlier. Guns with rifled barrels had been in constant use from the 17th century, but around 1750 the military importance of rifling began to be recognized, even if the smooth bore was not generally replaced until about 1870.

Particularly in Germany, Austria, and Bohemia, a gun with a rifled barrel was widely used: this was the sporting gun, the Jaeger, distinguished by its heavy butt and a short barrel of octagonal section. During the first part of the 18th century Swiss and German emigrants took the Jaeger to America, and it was on those same Jaegers that the famous "Kentucky rifles," widely adopted in the American Revolution, were based. This weapon was manufactured mainly in Pennsylvania, in the counties of York, Lancaster, and Berkshire; stock and barrel were the work of local craftsmen, but the flintlocks were imported from Germany and Britain. The classic Kentucky rifle had an octagonal barrel about 92 cm. (36 in.) long, a maple stock, brass fittings, and ornamental openwork mounts. Guns of this type were manufactured from the Revolution until late in the 19th century.

The main reason for the slow adoption of the rifle for military use was the difficulty in combining muzzleloading with a bullet that had to be adapted to the rifling. In France in 1826 Delvigne made a rifle with a chamber of smaller diameter than the barrel, in which the projectile was pressed into the chamber with an iron ramrod. In 1849

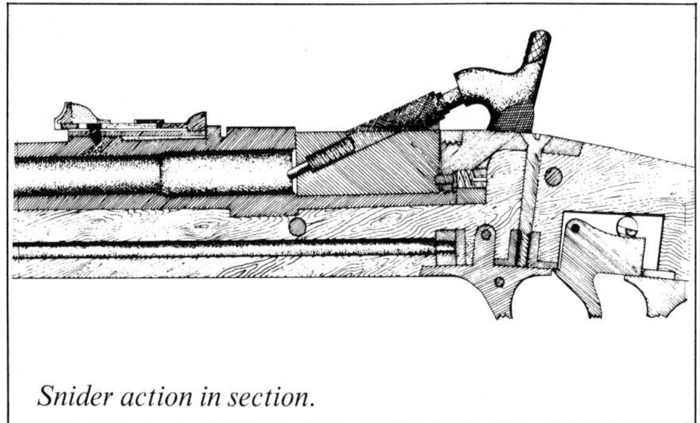

*Snider action in section.*

Minié made a projectile which expanded into the rifling when it was fired. The Brunswick rifle of 1849 had rifling in two grooves made to take a round projectile in a raised belt.

It has been said that the flintlock was brought to its highest level of perfection in Britain in the last quarter of the 18th century, and the first quarter of the 19th, thanks to famous gunmakers like Henry Nock, the Mantons, and Durs Egg, a Swiss immigrant who became the Royal Gunmaker. It is not surprising, therefore, that the percussion mechanism was slow to replace the flintlock, though that was bound to disappear eventually. In 1812 the Swiss firearms designer Samuel Johannes Pauly patented a breechloading system using a paper cartridge with a metal base which could be reused. Even though this invention attracted little attention at the time, the time was ripe for the advent of the breechloader.

*Breechloading Guns (up to c. 1850).*

"Breechloader" is a term used to describe a firearm which is loaded from the rear end, i.e., the breech, of the barrel. The invention of a breechloading system appears surprisingly early in the development of firearms, perhaps even from the beginning of their history. One of the earliest references to a firearm fitted with a separate chamber inserted into the breech can be found in an inventory of artillery in the castle of Rihout in Artois dated 1342. An arrow-firing cannon is described in it as being made in two separate parts—a chamber to contain the powder and a barrel for the missile. An early English reference to breechloading cannon is to be found in a Wardrobe Account of Edward III dated 1372 which refers to *uno gonne de latone cum iii pots* ("a brass gun with three pots"). The three pots were almost certainly separate chambers for the powder, which were probably held in place by means of a wedge, the chambers tapering toward the front to form a tight fit with the barrel. The simplicity of this breechloading system made it very popular, and it was used until well into the 18th century. An alternative system also found on early cannon was the use of a chamber which could be screwed into the barrel. The well-known Edinburgh Castle bombard, cast in Mons by Johan Cambier for Duke Philip the Good of Burgundy in 1449, is an example of a gun made in this way.

In a manuscript in the library of the University of Erlangen (West Germany) dating from 1460–80, handguns are illustrated with what appear to be reloadable metal cartridges. In one of the drawings, these slot into a recess in the breech and are held in place by a pin. Also shown is a breechloader with a chamber which could be inserted into the end of the breech and is fitted with a cover for the touchhole. As far as is known, however, no actual examples of 15th-century handguns based on this system have survived. Breechloading guns are illustrated in Leonardo da Vinci's *Codex Atlanticus* (c. 1500), one of which is a breechloading Hakenbüchse attached to a pole so that the breech could be unscrewed from the barrel, although it seems that this system was not actually to come into use until the 17th century.

The principle of the separate chamber is used in the earliest surviving specimens of breechloading guns. A carbine and gun made for Henry VIII of England (1491–1547) are preserved in the Tower of London. The carbine is fitted with a short barrel about 66 cm. (26 in.) long and bears the initials "H.R." and the date "1537." The maker's mark could well be that of William Hunt. The large gun is fitted with a long barrel measuring 1.1 m. ($43\frac{1}{2}$ in.) and was probably used for game or target shooting. Both guns have breeches fitted with a short hinged section which, when raised, allows a metal chamber to be placed in the barrel. Unfortunately, the original wheel-lock mechanisms of these guns are missing.

Another rare form of breechloading device is also connected with Henry VIII. A number of round metal shields, called targes, in the Tower of London Armouries are lined with wood and fitted in the center with breechloading matchlock pistols. The charge is placed in a separate iron chamber, and the breech is then pivoted to allow the chamber to be inserted and held in place by means of a latch. It has been suggested that these shields are the "several round shields ... containing firearms" mentioned in a letter dated 1544 from a painter, Giovanbattista of Ravenna, to Henry VIII.

Various attempts were made from the mid-16th century to develop satisfactory breechloading systems, and these are dealt with under separate headings.

*Breechloaders with movable barrels.* One solution to the problem of breechloading was to make the barrel separate from the breech. Although this had been done in the 14th century, as we have seen, with artillery, this method of construction did not become common until the 17th century, with the invention and development of the flintlock. One wheel-lock gun is certainly known to be extant; it is in the Kunsthistorisches Museum in Vienna. Its barrel unscrews to permit loading at the breech. In order to facilitate the removal of the barrel, the cock has been arranged to work from the opposite side of the wheel, i.e., behind it, on this particular gun. It dates from the middle of the 17th century and is signed on the top of the breech by Michael Gull of Vienna. One of the advantages of this system was that, by boring the chamber slightly larger than the barrel, the bullet fitted the sides of the barrel more tightly, thus increasing accuracy and range. This system was particularly advantageous when the

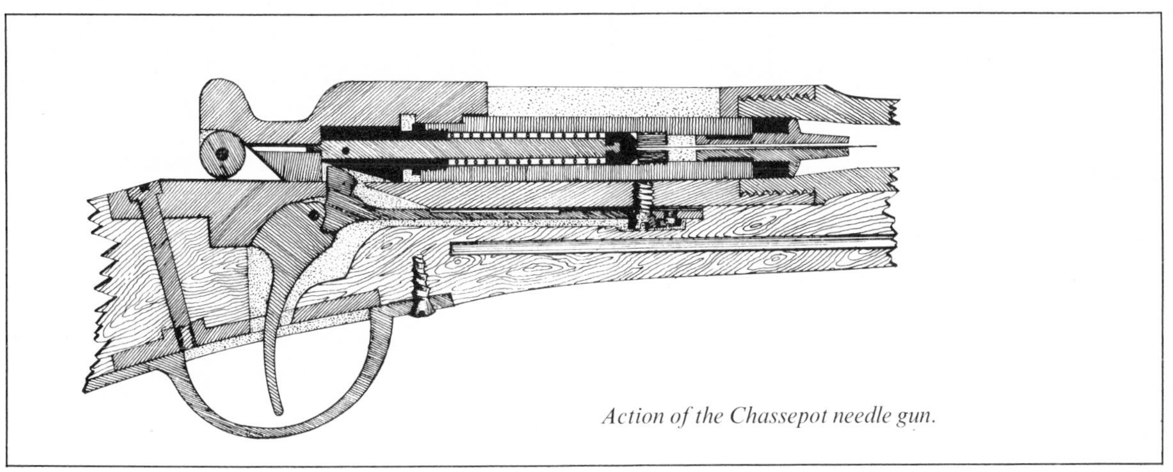

*Action of the Chassepot needle gun.*

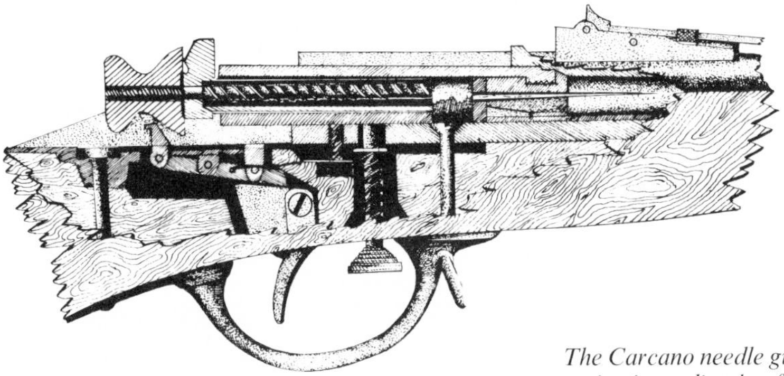

*The Carcano needle gun.* (above) *Sectional view of the action immediately after firing;* (below) *bolt with breech open.*

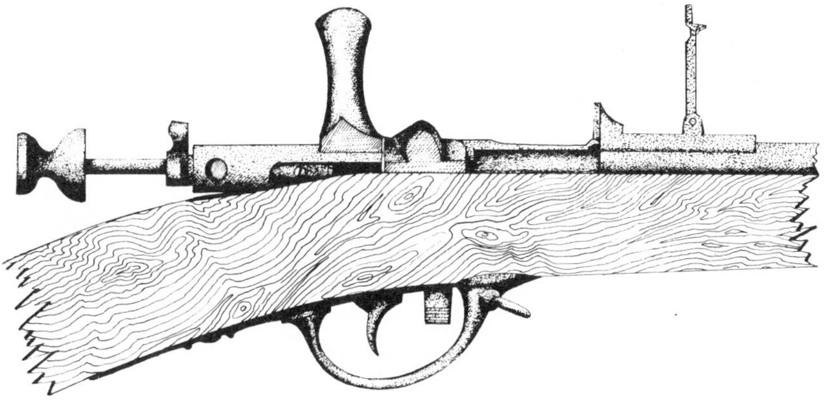

barrel was rifled, as the bullet was driven into the grooves and "lands" of the rifling at the outset.

Pistols fitted with a barrel which unscrewed for breechloading were known in England as "turn-off" pistols. In order to facilitate the removal of the barrel, some were made with a lug underneath the barrel at the breech which fitted a spanner, but other firearms had keys which fitted into recesses in the muzzle so that the barrel could be easily turned and separated from its breech. A flintlock turn-off pistol in the Victoria and Albert Museum, London, dating to about 1690, is fitted with a link which, while allowing the barrel to be separated from the breech, prevents it from becoming totally detached.

During the 18th century some breechloading guns had the barrels attached to the breech by means of a spring catch, the barrel sliding forward on a rod for loading. Breechloaders with movable barrels never gained universal recognition, perhaps because once the threads on the barrel–breech joint were damaged, it was impossible to obtain a gas-tight seal. They also took a considerable time to load.

*Guns with pivoted chambers.* With this system the breech was made as a separate feature but was hinged to the barrel at the rear to allow it to be moved for loading. Although guns working on this system had been known from the late 17th century, the system was used with more success on the carbine developed by Giuseppe Crespi of Milan in 1770. The breech was locked by a lever engaging in raised flanges on the outside of the breech, but because the breech simply butted against the barrel, there was a considerable escape of gas. In spite of this fault, it was adopted by the Austrian cavalry. It was also copied by Durs Egg for British Army trials in 1788, but was not adopted. The same system was patented in America in 1811 by Hall and Thornton. The lock mechanism and pan were mounted on top of the breech, the breech being tipped upward for loading. Officially adopted by the U.S. Army in 1817, rifles and carbines on the flintlock and the percussion systems continued to be made until the middle of the 19th century.

Various ways were tried to overcome the problem of obturation, that is, a closure preventing the leak of gas from the joint between breech and barrel. In 1817 an Italian inventor, Urbanos Sartoris, patented a breechloader with a chamber and barrel linked by an interrupted screw, although this system had been known since the end of the 17th century. A folding lever was attached to the barrel to turn and shift the barrel forward to reveal the breech. Although a few firearms were made with this system—principally for volunteer units in England—it never gained much popularity. Throughout the 19th century further attempts were made to produce a breechloading system of the Crespi type. These included that of the Danish inventor Nicolaj Johan Løbnitz in 1833, which employed the principle of a hinged chamber moving backward and upward; the Scheel system, adopted by the Norwegian Army in 1842; the Mont Storm system, which had a chamber hinged at the front and a locking bolt at the rear; and the Leetch system, developed in 1861 incorporating a chamber which was hinged sideways.

*Guns with separate reloadable chambers.* The gun and carbine belonging to Henry VIII, mentioned earlier, are of this type. Another interesting example, which is in the Historical Museum in Bern, is a German matchlock breechloader (c. 1600) with an iron chamber made in one with a plug and handle; this device can be placed into the open breech and retained by a flat peg fitting through the barrel and chamber.

A fine break-action flintlock breechloader made by Matteo Acqua Fresca of Bargi, Italy, dated 1694, is now in the City Museum of Birmingham, England; this breaks open sideways to take the loaded chamber. The English gunmaker Henry Nock devised an outstanding breechloading musket in 1786, an example of which is preserved in the Tower of London Armouries. In this, the breech is attached to a pivoted slide and, when in the barrel, held secure by an iron pin; when the pin is pulled back, the breech is unlocked and comes into the upright loading position, ready to receive a loaded chamber.

The separate chamber system was used throughout the 17th and 18th centuries.

*Guns with movable breech plugs.* In the Bayerisches Nationalmuseum in Munich there is a gun barrel with a pierced breech, the hole being filled with a large screw. This barrel was made by von Sprinzenstein of Munich in 1593 and is one of the earliest extant examples of this form of breechloader. After the screw or plug had been removed, the barrel could be loaded with powder and ball through the recess and the screw or plug replaced. Although various firearms were produced in the 17th century using this system, the best known was that invented by a Frenchman, Isaac de la Chaumette, in about 1704. A number of guns with the La Chaumette action have survived, most of them by a London gunmaker, George Bidet. In the breechloader of 1704, the screwed plug passed through the breech, which was opened by turning the trigger guard one complete revolution; this unscrewed and lowered the plug until its top was level with the base of the chamber. The gun could then be loaded from the aperture in the breech.

Although La Chaumette was granted a patent in England in 1721, this did not prevent Captain Patrick Ferguson from taking out a patent in 1776 for a breechloading system of exactly the same type. Ferguson made some improvements to the breech plug by cutting a smooth recess into it to form the breech end and cutting vertical grooves across the threads of the screw to clear fouling. After a successful trial, the Ferguson was given "limited service" by the Board of Ordnance, one hundred rifles being made and a company of riflemen trained to use the gun. After some success in the American Revolution, the rifle was withdrawn after the battle of Brandywine in 1777 (in which Ferguson was severely wounded). Several sporting rifles were produced on the Ferguson system by Durs Egg, a fine example made for the Prince of Wales in 1782 being preserved at Windsor Castle. As late as 1860 the same breechloading principle was employed on the cartridge breechloader patented by another English gunmaker, Charles Reeves.

*Breechloaders working with cartridges.* Leonardo da Vinci made a number of references to cartridges in his notebooks and advised carabineers to carry "pouches full of rolls of plain paper filled with powder." By the second half of the 16th century, gunpowder was carried in a made-up charge, wrapped in paper. After 1650 it was customary to include the ball within the made-up charge, thus making a primitive form of cartridge. However, the credit for the invention of a cartridge containing its own priming is usually given to Pauly, who took out a patent in Paris in 1812 for a breechloading system with a paper cartridge fitted with a reusable metal base, the center of which had a recess in which detonating powder could be placed. A striker, operated by a spring, caused the ignition. Pauly's patent shows two kinds of breech action—a drop-barrel type and a lifting-block type. In 1814 Pauly patented a gun which had an ignition system based upon an old-fashioned fire-making device founded on the principle that when air is compressed suddenly, great heat is generated. The gun had a spring-operated compressor which brought heat to bear upon the central part of the cartridge base. In its essential details this patent was the direct ancestor of the modern center-fire breechloading system. Pauly never enjoyed the success his invention deserved, but his ideas were taken up by others with better fortune.

A former employee of Pauly's, Johan Nikolaus von Dreyse (1787–1867), produced a bullet in 1827 containing fulminate in its base. It was detonated by a needle, connected to the cock of a modified flintlock, which passed through the breech plug. After a series of experiments, von Dreyse developed a bolt-action breechloader in 1835 in which the striking needle worked by means of a spring. This system, with a few modifications, was adopted by the Prussian army in 1840. In France, Lefaucheux produced an improved version of a pinfire cartridge which he had developed earlier, and in 1847–49 he took out a series of patents for breechloading systems using this cartridge. The modern center-fire cartridge was first patented in 1855 by Pottet.

A number of breechloaders were developed during the American Civil War. The Sharps of 1848 had a breechblock which moved vertically, the trigger guard operating as a lever. The Remington rolling block, however, was not developed until the end of the Civil War; its breech action worked by cocking the hammer, the breechblock being rolled back by the thumb. Another American breechloader of the same period—the Springfield—had a breechblock hinged at the front, the firing pin passing through it.

In England, the firm of Westley Richards developed the famous "monkey-tail" breechloader in 1858, the moving breechblock of which was attached to a lever on top of the stock. This was used with special ammunition incorporating a wad at the base which, by being blown through the barrel by the next bullet, operated as a cleansing action. The falling-block breechloading system developed by Henry Peabody of Boston in 1862 had a block hinged at the back and, by pulling the trigger guard down, the chamber was exposed for loading. This led to a host of variations on the Peabody theme, including the British Martini-Henry, the Werder of Austria, and the Winchester of the United States, but the stage was already set for the modern breechloading gun, discussed in the next section.

*Modern Breechloading Rifles*

*Single-shot Rifles*

*Bolt action.* What may be regarded as the first modern breechloading rifle was that invented by von Dreyse in 1835, which was mentioned in the preceding section. The best-known version of the Dreyse action, which was mainly used to convert and modernize existing muzzle-loading rifles, was assembled as follows. A cylinder forming the receiver was screwed onto the breech of the barrel, which tapered to a flat truncated cone. Screwed to the bottom of the receiver was a long laminar spring with a sear that engaged the striker. The trigger acted directly on the free end of the sear spring. The closure device was formed by a cylindrical bolt fitted with a handle having a rectangular base, which both guided the bolt as it slid forward within the slot in the receiver and locked the breech end of the barrel when turned to the right. The front face of the bolt was flared so as to fit onto the tapered breech, so that, in theory, the system was fully sealed. The bolt was hollow, and contained the striking mechanism, with the needle and a coil spring pressing on the striker. The cartridge consisted of a roll of paper holding the ovoid lead ball, with the percussion cap immediately behind it, and the powder charge at the rear end of the cartridge. To strike the cap the needle had to pass through the base of the cartridge and through all the black powder.

A number of the other rifles in use in the second half of the 19th century were derived directly from the Dreyse system. Outstanding among them was the Chassepot, which had a big rubber seal on the front face of the bolt to ensure obturation. While it was an improvement on the Dreyse rifle on the whole, the Chassepot was delicate and hard to strip; the "miracles" it performed at Mentana (1867) against muzzleloaders were not repeated in the

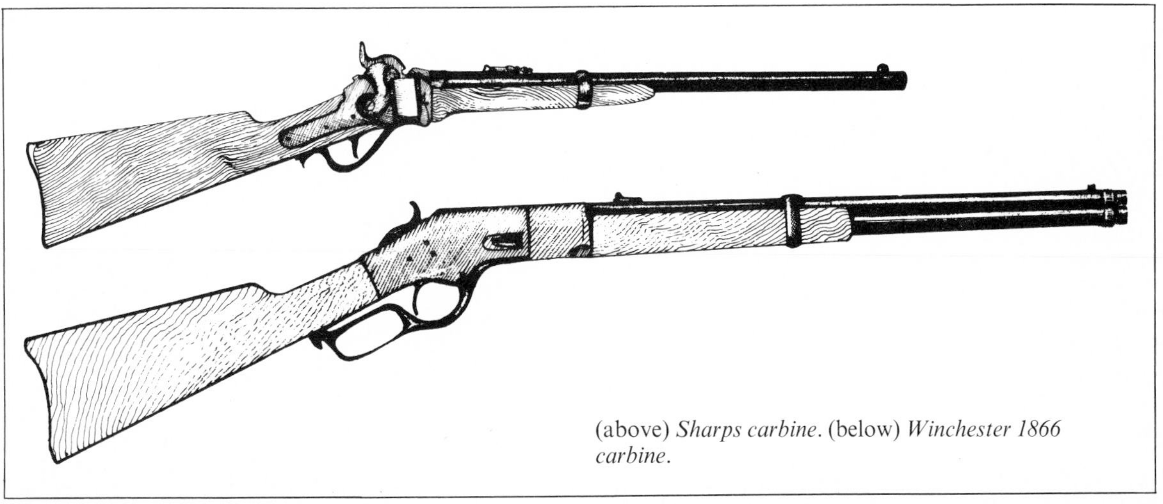

(above) *Sharps carbine.* (below) *Winchester 1866 carbine.*

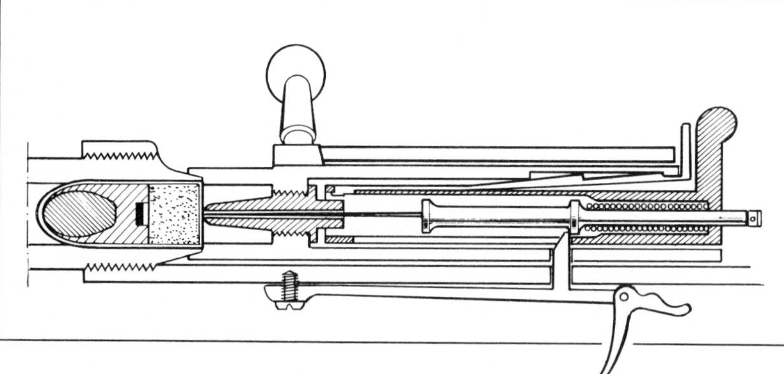

Breechloader. *Diagram of the Dreyse needle action. From* Die Rückladungs-Gewehr *(1876) by A. Mattenheimer.*

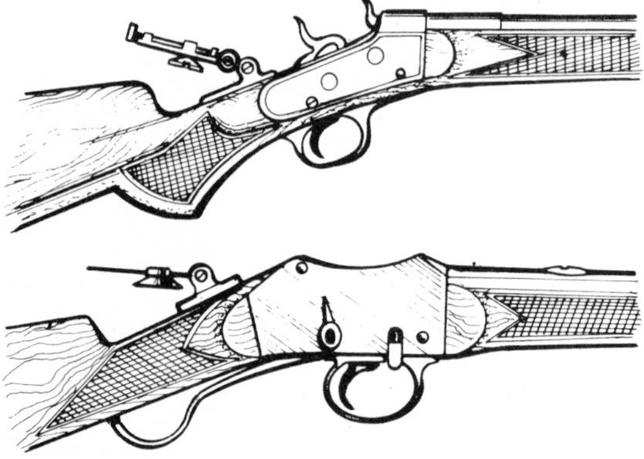

Breechloader. *1. Peabody-Martini system, United States, 1870. 2. Remington Rolling Block system, United States, c. 1880.*

Franco-Prussian War of 1870–71. Other rifles of interest were the Italian Carcano, the Luck, and the Döersch-Baumgarten, the latter being the first rifle with a turning and sliding bolt provided with locking lugs. The introduction of cartridges with expanding metal bases paved the way for a great number of single-shot breechloading systems, some intended for the conversion of old arms of relatively small caliber (the conversion of larger-caliber weapons would have meant using heavy and bulky ammunition), some for entirely new designs.

Among other early slide actions was the American breechloader designed in the 1850s by J. H. Burton. This had interrupted threads inside the end of the breech, which were engaged by corresponding threads on the bolt closing the breech. The striker, with its spring, was inside the bolt; when the bolt was pressed home, the sear, connected to the trigger, intercepted the striker, which compressed its spring. The arm was then ready to fire. A metal-based cartridge was used; it expanded at the moment of combustion and stuck to the walls of the chamber, thus preventing the gases from escaping backward. Another very important system, both historically and technically, was that patented by Samuel Norris, together with Paul and Wilhelm Mauser, in 1868. Some of the main features of this system were: (1) the striker was automatically cocked when the bolt was closed; (2) the cylindrical bolt had a head independent of the rotating movement of the bolt itself (this detail was useful with paper ammunition, which was subject to tearing as the bolt was turned, and with metal ammunition it allowed the use of an extractor fitted firmly to the head); (3) a valuable "primary extraction," a short but powerful movement, freed the base of the cartridge from the chamber before the full extraction; (4) when the action was open, the striker was

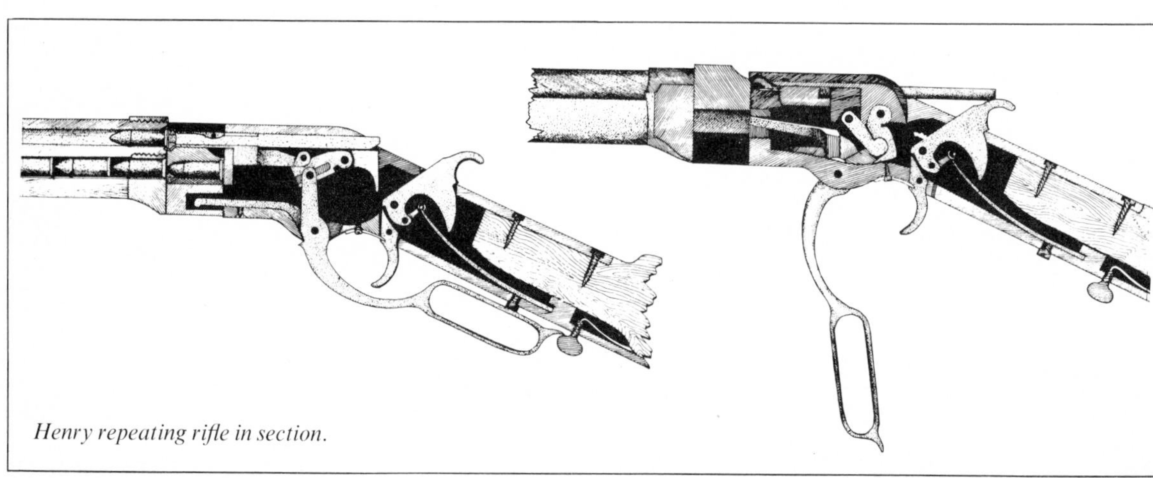

*Henry repeating rifle in section.*

held back within the head, preventing a premature discharge while loading; (5) a movable ejector, operated by the bolt, acted on the base of the cartridge case at the right moment; (6) the closure of the action was carried out by a strong locking lug integral with the bolt; when the bolt was closed, the lug engaged in a slot on the right side of the receiver.

Other systems with sliding bolts were the French Gras (used after 1874 for the conversion of the Chassepot to fire metal cartridges); the Beaumont, adopted in the Netherlands (1871); the Swiss Vetterli (1874); and the Russian Berdan No. 2 (1870). In the Berdan, as the bolt was turned to close the breech, the locking lugs entered circular grooves inside the breech, ensuring the best possible obturation. One of the first military rifles to be fitted with this action was the German Gewehr 1888, combining the Mannlicher magazine with the Mauser bolt fitted with locking lugs.

*Hinged breechblock*. The best known of these systems is undoubtedly that patented in 1866 by Jacob Snider and adopted by Great Britain and many other countries. In its basic principles the Snider recalls systems used as long ago as the beginning of the 16th century, but it had features that made it particularly suitable for the conversion of muzzleloading rifles. A section was cut out of the rear end of the barrel, leaving flat surfaces at each end at right angles to the axis. In this space a cylindrical breechblock was fitted, hinged on the right side of the barrel. A grip was fitted to the breechblock, and a hole was drilled obliquely through the block for the striker. An extractor was actuated by the breechblock when it was open and pressed backward. The original percussion lock was used, with slight modifications; the hammer struck the top of the striker, which ignited the cap of the chambered cartridge.

Another well-known system is that patented in 1865 by the American E. S. Allin and widely used, particularly in the United States, for modernizing muzzleloading long arms. The breechblock was hinged at the front to a base on the barrel, so that it opened forward. A catch controlled by an external plunger locked the breechblock when closed; the striker passed through the block and was actuated by the hammer of the original percussion lock. Similar systems were patented in the 1860s by other designers, among them A. Albini (Italy), I. Milbank, A. Ball, and S. Marsh (U.S.).

The breechblock designed by Joseph Werndl and adopted in 1867 by the Austro-Hungarian Army consisted of a metal cylinder pivoted below the breech. The rear of

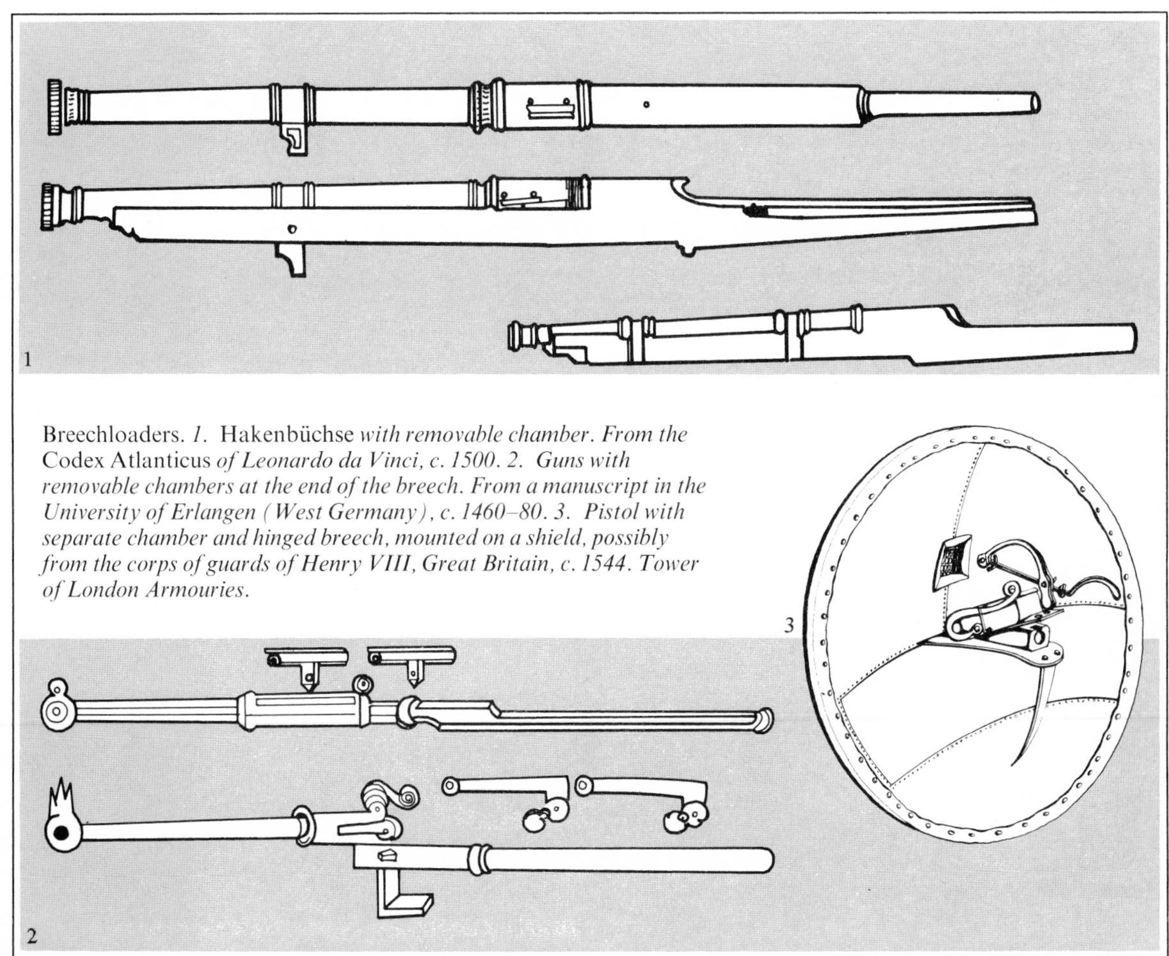


Breechloaders. *1.* Hakenbüchse *with removable chamber. From the* Codex Atlanticus *of Leonardo da Vinci, c. 1500. 2. Guns with removable chambers at the end of the breech. From a manuscript in the University of Erlangen (West Germany), c. 1460–80. 3. Pistol with separate chamber and hinged breech, mounted on a shield, possibly from the corps of guards of Henry VIII, Great Britain, c. 1544. Tower of London Armouries.*

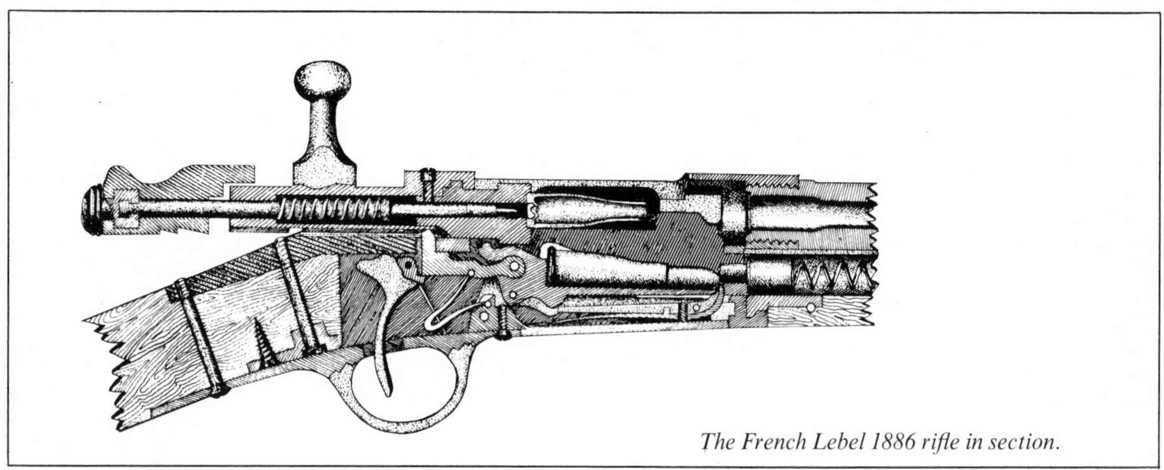

*The French Lebel 1886 rifle in section.*

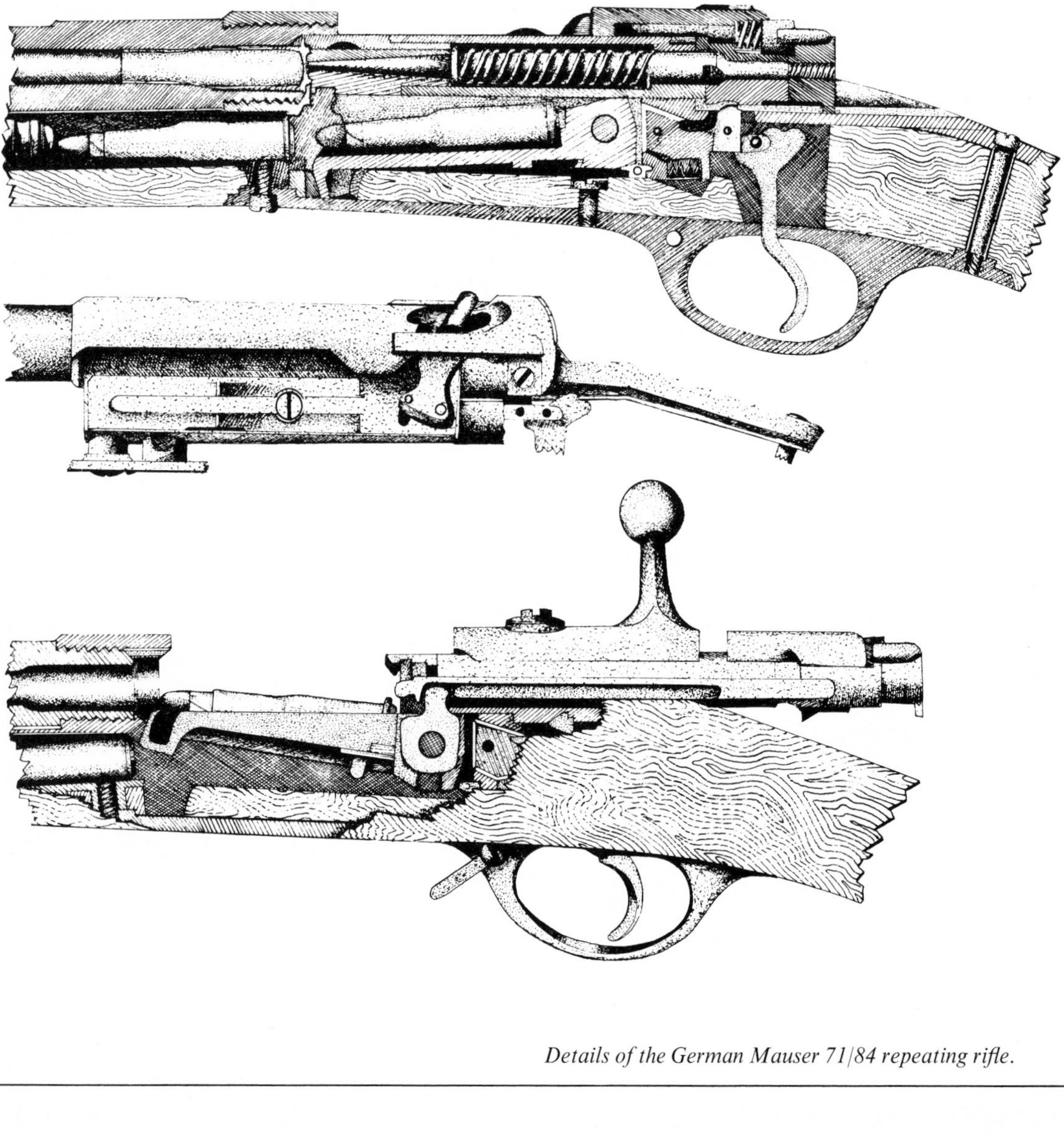

*Details of the German Mauser 71/84 repeating rifle.*

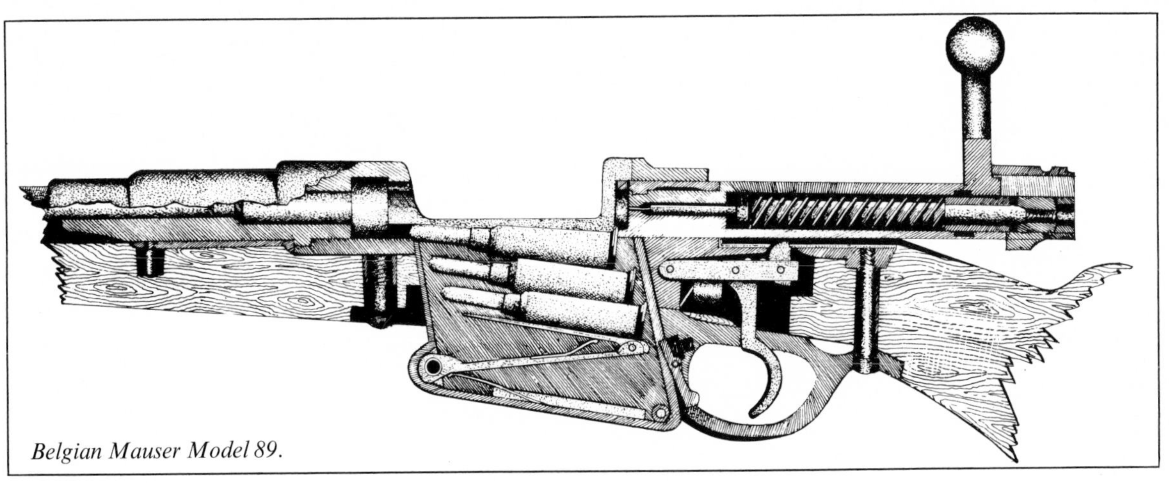

*Belgian Mauser Model 89.*

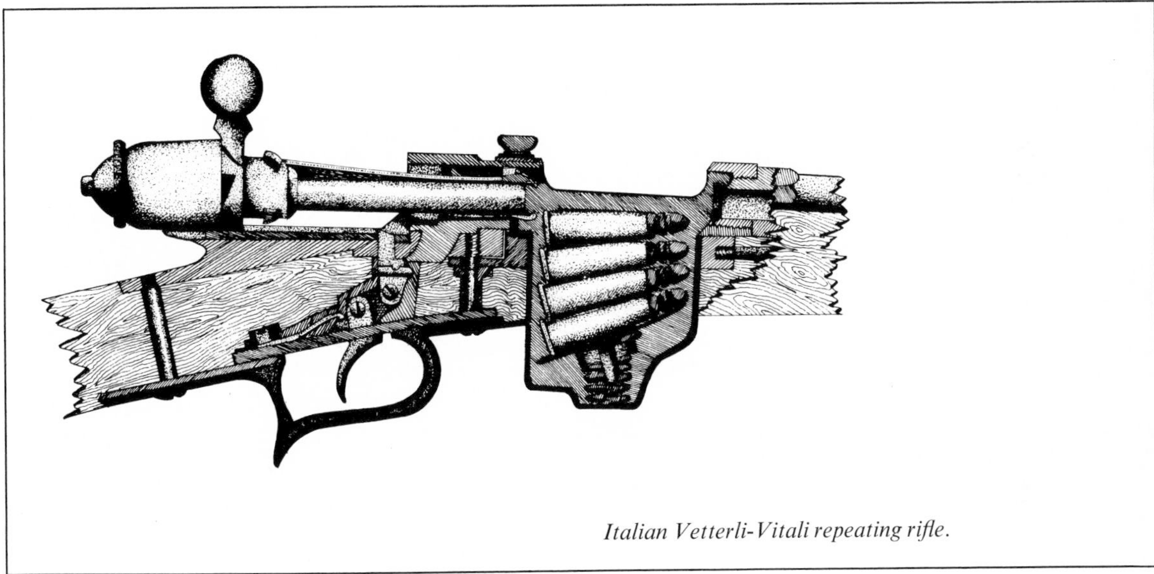

*Italian Vetterli-Vitali repeating rifle.*

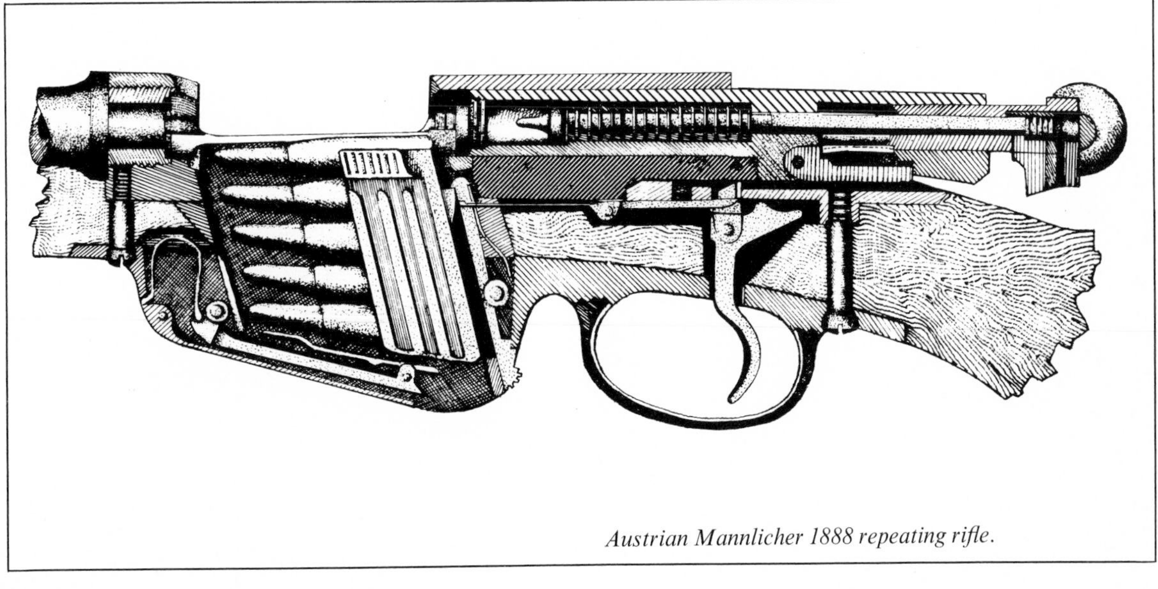

*Austrian Mannlicher 1888 repeating rifle.*

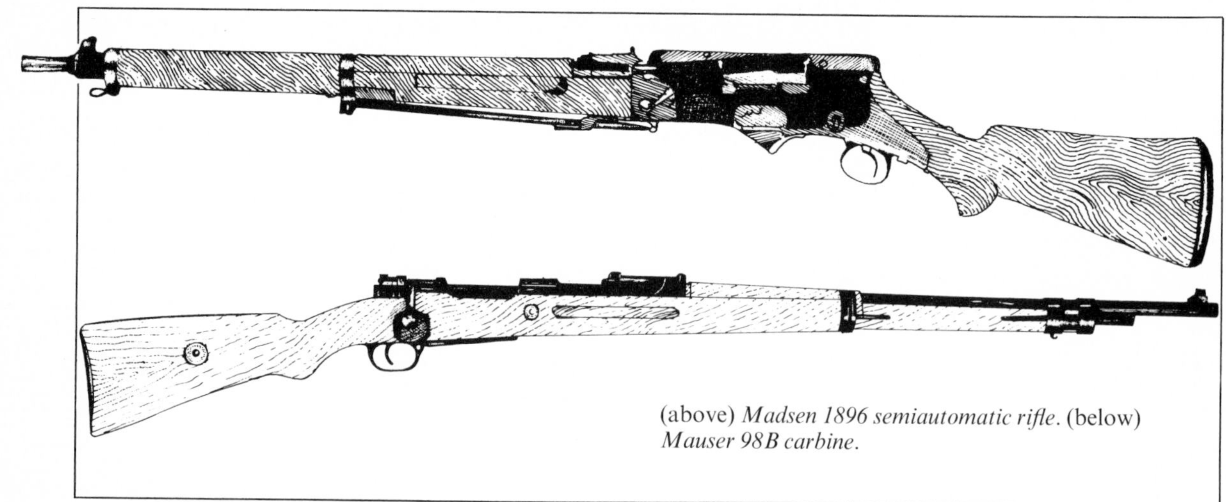

(above) *Madsen 1896 semiautomatic rifle.* (below) *Mauser 98B carbine.*

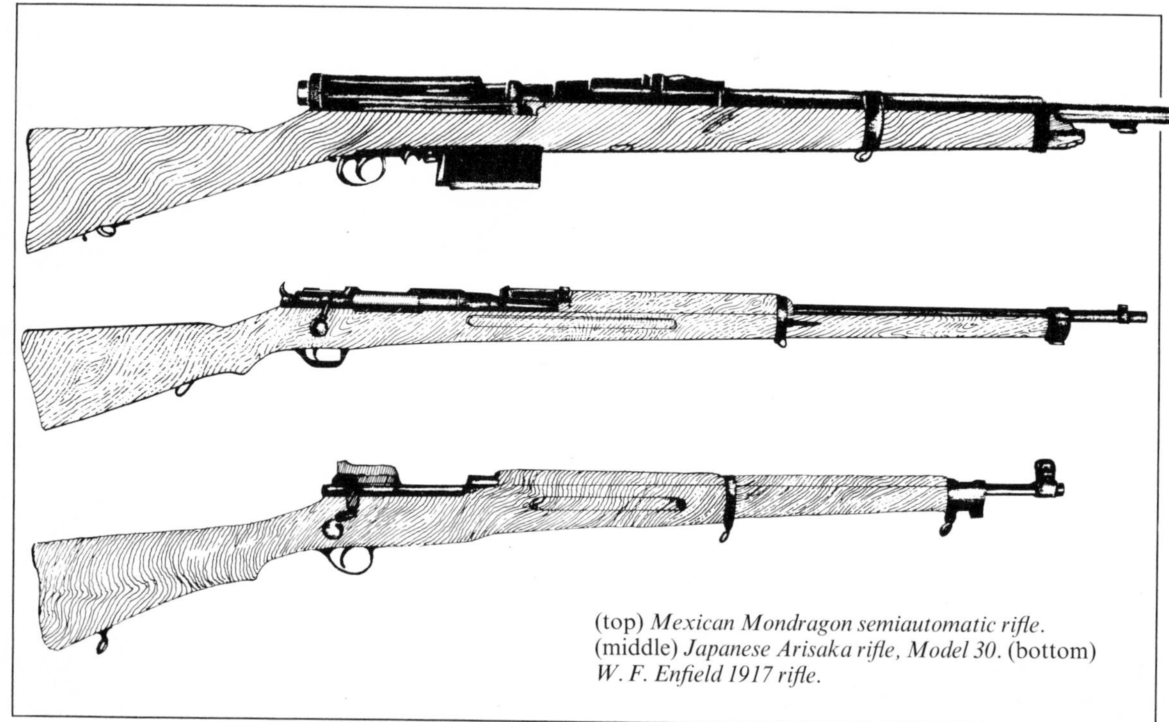

(top) *Mexican Mondragon semiautomatic rifle.* (middle) *Japanese Arisaka rifle, Model 30.* (bottom) *W. F. Enfield 1917 rifle.*

the breechblock was shaped in a spiral which fitted into a similar spiral on the back wall of the receiver. This arrangement forced the block forward as it was closed by turning a handle, and thus ensured the system's perfect seal. The striker passed through the block, and in the oldest specimens the original percussion lock was used, with some modifications to the hammer of the converted firearm.

*Rolling block*. The system used most widely was that patented in 1863 by Leonard Geiger and improved by Joseph Rider. From the name of the manufacturers, it became known as the Remington Rolling Block. Simple and strong, it had both the breechblock and the hammer hinged on strong center pins at right angles to the axis of the barrel; a perfect seal at the moment of firing was ensured by the action of the two against each other. The face of the breechblock, hinged at the front, was designed to fit closely against the breech and the chambered cartridge. The striker passed through a hole in the breechblock, which was curved at the back so as to engage with a corresponding curve on the front face of the hammer, which was hinged a little farther back and lower down. When the breechblock was closed and the hammer was brought down, the two pieces fitted together so that the face of the hammer supported the breechblock against the recoil force. The action could only be opened with the hammer cocked. The Remington Rolling Block system was adopted in the United States, Spain, Switzerland, Egypt, Cuba, Mexico, Chile, Turkey, and Italy.

*Oscillating block*. First in this very important category was the system patented in the United States by H. O. Peabody in 1862 and used in a number of countries. In arms constructed on the Peabody principle, a box-shaped receiver was screwed to the breech end of the barrel. The steel breechblock had a hinge at the rear end, connecting it to the receiver; a depression on the upper surface of the block made it easy to load the cartridges or extract the spent cases when the action was open. A simple lever system operated by the hinged trigger guard actuated the opening and closing of the breech. The striker, running in a groove of the breechblock, was struck by a hammer of conventional percussion-lock design. This outstandingly simple and robust system was improved in the Westley Richards, the Werder, and the Martini. Of these, the Werder was adopted by the Bavarian Army and, despite its complicated design, gave good results during the Franco-Prussian War of 1870–71. F. von Martini, who fitted a firing pin inside the breechblock in 1868, produced a system so simple and so ingenious that it was still used until quite recently in expensive shotguns.

*Falling block*. Among the systems in which the breechblock slides vertically in a slot of a strong receiver, the best known is undoubtedly that designed and perfected in the early 1860s by Christian Sharps, first for paper ammunition and later for metal cartridges. As in many U.S. arms, the movement of the breechblock was actuated by the trigger guard. One of the few European systems of this type was the Treuille de Beaulieu, used in the carbines for Napoleon III's Cent Gardes. In this system the breechblock was closed by the action of a powerful spring and at the same time fired the cartridge by means of a stud that struck the firing pin. While Sharps's arms always worked very well, the Cent Gardes' carbines soon disappeared.

*Systems with mixed actions*. The only notable arm in this category was that designed by H. J. Comblain of Liège in 1871, in which the block slid vertically and was finally slightly rotated. Adopted on a vast scale by the Belgian Army, this system was generally simple and strong, though it could not be produced very rapidly.

**Main Obturation Systems**

| | |
|---|---|
| Sliding bolt | Sliding (Mannlicher 1886, 1890, and 1895, Ross, Rubin-Schmidt)<br>Sliding and rotating (Dreyse, Lebel, Enfield, Mauser, etc.) |
| Externally hinged block | Side-hinged "trapdoor" block (Snider, Joslyn, Strong, Gunn, etc.)<br>Front-hinged "trapdoor" block (Berdan I, Allin, Milbank, Albini, etc.) |
| Internally hinged block | Pivoted at barrel (Werndl)<br>Back rotation (Remington Rolling Block, Spencer, etc.)<br>Oscillation (Peabody, Werder, Westley Richards, Martini, etc.) |
| Falling block | Sharps |
| Mixed action | Comblain |

### *Repeating Rifles*

Repeating rifles are fitted with a magazine containing a number of cartridges and allowing several shots to be fired without reloading manually after each shot. There are a great number of feed systems; the main types are (a) a tubular magazine parallel with the barrel; (b) a tubular magazine in the butt; (c) a fixed vertical magazine; and (d) a detachable vertical magazine.

The first rifle with a tubular magazine under the barrel was patented in 1849 by Walter Hunt and designed to use the special self-propelled bullets (rocket balls) that Hunt had patented the year before. As adapted later by Lewis Jennings, Daniel B. Wesson, Horace Smith, and Benjamin Tyler Henry, this arm was the ancestor of the famous Volcanic and Henry rifles and the Winchester rifles of 1866, 1873, and 1876. The Winchester 1866 rifle, which we take as our example in this category, had the rear end of the barrel screwed into a strong brass receiver. It contained the mechanism for closure, repetition, and firing; in its front, below the barrel, a steel-tube magazine was fitted. A long coil spring in the tube, at the front end, forced the cartridges back to the receiver by a cap called the follower; the cartridges were inserted into the magazine through a trap on the right side of the receiver. The cartridges were pressed out of the magazine into the carrier, which rose when the action was opened and aligned the next round behind the chamber. The horizontal sliding breechblock was controlled by a trigger-guard lever. This magazine system was used in many arms, including the Swiss Vetterli, the Früwirth, the Kropatschek, the 1871 Mauser, the Bertoldo, and the Lebel.

One of the most famous of all rifles with a tubular magazine in the butt was the Spencer. In this arm, used extensively by the Union Army in the Civil War, obturation was obtained by an ingenious rotating block actuated by the trigger guard. The cartridges—generally seven—were inserted in a sheet-steel tube with a coil spring and a follower; this tube fitted into the butt. The cartridges were picked up by the breechblock one at a time and loaded into the chamber as the breech was closed. Simple and very strong, the Spencer system still had an external

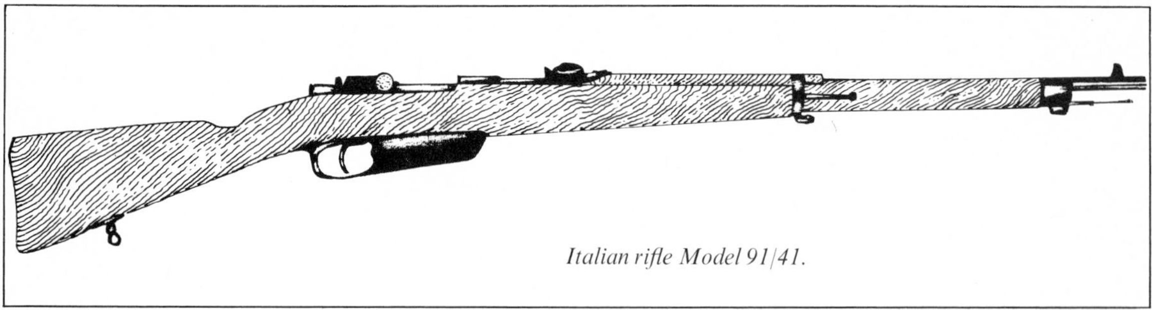

*Italian rifle Model 91/41.*

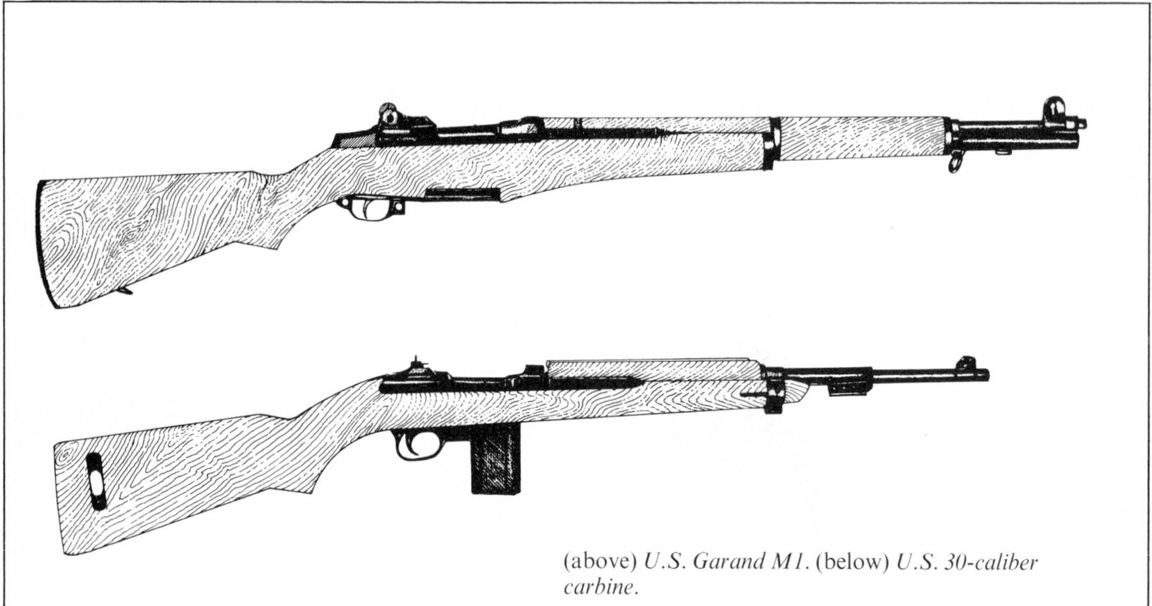

(above) *U.S. Garand M1.* (below) *U.S. 30-caliber carbine.*

hammer that had to be cocked by hand. The rifle could not stand up to competition from more modern weapons once the war was over and soon disappeared from circulation. The tubular magazine in the butt persisted in a number of later arms, among them the Hotchkiss of 1877, the Mannlicher of 1881, the Sporer-Härl of 1882, and the Schulhof of 1883.

The main defects of tubular magazines, the continuous shifting of the center of gravity of the weapon and the long time taken to change the magazines, were eliminated with the vertical magazine fitted below the breechblock. The first efficient vertical magazine was that designed and patented in the United States by the Scotsman James P. Lee in 1879. It consisted of a sheet-metal container open at the top, with a laminar spring inside acting on a follower; once inserted, the cartridges could not escape because they were retained by ridges on the top of the magazine. The Lee magazine was detachable; a further great advance was the adoption of chargers with which the magazine could be quickly filled instead of having to be changed.

Fixed vertical magazines were also produced. In the 1886 Mannlicher the cartridges had to be inserted in a sheet-metal "packet" (clip), but in the Mauser, adopted in 1889–98 by various countries, they could be loaded one at a time or slid in from a charger. Though many types of magazines were tried out and used, perhaps the only one that has stood the test of time is the Mannlicher-Schoenauer rotating magazine, developed after 1887. Mauser-type magazines are generally used in modern sporting rifles; for military rifles vertical magazines of light sheet metal are preferred, with the cartridges arranged in a double row, quickly replaceable—directly derived from the Lee system.

### *Semiautomatic and Automatic Rifles*

Between 1881 and 1883 an American-British inventor, Hiram Maxim, seeing the possibility of exploiting the recoil force, produced what was probably the first working semiautomatic firearm. It was a Winchester carbine fitted with a system of levers, which reloaded the weapon when it was fired. In 1885 F. von Mannlicher patented a short-recoil rifle also capable of automatic fire; in 1891 he produced two more weapons that showed some advance on the earlier model. This prolific Austrian inventor produced other automatic rifles in 1894, 1895, and 1900.

At the end of the 19th century and the first decade of the 20th there were a great number of new developments in this field, not all of them equally successful. Among the inventors concerned were the Italians Gaspare Freddi, Amerigo Cei-Rigotti, and Filippo Genovesi, the German Mauser, the French Clair brothers, the Englishmen Griffiths and Woodgate, and the Swedes Friberg and Kjellman. Almost the only weapons of the kind used to any effect in the First World War were the French 1917 and 1918 model semiautomatic rifles and, by the Germans, the excellent Mondragon, designed by the Mexican general of that name and patented in 1908.

Research and experiments continued after the war, but only one weapon was adopted officially. In 1936 the U.S. Army adopted a semiautomatic, gas-operated rifle with a sliding and rotating bolt, designed by John C. Garand; it was fed by a Mannlicher-type clip holding eight rounds in two rows. The Garand, a robust and effective weapon, gave the Americans a considerable margin of superiority over enemy forces armed with rifles that had to be reloaded manually. In the course of the Second World War the Germans produced some exceptionally important arms in the same field, notably the Gewehr 41M and Gewehr 41W semiautomatic rifles, the famous assault rifle FG-42, the Gewehr 43 and, later, chambered for the intermediate Kurz (short) 7.92 mm. cartridge, the assault rifles MP-43 and M-44 and the Volksturmgewehr (Sturmgewehr). The FG-42 (Fallschirmjäger Gewehr 42), produced for the parachute troops, could fire automatically, with the open-bolt action: when the trigger was pressed, the bolt went forward from its rear position, loaded and fired a cartridge, and remained in the open position when the trigger was released, thus allowing ventilation of the barrel. Single aimed shots were fired with the bolt closed, thus avoiding the vibration due to the movement of the bolt at the moment of firing. Like the Gewehr 41 and 43, the FG-42 was gas-operated.

The Germans recognized from their first military encounters in the Second World War that most exchanges of fire using personal weapons would take place at ranges of not more than 400 m. (440 yds.), so that the considerable power of the traditional rifle cartridges was

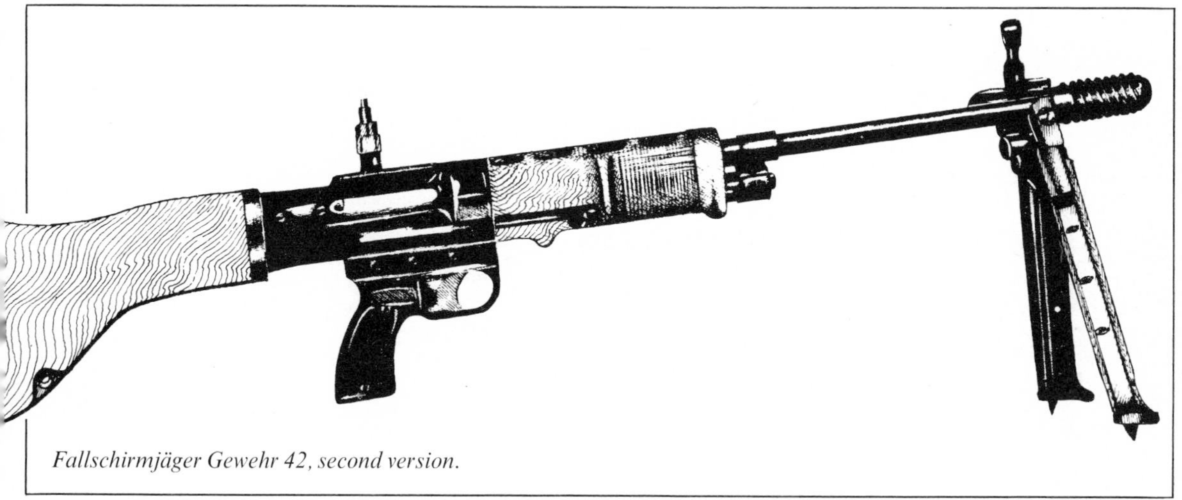

*Fallschirmjäger Gewehr 42, second version.*

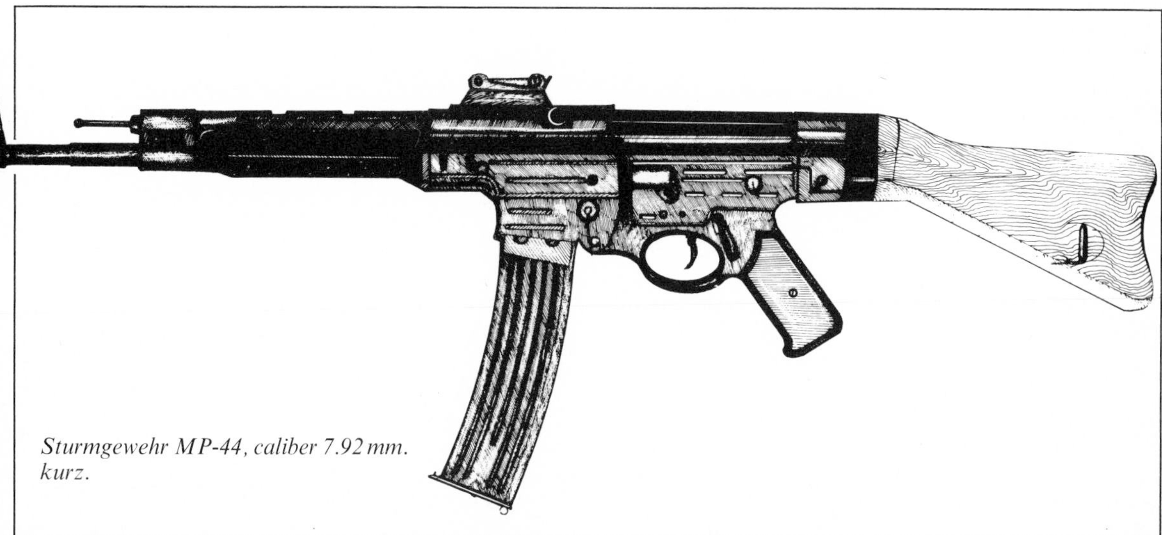

*Sturmgewehr MP-44, caliber 7.92 mm. kurz.*

*Some contemporary assault rifles. 1. Russian AK-47. 2. German-Spanish CETME Model 58. 3. American AR-15. 4. Belgian FAL, old version. 5. Italian Beretta 70/.223 carbine.*

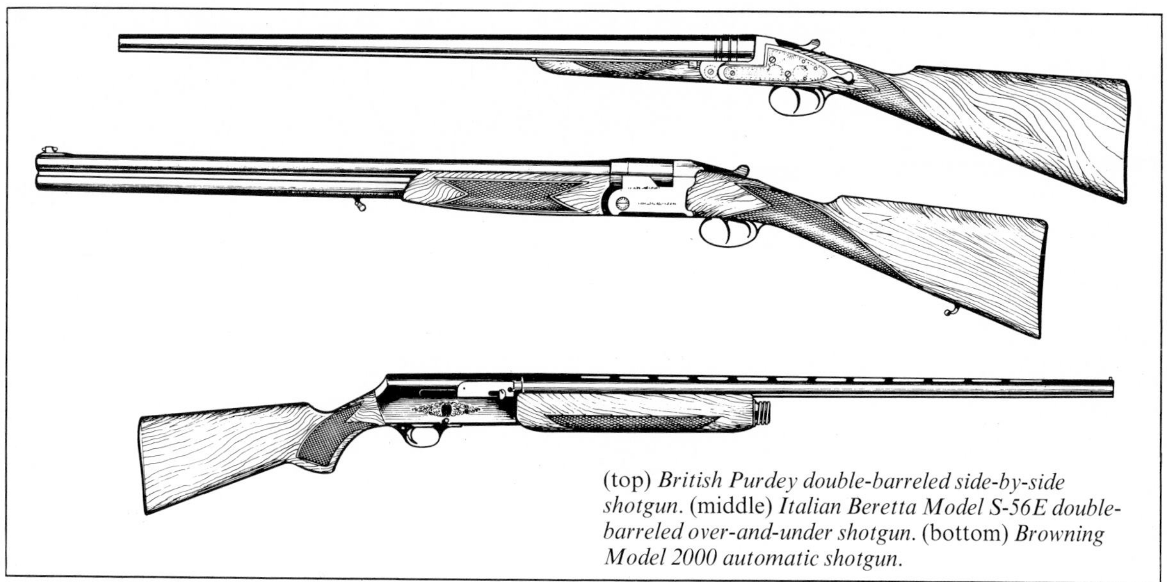

(top) *British Purdey double-barreled side-by-side shotgun.* (middle) *Italian Beretta Model S-56E double-barreled over-and-under shotgun.* (bottom) *Browning Model 2000 automatic shotgun.*

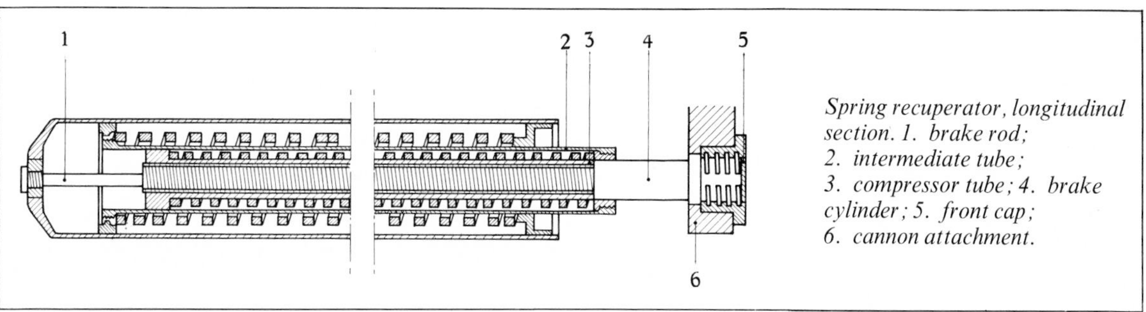


*Spring recuperator, longitudinal section. 1. brake rod; 2. intermediate tube; 3. compressor tube; 4. brake cylinder; 5. front cap; 6. cannon attachment.*

largely wasted. This led them to adopt the "intermediate" 7.92 × 33 mm. short cartridge, powerful enough for firing at ranges up to 500–600 m. (550–650 yds.). The first weapon firing this cartridge, the assault rifle MP-43 (later modified as the MP-44), was gas-operated, with a sliding bolt actuated by a rod driven by a piston. Relatively easy to produce (it was largely manufactured from stamped sheet steel) and fitted with a magazine for thirty rounds, the MP-44 was a starting point for several modern assault rifles, including the widely used Soviet AK-47. The semiautomatic Sturmgewehr, which went into production in 1944–45 and was issued in limited numbers, aroused great interest with the principles of its design. When this gun was fired, the sliding bolt was prevented from opening by the force of part of the gas, directed through four ports in the barrel into a mobile sleeve, coaxial with the barrel, giving the bolt (attached to the back end of the sleeve) a powerful thrust forward and so overcoming the blowback force until the bullet left the muzzle.

The adoption of the AK-47 assault rifle by the Soviet Army was an event of great significance; the Western nations were compelled to design rifles that could fire equally rapidly if they were not to be left behind. Since the cartridge standardized in the NATO countries, the 7.62 mm. Nato, differed very little from the powerful U.S. 30/06, the results achieved were not too brilliant. Certainly some excellent rifles were produced—notably the Belgian FAL F.N.—but the excessive power of the cartridge made rapid fire with them extremely unpleasant for the firer. In the AK-47, on the other hand, designed by the then Sergeant Major Mikhail T. Kalashnikov, we find the perfect symbiosis of weapon with cartridge. The designer's greatest merit lay in his having cleverly adapted and united the best features of existing arms to obtain an assault rifle which, while by no means revolutionary, was a fine, efficient weapon from every point of view. Without going into too much detail, it is worth noting that the bolt action, in which a bolt carrier actuated by a piston rotates the bolt, unlocking it as it is forced back and locking it again as the next round is loaded, recalls that patented by Bjorgum as long ago as 1911. The employment of the 7.62 × 39 (M-43) intermediate cartridge, similar in design to the German 7.92 short round, made an effective rapid fire possible with the firearms in this series—the AKN assault rifle and the similar RPK light machine gun.

In the United States, where the heavy M-14 (derived in principle from the Garand, but with a vertical magazine and capable of rapid fire) had been adopted for the 7.62 mm. Nato cartridge, a start was already being made by the end of the 1950s on experiments with an automatic firearm chambered for the light and fast .223 Remington cartridge. Today this cartridge, adopted officially as the

5.6 M-193, seems destined to replace the 7.62 Nato in the whole of the Western world. Arms of this caliber already in use in the U.S. armed forces are the M-16 and M-16A1 assault rifles, designed by Eugene Stoner of the Armalite company and produced by Colt. In Stoner's system the gas, instead of acting on a piston, is directed to act on the bolt. The bolt consists of a solid block with a rotating head having eight locking lugs at the front; it is rotated for the open and closed positions by a stud that runs in a spiral groove on the top of the bolt carrier.

Firearms of the new caliber are being designed and tested in Austria, Belgium, Finland, France, Israel, Italy, Sweden, Switzerland, the United Kingdom, and West Germany. Of particular interest are the short French MAS rifle and the Beretta 70/.223 group in Italy. These last, designed under the direction of the engineer Vittorio Valle, include the AR rifle, the SC carbine, and the 70/78/.223 light machine gun. Although experiments are going on in several countries with cartridges of even smaller caliber (between 3 and 5 mm. in the United States; 3.5 and 4.8 mm. in Belgium; 4 mm. in Spain; 4.84 mm. in Great Britain; 4.3 and 4.6 mm. in Germany) and ammunition of special types is being tried, it seems fairly certain that the admirable 5.6 × 44.5 mm. will be the essential choice for a few years to come.

*Sporting Guns*

This term is commonly used to refer to smooth-bore guns firing cartridges loaded with SHOT. Historically, the development of sporting guns, which for a long time were the weapons of the privileged classes, kept ahead of the evolution of military long arms, until the beginning of this century, which saw a general divergence between their respective lines of development. Modern sporting guns can be divided into smooth-bore shotguns for small game (game birds, hares, and so on) and sporting rifles firing bullets for big-game shooting or for target shooting.

In shooting game birds and small game, which can move suddenly and quickly, it is essential that the pellets spread over a certain area, the KILLING CIRCLE. To obtain a clearly defined killing circle there is a CHOKE in the barrel, which, according to its type, has a greater or lesser effect in concentrating the pellets. (Generally speaking, the choke is between 0.2 and 1.2 mm.) Sporting guns, which are usually double-barreled (side-by-side or over-and-under), often have two differently choked barrels so as to give a similar killing circle at different ranges. Modern smooth-bore sporting guns, both side-by-side and over-and-under, are generally "hammerless" (i.e., with internal striking mechanism), cocked by the dropping of the barrels, and fitted with automatic extractors.

Single-barrel, semiautomatic guns are also not uncommon, though these are liable to jam; also simple repeating "pump action" guns, in which a handle or "pump" that slides longitudinally beneath a fixed barrel is worked with hand to chamber the cartridge. The pump-action system is used quite widely for large-caliber sporting guns. Designed so as to obtain a flat trajectory with high muzzle velocity, these have smooth-bore or rifled barrels and may be fitted with special sights—telescopic, dioptric, micrometric, etc.—which make them very effective weapons.

Among special types of multibarreled sporting guns are the specimens which have different barrels in one cluster. One type has two barrels, one under the other; the upper barrel, generally 12-bore, is smooth and the lower is rifled for firing bullets. The three-barreled gun has two smooth-bore barrels side by side, with the rifled barrel below them. These guns are designed for use where small and big game may be found at the same time.

Another special shotgun, which appeared in the early 19th century, was the pigeon gun. It was usually single-barreled, with a large bore (gauge 10, 8, and even larger), using quite a heavy shot. After having been in vogue, particularly in England, for some fifty years, it was replaced, for pigeon shooting, by ordinary fowling pieces. The duck guns were similar to the pigeon guns in calibers but used still heavier loads and weighed $5\frac{1}{2}$–7 kg. (about 12–15 lbs.). The largest among shotguns were the punt guns, which had calibers from 9 to 1 gauge (20 to 45 mm./$\frac{2}{3}$–$1\frac{3}{4}$ in.). Weighing between 30 and 55 kg. (70–120 lbs.), they were mounted on specially built punts and boats for shooting ducks and geese on water and in marshy country. The punt guns were used since the 17th century and still enjoyed popularity in the 19th.

For big-game hunting and target shooting, rifles have been used from the second half of the 16th century. Very soon the target rifles started developing features of their own, particularly in the construction of the sights and the shape of the stocks, which were often furnished with special butt plates, hand rests, and lead beams in order to properly balance and hold the weapon. During the 19th century the three basic types of the target rifle for competition were established: the so-called Schuetzen rifle, of German-Swiss origin, historically going back to the early 17th century, for off-hand shooting; the Creedmore, a long-range rifle developed in the United States by the 1870s; and the bench-rest rifle. These types have been used up till the present time.

The useful range of a smooth-bore shotgun is not more than 40–50 m. (44–55 yds.); single pellets will of course travel a good deal farther, but beyond a certain distance the killing area becomes scattered, growing wider and longer. Rifles have a range, marked by the calibration on the backsight, of up to 300 m. (330 yds.), though the range of military versions of the same rifles may be 2000 m. (2200 yds.) or more.

**guncotton** Trinitrocellulose, obtained by treating cotton with a mixture of nitric and sulfuric acids. *See also* EXPLOSIVE.

**gun mountings** and **gun carriages** Supports for the barrels of artillery designed and built for convenience of operation both in firing and transportation. When a gun mounting is associated with a more complex system, providing a platform for the gun and protection for the piece and its crew, it is known as an emplacement. The mounting includes parts on which the barrel rests in such a way that it can be pivoted on a lateral axis to adjust the angle of fire.

*Italian 149/35 gun with rigid carriage and Bonagente tracked wheels.*

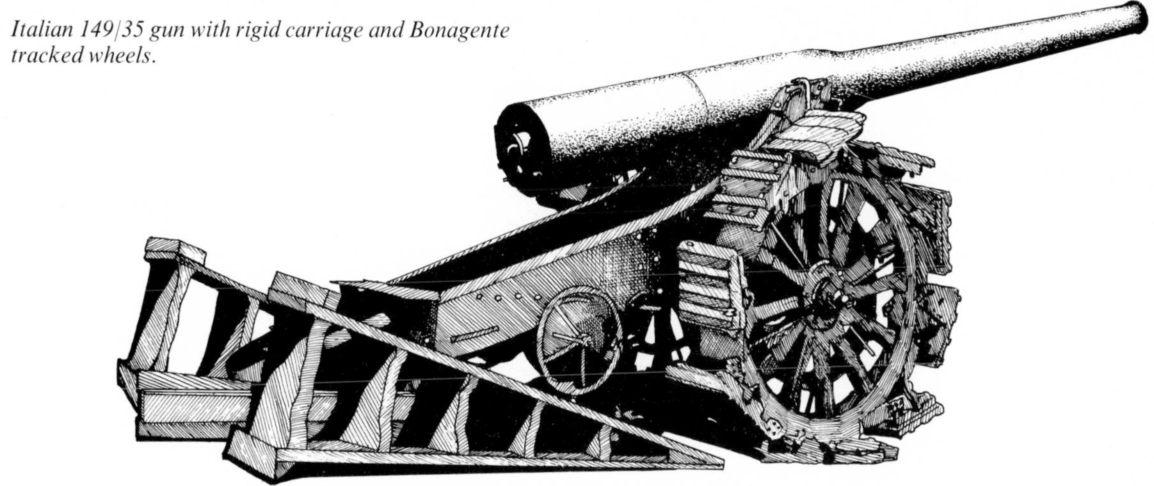

*Carriage for siege gun* (right) *and for coast defense gun* (below).

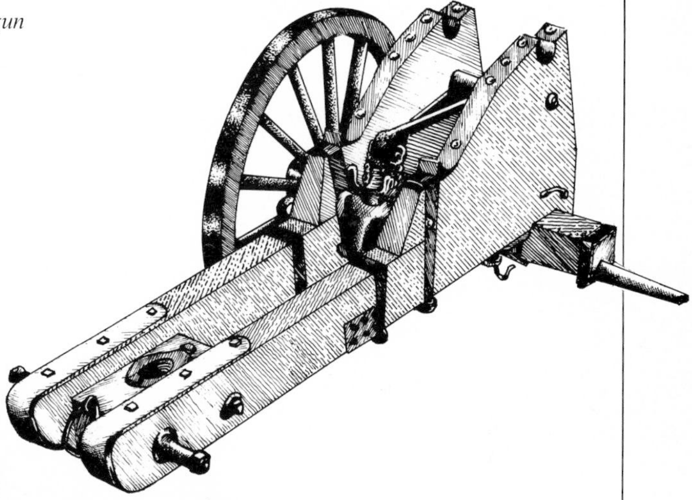

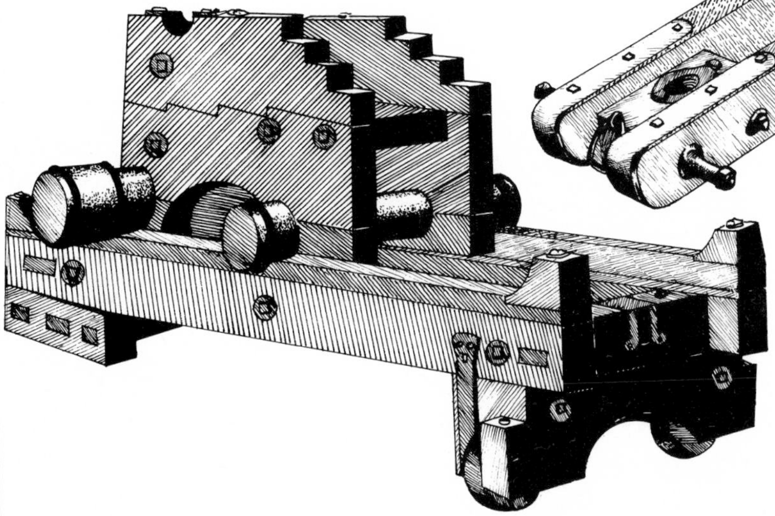

The axis is made up of two trunnions—cylindrical projections on each side of the cannon or mortar—which may either be built into the barrel itself or attached to that part of the mounting on which the barrel is supported. The trunnions are housed in special bearings on the upper part of the mounting, which allow the trunnions to rotate. The swiveling movement is obtained by means of an elevation device which also acts as a stabilizer for the barrel when this is positioned at different angles. To alter the direction in which the gun is to be pointed, the mounting is either completely movable on the platform or consists of two parts, one of which rests on the ground and the other being constructed to rotate on a vertical axis.

The following forms of gun mountings have been used: *Wheel carriages.* These consist basically of a center beam flanked by two securely joined lateral supports. The "tail" of the beam (the trail) rests on the ground, while the "head" is attached to an axletree for wheels. Gun carriages equipped with two or four wheels are extremely mobile and require no modification either to position them in a

*Diagram of the carriage of the Italian 75/27 Model 911 gun.*

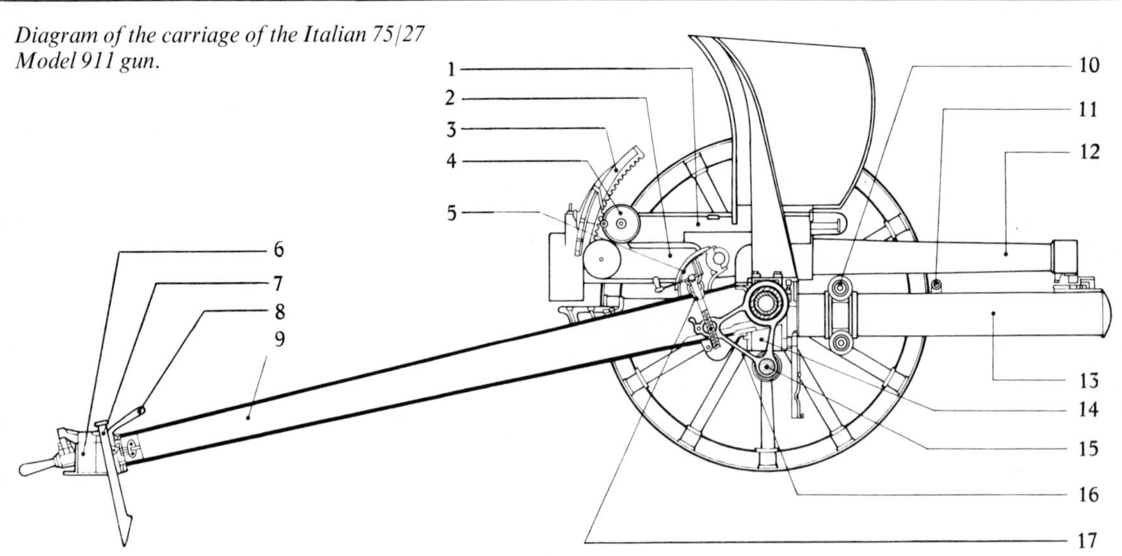


Side view: *1. cradle; 2. support; 3. toothed elevating arc; 4. elevating handwheel; 5. sides of the cradle; 6. trail bracket; 7. recoil spade; 8. spade lifting handle; 9. trail; 10. roller; 11. road brake lever; 12. piece; 13. carriage cradle; 14. axle housing; 15. oscillating crossbar; 16. aiming quadrant; 17 aiming quadrant screw.*

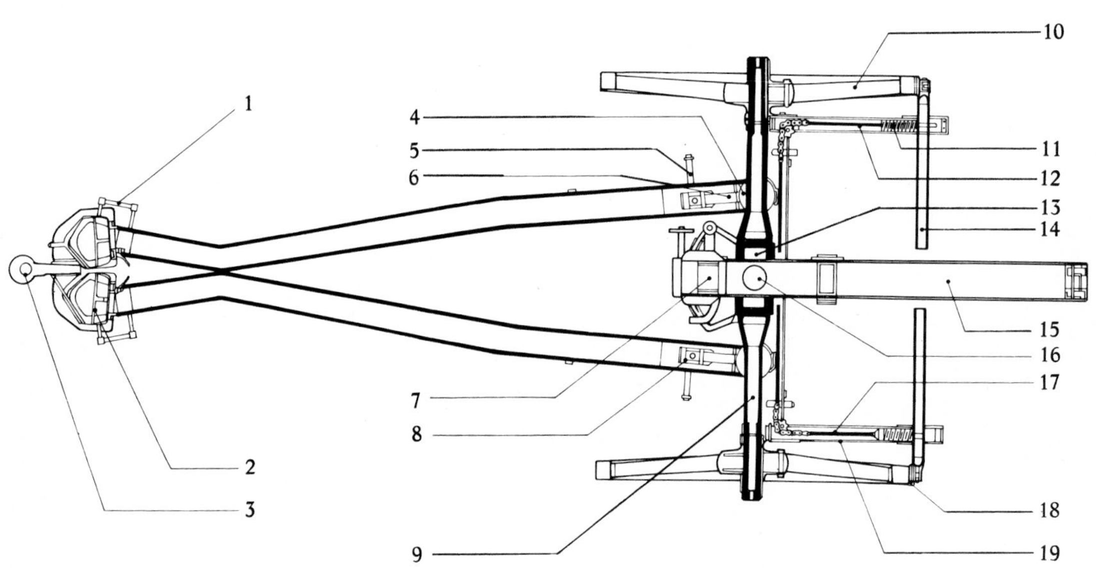


Top view: *1. lifting handle; 2. spade; 3. towing eye; 4. trail hinge; 5. locking bolt; 6. aiming quadrant; 7. roller; 8. aiming quadrant nut; 9. axle; 10. wheel; 11. brake lever spring; 12. brake lever tie rod; 13. axle housing; 14. brake lever; 15. carriage cradle; 16. carriage cradle pivot; 17. see 12; 18. brake shoe; 19. support arm.*

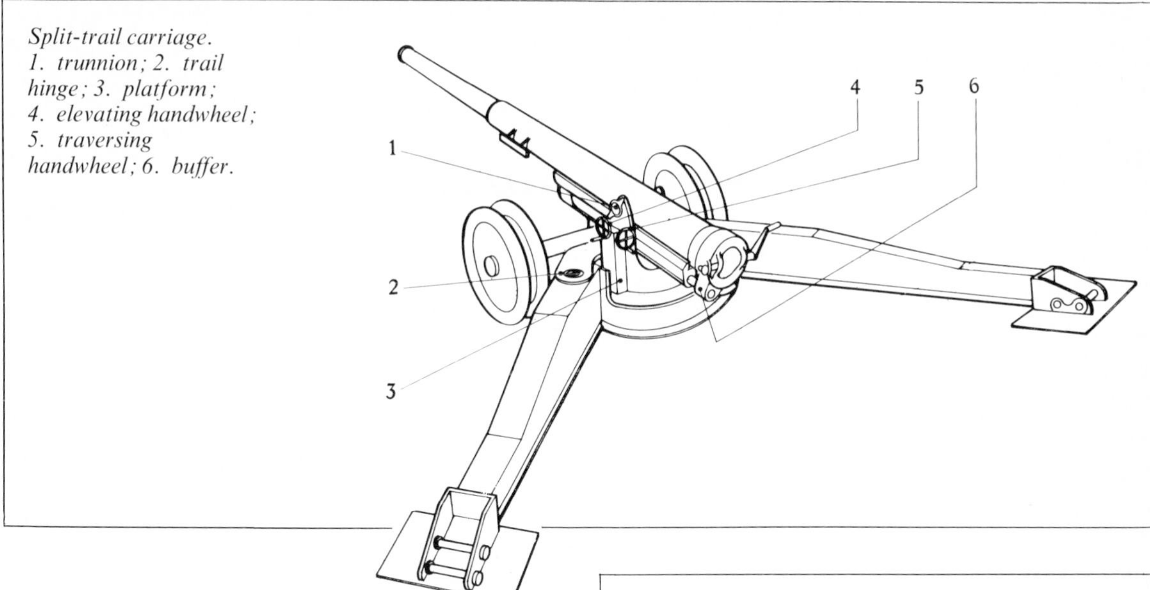


*Split-trail carriage. 1. trunnion; 2. trail hinge; 3. platform; 4. elevating handwheel; 5. traversing handwheel; 6. buffer.*

battery or for being drawn by horses or mechanized vehicles. The stability of the unit depends entirely upon its proportions and size.

*Block mountings.* These are built up by two rigidly joined side panels, in the form of a triangle or a trapezoid, which carry the trunnions on which the gun barrel rests. This "block" is attached to the bearing surface or platform, depending on where the gun is mounted, on which it can swivel on a vertical axis.

Block mountings may be used in various ways: (1) in movable emplacements, in which case they can be modified to facilitate trailing (or drawing, if horses are used), but they have limited efficiency and, in fact, became obsolete after the Second World War; (2) in self-propelled and railway emplacements when the mounting and gun are either installed on a vehicle or are an integral part of the vehicle; and (3) in permanent emplacements defending land or coastal fortifications.

*Pedestal mountings.* The main structure consists of two small side panels, joined at the base to a center column which swivels on a pedestal firmly fixed to the bearing surface, thus enabling the gun to be trained rapidly and to facilitate vertical firing. This type of mounting was extensively used at one time with small-caliber anti-aircraft guns.

Pedestal mountings may be "rigid" or "flexible," according to how the gun barrel is mounted. With rigid mountings, the barrel is held, by means of its trunnions, on trunnion bearings attached to the mounting. Thus, apart from the rotational movement around the trunnions to allow the gun to be trained or "laid," the gun barrel and its mounting become—so far as the impact of recoil is concerned—a single rigid unit. This system fell into disuse at the beginning of the 20th century.

In the case of flexible mountings, of which there are several variations, the principle is that on recoil the barrel of the gun, linked to a system of brakes and recuperator, is able to slide along the mounting, which does not move, and to return automatically to the firing position. The brakes consist of a cylinder with hydraulic fluid, closed at one end, in which a piston moves back and forth, the piston rod emerging from a watertight hole at the opposite end. This cylinder is connected to the gun barrel, while the piston rod is connected to the mounting (or vice versa). On recoil, fluid is forced either through inflow apertures in the head of the piston or into the recuperator cylinder. The recuperator contains heavy metal springs or compressed air geared by a floating piston. The recoil system restricts the barrel's recoil movement, returning it to the firing position when the recoil has played itself out.

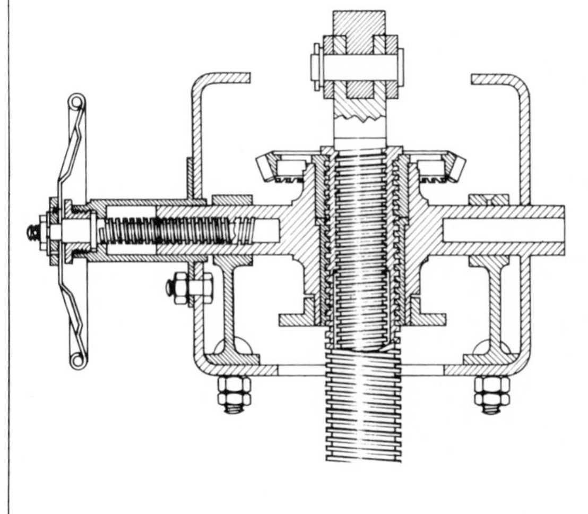

*Elevating gear with double screw and traversing gear with single screw.*

Flexible mountings can also be divided into *sliding mountings* and *cradle mountings*.

In the sliding mounting, the gun barrel rests on

trunnions mounted on bearings supported by a block which rotates on the mounting according to direction of fire. The bearings run on two rails, which are positioned over the side panels of the mounting. The brake cylinders are usually assembled inside the rotating block. The elevation mechanism acts on the assembly incorporating the barrel and rails, which are kept parallel on recoil.

In the cradle mounting, an intermediate part, the cradle with trunnions, is suspended on the mounting. The gun barrel is linked to the cradle by the brake and recuperator, and is thus able to slide over it. As the cradle is positioned by the elevation device, the barrel always recoils in the direction of the cradle axis. In most forms of cradle mountings, the cannon passes through the cradle, which is grooved on the inside to receive the guiding fins of the barrel (to prevent the barrel from rotating within the cradle) and the bronze bushings, which are intended to reduce friction between the barrel and the cradle.

**gunpowder** Also called black powder. An intimate mixture of saltpeter (potassium nitrate), sulfur, and charcoal, gunpowder is the oldest known and earliest used detonating and propellant explosive. Research into its origins has never yet produced any reliable answers. It cannot, however, be accepted that firearms, in the commonly understood sense of the term, were employed in the East as early as the 11th century, though it does seem certain that gunpowder, with a low content of saltpeter, was already used as an explosive by that time. Some interesting recent theories suggest that the mixture may have been known to the Alexandrine school of magic before the Christian era. One of the most firmly established traditions, going back to the 15th century, attributes the invention of gunpowder to a monk of Freiburg, Berthold Schwarz. However, Professor Partington, in his book *A History of Greek Fire and Gunpowder* (Cambridge, 1960), has collected all the available information about this character and reached the conclusion, which nearly all scholars accept, that he is a legendary figure invented, probably, to demonstrate the Teutonic origin of firearms.

For a long time the history of gunpowder was associated and confused with that of Greek fire, which is known to have been made by mixing saltpeter with incendiary mixtures already in use. In the *Liber ignium ad comburendos hostes* by Marcus Graecus (8th–9th century) we find descriptions of various incendiary mixtures, Greek fire, and rockets, and also of gunpowder. Recent research has shown, however, that this last recipe was added at a comparatively recent date. Roger Bacon (c. 1214–1292) in his *Opus majus* quotes, in an anagram that cannot be attributed to him with certainty, the formula of a powder made up of six parts of saltpeter, five of charcoal, and five of sulfur, which could certainly not have been used in firearms. Not so long ago some ancient chronicles collected by Lodovico Muratori in his *Rerum Italicarum scriptores* (1723–51) were adduced in an attempt to prove that the Italians were the first to use firearms. However, on closer analysis it turns out that all the chronicles in question were compiled by authors who lived centuries after the facts recorded, and therefore—from a technical point of view, at any rate—lose all credibility.

Among the oldest documents that certainly deal with the use of firearms and the use of gunpowder as a propellant are two manuscripts of 1326 by Walter de Milemete, chaplain to Edward II of England. The first of them is a copy of Aristotle's *De secretis secretorum* (in the British Museum), and the other is entitled *De nobilitatibus, sapientiis et prudentiis regum* (library of Christ Church College, Oxford); in the illustrated margins of both can be seen what are today unanimously agreed to be the oldest known depictions of firearms. After 1330 documents dealing with gunpowder and firearms became increasingly numerous in all parts of Europe, evidence of the rapid spread of this new and powerful means of destruction.

*Structure and Formula*

As already mentioned, gunpowder is a mixture of potassium nitrate (saltpeter), charcoal, and sulfur, a mixture made as intimate as possible by mechanical means. Saltpeter is a salt with a high oxygen content, and thus acts as a fuel providing the oxygen necessary for the combustion of the powder; the powder will be more powerful or less in proportion to the amount of saltpeter in it. The charcoal and sulfur are the combustibles; the explosive reaction is mainly due to oxidation of the charcoal (carbon), that is, the conversion of the solid substance into carbon monoxide and carbon dioxide, with the development of great heat. The actual explosion could therefore take place with only saltpeter and charcoal; in theory, the sulfur is not necessary for it. In practice, however, the sulfur acts as a kind of cement incorporating the other two ingredients; it burns at a lower temperature than carbon and thus promotes the combustion of the mixture; the heat developed as it burns assists the decomposition of the saltpeter and consequent oxidation of the carbon; and, as long as it is spread evenly through the whole mass, it helps the preparation of the combustion and has a definite effect on the regularity of it.

The percentage of the three ingredients in the mixture is called the "formula." The formula has to be such that the reaction gives the maximum quantity of gaseous products and the minimum of ash, and it is determined by consideration of what the powder is to be used for, bearing in mind that charcoal and sulfur accelerate combustion, while saltpeter retards it, and that charcoal produces great amounts of heat and gas, while sulfur makes the powder burn quickly and gives rise to solid residues. The formula is therefore different for powder for use in sporting guns, in blasting, and in warfare. But there are of course other things that influence the effects of the powder, such as the manufacturing process, the density, the grain, the addition of graphite, and so on.

The formula that in theory ensures complete oxidation on explosion, according to Berthelot, is 84 percent saltpeter, 8 percent sulfur, and 8 percent charcoal, which gives the reaction:

$$10\,KNo_3 + 3\,S + 8\,C = 2\,K_2CO_3 + 3\,K_2SO_4 + 6\,CO_2 + 5\,N_2$$

In comparison with powder made according to "practical" rather than theoretical formulae, it can be seen that the theoretical formula gives a smaller volume of gas and a larger amount of solid residues (potassium sulfate and carbonate), so that "practical" formulae have been preferred. In old times the formula was indicated in parts by weight of the three substances present in the mixture: 4-1-1 powder contained four parts by weight of saltpeter and one each of sulfur and charcoal. In the 1880s one of the commonest formulae used was what was called the "English formula": 75 percent saltpeter, 10 percent sulfur, 15 percent charcoal. The formula varied, of course, with the intended use of the powder. Powder for firearms has to be fairly slow-burning but very powerful, leaving a minimum of solid residues; it was therefore given a high proportion of saltpeter and not so much sulfur. For blasting powders (70 percent saltpeter, 18 percent sulfur, 12 percent charcoal) there is less saltpeter and more sulfur, which makes the powder burn quickly and produce a great volume of gas.

Gunpowder deflagrates at temperatures between 270° and 320°. It takes fire on contact with a body in flames and may explode if strongly detonated (e.g., by mercury fulminate). In the explosive reaction it may give rise to different substances according to the density with which it is packed. If well made and well preserved, it should be slate gray or shiny black in color, according to whether or not graphite has been added; if it is too black, that means either that it contains too much charcoal or that it is wet. Good powder will not make the fingers, or paper, dirty; if a small quantity is burned on a sheet of white paper it should not char it or leave any residue. Black stains would be a sign of too much charcoal, yellow stains of too much sulfur.

Gunpowder was used in firearms, both as a propellant and as a bursting charge inside the missiles, in mines, and in blasting work generally; nowadays it has been almost completely replaced for the first purpose by SMOKELESS POWDERS and for other purposes by the various EXPLOSIVES obtained by nitration of organic substances. It is still used for shooting with replicas of muzzleloading guns and period weapons, and is also used to some extent in making fireworks.

### *Raw Materials*

Saltpeter is obtained from the soil, either naturally or artificially, or by conversion of natural sodium nitrate. Saltpeter occurs in the natural state either in strata or impregnating the upper soil, but it can also be produced chemically by a process of decomposition of animal and vegetable detritus rich in nitrogen, hydrogen, and oxygen deposited in a porous, humid soil with a high content of potassium salts. In such conditions ammonia ($NH_3$) and carbon dioxide ($CO_2$) are generated. Microgerms present in the soil act on the ammonia to produce nitric acid and water: $NH_3+2O_2 = HNO_3+H_2O$. When the nitric acid comes in contact with ammonia not yet acted upon, it reacts to give ammonium nitrate: $HNO_3+NH_3 = NH_4NO_3$. If there is any kind of potassium salt in the soil, the ammonium nitrate reacts with it to form potassium nitrate; if for instance the salt is potassium chloride, the reaction will be: $KCl+NH_4NO_3 = KNO_3+NH_4Cl$. The potassium nitrate crystallizes readily in the cold, so there is no difficulty in extracting it. Given that urine, human and animal, has sodium chloride and potassium chloride among its main inorganic constituents and that its main organic constituent is urea ($H_2NCONH_2$), it is easy to see how this liquid can be used to produce saltpeter. Urea is actually hydrolized by certain microorganisms, such as *Micrococcus urea*, which accounts for the formation of ammonia in urine exposed to the air: $H_2NCONH_2 +H_2O = Co_2+2NH_3$.

The ancients, while not of course understanding the chemical process, were aware that saltpeter could be found in stables and wherever organic refuse was deposited. It was a short step from that to artificial production. Beds of loam and leaves were prepared in partially fenced-in and roofed enclosures, and large numbers of livestock, mostly cattle, were driven in. After some months, followed by a rest period, the "treated" earth was gathered into huge vats full of water, which was then boiled. The liquid obtained was filtered while still tepid and poured into other containers, in which the saltpeter crystallized as it cooled and could be extracted. The product thus obtained was not yet pure enough; it was only after two more crystallizations that it could be used for the manufacture of gunpowder (fine-baked saltpeter).

The preferred charcoal used in the early days was obtained artificially from thin branches of willow. From the 1800s on, charcoal was mainly obtained by the dry distillation of thin decorticated branches of willow, alder, or other soft woods, seasoned for at least two years, or of hemp stalks.

Sulfur for the powder used in firearms from the 16th century on was purified by sublimation (flowers of sulfur). The impurities generally found in this substance are arsenical compounds which give rise to corrosive emanations on deflagration.

### *Manufacture of Gunpowder*

The principle underlying the manufacture of gunpowder is as follows: reduce the ingredients to a very fine powder (trituration), mix these powders as intimately as possible (incorporation), compress the mixture to give it a certain solidity (compression), and then proceed to granulation. When powder was made by simply mixing the ingredients together (serpentine powder), the sulfur, charcoal, and saltpeter separated into three quite distinct layers when the mixture was transported for any distance, with the inevitable shaking up. To overcome this serious drawback, the masters began, probably from the second half of the 15th century, to use "corned," or granulated, powder, which had the great merit of burning with greater regularity.

A variety of processes and methods have been devised over the years to perform the different operations in the manufacture of gunpowder:

*Pestle method.* Apart from simply grinding the powder in a mortar by hand, this is the oldest method. The ingredients, carefully ground, were pulverized, mixed, and made into a paste by pestles operated mechanically in a row of bronze mortars. The powder produced by this method was porous, light, and of uneven consistency.
*Drum method.* The grinding and mixing of the ingredients was done in drums rotating on their own axis. This system was rapid, but produced powders that did not stand up to transport for lack of density and hardness.
*Mill method.* Trituration, incorporation, and compression of the ingredients were carried out at the same time under two heavy, hardened cast-iron runners above a bed of iron, or stone with iron tires, turning inside a big vat containing the ingredients.
*Drum and press method.* In this process the separate components, dried and pulverized, are mixed in iron drums containing a number of phosphor bronze balls some 25–30 mm. (about 1 in.) in diameter, two at a time, first saltpeter with charcoal, then charcoal with sulfur. The two mixtures so obtained, called "binary mixtures," are then incorporated in the "ternary drum," which is wooden and contains balls made of hard wood. This forms the "ternary powder." The expedient of preparing the two binary mixtures in advance and then the ternary mixture is imposed by reasons of safety; it substantially reduces the time needed to incorporate the three components, which are pretty dangerous once mixed together. The ternary powder, damped with water, is put into a hydraulic press and subjected to pressure of 100 kg. per mm.$^2$ (64.5 tons per square inch). The "mill cake" thus obtained is then broken up into small pieces and, after sifting, drying, and (in some cases) the addition of graphite, produces the different grains of powder, which range from fine powder to pellets.

**gunner's stiletto** A stiletto issued to bombardiers and used as a tool, a weapon, and a symbol of rank. The commonest form had a pommel in the shape of a spiraled pine cone and a cigar-shaped grip of bone or horn, decorated with inlaid ivory and copper wire. The guard had short quillons with swirled pine-cone-shaped or oval terminals, and the blade was usually triangular in section. These stilettos differed from other types by having on the blade a series of notches and numbers (the highest being 120, hence the name given the weapon in Venice, *centoventi*), which could be read by holding the stiletto point upward.

The gunner's stiletto could be used both as a weapon and as a means of measuring the bore of a cannon to determine the proper size of a cannonball; it was also used for slitting open the bag containing the powder charge, for cleaning the touchhole, and so on.

There are many different versions of the gunner's stiletto, with a wide variety of furniture and blades, and in the case of some of these it has been suggested that the presence of the notches and numbers was in order to disguise an ordinary stiletto, the carrying of which was

*Gusoku, 18th century.*
*Museo Orientale, Ca' Pesaro, Venice.*

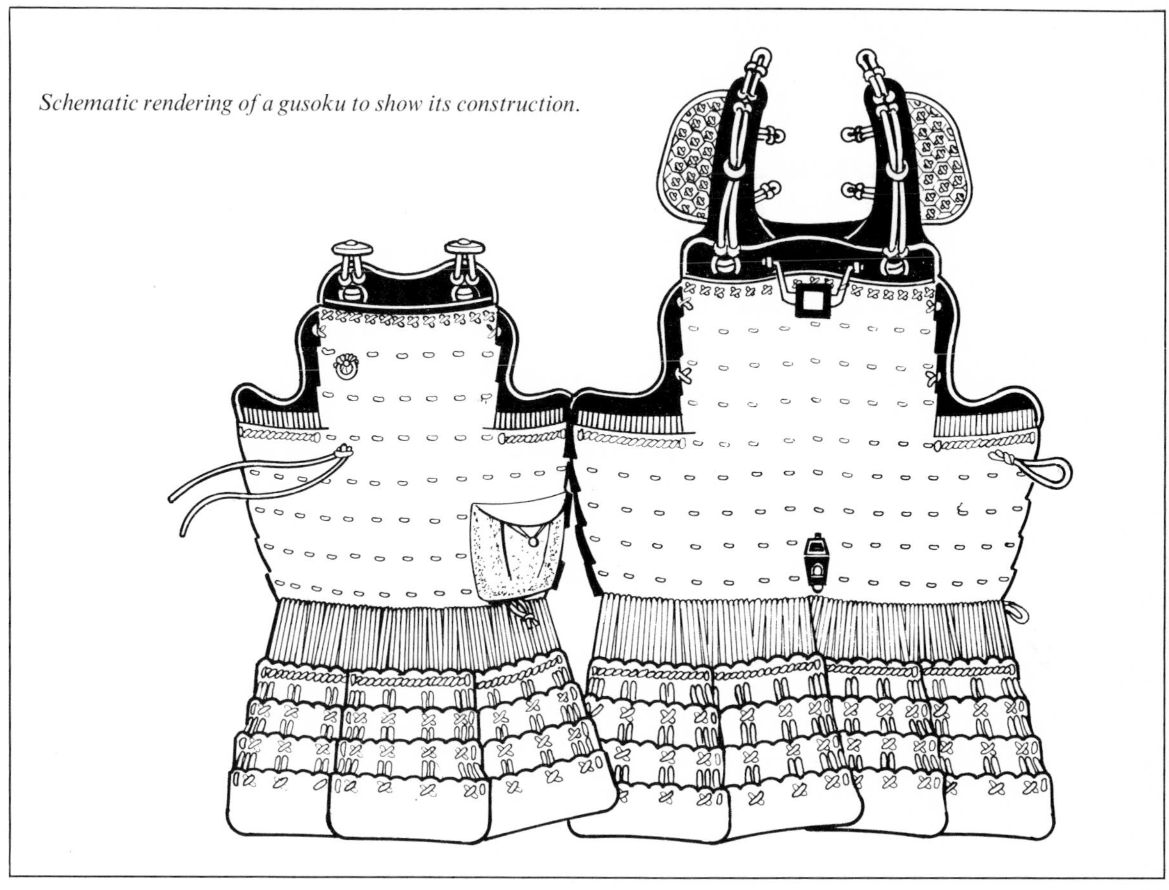
*Schematic rendering of a gusoku to show its construction.*

prohibited. In the Venetian republic, at least, these arms were used from the mid-17th century up until the end of the republic (in 1797).

**gupfe** German term for a 16th-century reinforcing piece which augmented the protection given by the helmet to the top of the head. It was mainly used in the Germanic countries, and in its simplest form consisted of a metal skullcap with two or more appendages by which it could be fixed with straps to the tail of the helmet. There were several variations, including iron frameworks rather like a cage, caps made of narrow iron bands, etc.

**gupti** An Indian sword stick, popular in northern and central India, not unlike those carried in Europe. Gupti blades were, in fact, frequently produced in Europe as well as being made in India. Although sharp-pointed and occasionally double-edged, they were sometimes screwed into the scabbard—that is, the cane itself—which meant they were inconvenient as weapons for immediate use. The handles were either straight, with a knob at the top, or curved; made of iron, wood, bone, or horn, they were often decoratively carved or inlaid with silver or gold. Stick-scabbards were of iron or wood, the wood occasionally being overlaid with leather and completed with a ferrule. Their length varied from about 40 cm. (16 in.) to 100 cm. (39 in.).

**gusoku** (or **tosei-gusoku**) The most modern style of Japanese armor, the gusoku was developed in the Momoyama period (1573–1602) and particularly during the Tokugawa (Edo) period (1603–1867). Several factors determined the shape and style of gusoku armor, the most important being the influence of European armor and firearms brought to the islands, first by the Portuguese and then by the Dutch; the long periods of peace during which armor tended to become more decorative and less functional; and the tenacity of the samurai tradition shown in the steady return to old patterns despite the technical progress in methods of warfare by the rest of the world. In fact, an immense amount of armor was produced during the Tokugawa period, and most of the examples preserved in Japan and in foreign collections originate from the 19th century.

There were many variations of gusoku armor, each with its own name, and some can be identified only by experts. All previous types of armor, such as *dō-maru*, *haramaki dō*, and *hara-ate*, were produced, with a few up-to-date modifications; even the ancient *yoroi* was imitated in the *sane-yoroi*. However, as frequently happens when modern civilization attempts to imitate original artifacts, the results were inferior to the prototypes and lacked many of their technical and decorative subtleties. Numerous workshops specialized in making particular types of helmets and armor, one of the most famous being that of the Myōchin family, which had been active since the 16th century.

A great many helmet types were associated with gusoku armor. The HOSHI-KABUTO, or knobbed helmet, was introduced in the late Muromachi period, in the "Age of Battles," during the second half of the 16th century. At the same time, the tall samurai EBOSHI CAPS were popular, while helmets consisting of three or four plates were produced by the Hineno and Haruta families. During the peaceful Tokugawa period, some ingeniously shaped helmets were devised, inspired by animals such as the stag or hare; dragons, birds, octopi, snails, and butterflies were also depicted, as well as plants and fruits such as poppies, bamboo shoots, pine cones, and chestnuts, and such other subjects as jewels, wooden gongs, bells, and even Chinese hats. Various masks were worn with these helmets.

As usual, the Japanese armorers displayed an inexhaustible and, sometimes, from a European point of view, a strange, even macabre, imagination which showed itself not only in the headgear but also in the cuirasses. Although the main pieces of gusoku armor consisted of lacquered iron lames, the cuirasses were often made—undoubtedly in accordance with European fashion—of large iron lames joined together horizontally (like the ANIME armor) or vertically. Full plates, separate for breast and back, were also used, and these would sometimes be molded like muscled cuirasses. Grotesque, almost surrealistic effects would be achieved by depicting the human face on the plates, perhaps putting the eyes in place of the nipples and the mouth over the navel.

In this type of armor, the backplate was usually a little higher than the breastplate and was furnished with shoulder straps fastening with toggles to loops on the breastplate. The two plates were joined by hinges on the left and straps or cords on the right. Typical European pieces of armor—especially collars and peascod-type cuirasses—were adapted for gusoku armor. Worn with morion helmets, slightly modified for Japanese use, these were known as *nanban-gusoku*.

In the 18th and 19th centuries, embossed cuirasses, *uchidashi*, were popular as well as those composed of several square, medium-sized plates joined with mail, *tatami-gusoku*. To complete a suit of gusoku armor there were also laminated tassets—consisting of four or five rows of laced lames attached by cords to the lower edge of the cuirass—to protect the abdomen and upper thighs, as well as shoulder, neck, thigh, and shin guards, sleeves, and special shoes covered with bearskin. In latter years, however, shoulder guards were often omitted. Various kinds of mail, *kusari*, were also introduced to give protection at joints and other vulnerable areas, and all the pieces were secured with straps or cords. During the last twenty-five years of the 19th century a great deal of armor was made entirely of lacquered leather.

**gusoku bitsu** A box in which Japanese armor was kept, usually of wood but sometimes of papier-mâché. These boxes were often lacquered and bound and hinged with bronze or iron mounts. The gusoku bitsu for light armor had loops on the front through which the person carrying the box on his back could put his arms. The more solid boxes for heavy armor were furnished with iron handles and stiff iron loops which stood up above the lid. When traveling, two men would carry the heavy gusoku bitsu on a pole passed through the loops. A family crest, the *mon*, was frequently painted on the front of the box.

**gusset** A small piece of the breastplate of an armor to protect the armpit. In general parlance, the word "gusset" refers to the edge of the breastplate that follows the line of the armpit; this was not normally an independent plate, being distinguishable only by a slight contoured depression and a reinforced roped edge. Specifically, however, the term is used to denote a lame riveted to the edge of the breastplate under the arm; this was also frequently reinforced with various styles of roping (round, boxed, twisted, etc.). Gussets were quite often used in the 15th and 16th centuries and were a distinctive feature of the cuirass in the 17th.

**guvia** Latin term for VOUGE.

# H

**habachi** Cloth leggings in Japanese armor. *See also* YOROI.

**habaki** A metal mount (ferrule) covering the base of the blade on a Japanese sword. When made in one piece it is known as a *hitoye habaki*, but a more ancient version, made in two pieces, is called a *nijiu habaki*, one piece fitting onto the blade and the other onto the scabbard. The habaki, which was either made in gold or in silver, copper, or brass with gilding, was usually quite plain. If there was any decoration, the design was generally analogous, such as a series of incisions called "cat's scratches" or representing rain, or sun and moon symbols or floral patterns were sometimes carved or inlaid on it. The habaki not only gave the weapon a very neat finish—so typical of Japanese work—but also had a functional purpose, since it held the blade steady in the scabbard and, by closing up the mouth of the scabbard, protected the blade from exposure to dampness.

**hachi** The skull of a Japanese helmet. *See also* KABUTO.

**hachi-manza** The brass rim around the hole in the top of a Japanese helmet. *See also* TEHEN.

**hachiwara** Although in Japanese this word means "helmet breaker," it refers, in fact, to a form of parrying weapon. Consisting of a slightly curved iron bar about 30 cm. (12 in.) long with a hook near the grip, it was very efficient for parrying sword blows and was even capable of breaking sword blades. The curved hilt sometimes resembled that of a typical dagger, with a small TSUBA and a sheath *en suite* of carved wood lacquered reddish or black; sometimes the sheath and hilt were made of horn. The sheath was often fitted with brass mounts and a hanging strap.

**hackbut** (or **hagbut**) An archaic English term for early long guns, derived from the German *Hakenbüchse*.

**hadome** A type of guard between the head and stave of a Japanese pole arm. *See also* YARI.

**haidate** An apron-like thigh protection worn under the tassets of Japanese armor from the Middle Ages. It was composed of two elongated rectangular pieces joined at their upper edges by a band, the ends of which extended to tie around the waist. The upper parts of the haidate, covered by the tassets, were of brocade or leather with two vertical slits like pocket openings. The lower sections consisted of plates, mail, or lames which were lacquered and laced together.

**haikuchi** *See* AIKUCHI.

**hair trigger** Also called set trigger, a device for a light-pull release of the firing mechanism often used from the second half of the 16th century on hunting and target rifles, and later also on dueling and target pistols. The hair trigger incorporates a spring trigger acting on the sear, which must first be pulled to be set in firing position. Another trigger, usually provided with a pull-regulating screw, requires then only a very slight touch to actuate the spring trigger and, thus, the firing mechanism.

**Hakenbüchse** Old German name for the ARQUEBUS, originally denoting guns with a hook under the barrel to serve as a rest to diminish recoil.

**halberd** From ancient times to the early Middle Ages the only arms available for foot soldiers in combat at close quarters were the sword, the shield, and the spear. A group of soldiers armed with spears could withstand a cavalry attack, because although horses were able to tolerate the effects of blows or wounds, they would rear up and flee when threatened by a spear. Consequently troops armed with this pole arm were invulnerable so long as their ranks remained unbreached. On the other hand, a close combat between a foot soldier and a horseman invariably led to the defeat of the former, whose sword was too short and inadequate against the weapons of a mounted opponent.

Between the 6th and 9th centuries the peoples of the North used a short single-edged sword 45–70 cm. (18–30 in.) long with a wide pointed blade. Grégoire de Tours (538–594) mentions it in his *Historia Francorum* and refers to it as a "scramasax." It is not known whose idea it was to fix the scramasax to the end of a staff, in the way that is depicted in the frescoes of St. John the Baptist Monastry at Münster (canton of Grisons, Switzerland), which are now in the Swiss National Museum in Zurich. From that time on, the foot soldier was equipped with a weapon with which he could both cut and thrust, a weapon particularly effective against the horseman, because it combined the advantages of both the spear and the ax.

The earliest examples of the weapon, which can be seen today in Zurich, and the drawings of different pole arms, ranging from the scramasax fixed to a staff to the halberd itself, clearly illustrate how the weapon developed.

The earliest mention of the halberd is contained in *History of the Trojan War* by a Swiss poet, Konrad Von Würzburg (d. 1287):

*Sechs tusend man ze fuoz bereit*
*Die truogen hallenbarten*
*Ser unde wol gesliffen*
*Swarz si damite ergriffen*
*Daz was ze töde gar verloren.*

(Six thousand men ready on foot
Armed with halberds
So finely honed
That any who was struck
Met certain death.)

Würzburg lived in Basel, where soldiers from all parts of Switzerland passed through with their arms. However, the fact that the first mention of the halberd was made by an inhabitant of Basel does not necessarily mean that the weapon originated there.

The word "halberd" comes from the German words *Halm*, a "staff," and *Barte*, "ax." In fact, the halberd is an ax of a very particular shape, intended for use in battle rather than for work. The inhabitants of ancient Helvetia (Switzerland), trained from an early age in the art of warfare, directed their efforts, to a greater extent than the people of other countries, to the search for weapons suited to their needs. This activity no doubt intensified in the course of the 13th century, at the height of their struggle for freedom, when they were in conflict with the mounted forces of the feudal lords. The manufacture of the earliest halberds, then, can be attributed with some certainty to the armorers and warriors of medieval Switzerland.

There is a type of halberd which can be classed as "primitive." It has a wide blade with a straight cutting edge, oblique or slightly convex, which curves backward to form the point. The staff, which is about 2 m. ($6\frac{1}{2}$ ft.) long, fits through two sockets at the back of the blade. The join between the blade and the point is by a rounded shoulder, and the point is outside the axis of the staff. These are the features which characterize this type of halberd, used in the late 14th and early 15th centuries and probably derived from the *gisarme*.

Toward the end of the 15th century, the design of the halberd was modified in order to increase its effectiveness. The halberds then being made were almost a different weapon, with a powerful spike within the axis of the staff, a fluke used to break open helmets or armor, and the join between blade and spike by means of a step of varying degrees. This "new" weapon was called a halberd, while the older type later became called a "Swiss VOUGE." The word "vouge" was never used in contemporary writings to refer to the halberd. It was applied to a different weapon, used in France, as well as in Germany and Spain, which is now known as the "French vouge" because it was in France in the 15th century that the weapon was most often mentioned or depicted. The first modern writer to employ the term "vouge" for a weapon which contemporaries called a "halberd" was Viollet-le-Duc (1814–1879) in his *Dictionnaire raisonné du mobilier français*.

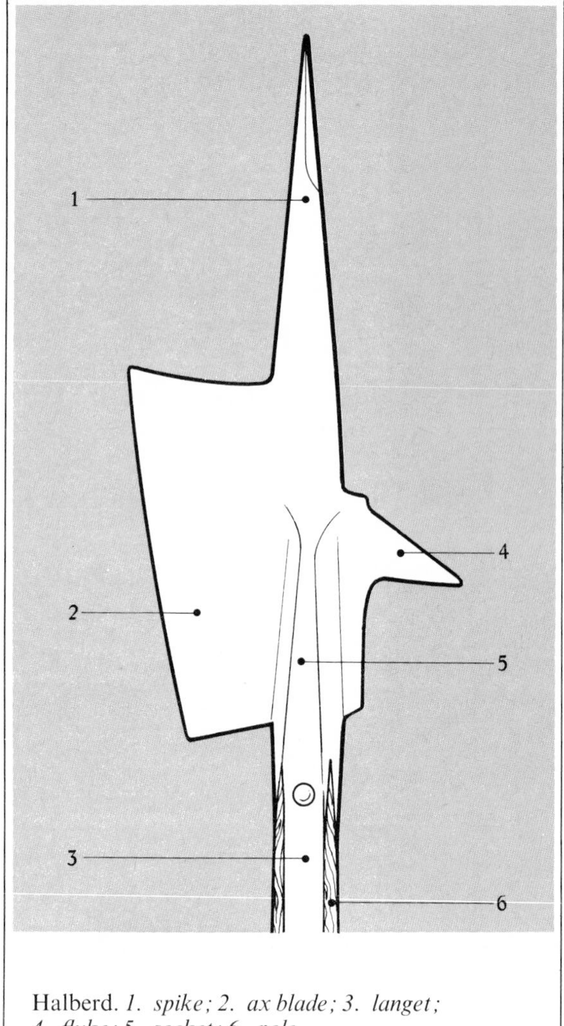

Halberd. *1. spike; 2. ax blade; 3. langet; 4. fluke; 5. socket; 6. pole.*

*The Halberd in War Chronicles*

The alliance signed in 1291 between the three Swiss cantons of Uri, Schwytz, and Unterwalden was not to the liking of the House of Hapsburg, which was unwilling to recognize the desire for independence shown by their inhabitants, who had taken the part of Louis of Bavaria against Frederick, Duke of Austria. The Hapsburgs decided to punish these rebellious people, and Duke Leopold (1290–1326), Frederick's brother, took the

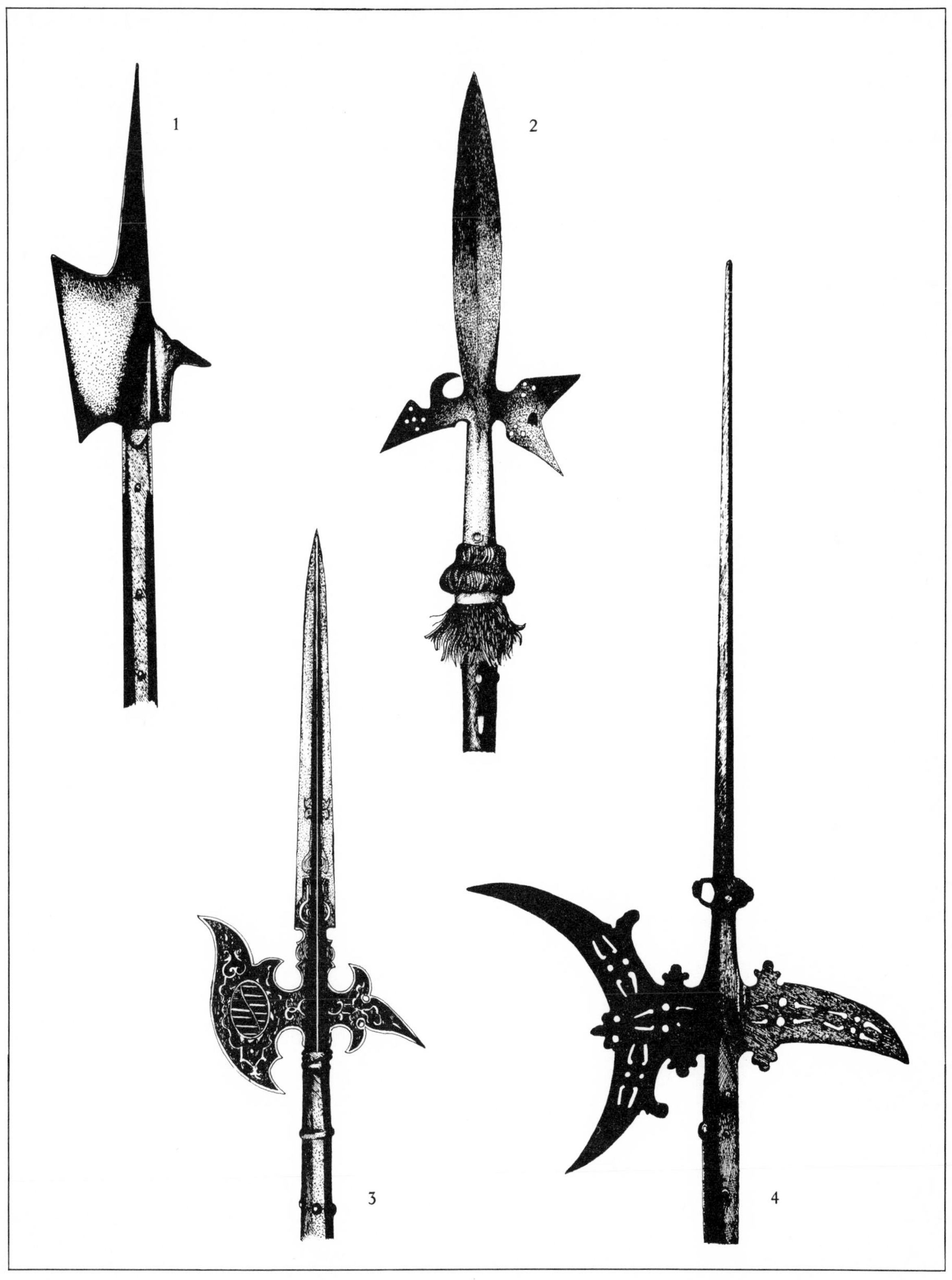


Halberds. *1. Swiss, end of the 15th century. Museo Civico L. Marzoli, Brescia. 2. Austrian, end of the 16th century. Museo Civico L. Marzoli, Brescia. 3. Saxon (Germany), 1580–90. Odescalchi Collection, Museo di Palazzo Venezia, Rome.*

matter in hand. The battle took place at Morgarten on November 15, 1315. Jean de Winterthour, whose father took part in the battle, has left an interesting account of it in his chronicle, written in about 1340: "The Schwytzois were armed with terrifying weapons, known as halberds, and although their opponents carried weapons almost as sharp as razors, they cut them to pieces."

At the battle of Sempach (1386) all the Swiss troops were armed with halberds. The young Duke Leopold III of Austria led his army and was in command of the second line himself. The confrontation was at first disastrous for the Swiss; they fell afoul of the lances of the cavalry, who had dismounted from their horses. Conrad Justinger (c. 1391–1420), secretary of the town of Bern, wrote an account of the battle thirty-five years later in his *Berner Chronik*. His account gives good grounds for supposing that the only weapon used by the Swiss on that occasion was the halberd: "They had gathered and taken up a formation for battle and they suffered terrible losses. Before long, however, they abandoned the formation and charged the lords, striking such devastating blows with their halberds that nothing could withstand the force of their attack."

From Switzerland and Germany the use of the halberd spread to neighboring countries.

*The Halberd in Italy and France*

The history of arms in Italy owes much to Niccolò Machiavelli (1469–1527), who began work in 1516 on his *On the Art of War*. He gives the following description of the Italian infantryman: "For defense he wears an iron breastplate and, as an offensive weapon, he carries a lance—which is called a pike—about 9 *braccia* [about 6 meters] long, with a sword at his side.... A few have their arms and back protected but all are bare-headed. Those few who are armed in this manner do not carry a pike but a halberd with a staff that is 3 *braccia* [about 2 meters] long."

The work of the historian Paolo Giovi shows that this weapon must have been of recent origin. It is apparent from his *Historiae sui temporis*, written in about 1520, that the halberd was not familiar to him. He describes the entry of Charles VIII and the Swiss battalions into Rome thus: "A quarter of them were armed with large axes with quadrangular heads. They held this weapon in both hands and used it for cutting and thrusting. In their own language it is known as a halberd."

It is reasonable to assume that the use of this weapon by the Italian infantry was introduced by the French, who had originally taken the idea from the Swiss.

The earliest mention of the halberd in France seems to be in a text written by the chronicler Jean de Troyes, a historian to Louis XI, in 1481: "At that time the King ... ordered all cutlers to make great quantities of pikes, halberds and large rondel daggers."

This new weapon was no doubt a consequence of military circumstances. In 1480 Louis XI had dissolved the "Francs archers" who had been established by Charles VII in 1448; the archers had failed to come up to expectations at Guignegatte (1479), where they were routed by the Flemish. The French king, realizing the need to establish a strong infantry, had—at the time of the fighting between the Swiss and Charles of Burgundy—grasped the full extent of the role that could be played by a well-trained, well-organized infantry on the battlefield. At Pont-de-l'Arche, near Rouen, he arranged for some 10,000 infantrymen and other soldiers to be assembled and trained by 6000 Swiss soldiers. The infantrymen were no doubt armed in the same way as their instructors, that is, with long pikes and halberds.

*The Decline of the Halberd*

In his memoirs, Blaise de Montluc (1499–1577) describes the composition of the army assembled by the Protestant leaders in Dauphiné, Provence, and Languedoc during the civil strife known as the Wars of Religion. "There were six thousand arquebusiers, all veteran soldiers ... and another six thousand who were less experienced ... Thus, of the seventeen-to-eighteen-thousand-strong army, most were arquebusiers, and the remainder were halberdiers and some pikemen."

By the last third of the 16th century the halberd had given way to firearms. A few contingents of pikemen remained, but by the end of the next century these, too, had disappeared from the battlefield. From the mid-16th century, the halberd underwent significant changes. Its massive wide blade, with forward-sloping edge, gradually developed a crescent-like form and became much lighter. Both the blade and the fluke were often pierced with ornaments, while the spike became much more slender, and longer. From now on, town militiamen and palace and church guards were to carry halberds mostly as parade weapons, although they continued to serve in European armies as a form of the LEADING STAFF up till the 19th century.

**half armor** *See* ARMOR.

**half-pike** A form of the LEADING STAFF used by infantry officers in the 16th and 17th centuries to give signals to their men. The half-pike had a small head and short shaft, about 2 m. (6½ ft.) long. It was also convenient aboard ships as a BOARDING PIKE. From the mid-17th century, the half-pike was called in France an *esponton*, hence English SPONTOON; this officer's staff derived from the half-pike.

**half-shaffron** A light type of the SHAFFRON.

**hambō** A type of Japanese war mask. *See also* MENPO.

**hamidashi** (or **hamidachi**) A Japanese short dirk which, like the AIKUCHI, is one of the TANTŌ range. Unlike the aikuchi, the hamidashi is furnished with a TSUBA, which is slightly larger than the grip. Its single-edged, slightly curved blade—usually with a groove along the back—is about 20–30 cm. (8–12 in.) long. Its hilt, like that of the sword, is covered with fishskin and bound with plaited cords. Its sheath, the SAYA, lacquered in red or black, is sometimes gadrooned (i.e., having inverted fluting) and furnished with brass, silver, or shibuichi alloy mounts with a hanging cord attached to a rigid loop on the saya. The KOZUKA is in its customary position.

**hammer** *See* WAR HAMMER.

**hammer** The spring-activated cock fitted with a striking

head used with the percussion system of IGNITION. In England during the 17th to 19th centuries the term "hammer" was also applied to the STEEL of a flintlock firearm.

**hammerless gun** Term (misleadingly) applied to guns in which the firing mechanism, including the hammer or striker, is inside the gun. The first "hammerless" gun in which the locks were automatically cocked as the gun was opened was that patented in Great Britain in 1875 by Anson and Deeley. Other well-known systems are the Holland and Holland, Greener, Purdey, etc.

**hamus** A Latin term meaning a hook or curved spur positioned horizontally at the base of arrowheads or javelin heads, or protruding from one of the cutting edges of the blade of the HARPÉ. The same term also applies to a spearhead fixed in the ground or to a wall as a defensive device.

**hanburi** A Japanese half-helmet of metal or leather, rather like the European skullcap. The hanburi was usually shallow, covering only the crown of the head, although there were also larger types which protected the forehead and temples, sometimes even associated with the *mempō* war mask (*see* MENPO). Hanburi helmets were often made of several plates connected by pins and were sometimes completed by a mail cap or coif. They were held on the head with bands.

**hand-and-a-half sword** *See* BASTARD SWORD.

**hand grenade** A small bomb consisting of a case, generally metal though nowadays special plastic materials are preferred, which contains the explosive and a detonator. It is sometimes fitted with a wooden handle, since it is intended to be thrown by hand, as its name implies.

The use of hand grenades in battle goes back some time: as long ago as the first half of the 16th century Gian Battista della Valle described small bombs being made for use by individual soldiers, and Du Belley records the production of similar arms in Arles in 1536. In the following century they were in general use; hand grenades were used in the assault on Wachtendonk in 1608 and in the defense of Regensburg in 1634 and of Vienna in 1683. During the siege of Namur the great Vauban used no fewer than 20,000 hand grenades. Seventeenth-century hand grenades were hollow cast-iron balls filled with black powder and fitted with a short fuze. Grenades fell into disuse about the middle of the 18th century, but returned to favor during the Russo-Japanese War (1904–5) and since then have been an integral part of normal infantry armament.

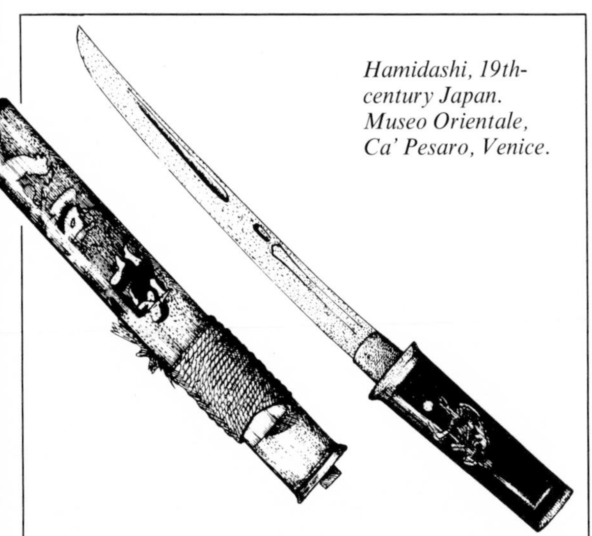

*Hamidashi, 19th-century Japan. Museo Orientale, Ca' Pesaro, Venice.*

Hand grenades can be divided into two main classes, offensive and defensive. Offensive grenades are designed for use in the assault phase; a powerful charge of high explosive in a case with very thin walls produces blast and a stunning noise, throwing out light splinters which are not dangerous beyond a few meters, so that the thrower, generally in the open, is not likely to be hit by fragments from his own grenade. Defensive hand grenades, intended for use by personnel under cover (in a trench, behind a wall, etc.), are designed to throw out a great number of heavy fragments for a considerable distance.

Until a few years ago the preference was for defensive hand grenades with a time fuze (the "pineapple" type, such as the British "Mills Bomb" (No. 36), the Russian "lemon" F1, the U.S. Mark 2, etc.) and a cast-iron case. Recently, however, it has been realized that the explosion of such grenades seldom led to proper fragmentation; when the grenade exploded, a few large splinters might be thrown as far as 200 meters, while the rest of the case broke down into particles harmless at a distance of no more than a yard or two. More modern defensive hand grenades either contain a number of steel pellets in a double plastic container (the Austrian Hd GR-69 has 3500 pellets, the German M-DN-11 3800 pellets, 2.5–3 mm. in diameter) or have a jacket of wire or a steel strip wound in a spiral with notches cut on the inside at regular intervals to cause fragmentation (the Belgian PRB-8, the U.S. M-26, etc.). The Belgian PRB-423 hand grenade is an example of the mixed use of both systems; it has a certain number of pellets at the bottom and top, and the rest of the case is wound with a tight spiral of rectangular-section steel wire with notches for fragmentation. Time or impact fuzes may be fitted, or often combined to ensure that the grenade explodes very soon after being thrown. Explosives used are of course chosen from among those least sensitive to shock, such as TNT, Composition B, lyddite, etc.

**hand guard** A detachable part of the stock of a gun that protects the upper part of the barrel from damage, and protects the user from burning his hand on the hot barrel when firing.

**hand mortar** *See* GRENADE LAUNCHER.

**handshar** *See* KHANJAR.

**hanger** A short hunting sword with a straight or slightly curved single-edged and pointed blade, often with a back edge. In the 17th century and first half of the 18th its hilt usually had quillons, a knuckle guard, a shell guard turned toward the blade, and a pommel, occasionally shaped like a bird's head. Hilts of later examples often have only short recurved quillons and a massive one-piece grip flaring toward a cap (instead of a pommel). The sheath sometimes was provided with small pockets for accessories such as a

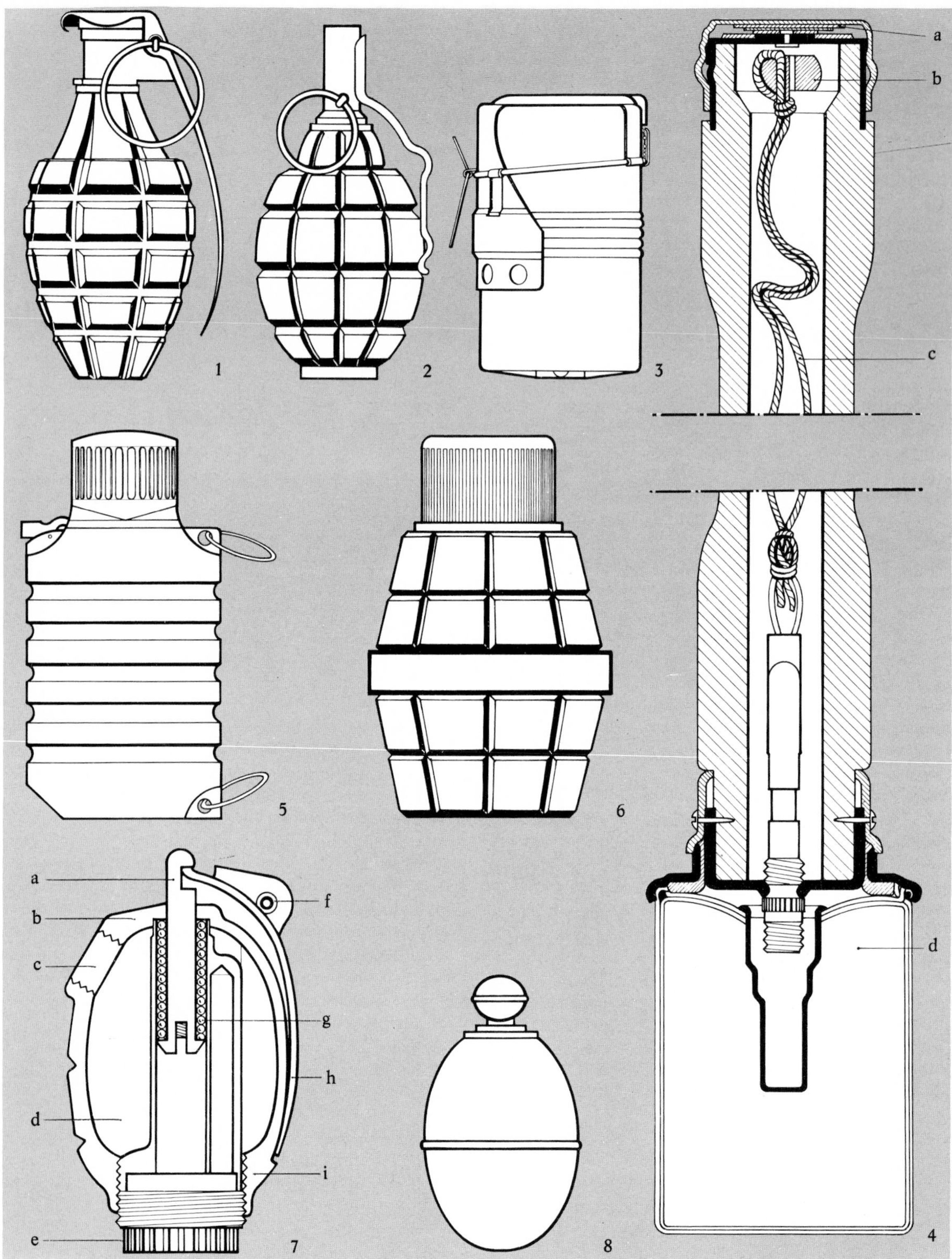


*Hand grenades. 1. Mark 2-A1 fragmentation grenade, United States. 2. F1 fragmentation grenade ("lemon"), USSR. 3. SRCM Model 35, Italy. 4. Steilhandgranate 39, Germany: (a) metal cap spring, (b) china sphere, (c) fuze cord, (d) explosive. 5. Pull type, Japan. 6. Fragmentation grenade, No. 69, Great Britain. 7. Hand or rifle grenade, No. 36 ("Mills Bomb"), Great Britain: (a) striker, (b) case, (c) closure screw, (d) explosive (Baratol 20/80), (e) base screw plug, (f) locking pin, (g) striker spring, (h) lever, (i) center block. 8. Eihandgranate 39, Germany.*

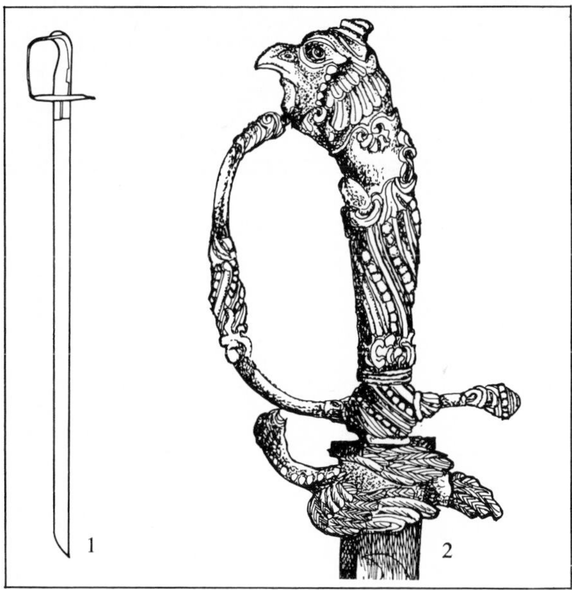


*1. Heavy cavalry sword (Pallasch), Great Britain, first half of the 19th century. Armémuseum, Stockholm.*
*2. Hunting hanger, Germany, mid-18th century. Museo Stibbert, Florence.*

little knife and a fork or bodkin. The hangers were often ornate, their blades being etched and gilded, while the hilts, made of metals, stag's horn, ivory, and semiprecious stones, were carved, encrusted, or chiseled. Mounts of scabbards were usually embellished to match the decoration of the hilts.

The term "hanger" is also applied to a short infantry soldier's regulation sidearm used in the 18th to mid-19th century (in Germany and Russia this military hanger was called, respectively, *Düsack* and *tessak*). "Hanger" can also refer to that pouchlike part of the girdle or sword belt, in use from the second half of the 16th to the middle of the 17th century, which housed the sword scabbard, holding it firm with several straps and buckles. Finally, a small strap with a hook, attached to a sword belt and used to suspend the sword or the dagger in vertical position, is also called a hanger.

**happuri** A type of Japanese war mask. *See also* MENPO.

**hara-ate** Japanese protective armor covering only the front of the body from neck to knees. Consisting of laced lames, hung on straps from the shoulders and tied with thongs and loops at the back, it was usually worn under ceremonial dress. The top plate was covered with tooled leather, the lower part had four tassets, and the lining was of silk damask with brocade-decorated suspender straps.

The terms *hara-ate* or *hara-ate-gawa* also referred to a primitive leather corslet worn by servants.

**haramaki** A Japanese light armor which developed, like the DŌ-MARU, in the 14th century but opened at the center back instead of at the right side. It was primarily designed for foot soldiers but was soon transformed into full armor, also known as *haramaki-dō*, and equipped with shoulder

*Hunting hanger, Italy, late 16th or 17th century. Museo Nazionale del Bargello, Florence.*

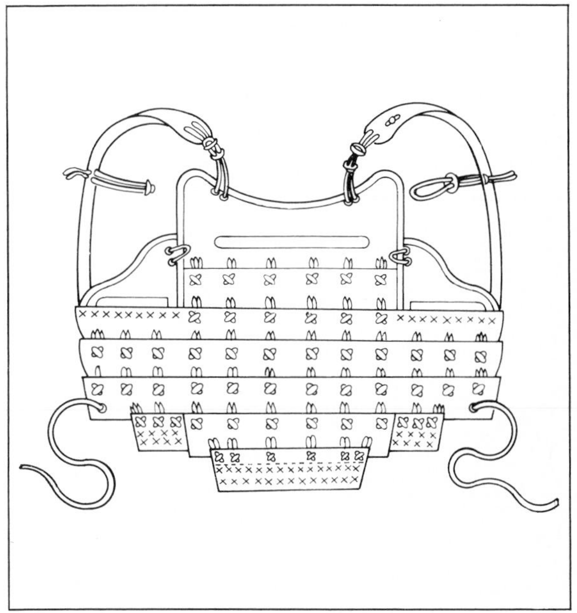

*Diagram of the upper part of a hara-ate.*

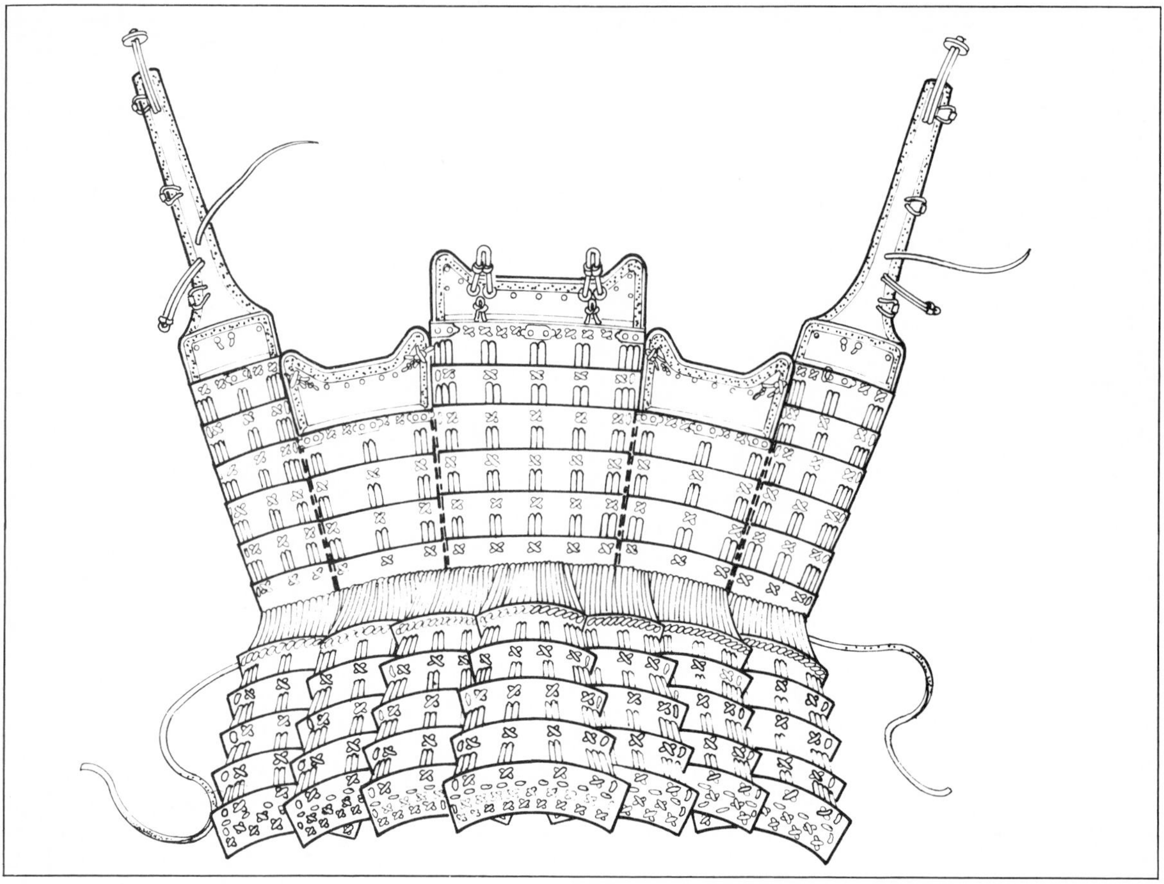

*Diagram of an early 16th-century haramaki.*

guards, helmet, and all the traditional pieces worn by the samurai.

A typical early 16th-century haramaki consisted of five pieces to protect the upper torso: the largest was for the breast, while two covered the sides and two the back, with shoulder straps attached to loops at the top of the breastplate. Seven tassets, the KUSAZURI, protected the lower torso. The haramaki (the word literally means "wrapping the belly" was constructed entirely of laced lames, except for the top parts, which were made of solid plates.

**harness** A general term for a suit of armor or for a set of horse armor and trappings.

**harpé** A Greek curved sword with a large spur on the concave cutting edge of the blade; the term was applied to a large sickle-shaped knife with a concave cutting edge. It is depicted in both forms in the Perseus cycle, when the hero kills the Gorgon. In the first instance—the *ensis hamatus* or *falcatus*—it appears as a sacrificial weapon used to slaughter the bull. *See also* FALX SUPINA.

**harpoon** A hunting weapon consisting of a fixed or detachable hooked head connected to a supporting shaft and extensively used by primeval man for hunting marine mammals and large fish. It was an artifact that depended, more than any other weapon, on environmental conditions and on the level man's evolution had reached. At first it was merely a simple pointed stick, but this was

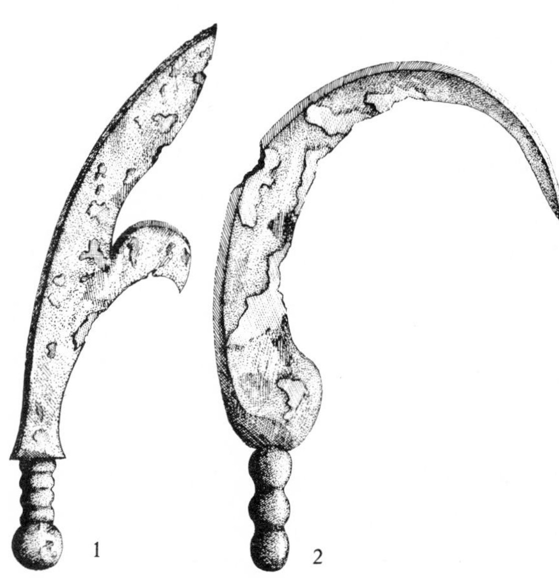


*Illustrations of harpé, associated with the cult of Perseus. 1. From a Capuan vase painting. 2. From a Neapolitan amphora.*

soon followed by the use of a bone or horn head, with one or more hooks cut into it; the head was either attached to or fitted into the end of the shaft and tied in place with animal sinews. To facilitate this, the haft frequently broadened at the shaft.

Then came the metal harpoon with a pointed and barbed head, into the end of which the shaft was inserted (like a walking stick into its ferrule); the head was detachable but remained connected to the hunter by a cord attached to it between point and barb.

For whale hunting, an iron head shaped like a lance was used, which had an extremely sharp point and good cutting edges. The head was attached to a wooden or cylindrical iron shaft about 2 m. ($6\frac{1}{2}$ ft.) long, ending in a ring to which the recovery cord was tied; the head was either fixed or mobile on the shaft.

Some harpoons were made with more than one point. Initially, the harpoon was thrown by hand and, when the weapon had found its mark, the whaler would follow his prey, paying out the rope as he went. In recent times mounted guns or small cannon have been used, enabling the harpoon to travel farther. Harpoons with explosive heads are also sometimes employed—although in the face of severe opposition.

In an exception to hunting marine mammals, it used to be the custom in the Philippines to hunt wild boar with harpoons.

**hasta** Latin general term for a *hafted weapon*, that is, a staff weapon or pole arm.

**hatchet** A short-handled implement with a blade similar to that of a small AX, used for cutting, chopping, or hewing. A common work tool, it was also used in warfare.

**hatomune-dō** A type of Japanese armor. See also DŌ-MARU.

**haubergeon** A shorter type of the HAUBERK.

**hauberk** A medieval term generally denoting a shirt of mail protecting the head, trunk, arms, and legs to below the knees. The hauberk, also called a byrnie, constituted an armor in its own right, and an early form consisted of a coif and long shirt with sleeves ending just below the elbow. From about the 1320s, shirts of mail were often provided with flared sleeves covering to the middle of the forearms. It was also a period when a shorter type of hauberk, the haubergeon, began to be increasingly used, its lower edge reaching to just above the knees. The haubergeon sometimes had a flaplike extension at the center of the rear edge of the skirt that could be pulled up between the legs and laced in front to form a BREKE OF MAIL to protect the genitals.

Up until the 14th century, armor had largely consisted of a mail shirt with helmet, mail CHAUSES or leggings, and sometimes mail gauntlets with flared cuffs. However, the sleeves of the hauberk itself were often extended to form mittens. Generally, the hauberk and haubergeon had no lining but were worn over a close-fitting quilted shirt, short breeches, and hose. A few types of hauberks appear to have been made of quilted fabric or leather to which were sewn rings, lames, scales, etc.

By the 15th century the mail shirt had become standard equipment, although in a secondary capacity to the armor itself, underneath which it was worn. Its main purpose by now was to fill in any possible gaps between one plate and another or where the plates did not adequately cover the body (e.g. the armpits or elbow joints inside). Mail shirts or fairly large pieces of mail retained defensive importance during the 16th century with light-horse and infantry armors, especially in conjunction with small pauldrons or spaudlers and elbow-length gauntlets which left part of the arms uncovered. In such cases, the sleeves of mail were attached to the ARMING DOUBLET worn under the armor. This precaution was unnecessary in suits of armor with well-developed arm defenses.

The term "hauberk" was also applied to other types of armor. Early plate defense for the trunk was sometimes called "hauberk of plate," and the expression "coat of mail and plates" is used to describe a hauberk in which plates or lames are incorporated (*see* BEKHTER and YUSHMAN).

**haute-piece** A piece of armor for a horseman, in use from about the middle of the 15th century. It consisted of a more or less high flange riveted to the PAULDRONS or forged in one with the GARDBRACES. Its purpose was to protect the neck against an opponent's lance or sword thrust, and it was used in the 16th century in field armor, tourney armor, and armor for the foot combat. In some instances the haute-piece was present only on the left pauldron or

*Hauberks, or shirts of mail, as depicted in a miniature from the Psaltery of St. Louis, France, 1256. Bibliothèque Nationale, Paris.*

gardbrace, used as a double piece to equip a field armor for a tourney.

**hayago** A Japanese powder flask or priming flask in lacquered papier-mâché or wood, sometimes overlaid with leather. Cow's horn, ivory, and metal were also used. It was made in various forms, the most usual being gourd- or pear-shaped—sometimes very elongated—or even boat-shaped, with an outlet tube closed by a bone or ivory cap. The priming flask was similar to the powder flask but smaller. Gilded lacquer crests, *mon*, were often displayed on the hayago.

**head** The striking part of any staff weapon, most often made of metal; in primitive weapons, it was made of wood in one piece with the handle, preferably with knots, and in later periods reinforced with a metal strap or hoop (bronze in the classical period) studded with pyramidal or conical spikes or points arranged alternately in two or three rows.

**headstall** A general term for that part of the BRIDLE that goes over the horse's head. It consisted (as it does today) of the brow band running horizontally in front of the ears, the CHEEK STRAPS going behind the ears and extending down to support the BIT, and the THROAT LATCH buckling loosely under the jowl. It might also include a noseband, attached to the cheek strap at each side about midway between the eyes and the nostrils.

**helm** (or **great helm**) A heavy helmet completely enclosing the head, which developed in the early 13th century from conical and round- or flat-topped helmets supplemented with a large oblong face guard and a neck guard. By the 1220s the helm structure comprised several solid plates joined together by strong rivets to form a barrel-shaped headpiece having, most often, a flat top. The face guard, sometimes reinforced with a riveted metal cross, had an eye slit and ventilation holes. Although this basic construction remained unchanged up to the late 14th century, several other forms were evolving over that time. After c. 1250 the skull of the helm tended to taper and during the next century became conical, with a flat or rounded top. A heavy helm was deep enough to rest on the wearer's shoulders, but to protect the head from shocks caused by blows, a system of buffers had been devised. The helm itself had a padded lining and a wide leather band with festoons pulled together on the top by a cord (a device still present in modern helmets), and an ARMING CAP, a basnet, and a coif of mail (or a combination of these) were worn under the helm. It was also provided with a chin strap to secure a tight fit.

Since the face of the knight was hidden by the helm, the CREST as a means of identification was often worn with this headpiece, particularly from the 13th century up to the mid-1500s. From the late 13th century some helms were fitted with a VISOR pivoted on the sides of the skull and a reinforcing bevor attached with straps behind the neck, but these modifications did not last long, for the helm was gradually replaced by other types of head defense for use in battle and remained, after the late 1300s, mostly as part of armor for jousts and tournaments. By this time a quite spectacular and lasting form, known as the "frog-mouthed" helm, had developed. It had a low rounded skull curving in front to the upper edge of a high face guard; a gap between these two parts served as an eye slit. Numerous holes were pierced in the metal for the laces of a thick arming cap, and the lower edge of the helm was provided in the front and back with massive hinged loops for attachment to the cuirass.

German jousting helms (*Stechhelm*) usually had gracefully curved contours, while Italian-style helms were somewhat squarish in appearance. A rectangular opening or a trapdoor for fresh air was sometimes arranged on the face guard's right side, safe enough for such a device, since in jousts all blows were aimed at the left side of each contestant. The "frog-mouthed" helms weighing up to 9–10 kg (20–22 lbs.) lasted in Germany to the second quarter of the 16th century and were then replaced by a less heavy type of jousting helm, constructed on the basis of the CLOSE HELMET, rotating on the collar but fitted with an enlarged bevor screwed onto the breastplate.

**helmet**

A general outline of the subject, from antiquity to the mid-20th century, is given under this heading. For particular types of helmets, see ARMET; BASNET; BARBUT; BURGONET; CLOSE HELMET; ENGLISH POT; GALEA; HELM; MORION; SALLET; ZISCHÄGGE. For the Middle East, see SHISHAK, and for Japan, KABUTO.

**helmets** The word used, in a general sense, to describe any type of protective headgear. Even from the Bronze Age, there is ample evidence to show that the styles of the first leather and bronze helmets, which are known to have been worn by the fighting men of Mesopotamia, derived from even earlier ones made of cloth. One of the best-known and important examples that has survived from this civilization is the gold helmet discovered in the tomb of Prince Mes-Kalam-dug, a royal warrior of Ur, dating from the third millennium B.C. Made from a single sheet of gold, its whole surface is skillfully embossed and engraved to represent beautifully dressed hair, with ears modeled at the sides.

No protective headgear seems ever to have been worn by the ancient Egyptians in combat; it is only foreign soldiers who are depicted wearing helmets in Egyptian tomb paintings, sculptures, etc. From the second millennium B.C., however, the Hittites are known to have worn various types of bell-shaped helmets, with or without cheekpieces, a distinctive feature of which was often an imposing crest. Assyrian warriors wore a particular type of conical bronze helmet, generally made with cheekpieces and sometimes with a lamellar AVENTAIL suspended from its lower edge to cover the neck and most of the face.

In the Minoan-Mycenaean civilization the helmet is known to have been in use from about the middle of the second millennium B.C., as it was depicted in various forms on excavated vases, weapons, jewelry, etc. Among such discoveries were found, in Mycenae and Knossos, helmets in the form of leather skullcaps with cheekpieces. These were reinforced with overlapping rows of wild boars' tusks strung together, just as described in Homer's poems.

Another type of protective headgear in the Mycenae

*Bronze helmet, N. Europe, early 9th century* B.C.

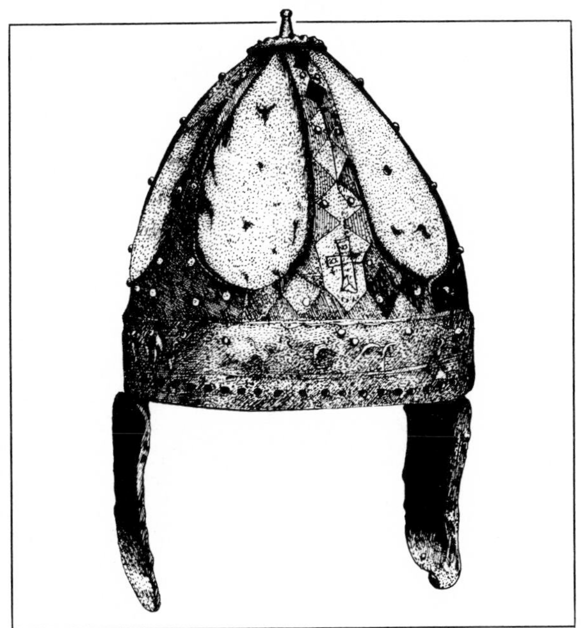

*Segmented helmet* (Spangenhelm), *N. Europe, 6th century.*

area was the so-called *phalerae* helmet. This consisted of a leather skullcap strengthened with round bronze bosses or studs which were the enlarged heads of the reinforcing rivets. There were also combed helmets in metal or leather and helmets on which animals' horns and plumes were mounted, such as those depicted on the famous Mycenaean "Vase of the Warriors" (c. 1200 B.C.).

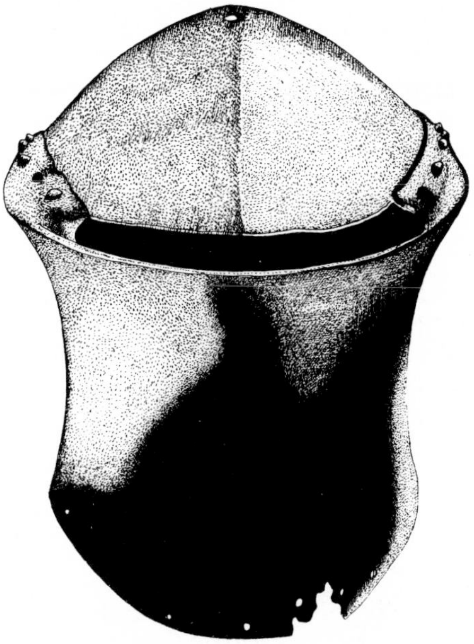

1

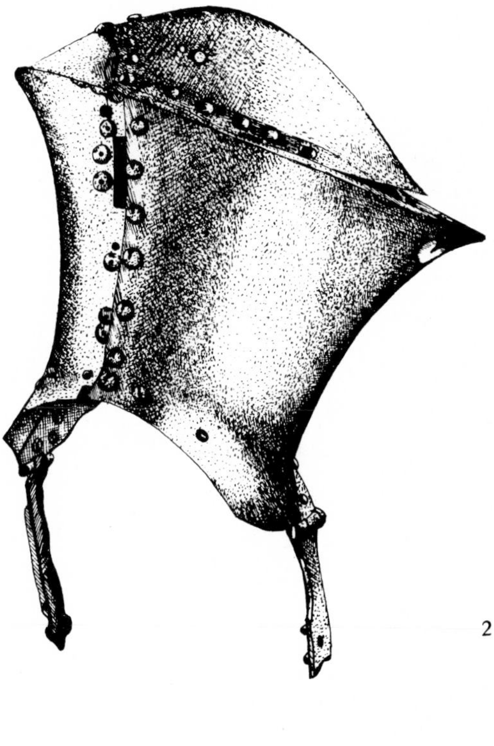

2

*Jousting helms. 1. England, probably late 14th century. Wallace Collection, London. 2. Innsbruck, c. 1483–85. Waffensammlung, Vienna.*

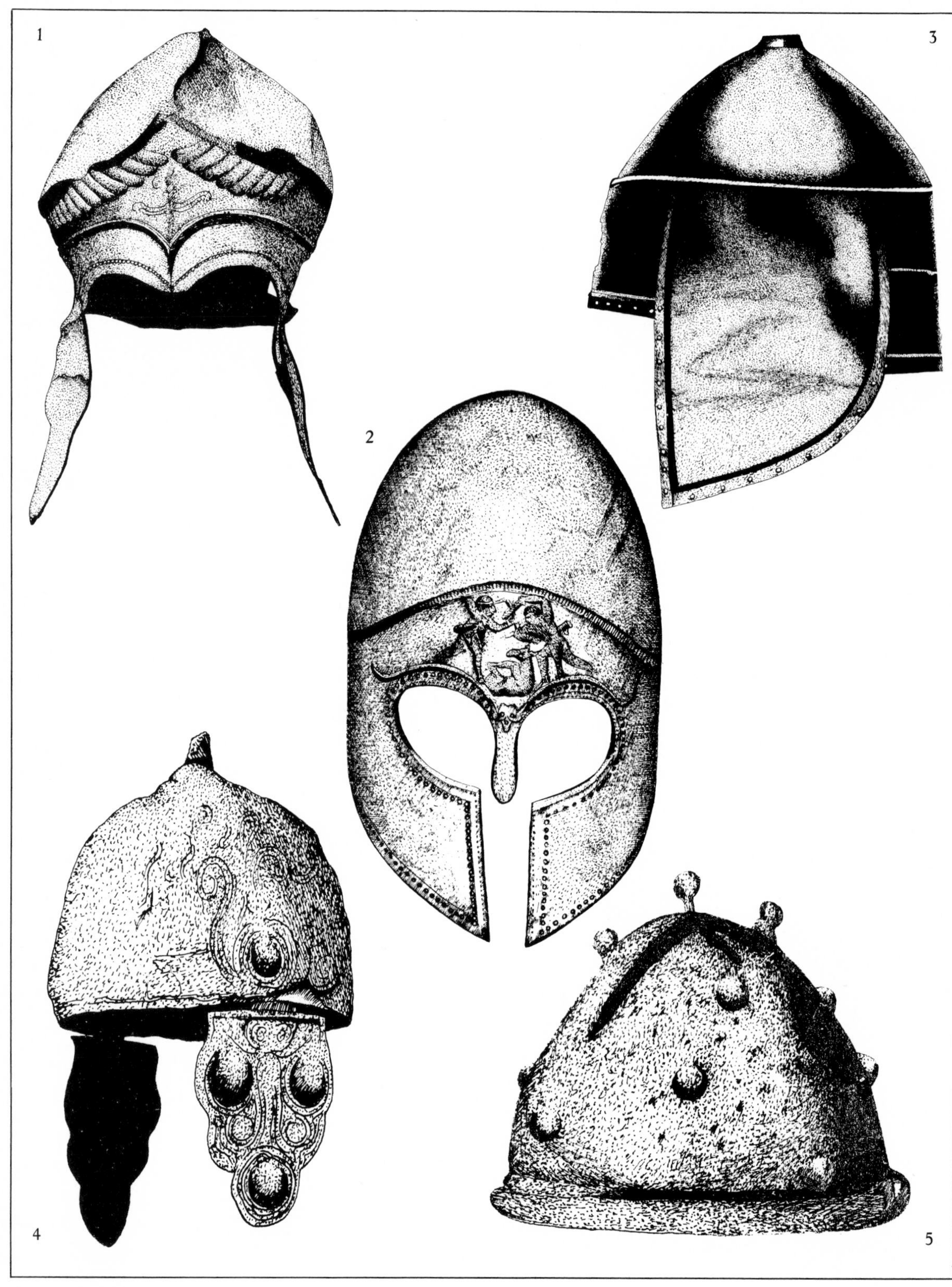


*1. Chalcidice helmet, Greece, 6th–5th century* B.C. *Olympia Museum. 2. Corinthian-type Etruscan helmet, Italy, 6th century* B.C. *Bibliothèque Nationale, Paris. 3.* Kegelhelm-*type leather helmet, c. 700* B.C. *Olympia Museum. 4, 5. Italic helmets. Staatliches Museum, Berlin.*

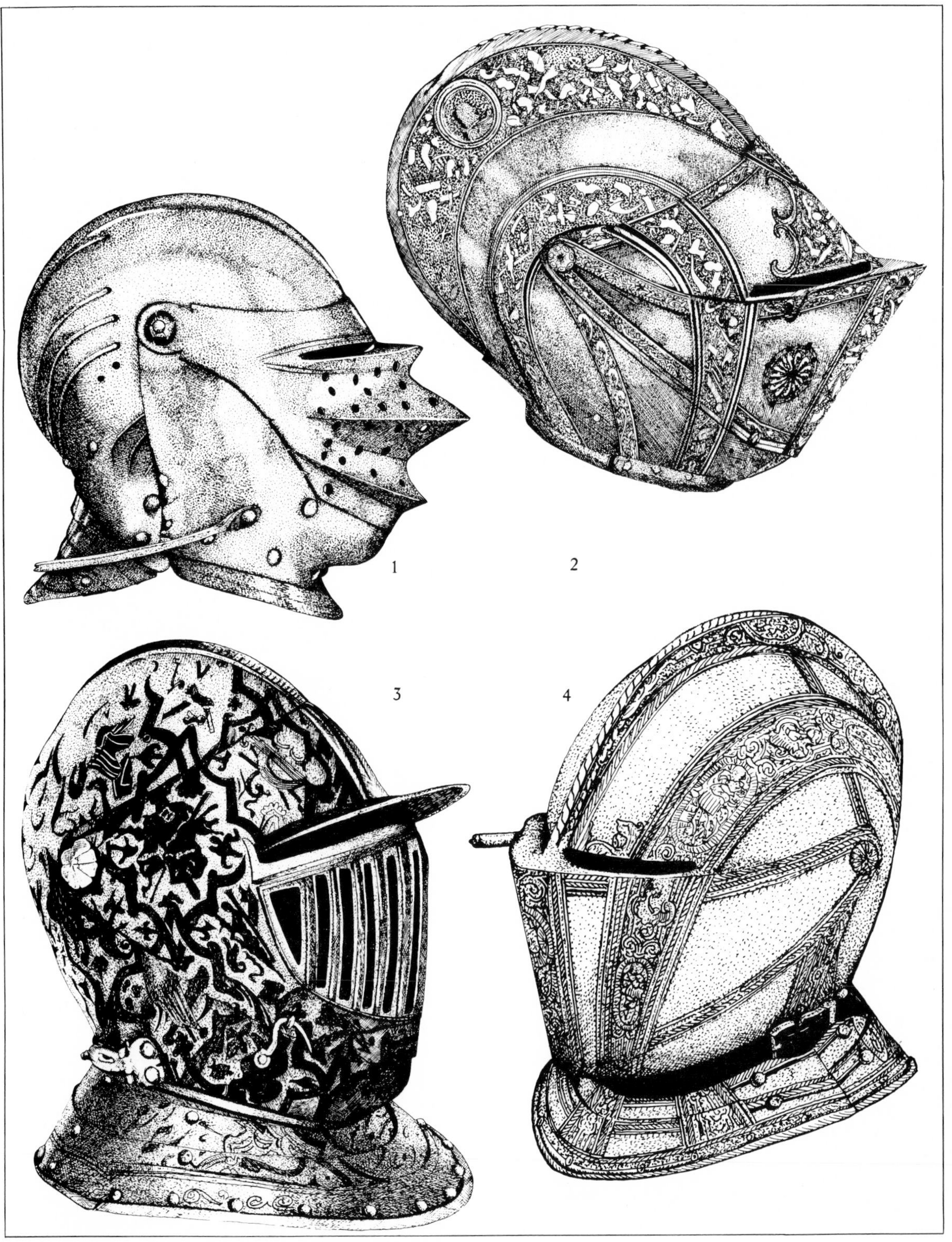


*1. Close helmet with bellows-style visor, S. Germany, c. 1510. Odescalchi Collection, Museo di Palazzo Venezia, Rome. 2. Close helmet to lock over rim of collar, N. Italy, c. 1550–60. Museo Stibbert, Florence. 3. Cuirassier closed burgonet with barred visor, Italy, c. 1600. Museo di Capodimonte, Naples. 4. Close helmet, N. Italy, c. 1580. Museo Stibbert, Florence.*

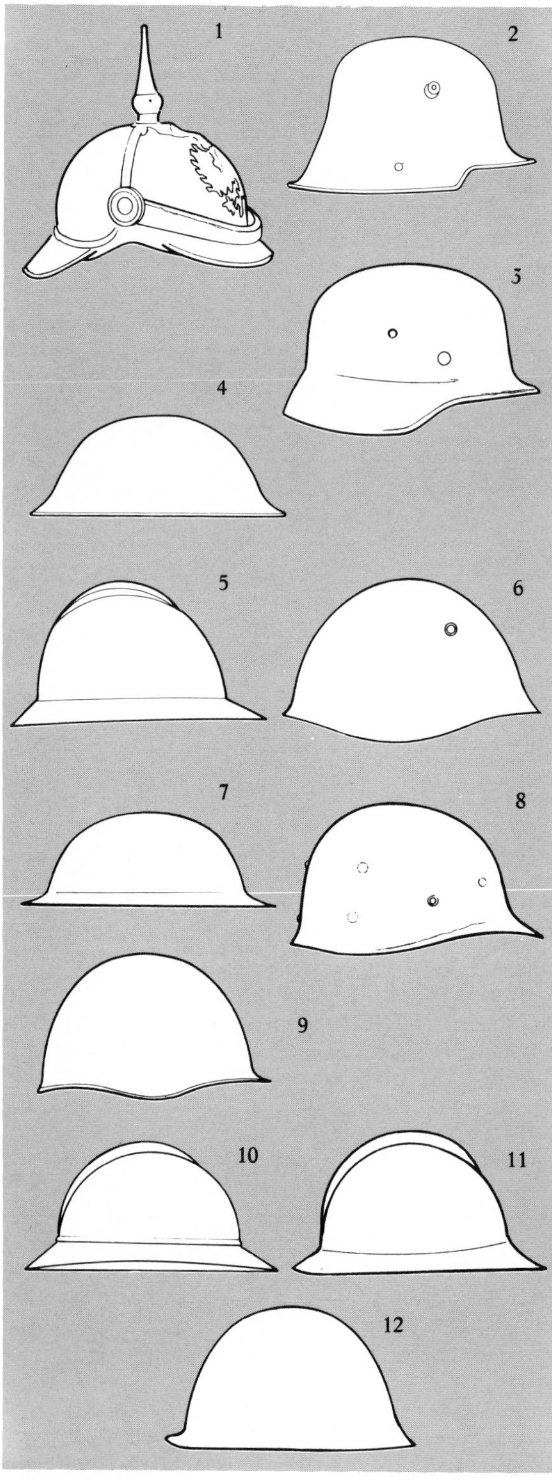


*Helmets of the First and Second World Wars. 1. Austria* (Pickelhaube). *2. Germany, 1918. 3. Germany, 1935. 4. Great Britain, design of 1915. 5. Italy, 1915–16. 6. Italy, 1933. 7. United States and Great Britain, 1917. 8. United States (Mark I), 1941. 9. Russia, 1940. 10. France, 1915. 11. France, 1935. 12. Japan, 1930–32.*

Leather and metal skullcaps were widely used in ancient Greece. These were fitted with cheekpieces, a chin strap, and sometimes a high crest. During the Geometric Period (10th–8th centuries B.C.) some helmets were conical, which may have been a result of Eastern influences, probably Assyrian. The most widespread type of head protection in classical Greece, however, was the "Corinthian" helmet, recorded from about the middle of the 8th century B.C. This helmet ensured the fighting man almost complete protection for his head and face. The skull extended downward at the back into a tail that entirely covered the nape and, at the sides, into two large cheekpieces shaped so as to leave only the eyes and part of the mouth uncovered. The nose was protected by a fixed bar projecting down from the brow. The Corinthian helmet often displayed a high crest and was sometimes richly decorated in relief with figures of animals, fighting men, deities, etc.

A type similar to the Corinthian, the "Chalcidice" helmet—so called because it has been found depicted on vases from the Peninsula of Chalcidice—had fixed cheekpieces separated from the tail by an opening at each side for the ears. The Chalcidice helmet sometimes carried a crest, which, as with the Corinthian, could either be attached directly onto the skull or mounted on a special support.

The "Attic" helmet, used in Greece from about the middle of the 6th century B.C., consisted of a skull with a short neck guard and two movable cheekpieces hinged to the skull. Attic helmets were frequently richly decorated, and we know from iconographic evidence that they were often surmounted by elaborate crests. Two other types of helmets were also extensively worn throughout Greece: the "Illyrian," typified by its hemispherical skull and fixed, pointed cheekpieces, and the "Thracian," with long hinged cheekpieces, a prominent tail, and quite often, a short peak to protect the eyes.

Various helmets were worn in pre-Roman Italy, some being of Italic origin and others of Greek derivation such as the Corinthian, which is known to have been used in Etruria from the beginning of the 6th century B.C. Prior to this innovation, only two kinds of helmets had been known to the Etruscans: one was a simple leather or bronze skullcap of Italic origin that was made in a number of variations, as we know from both iconographic evidence and archeological discoveries; the other was a helmet with a large triangular crest—a style that had already been created during the Villanovian culture of the early Iron Age. A later type of Etruscan helmet derived from Corinthian models is called the "Pseudocorinthian"; its skull covered the head to the eyes only, and it had a short tail at the back or flared circular brims protecting the nape and cheeks.

During the early centuries of Rome's history, many types of protective headgear in leather and metal were worn, derived from Italic-Etruscan styles. During the 5th and 6th centuries B.C., however, another influence—brought over the Alps by the invading Gauls—was to make its mark. A new type of helmet was introduced, the use of which was to spread throughout Italy. This was a "jockey cap" helmet, at first made of bronze but later of iron. Its hemispherical, slightly bulbous skull was topped by a button, and there were cheekpieces, hinged to the sides and tied under the chin. It was from this basic form that the numerous variations were to evolve which came to be worn by the legionnaires and cavalry of the Roman armies right through to the late Roman Empire. During the period of imperial grandeur, however, many types of helmets came into being that were not for war service. These included gladiatorial, masked, and parade helmets, which developed characteristics of their own according to the purposes for which they were used, and had little in common with the purely military helmet. A famous example of one of these, dating back to about 800 B.C., was discovered at Vigsø in Denmark; it is decorated with horns and two bronze studs to resemble eyes, in what appears to be a symbolic religious or amuletic manner.

Throughout almost the entire European continent—and especially in Gaul—the most widely used defensive headgear was the "jockey cap" helmet originally introduced to the Romans through Gallic influence. There is no doubt, too, that Roman armor had a considerable effect on the style of armor in other countries. For instance, archeological evidence shows that the masked helmet with cheekpieces used in northern European countries derived from the masked helmet of the Roman cavalry.

Apart from specific instances such as the one just quoted, most of the European helmets in the early Middle Ages derived from styles brought from the north by migrating "barbarians." The two basic types were the "segmented" and the "banded" helmet. In the former, an iron or bronze framework formed a headband which supported vertical triangular bands (usually six) that converged into a metal plate at the apex of the skull, the resulting segments then being lined with iron, bronze, or horn. In the "banded" type, the metal headband was also used but only two metal semicircular strips formed the framework for the skull, crossing at right angles at the apex. Four equal-sized segments were then overlaid with metal plates to form a fairly rounded shape. Both types sometimes had cheekpieces hinged to the skull and a short strip of mail attached to the back edge to protect the neck. Such helmets worn by chiefs and the more valorous warriors were often made from finer, costlier materials. The strips, for instance, would have been of bronze or gilded copper, engraved with designs inspired by provincial Roman art or by the rich traditional representational art of the "barbarians." Nor would it have been unusual for the overlying plates to be made of silver or gold.

This type of helmet remained in use for a very long time and over a very wide area without undergoing any major modifications. The Vikings, those great warriors of the north, certainly elaborated on several types of helmets, adding extra protection to the basic structure for various parts of the head, such as a tail, cheekpieces, and quite often, a face mask.

The banded conical helmet is portrayed in the famous Bayeux Tapestry (c. 1066–77), worn by Norman soldiers, with a nasal bar riveted to the lower edge of the brow. Some of the helmets in the tapestry, however, appear to have been forged in one piece, with a reinforcing strip and separate nasal bar, and two of these have survived to confirm that this type of construction did exist. The older of the two is in the Cathedral at Prague; it dates to the 9th or early 10th century and is traditionally regarded as having belonged to the sainted King Wenceslaus. The other helmet, now in the Waffensammlung in Vienna, was found in Moravia and is usually dated to the 11th or 12th century.

From the middle of the 12th century, many types of protective headgear evolved, one of which was a helmet that was rounded at the top and frequently had no nasal bar. Another, which was approximately cylindrical, had a flat top and tapered slightly toward the base. Such helmets, including the conical ones, were sometimes fitted with a face guard, rather like a modern welding mask, with ventilation holes and two eye slits. The early part of the 13th century saw these separate forms merging into a single structure, the HELM, or great helm, which was to remain in use without major modifications until about the end of the 14th century. While the helm was later replaced in field armor by other forms of helmets, special helms continued to be used with jousting armor until the second quarter of the 16th century.

From the 1300s the most widely used type of helmet was the BASNET, supplemented with an aventail or a visor to protect the neck and face. The basnet had various forms, one of which, called the great basnet, had a neck guard overlapped in front by a large bevor, both reaching to the cuirass. Basnets were still used during the 15th century, along with other helmets. The BARBUT, which had appeared in the 14th century, was a heavy closed helmet completely covering the head and face, with only a T-shaped opening in front for the wearer to see and breathe, One of the most popular helmets from the 1430s was the SALLET, with a tail to protect the nape and a detachable bevor to cover the face. By the late 15th century the sallet was often provided with a pivoting visor, and it was this type that soon developed into the CLOSE HELMET, complete with pivoted visor, bevor, and circular gorget. This form of head defense, worn with heavy-cavalry armor, was widely used in many variations until the 1640s. A helmet which since c. 1425 had coexisted with the sallet and later with the close helmet was the ARMET. It had a rounded skull supplemented with large hinged cheekpieces, a pivoted visor, and a mail fringe to protect the otherwise uncovered neck. During the 16th century the armet gradually conceded importance to close helmets and lighter types of headwear like the BURGONET, known in many versions and used by lightly armored horsemen and infantry soldiers. Another popular helmet of this period was the MORION, a light helmet with characteristic curved brims and laminated cheekpieces; the skull was either rounded with a prominent comb or pear-shaped with a spur on the apex.

Some types of steel helmets were still in limited use after the middle of the 17th century, but they were finally replaced by military headwear made of felt, fur, leather, brass, and tombac.

The dramatically increased effectiveness of firearms by

the First World War led to the revival of some forms of body armor, like the breastplate and the helmet. Although sometimes made of special synthetic materials when intended for particular purposes where metal is not appropriate, modern helmets are generally made of bulletproof steel. Every nation's forces have their own distinctive style, often going back to particular historic forms. Because the shining steel has to be camouflaged, they are either painted or covered with some kind of fabric in unobtrusive designs and colours. It may be of some historical interest to record that the British steel helmet, nicknamed "tin hat," strongly recalls by its shape, the English "shapewe" of the 15th and 16th centuries (*see* KETTLE HAT).

**hiki-gane** An elbow guard in Japanese armor. *See also* KOTE.

**hilt** The whole of the grip and the guard in a bladed weapon. Hilts come in a wide variety of forms, depending on the particular use of the weapon in question and on the fighting techniques being practiced at any given time. The hilt first made its appearance on bronze swords dating back to the period of transition to the Iron Age, when the blade of the short sword was joined to the grip by rivets; but it did not become a true protective element until the period of the "barbarian" migrations. A clearly defined protective hilt started to appear in Viking swords, although the CROSS GUARD did not protrude far from the grip. In the Carolingian sword, however, the cross guard became more pronounced, and after the 10th century it started to become longer, often flattening out at the ends and also curving forward toward the blade.

The earliest blades, cast or forged in bronze and iron, were made for fighting techniques based entirely on the thrust; in this period the hilt was no more than embryonic. Before long, and not least because of the great progress in metallurgy and constructional techniques, swords were designed for delivering cutting blows, and it was soon clearly necessary to extend the QUILLONS, or cross guard, to ward off blows from the enemy's blade. During the Middle Ages the quillons became gradually longer, and the whole format of the sword was modified; it now sported a fairly broad blade, grooved at the center and often rounded at the tip. Throughout the 14th century the various modifications only applied to the length of the quillons; these varied from country to country as a result of local preferences, but they invariably remained perpendicular to the blade, were fairly round or four-sided in section, and often flattened out at the ends. They were frequently curved toward the blade, but sometimes toward the handle, although this was rare, being quite unsuitable for the hand when a wide motion was required to deliver a powerful cutting blow. After the 15th century the hilt became progressively smaller in size, not least because of the wide use of new protective elements: the arms of the hilt and various additional parts (loops, rings, bars, and so on).

In weapons with a single cutting edge, the most suitable shape for the quillons was that of an *S*, in the plane of the blade; long, straight quillons would only be able to block the cutting blow without at the same time offering an

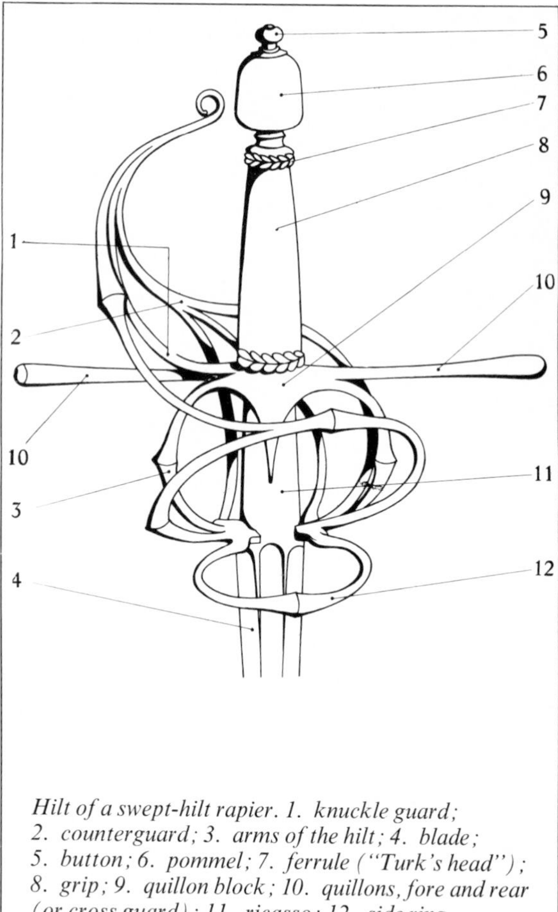


*Hilt of a swept-hilt rapier. 1. knuckle guard; 2. counterguard; 3. arms of the hilt; 4. blade; 5. button; 6. pommel; 7. ferrule ("Turk's head"); 8. grip; 9. quillon block; 10. quillons, fore and rear (or cross guard); 11. ricasso; 12. side ring.*

effective protection to the hand. In daggers the quillons were either straight and short, or curved toward the blade—especially in parrying weapons. The two-handed swords of the 15th and 16th centuries had larger quillons and GRIPS; in fact everything in these weapons was on a large scale, from the blade, which was often more than 1.3 m. (50 in.) long, to the grip, which had to be long enough to accommodate both hands, to the heavy POMMEL, which had to act as a counterweight to the long blade. The quillons in these fighting swords came in various shapes, and were even more ornate in those used for ceremonial purposes.

With the 17th century the quillons once more became straight, owing to new fencing techniques which introduced various thrusting blows. The sword itself had been considerably modified, its blade having become narrow and long, with a fairly flattish rhomboid section, often grooved, at least in the rear section (forte). The quillons of the Spanish-type sword protruded far from the SHELL GUARD or CUP GUARD, and were very efficient at parrying. In the smallsword and dress sword, the quillons were short and lobed at the tips, and barely protruded from the shell guard.

In the meantime swords were becoming more and more

specialized, being made in different ways, depending on whether they were to be used on foot or on horseback, either solely as weapons or as beating implements on the hunt; then there were the various ceremonial swords, which must be looked at separately. On the whole, swords for use on horseback were bulkier and heavier, whereas those for use on foot had a narrower blade and a lighter hilt; swords used by infantrymen were altogether more simple and functional.

The ceremonial swords were quite different; here, the construction involved not only the armorer but also the artist. The ceremonial function was paramount, although, constructionally speaking, these weapons often remained quite valid fighting pieces and generally reflected all the features of weapons in current use. These clearly defined forms were retained even when the original model was already out of date or obsolete. Typical examples are the papal sword, which for a long time retained abandoned forms.

An important step in the evolution of the hilt was the addition of the KNUCKLE GUARD in the 15th century. This protection was essential in any fight with cutting swords and permitted abandoning the bulky steel gauntlet in favor of a lighter and more comfortable leather glove. After the mid-16th century the knuckle guard was almost invariably present in the hilt of swords. A further step toward almost complete protection of the hand came with the adoption of the "two-bar" and later of the "three-bar" knuckle guard; the main guard bow split into three bars which joined up with the quillon or with the archetto. Also, the SIDE RINGS or loops were increased in number, to as many as eight or nine in some hilt types. With the introduction of the shell guard, which gradually became larger until, in the mid-17th century Spanish sword, it formed a complete "cup," the hand was completely protected. However, for use in battle, as well as for everyday wear, the sword now returned to simpler forms, relegated as it was to secondary functions, due to the effectiveness of firearms. The edged weapons still remained part of military equipment, but they grew less and less important, finally becoming more of a symbol, which is their role today.

**himogatana** A tiny Japanese dagger, mainly used by women. Made entirely of steel, it had a straight, narrow, diamond-sectioned blade about 15 cm. (6 in.) long and a straight handle round in section. The himogatana sheath consisted of a piece of cane with fittings at each end and a hanging cord.

**hind tasset** *See* TASSETS.

**hineri** Also called *neji*, a staved weapon used by the Japanese police. It consisted of a multispiked metal head with teeth and hooks fitted to a long wooden shaft, and was used to capture suspected wrongdoers by entangling the loose sleeves of their kimonos. Similar weapons, varying only in the distribution of barbs and hooks, were termed *tsukubō*, *mojiri*, and *sodegarami*. When police control over citizens was particularly keen, especially during the Tokugawa (Edo) period (1603–1867), such weapons were always kept readily at hand at city and provincial borders.

**hirumaki** Also called *ishizuki*, the metal shoe at the bottom of the stave of a Japanese pole arm. *See also* YARI.

**Hispano-Moresque swords** Also known as *espadas á la jineta*, this ancient class of Moorish swords had already been established for centuries when they became associated with the name of the last king of Granada, Boabdil, a member of the Nasredes dynasty in the late 15th century, who had owned a fine specimen. Such swords are depicted in the late 14th-century frescoes in the Alhambra, in Granada.

The one-edged blades of the Boabdil swords were long and broad, tapering slightly and having a fuller built into each side of the FORTE. Sometimes they bore the mark of a running wolf, which was the signature of Juan del Rey, a sword cutler in the service of King Boabdil (the same mark has also been used in Germany at Passau and Solingen). The swords had a swelling grip surmounted by a spherical or discoid pommel. The large quillons were sharply downcurved and often depicted weird animal forms such as monsters with elephants' trunks. Overall, the hilt was decorated with sophisticated arabesques and Arabic inscriptions, and the scabbards and sword belts, too, were given sumptuous ornamentation. The fittings on these swords were of a very high artistic standard, involving all the craft skills for which Granada was renowned, with lavish application of gold, ivory, and enamels. Some of the best examples can be seen in Madrid at the Museo de Ejercito and the Museo Archeologico and in Paris at the Bibliothèque Nationale.

**hitsu** The central hole for the tang in a Japanese sword guard. *See also* TSUBA.

**hi uchi bukuro** A Japanese fire lighter, also used to ignite the match of a gun. A Dutch type of snaphance flintlock (which itself was never fitted in Japanese firearms) was fitted into a round case containing a tinder. This tinderbox was usually hung from the match.

**hōate** A type of Japanese war mask. *See also* MENPO.

**hoko** A general term used to describe any Japanese spear up to and including the Nara period (c. 650–794), although earlier they had been called *rikken* and *tenchō*. The hoko was made of bronze or iron, with or without a side blade or spike, and was socketed or partially tanged. It was extremely efficient in parrying and turning aside an opponent's weapon, as well as inflicting damage to the shaft of the other's weapon.

The weapon that appeared in the late 15th–early 16th century was based on the forms of the Nara period and was also called hoko. It had a projecting side blade below the central one and was always tanged. During the Tokugawa (Edo) period (1603–1867), the hoko underwent an extravagant transformation and was used mostly for parades and ceremonies. In appearance, its side blade was often either exaggeratedly large or disproportionately short and stumpy. In some examples of 17th-century hoko, the main blade was extremely short and spikelike, the emphasis being on the horizontal blade forming a heavy, four-sided beak, similar to that of the European war hammer of the 16th and 17th centuries.

The hoko shaft, which was about 120–140 cm. (47–55 in.) long, was usually oval, lacquered, and fitted

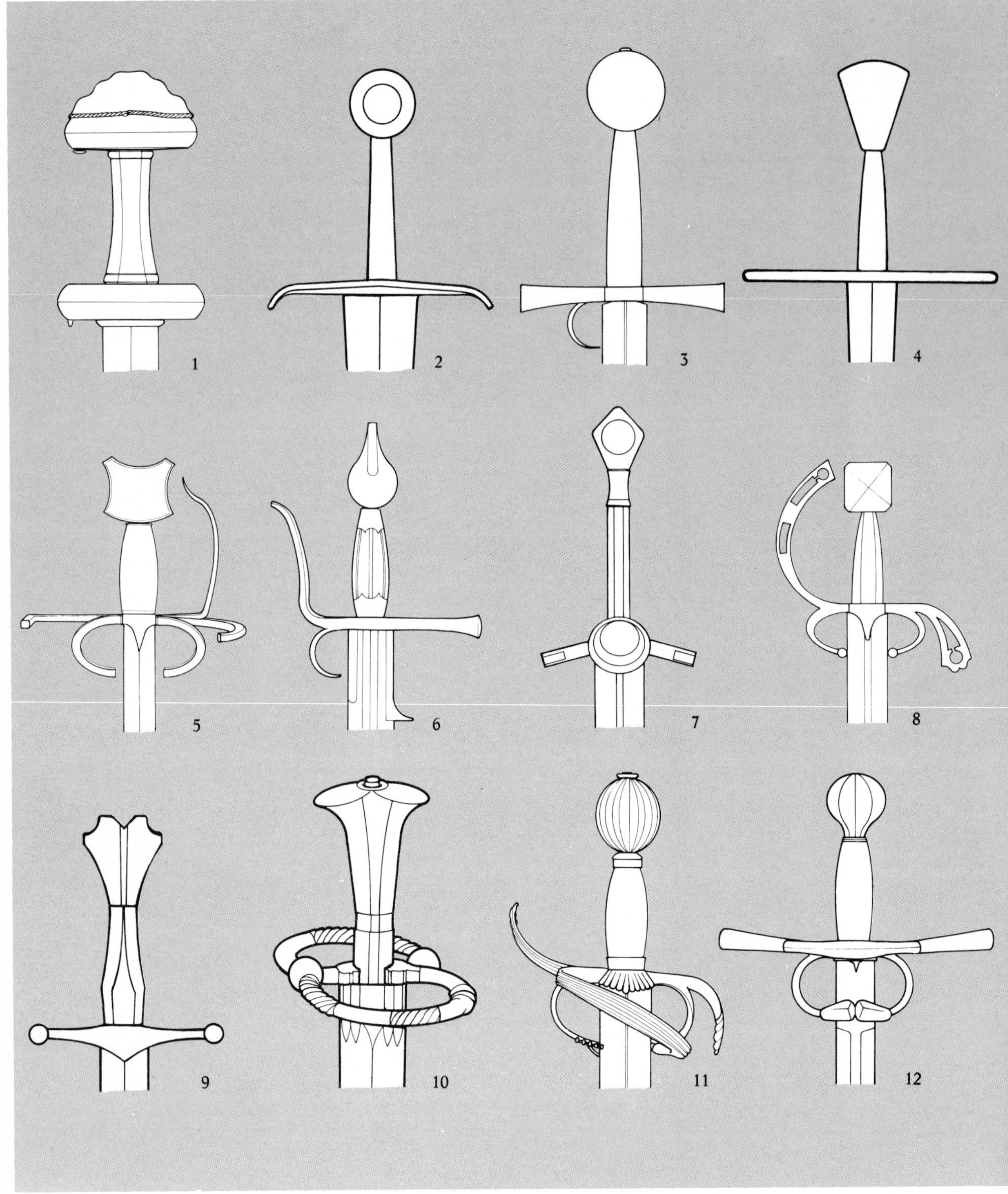


*Types of hilts. 1. N. Europe, 9th century (Viking sword). 2. W. Europe, c. 1350–1450. 3. W. Europe, mid-14th century to c. 1500. 4. Europe, c. 1360–1430. 5. N. Italy (Veneto) c. 1480–1520. 6. Italy, c. 1450–1500. 7. S. Germany, c. 1440–60. 8. N. Italy, c. 1480–1520. 9. W. Europe, c. 1440–80. 10. S. Germany, c. 1520–50 (landsknecht sword). 11. Italy, c. 1530–1620. 12. W. Europe, c. 1550–1630.*

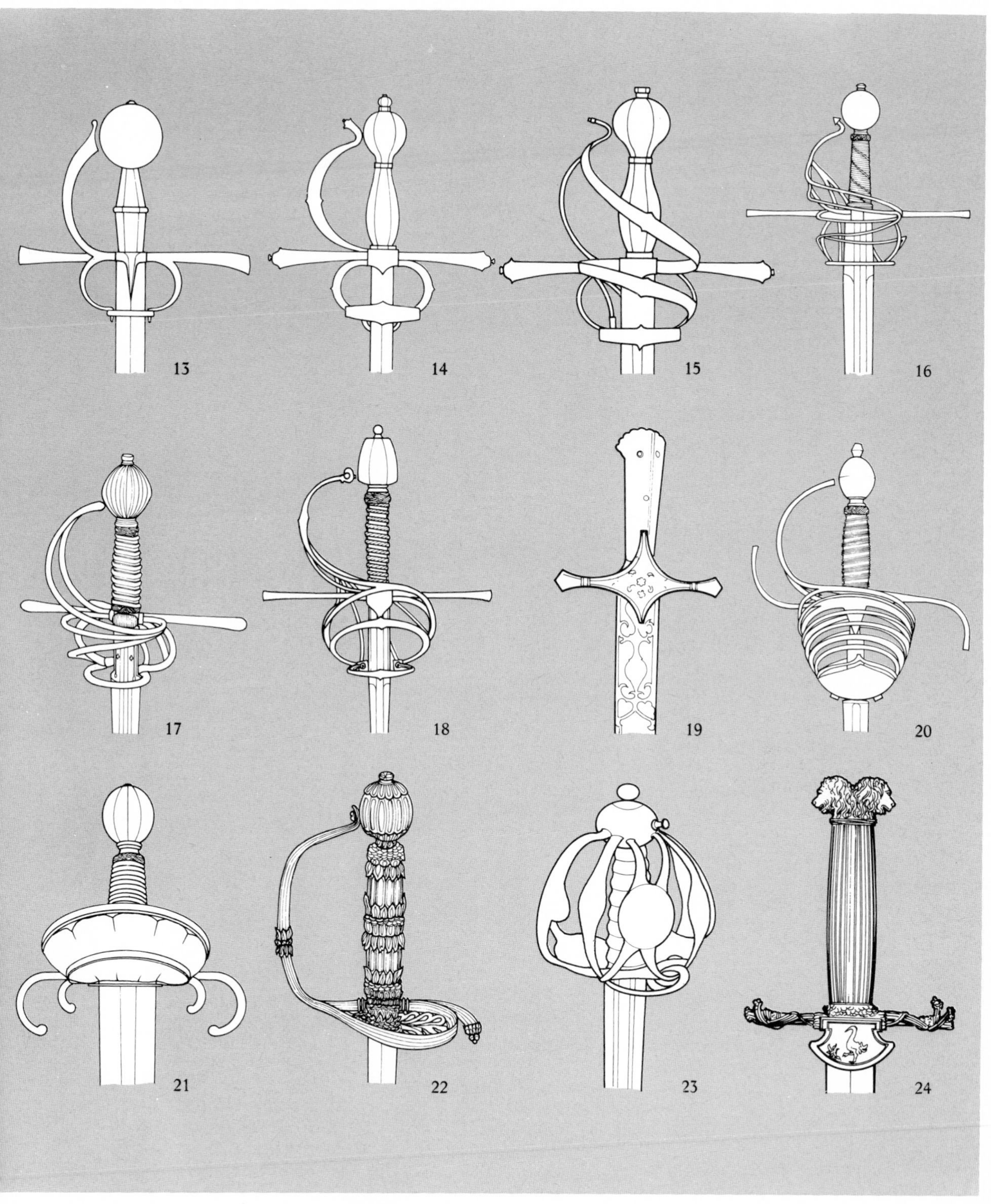


*13. N. Italy, c. 1480–1550. 14. Italy, c. 1500–1600.*
*15. W. Europe, c. 1550–1620. 16. Italy, c. 1540–1610.*
*17. Italy, c. 1530–1620. 18. W. Europe, c. 1600–40.*
*19. E. Europe, 17th century. 20. W. Europe, c. 1630–50.*
*21. Italy, c. 1600–1650. 22. W. Europe, c. 1620–1700.*
*23. Scotland and England, c. 1610 onward.*
*24. France, early 19th century.*

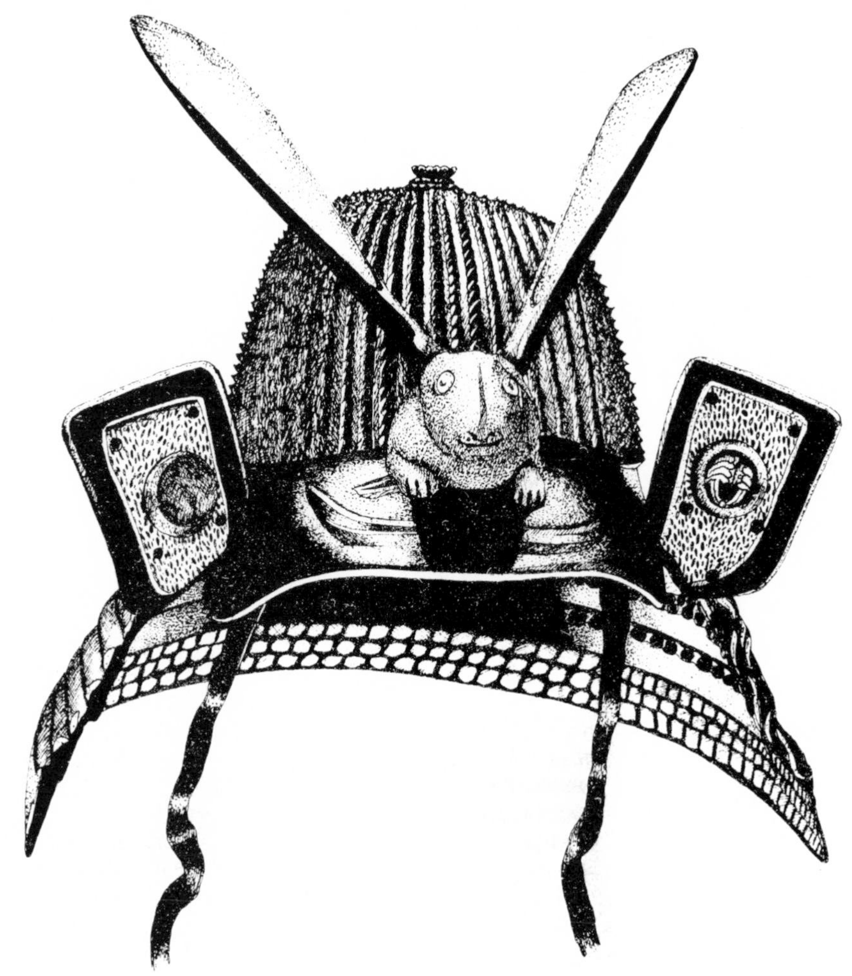

*Hoshi-kabuto, 19th-century Japan. Museo Stibbert, Florence.*

into a metal shoe, *hirumaki*, at the bottom. Some hoko blades were signed by their maker. The sheath was either a SAYA of decorated lacquer or a plain wooden SHIRAZAYA, which usually bore various inscriptions.

**holbein dagger** *See* DAGGER.

**holster** A hand-firearm accessory introduced in the 16th century, initially for horsemen. It consisted of a *cuir-bouilli* (hardened leather) or metal case shaped to the pistols or short arquebuses it was intended to contain, preserving them from dampness, and was carried in front of the pommel of the saddle. It was open at the top, often provided with a flap, and broadened out slightly to make room for the lock and the grip; the bottom was usually closed. The holster was frequently painted or decoratively stitched, and sometimes ornamented with metal appliqué. Belt holsters were introduced in the second quarter of the 19th century.

**holy-water sprinkler** An ironic slang name given in England, in the 16th and 17th centuries, to a weapon consisting of a stout staff, the end of which was bound by an iron sheath with spikes. This weapon is akin to the MORGENSTERN.

**horo** An accessory worn with Japanese armor mainly in the 15th and 16th centuries, which can be classified as "soft armor." It consisted of a square or trapezoidal cloth loosely fastened to the back of a mounted warrior; as it billowed in the wind its purpose was to protect the wearer against arrows shot from behind. Sometimes it was padded with cotton or partially distended by a wicker frame. Generally about 180 cm. (6 ft.) long, it was made up of five strips sewn together which bore inscriptions or the wearer's crest. The top of the horo was fastened to either the helmet or to a ring on the back plate, the bottom being held by cords tied around the waist.

**horse armor** *See* BARD.

**horse harness** All the equipment, in leather and cloth, needed to control and direct a horse. The term covers the bridle with all relative pieces such as the headstall, bit and reins, breast strap (pectoral), saddle, girth, stirrup leathers and irons, crupper, and breeching.

# Arms and armor from Japan and India

**Plate 35 Japanese armor** *Yoroi with red silk lacing, Fujiwara period (c. 898–1185). Mitake Jinja, Tokyo.*

**Plate 36 Japanese armor** *Yoroi with red silk lacing, Muromachi period (c. 1392–1573). Kushibiki Hachiman-gū Shrine, Aomori Prefecture, Japan.*

**Plate 37 Japanese armor** *Dō-maru with white silk lacing, early Muromachi period (c.1392–1573). Kushibiki Hachiman-gū Shrine, Aomori Prefecture, Japan.*

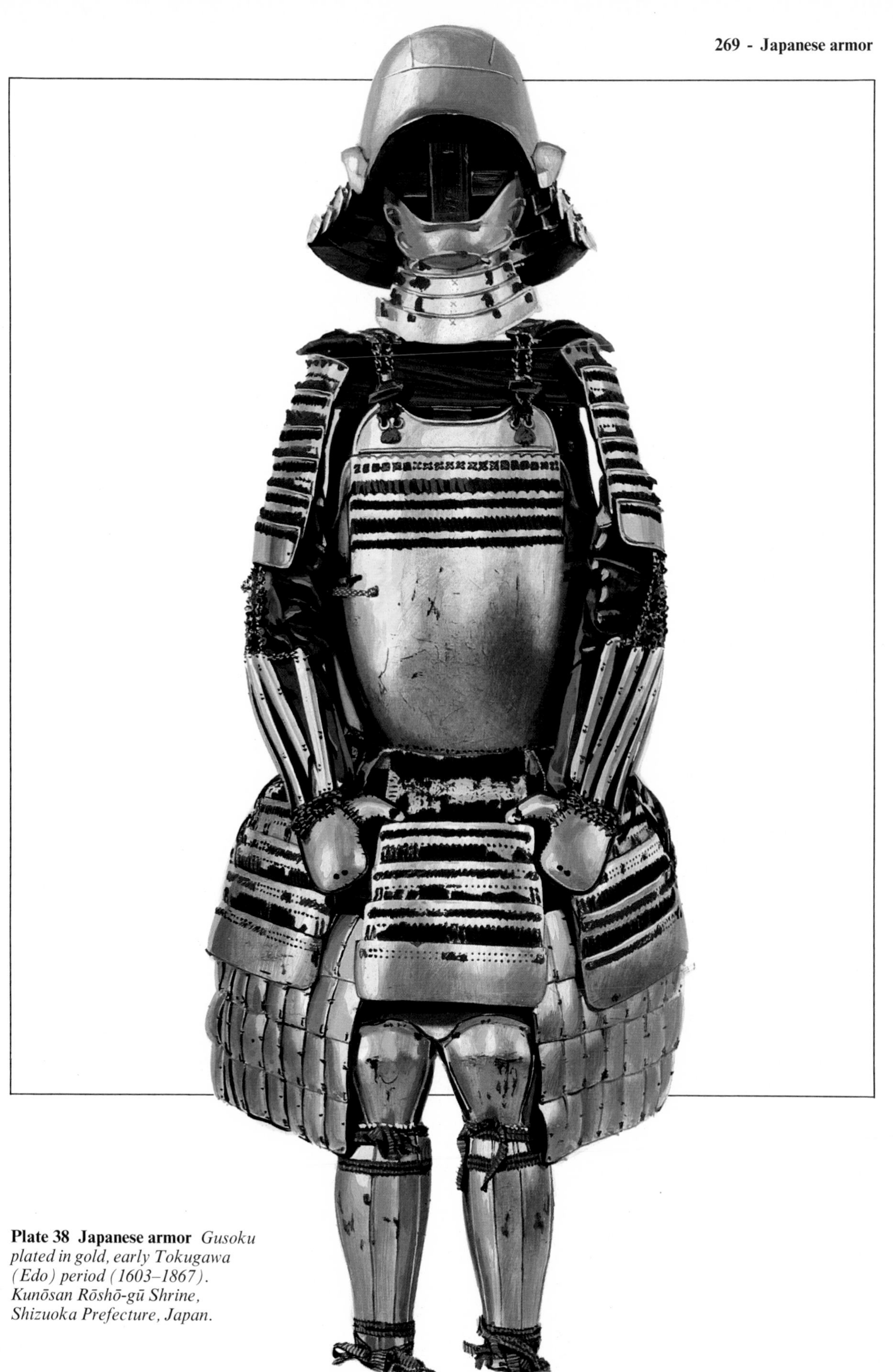

**Plate 38 Japanese armor** *Gusoku plated in gold, early Tokugawa (Edo) period (1603–1867). Kunōsan Rōshō-gū Shrine, Shizuoka Prefecture, Japan.*

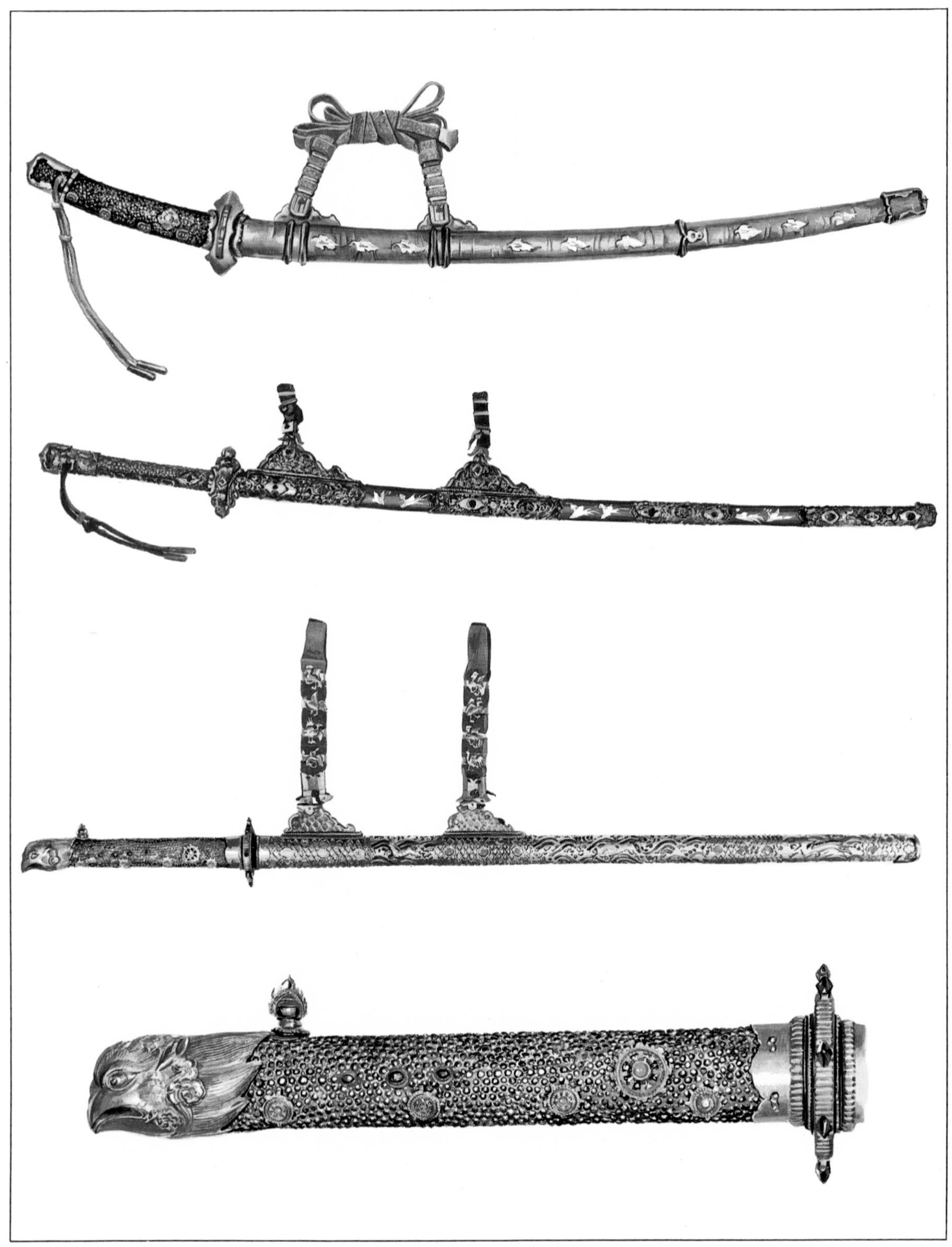

**Plate 39 Tachi** (top to bottom) *Tachi with furniture and scabbard decorated with mother-of-pearl on a gold background; this was a votive object at the Tsurugaoka Hachiman-gū Shrine, from the school of Kenyu. Kanagawa-Tsurugaoka Hachiman-gū Treasure House, Kanagawa Prefecture, Japan. As above but on a gilded background. National Museum, Tokyo. Tachi with furniture and scabbard decorated in gold and silver, and close-up of its handle in the form of a bird's head. Kumano Hayatama Taisha Museum, Wakayama Prefecture, Japan.*

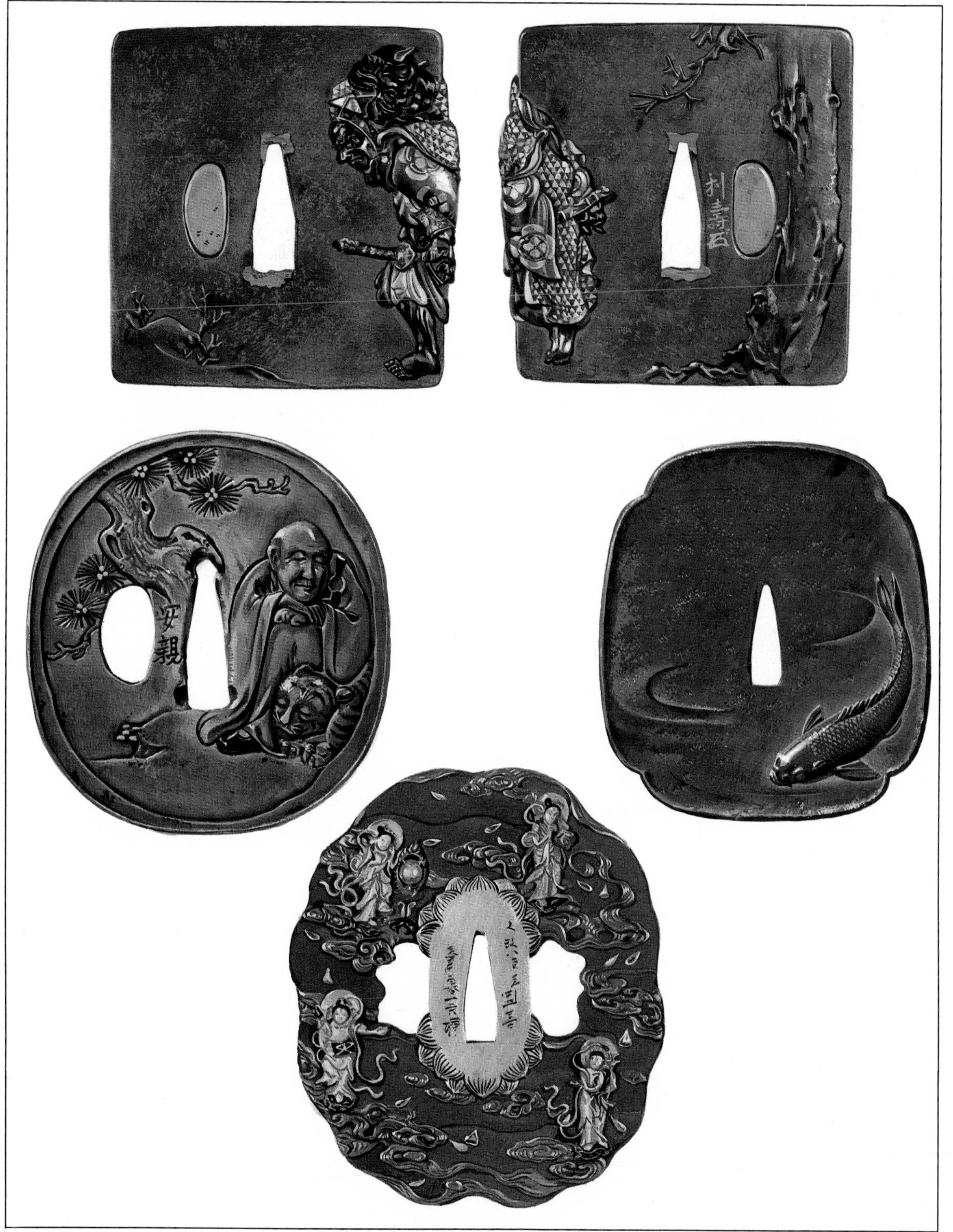

**Plate 40 Tsuba** (top) *Tsuba for the tachi, seen from both sides, by Toshinaga; on it is depicted a well-known character of folklore, Omori Hikoshichi. Taguchi Collection, Osaka.* (middle left) *Tsuba for the tachi by Yasushika. Kurakawa Kabunka Institute, Hyogo Prefecture, Japan.* (middle right) *Tsuba for the tachi by Natsuo depicting a carp. National Museum, Tokyo.* (bottom) *Tsuba for the tachi by Gotō Ichijō depicting Buddha descending from heaven with his disciples. Taguchi Collection, Osaka.*

**Plate 41 Japanese helmets** (top) *Kabuto, Kofun period (5th–6th centuries). National Museum, Tokyo.* (middle) *Kabuto, end of the Muromachi period (c. 1392–1573). Sata Jinja Shrine, Shimane Prefecture, Japan.* (bottom) *Hoshi-kabuto, end of the Fujiwara period (c. 898–1185). Oyamazumi Jinja Shrine, Ehime Prefecture, Japan.*

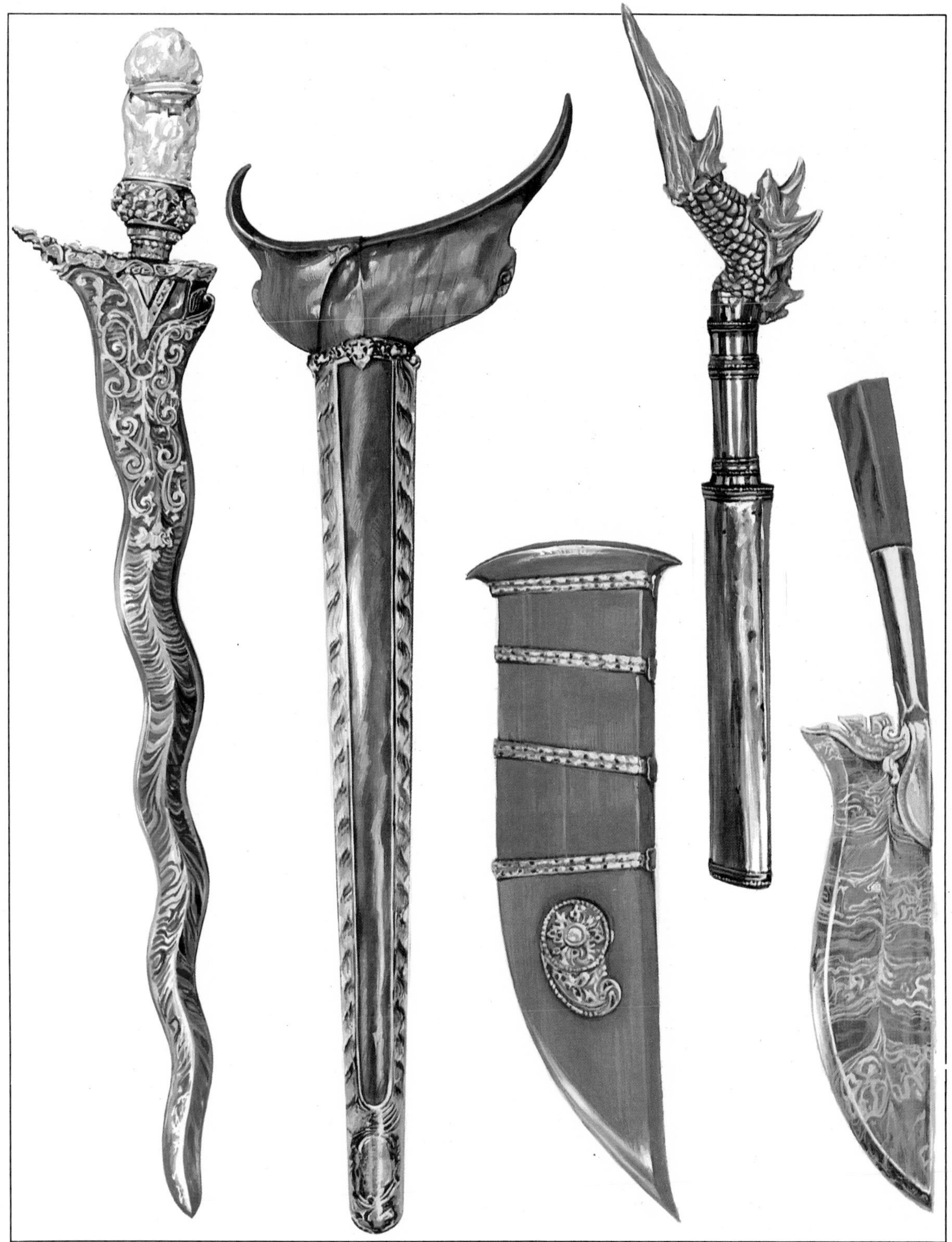

**Plate 42 Daggers of Southeast Asia** (left) *Kris with ivory handle and gold decorations and its lacquered wooden sheath, central Java.* (upper right) *Dagger, with handle shaped like a stag's antler, in its metal sheath, Thailand.* (lower left and right) *Wedong with gold decorations and red lacquered wooden sheath also mounted in gold, central Java. All in Rijksmuseum voor Volkenkunde, Leiden, Netherlands.*

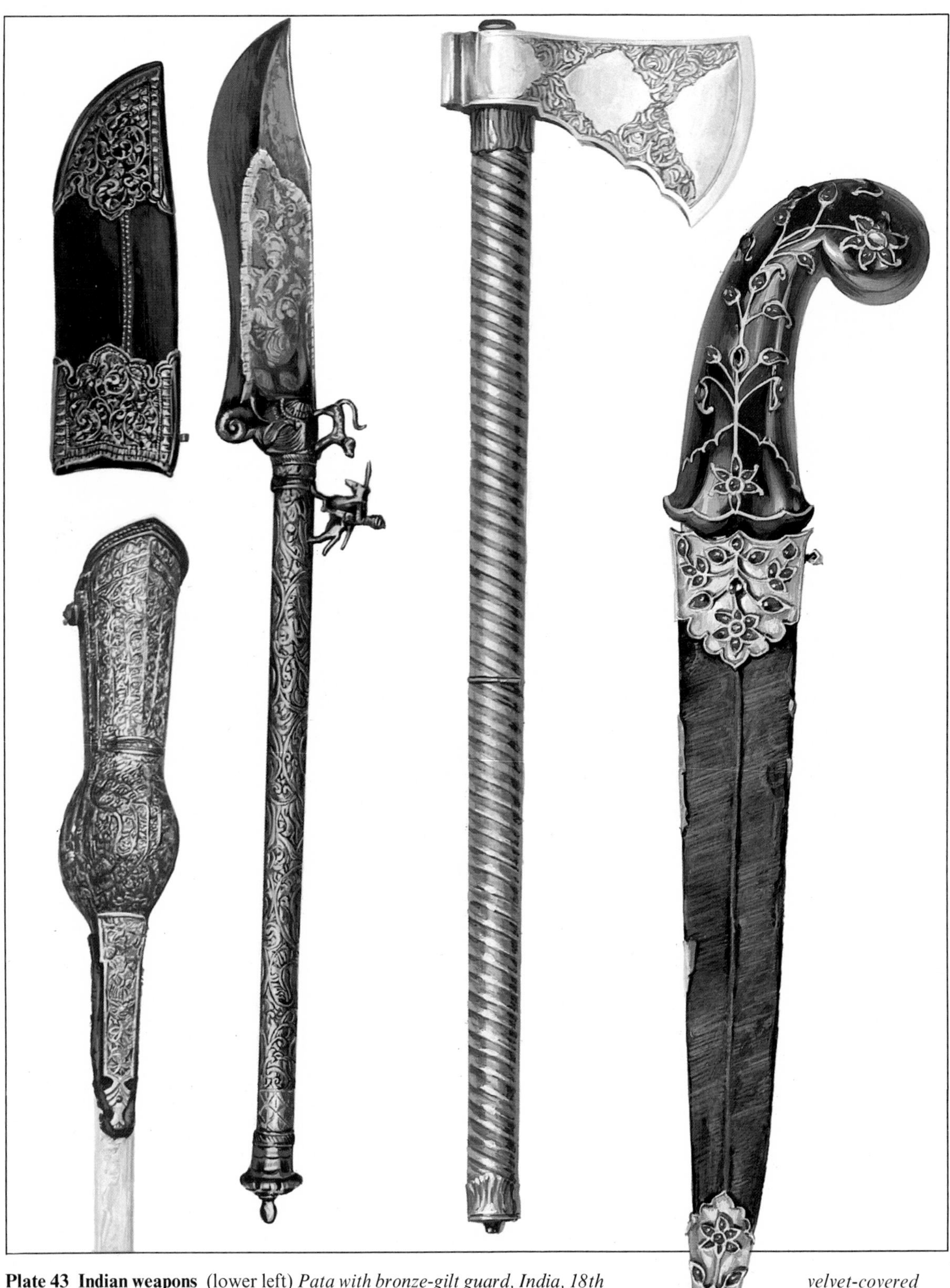

**Plate 43 Indian weapons** (lower left) *Pata with bronze-gilt guard, India, 18th century. Museo Stibbert, Florence.* (second from left) ***Bhuj** with velvet-covered wooden sheath* (top left), *N. India, early 19th century. Museo Stibbert, Florence.* (second from right) *Tabar with steel blade, India, 18th century. Wallace Collection, London.* (right) *Khanjar with jade handle and velvet-covered sheath, N. India, 18th century. Museo Stibbert, Florence.*

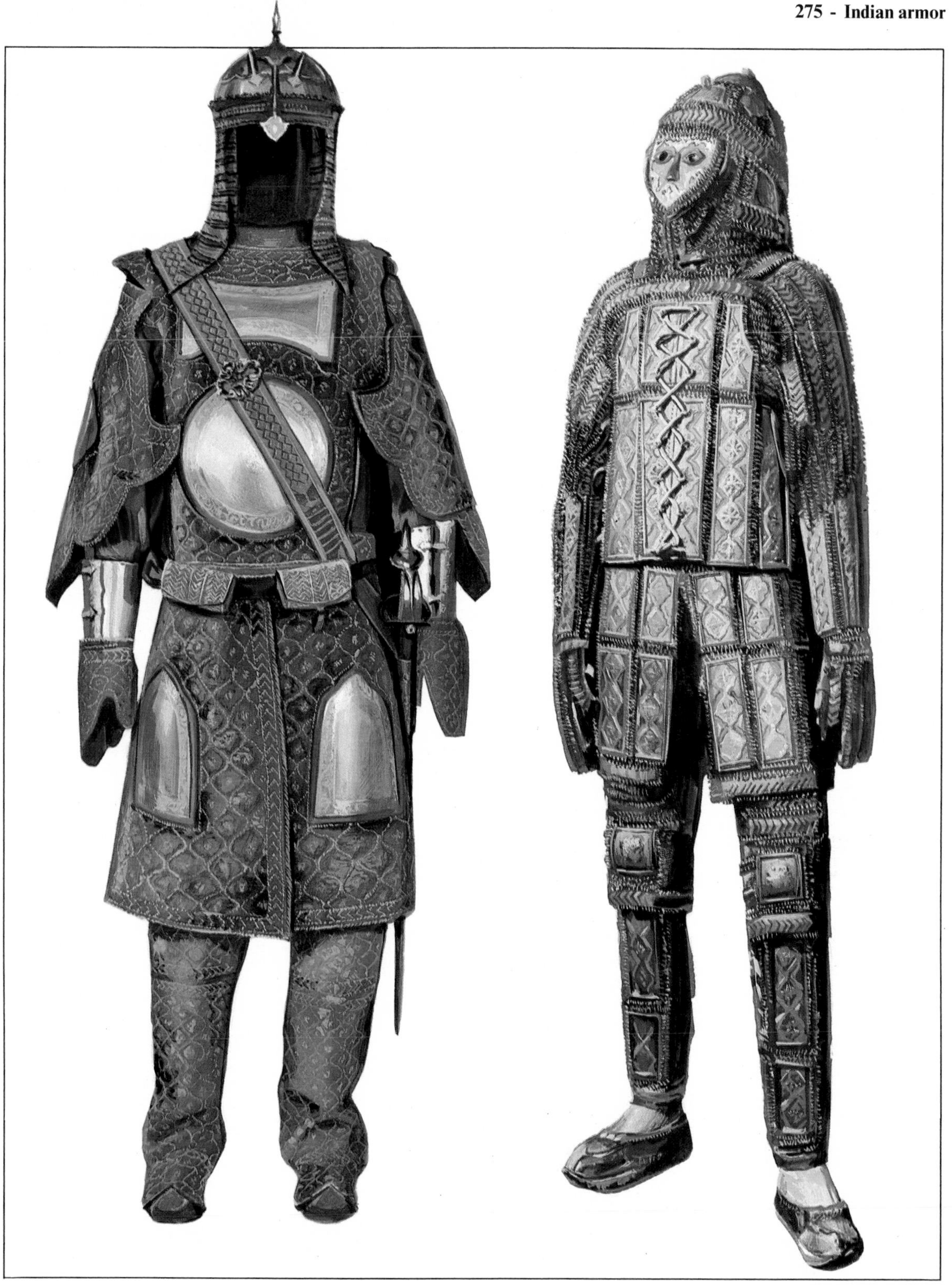

**Plate 44 Indian armor** (left) *Armor of a noble Rajput (member of the warrior caste), India, end of the 18th century. Wallace Collection, London.* (right) *Complete mail-and-plate armor, India, end of the 18th century. Museo Stibbert, Florence.*

Oriental harness differs greatly, as it leaves the horse much more freedom. Its main feature is the high packsaddle carried forward over the horse's shoulders; the breeching is replaced by a light crupper strap looped under the tail.

In reinforced harness or armored caparison, some protection was given the horse by reinforcing the normal harness with iron plates or pieces of specially prepared leather hardened by soaking them in heated wax (*cuir-bouilli*). The leather headstall was sometimes reinforced by a single plate attached to the brow band which went over the top of the animal's head to form a neck lame or poll plate; this extended into the neck guard or crinet, made of iron lames or overlapping pieces of hardened leather. To protect the horse's forequarters, the breast strap was considerably broadened by reinforcing it with another leather strip. The reins, too, were covered with another layer of leather. The crupper and loin strap were frequently armored with metal pieces and integrated with a tail guard.

**hose of mail** *See* CHAUSSE.

**hoshi-kabuto** One of the original forms of Japanese helmet, developed from earlier types dating from between the 4th and 6th centuries. It consisted of several curved plates set vertically, enclosed at the bottom by a single band, with a kind of peak or decorated reinforcing plate in the front and a hole, the TEHEN, in the top. The distinctive feature of this type of helmet was the method of riveting the plates, with the fairly large rivet knobs visible, in rows, on the surface. The same construction can be seen in some types of helmets of late antiquity, e.g., in Sassanian Persia, and in Europe during the periods of barbaric invasions, as well as in the great helm of medieval times.

In Japan, however, there was a continuity of type through the centuries until the Tokugawa (Edo) period (1603–1867). Early forms of the hoshi-kabuto, from the 10th and 11th centuries, were primitive and almost conical, constructed of large plates joined together with a few clumsy rivets and with a large tehen in the top. Between the late 13th and early 15th century the hoshi-kabuto, also called *ō-boshi*, became almost hemispherical and was made of numerous lames, with a tiny brim worked out of the lowest band. A huge laced neck guard, the SHIKORO, was attached to the back of the brim and protected by large, upstanding guards, the FUKIGAYESHI.

The hoshi-kabuto was particularly popular during the 16th century, in the late Muromachi period, when it consisted of anything from 32 to 72 plates with as many as 30 small conical rivet heads on each plate, carefully graded in size with the largest at the bottom and the smallest at the top. Each rivet passed through two overlapping plates so that the construction was particularly secure. This type of

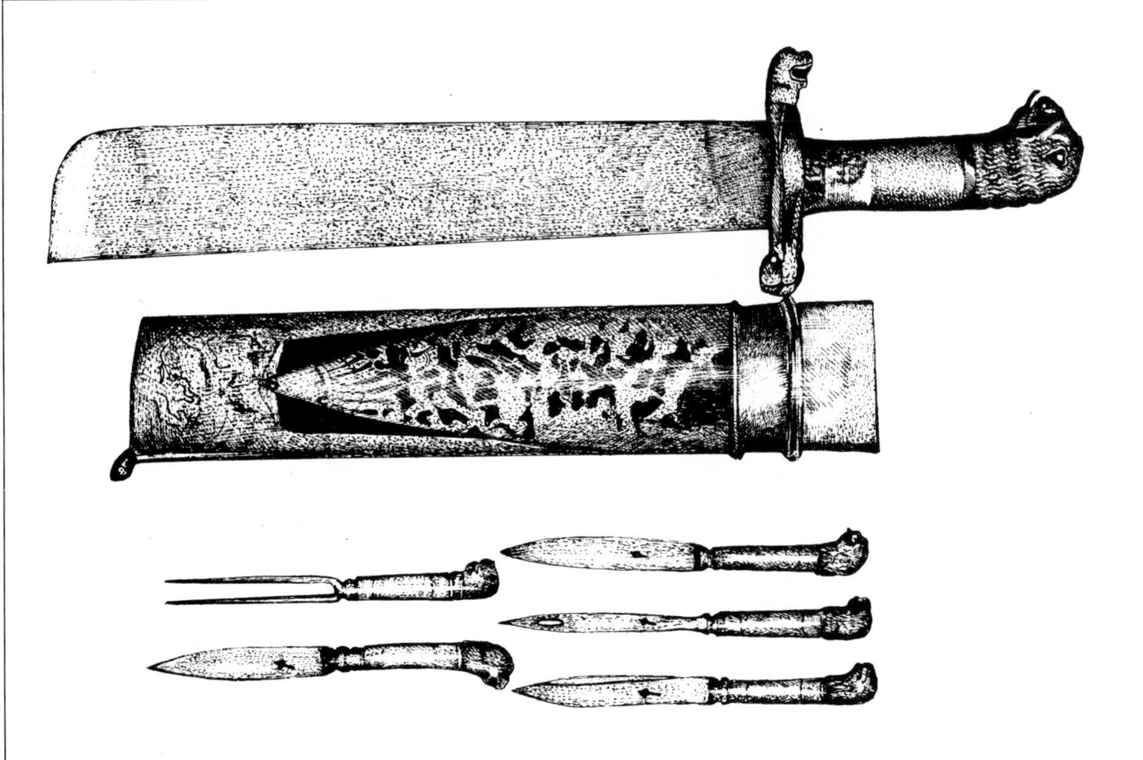

*Hunting garniture consisting of a large carving knife with sheath, three small knives, a bodkin, and a fork. Germany, 17th century. Odescalchi Collection, Museo di Palazzo Venezia, Rome.*

knobbed helmet was still being produced as late as the 19th century, in various forms.

**hotoke-dō** A type of Japanese armor. *See* DŌ-MARU.

**houfnice** Bohemian word from which the word "howitzer" is derived.

**housing** Also called *coverture,* a type of medieval caparison for the horse's protection. It consisted of two large pieces of thick cloth, often lined with fur, one of which was draped over the horse's head and forequarters and the other over its hindquarters.

**howitzer** A word derived from the German *Haubitze* (which in turn probably comes from the Bohemian *houfnice*), describing a large, comparatively short piece of artillery—12–25 caliber, halfway between a cannon and a mortar—able to fire with a curving trajectory but with rather longer range than a mortar. The German word seems to have been used for the first time during the wars in Flanders in the 17th century, to refer to guns which, while bigger than mortars, like them fired large bombs with a marked parabolic trajectory. The term "howitzer" was already in use all over Europe by the 18th century, in place of the term "short cannon" used previously. As field fortifications were continually improved, these guns increased in importance; with the great elevation of which they were capable (up to 75 degrees from the horizontal) they had no difficulty in firing over any kind of obstacle. The great tactical versatility of the howitzer was fully appreciated in the two world wars, and this kind of gun still forms the nucleus of the support artillery of the great powers. Among howitzers in service at present are the Italian 105/14, which has been adopted by several armies, and the self-propelled U.S. M-109 of 155 mm. and the M-110 of 203/25.

**Hungarian visor** A modern term for FALLING BUFFE.

**hunting garniture** A set of implements including a large knife, smaller knives, and other accessories which might be of use when hunting, all kept in a large scabbard with several pockets. Essentially it was a kit designed for cutting and deboning animal flesh. The principal knife, or chopper, had a massive single-edged, ribbed blade; it was rounded and sharp at the point, with its center of gravity situated well forward to make the weapon easier to use for cutting blows. The smaller knives, forks, and a bodkin were used for the *curée* ceremony (when parts of the stag—usually the innards—were handed to the hounds after its death, and the hunter who bagged the stag was rewarded with the front-right hoof) and for the immediate preparation of dead game. Various kits included a cleaver, a saw, chisels, and a serving knife (*presentoir*). The iconography of the 15th and 16th centuries often shows beaters wearing a special large knife at their side. The garnitures, with a number of knives and implements, were largely used by the hunting parties of noblemen in the 15th to 18th centuries, mainly north of the Alps.

# I

**ichi-no-ashi** Lockets for the sling on the scabbard of the TACHI.

**ignition** The first stage of combustion in muzzleloading firearms, in which the fine priming gunpowder in the pan and touchhole is ignited. Early hand and artillery guns were ignited manually by holding a slow match, tinder, or firebrand to the touchhole. Various methods were tried out based on this system, their main purpose being to improve the speed of firing and the operator's safety.

The basic technique, common to all systems, consisted of having a pan i.e., a dish-shaped container adjoining the touchhole, into which the fine powder was put; this powder was ignited and through the touchhole made contact with the explosive powder rammed into the barrel. The difference in the various methods of ignition lay in the method of igniting the priming powder in the pan. The three main methods which had evolved—each of which had several variations—were the serpentine (matchlock), the wheel-lock, and the snaphance (flintlock), and these remained in use until the beginning of the 19th century, when percussion mechanisms began to emerge.

*Matchlock with Serpentine Device*

The early method of ignition was still based on the slow match but brought into contact with the priming powder by a process of levers rather than manually, as hitherto. An illustration of a handgun operated by such a system appears in a German manuscript dated 1411 in the National Library, Vienna. The handgun is shown with a simple pole stock with a Z-shaped lever pivoted to its left side, with both arms extended. As the lower arm was pulled up toward the stock, the upper arm was lowered onto the pan. This simple but effective trigger device, which became known as the serpentine lock because of the shape of the lever, probably originated from the principle of the trigger mechanisms of contemporary crossbows, which were somewhat similar. Although the serpentine lock continued to be used on firearms until the end of the 15th century, no example is known to be extant today.

*Snap-matchlock*. The mechanism was attached to a metal plate. It consisted of a cock, or serpentine, which was kept pressed onto the pan by a spring. The jaws of the cock held a slow match or fuse. On the inside of the lock plate a Z-shaped lever, with a spring behind it, was pivoted laterally. A stud, or sear, at one end of the lever protruded through an aperture in the lock plate. As the cock was raised from the pan a projecting section at its lower end, the heel (if pointing backwards) or the toe (if pointing forward), was caught and held by the sear. At the rear end of the sprung lever was a button which either projected through the lock plate or through a slot in the butt. When the button was pressed, the sear was withdrawn, permitting the cock to snap down onto the pan.

The snap-matchlock was rarely used in Europe after the second quarter of the 16th century. However, it is found,

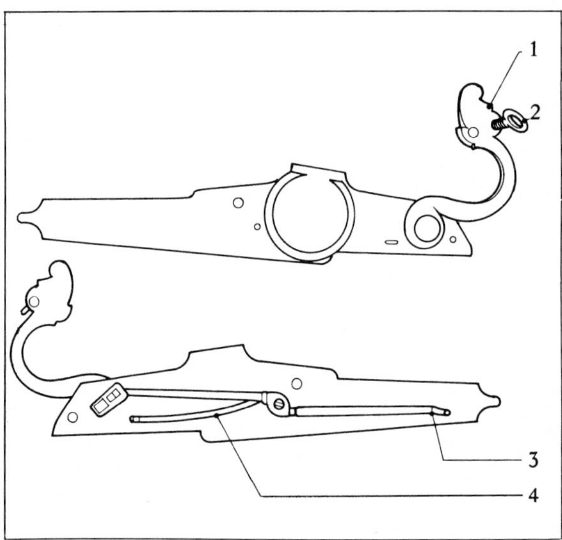


*Serpentine. 1. match holder; 2. thumb screw; 3. sear lever; 4. spring.*

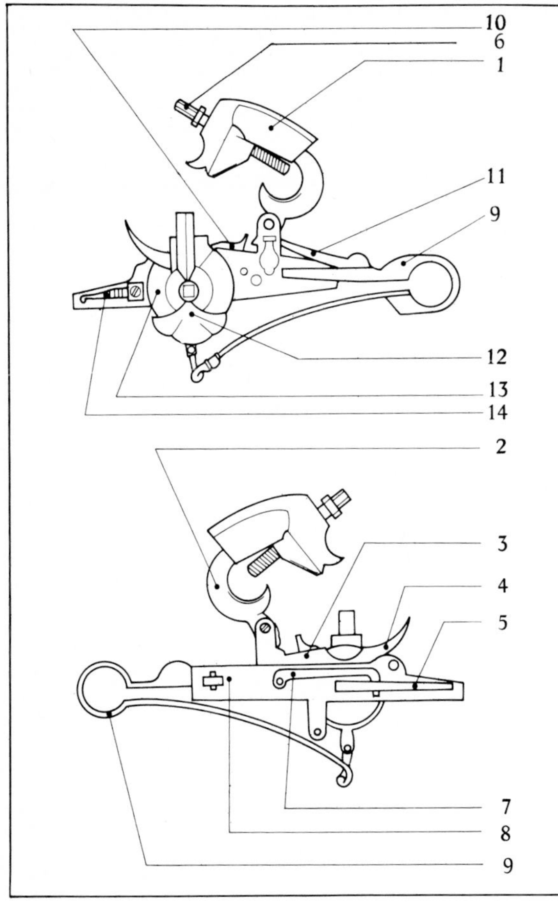


*Wheel-lock of archaic form (Museo d'artiglieria, Turin). 1. cock; 2. neck of the cock; 3. priming pan; 4. fence (flash guard); 5. sear lever; 6. jaw screw; 7. sear spring; 8. lock plate; 9. main spring; 10. pan cover; 11. cock spring; 12. wheel bridle; 13. wheel; 14. safety catch.*

although rarely, on some guns of the 17th century. Snap-matchlocks incorporating a hair trigger were made from about 1570 until c. 1635. The "snap" effect was increased by a spring-operated link between the sear and the trigger. When the main trigger was pulled, the second spring trigger struck the sear.

The snap-matchlock was used in Japan until the 19th century. Characteristic of Japanese matchlocks was the use of brass for the spring. The Japanese almost certainly copied the locks of guns which were introduced into Japan by the Portuguese in 1543.

*Sear-lock*. The mechanical action of this form of lock operated in the opposite manner to the snap-matchlock, that is, the serpentine or cock with the slow match was held back from the pan. The cock was pivoted on a spindle and linked by levers to a long lever-shaped trigger which ran parallel and underneath the stock. When the trigger was pulled toward the stock, the cock or serpentine was lowered into the pan. The sear-lock was introduced in the last quarter of the 16th century and remained in use for military guns until the close of the 17th century, principally because it was cheap to manufacture as well as being mechanically reliable.

### *Wheel-lock*

The wheel-lock system of ignition consisted of a lock plate shaped to fit a wheel, with a pan attached to the top edge. At the bottom of the pan was a slot through which the grooved rim of a rotatable wheel, mounted below, projected. On the inside of the lock plate and attached to the wheel spindle was a short chain which was linked to the end of a strong V-shaped mainspring. Pressing on the back of the wheel through an aperture in the lock plate was a sear carried on a horizontally pivoted lever, held in position by a spring. In front of the wheel the cock was pivoted, fitted with jaws secured by a screw, which held a piece of iron pyrite. The cock could be moved manually either onto the pan or away from it, and was held in the selected position by means of a strong V-spring. The pan cover—also spring-operated—could be pushed back over the pan, to be held by a spring catch. The wheel-lock was spanned by means of a spanner, which was fitted over the square-ended wheel spindle. The wheel was turned until the sear clicked into position in a notch on the reverse side. With the sear engaged, the sear lever moved to engage, and be wedged by, a spring-operated trigger lever. After priming and loading, the pan cover was closed and the cock brought down to the pan cover. When the trigger was pulled, it disengaged the trigger lever from the sear lever, and the wheel was then free to revolve, pulled by the main spring. As the wheel moved, a cam opened the pan cover and the wheel came into frictional contact with the pyrite, causing ignition.

Neither the date of the invention of the wheel-lock system of ignition nor its geographical location is known. The earliest datable wheel-lock is to be found on a combined gun and crossbow preserved in the Bayerisches Museum, Munich. This weapon is German and can be dated, on the basis of heraldry appearing on it, to between 1521 and 1526. The earliest documentary evidence which can be dated definitely is also German. A manuscript of drawings collated by Martin Löffelholz of Nuremberg in

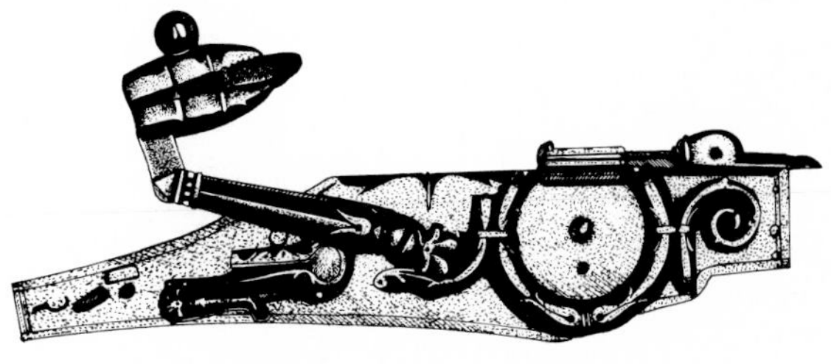

*Wheel-lock, S. Germany, c. 1540–50. Victoria and Albert Museum, London.*

1505 includes drawings of tinder lighters operated by a wheel-lock. In a document dated 1507 a servant is instructed to buy "a gun of that kind that is ignited with a stone" when on a visit to Germany. The mechanism at this date presumably refers to a wheel-lock. There are also other references to self-igniting guns from Germany and Switzerland dating from about 1515.

However, in spite of the above evidence for a German Origin for the invention of the wheel-lock, on folio 56b of the *Codex Atlanticus* by Leonardo da Vinci is what appears to be a design for a wheel-lock. The drawing dates probably from about 1500, and certain internal evidence suggests that it is a design for rather than a drawing of an existing lock. Significantly, three combined guns and crossbows in the Palazzo Ducale, Venice, which have been dated to 1510–20, show features which relate to the Leonardo drawing. There is thus a strong case to be made for the Italian origin of the wheel-lock. (All the evidence for both origins is discussed by C. Blair in *Journal of the Arms and Armour Society of Great Britain*, Vol. III, No. 8, Dec. 1960, Pl. 221, and Vol IV, No. 1, Pl. 187.)

By 1530 the wheel-lock was in use all over Europe. Certain national forms of wheel-locks were developed alongside the usual type discussed above. During the 16th century Italy employed a wheel-lock mechanism with a large external mainspring. In Spain, a very similar lock construction was used until the 17th century. In France, a wheel-lock construction was adopted which was characterized by having the mainspring set in a recess in the stock, the wheel spindle being held by a metal plate on the opposite side of the stock. This construction is found occasionally on certain German firearms. Except for Germany and those countries under German influence which used the wheel-lock for sporting and target guns until the 18th century, by the middle of the 17th century the flintlock had replaced it as a more satisfactory system of ignition.

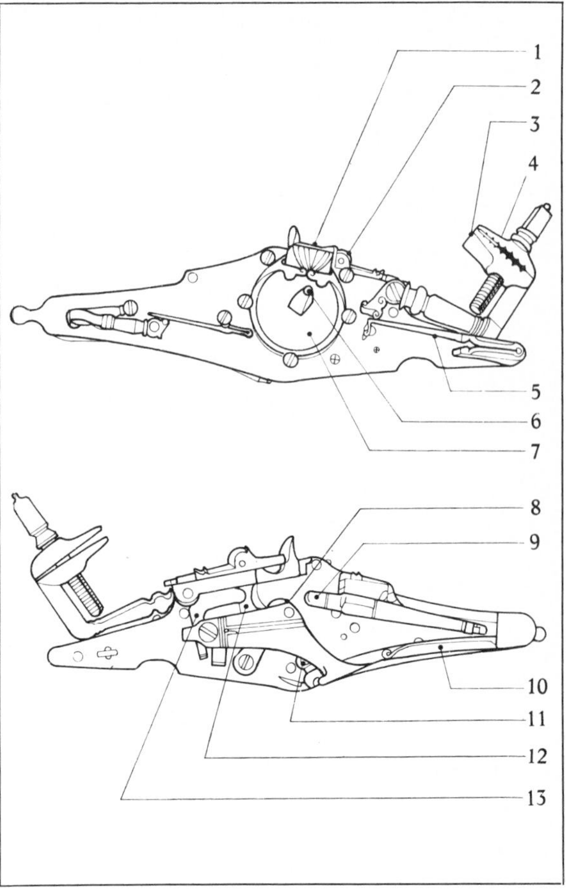


*Wheel-lock. 1. priming pan; 2. sliding pan cover (to hold priming powder in pan); 3, 4. jaws of the cock; 5. cock spring; 6. wheel spindle; 7. wheel; 8. wheel bridle; 9. sear lever; 10. main spring; 11. chain; 12. arm of pan cover; 13. pan-cover spring.*

*Snaphance Lock or Snap-lock*

The snaphance system of ignition belongs to the flintlock group and consists of a spring-operated cock, with flint held in its jaws, which strikes a steel plate hinged vertically over the pan, thus creating sparks; pyrites may also have been used during the early stage.

The earliest documentary evidence for the snaphance occurs in a Swedish document dated 1547, where it is referred to as a *snapplås* (snap-lock), and in a Florentine document, where it is described as *archibusi da focile* (the word *focile* was used at a much earlier date to describe the steel used together with a flint and tinder for striking fire). The earliest datable snaphance is to be found on a gun with a Nuremberg barrel in the Royal Armory, Stockholm, thought by most authorities to be one of thirty-five Nuremberg arquebuses known to have been fitted with snaphances in 1556 at Arboga, the Swedish royal workshop. The short cock of this lock has long, split jaws held together with a screw. As the cock is pulled back, the toe pushes against the end of a flat mainspring fitted to the outside of the lock plate. At full cock, the heel is caught by a sprung sear which projects through an aperture in the lock plate, from the inside. As the trigger is pulled, this sear is withdrawn, thus allowing the cock to fall toward the

*Florentine snaphance, central Italy, c. 1725–50. Odescalchi Collection, Museo di Palazzo Venezia, Rome.*

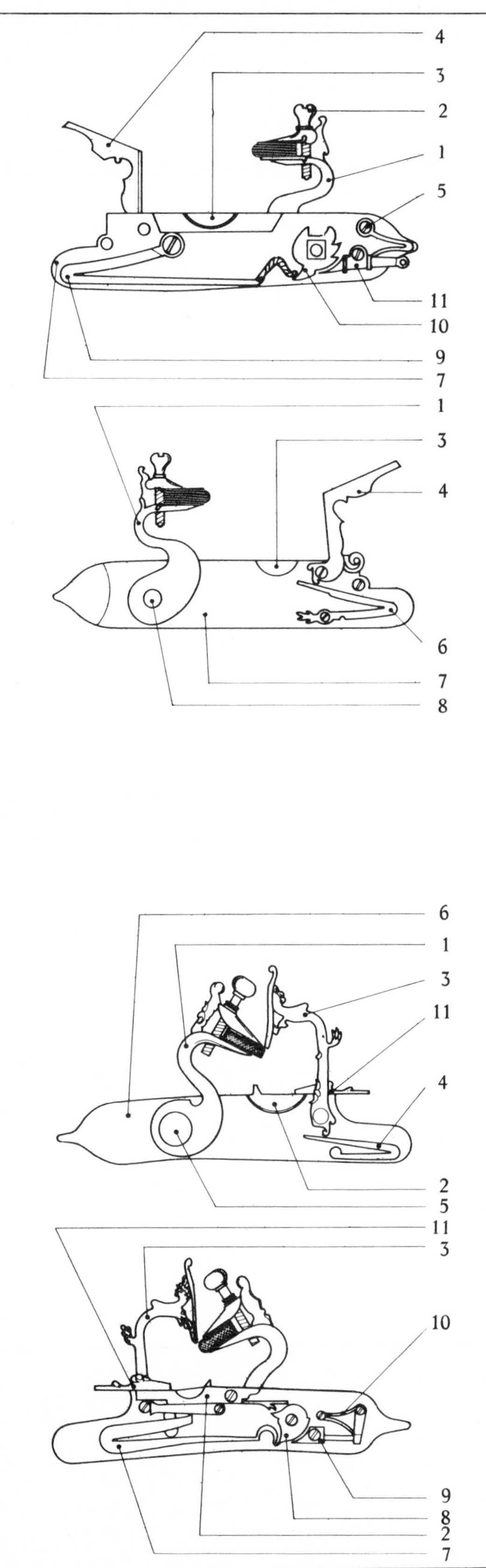


*Flintlock. 1. cock; 2. jaw screw; 3. priming pan; 4. steel (frizzen); 5. sear spring; 6. steel spring; 7. lock plate; 8. cock screw; 9. mainspring; 10. tumbler; 11. sear and trigger lever.*

steel. The steel is formed at the end of a long arm and consists of a square, slightly concave plate, at right angles to the arm. Although this basic form of snaphance is often referred to as the "Baltic" lock, there is every reason to suppose that it was invented in Germany, perhaps in Nuremberg.

The snaphance lock had been rapidly adopted over a wide area by the last quarter of the 16th century. By about 1570 certain national types of snaphance locks were beginning to emerge. An improved lock found on some guns combining both match and snaphance systems of ignition, associated with Saxony and dating from about 1570, had a mainspring inside the lock. This operated on a tumbler attached to the cock pivot, against which the sear engaged. Instead of long, split jaws, the cock was now in the form of an S-shaped arm with jaws to hold the flint.

Locks of similar form were used in England and the Low Countries by the 1580s, and they were widely used in Russia in the 17th century. A snaphance lock, based on the English version, was employed on Scottish firearms from about 1580 until about 1650. Italian gunsmiths produced a version of the snaphance characterized by a steel combined with the pan cover and an external mainspring acting on the toe of the cock. This was in use until the second quarter of the 17th century. In central and southern Italy an improved version of this type was made until the early 19th century. It was known as the "Roman" lock. A lock in the Artillery Museum in Turin, dating from about 1580—which consists of a wheel-lock combined with a snaphance—shows two interesting technical features found on all later flintlocks: the steel and pan cover are constructed as one element, hinged on the front edge of the pan, and the cock is provided with a safety position, in this case ensured by a small pivoted catch behind the cock that engaged in a recess in the back of the cock.

A much neater answer to the problem of holding the half-cock, or safety, position was introduced on flintlocks from about 1600 in Italy. It consisted of fitting a secondary sear within the lock plate, and was used on the Roman and Spanish forms of snaphances as long as they were made. The "patilla" lock had a mainspring operating on the heel of the cock, instead of the toe, and the front of the cock was cut to a chisel edge which engaged with two sears. "Patilla" was the term used in the 17th century in Spain to describe the lock now known to collectors as the Spanish miquelet or "Mediterranean" lock. The patilla was probably based on the early Italian snaphance, but this is by no means certain. It reached its fully developed form by the 17th century and was used in Spain until the 19th century.

*Snaphance. 1. cock; 2. priming pan; 3. steel (frizzen); 4. steel spring; 5. cock screw; 6. lock plate; 7. mainspring; 8. tumbler; 9. sear and trigger lever; 10. sear spring; 11. priming pan cover.*

During the 18th century a sophisticated miquelet lock was produced by the gunsmiths of Madrid which had an internal mainspring and a sear operating through an aperture in the lock plate, its outward appearance resembling the standard flintlock of French style. Variations of the patilla were widely used in the Caucasus, Turkey, Persia, and other Middle Eastern countries well into the 19th century.

*Flintlock*

The flintlock can be defined as the form of snap-lock which has the steel and pan cover made as one element and a vertical sear engaging in two recesses in the tumbler, which is attached to the inner side of the cock spindle. This allows the cock to be pulled to the half-cock position for safety as well as to the full-cock position.

The flintlock was probably invented in France in about 1620, and there is evidence to suggest that the inventor may have been Marin le Bourgeoys (d. 1634) of Lisieux, in Normandy. This artist-mechanic came from a family specializing in the manufacture of locks, watches, crossbows, and guns. His mechanical inventions include a terrestrial globe made for Henry IV of France, an air gun, and musical instruments.

The earliest flintlock mechanism as described above is a subject of some discussion among authorities. One of the earliest examples is thought to be the lavishly decorated sporting gun which belonged to Louis XIII of France and is now in the Hermitage in Leningrad. On a round plate on its stock are the arms of France and Navarre used by Henry IV of France and his successors. The metal mounts beneath the stock are inscribed with the name of Marin le Bourgeoys of Lisieux. This gun appears to have been made around 1620, while the next earliest firearm with the flintlock of the same construction was produced about 1625 in Moscow by Pervusha Issayev, recorded in 1616–25 as a gun maker at the Kremlin Armory.

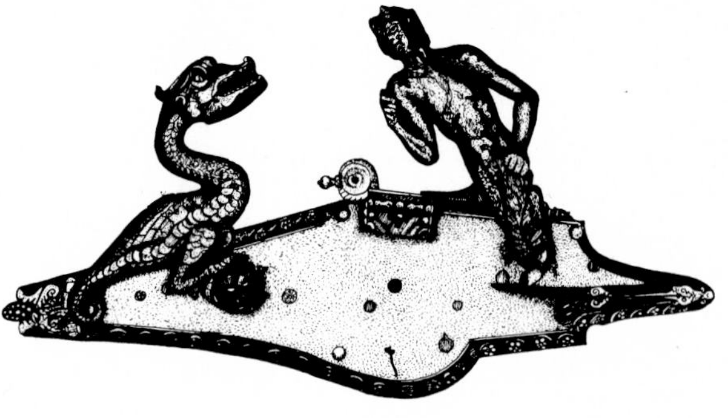

*Florentine flintlock, signed by Matteo Acqua Fresca of Emilia, Italy, late 17th century. Odescalchi Collection, Museo di Palazzo Venezia, Rome.*

By the 1640s the flintlock had already been fitted on military firearms, which is documented by some dated Flemish paintings. Flintlocks of the same basic design, improved only in functional details, were used on most European and American firearms, both civilian and military, until the second quarter of the 19th century.

*Percussion locks.* The first percussion system of ignition consisted of a cock shaped like a flat hammer and a bottle-shaped magazine containing detonating powder. Mechanically the percussion lock operated like the flintlock; however, ignition was produced by striking a volatile chemical detonating powder, or fulminate. A steel plug was screwed into the side of the barrel on the site of the old touchhole. At the top was a miniature pan with a channel joining it to the chamber. The bottle-shaped

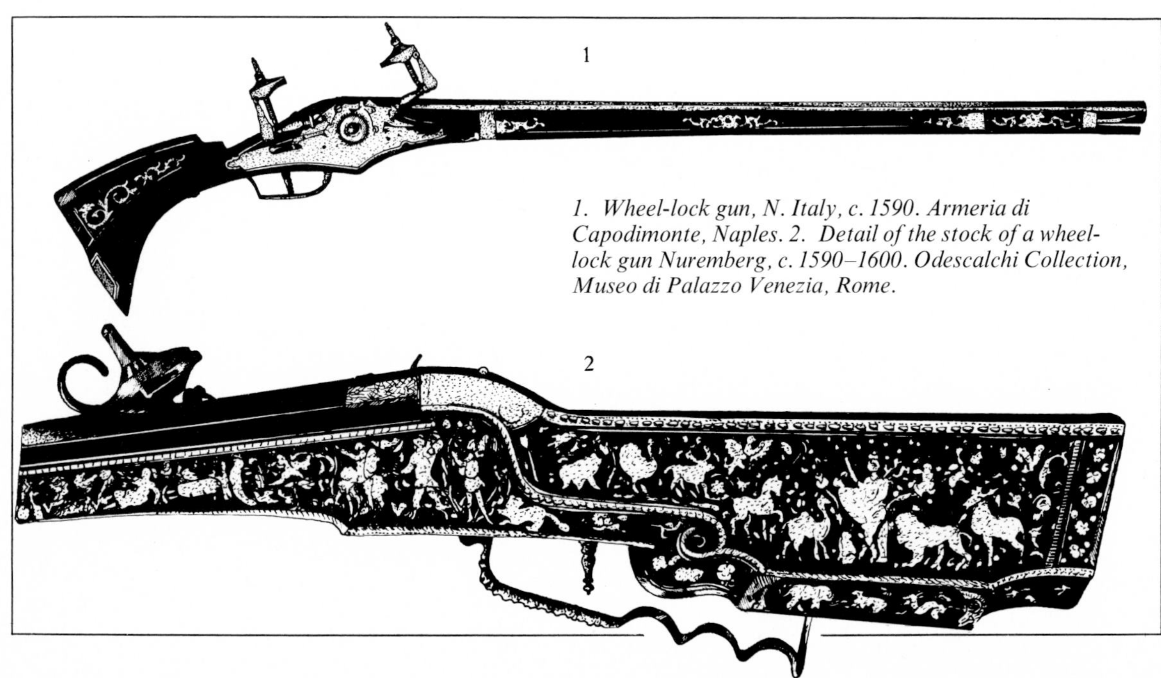


*1. Wheel-lock gun, N. Italy, c. 1590. Armeria di Capodimonte, Naples. 2. Detail of the stock of a wheel-lock gun Nuremberg, c. 1590–1600. Odescalchi Collection, Museo di Palazzo Venezia, Rome.*

magazine fitted over the steel plug and could be rotated. The bottom of the magazine contained fulminate, and the top was fitted with a spring-loaded striker. The magazine was rotated on its axis so that a quantity of powder fell into the pan. It was then returned to its former position so that the striker was positioned on top of the powder. As with the flintlock, the cock fell as the trigger was pulled, driving the striker onto the fulminate, thus causing ignition.

The principle of fulminate had been known since the 17th century. However, the idea of using it to detonate ordinary gunpowder was developed by Alexander John Forsyth (1768–1843) of Belhelvie, Scotland. Although the first percussion lock is said to have been invented in 1805, Forsyth conducted a number of experiments in the Board of Ordnance at the Tower of London and his invention was not patented until 1807. He established premises in London after 1811, and manufactured a number of pistols and sporting guns using the percussion system. It was not until some years after the patent had been taken out that the percussion lock began to replace the flintlock, that is, after about 1820, when the method of using the fulminate in percussion locks was radically improved.

Some experiments had been made in the intervening period with methods of containing the fulminate: in pellets, paper patches, copper tubes, and finally, in small copper caps. The percussion cap was first employed just before 1820, but the earliest known patent for the copper cap was granted to François Prélat, a Parisian gunmaker, in 1820. However, it is known that other gunmakers were experimenting with copper caps before this. Joshua Shaw claimed to have made an iron cap in 1814, although Colonel Peter Hawker, James Purdey, and Joseph Egg all laid claim to this very important invention, which not only made the percussion cap lock a complete success but also laid the foundation for the self-contained cartridges used from the mid-19th century to the present.

Forsyth also devised a percussion lock which used the principle of a sliding magazine, linked to the hammer, which automatically primed the lock as the hammer was pulled back. Firearms fitted with these sliding locks are, however, comparatively rare.

**ikada** Forearm guard in Japanese armor. *See also* KOTE.

**incendiary bottle** *See* MOLOTOV COCKTAIL.

**inner guard** *See* COUNTERGUARD.

**inoshishi-no-yari** A Japanese boar spear with a very wide, heavy blade and thick shaft, often equipped with a stout crossbar, the *hadome*, to prevent the beast from bearing down on the shaft and reaching the hunter. This construction was similar to European boar spears, which were in use during the 15th and 16th centuries, and the possibility, therefore, that the inoshishi-no-yari was the result of European influence cannot be discounted.

**ishizuke** The long locket near the mouth of the scabbard of the TACHI.

**ishizuki** (Also called *Hirumaki*) The metal shoe at the bottom of the stave of a Japanese spear. *See also* YARI.

# J

**jack** Common soldier's armor worn during the 15th and 16th centuries, if not earlier, consisting of a canvas jacket with small overlapping iron plates fixed inside between layers of fabric by trellis-pattern stitches. It was, in fact, a simpler and less expensive version of the BRIGANDINE. A similarly made protective garment of Mongolian origin was called KUYAK in medieval Russia.

**jacket** A fixed casing around bullets for small arms, made from some metal harder than lead. The jacket, which is necessary in small-caliber ammunition to avoid lead fouling of the barrel and tearing of the bullets, with consequent loss of accuracy, may be made from copper, brass, nickel steel, nickel silver, etc. It is essential in ammunition for automatic and semiautomatic weapons to avoid possible deformation of the bullet in the feed process. The jacket is fixed to the core by compression; such bullets are called composite or Lorenz bullets, from the name of the Karlsruhe firm that first produced them.

**jambiya** An Arabian dagger, also used in the Ottoman Empire, Persia, and India, particularly in the 17th and 18th centuries. The typical jambiya blade was double-edged and curved, with a central fuller. Hilts and sheaths varied in shape, and the type of decoration depended on the country or even the district of origin. In the Arabian Peninsula the jambiya was especially venerated as the symbol of a free man: to take his dagger away from a man was a degrading punishment. Not only was it an instrument of war but also of ceremony, being worn at circumcision feasts and weddings. The sheath was much longer than the blade, strongly curved, with a bulbous finial. Some truly beautiful examples can still be found, with silver or gold chasing, filigree work, and rosettes inset with colored stones, the hilt often being of horn, even giraffe horn—appreciated for its yellow color. Some 19th-century Arabian jambiya had U-shaped sheaths, but this was a degenerate form. A richly decorated leather belt usually accompanied the dagger.

In Morocco, jambiya blades were straight and single-edged for about half their length from the hilt and curved and double-edged for the remainder, seldom with fullers.

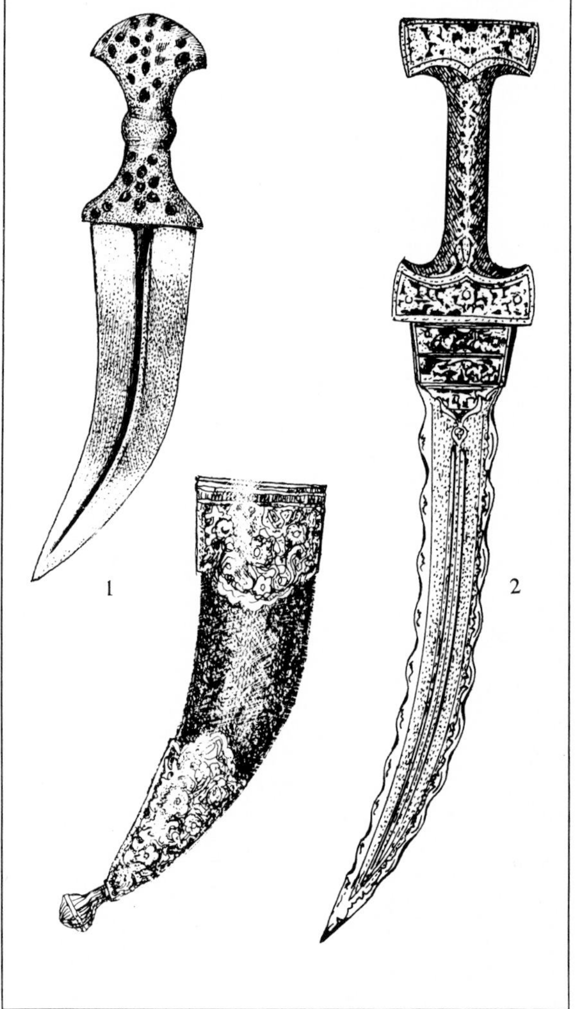


*Jambiya. 1. Delhi, 19th century. Wallace Collection, London. 2. Persia, 18th century. Museo Stibbert, Florence.*

*A javelin thrower depicted on an Attic amphora of the 5th century* B.C. *Museo Nazionale, Naples.*

The hilt had a large, flat pommel of the form known as a "peacock's tail."

In Turkey, jambiya blades were slightly curved, with or without fullers, and the sheaths did not have turned-up ends.

The most beautiful jambiya daggers came from Persia and India. Their blades, of watered Damascus steel, were of excellent workmanship, chased and inlaid with gold, with hilts of carved ivory and jade. They were often inset with semiprecious stones, and the pommels sometimes carved to represent a horse's head. Indo-Persian sheaths were of embossed silver lined with wood or of wood covered with embossed leather or silk brocade.

**jarid** (or **djerid**) An Oriental javelin used from antiquity for war and particularly for hunting, especially in India, Persia, Armenia, Turkey, Arabia, Africa, and occasionally in Poland and Russia. The French painter Eugène Delacroix depicted tigers being hunted with jarids in the first half of the 19th century. Jarids were also used for a form of jousting known as *jarid bazi.*

There are several forms of the jarid, but its basic features are constant: a square steel head about 15 cm. (6 in.) long set in a 70–90 cm. (27–36 in.) shaft with either a ferrule or, more often, a metal flight on the butt to act as a kind of stabilizer. The jarid is finely balanced, and can be thrown with great accuracy. Two or three jarids were usually carried in a flat, leather-covered case decorated and strengthened with metal mounts. In India and Persia, jarids are frequently made entirely of steel, often inlaid with gold.

A number of these weapons were captured from the Turks in the 17th century and have been preserved in Kraków, Dresden, and Vienna. Although some had square heads, most were triangular in section, and typically Turkish features were their hollow sides and horn-covered shafts. African shafts, however, were sometimes overlaid with snakeskin.

**javelin** A light spear, sometimes utilized as a throwing weapon, used on horseback and on foot for hunting and in war from very earliest times. The leaf- or lancet-shaped head could vary a great deal, but was usually not very large, with or without barbs.

Depending on the shape and the people using the javelin, it assumed different names. The Teutonic (Frankish) FRAMEA had a long leaf-shaped head, with a pronounced central rib which sometimes extended downward and reinforced the socket. The ANGON—also Frankish—had a small-tipped head with barbs mounted on a long shaft; it was not used in war beyond the 15th century, but in the 16th century it was used sporadically for hunting. In some countries, such as France and Spain, it remained in use for sporting purposes for some time, and featured in local competitions. Quite often, the javelin also served as a ceremonial weapon of bodyguards. In the Middle East there is evidence of the javelin dating back to antiquity; Assyrian bas-reliefs and artworks of various Mediterranean peoples show it being used for hunting and for combat, by foot soldiers and from chariots. Javelin-throwing was one of the contests in the ancient Olympic Games, and remains an event in the modern games.

**jaws** The two parts of the cock in wheel-lock and flintlock guns which hold, respectively, the pyrites or flint. One jaw is an integral part of the cock, the other, attached by a strong screw, can be screwed up or down to hold the stone firmly.

**jazeran** (or **jazerant**) An alternative term for the KAZĀGHAND.

**jelman** An alternative, but incorrect, spelling of YALMAN.

**jezail** An old type of Afghan gun. Its original matchlock has a serpentine match holder which operated in a slit of the stock with the trigger underneath. The European flintlock was also frequently adapted to the jezail.

The jezail had a very long barrel, usually at least 120 cm. (47 in.), with a smooth or rifled bore which was sometimes as large as 2.5 cm. (1 in.). The length of the barrel increased the effective range of the gun, which was between 200 and 300 m. (218–328 yds.), although this depended on the quality and quantity of powder, type of bullet, and weather conditions. The wooden stock was slender with rawhide, brass, or iron bands and a small curved butt broadening at the end. The gun was quite often decorated with bands and plates in brass or silver, occasionally inset with turquoises. A leather strap was usually attached to

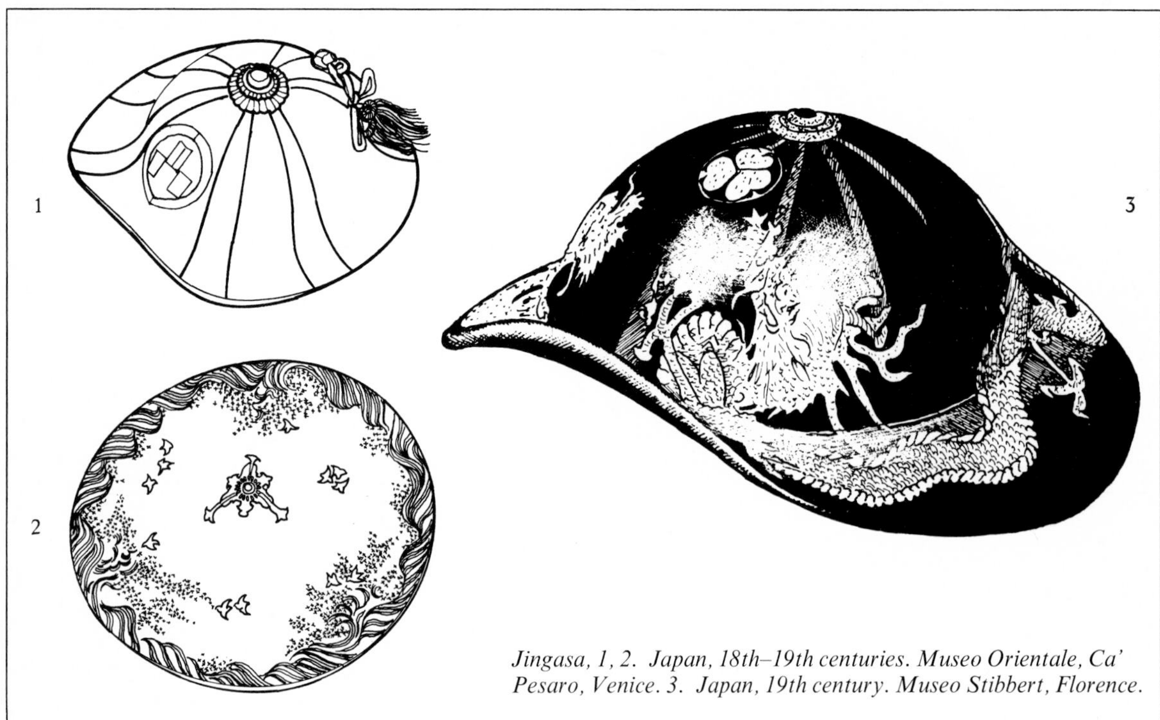


*Jingasa, 1, 2. Japan, 18th–19th centuries. Museo Orientale, Ca' Pesaro, Venice. 3. Japan, 19th century. Museo Stibbert, Florence.*

the stock, together with an A-shaped rest pivoted to a lug at the forestock. The rest served to fix the gun on the ground to fire from the sitting position. A gun rest of the same type was used in Central Asia and Siberia (*lamut* guns) as well as in Tibet.

**jigane** The main body of a Japanese blade. *See also* BLADE: Japanese.

**jineta, espadas á la jineta** *See* HISPANO-MORESQUE SWORDS.

**jingasa** Also called *kasa*, the jingasa was a Japanese war hat, an open helmet worn mainly by foot soldiers and the retainers of noble families. Made of iron, copper, or wood, it imitated the conical straw hats so typical of the Far East; sometimes it was constructed from several plates riveted together, though parade and ceremonial versions of the jingasa were made of lacquered wood.

The exact period in which the jingasa was introduced is not known, but it is represented in old pictures, and surviving examples are dated to the 16th and 17th centuries. These are made in one piece, deeply conical in shape and with a TEHEN opening in the top. Later helmets, from the 18th and 19th centuries, were often of embossed russeted iron decorated with a crest at the front and a bow (*agemaki*) at the back. These were either flat or made with a high, cylindrical crown, usually with a wide brim which generally curved upward in front to improve visibility. Although some were octagonal, they were usually round. Jingasa were lined with pads, and padded loops hung down on each side, below the ears, through which a soft cord or folded cloth was passed so as to be tied under the chin.

**jitte** A Japanese club which was used as a parrying weapon and was also carried by police as a truncheon. It was normally an iron, fan-shaped club, about 25–30 cm. (10–12 in.) long, with a simple handle and a belt hook on one side. One variety of the jitte had three folding blades—two knives and a saw—while another version, although made and mounted like a sword, had a curved iron bar, about 45 cm. (18 in.) long, in place of the blades.

**jousting sockets** *See* TILTING SOCKETS.

**jumon-ji-yari** Another name for the MAGARI-YARI.

**jupon** *See* COAT ARMOR.

*Jezail, Afghan gun. Bernisches Historisches Museum, Bern.*

# K

**kabuto** A general term for a helmet in Japan. There is no particular application of the word, for each type of helmet has its own supplementary definition, which locates it in a definite period or even to an armorer's school. The first Japanese helmets have been traded to prehistoric times, and their development continued until the 19th century, innumerable examples have been produced over the centuries. Nevertheless, a typological order can be established: the basic part of a helmet is the bowl, the HACHI, in which materials, construction, and shape are decisive factors in its value. Japanese helmet bowls have traditionally been made of riveted plates. From the 4th to the 10th centuries, hemispherical bowls with horizontal plates or with intermediate rows of vertical plates, SHŌKAKUFU-HACHI, predominated, but occasionally the Mongol type of bowl, which was also riveted but more conical,—the *Moko-hachi-gyo*, was adopted. In the late 10th century the *hoshi-kabuto* with a large top opening, the TEHEN, appeared, the surface of its bowl being ornamented with large rivet heads, *hoshi* ("stars"). In the front of the hoshi-kabuto was a steep peak, the MABEZASHI, which was to become a permanent feature of Japanese helmets.

In the 14th century a new, purely Japanese design, the SUJI-KABUTO, combined a fine shape and excellent technical features. Small vertical plates were riveted together, and because they overlapped to the extent of providing almost a double layer (the outer ones being convex), they trapped a thin layer of air between the plates,

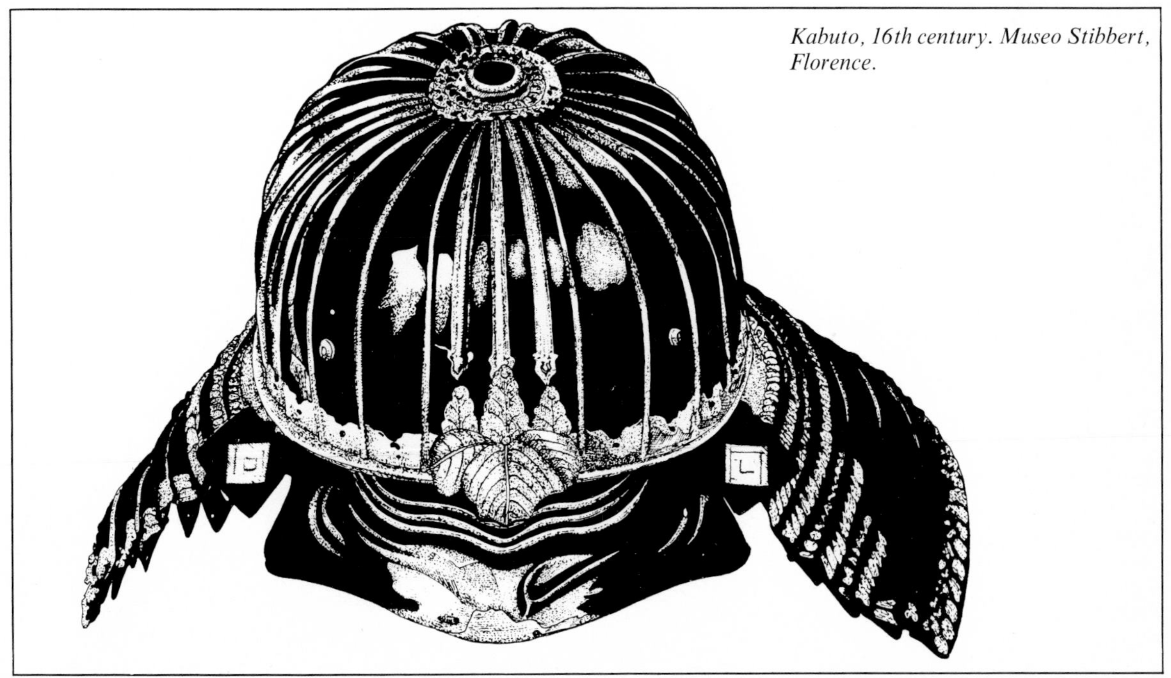

*Kabuto, 16th century. Museo Stibbert, Florence.*

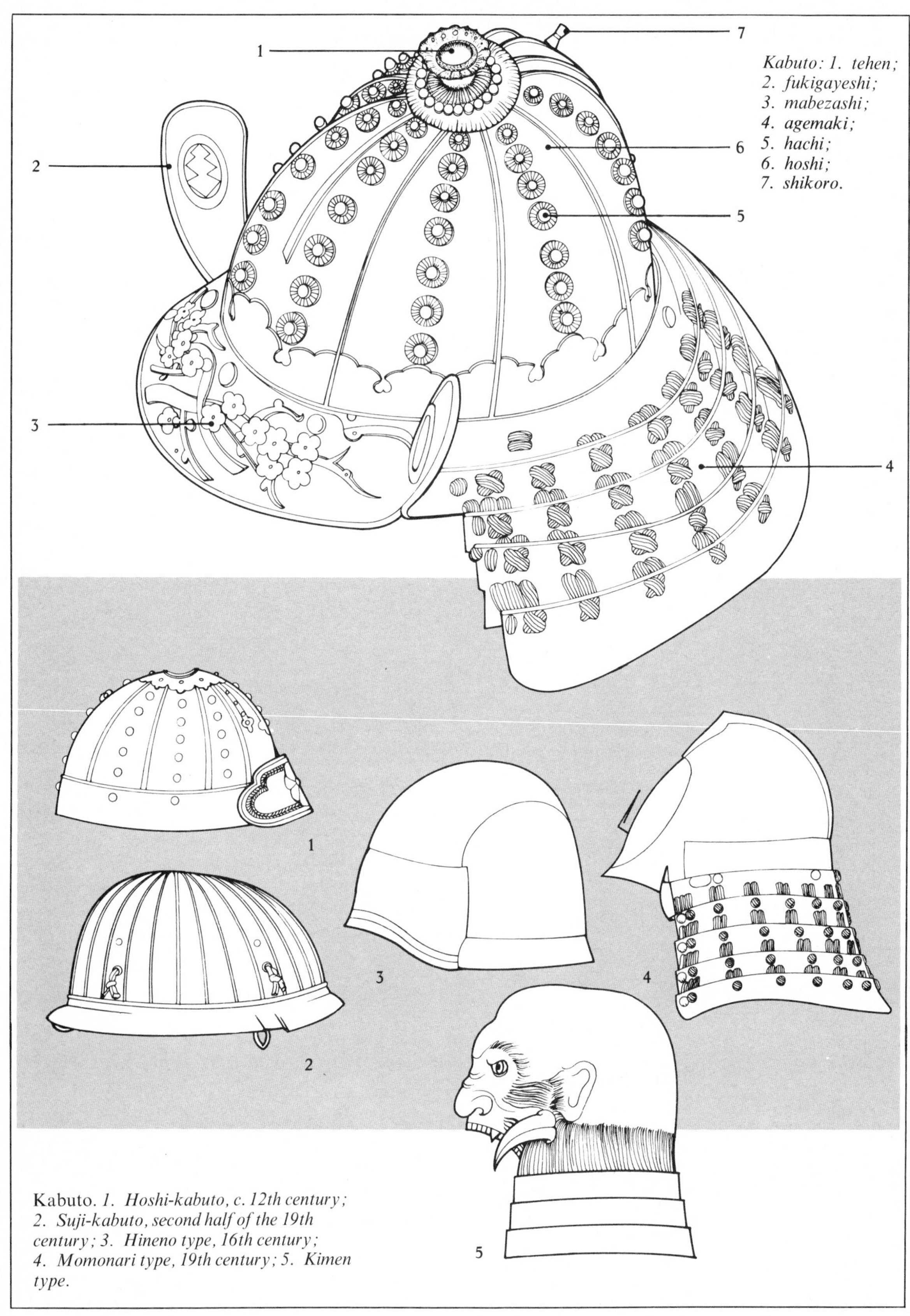


*Kabuto: 1. tehen; 2. fukigayeshi; 3. mabezashi; 4. agemaki; 5. hachi; 6. hoshi; 7. shikoro.*

Kabuto. *1. Hoshi-kabuto, c. 12th century; 2. Suji-kabuto, second half of the 19th century; 3. Hineno type, 16th century; 4. Momonari type, 19th century; 5. Kimen type.*

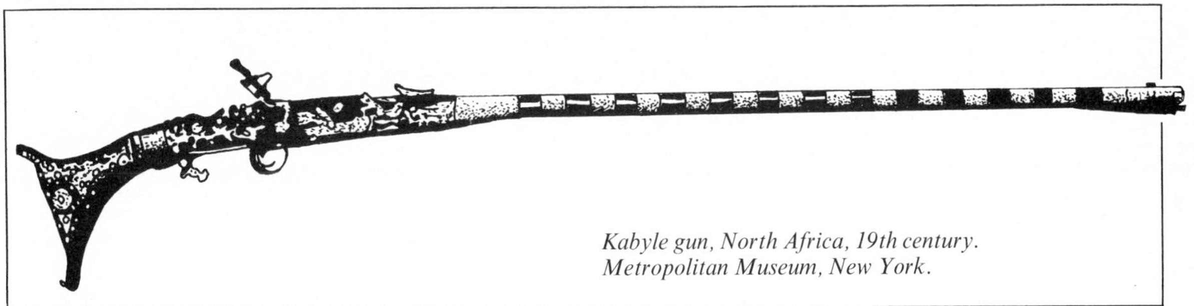

*Kabyle gun, North Africa, 19th century. Metropolitan Museum, New York.*

which produced a cushioning effect against the blows of an opponent's weapon. The large rivet heads were omitted, but the flanged edges, the *suji*, of the plates stood up, forming a ridged surface that resembled that of European fluted armor. The form of the suji-kabuto was extremely sophisticated, almost modern. It followed the shape of the skull but was a little higher at the back and depressed at the top. Brass, silver and gold, and leather and lacquer were used to decorate the hoshi-kabuto, the suji-kabuto, and later types. Beginning in the 16th century, helmets of large plates, such as those of the Hineno and the Haruta schools, were constructed, while, under European influence, helmets made of one piece also came into use. Some very heavy bowls were made for special purposes, for they were resistant to firearms, and some Portuguese and Dutch cabassets were adapted for the kabuto.

During the Tokugawa (Edo) period (1603–1867) the hachi took on various shapes, each of which was named for the object it was intended to represent, for example, the *momonari*, a peach; the *to kamurai*, imitating the *kamuri*, a ceremonial hat; and the *kimen*, a demon's head. Some bowls of this decadent period were embossed with grotesque masks, which created a theatrical effect; others represented the god of good luck, Fukuroku-Ju. The TATAMI KABUTO was a folding helmet made of horizontal rings that were laced together so that the helmet could be shut down almost flat. In the front of the hachi, crests or other ornaments, MAIDATE, usually horn-shaped, were fixed on a socket, the *haridate*. At the back there was usually a ring to attach the ritual *agemaki* bow or another badge, the *kasajirushi*. A very important part of the kabuto was the neck guard, the SHIKORO with wings or protective flaps, the FUKIGAYESHI. This laminated neck guard was usually very large; it consisted of three or five lames, hence the terms *sammai-kabuto* (three-plate helmet) and *gomai-kabuto* (five-plate helmet).

The ancient kabuto had no lining; a headcloth, the *hachimaki*, was wrapped around the head to act as a shock absorber. Later the helmet lining was made of leather or closely stitched fabric, attached to the inside edge of the bowl and with crossed reinforcing straps over it. The kabuto cord was attached to three, four, or five rings or cord loops on the brim of the helmet; it varied in length from 180 to 270 cm. (71–106 in.) according to the method employed for securing the helmet to the head. It was customary for a kabuto helmet, which was usually worn with a face defense or war mask (*see* MENPO), to be compatible with the accompanying armor.

**kabuto gane** The pommel on a particular type of Japanese sword. *See also* TACHI.

**Kabyle gun** A conventional term for a gun of a particular form that was popular in North Africa, especially among the Kabyles—a tribe of Berbers intermixed with Arabs in Algeria, Tunisia, and Morocco. A Kabyle gun was exceptionally long, 180 cm. (71 in.) or more, with a plain barrel linked to the stock by about twelve iron, brass, or silver bands. When silver was used, it was often nielloed. The stock and trumpet-shaped butt might be inlaid with ivory and silver plates.

Two systems of flintlocks prevailed in Kabyle guns. One, which derived from Dutch and English types of "snaphance" lock, was made heavier than the original patterns. It had a thick plate, a massive cock, and a large circular pan fence, which was often a feature of 17th-century Dutch locks. Another mechanism was the so-called Arab dock lock, or Kabyle lock, a form of the "miquelet" group of flintlocks. It had a curved plate and a small cock with long, massive jaws topped by a screw with a spherical head and a V-shaped finger grip. The external mainspring acted on the toe of the cock (as in another Mediterranean mechanism, the "alla romana," or Italian, lock). Half cock was provided by a dog catch behind the cock, while the sear, passing through the plate, engaged a recess in the heel of the cock in firing position. The steel and pan cover were combined in one piece. Besides these mechanisms, which were introduced in the 17th century, other types of locks, including discarded military locks, imported from Europe, were occasionally fitted to Kabyle guns at a later date. During the first half of the 19th century, "Kabyle" guns for the Arab trade were extensively reproduced in Liège—hence their nickname "Mahomet trade guns."

**kaddara** A Persian infantry sword, sometimes also used in Turkey. It had the form of a KAMA but was much larger. The sides of its broad, double-edged blade, which had a total length of about 75 cm. (30 in.), were almost parallel and met in a sharp point.

**kalkan** A light, round shield typical of many countries of the East, from India and Persia to Arabia and Turkey, and west to Hungary and Poland. Its basic wickerwork structure often consisted mainly of fig wands interwoven with threads of wool, cotton, or silk, with a large metal boss or UMBO in the center. Several rivets with decorative heads fixed the loops for the carrying cord on the inside. A stuffed pad was usually worked into the cloth lining to serve as a hand rest. A battle kalkan was invariably quite plain, with an unadorned iron boss, but there were also many costly examples set with jewels, covered with samite (silk fabric interwoven with gold thread) and plates of silver gilt encrusted with semiprecious stones and lined with velvet or other rich fabrics. A kalkan such as this must have been very colorful, for different types of thread were used to weave the geometric or floral motifs on the outside. Sometimes simple scroll ornamentations with inscriptions were also painted on them.

The kalkan can be traced as far back as Achaemenian Persia: it is shown in the bas-reliefs of Persepolis. It gained popularity throughout the Islamic world as a cavalry shield because it was light yet resistant and gave protection even when complicated turns were being executed in mounted combat as well as in real or feigned flight.

The kalkan was depicted many times in Persian miniatures of the Safavid Dynasty (16th to early 18th centuries), but very few of the shields have survived. Many Turkish kalkan, however, are preserved in the museums of Istanbul and in some European museums where Turkish booty is kept (e.g. in Kraków, Warsaw, Dresden, Vienna, Leningrad, and Moscow).

**kama** A Caucasian dagger, the kama was used by various peoples and tribes of the Caucasus and the surrounding area of southern Russia, especially by the Cossacks. The double edges of its broad, straight blade ended in a long, sharp point. Kama blades varied in length from about 10 cm. (4 in.) to 50 cm. (20 in.) and usually were multifullered on each face. Quite often, there was only one deep groove on each face; the grooves were decentralized to avoid the weakening of the structure that would have resulted from putting fullers in the middle of both faces.

The hilt, which swelled out at the base to take the blade, was straight with a broad, oblong pommel, and was riveted to the tang. It was made of two pieces of wood, black horn, ivory, or bone. Velvet or black leather covered the wooden sheath, which was furnished with silver, iron, or brass chapes and lockets, although it was sometimes entirely overlaid with decorated metal. Nielloeing of all the silver parts was quite common, and some kama were decorated with embossed silver inset with coral, as in the Turkish style.

The kama has remained part of the Caucasian national costume and used to be worn by some Cossack regiments of the Russian Imperial Army.

**kaman** A characteristic Indian bow belonging to a large category of Oriental reflex composite bows. It is also referred to as a "Tartar" bow. A typical example was constructed with a wooden core, a sinew back, and a horn belly. Great care was taken in gluing the pieces together. The convex handle was painted or lacquered all over in red and gold or black and yellow, although it was sometimes covered with brocade. When the bow was unstrung and the ends curved back because of the tension of the sinew backing, the kaman's total length was about 1 m. (39 in.). It took great skill to string a reflex bow, for the ends had to be bent downward. A few kaman were made entirely of steel, as in the Persian style.

**kama-yari** A Japanese spear with a picklike head set at right angles to a straight shaft. The slightly curved blade was usually tanged, but a socketed version was not uncommon. There was a small and a large version of this weapon; the latter was known as *ō-kama-yari*. The cutting edge varied from about 15 to 25 cm. (6–10 in.).

**kampilan** (or **campilan**) A Malayan sword, the national weapon of the Sea Dyaks of Borneo. Its blade, which may vary from 45 to 70 cm. (17–28 in.) in length, is straight, single-edged, and wider at the point than at the hilt, often with a scroll-like projection from the back near the point. Its carved hardwood hilt has a bifurcated pommel and a simple trapezoidal guard. The grip is bound with wire, and the pommel is decorated with tufts of hair dyed red or black. The scabbard is made from two pieces of wood held together by two fastenings which have to be undone in order to sheathe or draw the sword. In an emergency, a blow can be struck while the weapon is still sheathed; the blade will cut through the lashings, and the two halves of the scabbard will fall away.

Another type of kampilan scabbard consists of a solid single piece of hardwood that broadens at the center; a loop handle carved out of the wood itself enables one to use the scabbard as a parrying shield.

**kamuraita** A shoulder plate on a Japanese armored sleeve. *See also* KOTE.

**karabela** A type of saber with a characteristic hilt whose curved pommel was a symbolic representation of an eagle's head. The karabela had probably developed by the early 17th century in Ottoman Turkey and soon spread

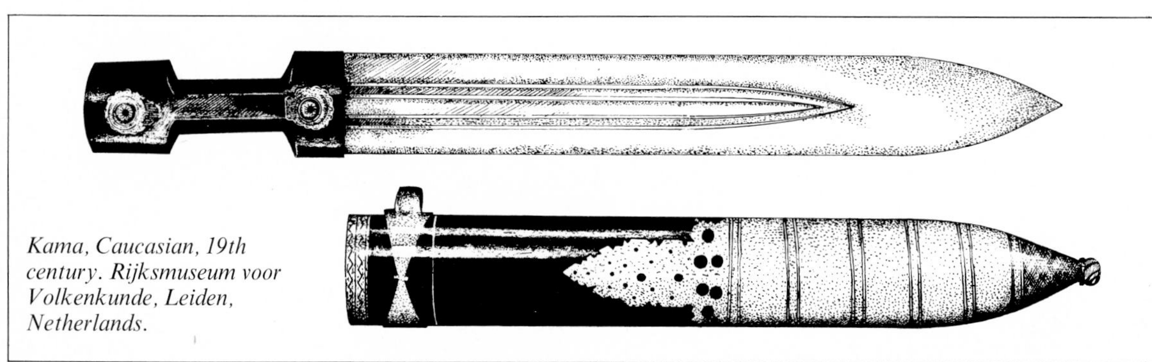

*Kama, Caucasian, 19th century. Rijksmuseum voor Volkenkunde, Leiden, Netherlands.*

throughout the Islamic countries, from Persia and India to North Africa as well as eastern Europe. A number of variations evolved in many areas, but none achieved widespread popularity. Perhaps the most outstanding variation was the pommel that curved at a right angle to the grip, which acted as a support for the hand.

There were two kinds of karabela. The one for use in battle usually had an imported blade (from Austria or other European country) and a hilt made of two pieces of dark horn mounted in iron or brass with very scanty decoration. The other was used for display occasions and was normally fitted with a blade of Damascus steel inlaid with gold and a hilt of ivory or of gilded, chased, or nielloed silver; sometimes grip plates were set with semiprecious stones, and in a few instances these plates were of pure gold.

The karabela was adopted in Poland at the end of the 17th century, where it was subsequently developed as the saber worn with the national costume and for combat. The karabela was produced in Poland in large quantities and was even defined by some 19th-century scholars as a typically Polish weapon. At first this type of saber was primarily made of imported parts, but everything was made locally at a later date. Karabela were manufactured in Kraków, Lublin, Lvov, and other cities. Even in the late 19th and early 20th centuries, they were worn by city dignitaries and other important citizens on national occasions.

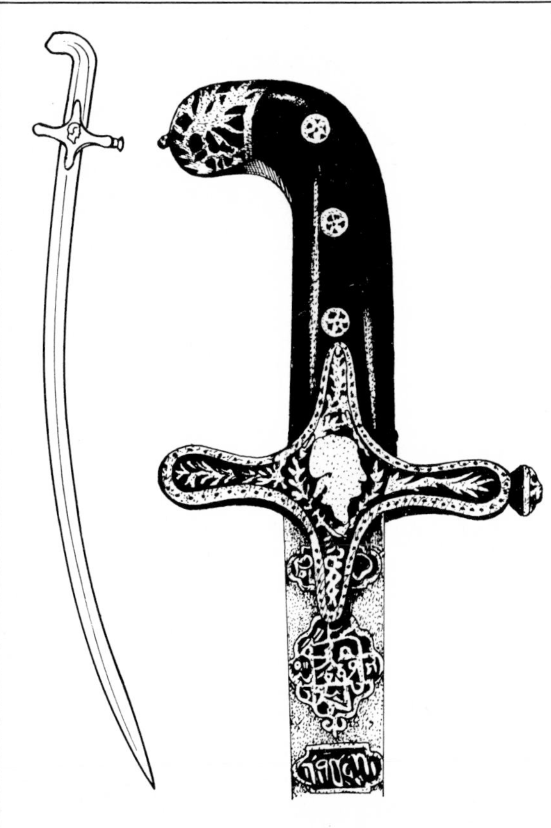

*Karabela dating from the second half of the 18th century, presented to King Stanislav August Poniatowski by a Turkish ambassador. Muzeum Wojska Polskiego, Warsaw.*

*Kard, Persia, 18th century. Museo Stibbert, Florence.*

**karacena** Polish term for the KORAZIN, a type of scale armor especially popular in Poland during the 17th century.

**kara-shino-suneate** An alternative word for SUNEATE.

**kard** An Islamic knife widespread in Persia, Armenia, Turkey, Central Asia, and India. Although the kard was made before and after the 17th and 18th centuries, most examples date from this period. It had a straight, single-edged blade averaging 20–40 cm. (8–16 in.) in length, usually of fine watered steel, which sometimes had a thickened point to enable it to pierce mail. The forte was frequently chiseled and inlaid with gold. It had no guard, and its straight hilt widened slightly toward the end; the grip was of bone, horn, or ivory. If the hilt was made of decorated copper gilt, the sheath too would have been mounted in copper gilt, and covered in red velvet; silver was also used, for pierced or embossed lockets and chapes. The wooden sheaths were covered with tooled leather and embossed mounts. A characteristic of a kard sheath was that it only partially covered the hilt.

A Turkish kard, with a whetstone attached on a band, is among the Turkish booty from the battle of Vienna (1683) preserved in the Czartoryski Collection in Kraków.

**Kardiophylax** A type of armor, of Italic origin, for the torso. *See also* CUIRASS; LORICA.

**karwasz** (pronounced "karvash") Polish word for BAZUBAND.

**kasa** An alternative word for JINGASA.

**kashira** The pommel cap of a Japanese sword or dagger, nearly always made of metal such as copper, iron, silver, gold, and various alloys, although occasionally made of horn. A cord, which passed through two openings in the bottom of the kashira, secured it to the handle. The kashira and the FUCHI were decorated *en suite*; the two mounts linked an allegorical theme, part of the story appearing on one and the remainder on the other.

Because of their imaginative designs and embodiment of a wide range of techniques, kashira, like fuchi and MENUKI are often objects of collectors' interest.

**kashira-date** A type of MAIDATE.

**kaskara** The sword carried by some Saharan tribes, especially related to the Barghirmi Sultanate, a powerful Moslem state that extended over a wide area near Lake Chad in the 16th and 17th centuries. Barghirmi warriors,

*Karacena, Poland, early 18th century. Wawel Collection, Kraków.*

like the European knights of the early Crusades, wore mail armor and were armed with lances and swords; their horses were protected by armored caparisons.

The kaskara was used in many other African regions, including the Sudan, until recent times. Its form was consistent throughout the region, although the blades varied in quality from place to place. The original Arab blades date from as far back as the 10th century, but a few hundred years later blades for the kaskara were being imported from Europe, usually from Solingen or Toledo. Local blades continued to be produced, but they were usually of inferior quality and carried faked old Arabic inscriptions.

The kaskara blade was straight, between 80 and 100 cm. (31–39 in.) long, double-edged, and with a central fuller. The hilt followed the European pattern, but it was much more primitive: the cross guard was always straight and made of poor-quality iron, although some examples were gold-plated; the grip was bound with thongs; the flat, mushroom like pommel was flat and sometimes gold-plated, like the cross guard, or overlaid with leather. The leather scabbard, which widened towards the lower end purely for the sake of appearance, was furnished with iron chapes, lockets, and a sword belt. For swords of better quality, the scabbards were sometimes covered in velvet.

**kastane** The national saber of Sri Lanka (formerly Ceylon). Most of the blades were imported from Europe; from the 18th century, many bore the mark of the Dutch East India Company. In fact, it was customary for officials of the company to be presented with a miniature kastane as a token of respect. The blade is generally curved, single-edged, and heavy, although averaging only 55–70 cm. (21–28 in.) in length, but straight, single-edged PALLASCH-type blades, about 75 cm. (30 in.) long, are not unknown. Some kastane blades are decorated with engraved brass plates on the forte. The hilt, of local make, is usually made entirely of brass and decorated with chiseling and inlaid silver, although the grip is frequently of ivory or horn. The hilt is furnished with one pair of quillons with a knuckle guard and a second pair that turn down toward the blade. The pommel and finials of the quillons are made to represent the heads of monsters. Sabers of better quality are lavishly ornamented with gold or set with stones. The carved wood or horn scabbards are overlaid with embossed brass, silver, or gold.

**kataha** The specially fused steel bar from which Japanese blades were forged. *See also* BLADE: Japanese.

**katana** One of the most important Japanese swords. The first Japanese swords were straight and single- or double-edged. These swords were followed by the TACHI, a single-edged curved sword, which was more like a saber and hung, edge downward, from the belt. Over the centuries, the tachi became a ceremonial sword that accompanied the katana, the fighting sword, which was similar in form but less curved; it was also a little shorter, about 60 cm. (24 in.) long, was mounted differently, and was carried thrust through the belt, edge upward. It was normally worn with the WAKIZASHI to form a DAI-SHO. The blades of the tachi and the katana did not differ greatly, but they were signed on opposite sides of the tang, always on the side that was

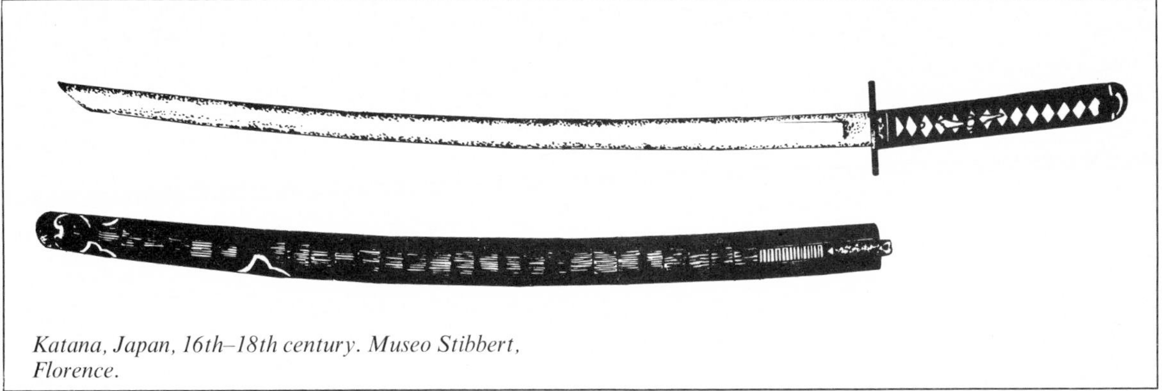

*Katana, Japan, 16th–18th century. Museo Stibbert, Florence.*

on the outside when the sword was carried.

The blade was, of course, of principal importance in the katana, as it was in other Japanese swords and daggers. The old tested steel blades were costly and highly valued; they were handed down from generation to generation but were often fitted with new mountings, hilts, TSUBAS, and scabbards. The katana hilt consisted of a wooden grip, about 20–25 cm. (8–10 in.) long, oval in section, pierced for the tang, and covered with SAMÉ (fishskin) or sometimes with metal plates; it was always bound with cord, flat braid or whalebone and fitted with the KASHIRA pommel, MENUKI ornaments at the sides of the grip, and the FUCHI ferrule next to the guard. Between two oval washers, and *seppa dai*, the tsuba guard was mounted on the tang, and beneath it was another collar, the HABAKI made of colored metal; it fit tightly to both blade and scabbard to prevent the edge from rubbing against the latter and to protect the blade against humidity. A bamboo peg, the *mekugi*, was passed through the holes of the grip and the hole of the tang, thus fastening the hilt to the blade; it could easily be removed if the sword had to be dismantled. The menuki metal ornaments were originally used to cover the ends of this peg. The cord binding of the hilt held the menuki and the kashira in place, and there were several patterns according to which the cord was arranged.

The katana scabbard was usually made of lacquered *honoki*, a fine-grained light magnolia wood, and was frequently decorated with its owner's crest or other ornamental features. Black lacquer was often used because it accorded with the highest criterion of beauty, *shibui*, meaning austere, dark, or toned down; however, red and rust-colored lacquers were also favored. In the Tokugawa (Edo) period (1603–1867), polychromic lacquer with marbling effects was in fashion, and sometimes the whole scabbard was covered with fishskin. Quite modern katana, made for the foreign market as expensive souvenirs from Japan, have hilts and scabbards in carved ivory or, in inferior specimens, bone, but this sword has nothing to do with the noble tradition of Japanese swords. In a good-quality katana, one or two small sheaths were sometimes hollowed out in the sides of the scabbard for the KOZUKA knife and the KŌGAI head pin, but these usually accompanied short swords. The edge of the opening for the kozuka was protected by a flat piece of metal, the *uragawara* (*see* SAYA), and that for the kōgai by the *kurikata*, made of horn, lacquered wood, or metal. The kurikata was a projecting lug with an opening through which a flat silk cord, the *sageo*, was passed in order to fasten the scabbard to the belt. Occasionally a hook of horn or metal, the *soritsuno* (*see* SAYA), was attached to the scabbard a few inches below the kurikata to prevent the scabbard from being pulled through the belt when the sword was drawn. A ring, the *kuchi-kane*, was often fitted around the mouth of the scabbard; its tip was either lacquered, in keeping with the main part, or a piece of horn was glued to it; metal chapes, *kojiri* (*see* SAYA), were also used. All the metal mounts were decorated with engraving or inlay *en suite*, although in general the katana was not lavishly decorated.

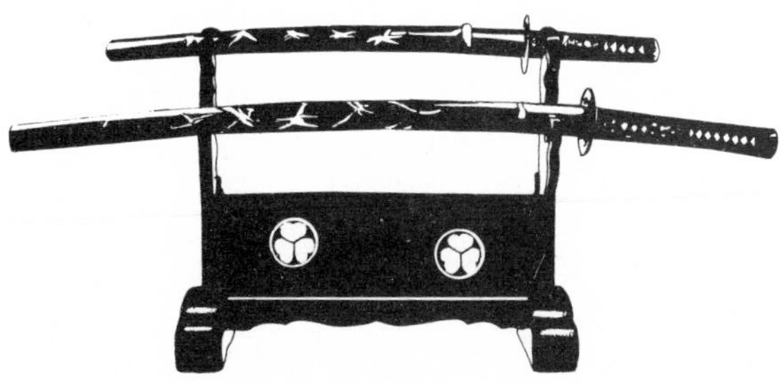

*Katana-kake with dai-shō sword, Japan, early 19th century. Museo Stibbert, Florence.*

There were various methods of testing the quality of a katana. Because a fighting sword was supposed to be capable of cutting off a man's head at a single stroke, the katana was tried out on criminals condemned to death or on dead bodies. Various types of cuts perfected during these tests were recognized. The katana, along with the tachi and other types of swords, was the object of an elaborate code of etiquette. The KATANA-KAKE, the stand on which the sword was laid, edge up, the hilt to the right, was a fine lacquered accessory and stood in a place of honor in the house. The sword was usually transported in a special case, the *katana zutsu*, made of lacquered wood decorated with the owner's crest. There was a prescribed code for handling, presenting, and admiring a katana; a different ritual was followed to provoke an opponent to combat.

**katana-kake** A Japanese sword stand or rack used not only for the katana but also for other types of edged weapons. At one time the racks were commonly made from a pair of deer horns set in a block of wood, but were later constructed of lacquered wood, in various animal and other forms, to hold a single sword, a pair of swords, or a set of edged weapons. Two kinds of racks exist: the vertical, in which each sword is placed with the point upright, and the horizontal, in which each sword is placed horizontally with the hilt to the right. TACHI are always positioned with their edges facing downward, but the edges face upward in all other cases.

Sometimes a small cabinet, with drawers for extra fittings, was built into the katana-kake. Folding racks could be used for traveling.

**katar** (or **kutar**) An Indian (Hindu) thrusting dagger, seldom used by Moslems and never encountered outside India, although European blades were often adapted to the katar. Its handle, a particularly unusual feature, consisted of two parallel bars connected by one or two crosspieces to form the grip. To strike a blow with this weapon, all that was required was to push the arm forward. Some katars were furnished with an S-shaped, convex plate guard, which were either plain or elaborately pierced and embossed. The typical katar blade was straight, broad, rather short (30 cm./12 in.), double-edged, and either fullered or ribbed. Other blade forms existed, however, including curved, bifurcated, and extremely long (70 cm./27 in.). Other types had scalloped edges, and there was even a blade type that folded into three parts; it was opened by squeezing a spring grip. Another variation, which demonstrated the extent to which Indian swordsmiths exercised their skill and imagination, was the sliding katar, whose blade was divided into two parts; the shorter was nearer the handle, and the longer was hollowed out so that the smaller part could be inserted into it. Some blades were thickened at the point so as to pierce mail.

Katar sheaths were usually leather, mounted in metal or wood and covered with velvet. From the katar the Mahratta gauntlet sword, the PATA, evolved.

**Katzbalger** A type of broadsword used in the late 15th and 16th centuries, particularly by the landsknechts of Switzerland and Germany. In its classic form, the Katzbalger was comprised of a broad, double-edged, straight blade with almost horizontal S-shaped quillons and a faceted grip widening at the pommel. The central part of the quillons extended to form a short socket into which the grip—usually wooden—was fitted. The pommel cap also extended down the grip, leaving exposed only a short section of the grip. The leather scabbard sometimes contained a pocket at the top in which small knives were kept. Perhaps the most famous example of a Katzbalger is that of the military leader Ulrick von Schellenberg, dating from about 1515; it is preserved in Vienna. In almost perfect condition, the hilt is of gilded iron, engraved and chased, and the scabbard contains its original set of small knives. As with other examples, the S-shaped quillons are decoratively roped at intervals and terminate in large spheres.

The Katzbalger was depicted in many engravings of landsknechts, which show the broadsword worn parallel to the ground and the point slightly raised. Another example of this form of sword can be seen in the London Museum; it dates from about 1520. The hilt bears an escutcheon engraved with the imperial eagle. It was excavated from the bank of the Thames during building operations in the last century. It has been suggested that the original wearer might have been one of the German mercenaries employed by Henry VIII.

Two theories have been advanced to explain the name. First, that this type of sword was carried by the landsknechts without a scabbard, but instead, was covered with the skin of a cat (*Katzenfell*) so that it could be drawn swiftly. The much more reasonable theory is that the name comes from the German slang verb *Katzbalger*, meaning to fight at close quarters, to tussle.

**kawagasa** A Japanese leather helmet worn by foot soldiers and servants of the nobility. Usually made of a special kind of leather known as *neri-gasa*, it was lacquered black on both sides. The kawagasa bowl was low and rounded with ribs, in imitation of the SUJI-KABUTO, and had a large peak in the front. Some leather helmets are known to have had pointed bowls.

**kazāghand** An Arabic word for a type of Oriental mail armor used in Turkey, Persia, and Arabia from the 11th century onward. It consisted of a mail shirt, cloth-lined and covered with good-quality fabric—often silk—which was sometimes colored, patterned, and padded. Although expensive, it must have been quite a popular type of armor because it was comfortable to wear and attractive in appearance. It was not durable, however; the cloth soon wore out, especially under conditions of war. Only a few examples are well preserved, one of which is in the Topkapi Sarayi Museum in Istanbul. This kazāghand has

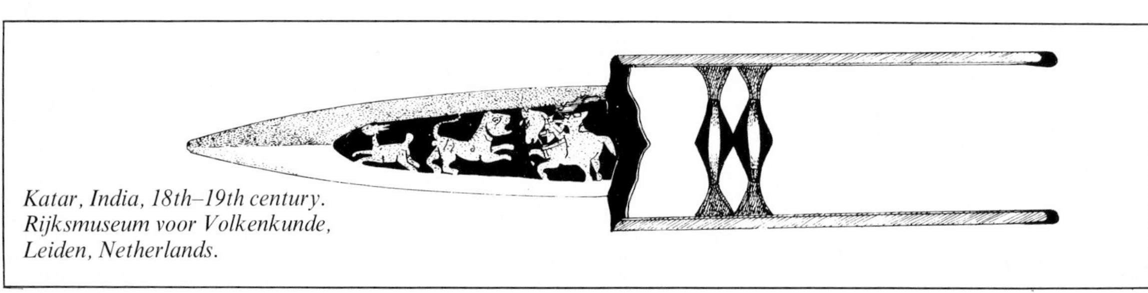

*Katar, India, 18th–19th century. Rijksmuseum voor Volkenkunde, Leiden, Netherlands.*

*Keiko armor, as worn by a Japanese warrior, 6th–7th century. Archeological Museum, Aikawa Prefecture of Gunma.*

long sleeves, mitten-like extensions for the backs of the hands, small buttons with corresponding loops to close the center front and the sleeves at the wrists, and two pocket-like patches for the attachment of cartridge clips across the top on each side of the breast. The term *jazerant* is a national name derived from *kazāghand* for the same type of mail armor.

**kebiki** A style of lacing of the plates in Japanese armor. *See also* ODOSHI.

**keikō** Early Japanese armor, used mostly between the 5th and 8th centuries, showing a strong influence of the Chinese and Korean cultures. The keikō, made entirely of laced lamellae, was soon adapted to the form of the earlier TANKŌ as far as the new method of construction would permit. A new form of helmet, with a rounded bowl and a broad flat peak, was introduced to accompany the keikō. The bowl was constructed of horizontal hoops alternating with rows of triangular segments riveted together, the top being surmounted with a cuplike finial with pierced holes for the fastening of a crest of hair or feathers. The neck guards of the helmet were of curved iron strips like those of the tankō helmet. The lamellar body armor of the keikō was in the form of a sleeveless jacket opening at the front, with a skirt reaching to the upper part of the thighs; a waist was formed by using narrow concave lamellae, while a row of shorter concave plates gave rigidity to the bottom edge of the skirt. The armor was held on the body by means of cotton shoulder straps. Neck and shoulder guards for the keikō were also made of laced lamellae, and the arm defenses were constructed of splints, shaped to fit the forearm closely, without hand guards, or in the tubular style, as in the tankō. Keikō armor was still used in the early Heian period (794–896); it became more and more squared in outline and was the starting point for the Japanese great armor, the *ō-yoroi* (*see* YOROI).

**keikō-naginata** A Japanese pole weapon used in training. *See also* NAGINATA.

**keikō-yari** A Japanese wooden lance used in fencing. *See also* YARI.

**ken** A very ancient type of Japanese sword going back to prehistoric times. Examples found in burial mounds were reproduced as ceremonial temple swords; surviving specimens date mainly from the 15th and 16th centuries. The ken had a straight, double-edged iron blade that sometimes widened slightly close to the point. Its iron hilt was equipped with a long ribbed grip, a ring pommel, and quillons with finials turned back to form small rings.

No scabbards of the early ken have been preserved, but they were certainly made of wood. Those of later specimens—particularly of the temple swords—were of lacquered wood decorated with floral motifs and sacred or symbolic animals such as dragons.

**kettle hat** Also called the shapewe, a helmet worn by common infantry soldiers and besieging forces from the 12th century to the end of the 17th. It was also worn by the knightly classes (one is known to have been lent to King Louis in Jerusalem to give some relief from his heavy, airless helm). It consisted of a spherically skulled iron hat, sometimes drawn up to a small point at the apex, with a broad brim running all the way around, which was either horizontal or downward sloping. There was sometimes an eye slit pierced through the thick iron.

In the early 16th century a further thickening of the skull took place, the width of the brim was reduced, and a low comb was sometimes formed on the skull. These modifications tended to render the helmet more resistant to hits coming from city walls during a siege.

A lighter form of steel hat appeared in the second half of the 16th century; it was widely adopted in northern European countries. Still in use by the infantry in the 17th century, it was also being worn by some cavalry units. The skull, which had become a great deal lighter than its predecessors, was either foreshortened and conical or

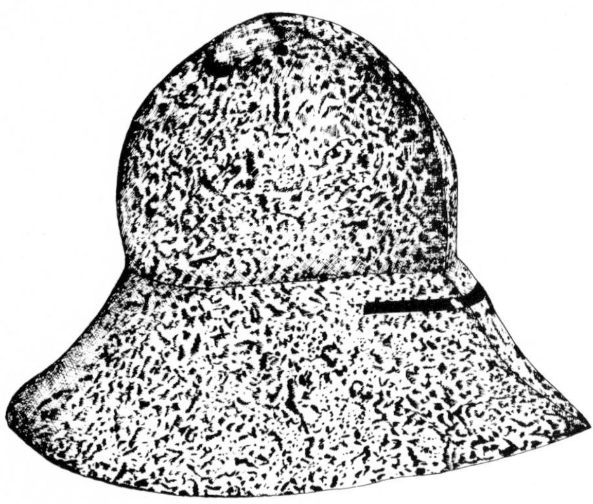

*Kettle hat, Germany, c. 1440. Museo Civico L. Marzoli, Brescia.*

round and had a narrow, straight brim; sometimes a slot was pierced at the center front of the brim for a movable nasal bar.

Apart from line incisions and rows of brass rivets, kettle hats were usually not decorated. There were some exceptions in the 17th century, however, when they were sometimes russeted and even gilded, and crest holders too were not unusual. Similar to the kettle hat was the PIKEMAN'S POT.

**khanda** A traditional Indian sword, the national weapon of the state of Orissa; also used by the Rajputs and the Mahrattas. Its straight, broad blade widens toward the blunt point and is usually single-edged (though double-edged khanda are sometimes found) with a decorated metal border on the back. The grip curves slightly forward and has a broad closed guard, which continues up to the large, flat, circular pommel and is comfortably padded for the hand. A slightly curved spike projects from the center of the pommel, which acts not only as an additional guard but may also be used as a grip for the other hand when a two-handed blow is needed. The khanda scabbard is usually leather with an embossed silver chape.

**khanjar** (or **kanjar, kinjal, handshar**) A word applied in various countries to denote the dagger in general, although in Arabic it means "knife." In Turkey and Yugoslavia the YATAGAN is often referred to as a khanjar. In Persia and India the typical khanjar has a slightly recurved double-edged blade, generally of watered steel and often fullered or ribbed, with inlays of gold. The so-called pistol hilt may be of jade, crystal, ivory, or metal and is frequently inset with colored stones and gold. The sheath, shaped to the blade, is furnished with pierced and chased metal mounts. In Russia *kinjal* is a general term for daggers.

**khanjarli** An Indian dagger not unlike a khanjar, with a recurved blade, usually fullered, about 12.5–25 cm. (5–10 in.) long. The hilt is frequently exquisitely worked in ivory and topped by a large, fan-shaped pommel, with or without a knuckle guard. The sheath is generally covered with velvet and furnished with silver mounts.

**khotun** An ancient Chinese gun. *See also* TUKHOTSIAN.

**Khyber knife** An Afghan knife, the national weapon of the Afridis and other tribes, who live near the Khyber Pass, between Afghanistan and Pakistan. The Khyber knife shows an affinity to the KARD. Its blade is straight and single-edged, and tapers gradually from the hilt to the point, with a wide rib at the back; its length varies from about 35 to 70 cm. (13–28 in.). The hilt normally has no guard, but in some examples there is a kind of knuckle guard. The grip consists of two pieces of horn, bone, or ivory riveted to the tang. The leather sheath is long enough to conceal the entire weapon, including the handle, and it is worn thrust into the belt.

**kia** A Chinese cuirass made of hide. *See also* ARMOR: Chinese.

**kiai** A Chinese armor made of leather scales. *See also* ARMOR: Chinese.

**kidney dagger** A modern term for the ballock knife. *See also* DAGGER.

**kikko** A light Japanese armor structurally similar to the European BRIGANDINE of the 15th and 16th centuries. It consisted of a cloth jacket reinforced with small plates of iron or steel; hard leather plates were also used. The plates were generally small hexagons, with a hole in the middle, quilted between layers of cloth and frequently tied with a thread through their central holes.

The kikko was worn in the form of a short jacket for particular occasions when security precautions were needed, for example, while traveling or walking in wild

*Khanda, India, 18th century. Wallace Collection, London.*

*Khanjarli, India, 19th century. Museo Stibbert, Florence.*

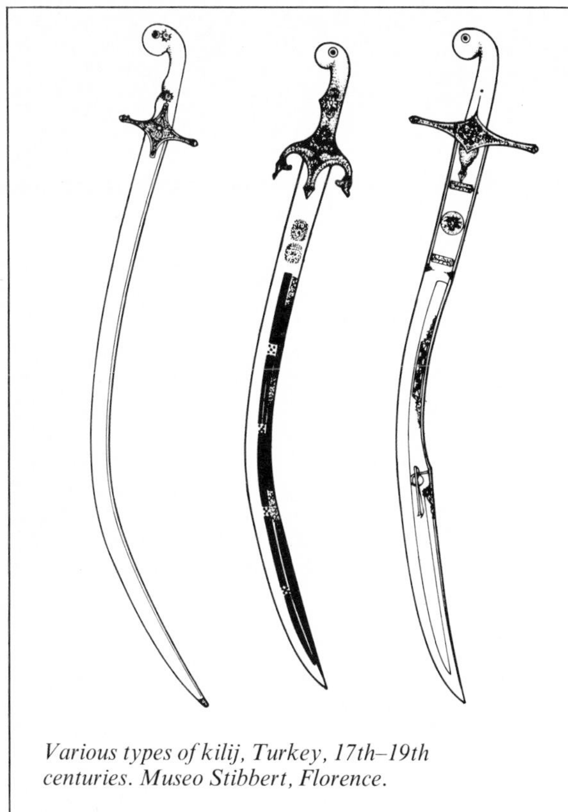

*Various types of kilij, Turkey, 17th–19th centuries. Museo Stibbert, Florence.*

country. Minor pieces of armor, such as neck guards or arm defenses, were also often made in this way.

**kilij** Turkish generic term (from *kilic*, "sword") conventionally used to denote certain types of Middle Eastern sabers with a blade double-edged at the point. They had evolved by the 17th century from earlier types. The kilij in its various forms was found throughout Ottoman-dominated lands and in adjacent areas. Some early blades—originating, for instance, in the 16th century—were later stripped for their furniture and refitted, which means that they cannot be used as a guide in dating the whole saber. However, a convention has arisen among scholars that it is not the blade but the furniture—especially of the hilt—that is the determining factor in deciding the origin and age of any kilij extant today. The typical kilij blade was of plain steel or various kinds of Damascus steel, black Khorassan being the most frequently used. The blade in its upper part continued the same line as the grip, but about halfway along it arched backward and sometimes became thinner, finally widening at the last third or quarter into a double-edged pointed YALMAN.

The blade was often richly decorated, inlaid with gold medallions, cartouches, floral designs, magic symbols, and inscriptions in Kufic or elegant cursive characters. These writings were mostly taken from suras of the Koran. Sometimes the blades were not only heavily overlaid with gold but also inset with jewels and gemstones, especially rubies, garnets, and almandines. In a much older type of kilij, the grip was rounded and made of metal or ivory—often colored and inlaid—with a small pommel turned forward and straight quillons with langets, i.e., prongs over the blade, which formed an additional stopping device for an opponent's blade. On some versions, a chain linked the pommel to the front quillon.

The wooden kilij scabbard was sometimes covered with velvet or, more frequently, embossed brass or silver, which was also chased in floral motifs. It was always fitted with two ringed lockets for the hanging bands; in the Turkish style these rings were loose, but in the Persian they were rigid, although the latter form was also popular in Turkey. The saber-belt was made of leather, cloth, or cord, with metal buckles and clasps.

Kilij of the 18th and 19th centuries had hilts made of boiled buffalo or rhinoceros horn, exquisitely shaped in two pieces to taper upward and broaden into a powerful, ball-like pommel that curved forward and is sometimes likened—if not very accurately—to a pistol butt. The grip was riveted twice, and there was a hole in the pommel for a cord to be attached. The other elements of more recent kilij—blade, quillons, and scabbard—did not differ radically from the earlier ones, although it is worth remembering that there are no two identical sabers in the Moslem world.

Sabers of the kilij type were also widely used in eastern Europe, and they were especially popular among the Cossacks of the Ukraine and southern Russia. Such sabers were officially adopted as regulation weapons (called *klych*) in the Russian Imperial Army's Cossack regiments.

**killing circle** The extent of the lateral spread of the pellets from a shotgun within which the concentration of pellets is sufficient to kill the game.

**kinjal** An alternative spelling for **khaujar**.

**kirrie** *See* KNOBKERRIE.

**kisaki** The point of a Japanese blade. *See also* BLADE: Japanese.

**klewang** (or **kleewang**) A typical Malayan saber, widely used throughout the archipelago, that has evolved into many local forms. Its single-edged blade is straight or very slightly curved and widens toward the point, which is either cut sharply or rounded toward the back; it is usually about 50 cm. (20 in.) long and often made of watered steel. The klewang hilt is of hardwood, horn, or bone, turned forward, with a protruberant—sometimes weirdly carved—pommel that may be decorated with hair. Tin or lead furnishings are often applied. The wooden scabbard is wide enough to accommodate the hatchet-shaped blade and is not infrequently bound with silver bands, tinfoil, or rattan.

**knife** A tool and weapon consisting of a single-edged pointed blade and a handle mounted asymmetrically in relation to the axis of the blade, closer to its back. Domestic and martial use of the knife dates to earliest times. Among the instruments of the Stone Age, the term "knife" is applied to flint blades with one or two cutting edges. But the real knife actually appeared with the discovery of metals; in the Bronze Age a knife was cast, often in a single piece, with a single-edged, usually straight,

*Hunting knife, Italy, 18th century. Victoria and Albert Museum, London.*

or slightly curved, blade. The curvature was sometimes accentuated near the point where the blade became crescent-shaped; the high point of this development came with the razor knives of the Villanovian culture (1000–600 B.C.).

The art of making knives from one piece of metal, as practiced thousands of years ago, has been revived for modern household and table knives. Once man had mastered iron, the handle became different, for the plasticity of the new metal not only made it possible to make stronger and more durable blades but also enabled the blade to be extended to form a flat tang, which was then covered with sidepieces made of horn, wood, or some other material that was easier to carve and to decorate in general. In the classical period, knives were commonly used for day-to-day activities in the home, on the hunt, and as a sacrificial tool. Of the latter use we have evidence dating to earliest times: the sacrificial weapon had a very broad blade in the shape of a triangle.

At the time of the barbarian invasions during first centuries A.D., new forms of knives, introduced to the various regions by peoples who used knives for all their vital activities, became common throughout Europe; small knives for domestic purposes, larger knives for hunting and martial use. But it was the large war knives (*see also* SAX; SCRAMASAX) that were the most impressive. The smaller knives, made for domestic use, underwent various changes dictated by purpose, means, and fashion, with the result that the man in the street sported a knife with a simple handle made of horn or bone, whereas the influential citizen's knife often had a handle made of rock crystal or other stone mounted in silver or some other precious material—this being a popular combination in the 15th century in particular. Handles made of cast silver were common in the 16th century; inlaid mother-of-pearl handles were *à la mode* in the 17th century, and porcelain handles were popular in the 18th century; in the 19th century handles made of carved ivory and bone and fine silver plate were favored. Modern handles are often of sophisticated design based on anatomical research.

The knife used for activities outside the home was completely different. It usually had a stronger blade and a sharper point, a vital feature for pilgrim, traveler, and hunter alike. It came with a proper sheath or was kept in the scabbard of a larger weapon, particularly that of a sword or a hunting dagger, thus making up a specialized hunting "set." Every country produced knives with blades and handles of particular shapes as expressions of its own culture and to meet day-to-day requirements or customs. For instance, a type of knife common in southern Europe had a blade that folded toward the handle; the cutting edge was housed in a special groove. The best-known and commonest type was the Spanish NAVAJA; in Italy these jackknives or clasp knives were known as *serramanico*.

Because people tried to sell weapons with dangerous blades in the shape of olive or willow leaves, like the blade of Spanish *punctillas*, decrees often forbade the carrying of such knives because of their offensive nature. Among the knives commonly used in Europe, the so-called Genoese knives deserve special mention. They had handles decorated with fluting and metalwork, and a chiseled blade with a faceted baluster at the base, near the grip. The most common type had a broad blade with a single edge for half or two-thirds of its length, which then narrowed abruptly to a pointed bodkin with an eyelet near the tip. Another type had the blade threaded onto the handle; the bodkin extended from the handle into a long slot chiseled in the blade. A third type had a blade that could also be unscrewed from the handle, but the bodkin was fashioned from the tang and placed inside the grip.

Possibly the most famous knife of the last century was one with a heavy, single-edged, and sharply pointed blade and a small handle with wooden sidepieces. This was a weapon designed for hand-to-hand fighting and used by the trappers and hunters of the American West. Between 1827 and 1830, it was perfected for and named after the frontiersman who made it famous: Colonel James Bowie of Arkansas. *See also* BOWIE KNIFE.

**knobkerrie** (or **kirrie**) A throwing knob club used by the Kaffirs and Hottentots of South Africa. It is cut from a solid piece of hardwood or, more rarely, rhinoceros horn. It consists of a short handle with a large knob on the end, which, although usually spherical, is sometimes elliptical. It varies in length from 45 to 52 cm. (18–21 in.). Its name comes from the Dutch *knop* ("knot") and the Hottentot *kirri* ("stick"). A longer version is used by the Zulus as a mace in close combat. The knobkerrie is carried by means of a thong, which passes through a hole drilled in the end of the handle, with the knob hanging downward.

**knuckle guard** An important part of the hilt of swords and sabers in the form of a bow extending from the cross guard toward the pommel. As can be adduced from several English swords, it appeared no later than the mid-15th century, first as an extension of the cross guard strongly bent upward to protect the hand from cutting blows. Later the knuckle guard became a central piece of the sophisticated system of side bars forming the guard of swords and rapiers. Although it gradually lost its importance with the introduction of light thrusting smallswords in the second half of the 17th century, some examples of this weapon preserved the knuckle guard as a traditional pattern up to the 20th century. In most types of military swords and sabers, the knuckle guard has always retained its role of protecting the hand from cuts, and it is still a feature of fencing sabers and of swords of historic form worn with full-dress uniforms.

**kōgai** A characteristic Japanese stiletto-shaped skewer, which was carried in a special pocket of the sheath of a dagger or sword scabbard. Made in one piece, generally either of SHAKUDŌ or SHIBUICHI alloys or of iron or copper with gold or silver inlays, it had a narrow blade, which was rounded off at the point, and a flat handle usually completed with a knob finial. The two flat surfaces of the handle allowed room for engraving or inlaid decoration with the owner's *mon* (family crest) and representations of animals, such as rabbits and wild boar, or of plants, such as bamboo shoots, as favorite motifs; human figures or Fukuroku-Ju, the god of fortune, were also depicted. Another form of kōgai was split lengthwise into two pieces, like chopsticks, and known as a *hashi*.

A popular name for the kōgai was "head pin" because it could be used to arrange the hair or to search for parasites. It has been said that the samurai of olden days used their kōgai to make distinguishing marks on their slain enemies or, after beheading them, to carry off their heads by thrusting the kōgai blade into an eye or an ear. Kōgai could also be used to open the veins of wounded comrades in order to shorten their suffering.

Although the kōgai could be put to a variety of purposes, as time passed its practical applications diminished. It continued traditionally to accompany short swords, such as the WAKIZASHI, but not the long ones, such as the KATANA.

**kogatana** This Japanese term is sometimes used to refer to the small knife, the KOZUKA, carried in the scabbard of a Japanese sword or the sheath of a dagger, in which case the word *kozuka* is applied only to the handle. Such semantic imprecision is not unusual in old Japanese culture.

**koiguchi kanagu** The locket at the mouth of the SAYA.

**kojiri** The chape over the point of the SAYA.

**koleos** The Greek term for SCABBARD.

**kopis** The etymology of this term is from the Greek *kopto*, meaning "cut." The word indicates a weapon designed for cutting blows. It is of nonclassical derivation, and there is evidence of this weapon in Greece among the remains of vanquished foreigners. It is often associated with the MACHAIRA, which was a war knife with a curved blade; but the two types can be distinguished by observing the curvature of the cutting edge of the blade: concave for the kopis, convex for the machaira. A version that combined features from both weapons was probably known as the "kopis-machaira." It was in use in ancient Greece and was depicted on vase paintings.

**kora** The national sword of the Gurkhas of Nepal, probably established in the 9th or 10th century and possibly descended from the KOPIS. It is an extraordinarily effective weapon that has played an important part in the military successes of these proud hill people. The kora's heavy, single-edged blade is about 60 cm. (24 in.) long, strongly inward-curving, and usually terminating in two concave cuts in the very broad end. Near the lower tip is a black-filled, engraved pattern of a lotus flower enclosed in a circle—a Buddhist symbol (like the notch in the blade of the KUKRI)—with ornamentation along the back edge of each face. The steel hilt, which sometimes incorporates brass elements, consists of a grip between two discs, that is, the guard and the pommel, which is usually topped with a dome and, frequently, a decorative knob.

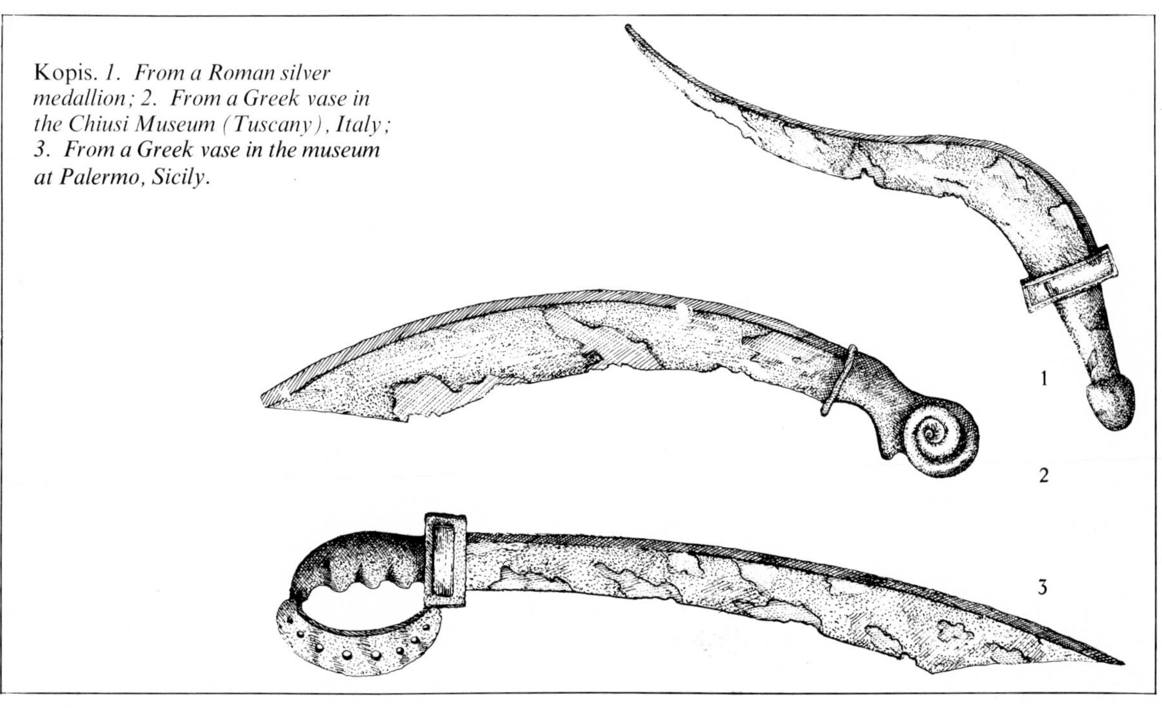


Kopis. *1. From a Roman silver medallion; 2. From a Greek vase in the Chiusi Museum (Tuscany), Italy; 3. From a Greek vase in the museum at Palermo, Sicily.*

The kora scabbard is of two kinds, the more common one being a wide sheath into which the blade can be slipped. The second type is shaped with a wide end to fit the blade and fastens with buttons along the back. These leather scabbards are sometimes covered with velvet, which may be embroidered with silk or furnished with silver mounts.

Many of the Nepalese weapons in British collections originated from the 1814–16 Gurkha War.

**korambi** A Sumatran knife, the korambi has a sickle-shaped, double-edged blade and a fluted or diamond-shaped cross section; it is usually about 15–20 cm. (6–8 in.) in length. The horn hilt has a large round pommel, which is more bulbous toward the inward-curving side of the blade. The sheath, also made of horn, broadens at the mouth.

**korazin** Oriental armor made of small scales of metal or pieces of horn fastened to cloth or leather, popular in late antiquity and the early Middle Ageş. Being heavy and slumsy and not very practical in use, it was supplanted by other forms of armor, particularly by mail or combinations of mail and small plates. It was usually in the form of a tunic with short sleeves. Almost certainly this type of armor—the lorica squamata (*see* LORICA)—was adopted by the Romans from countries of the East and was popular among legionnaires, for it was easy to manufacture and repair. But it was also associated with the scale aegis of Pallas Athene (Minerva) and hence considered a high-rank protection fit for emperors, often adorned with a gorgon's or lion's head. The scales used for armor by the Romans were of bronze or iron, pierced with small holes through which they were laced or stitched with fine thongs to the lining of leather or cloth and imbricated like the scales of a fish or roof tiles.

During the so-called Sarmatian period of Polish culture in the 17th century, when Oriental and Roman styles were adapted to suit the requirements of Polish noblemen, this type of armor, under the name *karacena*, became popular. Tracing ancestors among the ancient Sarmatians, the Polish nobility also tried to imitate their armor as shown on Roman monuments, especially Trajan's Column and the Arch of Galerius at Salonica; even more probably they were inspired by sculptures and coins showing Roman emperors clad in parade scale armor.

The karacena was always made of iron scales, flat or embossed, riveted onto a foundation of leather, usually of deerskin or elkskin, with ornamental brass-headed rivets.

Typical karacena armor consisted of a breastplate and backplate; sometimes it was comprised of a large beastplate fixed by straps and a metal boss at the back. It was supplemented with a collar, pauldrons, tassets, and forearm defenses in Oriental style but rarely with full leg defenses. The arms and sometimes the knees were decorated with grotesque masks or lions' heads in brass or copper gilt. The Polish "knight's cross" was frequently applied on the collar. The armor was combined with a scale helmet, in either of two forms—like a hussar's ZISCHÄGGE or like a turban. A leopard skin was often worn with the karacena, which was suitable for parades. For more warlike purposes, however, hussar plate or mail armor was preferred. The karacena was at its most splendid in the reign of King John Sobieski (1674–96), continuing until the middle of the 18th century.

**(1) koshiate** The Japanese sword carrier, a device for holding the sword scabbard firmly in the belt. The most common type of koshiate consists of a large piece of leather with crossed thongs going through it to fasten the sword in its correct place. There are also tube-shaped koshiate, to hold the sheathed sword inside, and double carriers for two swords, such as the KATANA and the WAKIZASHI.

**(2) koshiate** A kind of shield worn over the loins to protect the body from the tips of the arrows carried in a quiver on the back (*see* illustration 21 under YOROI).

**kote** An armored sleeve, an important part of Japanese armor, mentioned in documents mainly from the 14th century but also earlier. Most examples to be seen today, however, are on "modern" armor. The kote consists of a close-fitting sleeve of padded cloth, silk, or leather, laced over the arm and tied by strings around the chest. Some parts of the kote are covered with mail and others with metal plates of various size and splints, terminating in a hand guard or half-gauntlet called the *tetsu-gai*.

The kote is one of the most complicated of composite defenses, each element and variation in design having a specific name. The uppermost plate of the kote, covering the shoulder, is called the *kamuraita*, to which are attached cords for tying. Below this, for the protection of the principal muscles of the upper arm, is a large metal plate or

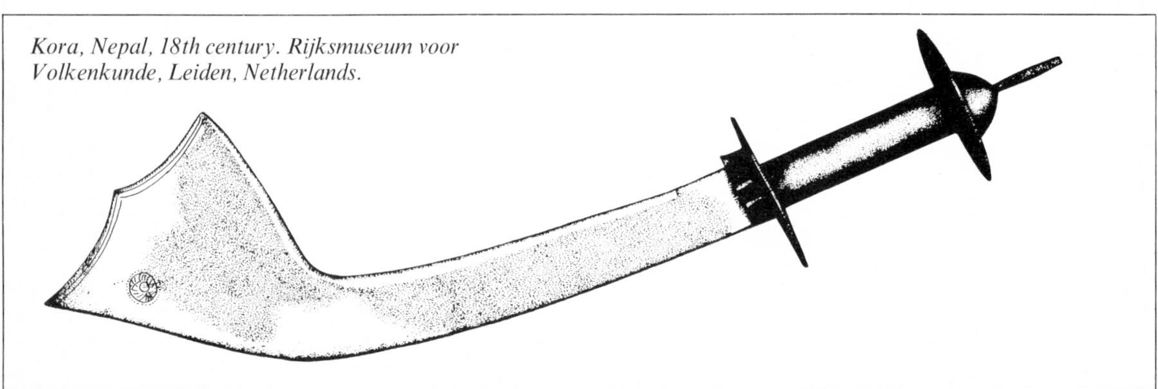

*Kora, Nepal, 18th century. Rijksmuseum voor Volkenkunde, Leiden, Netherlands.*

a group of scales connected by mail called the *gaku-no-ita*. At the point of the elbow is a circular plate of metal, the *hiki-gane*, or elbow cap. The lower part of the forearm is protected by a plate called the *ikada*, which sometimes consists of parallel splints of metal joined by mail and sometimes of one piece of embossed and pierced metal. The hand guard, the tetsu-gai, is a rounded lacquered plate following the shape of the back of the hand above the fingers. It is lined with leather and has loops on the inside through which the fingers pass; in addition to hand guards, leather gloves were worn.

Every specific combination of mail, plates and splints, lining, and various ways of tying has a specific name and plays its part in the large range of the kote. It is often decorated with the owner's *mon* (family crest), figures in high relief, and other gilded ornaments.

**koto** A type of pre-17th-century Japanese blade. *See also* BLADE: Japanese.

**kozane** Small plates used in the making of Japanese armor.

**kozuka** A Japanese knife carried in the pocket of the sheath of a dagger or a sword scabbard; it is sometimes termed a KOGATANA, in which case "kozuka" refers only to the handle, often regarded as a collectible object in its own right. The kozuka knife is usually about 15–25 cm. (6–10 in.) long. Its blade is straight, chisel-edged, and made of *kataha*, i.e., a bar produced by welding together a plate of iron and one of steel (*see* BLADE: Japanese). The steel side is flat and highly polished, whereas the iron one is usually left rough and tapers towards the edge; sometimes the iron side is engraved or inlaid and may be signed by the maker.

Kozuka handles are generally metal; the back and the front are frequently made of different metals, SHAKUDŌ and SHIBUICHI alloys being the favorites; occasionally they are of wood, bone, ivory, or stag's horn. Next to the TSUBA, the Japanese considered the kozuka handle to be the most important fitting of the sword and decorated it with carving, engraving, inlaying, and enameling, usually using a combination of methods. The decoration was confined mostly to the front, but not infrequently it extended to the back, where a short poem, proverb, or amusing maxim was sometimes inscribed. Motifs of figures in high relief were often continued on the back in engraving.

**kris** The characteristic Malay dagger, one of the world's most sophisticated weapons, with a long history and many complicated features of structure, decoration, and significance. It is an important feature of old Malay culture that is bound up with mythology, secret beliefs, and the mysticism of the Malay peoples. According to tradition, the kris originated in Java, its invention being attributed to Inakto Pali, king of Janggolo, in the 14th century. It was gradually adopted in all parts of the archipelago and evolved into countless variations. Every island—or even every district—has its own forms of blade, hilt, and sheath, and a kris may even include elements coming from various places. A real knowledge of the kris is therefore confined to a few great experts. Nevertheless, there is a general form, an ideal structure of this weapon, which unites all existing specimens and enables one to

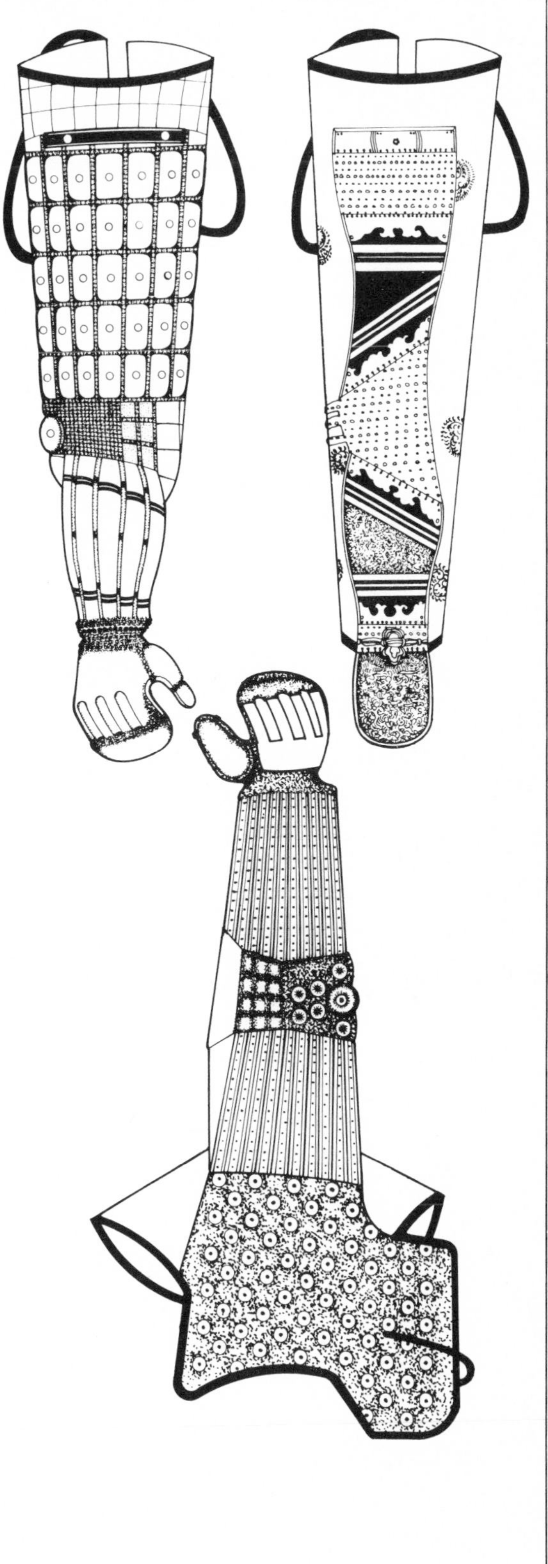

*Various types of kote. L. J. Anderson Collection, London.*

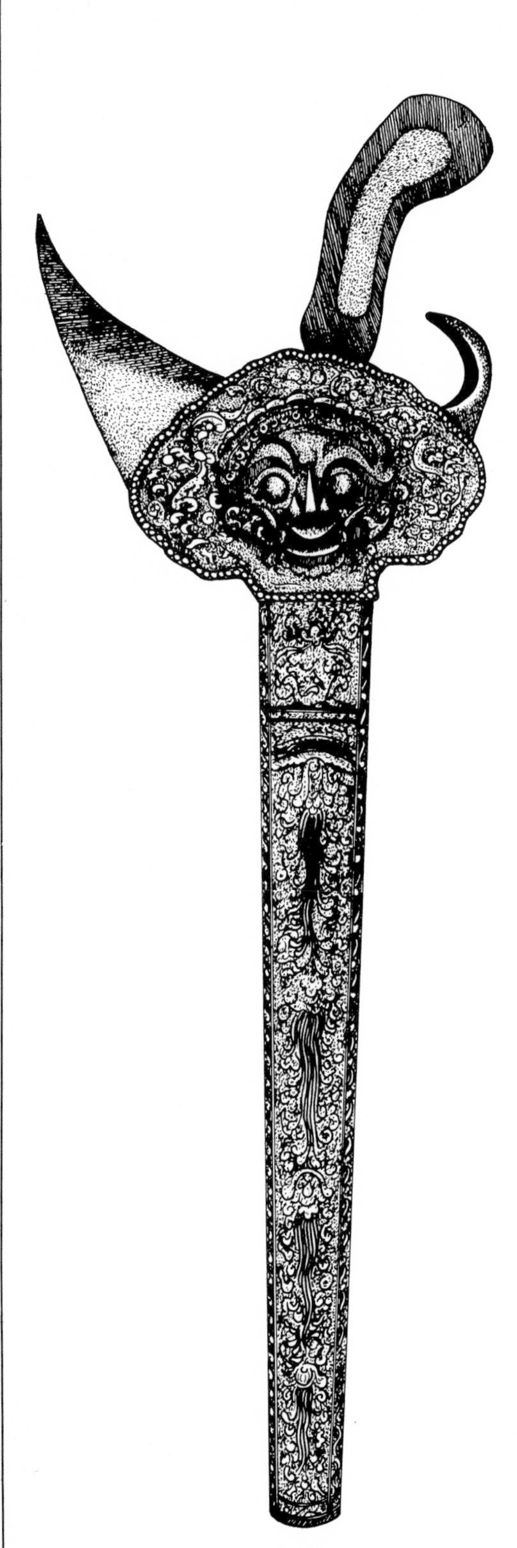

*Kris in its sheath, Java. Rijksmuseum voor Volkenkunde, Leiden, Netherlands.*

recognize the type immediately, even without understanding all its pecularities.

Among the constants are the material and techniques used in the making of the kris blade. Skilled metallurgists manufacture it by laminating three layers of iron or soft steel, separated by thinner layers of meteoric iron, called *pamir*, containing about 3 per cent nickel. In modern times the meteoric iron has been replaced by nickel steel or pure nickel. The bar is welded, beaten out, doubled, and twisted in various ways to produce the pattern of watered steel. It is then divided into three parts—one for the upper part of the blade, the *ganja*, the other two for the lower part and the point—and forged anew to get the desired straight or, usually, wavy shape.

The blade is decorated with engraving and gilding, often in the form of a dragon whose undulations correspond to the waves. The ganja widens and forms a sharp point next

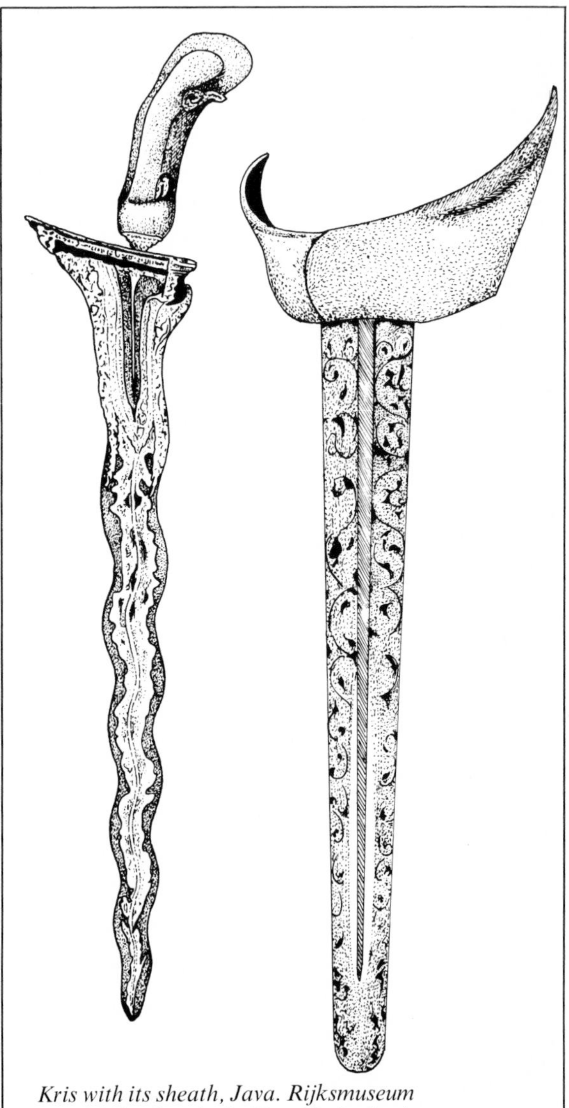

*Kris with its sheath, Java. Rijksmuseum voor Volkenkunde, Leiden, Netherlands.*

to the hilt, usually on one side only but occasionally on both, and there may also be a hook-shaped projection called the "elephant's trunk." These lugs form the guard but can also be used for strikes. Finally, the blade is etched with a mixture of arsenous acid and lime juice; the watering is brought out as the arsenic blackens the iron and leaves the meteoric iron or nickel bright. The blade is double-edged and sharply pointed; its average length is 30–40 cm. (12–16 in.). The ring between the blade and the hilt, called the *mendak* or *uwar*, is often made of gold or silver and is an elaborate piece of jeweler's craftsmanship, being frequently set with precious stones. The tang attaching the handle is rather small, weak, and easily bent (which is a defect of the weapon). The hilt is made of wood, bone, ivory, horn, or stone, occasionally overlaid with silver or gold or set with jewels, and often elaborately carved. Malayan imagination runs riot in the design of countless shapes for the hilt, although the purpose of the grip, to fit comfortably to the hand, is always maintained. The figure of Garuda, the eagle—the steed of Vishnu—is a favorite subject in a naturalistic or schematic version; another is the Raksha or demon, a grotesque human figure with terrible tusks. A form of the Garuda hilt is known in England as the "kingfisher kris."

Kris sheaths are made of wood, mostly of two or three pieces (although occasionally of one), their decorative value mainly deriving from the special graining of the wood and their graceful shape. They are often covered with tortoiseshell, embossed brass, silver or gold, painted figures, or other designs. They have exaggeratedly extended upper parts, ostensibly to hide the ganja lug but also for decorative effect, imitating some forms of Malay orchids; in Europe they are called boat-shaped sheaths. The Malays believe that a soul lives in some krises, which gives this type of dagger almost supernatural properties. Old family krises are highly venerated and are passed down through the generations. Every man keeping the tradition has a number of krises, among them one inherited from his forefathers, one given by his father-in-law, and one that he considers particularly his own. There are also executioner's krises with longer blades of about 50–60 cm. (20–24 in.). In the rich houses of Bali there used to be kris stands, grotesquely carved human figures about 60 cm. (24 in.) high in the open hands of which a visitor left his kris.

**(1) kuda-yari** The Japanese spear pipe, a device for directing the spear when thrusting. It consisted of a short iron tube with a wide flange at one end, which was placed over the shaft and grasped in the left hand to guide and steady the spear. A cord, the *kuda-no-utomo*, was attached to the tube and wound around the hand.

**(2) kuda-yari** A deceptive Japanese weapon, invented by Hōzōin Inei, a priest, in the mid-16th century. It consisted of a spear contained in a hollow outer shaft, giving the weapon the appearance of being shorter than it was.

**kukri** (or **khukari**) The national knife and principal weapon of the Gurkhas of Nepal. Its form, especially the forward-angled blade, shows that it is closely related to the ancient Greek swords MACHAIRA and KOPIS, which almost certainly accompanied Alexander the Great to India. It is

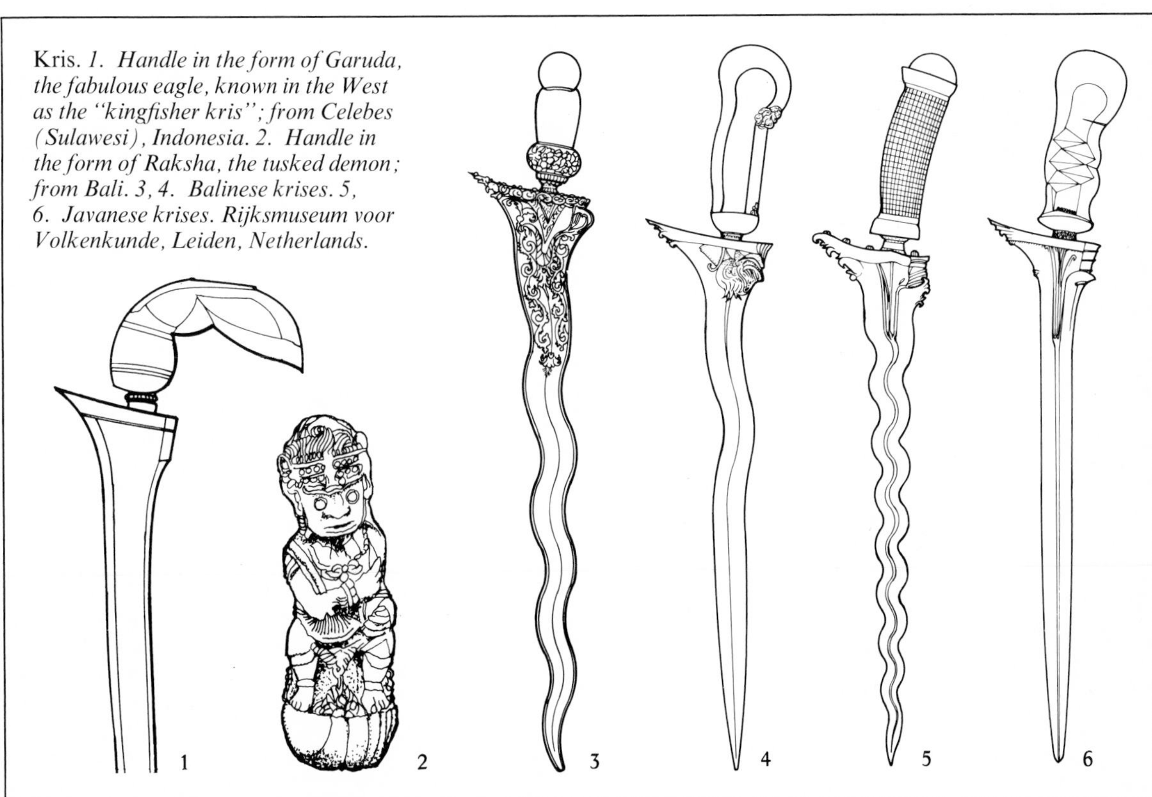


Kris. *1. Handle in the form of Garuda, the fabulous eagle, known in the West as the "kingfisher kris"; from Celebes (Sulawesi), Indonesia. 2. Handle in the form of Raksha, the tusked demon; from Bali. 3, 4. Balinese krises. 5, 6. Javanese krises. Rijksmuseum voor Volkenkunde, Leiden, Netherlands.*

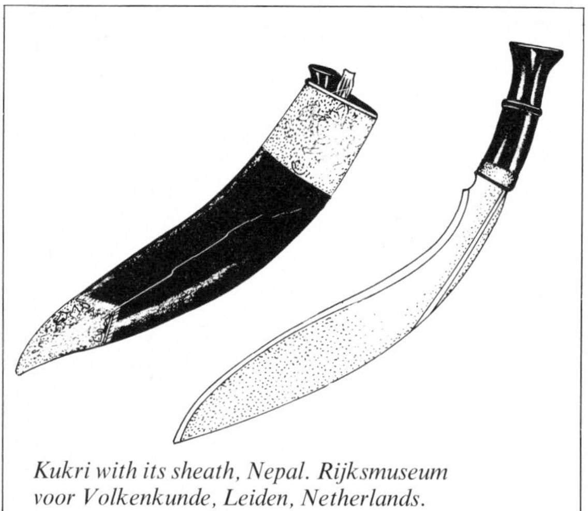
*Kukri with its sheath, Nepal. Rijksmuseum voor Volkenkunde, Leiden, Netherlands.*

not very different from the Indian SOSUN PATTAH a version of the Turkish YATAGAN.

The kukri is highly regarded by all classes of Nepalese society; its quality and decoration indicate the wealth of the owner. It is carried in a belted sheath containing one or two small knives of kukri shape and, at one time, a purse holding flint and steel for making fire. The kukri is also a useful implement for cutting through dense jungle, but above all it is a formidable weapon, mostly on account of its shape. Its blade is heavy, curved, single-edged, and sharp on the concave side. The weight of the blade is toward the point, and a tremendous blow can be struck using little muscular exertion. The base of the edge of a kukri blade contains a semicircular notch, which, like the lotus of the blade of the KORA, represents the female genital organ, intended to render the blade "effective."

The kukri hilt is usually made of dark wood or ivory; it is straight and has no guard; occasionally it has a disc pommel and a guard (like the kora) and often a ridge ring in the middle—a survival of the earlier handle with a plaited cane band and iron ring. Kukri sheaths, usually made of velvet-covered wood, are very ornate, embroidered or furnished with embossed and pierced mounts of silver or gold. Kukri belts match the decoration of the sheaths.

**kulah khud** A characteristic Persian helmet, extensively used from the 16th century, with a hemispherical skull, usually made of watered steel. It was either engraved or inlaid with gold or silver and often had applied decorative ribs and border, a square-section spike at the apex, and two sockets for plumes—generally of eagle feathers—at the front. A sliding nasal bar was always fitted, and in a few cases there were three nasals—one in the front and one on each temple—although this style seems to have been adopted from an Indian helmet. A mail AVENTAIL was attached to the skull; it had an opening at the center front to leave the face uncovered and a slit on each side to clear the shoulders, the two front pieces hanging down in long points. The best aventails were made of small riveted mail, often with patterns worked into the mail with brass links, whereas the aventail on poorer-quality helmets had open links. The skulls of some kulah khud—mainly of the 19th century—were decorated with metal horns and demons' heads.

**kumade** A Japanese weapon used in combat at sea, in pulling down barricades, in assaults on castles, and so forth. It is a grappling hook usually consisting of a curved blade backed by one or two hooks, which may be left unpolished, although the blade itself is properly finished. The head is mounted by a strong tang onto a long shaft of up to about 250 cm. (8 ft.).

*Kulah khud, Persia, 17th–18th century. Museo Stibbert, Florence.*

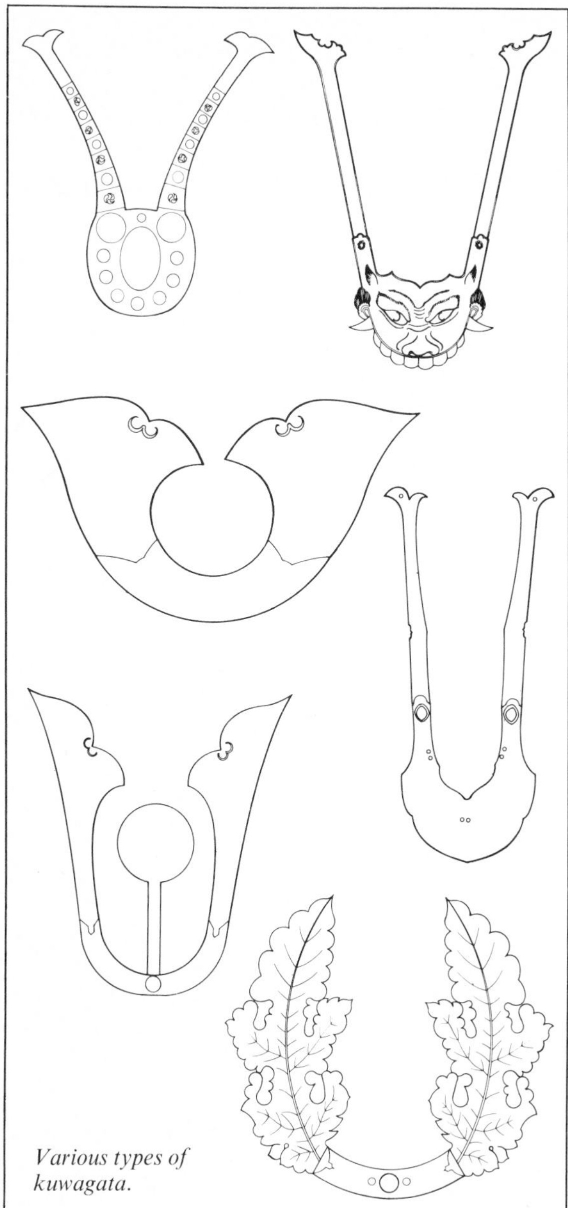

*Various types of kuwagata.*

**kummya** A dagger used mainly in Morocco by lower-ranking officers of the Mokhazni tribe. Its characteristic single-edged blade, which is of good quality, originates in Europe, as is borne out by the Solingen, Birmingham, and Sheffield marks. The wooden hilt is either partly or completely covered with silver, brass, or copper; it is wide at the base, has a very narrow grip, and is surmounted by a large pommel in the shape of a peacock's tail. The kummya sheath is of wood covered with metal, usually in keeping with the furniture of the hilt, and chased in dense floral designs. It turns backward strongly at the tip and terminates in a knob. There are two suspension rings at the same level on each side of the upper part of the sheath, and the hanging cord is made of plaited wool.

*Kusazuri in four sections. L. J. Anderson Collection, London.*

**kurimata** A variation of the YANO-NE.
**kusarigama** Another term for the NAGEGAMA.
**kusazuri** The laminated tassets of Japanese armor, consisting of strips of metal or lacquered leather laced together and hung by cords from the cuirass. In the more ancient armor, the YOROI, there were four sets of tassets—one for the front, one for the back, and one for each side. These tassets widened considerably toward the lower edge, which sometimes was slit in the middle to facilitate movement. In later armor, the tassets became narrower and more numerous, sometimes as many as eight or nine. These were more convenient for walking and riding but did not give as much protection as the earlier combination of four, hence the introduction of an additional defense, the apron-like HAIDATE.
**Kuse** *See* GLAIVE.
**kusungobu** *See* AIKUSHI.
**kutar** An alternative spelling of KATAR.
**kutti** *See* BHUJ.
**kuwagata** A forecrest ornament for a Japanese helmet made of either thin metal plates or whalebone; it was gilded and, although usually shaped like flat horns, it sometimes took the form of the unfolded leaves of the water plant sagittaria. Some ancient kuwagata were enormous. There has been much speculation about its significance, but in most civilizations horns have symbolized power and good fortune.

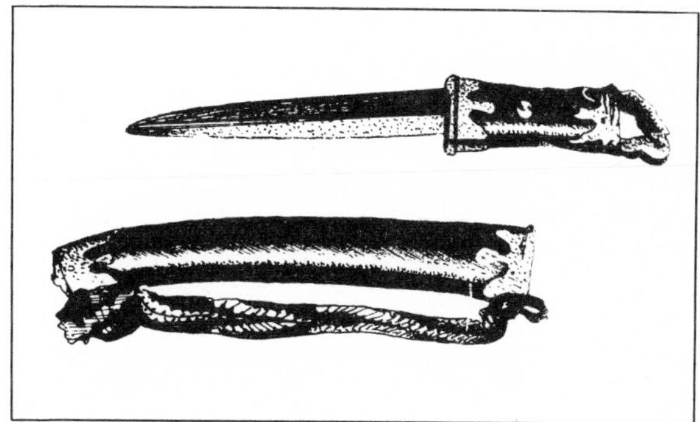

*Kwaiken, Japan.*

**kuyak** (or **khuyak**) A term for a type of armored garment of Mongolian origin, which was widely used in medieval Russia. The construction of the kuyak was similar to that of the European JACK.

**kwaiken** An old style of Japanese dagger carried by women, used to perform ritual suicide by cutting the veins in the left side of the neck. The kwaiken was usually about 20–25 cm. (8–10 in.) long, with a slightly curved single- or double-edged blade. Its simple hilt and sheath were of lacquered wood, with plain silver or horn mounts; it was sometimes covered in brocade. The kwaiken had no TSUBA or other fittings usually mounted on portable daggers.

# L

**lame** A fairly pliable iron or steel plate used in making up parts of an armor. Being lighter and less protective than the iron plates used for helmet skulls, breast- and backplates, the lames were incorporated in the structure of various pieces of armor which required substantial mobility. The most frequent use of them was made in articulated parts such as the pauldrons, vambraces, skirt, rump guard, greaves, tassets, etc. Flexibility was achieved by attaching the lames with sliding (loose) rivets or onto leather strips.

**lamella** A small, thin, oblong LAME, quite pliable, and of various contours. Many types of lamellae were attached in overlapping rows onto leather or canvas supports to form such armors as the BRIGANDINE.

Interlaced lamellae form the basic structure in Japanese, Chinese, and other Far Eastern body armor and helmets. Lamellae linked by mail were used in some types of armor in the Middle East and eastern Europe.

**lance** A word derived from Latin *lancea* ("spear") and originally synonymous with the more popular term "spear," both being applied to the spears of either foot soldiers or horsemen. The word "lance" was used from the 6th century in France and at least from the 13th century in England ("launce"). After the 16th century, however, the term "lance" was increasingly applied only to the cavalry spears, and is now accepted in this connotation even for description of these weapons used before the 16th century (in Russia, however, the lances were called "pikes," like the long spears of western European infantry of the 16th and 17th centuries).

One of the oldest weapons, the lance can be traced to the ancient Middle East and was widely used by mounted warriors of Greece and Rome. The lance head had various shapes, depending on the historical period, the place, and the specific use of the lance. As a rule the point was designed to penetrate, and was mounted on a long shaft made of tough wood, usually ash. The commonest forms have an iron head in the shape of a willow or laurel leaf with cutting edges and a sharp point. The length of the shaft also varied a great deal. From the late 13th century, for use in contests and tournaments the head of the "courtesy lance" was specially shaped, like a CORONEL, since the knight had to demonstrate his skills without causing too much harm to his opponent; in the "full tilt," which could cause fatal injuries, the head had a bluntish tip.

A distinctive feature of the lance was that it was gripped well to its rear, with the point advanced as far as possible, the purpose being to keep the foe at a safe distance, blocking his advance with a long-hafted weapon and striking him at a distance without losing the weapon. The common practice, at least from the early 13th century, was to aim the lance diagonally above the neck of the horse in such a way that contenders faced one another left side on.

Together with the sword, the lance has long been the best form of offensive weapon carried by cavalry; the mounted soldier has often been depicted on foot with the lance held out straight with the right hand. The lance continued to be used by the light cavalry up until the 19th century and many European armies did not abandon it until after the First World War. The last cavalry charge with lances and swords appears to have been the one by the Italian cavalry during the Russian campaign of 1942.

The length of the lance shaft varied over the centuries, depending on the country and the terrain in which battles were fought; the shape of the head varied as a result of cultural influences. In the Bayeux Tapestry, with its depiction of war (it was made between 1066 and 1077 to celebrate the Norman conquest of Britain), one can clearly see the essential characteristics of the mounted warrior armed with the lance, even his keeping it by his side, almost as if it were his symbol, when he dismounted. Here we see leaf-shaped points, and forms with barbs, which were used mainly on missile weapons. Another detail brought into prominence by the Bayeux "story" is the presence of a small pennant made of fabric and attached near the lance head. These ensigns were usually square or rectangular in the case of the gonfalon, bearing the seigneur's insignia, and flame-shaped or triangular in the case of the pennon, with the arms of the knight who was being followed into battle by his retinue.

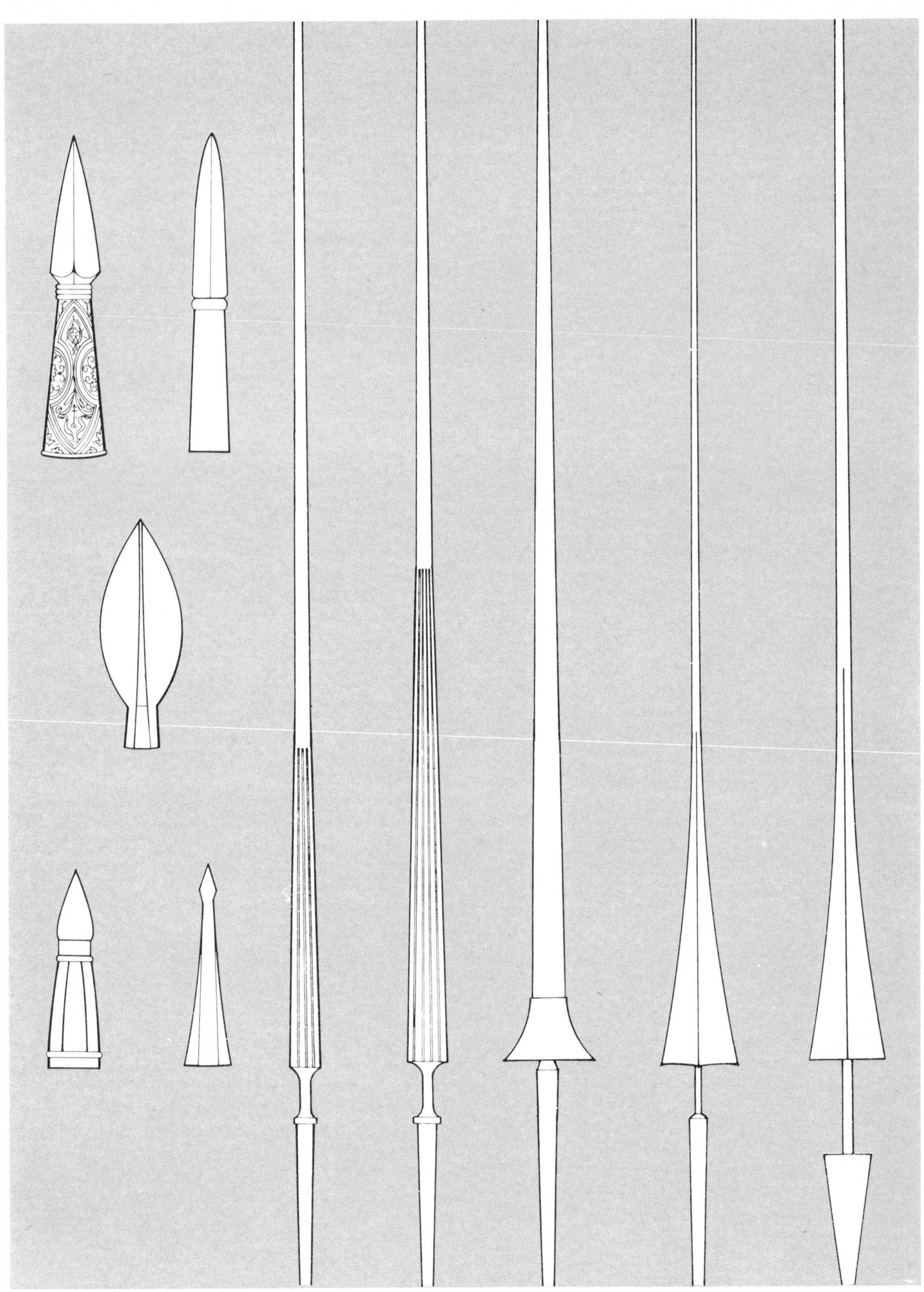

*Various heads and types of jousting lances of the 15th and 16th centuries.*

When in battle the lance was held aimed at the target, but in a parade or procession it was carried vertically, with the butt lodged in a stirrup or on the right thigh of the horseman; on the march it was carried across the shoulder, across the saddlebow, or held by the hand in a horizontal position alongside the horse. In the 13th century, with a view to increasing the force of the thrust, lances were made heavier and longer.

One of the problems when using the lance was the movement to the rear, beneath the armpit—not unlike a recoil—caused by the impact with the opponent. From the beginning of the 14th century a RONDEL or a thick leather ring called the GRAPER was fitted to the shaft behind the hand; this acted as a stop against the armpit, and thus checked the rearward jerk of the lance. To the same effect, the last quarter of the century saw the introduction of a new important device called the REST. This consisted of a small, and often folding, bracket fixed to the right side of the breastplate; the graper was leaned against this bracket when the lance was aimed at its target. The lance rest remained in use into the 17th century.

It was not until the invention of the rest that the whole might of the magnificent attacking unit formed by the knight and his galloping steed was focused on the point of the lance. In action, the horseman positioned his body well forward, wedged firmly between the high arsons, i.e., the saddlebow and canticle. With his left hand he controlled his mount and protected the upper part of his body with a shield; his right arm, held tightly bent with the hand almost beneath the armpit, aimed the lance at the foe.

Lances with specialized shafts were made for war, jousts, pageants, and tournaments. From the early 15th century, at the butt of the shaft a section was cut out of the wood to form a grip for the hand, which was protected by the VAMPLATE. The formerly thick and heavy shafts were made lighter, and were sometimes pierced or perforated for much of their length. In the 15th century the shaft was between 3.6 and 4.2 m. long (12–13¾ ft.), and a special lance (*gialda*), carried by the Italian *gialdonieri*, was even somewhat longer.

In the 14th century horsemen and knights in Europe adopted the combat on foot in use in England for their trials of valor and skill, but for this type of contest the lance was an awkward and bulky weapon for men already weighed down by their specialized suits of armor. If the lance enabled blows to be delivered in open terrain, where the cavalry could maneuver easily, in rough and wooded country it became a clumsy instrument which hampered much of the soldier's movement. The French cavalry had thus found itself in great difficulty in the battle of Agincourt in 1415, so much so that they were forced to shorten their lances by holding them halfway down the shaft.

The largest lances were made for tilting and jousting; these were very long and had a large diameter. Previously made of ash, they were later made with the lighter wood of the fir tree, and even hollow inside. Deep grooving ran from the vamplate almost as far as the socket of the rook-shaped head, making the lance easier to wield; a violent thrust would snap it, and it would be promptly replaced by another. The custom of decorating lances with many-colored spiral designs, based on the livery of the knight or the seigneur in whose honor the joust was being held, was already being practiced in the 14th century.

From the 14th century the term "lance" was also used to describe a unit formed by three men and three horses (in France the *lance fournie* consisted of six men and six steeds); these men were called the corporal (or lance corporal), the horseman (or trooper or ranker), and the page (or lad or garçon). The horses were similarly graded, the garçon's being the nag. Broadly speaking, the relationship between the members of the lance or *lance fournie* harked back to the days of the Crusades, when the knight was attended by two grooms.

By the beginning of the 17th century the war lance had disappeared from the equipment of the heavy cavalry, having been replaced by firearms; the tilting or courtly lance still remained in use for tournaments and equestrian contests. The Thirty Years War (1618–48) consolidated the distinctions in insignia between the two branches of the mounted troops: the cuirassiers—heavy cavalry—had their lances decorated with a four-sided standard, and the light cavalry had their lances bearing the roughly triangular guidon.

Though outdated by firearms around 1600, the lance was never completely discarded, especially by the light cavalry in eastern Europe and the Middle East. Poland and Russia even led a revival of the lance following the Napoleonic Wars, when special regiments of lancers (patterned after Polish uhlans) were formed in major European armies. They were active, if not particularly efficient, on the battlefields up to the end of the First World War and Russian Civil War. The 19th-century lances were somewhat different from the earlier models. Their shafts were about 3 m. (10 ft.) long, with a small, often pyramidal or lancet-shaped head and a heavy shoe, rounded or spiked; on some models, there was a rondel between the head and the socket to prevent too deep a penetration of the target. To the shaft was attached a leather sling for the right arm, to carry the weapon vertically on horseback with its shoe in the lance bucket of the stirrup. From 1890, first in Germany and later in France, England, and some other countries, the lances were issued with metal tubular shafts.

In recent times, the most famous use of lances in battle occurred in 1939, when Polish uhlans attacked German armored troops. As a part of military pageantry, lances are still carried with full-dress and historical uniforms by a few cavalry regiments in Europe and Asia.

**lance armor** *See* ARMOR.

**lance bucket** Also called portelance, an accessory of cavalry harness for light-horse troops, used from the 17th century on. It consisted of a small metal or leather socket hung at the right stirrup, in which the lance rested when the men were on the move.

**lancegay** A term used from the 14th to 17th centuries for a light spear, which was sometimes described as having a steel head on both ends of the wooden shaft. It was occasionally used as a missile weapon, like a dart or javelin. It is possible that the word "lancegay" originated from a contraction of "lance" and "assegai," the latter being an Arab term for a similar missile weapon in use by some South African tribes.

**lance rest** A modern term for the REST.

**landsknecht dagger** *See* DAGGER.

**langdebeve** (from French *langue-de-boeuf*, "ox tongue"). A 15th-century term for a spear of Italian origin. Its head had a long, triangular, double-edged blade, wide at the base and tapering toward the point. Its variation, the spear *alla bolognese*, had two laterally curved scrolls forged at the blade base, which served as a guard to block an opponent's weapon.

**langet** In staff weapons, the langet consisted of an iron strap, usually straight but sometimes of zigzag shape, extending from the socket down the wooden part of the shaft and attached to it by nails or screws. There were usually two langets, in line either with the cutting edges or with the flat faces of the head. They carried out the dual task of increasing the strength of the attachment of the head to the staff and of protecting the most exposed part from blows; in hafted combat weapons, therefore, the other two sides of the wood were sometimes protected by "false langets," with one end fitted into the socket or into a square ring under the socket, thus protecting the other two sides of the wood.

In sabers and, less often, in Pallasches, the langets are extensions of the cross guard going symmetrically from its center into the grip and over the shoulder of the blade, on both faces of the blade. In most cases, there is a small space between the blade and the langets, which tightly fit the locket or the mouth of the scabbard, thus preventing an accidental unsheathing. There is a possibility that strong langets were also used by experienced swordsmen to stop and catch an opponent's blade at a sliding lateral strike. Examples of langets can be found on the KILIJ and the SHAMSHIR, as well as on many European derivations of these sabers.

**lash** (or **latch**) *See* THROAT LATCH.

**leading staff** A light staff, about 2 m. ($6\frac{1}{2}$ ft.) long, carried by infantry officers in the late 16th and 17th centuries to give signals to their companies. The small head of this accessory, which was also called a feather staff, was rather a decoration than a weapon, although it had the form of a halberd, bill, partisan, or pike (hence the name of the HALF-PIKE). With the adoption of the bayonet and resulting disuse of long pikes, toward the end of the 17th century, officers in almost all armies of Europe were issued such small versions of staff weapons to mark their rank and to give commands to their men. These staffs most often had the form of SPONTOON or halberd, and in some armies the color of the head indicated the officer's rank: gilded all over, a colonel; half-gilded, a lieutenant colonel; silver all over, a captain; blued, a lieutenant; and polished steel, an ensign.

**left-hand dagger** *See* PARRYING DAGGER.

**legharness** Leg armor for mounted troops which replaced mail chausses and hose of mail about the middle of the 14th century. It covered the whole length of the leg and was made up of three main parts: the GREAVE, POLEYN, and CUISSE. At this stage the SABATON was not yet an integral part of a legharness. Sometimes, especially in 15th-century armor, leg defenses of plate included only a cuisse and poleyn, with an extension of the poleyn as a shin guard.

Toward the end of the 16th century, light-horse and cuirassier armors no longer included the complete legharness but were replaced by long TASSETS with poleyn to protect the thighs and knees and by high boots instead of greaves. Subsequently, legharness completely disappeared from cuirassier and carabineer armors.

**lifting peg** A small metal rod screwed into a threaded hole on the right side of some helmets, from the late 15th to the second quarter of the 17th century, and usually finished off with a little knob. Armets dating to around 1500 were equipped with lifting pegs so that the full visor could be raised. On 16th-century helmets, such as the close helmet with gorget plates or with rotating rim, a lifting peg would have been fitted on the visor for the same purpose. On field helmets a special notch had to be made in the top edge of the upper bevor to accommodate the peg as it projected from the visor.

**line of sight** Theoretical line marking the direction in which a gun is aimed and passing from the shooter's eye through the rear sight and foresight. *See also* SIGHTS.

**lingula** A term used to describe the Roman sword which preceded the GLADIUS and which, in its classical form, was of Celto-Iberian derivation. It probably refers to the short sword of the late Bronze Age, with a pistil-shaped blade which broadened out before the tip and was designed principally for cutting.

**lining** Used on all types of helmets and other parts of armor from the 13th century, the lining consisted of an internal covering made of linen canvas, wool, or fine leather which was either quilted or padded; it was glued into place or laced through a row of small holes in the metal. From the 15th century the lining was stitched to leather bands riveted to the borders inside. Its purpose was mainly to prevent the iron from chafing the wearer's skin and to alleviate the build-up of heat.

**linstock** An instrument used to ignite the charge in early pieces of artillery. It was easy to handle, consisting of a red-hot iron which was brought down to the vent of the gun to ignite a trail of gunpowder. Later, when the slow match was introduced, a new version of the linstock came into use which allowed the firer to stand a little farther from the gun. A common form was a pole with a steel leaf-shaped head with two lateral clips to hold the slow match. The linstock was replaced in the early 19th century by the friction tube, which was fitted into the vent to ignite the charge.

**lip of the guard** *See* RIM OF THE GUARD.

**liquid air** A mixture of compressed and liquefied gases employed in the preparation of explosives.

**lobster-tailed pot** *See* ENGLISH POT.

**Lochaber ax** A Scottish staff weapon used in the 16th to 18th centuries. It had a large heavy head with a crescentic pointed edge and two sockets on the back for the shaft. A hook usually was either forged with the upper socket or fixed at the top of the staff. It resembles the BERDYSH and, like the latter, probably derived from the GISARME.

**lock** In firearms, the mechanism that provides ignition, generally fixed to the side of the stock. The commonest and most efficient types were the matchlock, the wheel-lock, the snaphance, the flintlock, and the percussion lock. For descriptions of these locks, *see* IGNITION.

**locking gauntlet** *See* GAUNTLET.

**locking lugs** On a breechloading firearm, projections on the bolt, breechblock, or obturator which, by fitting precisely into corresponding recesses in the breech, ensure that the action is completely closed at the moment of firing. Best results are obtained when these are fitted at the forward end of the breechblock or bolt as, for instance, in Mauser repeating rifles.

Besides the fixed locking lugs, there are also systems which employ mobile lugs which protrude into the locking position only when the obturator is fully extended. Examples of such systems are found in the German semiautomatic Gewehr 41W and Gewehr 43 rifles and in the Soviet Degtyarev light machine guns.

**longbow** *See* BOW.

**lorica** A generic Latin word used to describe several types of cuirasses worn by Roman soldiers. Initially it would have been only a simple protective leather garment—the word derives from *lorum* (a leather strap or thong)—covering the breast and back, with wide shoulder straps. Other types of body armor are known to have been used, however, even in the early period of Roman history. One of the earliest of these was the forerunner of the rectangular bronze breastplate, worn over a leather cuirass, of which there is documentary evidence from the 8th–7th centuries B.C. This was still being used in the 2nd century B.C., for the contemporary historian Polybius—referring to it as *kardiophylax*—mentioned it in his writings. It must certainly have been of Italic derivation, and there is proof of its having been used by the Etruscans up to the 3rd–2nd centuries B.C.

One of the most widely used types of protective harness in Rome was the so-called muscle armor (*thórax stádios* in Greek), which was modeled on the contours of the torso. Usually in bronze or iron—and leather versions are also believed to have existed—this type of cuirass consisted of a breastplate, a backplate, and shoulder straps. The style was of Greek origin, probably having reached the Romans by way of the Etruscans, who, as we know from their sculptures and other surviving evidence, were well acquainted with it. Muscle armor continued to be used by the Romans as late as the 4th–5th centuries A.D., as symbolic of the authority and power of the Roman Empire. From the time of the Republic, however, it was being worn almost exclusively by top-ranking military leaders and other high officials, and was to be adopted later by the Praetorian Guard. Heavily decorated loricae of this type were often depicted on statues of imperial Roman times, one of the best examples of which, dating to c. A.D. 14–29, is in the Vatican Museums. It is believed to represent Emperor Augustus (27 B.C.–A.D. 14), wearing a magnificently embossed lorica, depicting Emperor Tiberius (A.D. 14–37) receiving a standard from a vanquished barbarian, while disporting themselves in the heavens are various deities such as Diana, the morning star; Apollo, the sun-god; Aurora, goddess of the dawn; and Gaea, goddess of the earth, with her cornucopia.

Another type of cuirass was the *lorica squamata*, "scaled lorica." This was made of overlapping bronze or iron scales attached to a foundation of hide or strong cloth. The scales, joined to each other with metal wires, were usually positioned in horizontal rows and imbricated like roof tiles to ensure the wearer's complete protection. The scaled lorica derived indirectly from the scaled cuirass which was well known in the Middle East as far back as the second millennium B.C. By the 5th century B.C. it was widely used in Greece, and the probability is that from there it was introduced into Etruria, where the Roman armies would have seen it, for, almost certainly, the wealthier warrriors in Rome had adopted it by the 4th century B.C. As the Republic became more established, between the 3rd and 1st centuries B.C., even the mounted troops and legionnaires were equipped with the scaled lorica, and by the early days of the Empire it was being issued to the auxiliary units as well. On the Arch of Constantine, erected in A.D. 312–315, bas-relief figures can be seen wearing the scaled lorica, although by that time it had evidently become longer, partially covering the legs.

From about the 3rd century B.C., another type of body defense was being widely used by the Roman armies. This was the *lorica hamata*, or "hooked lorica," which consisted of small interlinked metal rings to form a kind of tunic or shirt of iron or bronze mail. Some of these were made with short sleeves and others with no sleeves at all. This type of metal protection was probably invented by the ancient Celts of western Europe, and the Romans adopted it from the Gauls around the beginning of the 3rd century B.C. From the time of the great soldier Marius (157–86 B.C.), who carried out sweeping reforms in the Roman army, the mail lorica seems to have become standard protective wear for foot and mounted soldiers alike. Like the lorica squamata, the mail version was sometimes reinforced with wide shoulder straps fastened to the breastplate with bronze rivets or metal studs. It is very likely that a leather or cloth garment was worn under the mail lorica, and there are a few, though rare, examples, depicted in bas-reliefs and on statues from the days of imperial Rome, showing a cloth garment worn over the lorica, like the surcoat of many centuries later. The mail lorica continued to be used by mounted troops until the latter part of the 3rd century A.D.

The best-known and most typical form of imperial Roman cuirass was, however, the *lorica segmentata*. Although this term was not used in ancient inventories or documents, it has become universally accepted as denoting a type of segmented body armor. Many knowledgeable enthusiasts have tried to reconstruct the segmented lorica, down to the minutest details of shape and structure. The most successful attempt to date has been made by H. Russell Robinson, a British scholar, whose efforts were concentrated on findings dated to the 1st century B.C. which have come to light in a Roman camp at Corbridge-on-Tyne, an English town whose Latin name was Corstopitum. From these and other finds a number of variations of the segmented lorica have been identified, particularly with regard to the different systems of lacing and the number and sizes of lames used. The basic structure of the segmented lorica—which protected the trunk—consisted of fourteen or sixteen semicircular iron lames, positioned horizontally and riveted onto straps. The lames were laced at the center of the breast and back in such a way as to encircle the trunk completely while still allowing the body considerable freedom of movement because of their articulation. The defense was completed with two large shoulder guards of articulated lames which were fastened to other lames that formed a neck guard. There were twenty-four lames in all, kept in place by a fairly complicated system of straps and buckles. Before the cuirass was put on, it had to be laced up at the back and then slipped on like a present-day jacket, finally being laced up the front. The segmented lorica became a standard component of a Roman legionnaire's protective equipment from the second quarter of the 1st century A.D. and remained in use at least until the end of the following century. There is so little evidence, either iconographical or archeological, regarding any later types of lorica that no reliable hypothesis can be formed.

Characteristic of many loricae were the leather strips, often reinforced with metal studs, suspended from the bottom edge of the cuirass to form a sort of skirt to protect the lower abdomen. These were known by their Greek name, *ptéryges*.

**lower bevor** *See* BEVOR.

**lower breastplate** *See* BREASTPLATE.

**Lowland sword** A type of Scottish sword similar to the CLAYMORE.

**"Lucerne hammer"** *See* WAR HAMMER.

**lyddite** An EXPLOSIVE consisting mainly of trinitrophenol (picric acid).

# M

**mabezashi** The visor of a Japanese helmet. *See also* KABUTO.

**mace** A hand weapon consisting of a strong rod or haft with a stone or metal head; the latter made it distinct from the primitive club which was made entirely of wood. In ancient times in the Middle East, maces with heads made of stone, bronze, and copper were in use. The Romans, who never adopted the mace as a standard weapon in their own armies, saw to it that their allies were equipped with bronze-headed maces. The mace can be divided into two main groups: the first type consisted of a ferrule from which extended knot- or node-shaped pieces in no particular pattern; the other, which was geometric in design, had vanes or conical or diamond-shaped flanges.

In the Middle Ages, the mace was used by soldier and knight alike, the latter carrying it slung over a hook on the saddlebow, often beside his sword. From the 11th century on, a type of mace, consisting of a stout wooden staff with a head varying greatly in shape, was seen all over Europe. The head of the Norman mace depicted in the Bayeux Tapestry (1066–77)—which was made in celebration of the battle of Hastings and the conquest of England—had three lobes. In Italy in the 14th century, there were maces with ribbed or flanged heads whose edges were parallel to

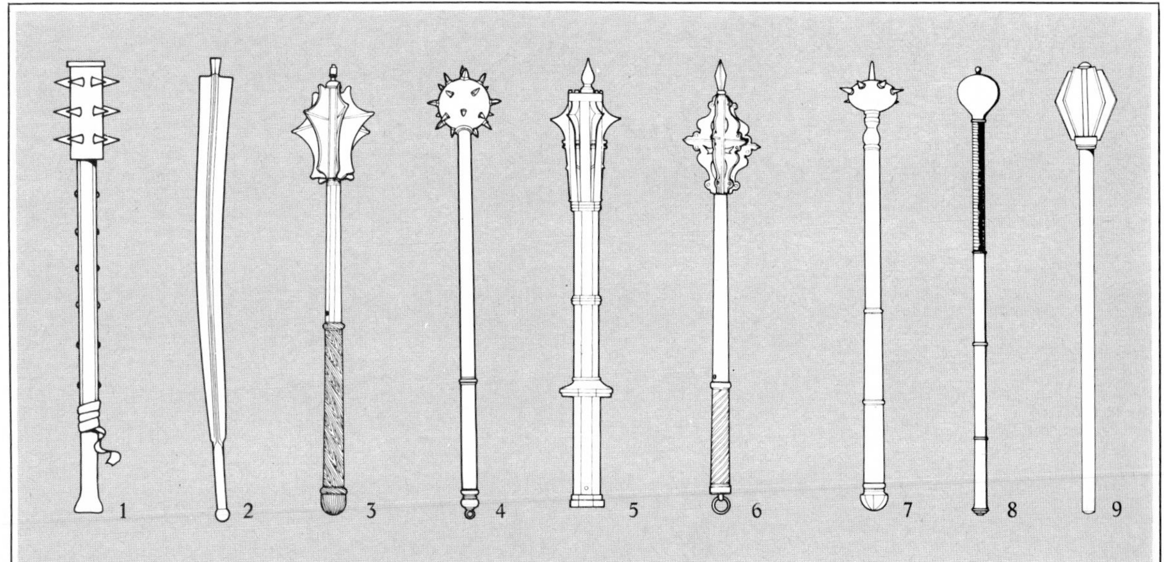


*Maces. 1. Europe, second half of the 13th century. 2. Italy, 14th–15th century. 3. Germany, early 16th century. 4. Italy, first half of the 16th century. 5. Austria, late 15th century. 6. Europe, mid-16th century. 7. Central or eastern Europe, early 17th century. 8. Eastern Europe, 16th–17th century. 9. Turkey, early 17th century.*

*Iron mace, 16th century, Museo Nazionale del Bargello, Florence.*

the handle, as well as a particular type of metal mace, apparently in use in central Italy: this weapon had a rounded grip, ending in a small pommel and a fairly long, narrow shaft formed by four or more ribs that broadened toward the top.

As combat weapons, maces varied a great deal in size, depending on whether they were used by foot soldiers or by men on horseback. The foot soldier's weapon can be clearly divided into two major categories, depending on whether it was an emergency weapon made by the village blacksmith (who was the first person to make certain simple forms of maces such as the MORGENSTERN and similar rustic weapons) or one made by an armorer who, though he might also equip local or peasant troops with the Morgenstern type of weapon, made weapons mainly for knights and professional soldiers. The knight's mace, which could be used with one hand, was fairly short and almost invariably made of metal; it played an important part in the knight's weaponry as early as the 13th century.

After the simplicity of the various maces made in the 14th century, the next century saw a wealth of highly complex maces, mainly owing to the influence which Gothic art had on all of man's expressions and products, particularly north of the Alps: spiraled or twisted grips with lobed discs at either end, decorated with scrolling and other designs around them; handles that were ribbed, fluted, straight, or twisted; heads with carefully shaped ribbing or flanges and a series of spikes ending in spire- or pinnacle-like tips. In the following century—the 16th—the lines of the mace took on an essentially combative appearance; only the wealthy seigneur's weapon was decorated and gilded. This was also the century in which, apart from the central and eastern European regions, where conflicts with the world of Islam caused the persistent use of the mace, the ribbed mace ceased to be used and gradually disappeared from the knight's armory. At the same time, some popular versions such as the Morgenstern, which from time to time was included even in the panoply of princes and knights, continued to be used. By then, however, combat between knights on horseback was virtually a thing of the past because firearms had become dominant. However, a wooden mace with deep fluting remained in use for a long time for courtly contests; this model was designed so as not to cause much injury to the contestants, whose main task was to demonstrate their skill and dexterity.

During the Middle Ages arming oneself with a mace had taken on significance among the nobility and commanding officers, and mace bearers became prominent in the retinues of influential and powerful figures. The king of France was preceded by a sergeant at arms with a mace bearing the royal lilies (*fleurs-de-lis*), and the pope was escorted by a corps of mace bearers that was still in existence until very recently. In eastern Europe, especially in Poland and Hungary, maces with "onion-shaped" heads, copied from Turkish models, were widely used until the 18th century (*see* BULAWA; BUZDYGAN). In time the

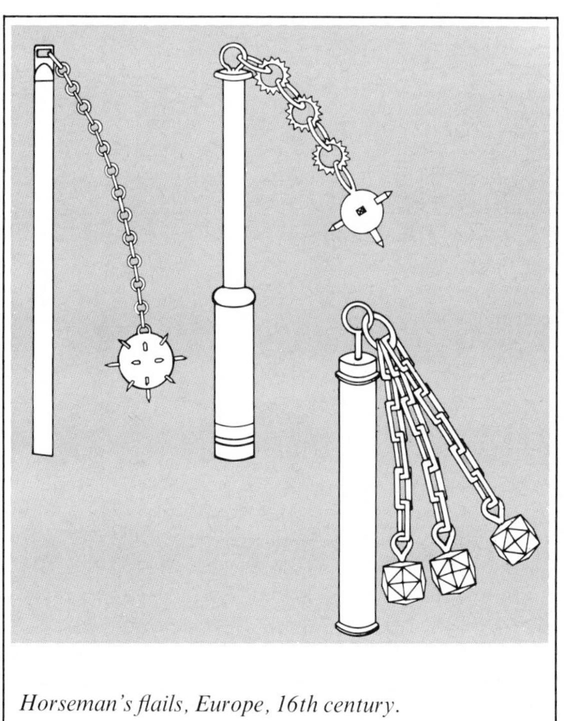

*Horseman's flails, Europe, 16th century.*

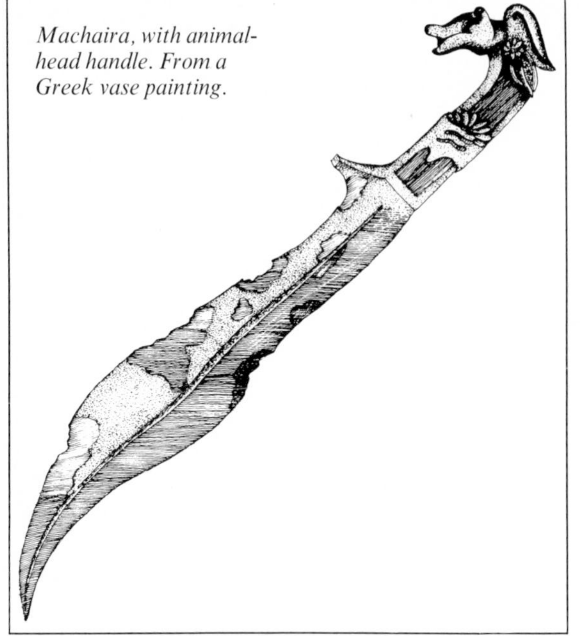

*Machaira, with animal-head handle. From a Greek vase painting.*

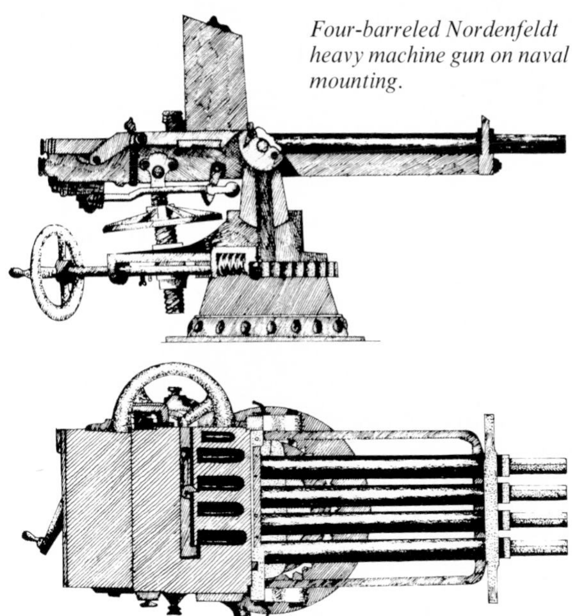

*Four-barreled Nordenfeldt heavy machine gun on naval mounting.*

mace became no more than a symbol of rank, with the number of ribs or flanges indicating the status of the owner.

**machaira** A single-edged, pointed war knife, carried by warriors in Homer's day and later, slung from a baldric or sword belt alongside the double-edged sword, the XÍPHOS. Authors writing after the Homeric period tended to confuse the two terms and sometimes even muddled them with KOPIS as well. The machaira was used by both infantry and cavalry. In fact, the Athenian historian and military chief Xenophon (c. 434–c. 355 B.C.) urged the cavalry to use the machaira instead of the sword because its cutting potential was greater. The machaira is distinct typologically from the kopis, which had a considerably more accentuated curvature and a concave cutting edge. It was also used for slaying sacrificial victims and for domestic uses. Among Latin authors, the term "machaira" is used to describe a single-edged, pointed sword for use with one or both hands. After the second Punic War (218–201 B.C.), it was issued to special corps known as *machairofóroi.*

**machete** A large knife with one entire cutting edge and the other sharpened for one-third of its length, used by sugarcane cutters in Central and South America. To make the knife easier to wield, the center of gravity is near the point. A military version was also made for use by American troops deployed in the Second World War in jungle operations in the Far East and Japan.

**machine gun** A rapid-fire weapon on a mount or a carriage, designed to use rifle cartridges or heavier ammunition and normally serviced by a crew of two or more men. Attempts to devise firearms capable of shooting a number of charges in rapid succession were made during the earliest phase in the history of firearms, resulting in the multibarreled batteries called RIBAULDS or organs, which were used until the 17th century. Other devices of the 15th to 18th centuries were based on the principle of the Roman candle, i.e., using superimposed loads connected by a fuse in one barrel. A battery of several such barrels could produce many shots in short time, but once the fuse was ignited the fire did not stop until the last charge was shot.

The invention of the percussion ignition and the percussion cap by 1820, which later made it possible to devise self-contained cartridges (by the 1860s), was one of the major factors in the development of machine guns. The first patent using the term "machine gun" was granted in 1829 to Samuel L. Farries in the United States. Other inventions using percussion ignition and, later, self-contained cartridges followed.

*Manually Operated Machine Guns*

The first modern machine gun was probably that designed by the Belgian engineer Fafschamps, a former captain in Napoleon's army. In 1851 Fafschamps went to the Montigny firm of Fontaine-l'Evêque for the necessary ammunition and to the Brussels firm of Fusnot et Montigny Fils for an assessment of his models. A Fafschamps machine gun was tested in Belgium between 1857 and 1859; it had a cluster of fifty breechloading barrels in nine alternating rows of five and six. The cartridges, with cardboard cases, were fired by a complex mechanism using long firing pins. The system was used again later, not only in Belgium in the Montigny-Christophe machine gun, but also in France.

The Montigny-Christophe consisted of a cluster of barrels (from seven to thirty-seven, depending on the caliber) mounted on a gun carriage, with mechanisms for loading, breech closure, and firing and a device for

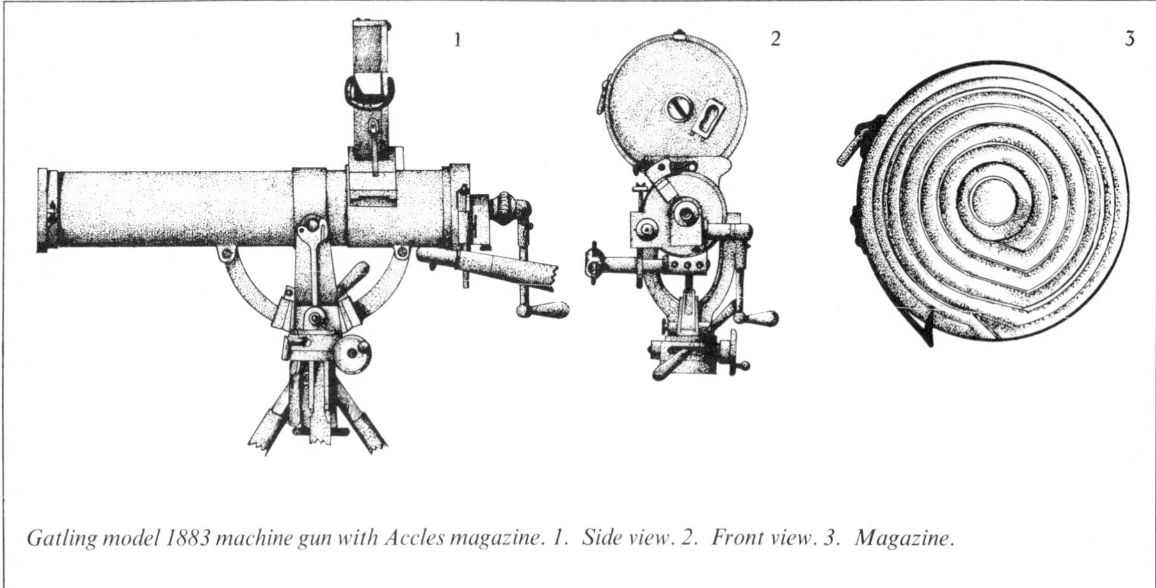


*Gatling model 1883 machine gun with Accles magazine. 1. Side view. 2. Front view. 3. Magazine.*

spreading out the shots sideways. The gun was loaded by pulling up a lever that withdrew the breechblock and inserting from the top a plate with cartridges. The plate was made of steel, with holes to hold the rear end of the cartridges; it was dropped between the breechblock and the barrel chambers, and as soon as it was fitted into the guides the percussion cap of each cartridge was aligned with an opening in the breechblock from which the strikers emerged on firing. When the breechblock was moved forward again, the plate also moved forward, enabling the cartridges to enter the chambers. By turning another lever, the firing pins were released one after another in order to fire all the barrels in turn. The Montigny-Christophe machine gun never worked very well, but the Austrian Montigny-Sigl, a development of the same basic design, met the challenge of every contemporary machine gun, including the Gatling.

Another arm developed from the Fafschamps was the French "mitrailleuse," the Meudon, also called the Reffye after the officer responsible for its production. Adopted in 1866, it had twenty-five 13 mm. barrels contained in a bronze casing and looked externally like an ordinary cannon; it was mounted on the carriage of a 4-pounder field gun. The gun was loaded and fired by two worm screws; one very big one, fitted along the major axis, moved the firing mechanism forward and back, while the other, operated by a wheel on the right-hand side of the breech, aligned the firing plate with the barrels.

During the Franco-Prussian War the Bavarian Army deployed the Feldl machine gun with a very fair measure of success. It was a comparatively light weapon, with four barrels chambered for the Werder rifle cartridge. A crankshaft set transversely actuated four individual breechblocks and released the respective strikers. Unfortunately, events moved too fast to allow this sensible and practical system to be fully developed.

*The Palmkranz-Nordenfeldt Machine Gun.* Another European multibarreled machine gun with separate breechblocks, the Palmkrantz, later known as the Nordenfeldt, was highly successful. Heldge Palmkrantz, a Swede, working with Unge and Winborg, approached his compatriot Thorsten Nordenfeldt, a well-known financier. Nordenfeldt recognized the value of the project and agreed to help on the condition that the gun be named for him. He set up a factory in England and very soon succeeded in getting a number of countries to adopt the new machine gun. The Nordenfeldt had from two to twelve barrels and could be chambered for cartridges of different calibers, from rifle ammunition to 25 mm. A rectangular iron frame enclosed the barrels and the action; it had two trunnions to attach it to a carriage. The barrels were arranged parallel at the front of the frame, and behind them the action could slide horizontally on guides. In the action block ran the bolts with the extractors and the strikers, driven by coil springs and having a catch on the underside. This mechanism was operated by the backward-and-forward movement of a hand lever. Two "locking studs" were fitted to the breechblock, and when the action moved forward they engaged in recesses in the frame and locked the system. After all barrels were consecutively discharged, the "carrier block" ejected the spent cases and lined up new cartridges from a hopper magazine opposite the chambers. The whole of this complex mechanism was operated by moving a single lever to and fro, resulting in up to100 rounds per minute fired by each barrel. It was this feature, together with the large number of barrels that could be fitted, that won for the weapon its outstanding reputation.

*The Gatling Gun.* In the United States, experiments with the production of rapid-fire weapons were often very successful. One interesting weapon was the hand-operated machine cannon patented in 1856 by C. E. Barnes of

Lowell, Massachusetts; the breech-closure system was operated by worm gearing worked by a crank. Outstanding among the many multibarreled weapons were the Ripley machine gun (1861), the Requa battery gun (1861–62), the Claxton with side-by-side barrels, the Claxton with a cluster of barrels (built and marketed later by the Lachaussée brothers in Liège), and the greatest of all hand-operated machine guns, the Gatling. Among single-barreled weapons of this period were the excellent Ager "coffee mill," the Williams, the Gorgas, and the Gardner.

The principle on which the Gatling worked is still employed in the Vulcan and guns developed from it; a brief description of one of the first models to use metal cartridges follows, although it must be remembered that Dr. Richard Jordan Gatling (1818–1903) designed his first weapon to use preloaded steel chambers that could be reloaded.

Fundamentally the Gatling gun consisted of a cluster of barrels that could rotate around an axis parallel with them, a magazine to feed them, and an action by which the cartridges were chambered and fired. The barrels—which varied in number according to the caliber of the weapon—were arranged in a circle around an iron arbor hinged at its two ends to the iron frame that enclosed the whole structure, extending to the rear to house a spiral-gear system. The barrels were fastened to each other (and to the arbor) by two bronze discs; their breech opening was flush with the rear face of the rear disc, to which they were screwed. Immediately behind this disc was a drum with grooves positioned to coincide with the chambers of the barrels. The cartridges were fed onto these grooves one at a time from a hopper fitted over the upper casing of the gun. Behind this drum was another, with a cast-iron cylinder around it for protection; there was a number of holes bored in it longitudinally, one for each barrel, for the bolts to slide in. When the mechanism was rotated, spiral cam tracks in a bronze outer casing interacted with studs on the bolts and the strikers to open and close the breeches, release each striker in turn, and extract spent cases. The whole system was worked by an endless screw hand turned by a crank on the right-hand side of the breech.

The Gatling machine gun, adopted by the U.S. Army in 1866, went through a great number of modifications over the years, and in 1893 was even powered by an electric motor, achieving a rate of 3000 rounds per minute. The feed system passed from the sloping hopper to the vertical prismatic magazine, from that to the radial-sector Broadwell drum, from the Accles drum to the long, straight, horizontal strip. The mechanics of the Gatling were so perfect that the system is still employed in powerful rapid-fire arms such as the Vulcan, the Minigun, and so on.

*The Hotchkiss Revolver Cannon.* Among the most successful machine guns invented in the United States was one known as the Hotchkiss revolver cannon. Built in France from 1875 onward by the American B. Hothckiss, it was another hand-operated weapon.

It got its name from the fact that its barrels were of exceptionally large caliber, from 37 mm. to 53 mm. The best-known model was the five-barreled 37 mm. gun; its barrels were arranged in parallel around an arbor that had

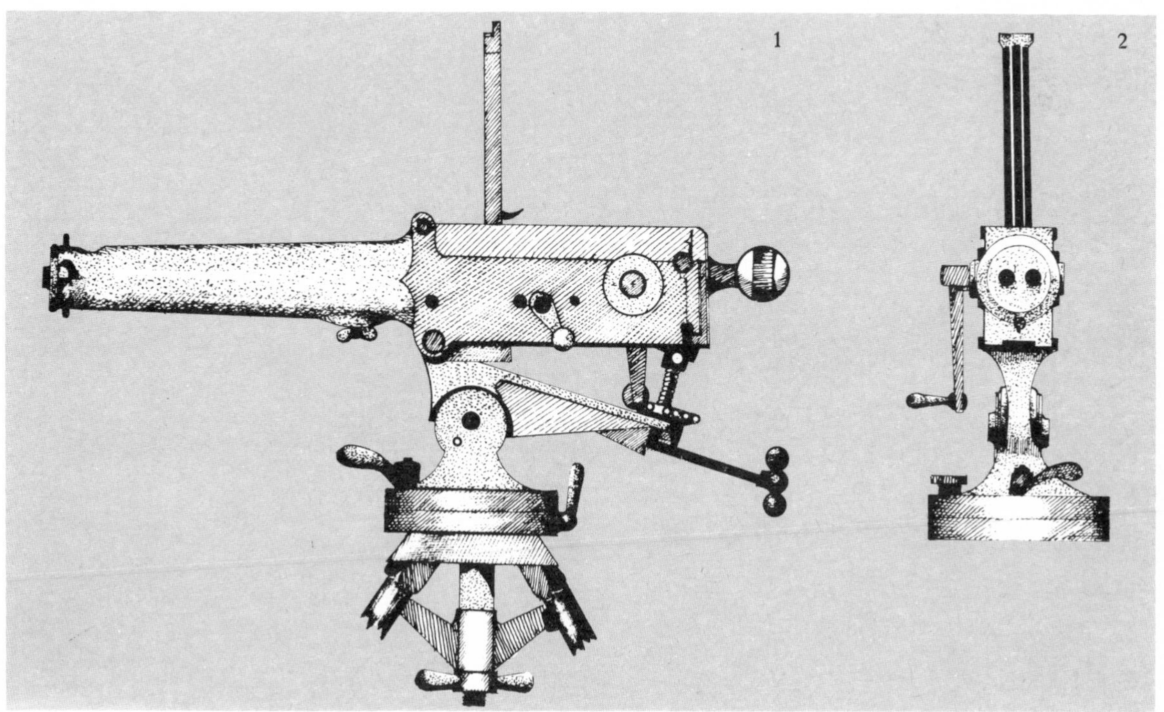


*Twin-barreled Gardner machine gun with water cooling. 1. Side view. 2. Front view.*

a gear wheel at its rear end that engaged with an endless screw operated by an external crank. The screw thread was interrupted so that the rotary movement of the barrels was not continuous, giving time for loading, firing, and the extraction of the spent cases. Feed was from an external hopper from which the cartridges fell into an opening in the metal casing around the mechanism.

The gun worked very simply: at the first turn of the crank a cartridge was loaded in the chamber of the barrel below the magazine opening. The barrels then began to rotate until, at the third turn, the cartridge just loaded came in line with the opening in the solid breechblock. Through this opening the striker, released in precise synchronization, struck the base of the cartridge case and fired the cartridge. At the end of the fifth turn of the crank, the empty case was extracted and ejected from the weapon. Because there were five barrels, one round was fired for every turn of the crank. The rate of fire depended, of course, on the strength of the firer; 60 rounds per minute was considered the optimum.

There was a range of mountings to meet different requirements, and the mechanism was fitted to control the laying of the gun. A pistol grip and a shackle were often fitted to make it easier to handle. Ammunition consisted of shells, armor-piercing shot, or machine gun ammunition.

Both the large-caliber Nordenfeldt and the Hotchkiss revolver cannon were used by the principal navies of the time. For a long time they were considered the best defense against the new danger represented by the torpedo.

*The Gardner Machine Carbine.* Another machine gun used extensively in Europe was the Gardner. The American inventor William Gardner of Toledo, Ohio, patented his weapon in 1874, but unable to obtain the capital necessary to manufacture and promote the weapon, he assigned manufacturing rights to the Pratt and Whitney company of Hartford, Connecticut. The fortunes of the weapon, and Gardner's fortunes as well, began to flourish when his machine gun was adopted by the Royal Navy; the British government opened a factory for its production under the direction of the inventor himself. A number of other countries hastened to follow the British example and adopted the Gardner. By far the most common model was the twin-barreled gun chambered for rifle ammunition. Externally the weapon looked like a small cannon: a slightly tapered bronze casing surrounded the two barrels, which were held in position by metal discs. There were two elliptical holes in the casing; the inventor's idea was that a current of air or water should be created through the holes for cooling or that the casing should be filled with water by closing a tap in the lower hole. Inside the bronze receiver were the feed, closure, firing, and extraction mechanisms. The cover plate, hinged to the receiver at the back, had an aperture for the magazine and two openings for the ejection of the spent cases. Inside was a bronze feeder with a steel bracket that guided a cartridge to the front of the bolt.

Inside the receiver were two steel bolts, working in guides. Each one worked as follows: (a) chambering the cartridge in the respective barrel; (b) firing the cartridge, ensuring that the breech was firmly closed; (c) extracting

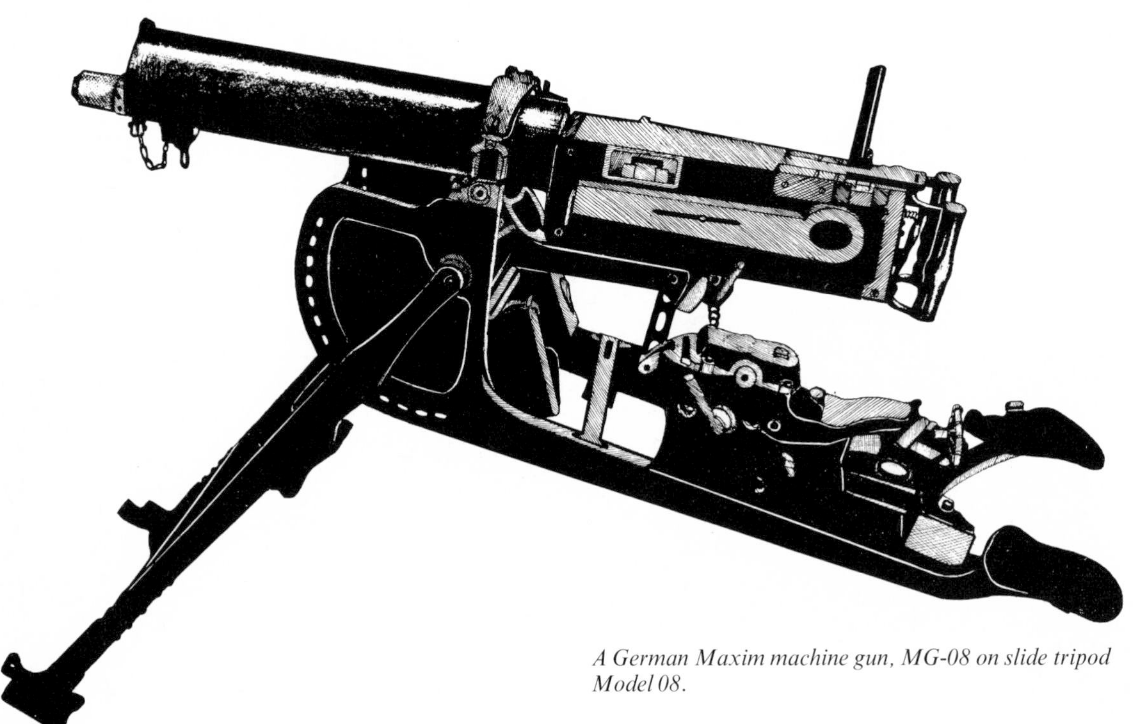

*A German Maxim machine gun, MG-08 on slide tripod Model 08.*

the case; (d) giving an oscillating movement to the cartridge guide and feeder; (e) operating the ejectors at the right moment.

The backward-and-forward movement of the two bolts was controlled by opposing cranks on a shaft attached to the inside of the receiver by bronze bearings and terminating outside with the firing crank and handle. There was a roughly U-shaped block at the back of each bolt and a steel bolt head at the front. A striker and a spring passed through each bolt in such a way that the point of the striker projected from the bolt head. Inside the bolt was a narrow tube with a rack on its underside; an opening in the bolt allowed the rack to engage the toothed head of a lever called the trigger ratchet. A steel sear with two arms was hinged in the U-block; the catch of one arm engaged the back of the striker, while the other arm was pressed against the respective eccentric on the crankshaft, releasing the striker at the right moment. As the firing crank was turned, one of the bolts moved forward, met the cartridge as it came out of the hopper, and loaded it into the chamber. While the crank was still being turned, the respective eccentric struck the arm of the sear, which released the striker. Still actuated by the eccentric, the bolt was withdrawn; it extracted the spent case and operated a long lever that acted as an ejector. This process was cyclical: as one bolt moved forward, the other was withdrawn so that two rounds could be fired with every turn of the crank. The rate of fire depended on the strength and quickness of the firer, 500 rounds per minute was considered the maximum if a five-barrel assembly was used.

Other mechanical machine guns worthy of mention are the British Lillie and Robertson, the U.S. Farwell, Lowell, Wilder, and Bailey, and the Swiss Albertini.

### *Automatic Machine Guns*

The first automatic machine gun was built by the American Hiram Maxim in 1884; a year before that, by fitting a Winchester carbine with a moving grip connected to the cocking lever, Maxim had produced a semiautomatic weapon operated by recoil. The inventor seems to have got the idea for the breech-closure action from the Gardner quick-firing gun. Maxim's first model had a crankshaft linked with the bolt action. On firing, the barrel and breechblock recoiled, locked together by a hook fixed to the barrel; after traveling about 2 cm. (0.8 in.), the barrel was halted and the unlocked bolt continued to the rear, extracting the spent case, recocking the firing mechanism, and compressing the return spring. Then the spring drove the bolt forward to chamber a cartridge already freed from the feed belt and positioned by a grooved reel. If the firing button was kept pressed, the action was repeated automatically until the ammunition was exhausted. This first model was followed almost immediately by a second, which proved to be the most famous and widely used machine gun for more than fifty years.

The Maxim soon demonstrated its offensive capacity. In the 1893 war against the Matabele, fifty Rhodesian police with four Maxims drove off 5000 warriors, leaving at least 3000 dead on the battlefield. There were similar episodes during the Chitral campaign of 1895 on the Afghan frontier and during the Sudan campaign. In the 1898 battle of Omdurman, more than 20,000 dervishes were killed; it was estimated that three-quarters of the casualties were attributable to the Maxim machine gun. The weapon was tested by nearly every country and adopted by many of them. Tactics that had been employed since the time of Napoleon were completely undermined; the advent of the Maxim marked the end of an era.

In 1889 Austria adopted the Maxim. Thirty of 8 mm. caliber were ordered for the defense of Kraków and Przemyśl. However, the Austrian government found three main faults in the machine gun. The first two were its excessive weight and the necessity of using black-powder cartridges; it was found that the breech-closure action did not stand up for long to the high pressure developed by smokeless cartridges, which the Austrians adopted in 1890. The third fault, probably the most serious, was the high cost of the weapon: a single Maxim, without stand or spare parts, cost no less than 3750 florins (about $1800 at the time). Consequently, the Austrian General Staff examined a machine gun designed by Carl Salvator and General Georg Ritter von Dormus. This weapon was ready for production in 1888; it worked on the delayed-blowback principle, was gravity-fed from a hopper, and cooled by water in a jacket around the barrel. In practice, many design faults came to light: the weapon was easily put out of action by fouling, and the gravity feed system severely limited vertical movement. The Salvator–von Dormus machine gun was soon relegated to fortresses and ships; it is nevertheless of interest because it was the first European effort to produce a machine gun in competition with the Maxim monopoly. It really was a monopoly; between 1883 and 1885 the shrewd American inventor had managed to patent almost every imaginable system that could be used in automatic weapons.

A gas-operated system used in the Hotchkiss machine gun was based on a patent obtained by the Austrian Baron Adolf von Odkolek; it employed a portion of the propelling gases in a cylinder with piston beneath the barrel—a feature found in all future models of the Hotchkiss machine gun. The first model was ready in 1895; tests carried out by the U.S. Navy made some modifications necessary, and these were incorporated in the 1897 model. In the 1900 model, poor cooling was corrected by fitting a radiator of steel fins. Other changes were made in later models, but for all practical purposes, the 1914 Hotchkiss, with which France entered the First World War, was merely a lighter version of the 1895 model. The Hotchkiss was first used in action during the Russo–Japanese War of 1904–05. The Russians were armed with Maxims, while their opponents deployed large numbers of recently acquired Hotchkiss guns. The Hotchkiss was apparently less efficient than the Maxim; an official Japanese report published in 1910 contained the statement that during the battle of Hei-kou-tai the Hotchkiss machine guns had a stoppage on an average after every 300 rounds.

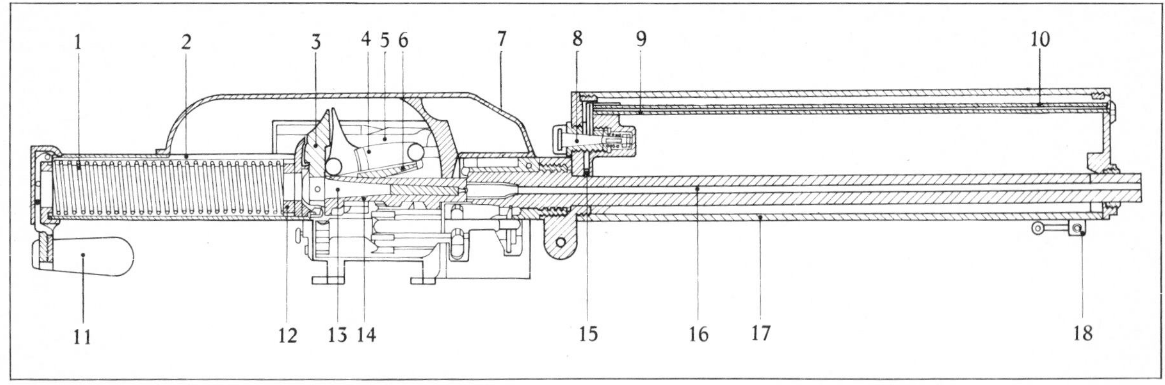


*Schwarzlose model 1907 machine gun, longitudinal section. 1. return spring; 2. release rod; 3. cocking arm; 4. interior toggle arm; 5. sear; 6. exterior toggle arm; 7. oil reservoir; 8. steam release valve; 9. steam release tubes; 10. steam tube port; 11. handgrip; 12. bearing nut; 13. striker; 14. bolt; 15. safety valve; 16. barrel; 17. cooling jacket; 18. drain tap.*

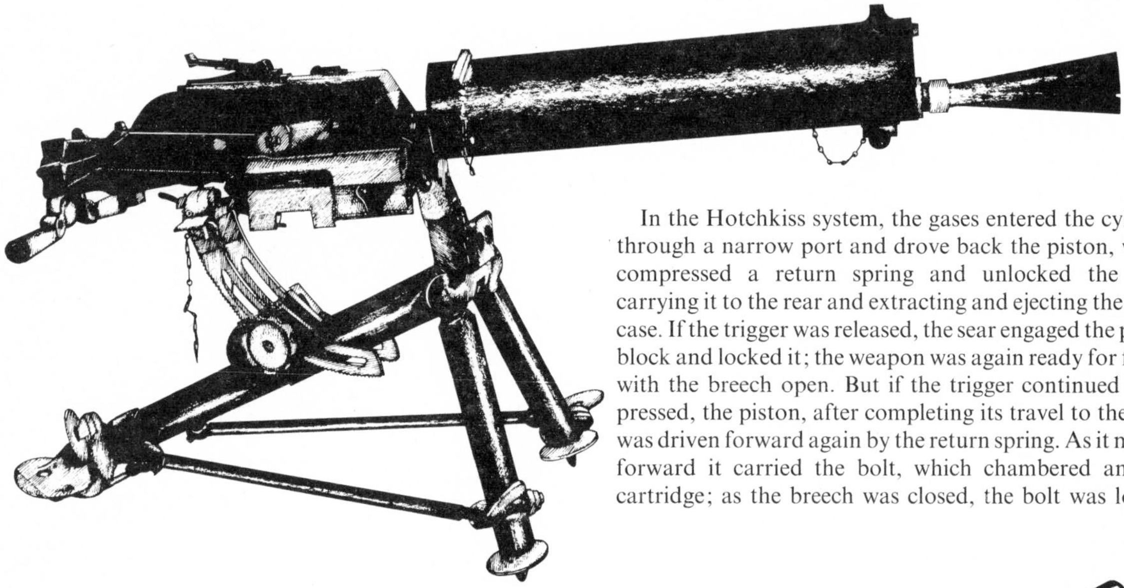

In the Hotchkiss system, the gases entered the cylinder through a narrow port and drove back the piston, which compressed a return spring and unlocked the bolt, carrying it to the rear and extracting and ejecting the spent case. If the trigger was released, the sear engaged the piston block and locked it; the weapon was again ready for firing, with the breech open. But if the trigger continued to be pressed, the piston, after completing its travel to the rear, was driven forward again by the return spring. As it moved forward it carried the bolt, which chambered another cartridge; as the breech was closed, the bolt was locked

*Austrian Schwarzlose model 1907* (above) *and model 1907/12* (below).

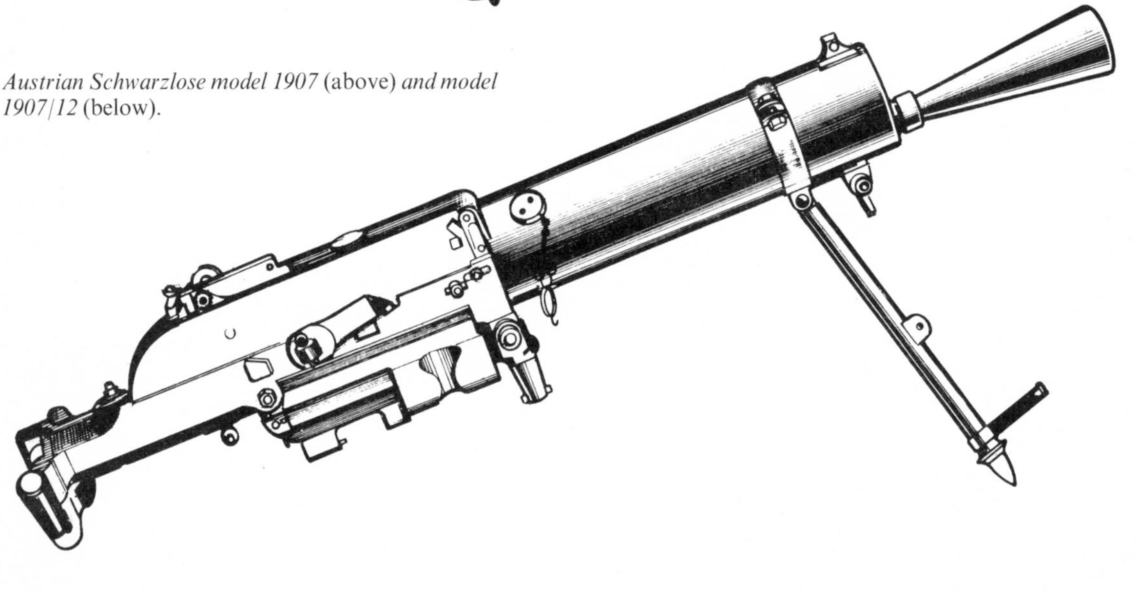

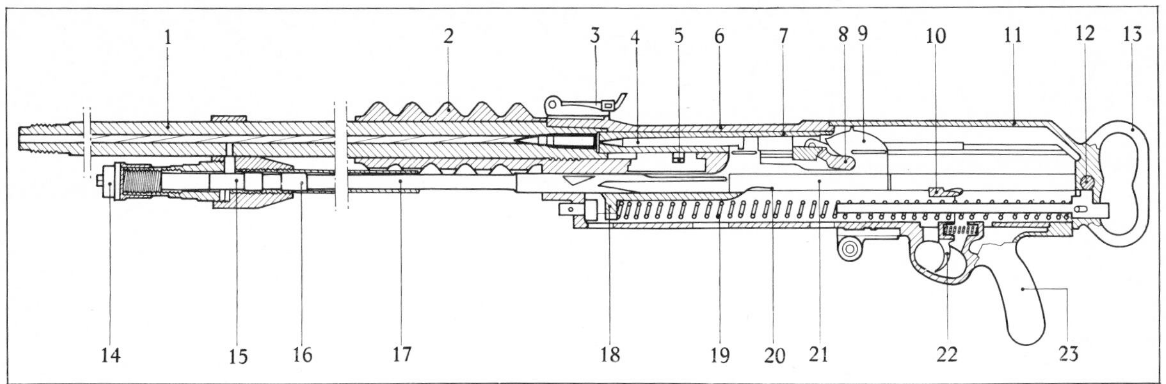


*Hotchkiss model 1914 machine gun, longitudinal section. 1. barrel; 2. radiator; 3. backsight; 4. striker; 5. cartridge lifter; 6. upper part of receiver; 7. bolt; 8. oscillating lug; 9. crank; 10. sear; 11. casing; 12. locking bolt; 13. handgrip; 14. regulator plug; 15. expansion chamber; 16, 17. piston; 18. spring base; 19. return spring; 20. stop catch; 21. piston rod; 22. trigger; 23. pistol grip.*

into the body by a lug hinged to the back of the bolt. Immediately after that, the striker fired the cartridge. Feed was accomplished by means of a metal strip fitted with clips to hold the cartridges.

*Principal Producing Countries*

*Austria.* After the disappointing performance of the Salvator–von Dormus, the military concentrated their attention on a machine gun acting on the blowback principle, with no breechlocking device, designed by Andreas Schwarzlose. All that held up the opening of the breech on firing was a hinged toggle arm and a powerful return spring. The barrel was relatively short so that the bullet could leave before the inertia and resistance of the breechblock were overcome; the action did not open until the internal pressure had fallen to the surrounding level. The Schwarzlose models 1907 and 1907/12, water-cooled and fed by canvas belts, always performed very well, and indeed were still in use by some African liberation movements seventy years after their introduction.

*Belgium.* The first machine gun developed in Belgium was the very modern MAG (*mitrailleuse à gaz*) produced by the Fabrique Nationale in the 1950s. It was a first-rate weapon, which combined the breech-closure system of the BAR (Browning Automatic Rifle) with the feed system of the German MG-42. The barrel could be changed quickly, and the rate of fire varied between 700 and 1000 rounds per minute.

*Czechoslovakia.* In 1922 the Československa Zbrojovka Akciova Společnost was formed at Brno and began production of the 1922 model Hotchkiss under license. As the result of research by a group of constructors, Vaclav and Manuel Holek, Anton Marek, and Antonin

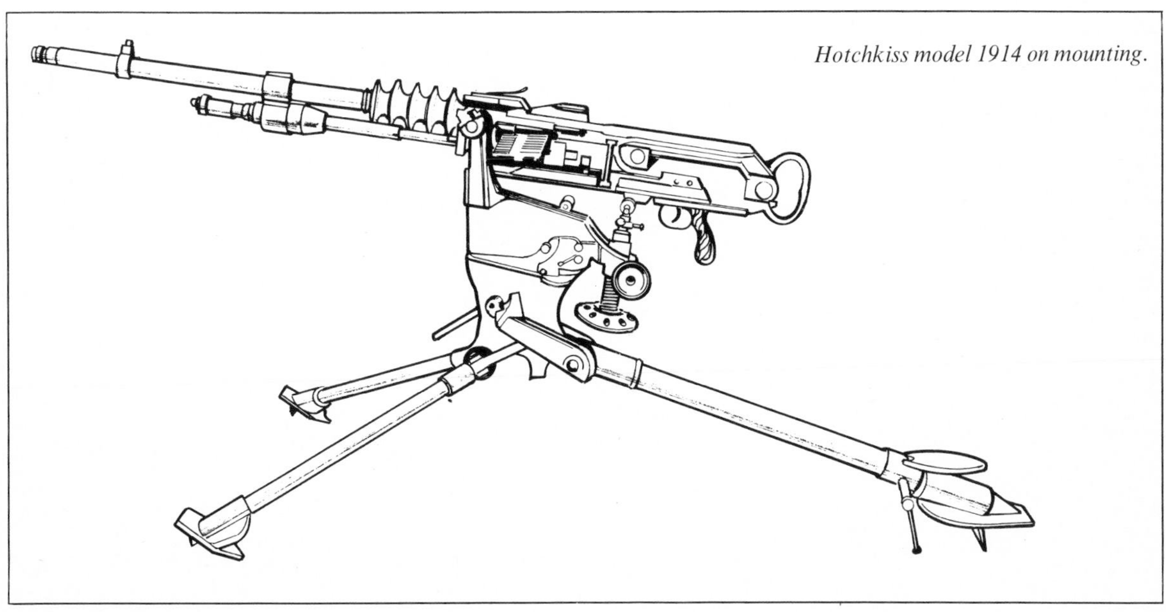

*Hotchkiss model 1914 on mounting.*

*Bren Mark I, 7.7 mm. caliber.*

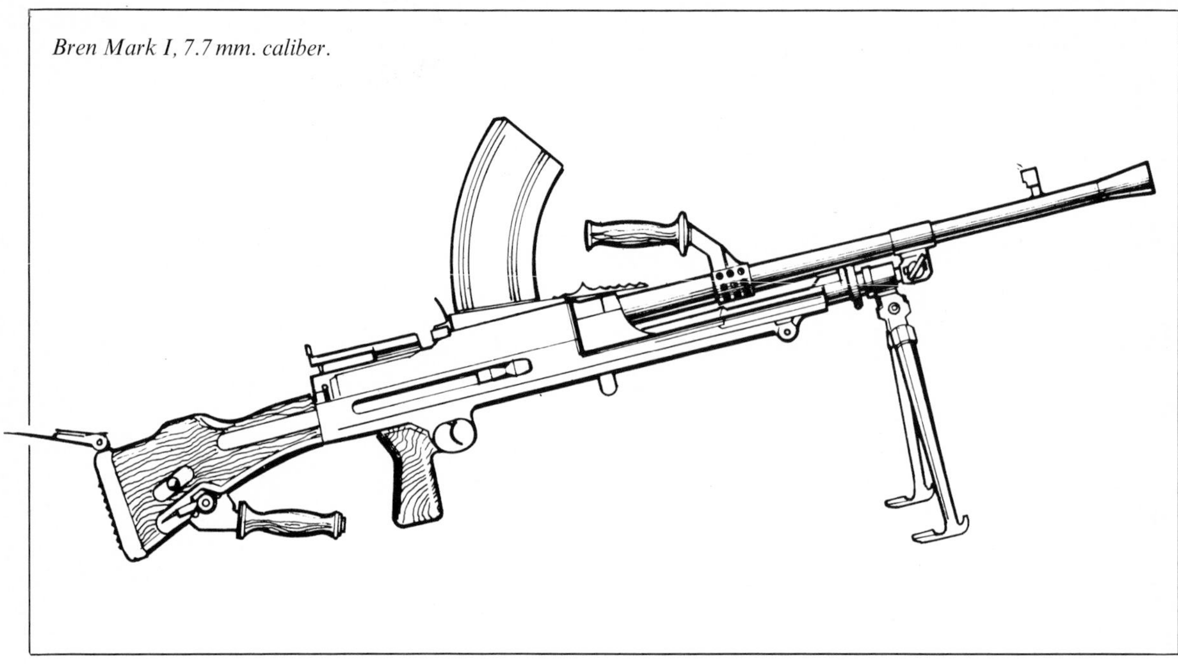

Podrabsky, the firm was soon able to demonstrate arms of its own design. Among these were the ZB-26 and its later modifications, the ZB-27, ZB-30, and ZB-34; from this series the famous Bren (Brno-Enfield) gun, adopted by the British, was developed. All were light, gas-operated maching guns with bipods. Feed was from pressed-steel box magazines fitted on top of the body; a quick-change barrel system allowed the guns to be fired for very long periods. Another remarkable machine gun was the 1937 Model ZB-53, designed under the direction of Vaclav Holek and adopted in Britain under the name Besa (Brno-Enfield Small Arms) with 7.92 mm. caliber (it had certain features that made it impossible to use the British .303 cartridge, which was rimmed). It should be regarded as a heavy weapon, although an even larger version was manufactured to fire a 15 mm. antitank cartridge. The VZ-52 and the VZ-59 machine guns, produced after the war and chambered for the Russian 7.62 mm. M-43 cartridge, were further improvements on the ZB series; fed by metal belts and simplified in design, they are among the best arms in this class.

*Denmark*. Production began in 1902 of an extraordinary machine gun, the Madsen, that in one or another version (there have been more than one hundred, of calibers between 6.5 mm. and 23 mm.) was adopted by many countries. Alone among automatic weapons in series production, the Madsen had an oscillating breechblock hinged at the rear, very much like the old Peabody rifle system. It was a short-recoil gun; the barrel and breechblock recoiled locked together on firing and after they had traveled a little over a centimeter, the breechblock was pivoted upward and the empty case was extracted and ejected by an independent, automatically operating extractor. The barrel and breechblock were driven forward again, the breechblock now pivoted downward; a cartridge was placed on its upper surface, and a lever pressed it into the chamber. As soon as the barrel was back in its original position, the breechblock was pivoted back to its middle position and closed the breech. The Madsen machine gun was fed from box magazines, generally curved, fitting over an opening in the upper surface of the body. Soundly built from excellent materials, it worked particularly well in the versions for rimless cartridges; the rate of fire was seldom more than 500 rounds per minute. Toward the end of the 1950s, the firm gave up the old system and introduced a gas-operated machine gun, the Madsen-Saetter, which had a breechblock with locking lugs. The new weapon could not compete with the German MG-42 and the Belgian MAG and never went into mass production.

*France*. Although the French Army had carried out trials of the Hotchkiss 1893 model, it did not acquire large numbers of them. In 1905 the state arsenal at Puteaux began production of a machine gun in which the gas tapped from the barrel was channeled through a complicated system of pipes toward the breech to drive a short piston forward from behind. As the piston was driven, a rack on its upper surface turned the pinion, which drew back the bolt and withdrew the spent cartridge. The barrel of the Puteaux had cooling fins right up to the muzzle; the weapon was also fitted with a control that enabled the rate of fire to vary from 8 to 650 rounds per minute. Although this weapon was adopted, it was never considered efficient, and in 1907 the Saint-Etienne arsenal produced a variant that seems to have worked a little better. The closure and feed systems in the 1907 model (also known as the Saint-Etienne) were the same as in the Puteaux, but there was a simpler and more reliable method

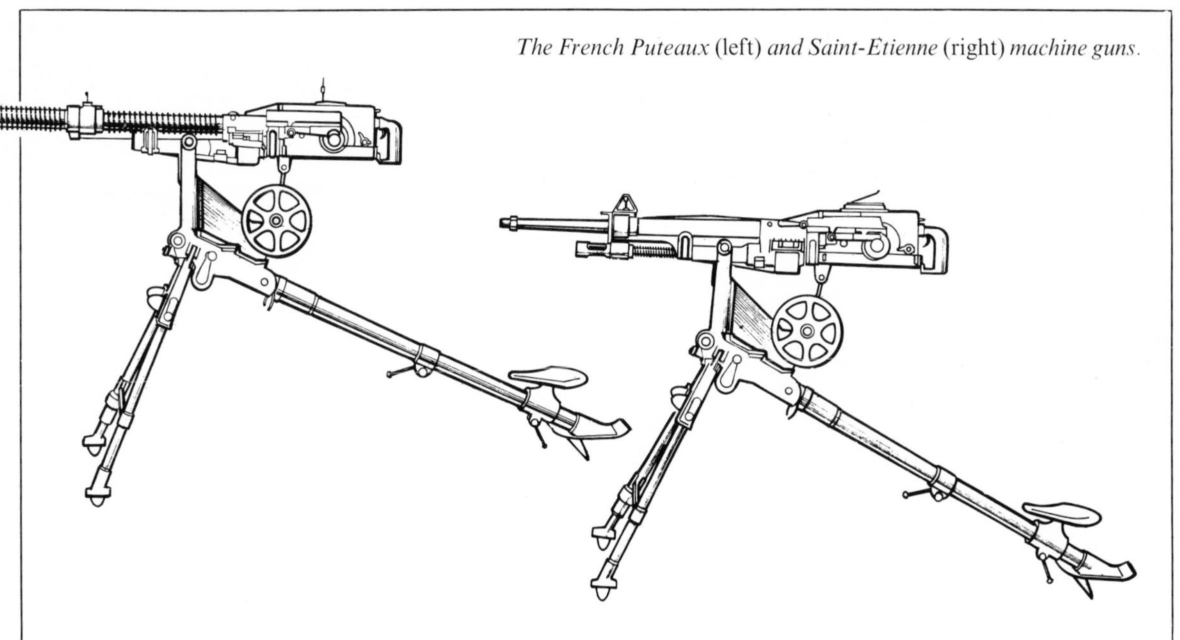

*The French Puteaux* (left) *and Saint-Etienne* (right) *machine guns.*

of tapping the gases. The cooling fins fitted on the Puteaux were scrapped; the Saint-Etienne had a radiator jacket around the barrel made of an alloy of 90 parts bronze and 10 parts aluminum. The Saint-Etienne was widely used in Italy as well as in France but does not seem to have acquired a good reputation; only the 1914 model Hotchkiss stood up to the German MG-08 during the First World War. In 1909 the Hotchkiss company introduced a new light machine gun, the Benet-Mercié; it was gas-operated, with a breech-locking system in which a cylindrical bolt, sliding and turning, had locking lugs that fitted into an interrupted thread inside a rotating collar around the breech, the "fermeture nut." This gun was adopted by the French and United States armies but saw little service, since in war conditions it proved awkward in use and its mechanism was delicate.

The need for relatively light automatic weapons that could be turned out quickly and cheaply impelled the French to adopt the Chauchat in 1915. This was a long-recoil, light machine gun fed from a curious crescent-shaped magazine. Constructed from a number of drawn tubes, the Chauchat earned the reputation of being the worst weapon employed in the First World War. As soon as the war was over, it was replaced; a light machine gun, similar mechanically to the BAR and the Berthier light machine gun, was developed at the Chatellerault Arsenal. The prototype, chambered for a 7.5 mm. cartridge derived from the Swiss 1911 model, was developed in 1921; it had become clear by that time that 8 mm. Lebel ammunition, with its large bore and pronounced rim, would never work properly in an automatic weapon. The first Chatellerault, the model 1924, officially adopted by the French Army, proved to have serious faults, which were attributed to the poor quality of the materials used in its manufacture and to an ineffective method of cooling the breechblock. After necessary modifications were made, the Chatellerault model 1924/29 proved to be an excellent weapon; it was reliable and had excellent ballistic properties.

After the Second World War the problem of equipping the armed forces with a modern machine gun arose again, and was resolved by adopting the AAT (Arme Automatique Transformable) model 1952. Fed from nondisintegrating metal belts, it worked on a delayed-blowback system with a bolt divided into two sections. The mechanism was similar to that of the CETME rifle and the SIG rifle; it was a fairly simple weapon that was cheap to manufacture, and seems to have performed very well.

*Germany*. The German Army adopted the Maxim at the end of the 19th century and standardized it in the versions known as MG-99 and MG-101; the Germans then produced a slightly lighter and improved machine gun known as the MG-08. This was followed by the still lighter MG-08/15, which was fitted with a pistol grip and a bipod. During the First World War another first-class machine gun, still based on the Maxim principle, was produced; this was the Parabellum, mainly used as an aircraft weapon. The Gast, the design of which was developed from the machine gun patented by Bethel Burton in 1886, came too late to be produced in quantity, but its performance made it clear that it was one of the best weapons ever produced. It had two barrels, with the breechblocks cross-connected by a strong beam so that the recoil from one barrel actuated the firing of the other; the breechblocks were locked in position by two pairs of rotating discs. Fed from two large drums each holding 180 rounds, the Gast was theoretically capable of a rate of fire of 1800 rounds per minute. A series of machine guns functioning on short recoil was produced between 1900

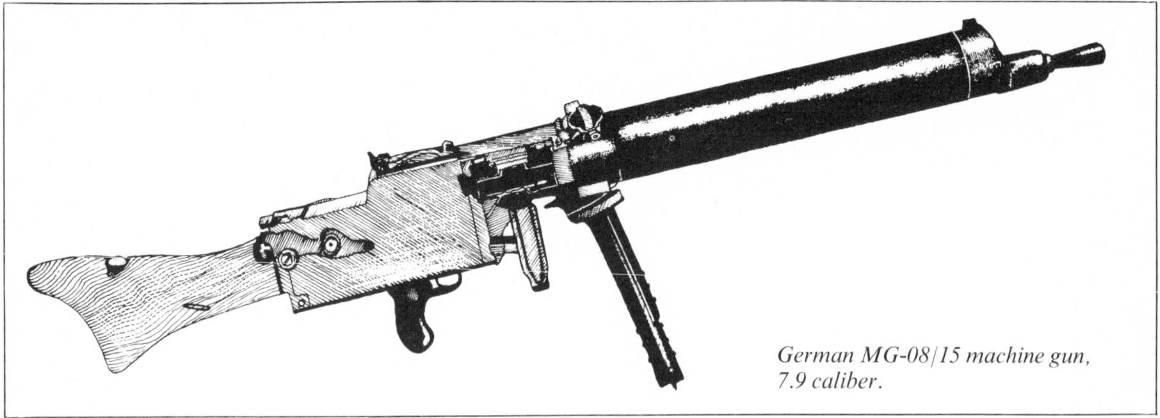

*German MG-08/15 machine gun, 7.9 caliber.*

and 1910 by Theodor Bergmann of Gaggenau. The Bergmann had a falling breechblock; it was fed from flexible aluminum belts with elastic steel clips to hold the cartridges.

Another interesting weapon was the Dreyse, designed by Louis Schmeisser and named after the inventor of the needle gun. It was patented in 1907 and produced until 1918. Its closure system, with a powerful hinged lever that exerted pressure on the rear of the breechblock to lock it firmly against the barrel at the moment of firing, was used again after the war in the MG-13, the first light machine gun for the new German Army. The MG-15, designed for use in aircraft but also widely used by the infantry, used a closure system with a rotating collar designed by Louis Stange, which had met with widespread approval in the various Solothurn machine guns. It was fed from a distinctive saddle magazine holding 75 rounds. Among other machine guns used in aircraft were the MG-17, MG-131, and MG-81. The latter was a development of the well-known infantry weapon, the MG-34. The MG-34, produced by Waffenfabrik Mauser A.G., was among the best designed and best constructed weapons of the Second World War. The barrel could be changed quickly, and feed was from a metal belt; it was a short-recoil machine gun with a bolt that had a turning head with retaining lugs. When mounted on the MG-Lafette-34 tripod, this weapon made a very effective heavy machine gun; used on the bipod, it was an excellent light machine gun. In service it was found to be very sensitive to dirt, and the crew had to be thoroughly trained to get the best results. With the MG-42, which came into service toward the end of 1942, the Germans had what is probably the best machine gun ever produced. It was another short-recoil weapon; the breechblock was a cylinder with a wider moving section at the front and two locking lugs that moved horizontally. When the round was fired, the lugs were pressed outward and engaged in slots in a mounting at the breech. The breechblock and barrel were thus firmly locked together, and recoiled for about 12 mm. (0.47 in.). The barrel was then halted while sloping ramps pressed the locking lugs inward, releasing the breechblock; the breechblock had acquired sufficient impetus to carry it farther back, extracting the spent case, compressing the return spring, and operating the feed system by means of a roller fitting at the rear. The firing mechanism was designed only for automatic fire, and there was a simple quick-change arrangement for the barrel. The MG-42 was remarkably cheap to produce; apart from the barrel and breechblock, nearly all the other parts were stamped from heavy sheet steel. The MG-42, under different names and with certain modifications—for example, to reduce the rate of fire (an increase of 400 grams in the weight of the breechblock changes it from 1200 to 700 rounds per minute) and to take different types of metal feed belts—is in service with a great many armies: Austria M-42/59, Chile MG-42/59, Denmark MG-G2, Iran MG-1A, Italy MG-42/59, Norway MG-3, Pakistan MG-1A3, Portugal MG-42/59, Switzerland MG-51, Turkey G-3, West Germany MG-3, Yugoslavia M-53.

*Great Britain.* Britain was among the first of the great powers to adopt an automatic machine gun but has always relied on foreign designs, preferring to choose the best foreign weapons rather than less good "homemade" designs. Nevertheless, the British have been responsible for improving the weapons they adopted from abroad, from the development of the Maxim into the Vickers medium machine gun to the various changes recognizable in the Czechoslovak Bren and Besa guns. Other foreign machine guns adopted on a large scale were the Lewis, the Vickers-Berthier (for the Indian Army), and currently the Belgian F.N. MAG (L-7A2).

The Lewis gun, British by adoption, was the design of an American, Colonel I. N. Lewis. When the Americans turned it down, Lewis set up a factory for its manufacture in Belgium, and in 1914, when Belgium was overrun by the enemy, he transferred production to the BSA factory in Britain, and the British Army subsequently adopted the gun. Few light automatics have generated such success and such widespread adoption as the Lewis: thirty-two models, adoption by a dozen countries, hundreds of thousands produced. It was a gas-operated gun that used a piston in a cylinder beneath the barrel; the breech-closure system used a sliding and rotating bolt. At the rear end of the piston were a strong piston post and a rack on the downward face that engaged the pinion attached to the helical clock-type return spring. The bolt was a cylindrical

# 16th-century arms and armor

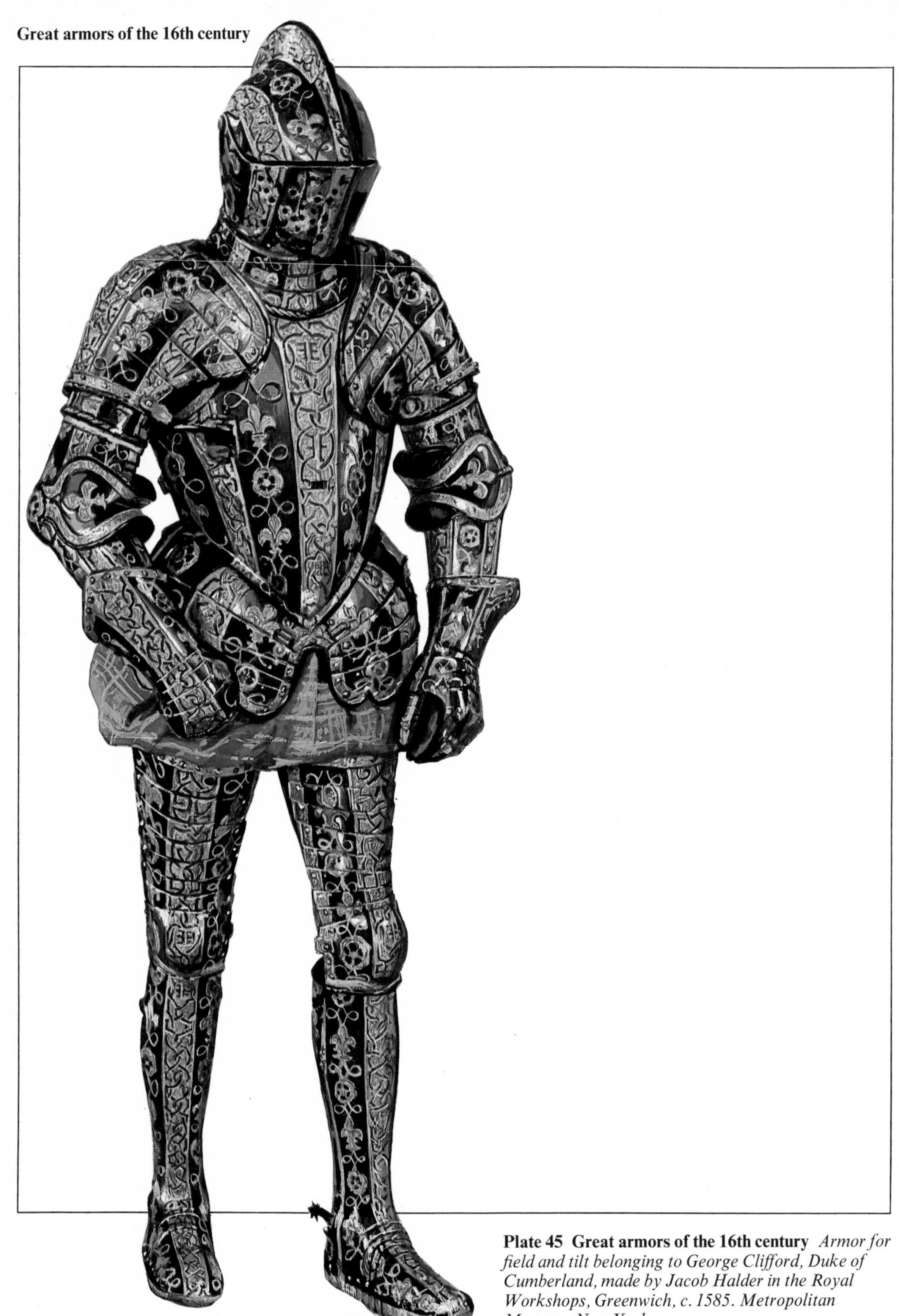

**Plate 45 Great armors of the 16th century** *Armor for field and tilt belonging to George Clifford, Duke of Cumberland, made by Jacob Halder in the Royal Workshops, Greenwich, c. 1585. Metropolitan Museum, New York.*

**Plate 46 16th-century helmets** (above) *Close helmet belonging to the so-called "blue and gold" garniture of Emperor Maximilian II of Hapsburg, S. Germany, c. 1550. Waffensammlung, Vienna.* (below) *Burgonet with detachable bevor-visor, worked in a diamond design, belonging to Emperor Charles V and made by Kolman Helmschmied, Augsburg, c. 1520–30. Armería Real, Madrid.*

**Plate 47 16th-century helmets** (above) *Parade burgonet mounted with tilt visor, France, c. 1540. Tower of London Armouries.* (below) *Gold morion with enameled decoration belonging to Charles IX of France, made by the goldsmith Pierre Reddon, Paris, 1572. Louvre, Paris.*

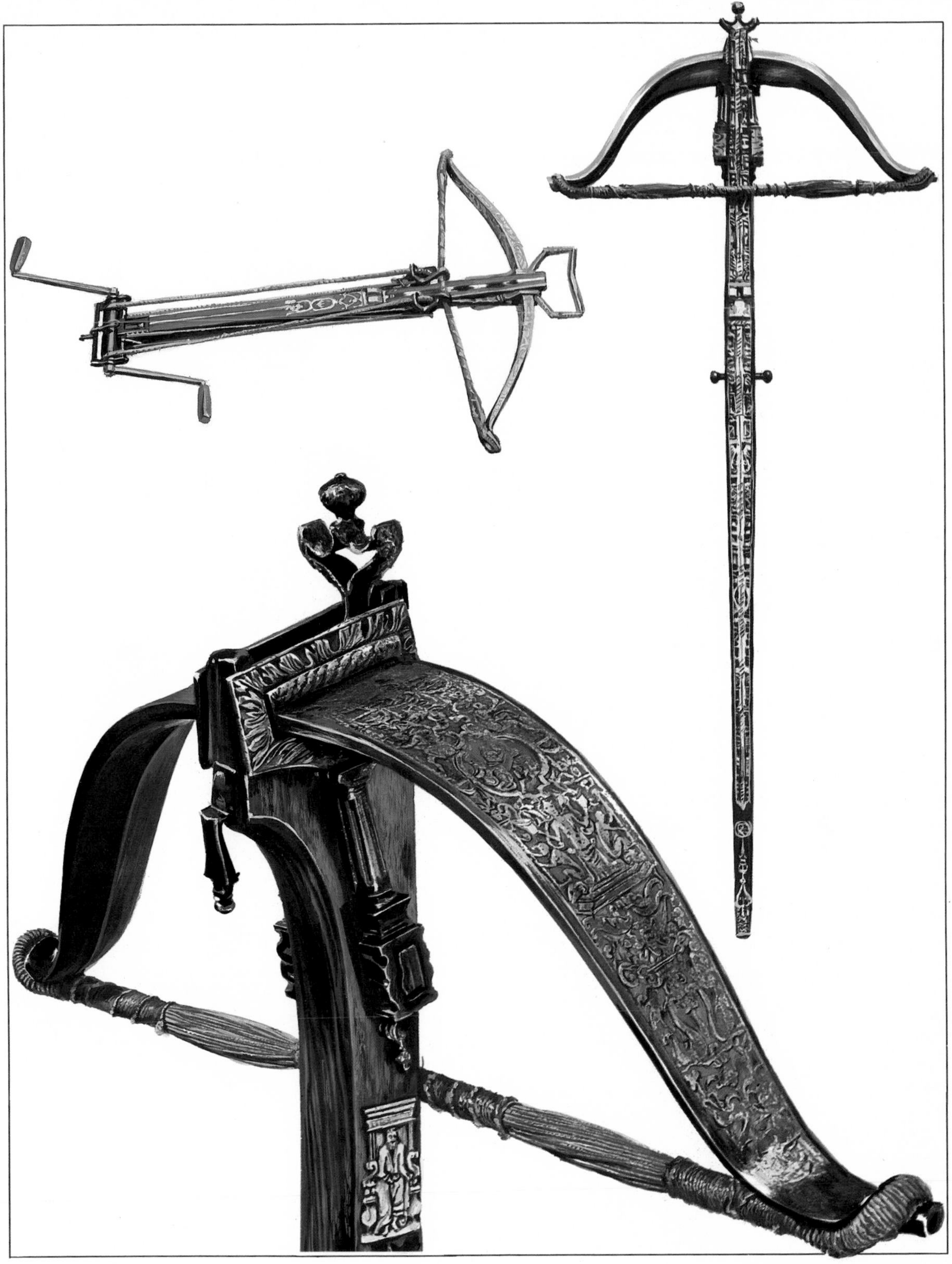

**Plate 48 16th-century crossbows** (top left) *Windlass crossbow which belonged to Louis XII of France, Spain, early 16th century. Waffensammlung, Vienna.* (top right) *Crossbow with "goat's foot" lever, France, c. 1530–50, and* (below) *detail of the same crossbow. Museo Nazionale del Bargello, Florence.*

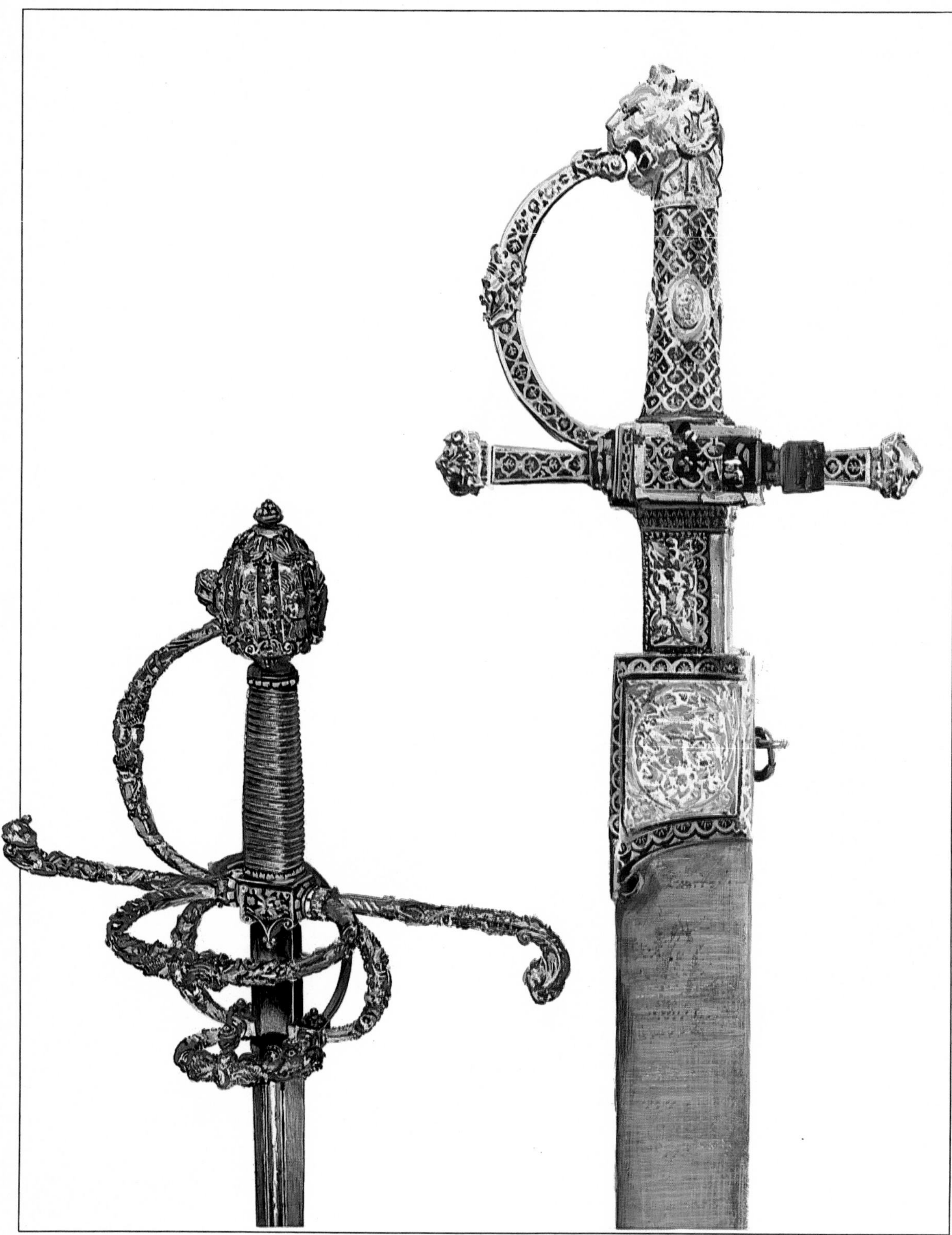

**Plate 49 16th-century swords** (left) *Rapier with gold and enameled furniture which belonged to Archduke Ferdinand of Tyrol, Spain, c. 1550. Waffensammlung, Vienna.* (right) *Falchion combined with a wheel-lock pistol, possibly belonging to Henry II of France, France, c. 1555. Waffensammlung, Vienna.*

**Plate 50 16th-century swords** (left) *Horseman's sword with gold-damascened hilt, Milan, c. 1560. Waffensammlung, Vienna.* (right) *Rapier, Italy, c. 1570. Museo Stibbert, Florence.*

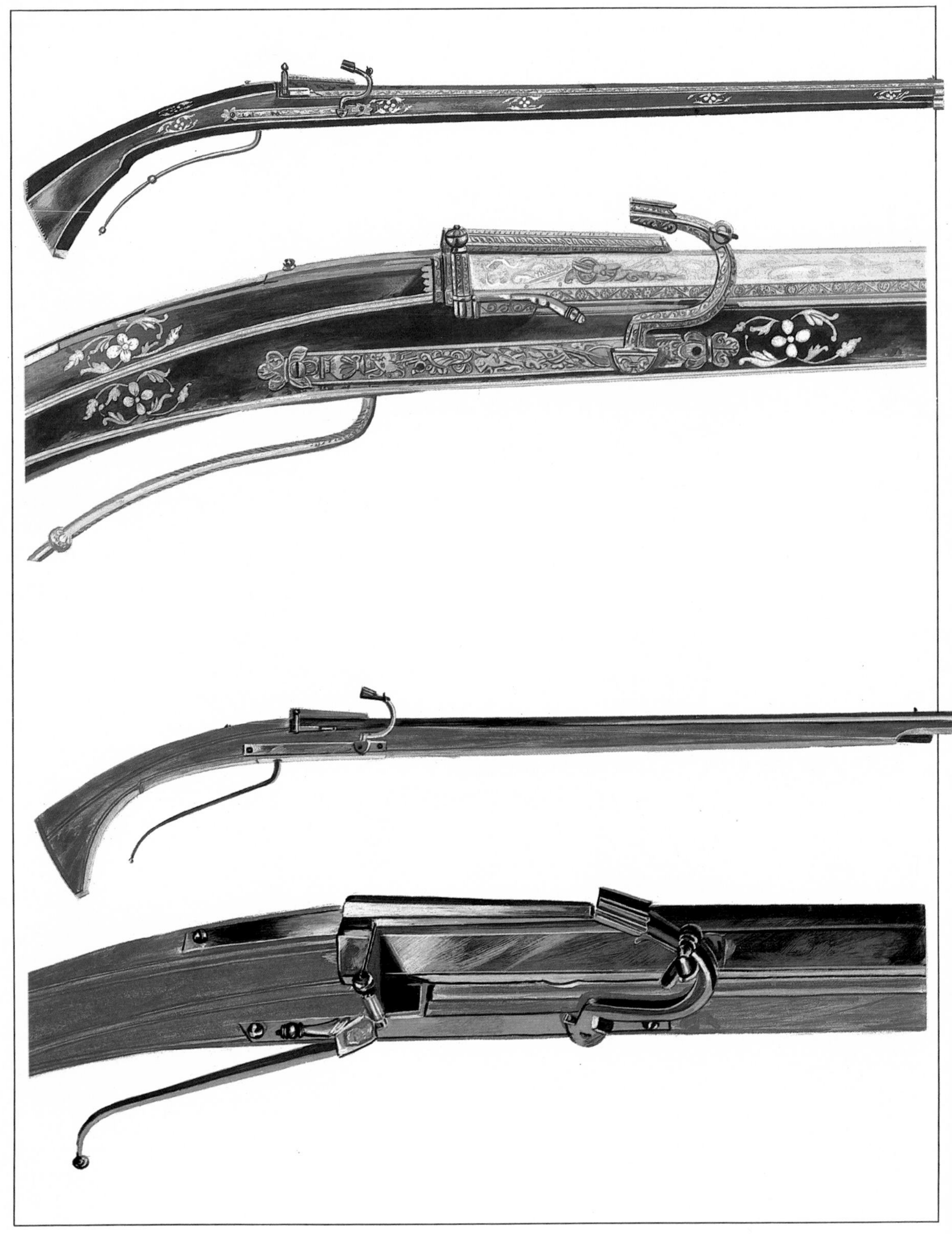

**Plate 51 16th-century matchlock firearms** (top) *Matchlock gun and detail, Italy, c. 1570 (stock of later date). Armeria Reale, Turin.* (below) *Matchlock gun and detail, Italy, c. 1570. Museo Nazionale d'Artigliera, Turin.*

**Plate 52 16th-century wheel-lock firearms** (top) *Pair of wheel-lock pistols, Augsburg, last quarter of the 16th century. Private Collection.* (bottom) *Double wheel-lock pistol for two superimposed loads, Nuremberg, c. 1570. Private Collection.*

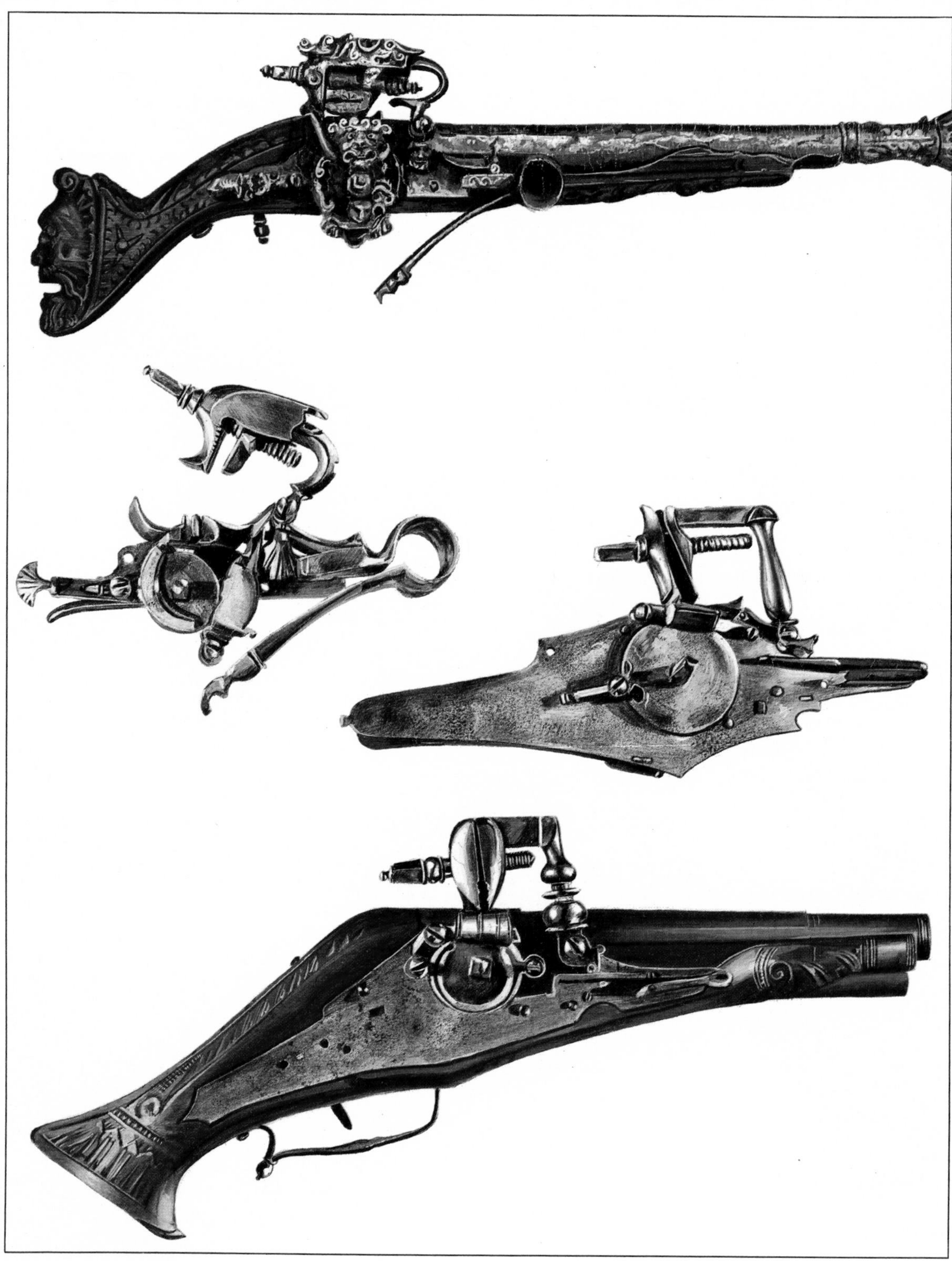

**Plate 53 16th- and 17th-century wheel-lock firearms** (top) *Wheel-lock pistol, probably Italian, c. 1570.* (middle left) *Wheel-lock, southern Europe, late 16th or early 17th century, and* (right) *wheel-lock, Italy, first quarter of the 17th century.* (bottom) *Wheel-lock pistol, Italy, last quarter of the 16th century. All in private collections.*

**Plate 54 16th-century artillery** (top to bottom) *Bronze cannon, France, 1590. Musée de l'Armée, Paris. Howitzer cast by Hanns Dinckelmeier, Austria, 1594. Cannon known as Amsel ("blackbird"), cast by Martin Hisger, Austria, 1579. Both in Heeresgeschichtliches Museum, Vienna. Bronze cannon named Greif ("griffin"), Germany, 1524. Musée de l'Armée, Paris.*

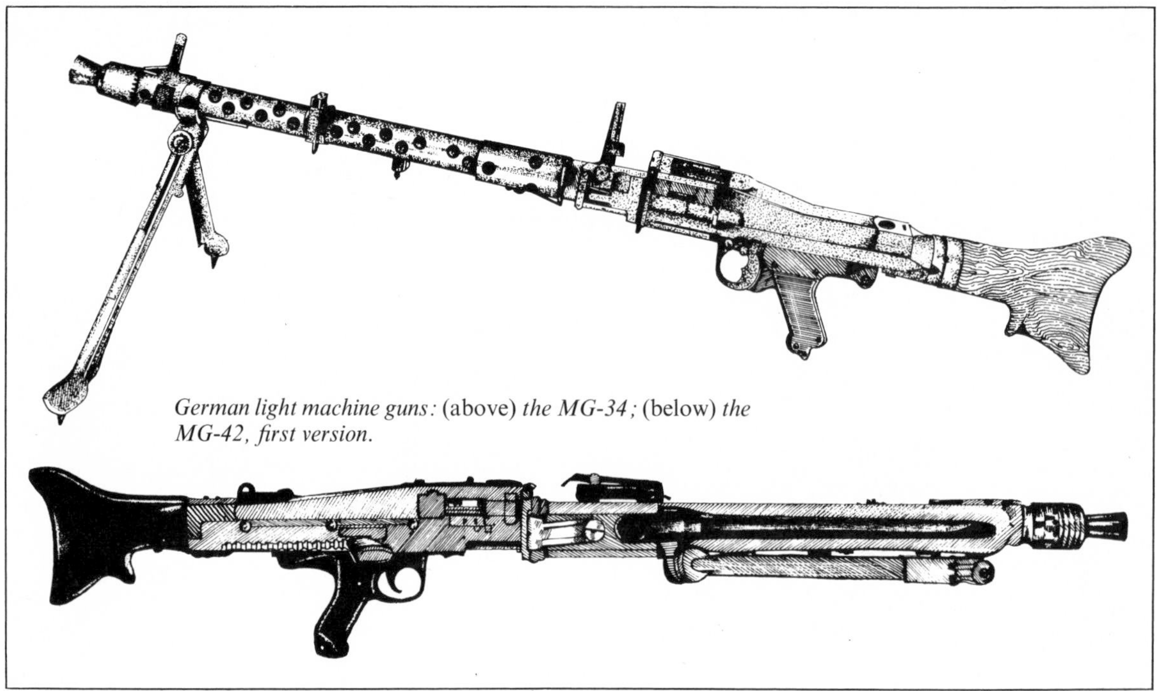

*German light machine guns:* (above) *the MG-34;* (below) *the MG-42, first version.*

steel block with four solid retaining plugs at the back; it had two extractors at the front and a groove underneath, spirally shaped at the rear end, in which the piston post ran. With the weapon cocked, the pressure of the trigger released the spring to carry the piston forward, drawing the bolt with it. The front face of the bolt struck the first cartridge in the magazine and pushed it into the chamber; the bolt was rotated by the movement of the piston post in the spiral groove so that the locking lugs engaged in recesses in the barrel extension. The firing pin, projecting from the bolt, struck the cartridge and fired it. When the bullet reached the gas port leading to the cylinder, some of the gases activated the piston and thus drove back the bolt, extracting and ejecting the spent case. In the first models, the barrel was completely surrounded by an aluminum radiator with longitudinal fins enclosed in a tubular steel casing. The feed system consisted of a drum magazine with a rotor arm actuated by an attachment on the bolt.

Among machine guns designed in Britain but for one reason or another not adopted, one interesting weapon was the 1909 Beardmore-Farquhar, a very light gas-operated gun. The piston did not act directly on the bolt but compressed a spring that unlocked the bolt when the pressure fell and opened the system in a remarkably smooth operation.

*Italy.* The Maxim was adopted at the beginning of the century, first in 10.35 mm. caliber, later in 6.5 mm. Then came tests on a weapon designed by the chief technician of the artillery, Giuseppe Perino, but it had not been perfected by the time war broke out and did not go into series production. The Perino machine gun, produced in a heavy version in 1908 and a light version in 1910, had several interesting features. It was a short-recoil weapon with a recoil intensifier at the muzzle and had a breechblock locked in the closed position by a rotating block. Feed was by metallic strips holding twenty cartridges; a box holding five connected strips could be attached to the left-hand side of the weapon so that as many as 100 rounds could be fired without a break. Properly tested, the Perino might have been an acceptable alternative to the costly Maxim, but it was abandoned when the war erupted, and the mediocre Fiat 1914, designed by Abiel Bethel Revelli and produced by the Turin motor-car factory, was adopted. The Fiat Revelli 1914, developed from a 1910 model, worked on a delayed-blowback system and was similar in structure and function to the semiautomatic Glisenti pistol. Feed was from a metallic box divided into ten vertical compartments, each holding five cartridges; the box fitted over an opening at the back of the body of the weapon, and each loaded compartment was automatically aligned with the bolt when the previous one was empty. Thousands of the Fiat 1914 were turned out; on the whole its performance was satisfactory, although better weapons were being produced in other countries. The Fiat 1935 was nothing more than an unsuccessful attempt to bring the 1914 model up to date; the belt feed and the quick-change barrel managed to produce a poorer performance than that of the original version. Two thousand of the Fiat 1926, a light, air-cooled weapon fed from a side magazine, were produced, though it was only a partially successful attempt to improve the basic system. The 1928 model used the closure system designed by Giuseppe Mascarucci but was adopted only on a limited scale. In 1914 Giovanni Agnelli patented an automatic weapon of which approximately 5000 were manufactured toward the end of the war.

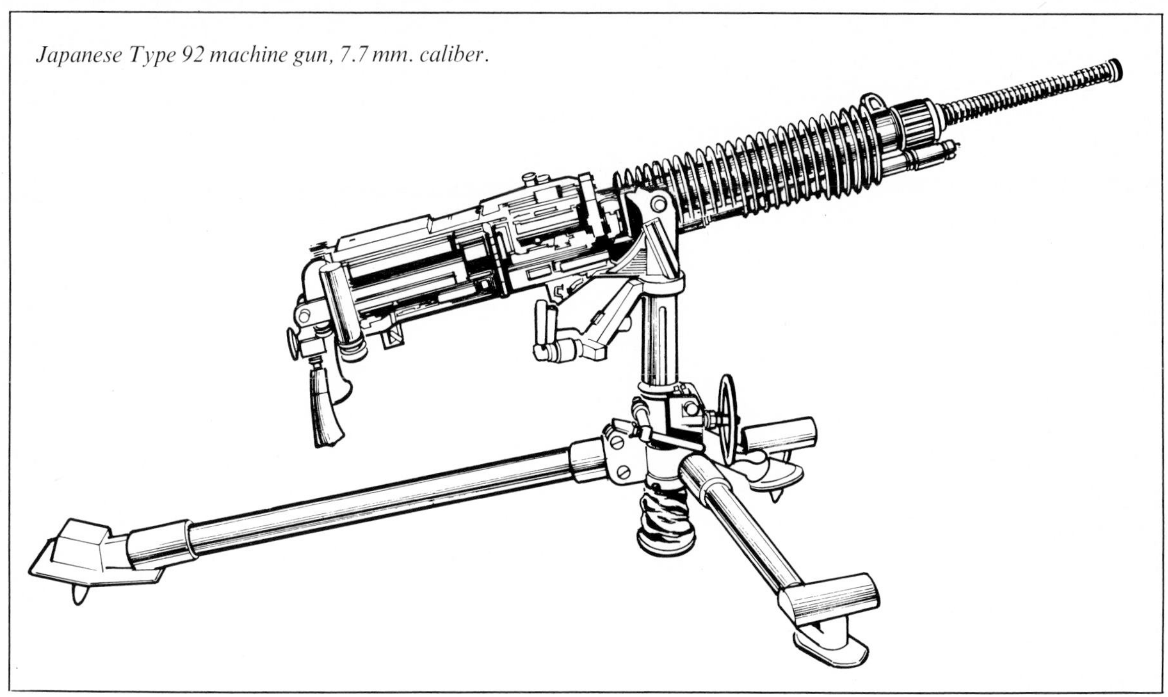

*Japanese Type 92 machine gun, 7.7 mm. caliber.*

Known as the SIA, it was a delayed-blowback weapon fed from a steel magazine shaped like the segment of a circle; it was capable of holding fifty cartridges. The weapon was soon discarded but was dug out again, together with other old junk in the army's stores, during the Second World War. The Brixia machine guns were of some interest; one model worked by short recoil, while another, the Brixia 30, had a fluted chamber and a closure system that worked by compressed air.

Far more important was the Breda machine gun. This large company produced a short-recoil light machine gun in 1924. Its bolt was locked to the breech by a fermeture nut, a threaded, rotatable collar around the breech. The same system was used in the Breda 30, great numbers of which were issued to the Italian Army during the Second World War. Even though it was carefully produced, the Breda 30 had many serious faults, among which were the poor forward support of the barrel, an easily damaged side

*Italian Fiat 1914 machine gun, 6.5 mm. caliber.*

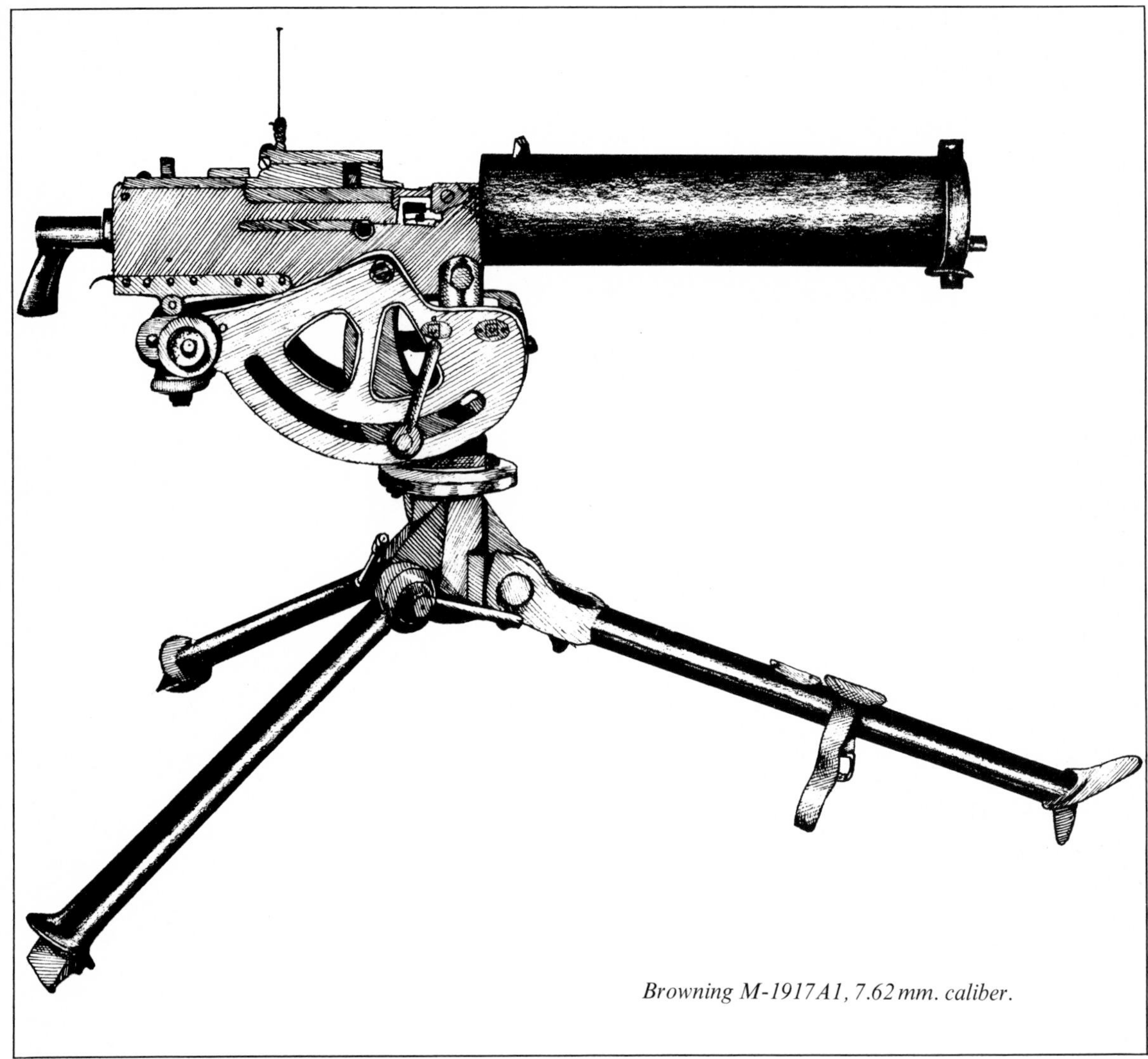

*Browning M-1917A1, 7.62 mm. caliber.*

magazine, and extraction problems that required permanent oiling of the cartridges. In the Breda 31, the earlier designs were abandoned. It was a gas-operated heavy machine gun of 13.2 mm. caliber for antiaircraft use that performed well in various trials. It was then proposed that it be adapted for smaller-caliber cartridges, a new 8 mm., the model 35, and that led to the approval of the Breda 37. Its closure system was based on a vertically moving breechblock actuated by two ramps at the rear of the piston; in the firing position, this device locked the breechblock, lifting its end into locking recesses in the body. When the gases passed through the gas port into the cylinder beneath the barrel and drove back the piston, the same device lowered the breechblock and carried back the bolt. The weapon was fed from metal strips; the empty cases were put back after firing. A modification of the Breda 37, the Breda 38, became the standard Italian tank machine gun; it was also used extensively by the infantry. Unlike the 37 model, it had a pistol grip and was fed from top-mounted box magazines. The Breda-Safat 1935 was a short-recoil gun with the Mascarucci bolt system. Belt-fed and chambered for the rimmed 7.7 mm. cartridge, it was used widely in the aircraft of the Regia Aeronautica. The Regia Aeronautica also used Scotti gas-operated machine guns in both 7.7 mm. and 12.7 mm. caliber, but not in large numbers.

*Japan.* The first machine gun adopted by the Japanese was the Hotchkiss 1897 model, which was produced under license in Tokyo. It was extensively used during the Russo-Japanese War of 1904–05 and performed very well, although it was inferior to the enemy's Maxim. The first Japanese machine guns of local design still employed the Hotchkiss system. General Kirijo Nambu, famous for his pistol, produced a modification of the Hotchkiss 1914 model, which was adopted as the Type 3. In 1922 the Type 11 light machine gun, also designed by Nambu, was introduced; it had a peculiar feed system with a hopper that took six rifle chargers, each holding six 6.5 mm. cartridges. The Type 92 of 1932 was a heavier weapon that was mounted on a tripod and chambered for the new

7.7 mm. cartridge; the Type 1 of 1942, fairly similar to the Type 92, was at least 15 kg. (33 lbs.) lighter. In 1936 the Japanese began to replace the "11" with the Type 96, which had an improved feed system with a 30-round magazine and a quick-change barrel. This weapon was further developed in 1939 as the Type 99; it served as the standard Japanese light machine gun until the end of the war.

In 1962 a new machine gun, designed by Masayi Kawamura and chambered for the 7.62 Nato cartridge, was adopted. It was gas-operated and had a breechblock that first pivoted in the vertical plane and then slid back. The breechblock had two locking lugs on the sides that fitted into corresponding recesses when the breech was closed. On firing, the movement of the piston first lowered the front end of the breechblock, so that the locking lugs were disengaged, and then drove back the block. Extraction was effected by a fixed claw on the front face of the breechblock above the aperture for the striker. Fed from disintegrating metal belts and capable of firing 530 rounds per minute, model 62, despite its complicated design, proved an excellent, reliable weapon.

*Russia.* As early as 1871 the tsarist government purchased more than 400 Gatling guns in the United States, and they remained in service until the outbreak of the First World War. In the last years of the 19th century, Russia's attention was drawn to the Maxim, and after trials a small quantity was acquired. In 1905 production of the Maxim began in the Tula arms factory; in the meantime further supplies had been ordered from overseas. Russia also acquired a number of Danish Madsen light machine guns, which were used to arm cavalry units in the war with Japan (1904–05), thus becoming one of the first countries to use such weapons. Despite the harsh lesson they got from the Japanese, the Russians still had a very limited number of automatic weapons in 1914 and had to order from the United States a great number of Colt Model 95 and Vickers machine guns chambered for the 7.62 mm. cartridge. Starting in 1921, a team of technicians devoted themselves to developing machine guns; one of these was the Degtyarev gas-operated machine gun, with a bolt locked by two moving flaps. Since 1926 it has been adopted in several versions: DP (infantry), DA (aircraft), DT (tanks), DPM (infantry, modified), DTM (tanks, modified), DS (medium machine gun), and the DShK (the Degtyarev-Shpagin heavy machine gun, introduced in 1938). The first five were fed from a flat drum magazine, whereas the two heavier guns were belt-fed. The Goryunov SG-43 machine gun, one of the best medium machine guns ever produced, was adopted in 1943 and was used by the Soviet Army until a few years ago. It was gas-operated and had a solid post on the back of the piston that engaged a cam slot in the breechblock to lock it. The bolt in the closed position was turned slightly to the side so that the right-hand side of the rear section was locked in a recess in the body. It was a reliable weapon, with a metallic belt feed and a quick-change barrel system that allowed prolonged sustained fire. The most important aircraft machine guns were the ShKAS (KM-33, KM-35, KM-36, the latter modified in 1941), the ShVAK (MP, KP, TP, SP), and the Beresin (BS, UBT, UBK, and UBS). After the Second World War the AK-47 assault rifle, chambered for the new intermediate 7.62 mm. M-43 cartridge, was adopted, and a new light machine gun was produced based on the same mechanism, the RPK, which has performed very well despite having no quick-change barrel system. The RPK was designed as a replacement for the SG-43, but it is a general-purpose weapon, combining the Kalashnikov breech-closure system with the Goryunov feed system.

*United States.* On April 6, 1917, the day on which it entered the First World War, the United States had available 670 Benet-Mercié, 282 Maxim, 143 Colt, and 353 Lewis machine guns. At the close of hostilities nineteen months later, the vast resources of American industry had produced 58,760 Lewis light machine guns and 87,848 Brownings.

The first machine gun designed by John Moses Browning was known as the Colt Model 95. Browning designed this weapon after studying for approximately a year the possibilities of using the gases produced when a cartridge was fired. Feed was from a hemp-fiber belt holding 250 cartridges, and the breech closure was by a hinged and recoiling bolt. The method by which the gases were used was unusual: a little more than 18 cm. (7 in.) from the muzzle there was a gas port—a small tube pointing downward, which was closed by a small piston in a gas cylinder. The piston was linked to a lever that worked the bolt by a simple mechanism and compressed the return spring. As soon as the bullet passed the tube, some of the gases acted on the piston and through it on the lever, which moved downward and upward, lifting the bolt free from two symmetrical locking lugs in the walls of the body. This ingenious device resulted in a substantial inconvenience. When the weapon was fired in the field, the legs of the tripod tended to sink into the ground, and the lever hinged to the piston struck the soil and dug deeper and deeper into it—hence the gun's picturesque nickname, the "potato digger."

As early as 1901, J. M. Browning patented a design for a short-recoil machine gun, but the weapon was not adopted until 1917, when mass production began. The mechanism was extremely simple and practical. The bolt was firmly locked to a frame fixed to the barrel by a vertically moving block; on firing, the bolt and barrel recoiled together. After about 18 mm. (0.7 in.) of recoil, which gave enough time for the projectile to leave the barrel, the barrel was halted and the block was lowered so that the bolt was free to recoil farther, extracting the spent cartridge. Belt-fed and chambered for the .30/06 cartridge, the Browning Model 17 was slightly modified time after time in the course of the years (M-1917A1, M-1918, M-1918 M1, M-2, M-1919A1, etc.); the M-1919A4 and A6 versions are still used by several armies.

The need for an automatic weapon that could pierce light armor led to the production of a machine gun similar in structure and mechanism to the smaller-caliber Browning but chambered for a more powerful cartridge, derived from the one that the Germans used in the Mauser antitank rifle. The water-cooled model adopted as the M-1921, was followed by the M-1921A1 and the M-2; the

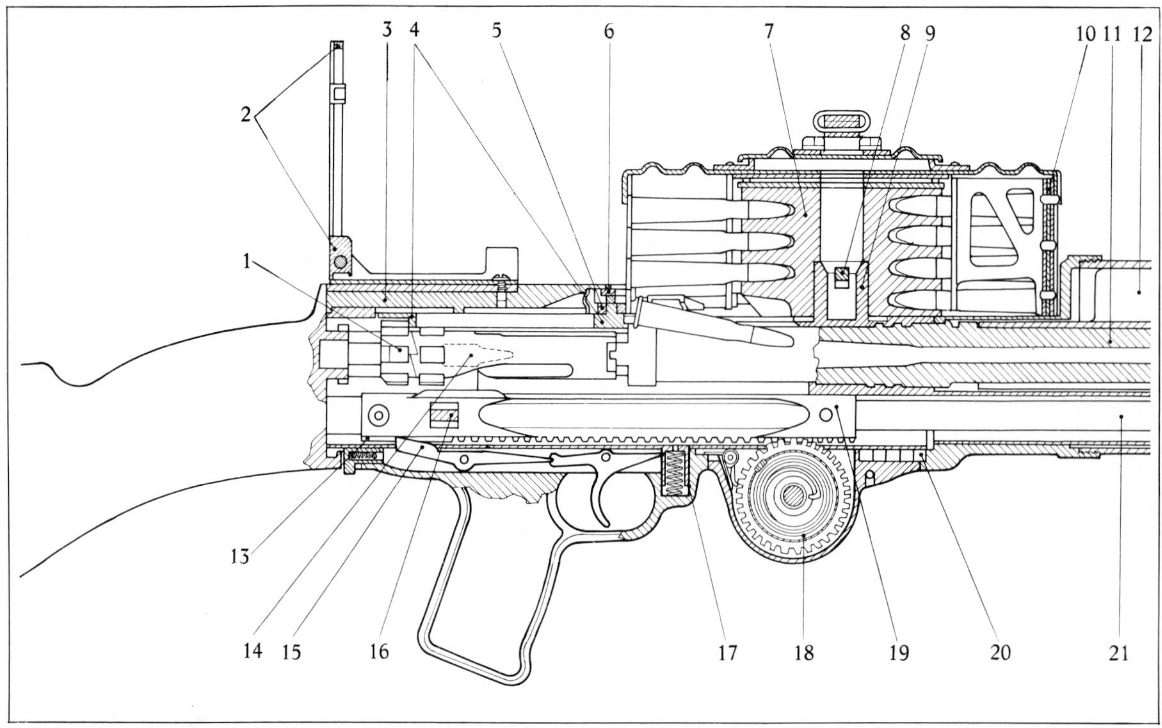


*Lewis light machine gun, 1915 model, longitudinal section of rear half. 1. feed-operating stud; 2. backsight; 3. fixed feed plate; 4. moving feed plate; 5. magazine operating pawl; 6. magazine stop pawl; 7. aluminum drum; 8. spring release catch; 9. magazine post; 10. magazine; 11. barrel; 12. cooling fins; 13. sear notch; 14. striker; 15. sear; 16. slot for cocking handle; 17. trigger spring and plunger; 18. spiral return spring; 19. rack; 20. locking key; 21. piston.*

*Lewis Mark I, air-cooled.*

latter, air-cooled, is still widely used, particularly in armored vehicles.

The BAR (Browning Automatic Rifle, first designed in 1917) was a gas-operated light machine gun, having a breechblock with a locking rod that moved vertically. The weapon was fired from the open-breech position to obtain better cooling; when the trigger was pressed, the return spring drew forward the breechblock and the bolt. During this closing movement a cartridge was extracted from the metal box magazine and fed into the chamber; finally the locking rod was pressed upward into a recess in the top of the body. The striker then moved forward and fired the chambered cartridge. The BAR went through a number of modifications, mostly slight, and remained in service until a few years ago.

The Lewis light machine gun was also an American

design, but as we have seen, it was first produced in quantity in England. It was adopted by the British, Canadian, Belgian, and Italian armies and, after the First World War, by the U.S. Marines and Army Air Corps; the U.S. Army used it only as a training weapon. Large numbers of the Lewis were used by ground forces during the Second World War.

After 1945 the United States considered adopting a weapon that, like the German MG-42, could serve as a general-purpose weapon, i.e., as both a light and a medium machine gun. After several years' research and trials, the United States adopted the M-60, which had a breech-closure system similar to that of the German FG-42 automatic rifle and a feed system like that of the MG-42. It is a weapon that can be produced very quickly, but certain errors in its design have come to light and it is likely to be replaced.

**machine pistol** A term applied to the SUBMACHINE GUN in some countries (e.g., German *Maschinenpistole*). Although many submachine guns have been designed for pistol cartridges, only a few of these firearms have both the size and the form of a pistol combined with a capacity for full automatic fire (as, for instance, the Soviet Stechkin pistol or the Czechoslovak VZ-61).

**madu** A rare form of Indian thrusting weapon combined with parrying shield, related to the FAKIR'S HORNS. Two horns of the black buck are fastened together with their points in opposite directions, sometimes with the tips armed with steel spikes, and a small shield of steel or leather is fastened in the middle to parry blows from the enemy's weapon.

**magari-yari** A Japanese spear with a cross-shaped blade, sometimes called the *jumon-ji-yari* because of its similarity to the figure 10, written in Japanese as a cross. According to a Japanese chronicle of the 8th century, the cruel Emperor Muretsu forced people into a swift stream, then killed them with a magari-yari as they flowed past him; but extant specimens of this three-bladed spear date from the 15th century. The earliest blades are well proportioned and are not thick in section. The magari-yari was enthusiastically adopted by the mounted warriors of the Momoyama period (1574–1602). In the course of time, this fighting weapon became an elegant processional pole arm, which in the Tokugawa (Edo) period (1603–1867) had a distinctive form of SAYA (sheath) and bore the clan crest, the *mon*. The retainer who carried the ceremonial magari-yari preceded his lord, the daimyo, or other persons of quality. Most of the magari-yari that are extant have come from this late period and belong to the class of ceremonial weapon.

Various types of magari-yari differ considerably in head size, the smallest blades being less than 10 cm. (4 in.) in length. There was also wide variation in the positioning of the blades of the head, some of them being of quite unusual form: a very long and slender central blade set at right angles to the side ones; the side blades strongly curved upward; the side arms crescent and L-shaped; a three-sided and grooved central blade; and asymmetrical side arms, one much longer than the other. The magari-yari head was furnished with a long tang fitted into the shaft, which was embellished with raised rings of red sprinkled lacquer and copper mounts. The shaft was usually about 2.1–2.7 m. (7–9 ft.) long.

**maidate** A generic word in Japanese for all kinds of crestlike objects on the helmet, particularly in the front. If the ornament was worn at the back, it was called *ushiro-date*; if worn at the top, *kashira-date*; and if there were two (one on each side), *waki-date*. The maidate was usually in the form of an animal, insect, or mythical creature—such as a dragon, or *kirin*—whose characteristics the wearer was supposed to imitate. It was usually made of metal, whalebone, or lacquered wood and gilded.

**mail** (from French *maille*, derived from Latin *macula*, "mesh of a net") A protective metal fabric, the European styles of which were based on a system known in antiquity and probably invented by the ancient Celts before the 5th century B.C. It involved the linking of iron or steel rings,

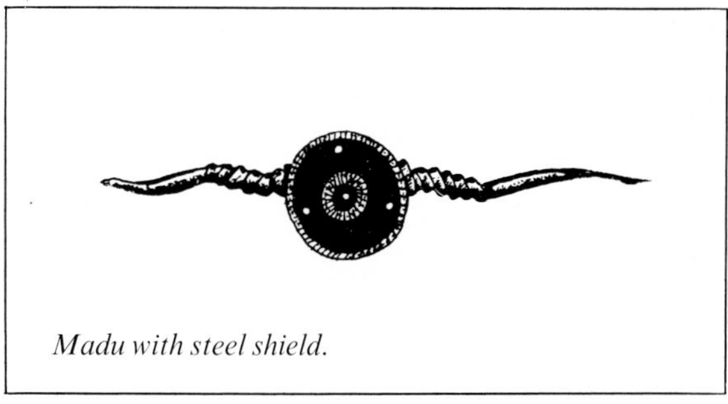

*Madu with steel shield.*

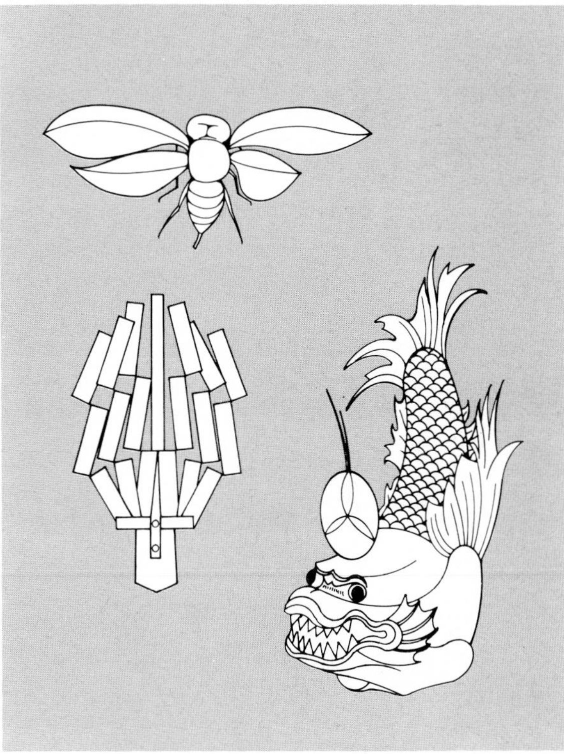

*Various types of maidate for Japanese helmets.*

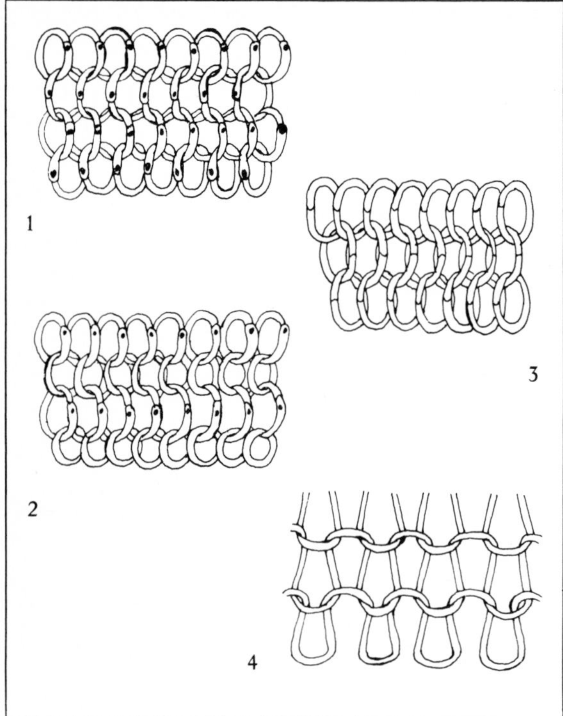


*Mail. 1. Mail with riveted links. 2. Alternate rows of riveted and solid links. 3. Links with ends butted together. 4. Interwoven wire mail. From the* Glossarium Armorum.

the ends of which were either pressed together or riveted, i.e., flattened, overlapped, and joined by a rivet. When solid links stamped out of sheet iron were used, each row was alternated with a row of riveted links. The most common system, however, was to arrange the rings so that each one had four others linked and riveted through it.

Each piece of mail was fashioned specifically for whichever part of the body it was intended to protect. For the head there were the coif and ventail, aventail, mail fringe, and "bishop's mantle"; for the torso, the hauberk, skirt, and breeches; for the upper limbs, mail sleeves and mittens; for the lower limbs, chausses and sabatons.

In the 14th century, mail tended to have a subordinate role in relation to plate armor, first as a linking element for various plates and then, in the following century, to protect the more vulnerable parts such as the neck, elbow, and knee joints. By the 16th century, mail was being used in western Europe mainly in an accessory capacity as under-armor, such as the ARMING DOUBLET or mail shirt. However, in eastern Europe and the Middle East, mail often served as the main defense until the late 17th century (in the Caucasus, some highlanders used mail shirts and coifs until the early 1900s).

**mail breaker** A modern term for a dagger of the late medieval and Renaissance periods, with a very strong blade, often square or triangular in section, sometimes reinforced at the point. It was essentially a weapon designed to penetrate the coat of mail and leather protecting the opponent's body.

**mail shirt** *See* HAUBERK.

**main gauche** A modern French term (meaning "left hand") somewhat misleadingly applied to the PARRYING DAGGER. The dagger was held in the left hand only by a right-handed swordsman, whereas a left-hander parried with the dagger in his right hand.

**malleolus** A Roman term for a large incendiary bolt fitted at the front with a ring in which tow soaked in pitch or some other combustible material was fitted; it was ignited before being fired.

**mandau** A Malayan sword used mostly by the Dyak tribe. Although *mandau* means "headhunter," the weapon is used mostly as a jungle knife and tool. Its single-edged blade is slightly curved, widening toward the point and convex on the cutting side. It is generally about 50 cm. (20 in.) long. Its hilt is made of hardwood or horn, without a guard; the long one-sided pommel is carved with grotesque masks or other ornamentation and decorated with tufts of hair, as are so many Malayan swords.

The mandau scabbard consists of two pieces of wood, carved and bound together with bands of braided cane. Tassels of colored hair and beadwork are attached to the scabbard; there is also a pocket of bark or cloth at the back to hold a very long handled knife.

The *mandau pasir* is similar but has a much larger blade.

**manifer** (from French *main de fer*, "iron hand") A reinforcing piece for the left gauntlet used in the 15th and 16th centuries for jousting and tourneys. Attached to the gauntlet cuff by means of a stud and staple, it was made of one plate shaped to cover the cuff, the backplate, and the adjoining part of the fingers.

**mantelet** (or **mantlet**) A type of PAVISE used during the

*Mandau, Borneo. Museo Orientale, Ca' Pesaro, Venice.*

late medieval period by besiegers as a movable protection against missiles. The term now denotes a bulletproof screen for gunners.

**manuballista** Another term for ARCUBALLISTA.

**martel de fer** (or **marteau de fer**) *See* WAR HAMMER.

**match** A cord made of twisted flax, hemp, or cotton soaked in a saturated solution of saltpeter (potassium nitrate), which was used to ignite the priming powder in the matchlock system of ignition. The match did not burn but smoldered; the musketeer blew the match into a healthy glow just before firing. The rate of burning could be varied by preparing the match accordingly, for example, for quick burning, the prepared match was also rubbed with gunpowder. In order to prevent accidents and to protect the smoldering cord from getting wet, the match was sometimes carried in a hollow iron or brass tube pierced with ventilation holes at one end.

A Dutch military leader, Prince Maurice of Nassau, in a manual first published in 1607 and illustrated by Jacob de Gheyn, spoke of musketeers using comparatively long, looped matches that were lighted at both ends and held between the fingers of the left hand during firing preparations. Military writers of the 17th century described several accidents caused by musketeers carrying their lighted matches too near the powder train in the heat of the battle. Great efforts were made to keep them apart. The use of the match for firearms became obsolete after the matchlock was abandoned in the latter part of the 17th century.

**meguriva** A type of NODOWA.

**melinite** The French name for trinitrophenol. *See also* EXPLOSIVE.

**mempo** A type of Japanese war mask. *See also* MENPO.

**mendak** A part of the furniture of a Malaysian dagger. *See also* KRIS.

**menpo** A mask used with the Japanese helmet since the 10th century; made of molded sheet iron and lacquered on both sides—usually red on the inside and black on the outside—it was attached to the helmet by a cord. The early *happuri* mask, which was still in use during the 14th century, covered the forehead and cheeks. The *hōate* mask, popular between the 14th and 16th centuries, and the *hambō* mask, used between the second half of the 16th century and the 19th, protected only the chin and the cheeks, whereas the *mempō* mask, like the hōate, was fitted with a detachable nasal bar. There was also a full mask, the *somen*, which was molded into terrifying facial features with eyeholes; this mask was used from the late 15th century until the 19th. Some masks were even furnished with long hempen mustaches. Although one of the functions of the mask was to secure the helmet more firmly to the head and give extra protection to the face, it was also designed to instill fear in the opponent and exploit his superstitious tendencies.

**menuki** Metal ornaments on the sides of the hilt of a Japanese sword or dagger. They were originally intended to conceal the peg, or *mekugi*, that fastened the hilt to the blade. They were held in place by a projecting lug on the back that fit into the side of the hilt and by the braid with which it was usually bound. The menuki were often beautiful pieces of jewelry made of gold, silver, copper, or shakudo and shibuichi alloys; they represented gods, demons, dragons, human figures, various animals, birds, insects, plants, and man-made objects. They were

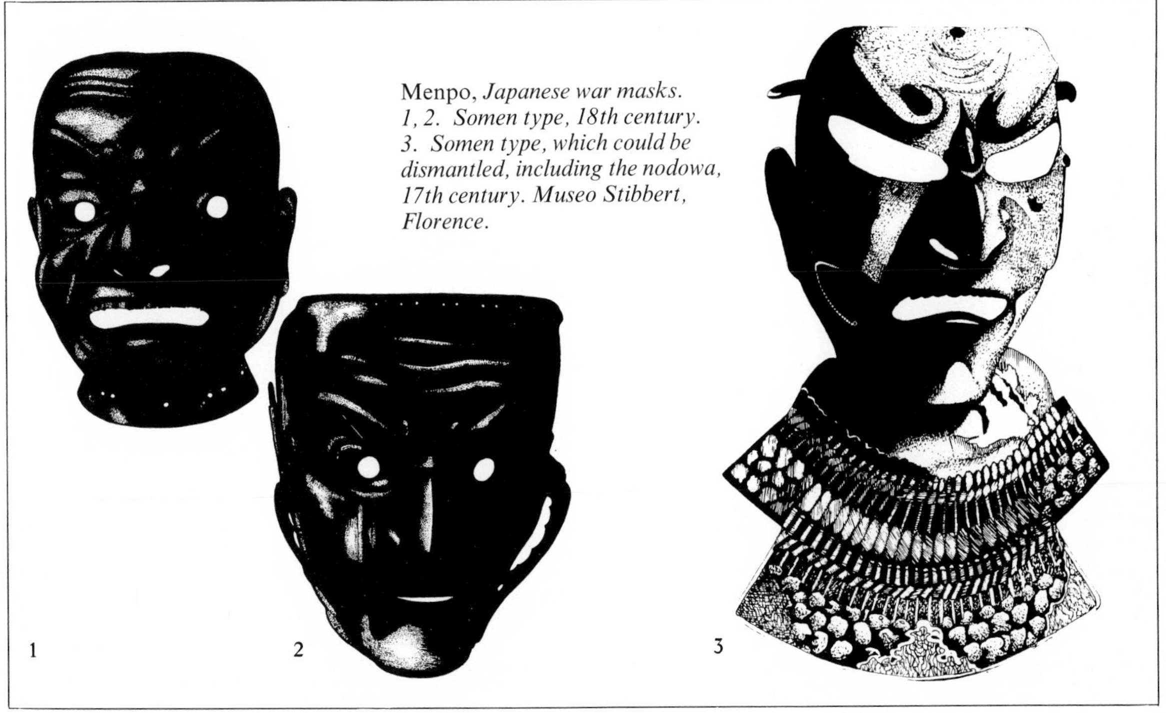


Menpo, *Japanese war masks. 1, 2. Somen type, 18th century. 3. Somen type, which could be dismantled, including the nodowa, 17th century. Museo Stibbert, Florence.*

*Menuki of the Tokugawa (Edo) period (1603–1867).*

manufactured by specialized master craftsmen and were frequently signed. As with other sword furniture, they have become collectible items.

**mimi** The border of the guard on a Japanese sword. *See also* TSUBA.

**mine** A term that in old military terminology meant the underground passage or "gallery" dug by the besiegers of a town or fortress either to make a surprise entry or to blow up defense works on the surface by means of an explosive charge. The "mines" widely used beginning in the 15th century were countered by the defenders with "countermines," sometimes prepared during the construction of the surface defense works.

On the battlefield the term is now used for a variety of explosive devices, underwater (naval mines) or on land (land mines), generally comprised of a powerful charge contained in a case fitted with an impact, pressure, magnetic, acoustic, or thermal fuze. Mines were used very widely during the Second World War, both to block roads and to deny extensive areas to the enemy. Land mines can be broadly divided into antipersonnel and antitank mines, according to use; among the former was the U.S. M-14, which, with a charge of just under 50 g. ($1\frac{3}{4}$ oz.) of tetryl, could blow off the leg of anyone who stepped on it; the tricky M-16, which, when activated on contact, was blown into the air from its camouflaged site and exploded waist high; the Italian V.1, with a trip wire, and R type, with a pressure fuze. Among antitank mines were the Italian C.S., the French Model 36, the British Mark I, II, III, and IV, the U.S. M-6, M-7, M-15, and M-19, and the German Teller mines 35, 42, and 43.

The traditional procedure of laying mines in advance has been supplemented since the Second World War by the new RDM (Remotely Delivered Mine) system, by which mines are laid by helicopter or artillery fire. This makes it possible to lay minefields quickly and secretly even in territory held by the enemy. Among the latest mines, an outstanding place has been accorded to the British bar mine, which will replace the Mark 3 antitank mine; other interesting designs are the Dingbat and the Ranger, also British, which can be sown by a launching system with seventy-two tubes, each containing eighteen mines.

*Morgenstern, or morning star, Switzerland, 17th century. Cantonal Museum at Thurgau.*

**misericorde** A term for daggers found in French and English texts of the 14th and 15th centuries; it probably referred to the daggers carried in combat by knights. It subsequently became a romantic term for a dagger with a thin, pointed blade designed to penetrate mail or the joints between plates of armor. It was thought that a victim knocked to the ground or wounded pleaded for *misericordia* ("mercy") from the warrior closing in to finish him off; hence the modern name of this dagger.

**missyurka** A type of head defense—its name comes from the Arabic *Misr* meaning "Egypt"—popular in many parts of the Ottoman Empire. It was also worn in Hungary, Poland, and Russia as well as in the Caucasus. It consisted of a shallow skull, just covering the top of the head, to which was attached a deep AVENTAIL of mail, and was worn over a cap or small turban. The earliest surviving specimens come from the late 13th or early 14th century and are in the Topkapi Sarayi Museum in Istanbul and in the Tower of London Armouries. The missyurka usually accompanied the mail armor worn by the medium cavalry, each of whose members carried a shield (*see* KALKAN), saber, and a bow, or light spear. The Turkish missyurka was often handsomely decorated with gold and the Georgian type with silver and niello, frequently with inscriptions. A Polish missyurka was usually made of plain steel, sometimes with scanty brass ornamentation.

**mitten** A type of GAUNTLET used throughout the 15th century and most of the 16th. It consisted of a tubular plate cuff, a back plate, and finger defense made of one plate, sometimes embossed to the shape of the fingers.

**mojiri** A Japanese pole weapon, similar to the HINERI.

**mokko** A four-lobed TSUBA.

**Molotov cocktail** An incendiary device named for the Soviet foreign minister during the Second World War. It consists of a bottle filled with highly combustible liquid and fitted with some form of fuze. In its simplest form, the bottle is filled with gasoline and plugged with a rag. The rag is ignited, and when the bottle is thrown the glass breaks on impact and the gasoline splashes out and alights.

More modern forms of such incendiary devices make use of reactive substances, one mixed with the combustible fluid and the other fixed to the outside of the bottle; when the bottle is broken, the two components react and set fire to the liquid. The two substances used most often are sulfuric acid and potassium chlorate.

**moluodis** The Greek term for GLANS.

**monnions** (or **munnions**) A 17th-century English term (derived from the French *mognion*) denoting SPAUDLERS.

**Morgenstern** (German, "morning star") A type of combat weapon akin to the HOLY WATER SPRINKLER and MACE. It was fitted with a round, oval, or cylindrical head studded with spikes; extending from the top of the head was a long point. Some had short handles for single-handed use; others had long, sturdy handles, requiring both hands to deliver the blow. The name was coined later than the period in which the weapon was actually used; it was probably derived from the appearance of the head, which resembled a star.

The Morgenstern was made either with a long staff for use on foot or with a short handle for mounted warriors. Because of its effectiveness and simplicity of production, it was a popular weapon from the Middle Ages to the 17th century, particularly among peasants and poor urban militiamen, who occasionally used it as late as the 19th century.

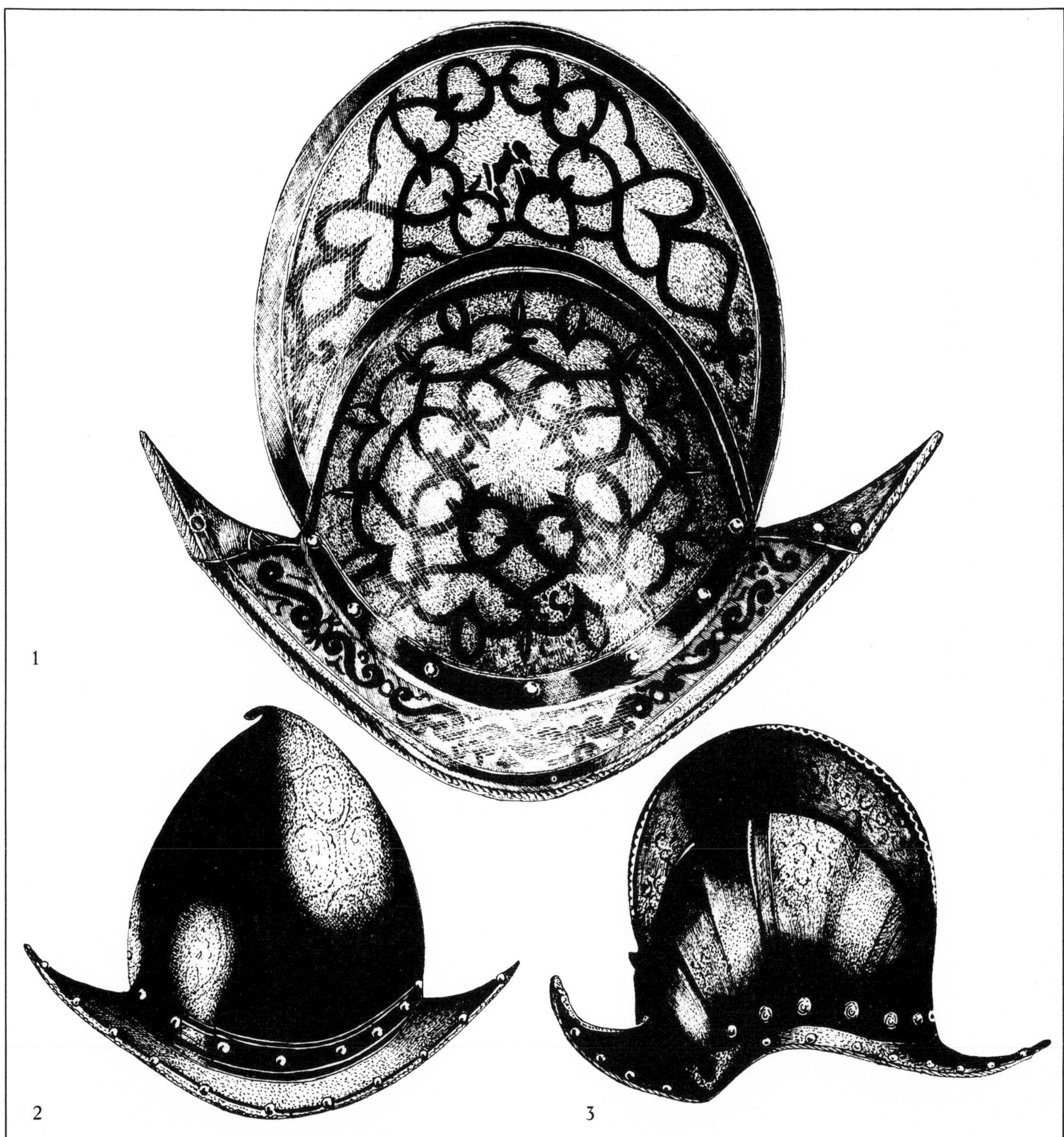


*1. Comb morion, Italy, late 16th century. Odescalchi Collection, Museo di Palazzo Venezia, Rome. 2. Peaked (or "Spanish") morion, Italy, last quarter of the 16th century. Wallace Collection, London. 3. Burgonet, Italy, second half of the 16th century. Wallace Collection, London.*

**morion** A helmet mainly used in the 16th century by light cavalry and infantry soldiers, particularly musketeers and archers. For common helmets, the skull was made from two plates joined by riveting and hammering overlapping edges of the comb and brims. Broad curved brims met in a point at the center front and back. In better-made and more expensive morions, the skull, comb, and brims were made of one plate even if the helmet had a fairly high comb. Unlike the comb morion, the Spanish morion had a pear-shaped skull, often with a backward-pointed "spur" on the apex. A rare variation was the three-combed morion, the middle comb being higher than those on its sides. Another uncommon version was the helmet whose brim appeared undulating, with both the front and the rear curving upward, while the sides were concave (this type resembled the shape of a burgonet and sometimes was called the combed burgonet).

A row of rivets on the skull along the brims attached triangular laminated cheekpieces and an internal band of leather, to which the lining was stitched. The rivet heads were often embellished with decorative chiseled rosetttes in iron or brass. A plume holder, eventually covered by an escutcheon with a coat of arms, was riveted at the rear of the skull. Whereas parade morions, including the helmets of palace guards, were richly ornamented with embossing or etching, those made for purely military use were usually quite plain.

**morning star** The modern English term for MORGENSTERN.

**mortar** From the 16th century the word "mortar," evidently a reference to the shape of the weapons (the word is derived from the Latin *mortarium*, the mortar used with a pestle to grind substances), was applied to those pieces of artillery, short and squat, that could fire large balls, later filled with explosive, with a very high trajectory over walls and earthworks. One of the first documents giving evidence of the existence of such weapons dates from 1453; it is a letter written to the pope by the Venetian Leonardo Giustiniani, who was present at the siege of Constantinople. An indisputable confirmation of the use of mortars is further found in Agostino Giustiniani's *Annali Genovesi* of 1506: "The commander of the fort fired on the houses in the town by night with mortars, but with these mortars brought death to no one." The use of mortars firing explosive bombs became general during the wars in Flanders in the late 16th and early 17th centuries. Their importance stemmed not only from their trajectory, which allowed them to fire on targets defended by walls or earthworks, but also from the fact that they were the only pieces of artillery with which it was possible to fire explosive projectiles of any power.

The old muzzleloading mortars might have two trunnions halfway up, like the old cannon, or a single double trunnion at the base of the breech. The latter arrangement was generally preferred because the great recoil force to which they were subjected and the rigidity of their mountings often caused trunnions fitted halfway up to bend or split. The remarkable elevation at which the projectile was fired meant that the recoil force was transmitted to the mounting almost vertically, so that it was subjected to very considerable vertical pressure, whereas the horizontal component was relatively small. That made it necessary to make the base of the mounting or mortar bed as wide and as static as possible, and it was thus impossible to fit wheels.

Mortars were developed along the same lines as the other pieces of artillery; from the end of the 19th century they were constructed with breechloading and rifled barrels, which improved their performance considerably. They were widely used in their heavy form in the First World War; notable designs were the excellent 310/10 Model 11 from Skoda and the Italian Models 911–916, of 305/8. This last type had a steel barrel rifled with sixty-eight spiral grooves of a constant right-handed pitch of 9150 mm. (30 ft.); a total length 3050 mm. (10 ft.); a length of the rifled section of 2031 mm. (6 ft. 8 in.); a weight of 5936 kg. (13,075 lbs.); obturation by a horizontally sliding wedge; sealing of the breech by expansion of the metal base of the cartridge case. The mounting had two side plates, with a base plate fixed to a wooden platform reinforced with iron. The cradle was a tube lined on the inside with bronze; on recoil, the piece ran along its center line. It had two hydraulic brake cylinders (two separate pieces, each containing 25 l. [5.5 gal.] of a 50–50 mixture of water and glycerin), at the top and inside, the hydropneumatic recuperator (with 18 l. [4 gal.] of the water-glycerin mixture and air compressed from 58 to 65 atmospheres), with two toothed arcs for elevation. This weapon, with a charge of 13 kg. (28.7 lbs.) of ballistite, threw the short rear-fuze shell weighing 287 kg. (630 lbs.), with a bursting charge of 32 kg. (70 lbs.) of toluolammonal for a distance of 11 km. (7 mi.).

During the Second World War the Germans used, among others, the enormous 60 cm. (23.6 in.) mortars of the Thor class (Gerät 040). Mounted on a special self-propelled tracked carriage, the 60 cm. mortar had a barrel 5068 mm. (16 ft. 8 in.) long, rifled with 112 grooves; it could throw shells weighing 2200 kg. (4546 lbs.) for more than 6 km. (3.7 mi.). The piece, complete with breechblock and cradle, weighed over 28 tons. *See also* HOWITZER.

*Infantry mortars.* Light, portable, muzzleloading infantry mortars firing subsonic bombs with stabilizing fins have been very widely used since the start of the First World War. The 76 mm. (3 in.) mortar invented by Wilfred

*Nineteenth-century motar.*

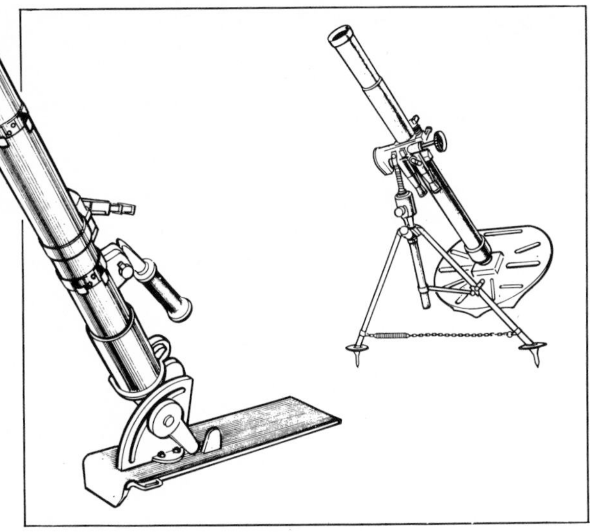

(left) *British 2 in. mortar;* (right) *Russian 1937 model 82 mm. mortar.*

Stokes is regarded as the progenitor of the present generation of mortars. It was no more than a very simple muzzleloading gun consisting of a launching tube, base plate, stand, and sights. The launching tube was actually a barrel closed by a breechblock at the bottom; a hollow hemisphere with the striker at its center was screwed to this block. The bomb, a cylinder with no fins, had a 12-caliber shotgun cartridge charged with ballistite at its base; when it was inserted and slid down the barrel, the cartridge hit the striker and was detonated, and the bomb was driven out by the gases of deflagration and described a parabola. The maximum range of the Stokes mortar was not more than 1 km. (0.6 mi.), even under the most favorable conditions. The basic design of the Stokes was notably improved in the 1930s by a Frenchman, Edgar Brandt; it is probably safe to say that all infantry mortars used in the last forty years have been derived from his models.

Infantry mortars are now divided into "light" (with caliber of up to 60 mm. [2.36 in.] and a total weight of not over 18 kg. [40 lbs.]); "medium" (caliber of up to 100 mm. [4 in.] and a weight of not over 70 kg. [154 lbs.]), and "heavy" (with caliber and/or weight greater than the medium). Infantry mortars consist of the barrel, the base plate, the bipod, and the sights. The most modern designs may also incorporate improvements that make them safer to use (a moving striker that can be cocked), more comfortable (springs or hydraulic shock absorbers between the barrel and the bipod), and more accurate (optical sights).

Apart from the Eastern bloc, the world market is today almost exclusively supplied by the French Hotchkiss-Brandt Company and the Finnish Tampela; however, for political reasons, the Finnish company markets its products through the Israeli Soltam Company. Hotchkiss-Brandt produces a huge range of mortars, from the very light (7.7 kg. [17 lbs.]) Commando V of 60 mm. (2.36 in.), with a maximum range of 1 km. (0.6 mi.), to the complex and heavy (582 kg. [1283 lbs.]) rifled 120 mm. (4.72 in.) mortar MO-120-RT-61, which can throw the effective PRPA (*projectile rayé à propulsion additionnelle*) bomb a distance of 13 km. (8 mi.). Tampela produces the excellent if conventional 81 mm. (3.2 in.) mortar made with three types of barrel: short (115.5 cm. [45 in.]), long (145.5 cm. [57.3 in.]), and long with a barrel that can be broken down into two parts. Also from Tampela comes a very interesting weapon, the 160 mm. (6.3 in.) mortar, which can throw a 40 kg. (88 lb.) bomb more than 9 km. (5½ mi.).

Among the best mortars made in the Eastern bloc was the Soviet 120 mm. (4.7 in.) M-38 that, slightly modified and now called the M-43, is still in service. The Germans in the Second World War appreciated the qualities and the features of the M-38; they produced an exact copy, which was adopted as the 12 cm. Granatwerfer 42. The M-38 has a barrel 185.4 cm. (6 ft.) long and weighs, ready to fire, 275 kg. (600 lbs.). It can throw a 15.5 kg. (34 lb.) bomb for a maximum of 5700 m. (3½ mi.).

**mouth** The opening in the scabbard or sheath through which the blade is inserted. The mouth of a leather or wooden scabbard or sheath is often reinforced with a metal ring referred to as a MOUTHPIECE.

**mouthpiece** A metal ring covering the mouth of a scabbard or sheath, which served both as a reinforcement and ornamentation. The upper edge of the mount was often shaped to the blade shoulder and to the casing of the handle, both to enable the weapon to be slipped in more easily and to be retained firmly in the scabbard.

**muffler** Mail mitten formed by extension of the sleeve of the HAUBERK.

**mukade tsuba** A variation of the TSUBA.

**multibarreled gun** A gun with several barrels. In modern three-barreled sporting guns, one of the barrels, smaller than the others and rifled, is intended for firing bullets. The double-barreled gun has one smooth-bore and one rifled barrel. *See also* GUN: sporting.

**musket** This name, derived from *moschetto*, an old Italian word for the sparrow hawk, was given at the end of the 15th century to the smallest of the culverins. The barrel was 40 to 50 calibers long, sometimes even longer (80 calibers in the specimen at the armory of the Council of Ten in Venice) and fired projectiles 3.5 to 4.5 kg. (8–10 lbs.) in weight; the mounting, although proportionately lighter, was the same as that used for other contemporary guns. This type of gun became outdated by the second half of the 16th century and fell into disuse; its name was used in Venetian artillery for a small culverin of one pound used by the "bombardiers" (gunners) for practice or sometimes used on board ships instead of falconets (*moschetto da zuogo*). "Breach muskets," small breechloaders of one pound constructed similarly to the perriers of the same name, were used in Venice. Relative data for these latter two types of Venetian muskets are: the piece of the musket "da zuogo" weighed about 93.3 kg. (206 lbs.) and was 34 calibers, or 148 cm. (58 in.) long; the piece of the "breech musket" weighed 24 kg. (53 lbs.) and was 25 calibers, or about 87 cm. (34 in.) long. The approximate calibers were, respectively, 4.3 cm (1¾ in.) and 3.5 cm (1⅜ in.)

The word was also used for a heavy handgun which

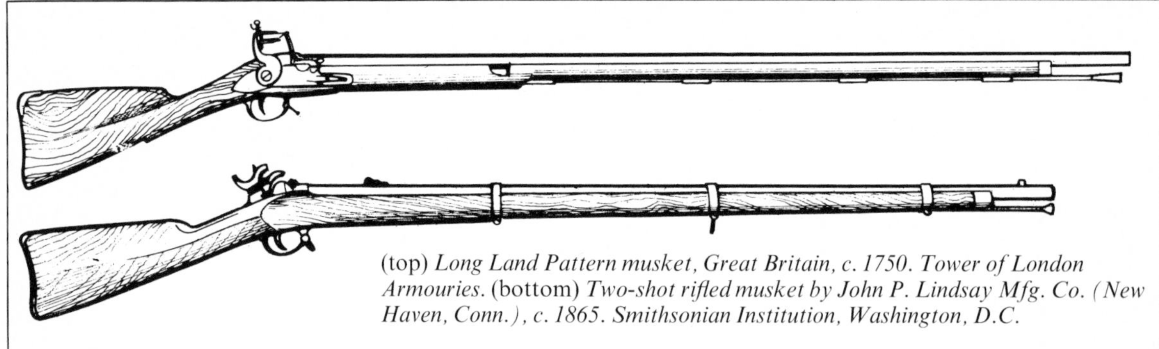

(top) *Long Land Pattern musket, Great Britain, c. 1750. Tower of London Armouries.* (bottom) *Two-shot rifled musket by John P. Lindsay Mfg. Co. (New Haven, Conn.), c. 1865. Smithsonian Institution, Washington, D.C.*

gradually began to replace the ARQUEBUS during the last decades of the 16th century. The favorite arm of the infantry throughout the 17th century, it fell into disuse in the first decades of the following century, when it was replaced by the much more manageable long arm, which inherited the name "musket" in England and other countries. With a few exceptions, muskets were fitted with a matchlock and needed a special support, the MUSKET REST, when they were fired. The following example illustrates the difference in size between an arquebus and a musket: a barrel made in Brescia for the former was 87.5 cm (34 in.) long and fired balls of lead weighing 20 g. (0.7 oz.); the barrel for the latter was 110 cm. (43 in.) long and fired lead balls weighing 35–40 g. (1.2–1.4 oz.).

In certain countries only (France, Italy) the word "musket" is still used for certain individual small arms derived from the individual firearms of the same name, but these derivations are much shorter and lighter. Thus in France we find the Mousqueton d'Artillerie model 1874, which was at least 30 cm. (12 in.) shorter and 900 g. (2 lbs.) lighter than the famous Gras rifle from which it was developed; and in Italy the various muskets (for special troops, cavalry, etc.) derived from the 1891 model rifle. In Italy, too, the term "automatic musket" is used to indicate heavy submachine guns with solid wood stocks (e.g., the MAB-38/a, Moschetto Automatico Beretta 38/a).

**musket rest** A long, stout wooden pole fitted with a wide pronged fork at the top and, at the bottom, an iron ferrule and spike that could be stuck into the ground. This fork was used to support the long, heavy barrel of a musket. Martin du Bellay, writing in 1569, stated that forks were employed for muskets at the battle of Chiara in 1521, but it is likely that similar devices to support heavy guns were in use much earlier. The wooden poles of some 17th-century forks were elaborately inlaid with mother-of-pearl and stag's horn. On some types, one prong of the fork extended to form a spike, while others concealed short blades, enabling the rest to be used as a weapon. With changes in the design and the weight of muskets in the second half of the 17th century, the rest fell into disuse.

**muzzle** An accessory used with the bridle in the 16th century. It consisted of a kind of cage made of small iron bars and pierced plates that were hooked onto the leather cheekpieces to cover the front part of a horse's face (also known as the muzzle) from just below the eyes. The whole "cage," which was quite light, curved downward to cover the animal's nostrils and mouth, leaving only the back open to permit the bit and its attachments to move freely. Although the muzzle probably helped to protect both people and horses from a "biter" in parades and on ceremonial occasions, its other function was mainly ornamental; the elaborate decorative designs worked into it included people and animals, family crests and mottoes, scenes of heroic deeds, and so on. The whole muzzle was often gilded. A similar accessory was used in the 17th century in Japan.

**muzzle** In a firearm, the open frontal end of the BARREL.

**muzzle band** A fitting on a rifle that anchors the barrel to the stock at the muzzle end so that the vibration of the barrel in firing will be as little as possible. It also protects and strengthens the front end of the stock and, in military arms, carries the boss for the bayonet. It often used to have an opening at the front to take the ramrod. A muzzle band may be attached to the stock either by a screw or by a retaining spring.

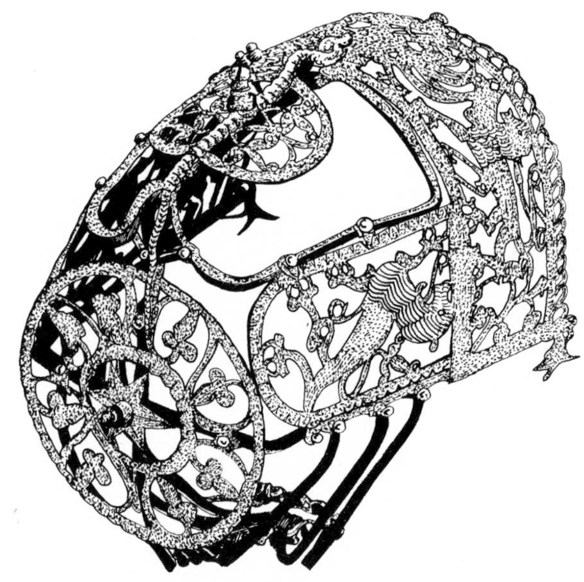

*Muzzle, Austria, c. 1560. Museo Stibbert, Florence.*

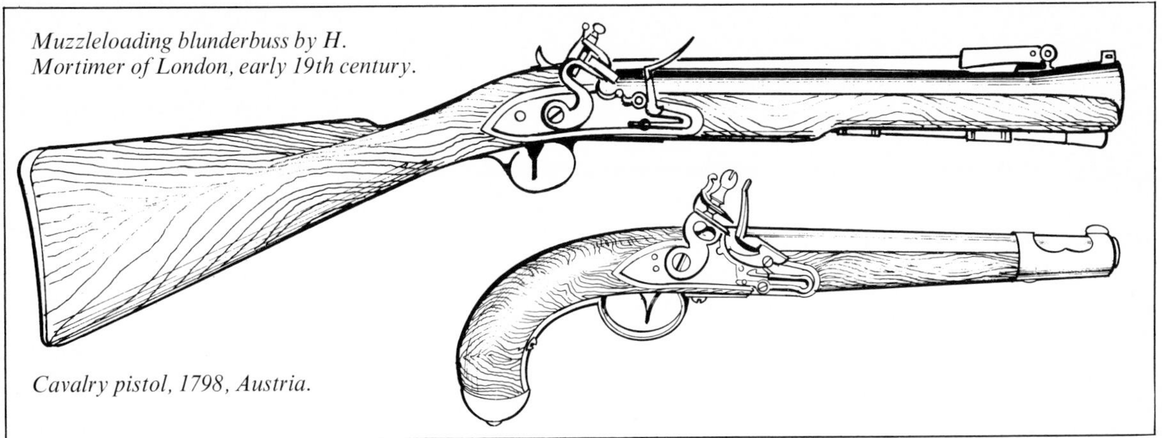

*Muzzleloading blunderbuss by H. Mortimer of London, early 19th century.*

*Cavalry pistol, 1798, Austria.*

**muzzleloader** A term used to describe a GUN or PISTOL that is loaded from the front end of the barrel—the most common form of loading used internationally from the origins of firearms until the adoption of the cartridge breechloader in the later part of the 19th century.

The process of loading the standard 18th-century flintlock musket or fowling piece was time-consuming. First the cock was set at the safety position, the cover of the pan was opened, and a small quantity of fine-grain priming powder was poured from the priming flask or torn paper cartridge into the pan. The pan cover was then closed, and any excess priming powder was blown away. The correct measure of powder was then poured from the paper cartridge of a powder flask down the barrel. The ball, often wrapped in a wad, was rammed down the barrel, thrusting it on top of the powder. This maneuver was achieved with the aid of the RAMROD which was usually housed underneath the barrel. The musket was then fully cocked and fired.

Celebrated muzzleloaders include the English "Brown Bess" or Long Land Pattern musket (illustrated on p. 348) that the British Army used in various patterns from the 1730s to the 1830s and the so-called Kentucky rifle, that was made in Pennsylvania and surrounding regions of the United States in the last part of the 18th century and throughout the 19th century.

# N

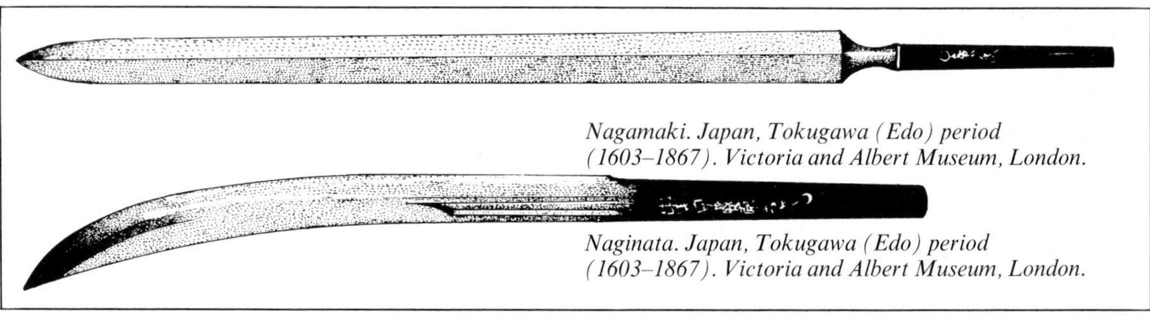

*Nagamaki. Japan, Tokugawa (Edo) period (1603–1867). Victoria and Albert Museum, London.*

*Naginata. Japan, Tokugawa (Edo) period (1603–1867). Victoria and Albert Museum, London.*

**nagamaki** A Japanese staff weapon and two-handed sword with a blade shaped midway between a sword and a NAGINATA, often termed a "straight naginata." Also called *nagatsuka-no-katana*, the nagamaki probably derives from the exceptionally long TACHI and NO-DACHI swords of the late Kamakura (13th–14th centuries) and Yoshino (1337–92) periods, but it may also have originated from the long naginata of the Kamakura period with its 1.2 m. (4 ft.) blade. The Japanese historian, Arai Hakuseki, mentions the names of various well-known warriors who wielded long swords with blades of the nagamaki type, some being more than 2 m. (6½ ft.) in length, and it is on record that the famous general Oda Nobunaga armed his front-rank warriors with formidable swords of this kind. Although sword blades were often mounted on long shafts as spears, nagamaki swords must not be confused with the true long-tanged blades that were actually made for spears. The nagamaki blade was almost always built like a slightly curved sword blade, with a rib and a *yokote*, a short transverse ridge at the top of the blade forming the base of the point section. The blade had a very long tang, usually about 50–60 cm. (20–24 in.), which was mounted on a shaft or a very long handle. There was also a TSUBA-like guard, and the blade was housed in a SAYA of lacquered wood. Special training was needed for wielding a true nagamaki.

**nagari** An alternative term for the NAGE-YARI.

**nagatsuka-no-katana** An alternative term for the NAGAMAKI.

**nagaye** The shaft of a Japanese spear. *See also* YARI.

**nagegama** A Japanese weapon with a short sickle-like blade fixed at right angles to a short handle with a long chain attached. It was used particularly in the defense of forts and castles, as it could be thrown down from the walls and drawn back by the chain. Another word for this weapon is *kusarigama*.

**nage-yari** A Japanese javelin, with a short heavy head, like a regular YARI, and a short shaft tapering toward the butt. It was carried for defense when traveling in a palanquin. The alternative word for this javelin is *nagari*; *uchi-ne* is also used to denote a short javelin with or without a feathered flight.

**naginata** A Japanese spear with a ribbed blade without a *yokote*, i.e., a transversal rib near the point, strongly curved and slightly widening toward the point. Its long tang was mounted in a long, oval-sectioned shaft terminating in a flared shoe. It is comparable to the European glaive and was most probably developed in the early Heian period, about the 9th century, from an agricultural implement. On the island of Kyūshū in the early part of the 10th century, a socketed naginata known as a *tsukushi-naginata* was used, with its blade fitted onto the shaft with a ring socket; this type was still being used in the late Heian period (12th century). In the Kamakura period (1186–1333) the naginata became a widely distributed weapon among both mounted and foot soldiers. At that time naginata blades were extremely long, up to about 1.2 m. (4 ft.), with a very long tang; these were called *shōbuzukuri-naginata*. Illustrations of the Mongol invasions of Japan in the late 13th century show many *bushi* (knights) armed with formidable long-bladed naginata spears. It was above all a most effective weapon for mounted troops, taking precedence over the sword. In the mid-14th century naginata blades became wider and more curved toward the point; this was when Hōjoji Kunimitsu, the most celebrated maker of naginata spears, was at the height of his activities. Some surviving naginata blades signed by Kunimitsu are finely shaped and heavy, about 40 cm. (16 in.) long.

A temporary wane in demand for the naginata may have been due to the increase in fighting on foot during and after the Great War of Ōnin (1467–77). In the following century, however, constant civil wars caused a rising demand for various arms, and naginata spears were re-created in new forms and extensively used, along with the straight spear called YARI and the sword. This period saw the introduction of the short-shafted naginata—though it is probable it had been conceived before this—with a normal curved blade, long tangs for setting in the shaft, and in many cases, the sword TSUBA. At the same time a rare form of socketed naginata, the *naginata-no-sake*, made its appearance; it had a long socket secured on the shaft with a nail.

With the arrival of peace in the Tokugawa (Edo) period (1603–1867), polearms lost some of their usefulness. Naginata blades become shorter and were sometimes chiseled or engraved, a dragon being a favorite motif. Their shafts were beautifully embellished or lacquered in floral motifs, occasionally overlaid with mother-of-pearl and mounted in brass. Such elaborate naginata were used mostly for display in ceremonial parades. The naginata shaft was always oval in section. It was an old tradition to keep the naginata blade in a wooden sheath. This was usually made of lacquered magnolia wood, decorated with crests and housed in a silk cover. The blade was always associated with the sword, and their evolution followed a parallel course. Various features of sword blades may also be studied in naginata blades, above all the YAKIBA. Naginata blades of the Tokugawa period were about 40–50 cm. (16–20 in.) and the shafts 1.8 m. (6 ft.) long, but there was also a lighter version, generally known as the woman's naginata, with a smaller blade mounted on a narrow shaft. Special spears known as *keiko-naginata* and *shiai-naginata* were used for training and contests. *See also* BLADE: Japanese.

**nahar-nakh** *See* BAGH-NAKH.

**nakago** The tang of a Japnaese blade. *See also* BLADE: Japanese.

**namban tsuba** *See* TSUBA.

**nanban-gusoku** Japanese armor showing European influence. *See also* GUSOKU.

**nasal** An integral part of many types of helmets to protect the nose. In the medieval conical helmet it was simply a fixed bar, either made in one with the skull or riveted to it, the bar sometimes broadening out to cover part of the face. This form survived until the first half of the 15th century, when the nasal was incorporated into the early types of BARBUT. There were several variations, some nasals being attached by screws and others by rivets just above the eye line and sometimes extending down below the mouth. One derivation of such a style can clearly be seen in the "Corinthian"-style barbut, in which the nasal extends down to cover the nose between two upward-sloping oval sights in the T-shaped face opening.

By the 16th century the nasal had completely disappeared, but it was to return in many types of 17th-century helmets such as the German Zischägge, Dutch and English pots, and the steel hat. In these, it consisted of a narrow vertical bar passing through a special slot in the fixed fall and secured through a staple on the brow by a wing screw, which enabled the wearer to adjust its position as circumstances demanded. The bar was frequently augmented by a small plate in various shapes, such as a leaf, trefoil, shield, or spearhead, whose purpose was to increase the protection given to the face.

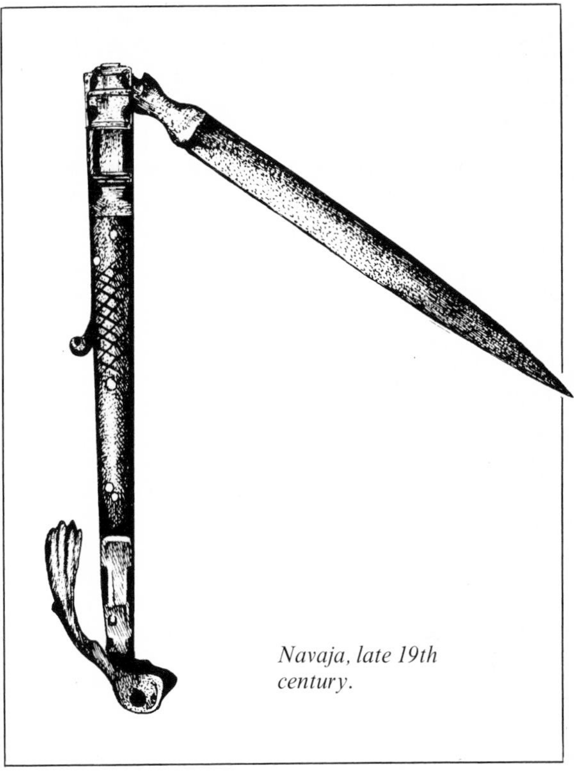

*Navaja, late 19th century.*

**navaja** A large knife with a folding blade, either single- or double-edged, made in many different forms. When the blade was open, a catch on the back held it in position and it was necessary to raise the catch spring to close it again. The size of the navaja also varied considerably; normally, when open, it was about 40 cm. (16 in.) long, but there are examples that are more than 1.3 m. (50 in.) in length.

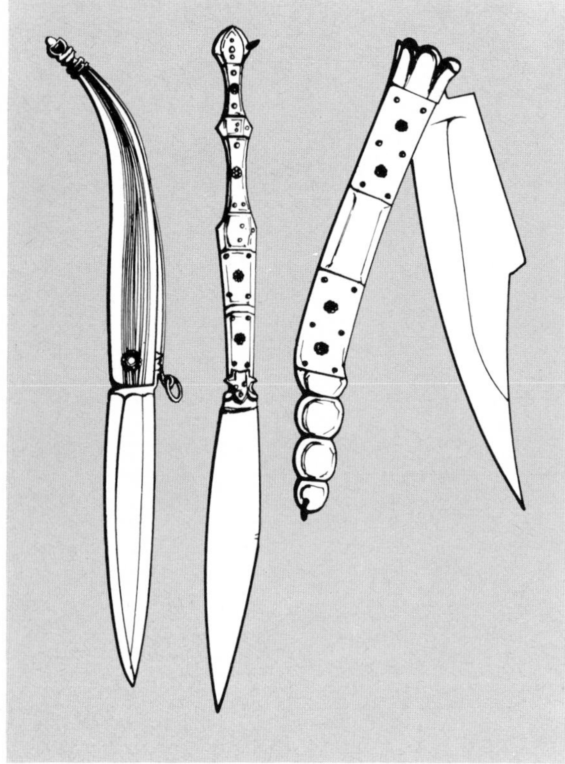

*Various types of navaja, Spain, 18th century. Livrustkammaren, Stockholm.*

Of Spanish origin, the navaja was in use from the 16th (and possibly even from the 15th) century. It had distinctive forms of handle and blade which remained regionally consistent for long periods, and almost up to the present day. Although it was a humble weapon, toward the mid-19th century its use was laid down in a fencing manual which dealt with every possible use of it in hand-to-hand combat and also as a throwing weapon (specifying, however, that this latter use was almost exclusively for sailors).

**neck guard** (in horse armor) *See* CRINET.

**neck guard** The part of a helmet which protected the nape. In some types of SALLET, CLOSE HELMET, BURGONET, and ENGLISH POT, it was an integral part of the skull, but in other types it was an appendage to the skull consisting of one or more articulated lames. The true neck guard appeared on German-style sallets toward the middle of the 15th century, the lame or lames being quite distinct from the skull, though attached to it. The Italian-style sallet was soon to adopt a similar form, with a combination of several lames articulated on sliding rivets.

The neck guard began to be fitted to close helmets in the latter part of the 15th century. By the early 16th century a long neck guard with articulated lames had been introduced on close helmets with full visors, especially in the Germanic countries. It continued to be fitted to field helmets and helmets for special purposes throughout the 16th century and most of the 17th as a combination of two or three lames forming part of the gorget plates.

Most types of burgonets did not have a separately made neck guard; rather, the lower rear part of the skull was extended to form one. There were some burgonets, however, which did have separately made neck-guard lames as a part of the gorget plates, but these helmets were mostly of the closed type.

**neck strap** A part of the bridle consisting of a broad leather strap which passes from left to right behind the horse's ears to join the brow band on each side, where it is connected to the CHEEK STRAPS and THROAT LATCH.

**neji** An alternative word for HINERI.

**neri tsuba** An ancient type of TSUBA, lacquered on both sides.

**niello** *See* DECORATIVE TECHNIQUES.

**nimcha** An Arab saber, used mainly in Morocco, which probably achieved its definitive style in the 16th century. Its forms originated in Europe, in Austria, Germany, or France, and this type can be seen in Polish and English art from the 17th century, as, for example, in the *Portrait of Adam Kazonowski*, in the State Collections of Art in Wawel Castle, Kraków. The blade of a typical nimcha was slightly curved and fairly wide, sometimes with a YALMAN. It was often fullered and bore the bladesmith's marks as well as symbols such as the moon, sun, the Seal of Solomon, or the Star of David; the decorator's name was sometimes given too, but signatures like "work of Ahmed" or "work of Hassan" throw little light on these artist-craftsmen.

The grip was made of a single piece of buffalo or rhinoceros horn, though hardwood was also occasionally used. It was cylindrical or square in shape with a large one-sided pommel representing a lion's head, whose curved neck served as a rest for the little finger. The tang was riveted into the grip. The knuckle guard, undoubtedly inspired by some 16th-century European swords, was rectangular at the base with drooping quillons terminating in pear-shaped knobs. Two of the quillons formed an additional guard, curving toward the blade like the arms of

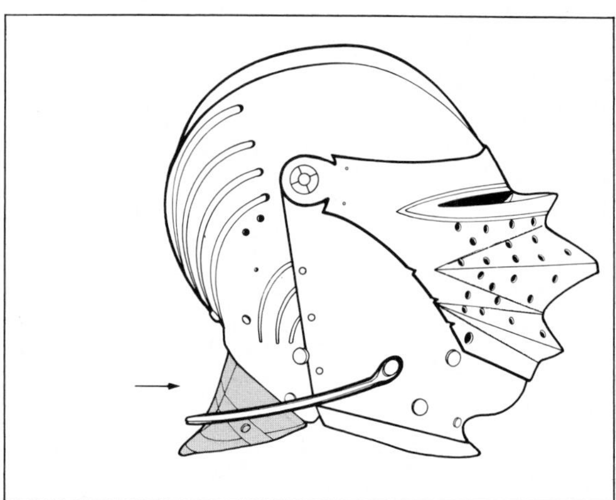

*Neck guard on an early close helmet.*

*Method of carrying the no-dachi. From an ancient Japanese print.*

the hilt. The guard was made of iron, brass, or iron inlaid with gold.

Nimcha scabbards were made of wood and covered with velvet or leather, sometimes mounted in silver with engraved floral motifs. The two suspension rings were set fairly high. A particularly sumptuous nimcha might have an ivory grip or one made of Sahara amber inlaid and mounted with gold or gilded brass.

Sometimes the nimcha was made with a straight, single-edged blade like that of a PALLASCH.

**nipple** A small stud, bored, tapped, and appropriately shaped, which was screwed to the top of the vent in the commonest types of percussion gun to take the percussion cap.

**nitrocotton** Term commonly used for dinitrocellulose. *See also* EXPLOSIVE.

**nitroglycerin** Oily liquid used as an EXPLOSIVE.

**nock** (or **nocking**) *See* ARROW.

**no-dachi** A Japanese field sword of enormous size and weight which could only be carried by exceptionally strong soldiers. The no-dachi, which sometimes measured as much as 1.8 m. (6 ft.), was carried on the back, slung on a narrow belt passed over the left shoulder. The hilt rose above the warrior's head, and the edge of the blade faced to the left. The no-dachi, made solely for fighting, seldom had elaborate furniture, having only a plain iron TSUBA and a simple wooden scabbard.

**nodowa** A gorget or throat ring in Japanese armor, fastened at the back of the neck by cords. There were two kinds of nodowa: the *meguriva*, secured by hooks, and the *eriva*, fastened with a buckle. Early nodowa were made of hide from the neck of oxen and covered with SAMÉ or soft morocco-like leather from India. The back was usually lined with brocade. On later versions, lacquered and laced plates were regularly used, although occasionally nodowa were constructed of mail on brocade or of small hexagonal plates which were quilted and sewn in.

**noseband** One of the straps on a horse's bridle, attached at each end to the lower part of the leather cheekpieces. It runs horizontally across the nasal bone about midway between the eyes and the nostrils. Its main purpose is to hold the leather cheekpieces in position and thus, indirectly, the bit as well. It also assists in controlling the horse, particularly for stopping it. Although the modern noseband also fits this description, it was used in the same way as part of the harness with full bard or light horse armor.

**nu-boko** The mythological "Jewel Spear of Heaven" which the gods Izanagi-no-Mikoto and Izanami-no-Mikoto thrust into the ocean in the act of creating the Japanese islands. It is said that this heavenly jewel spear was in the form of a *wa-bashira*, which literally means "male pillar," and is evidence of certain phallic cults practiced in prehistoric Japan. The word *wa-bashira* is still a current expression, usually applied to the end posts or pillars of a railing or balustrade, particularly of a bridge.

**nuclear bomb** *See* BOMB.

**nut** Part of the mechanism of the CROSSBOW, shaped in the form of a strong disc which, positioned in the tiller at a variable distance depending on the curvability of the bow, served to block the spanned bowstring and release it. In this disc, which had its axis of rotation crosswise to the stock—hence parallel to the bow—there were several notches, each with its specific function: the upper one was

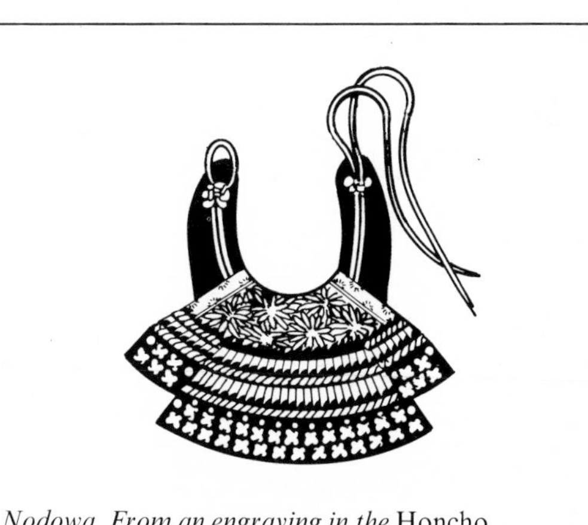

*Nodowa. From an engraving in the* Honcho Gunkiko *(a treatise on Japanese armor written by Arari Hakuseki in the late 17th–early 18th century).*

for holding the bowstring; a deep groove in the front was designed for centering the quarrel at the spanned bowstring; a notch on the opposite side was for the blocking tooth (sear) of the release mechanism.

The nut is a feature of European crossbows, although it was not the first type of catch; the peg system appears to be earlier. Here a small wooden dowel, pushed through a special hole in the stock, expelled the spanned bowstring from the nock, thus releasing the bolt. This release system shared many similarities with those adopted by the Chinese and Indochinese, which were apparently in use as early as the second millennium B.C. To make the nut it was necessary to use a hard material; boxwood and deer antlers were often preferred to bronze or iron.

**obitori** The suspension rings on the lockets of the Japanese TACHI scabbard.

**o-boshi** The 14th-century version of the Japanese HOSHI-KABUTO helmet.

**obturator** In breechloading firearms, the part of the mechanism that ensures the closure of the breech at the moment the gun is fired. For different systems and types, see ARTILLERY; AUTOMATIC WEAPONS; GUN; MACHINE GUN; MACHINE PISTOL; PISTOL.

**odoshi** The system of lacing small plates (lamellae), called *kozane*, which was of fundamental importance in the construction of Japanese armor. There were never more than three styles of lacing in the early, middle, and modern periods of the history of Japanese armor: the *kebiki*, the *sugake* (or *arame*), and the *shikime* (or *chikiri*). In the kebiki style each oblong kozane had two columns of seven holes, the three upper holes on each side being larger than the four lower ones. Diagram 2 (overleaf) shows how the kozane overlapped when laced with silk cords or leather thongs. The outer lace, *mimi-ito*, ran from one end of the upper kozane down to the lower one through the larger holes, while the lower lace, *hishi-nui*, tied the kozane together through the smaller holes. The large number of holes was an obvious source of weakness, and the sugake, or "sparsely pointed," style overcame this by having fewer perforations (Diagram 1). In this case, the kozane were in groups of two pairs, the first two kozane having three larger holes at the upper right edge and eight smaller ones in two rows at the bottom, while the next two kozane had only the eight bottom holes. In the shikime (Diagram 3), the kozane were wider and shorter than in the other two styles of lacing and the perforations were in three columns (18, 21, and 12 holes in different specimens), enabling each kozane to overlap two others instead of one other, to give

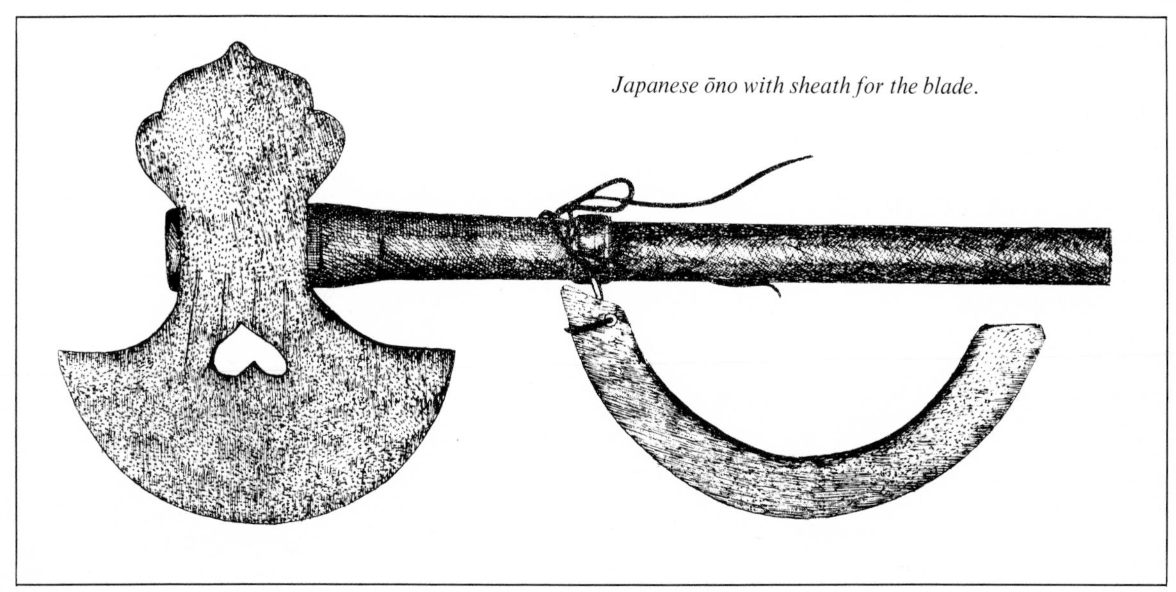

*Japanese ōno with sheath for the blade.*

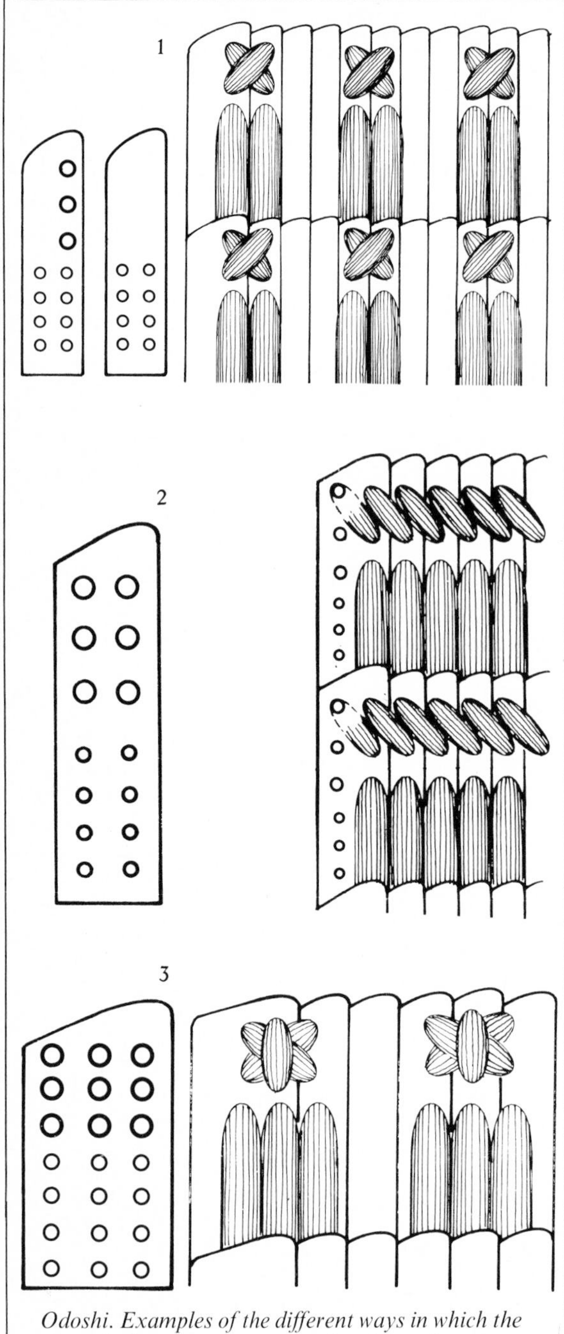

*Odoshi. Examples of the different ways in which the plates in Japanese armor were laced together: 1. sugake (arame); 2. kebiki; 3. shikime (chikiri).*

triple thickness throughout.

Various materials were employed for the laces, the most usual being silk and other textile braids in an infinity of colors. It is said that, in the time of the emperor Seiwa (A.D. 859–876), the great families had their own colors: the Taira family's was purple, the Fujiwara's light green, the Tachibana's yellow, and so on.

**ogive** The front part of a SHELL, which has to take the greater part of the wind resistance. It can be cast with the body ("monobloc" type) or screwed onto the body ("composite" type). The shape and thickness of the ogive are directly related to the purpose for which the shell is designed. Apart from certain special-purpose shells, the profile of the ogive is generally obtained from a single arc of a circle, though some are obtained from two arcs, that of the smaller radius at the point. For long-range artillery the shell may be cut off square at the base of the ogive, or have an ogive of small radius, to give the shell stability; in such cases a sheet-metal ballistic cap or "false ogive" may be fitted to preserve the streamlined form.

**ō-kama-yari** A larger variant of the KAMA-YARI.

**ōno** A Japanese poleax, which was mounted on a shaft up to 2.1 m. (7 ft.) long. Its large head consisted of a convex cutting edge of about 25 cm. (10 in.) on one side and a proportionately large scroll-shaped hammer or peen on the other. In some instances it looked like an ordinary European ax. The ōno was sometimes combined with a SU-YARI to make a type of halberd. Its sheath, the SAYA, covered only the edge of the blade.

**"organ"** A nickname since late medieval times for a multibarreled gun on a carriage. *See also* RIBAULD.

**over-and-under** Term normally used to describe sporting guns or shotguns with two barrels, one above the other. *See also* GUN: sporting.

**o-yoroi** An alternative term for YOROI.

# P

**pair of plates** Medieval term for the COAT OF PLATES.

**palà** A type of Turkish saber, mostly of the 18th or 19th century, very similar to the KILIJ but with a large, heavy, fairly short blade about 70 cm. (27 in.) long that had a strong curve and an enormous YALMAN. It was mainly intended for use on foot. Blades were frequently of black Khorassan Damascus steel with single or double fullers and often decorated with line engraving, gold damascening in floral motifs, palmettes, medallions, and inscribed cartouches. Also displayed were such symbols as the Star of David and the Lion of Ali (the Lion of God). The palà hilt was usually made of two pieces of rhinoceros or buffalo horn riveted to the tang, with a spherical scroll-like pommel turned forward, in which there was a hole for a sword knot. The horn was prepared by boiling it in oil and modeling it. The finished product was a transparent honey color. Straight quillons terminated in knobs with a lozenge-shaped escutcheon in the middle extending its langets over both grip and blade.

The palà scabbard had to be large enough to allow the weapon to be drawn, for which purpose the back of the upper part was often slit. Made of wood, it was covered with leather, velvet, brass, or silver, embossed and chased, mounted with lockets and chape, and fitted with two suspension rings. A particularly sumptuous group of palà, probably manufactured in Trabzon, had the outer side of the hilts and scabbards completely decorated with almond-shaped pieces of coral and round turquoises, and the inner side was made of brass chased in floral motifs. In this elaborate type of palà the quillons curved sharply downward.

**Pallasch** (German; Polish *pałasz,* Hungarian *pallos*) A term derived from the Turkish *palà* (meaning "straight") and used in Germany and other eastern European countries to denote a backsword with a straight, heavy blade, usually single-edged, and a closed (i.e., with a knuckle guard) or, more rarely, an open hilt. It was designed mainly for cutting, although thrusts with the point were also possible; occasionally the blade was double-edged and was grooved and ridged on both faces. As a weapon of the heavy cavalry, it was used at least from the beginning of the 17th century, and its typological derivations are still used today (e.g., the Soviet Navy *palash* worn by cadets in full-dress uniform).

It was also adopted in smaller forms by sailors, special corps, and irregular troops, and it found considerable favor among hunters. The hunting version of the Pallasch was in fact one of many types of the hunting HANGER. Its handle was made in a wide variety of materials (bone, horn, ivory, porcelain, semiprecious stones, metals), usually carefully decorated, and surmounted by a cap with a button. Unlike the military prototype with a closed hilt, the guard of the hunting weapon had only two short quillons, whose finials were occasionally shaped like an animal's foot or head; a shell of the guard, when it was present, usually pointed toward the blade. The blade was sharply pointed and sometimes had a fuller running almost the entire length; it was decorated with ornamental patterns and gilding. Along with other types of hunting hangers, such weapons were still used in the 19th century.

**pan** The small dish-shaped container, fitted to the barrel or the lock of a firearm, that holds the priming powder. The need to have some form of container for powder adjacent to the touchhole, in order to prevent the powder from being blown away and to improve ignition, was appreciated very early in the history of firearms. The bronze gun from Loshult, dating from the early 14th century and now in the National Historical Museum in Stockholm, has a recess cut around the touchhole on top of the barrel to take the priming powder. On the bronze hand cannon from Mörkö, also in Stockholm, dating from the late 14th century, the pan consists of a raised square dish surrounding the touchhole.

In the early part of the 15th century a cover for the pan was introduced. This consisted of a flat plate held by a pin to the edge of the pan, which could be moved aside by means of a small handle. It not only protected the priming powder from the damp but also allowed the firearm to be kept primed. Preserved in the Wozska Polskiego Museum in Warsaw is a 15th-century handgun with a recessed pan set on top of the barrel and fitted with a narrow rectangular pan cover operated by a lever.

Sometime during the later part of the 16th century, the touchhole was moved to the side of the barrel, where the pan projected like a shelf. The pan was retained in this position until the development of the percussion lock in the early part of the 19th century. With the invention of the wheel-lock in about 1500, the pan was fitted over the wheel, which operated through a slot cut in the base of the pan. For priming, the pan cover was slid forward until retained by a spring catch. It could be turned back over the pan either by hand or by means of a button release protruding through the lock plate. When the wheel revolved, a cam on its spindle pushed forward the lever of the pan cover and caused the latter to open, allowing the revolving wheel to strike the pyrite. A pan of similar construction was used on most "snaphance" locks. An important technical innovation in the flintlock system of ignition was the steel and the pan cover combined as one element. In the Artillery Museum of Turin there is a detached mechanism mounted with both a wheel-lock and a snaphance, whose steel is shaped to a right angle, one end of which is hinged over the pan. This lock is probably Italian; it has been dated to about 1580 or somewhat later and is the earliest known example of the combined steel and pan cover. It was probably invented sometime in the latter part of the 16th century. In the last quarter of the century, the pan on a number of snaphances was fitted with a flat plate set vertically at the outer edge, known as the "fence." It was frequently fitted on the locks of English, Scottish, Dutch, and Russian firearms in the late 16th and 17th centuries.

With the introduction of the flintlock, the form of the pan altered very little. From about 1780, high-quality firearms were fitted with waterproof pans, a raised rim on the pan being fitted into a recess cut into the pan cover to form a seal. A hole was drilled in the fence behind the pan to take away any water that had accumulated. The pan and touchhole were particularly susceptible to the corrosive effects of gunpowder, a problem that gunsmiths overcame by lining the pans and touchholes with gold. Some fine Spanish firearms had been fitted with gold-lined pans since the 17th century, but it was not until about 1725 that this feature became more widely adopted in Europe. An English gunmaker, Joseph Manton, claimed to have invented the technique of lining touchholes and pans with platinum instead of gold, a method introduced about 1805. Platinum was thought to be more satisfactory than gold, which was soft and easily damaged by ignition. With the introduction of the percussion lock by a Scottish minister, Alexander John Forsyth, in about 1806, the pan and the pan cover were replaced first by the roller primer and later by the self-contained cartridge.

**pan cover** The cover of the pan holding the priming powder in early firearms. *See also* PAN.

**panoply** Originally meaning the full armor of the heavily armed foot soldiers of ancient Greece, the hoplites, "panoply" later came to denote a complete suit of armor, especially worn by mounted troops. Today its use is restricted to a display of weapons for ornamental purposes.

**Pappenheimer** A sword whose modern name derives from that of Gottfried Heinrich, Count of Pappenheim (1594–1632), colonel of a cuirassier regiment and later the general in command of the imperial cavalry. During the Thirty Years War (1618–48) he adopted and encouraged the use of a sword that was *à la mode* among the officers of the day, and which was subsequently named after him.

The Pappenheimer had quite a large cut-and-thrust blade and a closed hilt comprising a pair of symmetrical shell guards enclosed in rings and pierced with holes, wide recurved quillons, and a knuckle guard with side bars. Some types of hilts had a pair of ring guards below the shells for additional protection. The heavy pommel was most often urn-shaped and also surmounted by a button on which the tang was riveted.

**parabellum** A word derived from the Latin motto *Si vis pacem para bellum* ("If you want peace, prepare for war") and used as a telegraphic address by the Deutsche Waffen und Munitionsfabriken of Berlin. It was later used as a trade name for various weapons, notably the Luger pistol of 1900 and its derivatives, and for the ammunition for these weapons.

**paragnatide** The Greek term for the side flaps on ancient helmets made of leather or metal to protect the cheeks. They were usually tied together under the chin.

**parang** A Malay jungle knife, of which there are numerous varieties. Its blade generally widens toward the point. Old parang blades were forged from local iron frequently inlaid with brass studs, but more modern blades are of European or Chinese iron. The *parang-dedak* is a Bornean knife with a heavy single-edged blade that is convex on the cutting side, while the back is concave at the point. The *parang-ginah* is a sickle-shaped knife. The *parang-jengok*, a weapon used by thieves, has a sharp extension at the tip set at right angles to the rest of the blade. The *parang-latok* is specifically a jungle knife, characterized by a blade that is bent at an obtuse angle, like a dog's leg, at about one-third of its length from the handle and widening considerably toward the point. The *parang-nabur* is a kind of saber with a curved blade; the hilt is furnished with a nuckle guard. The *parang-negara* has a grooved blade.

**parazonium** A Roman edged weapon of Greco-Macedonian origin, which, in terms of classification, falls somewhere between a short sword and a large dagger. Carried by the emperor and senior officials, it was hung from the CINCTORIUM (belt), or sometimes from the BALTEUS or BALDRIC, in an almost horizontal position. Pictorial evidence shows a Greek type of short sword with a spherical pommel and a rectangular guard. The blade was not visible because it was invariably sheathed; the sheath had parallel sides and a semicircular or pelta-shaped chape (a PELTA was a small shield).

**parma** A round bronze shield equipped with a sturdy boss, or UMBO, used by Roman mounted troops from the 7th or 6th century B.C.; it was derived from the much older CLIPEUS. One of the results of the reorganization of the Roman cavalry toward the end of the 4th century B.C. was that soldiers no longer had to engage in foot combat. The round parma was therefore replaced by an oval leather shield that, although lighter and more manageable, was less efficient. The parma continued to be used, however, as a parade weapon and as the insignia of the *ordo equestris* (the knightly class). Beginning in the latter part of the 3rd century B.C., lightly armed foot soldiers, the velites, were equipped with a type of parma that, althouth smaller (91 cm or about 3 ft.) in diameter, was similar to that of the cavalry; its framework of wood or plaited osier was covered with leather, and it was fitted with an umbo.

A small square shield, called a *parma thracidica*, was used by certain gladiators who were known as *thraces* (that is, Thracians).

**parrying dagger** A dagger used along with a sword in personal combats in accordance with the rules of the Spanish and Italian schools of fencing. It had a robust blade and was often made to match the sword in construction and in decorative features. The parrying dagger, which appeared toward the end of the 15th century, was fitted with special defensive devices. Long straight or curved quillons extended from the hilt in the plane of the blade or slightly bent in front of it. A strong side ring protruded from the hilt perpendicular to the blade to protect the fingers. There were many varieties of blades. Spring blades could be split into three when a button was pressed by the thumb. Other blades had the form of a comb designed to catch and possibly even break the tip of the opponent's sword.

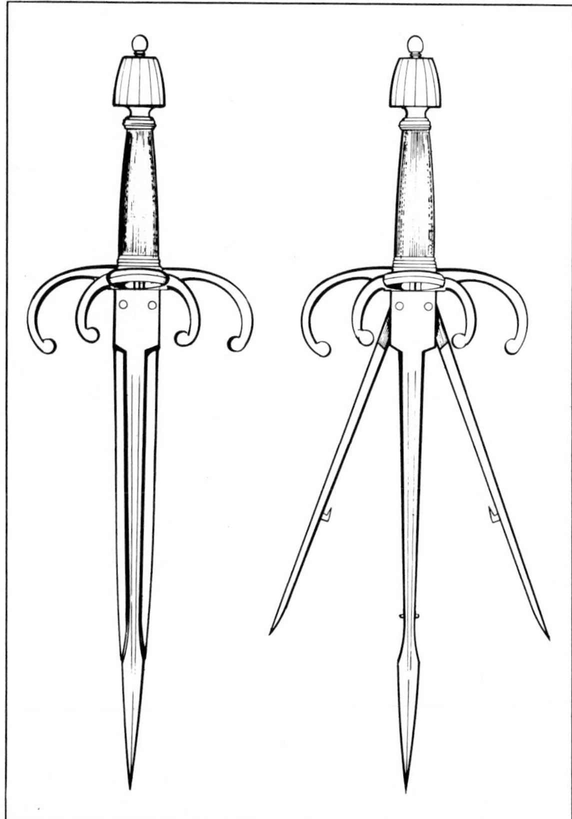

*Parrying dagger with triple blade, Italy, c. 1620–30;* (right) *the same dagger opened. Odescalchi Collection, Museo di Palazzo Venezia, Rome.*

Because the method of settling quarrels between gentlemen by formal armored combat in the lists was discontinued in the early 16th century, the private duel to settle disputes became fashionable with noblemen and soldiers. Since such an encounter could happen at any time, a light sword and a rapier became part of everyday dress; they were accompanied by a parrying weapon such as a buckler or, more often, a dagger of proper design. In the absence of a parrying weapon, a glove, a cloak, or even the scabbard of a sword were used to deflect the opponent's sword and protect the side of the body not covered by the fencer's own sword. The parrying dagger was usually worn on the belt opposite the side where the sword was suspended from its hanger.

A special form of parrying dagger was developed in Spain about the middle of the 17th century to accompany the sword with a cup guard. This dagger had very long straight quillons and a large convex guard of triangular shape (if viewed from the front) that completely covered the hand. The guards of both the sword and the dagger had a strong rim, often raised, to deter the opponent's blade. Some daggers had a blade with a very large base from which two prongs ran parallel to the blade to catch and block the sword. Cup-guard swords and daggers in the Spanish fashion were also widely produced in Italy and, to a much lesser extent, in Germany. Their guards were often intricately decorated with chiseling, piercing, and applied decoration.

Although fencing with both hands ceased to be the predominant mode in the second quarter of the 17th century, it survived in Spain, southern Italy, and other areas of Spanish influence until the third quarter of the 18th century. However, when they became part of the uniform of cadets at military academies, production of daggers of the classical Spanish form was revived in Toledo in the second half of the 19th century.

**partisan** A hafted weapon with a broad-pointed head, which had tapering, cutting edges. The flats of this weapon often had two lengthwise ribs that extended down to the socket. At the base of the point protruded two sharp lugs, symmetrical in the plane of the cutting edges. A strong socket, with two langets often extending from it, guaranteed a tough join with the shaft. The partisan could be used for both cutting and thrusting, the two lugs also playing part of a guard.

Deriving from the LANGDEBEVE, a broad-bladed spear, by the mid-15th century the partisan was probably identified with a variation of the langdebeve listed in old inventories as *spiedo alla bolognese* (Bolognese spear). The name "partisan" seems to have derived from the partisans who used it as a weapon toward the end of the 15th century in France and Italy; in the next centuries, it was used throughout Europe.

The large flats of the head, which lent themselves to ornamental engraving and other decoration, including the coats of arms of noble families, ensured the choice of the partisan as the pole arm carried by princes' personal guards and by palace guards. In military circles, from the mid-16th century onward, it was carried by officers as an emblem of their rank; it was later replaced by the SPONTOON. It remained in use as a ceremonial weapon for a long time after it was discontinued as a weapon of war. In the French court, partisans decorated with the royal coat of arms were issued to bodyguards, among them the Cent Suisses, and were used until the end of the *ancien régime*; at the Bourbon court in Naples the partisan was used until the dissolution of that kingdom. Today the Swiss Guards in the Vatican when in full dress carry not only their traditional weapon, the halberd, but also the partisan. The Yeomen of the Guard and the Yeomen Warders of the Tower of London still carry partisans on state occasions.

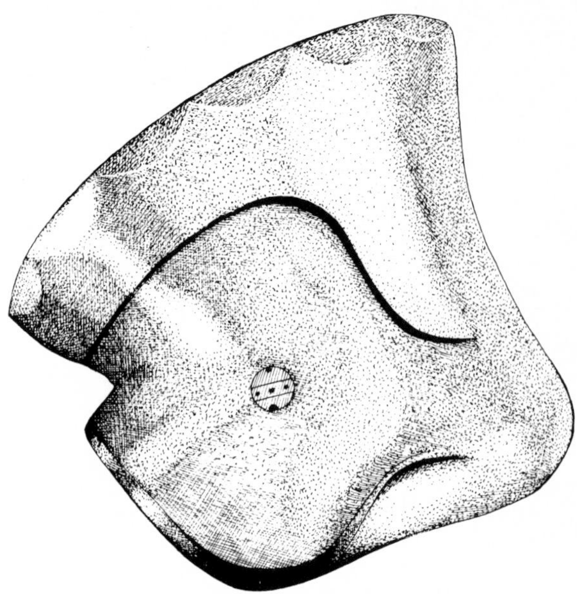

*Pasguard, worn on the left arm in the Italian joust, Augsburg, c. 1600–1610. Museo Stibbert, Florence.*

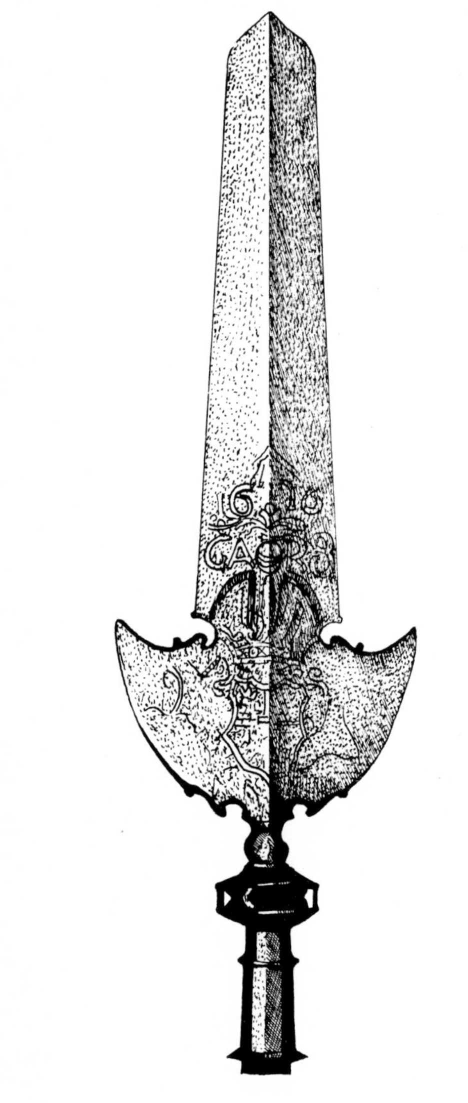

*Partisan carried by the Trabants (bodyguards) of King Gustav II of Sweden, 1626, Livrustkammaren, Stockholm.*

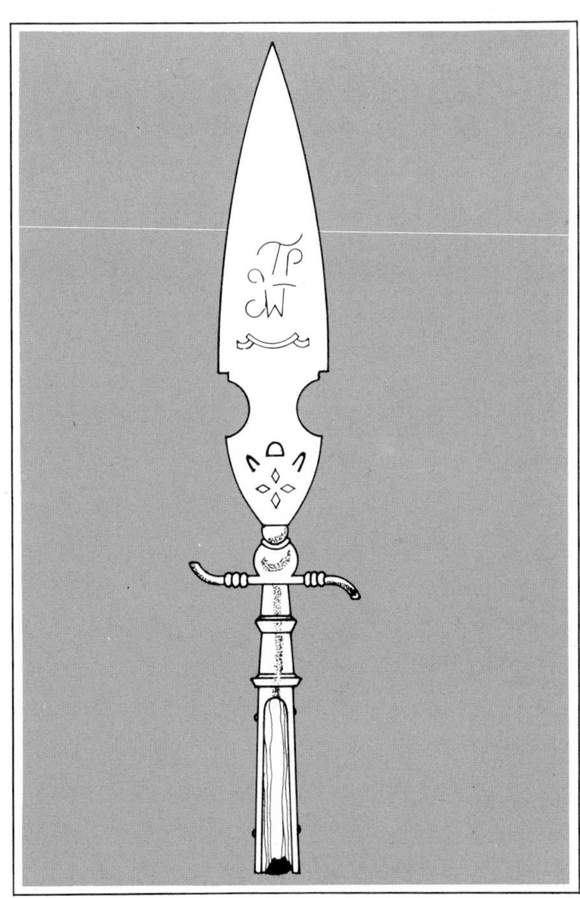

*Partisan of the Gardes du Corps of Louis XIV of France (1643–1715). Museo Stibbert, Florence.*

**pas d'âne** A term of French origin, used fairly widely but incorrectly since the 19th century to describe the ARMS OF THE HILT. As mentioned by La Touche in his *Les Vrais Principes de l'espée seule* (1670), this term in the 17th century was used to describe one of the oval shells forming the sword guard.

**pasguard** A reinforcing piece introduced in the 15th century for tilt armor to protect the left arm, particularly the elbow. It consisted of a heavy plate shaped to the bent arm, thus doubling the protection given by the VAMBRACE and the COWTER, to which it was either screwed or attached by a peg and staple. The size of the pasguard varied a good deal; some covered only the cowter, while the grand pasguard also reinforced a major part of the vambrace. The pasguard was one of the most widely used reinforcing pieces, employed in association with the reinforcing PAULDRON, the GRANDGUARD, and the MANIFER.

**passavolant** A term used at the end of the 15th and in the 16th century in France and Italy for various types of long, light artillery pieces. In the 16th century the demiculverin was a culverin of 9 pounds. Writing in the 17th century, Tomaso Moretti (*Trattato dell' artigliera*, 1672) stated: "The demiculverin (*passavolante* or *lebratana*), 48 to 50 calibers long, is poor in metal, throwing an iron ball of 8 to 9 pounds, but no more are made now."

**pata** A special form of the long, straight sword used exclusively in India and developed by the Mahrattas. It has a flat, usually double-edged blade and a gauntlet hilt. The blade is often European, generally Italian or Spanish. The hilt of the pata is attached to the blade by a pair of riveted plaques that run down the faces of the blade for a few inches. The hilt is in the form of a combined grip and gauntlet; it is usually chased and gilded with floral and animal motifs, mainly lions, tigers, and deer. Across the interior of the gauntlet is a transverse grip, and at the top of the gauntlet is a metal loop to fasten the forearm. The interior of this gauntlet hilt is padded. The pata, which evolved from the KATAR, would be difficult to use without training but was a very effective weapon for an experienced swordsman.

**pattern** The diagram made on a target by the pellets fired from a shotgun at any point short of extreme range; it is normally ascertained by firing the gun at a large sheet of paper with the standard charge for its gauge. Close patterns result when the pellets are traveling at high velocity, and thus indicate that the gun has killing force at that range. *See also* KILLING CIRCLE.

**pattisa** A type of sword used in southern and central India, the pattisa has a very broad, heavy, double-edged blade reaching 1 m. (39 in.) in length, often with decorative applications on both edges, and widening toward the point, which is occasionally rounded. It is fitted with either the Hindu hilt, which has a closed guard, or with the saucer-pommeled open hilt and short quillons with down-turning finials. Its leather scabbard follows the shape of the blade.

**pauldrons** The shoulder and upper-arm defense in a suit of armor worn from the 14th century to the middle of the 17th. In its complete form, it consisted of a series of lames articulated on sliding rivets and either buckled onto the

*Pasguard, Augsburg, c. 1559. Museo Stibbert, Florence.*

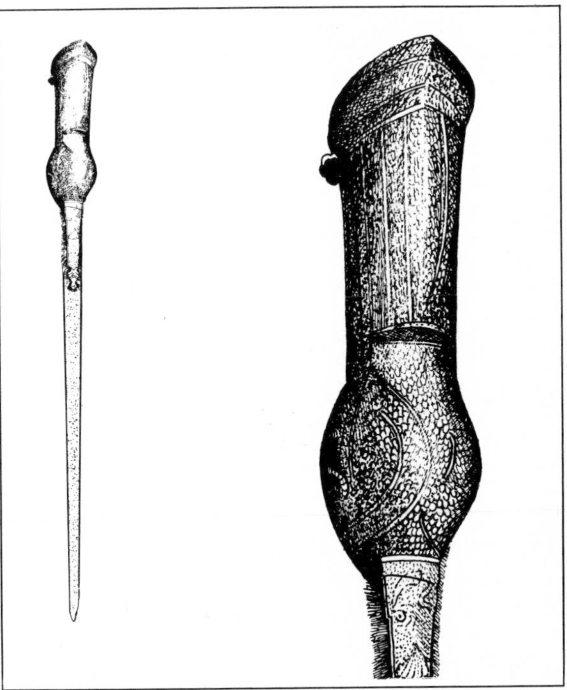

*Pata, India, 18th century. Museo Stibbert, Florence.*

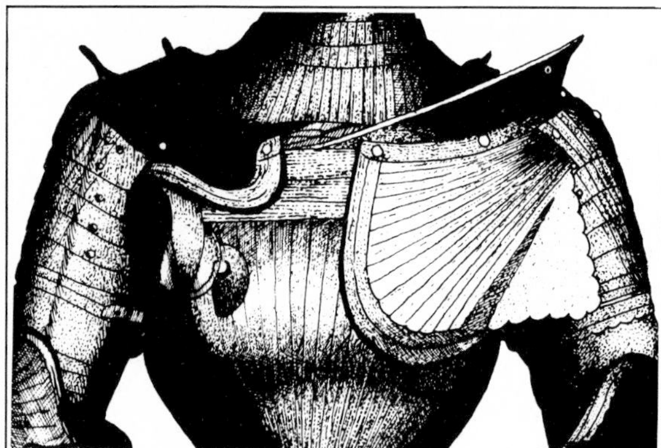

*Left pauldron with a haute-piece on a field armor, Nuremberg, c. 1525. Waffensammlung, Vienna.*

collar or GORGET or, occasionally, attached by means of a peg with a spring-loaded catch. The lames extended downward until they overlapped—or slotted into—the upper CANNON of the VAMBRACE. In the 14th century, each pauldron was a separate plate attached by laces to the COAT OF PLATES or to the mail. Some versions were made with more than one lame that had a reinforced border at the lower edge.

The developed form of the pauldron, consisting of three lames set parallel to and overlapping each other to give a squared contour, appeared somewhere around the 1390s. The lames were curved to the shoulder, but there was little difference between the front and the back. The lower of the front lames, which was usually the longest, was often equipped to take a reinforcing piece, the GARDBRACE, and was itself made with various types of reinforcement such as fluting, ridging, or a turn edge. This style, with some modifications, none of which was structural, lasted until about 1430. There was by then a noticeable trend toward enlarging the pauldrons and shaping them more carefully to the shoulders. The number of lames was increased, with a consequent improvement in articulation and a greater difference between front and back, the latter being considerably larger and squarish in general contour. The upper lame of the pauldron was now reinforced by an important part, the HAUTE-PIECE, which protected the gorget. This design was used into the first decades of the 16th century.

By the 15th century there was already a difference between the right and left pauldron, hence the term "asymmetrical" used when referring to them. The right pauldron was cut away at the armpit to facilitate the use of the lance. Pauldrons for foot combat or for mounted use without a lance remained symmetrical.

For the field and various types of courses both pauldrons could be reinforced with gardbraces, which were usually attached with screws or pegs and staples. For the Italian joust, the left pauldron was equipped to take the GRANDGUARD which was screwed into place. Fairly common variations were: symmetrical SPAUDLERS; large, multilamed pauldrons in armor used for the barrier; the symmetrical "à la Romana" pauldron consisting of three short lames shaped to the top of the shoulders and terminating in strips of laminated leather; and a type of small pauldron attached on both sides of the collar.

Pauldrons remained in use until about the 1650s, having been incorporated into cuirassier and light-horse armors. However, they were to disappear when it became the custom to wear the cuirass without pauldrons or vambraces.

**pavise** A large, oblong shield used mainly by archers and crossbowmen from the 14th century to the beginning of the 16th. It was also widely used by other foot soldiers. A typical feature was the central groove on the inside to hold a stake that was inserted in the ground to act as a prop; this groove was nearly always emphasized on the outside by a raised panel running the full height of the pavise. The purpose of the support was twofold: it freed the bowman's hands to enable him to shoot and provide the crossbowman with temporary shelter while spanning and loading his weapon.

There is evidence that the shield, and hence its name, originated in the city of Pavia in northern Italy. Soon thereafter the pavise was extensively used throughout Europe. The shield was generally rounded at the top and sometimes at the bottom too, with straight sides widening slightly toward the base. The central groove was either straight or broadened out toward the bottom. The whole shield tended to be concave on the inside, and two straps, called GUIGES, or chains were fitted there so that the soldier could carry it on his back from place to place. The

*Hand pavise, Tyrol, 15th century. Odescalchi Collection, Museo di Palazzo Venezia, Rome.*

*Pavise. 1. With coat of arms of the city of Nuremberg, 15th century. 2, 3. With the Austrian coat of arms and emblems used by Tyrolean crossbowmen in the service of the town of Klausen. Tyrol, mid-15th century. Odescalchi Collection, Museo di Palazzo Venezia, Rome.*

framework was generally made of wood and faced with cloth, parchment, or *cuir-bouilli*, although a few were reinforced with iron bands.

The pavise was also used as an assault defense, and for this purpose special spikes were fitted along the bottom edge to enable the shield to be thrust into the ground as the attacking force advanced. There was also a metal observation grille at the top. A hand pavise was a smaller version of the pavise, fitted on the inside with the ENARMES.

It was customary for the front of the pavise to be decoratively painted in a wide variety of designs, including city or personal armorial bearings.

**peak** *See* FALL.

**pectoral** The breast strap in horse harness and caparison. It served as a support for other attachments and, in caparisons, as a slight deterrent against light weapons or animals. In the harness it consisted of a band of leather, which in armored caparisons was large and reinforced with metal plaques, running across the front of the chest and fastened either to the saddle (in the harness) or at the base of the crinet (in armored caparisons). In ordinary harness, the breast strap was sometimes elaborated with fringes of cloth or fur.

In bards, the breast strap was replaced by the PEYTRAL.

**pedrero** A late medieval term (loan word from Spanish) for a breechloading piece of artillery designed to throw stone balls or bags full of rocks; it was also called a perrier or peterara. Used often in ships, the pedrero was loaded by means of a chamber with a handle; the chamber was inserted in an opening in the breech and held in place by a wedge forced between the base of the chamber and the frame or the mounting of the gun. The chamber contained the powder and had a vent for ignition, but the missile was put into the breech as the first step in loading. Pedreros were used with little or no modification from the 15th to the 18th century; because their recoil was relatively slight, they were commonly fixed to the side of a ship by a forked pivot, the swivel, and discharged from there during boarding operations. Three reloadable chambers were usually supplied for each gun. These weapons made up for their poor range by a rate of fire remarkable for the period.

**peen** The pointed, curved, or hooked FLUKE, of varying length, opposite the FACE of the battle-ax, war hammer, and other staff weapons. In some forms of battle-axes showing Eastern influences, the peen counterbalanced the ax head itself.

**pei k'uei** A round shield carried by Chinese mounted troops, usually made of leather and lacquered in red. The painted decoration usually depicted the heads of dragons and tigers. The pei k'uei was handled by means of double cord enarmes fitted on the back. Foot soldiers used a larger shield, the PU TUN.

**pelekus** Greek term for the BIPENNIS.

**pelta** The Greek and Latin word for a light, half-moon-shaped shield made from woven osier wands (wicker) and covered with leather. From classical Greek sculpture, vase paintings, and literary sources such as Virgil and Livy (1st century B.C.–1st century A.D.), it is known to have been regarded as the typical defensive weapon of barbarous people such as the Thracians, who probably developed it, and the Macedonians. It was also regarded as the weapon of the Amazons, who were often referred to by the poets as *peltiferae*, "pelta carriers," and their shield was usually represented as a double crescent. Thracians who fought in the ranks of the Greek armies used the pelta and were known as *peltastai.* (The word has been absorbed into English in the botanical term "peltate," which refers to shieldlike structures.)

**penetrating cap** A metal cap on the nose cone of an armor-piercing shell to prevent it from disintegrating on impact. The shape of the cap also tends to correct the path of the projectile at the moment of impact. To avoid any change in the shell's aerodynamic form, a second sheet-metal cap, called a ballistic cap, may be fitted.

**pennon** (or **pannon**) A long triangular or swallow-tailed streamer fixed below the head of the lance as an ensign of the knight during the Middle Ages and the Renaissance. The pennon usually bore the arms of the knight, who commanded a small unit of men-at-arms and their attendants. From the pennon derived the small streamers of the lancers, dragoons, and other mounted troops (*see* PENNONSEL). A similar flag used in the navy is called a pennant or pendant.

**pennonsel** (or **pensel**) A small narrow streamer, i.e., a length of colored ribbon tapering to a point, fixed under the head of the lance carried by knights during the Middle Ages and the Renaissance. A smaller form of the PENNON, the pennonsel was revived in the Napoleonic period; it is still used by some mounted troops in various armies (in England, for instance, H.M. Household Cavalry carry lances with pennonsels, while Dragoons and Royal Horse Artillery carry lances with guidons, a variant of the pennonsel).

**pepperbox** The name given to a pistol with four or more barrels arranged in a circle in order to rotate around a central axis. The oldest pepperboxes, derived from older weapons with rotating barrels, date from between 1820 and 1830; they were muzzleloaders with percussion ignition, and the barrels had to be rotated and aligned manually. A great advance was made around 1830 with the introduction of a mechanism that rotated the barrels automatically when the gun was cocked. The use of these weapons became widespread in 1837, when the American Ethan Allen patented a double-action firing mechanism. The pepperboxes made thereafter by the Allen and Thurber company and the Allen and Wheelock company had a faster rate of fire than any other pocket weapon, and for many years their reputation exceeded that of the famous Samuel Colt revolver. In Europe successful pepperboxes were produced by the Belgian Mariette; they were easily recognizable by their ring trigger and by a hammer that was located underneath and struck upward, leaving the sight line unimpeded. Also produced in Europe were VOLLEY GUNS of this kind that were breechloading, particularly for pinfire cartridges.

**pernat** Slavic term for a metal mace with more than six flanges ("feathers"). *See also* BUZDYGAN.

**perrier** *See* PEDRERO.

**pesh-kabz** A special type of dagger used in Persia, northern India, and occasionally in Turkey. It was designed mainly for penetrating mail. Its T-sectioned blade, usually of watered steel and about 28–36 cm. (11–14 in.) in length, was wide at the hilt but narrowed almost immediately on the cutting side by about a quarter of its width and then tapered to a very fine point. The grip of ivory or horn was heavy, with a rounded top.

**petard** After the end of the 16th century, the word "petard" denoted a special explosive device used to breach

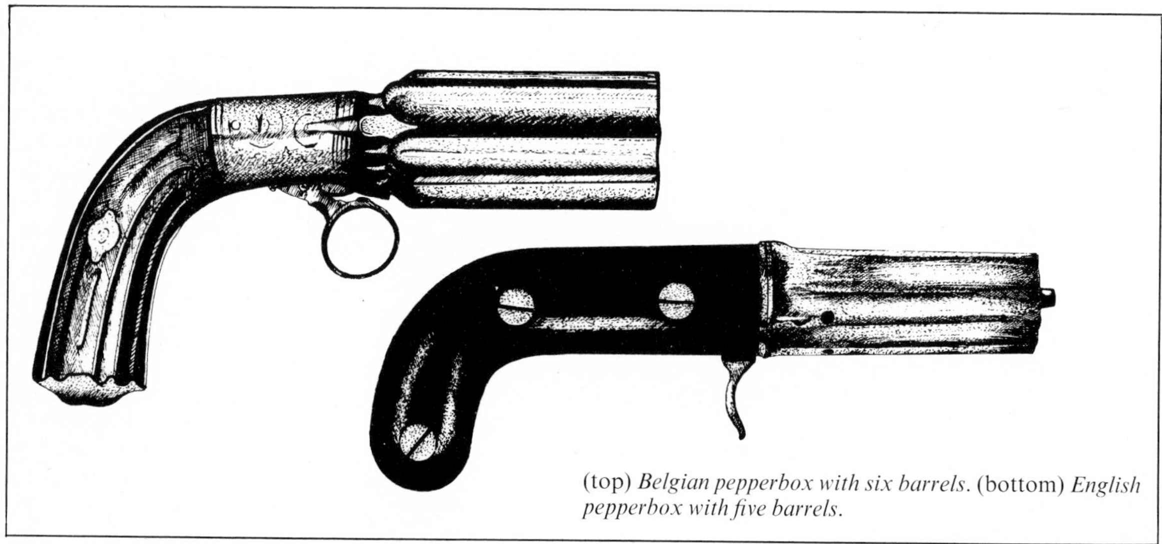

(top) *Belgian pepperbox with six barrels.* (bottom) *English pepperbox with five barrels.*

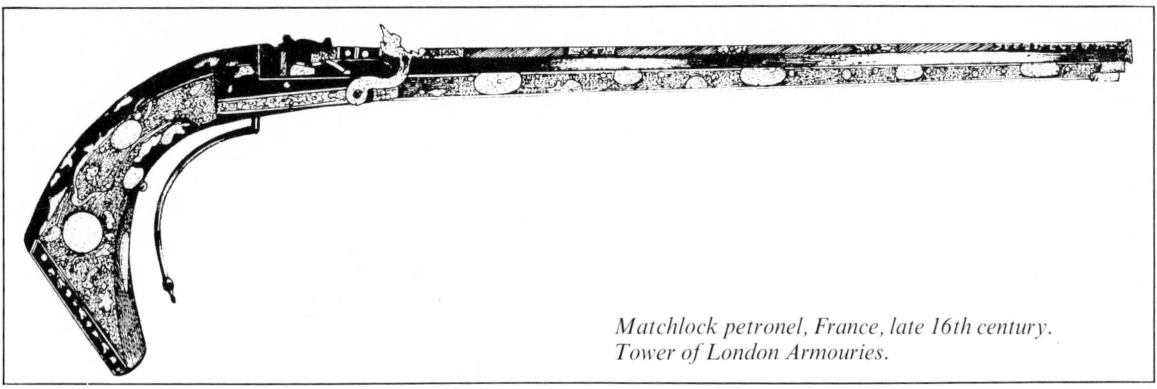

*Matchlock petronel, France, late 16th century. Tower of London Armouries.*

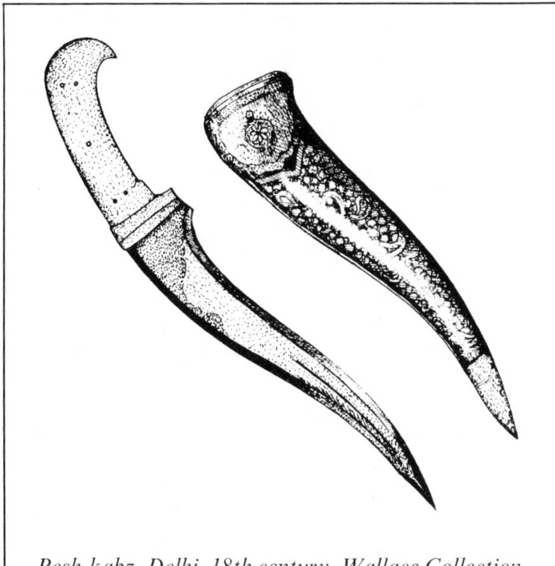

*Pesh-kabz, Delhi, 18th century. Wallace Collection, London.*

the gates of fortresses or walled towns. It consisted of a huge bronze container of tapered form, filled with fine gunpowder and supported firmly against the section of the gate it was intended to unhinge. Sometimes a big board reinforced with iron plate was put between the petard and the gate to increase the area on which it was to act. The vent was at the bottom of the container, as in artillery barrels of the period, and a piece of slow match or fuze was inserted to ignite the charge. The finest available powder was chosen to load the petard; it was packed firmly, so that the container held one and a half times more powder than of uncompressed powder. The powder was covered with a wad of felt topped by a piece of wood, and the whole was then covered with unpurified wax or pitch.

**peterara** *See* PEDRERO.

**petn** Abbreviation for pentaerythritol tetranitrate. *See also* EXPLOSIVE.

**petronel** This word, derived from the French *poitrinal*, was used in the 16th century to describe a light gun with a sharply curving stock which could be rested against the chest (*poitrine*) when being fired. Apparently originating in France about the middle of the 16th century, it was being used throughout Europe before 1600. During the 16th and 17th centuries the word "petronel" seems to have been reserved in England for a medium-caliber short gun mostly used on horseback. The English Council of War Order of 1630 listed the petronel with the carbine, and it seems clear that by that date the two weapons were regarded as one and the same thing. The dimensions of the petronel were given in 1630 as: length of barrel, 76 cm. (2½ ft.); overall length, 91 cm. (3 ft.); bore, 23. Before the middle of the 1600s the term "petronel" was abandoned in favor of "carbine."

In Spain the word *pedrenãles* was used to describe the type of wheel-lock pistol made in Ripoll; it derived from the Latin *petra* ("stone").

**peytral** A breastplate which from the 13th century was part of the full BARD and of light horse armor. In full bard, it consisted of plates attached to the sides of the CRINET that hung over the shoulders and chest but jutted out below to allow freedom of movement for the forelegs. The peytral was frequently provided with large bosses designed to deflect blows.

In the 15th century the peytral was generally composed of three large plates riveted together vertically, and extending up to the crinet. Protection of the forequarters

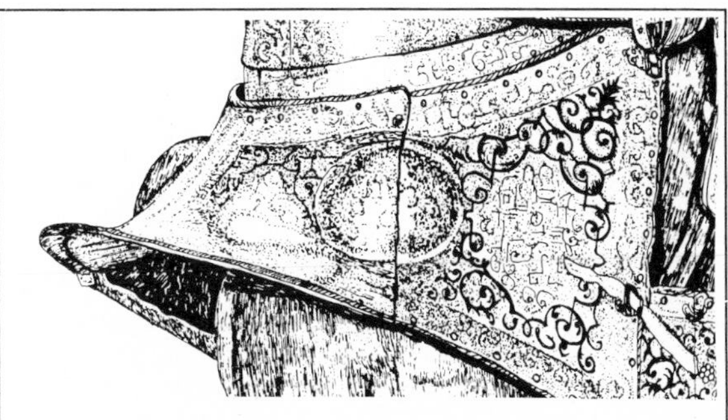

*Peytral of a bard made by Kunz Lochner of Nuremberg for King Sigmund II of Poland, c. 1550.*

was thus complete. In the following century the peytral was simplified and made lighter: the usual type consisted of a wide plate that curved to the shape of the chest; this plate was slung around the neck and withers by means of a strap. All the edges were reinforced with a roped finish. Peytrals of this kind were flared below to give greater freedom of movement to the horse. They were sometimes made with an added plate on each side that extended up to the crinet. In light horse armor, the peytral consisted of a large leather strap covered with riveted metal plates and bosses. The German style of peytral consisted of several horizontal lames articulated on sliding rivets.

In caparisons as in all harness, the peytral was replaced by the PECTORAL.

**phasganon** Poetic Greek term for a type of sword, dagger, or knife. It is the earliest literary evidence, deciphered from ideograms of the Linear B Cretan-Mycenaean language dating to about 1500 B.C., that documents an edged weapon in the eastern Mediterranean region. Originally the term referred to a straight-bladed sword, the blade being quite broad, double-edged, and pointed. It was used for a fairly long period of time: Homer mentioned it as a long weapon, that is, a sword rather than a dagger.

**phirangi** *See* FIRANGI.

**phurbu** A sacred knife of the Tibetan lamas, who used it in the ritual exorcising of evil spirits. Made of brass, brass and iron, or wood, it varies in length from about 15 to 60 cm. (6–24 in.). Its blade, usually of iron, resembles a dart head and is much shorter than the handle; its three edges in cross section form a triangle with concave sides. The phurbu hilt is always heavily decorated with symbolic figures, and the pommel is frequently a three-faced head surmounted by an animal figure with dragons and thunderbolts.

**pichangatti** A knife used in southern India by the Coorg tribe. In the Tamil language, *pichangatti* means "hand knife." Its single-edged blade is straight, broad, and heavy; it is about 20 cm. (8 in.) long. The hilt, usually of the "pistol grip" form, leaning slightly toward the cutting edge, has a protuberant, rounded pommel and is made of two pieces of horn or silver riveted to the tang. The large wooden sheath has silver or brass mounts and a suspension chain to which even a manicure set is sometimes fitted. Some particularly fine pichangatti knives are decorated with gold.

**pieces of exchange** Also called double pieces, the alternative parts and reinforcing pieces of armor introduced in the early 16th century to form variations for different uses, e.g., to convert full field armor into tilt armor or into foot soldier's armor. *See also* GARNITURE.

**pigeon gun** *See* GUN: sporting.

**piha-kaetta** (or **pia-kaetta**) A Sinhalese knife of Ceylon (Sri Lanka). It has a heavy, sometimes slightly incurving blade with a sharp point. Averaging 12.5–20 cm. (5–8 in.) long and 2.5–5 cm. (1–2 in.) wide, the blade has an elaborately decorated panel that is usually of silver, brass, or both. The blade is often engraved and inlaid with these metals. Its hilt is of elaborately carved wood, horn, ivory, or crystal, not unlike the Malayan KRIS hilt, and mounted in silver and brass. The wooden sheath is usually fluted and partly covered with brass or silver. It often contains a short, silver-handled stylus.

**pike** A term of French origin (*pique*) denoting from the late 15th century an infantry spear about 5–6.75 m. (16–22 ft.) long with a leaf- or lozenge-shaped steel head. The pike was in use until the latter part of the 17th century, when it was gradually abandoned because of the introduction of the bayonet. A distant predecessor of the late medieval pike was the Macedonian sarisa, which had been practically forgotten until the Swiss revived the use of infantry spears of such extraordinary length.

The battle of Sempach (Switzerland) on July 9, 1386, brought into conflict the forces of the Swiss Confederation and the army of Duke Leopold of Austria (1351–86). Acting on Leopold's orders, the cavalry advanced on foot. The Swiss attacked with their halberds and axes, which proved too short against the Austrian lances. It was probably on this occasion that Arnold Winkelried's famous exploit took place. He is said to have hurled himself amongst the impenetrable lances and grasped as many as he could hold, thereby opening a gap in the enemy ranks through which the Swiss surged to attack the Austrians with their axes and halberds.

The deficiencies of short arms were manifest again at the battle of Arbedo, near Bellinzona, on June 30, 1422, which brought together the Swiss and the army of the Duke of Milan, under the command of Francesco Carmagnola; the duke's cavalry was reputed to be the best in Italy, and the Swiss, having only their pikes with which to combat the lances of their opponents, were forced to retreat and seek refuge in the mountain passes. As a result, the Swiss

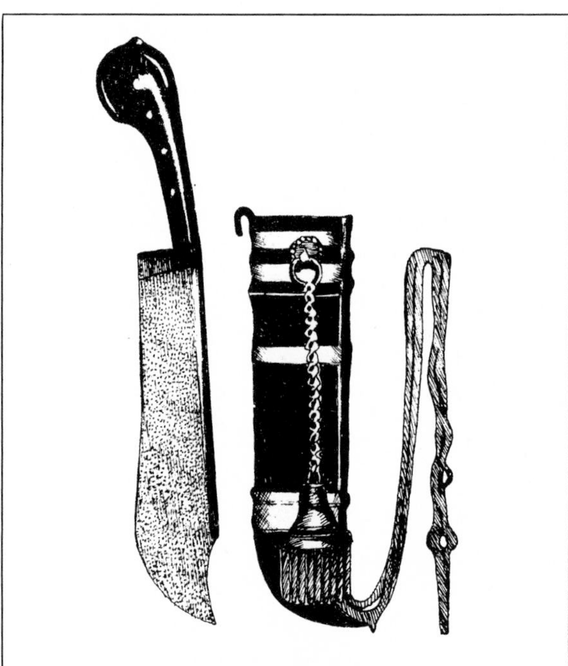

*Pichangatti with sheath mounted in silver.*

*Four-sided pike head, Italy, first half of the 17th century. Museo Nazionale Medioevale e Moderno, Arezzo.*

adopted the long pike as their national weapon; it had a shaft of ash about 5.5 m. (18 ft.) long with a 25 cm. (10 in.) steel head. The main difference between the pikemen of the 15th century and those of earlier times concerned the tactical use they made of their weapon. The Swiss pikemen took the offensive and attacked their opponents with their "long shafts." Raymond de Fourquevaux (1511–74), a French authority on military matters, provided details on the use of the pike after its "rediscovery" by the Swiss: "To defend themselves against the cavalry of their enemies, the Swiss had no option but to revert to the weapons of former times.... They used the pike not only to sustain the attacks of their opponents but also to counterattack and overpower their enemies.... The prowess demonstrated by the Swiss in their use of these weapons led other nations, notably Germany and Spain, to follow their example, after the voyage made by King Charles VIII to Naples in 1495.... The Italians and, finally, the French later did likewise."

In preparation for battle against the infantry, pikemen massed ranks, shoulder to shoulder, and advanced at a slight angle. When repelling a cavalry charge, they took up a position in which the left knee was bent and thrust forward, and the pike was held in the left hand at knee height, the base of the weapon resting on the right foot; the sword was held in the right hand. The pikemen were also regularly employed to protect the cavalry and halberdiers who were retreating and regrouping; the pikemen also provided essential protection for musketeers in the process of reloading or formation.

The pike continued to be an important weapon until the end of the 17th century, when the combination of infantry muskets and bayonets rendered it obsolete.

**pikeman's pot** A type of 16th-century infantryman's helmet. Although it was a variation of the MORION, it had a special feature: a straight, large brim. The skull was spherical or pear-shaped, terminating in either a "spur" or a low comb. The position of the plume holder and other technical details were similar to those on the morion, and it was not unusual for there to be cheekpieces at the sides.

**pile** The head of the ARROW.

**pilgrim's staff** The staff used by wayfarers and pilgrims on their journeys. It often concealed a sword blade, and in those instances such staffs were similar to the BRANDISTOCK. Staffs and sticks concealing a blade date to the early 15th century, according to records and inventories.

**pilum** (Greek *ussos*) A javelin, that is, a throwing spear, of Etruscan origin issued to Roman soldiers, from the republican period onward, generally carried two of

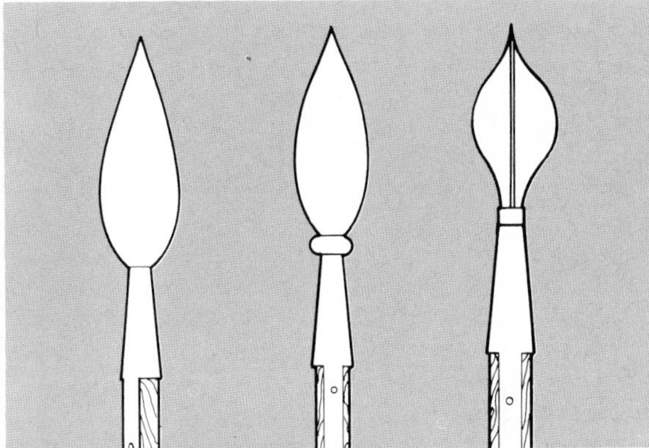

*Various types of pike heads, Switzerland, 15th century. Landesmuseum, Zurich.*

different weights. In its oldest form—the pilum was first used in the early 4th century B.C.—it had a long round or polygonal pointed head, which was inserted in the wooden haft. The long head of the pilum was particularly useful in combat against a foe wielding a long sword (the Gauls, for example) because it could cut the wooden shaft. The classical pilum came in two forms. The heavy type consisted of a head about 70 cm. (27 in.) in length, in the shape of a flattish leaf or a round or polygonal spike, and a haft made of ash with a diameter of 7.5 cm. (3 in.) and a length of about 1.4 m. (55 in.), often fitted with a shoe (*see* SAUROTER); in the late empire, the shafts reached 2 m. (7 ft.). The head was attached to the haft either with a flange (which was fitted into a special slot in the staff and was fixed there by two nails) or with a complete or half socket. Immediately below the head attachment was a four-sided, truncated conical or spherical weight designed to improve balance and trajectory. In the light pilum, the head and the haft were the same length as in the heavy version, but the head, having a diameter of 3 cm. (1.2 in.), was considerably slimmer, and was usually fitted with flanges inserted in the haft.

During the long period in which this type of javelin was used, it underwent two specific modifications designed to prevent the enemy from using the weapon once it had been launched. The first was introduced during the time of Gaius Marius (158–86 B.C.), who had the forward nail used for attaching the head to the haft replaced by a wooden rivet. When the enemy's shield was struck, the rivet broke; the haft turned on the remaining nail, rendering the javelin useless and at the same time throwing the enemy off

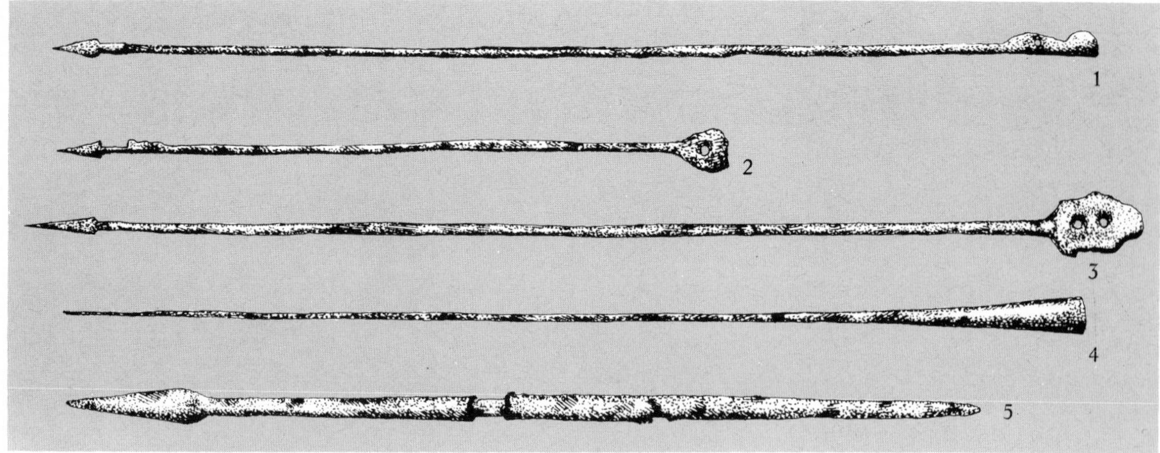


*Pilum. 1, 4. With socket. 2, 3. With flange. 5. With a breakable section.*
*Pilum. 1, 2. Reconstructions on the basis of descriptions given by Polybius; a and b depict movable weights. 3. An example of a head with flange (view on the right shows the rivets).*

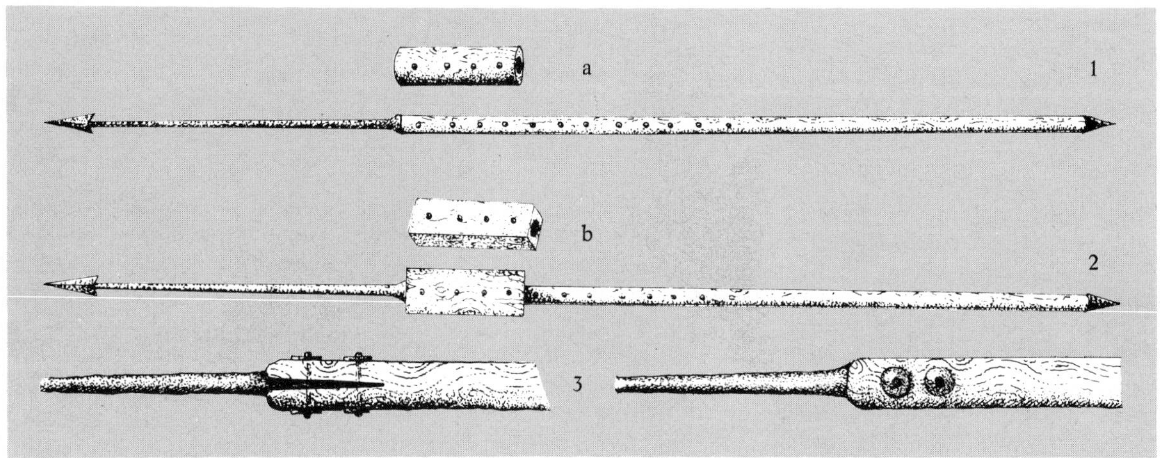


balance. The other modification was made at the time of Julius Caesar (100–44 B.C.). The change involved the head, the central part of which was made considerably narrower and of soft metal, thus weakening it and making it easy to bend. So the pilum retained its strong metal tip, joined to the rest of the head by a deliberately weaker section, which even seems to have been made of a different metal in some cases. In the time of Marcus Aurelius (A.D. 160–180), the head was lengthened considerably.

The pilum gradually disappeared from the battlefield in the 4th or 5th century A.D. and was replaced by the VERUTUM.

**pin** Known variously as a percussion, firing, or striking pin, this long, pointed device was used to touch off the PRIMER and to extract a pinfire cartridge from the chamber. When the primer was placed in the "heel" of the bullet, as in the systems of Dreyse and Carcano, the pin had to penetrate the entire charge of black powder in the cartridge to complete its task. The first pin-firing system was produced by Nicolaus von Dreyse (*see* GUN). The term is also applied to a small metal pin projecting radially from the base of a pinfire cartridge, which worked as a striker and was used for extraction.

**pistol**

This entry deals with all aspects of the historical development of the pistol, which was parallel to that of shoulder arms. There are detailed illustrations of modern pistols, especially of semiautomatics and some automatics (machine pistols). For further information, see AIR GUN; BREECHLOADER; CARTRIDGE; DUELING PISTOLS; GUNPOWDER; IGNITION; PEPPERBOX; VOLLEY GUN.

**pistol** A word of uncertain origin, that came into use by the mid-16th century to describe a portable firearm, generally with a very short barrel, that can be fired with one hand. Although at least two European matchlock pistols are known (and such pistols were common in Japan), it has been reckoned that the development of this type of weapon began with the wheel-lock in the early 16th century. A matchlock pistol was not of much practical use because it was impossible to fire without using both hands, if only to keep adjusting the position of the lighted match. The wheel-lock, with its instant automatic ignition, made it possible to produce short arms that could be used by cavalry; being relatively small and needing no open flame, they could be carried under the cloak or tucked into the belt.

The invention of the pistol had a profound effect on the social life of the period. Among civilians the pistol became the weapon most commonly used for personal attack and defense. It proved to be a remarkable leveler, for it enabled the weak to confront the strong on equal terms. In the military field, the pistol restored some of the cavalry's effectiveness; the weapon gave them an adequate means of response to the long pike and the murderous fire of the arquebus. The German *Reiter*, armed with two or more pistols, introduced a new tactical maneuver, the caracole: instead of the traditional charge, the columns of horsemen advanced abreast in close ranks; each rank, after discharging their pistols at the enemy "square," wheeled to a flank and fell in again at the rear, while the next rank advanced and repeated the maneuver.

Among the oldest wheel-lock pistols known are those that belonged to Emperor Charles V. They were made in southern Germany during the period 1535–50 and are now in the Royal Armory in Madrid. The angle between their

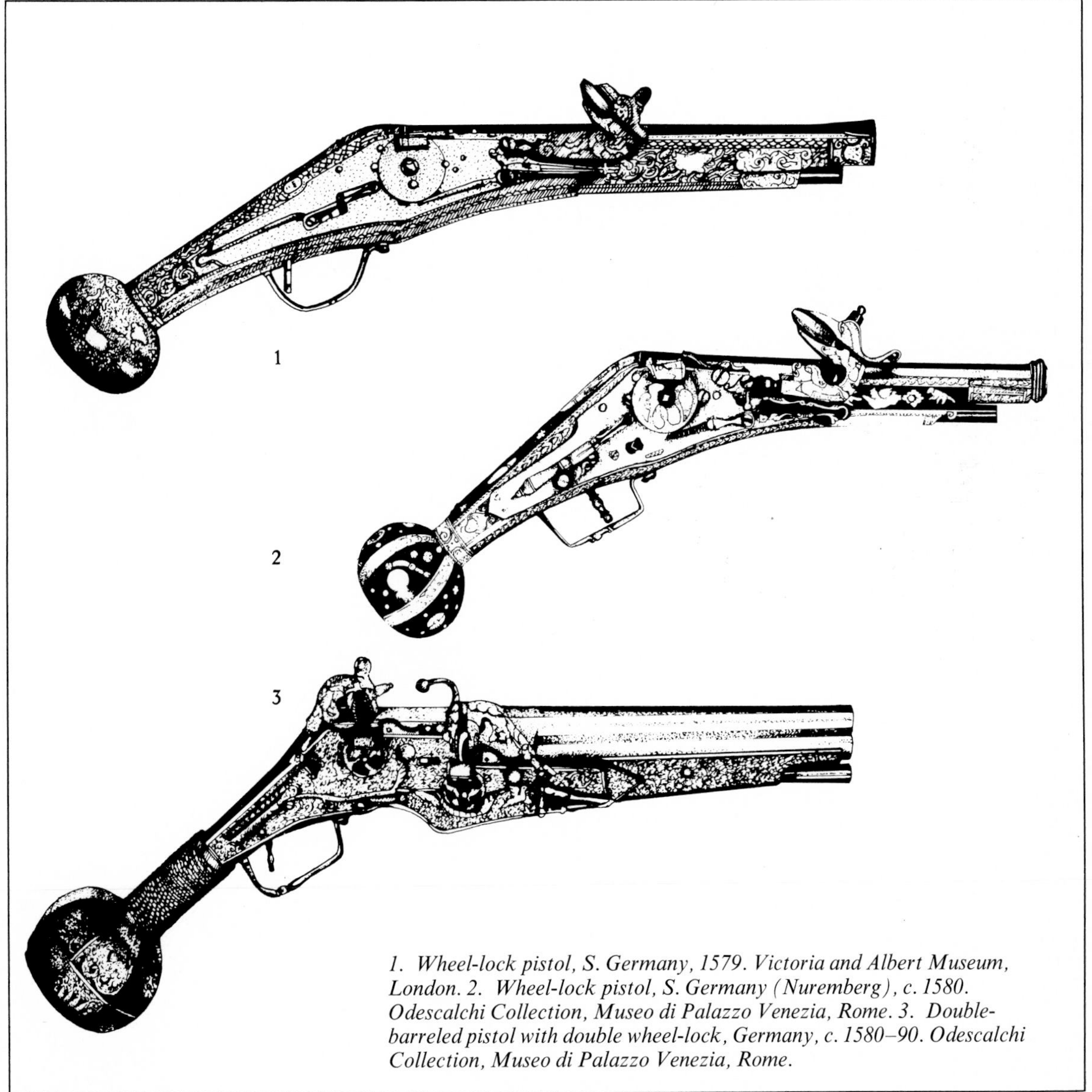


*1. Wheel-lock pistol, S. Germany, 1579. Victoria and Albert Museum, London. 2. Wheel-lock pistol, S. Germany (Nuremberg), c. 1580. Odescalchi Collection, Museo di Palazzo Venezia, Rome. 3. Double-barreled pistol with double wheel-lock, Germany, c. 1580–90. Odescalchi Collection, Museo di Palazzo Venezia, Rome.*

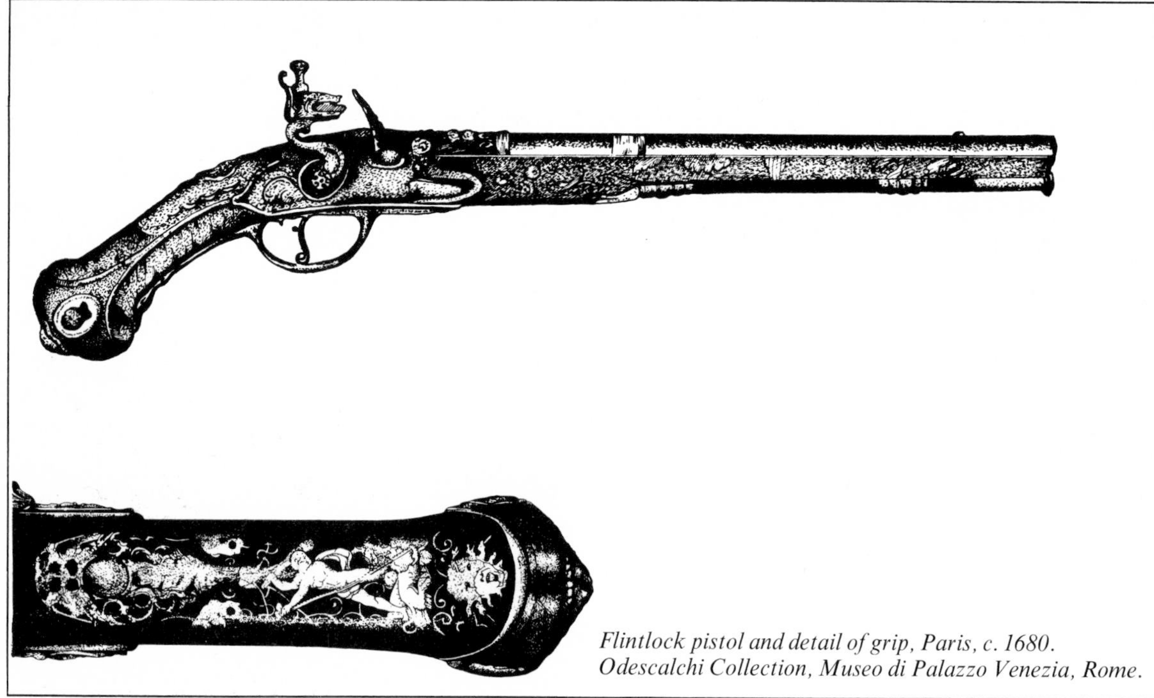

*Flintlock pistol and detail of grip, Paris, c. 1680. Odescalchi Collection, Museo di Palazzo Venezia, Rome.*

butt and barrel is very small, sometimes almost zero; they have a rather long lock with an external safety catch and a cock spring around the wheel (which underwent a remarkable evolution, described by Arne Hoff; see Bibliography).

For most of the 16th century the great mass of pistols was produced in Germany, while elsewhere, partly because of restrictive legislation, local differentiation did not become evident until the latter part of the century. In the German wheel-lock pistol, the angle between butt and barrel was greatly increased, the barrel was lengthened, and the lock was improved by the adoption, among other things, of a V-spring for the cock. In the second half of the century, the "puffer," characterized by a big ball on the butt, became the favorite cavalry weapon; the ball gave the horseman a solid grip as he drew the weapon out of the holster. Of interest in that period was the production, also centered in Germany, of all-metal pistols; the wooden stock was replaced by a stock of steel or brass, which made the weapon stronger, though more expensive.

For decoration, in addition to the chiseling or etching on the metal parts, the manufacturers used inlays of mother-of-pearl, carved stag's horn, and rare wood. From the beginning of the 1600s the external safety catch disappeared and the lock plate was rounded, while the butt acquired a pronounced belly to which the trigger guard was fixed. This form was also found in Dutch, Russian, Swedish, French, and German pistols of the time; the French pistol, with a specially constructed wheel-lock, had a metal side plate that had a hole at the center for the left-hand end of the axle of the wheel; it also acted as a support for the side screws of the lock and a hook for the belt.

The Italian wheel-lock, unlike those built north of the Alps, never had the external safety catch or the button that

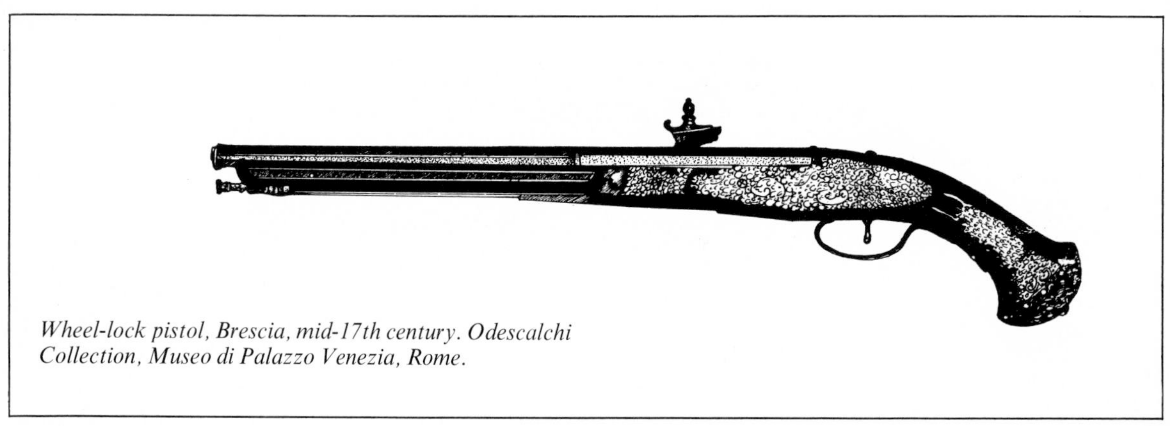

*Wheel-lock pistol, Brescia, mid-17th century. Odescalchi Collection, Museo di Palazzo Venezia, Rome.*

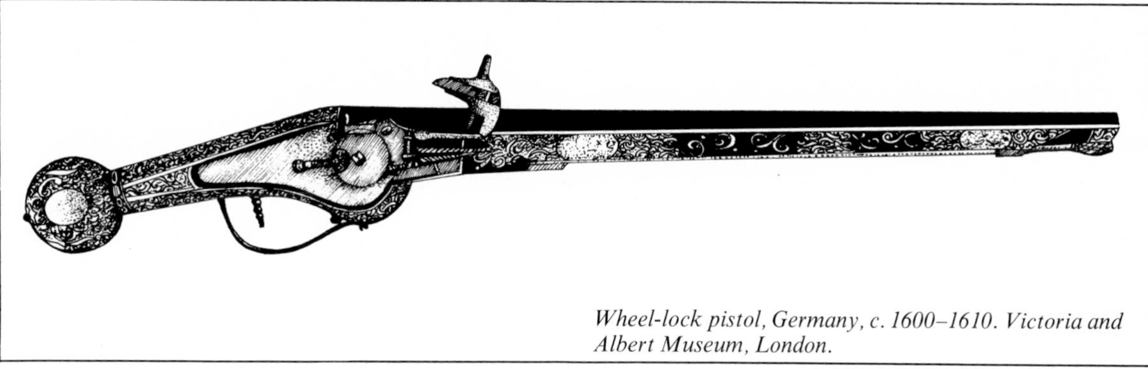

*Wheel-lock pistol, Germany, c. 1600–1610. Victoria and Albert Museum, London.*

automatically closed the pan cover. Pistols made in Brescia, built with German locks for the military, were distinguished not only for their excellent barrels but also for their elegant shape and all-metal decoration.

In the Iberian Peninsula, besides the fine weapons of Ripoll, there were small pistols with wheel-lock systems characterized by large external springs.

On the strength of present knowledge it is generally believed that the snaphance ignition (a flintlock system) was first applied to pistols on a wide scale in England; it remained in use there for a number of decades after its introduction in the last twenty years of the 16th century. The snaphance lock was also used in Scotland, Russia, Holland, Sweden, and Italy; under the name "Florentine lock," it was fitted to Italian pistols until late in the 18th century.

The "true" flintlock, which for practical purposes soon replaced all other systems in most European countries, was almost certainly first developed in France; the oldest pistols with this form of ignition are of French origin.

The different breechloading systems—the multibarrel and repeating systems, and so on—that were tried out on long arms were almost always applied to pistols as well. Thus there were pistols with chambers, multibarreled pistols, repeating pistols, etc. The later developments similarly paralleled those of long arms: rifling of the barrel, gold or platinum plating of touchholes and pans to prevent rust, roller bearings on the combined pan cover and steel. The same is true of the percussion systems; there were pistols with Forsyth's "scent bottle" lock, with the Pauly breechloading system, and so on.

*Revolvers*

Revolvers are firearms, both pistols and guns, that can fire a succession of cartridges (or charges) from a cylinder turning (revolving) on its axis. The revolver is fairly old—one of the first weapons of the kind is a 16th-century revolving pistol in the Bayerisches Armeemuseum in Munich—but its use on a broad scale dates from the first half of the 19th century and has been attributed to the genius and promotional skill of an American, Samuel Colt (1814–62), who with his British patent of 1835 acquired the industrial ownership of any weapon with the following features: nipples placed centrally at the rear of the cylinder; each nipple separated from the others by partitions to prevent neighboring charges from being ignited at the same time; rotation of the cylinder by the action of the hammer (cock); locking of the cylinder in alignment of each chamber with the barrel.

Until 1850, when the patent expired, Colt defended his rights so successfully that virtually no other weapon could compete with his revolvers. Substantial improvements were subsequently made in the lock (the Beaumont lock, incorporated in the Adams revolver, which made an excellent double-action system possible) and in the structure (the Deane-Adams revolver with the frame closed at the top). It was not until 1857, however, that a

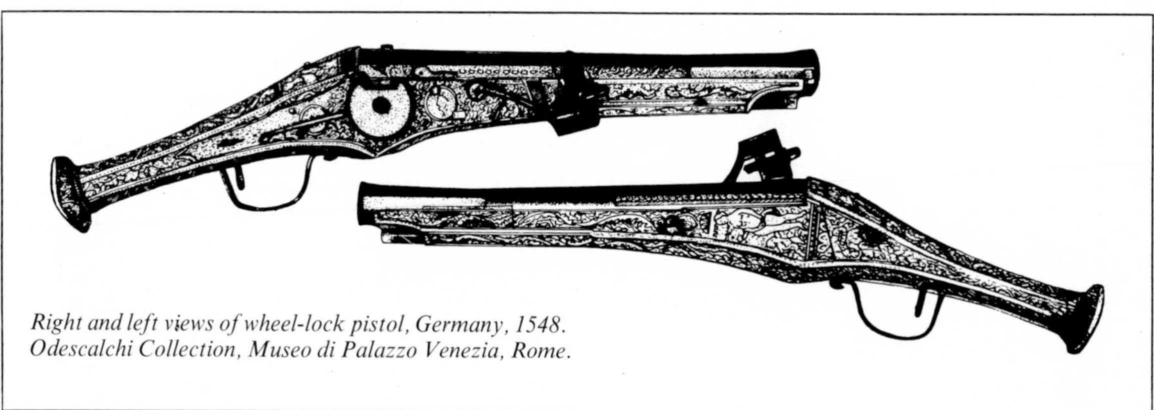

*Right and left views of wheel-lock pistol, Germany, 1548. Odescalchi Collection, Museo di Palazzo Venezia, Rome.*

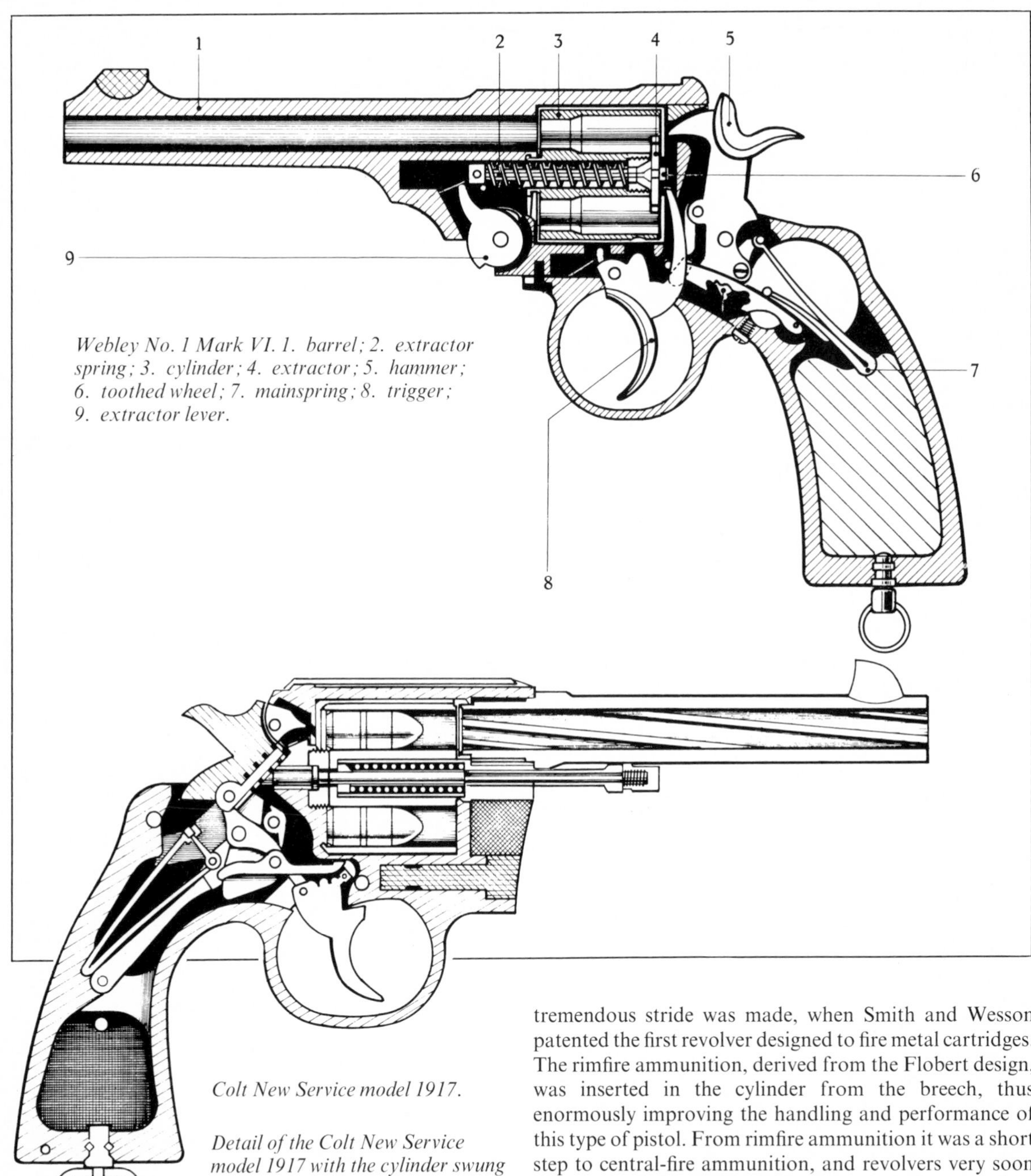


*Webley No. 1 Mark VI. 1. barrel; 2. extractor spring; 3. cylinder; 4. extractor; 5. hammer; 6. toothed wheel; 7. mainspring; 8. trigger; 9. extractor lever.*

*Colt New Service model 1917.*

*Detail of the Colt New Service model 1917 with the cylinder swung out.*

tremendous stride was made, when Smith and Wesson patented the first revolver designed to fire metal cartridges. The rimfire ammunition, derived from the Flobert design, was inserted in the cylinder from the breech, thus enormously improving the handling and performance of this type of pistol. From rimfire ammunition it was a short step to central-fire ammunition, and revolvers very soon acquired much the same appearance and mechanical features that they exhibit today.

From a structural point of view, revolvers can be put into the following categories: (1) hinged frame and tip-down barrel with simultaneous automatic extraction; (2) open frame—a rigid frame open at the top; (3) rigid frame closed at the top with (a) a fixed cylinder and manual extraction and (b) a swing-out cylinder and automatic simultaneous extraction.

According to what ammunition is used, there can be: (1) weapons with the cylinder loaded from the front and ignition by cap and nipple (19th-century revolvers and modern replicas of them); (2) weapons with the cylinder

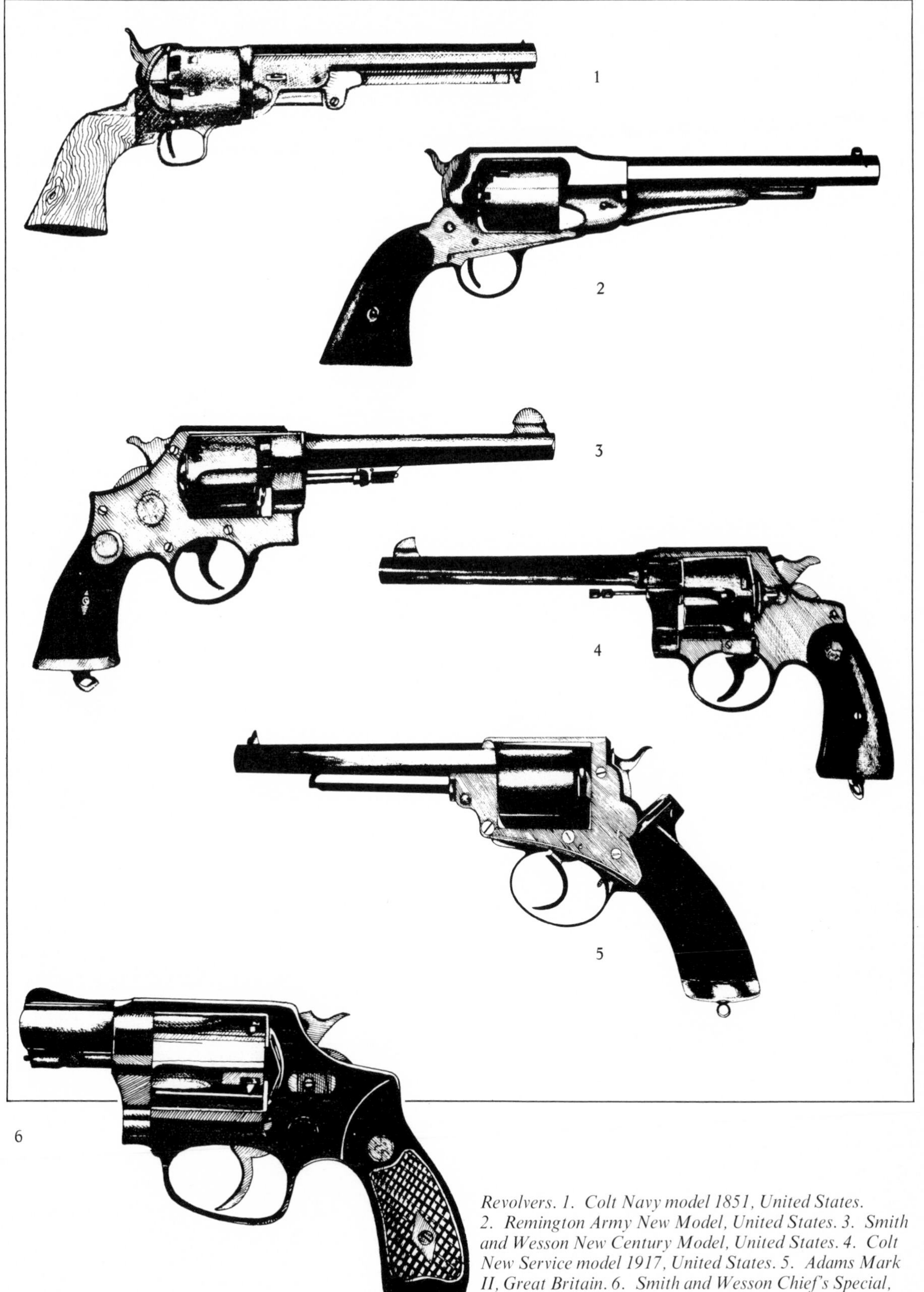


*Revolvers. 1. Colt Navy model 1851, United States. 2. Remington Army New Model, United States. 3. Smith and Wesson New Century Model, United States. 4. Colt New Service model 1917, United States. 5. Adams Mark II, Great Britain. 6. Smith and Wesson Chief's Special, United States.*

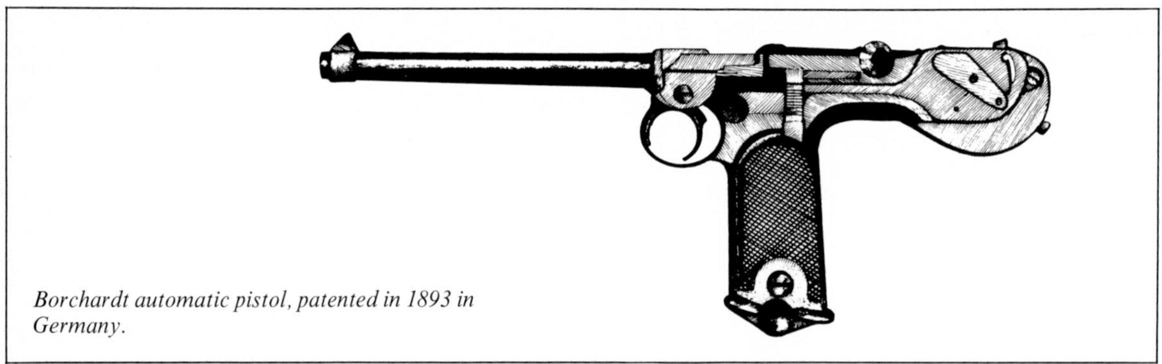

*Borchardt automatic pistol, patented in 1893 in Germany.*

loaded from behind with metal cartridges (from the first Smith and Wessons of 1858 to the present-day .22); (3) weapons with the cylinder loaded with metal cartridges from the front—mostly attempts to get around the Smith and Wesson patents (e.g., the Moore revolver with teat-fire cartridges patented in 1864 by D. Williamson).

The different forms of action are (1) single-action weapons in which the external hammer has to be cocked manually for each shot, and (2) double-action weapons, which can be cocked and fired by a single press of the trigger. In many modern weapons both actions coexist; the single action, which requires less pressure on the trigger, is preferred for accurate shooting, while double action is used when a higher rate of fire is needed. However, there are still some revolvers which work only on double action, such as the Smith and Wesson .38 Safety with internal hammer, the Enfield .380 Pistol No. 2 Mark I, and the Japanese Type 26.

Most of the revolvers used today are those with rigid frame and swing-out cylinder; the United States is still the most important center of production of high-class weapons (Colt, Smith and Wesson, Ruger, Dan Wesson, etc.). The most common calibers, besides the .22, are the .38 Special and .357 Magnum.

Notable European military revolvers of the past include the French 1873, 1874, and 1892 models, the Austrian model 1898, the Italian model 1889, and the various Webley and Scott models from Britain. The Webley-Fosbery Automatic deserves special mention. The upper part of the frame, together with the barrel and cylinder, recoiled across the complex grip which formed the lower part of the frame. This movement automatically cocked the hammer, rotated the cylinder, and compressed the return spring to drive the moving part forward again. Another interesting revolver was the Nagant of the last decade of the 19th century, in which was resolved the persistent obturation problem that, if the cylinder is free to turn, there must be a certain space between the face of the chamber and the barrel which allows some of the propellant gases to leak. This revolver, designed by the Belgian Léon Nagant in 1892 and adopted by the Russian Army in 1895, used special cartridges with an elongated bottleneck case completely enclosing the flat-nosed bullet. When the hammer was cocked, the cylinder was thrust forward so that the beveled mouth of the chamber engaged the tapered rear of the barrel. On firing, the gases expanded the case, which acted as a seal at the joint between barrel and cylinder and prevented any escape of gas. This system, designed to exploit the energy of the propellant charge, also made possible the use of silencers, which had been impossible with pistols with ordinary cylinders.

### *Semiautomatic and Automatic Pistols*

Among the first breechloading pistols were the Dreyse, Werder, Werndl, Remington, and Berdan, all built in the second half of the 19th century to make use of the closure mechanisms of corresponding rifles. Repeating pistols such as the U.S. Volcanic and the Belgian Harman (incorrectly called the Collette), both with self-propelled bullets, and the Bittner, Schlegelmilch, Kimball, and many others were fairly successful. In all these weapons, loading, cocking, and ejection of the spent case were carried out manually.

The great increase in the use of pistols did not occur until practical and efficient semiautomatic weapons were produced, most of them using one of the following systems: (1) "blowback," in which the bolt or breechblock is not locked to the barrel, and (2) locked breech, which may be subdivided into short recoil, long recoil, and gas-operated.

For less powerful ammunition (.22, 6.35, 7.65, 9 short, etc.), the blowback system continues to be employed; simple and cheap to manufacture, it has always proved adequate to deal with the forces developed in firing. For more powerful ammunition, from the 7.65 Parabellum upward, it has nearly always been thought advisable to give pistols a locked breech system, most often a short-recoil system. Long recoil has been used only in a very few models, among them the Hungarian Frommer, while attempts to use gas operation—the French Clair and U.S. Philipps pistols—were never completely satisfactory; the Roth system, in which the percussion cap (fitted in a deep cavity at the cartridge base) was driven back to strike the bolt head, was never fully developed.

The first semiautomatic pistol on the commercial market was probably the Schönberger, derived from the Laumann patents of 1890–92 and produced during the next two years by the Steyr arms factory in Austria. A very

(left) *Browning Baby.*
(right) *Browning H.P., Belgium.*

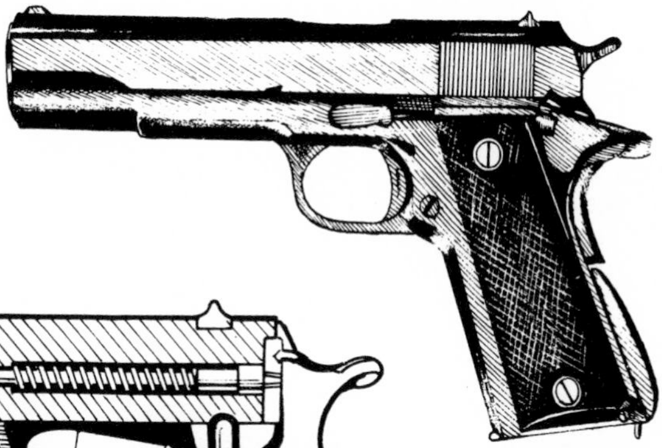

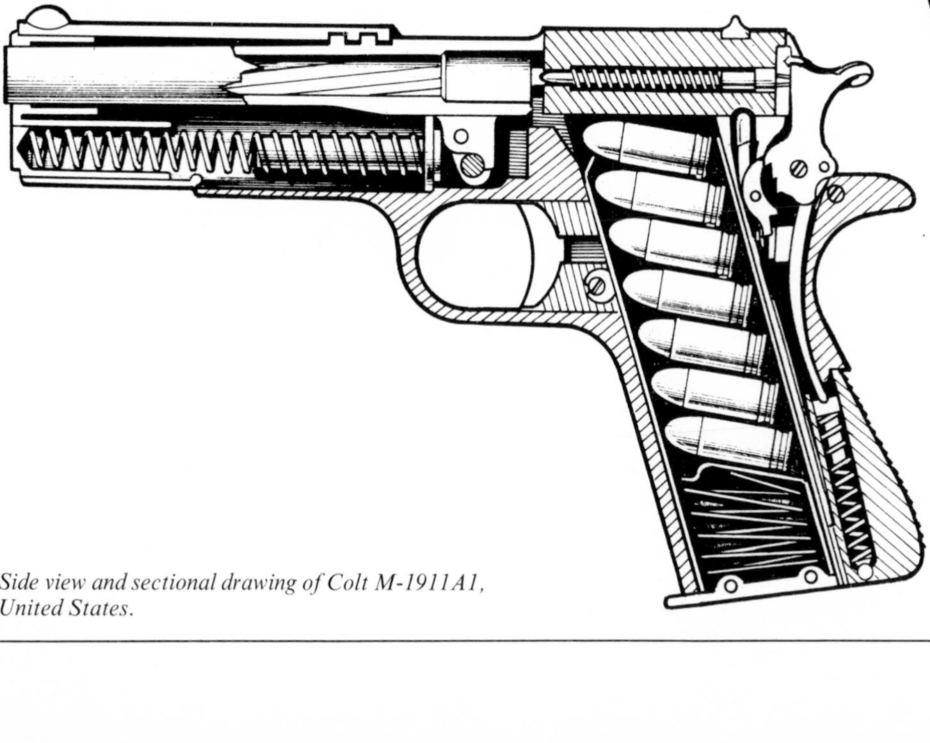

*Side view and sectional drawing of Colt M-1911A1, United States.*

rare weapon nowadays, the Steyr used a blowback system with a delay lever in front of the trigger unit. In 1893 the famous Borchardt, produced by the German Ludwig Löwe company, appeared on the market. It was a large short-recoil pistol, with a toggle lock on the lines of that of the Maxim machine gun; the magazine was in the butt. Chambered for a special bottleneck cartridge, the Borchardt can fairly be called the first semiautomatic pistol that was really practical (apart from its size) and functional. In the same year the prototype of the semiautomatic pistol designed by Andreas Schwarzlose was produced; it was a very odd firearm with a short recoil using a blowback system, with seven cartridges contained in a tubular magazine under the barrel.

In 1894 von Mannlicher designed a blow-forward pistol, but it had little success. On firing, the pressure of the bullet on the rifling pushed the barrel forward so that the case, which remained stationary, was made to project automatically to the rear.

Also in 1894, Theodor Bergmann began production and marketing of the blowback pistol, chambered for a special 6.5 mm. cartridge—one of the first fruits of the research begun by Louis Schmeisser in 1892. A larger Bergmann pistol, intended for military use, was produced in 1896; this weapon operated on the blowback principle and was chambered for an 8 mm. cartridge. Its performance proved disappointing, so the next year a short-recoil pistol was brought out, firing a 7.65 mm. cartridge with a bottleneck case.

In 1896 the Mauser company patented the famous pistol designed by the Federle brothers; solid and heavy but perfectly engineered, its exceptional performance made it for a long time the most widely used pistol in half the world. On firing, the barrel and breechblock recoiled together, firmly joined by heavy locking lugs. After a few millimeters, the lugs fell, the barrel was halted, and the bolt continued to the rear to extract and eject the spent case and to cock the hammer. The weapon had an external hammer and a fixed magazine in front of the trigger. Produced with only small modifications for forty-three years, this Mauser marked a fundamental stage in the evolution of pistols.

In 1898 Andreas Schwarzlose produced an interesting short-recoil pistol with a rotating bolt with four locking lugs on the head and a device to hold the bolt open after the last cartridge was fired. In the same year Georg Luger left the Borchardt firm and designed the first of his famous pistols (*see* PARABELLUM), a weapon that was at first manufactured by the Deutsche Waffen und Munitionsfabriken of Berlin, starting in 1900. The opening of the breechblock, held up by a three-part toggle arm as in the Borchardt, was effected by breaking the alignment of the hinges when two external cylindrical parts struck a symmetrical ramp on the frame. This occurred when the barrel and the breechblock had recoiled locked together for a little over 10 mm., which gave time for the bullet to leave the barrel. The perfection of the system, the magnificent workmanship carried out with materials of the highest quality, and the elegant shape of the pistol all contributed to the extraordinary fame that it won. The Luger, in various versions, is still the enthusiast's

*Steyr model 1912, Austria.*

*Glisenti model 1910, Italy.*

*Walther PPK, Germany.*

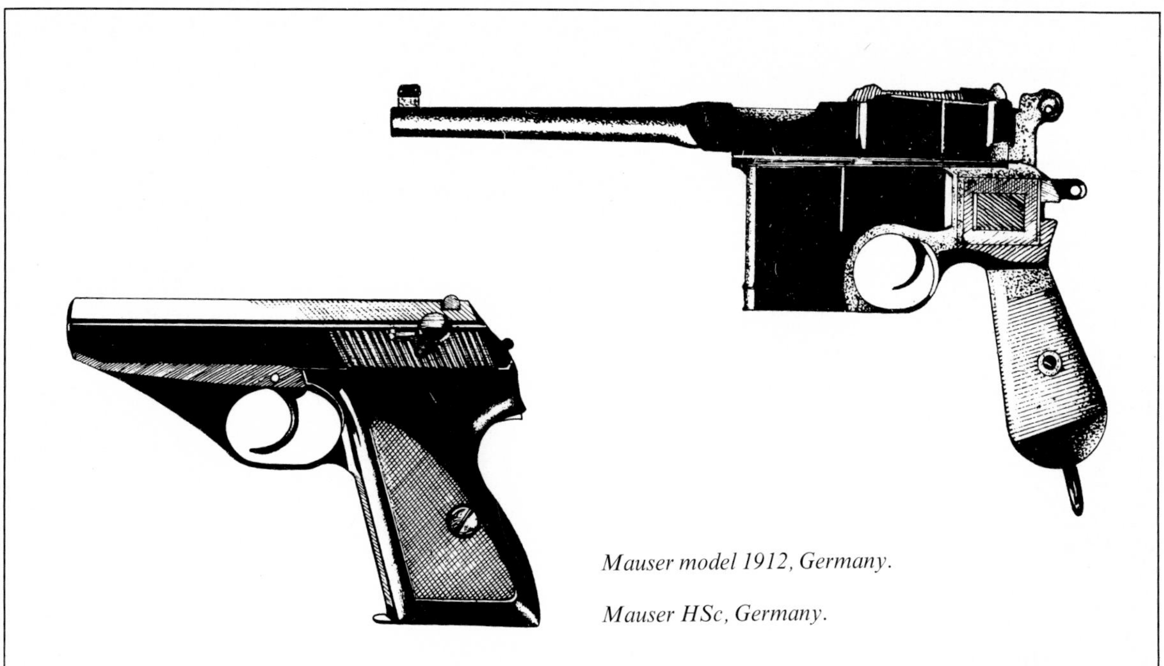

*Mauser model 1912, Germany.*

*Mauser HSc, Germany.*

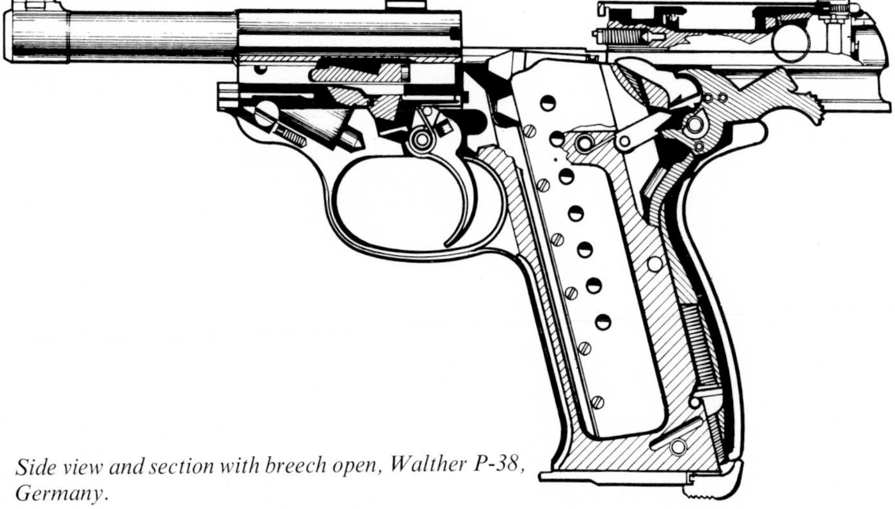

*Side view and section with breech open, Walther P-38, Germany.*

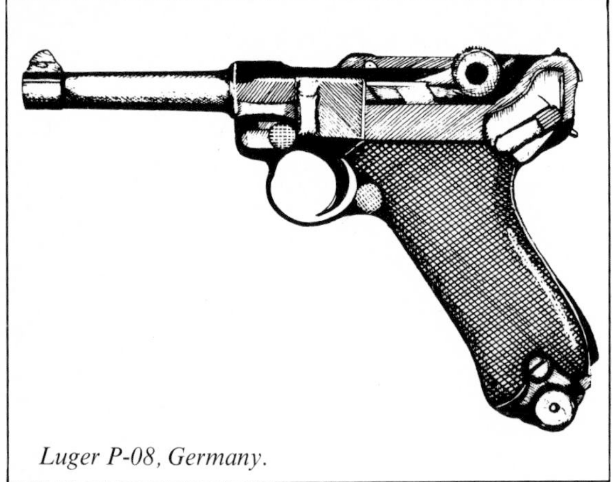

*Luger P-08, Germany.*

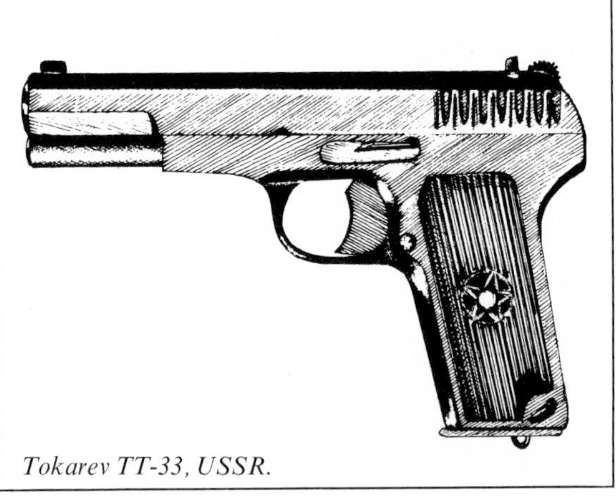

*Tokarev TT-33, USSR.*

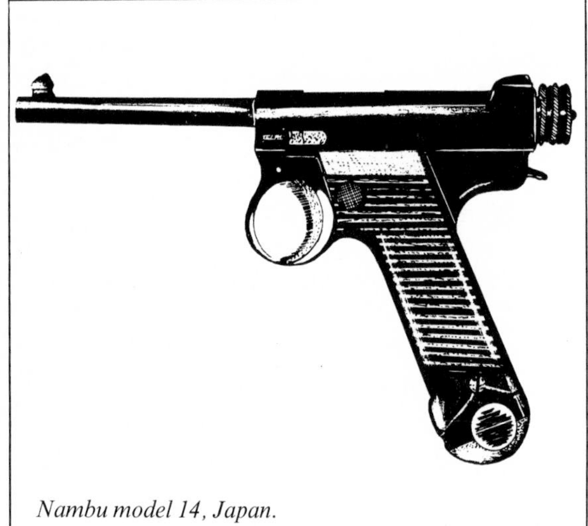

*Nambu model 14, Japan.*

favorite, although it is now considered hopelessly obsolete as a military arm.

In 1897 John Moses Browning, already famous for his rifles, patented a "hammerless" pistol (i.e., with the striker operated internally) that worked on a blowback system; it was chambered for a new cartridge, the .32 ACP, which soon became famous in Europe as the 7.65 mm. Browning. This weapon, not at first highly regarded in the United States, perhaps because it was of so small a caliber, was manufactured by the Fabrique Nationale at Liège and marketed as Model 1900 in January 1899. It was enormously successful; by 1912 the factory was able to celebrate the production of the millionth pistol. This pistol was not the first designed by Browning; as early as 1895 he had patented a .38 gas-operated semiautomatic pistol with the slide articulated in three sections. In 1897 Browning also patented a short-recoil pistol in which, on firing, the barrel was locked to the slide by three semicircular lugs on

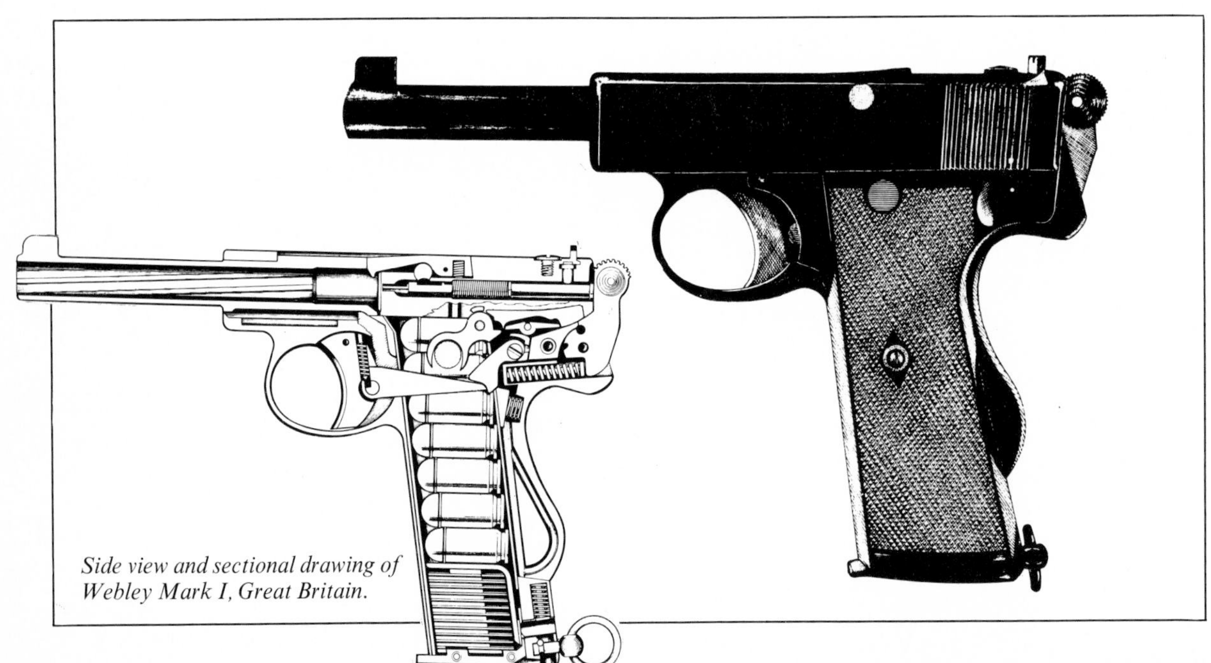

*Side view and sectional drawing of Webley Mark I, Great Britain.*

*Beretta model 1915, Italy.*

*Beretta model 92, Italy.*

the top, engaging in corresponding grooves. The barrel and slide recoiled together for a few millimeters; then the barrel, which was attached to the frame by two hinges, moved downward and released the slide to continue to the rear and extract the spent case, compress the return spring, and cock the gun. With some slight modifications, this system is still employed in all large-caliber Colt and FN pistols (including the model 1911 used in the U.S. Army and the HP adopted in Australia, Belgium, Canada, Denmark, Indonesia, Holland, the United Kingdom, and Taiwan) as well as in the Polish Radom Vis and other pistols. Browning was equally successful with his cartridges, which were adopted in many countries—the .25 (6.35 mm.) ACP, the .32 ACP mentioned above, and the .38 ACP, known in Europe as the 9 mm. short Browning.

Two particularly interesting pistols were the 1907 and 1911 models of the Steyr company. The first, which was adopted by the cavalry of the Austro–Hungarian Army, had two pairs of locking lugs on the barrel; those at the front controlled the rotation of the barrel, which disengaged those at the back from grooves inside the breechblock. This rotary opening movement did not, of course, take place until the locked barrel and breechblock had recoiled together for the short distance (8 mm.) necessary to allow the bullet to leave the barrel. In the 1911 model, the same short-recoil system was operated by a different arrangement; the locking lugs on top of the barrel engaged in grooves on the face of the breechblock (as in the Browning system), while the rotary opening and closing movement was obtained by interaction between a helicoidal cam running in a groove in the frame. Both pistols had a fixed magazine in the butt, which had to be reloaded at the top from a charger.

Another military short-recoil pistol was the Italian model 1910 (also known as the Glisenti), which used the Revelli turning-lever system; its frame was not very strong, and its performance was disappointing. The version that followed it, known as the Brixia, was another pistol that could never compete with similar weapons from other countries.

A notable step forward was made in 1929 when the Waffenfabrik Walther of Zella-Mehlis produced its famous 7.65 mm. PP (Polizei Pistole) and PPK (Polizei Pistole Kriminal). These first-class weapons had one feature which, if not actually new, was incorporated in a series-produced pistol for the first time: double action. With double action, already a feature of the Austrian Little Tom (in production between 1908 and 1918), the pistol could be carried with a round in the chamber and the hammer closed, absolutely safe and ready for use. In case of need, a single trigger pressure would raise the hammer and then let it fall on the striker. To enable the hammer to be lowered on the loaded chamber without firing, the PP and the PPK were fitted with a special safety device, by which a steel plate was interposed between the head of the striker and the hammer, and afterward the hammer was released and fell harmlessly onto the partition plate. The safetycatch was raised when needed, and the weapon was ready to fire. Other pistols with double action were the Mauser HSc (Hahn-Selbstspanner, i.e., self-cocking), the Sauer 38(H), and of course the world-famous Walther P-38. The latter, so called for the year in which it was adopted by the German Army (1938), had a closure system considered among the strongest in existence. The barrel had two attachments on the underside; the breechblock was hinged laterally to the front one and actuated by a small piston fitted longitudinally into the back one. The block was provided with two symmetrical lobes that fitted into grooves in the slide when the breech was closed. On firing, the barrel and slide recoiled locked together for a little over 6 mm., when the rear end of the piston struck a cam on the frame and rotated the block downward, thus disengaging the lobes. The barrel was halted, while the slide continued backward to extract the case and cock the gun.

After the Second World War, the Walther obturation system, with some small modifications, was used again by the Beretta firm in its Models 51, 92, and 92S pistols, each of which had an excellent double action and a double-row magazine of very large capacity. Other military pistols in use up to the Second World War were the Finnish Lahti M-35 with a vertically sliding block, the Japanese Nambu of 1904 and Model 14 (of 1925) with a rotating block, the Japanese Model 94 (1934) with a sloping block movement,

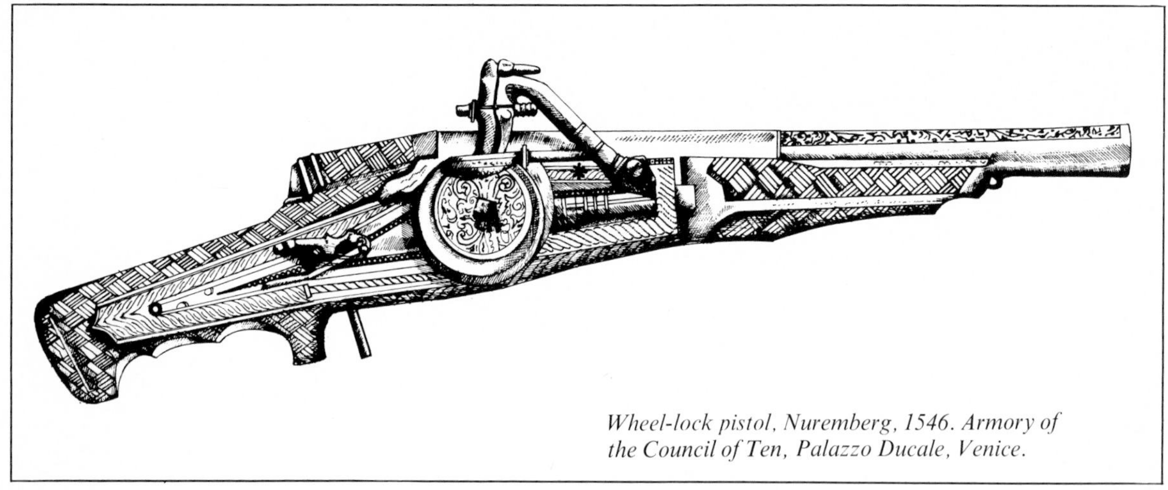

*Wheel-lock pistol, Nuremberg, 1546. Armory of the Council of Ten, Palazzo Ducale, Venice.*

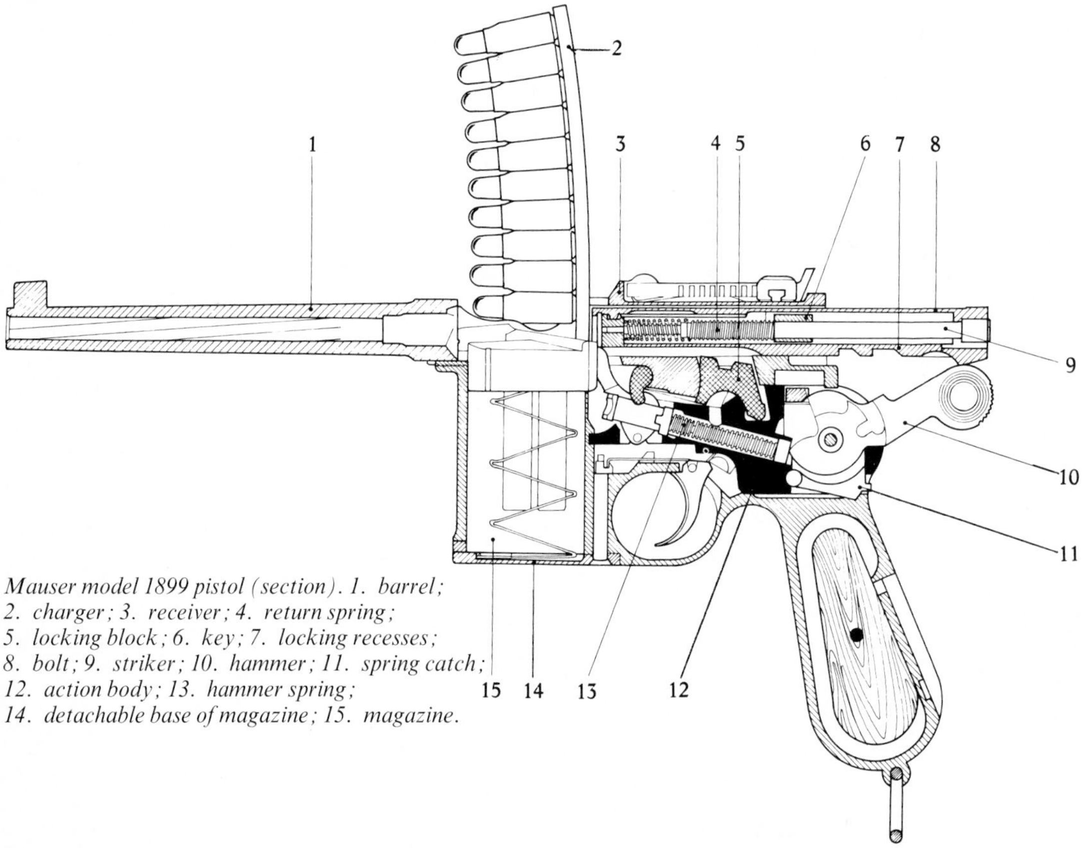

*Mauser model 1899 pistol (section). 1. barrel; 2. charger; 3. receiver; 4. return spring; 5. locking block; 6. key; 7. locking recesses; 8. bolt; 9. striker; 10. hammer; 11. spring catch; 12. action body; 13. hammer spring; 14. detachable base of magazine; 15. magazine.*

the Russian Tokarev TT-33, and the French model 1935, the latter two incorporating the Browning closure system.

Since the war, as far as "civilian" pistols are concerned, progress has been confined to improved manufacturing techniques and some refinement of already well known systems. Some attempts—some of them revolutionary—to break free from conventional designs have not, or not yet, proved very successful. There is the Kimball pistol chambered for the powerful M-1 carbine cartridge, the Dardick with its curious rotary feed and special triangular plastic cartridge cases, the Gyrojet with self-propelled projectiles, and the big Auto Magnum, which has revived the old Schwarzlose system and is chambered for the powerful .44 cartridge. In the military field, apart from the exploitation of well-tried systems—the Walther in the Beretta Models 51, 92, and 92S mentioned above and the

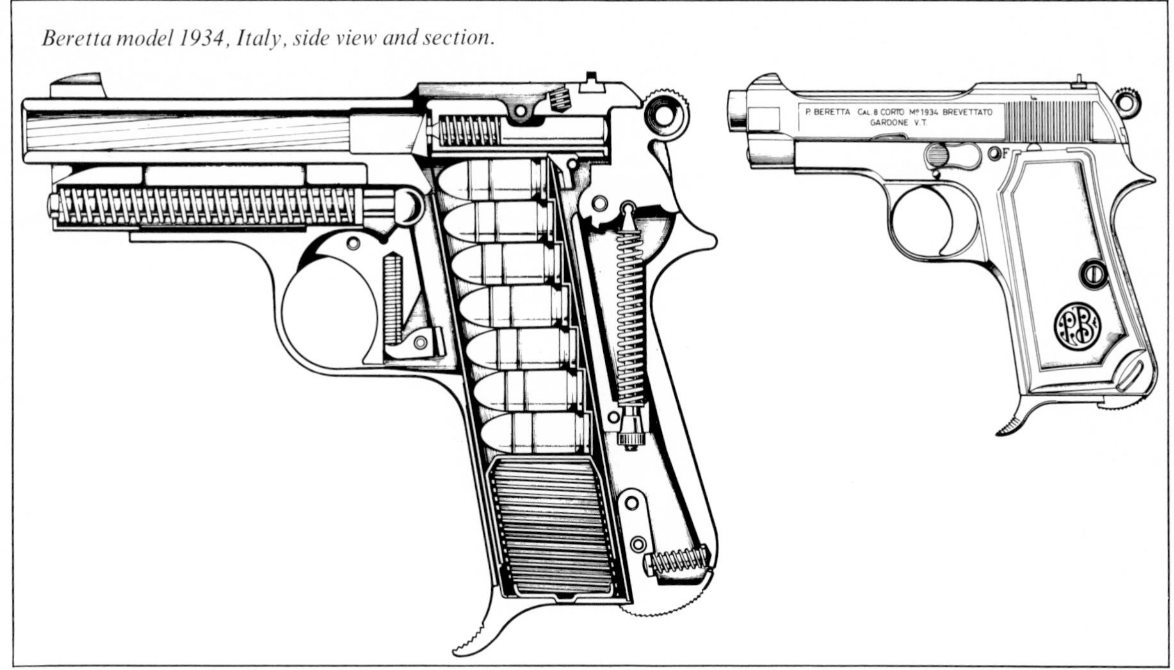


*Beretta model 1934, Italy, side view and section.*

Browning in the French MAS 1950 and the Swiss SIG P-210—there are only a few notable innovations: the Czechoslovak M-52 with a closure similar to that of the German MG-42 machine gun, and the Heckler und Koch and the P-95 with the delayed-blowback systems already perfected in the Mauser StG-45(M) and widely used in the G-3 assault rifle and MP-5 submachine gun. In the Warsaw Pact countries, which use many Soviet-designed weapons, the Tokarev TT-33 has been replaced by the Makarov SL pistol, a blowback pistol with double action chambered for a special 9 mm. cartridge (Makarov 9 × 18). The Stechkin is chambered for the same cartridge; it is a genuine machine pistol, fitted with a selector for semiautomatic and burst fire and a magazine holding twenty rounds. Finally there is the very effective Czechoslovak machine pistol VZ-61, also called the Skorpion; chambered for the 7.65 mm. Browning cartridge, it is capable of automatic fire and has a folding metal butt.

**pistoletto** An Italian term used in the 16th and 17th centuries to describe a small pistol. At first the word *pistoletto* seems to have been applied only to wheel-lock pistols; Pistofilo Bonaventura, in *Oplomachia* (Siena, 1621), stated: "Wheel-lock arquebuses, of which there are three types, long, medium, and small, can be distinguished as follows: first, the long arquebus; second, the pistol or rather TERZARUOLO; and lastly the archibusetto or rather pistoletto." According to some authorities, the term *pistoletto* was also applied to the small snaphance and flintlock pistols made in Italy during the 17th and 18th centuries.

**pitch** *See* RIFLING.

**pizaine** *See* AVENTAIL.

**placate** An over-breastplate, that is, a reinforcing piece of armor for the field and the tournament to give extra protection to the breast. A type of reinforcing steel plate worn over the COAT OF PLATES is recorded from the middle of the 14th century, and it was widely used from the late 15th to the early decades of the 17th century. It extended up from the waist to cover the whole of the breastplate, thus doubling its thickness. The placate was usually screwed and buckled to the breastplate of the field armor, although occasionally riveted to it. To meet the increasing power of hand firearms it became commonplace from the middle of the 16th century to reinforce field armor with placates, a practice that continued until the final decline of armor in the second half of the 17th century.

**plançon-à-picot** (or **plançon-à-broche**) A Flemish staff weapon used from the late 13th to the early 15th century. It was a wooden club about 150 cm. (5 ft.) long; the upper end was reinforced with an iron band, often with a flange, and topped by a spike—its appearance earning it the nickname "chandelier."

**plug bayonet** *See* BAYONET.

**plume** An accessory of almost every type of helmet from the 15th century to the 17th. It was also worn with horse armor on the shaffron or half-shaffron and with parade caparison. The plume was entirely ornamental and always made of relatively delicate materials, such as colored silks or, more frequently, feathers, which were inserted in the PLUME HOLDER. It can be regarded as merely a relic of the CREST, having no warlike purpose. As an accessory worn in parades, ceremonial displays, and tournaments, it was not only colorful but enabled onlookers to distinguish individuals by their personal colors. No original plumes have survived, but there is abundant evidence of them in paintings, sculpture, etc., throughout the centuries.

**plume holder** An accessory fitted to various types of

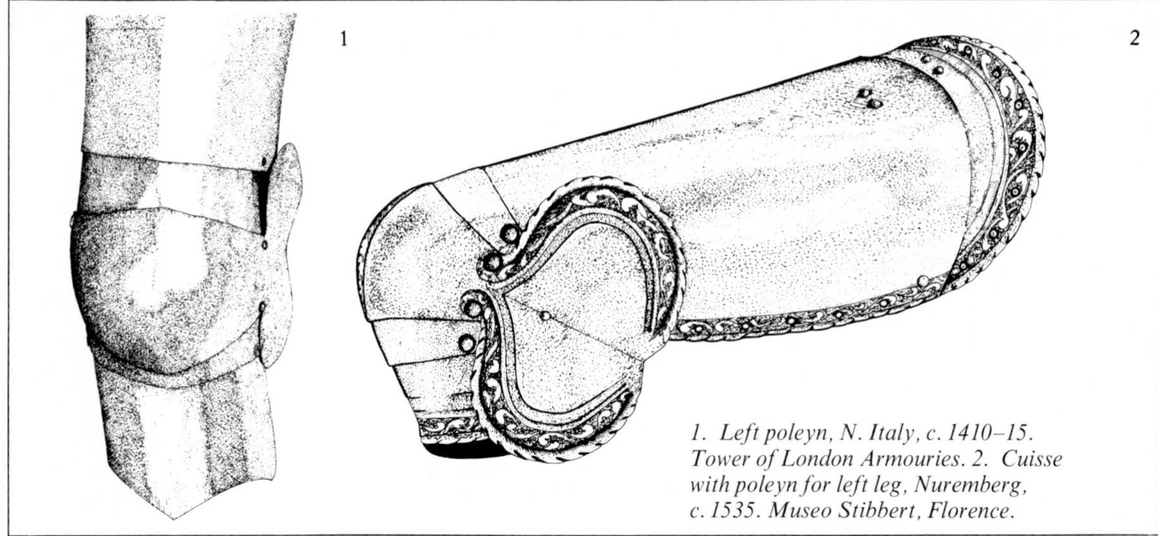


*1. Left poleyn, N. Italy, c. 1410–15. Tower of London Armouries. 2. Cuisse with poleyn for left leg, Nuremberg, c. 1535. Museo Stibbert, Florence.*

helmets to support a plume. It consisted of a metal tube—generally of iron but also of brass, silver, and so on—usually riveted to the bottom edge of the back of the skull (or, more rarely, at the front or side) and covered by a small plate which, in itself, was to become a decorative feature. This plate was made in various forms over the years, including that of an ornamental or symbolic plaquette emblazoned with heraldic crests. A similar plume holder was riveted to the center front, slightly above eye level, of a SHAFFRON in horse armor. It was invariably concealed behind a rondel or small shield.

**pneumatic guns** *See* AIR GUNS.

**Poldermitton** A combination of a special stiff mitten (manifer) with a reinforcing piece used in the 15th century and first half of the 16th to give extra protection to the left armpit. This piece consisted of a large, heavy plate shaped like a great wing or shell and riveted to the inside of the lower cannon of the VAMBRACE. When the arm was bent, holding the reins, the shell was positioned in front of the armpit. A similar shell was forged on the right lower cannon to give additional protection to the right armpit. The Poldermitton was characteristic of German-style jousting armor.

**pole arms** An alternative generic term for STAFF WEAPONS.

**poleax** A staff weapon whose head had a Danish-type AX offset by either a thick fluke, straight or curved, or a flat ridged hammer; at the top of the haft was a sturdy spike. The term "poleax," which came into use in the early 15th century, was also applied to a similar staff weapon (called the pole hammer by modern writers) with the head formed by a heavy ridged hammer instead of an ax, balanced by a massive fluke. The upper part of the shaft of the poleax was protected by a metal reinforcement, below which was fixed a broad rondel serving as a guard against the opponent's blows. As a foot soldier's two-handed weapon, the poleax was quite a match for the mounted man protected by armor and wielding a battle-ax or a war hammer. The poleax was popular for fighting on foot in the lists during the 15th and 16th centuries. Poleaxes were sometimes used by infantry officers in the field.

**pole hammer** *See* POLEAX; WAR HAMMER.

**poleyn** A part of a horseman's armor protecting the knee in legharness. The whole structure comprised a series of articulated lames, fastened inward on each other with sliding rivets, and the main cup-shaped plate, which fitted over the others, to protect the kneecap; this plate carried a side WING, a small shield worn on the outer side of the knee. The top lame was riveted to the CUISSE, and the bottom plate to the GREAVE. This structure had evolved by the beginning of the 14th century, although the number of secondary lames had not been fixed at that time. The typical features of the poleyn of the second half of the century were the shallow, V-shaped "pucker" running vertically across the knee guard, i.e., the cup-shaped plate, and the bottom lame with an attached mail fringe.

In the late 14th and 15th century the lowest lame of the poleyn was often made long enough to overlap the top edge of the greave, to which it was attached with either rivets or turning pins. This extension of the poleyn was no longer used in the 16th century, but it reappeared in some 17th-century armor worn with the top boot, which by then had replaced the greave.

By the 16th century each poleyn consisted of five lames. The side wing was relatively smaller than before and was slightly bent around the knee—a style that remained unaltered. An important variation occurred in the late 16th century with the introduction of long TASSETS ending with the poleyn, sometimes referred to as "lobster-tail" tassets. In this form the knee guard was an extension of the thigh guard, i.e., tassets with a few small lames, which were shaped to the knee. This type of poleyn did not carry a side wing.

**pommel** The end of the grip in swords and daggers, which served either to give a better hold on the weapon or to balance it.

The need to fit weapons with a suitable grip that would give a firm hold must have been felt very early. But it was not until metal came to be used that edged weapons were fitted with a pommel, as shown by specimens from the Bronze Age and the Hallstatt and La Tène cultures, and subsequently by Roman arms. The earliest of these were characterized by a grip ending in a disc, a piece shaped like a truncated rhomboid pyramid, or a metal strip that formed two curled ends. In the early Hallstatt period, a lens-shaped pommel was used; at a later date, the pommel became more elaborate, adopting a cylindrical form with anthropomorphic or geometric decorations which were often an integral part of the grip, cast in bronze in a single piece. The Roman gladius, which had the first orthopedic "ringed" grip, usually had a fairly flattened spheroidal pommel.

The pommel of Viking swords was in the form of a pyramidal piece on a rectangular base, which developed into three and then five lobes; it also took the form of a crosswise rod on which was mounted a pyramidal piece of varying lobed and curved shapes, depending on the place and time; weapons with pommels of this type were commonplace throughout central and northern Europe between A.D. 800 and 1050. For two centuries after the year 1000, the pommels of swords used throughout Europe took on a paraboloidal form with mushroom- or pagoda-shaped designs. In the beginning of the 13th century the discoidal pommel was introduced, and this type spread throughout Europe. In Italy it was in use until the first half of the 14th century, in an almost flat or slightly tapered form, but had a longer vogue north of the Alps.

From the second half of the 14th century, pommels tended to become smaller and more refined as a result of adaptation to developing combat techniques. Thus in this period we find faceted, pear-shaped pommels, flat, oval pommels, and fin-shaped and rhomboid pommels. In addition to these forms there were pommels peculiar to various countries: the "Moorish" pommel in use in Spain throughout the 13th century; the four-sided pommel with a central bulge and distinctive point found on Venetian swords in the 15th century; disc-shaped pommels with a central swelling and a button at the top. A feature of the Swiss dagger and Katzbalger of the 15th and 16th centuries was the pommel with a rhomboid base that flared into a mushroom shape. The pommel of 16th-century Irish swords was in the form of a ring with the tang passing through it.

In the 15th and 16th centuries, the Spaniards and Venetians produced daggers of Levantine design; along with decoration of Eastern inspiration, these weapons had a specific shape: the pommel had two earlike projections, hence the term "eared dagger." The swords given by the popes to those admitted to the Knighthood of St Peter also had a particular shape, almost like a scroll. The pommels of swords in the 16th and 17th centuries tended to be smaller and slimmer. In this period characterized by the increased use of firearms, the sword started to become a distinctive part of the attire worn by noblemen, the military, and wealthy individuals. This meant that some types of weapons were kept in circulation because of fashion and tradition. In the 18th century, the pommel of swords was frequently spheroidal, with vertical or spiral fluting, or with medallions; after the 1750s it was common to find urn-shaped pommels, either round or four-sided and sometimes faceted; the pommel and other parts of the hilt were often decorated with cut-steel studs.

Short-bladed weapons also had particular types of grips with local characteristics, but in the case of the dagger the pommel did not serve the function of counterbalancing the long blade, as it did in the sword; its purpose was to ensure a better hold of the weapon. Thus there were roundel pommels with a matching roundel guard and I-shaped forms, as in the baselard and the Swiss dagger. For the daggers which matched swords in the Spanish and Italian schools of fencing, the pommel of the PARRYING DAGGER, and the rest of the hilt, was usually made *en suite* with the larger weapon.

In the 19th century, the pommel in the various standard weapons became like a small cap covering the top of the grip, sometimes in the form of an animal's head, or with an extension on the back of the handle.

**poniard** (also **poyniard, puniard)** A term derived from French *poignard* and introduced in England in the late 16th century, denoting a light dagger that had a strong blade, usually squarish in section, and a reinforced point, beadlike in shape. Some blades were deeply grooved and ridged, such a structure adding to the rigidity of the blade. Most poniards were only thrusting weapons—unlike the daggers of the time, which had larger, double-edged blades for making cutting strikes as well. When provided with a sizable cross guard and, particularly, a strong side ring for protection of the hand, the poniard served as a light parrying weapon used in conjunction with the rapier in personal combat. Both weapons were therefore often made *en suite* as a garniture, supplemented by a waist belt (the girdle) having a sword hanger and straps whose mounts and buckles were decorated to match the ornamentation of the hilts and scabbards. From the 16th to the middle of the 17th century, the poniards were carried—like most daggers—on the girdle, often horizontally behind the waist, on the right side by right-handers and on the opposite side by left-handers.

With the disappearance of sword-and-dagger fencing in England and most other European countries (except Spain and Italy) in the mid-17th century, the word "poniard" gradually became obsolete, and "dagger" has remained a general term covering all variations of the weapon. *See also* PARRYING DAGGER.

**portelance** Another name for the LANCE BUCKET attached to the right stirrup to carry a cavalry spear, lance, or standard.

**potato digger** Nickname for the Browning-designed Colt 95 MACHINE GUN.

**poudre B** Name of the first SMOKELESS POWDER.

**powder** *See* GUNPOWDER (black powder); SMOKELESS POWDERS.

**powder flask** A container made from wood, horn, or metal used to hold the powder for a firearm. The earliest form of portable container for powder, used in the 15th century, seems to have been a leather bag. At some time

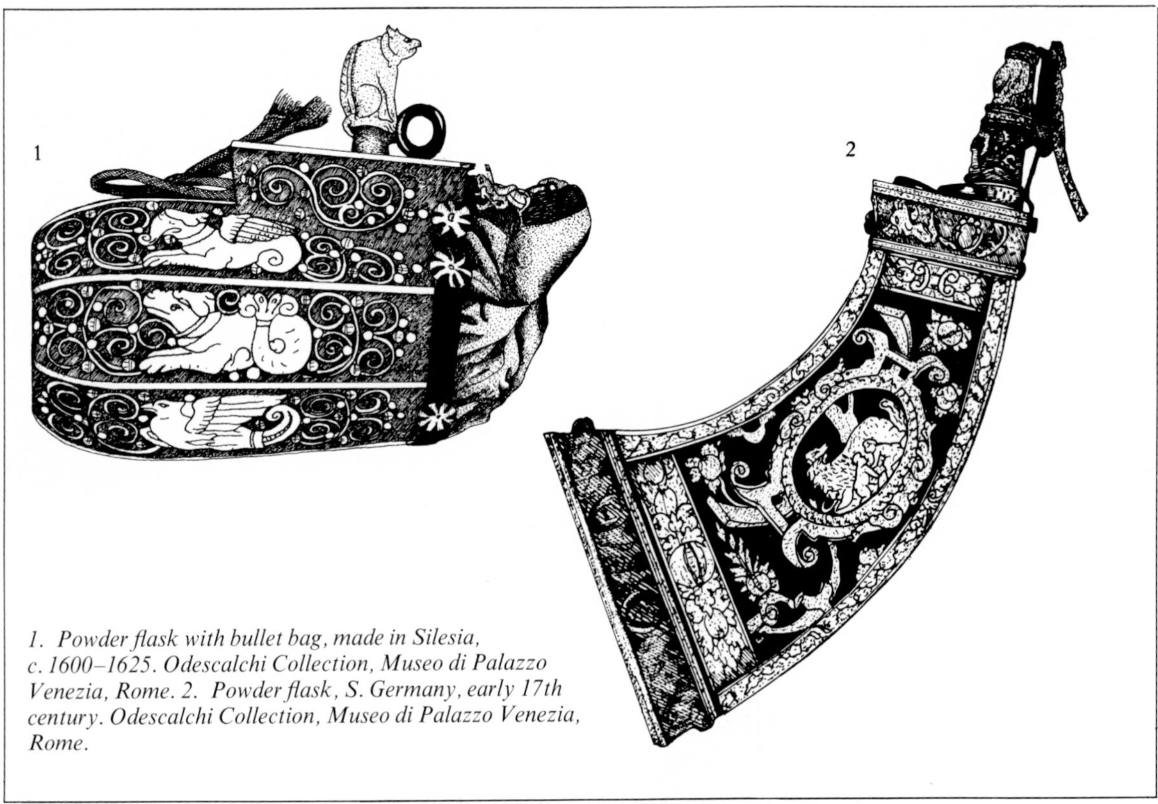


*1. Powder flask with bullet bag, made in Silesia, c. 1600–1625. Odescalchi Collection, Museo di Palazzo Venezia, Rome. 2. Powder flask, S. Germany, early 17th century. Odescalchi Collection, Museo di Palazzo Venezia, Rome.*

later in the century it was found more convenient and safer to carry powder in flasks made from cow's horn, and early 15th-century illustrations indicate that the first powder flasks consisted simply of a section of cow's horn with a fitted wooden cover. Later the horn was worked into a flatter shape so that it could be more conveniently carried on the belt. The bottom of the flask was sealed with wood, and a small tubular nozzle was fitted to the top through which to pour the powder. Some of the most attractive early powder flasks were made from stag's horn; an early example of such a horn can be seen in the Czartoryski Museum in Kraków. Said to have belonged to Henry VIII of England (1509–47), this elaborately carved flask, dated 1531, is mounted in silver gilt and iron damascened in gold.

The original tapered cow's-horn shape was still retained, particularly in Germany, in the 16th century, although powder flasks were by then also being made in bronze and copper. A German flask, dated 1547, in the Victoria and Albert Museum has the tapered cow's-horn shape of the earliest flasks but is made of copper gilt with chased and engraved decoration. A variety of metal flasks were produced in the 16th century; some of the German examples were of bronze gilt with panels based on the designs of such artists as Peter Flötner (d. 1546). Many horn flasks were engraved with scenes from classical mythology drawn from the work of such artists as Virgil Solis (1514–1562) and Jost Amman (1539–1591), and the metal mounts were elaborately chased and engraved. At some period during the 16th century, a spring-operated valve was attached to the nozzle to allow a quantity of powder sufficient for one loading to be taken from the flask. Wooden powder flasks, usually mounted in metal, with elaborate stag's horn inlays on the front panel, were common during this century. Flasks were often made *en suite* with the firearms, the same inlaid designs being used on the flask as were employed on the stock. Several powder flasks that combined the powder container and a box with a hinged lid to hold bullets have survived from the late 16th century. A group of these combined flasks and bullet boxes were preserved in the armory of the elector of Saxony in Dresden; several are now in public and private collections. Toward the end of the 16th century, the iron mounts were often etched in foliate designs.

A number of powder flasks were made in Silesia, possibly in Teschen, in the mid-17th century, most likely for use with the TSCHINKE; these German flasks were round in shape with a central panel of ivory, and the walnut body was inlaid with brass wire and colored stag's horn. During the late 17th and 18th century some small, round German flasks were made in metal and enameled with hunting scenes, although they must have been too fragile to withstand hard usage. In certain areas, however, the traditional cow's-horn shape was retained. During the 17th and 18th centuries, Scotland, for example, produced some fine powder flasks, the surfaces of which were engraved with elaborate Celtic motifs and mottoes. Horns of this shape were also made in Scandinavia. In America,

# Armor's final flourish and 17th-century swords and guns

**Plate 55 16th-century armor** *Infantryman's armor, with side view of the burgonet, Innsbruck, 1550–60. Odescalchi Collection, Museo di Palazzo Venezia, Rome.*

**Plate 56 16th-century armor** *German medium-cavalry armor, made in Nuremberg, c. 1560. Museo Stibbert, Florence.*

**Plate 57 The final period of armor** *Cuirassier armor, N. Italy, first half of the 17th century. Museo Stibbert, Florence.*

**Plate 58 The final period of armor** *Armor of a winged hussar belonging to S. Skórkowski, secretary to King Ladislaus IV of Poland, first half of the 17th century. Wojska Polskiego Museum, Warsaw.*

**Plate 59 The final period of armor** (left) *Equipment of a cavalryman in England, c. 1645. Tower of London Armouries.* (right) *Arquebusier armor with the initials of James II of England, made by Richard Hoden, London, 1686. Tower of London Armouries.*

**Plate 60 Decorated swords c. 1600** (left) *Hunting sword with hilt and scabbard mounted in gilded silver and decorated with precious stones, from the so-called Hungarian garniture which belonged to Duke Maximilian I of Bavaria, made by Johann Michel, Prague, c. 1610. Bayerisches Nationalmuseum, Munich.* (right) *Curved sword with a grip made of coral which belonged to Emperor Rudolf II of Hapsburg, with a small knife, also with a coral grip, in the scabbard, N. Italy, c. 1590–1600. Waffensammlung, Vienna.*

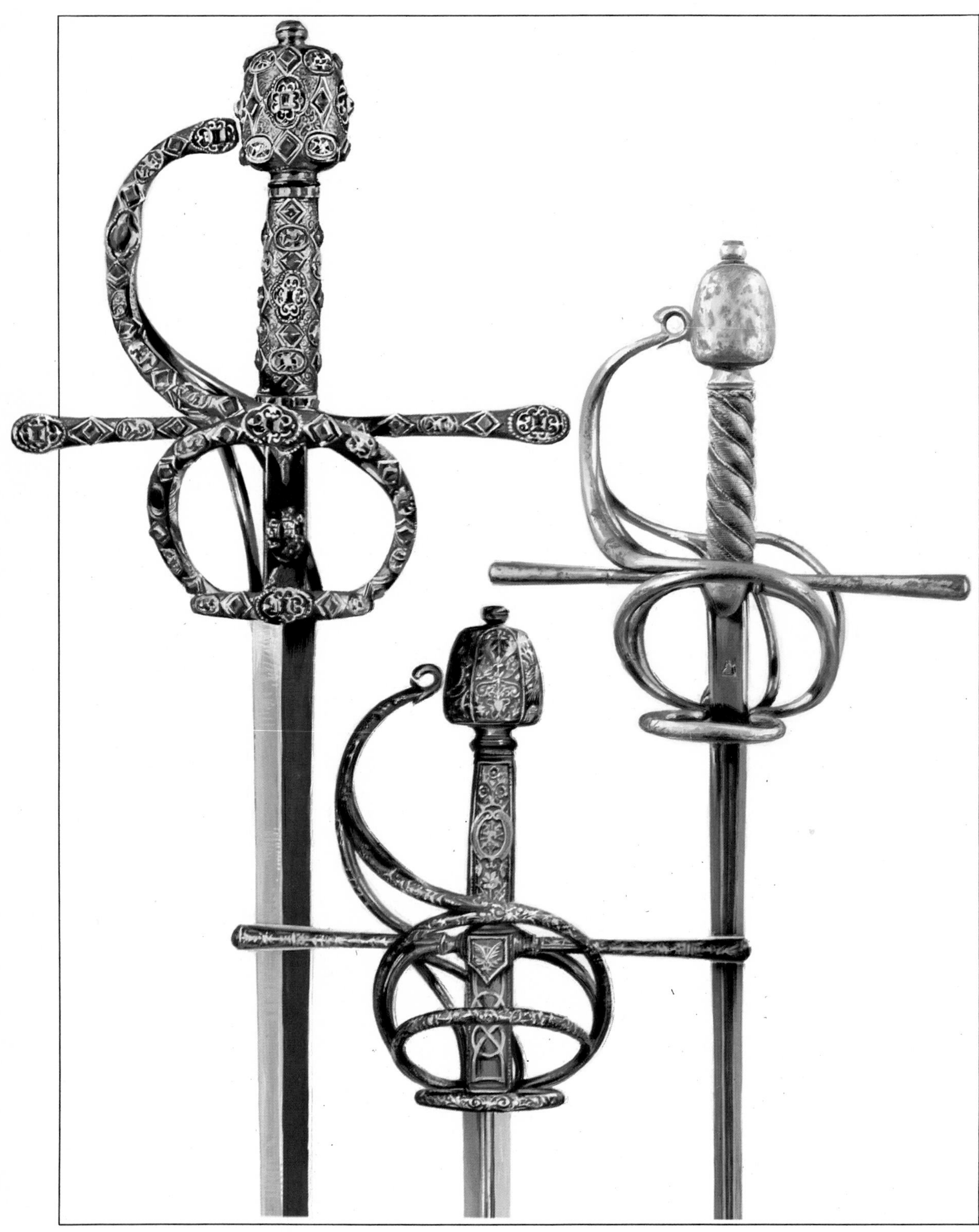

**Plate 61 17th-century swords** (left) *Rapier with gold-damascened hilt decorated with diamonds and rubies, the blade made by Federico Piccinino, Milan, c. 1600–1605. Historisches Museum, Dresden.* (middle) *Rapier with gold and silver damascening on the hilt, Italy, c. 1600. Metropolitan Museum, New York.* (right) *Rapier with gilded guard and pommel, Italy, c. 1600. Museo Stibbert, Florence.*

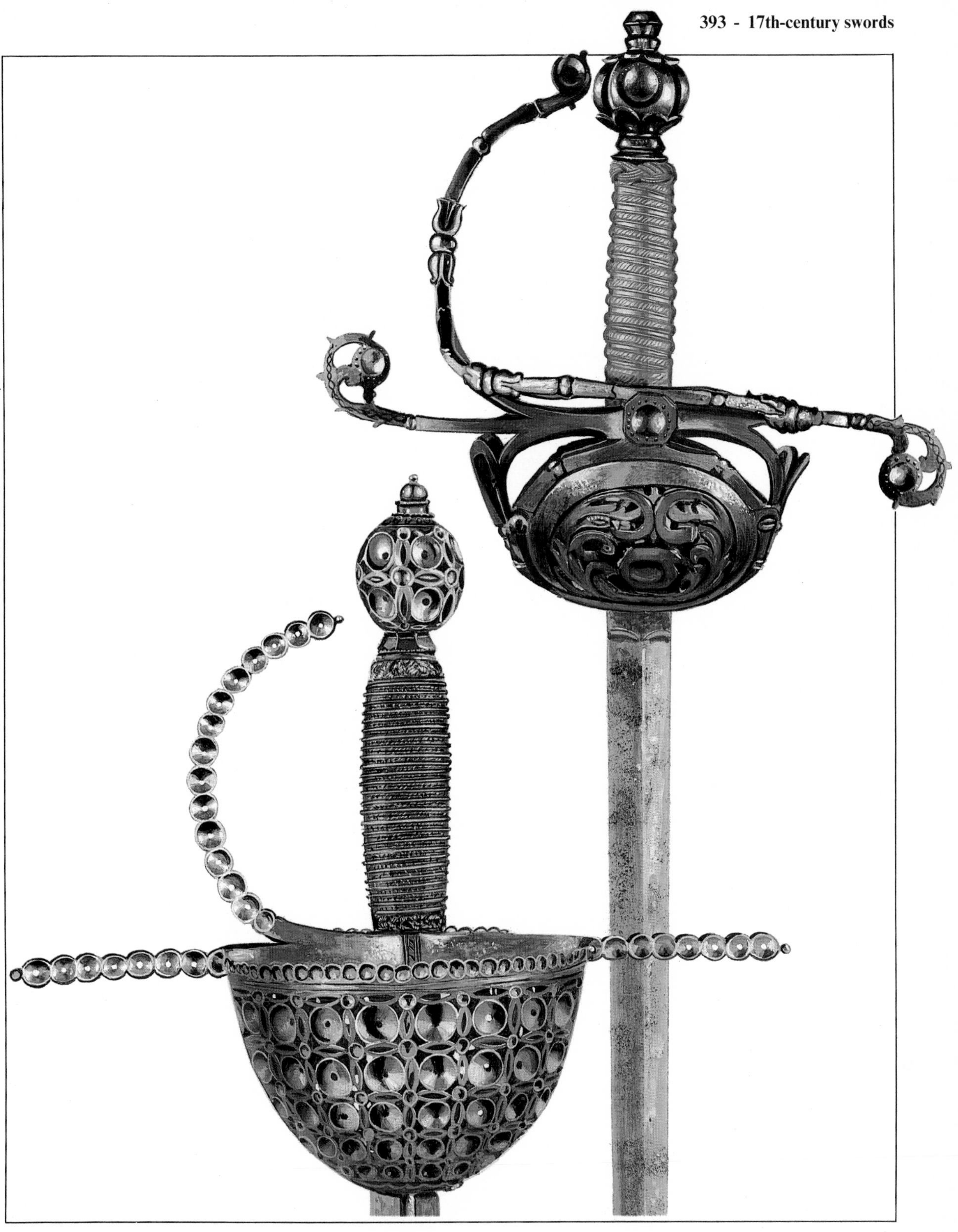

**Plate 62 17th-century swords** (left) *Cup-hilted rapier, Spain, c. 1670. Museo Stibbert, Florence.* (right) *Rapier with shell guard, Netherlands or Flanders, c. 1630–35. Museo Poldi Pezzoli, Milan.*

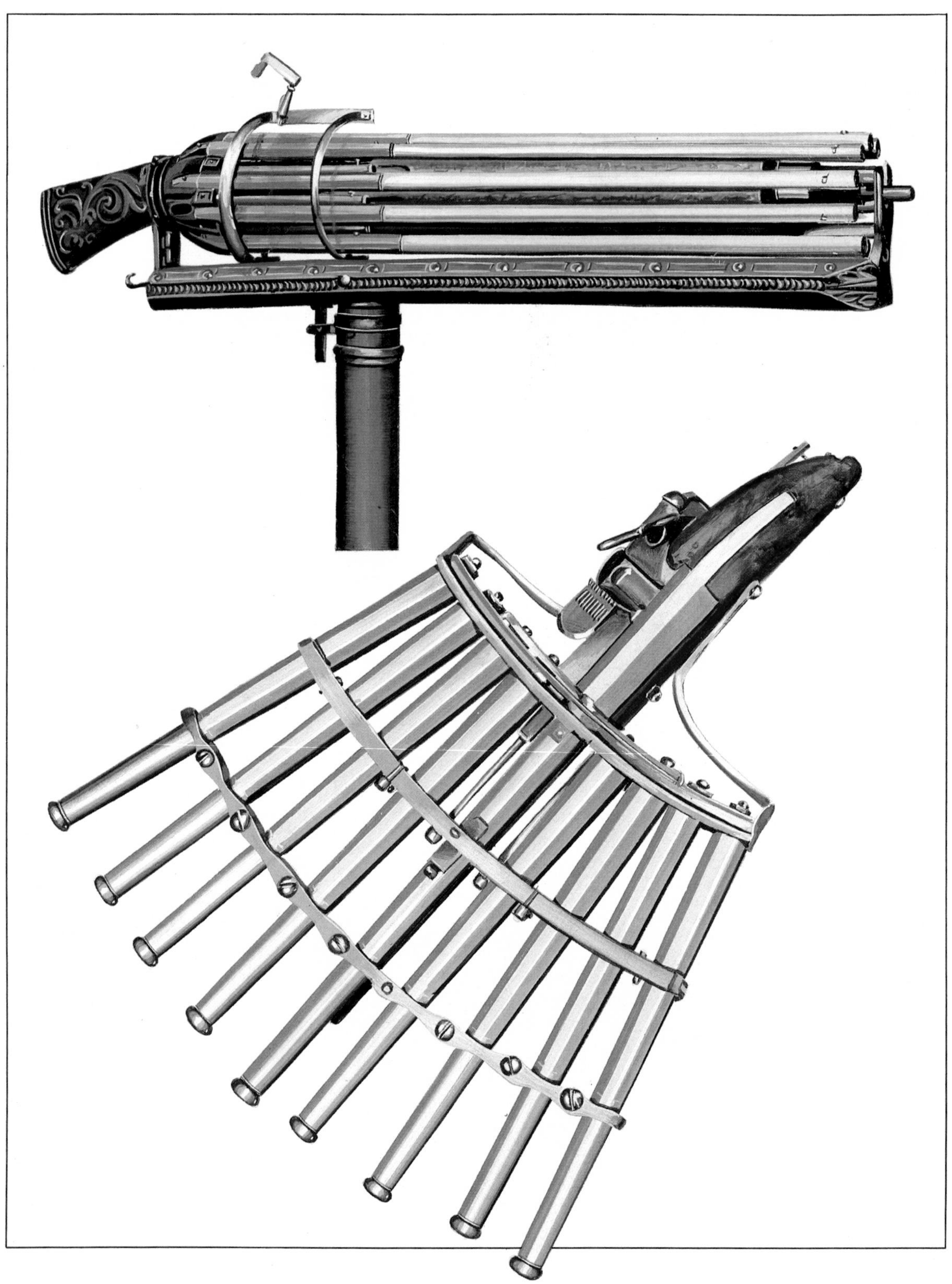

**Plate 63 17th-century multibarreled guns** (top) *Matchlock revolving gun with ten rotating barrels, by G. B. Bergamin, Italy, 1625. Armory of the Council of Ten, Palazzo Ducale, Venice.* (bottom) *"Duck-foot" nine-barreled flintlock volley pistol, Italy, c. 1630. Museo Nazionale del Bargello, Florence.*

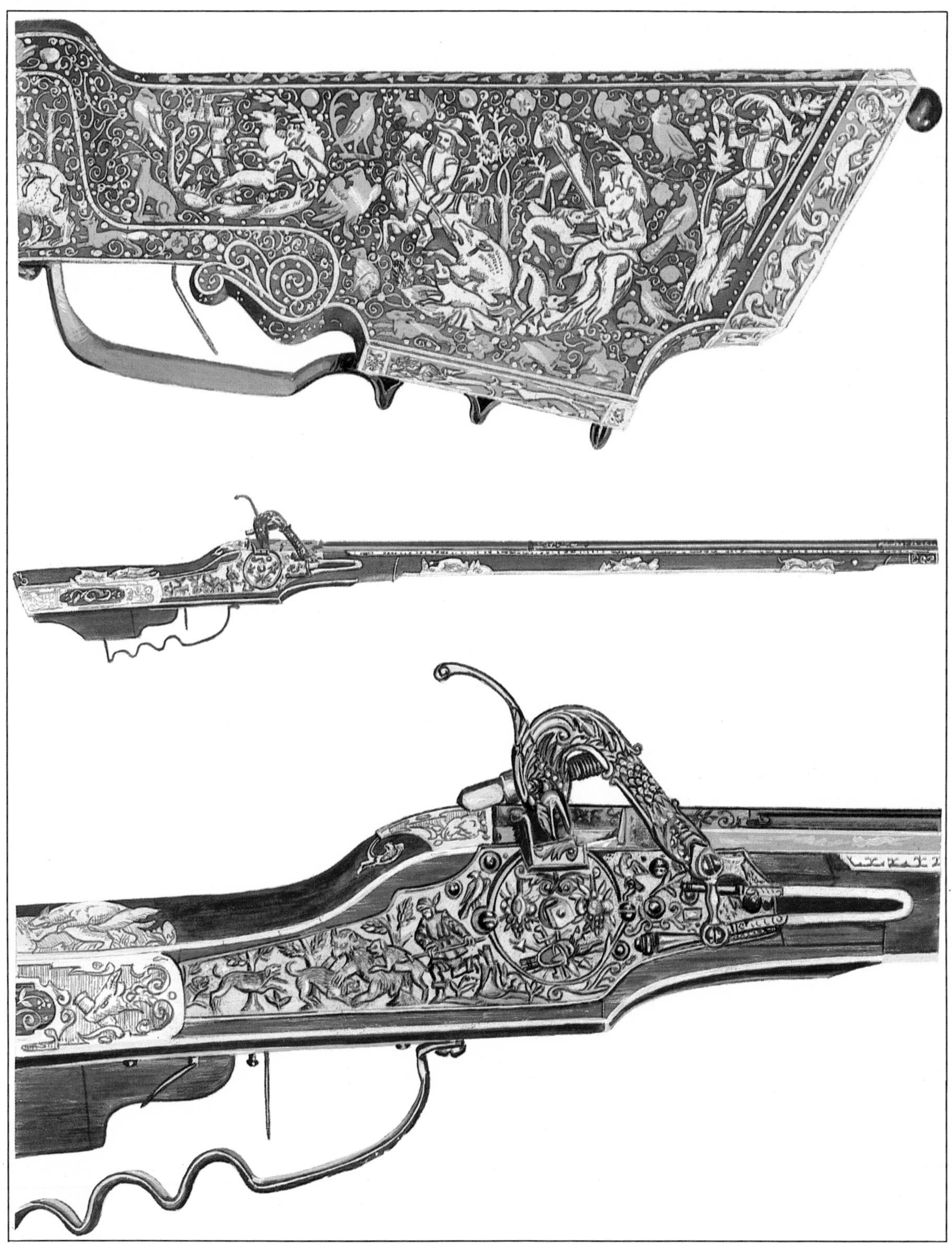

**Plate 64 Wheel-lock sporting guns** (top) *Detail of the butt of a wheel-lock rifle by Johannes Harrtel, Teschen, 1666. Museo Poldi Pezzoli, Milan.* (middle) *Wheel-lock rifle by D. Sadeler and H. Borstorffer that belonged to Grand Duke Ferdinand II of Tuscany, and* (bottom) *detail of the same rifle, Munich, 1626. Museo Nazionale del Bargello, Florence.*

particularly after 1750, it was customary to engrave maps of the local territory, together with patriotic mottoes, on such surfaces.

In addition to flasks made to contain the powder for the main charge, from the 16th century smaller flasks were made to contain the finer priming powder; these priming flasks were often made of metal. A number of triangular-shaped flasks of gilded brass have survived; decorated with plaquettes after Flötner, these are all dated 1574 and bear the arms of the prince-bishop of Würzburg. It is thought that they were made for the bishop's guard. Priming flasks of the 17th and 18th centuries were usually circular and, being small, were sometimes combined with a spanner and a screwdriver to make a combination tool. There is an elaborate example of one of these flasks made of iron, with the crest of the Duc de Sully (1560–1641) inlaid with silver, in the Hermitage, Leningrad.

During the 19th century, after the introduction of the percussion system, metal flasks with die-stamped decoration became fashionable, particularly in England. Many Sheffield firms—especially James Dixon & Sons and Hawkesleys—produced illustrated catalogs showing a wide variety of these flasks. With the introduction of the self-contained cartridge in the 19th century, the powder flask became obsolete.

**powder tester** A device for testing the strength of gunpowder by igniting a measured quantity; the force of the explosion drove a wheel or a bar against a scale, thus enabling its relative strength to be read. It is not known when powder testers were introduced, but it is likely to have been in the 16th century. The earliest documentary account of one in English, entitled "Rare Inventions and Devices Very Necessary for All Generals and Captains," was published by William Bourne in 1587. The development of the powder tester was an essential response to the varying quality of early gunpowder. Impurities and exposure to damp greatly affected the efficiency of powder, and it was therefore essential for the quality of the powder to be known before being used.

Powder testers can be divided into three basic types. The simplest type worked on the principle of the explosion driving a wheel operating against a spring; another used the principle of the explosion driving a weighted vertical bar upward; the third type, of quadrant form, used the explosion to compress a V-shaped spring.

The earliest surviving example of a powder tester, of the type in which the powder operated a vertical bar, dates from the 16th century and is preserved in Vienna. The most common type was the one based on the rotation of a wheel, which seems to have been introduced in the 17th century. An example in the Victoria and Albert Museum, London, apparently dates from the latter part of that century. It consists of a flat plate in the center of which is mounted a wheel engraved with a scale with numbers ranging from 1 to 18. One side of the wheel extends to form an arm with a cap that fits over a small, cylindrical, brass powder container pierced with a touchhole. A strong spring is held against the wheel by means of a screw at the other side. The wheel is held in a bifurcated support, the arms of which are pointed and form indicators for the scale inscribed around the edge of the wheel. When the powder in the cylindrical container was ignited, the cap was forced upward and turned the wheel, thus registering the strength of the powder on the scale. Traces of what was probably a French coat of arms can be seen engraved on the base plate. Most powder testers of the wheel type had the stock and lock of the standard flintlock pistol and could be held in the hand. One early 18th-century Italian powder tester, preserved in a private collection, has the wheel concealed in a box and is operated by a flintlock mechanism.

The quadrant type operated on the basis of the explosion compressing a large V-spring that acted on a marker sliding along a curved bar with a scale. Most V-spring testers appear to have been either French or Belgian, and it was a Belgian, Guillaume Berleur of Liège, who was the most prolific producer of this type in the early 19th century. Most powder testers in this category seem to date from the end of the 18th or early 19th century. Powder testers continued to be made until about 1850, when the standardization of firearms and, more important, the introduction of the self-contained cartridge rendered them unnecessary.

**pricker** A long iron or brass pin for cleaning the touchhole when it became foul with burned powder. References to prickers being a necessary part of a musketeer's equipment can be found in England dated as early as 1590. The pricker was often attached to other tools and accessories; for example, the Spanish multipurpose tool known as an *eslabon* was usually fitted with an iron needle. Nearly every Scottish pistol at one time had a pricker screwed into its butt, the handle of which formed a decorative terminal. With the introduction of the percussion lock, however, the pricker was more or less discarded, apart from its occasional appearance in the 19th century as an accessory for sporting guns.

**prick spurs** *See* SPURS.

**primer** A general term for anything that initiates the decomposition reaction in an explosive mass. On the one hand, it must be proportionate to the degree of sensitivity of the charge to be detonated and, on the other, to the extent of the effect that one wishes to obtain from the explosion. There are various types of primers that work on different principles: impact fuzes, friction fuzes, electric fuzes. They are of different forms: percussion caps, screw-in tubes, priming tubes, blasting caps, slow match (fuze), tapers, etc. They serve different purposes: cartridge cases, fuzes for shells and bombs, mines, etc. Primers can also be divided into two main classes, deflagrating and detonating. The first of these, effected by combustion, is best suited for propellant charges, the second for bursting charges (*see* EXPLOSIVE). For primers used in hand firearms, see CARTRIDGE.

**priming flask** Also called the primer or touchbox, a small flask which contains the fine powder used in the pan of a firearm. *See also* POWDER FLASK.

**projectile** In military terminology, any object designed to be launched at a target by any kind of force.

The most effective shape for artillery projectiles (commonly called shells) is cylindro-ogival; driving bands and steadying bands or rings are fitted to the outer cylindrical surface to control movement through the barrel. The interior of the shell is usually hollow; it may be the same shape as the exterior or, for a variety of reasons, may diverge from it. There is a hole, called the fuze hole, that extends from the interior to the exterior. It may be at the point of the ogive (point-detonating shells) or at the center of the base of the shell (base-fuzed shells). Housed in the fuzehole is the fuze for exploding the bursting charge.

Artillery projectiles can be divided into direct-action shells and predetermined-action shells. The functions of direct-action shells are (a) penetrating ("cannonballs" and armor-piercing shells); (b) splintering (common high explosive shells, demolition shells, timed fragmentation shells); (c) highly explosive shells (nuclear warheads and, in the past, the mines and bombs thrown from mortars); (d) special types of shells (different types of smoke shells, incendiary, illuminating, irritant, or toxic gas).

For projectiles used in small arms, see BULLET. For further details, see CANISTER; FUZE; SHELL; SHRAPNEL.

**proximity fuze** A type of FUZE fitted with a radio transmitter, receiver, and aerial to detect when the projectile is within lethal distance of the target and detonate it.

**ptéryges** Greek term for the pendant skirt of straps, often reinforced with metal, on the LORICA to protect the abdomen.

**puffer** A typical German wheel-lock pistol of the latter part of the 16th century, with a large ball-shaped pommel.

**pugio** A small double-edged dagger with a sharp point worn without a sheath on the chest by Roman emperors as a symbol of the *jus vitae et necis*. Daggers of this type are also depicted being worn by senior officials and imperial bodyguards in various Roman works of art.

**pump action** The name for a mechanism in rifles and shotguns by which a sliding grip below the barrel is pulled back with the left hand (for right-handers) to open the breech and extract the case, and pushed forward to reload.

**punt gun** *See* GUN: sporting.

**pu tun** An ancient type of Chinese wooden shield, described in dictionaries compiled during the Han Dynasty (206 B.C.–A.D. 220). It was the foot soldier's only means of defense. Long and narrow, it had a central ridge and tapered off to a point at the top. The front was lacquered in red, and the back was fitted with a prop that could be set into the ground to protect the soldier, leaving his hands free to operate his weapon, like the European PAVISE. A smaller type, the *kie tun*, with no prop, was used in war chariots. A framework of bamboo covered with rhinoceros hide was sometimes used to make such shields.

# Q

**quadrant** Another term for the "gunner's square," an old instrument for setting the elevation of ARTILLERY.

**quarrel** A term referring to a crossbow BOLT and initially applied to bolts with a heavy quadrangular point, usually of rhomboid section. In Tuscany in the 16th century, certain stilettos with a strong blade of four-sided section were also called quarrels (*quadrello*).

**quarterstaff** The simplest of all staff weapons, the quarterstaff was a length of wood about 2–3 m. (6–9 ft.) long, round in section. Better pieces were made of oak and had both ends shod with heavy metal ferrules. Quarterstaves were very popular during the Middle Ages, particularly in Britain, both as a real weapon used for attack and defense and as a practice weapon instead of the long two-handed sword, halberd, spear, or similar pole arms. The quarterstaff was held in the middle with the left hand, while the right hand grasped it at one-quarter (of the whole length) from the end.

**queue** A horizontal bar screwed to the right side of the breastplate and projecting backward under the arm to terminate at the rear in a hook under which the butt end of a heavy lance could be lodged. It was positioned symmetrically to the REST. This fitting was used toward the end of the 15th century and beginning of the 16th and was characteristic of German jousting armor (*Stechzeug*) and armor for the German course (*Rennzeug*).

**quillon block** Part of the guard of edged weapons, consisting of a small block of metal with the tang passing through it, acting as a support for the shoulder of the blade and the base of the cross guard. This feature was absent throughout most of the Bronze Age, appearing in antiquity as an intermediate element between the grip and the blade, being slightly broader than the latter. With the appearance of QUILLONS and other elements of the guard, its form and function became more defined; in fact, the quillons extended from it, as did the knuckle guard and the arms of the hilt. The quillon block was also called the écusson.

**quillons** An extended cross guard of swords and daggers designed in the 16th century to parry or entangle the opponent's blade. The quillons extended from a base, the QUILLON BLOCK, below the grip, and were either straight, recurved in S-form, or bent toward the blade (especially in the PARRYING DAGGERS). In some types of hilts the forward quillon was curved toward the pommel, serving, in fact, as a knuckle guard.

**quiver** A container for holding and transporting arrows or bolts. Made of metal, wood, or leather, quivers were varied in form, though proportionate in size with the type of arrows or bolts to be used. Quivers for arrows were fairly deep so as to protect them for almost their entire length; only the vanes (feathers) and a small section of the shaft emerged from the top, enabling the archer to extract them without difficulty. The quiver was slung across the archer's back with an appropriate baldric or belt in such a way that the arrows protruded from it above his shoulder or to the side. The quiver worn with the composite or Turkish bow had two compartments: in one the arrows were placed, in the other the bow, at repose, with the bowstring completely slackened. The quiver designed for holding crossbow bolts was considerably less deep, often fitted with a lid, and in some cases had a series of compartments inside, each one for a quarrel, again with the head downward so that the vanes would not be damaged; the crossbowman wore it attached to a belt, often on the right-hand side. The rule about putting the bolt or arrow in the quiver head downward is a constant one for all vaned missiles; various coloration or decoration of the feathers usually helped identify the different types of heads. For bolts without vanes there was no hard rule about the direction of the head in the quiver; sometimes they were carried with the heads protruding from the quiver so that the most suitable arrow could be chosen in haste to shoot an animal.

As a complement to the bow and crossbow, the quiver followed developments in the respective weapon. It was tough and inexpensive when designed for use in battle; elegant and richly decorated for the hunting nobleman; makeshift and often made with scavenged materials, for the peasant. Today, archers still like to have their own particular quiver bearing the colors or emblem of their club.

# R

**rack** A 16th-century term for the CRANEQUIN.
**raentjan** *See* BATTIG.
**ram dao** A sacrificial sword of northern India, never used for fighting but for beheading animals—usually goats and occasionally buffalo—offered in sacrifice to the goddess Kali. It often bore an inscription in Bengali characters such as *jay Kali* ("victory to kali"), and the sword itself was regarded as the physical manifestation of the goddess's powers of severance. They were frequently donated by pious people who recorded the fact of their gift in an inscription.

The ram dao was mostly found north of the Ganges basin, over an area extending from Bengal to Assam. It was made in various shapes but consisted basically of a short, turned wooden handle with a very large, flat, single-edged blade shaped like a scythe or sickle, 60–80 cm. (24–32 in.) long. The blade was usually decorated along the back edge with simple line-engraved motifs filled in with red and, at the point, an eye with the eyebrow painted in red, yellow, and black. Most of the ram dao seen today date from the 19th century.
**rammer** A tool used in the loading of muzzleloading pieces of artillery and for cleaning the barrels. It consisted of a long pole, generally wooden, with a thicker section at the end to ram the charge home. The rod could be reversed and used to swab out the barrel with a sponge. A hand-firearm accessory with similar functions is usually called a RAMROD.
**ramrod** A rod of wood or iron used from the 15th century to drive the ball into the breech of the gun or pistol barrel. Initially ramrods were separate from guns, but by the last quarter of the century the ramrod was fitted into a recess underneath the barrel. Wooden ramrods were usually made of ash or walnut mounted with a horn tip. During the 17th century ramrods known as "scouring sticks" were often fitted at one end with screw threads to which a variety of special tools such as worms and cleaning rags could be attached. In the early 18th century an iron ramrod was again introduced for military firearms because the wooden ramrod had proved too fragile during sustained use in the field. In the early years of the following century the ramrod was often linked to the barrel by means of a revolving swivel.

Special ramrods were developed for certain firearms during the 19th century. The ramrod for the Lancaster pillar-breech rifle, for example, had a recessed head so as not to deform the bullet.

The ramrod became absolute with the development of the modern cartridge, but its position on a gun is now filled by the modern cleaning rod.
**rancoon** *See* RAWCON.
**ranseur** *See* RAWCON.
**rapier** A term borrowed in the 16th century from the

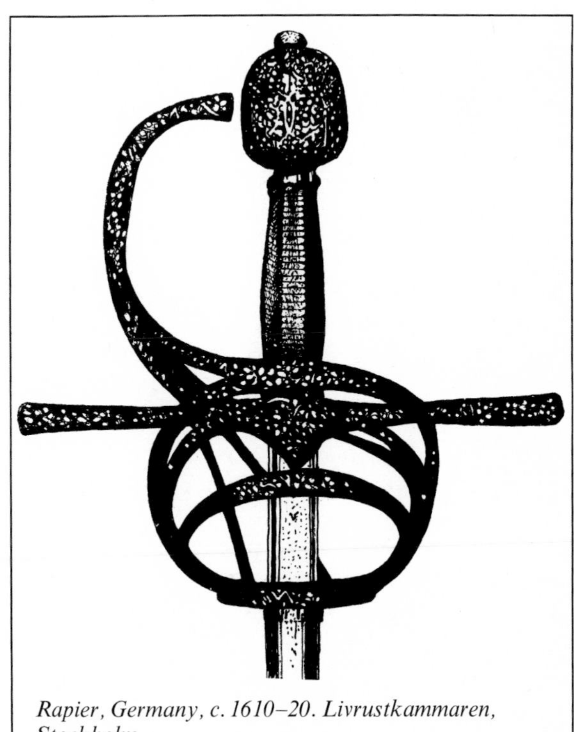

*Rapier, Germany, c. 1610–20. Livrustkammaren, Stockholm.*

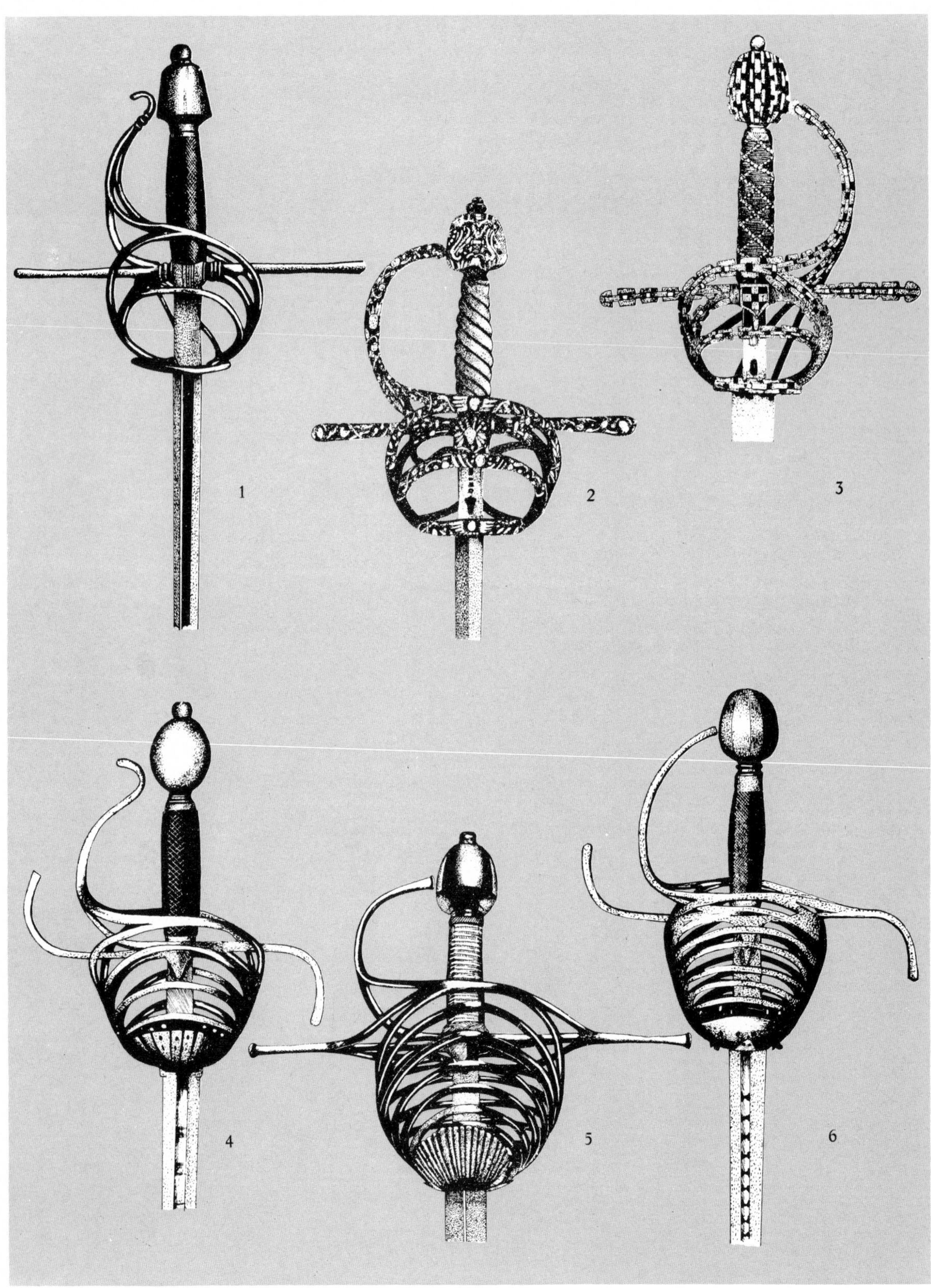


*Various types of rapier hilts. 1. Italy, late 16th century. 2. Western Europe, late 16th or early 17th century. 3. For left-hander (position of the guard being reversed), Italy or Spain, c. 1600. 4. Spain, early 17th century. 5. Spain or Italy, c. 1620–30. 6. Italy or Spain, c. 1620–40. 7. Western Europe, c. 1630–40. 8. Spain or S. Italy, c. 1670–80. 9. Spain or*

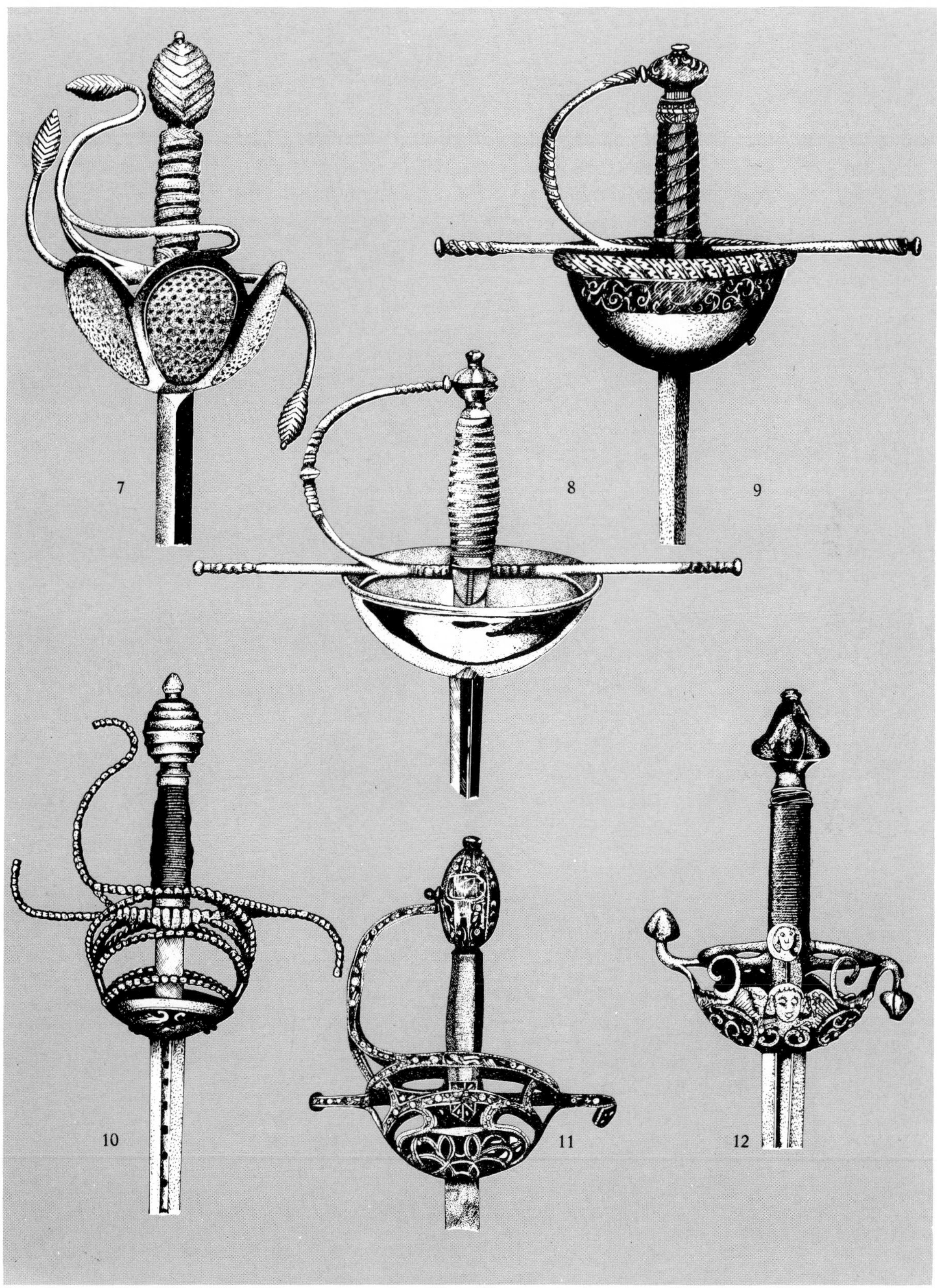


*Italy, third quarter of the 17th century. 10. Italy or Spain, c. 1620–40. 11. England, c. 1630–50. 12. England, c. 1640–50.*

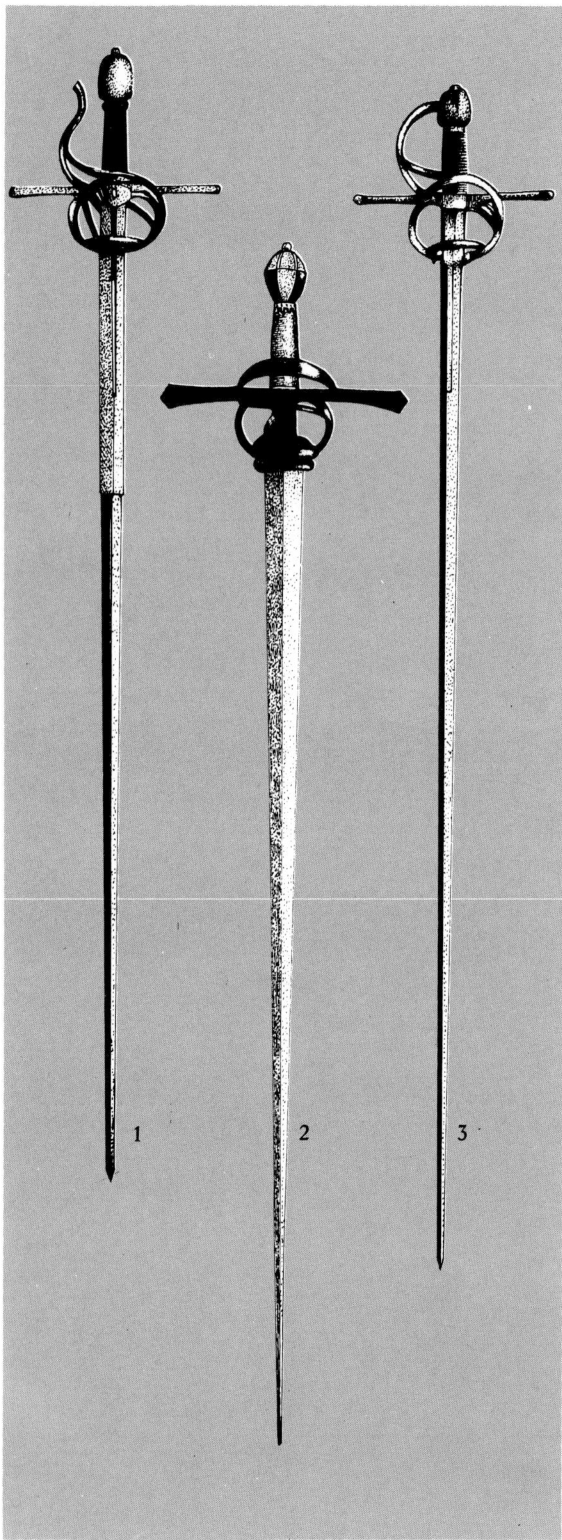


*Rapiers. 1. With extendable blade, Germany, c. 1610. 2. Germany, late 16th century. 3. Italy, late 16th century.*

French (*rapière*), where it was first recorded in 1474 in the phrase *épee rapière*, which itself derived from the contemporary Spanish *espada ropera*, "dress sword," carried daily by gentlemen. If compared with the arming sword, the rapier was a much lighter weapon with a straight double-edged and pointed blade, which, with the development of the art of fencing in the 16th and 17th centuries, finally became narrower and lighter, and thus suitable for thrusts only. The word itself was subject to various definitions with time and place. It soon became obsolete in Spain, where the general term *espada* prevailed to cover almost all sword forms, and it never was used in Italy. In English and French, it has retained its classical connotation of a light thrusting sword used in the 16th and 17th centuries. The German *Rapier* had the same meaning in that period, but from a later time up to the present has denoted a fencing foil or fleuret. In this latter meaning the word *rapira* was also, and still is, used in Russia.

When the blade and the hilt of rapiers underwent great changes in size and form in the late 17th century, the English language reacted to this development by introducing a new term, SMALLSWORD.

The new technique of swordplay, introduced in the mid-16th century, with the emphasis now on the point of the blade as the main instrument of attack, brought about the changing structure of the sword's guard. In order to point the blade more effectively, some swordsmen preferred to place one or two fingers in front of the QUILLONS, and these fingers had to be protected by ARMS OF THE HILT and SIDE GUARDS. And since ordinary gloves were usually worn during an encounter, an increase in all these elements of the guard became a necessity to cover the hand of the target nearest to the opponent. Finally, in Spanish dueling rapiers a CUP GUARD was developed by the mid-17th century, which completely protected the hand.

A different reason gave rise to the gradual lengthening of the blade: it was believed for a time that with a longer blade it was possible to hit the adversary more easily and at the same time stay out of reach of his weapon—unless it was of about the same length or longer. But this gave rise in turn to problems of balance and handling, which were resolved, in the 16th to the 18th century, by using a parrying weapon—a BUCKLER, a PARRYING DAGGER—a cloak, or even an unarmed hand. Some long rapiers had slender, still stiff, blades that were square, rhomboid, or rectangular in section, with a very sharp point. They were used exclusively by skillful fencers able to master these quite poorly balanced weapons and take advantage of their length. Rudolfo Capo Ferro da Cagli in his *Gran simulacro dell'arte e dell'uso della scherma* (1610) indicated that, for a dueling rapier to be well balanced, the point of balance had to be 8 cm. (3.1 in.) down the blade from the ricasso.

The rapier of the latter half of the 16th century usually had a hilt with straight or recurved quillons, side guards, arms of the hilt, and knuckle bows; additional rings and bars in ever increasing numbers were used in various types of hilts to improve the protection. But the sharp point of the opponent's blade often found a way through this sophisticated defense network, and the only foolproof way

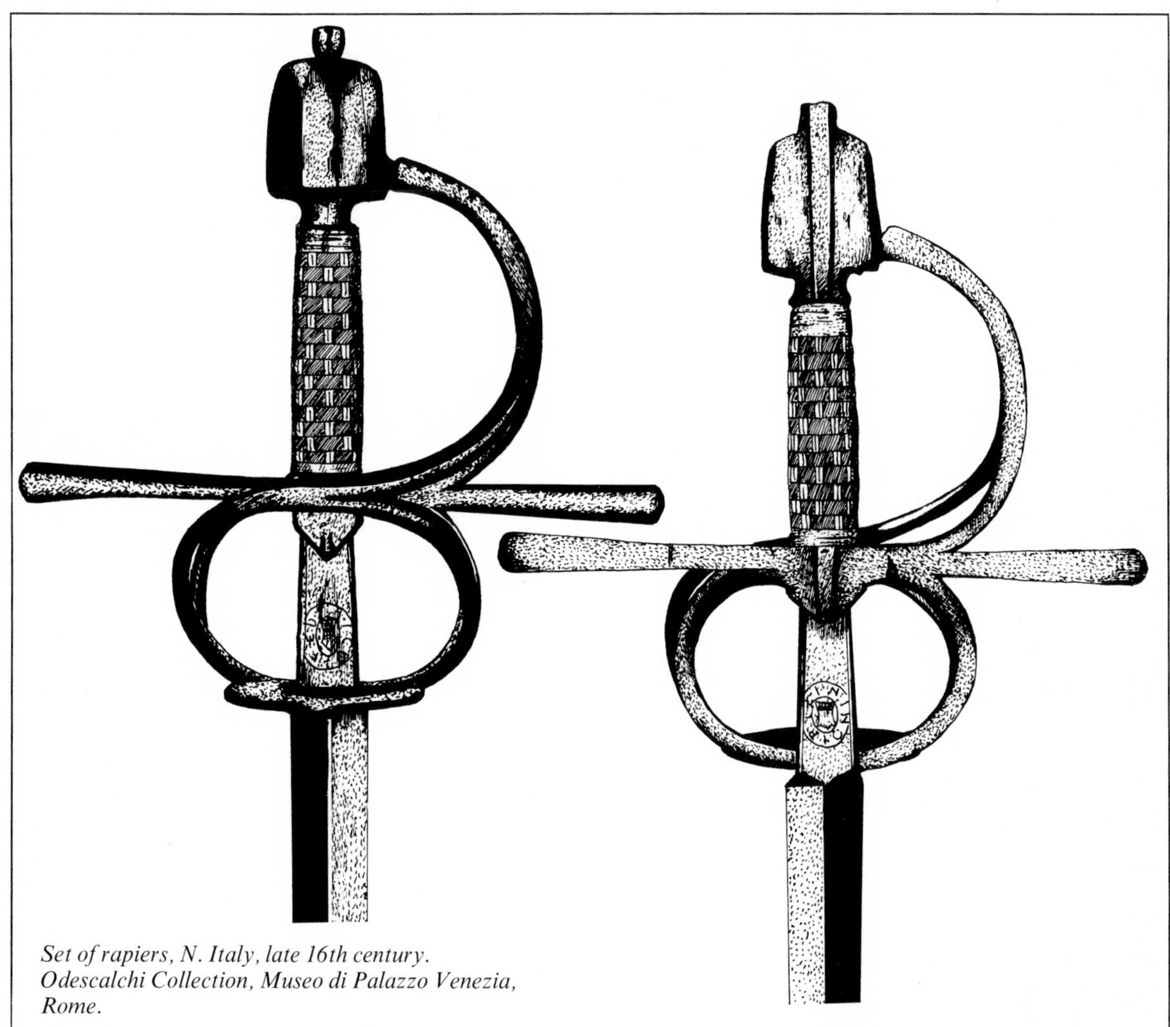

*Set of rapiers, N. Italy, late 16th century. Odescalchi Collection, Museo di Palazzo Venezia, Rome.*

of stopping it was the use of a metal plate. In the early decades of the 17th century the SHELL GUARD started to increase in size until this protection reached the form of the cup guard.

Not every swordmaker could make a good rapier blade; in fact, most of the blades seem to have been made in a number of highly specialized workshops in such centers as Milan and Brescia in Italy, Toledo and Valencia in Spain, Solingen and Passau in Germany. From these cities the blades were exported throughout Europe and mounted in accordance with local fashions and the fancy of the purchaser. The famous names and markings on these blades were often painstakingly forged on inferior blades made elsewhere.

In the closing stages of the 17th century the rapier fell out of favor throughout central and northern Europe, where it was being replaced by the smallsword. In Spain and Italy, it retained its glory for several decades to come; during this period rapiers were made there with elaborate decorative work. Although Milan, Naples, and Palermo were Spanish dominions, the decoration style was typically Italian. In southern Italy the dominant features were the fuller running down the blade and the decorative work using the *à jour* technique. In the north, Milan and Brescia ably met the market requirements with cup guards chiseled with concentric loops or spirals.

**rawcon** (also **rancoon**, **ranseur**) A term used in the 16th and 17th centuries to denote a staff weapon whose three-pronged head had a long double-edged spike flanked by two short upcurved blades. Its shape resembles the heads of the CORSESCA and PARTISAN, but the latter are more massive and sturdy.

**receiver** The metal component screwed onto the breech of a firearm and forming an extension of it. It contains and holds, wholly or partly, the breechblock and firing mechanism.

**recoil** The movement of a weapon (or of an artillery piece, in a gun mounted on a recoil carriage) in reaction to the movement of the projectile and the gases along the bore on firing. The "dynamic" system formed by the projectile, the weapon, being free to recoil, and the propellant charge is subject to no external forces;

consequently, by a well-known principle of mechanics, the sum of the different movements in the system projected along the axis must come to zero. In analytical terms, we have:

$$mv - MV + v'\frac{d\omega}{g} = 0$$

where $m$ is the mass of the projectile and $v$ its velocity, M is the mass of the weapon and V the velocity it acquires in recoil, $v'$ is the velocity of the propellant charge and $\frac{\omega}{g}$ the mass of the propellant charge. To calculate the integral (in which $v'$ is the velocity acquired by the element of mass $\frac{d\omega}{g}$), let us suppose, based on the expansion phenomenon of gases, that half the mass $\frac{\omega}{g}$ moves with the projectile and the other half recoils with the weapon thus:

$$v(m + \frac{\omega}{2g}) = V(M + \frac{\omega}{2g}) \qquad VM$$

Disregarding the weight of the charge, which is very small in relation to that of the weapon, and substituting for the masses $m$ and M the corresponding weights $p$ and G, we obtain the velocity of recoil in relation to that of the projectile:

$$V = \frac{p}{G}(1 + \frac{\omega}{2g})\, v$$

There are a number of accessory factors that complicate the theoretical and practical calculation of the recoil, so that, to simplify the problem, only three distinct moments have been considered: the reaction due to the acceleration of the projectile from rest to muzzle velocity; the reaction due to the acceleration of the mass of the gases generated by the decomposition of the propellant charge; and the reaction due to the expansion of the gases at the muzzle when the projectile leaves the barrel. On the problems arising from the recoil of artillery, *see* GUN MOUNTINGS; for small arms, *see* AUTOMATIC WEAPONS; PISTOL).

**recuperator** The mechanism in modern artillery that returns the piece to the firing position when recoil is completed. It is found in its simplest form on platform mountings, where the slope of the platform enables the piece to roll back to its original position. As the gun recoils, the recuperator reinforces the action of the buffer (hydraulic brake); to begin with, it has to be in a slight state of tension, so as to hold the piece firmly in battery. The chief types of recuperator are:

*(a)* Spring, consisting of a cylinder in which a piston slides as the gun recoils and compresses recoil springs. As the springs expand again, the piece is returned to battery.

*(b)* Compressed air, contained in a cylinder with an airtight piston sliding in it, which compresses the air strongly on recoil.

*(c)* Hydropneumatic, consisting of a hydraulic buffer with a liquid (oil) connected at one end to a recuperator cylinder parallel with it, which contains a floating piston and compressed air. As the gun recoils, the liquid that gives resistance to the buffer is forced into the recuperator and compresses the air still further. When the recoil is complete, the air expands again and forces the piston and the liquid back into the buffer cylinder, returning the piece to battery.

**reinforcing pieces** A generic term which covers a number of pieces of armor which could be added to the basic suit, especially for the joust and tourney. The most commonly used were the reinforcing bevor, pasguard, grand guard, tilting targe, stomach lame, gardbraces, tilting cuisses, and shield-style jousting sockets. Another term used occasionally in writings on armor is "pieces of advantage."

**reins** Part of the bridle, used for controlling and directing the horse. The main or curb rein consisted of two long strips of leather attached to rings at the top of the metal BRANCHES of the bit, which brought the CURB CHAIN into action. By pulling back or releasing the rein or by bearing more to the right or to the left, the rider could check or guide his mount in conjunction with other aids—use of legs, spurs, etc. While the rein for the battlefield or tournament was often armored, for parades, ceremonial occasions, and various courses it was decorated with fringes, often of leather or velvet, and embellished with precious metals and stones.

In a full bard, the curb rein was nearly always covered with reinforcing lamellae or even made of linked metal plates. In this case, a second rein was often used which acted directly on the mouthpiece of a single bit (snaffle) and was known simply as the "rein" or "false rein." When not in use, the reins were fastened to the saddlebow.

**repeating firearms** Those firearms whose design enables the shooter to fire several shots in succession, manually reloading the weapon with the cartridges contained in its magazine. The functioning of the mechanism varies according to the weapon concerned. *See also* GUN.

**rerebrace** A medieval term for upper-arm armor made of iron plate and worn over the sleeve of mail. Its early types were gutter-shaped and protected the outer side of the arm, to which they were attached with straps and buckles. *See also* VAMBRACE.

**rest** (from *arrest*, "stop") An accessory attached to the breastplate of armor worn by mounted soldiers or contestants armed with lances. Its purpose was to ease holding the lance and to prevent it from being jerked backward under the arm on impact when it was couched for the charge, both on the battlefield and in the joust or tilt. The rest took two main forms: "bracket style," in which the arm of the rest, seen in section on page 405, had the form of a reversed "L"; and the hook-shaped rest. A thick piece of leather nailed around the butt of the lance behind the hand (*see* GRAPER) was engaged against the rest to provide a "hold" for the lance. The term "rest" was at first occasionally applied to the graper, but from the late 14th century referred to the support on the breastplate.

The rest consisted of a small base plate attached to the right side of the breastplate from which a short stout arm projected to support the lance. In the 14th and the first half of the 15th century, rests were almost always fixed but later became hinged to the base plate—which was riveted or screwed onto the breastplate—and fitted with a spring lock. In the latter period, adjustable rests were introduced;

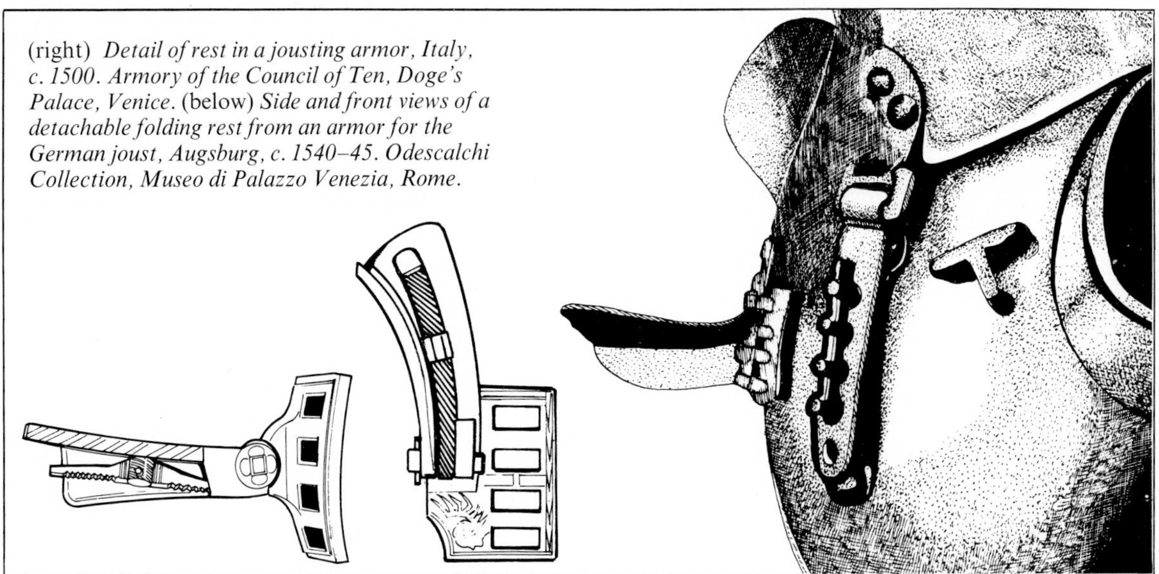

(right) *Detail of rest in a jousting armor, Italy, c. 1500. Armory of the Council of Ten, Doge's Palace, Venice.* (below) *Side and front views of a detachable folding rest from an armor for the German joust, Augsburg, c. 1540–45. Odescalchi Collection, Museo di Palazzo Venezia, Rome.*

these fixed the base to the breast by means of a removable pin inserted through pierced pegs of the breastplate protruding from the holes in the base. This system was particularly favored in Italy, but was used also in English armor. It remained in occasional use for the joust in the 16th century.

The most widespread use of the rest occurred during the 1400s and up to about 1550, when military operations were tactically based on the charge with lances. It survived into the second half of the 16th century almost exclusively for use in the joust. Its larger version included the QUEUE for armor used in the German joust (*Gestech*) and the German course (*Rennen*).

**rest of advantage** An English 16th-century term for the REST and its rear extension with a hook, the QUEUE, used in armor for the German joust (*Stechzeug*) and that for the German course (*Rennzeug*) to place the butt of a heavy lance before charging the opponent.

**return spring** Also called recoil spring; in semiautomatic and automatic weapons, the spring used to absorb part of the energy imparted to the breechblock or bolt as the breech is opened. This energy is then used to drive the breechblock forward again to the closed position, carrying out various connected processes—detaching and chambering the next cartridge, rotating and locking the bolt head, etc.—on the way. The return spring (or, in some cases, springs) may be behind the breechblock or bolt, beside it, or even in front of it; in this last case, connection is made by way of some moving piece or pieces in the mechanism, such as the piston in the Garand rifle or the Beretta AR70/.223. Contrary to common belief, it is only in exceptional cases (in the Schwarzlose machine gun, for instance) that the return spring plays any appreciable part in holding the breechblock in the closed position in blowback systems.

**revolver** A general term denoting the firearms in which several barrels, or a cylinder with several chambers, rotate in such a way that each load is positioned in turn in front of a firing device. The term is commonly applied mainly to pistols whose construction incorporates a cylinder revolving around the axis parallel to the barrel. *See also* GUN; PISTOL.

**rib** (or **ribbing**) Part of the blade of edged side weapons and also, in some cases, of hafted weapons; more specifically, it was a thicker section on the back of the blade which gave the blade greater rigidity. It appeared first on knives and other weapons made exclusively for cutting, but then spread to sabers, cavalry sabers, smallswords, etc. Not until the 19th century did the ribbing become a consistent T-shaped part of the blade of cavalry sabers and bayonets. The progressive lightening of the blade, which had been taking place for more than a century due to the reduced strength of protective wear, had now reached such a stage that only strong ribbing could provide the blade with the required balance between flexibility and rigidity.

**ribauld** (or **ribalde**) Also called ribauldequin or organ, from its resemblance to the pipes of an organ, this ancient firearm consisted of a number of guns joined together as a bundle or side by side in a wooden frame, so that they could fire a volley (*see* VOLLEY GUN). Ribaulds were used from at least the mid-15th century and were still in use in the 19th (the Danish *orgelespignål*, for example, was used in 1864 in the war against Prussia).

**ricasso** The blunted base of the blade beneath the tang and the grip. It appeared regularly from the 15th century as a result of the extended protective parts added below the quillons and of the new technique of holding the sword to deliver thrusts. From the early 17th century it also frequently served as a mounting for the shell guard. Sword-makers often engraved their mark on the ricasso.

**rifle** *See* GUN.

**rifling** System of helical grooves cut along the bore of the barrel of a firearm and making about one full turn to give

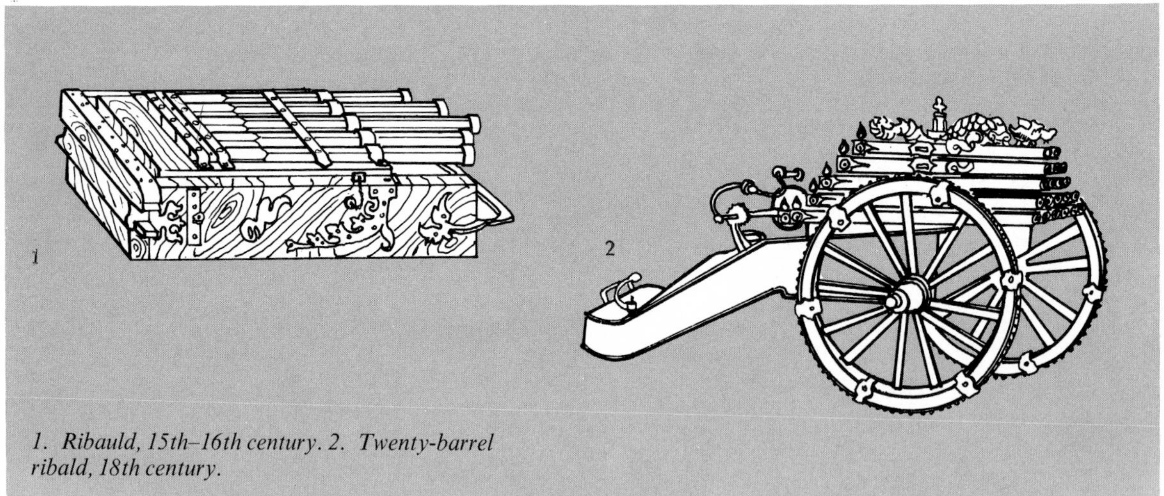


*1. Ribauld, 15th–16th century. 2. Twenty-barrel ribald, 18th century.*

the projectile a rotary motion around its longitudinal axis, ensuring stability in its trajectory. The oldest extant gun with rifling appears to be the one made between 1493 and 1508 which belonged to Emperor Maximilian I. Rifled guns did not come into wide use until the latter half of the 16th century, from which time rifled barrels were increasingly mounted, especially in central Europe, on sporting and target guns, as well as on military firearms issued in limited number to selected units and well-trained marksmen. Dueling and target pistols were often fitted with rifled barrels, particularly those produced by French, Belgian, and German gunmakers in the late 18th and 19th century.

The following are the main elements in rifling:

*(a)* The profile, i.e., the geometrical figure obtained from a cross section of the barrel. The profile of a groove has a "base," normally concentric with the bore, and two "sides" flanking the base and running from it to the inner surface ("land") of the barrel. The side against which the projectile pressed more strongly as it passes down the barrel is called the "guiding edge" and the other side the "counterside."

*(b)* The direction, i.e., the way the groove turns to spin the projectile. It makes no difference in the accuracy of the shooting or in the recoil of the weapon whether the grooves turn clockwise or counterclockwise; clockwise rifling is generally preferred in small arms to compensate for the tendency to pull off to the left in pressing the trigger. The guiding edge of the groove is on the side opposite to the direction of turn of the rifling.

*(c)* The pattern made by the rifling if the cylindrical surface of the bore is traced on a flat surface.

*(d)* The pitch of the groove, i.e., the distance between one turn and the next measured along the same generatrix. It is determined by the degree of twist as expressed by an acute angle made by a tangent to the groove at a given point with the generatrix of the bore. Rifling may be "spiral," when the twist is constant, or "progressive," when it increases from breech to muzzle. In spiral rifling, since the pitch is given by the value $p = \pi a / \tan \delta$, where $a$ is the caliber and $\delta$ the acute angle made with the generatrix of the bore by a tangent to the groove at a given point, it follows that the pitch is constant for every section of the rifling. In progressive rifling, the pitch at any given point is the pitch that would correspond to a groove with a constant degree of twist equal to the degree of the progressive rifling at the point in question. The pitch is consequently variable, diminishing as the angle $\delta$ increases; such rifling is called "variable pitch rifling."

**rikken** An ancient Japanese term for the HOKO.

**rim** The circular ring around the bottom end of a cartridge case, made either by simply folding back the metal of which the case is made or by stamping if the metal of the base is thick. Its basic purpose is to provide a grip for the extractor, but it also serves to locate the cartridge exactly when it is pressed against the face of the breech or into a special circular groove at the mouth of the chamber.

**rim** (or **lip**) **of the guard** A swelling on the border of the shells, plate, or cup of the sword guard designed to protect the hand; it helped to block the thrust of the opponent's blade which might otherwise slide over the curved surface of the guard and wound the hand. In Spanish-type cup guards the lip was turned outward to form a groove all around the guard.

**ring guard** *See* SIDE RING.

**rod holder** In old firearms, the housing in the forestock for the ramrod, lodged underneath and parallel with the barrel.

**rolling block** Term used for the firearms obturation system patented by L. Geiger in 1863, improved by Joseph Rider and manufactured by Remington. *See also* GUN.

**romphaea** A classical Greek staff weapon of Thracian-Illyrian origin; it was more than 2 m. ($6\frac{1}{2}$ ft.) long with a large head in the form of a curved, double-edged blade (like the HARPÉ or SICA curved daggers), which was mounted on a sturdy shaft.

**rondache** A French term often used to denote a large circular TARGE. Known at least from the Bronze Age, such heavy round shields made of iron or steel were used in Europe by horsemen and men on foot until the 15th

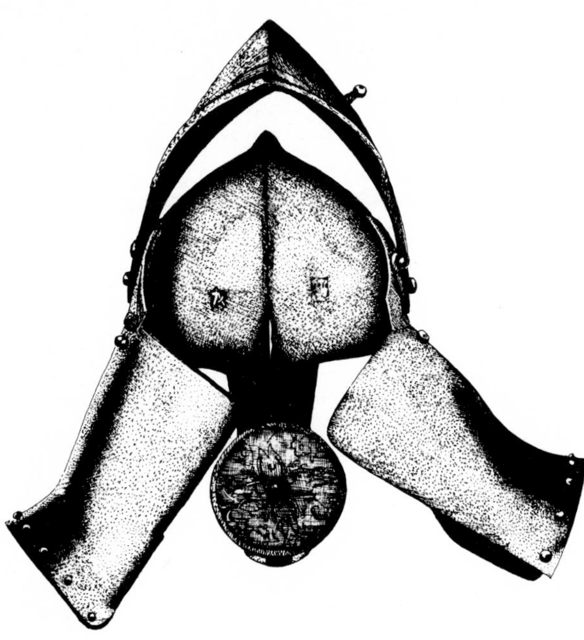

*Rondel on an armet, N. Italy, c. 1490–1500. Museo Nazionale del Bargello, Florence.*

century, when they were gradually discarded by mounted warriors but were kept in service for a few more decades by some infantry swordsmen. A steel bulletproof shield designed in the late 16th century was occasionally used even in the 17th.

In the 16th century rondaches made of wood, steel, or leather became popular as parade shields. They were richly decorated in various techniques, depending on the main material, and usually had a padded velvet lining with gold or silver embroidery and trimmings. Particularly superb rondaches were produced in Milan by great artist-craftsmen, the famous Negroli family among them.

**rondel** An accessory of certain types of helmets, especially the ARMET, consisting of a small, round iron plate attached to the neckpiece by means of a short rod. It was seldom decorated, but occasionally was cut in a decorative shape. The rondel was used from the middle of the 15th century through the first few decades of the 16th. One likely explanation of the purpose of the rondel is that it acted as an anchor for the supporting straps of the reinforcing BEVOR, which made its appearance at about the same time, as well as protecting the buckle by which the straps were fastened.

**roundel dagger** *See* DAGGER.

**rowel spurs** *See* SPURS.

**rump guard** A piece of armor worn in both foot and mounted combat to protect the buttocks, consisting of several articulated lames loosely riveted together. It extended from the waist edge of the backplate, curving around the lower back of the wearer. Also called a culet, the rump guard followed much the same evolutionary pattern as the SKIRT toward the end of the 14th century. The rump guard actually formed the rear half of the skirt and was usually fastened at the sides with hinges (generally on the left) and buckles (on the right), although press studs and holes were sometimes used as an alternative. In the 16th century the joins between the skirt and rump guard were often achieved with a waist belt.

During the second half of the 15th century, the rump guard tended to get smaller and, by the end of the century, consisted of one or two lames fewer than the front of the skirt. In the first quarter of the 16th century, its place was sometimes taken by a single lame, either straight or scalloped, projecting from the lower edge of the backplate. In the early 17th century, the full rump guard of a large size made a brief reappearance in cuirassier armor.

**runca** (or **runka**, from Italian *roncone*) English term of the 16th and 17th centuries for an Italian-made BILL.

**russeting** Also called browning, a method of coloring metal surfaces by applying various chemical solutions, according to the color desired. Armour was sometimes treated in this way, which not only gave it a striking appearance but also made it rust-resistant.

**ryo-shinogi-yari** A type of Japanese spear with a diamond-sectioned blade. *See also* YARI.

# S

**sabatons** Part of the armor protecting the feet. The earliest type were mail shoes, introduced in the Middle Ages and still being used, with minor variations, in the 15th and 16th centuries. Made from fine mail, they covered the whole of the top of the foot from the ankle to the toes and were attached with pins or rings to the mail leggings, or CHAUSSES, and, later, to the GREAVES. During the middle of the 16th century, the toe-capped mail shoe or "mail sabaton" became popular, consisting of a strip of mail over the instep and an attached small plate toe cap.

In the early 14th century, sabatons of articulated lames were introduced whose structure was to remain almost unaltered for about three centuries. A group of small, properly shaped articulated lames were clipped onto the lower edge of the greaves; a second group of lames then covered the foot and broadened out slightly to link up with a plate toe cap which fitted over the last lame. Articulation was achieved by means of rivets along the lower edges, while the lames over the instep were free to flex. The same system was applied to sabatons for greaves which terminated at the ankle instead of extending to the ground at the back and sides of the heels, with the addition of an ankle guard generally made of two hinged lames; this protection was not always present, however, and the sabatons would then have been buckled onto the greaves.

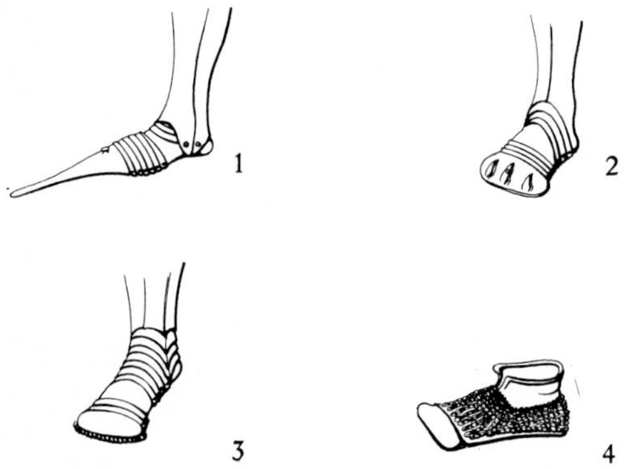

1 2 3 4

*1. Pointed sabaton, with removable point. 2. Broad sabaton. 3. Broad sabaton. 4. Mail sabaton with plate toe cap. From the* Glossarium Armorum.

Within this basic structure, a range of features can be discerned which can be categorized chronologically, especially in the styles of the toe cap. In the 15th century, the commonest type of sabaton had a short, ogival toe cap. A variation of this form, typical of the middle of the century, was the sabaton with an exaggeratedly long, pointed toe cap, often articulated along its entire length and usually detachable. Toward the end of the century, however, the toes became shorter and broader, with further variations in which the toe cap was slightly raised and considerably broader than the instep. By the end of the 1500s, the top boot had begun to replace the legharness in light-horse and cuirassier armor and the iron shoe became obsolete.

**saber** A weapon with a long, curved, single-edged blade designed for use mainly on horseback. The term, which seems to be of Slavic-Hungarian origin, was adopted by all European languages with few phonetic variants. Among the single-edged blades of the Middle Ages, the saber represented a pattern of Eastern derivation, and modern research has suggested that this weapon developed initially in regions of Central Asia. From the 9th century the saber was already used by the Slavs, who probably had adopted it from their opponents, the tribes of nomadic horsemen from the Steppes. During the same period, in northern Europe the SAX was developing into a peculiar weapon, the curved sword later known as the FALCHION.

Another European form of the saber was the *Schweizersäbel*, a variant of a BASTARD SWORD developed and used mainly in Switzerland in the 16th and 17th centuries. It had a long curved blade with a back edge and a hilt of various forms, with long recurved quillons, a ring guard, and a fairly developed knuckle guard with a main bow and several side bars. Contemporary German sabers were similarly provided with long quillons and a knuckle guard, but as additional protection they used a large shell guard covering the grip and, from the late 16th century, various forms of the basket hilt. Some of these weapons were nicknamed "Sinclair" sabers in the 19th century because of a resemblance of their hilts to those of typical Scottish broadswords (G. Sinclair was a colonel in a Scottish mercenary force destroyed in Norway in 1612).

The popularity of the saber in central and eastern Europe, particularly from the 16th century, was enhanced by the fact that German fencing schools were developing

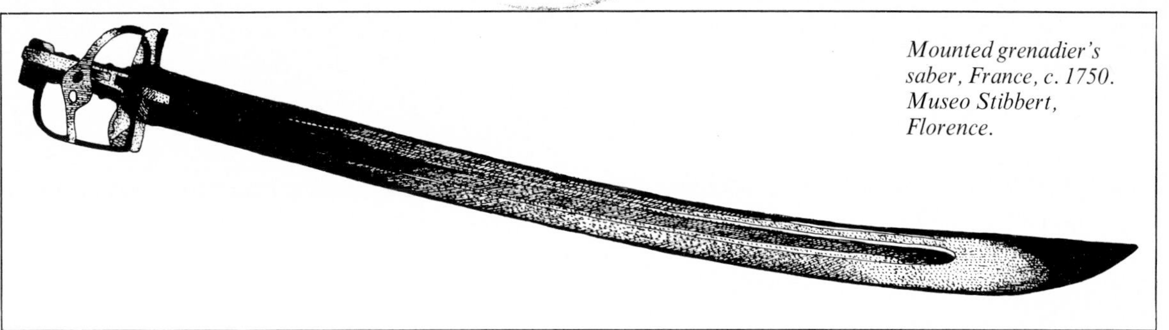

*Mounted grenadier's saber, France, c. 1750. Museo Stibbert, Florence.*

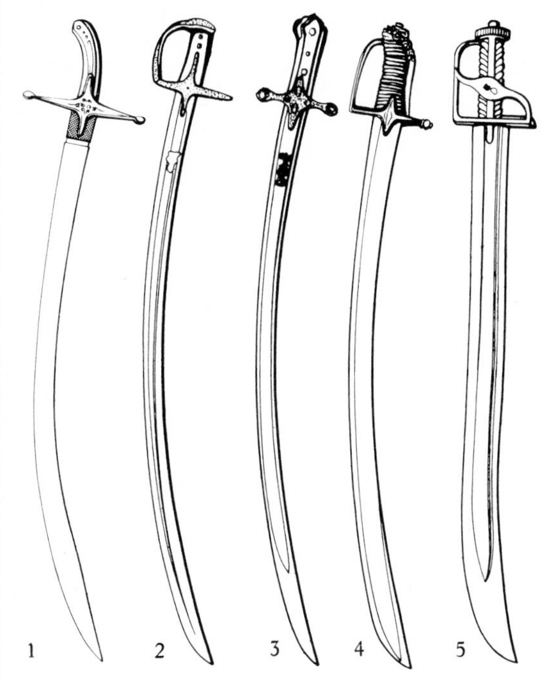


*Sabers. 1. With Turkish-type blade* (kilij), *Sweden, late 16th or 17th century. 2. Batorowka type, Poland, 17th century. 3. Karabela type, Poland, first half of the 18th century. 4. Hussar's saber, Austria, mid-18th century. 5. Mounted grenadier's saber, France, 18th century.*

*The saber of honor presented to Viceroy of Italy Eugène de Beauharnais, Milan, c. 1806. Musée de l'Armée, Paris.*

special training methods for this weapon using a practice saber, the *Düsack*, which later evolved into the infantry soldier's hanger (hence the Russian loan word *tessak* for this weapon in the 18th and 19th centuries).

The great Turkish invasions in the 16th century made the saber of Turkish form, the KILIJ, very popular, though the period of its greatest distribution came toward the end of the 17th century. Its influence remained undisturbed up to the end of the 18th century, that is, until Napoleon's troops, on their return from the Egyptian campaign, spread the word about the Persian version, the SHAMSHIR or scimitar, which had a considerably more curved blade with an elongated point. Still, the influence of the Turkish weapon lasted for a much longer period, at least as far as Europe was concerned.

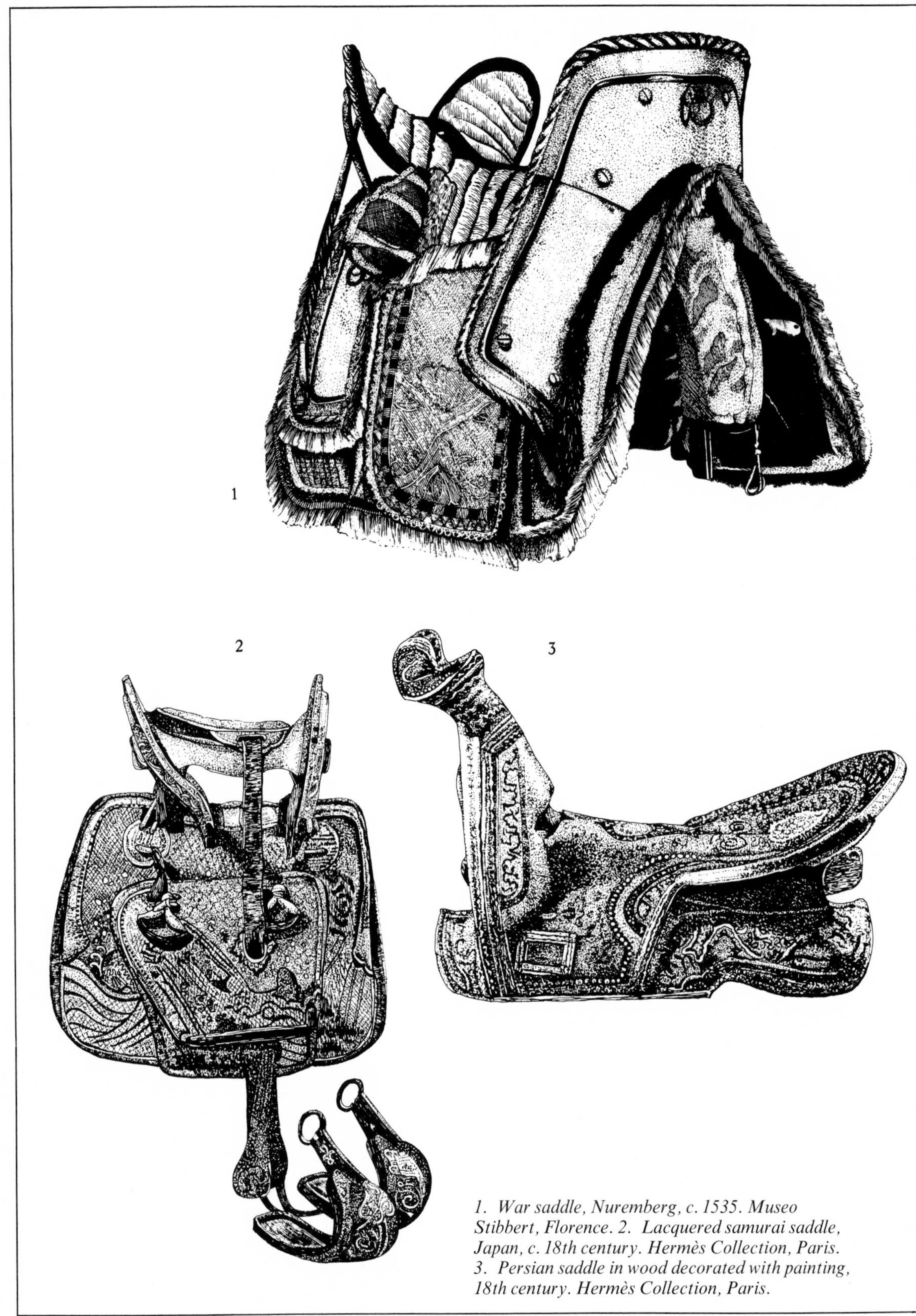


*1. War saddle, Nuremberg, c. 1535. Museo Stibbert, Florence. 2. Lacquered samurai saddle, Japan, c. 18th century. Hermès Collection, Paris. 3. Persian saddle in wood decorated with painting, 18th century. Hermès Collection, Paris.*

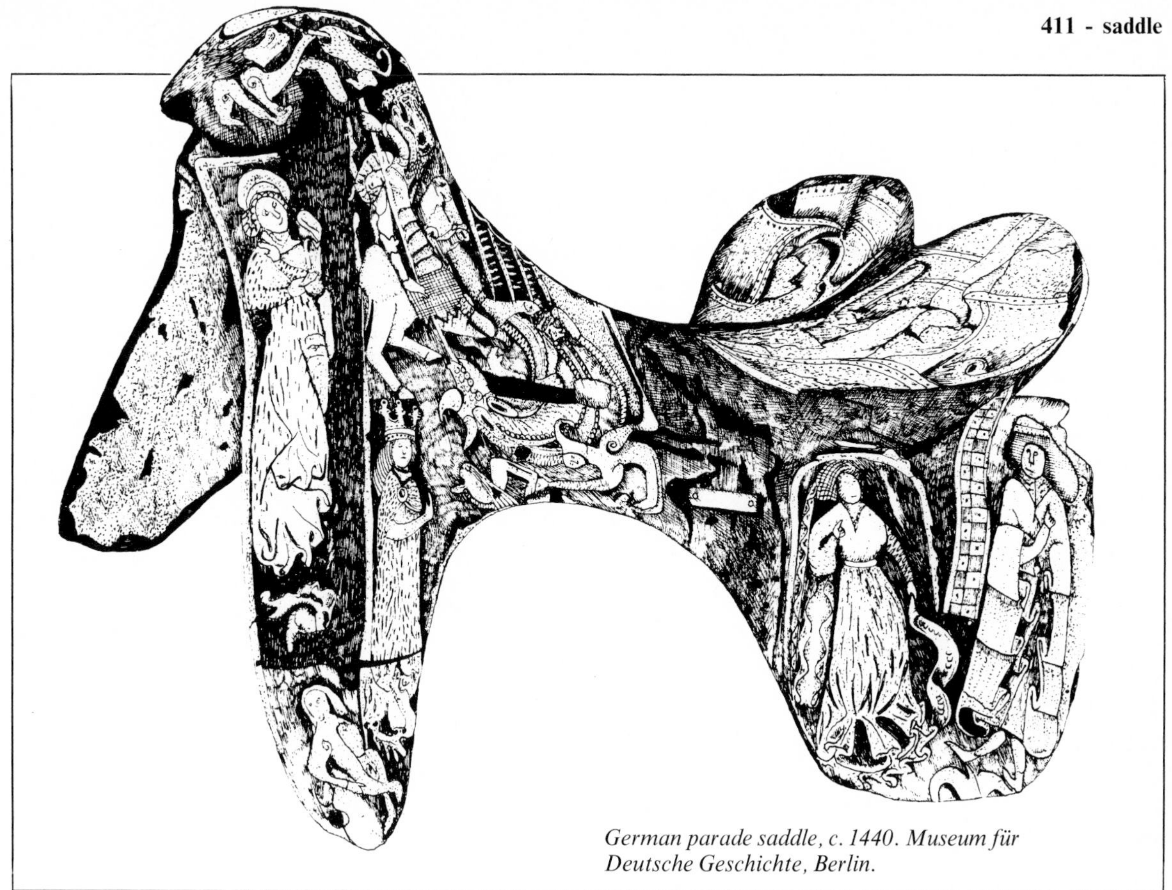

*German parade saddle, c. 1440. Museum für Deutsche Geschichte, Berlin.*

Little by little the saber became the main edged weapon of European light cavalry and virtually a symbol of the Hussars; by the mid-19th century it was issued to almost all mounted troops.

A peculiar kind of saber, the SHASHKA, was developed in the Caucasus; it had a grip without a guard, which partly entered the sheath. The blade was fairly curved, single-edged with a back edge, and often with a broad central fuller which ran almost to the tip.

Many European sabers made from the 17th century on were fitted with Middle Eastern blades, often of a high quality. Some military regulations did not forbid this if the outward appearance of the sheathed weapon was kept in line with a formal pattern.

The term "saber" is now also applied to a fencing cut-and-thrust weapon with a large closed hilt, although its blade is not curved, being rather a very light version of the PALLASCH blade.

**saddle** The part of a complete horse harness on which the rider normally sat—although some forms of tilting saddles were specifically made to keep him in a standing position. In most saddles the main feature was—as it still is—the seat, often padded, forming a kind of valley between the front bow, known as the front ARSON, and the hind arson, or cantle, which helped to steady the horseman and prevent him from falling. The whole structure—which has changed little in Europe during the last thousand years—was made on a wooden framework, the saddletree (usually of beechwood), often reinforced at the front by a steel gullet plate and covered in pigskin or cowhide. On the underside of the saddle were well-stuffed panels lined with linen, serge, or leather. A cloth was usually placed over the horse's back before saddling up, and a wide strap, the "girth" or "surcingle"—already buckled onto the underside of the saddle on the left—passed under its belly and buckled securely on the right. Stirrup leathers, to which the stirrup irons were attached, were then hooked through their supporting bars, and accessories such as a saddlebag or lance bucket were attached, according to the type of equipment used. It was often the custom, especially in the 18th and 19th centuries, to cover the whole saddle in rich fabrics and elaborate trimmings such as braid or fringe.

From the late 15th century, special saddles were brought into use for the joust, particularly in the Germanic countries. In addition to the war saddle (see below), which was the most widely used, there were several types of tilting saddles, including the "high" saddle with its elevated front bow which was linked by straps to the rear bow, and the "large-bowed" saddle with its broad, flat seat and very high, often elaborate front bow which gave protection to the contestant from his chest down to his legs. These two variations, while providing excellent frontal protection, did not trap the rider between the two bows, as some styles did, and was thus particularly suitable for the German joust, in which it was preferable to be unseated by the violent impact of an opponent's lance than to meet it in a position of unyielding rigidity, with every probability of a resulting broken back.

In the steel or war saddle, used during the 16th century and first half of the 17th in both the field and the joust, the main features were its high, plated front and hind arsons. In a full bard it was placed between the CRINET and the CRUPPER and was sometimes equipped with sabaton stirrup irons and a laminated curb rein.

**safety catch** A device which, when applied, prevents accidental discharge of a firearm. In modern weapons the safety catch generally acts on the striker or the hammer.

**saguntine spear** *See* FALARICA.

**saker** A 12-pounder culverin used from the end of the 15th century to the end of the 17th. According to Robert Norton (*The Gunner*, London, 1628), the saker was a gun 12 ft. (3.7 m.) long which threw iron balls weighing between 5 and 5½ lbs. (2.5 kg.).

**sàkos** The typical early Greek shield, referred to in Homer's *Iliad*, forerunner of the ASPÍS.

**sallet** A type of helmet used from about 1430 to the end of the 15th century, with a few known examples appearing even later. The basic form consisted of a rounded skull, curving in and out again at the nape of the neck to form a small tail. As the sallet afforded protection only to the head and upper part of the face, leaving the chin uncovered, a BEVOR was usually worn with it. Made from a single piece of iron, the sallet was provided with holes, pierced on a line corresponding to the base of the wearer's skull, for attaching the lining. The skull generally had a low keel-shaped comb, pierced at the top with a keyhole slot for a crest holder.

There was a distinct difference between the Italian and German style of sallet, although this did not necessarily relate to their source of origin. The skull of the Italian-style sallet was hemispherical, with a comb, the tail continuing the line of the skull. In the second half of the 15th century, the tail was sometimes made of one or more lames on loose rivets, fixed by pivots to the lower edge of the skull. About this period, a BROW REINFORCE, often with cusped upper edges, was usually attached to the helmet. This was either fixed or movable.

A little later, about 1490, another version was introduced—or earlier helmets transformed into it. This sallet was provided with a so-called bellows visor, made with reinforcing horizontal ridges and flutings; the visor protected the whole of the face and was pivoted to each side of the brow. This type of sallet, with the addition of the pivoted bevor, was to evolve into various types of CLOSE HELMETS. Another style of sallet, which probably originated about 1430 in Italy, had a long one-piece tail and was fitted with a movable visor. Sallets of this form were used both in Italy and Germany up to the late 15th century.

The German-style sallet had a slightly flattened skull with a well-defined comb ending in a straight line over the brow. The tail was very pronounced and sloped outward, while the sides of the skull, continuing the line of the tail, extended to cover the face to the chin; an eye slit with ridged edges was made in these fairly deep skulls.

The second half of the 15th century saw the introduction of the "visored sallet," a modification of the Italian style with the addition of a short pivoted visor which gave this helmet the appearance of a German sallet. A variation of this is described in modern terminology as a "black sallet." This, too, had a movable visor with a double eye slit. The skull, flattish on top, extended straight to the point of the tail, instead of curving to the shape of the head, while the lower edge followed a convex curve. The black sallet was so called because it usually had a rough unpolished surface, which was sometimes painted or covered with fabric; it was chiefly used by men-at-arms, and the workmanship was generally shoddy.

The sallet was usually of plain metal, although it was sometimes russeted. A few extant examples have light etched or engraved gilded ornamentation, and it was quite common for the rivet heads and visor pivots to be chiseled.

The so-called Venetian style was merely the transformation of a sallet by covering it in velvet with decorative metal mountings, such parade modifications often being added long after the battlefield lifetime of the helmet. Fifteenth-century documents relating to the dukes of Burgundy contain references to sallets decorated with silver mountings—which can clearly be seen, for example, in the reliquary of Charles the Bold in Liège Cathedral. In various museums are Venetian parade sallets profusely decorated with embossed and gilded bronze mountings; some helmets are crested with the Lion of St. Mark as well.

The sallet virtually disappeared from field armor toward the end of the 15th century, only certain special forms being retained for jousting, such as the sallet for the German course (*Rennen*), derived from the German-style sallet.

**samé** The skin of various types of rays and small sharks used in Japan to cover the hilts and scabbards of swords and other weapons. Sword handles have been covered with fishskin since ancient times, and the custom is mentioned in a number of very old Chinese writings. The various types of rays found in the surrounding seas, such as the *Rhinobatus armatus*, *R. granulatus*, and *R. schlegelli*, have skin that is densely covered with a calcareous material in rounded tubercles. This is particularly hard-wearing, clings to the hand, and is very attractive in appearance. Another variety of ray is the *Urogymnus asperrimus*, whose skin is especially sought after since it possesses all these qualities to an exceptional degree.

The quality of samé is judged according to its color and the size of its protuberances. Although white, bluish-white, yellow, reddish-yellow, gray, and black samé each has its specific name, classification also depends on the shape and distribution of the grain, the larger nodules being more valuable. Originally the preparation of samé for sword furniture was in the hands of the scabbard-makers, but it later became a separate trade and specialists in the craft were called *sameshi*. The fishskin was first softened in water, scrubbed with a bamboo brush until its true color was obtained, and then lined with slips of willow. Great care was taken to ensure that the grain was evenly distributed over the handle, thin wood packing being inserted at the back where needed. The skin was then

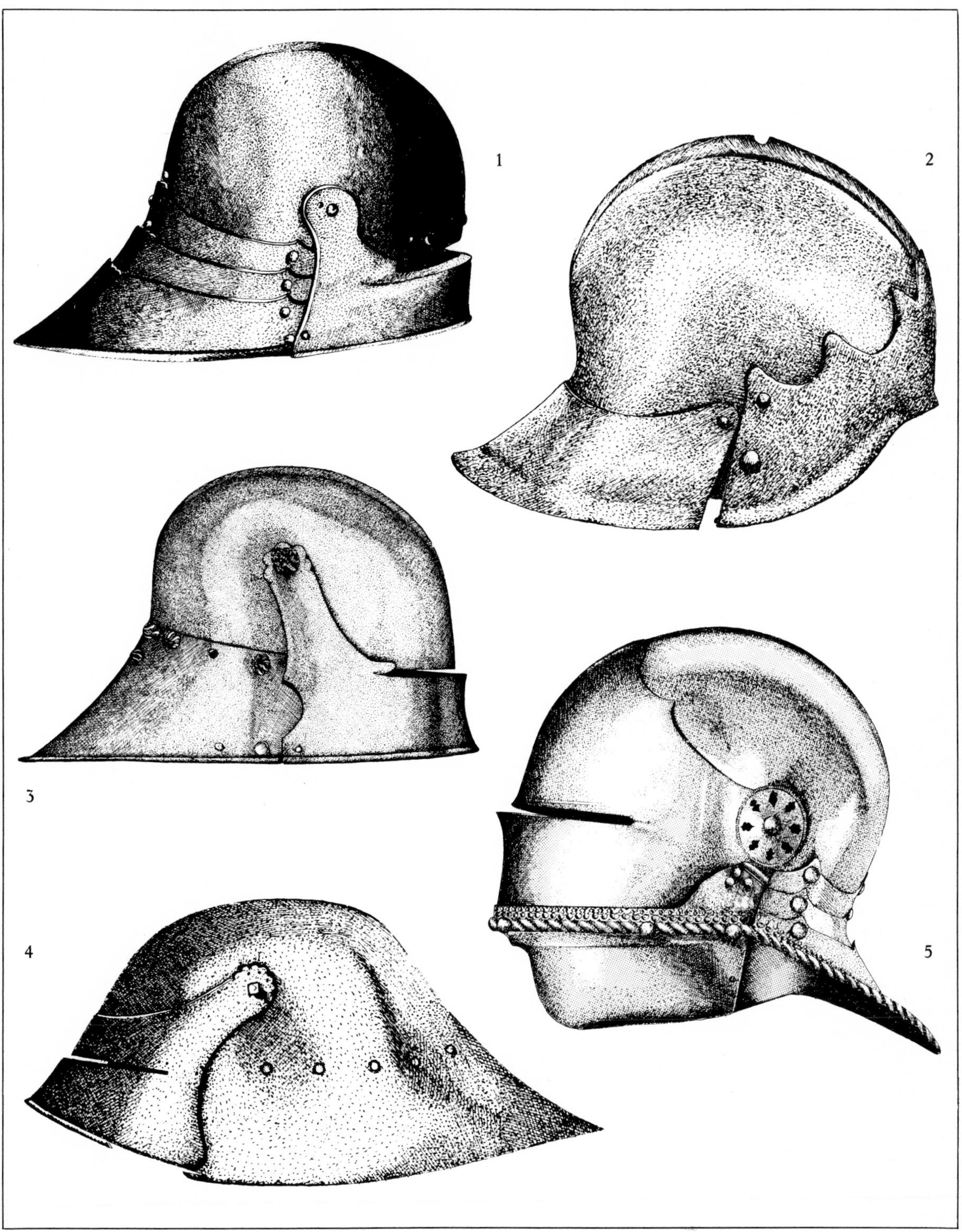


*1. Sallet with pivoted visor and laminated tail, by Kaspar Rieder, Innsbruck, c. 1490–95. Waffensammlung, Vienna. 2. Sallet with tail and brow reinforcement, N. Italy, end of the 15th century. Odescalchi Collection, Museo di Palazzo Venezia, Rome. 3. Sallet with pivoted visor, Augsburg, c. 1490. Odescalchi Collection, Museo di Palazzo Venezia, Rome. 4. Sallet with pivoted visor, Germany, c. 1500. Odescalchi Collection, Museo di Palazzo Venezia, Rome. 5. Sallet with pivoted visor and a bevor for foot combat, belonging to Emperor Maximilian I, Augsburg, 1492. Waffensammlung, Vienna.*

polished to bring out its luster.

For covering scabbards, the skin was often lacquered black or green and the tops of the nodules ground down to give them the appearance of ivory. This kind of work is known as "inlaid ivory." Particularly good samé, sometimes mounted on wood and framed in brocade, was made for use as presentation pieces or to sell. Attempts were often made to sell imitation samé, and special tests were devised to discover such forgeries.

**sammai-kabuto** A type of Japanese helmet. *See also* KABUTO.

**sang de dez** French term for CINQUEDEA.

**sankaku-yari** A Japanese spear with a blade triangular in section. *See also* YARI.

**sapara** The Assyrian bronze sword, which may well be described as one of the oldest types of sabers. A unique specimen of the sapara can be seen in the Metropolitan Museum of Art in New York. The single-edged blade of this sapara is straight for about one-third its length below the hilt and then strongly curved, the cutting edge being convex. The blade is decorated with an engraved symbol of a horned animal and cuneiform writing. Of the handle, only the tang has survived; this is of bronze in one piece with the blade, leaning slightly toward the cutting edge, narrow in the grip and widening toward the pommel with a beaklike protrusion.

**sarisa** (or **sarissa**) A type of infantry spear, characteristic of the Macedonian phalanx and similar to that used by other peoples inhabiting the coast of Pontus. This exceptionally long pole arm—its shaft measured about 5–7 m. (16–24 ft.)—played an important role in many battles and achieved lasting fame following the victories by the Macedonian armies led by Philip II and Alexander the Great in the 4th century B.C. It had a short, leaf-shaped iron head and a shoe which could be plunged into the ground to help withstand the impact of an attack. Sometimes there was a point at each end. Normally sarisa were held vertically, with the head uppermost, until the moment before contact of the phalanx with the enemy, when they were lowered in one quick movement, to confront the foe with a veritable iron hedge, sixteen ranks deep. It has been calculated that the sarisa must have weighed over 5.5 kg. (12 lbs.).

**sashimono** A Japanese device worn on the back as a badge to indicate under which feudal lord a man was serving. The lord himself would wear a large sashimono on which his personal emblem, the *mon*, was displayed, while that worn by his retainers would be a smaller version of it. The sashimono consisted of a small rectangular flag on a thin bamboo pole, with a short rod set at right angles at the top to keep the fabric stretched out to assist identification. The sashimono was attached to the samurai's cuirass by means of short metal sockets at the small of the back and a loop between the shoulders. It was introduced in Japan after 1573, in the Momoyama period, and was used until the Meiji Restoration in the mid-19th century.

This device was also used in China during the Ming Dynasty (1368–1644), mainly as an aid for keeping soldiers in formation while marching or attacking.

**sasumata** A Japanese spear, also called *futomato-yari* (*see* YARI), with a forked (or, occasionally, crescent-shaped) head, rather like a pitchfork but with blades instead of prongs. The head was attached to the lacquered shaft, which was about 2.5 m. (8 ft.) long, by means of a narrow tang and secured by a peg. There were sometimes barbs near the head, and binding around the shaft acted as a grip to prevent the hand from slipping. The sasumata was widely used as a weapon in the 16th century, but by the late Tokugawa (Edo) period (1603–1867) it was being used mainly as a piece of fire-fighting equipment.

**saunion** Greek term for VERUTUM.

**sauroter** A generic ancient Greek term that describes the SHOE of a hafted weapon. It was normally conical, ending in a sharp point, cylindrical or polygonal, made of bronze or iron, and often heavy in order to counterbalance the weight of the head. The fact that the sauroter was often very long and conical suggests that it was itself used as a weapon; in effect, if the thrusting head were sheared off, by reversing the shaft the tip of the shoe would provide the combatant with a substitute weapon. The length of the sauroter was proportionate to the length of the head of the weapon, but invariably shorter.

**sax** A large war knife with a blade having a straight back, a single cutting edge, and a point of varying shape. In many cases the grip was set slightly to the rear, toward the back of the blade. Its size varied a great deal, ranging from that of a dagger (about 30–40 cm./12–16 in.) to that of a sword (85–100 cm./33–40 in.). This large knife—which in regions north of the Alps was used as a domestic implement, a weapon of war (*see* SCRAMASAX), and, according to some experts, as a throwing weapon—derived from a very similar weapon made of bronze and widely used in the Hallstatt period (900–500 B.C.) and then in the La Tène culture (from 500 B.C. to the beginning of

*Several examples of sashimono.*

the Christian era) in an iron version. It was one of the national weapons of the Saxons, who at the time of the migrations (4th–6th centuries) carried it in a sheath on their left side and, at least up until the early Middle Ages, alongside the sword. Examples have been unearthed in the warrior tombs of various Germanic peoples, which clearly shows its wide distribution.

With the advent of cavalry, the large sax disappeared from the warrior's armament and was relegated to the tasks of a domestic implement; the smallest type became a knife which, together with the sword and the spear, was part of the horseman's weaponry in the field. In an intermediate version it survived throughout the Middle Ages as a hunting knife.

**saya** The scabbard of a Japanese sword or the sheath of a dagger, nearly always made of wood—preferably magnolia (*honoki*) wood—although occasionally metal was used with a magnolia lining. The saya was generally lacquered, its mountings in keeping with those on the hilt. A silken cord, passing through a slotted projection, the *kurikata*, on the side of the scabbard, secured the sword in the girdle. The TACHI and some small daggers, however, had no kurikata. Other fittings consisted of the *koiguchi kanagu*, a locket forming the top mount; the *uragawara*, a strip of horn or metal protecting the opening for the KOZUKA; the *soritsuno*, a hook below the kurikata to keep the scabbard from being pulled through the belt when the weapon was drawn; and the *kojiri*, a chape. Ornamental MENUKI were also sometimes attached to the scabbards.

One sword often had several saya: a plain case of natural wood in which the blade was kept when not in use; a simply mounted saya for everyday wear; a plain, iron-clad one for war; and an ornate one for ceremonial occasions. Each one had a corresponding hilt. Double scabbards also existed, one fitting inside the other; the reason for this was that when a blade had to be reground a new inner saya could be made to fit it and the more costly outer one reused.

**sayf** Both a general term for the sword in the Arab world and a name for a characteristic type of saber created by the Arabs, closely resembling the NIMCHA of Morocco. There are various types of sayf blades, often imported from other countries. The most frequent type has a curved, fairly short blade, about 65–75 cm. (26–30 in.) long, with a back edge and one or two grooves along the back. The very distinctive hilt is made of ivory or horn, with a large hooked pommel tilted forward and having the shape of a lion's head. When ivory is used, it is usually ornamented with decorated brass studs. Occasionally there is a knuckle guard; but more often the hilt is open, with a cross guard extending two langets over the blade and two langets over the grip.

The scabbard is covered with leather and mounted in brass or silver, and there are rings in the locket or band for attaching to the belt.

**scabbard** A rigid sheath made of wood, metal, or leather—often *cuir-bouilli* (hardened leather)—used to

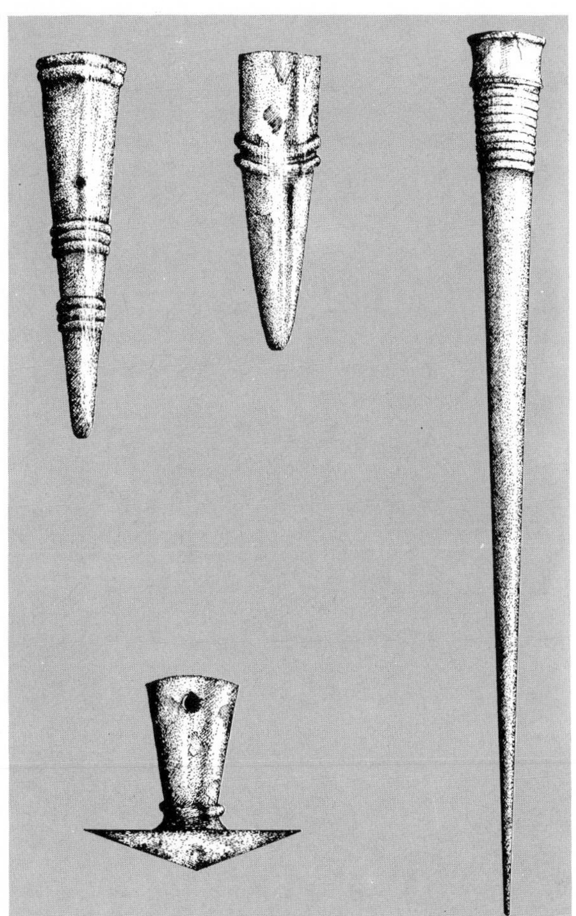

*Sauroter. Shoes for Etrusco-Italic hafted weapons.*

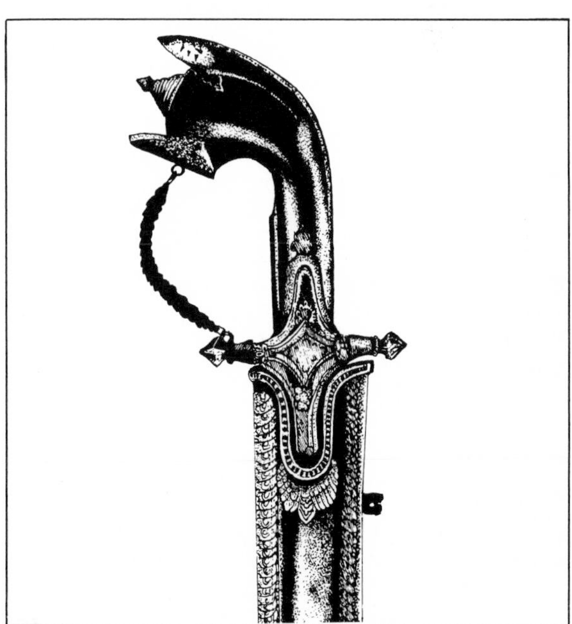

*Sayf (saber). Arab, 18th century. Kunstsammlungen der Veste, Coburg, West Germany.*

enclose and carry the blade of an edged weapon, both to protect the wearer and to keep the blade clean and sound. In the protohistoric period it was often made with plaques of cast bronze; later it was made with small wooden plaques which were covered with leather or fabric and then fitted with bindings and metal mounts. The edged weapon has always been something of a status symbol, and the scabbard was therefore of great importance to keep the weapon in good order.

The ways in which scabbards have been made down the ages vary a great deal, but they have been generally simple for weapons of war, and richly decorated and ornate for weapons carried by leaders and princes, and for presentation and ceremonial weapons. The scabbard was also the part of the weapon on which artistic skills could best be expressed. Metal mounts were often decorated with engraving, niello, gilt and other techniques, and the large surfaces covered with hide or colored fabrics.

**scales** Small metal plates used from classical antiquity to make up a type of armor. They were usually shaped like tiny shields and were sometimes ridged to make them more rigid. Scales were sewn onto the supporting material—leather or cloth—in such a way that they overlapped one another at the edges like roof tiles or, occasionally, were interspaced in rows.

**schiavona** Italian term (meaning "Slavonic") for a sword with a distinctive basket hilt, peculiar to the Slavonian corps whose task was to act as bodyguards to the Doge, until the end of the Venetian Republic in 1797. Back in the 15th century Slavic mercenaries from the Balkans had fought for Venice, and their loyalty was unswerving throughout the centuries.

In its earliest form the schiavona had a pommel made almost invariably of bronze or brass, in the shape of a cat's head with a central boss on each side. The grip was usually made of wood, wound around with cord or twine in broad loops and usually covered with leather, often gilded. In some cases the loops were of wire and overlaid the leather binding. The guard, arms of the hilt, and straight rear quillon all extended from the quillon block. A series of side bars, going from the knuckle guard to the rear quillon, and the arms of the hilt on both sides of the hilt offered good protection to the hand. As time passed, the bars of the guard increased in number until they formed a "basket."

Schiavona blades had various places of origin: Italy, Germany, Spain. The blade was usually double-edged and pointed, often with one or more fullers. The use of the ribbed saber blade was rare and usually of a later date. The swords which have survived do not usually date back beyond the 16th century, but even this dating has not been unanimously agreed upon, especially with regard to certain obviously older examples. We know that the swords called *schiavone* were in use as early as the late 15th century from a chronicle which refers to incidents which occurred during the 1493 carnival in Rome.

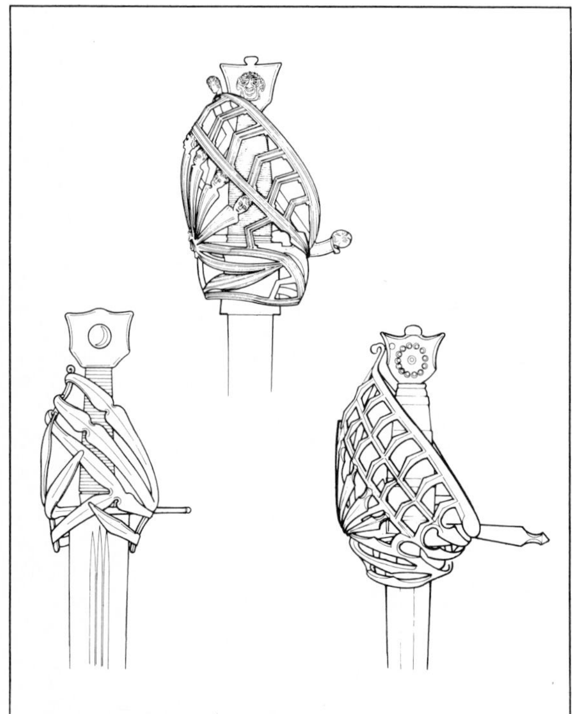

*Various types of schiavone from the 17th and 18th centuries.*

**schläger** A German term for a special cutting sword used in *Mensur*, a type of personal combat popular among German university students. The Schläger, developed in the 19th century from basket-hilted broadswords, was a light type of the PALLASCH, with a straight blade sharpened on both edges near the point only. The point itself was rounded, making thrusts impossible. The guard was of basket type, padded inside, and decorated with the colors of the student's college.

**schynbalds** (or **shynbalds**) *See* GREAVES.

**scimitar** An obsolete general term derived from the Persian SHAMSHIR and used to describe Middle Eastern and Oriental-looking sabers with a strongly curved blade gradually tapering to a sharp point.

**scouring stick** (or **rod**) *See* RAMROD.

**scramasax** A term used for the first time by Gregory of Tours (6th century), and later in various Visigoth legislative documents which list weapons and include the scramasax among the weapons issued to warriors. The etymology of the word (*scrama*, causing injury, and *sax*, [war] knife) suggests that it was a particularly offensive type of SAX. But the precise meaning of the term is unclear.

**scutum** A Latin term denoting the large, long shield, rectangular or oval, whose Italic origin is extensively documented in the art and literature of the period. The scutum was used by the Romans from the beginning of their monarchy in the 8th century B.C., although it probably had already been widespread in central Italy for a long time. The first scuti were made of wood or woven osier (wickerwork) reinforced by a central spine of wood which broadened toward the middle to form an UMBO, which was usually circular. From the end of the 8th century B.C. the scutum coexisted in the Roman soldier's equipment with the Greek-derived CLIPEUS, which was to disappear almost completely toward the beginning of the

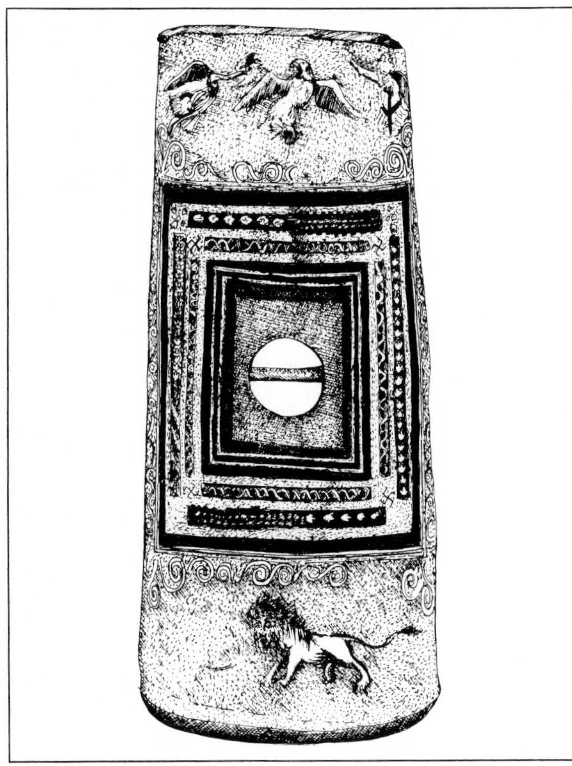

*Scutum of a Roman legionnaire, second half of the 2nd century* A.D., *discovered at Dura Europos (Mesopotamia). Yale University Collection.*

4th century B.C. The oval scutum thus became the classic shield of the Roman heavy infantry. From the Greek historian Polybius (c. 205–120 B.C.) we know that the usual specifications of this shield at that time were about 120 cm. (47 in.) in length and 75 cm. (30 in.) in width, with the typical longitudinal spine and metal umbo.

In the 2nd or 1st century B.C., the characteristic rectangular shield—which was semicylindrical to protect the body from neck to knees—was adopted as part of the legionnaires' defensive equipment. This is believed to have derived from a type of shield which had already been in use for centuries by the Samnites and was, in fact, known as the "Samnite shield." The rectangular scutum was made of one or more pieces of wood covered with leather and reinforced with a squared umbo with a hemispherical protuberance at the center, corresponding to the position of the handle. The handle was positioned in the center of the shield where a large opening was made, and a horizontal wooden rod passed across the opening to serve as a grip on the inside; the hand was, of course, protected by the metal umbo. These constructional details are well known because a unique specimen of a scutum has survived almost intact. It was found during archeological excavations in the Mesopotamian city of Dura Europos, on the outer border of the Roman Empire, and is datable to the second half of the 2nd century A.D.

The field and umbo of these shields often carried various types of decorative motifs; the scuti intended for parades were heavily ornamented, while those for combat were simpler and bore the emblems and colours of the legions to which they belonged.

The rectangular scutum, apart from being carried as a frontal defense, was also used to form the *testudo* (a word meaning "tortoise" and "tortoiseshell"), a formation in which the legionnaires held the scuti over their heads in such a way that they overlapped to form a movable screen or shell when attacking fortified positions.

The rectangular scutum gradually disappeared during the late Roman Empire. From the 3rd or 4th century A.D. the only shield used by the Romans seems to have been the oval type, which remained in use until the fall of the empire in western Europe (A.D. 476).

**scythe** An agricultural tool which was often used as a staff weapon, especially with the blade mounted vertically on the haft. It was a weapon popular among peasants, since it was easily converted by village smiths from the implement. The Poles successfully used such weapons as late as 1920 against the invading Soviet troops. The scythe with a pivoting blade, which could be locked in either position, was invented in France about 1740 for use by the army's foraging parties.

**secrète** *See* STEEL SKULL.

**securis** Latin term for the BIPENNIS.

**self-loading firearms** Semiautomatic and automatic weapons which utilize either the recoil or explosive gases to extract the case and to chamber the next round. *See also* GUN: semiautomatic and automatic rifles; MACHINE GUN; PISTOL; SUBMACHINE GUN.

**semiautomatic firearms** Guns and pistols which utilize either the recoil or explosive gases to extract the case and to chamber the next round, but requiring a pull of the trigger for each shot (while fully automatic weapons are able to fire as long as the trigger is pressed and there is ammunition in the magazine). Quite often semiautomatic pistols are incorrectly referred to as automatics. *See also* GUN: semiautomatic and automatic rifles; PISTOL.

**seppa dai** The surrounding collar of the TSUBA.

**serpentine** A mechanical device forming part of the matchlock (*see* IGNITION). It consisted of a lever in the form of an elongated Z or S, hinged at the middle to the stock or lock plate of the weapon and holding a piece of slow match at the top end. When the lower part of the lever was pressed up toward the body, the end holding the match was lowered toward the vent. The first picture of a matchlock is in a German manuscript of 1411, now in Vienna; it shows a lock of this type on a handgun. The match is held in a vertical hole at the top of the lever. It may well be that the idea of this system of ignition, simple but effective, was suggested by the release mechanism of the crossbows of the same period, which was in some ways similar.

**set trigger** *See* HAIR TRIGGER.

**sfendone** Greek term for the FUNDA.

**shaffron** (also **chamfron**, **chanfron**) The part of a full BARD or of a light bard that protected and decorated a horse's forehead and face. Although well known in ancient Greece, the shaffron made of metal plates was not used in Europe for many centuries until it reappeared after the

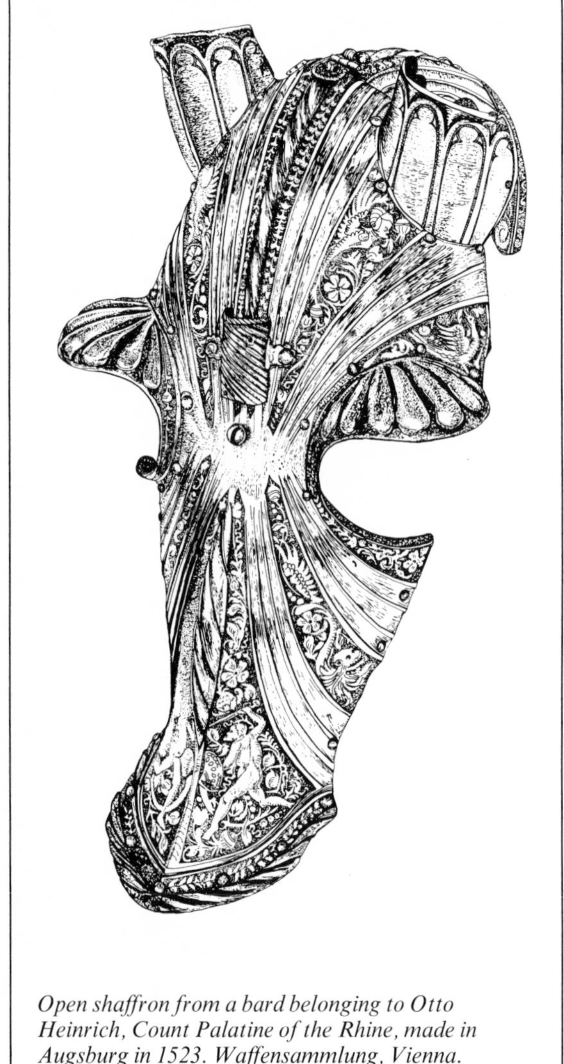

*Open shaffron from a bard belonging to Otto Heinrich, Count Palatine of the Rhine, made in Augsburg in 1523. Waffensammlung, Vienna.*

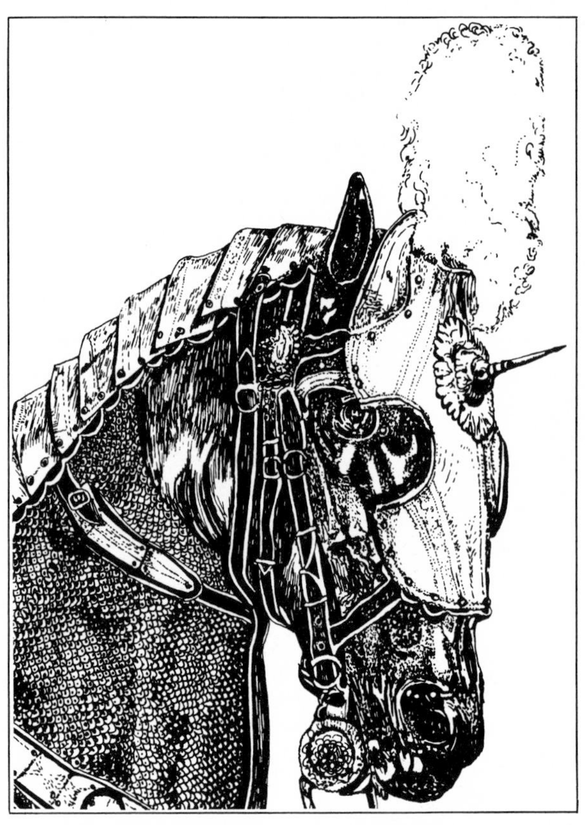

*Half-shaffron with spiked boss, Nuremberg, 16th century. Museo Stibbert, Florence.*

12th century, headstalls having previously been of mail or plates of *cuir-bouilli.*

The shaffron, having regained its importance in the early 16th century, did not change its definitive structure before becoming obsolete in the mid-17th century. It consisted of a plate contoured to the horse's forehead and face, from its ears to its nostrils, and was shaped around the edges to follow its facial contours. Normally two holes were cut at each side of the forehead for the ears, and earpieces were sometimes riveted around their edges. At the lower end, the nostril guards were roughly shaped to the outline of the muzzle. At each side of the face there were either holes for the eyes, which were often protected by shaped, overhanging flanges, or the edges of the shaffron itself were cut away at eye level, and these openings, too, were protected by special flanges. This type of shaffron is known as an "open shaffron."

In war or tournament bard, riveted or hinged extension plates were often incorporated to cover the cheeks (jowls). At the center of the shaffron's forehead a rondel or shield was nearly always superimposed, behind which a plume pipe was often concealed; this shield served a protective as well as decorative purpose, and there was frequently a spike projecting from the middle of it. The shield often bore the coat of arms of the owner.

The neck lame was usually incorporated with the shaffron and made of the same material. This was generally metal, but *cuir-bouilli* or leather was also used. The neck lame protected the top of the head and connected the shaffron with the CRINET.

In light bard, only the forehead and face to just below the horse's eyes were covered by a piece of armor, known as a "half-shaffron."

The shaffron was regarded, decoratively, as an integral part of a horse harness and a GARNITURE, and was certainly one of the most important pieces in parade and tournament trappings. The ornamental patterns were those normally seen on contemporary armor, and the artist-craftsman generally exercised all his skills in making the shaffron an outstandingly beautiful and ornate feature.

**shakudō** A Japanese copper alloy used extensively for sword mountings and other decorative metalwork. After being chemically pickled it becomes either bluish-black or deep velvety black. Although usually composed of 30 parts

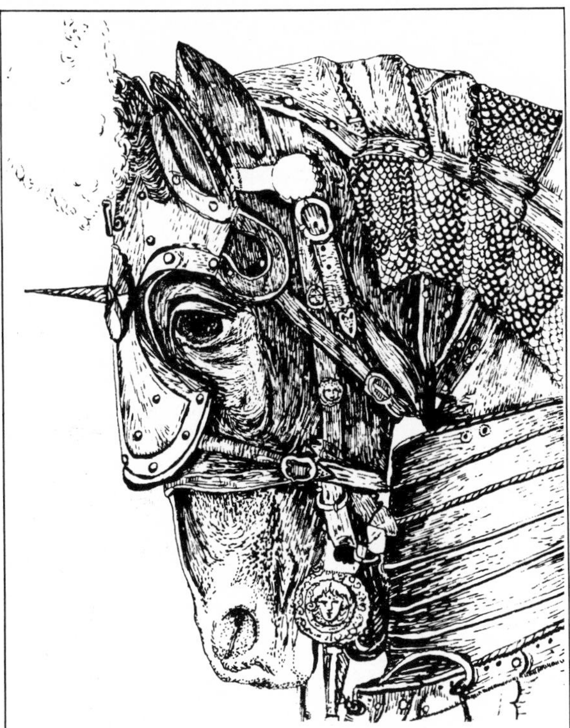

*Rondel with spiked boss on a half-shaffron, N. Italy, 16th century. Museo Stibbert, Florence.*

antimony, 7 of gold, and 100 of copper, its make-up varies a great deal.

**shakujō-yari** A type of disguised Japanese spear used mainly by mendicant priests or by samurai when traveling on secret missions. The normal pilgrim's staff was furnished at the top with a metal fitting with three interlocking rings, but on the shakujō-yari this was removable, since it really served as a sheath for a SU-YARI.

**shamshir** A generic Persian term for the saber, conventionally used in modern times to denote sabers of certain types. The Latin *simiterra*, French *cimeterre*, and English "scimitar" probably derive from this Persian name, which literally means "lion's tail." The shamshir blade has, in fact, a very pronounced curve somewhat resembling the tail of this royal animal which was prominent in Persian heraldry. The blade is straight from the hilt but, just over halfway to the point, it curves back to give a perfect line for the draw cut. It is usually made of high-grade watered steel, the quality of which is vital to the weapon's efficiency, and its weight, shape, and length are also important factors. The weapon has to be perfectly balanced, since its power in administering a blow largely depends upon its center of gravity. The shamshir blade is long, about 76–89 cm. (30–35 in.), and narrow but rather thick and heavy. It is of almost the same width from the hilt to the foible, where it tapers to a point, while the back is slightly rounded.

The flat blade of the Shamshir is rarely fullered or decorated except with an occasional inscription and

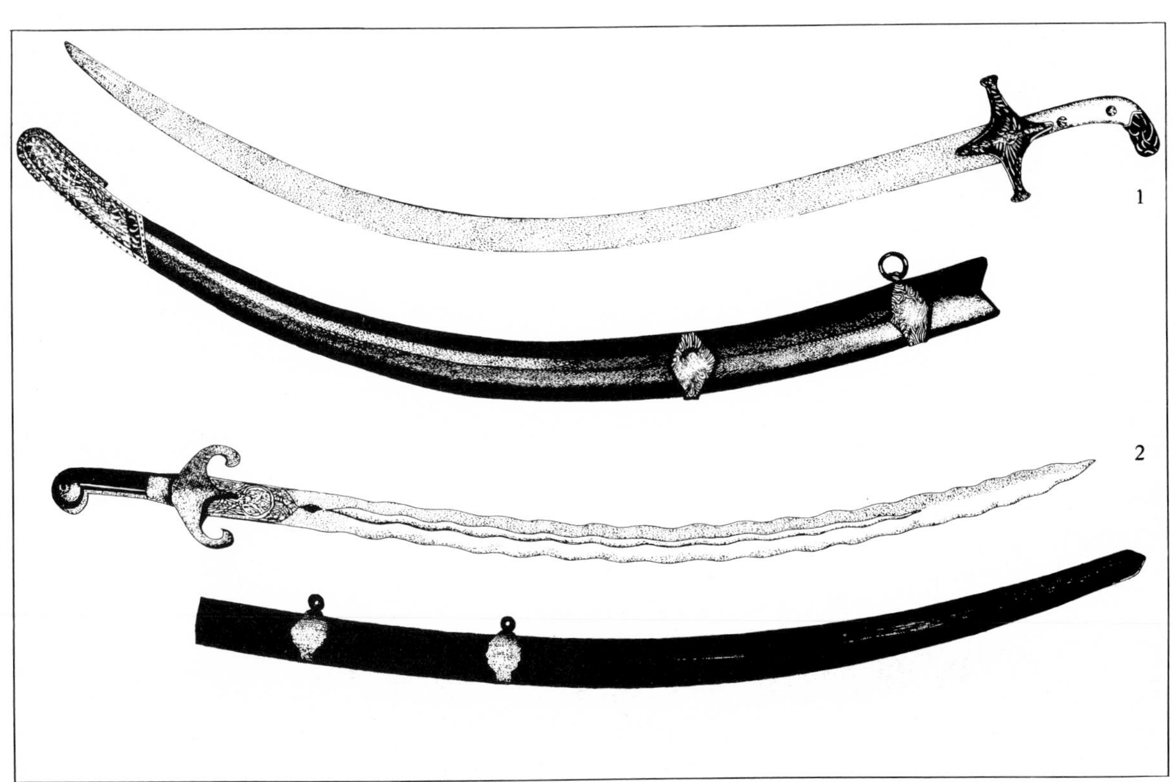


*Shamshir and scabbards. 1. India, c. 1855. Wallace Collection, London. 2. Persia, 17th–18th century. Wallace Collection, London.*

swordsmith's signature in a cartouche, inlaid with gold, and sometimes engraved. The inscriptions, in Arabic calligraphy, contain invocations to Allah, to the Prophet and his caliphs, while the signatures of the renowned craftsmen include "Assad Ullah [or Allah] Khurassani," "Kalb Ali," and "Assad Ullah [or Allah] Isfahani," who is known to have been the most talented of them all and probably lived during the reign of Shah Abbas I (known as "the Great"), 1587–1629. However, his signature has been imitated repeatedly over the centuries and it is impossible to assess the age and origin of a blade simply on the basis of such marking. The amuletic sign *Beduh* can also be seen on shamshir blades and consists of a square with four Arabic letters—*bā*, *dāl*, *hā*, *wāw*—which may denote the planet Venus and be a talisman to bring strength and courage as well as give protection against physical pain. The most highly prized ornamentation, however, is the pattern of the steel enhanced by etching and polishing.

The Shamshir hilt is equal, in its simplicity and elegance, to the blade. The grip is quite frequently made of two rounded plates of walrus ivory, riveted to the tang and tapering slightly toward the pommel. The latter, curving forward at right angles to the grip, is usually furnished with a metal thimble-shaped cap in steel, silver, silver gilt, etc., in keeping with the other mounts. The grips might also be made of horn or bone, and these are always slim and short, being adapted to the typically small hands of the Persians, especially the noblemen. The quillons are generally straight with a large escutcheon and langets and small terminal knobs, although down-turned quillons with "lion's head" terminals are also seen. Usually made of steel, they are often inlaid with gold or silver in simple floral designs.

The shamshir scabbard is usually made of wood covered in leather, with mounts made *en suite* with the hilt. These include one or two chapes and lockets with rigid suspension rings, but the mouth of the scabbard is sometimes not mounted.

**shapewe** An old English term for the KETTLE HAT.

**shashka** A typical Circassian saber, used by most of the tribes of the Caucasus and, from the early 19th century, by the Cossacks and other mounted troops of the Russian imperial army. The shashka was used for slashing and thrusting. It was worn on the belt, with the cutting edge rearward (unlike the saber). Its rather large blade was either hollowed or fullered, averaging between 76 and 86 cm. (30–34 in.) in length and very slightly curved. The blade's cutting edge, which was ground on the bias, was double-edged at the YALMAN. Shashka blades came from various sources, some being locally made and others imported from Russia. In the 19th century, many came from Germany too, and Solingen, in particular, produced a number of shashka blades displaying imitations of the "running wolf" mark of Passau. Persian watered-steel blades are also commonly found. Inscriptions, mostly in Arabic (or Russian) characters, are frequent on shashka blades, together with the date. The characteristic wooden hilt was often entirely covered with nielloed silver or silver gilt. There never was a guard in the Caucasian-type shashka, and the narrow grip had a large, crestlike pommel divided at the top like that of a YATAGAN. The wooden scabbard was generally covered in morocco leather, with mounts of nielloed silver in keeping with the hilt. The scabbard widened at the mouth and was long enough to contain most of the hilt. The mounts consisted of two lockets with suspension rings and a chape. The niello motifs were floral, and the Arabic inscriptions in ornamental NASKHI script.

This elegant weapon was often richly decorated with ivory and gold for special uniforms worn by court dignitaries and the tsar himself. Good-quality shashka were often made to his order for presentation to the Cossacks as a reward for bravery.

During the conquest of the Caucasus, Russian troops gradually adopted the native shashka, instead of their army-issue sabers, and from the 1830s it was officially allowed as a service weapon in the Russian Army's Caucasian Corps. However, from 1838 this original type of shashka was authorized mostly for Cossacks and officers stationed in the Caucasus. Other Cossack troops were issued a new type of the shashka, whose open hilt did not fit into the scabbard, and the latter was provided with a locket. Still another weapon was introduced in 1841 under the name of shashka. It had a knuckle guard and looked, strictly speaking, more like a saber (although it, too, was carried with the convex curve rearward). This so-called dragoon shashka had on its scabbard two rings with sockets for the bayonet. Later, other cavalry branches also received such "shashkas" but without bayonet sockets. All three types of the shashka remained in service until the end

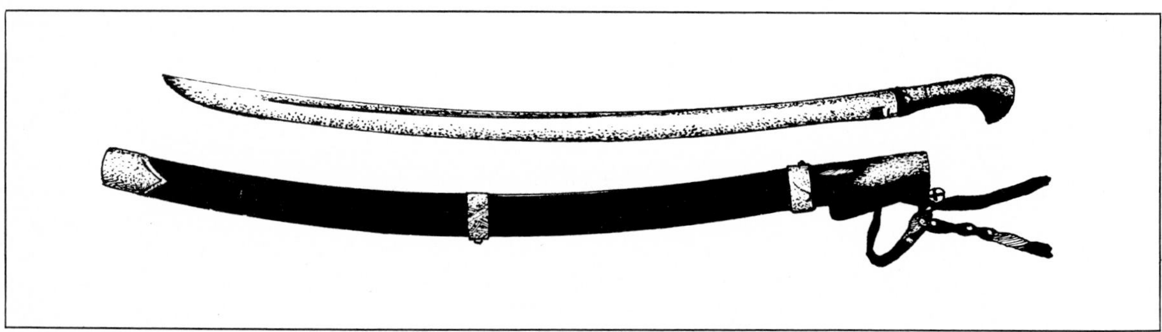

*Shashka and scabbard, Caucasus, 19th century. Metropolitan Museum, New York.*

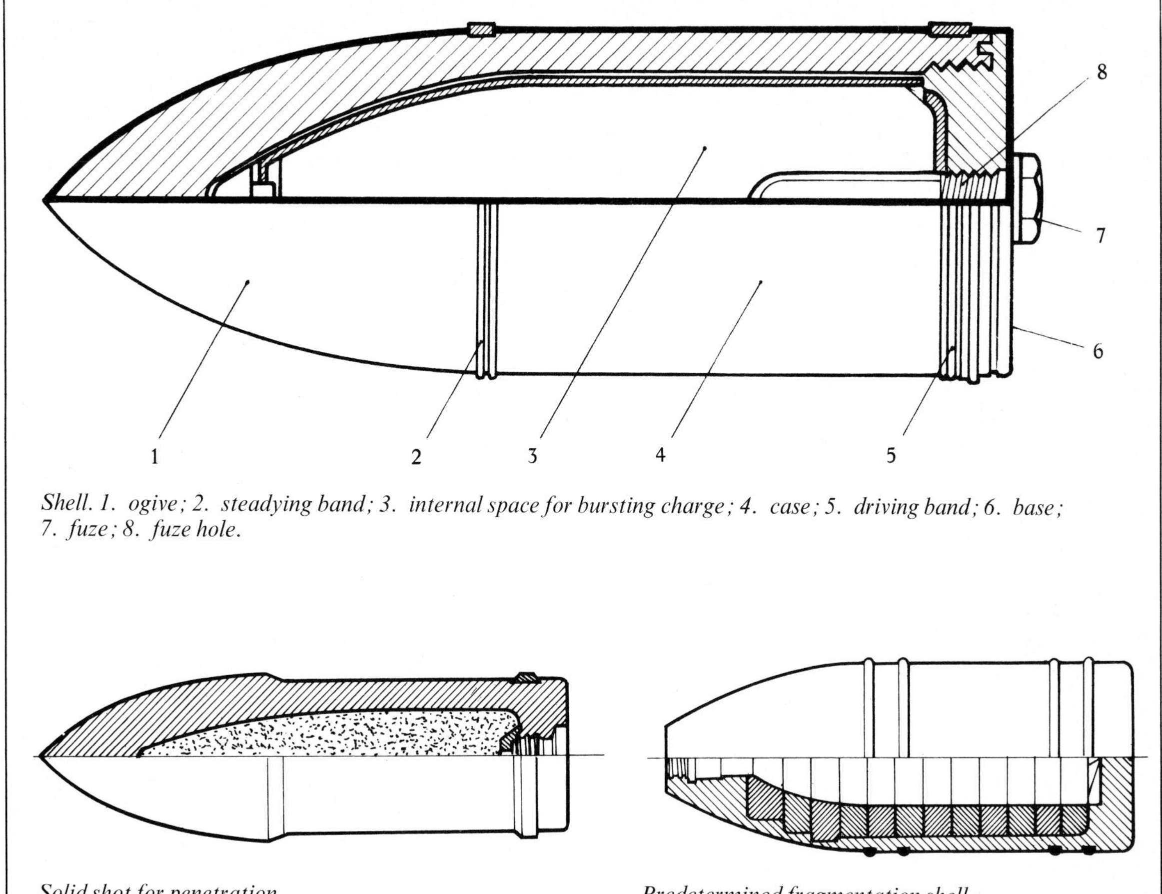


*Shell. 1. ogive; 2. steadying band; 3. internal space for bursting charge; 4. case; 5. driving band; 6. base; 7. fuze; 8. fuze hole.*

*Solid shot for penetration.*

*Predetermined fragmentation shell.*

of Russia's old regime, and the open-hilt Cossack shashka, stamped with the emblems of the new state, continued in service with the Soviet Cossack units and other mounted troops.

**sheath** *See* SCABBARD.

**shell guard** A type of the sword guard, roundish or oval, often bombé, in shape. It appeared in the early 17th century and was used in various swords, such as the PAPPENHEIMER or the WALLOON SWORD. By 1630 it had assumed the hemispherical shape and was widely used in Spanish and Italian swords. Shell guards were also fitted to smallswords and to various hunting and naval weapons.

**shell** Term covering the greater part of the explosive projectiles used in modern artillery. Small-caliber shells have the fuze in front, medium- and large-caliber shells either in front or at the base. Among the various types of shells are armor-piercing, antitank, high explosive, and those with time fuzes. *See also* PROJECTILE.

**sher basha** A heavy Turkish wall gun with an octagonal stub-twist barrel, often inlaid with gold, copper, or silver, and a very large backsight pierced with a number of holes for different ranges. Its heavy, pentagonal wooden stock was usually inlaid with silver or brass. The average sher basha was about 1.5 m. (5 ft.) long.

**shestoper** (Russian, "six feathers") Russian term of Persian origin for a mace with six flanges. *See also* BUZDYGAN.

**shiai-naginata** A type of NAGINATA used for contests.

**shibuichi** A Japanese alloy widely used for sword mounts and other decorative metalwork. Literally meaning "four parts," shibuichi consisted of silver—this was the constant factor—while the other three metals were either copper, tin, lead, or zinc. The composition varied considerably, the silver content ranging from 10 to 90 percent. Shibuichi, being a much harder alloy than SHAKUDŌ, was generally given a smooth, polished finish when used for fine engraving. When chemically pickled, it took on a particularly beautiful color and patina.

**shield**

This section represents a broad study of the general characteristics of this important piece of armor and the evolution of its various types, specific details for which can be found under the following headings: ASPÍS; BUCKLER; CLIPEUS; KALKAN; PARMA; PAVISE; PELTA; RONDACHE; SCUTUM; SIPAR; TARGE. For Chinese shields, see PEI K'UEI; PU TUN.

1

2

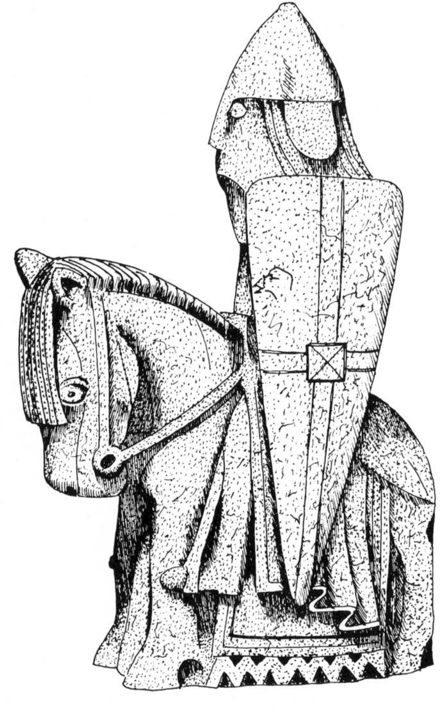

3

*Shields. 1. Assyrian, from a bas-relief of the 7th century* B.C. *found in Nineveh. British Museum, London. 2. Byzantine, 5th–6th century* A.D.*, from a mosaic in the Basilica of San Vitale, Ravenna. 3. Norman, 12th century, from a set of chessmen discovered on the Island of Lewis with Harris, in the Hebrides.*

**shield** A generic word covering all defensive weapons—of hide, wood, or metal—which are carried either on the arm or in the hand opposite to the one holding the offensive weapon. The fact that shields were in use as long ago as the Bronze Age is well established by both material evidence and pictorial sources over an extremely wide area, including Europe and the Middle East. Shields were used by the ancient Egyptians, Sumerians, Assyrians, and Persians in a variety of shapes—rectangular, oval, and round—and materials—leather, leather-covered wood, and wickerwork, often overlaid with decoratively embossed or engraved thin metal plates. Proof that several types of shields existed in Crete and Mycenae in the second millennium B.C. can be found in scenes with which other weapons were decorated. A particularly interesting example can be seen on a Mycenaean damascened dagger (Archeological Museum, Athens), dated to the 17th century B.C., which depicts scenes of a lion hunt and clearly shows two types of shields: rectangular, with an incurving upper edge, and bilobed. These were probably made from layers of oxhide, which was sometimes covered with metal plates; the edges were reinforced with decorated metal strips, and a wooden reinforcing spine ran down its entire length, broadening out in the middle to form a boss or UMBO.

Homer gave detailed descriptions of the shields employed by the heroes of the Trojan War and, of them all, the most widely used were either the great oval or the bilobed shields, the aspís, made from layers of hide and reinforced with metal fittings. As time passed, the aspís became smaller and circular, and was adopted by almost all the armies, in coexistence with a light wicker shield, introduced by the barbarians, known as a PELTA. From the inception of the aspís right up to the Hellenistic age (356–146 B.C.), the field of this shield was invariably richly decorated with geometrical motifs, hunting and battle scenes, family crests, mottoes, and amuletic symbols.

Before the rise of Rome's power, the shape of shields in Italy was strongly influenced by the forms prevailing in Magna Grecia, the area in southern Italy colonized by the Greeks. It is known that a round shield, similar to the aspís, was also used extensively by the Etruscans. The Samnites, however, used an elongated wooden shield, appropriately known as the "Samnite shield." From the beginning of Roman history, two basic types of shields were used by foot soldiers: the great scutum, in either its oval or rectangular form, and the round bronze CLIPEUS. Mounted troops, however, were equipped with a smaller round shield, the PARMA, which was soon superseded by a light oval shield of wood or leather. About the fifth century B.C., the round shield was almost completely replaced in the Roman army by the scutum, which remained in use until the fall of the western Roman Empire (A.D. 476). During the imperial period, however, many different types of shields were adopted, for use by the auxiliary military forces and in circus games. These ranged from the hexagonal one of German origin to the gladiatorial type, produced in a wide variety of styles and smothered in decoration.

In the Byzantine world, a large oval shield was extensively used. A good example can be seen depicted in the mosaics of San Vitale in Ravenna, held by a soldier in Emperor Justinian's retinue (c. 532–540), with the chrismon (a religious symbol signifying consecration with holy oil) occupying the whole field and richly decorated with gold and precious stones.

There is considerable evidence throughout the continent of Europe to show that predominantly round shields made of leather, wood, or wicker, with metal fittings and a metal boss or umbo, were being used from the time of the Bronze Age. Within the Germanic countries particularly, round or slightly oval shields with metal reinforcements were being employed. A variation was made which combined the shield with a weapon of attack; a sharp iron or bronze spike protruded from the center, in place of the rounded boss. The Celts of western Europe adopted a distinctive large oval shield, rather elongated, made of wood.

During the centuries following the fall of the western Roman Empire, the people of central and northern Europe were mainly using round shields which were frequently decorated in bright colors to distinguish between various ethnic and family groups. This type of shield, usually made of leather-covered wood and about 70–80 cm. (27–32 in.) in diameter, was equipped with a rather large boss, suitable to use as an offensive weapon.

It was not until about the 12th century that Europe was to see a new type of shield, which was kite-shaped. This became known as the "Norman" style, as it appears several times as a typical Norman weapon in the Bayeux Tapestry (1066–1077), that great piece of embroidery celebrating William the Conqueror's victory at the battle of Hastings. The Norman shield is shown as an elongated triangle, the top edge and sides being slightly convex. The field is occupied either by an applied cruciform metal fitting with a boss or by decorative painting. In addition to ENARMES, it was furnished with a GUIGE or looped strap at the top by which the shield could be suspended from the neck during fighting, thus giving greater protection and allowing more freedom of movement. The kite-shaped shield became the typical shield of mounted troops for about three centuries, since its elongated shape provided good protection for the left side of the body, the area most vulnerable to lance thrusts. In the course of the 13th and 14th centuries, it gradually evolved into a true triangle, becoming smaller in the process (sometimes described as "heater-shaped" because of its resemblance to the bottom of a flatiron). This was the period in which the field of the shield became emblazoned with heraldic devices, which, apart from serving decorative and symbolic functions, enabled the wearer to be recognized even when his face was completely covered by a helmet.

From the 15th century, a complex increase occurred in the types of shields—a trend which was to continue for several centuries. It is possible, however, to distinguish three different categories, each of which includes several types: (1) large shields able to stand on the ground as shelters for soldiers on foot (pavise); (2) shields to wear on the arm (targe); (3) shields to be held with the hand (buckler).

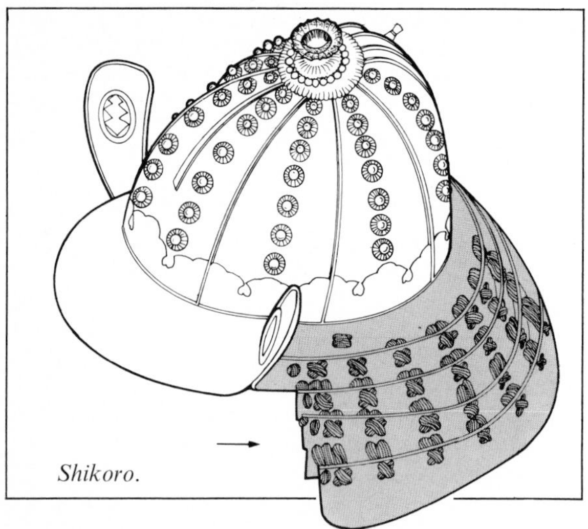
Shikoro.

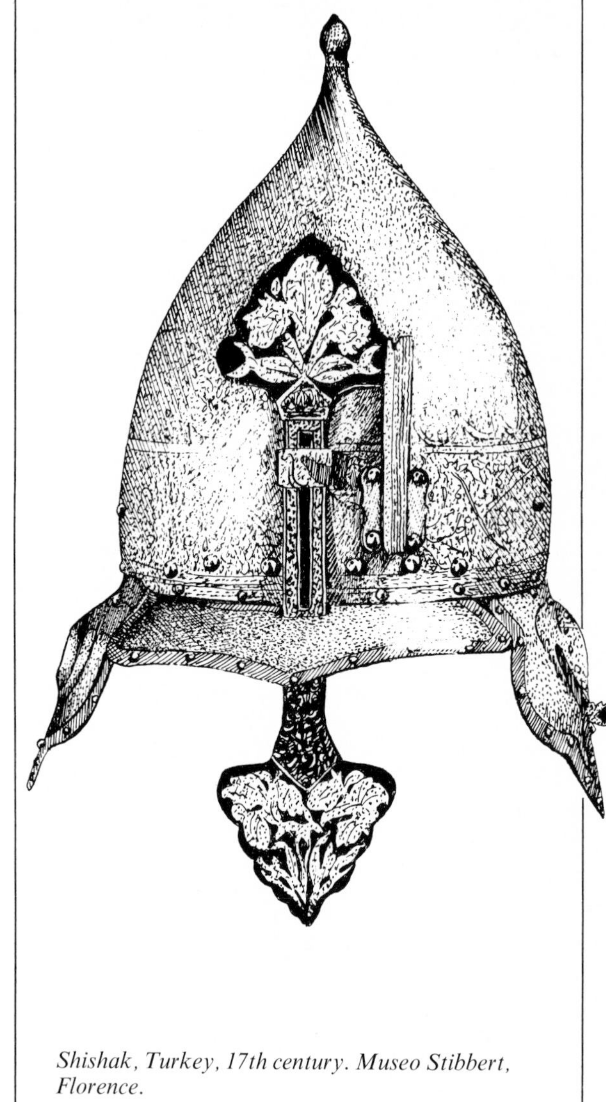
*Shishak, Turkey, 17th century. Museo Stibbert, Florence.*

**shikime** A method of lacing the plates of the ODOSHI.
**shikoro** The laminated neck guard of a Japanese helmet, consisting of lamellar bands—three to five rows, rarely more—laced together. The uppermost was originally attached to the crown with ornamental studs, but leather or braid fastenings were later used. The shikoro varied in shape according to the historical period, the most ancient being rounded. The four upper rows extended beyond the helmet at each side and turned back to form the side guards, the FUKIGAYESHI. By the mid-16th century only the top row was so treated, even though there were sometimes as many as six or seven lames. Shikoro made of leather or solid iron plates or laminations were occasionally used.
**shimose** Japanese word for trinitrophenol. *See also* EXPLOSIVE.
**shingen-tsuba** A type of TSUBA.
**shinogi** The back of a Japanese blade. *See also* BLADE: Japanese.
**shino-suneate** A type of SUNEATE.
**shinto** "New" type of Japanese blade, produced from the 17th century. *See also* BLADE: Japanese.
**shirasaya** A type of Japanese sword scabbard, the word literally meaning "white scabbard." The shirasaya consisted of a plain handle and sheath, made of magnolia (*honoki*) wood, in which good-quality blades were kept when not in use. The name of its maker and other information about the blade was frequently inscribed on it.
**shirizaya** A special type of scabbard for a Japanese sword, the TACHI, covered with the skin of a leopard, tiger, bear, boar, or deer. When the scabbard was covered in any of these animal skins, the whole sword was referred to as a shirizaya. It is said that court musicians wore their swords encased in tigerskin scabbards. At one time the shirizaya was carried only in warfare and when traveling, but it came to be worn later by high-ranking officials when out riding in fashionable dress or when in mourning.
**shirt of mail** *See* HAUBERK.
**shishak** Slavic term of Turkic origin for a type of helmet, which probably originated in the Hellenistic countries. Its definitive shape evolved in the Islamic world, the early examples being from the 13th-century Seljuk Turkish dynasty in Anatolia. Its popularity then spread throughout Ottoman Turkey and it was subsequently adopted in Hungary, Poland, Russia, and in western Europe, where it was called Zischägge. The word *shish*, from which the term derived, refers to the spike or sharp point on the top of the helmet's skull, and *Zischägge* is a 16th-century German transliteration of the word *shishak*. The shape of the cavalry helmet, or ENGLISH POT, of the Thirty Years War and the English Civil War was certainly influenced by the shishak. Its main features were a spherical or pointed conical skull with cheekpieces, a neck guard, and a fixed peak with an adjustable nasal secured by a staple and spring catch or wing screw.

Turkish and Mameluke shishak of the 15th and 16th centuries had skulls of both types, spherical and pointed;

these were sometimes fluted, engraved, or gilded, with a knobbed finial and a plume holder at the front, next to the sliding nasal. Their peak and neck guard were usually attached loosely by means of links or riveted leather straps, as were the cheekpieces, which were built up of several plates, the central one being embossed with a "kite" shape and pierced to facilitate hearing. These helmets were normally lined with quilted colored cloth.

In Hungary, by the late 15th century the most widespread type of shishak had a decorated pointed skull. Some "Hungarian type" Zischägge, lavishly ornamented with etched and gilded arabesques, were produced in Nuremberg in the 16th century. These were mostly for export to Hungary and Poland, where they were used by the hussars.

In early 17th-century Poland, a local variety of the hussar shishak was developed. This always had a hemispherical skull, sometimes with a comb like that of the Western MORION, cheekpieces with a heart-shaped cut in the middle, a neck guard of several plates secured by sliding rivets, and a peak pierced for an adjustable nasal terminating in a leaf-shaped plate, each piece being decorated with brass. Shishak for lower-rank hussars were blackened, as was their armor.

In Russia, the shishak was usually made with a pointed skull and was worn with various types of armor. Its shape was generally along the lines of the Turkish models. Many of these steel helmets were quite simple and undecorated, but there were also some that were sumptuously embellished with gold, pearls, and precious stones. One such helmet belonged to Tsar Mikhail Fiodorovitch, made by an armorer and decorator, Nikita Davydov, in 1621. It is kept in the State Armory at the Kremlin.

**shobuzukuri-naginata** An ancient type of NAGINATA.

**shoe** A ferrule on a staff weapon, designed to protect the butt end of the shaft when it is resting on the ground. Usually shaped like a conical or many-sided cap, it was sometimes fitted with a protruding spike to make it easier to stick into the ground. In some instances (for example, in the Italian cavalry lance of the mid-19th century), a heavy shoe also helped to balance the weapon.

The term "shoe" is also applied to a flange on the chape of a sword scabbard, or directly on the tip of an all-metal scabbard, for protection when the weapon is "trailed" on the ground. Such shoes have been used, particularly on saber scabbards, from the mid-18th century.

**shokakufu-hachi** Metal plates used in the making of the KABUTO helmet.

**shokakufu-no-hachi** A common term denoting the beaked form of the bowl of the TANKŌ helmet.

**shot** Spherical stone, lead, or iron projectiles fired from ancient artillery pieces. The so-called solid shot used much later, however, was designed to pierce highly resistant materials—the armor plating of ships, armored structures in fortifications, and so on—and was thus suitable for use in large-caliber coast defense and naval guns. These shells were cylindro-ogival in shape, and base-fuzed. The OGIVE was long, pointed, and specially hardened so as to give the necessary resistance on impact. The explosive charge was powerful but not too sensitive to shock, to ensure that it withstood the high initial velocities given to the projectile and that it did not detonate on impact, but only after penetration was complete. So-called blunt shot, completely solid with a flattened ogive, was also used up to the Second World War; it was intended to disintegrate the plates of armor by sheer force of impact.

**shot** Small spherical projectiles of soft or hard lead, used in shooting game. Sporting cartridges containing shot generally have a number on the case showing the diameter of the shot, from 12 to 0; the biggest number indicates the smallest shot, the difference from one number to the next being 0.25 mm. The pellets of shot numbered 0 are 4.25 mm. in diameter; there is also shot of larger diameter (double 0, triple 0), used for bigger game such as foxes. Finally, there is special shot of molded lead known as buckshot, of which there are four to seven pellets in each cartridge.

**shotel** An Ethiopian sickle-shaped edged weapon, generally, but not quite correctly, referred to as a saber. Its double-edged blade is diamond-shaped in cross-section, has a deep curve, and narrows to a point. The blade, from the base of the hilt to the point, is usually about 75 cm. (30 in.) long and up to about 100 cm. (39 in.) measured along the curve. Its wooden hilt is I-shaped and has no guard. The leather scabbard fits closely to the blade. The specific shape of the shotel was used to circumvent the opponent's shield by lateral and vertical strikes. Shotel carried with ceremonial dress are decorated with silver mounts and have velvet-covered scabbards and leather belts with matching silver furniture.

**shotgun** A smooth-bore gun used for sports and usually firing a load of pellets (shot). With shot of larger size (buckshot), it can serve as a big-game gun or an anti-riot weapon. In spite of its name, the shotgun is sometimes used to fire special bullets (often referred to as slugs). *See also* GUN: sporting.

**shoulder straps** Buckled straps linking the breast- and backplate of a cuirass. Introduced in the 14th century, they survived in the cuirasses of heavy cavalry to the 19th century and in parade cuirasses up to the present time. In later forms they consisted of two sturdy leather strips reinforced with metal scales, attached by means of studs

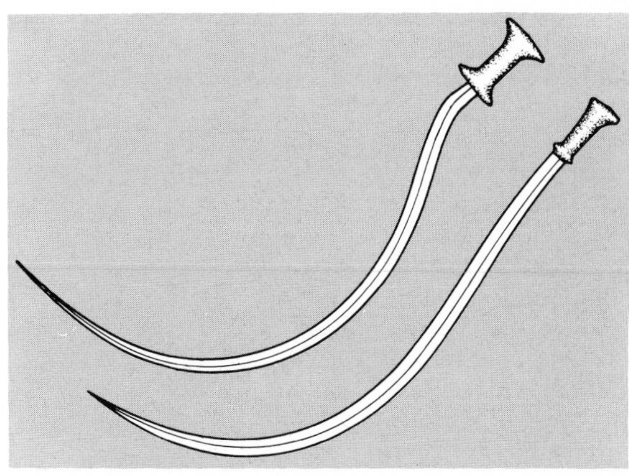

*Ethiopian shotel with wooden hilt.*

on the breastplate, the other end being riveted to the backplate.

**shrapnel** An artillery shell, named after its inventor, Lieutenant (later General) Henry Shrapnel of the British Army. Shrapnel, invented in 1784, consists essentially of a hollow shell filled with lead balls and fitted with a bursting charge and a fuze. Used with Bormann or Breithaupt fuzes, Shrapnel's "spherical case shot" used as an antipersonnel weapon became a terrible engine of destruction.

**sica** Greco-Roman term for a single-edged, pointed dagger, with a strongly curved blade forming a virtual right angle with the grip. Of Thraco-Illyrian origin, it was used by the Etruscans and the Ligurians, and particularly by the peoples living beyond the Rhine and the Danube. In those early times (6th–4th centuries B.C.) all weapons with curved blades were referred to by Greek authors as *machaira* or *kopis*. It was not until the Hellenistic period that the term *sica* was used, with reference to the atrocities committed by the Thracians and the Illyrian foot soldiers. As early as the 1st century B.C. the term *sicarii* was used to describe brigands (for example, the Illyrian pirates who roamed up and down the Adriatic shores) and professional assassins.

**side plate** A metal plate fitted on the outside of the stock of a gun opposite the lock, to provide a base for the heads of the screws attaching the lock to the stock.

**side ring** Also called ring guard, a part of the guard of swords and daggers for protecting the hand during parrying actions, first seen in the 15th century and particularly widely used in the 16th and 17th centuries. The side ring was positioned at the center of the cross guard, at right angles to the blade. It was made of a solid piece of steel welded or brazed to the cross guard and was sometimes fitted, for additional protection of the fingers, with an openwork metal shield. Occasionally a smaller side ring was placed inside another, both meeting at the cross guard. In other types, one side ring projected from the cross guard and the other from below it, both being linked by the arms of the hilt. The latter construction is frequently found on two-handed swords and rapiers.

**side tassets** *See* TASSETS.

**sight** An eye slit in the basnet, the armet, the close helmet, and some types of sallets. In many cases it consisted of a real slit in the visor; in other instances—such as on the armets and visored sallets—it was really a gap left between the brow reinforce or skull and the visor. In a number of 16th-century German helmets and in the Savoyard-type burgonets it was replaced by large, anatomically shaped eye sockets.

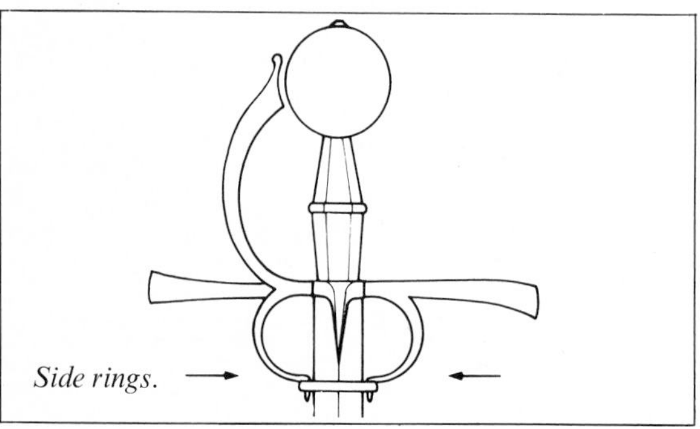
*Side rings.*

**sighting rib** A strip of metal on side-by-side double-barreled sporting guns that connects the two barrels at the top and fixes the line of sight. It is also found in under-and-over guns and in revolvers; in such cases it is often "ventilated," i.e., attached to the barrel so as to leave small oblong apertures, and serves essentially to fix the line of sight.

**sights** The system for sighting (or aiming) of firearms, consisting of an adjustable device with an aperture, known as the rear (or back) sight, and the foresight, which enable one to establish the lines of sight. The need to use a number of lines of sight is due to the curvature of the trajectory of the projectiles, which necessitates adjusting the elevation of the gun according to the distance of the target. Sights came into use as early as the mid-15th century, the foresight being a simple metal bead at the muzzle, while a notch on the breech served as an open rear sight.

Among the various types of sighting devices in use, the following are of particular interest.

*Flange rear sight.* This consists of a small metal plate fixed or hinged perpendicularly to the axis of the gun barrel, in which there are a number of small rectangular holes, referred to as notches. A simple idea, although not very practical, it was used in military guns during the second half of the 19th century. A fixed plate with several apertures was used on Turkish guns from the 16th century.

*Rear sight with "leaves."* This consists of several small metal plates of different height known as "leaves," one of which is fixed to act as a rest for the others swiveling on parallel hinges. Each leaf has a rear-sight notch, with an indication on it of the greatest distance it can cover. This type of open sight was used from the 17th century and is still used on some sporting shotguns.

*Rear sight with slide.* Used in the 19th century on many military rifles, this consists of a base with a curved surface and a leaf positioned over it which carries the slide with a notch. The slide can be stopped on the leaf by two side catches in various positions according to required ranges. A variation of this type of rear sight has a base with graduated steps for the slide.

*Folding rear sight.* This consists of a base and a bracket hinged at the base to take two positions: downward or at rest, and upright or aiming. The bracket is fitted with a slide, which has a bushing with a peep sight. Folding sights have been used on long-range rifles.

*Tubular sight.* One of the oldest types of rear sight, the tubular sight consists of a more or less long pipe fixed on the breech. It was used on hunting and target guns from the early 16th century.

*Rear sight with dial.* This consists of a bracket, with a notch at the top, turning on a hinge at the base, which is provided with a graduated dial.

There are many other types of sighting devices, the most noteworthy being the dioptric system whereby a lens is fitted into a small aperture. The rest are virtually all variations of the systems described above. There is a

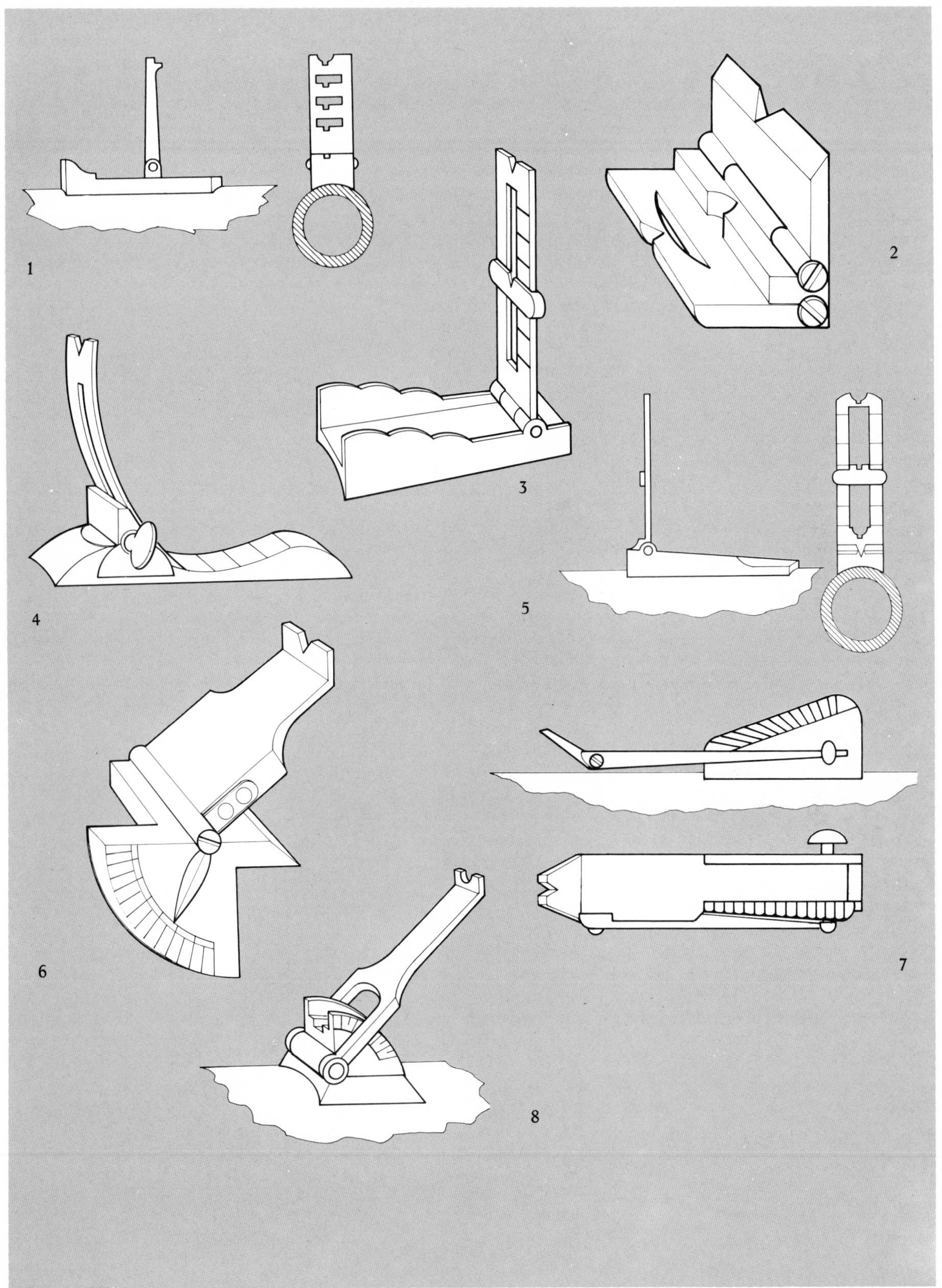


*Different types of sights. 1. Notched. 2. Leaved. 3. Scale and cursor. 4. Sliding leaf. 5. Cursor. 6. Quadrant. 7. Italian quadrant. 8. Quadrant.*

tendency nowadays for modern military firearms to be furnished with simplified sighting devices because, with the use of ammunition of low-angle trajectory, their lines of aim are restricted.

**silencer** Device attached to the muzzle of a personal firearm to reduce or suppress the noise of discharge. The first silencers were designed by Hudson and Hiram Maxim in the 1900s. For bullets that leave the barrel at subsonic speeds, the effect is produced by reducing the energy of the explosive gases by making them expand in a system of circular metal plates (baffles) with holes in the center for the passage of the bullet. In its simplest form the silencer consists of a metal tube, 30 mm. ($1\frac{1}{4}$ in.) or more in diameter, containing a number of baffles. The silencer is fixed to the muzzle of the gun and, when the gun is fired, the bullet emerges from the silencer through the holes, while the combustion gases following it are almost completely trapped and slowed down by the plates.

To silence supersonic cartridges effectively, the bullets must first of all be slowed down to avoid an audible shock wave. The simplest way is to extend the tube of the silencer to the rear so that it completely encloses the barrel and to bore a number of holes in the barrel, connecting its bore with the tube. Accurate calibration of the holes reduces the velocity of the bullet to the desired level by letting some gas off to the rear of the silencer, which acts there as an expansion chamber, while the front, fitted with baffles, works as the actual silencer.

**Sinclair saber** (or **Sinclair sword**) A name given by 19th-century collectors to a group of weapons whose hilts, provided with long recurved quillons and either a ring guard or a knuckle bow with a shell guard, bear some resemblance to Scottish swords. It was erroneously believed that these weapons had belonged to a Scottish mercenary band commanded by Colonel G. Sinclair that perished in Norway in 1612.

**single action** The mechanical arrangement in REVOLVERS by which the cylinder rotates automatically when the weapon is cocked manually. Single-action revolvers (and pistols) can be cocked only by pulling back the hammer by hand, not by pressing the trigger as in DOUBLE ACTION.

**sipar** A Persian steel shield, which probably developed its definitive form in the 15th century, having had various prototypes in antiquity. At one time it was used alongside the wicker-and-silk shield, the KALKAN, but almost totally supplanted it during the 18th century. A good-quality sipar was made of watered steel; it was nearly always round, measuring 20–60 cm. (8–24 in.) in diameter, although an occasional oval one can be found. While the shield itself was more or less convex, its edges were either flat or rolled back. It was held by two or three handles (*see* ENARMES) at the back, fastened to ring bolts passing through the shield and riveted to studs on the front. A small square pad was fitted close to the handles for the hand to rest against. Another strap (*see* GUIGE) was positioned near the edge, to carry the shield on the arm. The surface of the sipar was usually inlaid with gold or silver or nielloed, occasionally being set with stones and frequently decorated with engraved or etched inscriptions and designs, both floral and figural. There was often a metal crescent applied above the studs. Velvet or other decorative fabric was used to line the shield.

There was another type of sipar, made of leather—usually rhinoceros hide—and treated in such a way as to render it translucent; it was ornamented with painting, gilding, or enameling and with four or six metal studs, depending on the number of enarmes.

In the 19th and 20th centuries numerous sipars have been produced as souvenirs for tourists; they are of poor-quality iron, very carelessly etched and lacking the correct handles.

**skene dhu** (or **skean dhu**) The term is derived from the Gaelic *Sgian Dubh*, meaning "black knife." It is used to describe the small knife with a flat grip, of dark or black wood and usually set with a cairngorm (smoky quartz), carried in the top of the stocking as one of the accoutrements of traditional dress in Scotland. It is significant that the account of Highland dress given by John Campbell in *Description of the Highlands of Scotland* (1752)—although giving precise details of other arms, such as the broadsword and dirk—does not mention the skene dhu. Moreover, the earliest illustration of knives being carried in the stocking in Scotland appears in the portrait of Colonel Alistair Macdonald of Glengarry painted by Raeburn in 1812. This painting shows two small knives, one above the other, fitted into the top of the stocking. It seems likely, therefore, that the carrying of a skene dhu was a comparatively late tradition in Scotland, probably connected with the revival of Scottish dress which took place in the early 19th century.

The carrying of a small knife in the stocking is a custom of some antiquity elsewhere, however. In the 14th century Chaucer, describing the Miller in "The Reeve's Tale," wrote: "A Shefeld thivitel bare he in his hose" (A Sheffield knife he carried in his stocking). It is possible that the skene dhu may represent a revival of the custom of carrying a small knife. This was kept in a compartment,

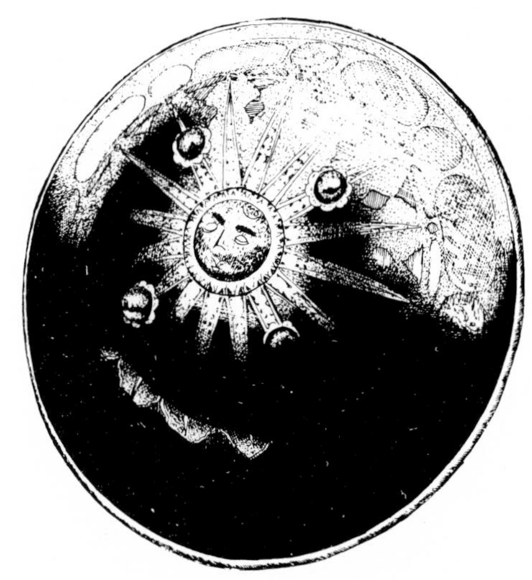

*Sipar, Persia, 19th century. Museo Stibbert, Florence.*

# Artillery, firearms and smallswords from the 17th to the 19th century and the first machine guns

**Plate 65 17th-century rapid-fire "organ"** *Multibarreled gun, Europe, c. 1670. Three groups of side-by-side barrels were mounted on a triangular frame, and each group fired through a single vent producing a volley. Liechtenstein Waffensammlung.*

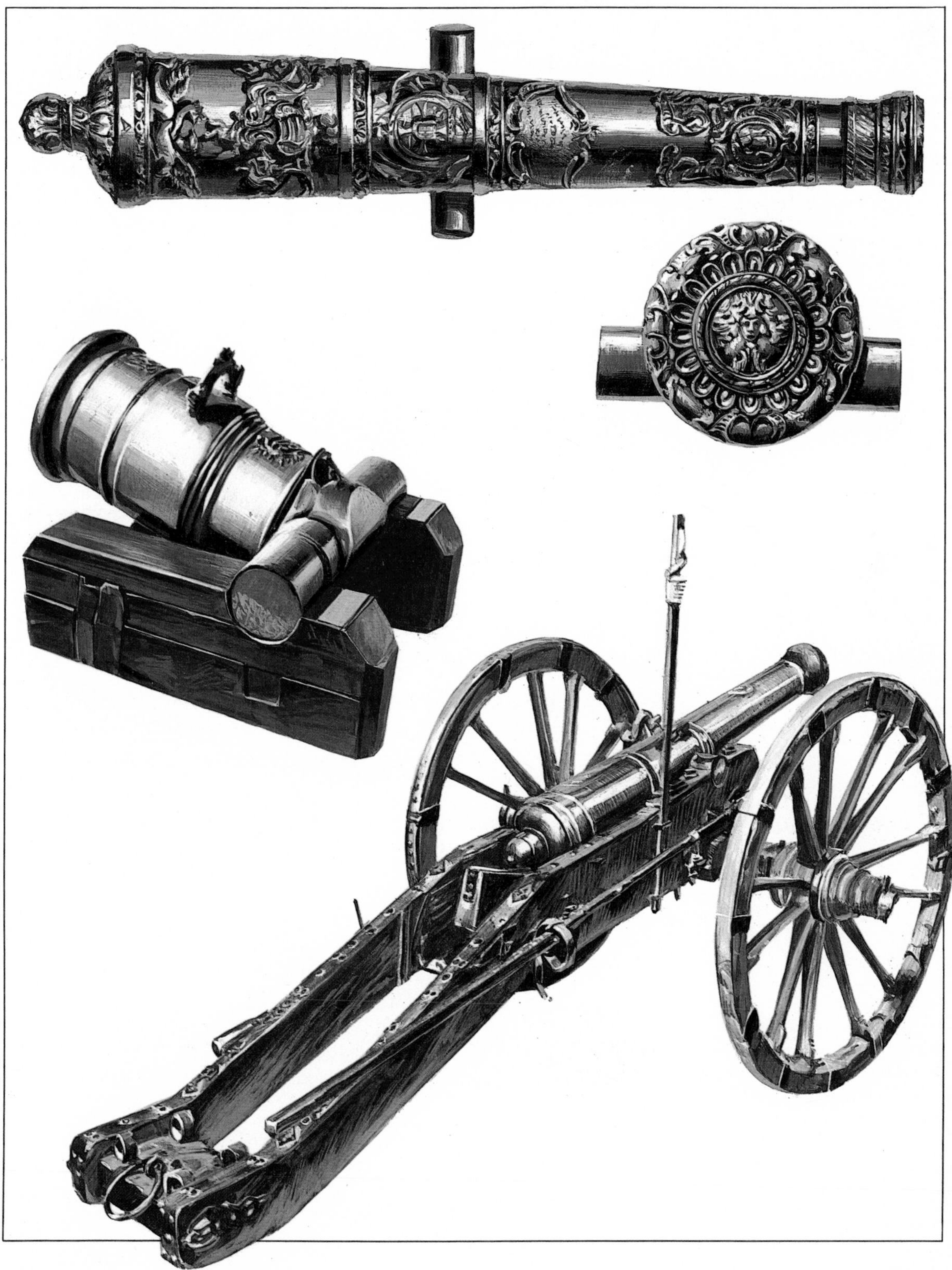

**Plate 66 18th-century artillery** (top) *Cannon cast in Venice in 1708 in the presence of Frederick IV of Denmark, and its rear view.* (middle) *Mortar known as Adler ("eagle"), 1764. Bernisches Historisches Museum, Bern.* (bottom) *Bronze cannon, 1732. Bernisches Historisches Museum, Bern.*

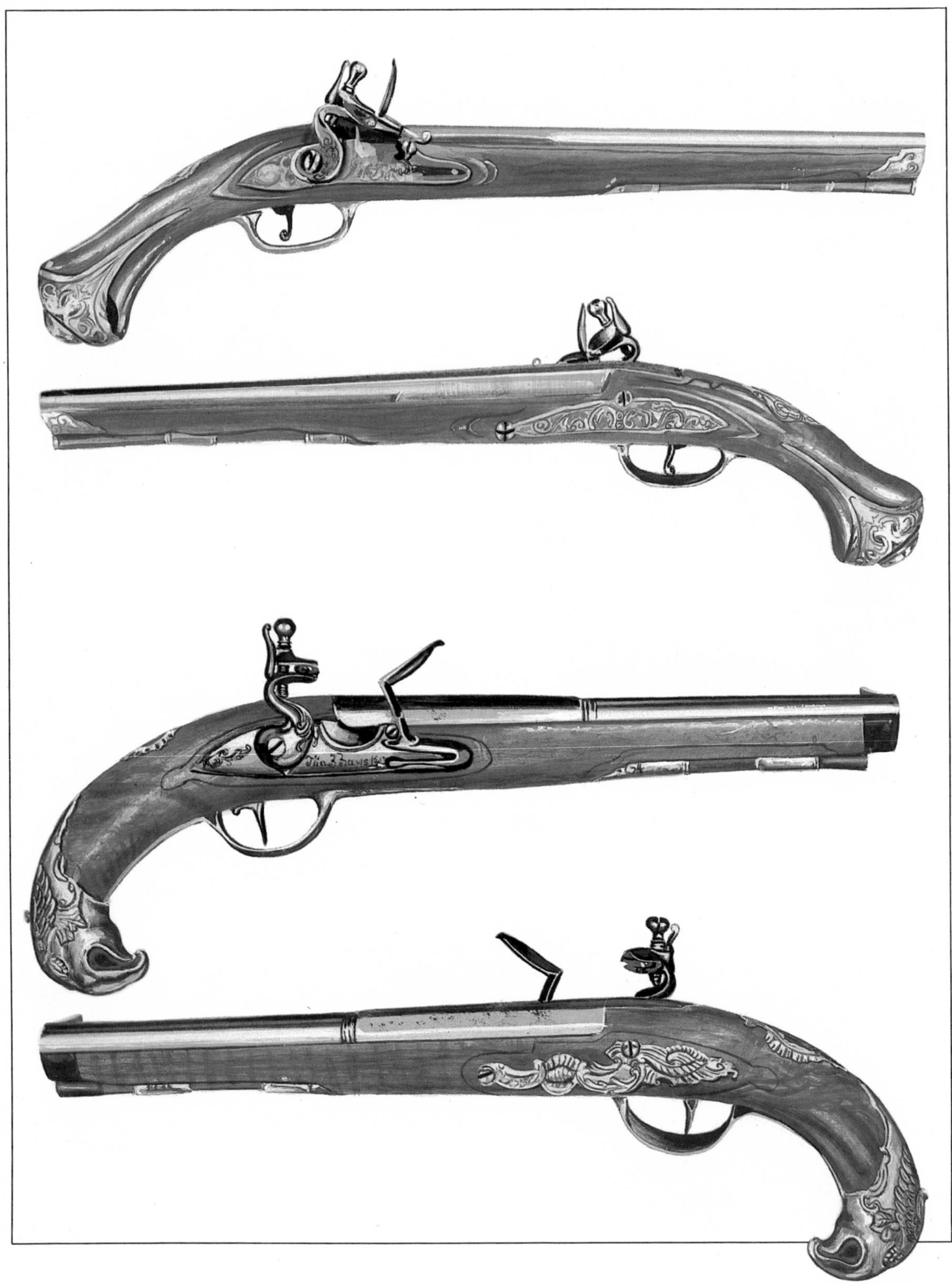

**Plate 67 18th-century firearms** (top) *Pair of flintlock pistols, Brescia, c. 1730. Armeria Reale, Turin.* (bottom) *Pair of flintlock pistols by Thaddäus Poltz, Karlsbad, c. 1760. Museo Sibbert, Florence.*

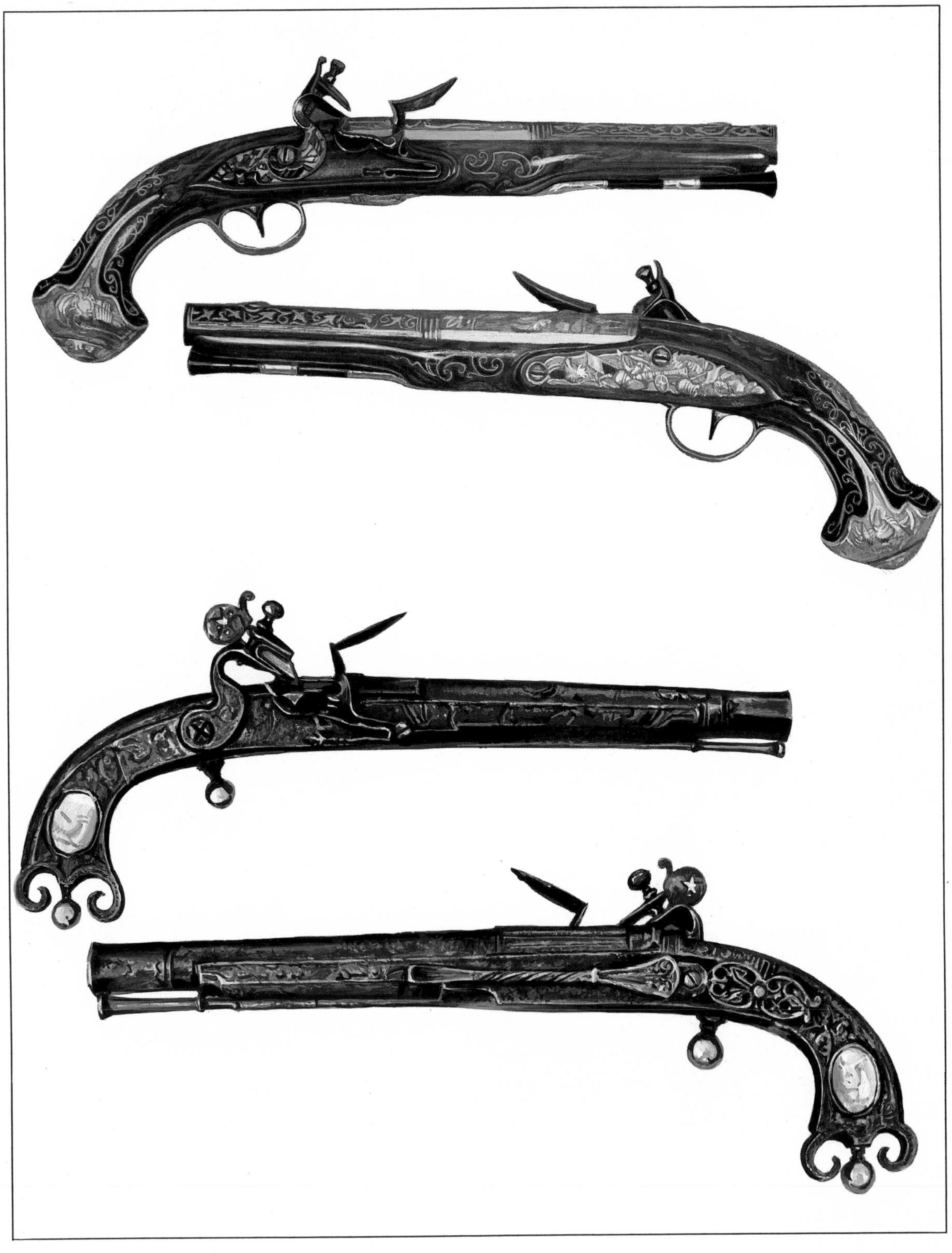

**Plate 68 18th-century firearms** (top) *Pair of pocket pistols by James Wilson, London, last quarter of the 18th century. Private Collection.* (bottom) *Pair of all steel pistols, Scotland, third quarter of the 18th century. Private Collection.*

**Plate 69 18th-century smallswords** (left) *Smallsword with porcelain grip, Saxony, c. 1750. Museo Sibbert, Florence.* (right) *Smallsword with gold furniture decorated with pearls and precious stones, France, c. 1760. Kungl Skattkammaren, Stockholm.*

**Plate 70 19th-century target and dueling pistols** *Pair of breechloading target and dueling percussion pistols, with accessories and case, Austria, c. 1860. Victoria and Albert Museum, London.*

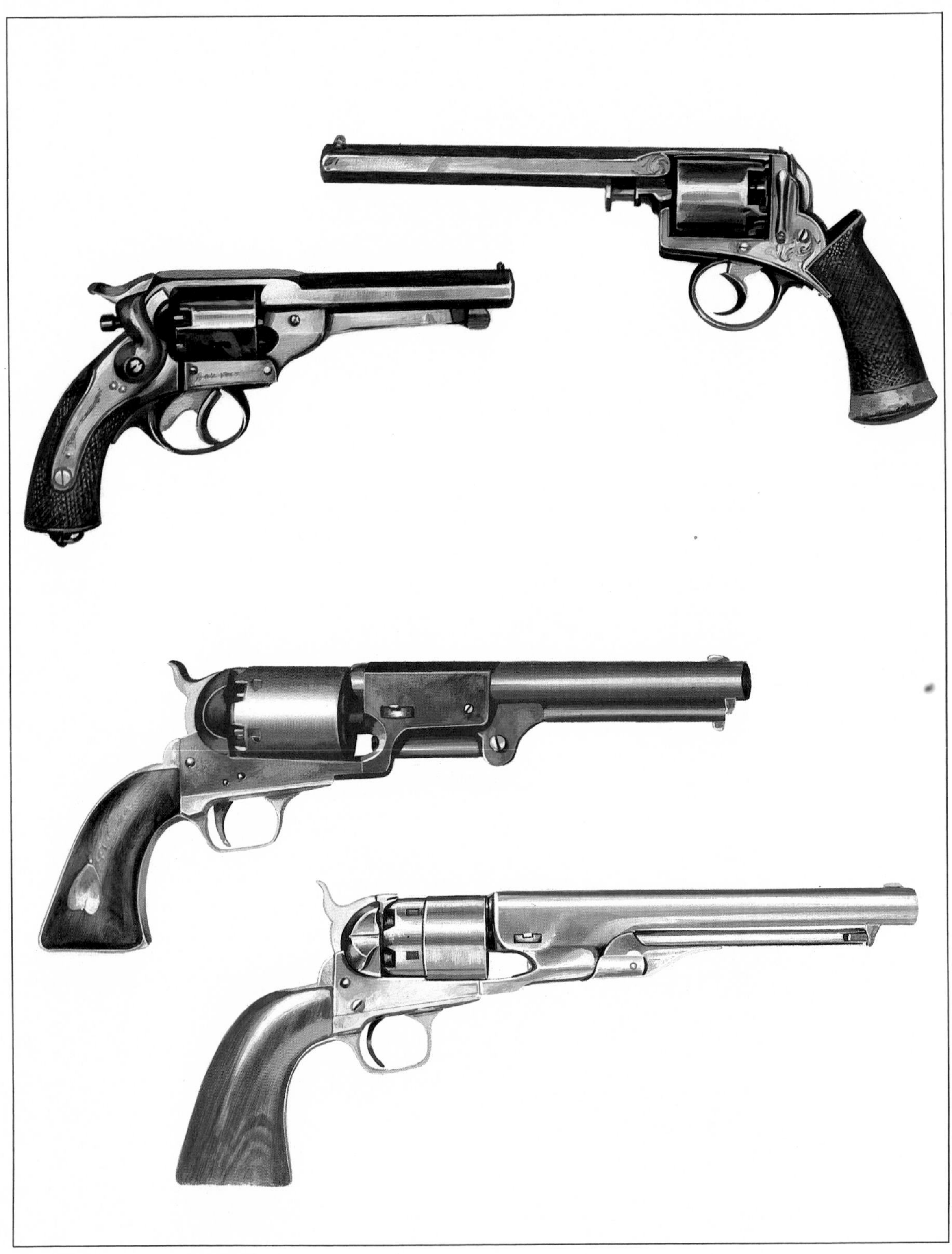

**Plate 71 Improvements to the revolver** (top to bottom) *Double-action Adams revolver, Great Britain, 1851, made by Royal Small Arms Factory, Enfield. Double-action Kerr revolver, Great Britain, 1858–59, made by Royal Small Arms Factory, Enfield. Single-action Colt Third Model Dragoon, United States, 1851–60. Single-action Colt model 1860 Army, United States, 1860–73.*

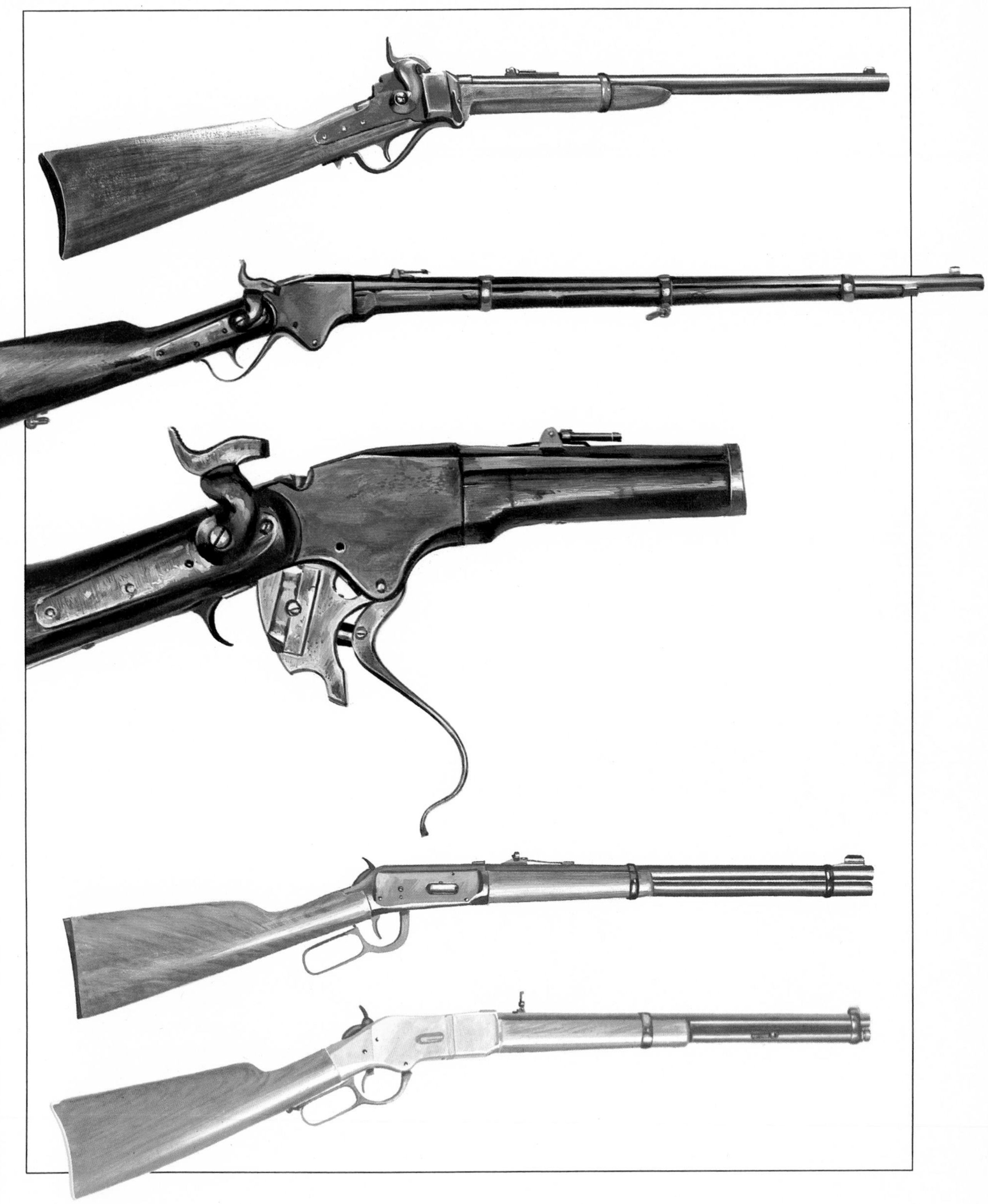

**Plate 72 Carbines and rifles in the New World** (top to bottom) *Sharps breechloading carbine, United States, patented in 1848. Spencer breechloading rifle, with detail of the breechblock in the open position, United States, patented in 1860 and 1862. Winchester magazine rifles model 1894 and model 1866, United States.*

**Plate 73 19th-century artillery** (top to bottom) *Armstrong gun used in the Civil War 1861–65. American heavy mortar known as the "Dictator," used in the siege of Petersburg, Virginia, in 1865. British 4.7 in. gun adopted during the Boer War (1899–1902) and used until the First World War. American model 1857 gun, known as the "Napoleon," used by the Confederate forces during the Civil War. German Krupp L-35 gun, 1871–1900.*

**Plate 74 The first machine guns** (top) *Gatling machine gun, United States, 1862.* (middle right) *The Gatling as field gun, and* (left) *the later model adopted by the French in the Franco-Prussian War (1860–61).* (bottom) *Montigny model 1851 mitrailleuse, Belgium.*

together with a small fork, on the sheath of the traditional Scottish dirk. A number of dirks are still in existence, dating from the end of the 17th century and later, which are fitted with their original knife and fork. The wooden handles of these knives, like the later skene dhu, are carved with interlaced decoration in the traditional Scottish manner and are similar in general form.

An account dated 1737 describes Highlanders carrying a knife called a "skeen ockles"—a "sleeve knife"—in addition to the dirk, although its exact form is unknown. Some short daggers with carved wooden handles which survive from, probably, the latter part of the 18th century do, however, differ in form from the dirk, and it has been suggested that these may be the "sleeve knives" referred to above.

**skirt** A piece of armor for foot or mounted soldiers consisting of a combination of articulated lames on loose or sliding rivets, extending from the waist to protect the abdomen and the hips. In the 14th century it was rather like an apron, made up of several articulated lames curved to the body and riveted to the breastplate. In the 15th century the skirt was supplemented by the corresponding rump guard of the same construction, while in front the TASSETS were attached to the skirt with leather straps and buckles. This lamellar skirt remained in use throughout the 15th century, the front and the rear halves of the skirt being joined with hinges on one side and buckles and straps on the other. Several technical modifications were made in the contouring, to achieve a better fit around the hips, and in the shape of the lames themselves, which became more sickle-shaped with a cusped center, where they were also frequently strengthened with ribbing. The lower lame often had a cutout, which with the tassets formed an arc over the fork. Sometimes a piece of mail was suspended at the fork, known as a breke of mail, to protect the genitals.

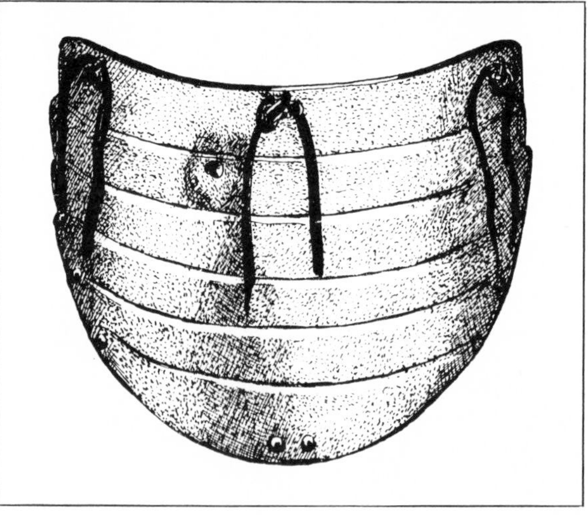

*Skirt for a foot soldier's armor, made in Brescia about 1650. Museo Stibbert, Florence.*

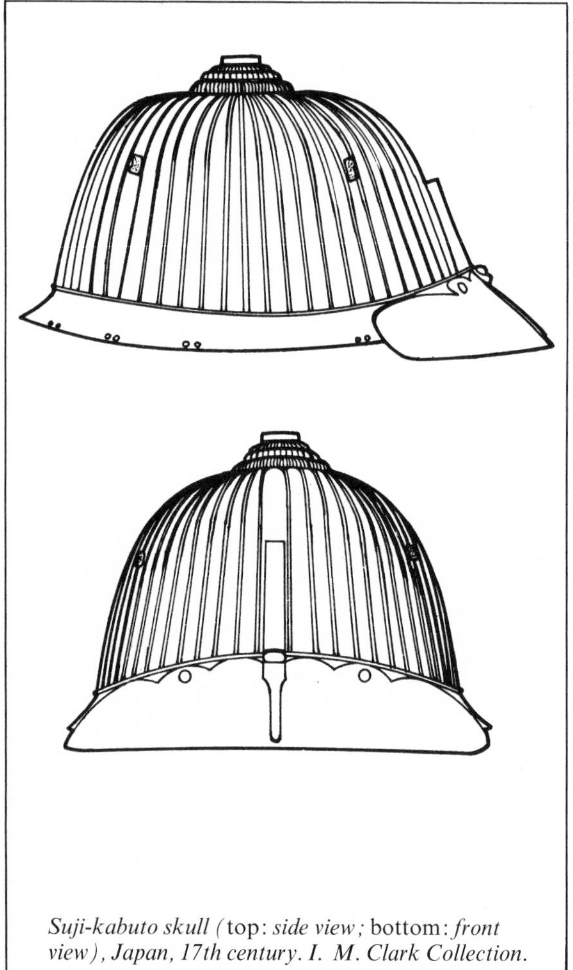

*Suji-kabuto skull (*top: *side view;* bottom: *front view), Japan, 17th century. I. M. Clark Collection.*

In the late 15th century a special type of skirt was designed for foot-combat armor. It was called the tonlet (from French *tonnelet*, "little barrel") and consisted of a flared lame skirt that completely encircled the body. In general, the skirt was a combination of only a few lames—sometimes only a single one, especially in the latter part of the 16th century—riveted to the raised lower edge of the cuirass or, more rarely, attached with turning pins. A variation of this was the skirt of the so-called "alla romana" parade armor, made in imitation of ancient Roman armor. Its lower edge was contoured in a convex curve under the stomach, and suspended from it were laminated strips of leather instead of tassets.

By the 17th century the skirt had become an integral part of cuirassier armor and consisted of two or more lames with clasps for long tassets. It continued to be used, in a particularly heavy form, with cuirassier and carabineer armors.

**skull** The generic term to describe that part of a helmet that directly protected the cranium. The outer shape varied considerably and may be described as conical, ogival, hemispherical, semi-oval, flattened, flat-topped, etc. Several types of helmets consisted solely of a skull, but in most cases this extended into the brow and into the NECK GUARD or tail at the back. In the 15th century skulls were generally made from a single piece of metal, reinforced on the top by a central keel, but in the 16th century they were often made in two overlapping halves which were then joined together at the comb by riveting and hammering.

The interior of a skull was fitted with a padded LINING, originally attached by means of small holes along its lower edge, but in the 16th century it was stitched to a leather band held in place by rivets.

**skull reinforce** *See* GUPFE.

**sleeves, mail** Shoulder and arm protection worn in the 16th century under plate armor. They were made of fine riveted mail, which was sometimes used double. Separate mail sleeves were probably intended for foot soldiers' armor, since the SPAUDLERS and elbow-length GAUNTLETS left parts of their arms vulnerable. In many instances, mail sleeves were edged with several rows of brass rings. Such sleeves were fairly short, reaching to just below the elbow, when they were worn under the PAULDRON–VAMBRACE combination, as they would have been an encumbrance if they extended under the (closed) lower CANNON.

**slide** Term commonly used for the mobile upper part of some semiautomatic PISTOLS. It runs along the top of the pistol frame and contains the firing and extraction mechanisms, the obturator, and part or whole of the barrel. The ejection port is found in its upper side, which also bears the sights—the backsight and, when it is not fitted on the barrel, the foresight.

**slide action** *See* PUMP ACTION.

**sling** A throwing weapon consisting of a strap made of leather or fabric at the center of which there was a pouch for holding the projectile. The throwing technique involved whirling the missle around the head, holding the two ends of the strap while so doing: when the greatest possible speed was reached, the missile was "launched" by letting go of one of the ends of the strap. Use of the sling dates back to very earliest times and was highly developed among various peoples around the Mediterranean basin; it seems almost too elementary to recall the biblical episode in which David, armed with a sling, slew the giant Goliath. In classical times the Romans never adopted the FUNDA for their own troops, but permitted the use of this weapon among the auxiliary troops, incorporated in their own armies from among allies.

Use of the sling in battle is depicted iconographically throughout most of the Middle Ages, and particularly by or against troops occupying fixed defenses; there is also evidence of its use for hunting waterfowl. In the late Middle Ages a type of sling mounted on a long handle was also in use, which made it possible to increase the range (*see* FUSTIBALUS).

Because the sling was a very economical weapon, its use as a hunting weapon lasted for a long time among the less prosperous classes, particularly among shepherds and herdsmen; in the 19th century, it was still used to good effect in depressed areas of central and southern Italy.

**slow match** *See* FUZE.

**small arms** A general term covering all weapons of individual soldiers, but also including the firearms manned by small crews, like machine guns and light mortars. The term is often applied now to military hand firearms only.

**smallsword** A civilian sword with a light, slender, moderately long blade, variously sectioned, and a simple small guard with one or two shells and the arms of the hilt; many but not all types had a knuckle bow. The smallsword developed in the first half of the 17th century from the arming sword and the short rapier.

By the late 17th or early 18th century, the typology of the various forms of the hilt had become international, and the place of production can often be identified only on the basis of the decoration. Thus, in Italian smallswords manufactured in Brescia the hilt and entire furniture consisted of delicately pierced and chiseled scrollwork; those made in Saxony have steel or gilded-bronze furniture and grips often made of ornate Meissen porcelain; brightly colored Baroque and Rococo decoration was generally typical of German work. The blades mounted on these smallswords were very varied indeed; although the commonest form was flattened, hexagonal-sectioned, rhomboid- or triangular-sectioned blades were also widespread, the latter with shallow grooves and pronounced edges. The manufacture of blades had by now become centralized in several centers which supplied the entire market. The initials and other signature marks often referred to the assembler or fitter rather than to the actual maker.

In the later decades of the 18th century a new fashion for decoration of the hilt spread throughout Europe from England. The entire hilt was covered with patterns of small studs made of faceted cut steel, looking very much like diamonds. The knuckle guard was often replaced by one or more small chains, with tassels, similarly decorated with cut-steel beads (a chain instead of a knuckle guard had already been used earlier in sabers showing an Eastern influence).

The custom of wearing the smallsword (also known as the "town" or "walking" sword) as part of the everyday civilian attire started to fade toward the end of the 18th

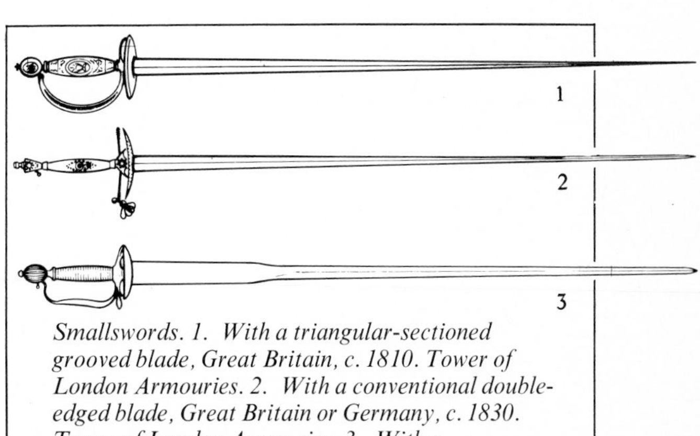


*Smallswords. 1. With a triangular-sectioned grooved blade, Great Britain, c. 1810. Tower of London Armouries. 2. With a conventional double-edged blade, Great Britain or Germany, c. 1830. Tower of London Armouries. 3. With a "colichemarde" blade, Sweden, c. 1680–1700. Livrustkammaren, Stockholm.*

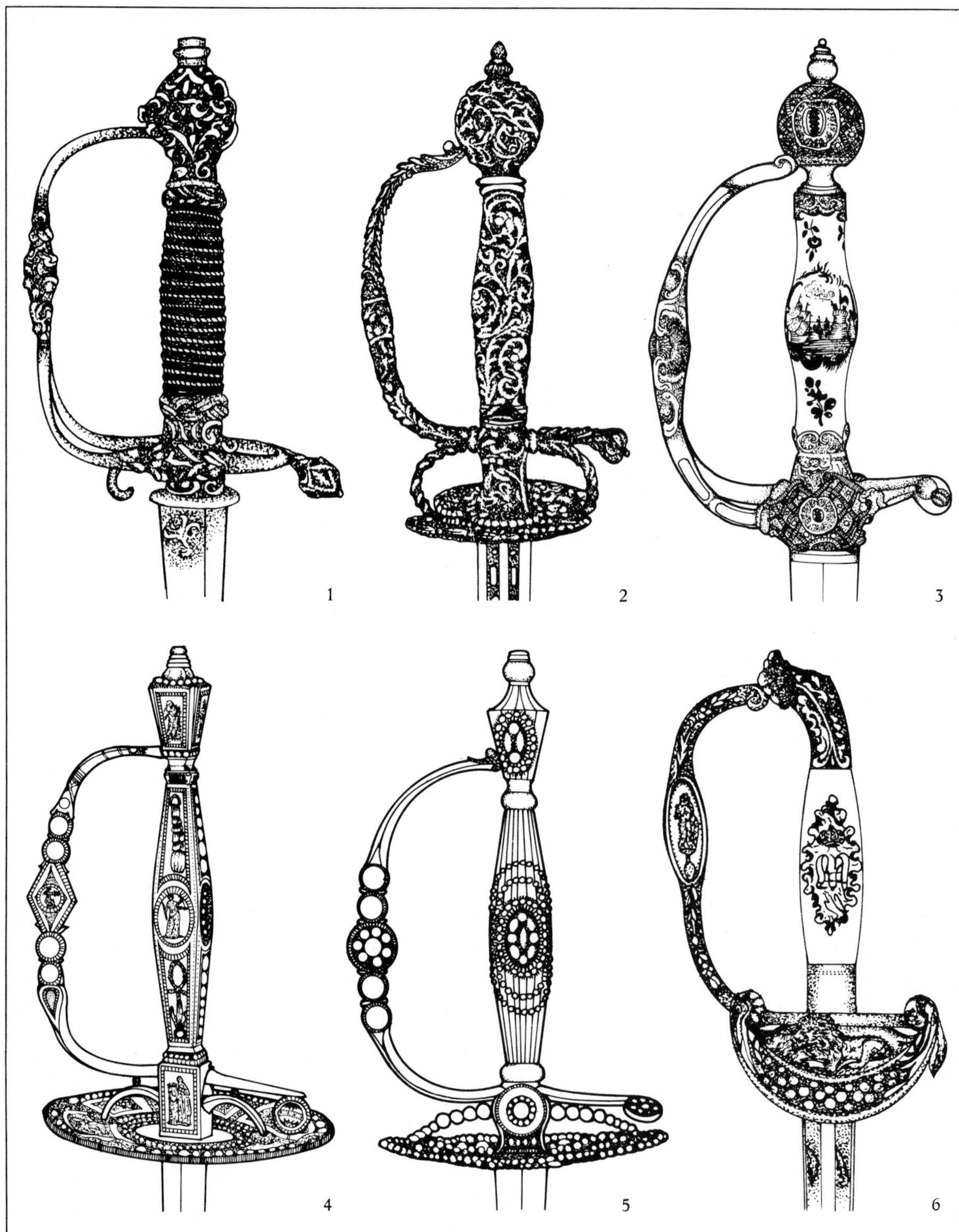

*Smallsword hilts. 1. Netherlands, c. 1650–55. Museo Stibbert, Florence. 2. With a Toledo blade, Italy, c. 1680–1700. Museo Stibbert, Florence. 3. Germany (Saxony), c. 1750. Museo Stibbert, Florence. 4. England, c. 1790. Metropolitan Museum, New York. 5. England, c. 1800–1810. Museo Stibbert, Florence. 6. Germany (Bavaria), c. 1820–25. Germanisches Nationalmuseum, Nuremberg.*

century, but in military circles, from the latter half of the 18th century onward, the dress sword, a military counterpart of the smallsword, served to round off the uniform and keep alive the decorative forms traditionally applied to swords. In the 19th century a type of hilt was adopted which lasted until the early 20th century. It consisted of a grip with rounded corners, covered with mother-of-pearl, and surmounted by a small curved cap; this was met by the knuckle guard, which ran from the quillon and the shell guard. The shell was broad and rounded, and turned toward the blade; it bore the insignia of the corps to which the bearer belonged, or a princely coat of arms.

**smokeless powders** General term used for powders whose explosive decomposition produces no—or hardly any—smoke. They may also be described as "colloidal powders," from the state in which their principal constituents occur. The colloidal structure taken on by smokeless powders in their preparation enables them to be made in a variety of different forms—threads, sheets, slabs, flakes, tubes, and so on. Thus, by varying the shape and size of the grains, and so the action of the powders, the speed of ignition can be varied at will. The seasoned "cake" obtained from the original raw materials is laminated, cut, dried, and sifted, and sometimes has graphite added to it to obtain the final granulation.

Historically speaking, the discovery of smokeless powders is generally attributed to the French chemist Paul Vieille (1854–1934), who in 1884 produced the famous "B powders." The Germans, however, declare that Max von Duttenhofer had already prepared a smokeless powder in 1883, using acetic ether to gelatinize nitrocellulose produced by the nitration of wood cellulose. In fact, the first smokeless powder—though it was not colloidal—seems to have been that produced by Captain E. Schultze of the Prussian Artillery in 1864.

The Schultze process was based on the use of sawdust, cleaned, boiled, lixiviated, and then treated with nitric and sulfuric acids. The product of this nitration was cleansed for another three weeks and then boiled in a dilute solution of potassium carbonate, followed by another wash that lasted for several days. The pulp was then impregnated with potassium nitrate and dried. The physical structure of the wood and the presence of material other than cellulose made this powder burn more slowly than guncotton. The speed of ignition was further lowered by the addition of the potassium nitrate, but Schultze powder was still too "fast" for rifled weapons. However, it was widely used in smoothbore sporting guns, and for blasting.

Later, Vieille discovered that when the nitrocellulose was dissolved in a mixture of alcohol and ethyl ether, an explosive was produced which, when used properly, transformed the destructive action of the nitro-derived explosives into propellant action. This was the origin of the French "B powders." In those powders collodion cotton was first gelatinized using the alcohol-ether mixture, in which it was completely dissolved to form a colloidal solution. Guncotton was then kneaded in this solution; not being gelatinized by either alcohol or ether, it remained in its original state, so that the powder was only partially gelatinized. Actually, it should be noted that guncotton can be slowly gelatinized in the later process of preparation of B powder if not more than 25 percent of it is added to the solution. Vieille's powder was followed by other powders using only nitrocellulose, such as the American Pyrocellulose, Dupont No. 15, T(a), etc., all of which contained a stabilizer (generally 0.5–1 percent of diphenylamine).

The second important type of smokeless powder was discovered by Alfred Nobel in 1888, by the gelatinization of collodion cotton with nitroglycerin in the presence of water: ballistite, as it was called, is normally made of 50 percent nitrocellulose and 50 percent nitroglycerin, and is thus a colloidal powder with a fixed solvent (nitroglycerin) which is not eliminated and so remains in the powder. It is a compact, homogeneous colloidal substance, more or less dark yellow in color. When ignited it burns completely with a bright yellow flame, leaving no solid residues; it explodes at 180° C. It is not greatly sensitive to shock and only slightly hygroscopic, but it is sensitive to temperature. Below 80° C. it exudes the nitroglycerin, which appears on the surface as small needlelike crystals. The extremely high temperature produced when it explodes (3300° C.) makes it very erosive, and it soon causes damage to the gun. To overcome this defect, what are called "diluted ballistites" were produced: in Italy, C.G.13 contained pyrocollodion (collodion cotton with a high nitrogen content) 60%, nitroglycerin 25%, dinitrotoluene 15%.

As the above shows, smokeless powders can be divided into two categories:

*Nitroglycerin powders*, using the nitroglycerin as a solvent which remains incorporated in the nitrocellulose, so that the powder contains two explosive substances. The ballistic effect is greater and more constant and reliable, since the solvent is not eliminated. Nitroglycerin powders are also more stable. They do, however, have two faults: they cause damage to weapons by erosion through the high temperatures generated by their explosion, and at low temperatures the nitroglycerin is exuded.

*Nitrocellulose powders:* the solvent used in the manufacture of these powders is not an explosive substance, but may be acetone, an alcohol-ether mixture, etc., which are substances eliminated by evaporation. However, the elimination is never complete, since the remaining solvent leaves the mixture slowly; the ballistic properties are consequently never reliable. This defect has been overcome by the addition of stabilizers such as diphenylamine or centralite.

Among the most important nitroglycerin powders is cordite, first produced in 1889 after a long series of experiments conducted in England under Sir Frederick Abel. It consists essentially of nitroglycerin and guncotton, made into a gelatin by the action of a volatile solvent (acetone). A small amount of petroleum jelly, originally added to prevent excessive corrosion of the barrels, slightly lowers the explosion temperature and helps to maintain stability in different climatic conditions. To avoid the erosion that occurs, especially in heavy artillery, as the result of an explosion temperature that is still high, "modified cordite" was later adopted, which contained 30% nitroglycerin, 65% nitrocellulose, and 5% petroleum jelly, as against 58% nitroglycerin, 37% nitrocellulose, and 5% petroleum jelly in ordinary cordite. Similar to modified cordite is solenite (36% nitroglycerin, 61% nitrocellulose, and 3% mineral oil), widely used in Italy for the cartridges of the Model 91 weapons.

Other nitrocellulose powders include Russian powder (Mendeleeff's pyrocollodion), the Austrian Schwab Model 92 powder, the Belgian Wetteren powder, Troisdorf powder, the commercial Dupont powders, etc. Among nitroglycerin powders, besides those already mentioned (ballistite, cordite, solenite), there are also the Austrian Model 95, $C_2$, and Maxim Schupphaus

*Ball (globular) powder.* At the beginning of the Second World War the Western Cartridge Company, now a division of Olin Industries Inc., developed a process, which immediately proved cheap and very practical, for the production of nitrocellulose powder in spherical grains. In this process the nitrocellulose (which can even be obtained from old unused powders) is pulverized in water and ethyl acetate. The mixture is heated with the addition of amide or gum arabic and, when it reaches the right viscosity, vigorously shaken. This makes it break down into little globules, the size of which depends on how long and how hard the mixture is shaken. When the solvent evaporates, the globules become dense, homogeneous, and smooth. When the suspension—the globules in water—cools, it is transferred to another still and treated with an emulsion of nitroglycerin dissolved in toluene. As the toluene evaporates, the globules are found to be covered with a film of nitroglycerin, and can be sifted while still underwater. The Ball Powder is then ready for use as soon as it is dry. The advantages of carrying out the whole process underwater without having to submit the powder to any mechanical action are obvious.

**snaffle** A form of the BIT. The mouthpiece carries a bar at each end, the BRANCHES, to form an H-shape with the bit, and it is to these branches that the reins are attached. The snaffle, which is still extensively used today, descends from the 5000-year-old prototype of all bits.

**snaphance** (or **snaphaunce**) A type of flintlock IGNITION system. *See also* IGNITION.

**snap-matchlock** A particular kind of matchlock. *See also* IGNITION.

**socket** In staff weapons, a hollow part of the head, in which the upper end of the shaft is fitted. It may be conical or truncated pyramidal, sometimes with chiseled decoration in the form of a ball, a baluster, or rings. As a rule, the socket is forged in one with the head and has two or more LANGETS for reinforcement of the shaft.

**sode** The shoulder guards of Japanese armor, YOROI. Although sode were generally worn with armor of earlier periods, they were regarded as too cumbersome and went out of fashion at about the same time as many other changes were being made in the 15th and 16th centuries to meet the new conditions of warfare. When the "modern" armor was introduced, however, they were restored. Sode are generally made of lacquered lamellae, scales of metal, laced together with silk cords, the top piece always being a strip of solid metal. Sometimes, though, they are made from a single metal plate or from a large one with one or two narrow lames below, in which case they are frequently embossed with figures. They vary in size and shape but are generally almost square, measuring from 15 to 35 cm. (6–14 in.) in width, and are secured to the armor with cords or bands attached to the upper lame.

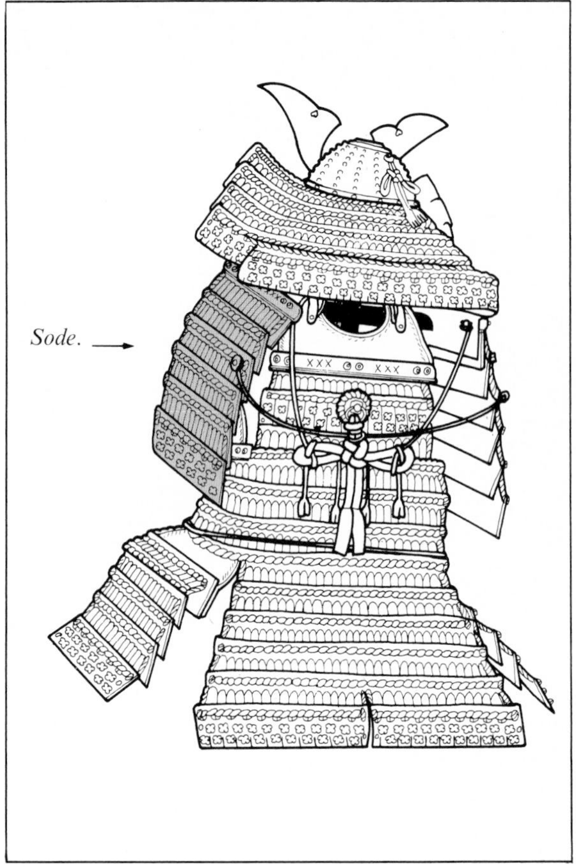


**sodegarami** A Japanese pole weapon, similar to the HINERI.

**somai** A type of two-balled BOLAS.

**somen** A type of Japanese war mask. *See also* MENPO.

**sori** The curve of a Japanese blade. *See also* BLADE: Japanese.

**soritsuno** An accessory of the SAYA.

**sosun pattah** A cut-and-thrust sword of northern India, with a blade closely related to that of the KOPIS and the YATAGAN. The word literally means "lily leaf," which is certainly apposite for the blade, which is broad, single-edged, and incurving. The typical Rajput sosun pattah has a padded basket hilt with a saucer-like pommel surmounted by an elongated curved knob, while the Islamic sosun pattah has an open hilt with a strong cross guard and langets, the grip being surmounted by a disc pommel.

**spadroon** Name given in the 18th and 19th centuries to a light, simplified version of the BROADSWORD. It had a fairly narrow cut-and-thrust blade and a closed hilt with a knuckle guard and rear quillon. The term was also applied to a fencing weapon (later called saber) in Germany and eastern Europe (the Russian rendering of the word being *espadron*).

**Spanish morion** A type of helmet which originated in Spain in the 15th century but was used in other European countries as well (where it was called the *cabasset*, from Spanish *capacete*). It had a deep almond-shaped skull with a very low comb and large curved brims. To protect the lower part of the face, the early cabassets were worn with a bevor attached to the breastplate. In the 16th century this helmet became much lighter and developed into a variant of the MORION. However, it preserved its basic original form, its skull terminating on the top in a kind of "spur" instead of a high comb typical for the combed morion.

**spanner** A flat key pierced with a square hole which fits the central spindle of a wheel-lock mechanism, enabling it to be "spanned," or wound up. In addition, spanners were used to unscrew and tighten the top jaw of the cock to replace the pyrites. Sometimes spanners were provided with a screwdriver to remove the lock from the stock.

The surfaces of the spanner afforded ample opportunity to craftsmen for pierced and chiseled work—some 17th-century Italian and German examples being extremely fine. It was usual for the spanner to be decorated *en suite* with the firearm, and some keys had swivel attachments enabling them to be fitted to a belt. Several of the Nuremberg wheel-lock pistols made for Emperor Charles V, dating from the second quarter of the 16th century, had spanners permanently fitted to the locks. Certain elaborate 17th-century keys were combined with other tools, such as priming flasks.

**sparth** A late-medieval English term for the battle-axes of Danish type. *See also* AX.

**sparum** A hafted weapon used by the Romans mainly for hunting; in emergencies it was also used as a weapon of war and sometimes as a missile weapon. The sharpened head had a blade with one curved edge.

**spaudler** A particular type of PAULDRON used from the mid-14th century. Each spaudler consisted of a series of articulated semicircular lames—usually five or six—the upper ones covering the top of the shoulder, while the lower lames were strapped over mail sleeves. From the beginning of the 16th century the lowest lame was sometimes grooved and provided with a buckled strap for attaching to the top rim of the upper CANNON of the VAMBRACE. From the late 15th century spaudlers were used mostly in Germany, often being associated with a GORGET such as the "Almain collar." To enable the collar to be opened, the spaudler on one side (usually on the right) was fixed only to the rear collar plate, the front articulating leather of the spaudler being elongated and fitted with a stud engaging in a keyhole slot in the front collar plate. The second spaudler was fixed to the collar plates with rivets and slots.

The two spaudlers, which were sometimes supplemented with BESAGEWS to protect the joint between shoulder and forearm, were symmetrical in armor for both the foot soldier and light cavalry. In armor for foot combat and the barriers, the spaudler was sometimes used on the right arm, while the left, unprotected by a weapon, carried an enlarged pauldron.

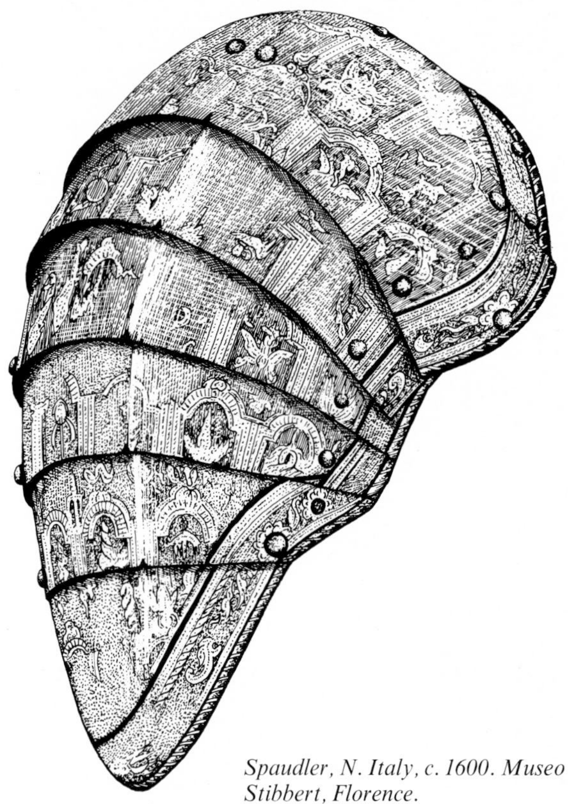

*Spaudler, N. Italy, c. 1600. Museo Stibbert, Florence.*

**spear** One of man's earliest and most widespread weapons, the spear, in its simplest form, was a wooden pole sharpened at one end with a stone or bone tool. After Paleolithic man learned to use fire (about 500,000 years ago), the point of the spear was hardened by charring. Still later, the point was reinforced with inserted splits of bone or stone, the method used up to the Upper Paleolithic period (about 8000 B.C.), or fitted with a stone head. Subsequent development of the spear produced many varieties and derivations, which in some instances led to the evolution of different kinds of pole arms.

The spear was a staff weapon mainly for thrusting, used in war and hunting, both on foot and on horseback, but many types were designed to serve primarily as missile weapons (from about 20,000–15,000 B.C.). These throwing spears were often used with special devices, spear throwers, which acted as a lever increasing the effective range of the weapon. The spear throwers were variously shaped pieces of wood, bone, or horn with a hook, hollow, or groove to engage the butt of the spear. Another kind of spear thrower was a leather thong hitched around the staff, with a loop, knot, or grip at the end held by the hand. A good example of such flexible spear throwers is the AMENTUM, used by the Greeks and the Romans up to the 2nd century A.D.

One of the most efficient weapons of the Roman infantry was a sturdy thrusting spear and, later, a special throwing spear known as the PILUM. The Greeks first introduced a very long thrusting spear, the SARISA, for use by foot soldiers in special large formations.

For use in war the Franks had a thrusting spear with a long leaf-shaped blade, also capable of cutting. At the socket the head was provided with two triangular lugs ("wings"), which prevented too deep a penetration of the weapon into a target and could also serve as a parrying guard. A version of this "winged" spear, with a somewhat shorter blade, was used for hunting, and this form survived until the 17th century. Another, and even more popular, type of hunting spear, also called the boar spear (although it was used for other big game as well), appeared toward the late 15th century, and could still be found in modern times. It had a sturdy, heavy, leaf-shaped blade with a crossbar inserted into the socket or a toggle attached to it with leather lace; such devices stopped the head from sinking too deep into a prey and prevented a wounded animal from reaching the hunter. The detachable toggle was also used to adapt a military spear for hunting purposes. The shaft of these spears was usually about the same as the average man's stature, for hunting

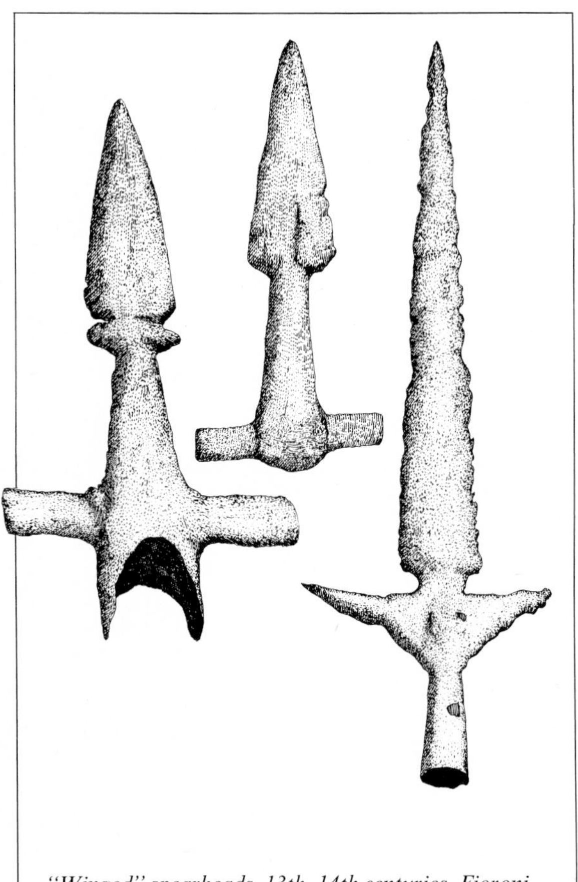

*"Winged" spearheads, 13th–14th centuries. Fioroni Museum, Legnago.*

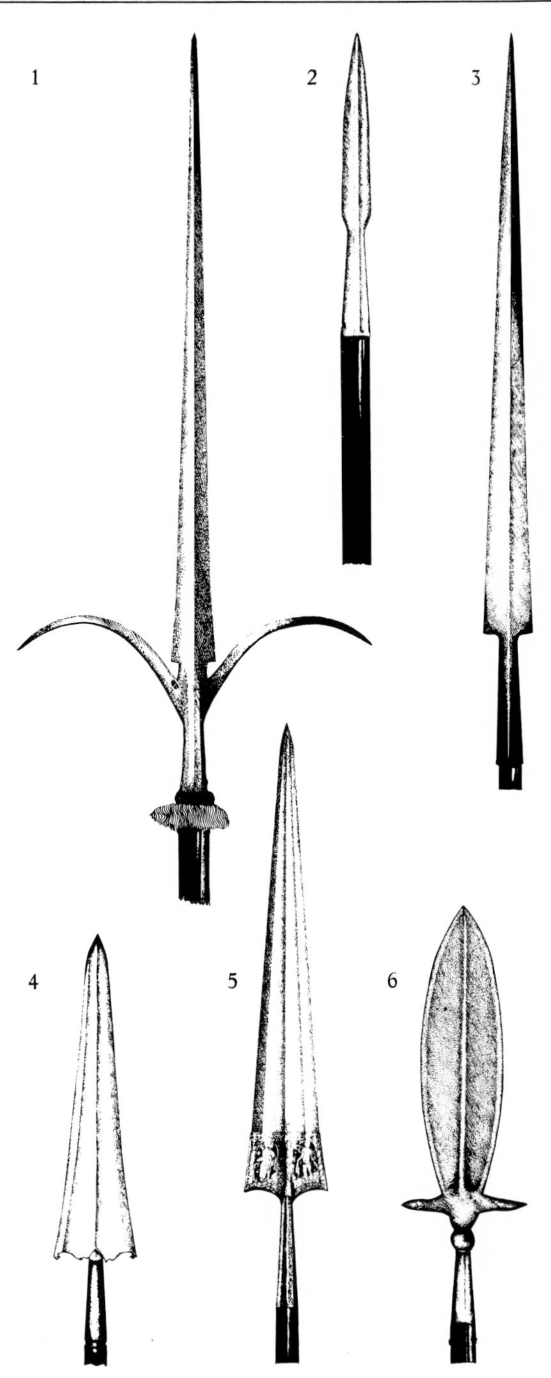


*Spearheads. 1. So-called Friuli spear, Friuli, c. 1480. Armory of the Ducal Palace, Venice. 2. Italy, c. 1480–1500. Tower of London Armouries. 3. Italy, c. 1500. The Hermitage, Leningrad. 4. Bolognese-type spear ("langdebeve"), Italy, c. 1500–1520. Musei Civici, Bologna. 5. "Langdebeve," Italy, c. 1500–1520. Tower of London Armouries. 6. Boar spear, Italy, second half of the 17th century. National Museum of Castel Sant' Angelo, Rome.*

on foot, and somewhat longer for use by mounted hunters.

In the 12th to 14th centuries, heads of European war spears usually had a leaf- or lozenge-shaped blade, but by the end of this period the Italians had introduced a new important form, which had a long, triangular, double-edged blade, fairly wide at the base and narrowing toward the point. Known as the LANGEDEBEVE or the Bolognese spear, this form, provided with lugs at the base of the blade, became a prototype for the PARTISAN, while the older "winged" war spear contributed to the development of the CORSESCA and its variations.

An interesting variant of the hunting spear was a type which had one or more gun barrels fitted alongside the blade. After the introduction of the wheel-lock mechanism in the early 16th century, which gave a reasonable guarantee of igniting the charge at the required moment, many edged weapons combined with firearms were produced in Europe. The spear-cum-firearm had the advantage of enabling the user to shoot an animal already struck by the spearhead, or even to bypass the use of the spear and shoot the animal outright. The hunting spears were often highly ornate, bearing the coat of arms or family crest of the owner.

*Folding spears. 1. N. Italy, c. 1560. Armeria Reale, Turin. 2. Italy, c. 1540. Waffensammlung, Vienna.*

A great deal of attention was always paid to the shaft of spears, which were made from yew or ash because of the excellent combination of strength and flexibility of these woods. In many cases, near the fastening of the head, hunting spears had a section of the shaft ridged with a knurling tool, carved with false knots, or covered with criss-crossed strips of leather to give the user a better grip on the weapon.

The folding spear was a special type of weapon, developed in Italy in the 16th century and later found throughout Europe. The head had a conspicuously long, straight, double-edged blade, often reinforced with ribbing; at the base of the head there were two long, curved wings, with the cutting edge on the inside. The wings could be folded in toward the head, which in turn could be folded in toward the haft; and in turn the haft could be folded two or three times, which reduced the size of the weapon and made it easier to carry. This spear served as a weapon for wealthy noblemen only, not least because of the high cost of manufacture and the expensive decoration which often embellished it.

The spears for mounted warriors underwent substantial improvements from the 14th century and became specialized cavalry weapons, now commonly called LANCES, for use either in battle or in contests. The next century saw the introduction of a special infantry spear, up to 5.5 m. (18 ft.) long, called the PIKE, which was to play an important role in the development of the art of war until the late 17th century.

**speed loader** *See* CHARGER.

**spiculum** A term used by the Romans to describe both the javelin (in this case it was synonymous with PILUM, but referred to a smaller version) and a spiked head designed for delivering blows: arrowhead, spearhead, and so on.

**spingard** According to Francesco di Giorgio Martini (Siena, 1439–1501), military architect and artist, the spingard (*spingarda*) was a piece of artillery 2.8 m. (8 ft.) long, which threw stone balls weighing between 4½ and 7 kg. (10–15 lbs.). By the early 17th century the term was applied to a light piece about 137 cm. (4½ ft.) long firing a load of "many bullets at once no greater than walnuts" (1626). Still later, and well into the 19th century, "spingard" was another word for the punt gun.

**spontoon** (or **espontoon**) Also called the HALF-PIKE, the spontoon was an infantry officers' staff weapon, with a head deriving from the pike. From the second half of the 17th century, it served as an officers' LEADING STAFF, with a shaft about half the pike's length, that is, approximately 2 m. (6½ ft.) long. The most widely used type of spontoon had a broad head, shaped like a pike's, and a crossbar (often S-shaped) in the socket. This term is sometimes also applied to smaller forms of the halberd, bill, and fork, which had the same function. Spontoons were used in

*Spingard, Italy, 15th century. Museo Nazionale d'Artigliera, Turin.*

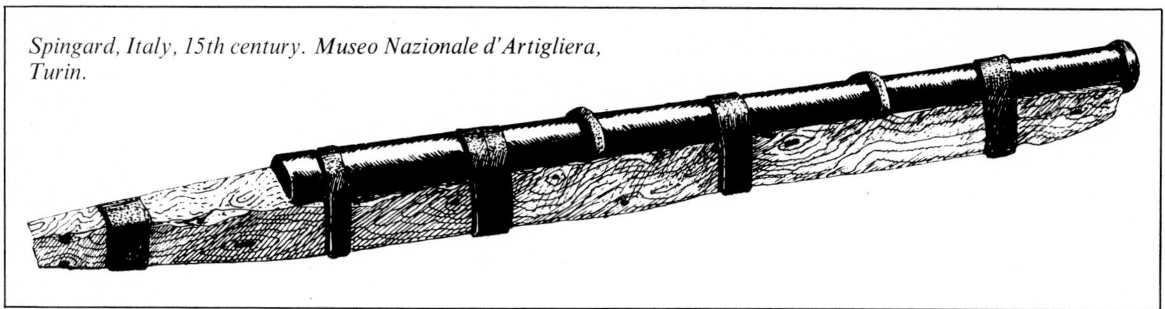

European armies until the first half of the 19th century. In England, for instance, sergeants carried them until 1830.

**spring** The earliest use of springs on firearms can be traced back at least to the mid-15th century, to the early serpentine locks. Surviving examples indicate that these springs were simply thin, flat bars of tempered steel, gradually tapering, attached to the inside of the lock plate to act against the edge of the tumbler and force the match holder to fall into the pan. On some mid-16th-century snap-matchlocks the mainspring was mounted outside the lock plate and acted on a lower extension of the match holder. The wheel-lock method of ignition, invented about 1500, required three springs—a large V-shaped mainspring which acted on the wheel by means of a chain, a smaller V-shaped spring attached to the outside of the lock plate which held the cock against the pan, and a small spring which operated the pan cover. The flintlock usually called the "snaphance," developed in the mid-16th century, required a long V-shaped mainspring, one branch of which was extended to operate on the heel of the cock or on the tumbler attached to the cock spindle. On the outside of the lock plate, at the front, a smaller V-shaped spring operated on the toe of the steel. The snaphance was also fitted with a small V-shaped trigger or sear spring, which was attached to the lock plate, on the inside of the sear. Springs were attached to the lock plate by means of a lug on the edge of the spring which fitted into a slot in the plate. This facilitated removal should the spring be damaged.

Some lock mechanisms were distinguished by their large springs. One type of wheel-lock—probably of Italian origin but often referred to as Portuguese—which is found from the mid-16th century onward, had a very large external mainspring, with the spring formed in a half-circle at the end, rather like a primitive pair of shears. The large external mainspring was a characteristic of the Spanish flintlock known as the "miquelet," developed in about 1580. In Italy the form of the miquelet known as the "Roman" lock had, in addition to the mainspring and pan-cover spring, a split trigger spring, one leaf of which pressed against the half-cock sear lever and the outer leaf pressed against the full-cock sear, both sears projecting through the lock plate. The French flintlock of the early 17th century required three springs, all of V-form—a large mainspring on the inside of the lock which operated on the tumbler, a smaller V-spring operating on the sear to give half-cock and full-cock positions, and the usual pan-cover spring. The same spring works are found on the percussion lock.

A spiral spring is found on a French gun of c. 1540 and on a group of guns made in Germany in the second quarter of the 18th century. In these guns the lock is completely concealed in the breech, the cock operating by means of a coil spring which drives it against the steel like a piston. In the late 18th century some firearms were fitted with a trigger spring, the tension of which could be altered by means of a small screw, thus allowing a "light" or "heavy" pull, as required.

Because of the need to preserve their strength, springs were never decorated on their working surfaces, but occasionally the edges were incised with simple geometric designs. The manufacture and fitting of a gun spring was always a specialized trade. Special vises were developed to facilitate their positioning and removal from a lock, as they were always under tension. These lock-spring vises were small and operated by means of a long screw with a large flat head, which could be easily turned. To remove a mainspring the gun was cocked and the vise locked over the compressed spring by means of the screw. After the cock was released the spring could then be removed from the lock plate.

In spite of the superb steel technology used on Japanese swords, Japanese firearms were invariably fitted with fairly weak brass springs. Many of the snap-matchlocks made in Japan from the early 18th century were fitted with spiral brass springs, with additional fastening holes on the sear to stretch the spring and increase its tension.

The development of the semi- and fully automatic firearms of the 20th century has involved the introduction of complex spring mechanisms, the 1908 model Mauser pistol being particularly notable in this respect. The tendency with modern automatics is to simplify the mechanism as much as possible for the sake of economy and reliability.

**spurs** Part of the equipment for a horseman, fastened to his heels to prod the horse into action. They were made of metal and usually consisted of two arch-shaped branches which straddled the heel, the end of each branch having a ring or two rings for attachment of straps and buckles; and the neck, fixed to the apex of the branches and terminating in a spike, the "prick," or a spiked wheel, the "rowel." The spurs were fastened to the feet by means of straps and buckles, except for those spurs which were worn with plate SABATONS.

*Spurs. 1. Prick spur, Europe, 12th century. 2. Prick spur, Europe, 13th century. 3. Rowel spur, Europe, second half of the 14th century. 4. Rowel spur, Europe, early 15th century. 5. Rowel spur, central or eastern Europe, second half of the 15th century. 6. Rowel spur, Germany, end of the 15th century. 7. Rowel spur, Germany, early 16th century. 8. Spur from an armour, Europe, 16th-17th century. 9. Rowel spur, western Europe, 16th-17th century. 10. Rowel spur, France, early 17th century. 11. Rowel spur, France, early 17th century. 12. Rowel spur, Italy, early 17th century. 13. Three-roweled spur, Germany, first half of the 17th century. 14. Rowel spur, England, first half of the 17th century. 15. Rowel spur, Spain, first half of the 17th century. 16. 32-pointed rowel spur, France, mid-18th century.*

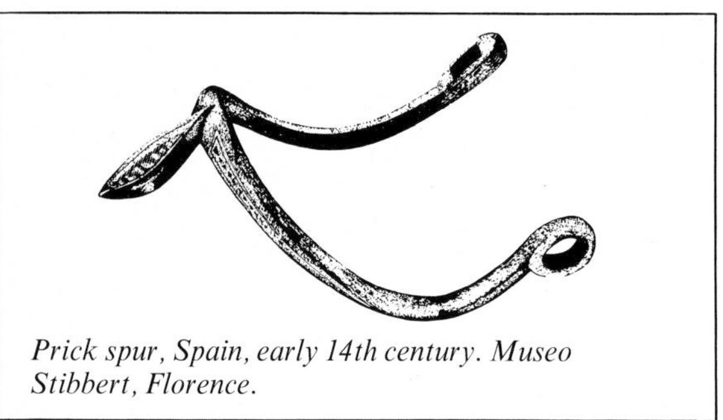

*Prick spur, Spain, early 14th century. Museo Stibbert, Florence.*

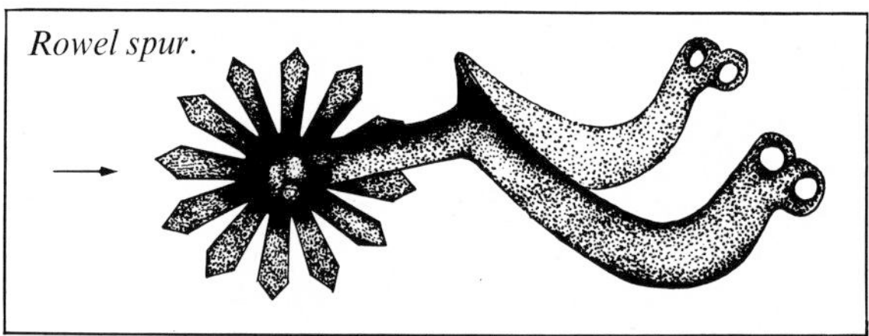

*Rowel spur.*

The oldest recorded type of spur, which remained in use from the time of ancient Greece and Rome up to the 17th century (and is still used today in African, Arab, and some South American countries), was the "prick spur," in which the branches were semicircular or ogival and the neck ended in a spike. The most highly developed spur—which was already in use by about the 1240s and was to become the most widely used type, even to this day—was the "rowel spur." Instead of a prick, it had a rotating spiked wheel installed between two prongs at the end of the spur neck, through which the axle of the wheel passed. Although this structure changed little over the centuries, countless variations of it were produced which, within certain limits, can be dated. Such variations were in the positioning and the form of the rowel, as well as in the shape of the branches and buckles. Initially, the rowel had many small teeth, but in the 14th and 15th centuries they became longer and fewer in number, six being widely used. Later, the number of teeth was again increased, to as many as thirty-two.

There were no hard-and-fast rules, however. In the 17th and 18th centuries, for example, the types of spurs most frequently worn had either a very small rowel or a rowel with indentations that hardly projected at all. During the same period a rowel with widely spaced spikes that were particularly strong and sharp-pointed was also being used, although it was reserved for exceptionally difficult horses. The length of the spur neck, which in the 14th century had been short and heavy, grew longer until it reached the imposing dimensions which can be seen in examples from about 1450–1500. The neck became more curved and heavily ornamented as the 16th century advanced, while the strap rings on the branches were sometimes doubled or even tripled; this inevitably necessitated altering the shape of the branches themselves, so to give more support on the top boot, and this was the trend from the 17th century onward.

As a rule, spurs were made of iron, but other metals were frequently used too, such as bronze—especially in the Middle Ages—and silver. They were freely decorated with chiseling and engraving, with inlaid work and damascening, mainly on the branches, buckles, and spur neck.

Spurs of special construction were worn with the complete GREAVE or with the iron sabaton. The most widely used type had considerably shortened branches without strap rings. The branch was fixed to the greave or sabaton by being passed through a staple and kept in place by a locking bar. Occasionally the spur had no branches at all, the spur neck being brazed directly onto a plate of the greave or sabaton.

A light type of spur was used from the 17th century. It had no branches and the spur neck carrying the rowel was either screwed directly to the boot heel or soldered to a large, curved rectangular plate shaped to the heel, to which it was fastened by two screws. The supporting plate was often decorated with engraving or piercings. A particular type of 17th- and 18th-century spur had another system of attachment to the foot. The neck with the rowel was usually short and fixed not to branches but to a thin metal plate shaped to the heel and partially going under the sole; to this metal plate were fitted D-shaped rings carrying a strap that passed over the instep.

**squama** Latin term for SCALE and, by extension, scale armor.

**staff weapons** A generic term for hafted weapons, that is, edged weapons mounted on a short handle or on a long two-handed shaft usually made of wood, but sometimes of metal. Depending on period and region, the head of a staff weapon was attached to the haft by various methods (lacing, nailing, riveting, socketing).

**standard** (of mail) *See* AVENTAIL.

**steadying ring** The section of a shell casing with increased diameter to perform the function of the steadying band (*see* DRIVING BAND).

**steel** In the snaphance and flintlock systems of ignition, the steel plate (also called the frizzen) against which the pyrites or flint strikes to produce sparks, thus enabling the charge to ignite. The earliest recorded steel is to be found on a snaphance musket in the Livrustkammaren in Stockholm, which was probably fitted with a snaphance lock in 1556. The steel of this lock is narrow and rectangular, and attached to a long arm. In Italy, by the late 16th century, the steel was combined with the cover of the pan to create a snaphance lock combined with a wheel-lock, an example of which—unfortunately detached from its original gun—dating probably from about 1580, can be seen in the Artillery Museum, Turin. The steel was attached to the pan by means of a screw, allowing the steel to pivot forward.

The steel began to develop its elegant rounded profile with the advancement of the flintlock in France during the early 17th century. The combined flintlock and matchlock gun made by François du Clos, dated 1636 (in the Musée de l'Armée, Paris), is fitted with a steel having a concave face and pointed profile, very similar to those in use some two hundred years later. In about 1775 the form of the steel underwent a further improvement with the introduction of the roller bearing. The end of the steel was extended on the opposite side of the buffer to take a small roller bearing. This speeded up the process of ignition by reducing the friction on the steel. Not all steels followed this line of development, however, and the Spanish gunmakers of Ripoll, for example, still employed the small square-shaped steel until the end of the 18th century. In some instances steels were made with a detachable striking plate on the face which could be replaced when worn out.

The introduction of the percussion lock in the early 19th century rendered the steel, and the flintlock itself, obsolete.

In the 17th to 19th centuries, the steel was also referred to as a "hammer" in England.

**steel skull** A form of protection used in the 17th century for the crown of the head. It consisted of a metal skullcap. made in one piece, worn under the felt hat of the period. Holes pierced all around the lower edge enabled a padded lining to be sewn inside. The skull was virtually invisible (for which reason it was also called a secrète) and could be worn by civilians as well as soldiers. A variation of the skull was made of riveted strips of iron, and specimens are known which could be folded when not in use. A few instances of a pair of cheekpieces having been fitted to the skull are also documented.

**stiletto** (or **stylet**) A short dagger with a triangular- or square-sectioned blade which was strong, slender, and sharply pointed. The name seems to stem from the word "stylus," a small pointed instrument used since ancient times for writing and drawing on wax tablets. Because this easily concealed weapon was designed exclusively for delivering thrusts, it was often prohibited in peacetime in towns and cities. Nevertheless, it was a very widespread weapon in the period when mail and leather were used in civil life to protect the body, because it could easily pierce these defences with a swift stabbing blow.

Blades of this sort have been used by all the European peoples, so the furniture tends to be very varied. In the 17th and 18th centuries, and particularly, though not exclusively, in central and northern Italy, the stiletto was made entirely of steel. The hilt included a small spherical pommel, somewhat flattened, or a pommel in the form of a spiraled pine cone. The handle consisted of rings and balusters, either smooth or twisted; the straight guard with short quillons had finials which echoed the form and pattern of the pommel. One specific type of stiletto was the weapon issued to artillery commanders, the GUNNER'S STILETTO. The compact size of the weapon made it possible to conceal it in a wide variety of larger arms. Stilettos were commonly found in sword sticks and sword handles, and even in the back of the sheaths of traveling or household knives.

**stirrups** Accessories of the saddle whose purpose was (and still is) to facilitate mounting and to give the rider greater security when riding. Their origins are believed to

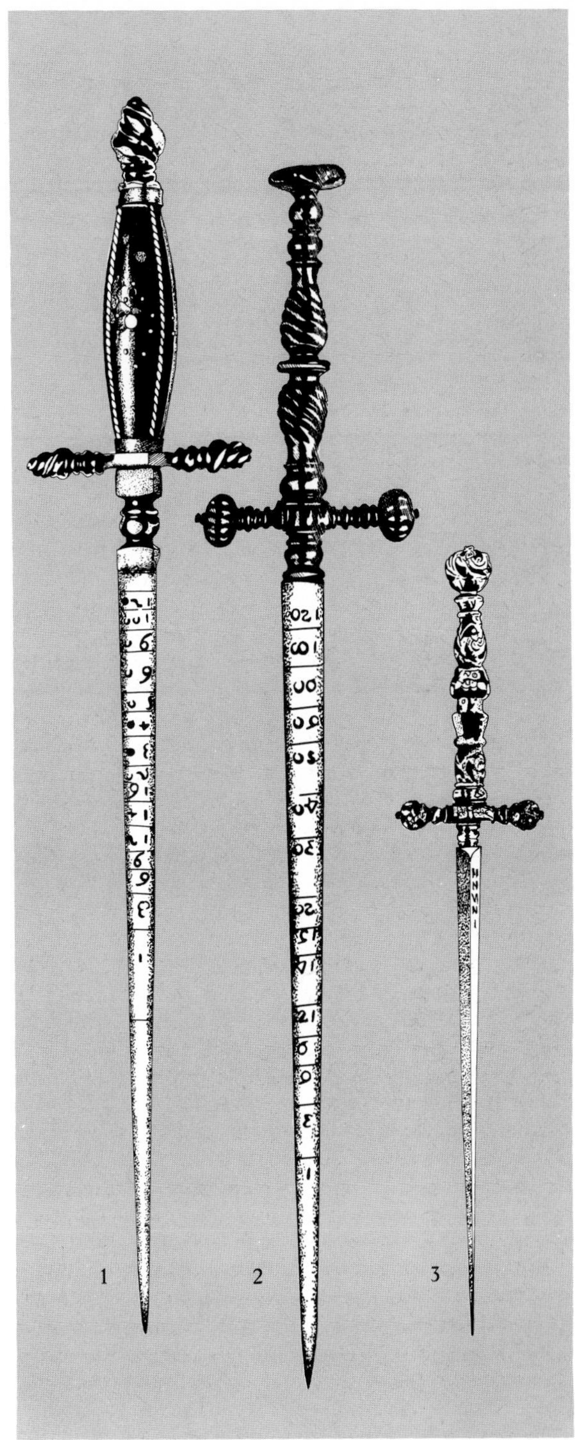


*Gunner's stiletto, N. Italy, second half of the 17th century. Odescalchi Collection, Museo di Palazzo Venezia, Rome.*
*2. Gunner's stiletto, N. Italy, second half of the 17th century. Museo Nazionale del Bargello, Florence.*
*3. Stiletto, N. Italy, second half of the 17th century. Museo Poldi Pezzoli, Milan.*

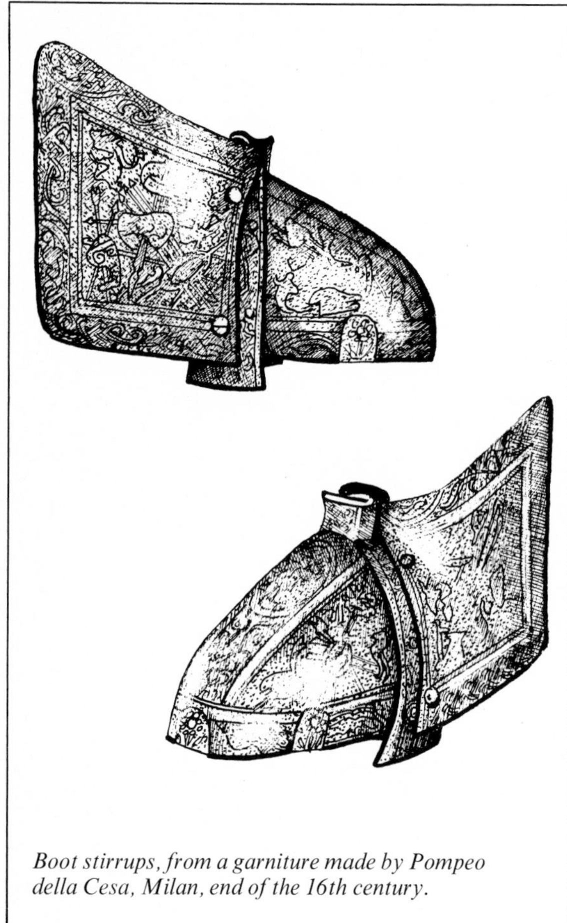

*Boot stirrups, from a garniture made by Pompeo della Cesa, Milan, end of the 16th century.*

have been in Asia (about the Japanese stirrup, *see* ABUMI) prior to the 3rd or 4th century A.D. They were probably introduced into Europe by the invading horsemen from the Steppes—a fact noted by the Byzantine emperor Maurice Tiberius (582–602) in his *Art of War*. Basically they consisted of a footplate or a bar on which the foot rested, with two sidepieces or branches, attached to each side of the footplate and curving up over the foot to meet at the apex, where a ring or pierced slit held the stirrup leathers by which they were suspended from the saddle. The stirrup leathers consisted of two straps with a buckle at one end and holes for adjusting the length at the other. After being threaded through the ring or slit of the stirrup iron, the leathers were slipped behind the metal bar at each side of the saddletree and subsequently adjusted to the correct length for the rider.

Metal stirrups had been used in western Europe, in their trapezoidal form, since at least the 10th century, when they replaced the simple double strap. Many modifications have taken place over the centuries, in order to adapt to changing types of footgear and styles of mounted combat, but the basic principle has remained the same. The modifications mainly affected the shape of the sidepieces, the width of the footplate, and the position of the ring for the leather. Instead of a footplate, in the early, simpler forms there was a horizontal bar of wood or metal attached to two sloping sidepieces. By the 15th century, more complex designs of the foot support were in use, such as the double-barred, ring-shaped, barred-and-ring-shaped, and footplates made from solid iron. Attachment to the sidepieces, which had by now become curved, was either by brazing, hollow rims and flanges, or with screws.

A particularly noticeable variation took place in the 16th century when broad-toed SABATONS were introduced, which caused the sidepieces of the irons to be opened up into a wide oval or rounded shape and the footplate to be lengthened. Some specialized types of stirrup irons appeared about this time, among which were the boot stirrup and the cage stirrup (*see below*). By the 17th century the shape of the stirrup iron had become relatively stable, with sides either cut from a metal plate or made of closely placed metal strips.

Stirrup irons were quite frequently decorated with engraving, embossing, chiseling, and sometimes even damascening. Such ornamentation was usually worked on the sidepieces and ring but seldom on the footplate.

The *cage stirrup* was a special form of iron used mainly from about 1500–1550 to accommodate the broad-toed (so-called bear's paw) sabatons. Its main features were the broad footplate and sidepieces combined with curved narrow bars running from the ring to the toe of the footplate.

*Stirrups "á la jineta"* were first used by mounted Arab troops, *jinete* being the Spanish name for a soldier in such a regiment, and were later adopted by horsemen in the Middle East and the Balkans. Their main feature was the slightly convex, oblong footplate. Each sidepiece consisted either of a solid plate attached to the footplate or was formed from the upward-bent sides of the footplate itself. These stirrups were particularly suitable for use with Eastern high saddles and short stirrup leathers, which meant that the rider's leg, being strongly bent, required a larger surface to maintain a firm foothold. It is interesting to note that the word *jinete* originates from "Zenāta," a Berber tribe in North Africa famous for its horsemen.

A European variation of the stirrup "á la jineta" was worn in the 16th to 18th centuries. Its slightly convex footplate was often made from a solid plate, while the sidepieces were either attached to it or made in one piece with it. They were quadrilateral, narrow at the top and broadening out to the footplate; they were joined at the top by a narrow bridge with a ring for the stirrup leather. Irons of this kind were frequently decorated with damascening, filigree, and chiseling.

The *boot stirrup* was used during the 16th century, mainly for jousting—particularly in the German style. In its complete form, the iron was shaped as the front part of a sabaton, open at the back to enable the foot to be slipped in easily. It had the arched sidepiece to provide a slot for the stirrup leather and a protective wing on the outside of each stirrup. A more common form, however, covered only the toe and had the arc with a slot for the stirrup leather. Boot stirrups were rarely decorated and were made from either an iron plate or several plates riveted together.

The *rowel-spurred stirrup* was a relatively rare design only occasionally made before the 18th century, when it gained some popularity in the Balkans. Basically it consisted of a common type of stirrup to which a rowel SPUR was brazed rather than being fastened onto the foot. It never achieved much success, since it was difficult to apply the spurs without jeopardizing the foothold.

**stock** In small arms, especially long arms, the stock contains or joins the various components so that the gun can be handled, aimed, and fired. Initially, before the 16th century, the stock was very simply shaped, often being only a polelike extension of the barrel. Improvements in the ignition methods and increased use of guns for aimed fire and target shooting led to the development of the stocks, particularly their rear part, the BUTT.

The stocks of long arms have been generally made of a close-grained wood, well seasoned and without knots. Walnut is the best; though expensive, it is very strong without being too heavy. There are three main parts to the stock of a gun: the forestock; the grip, or small of the butt; and the butt. The forestock protects the barrel and allows the firer to hold the gun without burning his hand as he fires. To give added firmness to the connection of the barrel to the stock and transmit the recoil directly to the butt, a metal cross-pin is often fitted in the stock, with a tooth from the receiver engaging with it. The grip is the waisted section of the butt, held by the hand that works the trigger; it is usually oval in section, with its major axis in the plane of symmetry of the weapon. Sometimes there is a conveniently shaped thumb recess where the butt joins the grip, to give the firer's hand a comfortable grip as he aims. The butt supports the weapon firmly against the firer's shoulder as he aims and fires. Its axis follows the axis of the grip; in modern guns it is almost elliptical in section, and elongated, with its major axis in the plane of symmetry of the weapon.

**stomach lame** A rare piece for the Italian joust, used in the first half of the 16th century. It consisted of a heavy, shaped plate screwed onto the lower left edge of the breastplate in such a way that it doubled the thickness of the SKIRT. It was frequently supplemented by a left over-tasset.

**stop rib** An accessory to the BREASTPLATE, added toward the end of the 14th century, as an extra safeguard to supplement the reinforced neck edge and prevent an opponent's weapon from sliding up into the throat. It consisted of a narrow strip of iron, square or round in section, fixed just below the neck edge with two or three screws or rivets. It was generally in the form of a wide V, although the shape varied a great deal, some being quite straight and others fairly curved. A stop rib was also sometimes fitted just below the upper border or pauldrons, vambraces, and cuisses.

**strap** Also called the back strap, a metal strip covering the back of the butt of a handgun and running from the rear of the barrel to strengthen the grip. It was mainly a military feature.

**stringing** The difference between the distances traveled by the first and last pellets in the discharge from a shotgun. The pellets leave the muzzle at substantially different velocities, so that probably not more that 40 percent of them represent the actual killing value of the shot.

**submachine gun** Individual portable weapon designed for rapid fire of pistol ammunition; known also as a machine pistol. From a mechanical point of view, the closure action of submachine guns is generally on the "blowback" principle; on firing, obturation is ensured only by the friction between the cartridge case and the chamber and by the inertia of the breechblock. With a few exceptions, submachine guns are extremely simple and easy to manufacture; they usually fire from the open breech position to avoid cook-off (premature ignition due to heat) of the chambered cartridge. A submachine gun generally consists of the following components: barrel; receiver; bolt or breechblock; feed system; firing mechanism, selector, and safety catch; butt stock.

The barrel, generally rather short, is fixed to the receiver, which may be either rectangular or, as in most cases, cylindrical, and may be pressed from sheet steel (as in the Madsen model 1950 submachine gun) or by milling from the steel block (as in all the Thompsons). The receiver, besides holding the barrel, contains the firing mechanism and the magazine housing. The breechblock or bolt, propelled forward by one or more return springs, travels inside the receiver, which has a longitudinal slot in the side or top for the cocking handle, which in most cases forms part of the bolt. At the front of the bolt is the extractor, and underneath it (or on the side, according to where the magazine is fitted) is a groove to make way for the magazine as the bolt is closed.

The firing pin may be (a) fixed, as in the Sten; (b) mobile, on its own mounting but moving together with the bolt, as in the M.P. 18/I; or (c) moving independently of, and not necessarily simultaneously with, the bolt, as in the Bergmann M.P. 34/I.

The ejector is normally fitted inside the receiver so that the spent cartridge strikes against it as it is extracted and is thrown out of the gun through an opening for that purpose. The feed system consists of a detachable magazine and the magazine housing on the gun. The magazines (sometimes incorrectly called "chargers") may be of various shapes; the commonest is still a rectangular box containing a double column of cartridges.

The firing mechanism consists of the trigger (in some guns, such as the MAB, there are two triggers) and, in the simplest actions, the lever and the sear; pressing the trigger lowers the sear and releases the bolt to move forward.

The most sophisticated weapons are designed for both semiautomatic and automatic fire and are therefore fitted with a selector, generally combined with the safety catch. We also often find an "automatic" grip safety which prevents firing if the weapon is not held properly (e.g., UZI, Madsen model 1950, etc.).

The firing cycle of a typical submachine gun is as follows. A magazine is fitted to the magazine housing, and the breechblock is pulled back by the cocking handle until it is caught and held by the sear. When the trigger is pressed the breechblock, propelled by the compressed

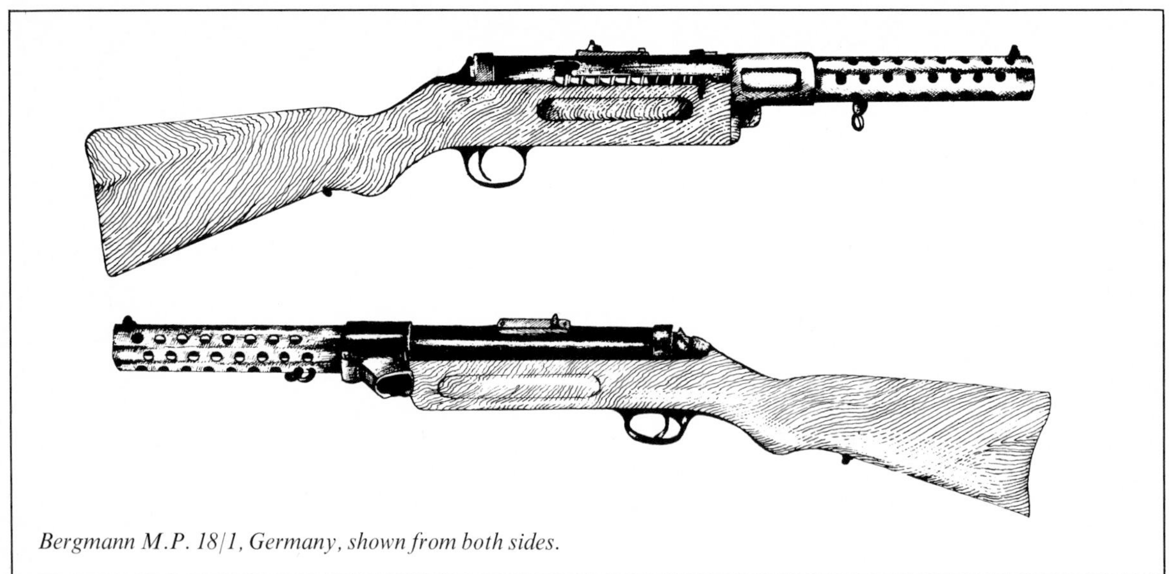

*Bergmann M.P. 18/1, Germany, shown from both sides.*

return spring, moves quickly forward. As it passes the magazine its face extracts the first cartridge and presses it into the chamber. A fraction of a second before closure is completed, the firing pin strikes the percussion cap and fires the charge. The gases produced act, naturally, in all directions; they drive the bullet forward, press the walls of the case against the chamber, and, through the base of the cartridge, press against the face of the breechblock. Friction between the case and the chamber, the inertia of the breechblock, and, in an almost negligible way, the resistance of the return spring delay the opening of the breech until the bullet has left the barrel and the internal pressure fallen to the surrounding level. The breechblock is then driven back together with the spent case, which strikes the ejector and is thrown out of the gun. Still traveling backward, the breechblock compresses the return spring. If the trigger is still pressed, the spring then drives the breechblock forward again, and the cycle described above is repeated, and will continue as long as the trigger is pressed until the magazine is empty.

*Origins*

The first submachine gun was perhaps the Villar Perosa, designed by Abiel Bethel Revelli and used by the Italian army in the First World War; but that was actually designed, and used, as a light machine gun, and as such was not a great success. In the form adopted, the Villar Perosa consisted of two independent guns joined rigidly side by side. It was chambered for the standard 9 mm. Glisenti model 1910 pistol cartridge and had a delayed-blowback action. A powerful return spring and light bolt combined to give it a very high rate of fire, in theory 1250 rounds per minute, or 50 rounds in 1.2 seconds. Feed was

*Beretta (MAB) Model 38A submachine gun, Italy.*

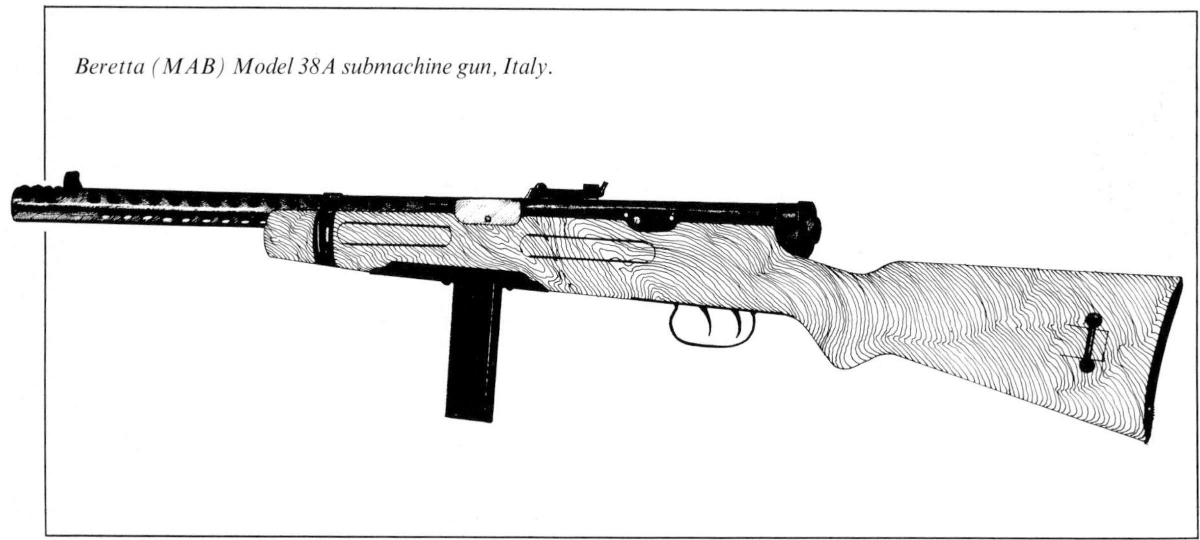

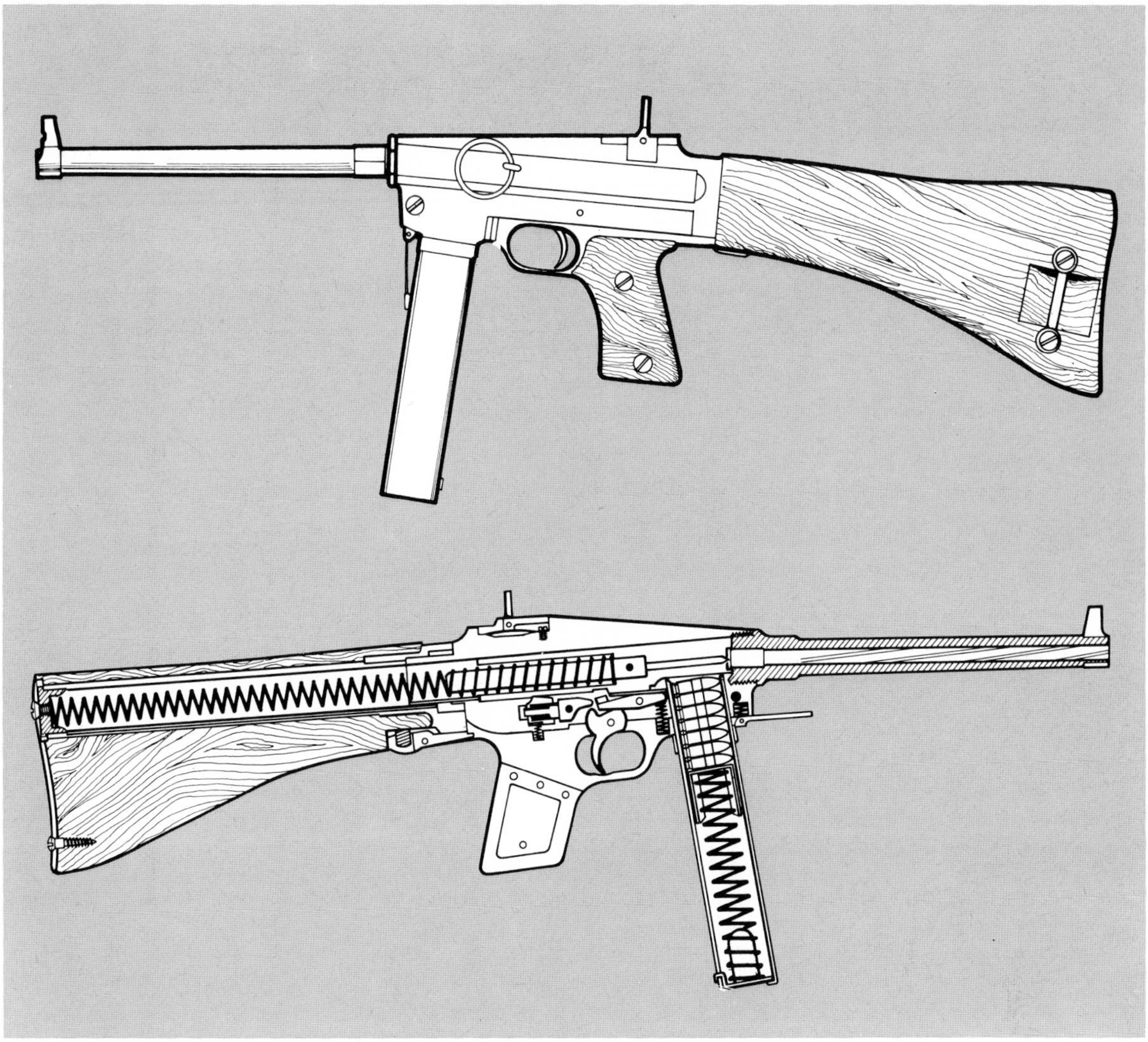

*MAS-38 submachine gun, France; below, the same in section.*

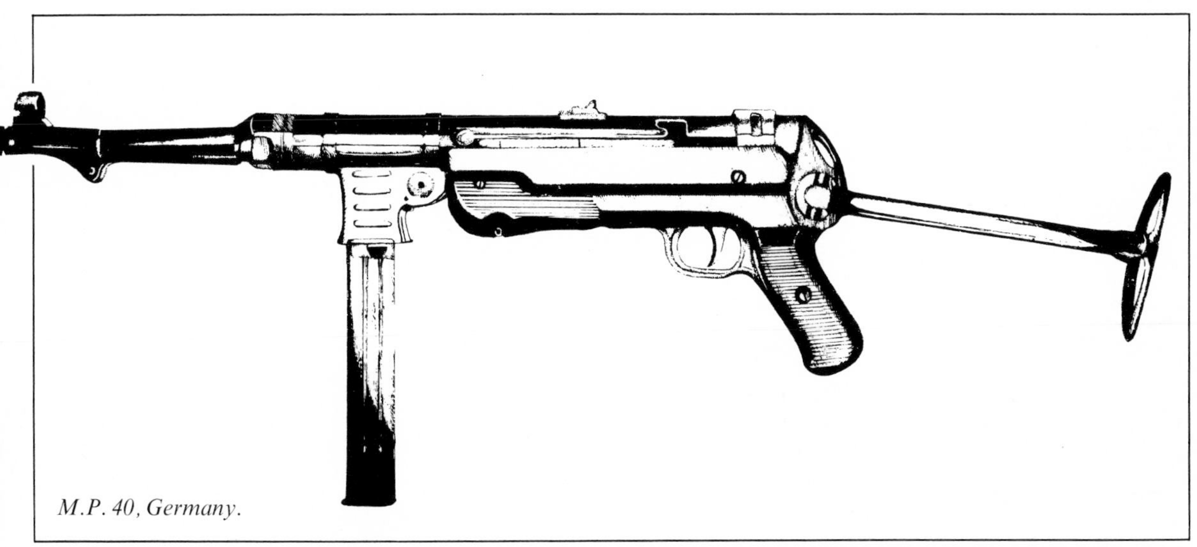

*M.P. 40, Germany.*

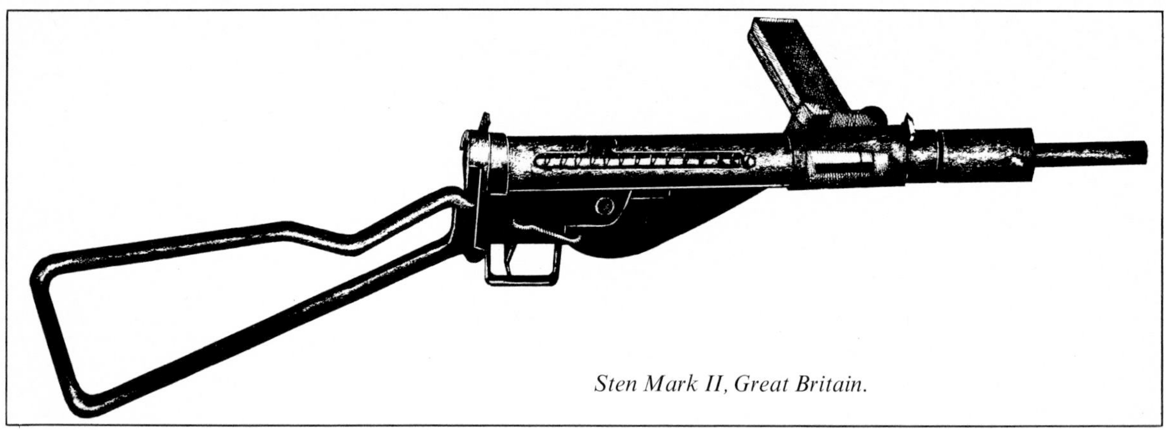

*Sten Mark II, Great Britain.*

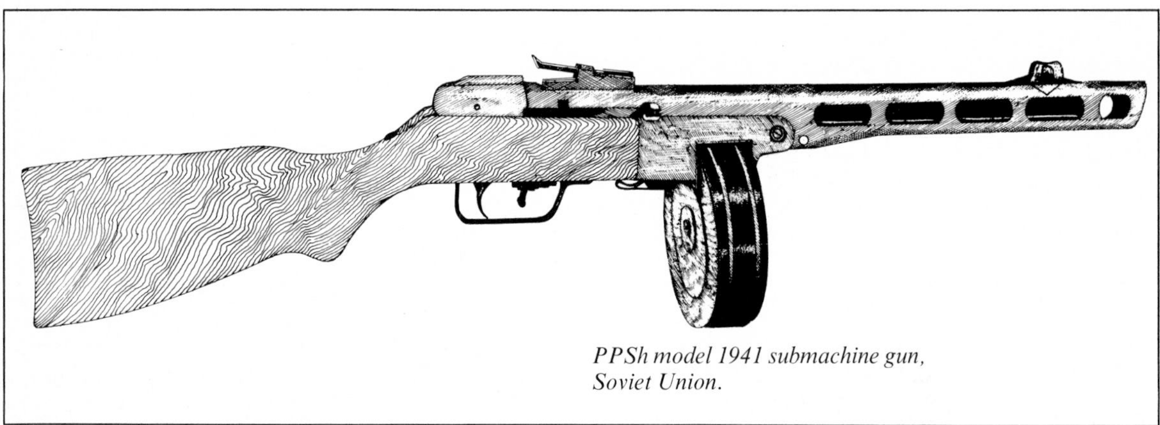

*PPSh model 1941 submachine gun, Soviet Union.*

by a curved box magazine holding 25 rounds.

The German Maschinenpistole 18/I (M.P. 18/I) was perhaps the first submachine gun with blowback action ever produced and adopted. The development of this very important weapon began in 1916 at the Bergmann factories at Gaggenau and Suhl. It may be that the Germans had been impressed by specimens of the Villar Perosa captured in Italy; warned how ineffective the gun was in the light-machine-gun role, they recognized its great possibilities as an individual small arm. Hugo Schmeisser, unquestionably the most famous and most gifted of all designers of this type of weapon, produced a prototype which was named after the year it appeared, M.P. 18. After some small modifications had been made to the prototype, mass production of the weapon, now named M.P. 18/I, began in the spring of 1918. Many features of it, both aesthetic and mechanical, were to be shared by almost every future design. It had a one-piece stock, a perforated barrel jacket screwed to the receiver, a very simple bolt, and an even simpler firing mechanism. Indeed, this submachine gun, which in every other way was a milestone in the history of the development of firearms, had only one weak point, the feed system, which used the clumsy "snail" drum magazine of the model 1908 Artillery Luger pistol. Around 1925 all existing M.P. 18/I guns were substantially modified by changing the feed system to take new pressed-steel box magazines which Schmeisser had designed; thus rejuvenated, they appeared again in the Second World War.

A series of submachine guns which became only too famous between the wars was that produced in the United States by the Auto-Ordnance Corporation and known by the trade name of Thompson. General John T. Thompson was in fact head of the company's design department, but credit for the actual design must go to O. V. Payne and T. H. Eickoff, who held the main relevant patents. After a series of prototypes had been produced between 1918 and 1920, mass production of the Thompson model 1921 began in that year, and it soon became one of the most famous of all guns of its type. The model 1921 had a delayed-blowback closure; an H-shaped bronze piece with two projecting lugs fitted to the bolt held up the opening of the breech and reduced the rate of fire. Feed was either by double-column box magazines of various capacities or by drum magazines, which were widely used and became one of the best-known features of the appearance of the gun. The model 1921 was followed by the model 1923, identical mechanically but intended for military rather than police use. The next model, the 1927, offered with or without the Cutts compensator, was only a semiautomatic; its production was justified by the desire to profit commercially from the tremendous notoriety won by the model 1921 during Prohibition, enhanced by the "St. Valentine's Day Massacre" (February 14, 1929), when Al Capone's gangsters, armed with two model 1921 Thompson guns, wiped out half the rival gang of "Bugs" Moran. The model 1928 differed from the model 1921 only in its lower rate of fire (700 rounds per minute as against 800), the result of a redesigned cocking mechanism.

With the outbreak of the Second World War the demand for these weapons grew out of all proportion, and it was necessary to simplify the design to speed up production. The new Thompson models, the M-1 and M-1A, lost the complex delayed-blowback system and used only the double-column box magazine.

### *Second World War*

The most important research into the improvement of the submachine gun, carried out in Europe between the wars, was done in Germany. Toward the end of the 1920s Hugo Schmeisser produced the M.P. 28/II, a weapon much like the earlier M.P. 18/I but fitted with a selector and quadrant sights. In 1932 Theodor Emil Bergmann patented a submachine gun which was produced as the M.P. 34/I and later, modified, as the M.P. 35/I; it was widely used in the Spanish Civil War and by the Waffen SS in the Second World War. Another interesting gun was that known as the ERMA (from the factory where it was made, the Erfurter Maschinenfabrik), designed by Heinrich Vollmer with the collaboration of Berthold Geipel. In 1936, in response to military requirements, the famous M.P. 38 appeared, which, together with the later M.P. 40, was to be the German submachine gun most widely used and admired in the Second World War. The M.P. 38, of a simplicity surpassed only by the M.P. 40 and the British Sten, had the outstanding feature of being the first gun of its kind completely made of metal and plastic. It had a practical folding butt, and the return spring was contained in a telescopic tubular casing which had the striker at the front. The bolt, like the rest of the very simple action, was much like that of the old M.P. 18/I. The M.P. 40 was a highly successful attempt to adapt the production of the new weapon to the exigencies of the wartime economy; the receiver, the pistol-grip frame, and other parts were stamped out of heavy sheet steel, cutting down remarkably on the cost and the time taken for manufacture.

Between the two world wars the submachine gun became established as the infantry weapon par excellence, and many countries set out to make their own.

In Austria, where even in the First World War they had used a pistol model 1911 with an enlarged magazine that was also capable of rapid fire, the admirable Steyr-Solothurn model 1930 was adopted by the police in 1930, and a few years later the army adopted the Steyr-Solothurn model 1934. Belgium meanwhile adopted an exact copy of the German M.P. 28/II under the name of Model 34.

In Czechoslovakia and Bulgaria they used the ZK-383, an excellent but complicated weapon with a bipod and a bolt whose weight could be adjusted to alter the rate of fire.

France remained faithful to the not very powerful 7.65 mm. long cartridge and chose the small but well-made MAS-38.

Italy had one of the best weapons in this class from any point of view (apart from weight and cost) in the excellent MAB (Moschetto Automatico Beretta) 38/a.

In Switzerland the Schweizerische Industrie Gesellschaft (SIG) first manufactured the M.P. 18/I under license and then produced its own excellent but expensive MKMO and MKPO.

The British Lanchester Mark I was only a copy of the German M.P. 28/II, and it was not until 1941, when the Sten gun was brought into service, that the United Kingdom had a cheap and efficient gun of its own. The Sten (so called from the surname initials of the designers, Reginald Vernon Shepherd and Harold John Turpin, and the first two letters of Enfield) was one of the simplest submachine guns ever made; the Mark I, II, and III, mass-produced, cost no more than $11 each. Roughly finished, with no great accuracy, the Sten had a selector and a very simple safety device that secured the cocking handle, a device first seen on the M.P. 18/I. It was one of the first guns of its kind with a fixed striker.

In Finland the designer Aimo J. Lahti designed some interesting submachine guns, including the Suomi models 1926 and 1931. The highly successful model 1931 was adopted by Finland, Sweden, and Switzerland.

The Soviet Union, after the not very convincing performance of the Tokarev model 1926 and the Mauser-Korovin model 1930, adopted a series of submachine guns designed by V. A. Degtyarev and known as the PPD 1934, PPD 1938, and PPD 1940. These guns, which combined the best features of the Schmeisser and the Suomi, turned out to be so expensive that they were soon replaced by the new PPSh 1941, a simple and robust weapon designed by Georgii S. Shpagin. By the end of the 1940s at least 5 million of these first-class submachine guns had been produced in Soviet factories. The PPSh had some extremely interesting features, including a perforated barrel jacket and a drum magazine holding no fewer than seventy-one 7.62 mm. cartridges.

### *Postwar Progress*

Progress in submachine gun design was by no means exhausted after the Second World War; it was channeled in two main directions, the production of weapons that would be cheap but still very efficient, and the construction of more sophisticated weapons capable of still better performance.

The first objective led to the production of guns like the Madsen models 1946 and 1950, the MAT-49, and the Vigneron M-2; improved stamping techniques and the technological advances made during the war made it possible to hold down the cost of production to a remarkable extent while still having what was in every respect a "finished" product. The second objective—which was not allowed to obscure the first—led to the design of such submachine guns as the Czechoslovak M-24, the Israeli UZI, and the Italian M-12. The Madsen model 1946 and a slightly improved variant of it, the model

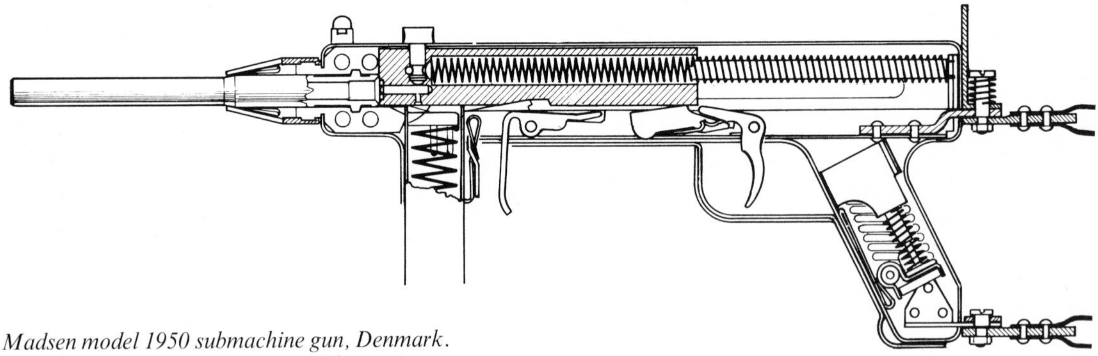

*Madsen model 1950 submachine gun, Denmark.*
Above, *in section;* below, *side and front views.*

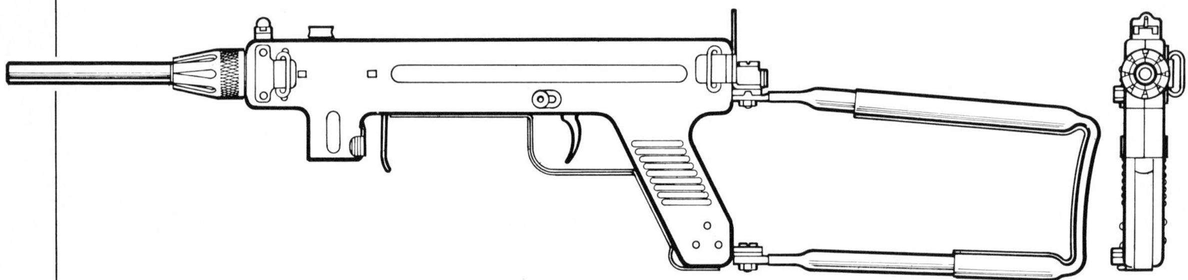

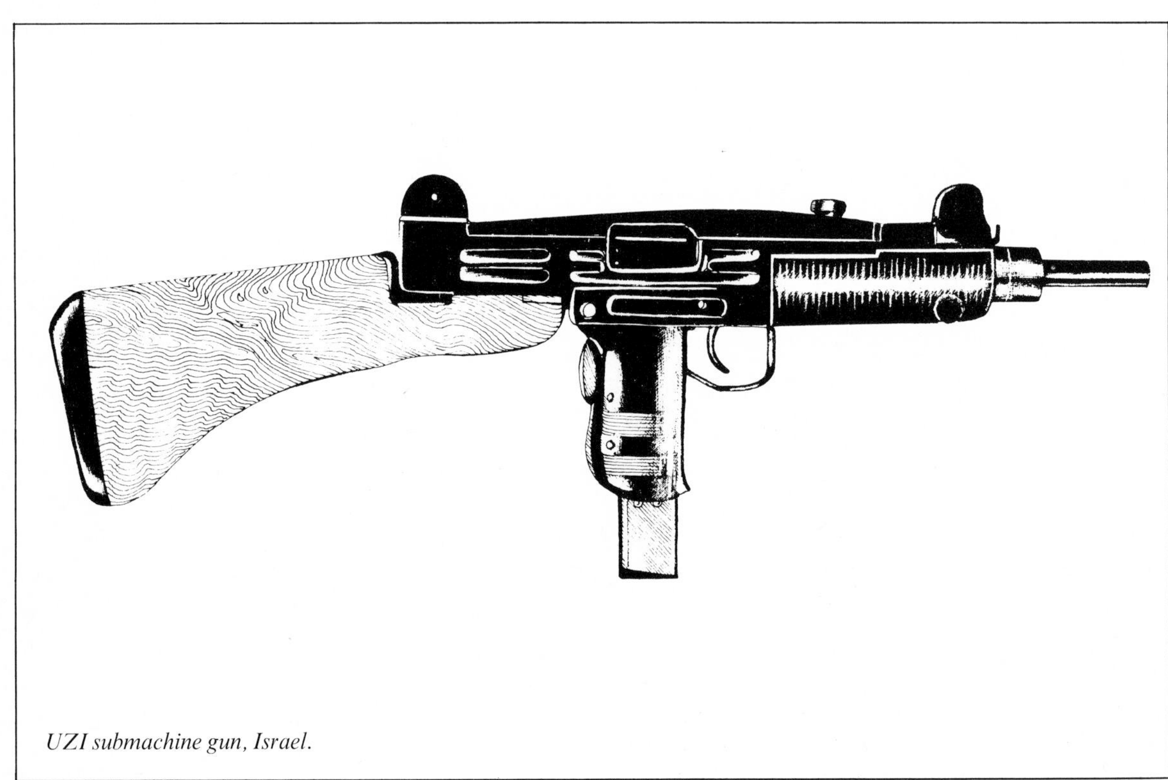

*UZI submachine gun, Israel.*

*MP-5, West Germany.*

1950, produced by the Danske Industrie Syndikat, Compagnie Madsen A.S., represented what was once described as "triumphs of stamping engineering design." And indeed those weapons, perfect as they were, were extremely cheap to produce. The pistol grip, the frame (receiver), and the magazine housing were stamped out of two pieces of sheet steel hinged together at the back of the gun. These two halves were joined together and with the barrel by a large retaining nut fixed in the barrel and screwed into the front of the receiver. The left side of this construction was actually a "lid" for the right half, which acted as the real frame and in which the simple rectangular bolt slid.

The MAT-49, produced by the Manufacture d'Armes de Tulle and still in service with the French forces, has frame, barrel jacket, firing mechanism and safety, ejection port and magazine housing all of pressed steel. Another feature of this gun is that the magazine housing, which also acts as the front pistol grip, can be turned forward to a position parallel with the barrel.

Moving on to more sophisticated weapons, we must first mention the Czechoslovak Model 23, designed by Vaclav Holek, which appeared in 1948. It was the first mass-produced weapon with an important new feature: the bolt was hollowed out in front so that it partly overhung the rear of the barrel on firing. This had a highly important

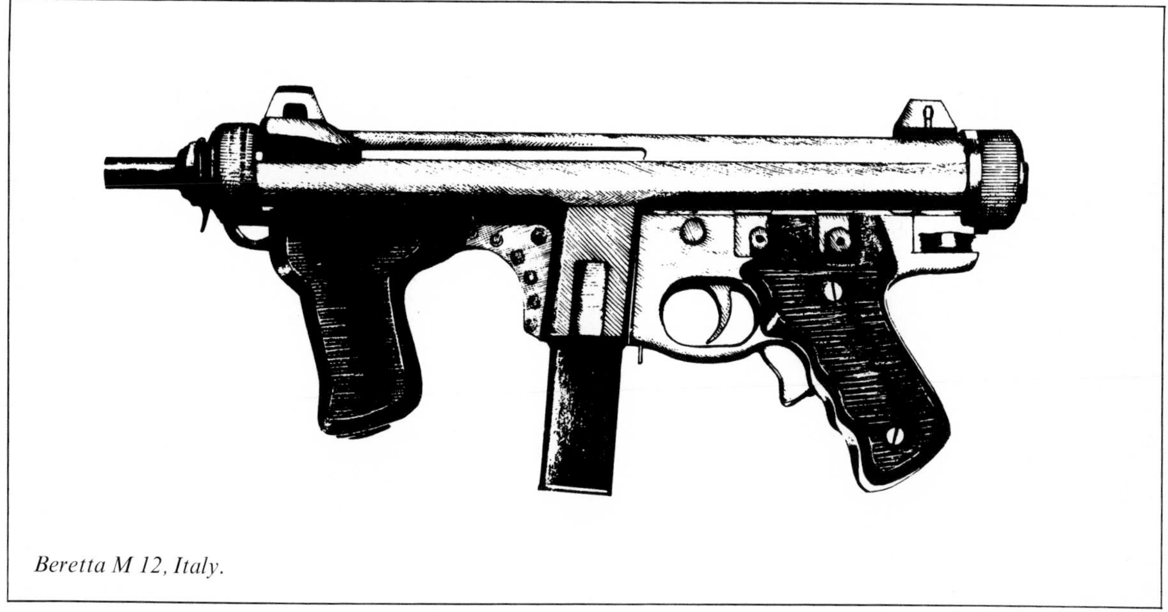

*Beretta M 12, Italy.*

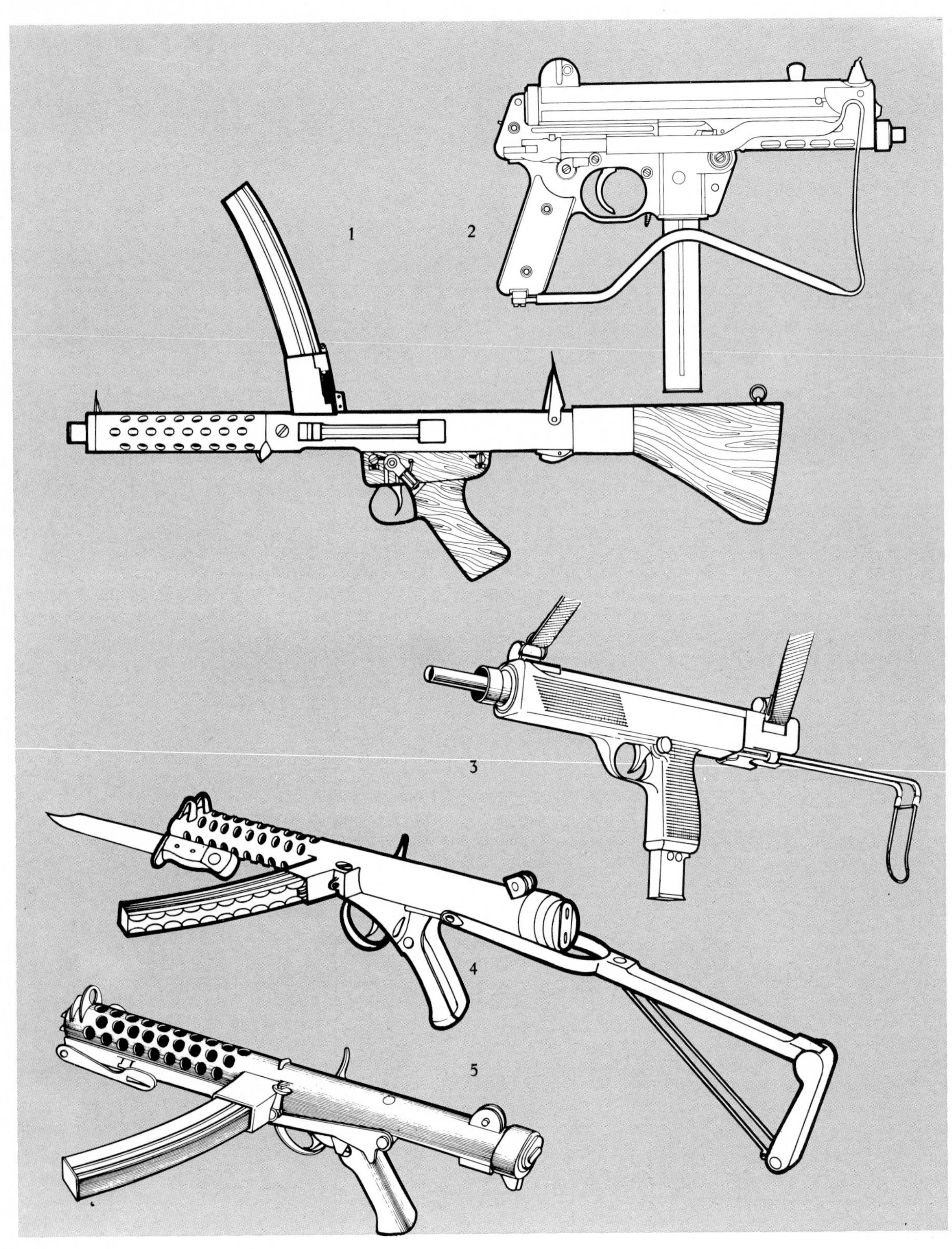


*1. Owen F-1, Australia. 2. Walther MP-K, West Germany. 3. Steyr 9 mm., Austria. 4. L2A3, Great Britain. 5. L2A1, Great Britain.*

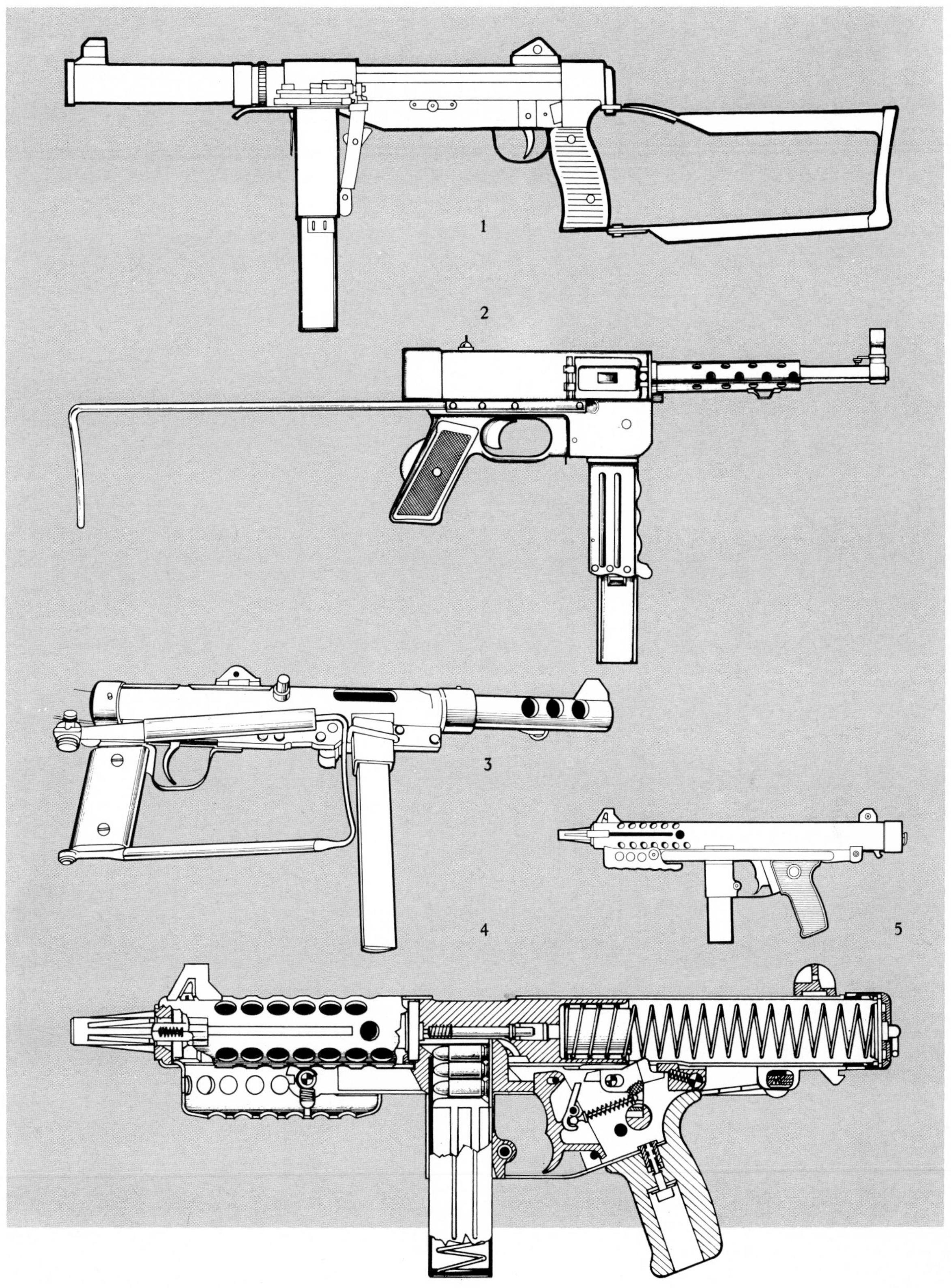


*1. Shin Chuo Kogyo, Japan. 2. MAT-49, France. 3. Carl Gustav Model 45, Sweden. 4. Star Z62, in section, Spain. 5. Star Z62, Spain.*

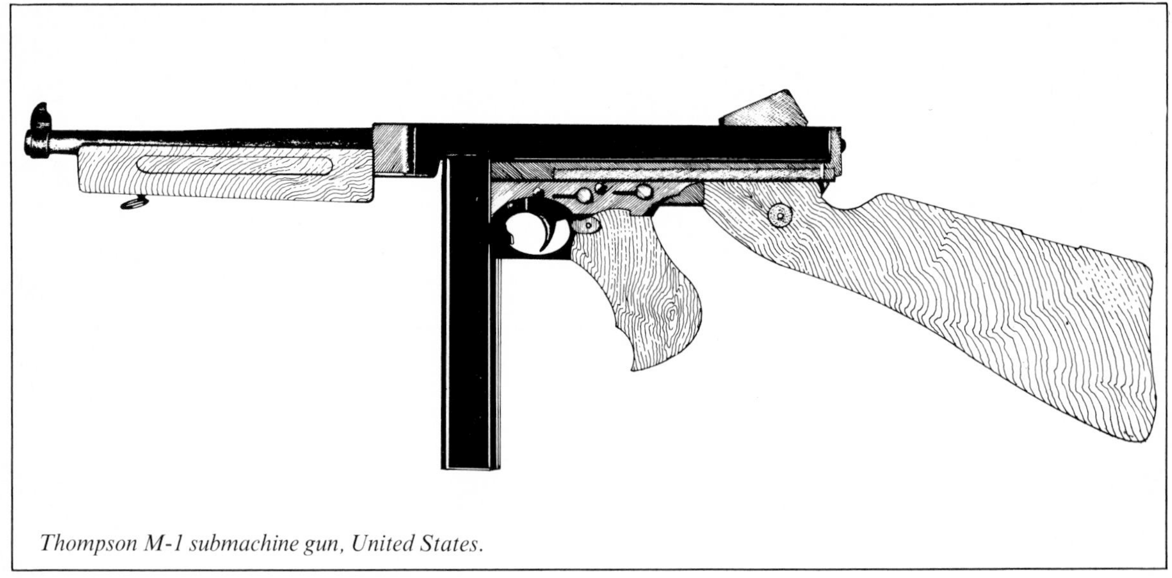

*Thompson M-1 submachine gun, United States.*

effect on the design; while the barrel was 29 cm. (11.4 in.) long, the gun was still extremely short and compact, and the kick in rapid fire was greatly reduced. This arrangement has been copied particularly by the Israeli UZI, one of the most widely used submachine guns in the Western world today. Designed by Major Uziel Gal, it makes great use of pressed steel and a special shockproof plastic. A few milled parts—parts of the trigger and firing mechanism, the magazine catch, the bayonet boss, and the barrel support—are welded to the pressed-steel frame. The recessed end of the rectangular-section bolt is open at the bottom, so that the rear of the barrel is surrounded by only three of its four sides on firing. This arrangement has the advantage over the Czechoslovak Model 23 that it considerably simplifies manufacture, even if it does cut down the reduction of the kick to some extent. The UZI has been adopted in West Germany, Belgium, the Netherlands, and a number of other countries.

Another very modern submachine gun using this principle is the Beretta M-12, designed by Domenico Salza and recently improved by Vittorio Valle (Model M-12S). Perfect calculation of masses has completely eliminated the kick in rapid fire, so that this gun can actually be fired from one hand, thus deserving the name "machine pistol."

*Principal Producing Countries*

*Argentina.* Among the submachine guns produced by the Halcon company of Buenos Aires, two of interest are the Model 57, a conventional weapon with a selector, sideways folding butt, and slightly curved box magazine holding 40 rounds, and the Model 60, which has two triggers, the front one for semiautomatic fire and the rear for rapid fire. The PA3-DM submachine gun produced by the Fábrica Militar de Armas Portátiles di Rosario is, in contrast, a highly modern weapon of the UZI type. The outer jacket is of pressed steel; the bolt, partly hollow, overhangs the rear of the barrel for about 18 cm. (7 in.). The 25-round magazine fits in the pistol grip.

*Australia.* Following the successful Austen and Owen series, Australia continued its research after the war with the aim of producing a submachine gun that would be both more modern and cheaper. Efforts to improve the experimental Kokoda were not really successful, and attention has been redirected to the F-1, a derivative of the Owen.

*Austria.* The Steyr-Daimler-Puch MPI is clearly derived from the UZI, though there are differences. It is simpler and cheaper than the Israeli weapon and has a particularly interesting firing mechanism which gives single shots or rapid fire by simply varying the pressure on the trigger.

*Great Britain.* The research carried out by George William Patchett, and resumed in greater depth after the war, led to the adoption in 1953 of the SMG L2A1, also known as the Sterling. With its slightly modified versions, the L2A2 and L2A3, it is still the standard British submachine gun—a first-class weapon, fairly conventional but accurately made and with some praiseworthy features. One of these is the ribs on the bolt which scrape up and collect any dirt or other extraneous material during firing and drive it into receptacles, so that the weapon can be fired even in the worst conditions.

*Japan.* Japanese forces use the SCK submachine gun, produced since 1960 by the Shin Chuo Kogyo company of Tokyo. It is a conventional weapon, not unlike the Swedish Carl Gustav, from which it differs chiefly in the absence of perforations in the barrel jacket.

*Spain.* The Spanish Star Z62 submachine gun gives unmistakable evidence of a great effort to cut down manufacturing costs. Ideas culled from the latest generation of submachine guns—such as the recessed or asymmetrical overhung bolt—have not been taken up, but every effort has been made to overcome the problem of accidental firing by a movement of the bolt resulting from a blow to the gun. With this in mind, the Z62 has been given an interesting firing mechanism fitted with a dog. It also has a trigger with double pressure; pressure on the lower part gives self-loading single shots, pressure on the upper part, rapid fire. The later Z70/B differs from the Z62 in having an orthodox selector instead of this special trigger.

*Sweden.* The armed forces in this country are issued the excellent Carl Gustav submachine gun. The Model M/45B, unlike earlier models which could use either their own magazines or the Suomi magazine, can take only the new and highly efficient rhomboidal-section magazine holding 36 rounds. The M/45B has been sold to Indonesia and has been adopted by Egypt, where it is produced under license. It has no selector, but is easy to fire in single shots by limiting the pressure on the trigger.

*United States.* The 5.56 mm. Armalite AR-18S is only a shortened version of the AR-18 assault rifle fitted with a second pistol grip under the stock.

Maxwell Atchisson, after producing the simple and cheap model 1957 (in which the magazine also formed the pistol grip), concentrated on transforming the M-16A1 rifle; the three versions produced, all with blowback action, fire with closed bolt, which gives them greater accuracy. The widespread adoption of the M-16A1 rifle soon led to a request for a shortened version, which was used by the U.S. Special Forces in Vietnam under the name Colt Commando. This submachine gun, still undergoing tests as the XM-177E2, differs from the M-16A1 only in the length of the barrel and in having a telescopic tubular butt stock.

The IMP .221, which is really halfway between a so-

*1. Ingram Model 10, United States. 2. XM-177E2, United States. 3. AR-18, United States.*

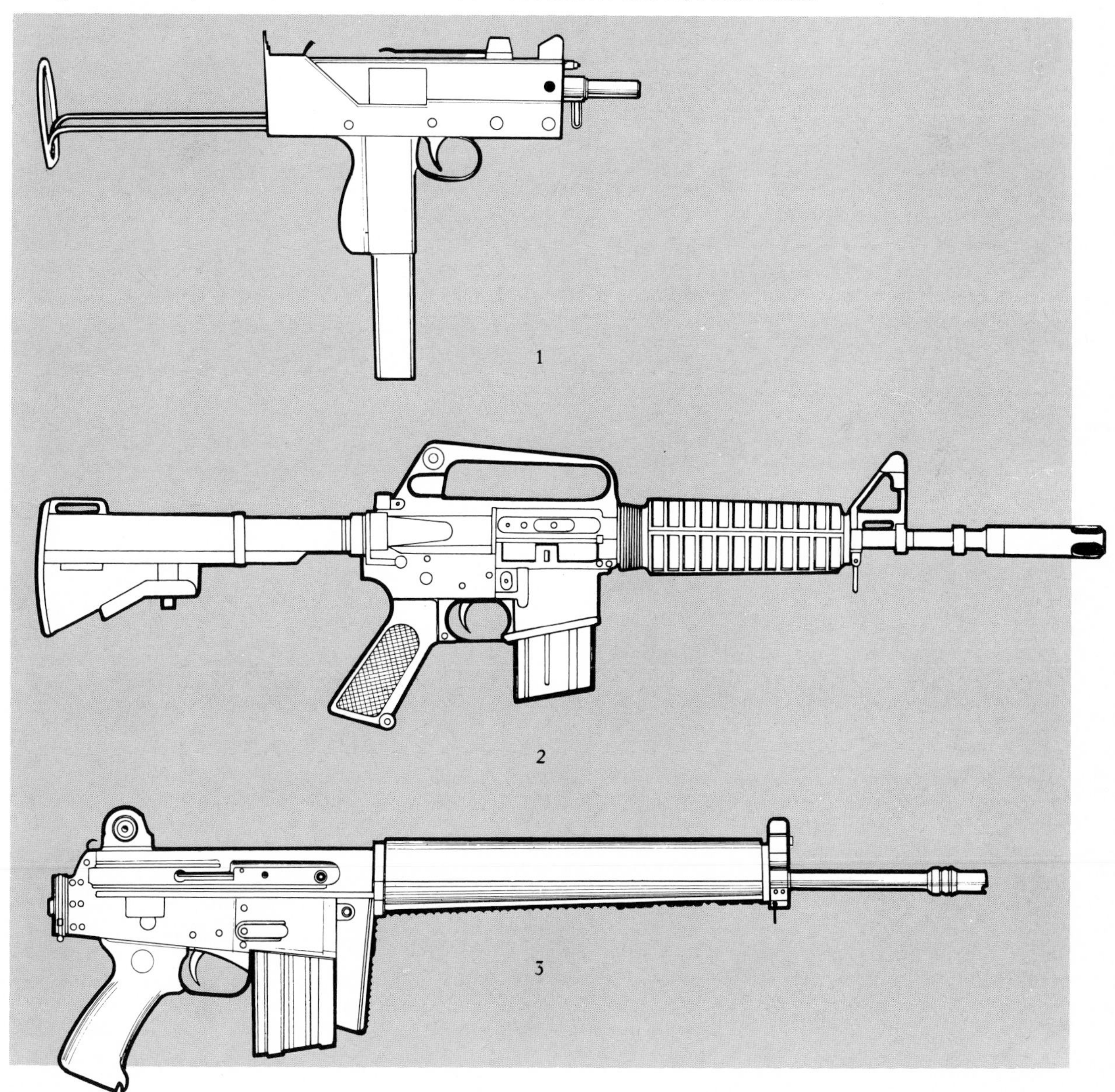

called survival rifle and a submachine gun, was produced in accordance with precise specifications from the U.S. Air Force. It is of the "bullpup" type, with the magazine at the extreme rear, chambered for the .221 Remington Fireball and gas-operated, with a sliding and turning bolt with eight locking lugs.

The submachine guns designed by Gordon B. Ingram have met with some success—including commercial success. His various models include the M-6, sold to Cuba, Peru, and other countries, and the recent M-10 and M-11. Of these last, produced by the Military Armaments Corporation of Powder Springs, Georgia, numbers have been sold to Spain, Chile, and Yugoslavia. The Ingram M-10, chambered for the .45 ACP and the 9 mm. Parabellum, is very much like the UZI, though much shorter (with the butt folded, it measures 27 cm. [10½ in.] as against the Israeli gun's 47 cm. [18½ in.]); the magazine forms part of the pistol grip, and the gun is cocked by a knob projecting from the top of the weapon. The Ingram M-11, even shorter and lighter, is chambered for the 9 mm. short cartridge (.380 ACP).

*USSR.* Since the long innings of the PPD and PPSh came to an end, nothing has been heard of any new Soviet submachine gun. It is perhaps relevant that one of the considerations that led to the adoption of the AK-47 assault rifle was that the new weapon would also replace the submachine gun.

*West Germany.* Toward the end of the 1950s the ERMA company produced some not very successful prototypes, including the ERMA Panzer, which could fire an antitank shell from the closed bolt position. The MP-58, 59, 60, 61, and 64 never got beyond the prototype stage. The Mauser company, after trying to produce an arm of particularly small size with the MP-57, produced the Model 60, their response to the ERMA Panzer. It gave excellent results in all its tests, but it has probably been realized that something more powerful is needed against tanks. A certain number of Walther MP-L and MP-K submachine guns, versions of the same model with different length barrels, somewhat similar to the Italian Franchi LF-57, have been sold.

A particularly interesting gun is the Heckler und Koch MP-5, produced on the mechanical principles of the G-3 rifle and adopted by the police, the frontier guards, and the customs service. Tried out for a long time in the MP-56 version, this submachine gun has a delayed-blowback system, which gives it greatly reduced recoil and an accuracy, especially in single shots, far greater than is normally found in weapons of this type. However, it has disadvantages that seem to cancel out its advantages: manufacture is rather more complicated and thus more expensive; and when it is fired in bursts, with closed bolt, there is insufficient circulation of air in the barrel between shots and a risk of premature ignition of the cartridge in the chamber due to excessive heat (cook-off). This is not normally a serious risk in northern and moderate climates, but it can be very troublesome in warm countries.

**sugake** A system of lacing Japanese armor. *See also* ODOSHI.

**suiba-abumi** A type of Japanese stirrup. *See also* ABUMI.

**suji-kabuto** A type of Japanese helmet, developed about 1325–50. The usual large rivet heads were not present, so that only the flanged edges, the *suji*, of the scales extended above the surface of the bowl. All other elements, such as neck guards, the SHIKORO, with the turn-backs, the FUKIGAYESHI, were the same as with the older HOSHI-KABUTO. The suji-kabuto was much stronger, however, because it was constructed of numerous narrow overlapping scales which almost doubled its thickness throughout. These lamellae—which were flat or slightly convex—were strikingly effective and, although the rivets holding them in place were arranged in both regular and irregular rows, they did not show on the surface, since the rivets had no heads. Suji-kabuto helmets, of various kinds, continued to be produced into the 19th century.

**suma** A Turkish ramrod for a pistol, also found in the Balkans and the Caucasus. The suma averaged 35–50 cm. (14–20 in.) in length and was made either entirely of steel or brass or, quite frequently, in various combinations of metals such as steel, brass, bronze, and silver. It was sometimes made of bronze covered in discs of green and white ivory and thinner discs of black horn. Occasionally there was a cap at the end of the rod which covered a worm for drawing the charges from an unfired pistol. The suma was often hollow and served as a sheath for a triangular-bladed stylet or for a pair of tongs for holding an ember to light a pipe. In this case the handle served as a grip both for the ramrod and the dagger. The rod itself was either round and smooth or with spiral molding, often with pierced slots, well suited to holding the rags necessary to clean a barrel. The handle was usually decoratively chiseled and was fitted with a suspension ring at the top for attaching to the belt, since the suma was carried separately from the pistol.

**sumpitan** A blowpipe used in Borneo, consisting of a wooden tube about 1.5–2.4 m. (5–8 ft.) long with a bore of about 1 cm. (⅖ in.). The hard, straight-grained wood of the jagang tree is mainly used, but there are also bamboo blowpipes. The darts, made from the wood of the wild sago palm, are usually about 25 cm. (10 in.) long and 5 mm. (⅕ in.) in diameter, with a pith cone on the end that exactly fits the bore of the sumpitan. These darts are poisoned with a mixture of ipoh-tree juice and various other substances such as scorpions' stings, snake venom, pepper, or arsenic. Special cases made of bamboo bound with rattan are used to carry the darts.

**suneate** The shin guards of Japanese armor. In the early days of protective armor, each shin guard was composed of three splints laced—not hinged—together, hinges probably not being introduced before the Tenshō period (1573–92). The splints were of iron or lacquered leather, and there was sometimes an extension consisting of an additional broad plate projecting upward and backward from the knee to protect part of the thigh when on horseback. The great changes that began to take place in armor in the medieval period affected the suneate as well, and lighter, more comfortable types were developed as fighting on foot gradually gained favor. These were the *shino-suneate*, with five to twelve splints—narrow metal strips joined vertically by mail; some had hinges in front at

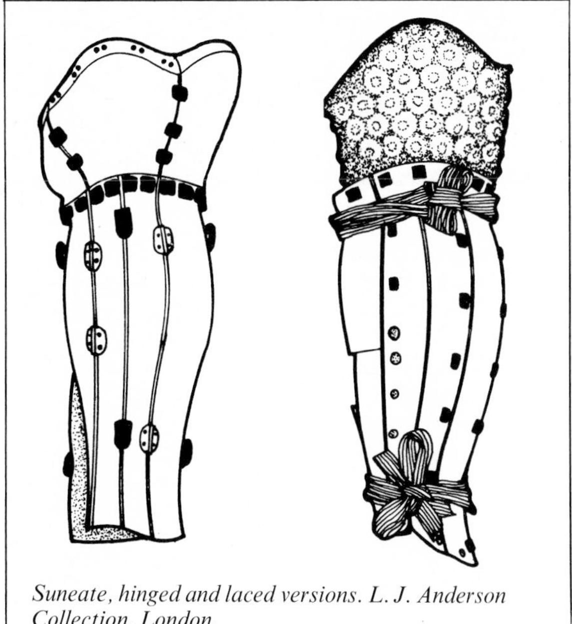

*Suneate, hinged and laced versions. L. J. Anderson Collection, London.*

**sword**

Under this heading the general typology of the weapon and its historical development, particularly in the West, are discussed and described. For specific types and the separate parts of swords, see:

| | |
|---|---|
| Arms of the hilt | kilij |
| backsword | knuckle guard |
| bars | mouthpiece |
| bastard sword | Pallasch |
| beidana | Pappenheimer |
| blade | pas d'âne |
| broadsword | pommel |
| button | quillon block |
| chape | quillons |
| claymore | rapier |
| colichemarde | rib |
| counterguard | ricasso |
| cross guard | rim of the guard |
| cup guard | saber |
| Dusägge | scabbard |
| épée | schiavona |
| falcion | Schläger |
| firangi | shamshir |
| flamberge | shaska |
| fleuret | shell guard |
| flissa | side ring |
| fuller | Sinclair saber |
| gladius | smallsword |
| grip | spadroon |
| guard | tang |
| hanger | tessak |
| harpé | tuck |
| hilt | two-handed sword |
| karabela | Walloon sword |
| Katzbalger | |

the ankle, and were lined with cloth and secured to the legs by cords or bands. Another variation was the *kara-shino suneate*, which did not have fabric lining and consisted merely of the metal splints and connecting mail.

**surcoat** *See* COAT ARMOR.

**su-yari** A Japanese spear with a long blade with straight, parallel edges. *See also* YARI.

**Swiss dagger** *See also* DAGGER.

**sword** An edged weapon with a long blade designed for delivering cutting blows or thrusts, or both. It first appeared in the prehistoric period; once copper had been mastered, the dagger was fitted with an increasingly longer blade, until it became in effect a short sword. This new weapon was clearly superior for combat at close quarters and, accordingly, led to the decline of the dagger, which took on a secondary, complementary role and remained in use for hand-to-hand combat.

The copper swords had been based on the forms of earlier stone daggers; later, bronze was cast to resemble the copper swords. This new metal easily satisfied the requirements for producing longer swords, and as a result their length increased from 70–80 cm. (27–31 in.) to more than 90 cm. (35 in.); the typology also changed, and both long and short swords were manufactured.

The shape of the blade also showed the influence of the dagger and was designed solely for thrusting. The strong central ribbing and the two smaller side ribs on both flats gave it total rigidity under the impact of a violent blow. The Mycenaean swords of the second millennium B.C. were likewise designed for delivering thrusts, but little by little the need was felt for swords capable of cutting blows as well, and as a result double-edged swords started to be made with more or less parallel cutting edges and a strong point. Changes in combat techniques obliged craftsmen to solve the problem of fitting the blade to the handle more solidly. As long as the blade was in alignment with the grip, the two or three small nails or rivets which held the two parts of the grip together were sufficient for the task. In the new type of sword, which was to be used for both cutting and thrusting, this join had to be made stronger. This was done by inserting the shoulder of the blade into a specially made slot in the grip and fixing it with several rivets. Another way of making a more reliable weapon was to cast the blade and the tang as a single piece, with the tang fashioned like a handle; this usually involved covering the sides of the tang with small plaques of wood, bone, or other material which was easy to shape and attach with rivets.

The different ways of fashioning the sword did not follow a chronological order in the European sphere; the availability of expensive metal, and the level of mastery of casting it, which gave rise to many a jealously guarded secret, meant that there would be local preferences for one system over another. In the south the bronze swords were decorated on the handles with gold, ivory, and semi-precious stones; in the north there was a preference for decorating the bronze with elaborate engravings. Even in this early period the pommel became an essential part of the grip, and from its original form as a simple projection or swelling it started to take on specific shapes depending on its function. In order to protect elaborately made swords, the blade was kept in a sheath made of wood,

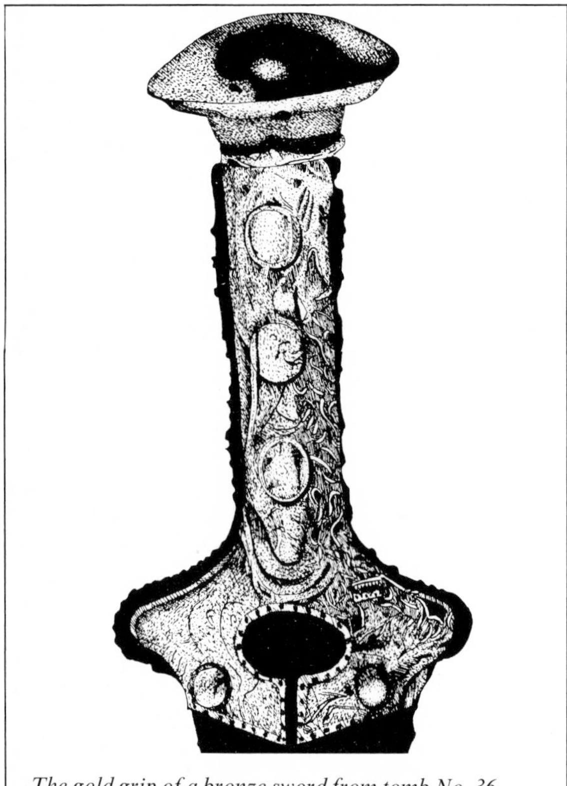

*The gold grip of a bronze sword from tomb No. 36 in the Zapher Papura necropolis near Knossos, late Minoan period, c. 1450* B.C.

leather, or sometimes bronze; chapes served to protect the point of the weapon; a metal mouthpiece was added to reinforce the sheath.

The discovery of iron, and how to work it, gave added momentum to the development of the sword, and in one and the same cultural environment swords made of bronze and of iron presented the same form and coexisted for a long period of time. Bronze was a rare material, imported for the most part from regions of the eastern Mediterranean; iron was more common, but it was more complicated to work. The transition from cast bronze to forged iron was neither speedy nor simultaneous in the European region as a whole; for three centuries at least the two techniques existed together, with preferences for one or the other based on the differing economic and technical possibilities.

In the Hallstatt culture (900–500 B.C.) swords made of bronze and swords with iron blades coexisted and were modeled after earlier forms. Swords with a long, lancet-shaped blade were typical of this culture; these blades had a broader section with the ridge beyond the center of the blade, and ending in a right-angled point. The grip was surmounted by a mushroom-shaped pommel, typical of this culture, which was often decorated with gold or other precious materials. An example from a Hallstatt tomb, with an iron blade, still had its magnificent grip made of

1. *Bronze Assyrian sword, c. 1310–1280* B.C.
2. *Bronze Italic sword, first millennium* B.C.
3. *Egyptian sword of the XXIII Dynasty, 893–870* B.C. *Metropolitan Museum, New York.*

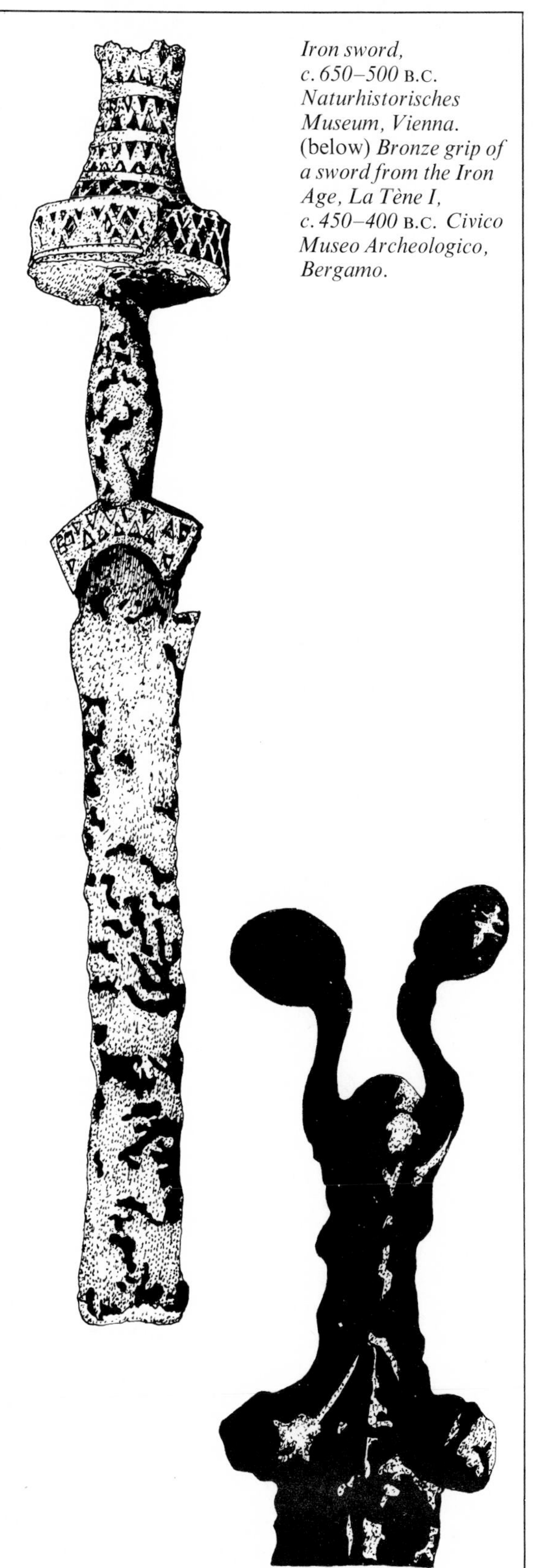

*Iron sword, c. 650–500* B.C. *Naturhistorisches Museum, Vienna.* (below) *Bronze grip of a sword from the Iron Age, La Tène I, c. 450–400* B.C. *Civico Museo Archeologico, Bergamo.*

ivory with carved bands of zigzag patterns and traces of the original coloration. Another grip typical of this culture was the "anthropomorphic" type: the lower limbs, carefully fashioned, were positioned on either side of the blade; the upper limbs, raised above the shoulders, shielded the head; the body formed the actual handle.

The pre-Roman iron swords were similar in form to those in use in the late Bronze Age, with the length in some cases exceeding 1 m. (40 in.). But as fighting techniques evolved, the Romans developed a preference for the short version of the sword called a gladius, which was better suited to their rigidly arrayed troops, who had to be able to maneuver swiftly and with precision. Their "barbarian" foes were for the most part armed with long swords, but the reason for the barbarian victories can be found in their strategic techniques and warrior spirit rather than in any intrinsic superiority of their arms.

In the La Tène culture (from 500 B.C. to the beginning of the Christian era), the somewhat angular lines of the sword blade typical of the Hallstatt culture were softened. The edges of the blades were parallel and the right-angled tip took on an ogival shape. In this period the sword changed from the elaborate object-cum-weapon into a simple and practical fighting weapon which was lighter and easier to wield. The swords which have survived to this day are all without handles and have a broad double-edged and pointed blade; the only surviving decorative element is around the mouth of the scabbard. This period also saw the addition, near the mouth of the sheath and on the back of it, of a metal ring or loop through which a carrying strap was passed. Some sheaths of the La Tène period are made entirely of bronze and decorated with engravings. In the last three centuries B.C. the most common sword in the European region was the long Gallic sword of the La Tène culture. Tombs of this period have produced examples of blades, spears, swords, and axes made of iron, found together with weapons made of bronze.

The eventual and definitive supremacy of iron for the manufacture of the sword blades and other arms relegated bronze to being used for accessory parts: grips, sheaths, and the reinforcing mounts for wooden sheaths, which were sometimes covered with hide and fabric. During the Hallstatt culture there had been a gradual lengthening of the sword; during the La Tène period the length was first reduced, then increased once more to between 80 and 90 cm. (31–35 in.), as progress in metalworking made it possible to construct lighter and stronger blades. In many instances the craftsmen who made swords impressed on the blade a "trademark" identifying the maker. The malleability of these blades meant that they could be twisted in such a way as to form a spiral of three or four turns without breaking; in fact, in the La Tène period there is evidence of the first examples of this type of metal-working, which is called "pattern welding." But the fact that the blade could become deformed on impact often meant that the combatant had to interrupt the fight to straighten the blade, with the help of his foot or with a rock. It was with these swords that the Teutonic and Gallic horsemen who fought against Caesar's legions were armed.

*1. Iron sword from the Hallstatt period, 7th–6th centuries* B.C. *(from a drawing published by E. von Sacken,* Das Grabfeld von Halstatt in Oberösterreich und dessen Alterthümer, *Vienna, 1868). 2. Single-edged sword of the early Viking period, 9th century. Universitets Oldsaksamlung, Oslo. 3. Double-edged sword of the early Viking period, 9th century, Nationalmuseet, Copenhagen. 4. Double-edged sword, central Europe, 12th–13th century. Bernisches Historisches Museum, Bern. 5. Double-edged sword, France, c. 1300–1350. Wallace Collection, London. 6. Thrusting sword, France, c. 1350–1400. Wallace Collection, London.*

*1. Double-edged sword, Europe, c. 1300–1350. Armeria Reale, Turin. 2. Double-edged sword, Europe, 1432. Tower of London Armouries. 3. Thrusting sword (tuck), Europe, c. 1400. Wallace Collection, London. 4. Spanish sword, late 15th century, Museo Nazionale of Castel Sant' Angelo, Rome. 5. Ear-hilted thrusting sword (tuck), Spain, c. 1500. Museo Nazionale del Bargello, Florence. 6. Hand-and-a-half sword belonging to Emperor Frederick III (1440–93), S. Germany, c. 1450. Waffensammlung, Vienna.*

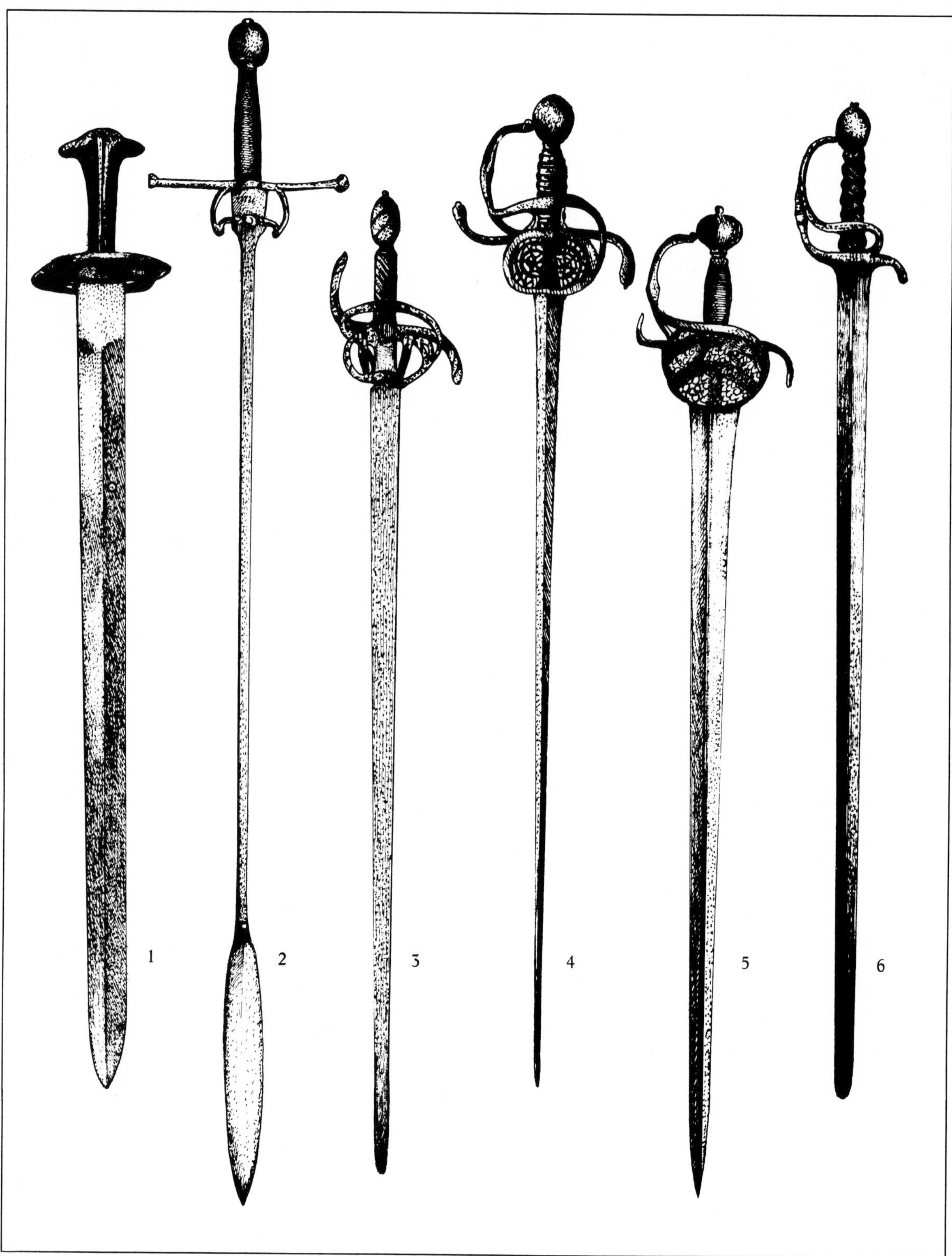


*1. Landsknecht's sword ("Katzbalger"), Germany, first half of the 16th century. Historisches Museum, Dresden. 2. Hunting or "boar spear" sword, Germany, c. 1560–70. Waffensammlung, Vienna. 3. Cavalry sword, Germany, c. 1600. Livrustkammaren, Stockholm. 4. Officer's rapier with so-called Pappenheimer hilt, Germany, period of the Thirty Years War, 1618–48. Livrustkammaren, Stockholm. 5. Cavalry officer's sword ("Pappenheimer"), Germany, period of the Thirty Years War, 1618–48. Armémuseum, Stockholm. 6. Cavalry sword, Germany, second half of the 17th century. Uppland (Sweden), in the church at Kungs-Husby.*

The Roman gladius, a development of the Hallstatt sword, had a double-edged blade with a strengthened tip; the grip was ringed, giving the soldier a good hold. The grip was made of wood, ivory, and bone, ending in a sphere-shaped pommel. The gladius was carried on the right side slung from a baldric which passed over the left shoulder. Although Rome defeated its foes who were armed with the long sword, because its army was so highly disciplined, the Romans nevertheless acknowledged the functional qualities of that weapon when used on horseback: accordingly the Roman cavalry was equipped with a similar sword. When the upper hand was eventually gained by the various Teutonic peoples migrating southward, the gladius, which had barred their passage on so many occasions, was replaced by the long sword, and the dagger by the short sax, which dated back to the Bronze Age and remained in use up until the Carolingian period.

During the great migrations the sword clearly showed the influences of the type in use in the latter stages of the La Tène culture. It had a broad, double-edged blade and a rather blunt point, and measured between 75 and 95 cm. in length (30–37 in.); a wide, shallow fuller ran down the blade in the center of both faces, almost to the point. The handle was shorter, but structurally similar: a small oval metal plate, between the shoulder of the blade and the grip, protected the latter from being damaged against the metal rim of the mouth of the sheath, and at the same time provided a better grip; in addition, because it was somewhat salient, it protected the hand. This in fact marked the beginnings of the guard, the hand-protecting device—although it was no more than embryonic at this stage. A second small plate rounded off the grip at the top, and this was surmounted by a point. The sword retained these forms in the Merovingian period; the only modification was a gradual thickening of the plate between the grip and the shoulder of the blade. The handles of these swords were richly decorated with gold and silver inlays. The blades were excellently made by forging soft and hard steel rods which were bent several times during the process.

Early narratives and documents have given us the names of various valiant knights and their swords, and sometimes the names of the craftsmen who forged them as well. Siegfried thus carried out his acts of valor with "Balmus"; Roland routed brigands and infidels with his faithful "Durandal," which was made by Madelger of Regensburg with such skill that when the hero was finally felled during the battle of Roncesvalles, he was unable to break it. In the *Chanson de Roland* we find the following words: "Roland felt that his life was about to end. Summoning his strength he raised himself to his feet. His face was pale. Before him lay a grey rock. With pain and rage he struck the rock ten times with his sword. The steel clashed but neither broke nor splintered." In another passage we find the following description of Charlemagne with his sword: "He was wearing his fine white coat of mail and his helmet with gold-studded stones; by his side hung Joyeuse, and never was there a sword to match it: its color changed thirty times a day. We know well the fate of the lance with which Our Lord was transfixed upon the cross. By the grace of God, Charles possesses the tip, and has had it set in the golden pommel of his sword. Because of this great honor the sword is called Joyeuse." The sword of King Arthur was made on the island of Avalon and was called "Excalibur." If one reads sagas and *chansons de geste* it is not hard to see the important difference between defensive and offensive arms; all the fights are reduced to a single well-placed blow which overwhelms the foe and pierces his mail, his shield, or his helmet.

In the Carolingian period the various parts of the grip became more defined and specialized in their function; the elongated small oval plate peculiar to the Merovingian period was turned into a small four-sided bar about 10 cm. (4 in.) long, i.e., the guard. The wooden grip ended in a pommel with a rectangular base which was larger and more massive at the center. The form of the Carolingian sword clearly shows that it was an excellent fighting weapon designed for cutting; larger and longer than the earlier swords, it measured 95–100 cm. (37–40 in.), the increase in length, and thus weight, being counterbalanced by a more massive pommel.

At the beginning of the Romanesque period (11th–12th centuries) the sword retained the form of the Carolingian period, but the blade became slightly broader and the name of the maker started to appear in the fuller; the quillons were lengthened; and the pommel—which had been made up of two parts, one flat and the other swelled, and which had been so common among the Nordic peoples—was replaced by a type which was hemispherical or paraboloidal in shape. Later, in the latter half of the 12th century, the blade was made broader still; the quillons measured 20–22 cm. (8–9 in.), although the length varied according to local preferences. In Italy and elsewhere south of the Alps the quillons remained considerably shorter than those found north of the Alps. The pommel, which up until this period had had a flat base, now adopted an upward-curving base and took on the form of a clove.

The sword was used in this period solely for delivering cutting blows. The Bayeux Tapestry (1066–77), whose various sequences depict the feats of William the Conqueror at the battle of Hastings, shows all the combatants wielding swords, busily cutting at their adversaries; none of them is making thrusts. In the *Hortus deliciarum* of the abbess Herrade of Landsperg (Alsace), an illuminated encyclopedia of the second half of the 12th century, almost all the warriors are smashing helmets and breastplates with cutting blows, but some are also thrusting with their swords. After many centuries the sword had reassumed this function and as a result the blade was modified; now it adopted a form which was suited both to thrusting and cutting: the pommel was clove-shaped, the long quillons were fairly flattened at the tips, and the blade was long with a sharp point.

In the Gothic period the sword became a more specialized instrument depending on whether it was to be used on foot or on horseback, or to be carried on parade or in ceremonies. Earlier blades were remounted with new hilts, especially in weapons for troops made up of vassals and peasants. Among these swords the type carried by the

14th-century knight was especially remarkable for its strength, beauty, and harmony of its lines. This sword was some 120 cm. (47 in.) in length, with the blade accounting for almost 100 cm. (40 in.); the blade was in the form of a long isosceles triangle. The robust hilt was straight, and the pommel, which was larger and heavier than previous types, was polygonal or disc-shaped. This latter form of the pommel became common throughout Europe, although it had variations from country to country. In Italy it was fairly flat or slightly convex when compared with examples from north of the Alps. A knight might well have several swords, according to his preferences and requirements: swords with blades having parallel edges and a point, for cutting; swords with stout triangular- or rhomboid-section blades, for thrusting; and swords designed for both cutting and thrusting. These forms developed as principal local types: in southern and western Europe there was a preference for thrusting weapons; elsewhere on the Continent cutting swords were preferred.

*Sword of honor presented by Pope Julius II to Emperor Maximilian I, attributed to Maestro Ercole, Italy, 1509. Waffensammlung, Vienna.*

The new battle formations and the important role taken on by the infantry in the 15th and 16th centuries meant that swords were now made for foot soldiers. This sword had a long, double-edged blade with a point, and a grip better protected by the guard than the horseman's sword. Hitherto the sword with a cross-shaped hilt could be held with either of the two cutting edges to the fore; now, however, with the development of the guard and the appearance of arms of the hilt, rings, loops, and knuckle bows, the sword came to have an outer and an inner edge, since it had to be held in a manner predetermined by its hilt. The most specialized swords for combat on foot were the two-handed swords; these huge weapons, wielded by mighty and fearless soldiers, were used in the fray and for opening up breaches through the enemy ranks. The horseman's sword, which could be used both on foot and on horseback, could have a long, slender blade or a short, broad blade; its hilt had long, straight, or S-shaped quillons, side rings, arms of the hilt, and a disc-shaped or polygonal pommel. Local types and forms flourished in this period; for example, the schiavona, the sword with "eared" hilt, and the Katzbälger. Hunting swords and rapiers appeared in all of Europe together with swords which showed the effects of contact with the East, where there was still a preference for cutting weapons, such as the saber.

In the 16th century the thrusting function of the sword became increasingly accentuated. The blades became more rigid, although they still remained broader in northern areas than they were in Italy and Spain; the hilt became a complex web of rings, bows, and bars designed to give the hand the greatest possible protection from the opponent's thrusts. In the 17th century a further effective defensive element developed in the form of two strong shells, either solid or pierced, which complemented the guard. The evolution of the sword's guard now followed a trend which led, in southern Europe toward the middle of the century, to the hand being completely protected by a hemispherical cup guard. It was no coincidence that this type of guard evolved in southern Europe: the Mediterranean countries had always shown a preference for thrusting swords and corresponding swordplay, wherein it was necessary to shield the hand against the long, sharply pointed rapier.

By the end of the 16th century firearms were playing an increasingly effective part on battlefields, and the sword found its role limited more and more to the dueling ground. Specialized swords were made for dueling, and from the end of the 15th century attempts had been made to standardize dueling weapons and the rules of the duel itself. In the first half of the 16th century the first treatise on fencing was published; this manual laid the foundations of the Italian school of fencing which subsequently became prevalent throughout Europe and which, together with the Spanish school, reached a very high level of accomplishment. There is documentary evidence that the custom of wearing the sword with everyday attire appeared in Spain in the 15th century. From Spain the fashion then spread throughout the rest of Europe, and until the late 18th century, a distinctive form of nonmilitary sword with a long, rigid blade and a sharp point, known as the rapier and the smallsword, became part and parcel of the attire of every gentleman as a status symbol. The fact that a man carried his rapier at all times meant that it could be used in a flash for self-defense or to settle a matter of honor.

In military circles, too, the sword was now carried in peacetime out of respect for tradition rather than for more practical reasons, for it had become too cumbersome and heavy compared with weapons regularly used in duels. The sword had come full circle, and a new military sidearm called the dress sword took its place to be worn with uniform in peacetime. The sword as a weapon of war was still widely used in the early 20th century, but later it was issued mostly in versions designed for uniforms, for ceremonial use, or for presentation.

*Presentation sword.* A sword of honor offered by sovereigns, princes, popes, associations, and admirers in general as an award or token of recognition to important figures for their achievements in war or political life. The Italian tradition in this respect is very old indeed: the Church had long rewarded princes, military leaders, and anyone else who had distinguished himself in the defense of Christianity with the gift of a papal sword which had been blessed on Christmas Day. Presentation swords were also given to persons admitted as members of the Knighthood of St. Peter, and two of these are now in the Waffensammlung in Vienna.

The custom of awarding a saber, a dress sword, or a smallsword spread in the 18th and 19th centuries to France, England, and America. Presentation swords were invariably elaborate objects worked on by designers, swordmakers, jewelers, and engravers, ending up as nothing less than works of art. The various surviving examples testify clearly to this: for example, the sword offered to King Frederick VII of Denmark (Rosenborg castle in Copenhagen), the sword given to General Lafayette (National Museum of Castel Sant' Angelo in Rome), and those presented to Major General William Scott and General Ricciotti Garibaldi (in private collections).

In Russia, there was an old tradition for the monarch to present a saber with a gold-inlaid dedicatory inscription to selected Cossacks as a reward for bravery and loyalty. In the early 19th century presentation swords for officers of the regular forces were introduced under the name "Golden Weapon" since the hilt and scabbard mounts were made of gilt bronze. In addition, the hilt was decorated with the motto "For bravery" and the badge of the Order of St. Anne, with the sword knot on the ribbon either of this order or that of St. George.

*Papal sword.* A long sword used by popes to reward princes and military commanders for their achievements as "defenders of the faith." The custom of presenting a sword to defenders of Christianity did not occur much before the year 1000. The first papal sword which can be dated with certainty goes back to 1386, when on the morning of Christmas Day, in Lucca, Pope Urban VI presented the city's gonfalonier with a papal sword and cap, both duly blessed. From the early 15th through the 17th century this tradition of blessing a papal sword and cap was continued. Few Christmases at the Vatican passed without some prince or general being rewarded with this gift. The last papal sword was presented by Leo XII in 1823, to the Duke of Angoulême for his successful

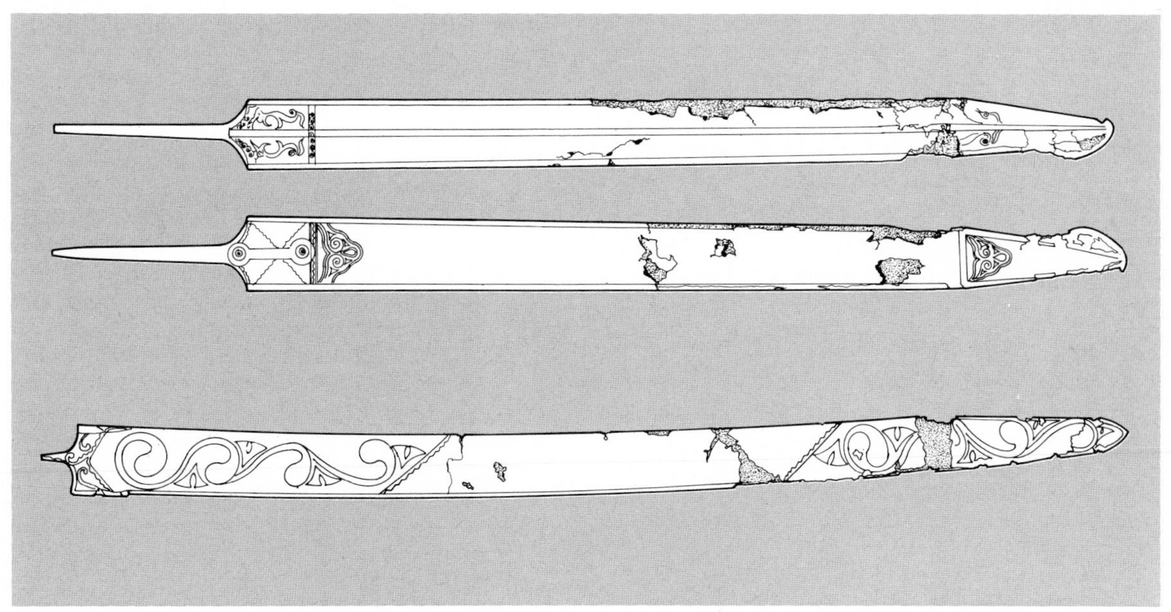

*Swords of the Late Iron Age (La Tène culture, 5th–4th centuries* B.C.*); the two illustrations at the top show both faces of the same sword.*

*Hilt and scabbard of a ceremonial sword which belonged to Emperor Frederick II (1220–50), and was later altered for Emperor Charles IV (1346–78), who had a pommel mounted on it with the arms of Bohemia and Germany. Made in S. Italy, c. 1220. Weltliche Schatzkammer, Vienna.*

storming of the Trocadero. A subsequent sword, which was never actually presented, is still in the Vatican. Only on one occasion was the papal sword presented to a whole nation rather than to an individual; this was the sword dispatched by Julius II in 1511 to the Swiss Confederation in recognition of the conduct of the Swiss Guard (the pope's bodyguards). This sword is now in the Landesmuseum in Zurich. If one runs through the list of people who received this gift, the historical and political relations between the papacy and the various other powers in Europe emerge clearly.

The manufacture of the papal sword and cap was entrusted to the best artists and craftsmen of the day. The grip was usually cast in solid silver, engraved and gilded, and in some cases the pommel bore the insignia of the pope. The broad, two-edged blade usually had a wide fuller in the upper section, with the name of the pope, the year of the papacy, and sometimes an exhortation to fight for Christendom, in addition to the year of presentation, on the forte itself. The wooden scabbard was mounted with embossed and gilded silver and covered in velvet. The papal gift included a special cap as well; this was a large dome-shaped hat embroidered with the figure of a dove—the symbol of the Holy Ghost—and a girdle.

The silver used in the furniture of these costly swords was stolen and plundered down the centuries; therefore few complete swords are extant. The Museo Civico at Bologna has the sword presented in 1454 to Giovanni Bentivoglio by Nicolas V. The Tesoro di San Marco in Venice has the sword presented by Pope Alexander VIII in 1686 to the doge Francesco Morosini. In the Armeria Ducale in Venice we find the sword sent in 1450 by Nicolas V to the doge Francesco Foscari, and the sword presented in 1463 by Pius II to the doge Cristofaro Moro. In Rome, at the headquarters of the Knights Hospitalers of St. John of Jersusalem we find the sword presented in 1774 by Clement XIV to the grand master of the order, Francisco Ximenes de Texada.

*Coronation sword.* The sword worn by a sovereign as a symbol of his authority at the investiture or coronation. Charlemagne, who was crowned in Rome on Christmas Day in the year 800 as emperor of the Holy Roman Empire, had his sword buckled to him in St. Peter's Basilica. The sword with which Frederick II of Swabia was crowned in 1220, again in Rome, is currently in the Schatzkammer in Vienna. The sword used at the coronations of the kings of France, dating back to the 12th century, is now in the Louvre in Paris.

Coronation swords represented the very best products of the goldsmiths, craftsmen, and armorers of the day. Modeled on a sword which had been in active use, the coronation sword had to retain the appearance of the true weapon and these various artisans would set to work on it, expressing the taste of the times with a wide variety of elaborate decorative techniques.

*Bearing sword.* A weapon carried during public ceremonies to signify the authority of the wearer. This ritual usage was derived from the Byzantine Empire, where an arms-bearer would follow the emperor with an unsheathed sword with the point pointing upward to

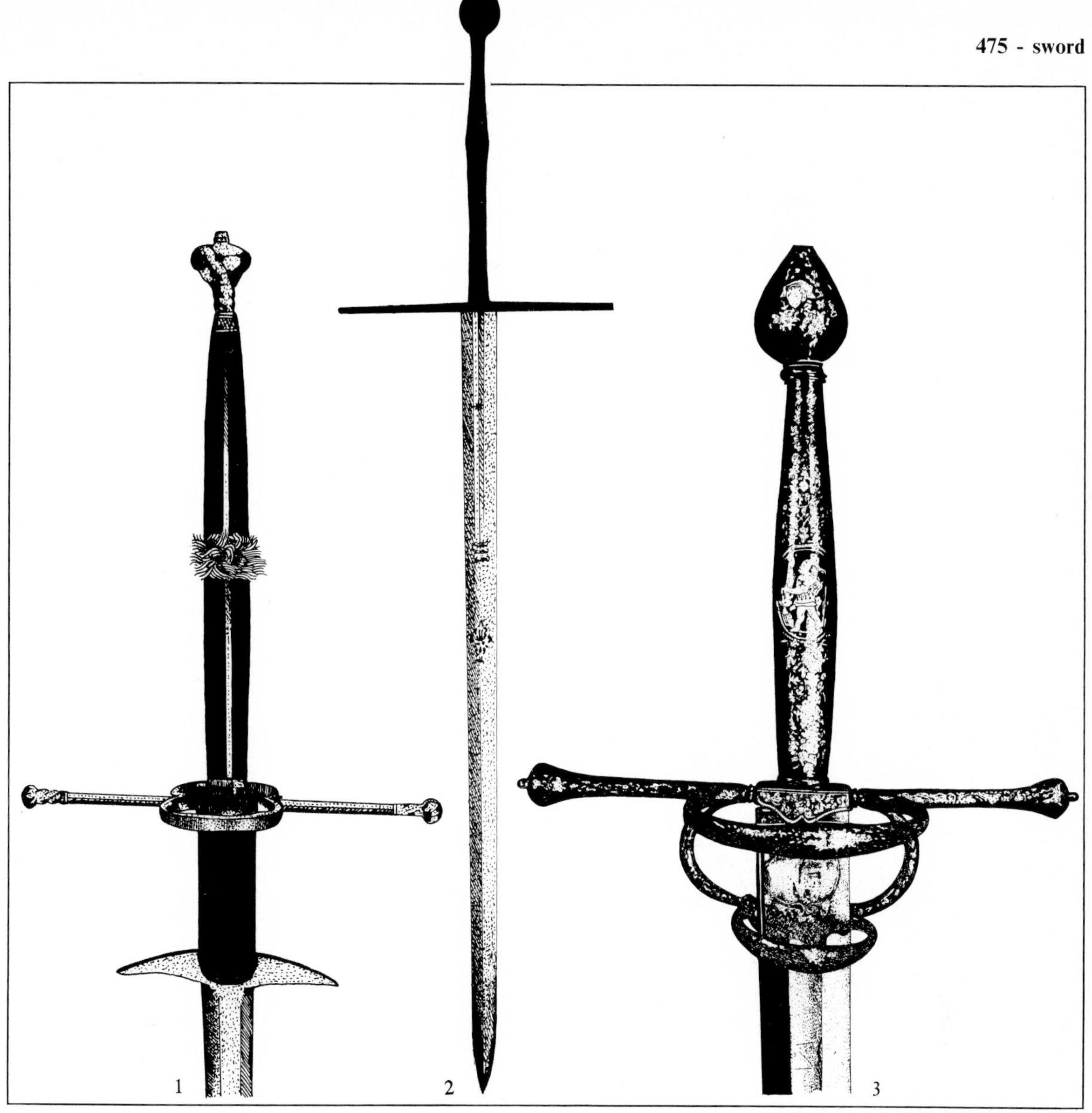

*1. Two-handed sword, Germany (Munich), c. 1580. Museo Stibbert, Florence. 2. Two-handed sword, of the bodybuard of Edward, Prince of Wales, England (blade German), 1475. Tower of London Armouries. 3. Hand-and-a-half sword, Italy, c. 1555–60. Waffensammlung, Vienna.*

testify to the emperor's powers. The papal sword given by the pontiff to princes who had fought for Christianity was likewise a bearing sword. A typical ceremony in the Venetian republic, from the end of the 16th to the early 18th century, was the presentation to distinguished persons of a broadsword, which then was displayed during public ceremonies as a symbol of the powers bestowed upon them. These large ceremonial swords had a broad blade in the form of an acute isosceles triangle, with a central rib. *Venezia* (Venice) and *Giustizia* (Justice), both legible when the point of the weapon was raised upward, were inscribed on the furniture. The hilt was made of cast bronze, gilded and engraved; the scabbard was covered with crimson velvet.

Many two-handed swords became ceremonial bearing weapons when they were no longer used for fighting purposes, and they continued to be made long afterward for their new role. The forms of the blades and the quillons are evidence enough of this: additional elements in the form of curls on the guard and decorative fringes on the grip turned these arms into a display of craftsmanship rather than a fighting instrument. For use at festivals and tournaments Duke Maximilian I of Bavaria had a sword made in 1626 with the blade embellished with the Bavarian coat of arms, highlighted in blue and gold.

The largest bearing sword that has come down to us would seem to be the one which Edward, Prince of Wales (later King Edward V), ordered for his bodyguard when he was created Duke of Chester (1475); this example is in the Tower of London Armouries. It had a German blade,

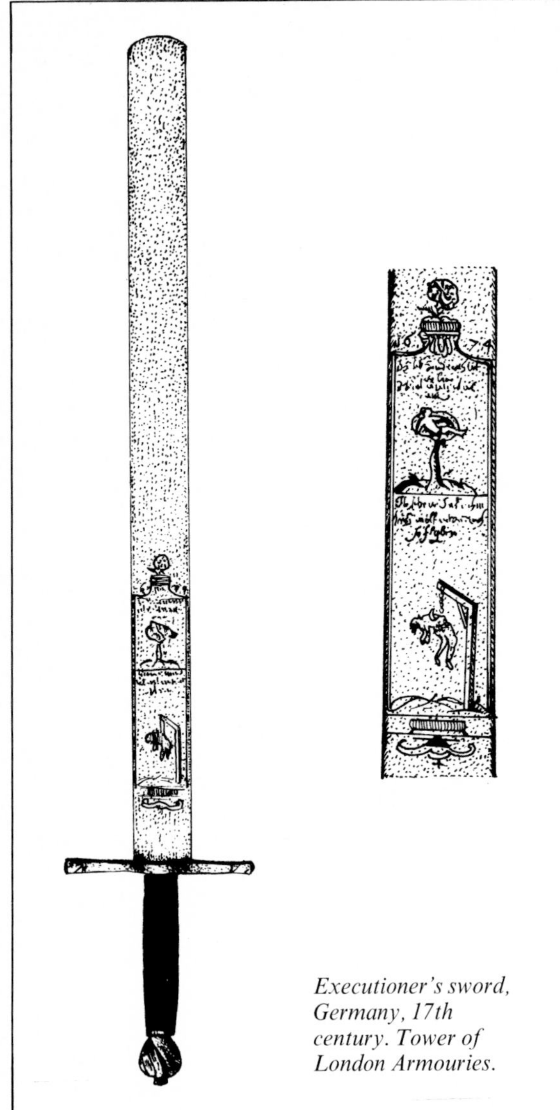
*Executioner's sword, Germany, 17th century. Tower of London Armouries.*

bearing the "running wolf" mark of Passau, that was double-edged and ribbed, with a central fuller and an ogival point. It had long, straight quillons, and the grip ended in a flat, octagonal pommel. The sword measured 226 cm. in all (89 in.).

*Executioner's sword.* A sword slightly more than 1 m. (40 in.) long, with a blade measuring 85–90 cm. (33–35 in.) in length and 6–7 cm. (2.5–3 in.) in width, with a rounded point. The quillons were quite short, and mainly straight, but sometimes curved in an S-form; the long grip was surmounted by a pear-shaped, mushroom-shaped, or faceted pommel. Throughout the 17th century it was widely used in central Europe for beheadings, but this use ceased altogether in the early 18th century. The earliest such sword dates back to 1540, although the form and lines of this example recall those of the two-handed sword in use in the late 15th century. The blades of executioner's swords were often decorated with designs representing Justice, the gallows, the rack, and the Crucifixion, or with moralistic inscriptions. When it was no longer used for executions, the sword sometimes continued to be used in ceremonies and processions as a symbol of power.

*Chinese Swords*

The evolution of the sword in China covers many centuries, dating from prehistoric times. A number of variations emerged, each shape being especially suitable for certain well-defined purposes, although the swords never acquired the same degree of refinement and precision as in Japan and some parts of medieval Europe. The straight, double-edged sword remained predominant in China as long as swords were worn, almost into the 19th century. Although blades made in China were used, they were often of mediocre quality, and consequently Indian and Persian blades were frequently mounted on Chinese hilts. European blades also became popular as the trade routes opened up. Some particularly fine blades of watered steel were among those imported, usually measuring about 60–70 cm. (24–28 in.) in length.

Chased and engraved brass was widely used for the hilt, especially for the pommel, quillons, and grip. Other parts of the hilt might be made of gold, silver, jade, ivory, or even of cloisonné enamel. The wooden scabbard was frequently covered in fishskin, and its metal furniture—which was always in keeping with the hilt—included two lockets and suspension rings for the straps by which the sword hung from the belt.

Characteristic for China were the twin swords used for fighting with both hands. Both swords, which were identical, were housed in the same scabbard.

A curved, single-edged sword, in fact a saber, also existed in China and, while imported blades were often used for this weapon, its mounting was typically Chinese. It had a fairly long, straight grip, a forward-bent cylindrical pommel, and a discoidal guard, all in unadorned iron. The Chinese executioner's sword, in particular, was an enormous saber. Measuring between 120 and 150 cm. (4–5 ft.) in length, its blade was curved and heavy, while its extremely long, straight hilt was either clad in leather or bound with silk cord, sometimes surmounted by a ring pommel. Of course, both hands would have been used to wield this mighty instrument. When not in use, it was housed in a scabbard covered in black leather. *See also* TAU-KIEN.

For Japanese swords, see BLADE: Japanese; CHIKUTO; CHIZA KATANA; DAI-SHŌ; INOSHISHI-NO-YARI; KATANA; KEN; NAGAMAKI; NO-DACHI; TACHI; TSURUGI; WAKIZASHI.

For other Eastern swords, see DHA; FIRANGI; KAMPILAN; KHANDA; KORA; MANDAU; PATTISA; RAM DAO; TALWAR; ZAFAR TAKIEH; ZULFIKAR.

**sword breaker** A modern name given to the devices found on many 16th-century BUCKLERS and to such shields themselves. It is also applied to certain PARRYING DAGGERS with an indented blade or with two narrow side blades that splayed out at the touch of a button, in which the

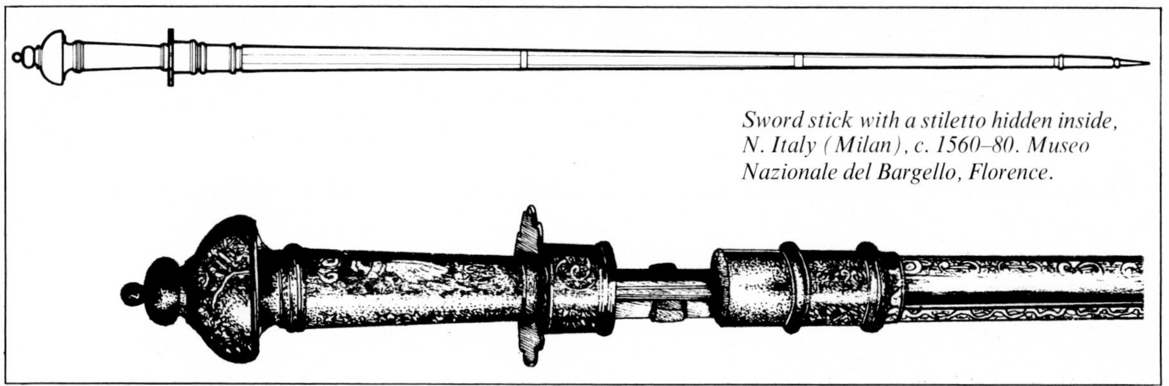

*Sword stick with a stiletto hidden inside, N. Italy (Milan), c. 1560–80. Museo Nazionale del Bargello, Florence.*

adversary's sword could be caught and jammed. In many cases, however, these devices must have been too frail to break a blade, though they would have parried the thrust.

**sword knot** A loop made of a strip of leather, ribbon, or twine, with both ends joined with a knot, tassel, or felt-covered ornament. It was tied to a quillon or to the grip of a sword or saber. The wrist was passed through the loop, thus preventing the weapon from falling if the wearer lost his grip on it, or if he had to take charge of his mount or draw a pistol. Small chains and thongs for attaching weapons to mounted soldiers are documented as far back as the Viking period; typical examples are the chains which attached the sword and the dagger—and frequently the helmet too—to the chest.

Nowadays horses are used by very few police units or ceremonial corps, and the sword knot has been kept simply as an ornament for full-dress or regimental uniforms. Different materials and colors help to identify the various corps and ranks, and, in some cases, the decorations awarded to the wearer.

**sword stick** A sword or dagger concealed inside a walking stick. The shape and size of the stick and the hidden blade varied a great deal: broad, flat blades were sometimes concealed within stout wooden sticks, whereas slender and fairly long blades could be hidden inside bamboo canes. A spring catch, a threaded socket, or proper friction formed a joint between the handle and the stick-cum-scabbard. The idea of concealing a weapon inside a harmless-looking, or less-offensive-looking, object is a very old one. It can be traced to the theatrical dagger of Roman times: to give the impression that the blade had entered the person struck, the impact of the blow caused the blunt blade to retract into the hollow handle. In the Renaissance and later periods, the staffs of pilgrims and wayfarers often concealed a long dagger (*see* BRANDISTOCK). But it was not until the late 18th century, when gentlemen stopped carrying swords at their side, that the sword stick became a frequent accessory of male attire outside the home.

In the kingdom of Naples, gendarmes in plain clothes were issued a "regulation" sword stick, but the carrying of sword sticks by ordinary citizens required a permit from the police. Riding whips sometimes also concealed a blade in their crops.

# T

**tabar** A generic Indian word for a battle-ax. The various forms of battle-axes existing in India are generally lighter than European ones and often have handles made from a flat steel plate with pieces of wood riveted to each side. Another type is made from a single piece of steel and has a round, hollow handle that sometimes conceals a dagger. On some, a sharp hook juts out from one side of the head and is used to sever the bridle of an enemy's horse. There are two basic forms of Indian tabars: one has a crescent-shaped blade, which may be as long as 35 cm. (14 in.) but is usually much shorter; the other has an elongated blade that has an almost straight upper edge and a slightly rounded cutting edge. Both most often have a square hammerhead opposite the blade. Quite common is the tabar with a double-ax head. The tabar averages about 50 cm. (20 in.) in length, although those with large, crescent-shaped blades are, of course, much longer.

**tabard** A short textile garment split at both sides, with very short flared sleeves, often worn over an armor during the 15th century, after the COAT ARMOR went out of fashion in the 1520s. The front, back, and sleeves of the tabard served to display the wearer's or his lord's heraldic devices. It remained in use at later periods as the official dress of heralds.

**tabi** Japanese defensive foot covering worn with sandals, tabi were made either of small iron or lacquered leather scales connected by mail or of mail alone, with or without soles. A separate covering was usually incorporated to cover the toes.

**tachi** The Japanese sword whose proud tradition goes back to prehistoric times. Although the tachi is single-edged and curved, like the KATANA, and might be classified as a saber according to European criteria, it is commonly referred to as a sword. The earliest blades were only slightly curved and about 60–70 cm. (24–28 in.) long, but in more recent times the tachi was shortened to about 50–60 cm. (20–24 in.). Produced by highly specialized swordsmiths, the tachi blade can be distinguished from the katana blade by the position of the maker's signature, which, because the katana was worn thrust into the girdle

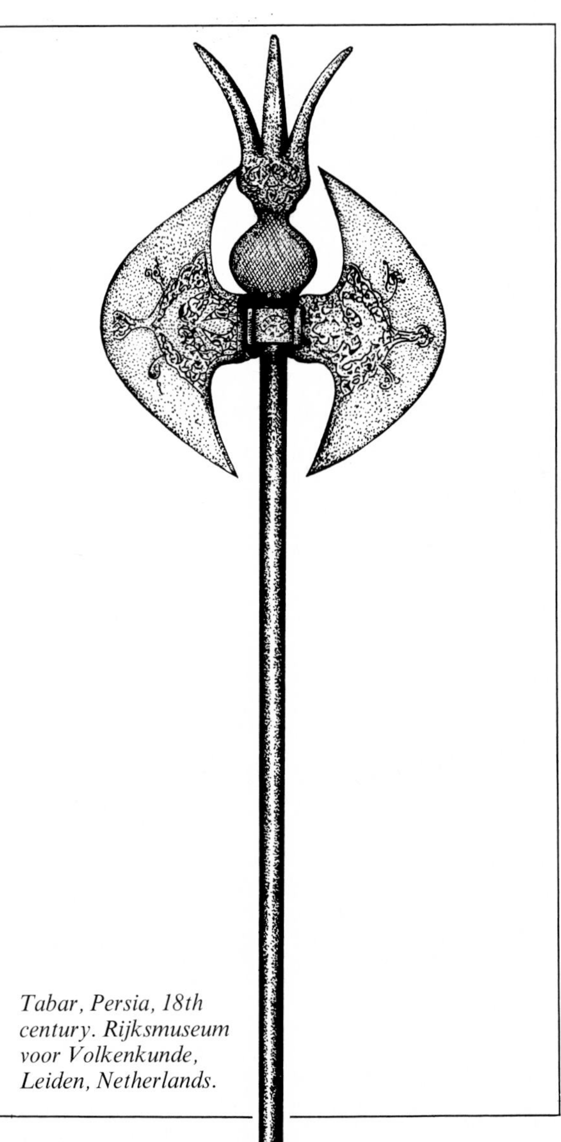

*Tabar, Persia, 18th century. Rijksmuseum voor Volkenkunde, Leiden, Netherlands.*

with the edge upward, came on the inner side. The tachi was hung edge downward from the belt by two straps, and the signature on its tang was on the outer side, away from the wearer.

Although as a war weapon the tachi ranked in importance alongside the spear and the bow over a long period, it was replaced in battle by the katana and WAKIZASHI. It remained, however, as the ceremonial sword worn at court and on formal occasions until, in 1877, it became illegal for swords to be carried in Japan. Most of the tachi mounts were individualized, each one having its own specific name that differed from the corresponding terms for mounts on other types of swords. For instance, the pommel was not called a KASHIRA but a *kabuto gane*; it had an opening at each side with a ring to take a doubled cord for the sword knot. The kabuto gane was occasionally shaped in the traditional form of the head of a phoenix, the Ho-o. SAMÉ was frequently used to cover the hilt, but it was seldom bound with braid. In place of MENUKI ornaments, it had main hilt adornments called *tsuk-ai* and a number of smaller ones, *tawara-byo*. The TSUBA guard was often made in a form said to be copied from the ceremonial rice cake and was known as the *shitogi*. In some cases there was an *aoi-tsuba*, a form of guard with heart-shaped perforations, embellished with a large, elaborate collar, the *seppa dai*. Nor was the KOZUKA or KŌGAI carried with the tachi.

The wooden scabbard was generally lacquered, with floral and representational motifs, as well as crests, for decoration. Tachi scabbards were sometimes completely overlaid with metal, and because this was a slung sword there was no *kurikata* (*see* KATANA) projection. There was a long locket, the *ishi-zuke*, near the mouth of the scabbard, and the other lockets, or scabbard bands, the *ichi-no-ashi*, each carried a suspension ring, the *obitori*, to which slings of cord, fabric, leather, or chain were attached. All the scabbard mounts were of either engraved or gilded copper or of SHIBUICHI, SHAKUDŌ, silver, or gold.

There were many variations of the tachi. Always treated with the greatest respect, it was often kept wrapped in brocade when not in use and put either in a special case or on a special rack, the KATANA KAKE.

**tail guard** A protective piece for a horse's dock (the root of the tail) in horse armor. It was an integral part of the CRUPPER in a set of bards, and in light horse armor and armored caparisons it took the form of a large strap, sometimes reinforced with metal scales. To protect part of the tail itself, a piece of thick cloth was tied below the root, forming a tube around the tail.

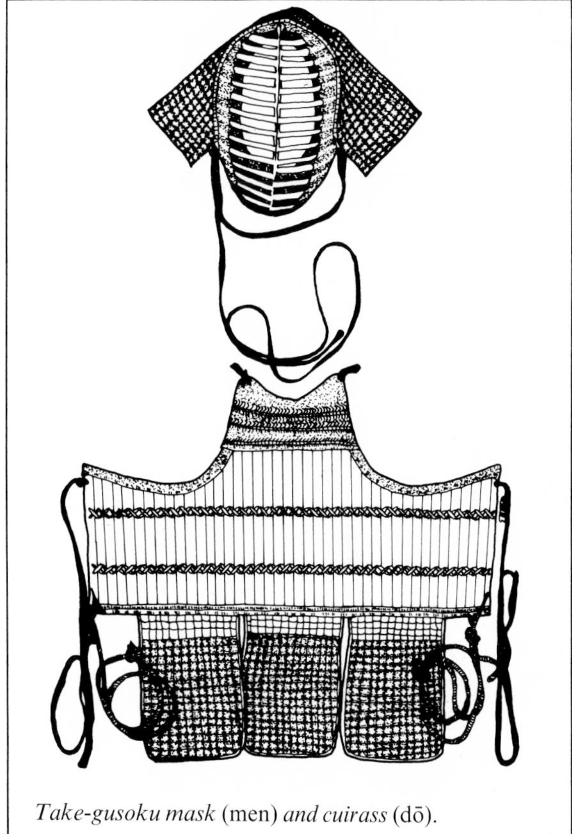

*Take-gusoku mask* (men) *and cuirass* (dō).

**take-gusoku** Japanese fencing armor, developed in the 18th century, originally made of small lengths of bamboo laced together with thongs. It consisted of a padded breastplate, DŌ; an apron-like protection, *tare*; gauntlets,

*Tachi, Japan, 18th century. Museo Stibbert, Florence.*

KOTE; and a fencing mask, *men*. A breastplate in this style of bamboo armor is used to this day under lacquered leather in most armors made for *kendō*—fencing with bamboo swords.

**take-yari** (or **take-hoko**) The most primitive kind of Japanese spear, it consisted of a bamboo pole cut to about 2–2.5 m. (6½–8 ft.). Although normally used by peasants, in an emergency it was sometimes wielded by samurai and was capable of inflicting nasty wounds, with its jagged end.

**takouba** A typical sword of the Saharan Tuaregs with a very old genealogy. It is known mainly from iconography, and the few extant specimens, preserved in Greece and Turkey, have a cruciform hilt resembling that of the Byzantine sword. Takouba blades, which are generally imported and often bear the marks of Toledo or Solingen, are straight, double-edged, broad, and rounded at the tip and often have several shallow fullers down the middle on both sides. The hilt, usually of copper, has a mushroom-shaped pommel, a slim, round grip, and a straight guard in the form of a broad, flat bar. Both the grip and the guard are covered with leather tooled in simple motifs. The scabbard is also of decorated leather, with copper mounts.

**talwar** An Indian saber developed in the 16th century under Mogul rule by combining various local and foreign features, chiefly Persian, Mongol, and Turkish. Although the prestige of Persian blades remained supreme, Indian swordmakers had no problems in developing a new form because their skills in metallurgy were advanced, particularly in producing the watered steel called *wootz*. During the reigns of Akbar (1555–1605) and Jehangir (1605–27), Mongol-style blades, shallowly curved and with a heavy YALMAN, were still popular. Later, similar but more deeply curved blades were used for an indigenous type of talwar, the *tegha*. In the 17th century, a deeply curved and continuously tapering blade was introduced both in Persia and India.

All blades, mostly of watered steel, were decorated by chasing, gilding, or etching, with floral or abstract motifs, cartouches, inscriptions (mainly in Arabic), and also with human or zoomorphic figures, sometimes in relief.

A significant difference between Persian and Indian blades was that no Persian blade was ever made with the so-called Indian RICASSO, that is, a short, flattened section of the edge at the shoulder for the index finger when it was hooked around the front quillon. European blades of various kinds were also used for some talwar.

There were several forms of talwar hilts. Early examples were in the Persian style with its characteristic long quillons and escutcheon all in one piece, together with a forward-rolled pommel often shaped into a lion's head. Under the Shahs Jehan (1627–58) and Aurangzeb (1658–1707), the Indo-Moslem hilt became the standard mounting for these sabers; it had a bellied grip running down into the quillons, usually terminating in flattened bulbs. Below the quillons two langets extended downward, standing slightly away from the blade to fit over shaped recesses at each side of the mouth of the scabbard. The grip was surmounted by a saucer pommel with a dome topped by a finial. A curved knuckle guard was often incorporated.

Many local variations of the general structure of the talwar hilt developed throughout India. Decoration, too, varied widely as different techniques and local styles were applied. A few examples that give an idea of their range are: the application of gold and silver to steel, enameling (mostly *champlevé*, although in Jaipur *cloisonné* was worked), gilding, chasing, repoussé, niello, and filigree. The decorative motifs had both abstract and naturalistic floral themes.

The wooden talwar scabbards, which had suspension rings, were usually covered with velvet and mounted in metal to match the hilt. Members of fighting castes were extremely careful of their swords and took as much trouble in looking after them as the Japanese.

**tang** The stem of the blade, which extends into the handle and serves to attach the hilt. Its form varies depending on the system that joins the handle to the blade. If pointed, the tang is driven in like a nail, a very simple system still used for tool handles (e.g., files, chisels, etc.). In order to achieve a stronger join, the tang is usually shaped like a tapering cylinder that slightly exceeds the length of the handle and is riveted onto the pommel or button. In the 19th century the end of the tang was often threaded, and the button was screwed onto it.

**tankō** An armor of protohistoric Japan, used mostly from the 4th to 7th centuries A.D. A development of earlier armors of hide and bamboo, the tankō consisted of a beaked, rounded helmet of horizontal iron plates joined by rivets or leather lacing, with a laminated neck guard of plates laced together on the inside and a plume of pheasant's feathers. A distinctive feature of the bowl of the helmet was its sharply rigid beak at the front known as the *shōkakufu-no-hachi*, or "battering-ram bowl."

The body armor somewhat resembled the Roman LORICA *segmentata*, although even indirect influence would be hard to credit. The similarity may, perhaps, be accounted for by the theory that similar objects are sometimes created in distant cultures for similar purposes.

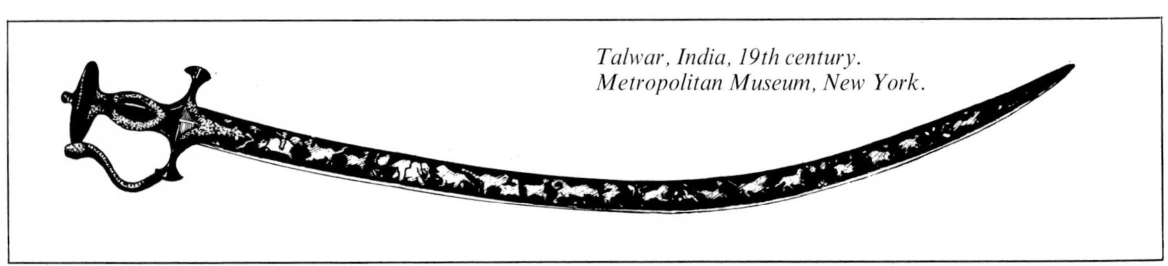

*Talwar, India, 19th century. Metropolitan Museum, New York.*

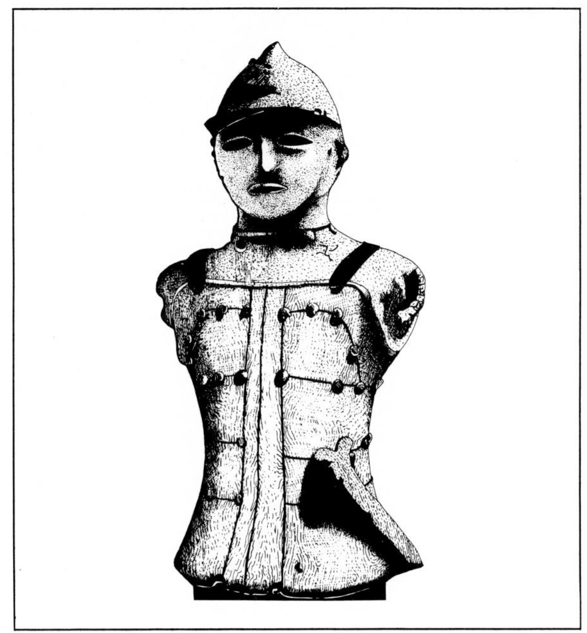

*Funerary statuette depicting a warrior wearing tankō armor, Japan, 6th–7th century (Kofun period). National Museum, Tokyo.*

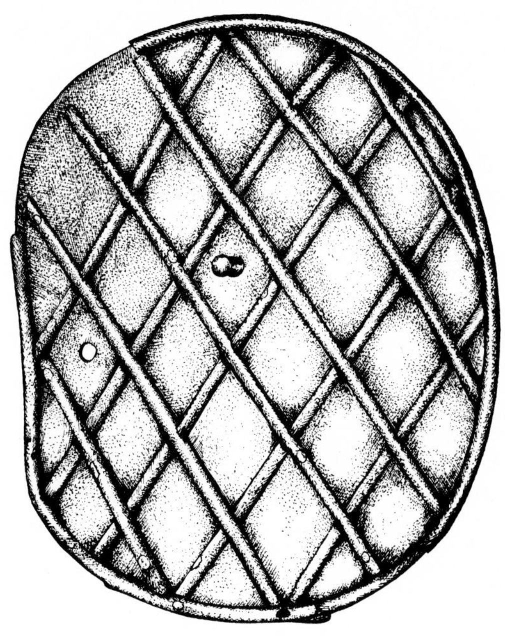

*Targe for tilting armor, Innsbruck, c. 1530–35. Odescalchi Collection, Museo di Palazzo Venezia, Rome.*

The tankō cuirass, shaped to the body, was built up of horizontal plates riveted or laced together within a framework. The opening was at the center front, and there was a hinge either on the right half of the breast or on both halves, at the side, to admit the body. In some types in which there were no hinges, the cuirass must have been sprung onto the body, rather like the ancient Greek bronze greaves. The front opening was fastened with leather thongs, and the shoulders of the cuirass were secured with fabric ties. The collar, the *uwa-manchira*, with its shoulder guards, was worn over the top; this consisted of two plates with ties at the center of the chest and back, permanently laced with laminated curved iron strips fitted to the outside of the shoulders and arms. The forearms were protected by tubular vambraces, KOTE, with rows of small laced lamellae for the back of the hands. The cuirass was completed with a large, hooplike skirt in two sections, one at the front and one at the back, comprising a series of narrow, curved laminations laced—like the neck guard and shoulder pieces—on the inside. There were no special leg defenses in tankō armor.

**tantō** A typical Japanese dagger with a small TSUBA. Its single-edged blade was similar to that of other edged weapons, measuring about 20–30 cm. (8–12 in.) and slightly curved, although a few were made that had a straight blade. The tantō was mounted in the same style as the KATANA and the WAKIZASHI. Its hilt, generally covered with SAMÉ and bound with braid, was fitted with a KASHIRA pommel, MENUKI ornaments, a tsuba, and its companion fittings.

The lacquered wooden sheath had all the appropriate mounts: *kojiri* (chape), *kurikata* (slotted projection), *uragawara* (top mount), *soritsuno* (retaining hook), and even menuki. A KOZUKA knife and a KŌGAI skewer were frequently carried with the tantō, and a cord passed through the kurikata to secure the dagger to the wearer's belt. In the days before it became illegal for civilians to carry swords (1877), the tantō was not one of those left at the door when visiting. For further details about the scabbard mounts, *see* SAYA.

**t'ao** A kind of Chinese armor. *See also* ARMOR: Chinese.

**targe** (or **target**) A general term used to cover various types of shields carried on the arm by infantry troops from the 13th to 16th century. Strictly speaking, however, the targe was a round or squarish shield, concave toward the body, fitted on the inside with two straps, ENARMES, through one of which, adjusted by means of a buckle, the left forearm passed, the other being fixed and held by the left hand. There was also an oblong pad against which the forearm rested. This type of shield was usually made of iron or of iron-plated wood. From the 15th century, when the use of targes by warriors notably decreased, the word "targe" was also applied to several types of variously shaped shields used for the German jousts.

A specific form of targe was the "Hungarian" shield, which was also used in Germany in conjunction with eastern European armor. It was rectangular at the bottom, but the upper edge sloped up to the left in a concave curve to form an elongated point with the vertical left-hand edge.

*Targes for jousts.* A small wooden shield of roughly rectangular form (*Stechtartsche* in German) was used in the 15th and first half of the 16th century to supplement a special heavy armor (*Stechzeug*) for a joust with lances (*Gestech*) popular in Germanic countries. Similar but higher targes were used from the early 16th century with somewhat modified Stechzeug for the tilts (*Plankengestech* or *Welschgestech*, "Italian joust") introduced into Austria and Germany from Italy. In these contests, the two opponents rode along the respective sides of a long barrier tilting toward it as they tried to score a hit.

In other forms of joust with lances known as *Scharfrennen*, special armors were worn in c. 1475–c. 1550 with quite a large targe, the *Renntartsche*, so shaped as to cover the breast and the bevor. Made of wood and leather, it was reinforced with metal strips and attached to the armor with two screws.

A steel tilting targe, introduced in Italy (*targhetta*) but also widely used in other European countries in the 16th century, had a concave surface with a trellis structure wrought or applied. Screwed to the armor, it covered the left side of the breast.

*Fencing targe.* A rare defensive piece for one arm and shoulder used as a sword-dueling accessory in the late 15th and 16th centuries. A mitten gauntlet, worn over the left forearm, was incorporated into a round or square shield. There were several accessories on these shields, although not all of them were necessarily present on the same piece. These included a spike in the center, a sword-breaking ring or hook, and two thin serrated blades of different lengths and set at varying angles protruding from the top of the gauntlet. There was sometimes a lantern, too, attached to the top edge of the shield.

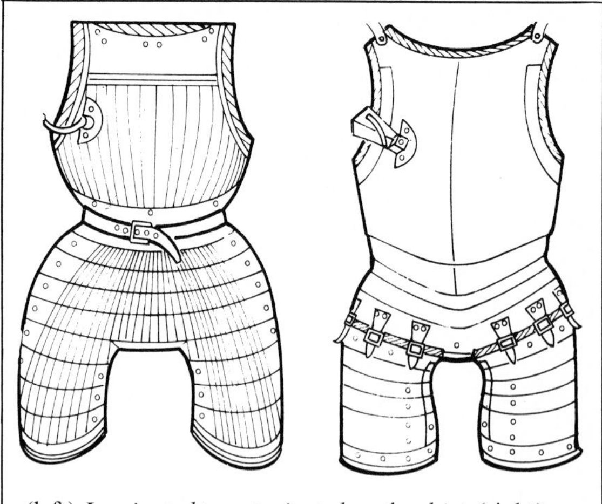

(left) *Laminated tassets riveted on the skirt.* (right) *Short tassets attached by straps and buckles.*

*"Hungarian"-style targe, Germany, second half of the 16th century. Odescalchi Collection, Museo di Palazzo Venezia, Rome.*

**targone** Italian term for a specific elongated 15th-century shield used for the joust and dueling on horseback. It measured a little over 2 m. (6 ft.) and was fitted with two rigid handles on the inside, although occasionally there was only one. Usually of wood, it was made in a variety of shapes. The targone continued to be used for a specific type of joust in Pisa, *gioco del ponte* ("games on the bridge"), even in the 17th and 18th centuries. It was generally painted in bright colors with armorial bearings, family mottoes, heraldic devices, and, occasionally, motifs depicting human figures.

**tasset** Worn from the 15th to the first half of the 17th century, the tassets consisted of a plate, or series of lames, suspended in front from each side of the lower edge of the skirt to protect the upper part of the thighs. They appeared around 1420, each tasset comprised of a single keeled plate attached to the skirt by two buckles and straps. These sturdy, compact plates were generally rectangular, their lower edges being turned and reinforced. This style was retained until the middle of the 15th century, although there was a tendency for the plates to get larger, both in width and length. In the second half of the century, the tasset took on the shape of an irregular trapezoid, with a cusped lower edge.

Tassets made up of several lames articulated on sliding rivets appeared in the late 15th century and were used for more than a hundred years. Serving also as cuisses, they were still in use in the first half of the 17th century, when they extended down to the knees and were joined there to the poleyns. These long tassets, which had the same basic structure as short ones—articulated lames on sliding rivets, with the upper lame buckled onto the skirt—were a characteristic feature of infantry and cuirassier armor. This was especially the case in the Germanic countries, where, in fact, they continued to be used long after they had ceased to be worn in Italy. In some suits of three-quarter armor, the laminated tassets combined with cuisses and poleyns were made in two parts, the lower section and poleyn being detachable from the tassets themselves. The long laminated tassets with poleyns, because of their appearance, are described as "lobster-tail" tassets in Italian terminology.

A special kind of tasset, called the *hind tasset*, was used in some 15th-century armors to protect the loins. It was a one-lame piece attached with straps and buckles to the lowest lame of the skirt in the back. It was flanked by two small plates, the so-called side tassets.

**tatami-dō** A type of Japanese armor. *See also* DŌ-MARU.

**tatami-gusoku** A type of Japanese armor. *See also* GUSOKU.

**tatami kabuto** A Japanese folding helmet, worn with the TATAMI YOROI, used mainly for traveling. The helmet, the KABUTO, was made of horizontal steel rings laced together so that it could be closed like an opera hat. An arched piece, hinged to the lower part of each side, could be turned upward over the top of the crown and locked to it by means of a pin. Another type of tatami kabuto, resembling a cap with neck and ear guards, was made of medium-sized four-sided lacquered leather plates connected by mail.

**tatami yoroi** Japanese armor, worn with the TATAMI KABUTO. The corslet of the tatami yoroi was constructed of lacquered leather plates joined by mail, the arm guards, KOTE, being in their usual form. Another type of armor, made of small octagonal steel plates connected by mail, is also classed as tatami yoroi.

**tate** The Japanese standing rectangular shield, like a European PAVISE, supported by a hinged prop at the back. This shield hardly altered in appearance from the 11th to the 19th century. The normal tate was made of wood, painted in black bands, and sometimes had a *mon* (family crest). Although some were made to fold at the center, they were generally rigid. On the march, soldiers carried them on their backs. Massed together, they were used to form defensive walls on land, on the ramparts of a castle, and even along the side of a ship.

**tau-kien** A Chinese sword bearing some resemblance to the European fencing rapier. Its blade, about 75–80 cm. (30–32 in.) long, consisted of a heavy metal bar, usually triangular or square in cross section, sometimes with transverse grooves or flutes. The straight hilt, either entirely of iron or with a wooden grip, had a plate guard and a round or polygonal pommel. Some of these weapons had blunt-tipped blades and were probably used for fencing exercises.

**tawarabyo** Mounts for the Japanese sword TACHI.

**tegha** A type of Indian saber (*see* TALWAR) developed in the 16th–17th centuries. It had a deeply curved blade, which either gradually tapered to the point or had a YALMAN.

**tehen** An opening in the top of some Japanese helmets, such as the HOSHI-KABUTO and SUJI-KABUTO, surrounded by an elaborate brass molding, usually in the form of a chrysanthemum, *hachimanza*. Japanese men used to dress their hair in a small pigtail, and this was passed through the tehen. However, there are several incorrect interpretations of the function of the tehen, one being that it was a ventilation hole and another that it was to allow the air from the bowl to pass through when the warrior had to dive, in full armor, into water. It was also thought that the hole was the opening through which heavenly influences could be brought to bear on the wearer. In fact, the tehen was tightly covered by the lining in modern helmets and no free passage, either for air or inspiration, was possible. When the pigtail went out of fashion, the tehen survived merely as a traditional feature having no practical function.

**telamon** Greek word for the BALTEUS.

**telek** A characteristic dagger of the Saharan Tuaregs, its straight, double-edged blade is 30–40 cm. (12–16 in.) long, diamond-shaped in cross section, and tapers to a sharp point. There is a small circular guard at the base of the hilt, which is often bound with brass wire. The pommel has the form of a cross and probably originates from the hilts of Crusaders' swords (which gave grounds to the belief that the Tuaregs had descended from Christian ancestors).

The telek sheath is made of decorated leather, mounted in brass, and furnished with a wide leather loop for the left wrist. It was carried flat against the inside of the left forearm and, when necessary, the telek was drawn with the right hand.

**tencho** An ancient Japanese word for the HOKO.

**teppo** *See* FIREARMS: Japanese.

**teppo yumi** A light Japanese sporting crossbow in horn or whalebone, about 70 cm. (27 in.) long. Its bow, made in two halves that fit into sockets on the sides of the wooden stock, measures a little over 60 cm. (24 in.) and is shaped like a gunstock.

**terzaruolo** (also **terzaruola, terzarolo**) An Italian term used to describe a type of medium-length wheel-lock—either a short arquebus or a long pistol. A Florentine

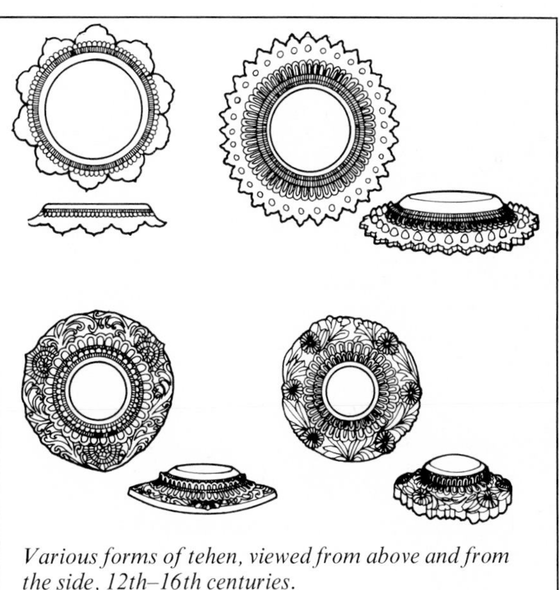

*Various forms of tehen, viewed from above and from the side, 12th–16th centuries.*

document dated 1638 refers to "three hundred light wheel-lock terzaruoli for arming the cuirassiers." Pistofilo Bonaventura, the author of *Oplomachia*, published in Siena in 1621, describes wheel-lock guns as being of three types: "first, the long arquebus; second, the pistol or rather Terzaruolo; and lastly the Archibusetto or rather pistoletto." Angelucci, in his *Catalogo dell'armeria reale*, published in 1890, states that the name *terzaruolo* derives from the fact that the barrel was "a third shorter than the long arquebus."

**terzett** A word used to describe a type of pistol having a long barrel, one-third the length of the standard musket. It is also used generally in Italy, where it is spelled "terzetta," to describe a short pistol. A reference in a 17th-century document describes the bullet of the terzett as "having the weight of ten ounces" (28 g.), which corresponds to a bore of 0.396.

**terzo** The middle section of a blade, between the forte and the foible.

**tessak** (from Czech *tésak* and German *Duságge*) A Russian name for the infantry soldier's hanger used in the 18th and 19th centuries. Most models look like a short saber with a large blade and a simple closed hilt, but some patterns issued in the 19th century were fashioned, under French influence, after the Roman GLADIUS and had a straight short blade and solid bronze hilt with a cross guard. In recent times, the nickname "tessak" has been applied to navy cutlasses worn with full-dress uniform by cadets of naval academies (the official name for this weapon being *palash*, the Russian derivative of PALLASCH).

**tetrahedron** *See* TRIBULUS.

**tetsu-gai** A half-gauntlet in the KOTE.

**tetsu-ten** A variation of the Japanese WAR FAN.

**thermonuclear bomb** *See* BOMB.

**thórax** Greek term for CUIRASS.

**three-quarter armor** *See* ARMOR.

**throat latch** (or **lash**) A narrow leather strap forming part of a horse's bridle. It passes from one end of the brow band under the horse's jaw to buckle at the other side of the brow band, helping to keep the bridle in position. It never fits tightly, however, and is quite separate from the controlling straps.

**thumb ring** *See* ARCHER'S THUMB RING.

**t'ie cha** Chinese lamellar armor. *See also* ARMOR: Chinese.

**tiger's claws** A typical Indian weapon, not unlike the European knuckle-duster. *See also* BAGH-NAKH.

**tiller** The wooden or metal stock of the CROSSBOW incorporating the release mechanism. In the primitive crossbow the tiller consisted of two small boards hinged at the front. The upper board had a nock set crosswise, to hold the spanned bowstring, with a hole in the middle. In the lower section, corresponding to the hole, there was fixed a dowel that, when the two boards were joined together, entered the hole in the upper board and pushed out the bowstring from the nock. At a later stage the stock was made from a block of wood in which a blocking and release mechanism was housed—the nut, controlled and operated by a trigger lever beneath.

The construction of the tiller differed in the various European countries and depended on two factors. One factor had to do with the use of the crossbow—either as a weapon of war or for hunting; the other had to do with the mechanism used to span the bow. Broadly speaking, in central and southern Europe a straight tiller with parallel sides was mainly used. Designed for use with a goat's-foot lever as a spanning mechanism, this system applied to both the combatant's and the hunter's version, although the two differed in their finish and decoration. North of the Alps, in Switzerland and Germany, a tiller with a swelling at the center was preferred. This was better suited for holding and blocking the loop of the CRANEQUIN. For use in battle there was a preference for a straight tiller to which the WINDLASS was fitted. Later, in the 17th century, a metal tiller came into vogue, which ended with a short butt. This type of tiller had a spanning lever incorporated in it: by raising the lever arm, the pivoted nut was moved forward until it caught the bowstring; then by pushing the lever and nut back to the shooting position, the bow was spanned. Such tillers were often used with the stone-throwing crossbows. Sometimes the tiller of the stone crossbow had a special shape; since this weapon did not need to support a bolt, the tiller was strongly curved downward between the bow and the release mechanism, which included a hook to hold the pouch for the missile, formed by the double bowstring. From the mid-17th century onward we find hunting crossbows, often of the stone or pellet type, with tillers or handles identical in their forms to the stocks of contemporary firearms.

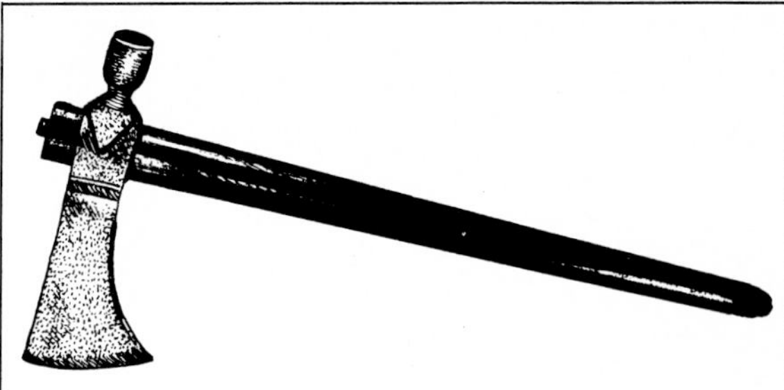

*Pipe tomahawk, made in England for the American market, c. 1850. Musée d'Armes, Liège.*

**tilting saddle** A special type of wooden saddle used for the tilt or joust. *See also* SADDLE.

**tilting sockets** (or *German* **Dilgen**) A pair of defensive pieces for the German joust to give protection to the thighs and knees. They consisted of large metal plates, either shield-shaped or thigh-shaped, one of which was hung on each side of the saddle or fastened to the combatant's thighs with a strap and buckle. Typical of German armor, they were in use in the 15th century and the first half of the 16th. Tilting sockets were used in the *Scharfrennen*, a course in which the aim was to unhorse one's opponent or at least to hit him.

**tilting targe** A piece of reinforcing armor for the tilt, characteristic of the Germanic style, which fulfilled a similar function to the GRANDGUARD used in Italian-style tilting armor. It was a heavy plate shaped to the contour of the left shoulder and also covering the left side of the breast and upper arm. It was screwed onto the breastplate, and its lower edge jutted out freely, partially covering the left forearm holding the reins. Many variations of this piece were produced, the modifications being chiefly in two areas: one was in the angle of the tilting targe in relation to the breastplate, to improve the possibility of an opponent's lance glancing off it; the other was in the reinforcing strips that were fitted on the whole surface in the form of applied trelliswork ("trellised targe").

**tinder** A term used to describe a form of tree fungus (*Boletus lignarius*) used as tinder in the 15th century and later. By soaking the material in saltpeter and then allowing it to dry, it acquired excellent qualities of combustion that made it ideal for the hand ignition used in early firearms. It was also used in TINDERBOXES up to the 19th century.

**tinderbox** Also called tinder lighter, a container in which a piece of steel and flint were kept, together with easily ignitable material, for example, charred linen or tinder. Tinderboxes were widely used, by hand or mechanically, until the invention of matches in the 19th century made them obsolete. Tinderboxes with ignition mechanisms similar to the wheel-lock had been known since the early 16th century and may have influenced the wheel-lock's inventors. In the same way, the old, widespread method of striking a piece of flint with a steel bar to produce sparks for tinder may have inspired the inventors of flintlocks.

**ting kia** A type of Chinese armor similar to the European BRIGANDINE. *See also* ARMOR: Chinese.

**Todenkopf** (German, "death's head") A modern term for a type of BURGONET that has a bevor shaped as a grotesque human face. This type is sometimes referred to as a "Savoyard" helmet.

**toe cap** *See* SABATONS.

**togari-ya** A variation of the YANO-NE.

**tomahawk** A fighting ax of the North American Indians, it originally had a stone head and short wooden handle. At this stage, it was still a kind of prehistoric weapon, used for striking as well as throwing. When Europeans began to settle in America, however, they supplied the Indians with iron heads for their tomahawks. These were of various types, the French ones being much more complicated than those of English make. Some heads had narrow hatchet blades, others were flat rhomboidal or triangular. Some even had a hook on the opposite side of the blade. A rather special variation was the pipe tomahawk, which had a hollow handle usually about 40–50 cm. (15–20 in.) long and an iron tobacco-pipe bowl on the other side of the blade. From the various shapes, each Indian tribe chose the one it preferred. In 1872–97, tomahawks, known also as boarding axes, were issued to the Royal Engineers (British Army); they were provided with leather cases.

**tonlet** (from French *tonnelet*, "little barrel") A special long, flared steel skirt of "tonlet armor" used for the foot combat during the late 15th and 16th centuries. The horizontal lames of the tonlet completely enclosed the wearer's body from the waist to just above the knees. The tonlet was hinged on one side and fastened with buckles and straps on the other. This defense assured adequate protection against blows from offensive weapons.

*Tonlet for the foot-combat armor belonging to Emperor Maximilian I of Hapsburg, made in N. Italy, c. 1500–1508. Waffensammlung, Vienna.*

**top** An Indian helmet, very similar to the Persian KULAH KHUD but with some features of its own. The Persian helmet of this kind generally had a definite form—an ideal combination of the functional with good design, with variations only in material and decoration. The Indian top was always more informal, giving scope to the individual imagination of its maker. Its solid plate skull was often fairly shallow or very small, almost like that of the Middle Eastern MISSYURKA. It normally had two plume sockets at the front of the skull, but a few tops had a third socket instead of a spike on the summit. There were often three nasals to protect the face, and the AVENTAIL was cut in a deep zigzag pattern in the lower edge.

**toradar** An Indian matchlock gun that came into being in the 16th century. It was made with Indian-built barrels, about 100–120 cm. (39–47 in.) long. Of fine twisted (Damascus) steel, the barrel was enlarged at the breech and tapered toward the muzzle, which was usually reinforced with molded rings. The barrel was occasionally square, even having a square bore. The backsight was generally V-shaped, although sometimes ogival in the Turkish style, while the front sight was worked on the front ring to look like the nose of a man or an animal. The barrel was frequently chased in high relief or inlaid with silver, gold, or precious stones, and sometimes there were also Sanskrit or Hindustani inscriptions. It was bound to the stock with wire or rawhide thongs and with barrel bands. The serpentine functioned in a slit of the stock, its lower end forming a bladelike trigger. The pan cover was hinged sideways on a pin or was lifted like a lid before pressing the trigger. The lock was provided with a pricker on a chain to clean the touchhole. The match cord was usually wound around the butt. Lock plates were made of silver or watered steel, and the stock—often of rosewood

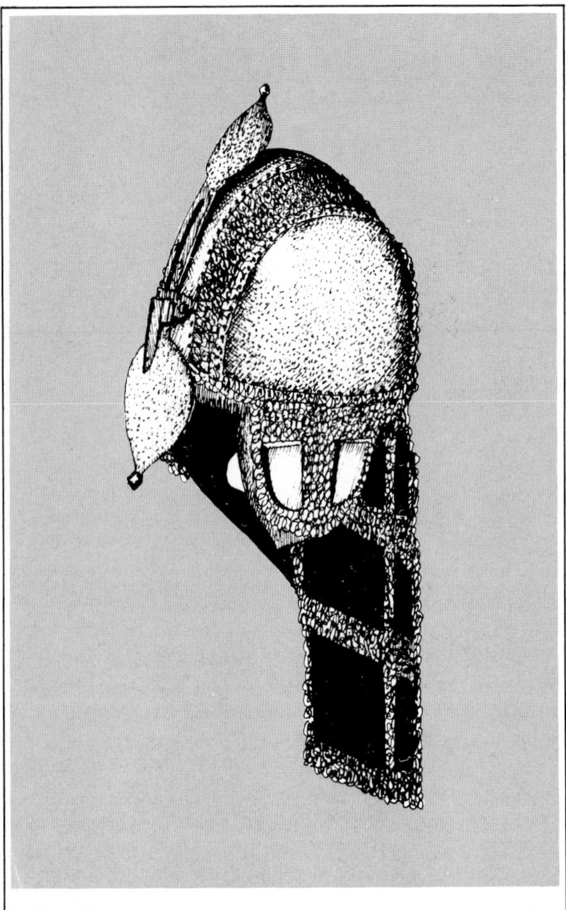

*Top, N. India, 17th–18th century. Museo Stibbert, Florence.*

or mahogany—was frequently lacquered green, painted with flowers, and inlaid with ivory or enameled silver.

There were two types of butts: one, popular in central India, was straight, slim, and pentagonal in section, while the other, used in the north, was curved and diamond-shaped in section. The toradar was usually fitted with a clevis—a U-shaped projection—for the sling strap, some even having two. A toradar was normally about 1.5–1.8 m. (5–6 ft.) long, but there were also much smaller models—perhaps intended for boys—no longer than 1 m. (39 in.).

**tosei-gusoku** Another name for "modern" Japanese armor. *See also* GUSOKU.

**touchhole** *See* VENT.

**tragula** (Latin; Greek *tragolas*) A javelin having a head sometimes fitted with a HAMUS (hook, tooth). Its shaft was fitted with a thong, the AMENTUM, and with this device it could be recovered at a short distance after having been thrown. It seems to have been used mainly by the Celtic peoples: Gauls, Celto-Iberians, Bretons. It was known in Rome in the time of Plautus (who died in 184 B.C.), and Caesar (100–44 B.C.) describes having ordered a Gaul to throw a *tragula cum epistula ad ammentum ligata* ("a javelin with a letter attached to the thong") into his camp. There is also evidence that it was used for hunting and fishing.

**trapper of mail** A type of medieval horse armor (*see* BARD), consisting of a large piece of mail extending to the knees of the horse and covering also its neck and head.

**tribulus** Also called a caltrop or tetrahedron, an instrument made of iron consisting of four or more sharp spikes, often barbed, joined at the center. These devices were strewn in great number on the ground in order to impede cavalry charges and infantry attacks. When on the ground, one of the spikes always remained turned upward, designed to damage horses' hooves and infantrymen's feet. In classical antiquity, from at least the 4th century B.C., it

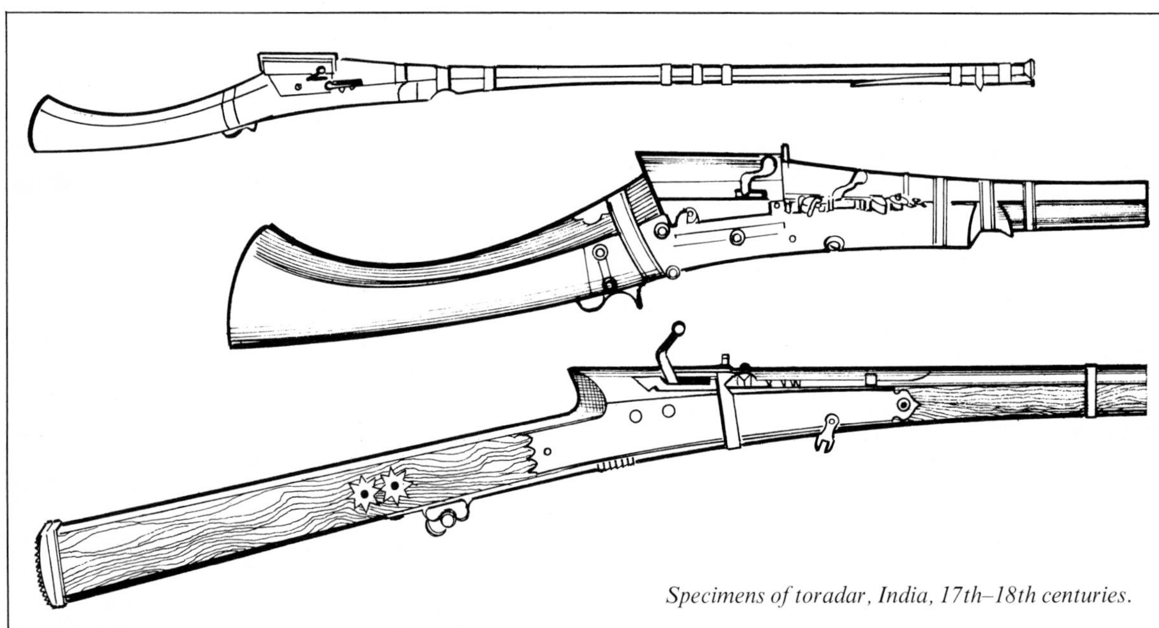

*Specimens of toradar, India, 17th–18th centuries.*

was simplified to one spike, sometimes with a hook, with the tang fitted into a conical piece of wood driven into the ground, leaving just the spike uncovered. As a result it was very hard to detect the tribulus by day and virtually impossible at night. During pitched battles and sieges, the tribuli were scattered widely along ditches and in breaches, often concealed beneath earth and leaves. They were also used aboard ship, with the intention of slowing down assaults and boarding parties. A modern version of the tribulus, termed the tetrahedron by the military, is used to prevent vehicles from crossing roadblocks and checkpoints.

**trident** A large three-pronged fork, probably originally fashioned from antlers but made of metal as soon as primitive technology made this possible. Used mainly for fishing, but also for hunting and certain agricultural tasks, it was never carried by regular armies, although occasionally it was used in guerrilla-type skirmishes. In the classical period it was the weapon of the *retiarius*, the gladiator in the arena who was armed with a net and trident and mimicked the movements of the fisherman as he tried to snare his opponent before slaying him. It was also used in naval battles as a boarding weapon. Mythology associates the trident with Poseidon (or Neptune), god of the sea, but it also appears in the hands of other deities. It was depicted on coins minted in the maritime cities of the Greek settlements in southern Italy. In central Africa the trident was often used for fishing, and by local sorcerers in propitiatory rain rites. The head of the trident sometimes has the three prongs with their flat faces rather than the cutting edges turned toward each other.

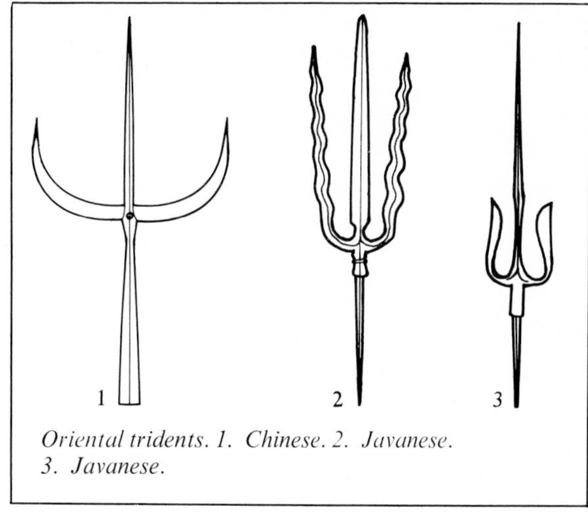


*Oriental tridents. 1. Chinese. 2. Javanese. 3. Javanese.*

*Trident, Urbino, c. 1530. Museo Nazionale del Bargello, Florence.*

**trigger** The part of the firing mechanism of small arms that when pressed actuates the firing. It is generally a hinged lever acting on the sear so as to release the firing mechanism when the lower end or "tail," projecting below the firearm body, is pressed.

**trigger guard** A rounded guard, usually of iron, that is screwed to the base of the stock of a firearm to prevent the trigger from being accidentally pressed. This safety device was introduced as early as the first half of the 16th century. A wheel-lock gun in the Bayerisches Armeemuseum in Munich, made for a Bavarian duke and dated 1533, is fitted with a large trigger guard, the rear portion of which is recessed for the fingers to provide a steadier grip. The trigger guard, found on most firearms from the 17th century to the present, is rarely found on Oriental firearms or on early Scottish firearms. In some breechloading systems the trigger guard acted as a lever used to open the breech.

**trigger matchlock** *See* IGNITION.

**trigger sear** The release lever of the CROSSBOW formed by a slightly curved metal bar beneath the tiller. On the forward end it has a tooth—the sear—which, when locked in the lower notch of the nut, blocks it. By pressing the trigger toward the tiller, the sear is moved out of the notch and enables the nut to rotate, thus releasing the bowstring.

A spring inside the stock acts on the trigger, keeping it in the lower position and the sear in the blocking position. This device was used up until the end of the 15th century on all types of hunting and war crossbows; later, it was also used on competition crossbows. In the 17th century, for sporting and hunting crossbows, the trigger sear was replaced by a release mechanism controlled by a trigger of the form already in use on hand firearms.

**trinitrotoluene (TNT)** Also called trotyl, a chemical substance used as an EXPLOSIVE.

**trombone** An archaic name for the BLUNDERBUSS.

**trousse** (or **trousse de chasse**) French term for a HUNTING GARNITURE and a WOOD KNIFE.

**trunnions** Strong cylindrical pivots projecting from the sides of old guns by which the pieces were mounted on the carriages, enabling the piece to be elevated or lowered. The introduction of trunnions, in the second half of the 15th century, was a notable step forward in the development of ARTILLERY. The shocks received when smooth-bore guns were fired (battering by the projectile, escape of gas at the vent, etc.) were not balanced by the inertia of the piece. Therefore it was found advantageous to locate the trunnions, with their axis perpendicular to the plane of symmetry, away from the center of gravity of the gun, leaving the bulk of the weight in the breech for cannon and howitzers and in the chase for mortars. The point at which trunnions were most likely to break was where they joined the barrel. In order to give that section additional thickness without making the trunnions too big, a system was adopted from the time of Gribeauval's reforms (1765–74) by which the trunnions were constructed in two cylindrical sections of different diameters, the base (with a diameter $1\frac{1}{4}$ to $1\frac{1}{2}$ times that of the trunnion itself) attached to the piece and the trunnion proper, on which the gun rested in the cradle.

**Tschinke** Name given to a small-caliber rifle used for shooting birds. Its principal characteristics included a wheel-lock with an external mainspring, a button to set the sear, and, usually, a characteristic sharply angled small butt. This type of fowling piece owed its name to the town of Teschen in Silesia, where, as early as 1580, the name of the town was already associated with a particular type of gun. The precise date of the invention of the Tschinke is unknown, although in the Waffensammlung in Vienna there is a Tschinke of classic form bearing the date 1610. Only a few examples are dated, but most of those surviving appear to have originated in the middle years of the 17th century, with a handful perhaps dating from the early 18th century. The stocks of many Tschinke were elaborately inlaid with mother-of-pearl and stag's horn, the locks often being coarsely engraved and gilded.

**tsuba** The plate guard of a Japanese sword, which was not only an essential functional fitting but also a most interesting piece of decoration. Since the appearance of the tsuba in the early centuries A.D., evidence of which has been found from excavations in dolmens and tombs, this part of the Japanese sword underwent a steady evolution, both in form and decoration. In fact, tsuba were finally produced separately from the swords by highly specialized artist-craftsmen and were then fitted to whatever sword the purchaser wished. As the mounting and remounting of a Japanese sword was a fairly easy process, each tsuba could be quickly replaced by another. An immense market developed, and the collecting of tsuba soon grew into a highly specialized field. So much relevant material has been amassed on tsuba that only the barest outlines of their history, construction, and interpretation can be covered in a work of this nature.

The tsuba found in burial mounds of the 7th century or earlier are of solid iron plate, kite-shaped, with a single hole in the middle for the tang of the blade; this central opening was occasionally surrounded by a series of smaller perforations. Some early tsuba were made of leather in an iron frame, lacquered on both sides to protect them from humidity; these were called *neri tsuba*. Most surviving tsuba are of iron or steel, SHAKUDŌ or SHIBUICHI alloys, copper, brass, silver, or gold but rarely of wood or ivory. The most usual tsuba forms are elliptical, round, or

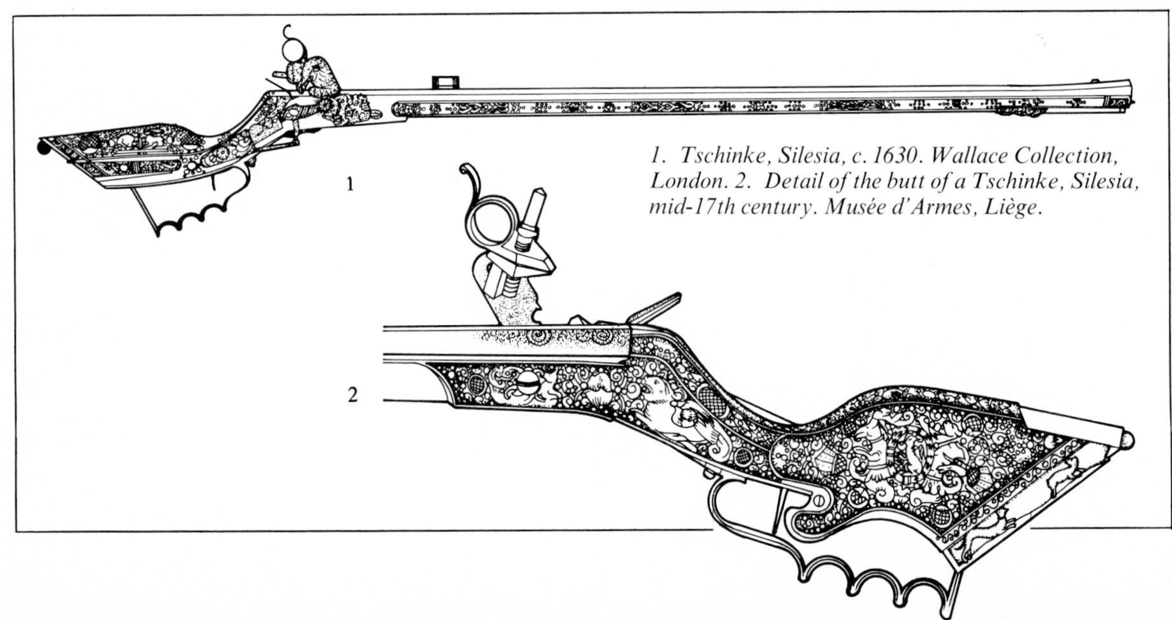


*1. Tschinke, Silesia, c. 1630. Wallace Collection, London. 2. Detail of the butt of a Tschinke, Silesia, mid-17th century. Musée d'Armes, Liège.*

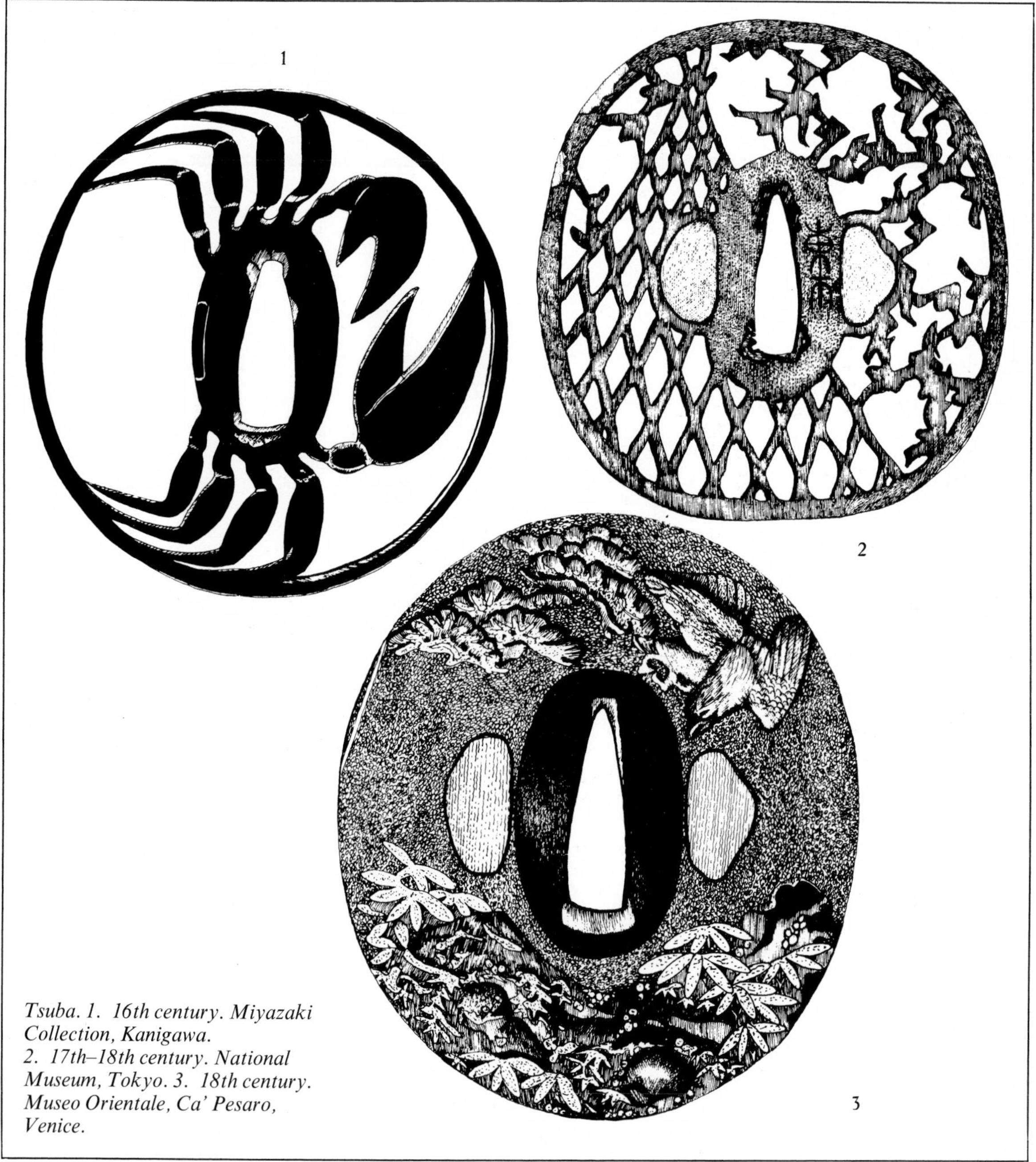

*Tsuba. 1. 16th century. Miyazaki Collection, Kanigawa. 2. 17th–18th century. National Museum, Tokyo. 3. 18th century. Museo Orientale, Ca' Pesaro, Venice.*

rectangular with slightly curved sides and rounded corners. There are, however, four-lobed tsuba, called *mokko*, because they resemble a section of tree melon, as well as octagonal, rhomboid, and three-lobed ones. Imaginative forms also exist, evidence of the analytical minds and subtle understanding of the Japanese, who seem to have a special ability to bestow on objects a certain spiritual quality. It is hardly surprising, therefore, to find that each part of the tsuba has a specific name: the edge is the *mimi*, the central hole for the tang is the *hitsu*, and the surrounding collar is the *seppa dai*. There are often openings called *riobitsu* at the sides of the seppa dai for the handles of the companion implements, the KOZUKA and the KŌGAI, which are attached to the sword scabbard. The riobitsu are usually finished with a different type of metal from that of the guard.

The tsuba, originally a strictly utilitarian hand protection in the form of a simple iron plate, in time became a field for the most exquisite decoration. On this limited space the whole mastery of composition and ornamental design was displayed, with a large choice of subjects, from geometric and abstract, to floral and animal

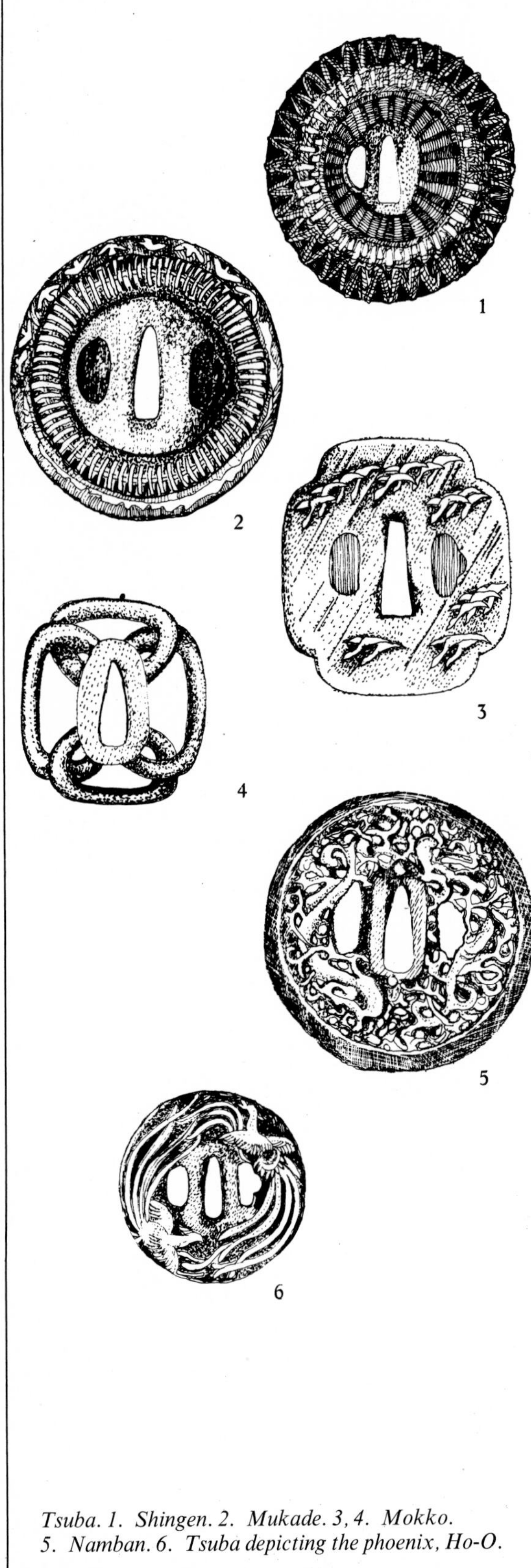


*Tsuba. 1. Shingen. 2. Mukade. 3, 4. Mokko. 5. Namban. 6. Tsuba depicting the phoenix, Ho-O.*

to human and divine, manifold symbolism being expressed everywhere. In the Kamakura period (1186–1333) guards were pierced in the form of the mythical jewel *magatama* or worked in low relief with a pagoda image. The plates were made by first welding together steels of different hardness and then twisting the bar in various ways so that, when lightly etched, it had the appearance of wood graining, *mokume hada*. Particular attention was paid to the edges by turning them over and then raising them.

It was not, however, until the late 15th century that tsuba makers established themselves as specialized craftsmen and particular families monopolized the profession by developing the technology, creating original styles, and passing on the secrets to the next generation. Master Nōbuiye (1486–1564), a member of the celebrated Myōchin family of swordmakers, created guards that were distinguished by their subtle designs in decorative openwork, and he was the first to sign the tsuba. The Myōchin workshop also produced articulated animals made from several little separate sections linked and riveted together.

Another outstanding decorator of the tsuba was Gotō-Yūjo (1440–1513), who worked for the shogun Ashikaga Yoshimasa. He introduced an alloy, shakudō, to embellish the guard plates, and by applying a system of lixiviation, he obtained a dark blue patina in the metal. His children founded the famous Gotō school, a dynasty of wonderful craftsmen who developed the techniques of metalworking to what was probably its highest point, especially with ornaments in gold and bronze.

The founder of another school was Kaneiye, whose exact dates are not known; some historians try to place him in the 15th century, and others at about 1600. His workshop was at Fushimi, near Kyoto. The tsuba of Kaneiye and his school are mostly of iron patinated red, with delicate low relief and inlays of various colored metals. Some motifs of the Kaneiye tsuba—miniature scenes—were certainly influenced by Chinese painting of the Sung Dynasty (960–1279). Chinese, and even European, inspiration is to be found in the decoration of the *namban tsuba*, popular in the second half of the 16th century (*namban* meaning "in the style of the southern barbarians"). These tsuba are ornamented with openwork, symmetrical in composition and often with interlaced floral scrolls and dragons. From the same period comes an original group of *mukade tsuba*, *mukade* meaning "wood louse," and, in fact, the decorative motif certainly recalls this creature. These guards also have another name, *shingen tsuba*, because they were eagerly acquired by the famous knight Takoda Shingen (d. 1573).

From among the many schools of the 16th century, the Umetada family and the school of Shōami should be mentioned, both distinguished for the elegance and decorative expression of their inlaid work in various metals. Several tsuba schools of the 17th and 18th centuries originated from the Gotō: the Nara school started by Toshiteru and the Hamano school founded by Shozui, whose pictorial subjects and humorous themes were famous. In the Soten school, episodes from civil wars crowded the tsuba with figures in high relief or in the

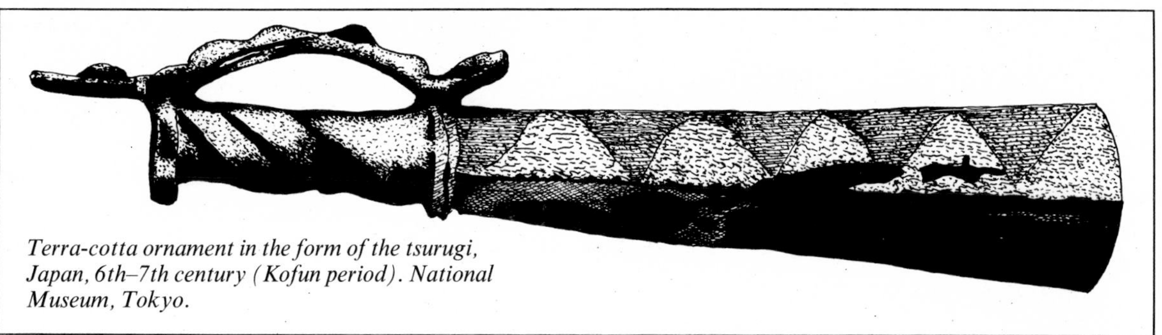

*Terra-cotta ornament in the form of the tsurugi, Japan, 6th–7th century (Kofun period). National Museum, Tokyo.*

round, minutely sculpted and inlaid, while the Yokoya school was celebrated for its high relief and engraving. In later periods, especially during the 19th century, schools and styles multiplied enormously. The tsuba became an illustration in miniature of the history, mythology, legends, customs, and fashions of old Japan. Every variety of technique was used: modeling in high, low, and medium relief; sculpting in the round; openwork both in simple silhouette and more or less elaborately chiseled; engraving and inlaying in a number of metals; encrusting with colored stones, pearls, and amber; inlaying with ivory; and enameling. The tsuba surface was usually polished or—especially when the black alloy, shakudō, was used—given a "dotted" finish known as *nanako* ("fish roe").

Somin, Higo, Hirata, and Akasaka were the most prominent centers of tsuba makers. The inexhaustible imagination of the Japanese artists produced a vast wealth of fresh motifs for the tsuba. Now far removed from their modest beginnings and original purpose, they still remain a strong manifestation of Japanese genius.

**tsuka-ai** A type of hilt for the TACHI.

**tsukubo** A Japanese pole weapon similar to the HINERI.

**tsurugi** Ancient term for a Japanese sword that was originally straight, single- or double-edged, and sometimes surmounted with a ring pommel. Some specimens of the tsurugi have been found in prehistoric burial mounds, but there are also several references to it in old Japanese chronicles. From these it has been learned, for instance, that swords worn by various gods when descending from heaven were called Kōtsuchi no Tsurugi. The chronicles also reveal that a sword called Ama no Murakumo no Tsurugi emerged from the tail of a dragon and became one of the three sacred treasures of Japan (the other two being the Sacred Mirror and the Sacred Necklace).

**tuck** (from French *estoc*, "thrust") A long thrusting sword usually with a fairly long grip and a simple cross-shaped hilt. The strong, rigid blade, designed for thrusting at armored opponents, was triangular, rhomboid, square or flat hexagonal in section. In some blades, toward the center, there was a smooth, edgeless portion that enabled the user to grip the weapon with his other hand and deliver a more powerful blow.

The tuck, carried hanging from the saddle, was in use as early as the beginning of the 14th century as an auxiliary side arm for the cavalry. Occasionally it was used by the horseman when he had dismounted. It continued to be used throughout the 17th century, particularly in eastern Europe (in Poland and Russia the tuck was called *konchar*, akin to *kinzhal*, "dagger"). The tucks were especially suitable for blows aimed between the plates of armor and at opponents protected by mail (hence the German term for the tuck, *Panzerstecher*, "mail-piercing [sword]").

Toward the end of the 16th century the simple cruciform hilt of earlier German tucks was replaced by a stout grip with a mushroom-shaped pommel and a fairly developed guard consisting of quillons, straight or curved, and a ring guard; occasionally a knuckle guard and a counterguard ring were used to protect the hand, no longer covered by a gauntlet.

**tukhotsian** *See* FIREARMS: Chinese.

**tumbler** In the locks of firearms, a steel cam fixed on the axis of the cock or hammer, on which the mainspring and the sear act. It had a deep recess on one side, against which the end of the free branch of the mainspring pressed, and two notches diametrically opposite for the sear to give the full cock and half cock (the arrangement introduced in the early 17th century). In guns with internal actions—not the oldest of them, but such guns as box-lock firearms, the Remington Rolling Block rifle, and revolvers—the cock and tumbler formed a single part.

**Turk's head** A modern nickname for rings made of twisted-wire braid sometimes used to finish off both ends of the grip of swords and daggers. It is so called because of its resemblance to a turban, a type of headdress typical of some Moslem peoples.

**two-handed sword** (German, *Zweihänder*) A large sword, up to 1.8 m. (6 ft.) in length, used by foot soldiers from the mid-15th to the late 16th century. The name is derived from the fact that this weapon required both hands to wield it. Its prototypes appeared in the 13th century and were probably of Teutonic origin. The long, usually double-edged blade, with a sharp or rounded point, was mounted with a hilt that had straight or slightly curved quillons. The grip was quite long, designed to accommodate both hands. The heavy pommel was triangular, faceted, or pear-shaped, and invariably larger toward the top, designed to balance the weapon.

The version of the two-handed sword in use in Germany and Switzerland in the first half of the 16th century often had a ribbed blade, a double-ring guard with slightly curved or straight quillons, and a pommel that was almost triangular in shape. At a later date the blade became broader, with fullers along the forte, and the pommel was usually faceted. An important feature of these blades was a long ricasso covered with leather, which protected the dress when the sword was carried on the shoulder and provided a more convenient grasp when the soldier had to move the hand forward for more powerful blows. To protect the hand on the ricasso, two strong parrying lugs were forged on the blade just in front of the ricasso.

At a later period the two-handed sword became largely a ceremonial or processional weapon. Its blade was often made with impressive wavy edges, and the grip was decorated with trimmings and fringes.

# U

**uchidashi** A type of Japanese armor. *See also* GUSOKU.
**uchi-ne** A type of Japanese javelin. *See also* NAGE-YARI.
**uchiwa** A variation of the Japanese WAR FAN.
**umabari** A Japanese knife, the so-called horse needle. Its blade was double-edged, flattened triangular or diamond in section, and forged in one with the hilt, which was usually inlaid with silver or gold with a heart-shaped opening at the top. The hilt was sometimes in the form of a Buddhist symbolic thunderbolt, the *vajra*. The total length of the umabari was about 15–25 cm. (6–10 in.). It was carried as a companion piece with the sword, in place of the KŌGAI, and one of its purposes was to incite a horse to gallop.

**umbo** A boss applied to the center of a shield. Usually made of iron or bronze, the umbo was in use since very early times as a reinforcement and, when appropriately designed, as an offensive device to be used at close quarters. It was generally more or less hemispherical and often supported on a ring base or truncated cone, while many old examples were integrated with a spike protruding from the center.

The umbo was secured to the shield by means of metal studs, often placed so as to form decorative motifs. It was sometimes heavily ornamented, especially on parade shields, with engravings and metal laminae molded to produce elaborate designs in relief which were then silvered or gilded. By the late Middle Ages, however, the umbo was gradually disappearing from the shield, but was still occasionally used as a decorative element.
**upper backplate** *See* BACKPLATE.
**upper bevor** *See* BEVOR.
**upper breastplate** *See* BREASTPLATE.
**uragawara** An accessory of the SAYA.
**ushiro-date** A type of MAIDATE.
**uwa-manchira** A gorget worn over the cuirass of the TANKŌ.
**uwar** Part of the fittings of the KRIS.

*Umbo of a silver-gilt shield, 1st century* B.C.*–3rd century* A.D.*, found in Den Helder, Netherlands. Rijksmuseum voor Volkenkunde, Leiden, Netherlands.*

# V

**vagina** (Latin; Greek *kóleos*) A term used to describe the sheath of weapons used in antiquity; the Greek equivalent refers, etymologically, to a leather sheath. Its form was of course closely linked to that of the respective weapon. In western Europe the metal mountings of sheaths for edged weapons do not date back beyond the latter stages of the Bronze Age, at the end of which we find examples made entirely of bronze, even when the blades of the weapons were made of iron. As a rule the ancient sheath consisted of a wooden framework, covered in various ways with fabric, leather, or thin, decorated metal plaques, held together by a chape, straps, or bindings.

**vambrace** Plate defense for the arm used from the 14th century onward. Each vambrace consisted of three distinct parts: the upper CANNON (or rerebrace), the COWTER, and the lower cannon (vambrace). However, from the last quarter of the 14th century, "rerebrace" usually meant the shoulder protection which, after about 1450, was generally described as the PAULDRON, and "vambrace" referred to the remainder of the arm defense, including the cowter.

In the oldest types, which were worn until about the end of the 15th century, the upper gutter-shaped cannon did not entirely enclose the arm and was made either of one lame or of several riveted together. It was quite

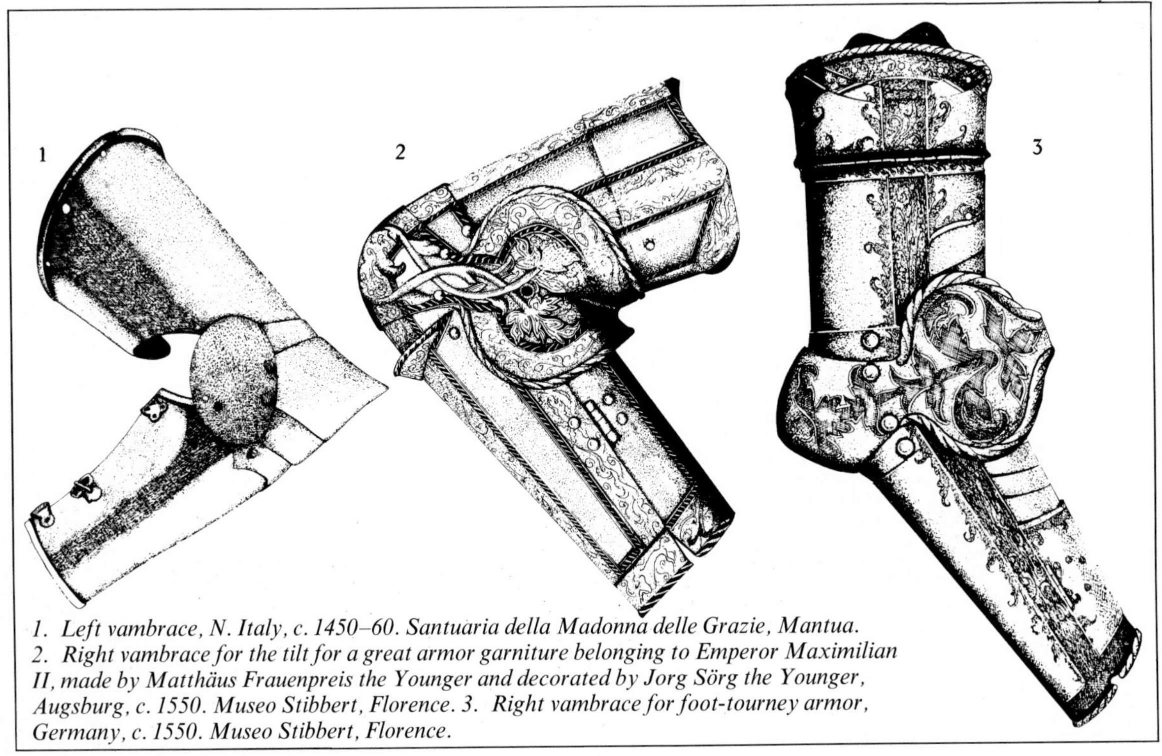


*1. Left vambrace, N. Italy, c. 1450–60. Santuaria della Madonna delle Grazie, Mantua. 2. Right vambrace for the tilt for a great armor garniture belonging to Emperor Maximilian II, made by Matthäus Frauenpreis the Younger and decorated by Jorg Sörg the Younger, Augsburg, c. 1550. Museo Stibbert, Florence. 3. Right vambrace for foot-tourney armor, Germany, c. 1550. Museo Stibbert, Florence.*

independent of the pauldron, being laced to the hauberk. The bottom and top lames of the cowter—which was either strapped around the hauberk's sleeve or riveted to it—overlapped respectively the upper edge of the vambrace and lower edge of the rerebrace, while the central part of the cowter was shaped to the elbow and equipped with a slightly incurving wing. The lower cannon was closed, that is, it completely encircled the forearm and consisted of two semicylindrical lames hinged together longitudinally and tapering at the wrist.

By the end of the 15th century, the rerebrace was made like a tube, and shortly after 1500 had, apart from rare exceptions, become almost closed. It now consisted of two parts, each shaped to encircle the arm, the upper of which could be connected to the pauldron and the other being riveted to the cowter. However, in 15th-century German vambraces the cowter was laced on separately to the elbow. The lower cannon remained much as it had always been, except that its locking device was usually changed to riveted studs in one half of the cannon which projected through corresponding slots in the other (inward) half.

A completely closed type of vambrace, giving a high degree of protection, was in use from the second quarter of the 16th century to the middle of the 17th. The basic cannon-cowter-cannon structure remained, but the two cannons were cut away and laminated inside the joint of the elbow, giving increased flexibility. In addition, the upper and lower parts of the rerebrace were joined by a groove-and-rim fitting, which gave the arm complete freedom to turn laterally without disturbing the vambrace-pauldron joint. This type of mobile joint was also widely used in other types of vambraces. Vambraces laminated inside at the elbow joint were particularly favored in the late 16th century in laminated armor used for the foot combat.

With the introduction of cuirassier armor in the mid-17th century, the vambrace disappeared.

**vamplate** A protection for the hand, introduced in the early 14th century, which fitted onto the lance. It consisted of a heavy funnel-shaped plate which was slipped over the shaft, narrow side toward the head, where it was firmly fixed in front of the grip. Most vamplates were circular, but that used with armor for the German course (*Rennen*) was a large semicircular shield covering both the hand and the arm (which was not protected by a vambrace). The vamplate continued to be used into the early 17th century.

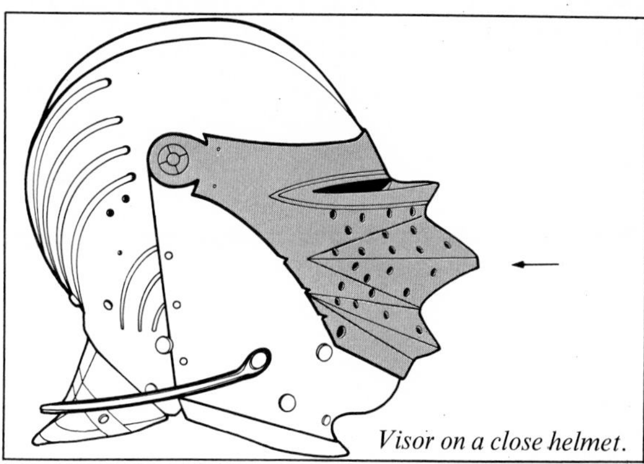

*Visor on a close helmet.*

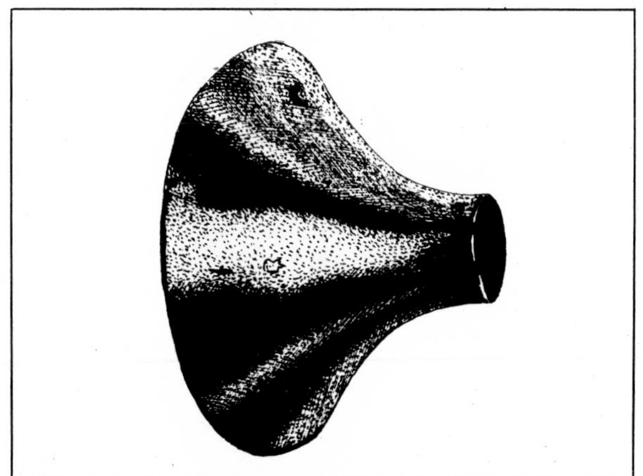

*Vamplate of a lance, Italy, c. 1490. Waffensammlung, Vienna.*

**vanes** *See* FEATHERS.

**vent** Also called the touchhole, a hole bored in the breech of the barrel of a muzzleloading firearm leading from the pan to the chamber, through which the propellant charge was ignited.

**ventail** Another term for the upper BEVOR.

**ventilation door** Part of some types of 16th-century jousting helms, such as the "frog-mouthed" helm. It consisted of a vertically hinged plate on the right side of the bevor—replacing the rosette of pierced ventilation holes seen on some lighter helmets—which could be opened by pulling a short thong.

**verutum** (Greek *saunion*) A javelin, that is, a throwing spear, of Sabine-Latin origin (though Greek writers attributed it to Celto-Iberian origin) which was sometimes fitted with a thong, the AMENTUM. There were two types: the head of the first was in the form of a sturdy curved blade, 60–70 cm. (24–26 in.) long, with the cutting edge on the concave face (like the KOPIS and HARPÉ). The other type had a long head which narrowed toward the point and was sometimes fitted with barbs. This weapon had been known from the 5th century B.C. but was introduced to the Roman light infantry in about the mid-4th century A.D.

**vireton** (from French *virer*, "to turn") A heavy bolt (quarrel) shot from a large, powerful crossbow. It was fitted with obliquely set feathers which made it rotate around its own axis in the air, thus giving the bolt more stability.

**visor** Part of basnet, armet, and close helmet used from the 14th to 17th centuries, consisting of a heavy, contoured plate positioned to protect the face below the forehead down to the BEVOR.

During the 14th and 15th centuries, the visor with sights and vents was an integral part of the basnet. It was hinged on the brow or, more often, hinged and pivoted on the sides of the skull, and could therefore be raised with a

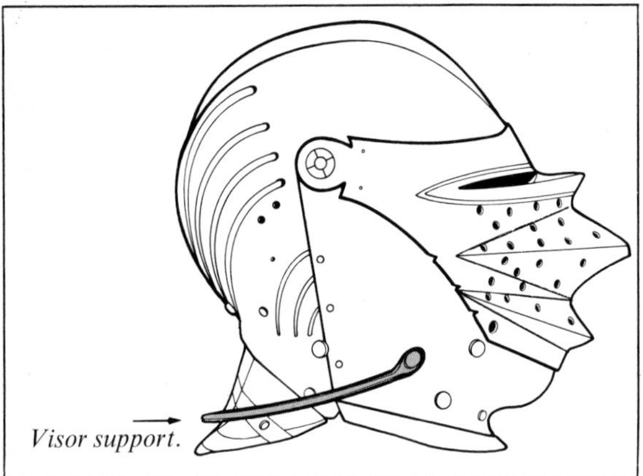


lifting peg. Large visors lasted up to the 1520s on the "visored" sallet and the armet. They were gradually abandoned, however, from the beginning of the 16th century when a system of face protection was devised consisting of a two-piece bevor and a smaller visor, all three parts being attached to the skull by the same pair of side pivots.

**visor support** An accessory of the 16th-century close helmet consisting of a bar with two small prongs at one end; its other end was attached by a pivot to the lower bevor. When the visor or upper bevor was raised, the forked end supported its lower edge to keep it open. It was also called the bevor support.

**volley gun** A general term used to describe a multibarreled gun or pistol which discharges several projectiles simultaneously.

The simplest way to create a volley gun was to group a number of barrels together which could be fired at the same time. As early as c. 1380, the English Wardrobe Accounts describe payments to a London cannon founder for a gun with eleven barrels. According to the description of the gun, one barrel fired a stone and the other barrels fired lead bullets or arrows. The weight of this gun, 302 kg. (665 lbs.), was very considerable, and this was one of the main disadvantages of the volley gun throughout its history. In an inventory of the Bastille taken in 1435 there is a reference to a seven-barreled gun described as being without a chamber. Illustrations of these volley guns can be seen in some early 16th-century German manuscripts. In the Munich State Library is a manuscript illustrating some of the guns made for Emperor Maximilian I in about 1500. The barrels are laid side by side, the touchholes upward, in a simple wooden cradle. With some three-barreled guns, the barrels are grouped in such a way that the muzzles form a trefoil shape. Contemporary 16th-century references describe the multibarreled guns as *ribauldequins* or *Orgelgeschütze* because of their similarity to the pipes of an organ.

The great weight of these volley guns in the early period of their development generally precluded them from being used as handguns. However, there are examples extant from the 17th century which were designed to be fired from the shoulder or chest, among them a seven-barreled volley gun in the Tower of London bearing the date 1612. The stock of this gun was replaced in the 18th century, but the barrels, which have been drilled out of a single block of steel, are light enough to enable the user to fire it from the shoulder. This particular gun was almost certainly designed for sporting purposes.

Like the BLUNDERBUSS, the volley gun was accurate only up to a limited range and was thus more suitable for using at close quarters; the discharge of a number of barrels in the close confines of a man-of-war, for example, could be particularly deadly. It is not surprising, therefore, that one of the best volley guns ever devised was the model invented by Captain James Wilson of the Royal Marines and adopted by the British Admiralty in 1779. Like so many of the earlier guns of this type, it had seven barrels and was designed to be used by snipers stationed in the "tops" of the rigging. The Admiralty commissioned the famous English gunmaker Henry Nock to make a considerable number of these guns from 1779 to 1788. The gun was designed to have six barrels arranged around one central barrel, all of about 51 cm. (20 in.) in length. The guns were reasonably portable, in spite of their size, and weighed about 25 kg. (12 lbs.). The problem of igniting seven charges simultaneously was solved by having radial channels drilled from the central barrel through the six surrounding barrels, connected to a central touchhole and chamber. Except for the early examples, which were rifled, the majority of the 655 volley guns made by Nock were

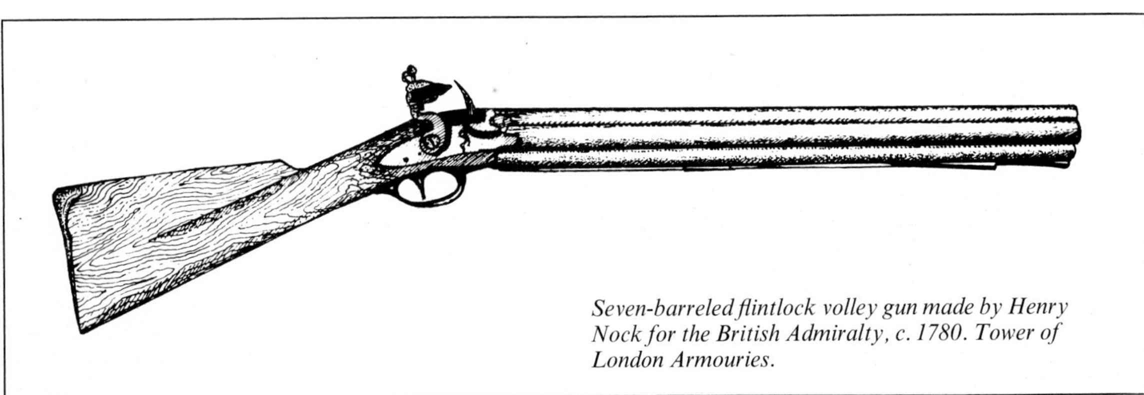

*Seven-barreled flintlock volley gun made by Henry Nock for the British Admiralty, c. 1780. Tower of London Armouries.*

smooth-bore. In spite of their technical superiority they do not appear to have been very successful and were considered obsolete by 1805.

The advantages of the volley gun for sport were recognized at an early date in its development. Preserved in the Arms Museum at Liège is the famous volley gun belonging to the English sportsman Colonel Thomas Thornton. The gun is fitted with two sets of seven barrels, used with a single stock. Both sets of barrels are inscribed with patriotic sentiments and with references to Colonel Thornton's favorite Scottish hunting ground, Glenmore Forest. The gun was made for Thornton about 1790, the two flintlocks being marked "Dupe and Co."

With the invention of the percussion system of ignition in the early 19th century, four-barreled volley guns became more fashionable. However, a few seven-barreled guns were still being made. A fine example—based on the cartridge system patented in 1814 by the Swiss gunmaker Samuel Johannes Pauly—is preserved in the Tower of London. This volley gun is a breechloader, the single brass cartridge filling all seven chambers. At the end of the 19th century the volley gun underwent a brief revival, owing to the suggestions of an American, General O. Vandenburgh, who tried to introduce a system of artillery consisting of 451 barrels, all firing musket balls simultaneously. Another late variant of the volley gun was produced by the Belgian gunmaker Henri Pieper. His gun had a rolling breech which fed .22 caliber rimfire cartridges into seven barrels.

One of the most dramatic volley guns, certainly in appearance, is the Billinghurst and Requa battery gun of 1862. Also known as the "Eureka," this gun had twenty-five barrels set alongside each other, of .50 caliber, and was automatically fired and reloaded by turning a hand crank set at the breech end. Its considerable size necessitated a substantial wheeled carriage. A fine example can be seen at the U.S. Armory in Springfield, Massachusetts.

Volley pistols are comparatively rare, principally because they offered little advantage over the larger volley guns. Most surviving volley pistols date from the late 18th century and are based upon the Henry Nock volley guns described above. Preserved at Windsor Castle is a seven-barreled volley pistol by Nock dating from about 1790, which is simply a reduced version of the volley gun he designed for the British Admiralty. Instead of having the standard construction of six barrels grouped around one central barrel, some so-called duck-foot or mob pistols were made in the early 19th century which have the barrels set alongside each other but splayed out like a webbed foot. Although examples of this type of pistol are known from early 17th century Europe, most surviving examples are English and date from the early 1800s. The introduction of the center-fire cartridge led to the development of several four-barreled volley pistols in the latter part of the 19th century. The most important of these include the Martin-Marres-Braendlin "Mitrailleuse" pistol and the pistols of John Bland and Charles Lancaster.

**volley pistol** *See* VOLLEY GUN.

**vouge** A term used, mainly in French texts of the 12th to 16th centuries, for a staff weapon whose exact form cannot be defined with certainty. It is possible that at different periods and places the term was applied to different, though somewhat similar, kinds of pole arms. Thus, a number of texts make it possible to associate the vouge with the weapon called the BILL in England. Another connotation of "vouge" (which has been also used in France for a tool to cut brushwood) might be a staff weapon with a slightly curved, knifelike head, in fact similar to, if not identical with, the pole arm classified as the GLAIVE. It is believed that such "French vouges," equipped with a rondel guard at the socket, were used by foot soldiers of Anthony, Great Bastard of Burgundy, who clashed in 1476–77 with the Swiss at Grandson, Morat, and Nancy. The Swiss themselves had developed a more versatile staff weapon, the so-called Swiss vouge, which had a large, long blade narrowing at the top to form a spike, with a hooklike fluke at the back of the socket. This form was, in fact, an early type of the HALBERD.

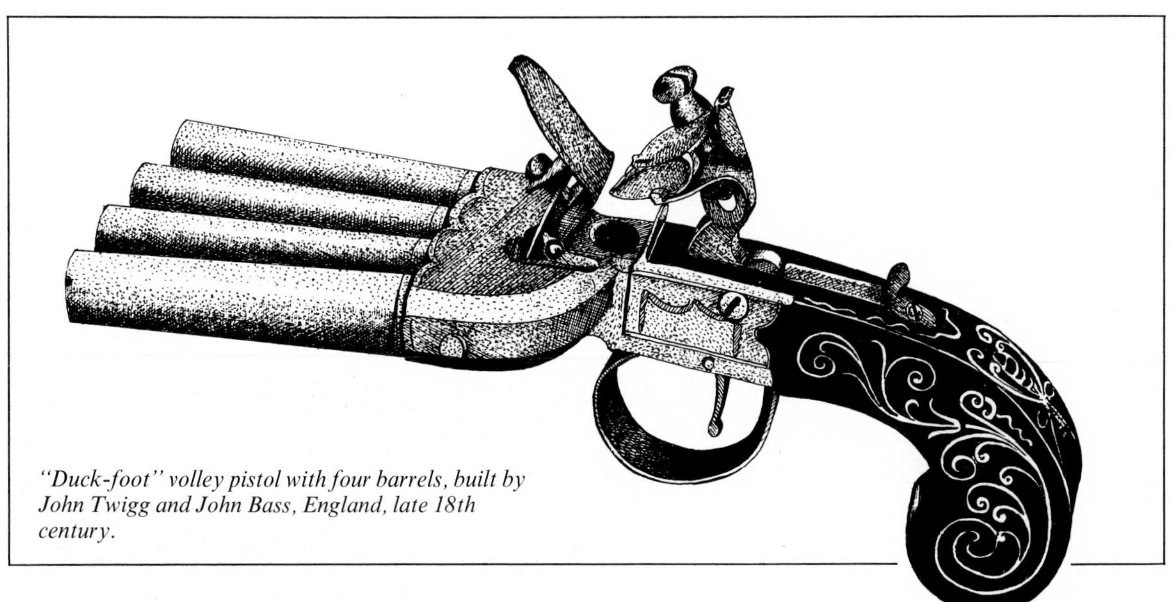

*"Duck-foot" volley pistol with four barrels, built by John Twigg and John Bass, England, late 18th century.*

# W

**wagh-nakh** An alternative spelling of BAGH-NAKH.
**wahar-nuk** An alternative spelling of BAGH-NAKH.
**waidate** Part of the cuirass of the YOROI.
**waki-date** A type of MAIDATE.
**wakizashi** A short Japanese sword normally carried by the samurai with the longer fighting sword, the KATANA; in fact, when their technical and stylistic features were the same, they became the companion pair known as the DAI-SHŌ. The wakizashi blade was a fine example of the unparalleled skill of Japanese bladesmiths. It was usually about 45 cm. (18 in.) long, and its fittings were even more elaborate than those on longer swords. It was nearly always accompanied by both the KOZUKA knife and KŌGAI pin, and its *soritsuno* and *kojiri* (*see* SAYA) were beautifully decorated. The owner of a wakizashi took great pride in it and always kept it with him; he regarded it as "the guardian of his honor." Although it served mainly as a supplementary fighting weapon, it was also used for ritual suicide, seppuku.

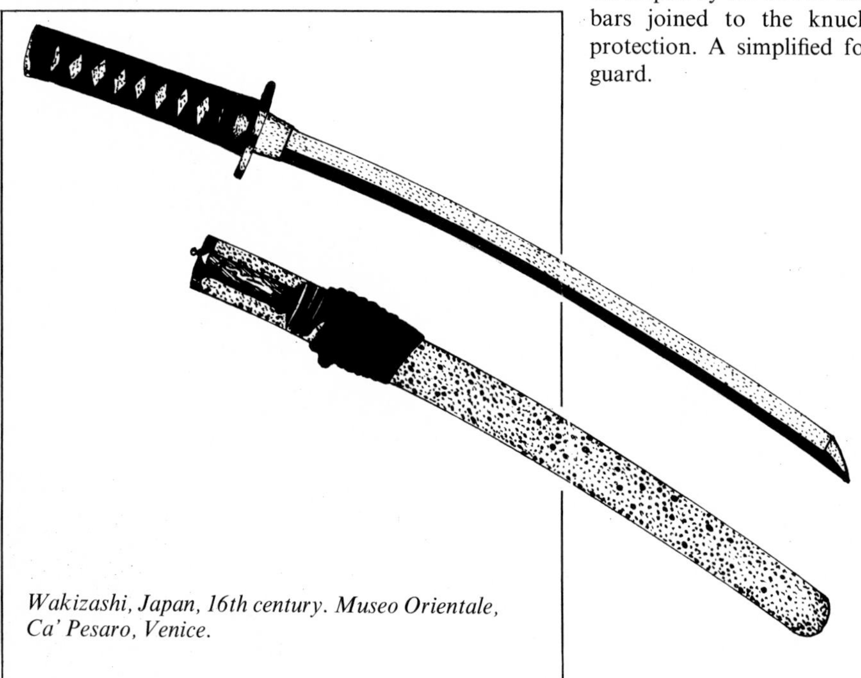

*Wakizashi, Japan, 16th century. Museo Orientale, Ca' Pesaro, Venice.*

**walloon sword** A broad-bladed sword in use from the middle of the 17th century, mainly in central and northern Europe. Its name derives from Wallonia, a part of modern Belgium. The guard, made principally of iron, had two oval rings perpendicular to the blade, which enclosed two flat or slightly convex shells with *à jour* holes and stars. The two rings joined near the knuckle guard, which was fixed to the pommel with a screw; the short rear quillon ended in a curled finial or a lobe, and on the inside shell there was a small thumb ring. Variations of the Walloon hilt, developed by the end of the century, had one or two side bars joined to the knuckle guard as an additional protection. A simplified form had only the outer shell guard.

*Sword with Walloon hilt, central or northern Europe, 1660. Armémuseum, Stockholm.*

**war fan** In old Japan, when it was the custom for everyone to carry a fan, it was also used as a military accessory, not only as a mark of rank but also for signaling and even as a weapon. There were two types of military fans. One was the *uchiwa,* a flat, open fan made of embossed or inlaid iron, lacquered wood, or leather. The body, which was usually violin-shaped, was decorated with applied ornaments of brass, silver, or gold as well as with crests, inscriptions, or symbolic figures. It was mounted on a handle with a cord attached, its total length being about 35–50 cm. (14–20 in.) The uchiwa was used by both high- and medium-ranking officers and officials; it was also carried ahead of wrestlers as they were about to enter the ring. The other type was the folding fan (shaped like a familiar fan) known as the *tetsu-ten,* or "iron fan," because its outer sticks—and sometimes all of them—were made of heavy steel. It was covered with parchment and had the Japanese "rising sun" symbol painted on a constrasting ground. Some tetsu-ten, however, were merely heavy clubs shaped like folded fans. The tetsu-ten was carried by lower-ranking officers and officials; it was also carried by civilians at night for their own protection, since it could be used as a parrying weapon until the person was able to draw his sword.

**war hammer** A staff weapon, known since Paleolithic times, when it had a stone head attached to a short handle. In medieval Europe, several forms of the war hammer developed. From no later than the 13th century, foot soldiers used war hammers of a simple shape, with a head of iron or lead mounted on a long shaft (about 2 m./7 ft.), often topped by a spike. A much improved version of this pole arm was used in the 15th and 16th centuries by

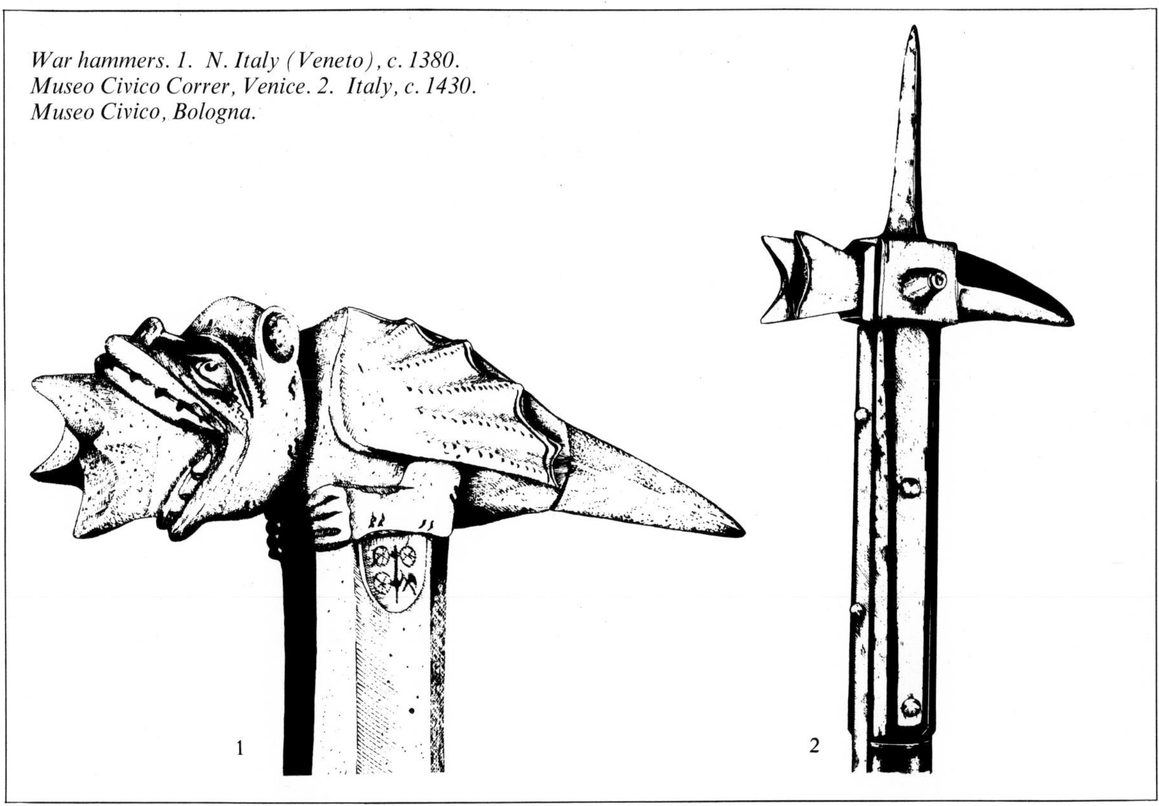


*War hammers. 1. N. Italy (Veneto), c. 1380. Museo Civico Correr, Venice. 2. Italy, c. 1430. Museo Civico, Bologna.*

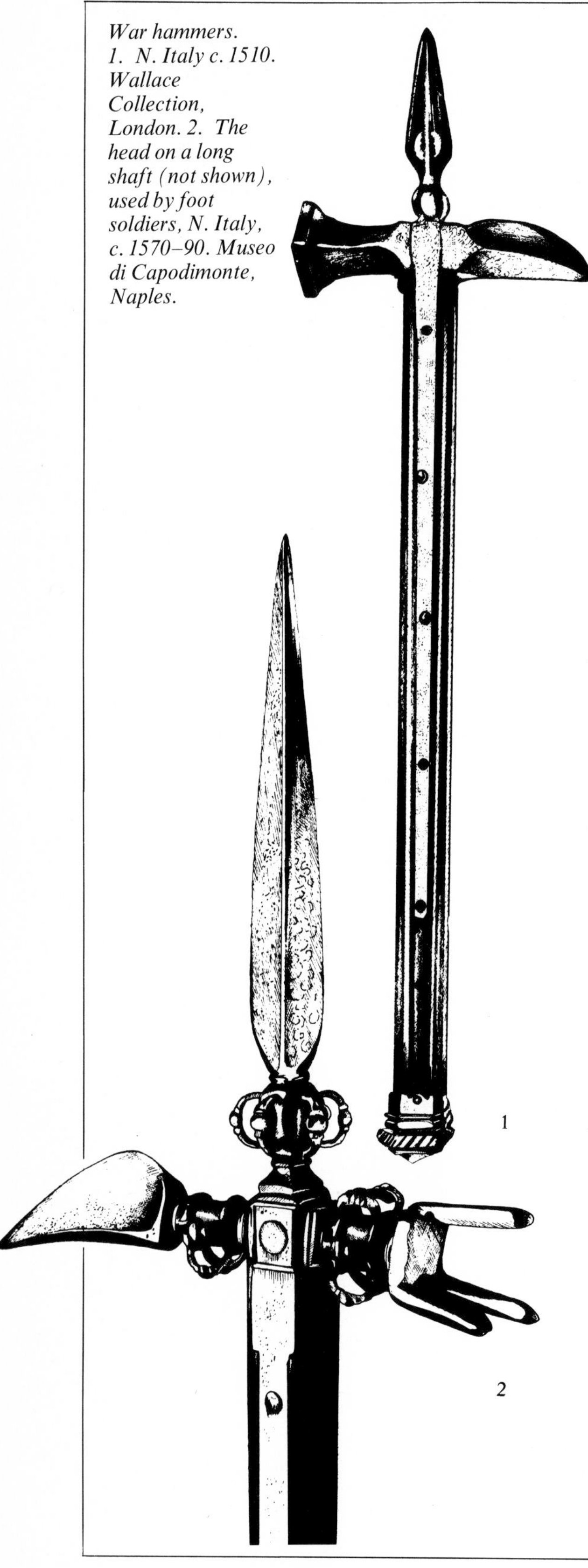
*War hammers. 1. N. Italy c. 1510. Wallace Collection, London. 2. The head on a long shaft (not shown), used by foot soldiers, N. Italy, c. 1570–90. Museo di Capodimonte, Naples.*

knights fighting on foot. In this form the hammer itself (*maul, martel*) was offset by a massive curved fluke, which gave the weapon the French nicknames *bec-de-corbin* ("crow's beak") and *bec-de-faucon* ("falcon's beak"); the usual term in England was POLEAX—by association with a similar staff weapon having an ax at its head (instead of a fluke or a hammer). Swiss militia used two-handed war hammers up to the 17th century, but later examples are of a very poor quality, with four ugly prongs instead of a ridged hammerhead. Judging from the contents of the armory at Lucerne, the war hammers were particularly popular in this canton, leading some modern writers to call this weapon the "Lucerne hammer."

A short-handled version of the war hammer was wielded with one hand by mounted warriors from the mid-13th century, but this form was only rarely provided with a spike on the top. In the 16th and 17th centuries, it was often made of steel, sometimes with rondels protecting the grip. A rare type of the horseman's war hammer, probably of German origin, had a cast-bronze head modeled like a hand grasping a steel dagger; it was used mostly in the 15th and early 16th centuries. A regional variation of the horseman's war hammer, with a light face and a long curved fluke, was popular in eastern Europe, where it was called *czákan* (Hungarian; Russian *chekan*).

From the 14th to early 16th centuries, a special type of the war hammer was used in central Europe as a missile weapon, which was given a spinning motion in flight. Functionally similar to the throwing axes, these war hammers had a conical pointed head with a spike and a fluke, and the steel handle was also sharply pointed at the bottom. In its simplets form, the throwing hammer had the form of a Latin cross whose four pointed arms were designed to inflict a wound however the weapon hit.

**watakusi** A particular type of YANO-NE.

**wazna-i-barut** A Persian term denoting a powder measure used in Persia, Turkey, and the Caucasus. It consisted of a round or polygonal tube of brass or watered steel, frequently inlaid with gold or silver and sometimes nielloed, with a close-fitting plunger on the end of a graduated stem. To obtain an accurate amount of powder, the stem was drawn out to give the required reading for the charge and the tube filled with powder, which was then poured into the gun. The tube was surmounted by a loop to enable the wazna-i-barut to be suspended from the belt.

**wedong** (or **wedung**) A ceremonial Javanese knife with a broad blade, usually about 25 cm. (10 in.) long, with an S-shaped cutting edge. The horn handle is square in section and narrow, tapering toward the blade. The wooden sheath is mounted with bands of horn or braided cane and has a large belt hook of horn.

**wheel-lock** *See* IGNITION.

**windlass** A spanning mechanism for a type of heavy CROSSBOW. The windlass consisted of a box-shaped base into which the butt of the tiller was fitted. A winding drum with a pair of pulleys and two opposing cranks with handles was mounted on the box. A system of cords connected the drum with another pair of pulleys provided with a double claw for the bowstring. When the handles were turned, the cords unwound until the claw could be hooked on the string. By reversing the rotation of the drum, the bow was spanned until the string reached the nut. The cords then were loosened, the claw taken off the string, and the whole instrument was removed from the crossbow, which was ready to be loaded and shot.

**wing** In armor, a part of the elbow and knee guards (respectively called the COWTER and POLEYN) for protecting the articulated joints. In the case of the cowter the wing was really an extension, although instances exist of wings having been made separately and riveted to the cowter or locked on it by means of projecting rivets and keyhole slots. The wings used on poleyns were similarly designed but were flatter and less elaborate in shape than the cowter wings.

**woodknife** An English term used in the 15th to 17th centuries for a heavy knife carried by hunters in a sheath often provided with small pockets for various tools necessary to cut up the kill. The term was also applied to a similar weapon, the HANGER.

**worm** A special steel screw used to extract an unfired ball from the barrel of a muzzleloading gun. It was generally fitted onto the end of the ramrod. By turning the rod, the screw was made to penetrate the lead ball, which could then be pulled out.

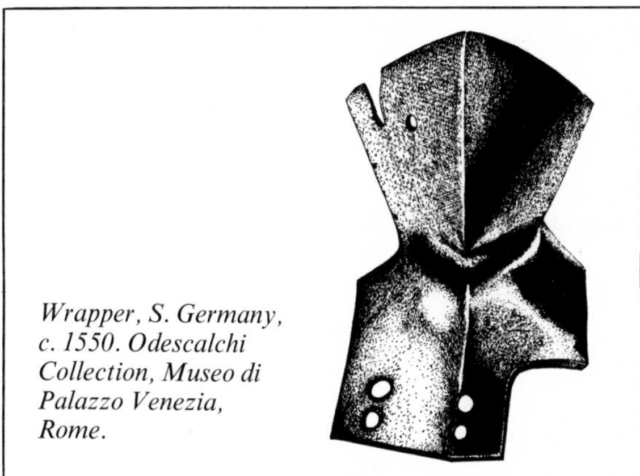

*Wrapper, S. Germany, c. 1550. Odescalchi Collection, Museo di Palazzo Venezia, Rome.*

**wrapper** A reinforcing bevor for an ARMET or a CLOSE HELMET. It consisted of a plate shaped to the lower half of the visor and to the chin, attached to the helmet by a strap around the neck and buckled at the back. The wrapper was one of various pieces used with armor for the tourney and joust.

# X

**xíphos** A term which appears in the ancient Cretan-Mycenaean language known as Linear B, used to describe a special type of large, pointed sword, the PHASGANON. This was the straight-bladed, double-edged sword of classical Greece which has been documented by archeological finds.

**yadzutsu** A type of Japanese quiver consisting of a long box of lacquered wood with a lid. Although the arrows were not easy to remove from the quiver, the lid completely protected them from the rain. The yadzutsu was often carried in a frame with a pair of bows.

**yakiba** The tempered edge of the blade of a Japanese sword or spear, which looks like a band of clouded pearly luster about 0.8–1.3 cm. (5/16–½ in.) wide along the cutting edge. The most important part of the bladesmith's work was in perfecting the yakiba. He first covered the whole blade with a mixture of ferruginous clay (*sabidore*, or "rusty earth"), sand, and a small proportion of powdered charcoal. When this coating had hardened a little, it was partially removed from the edge, on both sides, with a sharpened stick of bamboo to achieve the required contour. When the remaining coating was dry, the smith would hold the blade, edge downward, and run it back and forth over the fire until he could see by the color that the proper temperature had been reached. The blade was then plunged into water, the quality and temperature of which was of the greatest importance. The eighth month of the year was regarded as most suitable for this process, as water was then at its best natural temperature, and the figure 8 was therefore often put on the sword together with the year in which it was made.

The principle of hardening the edge while the body of the blade remained relatively soft is the main point of difference between Japanese blades and all others. Only in medieval Switzerland was a similar process adopted, in the making of halberd heads, in which a hard edge was combined with a soft core.

The form of the yakiba varied a great deal, according to the different "schools" and most prominent masters. There are considered to be thirty-two recognized principal classes, with further subdivisions, and the Japanese terms for these demonstrate this nation's love of metaphor, as, for example, the horse's tooth (*uma no ha*), the rose garden (*juzu*), the gourd (*hyōtan*), and the saw (*nokogiri*). The contours of the yakiba toward the point of the blade, the *bōshi*, were of particular importance, each variation having a name of its own. It is possible to deduce both the date and school of origin of a yakiba from its shape. *See also* BLADE: Japanese.

**yalman** Sometimes incorrectly spelled *jelman*, the Turkish term (meaning "pointed cutting part of a weapon") for the somewhat widened and edged section of the back of the saber blade extending from the point to about one-third or one-fourth of the blade length. This part of the blade thus has two cutting edges, which is useful for repeated slashing strikes carried out with both edges without changing the position of the hand and weapon.

**yano-ne** The Japanese arrowhead. As archery was a highly developed martial skill in Japan, there was a wide variety of arrows, some of which fulfilled special roles in battle or siege while others merely had a decorative or symbolic meaning. The yano-ne comprised the head itself and a pointed tang which was fixed to the shaft. Except in prehistoric times, the system of attaching the head to the shaft by means of a socket was not adopted in Japan.

The yano-ne, which was always made of high-quality steel, can be divided into four main classes. The typical fighting arrowheads were the *yanagi-ha* ("willow leaf"), with straight sides and of diamond cross section, varying considerably in size and shape but usually measuring 1–6 cm. (½–2½ in.) excluding the tang. *Togari-ya* arrowheads were pointed but wider than the yanagi-ha, up to about 15 cm. (6 in.) long and 6 cm. (2½ in.) wide; they were often heart-shaped and pierced with *mon* signs (family crests), inscriptions, or figures. *Watakusi* ("flesh-tearer") were barbed arrows and particularly dangerous since they were difficult to withdraw from the wound; they often had special names such as "sword's point," "sparrow's beak," "water plantain," or "dragon's tongue." *Karimata* were forked arrowheads, which, although sometimes called "rope cutters," were also used to carry fire during siege operations; varying greatly in size, they ranged from about 3 to 15 cm. (1¼–6 in.) across the points.

A special kind of whistling arrow was also used in Japan; this was for signaling and consisted of a large,

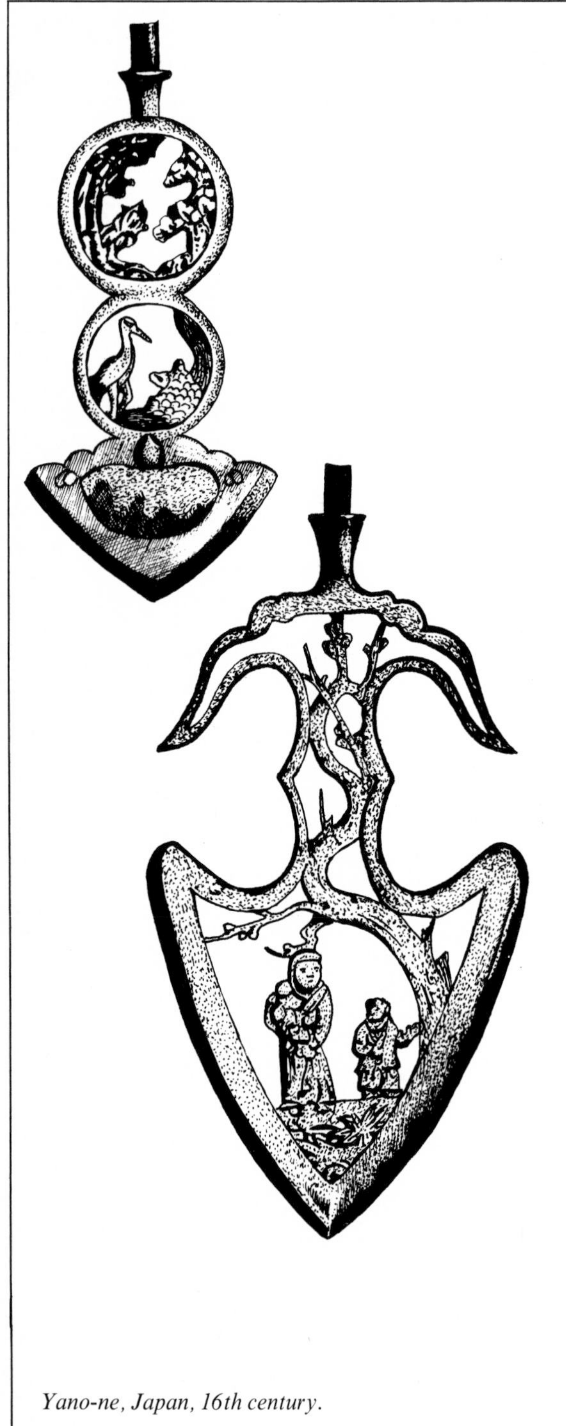

*Yano-ne, Japan, 16th century.*

hollow arrowhead with openings in the front and sides so that, when shot, the air rushing through the holes would make a whistling sound.

**yari** A generic Japanese term for spears, although it mainly refers to the straight-bladed spear mounted on the shaft by means of a long tang or, occasionally, a socket. The yari has a long tradition going back to prehistoric times when its socketed blade was made of bronze. In the Kamakura period (1186–1333) the yari was largely used by warriors, whether mounted or fighting on foot. It is recorded that in the third quarter of the 14th century Ise Muramasa, of Ise province, was the most celebrated yari-maker. Legends and superstitions have grown up around the blades of Muramasa; they were supposed to hunger after men's lives and to madden their owners so that they would kill indiscriminately or even commit suicide. The Muramasa school is particularly noted for the beauty of an undulating pattern, called *notare-ha*, of the tempered edge, which presents an identical pattern on both sides of the blade.

The intricate craft of the swordsmith applied to spear-making as well. The ordinary yari was in demand at the time of the War of Ōnin, in the second half of the 15th century, while the long-bladed yari was immensely popular in the later part of the Muromachi period (1337–1573). Great quantities of yari were produced under the Tokugawa shoguns (1603–1867); they were often made in identical form for detachments of soldiers, but these weapons were more for parade purposes than actual combat. In today's collections only a small proportion of yari have survived from before the Momoyama period (c. 1573–1602).

The extant yari are of two basic types: the *sankaku-yari*, with a blade of triangular section, and the *ryō-shinogi-yari*, of diamond section. However, there are further variations: the triangle-sectioned blade sometimes had grooved arms, i.e., side blades, or one blade longer with a groove and the other two blades flat. The cross section might be square or flattened rhomboid, the latter sometimes with two grooves at the flattened sides. The grooves were shallow or deep, narrow or wide, sometimes double, and with round or square ends.

The horseman's yari was furnished with a shorter blade, about 10–12 cm. (4–5 in.) long, which was either triangular or diamond in section, with or without grooves. The *su-yari* usually had a long blade, sometimes of more than 50 cm. (19 in.), with parallel straight edges. There were also the leaf-shaped *inoshishi-no-yari*, used for hunting, and the yari with a round socket. The yari shaft, the *nagaye*, was usually of white kashi, the close-grained Japanese evergreen oak, which, though hard and resistant, offered a certain amount of spring; red kashi and bamboo were occasionally used, too. The normal yari shaft can be round, pear-shaped, or many-sided in section.

Engraved ornamentation of various kinds, called *horimono*—such as flames, dragons, the god Daruma, flower sprays, stylized Sanskrit characters called *bonji*, or even short poems—is to be found on the yari. Yari makers occasionally cut their signatures on the blades. Sheaths of plain wood, *shirasaya*, as well as decorated lacquered sheaths, *saya*, were used with the yari.

The mounting of the head onto the shaft is always very precise: the tang is inserted in the shaft, which is then bound with cord and strengthened with a metal collar, the HABAKI. In the case of a socketed blade, the socket is put on the tapered end of the shaft and nailed from one side. The

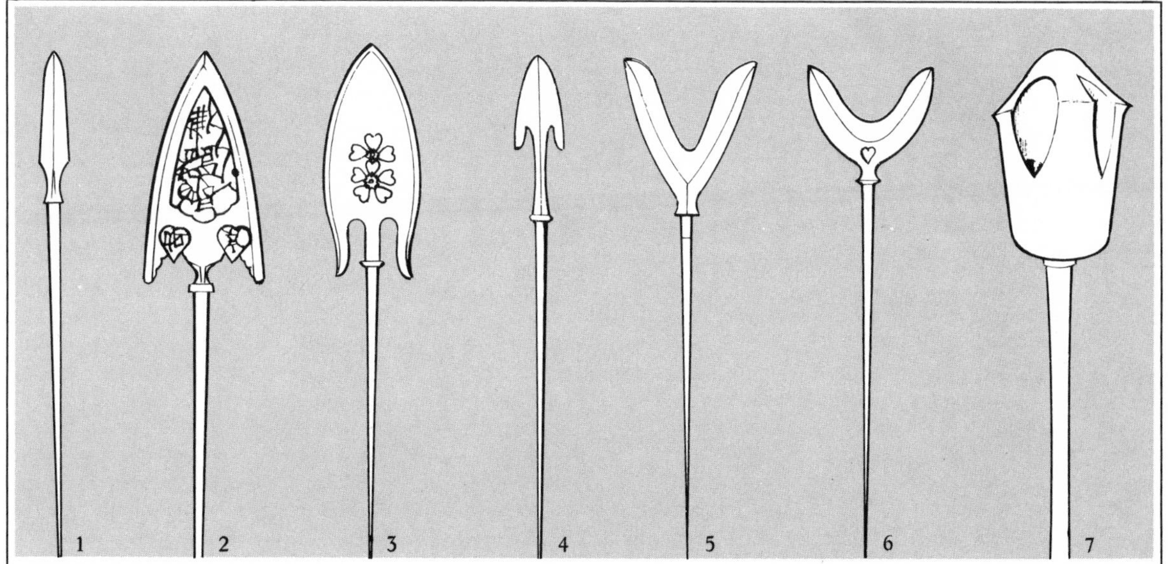


*Yano-ne, Japanese arrowheads, Tokugawa (Edo) period (1603–1867). 1. Yanagi-ha ("willow leaf"). 2, 3. Togari-ya. 4. Watakusi ("flesh-tearer"). 5, 6. Karimata ("rope cutter"). 7. Whistling arrow. Victoria and Albert Museum, London.*

shaft is also pierced for a peg or pegs, *mekugi*, and finished off with an ornamental whipping of rattan or cord, sometimes covered with lacquer. A metal sleeve, the FUCHI, slips over the top end of the shaft. The habaki and fuchi are made of various metals—iron, copper, shakudo alloy, brass, silver, or combinations of these—and often decorated with floral engravings or a *mon* (family crest); they are often signed or dated.

The bottom mount on the shaft is known as the *hirumaki* or *ishizuki*, and is made of iron, bronze, or brass; it may be lacquered or plain, short or long, stumpy or slender, or sometimes in the shape of two curved horns to which a lantern could be attached on night marches. The hirumaki acted as a shoe and also as a counterweight to the blade; it was sometimes even employed as an offensive part of the weapon. A special guard of steel or brass, the

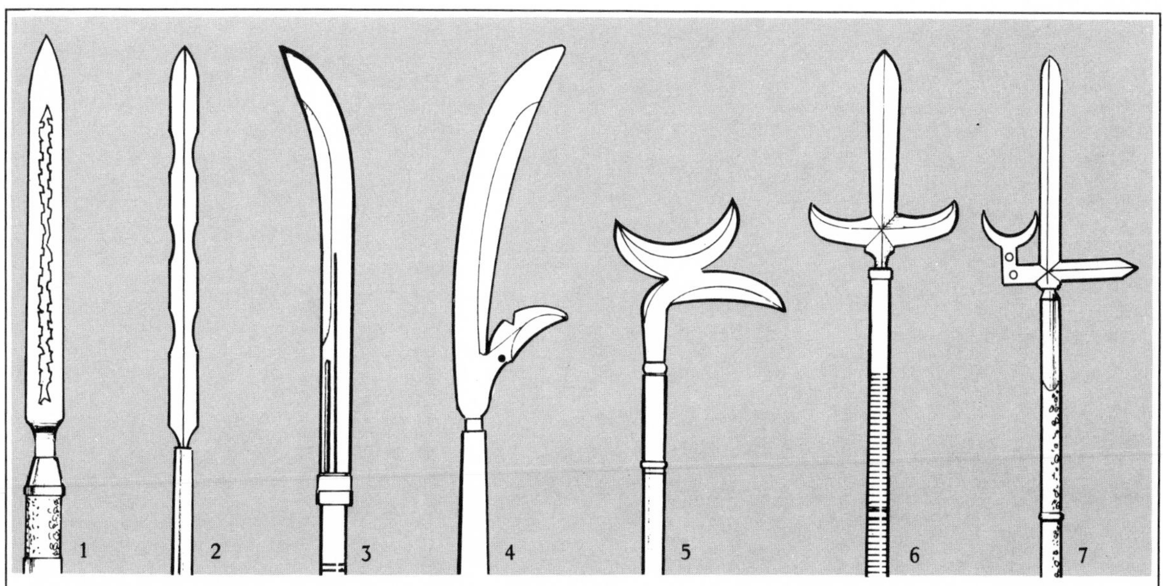


*Yari, Japanese spearheads, Tokugawa (Edo) period (1603–1867). 1. Hira-saukaku-yari. 2. Yari. 3. Naginata. 4. Hoko. 5. Hoko. 6. Magari-yari or jumonji-yari. 7. Magari-yari. Museo Orientale, Ca' Pesaro, Venice.*

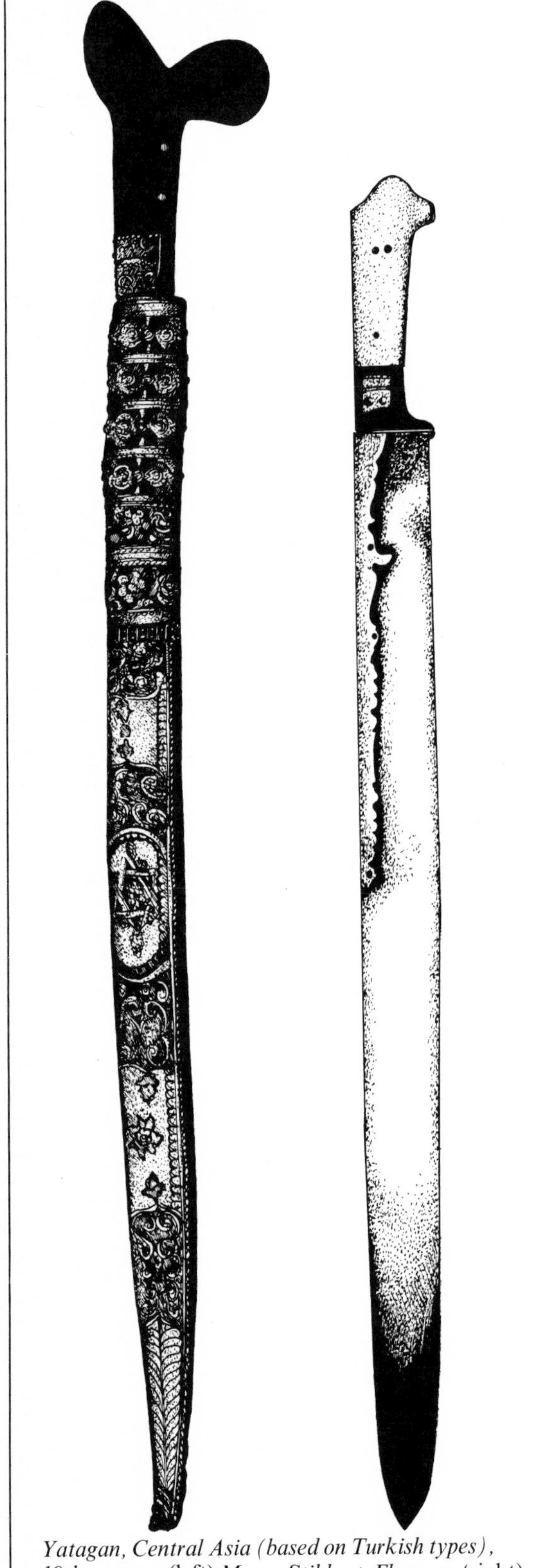

*Yatagan, Central Asia (based on Turkish types), 19th century.* (left) *Museo Stibbert, Florence,* (right) *Rijksmuseum voor Volkenkunde, Leiden, Netherlands*

*hadome,* is attached under the blade of the yari; its function was to parry the attacking pole arm or sword and to deflect the blow; it could also be used to break the opponent's sword. The hadome arms are generally irregular, one of them frequently being L-shaped. A corded hand stop can be found on some shafts, and a pennon was occasionally attached just below the head.

The art of spear fencing had a long tradition in Japan, and there were numerous schools and styles of this skill. At the end of the 8th century the Academy of Military Sciences was established in Kyōto, where the use of sword and spear was taught as well as tactics and classical Chinese strategy. Particular blows and thrusts had their own, usually poetic, names, which were incorporated into dramas of the Nō theater in the 13th and 14th centuries. Wooden spears with ball-like heads of leather, *keiko-yari,* were used for practicing fencing. Yari fencing was mostly left-handed, i.e., the left side of the body was toward the opponent, the left arm guiding the spear and the left leg forward. Fencers would travel around the country in search of worthy opponents, matches would be organized, and in this way, a high degree of skill was achieved. In the 16th century there was an important dispute between military experts about the advantages of long and short spears; it is said that the supporters of long spears prevailed.

**yari-ate** The Japanese spear rest, the equivalent of the European lance bucket, made of iron, copper, or leather. It was carried on the right-hand side, fastened either to the leg, saddle, or stirrup, and was sometimes hinged. In some cases a special hole in the stirrup (see ABUMI) served as a yari-ate.

**yari-kake** A Japanese spear rack, of which there were two main kinds, both made of wood. The first was an upright rack in which the shafts stood vertically; this was the military version, generally found in guard posts, castles, aristocratic homes, and at town and provincial barriers. The second was the domestic type, made in such a way that the spears could be laid horizontally between two rows of pegs, since the low-ceilinged houses precluded vertical storage. This rack was usually kept close to the outer door so that the weapons could be easily seized in the event of a sudden attack.

**yatagan** A single-edged cut-and-thrust sword typical of Turkey and the Balkan countries, which developed in about the 17th century, probably following the tradition of the Greek-Roman MACHAIRA. In the next two centuries the yatagan was popular in all lands under Ottoman domination, where numerous variations evolved. Various materials and decorative styles were applied, but the basic structure of the weapon remained unchanged, its true worth lying in its convenience of handling, comfortable weight, and fighting properties. The yatagan was still being used in the 20th century by the Serbian army in place of bayonets. Most of the surviving specimens, however, are from the 18th and 19th centuries, and are preserved in many museums.

The yatagan blade, like that of the Greek machaira, is incurving at the central part but turns toward the back again at the point. The surface of the blade is smooth but

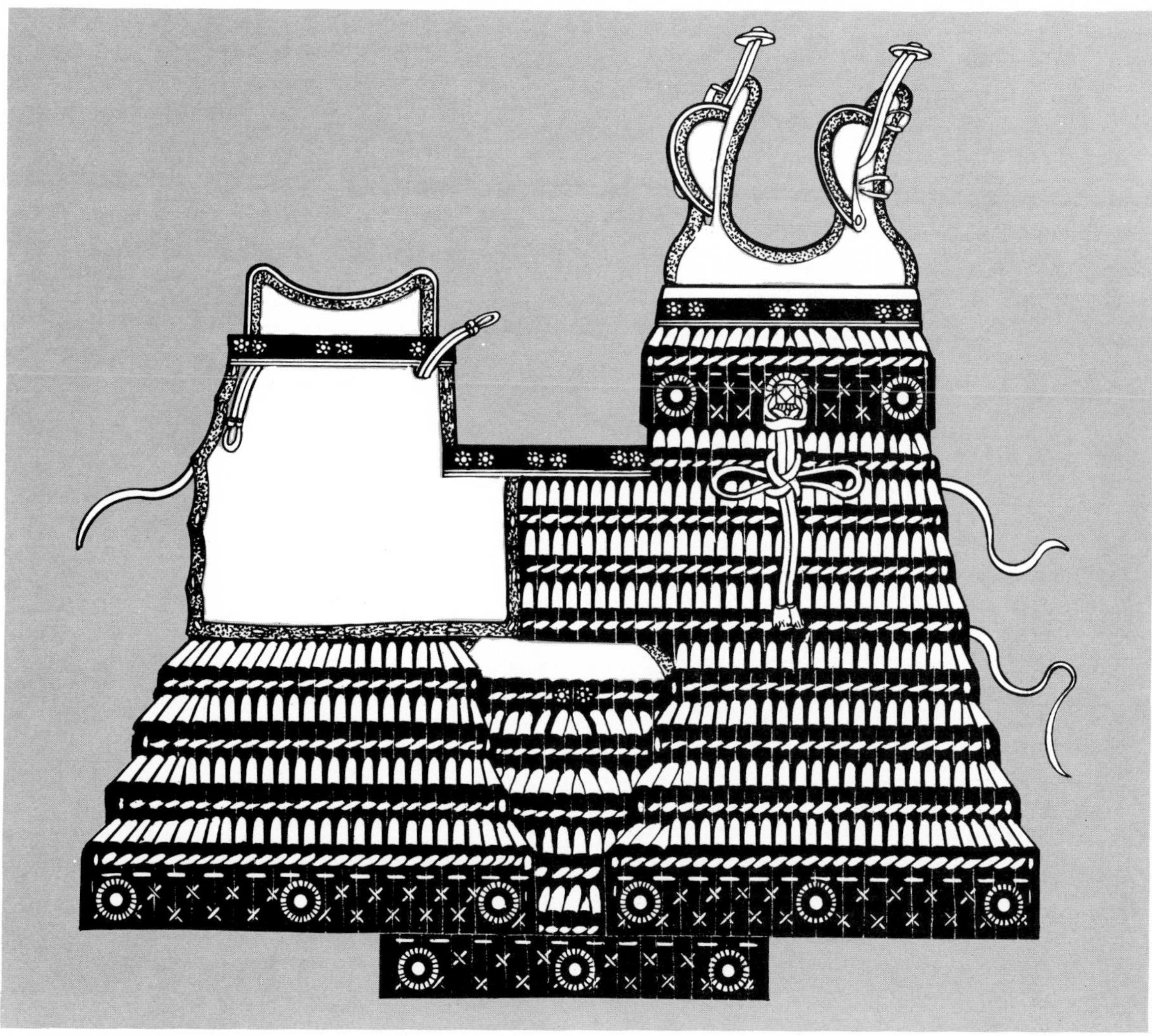

*Schematic drawing of a yoroi.*

very often decorated with inlays of brass, silver, or gold in various motifs popular in Turkish art, such as lambrequins, palmettes, obelisks, and cypresses, as well as inscriptions, sultans' *tughra* (monograms with the name and titles), and swordmakers' marks with dates and names.

The yatagan hilt has no guard. Its most outstanding features are the two "ears" of the pommel and the two metal decorative plaques extending over the blade. The peculiar form of the pommel may be explained by the early adoption of the sheep's thighbone for the hilt. Daggers with similar "ears" at the pommel may be found in the prehistoric Iranian culture of Luristan. In a Turkish yatagan the tang of the blade is usually covered with two plates of walrus ivory pierced with several rivets. Sometimes these are of true ivory, horn, or bone, but occasionally they are modeled in metal, brass or silver embossed and chased with scrolls and foliage, or filigree set with corals. Yatagan scabbards are of wood covered with leather, velvet, or brass or silver plaques, embossed and chased to match the hilt. There are no sling loops, since the yatagan is carried thrust through the belt or sash, but there is often a small loop near the top for a cord to fasten it to the belt.

**yokote** Part of a Japanese blade. *See also* BLADE: Japanese; NAGAMAKI.

**yoroi** (or **ō-yoroi**) The classical Japanese armor developed in the middle and late Heian period (858–1185) used by wealthy warriors, *bushi*, and by samurai, who were originally mounted bowmen, until the 15th century. Many features of this armor were determined by the necessities of cavalry tactics, and when the samurai adopted mostly infantry tactics this type of armor became obsolete. The term *ō-yoroi* means "great armor," and all its elements were indeed large; a knight clad in such armor took on the appearance of a supernatural being. Plate and lamellar elements were combined, but the lamellar technique had been improved, as now the lamellae were first laced together and then covered with lacquer, which made the structure strong and resistant against corrosion; this was of basic importance in the humid Japanese climate.

The typical helmet, the KABUTO, for the ō-yoroi had a

low, rounded bowl, the *hachi*, with a large hole at the top, the TEHEN, for the wearer's short pigtail to pass through. The bowl was made of a number of riveted vertical and rounded plates; the rivets had large conical heads, *hoshi*, which added ornamental qualities. Broad gilt strips were laid over the front plate, and sometimes the back plate, too, was secured with large rivets. A gilt ring was fastened to the center of the back to carry a tasseled cord bow, the *agemaki*. A convex iron peak was riveted over the face; this was covered with doeskin, and there was a gilt rim, the *fukurin*, at the lower edge. The neck guard, the SHIKORO, consisted of five curved laminations, with the ends of the upper four turned outward on either side of the face to prevent a sword from entering between the edges of the laminations and cutting the lacing. These turn-backs, FUKIGAYESHI, were covered with leather and ornamented with a gilt chrysanthemum-like motif. Kabuto linings were fitted with leather and silk cords which were knotted through holes in the plates and tied under the chin. The kabuto was often completed with a face guard, the *happuri* mask (*see* MENPO), made of thin molded iron plate which was either lacquered black on the outside and red inside or covered with stenciled leather.

The cuirass, the DŌ, was in two parts: one separate defense for the right side, the *waidate*, and another for the rest of the body. The upper part of the waidate was made of solid iron plate, covered inside and outside with leather and edged with a gilt rim, the lower part consisting of laminations. The waidate was put on the body before the rest of the cuirass, fastened with cords passing through eyelet holes in the center plates and tying around the body. The larger part of the cuirass, which protected the breast, back, and left side, was held by shoulder straps of padded rawhide, the *watagami*. The breast section of the cuirass was made of a large iron plate covered with leather, the lower section being a laminated skirt. The left-side and back defenses were constructed in a similar way except that the proportions of plates and laminations were different.

The yoroi was supplemented by various pieces, fastened mostly by colored cords and toggles. Shoulder guards, *ō-sode* (*see* SODE), were large and rectangular, made with rows of lamellae and a cap plate, while a fabric sleeve (*see* KOTE) was worn on the left arm only, with a rounded plate for the back of the hand, a forearm plate, and an elbow plate. Soft doeskin gloves were worn with the armor, the right one having an additional pad on the inside of the thumb for drawing the bowstring, instead of the thumb ring used for this purpose in other Asian countries. The shins were protected by greaves, SUNEATE, consisting of three lacquered iron strips joined by hinges and secured by two ties over fabric leggings, *habaki*, and the feet were covered with bear- or sealskin shoes. Generals and other prominent warriors wore on their kabuto helmets a crest in the form of straight, slender metal horns with bifurcated ends.

During the Kamakura period (1184–1333) the shape of the yoroi did not change much, although the details and decoration underwent some modifications. One of the most celebrated yoroi of the second half of the 14th century, now in the Kasugajinsha Shrine in the city of Nara, is decorated on the *sode* shoulder guards with a gilt figure of a tiger in a bamboo grove.

**yu gake** Japanese archers' gloves, of which there were several kinds. The second and third fingers were usually in a contrasting color and made of softer leather than the rest of the glove, while the thumb had a double thickness of leather on the inside to take the wear from the bowstring. There were long straps by which the gloves could be fastened at the wrist, and some had a heart-shaped opening in the palm for ventilation. A simpler yu gake covered only the thumb and one or two fingers and had a broad wristband; the thumb was lined with some very hard material to take the place of the archer's ring worn in most Eastern countries using the so-called Mongolian release—a method of drawing the string and placing the arrow—in which the thumb was particularly vulnerable. Another type of yu gake was the glove for the hand holding the bow; this was made of cloth lined with mail to protect the exposed hand.

**yumi** The Japanese bow, which belonged to a large family of Asian composite bows but was different from the Mongolian, Turkish, or Persian ones both in construction and length. The yumi was usually more than 2 m. ($6\frac{1}{2}$ ft.) long, sometimes reaching nearly 2.4 m. (8 ft.), about 2.5 cm. (1 in.) thick, and about 5 cm. (2 in.) wide. Its grip

*Japanese archer taking aim with a yumi.*

# Turn-of-the-century artillery, First- and Second-World-War weapons and modern firearms

**Plate 75 Weapons of the First World War** (top to bottom) *M-95 Mannlicher rifle, Austria. Lebel model 1886 rifle, France. Lee-Enfield Mark III rifle (1907, SMLE or Short, Magazine, Lee-Enfield), Great Britain. BAR (Browning Automatic Rifle), United States. Chauchat light machine gun, France. Mauser semiautomatic pistol, Germany.*

**Plate 76 Machine guns of the First World War** (top) *Vickers Mark I machine gun, Great Britain.* (middle left) *Villar Perosa twin machine gun of 9 mm. caliber, Italy.* (middle right) *MG 08/15 light machine gun, Germany.* (bottom) *Hotchkiss model 1914 machine gun, France.*

**Plate 77 Late 19th-century artillery** (top left) *150 mm. model 1884 howitzer, Russia.* (top right) *120 mm. Saint-Chamond gun, France.* (middle) *155 mm. model 1917 Schneider, France.* (bottom) *75 mm. Puteaux model 1897 gun, France.*

**Plate 78 Early 20th-century artillery** (top to bottom) *Field gun Mark II, Great Britain, 1906. Six-inch howitzer, Great Britain, 1915. Twelve-inch siege howitzer Mark IV, Great Britain.*

**Plate 79 Artillery of the First World War** (top) *120 mm. fortress gun, Austria.* (middle) *21 cm. mortar, Germany.* (bottom) *15 cm. model 1913 gun, Germany.*

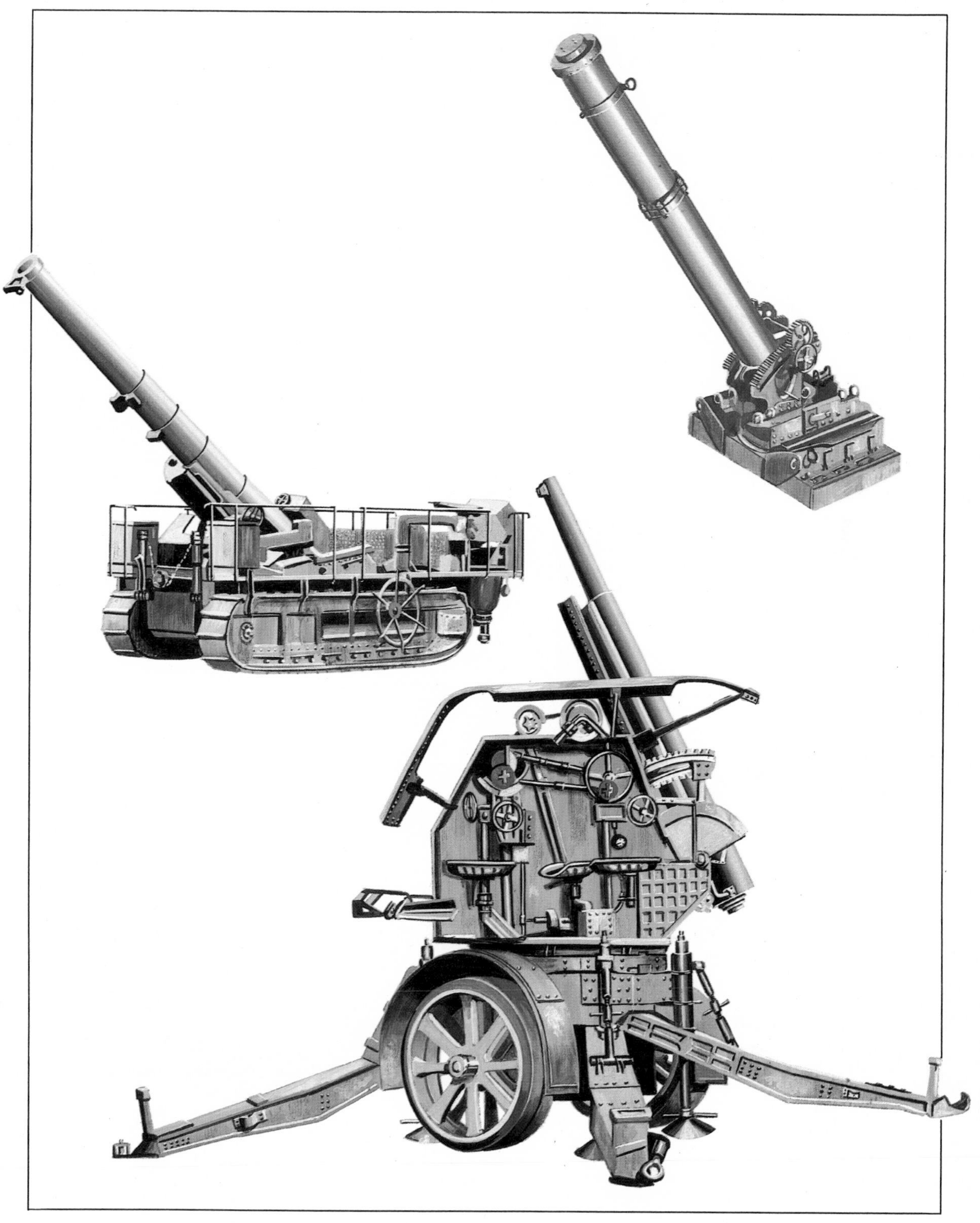

**Plate 80 Artillery of the First World War** (top right) *240 mm. bombard, Italy*. (middle) *194 mm. Saint-Chamond gun on self-propelled carriage, France*. (bottom) *75 mm. Schneider antiaircraft gun on special carriage allowing 360° traverse.*

**Plate 81 Firearms of the Second World War: Germany** (top to bottom) *Mauser model 1898 rifle. Sturmgewehr MP-43 assault rifle. MP-38 submachine gun. Luger P-08 pistol. Walther P-38 pistol.*

**Plate 82 Firearms of the Second World War: Italy** (top to bottom) *Mannlicher-Carcano Model 91/41 rifle. Beretta automatic rifle MAB 38/42. Breda Model 30 light machine gun. Beretta 9 mm. pistol model 1934.*

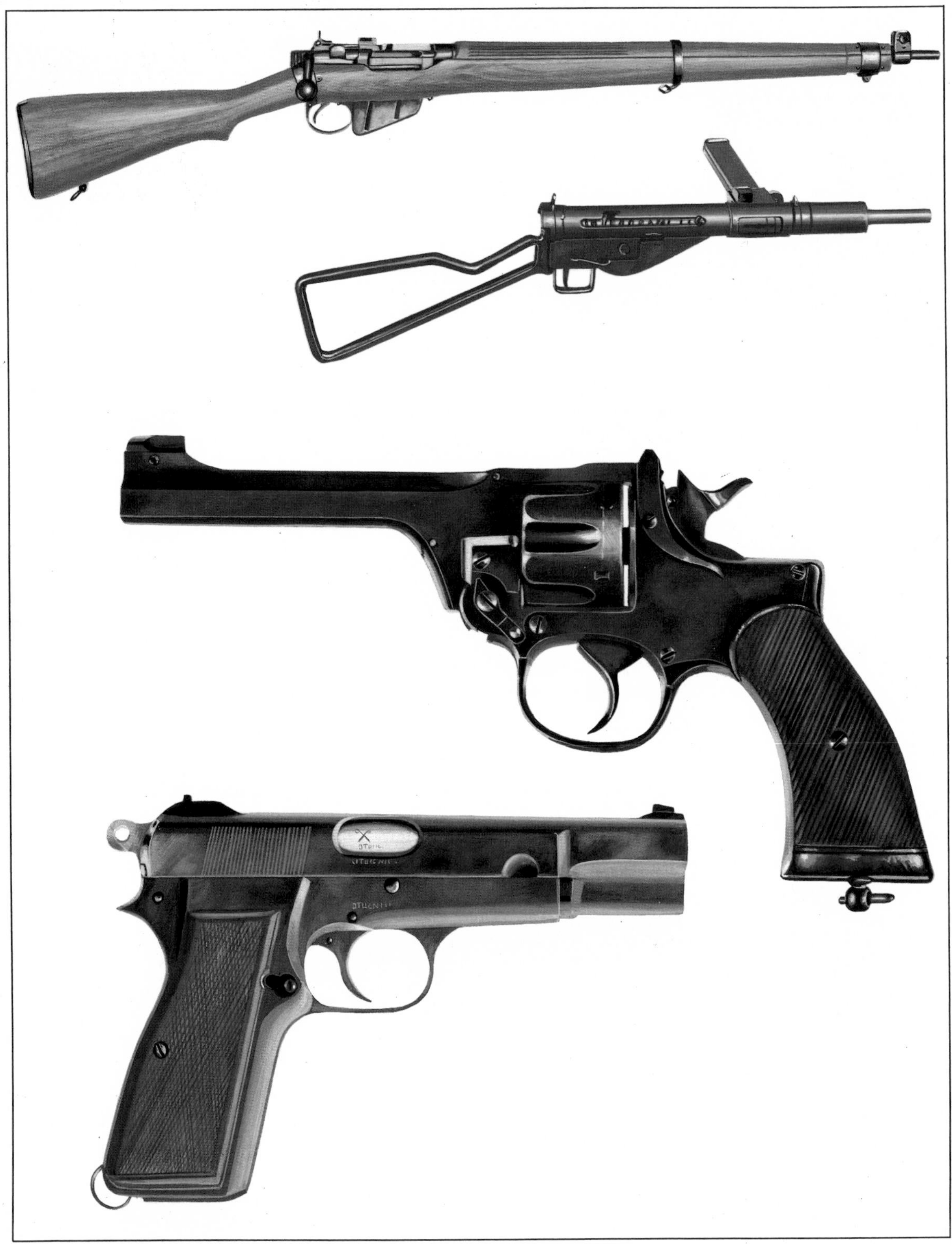

**Plate 83 Firearms of the Second World War: Great Britain** (top to bottom) *Lee-Enfield Mark I .303 in. rifle. Sten Mark II submachine gun. Enfield Mark I revolver. F. N. Browning 9 mm. pistol (Belgian designed, manufactured in Canada during the war and used by several of the Allies).*

**Plate 84 Firearms of the Second World War: United States** (top to bottom) *Garand M-1 semiautomatic rifle. Winchester M-1 .30 caliber carbine. Thompson M-1 submachine gun. M-3 .45 caliber submachine gun (the "Grease Gun"). Colt M-1911A1 .45 caliber semiautomatic pistol.*

**Plate 85 Firearms of the Second World War: Japan** (top to bottom) *Rifle Type 1, 6.5 mm. caliber. Nambu Type 11 light machine gun. 8 mm. Model 94 pistol. Nambu 8 mm. model 1904 pistol.*

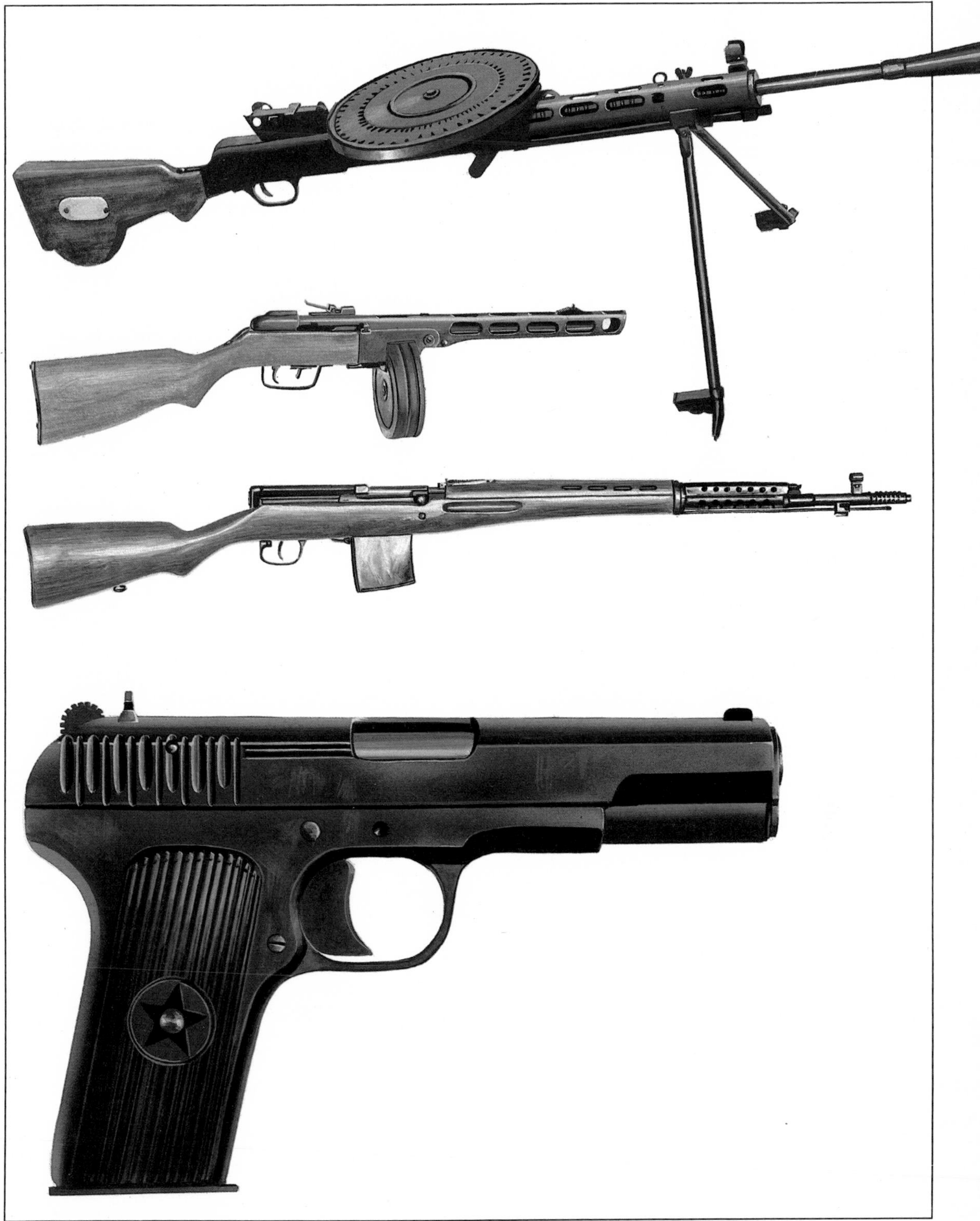

**Plate 86 Firearms of the Second World War: Soviet Union** (top to bottom) *Degtyarev DP light machine gun. PPSh 1941 submachine gun. Tokarev model 1940 semiautomatic rifle. Tokarev TT-30 7.62 mm. pistol.*

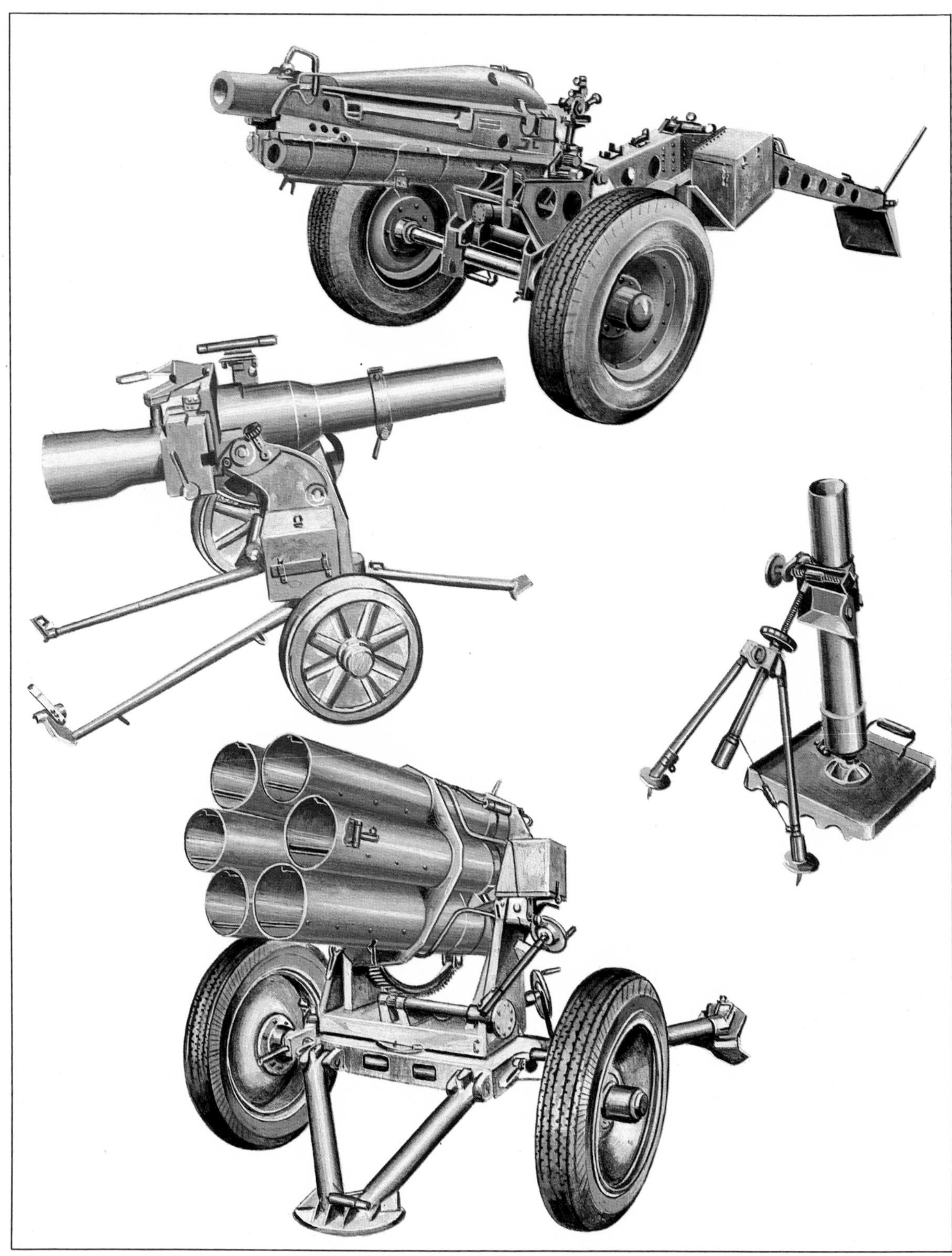

**Plate 87 Artillery of the Second World War** (top) *75 mm. light howitzer, which could be airlifted and parachuted, United States*. (middle left) *75 mm. recoilless gun, Germany*. (middle right) *Model 97 81 mm. mortar, Japan*. (bottom) *Nebelwerfer-41 15 cm. rocket launcher, Germany*.

**Plate 88 Artillery of the Second World War** (top to bottom) *British 25-pounder gun-howitzer; the platform under the wheels enabled the gun to be traversed. German 88 mm. antiaircraft gun. USSR 203 mm. howitzer, on which wheels were replaced by tracks to allow rapid laying in the snow. German Dora 80 cm. railway gun; this gun was transported in a number of separate loads, then assembled on dual tracks much longer than normal railway sidings.*

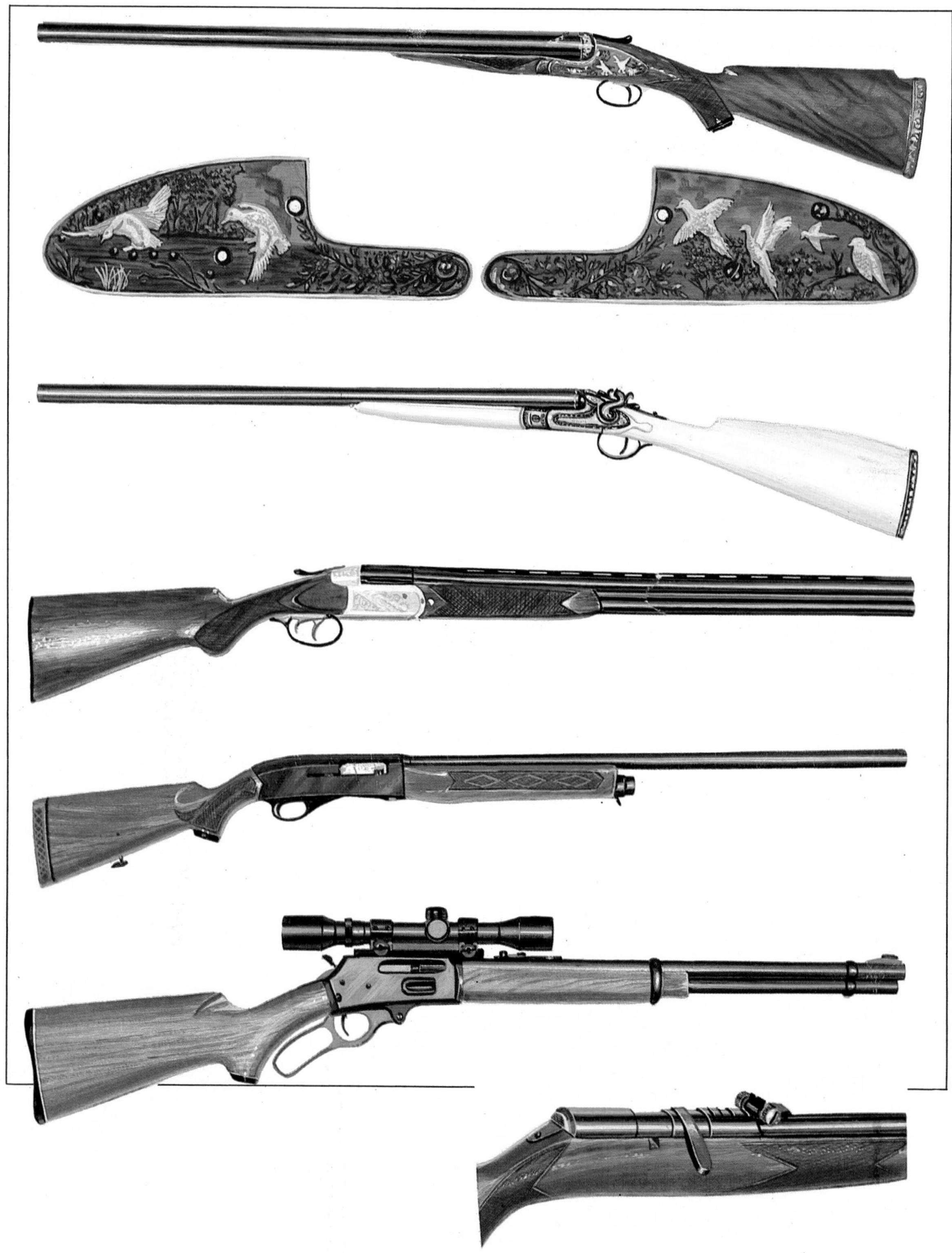

**Plate 89 Modern sporting guns** (top to bottom) *Purdey deluxe model double-barreled shotgun, Great Britain. Two lock plates for Purdy guns. Famars Castore EA double-barreled shotgun, with external hammers, Italy. Manufrance Falcon over-and-under hammerless shotgun, France. Winchester automatic shotgun, United States. Marlin 336C repeating carbine, United States. Detail of the Beretta Olimpia automatic carbine, Italy.*

**Plate 90 Modern target firearms** (top to bottom) *Taifun "free pattern" carbine, USSR. Hammerli Model 150 pistol, Switzerland. Ruger Mark I automatic target pistol, United States. Walther Olympia automatic pistol, Germany.*

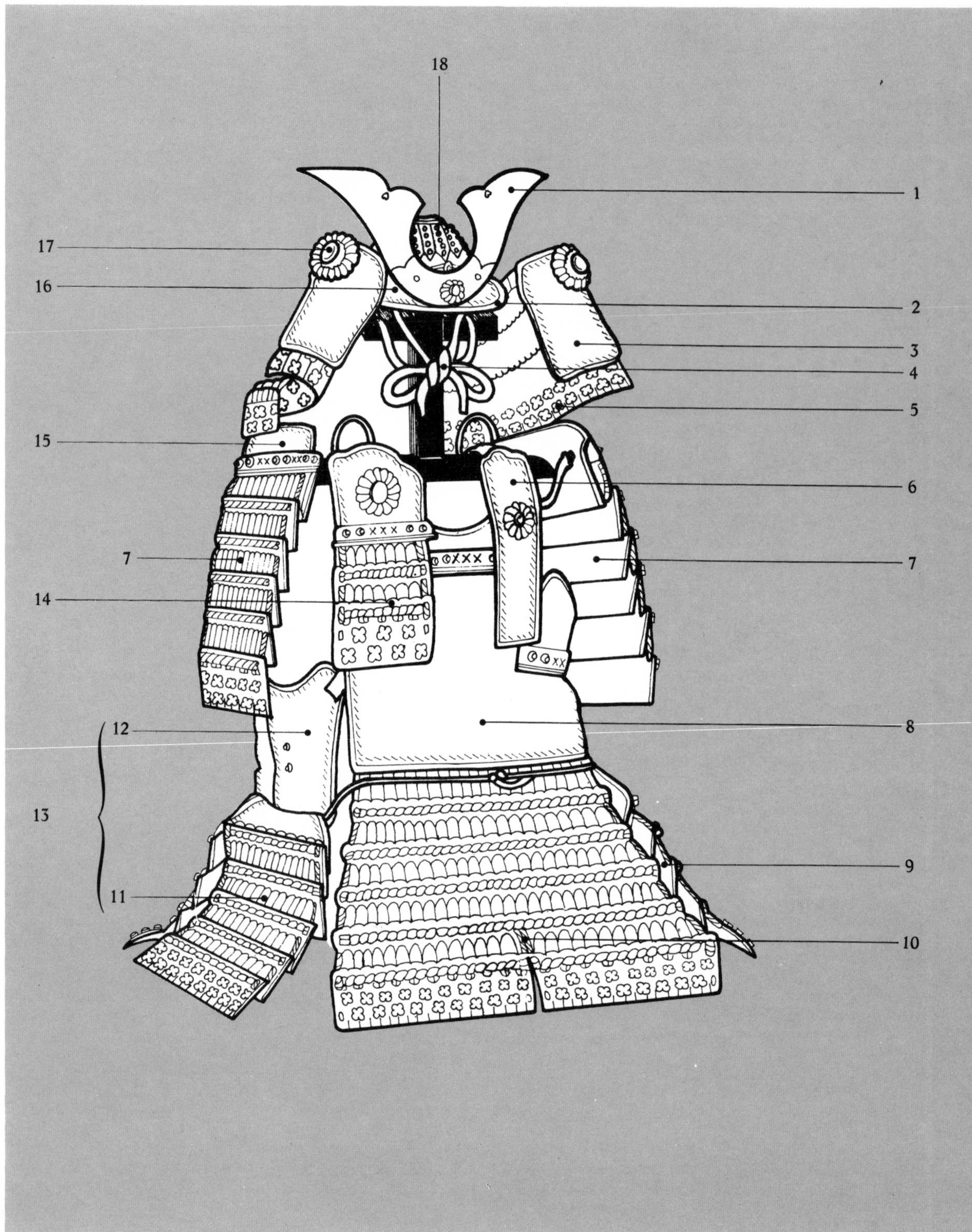


*Yoroi. 1. kuwagata (ornament and reinforcement of helmet); 2. fukurin (peak border); 3. fukigayeshi (side guards); 4. shime-o (chin straps); 5. shikoro (tail); 6. kyubi-no-ita (left pectoral); 7. o-sode (shoulder guards); 8. tsurubashiri (breastplate); 9. imuke-kusazuri (skirt, left side); 10. mae-kusazuri (skirt front); 11. komori-tsuke (skirt, right side); 12. tsubo-ita (right side plate); 13. waidate (combination of parts to protect right side); 14. sendan-no-ita (left*

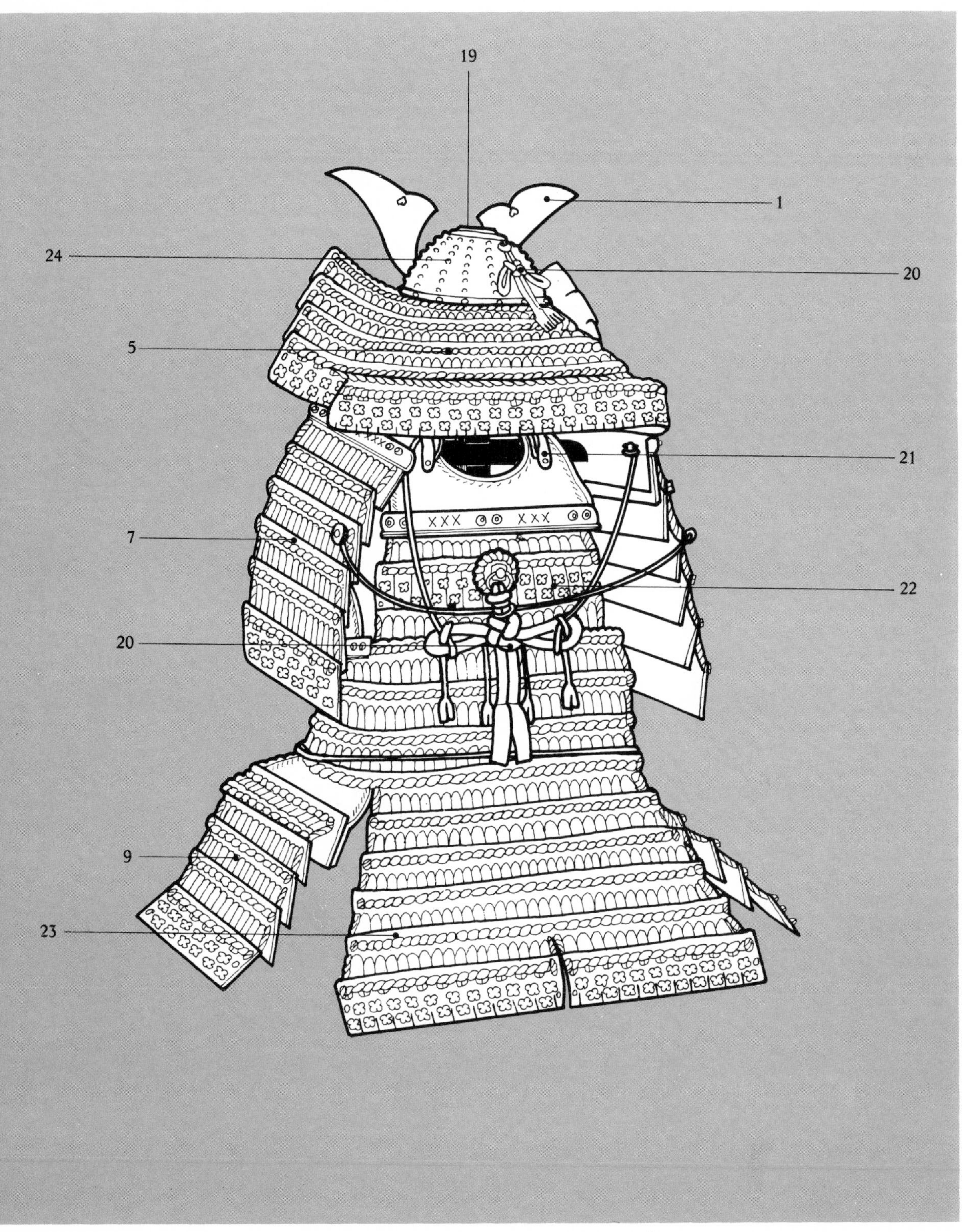


*pectoral); 15. kamuri-ita (top plate of shoulder defense); 16. mabezashi (peak); 17. mon (armorial crest); 18. kabuto-bachi (skull); 19. tehen (top opening); 20. agemaki (knot); 21 watagami (shoulder strap); 22. saka-ita (backplate); 23. hikishiki-kusazuri (skirt back); 24. hoshi (rivets).*

*Stages in the putting on of a yoroi armor and weapons, taken from the treatise* Yoshiiye Ason no Yoroi-chakyo-dzu *("How Yoshiiye Wore His Armor") by Vice General Yoshisada: (1) Over the loincloth (*tazuma *or* fudoshi*) is put (2) a kimono with narrow-wristed sleeves (*kosode*) and (3) a pair of short, wide breeches (*o-guchi*). The hair is loosened (4) and the cap (*eboshi*) fastened to the head with a band (*hachimaki*). The archer's gloves (*yugake*) are now put on (5). At this point (6) the under-armor tunic (*yoroi-hi-tatare*) and (7) matching breeches (*hakama*) are slipped into. Now (8) come the leggings (*habaki *or* kiahan*) and (9) the laces (*kukuri*) are tightened to anchor the breeches. The next step (10) is to put on the shin guards (*suneate*) and (11) the fur shoes (*tsuranuki *or* kutsu*). Now (12) the right side*

*of the cuirass (*waidate*) is put on and (13) the armored sleeve (*tegai *or* kote*) drawn onto the right arm. (14) The ends of the various cords now have to be secured, after which (15) the other armored sleeve (*tegai *or* kote*) can be drawn onto the left arm. The right sleeve of the tunic (*hitatare*) can now (16) be tied. Finally the actual armor (*yoroi*) is put on (17); this consists of the cuirass (*dō*) and shoulder guards (*sode*) with a decorative knot (*agemaki*) at the back (18) to hold them together. With the short sword (*koshi-katana*) (19), the long sword (*tachi*) (20), a roundel carrying the cord for the bow (*tsurumaki*), the quiver (*ebira*) (21) with the arrows and the bow (*yumi*) (22), the warrior completes his arming.*

was placed well below the center, so that the upper part was almost twice as long as the lower (because the archers shot mainly from horseback or in a kneeling position, they could not have used such long bows if the grips had been in the middle). The yumi was warped into permanent curves at both ends, which reversed when the bow was strung.

Some smaller bows, about 90 cm. (3 ft.) long, which were well adapted for shooting from a litter, were also used in Japan, but the big war yumi dominated the scene. It was always made of wood, originally of boxwood, but later bamboo was used exclusively, with the addition of waxwood (*Rhus succedanea*), fish glue, rattan, lacquer, and leather. Between the two thin strips of bamboo which formed the "back" and "belly" of the bow were set three additional strips of bamboo, edgewise, to give greater strength. The outer edges of the bow consisted of two strips of waxwood, the whole being secured with fish glue, lacquered, and bound at intervals with rattan. The grip was covered with deerskin. There was no notch for the string, but both ends of the bow were cut back to form shoulders which sloped from the back to the belly. The string, made from tightly wound grass fibers, was wrapped around the projecting end of the bow and rested on its shoulder. The bow was operated by drawing it well behind the ear; it shot long, heavy arrows over moderate distances with a flat trajectory.

The typical yumi arrow was about 90 cm. (3 ft.) long; it was made of a colored reed and usually set with three feathers. The iron war heads were small with a long tang fixed into the reed, but parade arrows had large flat heads decorated with pierced heraldic motifs. Ceremonial yumi were similar in construction but made in two pieces joined by a metal sleeve at the grip and decoratively lacquered. The small bows were often carried in a frame with a case for arrows (*see* YADZUTSU).

**yushman** Term of Tatar origin for the combined plate and mail armor which was in widespread use in various Islamic and Eastern countries such as Turkey, Arabia, Persia, India, and Russia. Most of the specimens extant today are from the 16th and 17th centuries, but it can be seen depicted in much earlier iconography. It consisted of a coat of mail with sleeves reinforced with fairly large rectangular plates built into the front, back, and both sides. It opened at the front, fastened with clasps or buckles and thongs. The best examples are in the State Armory of the Kremlin and in the Askeri Museum in Istanbul.

# Z

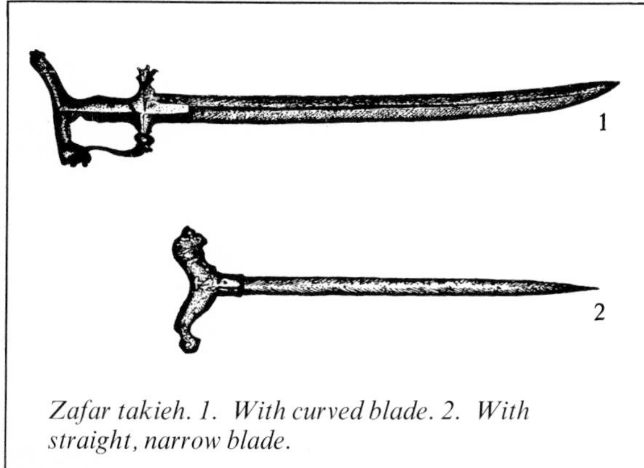

*Zafar takieh. 1. With curved blade. 2. With straight, narrow blade.*

**zafar takieh** An Indian term meaning "cushion of victory" and referring to a short sword, about 40–60 cm. (16–24 in.) long, once carried by Indian princes when seated on a cushion to give audiences. There are two types: one has a straight, narrow blade, oval or diamond-shaped in cross section, and a handle like a simple crutch at right angles to the blade; the other has a wide, slightly curved blade, often fullered, and a hilt like that of the TALWAR but with a crutch-shaped pommel to form a rest for the arm or hand. The zafar takieh, being a princely object, always had a fine watered-steel blade and was made of precious materials, with a handle of jade or other fine stone decorated with gold.

**zaghaya** *See* ASSAGAI.

**zertsalo** A Russian word (meaning "mirror") for the CHAR-AINA.

**Zischägge** A German word used from the 16th century to indicate a particular type of helmet, the SHISHAK, of Islamic origin. In the English-speaking world, a variation of this type of helmet became known as the ENGLISH POT.

**zone** Greek term for the CINCTORIUM.

**zoster** Greek term for the CINGULUM.

**Zulfikar** The sword of the Prophet Mohammed, known also as the sword of Ali, in Arabic *Dhū'l-Faqār* ("The Cloven Blade"). According to some Arabic sources, it was captured by Mohammed from an infidel at the battle of Badr (624), the first great victory for the Prophet. A legend was soon built around this victory and some miraculous properties were discovered in the trophy sword, which was supposed to be the work of an Arab swordmaker, Marzuq. Zulfikar became the Prophet's favorite weapon, carried by him in all later battles. After Mohammed's death it was inherited by Ali, his son-in-law, then by Ali's sons Hasan and Husein, and finally by the Abbasid caliphs (750–1000). Harun-ar-Rashid later presented it to his chief commander of the army, Jezid. Although the sword's subsequent fate is unknown, some historians maintain that it was passed to the Fatimids and then regained by the Abbasids, who kept it until the end of their rule in the mid-13th century.

Early representations of Zulfikar in miniatures date from the 14th century, particularly in Persia, depicting Ali with the sword. Under Ottoman domination the fame of Zulfikar continued to grow. It appeared both as a symbol on Islamic flags and in actual reproductions, modeled upon the legendary prototype. Old descriptions left room for imagination and free interpretation of how Zulfikar had really looked, its basic feature being the double ending of its blade. In the large Ottoman banners called *sanjak* of the 16th and 17th centuries, it was just a sword with a bifurcated blade, the turned-down quillons terminating in dragon's-head finials. Under the hilt, the Shield of David—sometimes identical with Solomon's Seal—was placed, and a crescent and star above the pommel. In smaller, regimental flags, *bayrak*, Zulfikar was depicted in the form of a saber with a double-ended blade.

A small group of actual sabers of this type has survived, mostly from the 18th century. The bifurcated blade served no practical purpose in fighting. A specimen of a sword of this kind, in the Czartoryski Collection in Kraków, has a blade with an inscription in Arabic which can be translated: "There is no hero like Ali, there is no sword but

Zulfikar." Some of the "Zulfikar" swords have a typical KILIJ hilt, such as the one in the Musée de l'Armée in Paris. Many scholars think these sabers were a sacred symbol of the janissaries, Turkish infantrymen, who also formed the sultan's guard, in the 14th to 19th centuries.

**zyhgyr** The Persian term for the thumb ring used by eastern European and Islamic archers. Wherever the recurved composite bow was used, its string was drawn with the right thumb, the knuckle being protected by a ring made of some hard material such as horn, bone, ivory, stone, or metal. This was the so called Mongolian release and was most probably invented somewhere in Asia. Various thumb rings are to be found from China, across Asia and Europe as far as Italy and into Africa, but only a few can be dated or have come from identifiable archeological sites. There were two basic Asian types: the ring in the form of a cylinder, which comes from China, and the lipped ring in which one side extends toward the tip of the thumb in a projection known in Turkish as the *dimagh*. The lipped zyhgyr was very popular in Moslem countries, and early specimens from the 8th century A.D. have been found in Fustat. Jade rings were used in India and ivory ones in Turkey. Zyhgyr were carried in special leather cases. *See also* ARCHER'S THUMB RING.

# Credits for Illustrations

## Color Plates

Nicola Arolse
Plates 7, 8, 10, 11, 12, 18, 21, 24, 25, 33, 34, 51, 53, 54, 62, 63, 64, 67, 69, 71, 75, 76, 77, 78, 80, 82, 83, 84, 85, 86, 87, 88, 89, 90

Carlo Carfagni
Plates 1, 2, 4, 5, 31, 32, 65

Vincenzo Cosentino
Plate 60

S. Kromos
Plates 3, 6, 13, 15, 16, 17, 19, 20, 22, 23, 26, 27, 28, 29, 30, 35, 36, 37, 38, 40, 41, 42, 43, 44, 45, 46, 47, 48, 49, 50, 52, 55, 56, 57, 58, 59, 61, 66, 68, 70, 72, 74

Mario Pedrazzi
Plates 9, 14

## Technical and Line Drawings

Maurizio e Paolo Riccioni
Daniela Dazzi

# List of Color Illustrations

# Select Bibliography

## Periodicals

Among the periodicals in the field of arms and armor, the following are noteworthy:

*American Blade*
*The American Rifleman*
*American Society of Arms Collectors*, Bulletin
*Ami-Armes-Militaria* (Italy)
*Armamentaria, uitgabe van de Stichting "Vrienden van het Legermuseum"* (Netherlands)
*Armes Anciennes* (Switzerland)
*Armi Antiche*, Bulletin of the Academy of San Marciano (Italy)
*Arms Cavalcade, the Journal of the Antique Arms Collectors Society of Australia*
*Arms Gazette* (incorporated by *Man-at-Arms* since 1981)
*Association Suisse pour l'Etude des Armes et Armures*, Bulletin
*Bullettin des Amis du Musée de l'Armée* (France)
*The Canadian Journal of Arms Collecting*
*Caps and Flints*, the official magazine of the Antique and Historical Arms Collectors Guild of Victoria (Australia)
*Deutsches Waffen-Journal* (West Germany)
*Diana-Armi* (Italy)
*Eserciti e Armi, Interconair* (Italy)
*Gazette des Armes* (France)
*Gladius* (Spain)
*The Gun Collector*
*The Gun Digest*
*The Gun Report*
*Internationaler Waffen-Spiegel* (West Germany)
*Journal of the Arms and Armour Society* (Great Britain)
*Journal of the Historical Firearms Society of South Africa*
*Journal of the Society of Archer-Antiquaries* (Great Britain)
*Kungl. Armémuseum Meddelande* (Sweden)
*Livrustkammaren, Journal of the Royal Armory* (Sweden)
*Man-at-Arms*
*Musée d'Armes*, Bulletin de l'Association "Les Amis du Musée d'Armes de Liège" (Belgium)
*Muzzle Blasts*
*Report of the Congress of IAMAM* (International Association of Museums of Arms and Military History)
*Svenska Vapenhistoriska Årsskrift* (Sweden)
*Tac-Armi* (Italy)
*Vaabenhistoriske Aarbøger* (Denmark)
*Varia, utgiven av Svensak Vapenhistoriska Sällskapet* (Sweden)
*Vesnik*, Bulletin du Musée Militaire à Belgrade (Yugoslavia)
*De Wapen Verzamelaar Tijdschrift van de Vereniging Nederlandse Wapenverzamelaars* (Netherlands)
*Zeitschrift für Historische Waffenkunde (ZHWK)*, since 1960 *Waffen- und Kostumkünde* (West Germany)

A detailed listing of new publications on arms and armor appears regularly in the *Journal of the Arms and Armour Society.*

# Works of a General Nature

Angelucci, A. *Documenti inediti per la storia delle armi da fuoco italiane*. Turin, 1869.

———. *Catalogo dell'Armeria Reale*. Turin, 1890

Askgaard, F. *Det Oldenborgske Rustkammer*. Copenhagen, 1961.

Aznard, J. C. *Las nuevas salas del Museo Lasaro Galdiano*. Madrid, 1957.

Bartocci, A., and L. Salvatici. *Armamento individuale dell'esercito piemontese e italiano 1814–1914*. Florence, 1978.

Blair, C. *European and American Arms c. 1100–1850*. London, 1962.

———. *The James A. de Rothschild Collection at Waddesdon Manor: Arms, Armour and Miscellaneous Metalwork*. Fribourg, 1974.

Blackmore, H. L. *Hunting Weapons*. London, 1971; New York, 1972.

Boccia, L. G. *Nove secoli di armi da caccia*. Florence, 1967.

———. *Il Museo Stibbert a Firenze–L'armeria europea*. Florence, 1975.

Boccia, L. G., F. Rossi, and M. Morin. *Armi e Armature Lombarde*. Milan, 1980.

Boeheim, W. *Handbuch der Waffenkunde*. Leipzig, 1890.

———. *Kunsthistorische Sammlungen des Allerhöchsten Kaiserhauses. Waffensammlung*. Vienna, 1894–98.

Brinckerhoff, S. D., and P. A. Chamberlain. *Spanish Military Weapons in Colonial America 1700–1821*. Harrisburg, Pa., 1972.

Buttin, F. *Catalogue de la Collection d'armes anciennes européennes et orientales de Charles Buttin*. Rumilly (France), 1933.

Carpegna, N. di. *Antiche armi dal secolo IX al XVIII (già Collezione Odescalchi)*. Rome, 1969.

Carré, J. B. L. *Panoplie*. Paris, 1797.

Cederström, R. *Livrustkammaren oc därmed förenade smalingar*. Uppsala, 1919.

Cederström, R., and G. Malmborg. *Den äldere livrustkammaren 1654*. Stockholm, 1930.

Clunie, F. *Fijian Waffen and Warfare*. Suva (Fiji), 1977.

Cockle, M. J. D. *A Bibliography of English Military Books up to 1642 and of Contemporary Foreign Works*. London, 1900.

Cortés, J.. *La Real Armería de Madrid*. Madrid, 1968.

Couissin, P. *Les armes romaines*. Paris, 1926.

Cripps-Day, F. H. *A Record of Armour Sales 1881–1924*. London, 1925.

Crooke y Navarrot (JUAN, Conde Valencia de Don Juan). *Cátálogo Historico-Descriptivo de la Real Armería de Madrid*. Madrid, 1890.

D'Aquino, C. *Lexicon militare*. Naples, 1702.

Dean, B. *Catalogue of a Loan Exhibition of Arms and Armor*. The Metropolitan Museum of Art. New York, 1911.

———. *Handbook of Arms and Armor, European and Oriental, including the William H. Riggs Collection*. The Metropolitan Museum of Art. New York, 1915.

Dean, B., and S. V. Grancsay. *Handbook of Arms and Armor*. The Metropolitan Museum of Art. New York, 1929.

Demmin, A. *Die Kriegswaffen in ihren geschichtlichen Entwicklungen*. Leipzig, 1891.

Diderot, D., and J. Le Rond d'Alembert (eds.). *Encyclopédie, ou Dictionnaire Raisonné des Sciences, des Arts et des Métiers*. Paris, 1751–77.

Dolleczek, A. *Monographie der K. u. K. O-U, Blanken u. Handfeuer-Waffen*. Vienna, 1896.

Dreger, E. H. M. *Waffensammlung Dreger*. Berlin, 1926.

Drummond, J. *Ancient Scottish Weapons*. London and Edinburgh, 1881.

Ehrenthal, M. von. *Führer durch das Königliche Historische Museum zu Dresden*. Dresden, 1899.

Estruch y Cumella, J. *Museo-Armería de Don José Estruch y Cumella Estruch*. Barcelona, 1896.

ffoulkes, C. *Inventory and Survey of the Armouries of the Tower of London*. London, 1916–17.

Fraga y Sorrondegui, J. M. de la. *Museo Militar y Castillo de Montjuich*. Barcelona, 1970.

Gaier, C. *L' Industrie et le Commerce des Armes dans les Anciennes Principautés belges du XIIIè à la Fin du XVè Siècle*. Liège and Paris, 1973.

Gamber, O. *Waffen und Rüstung Eurasiens: Frühzeit und Antike*. Brunswick (Germany), 1978.

Gardner, R. E. *Small Arms Makers*. New York, 1963.

Gelli, J. *Guida del raccoglitore e dell'amatore di armi antiche*. Milan, 1900/1968.

Gelli, J., and G. Moretti. *Gli armaioli milanesi*. Milan, 1903.

Gessler, E. A. *Führer durch die Waffensammlung des Schweizerischen Landesmuseums*. Zurich, 1928.

Gilchrist, H. J. *A Catalogue of the Collection of Arms and Armor Presented to the Cleveland Museum by Mr and Mrs John Long Severance*. Cleveland, 1924.

Gille, F. *Musée de Tzarskoe-Selo ou Collection d'Armes de Sa Majesté l'Empereur de toutes les Russies*. St. Petersburg and Karlsruhe, 1835–53.

Grancsay, S. V. *Loan Exhibition of Mediaeval and Renaissance Arms and Armor*. Los Angeles County Museum, Los Angeles, 1953.

———. *Arms and Armor*. Allentown Art Museum, Allentown, Pa., 1964.

Graziani, E. *Brescia nella storia delle armi*. Brescia, 1904.

Grose, F. *A Treatise on Ancient Armour and Weapons.* London, 1786.

Grosz, A., and B. Thomas. *Katalog der Waffensammlung in der Neuen Burg.* Vienna, 1936.

Haenel, E. *Kostbare Waffen aus der Dresdner Rüstkammer.* Leipzig, 1923.

Held, R. (ed.). *Arms and Armor Annual.* Northfield, Ill., 1973.

———. *Art, Arms and Armour. An International Anthology.* Vol I. Chiasso (Switzerland), 1979.

Hewitt, J. *Ancient Armour and Weapons in Europe.* Oxford, 1855 (reprint Graz, 1967).

Hoff, A., H. D. Schelepern, and G. Boesen. *Royal Arms at Rosenberg.* Copenhagen, 1956.

Jubinal, A., and G. Sensi. *La Armería Real ou collection des principales pièces de la Galerie d'Armes Anciennes de Madrid.* Paris, n.d.

Kalmár, J. *Régi Magyar Fegyverek.* Budapest, 1971.

Kelly, F. M., and R. Schwabe. A Short History of Costume and Armour. London, 1931.

Kienbusch, C. O. K. von. *The Kretzschmar von Kienbusch Collection of Armor and Arms.* Princeton, N.J., 1963.

Kienbusch, C. O. K. von, and S. V. Grancsay. *The Bashford Dean Collection of Arms and Armor in the Metropolitan Museum of Art.* Portland, Me., 1933.

Laking, G. F. *A Catalogue of The Armour and Arms in the Armoury of The Knights of St. John of Jerusalem.* London, n.d.

———. *The Armoury of Windsor Castle, European Section.* London, 1904.

———. *A Record of European Armour and Arms through Seven Centuries.* London, 1920–22.

Leitner, Q. von. *Die Waffensammlung des Österreichischen Kaiserhauses.* Vienna, 1866.

Lenz, E. *Imperatorskiy Ermitazh, Sobranie oruzhiya.* St. Petersburg, 1908.

Lucia, G. de. *La sala d'armi nel Museo dell'Arsenale di Venezia.* Rome, 1908.

Macoir, G. *Le Musée Royal d'Armes et d'Armures de la Porte de Hal à Bruxelles.* Wetteren (Belgium), 1928.

Malatesta, E. *Armi ed Armaioli d'Italia.* Rome, 1946.

Mann, J. G. *European Arms and Armour. Wallace Collection Catalogues.* London, 1962. Updated in "Amendments and Additions to the Catalogue of Armour in the Wallace Collection, London," by A. V. B. Norman, *Journal of the Arms & Armour Society.* Vol. II, No. 7/8 (Sept.–Dec., 1972).

Margerand, J. *Armement et Equipement de l'Infanterie Française du XVIè au XXè Siècle.* Paris, 1845.

Mariaux, General. *Le Musée de l'Armée: Armes et Armures Anciennes.* Vol. II. Paris, 1927.

Mavrodin, V. *The Hermitage, Leningrad: Fine Arms from Tula.* Leningrad and New York, 1977.

Meyrick, S. R. *A Critical Inquiry into Ancient Armour.* London, 1824.

Møller, Th. *Gamle Danske Militaervaben.* Copenhagen, 1963.

Neumann, G. C. *The History of Weapons of the American Revolution.* New York, 1967.

Nickel, H. *Ullstein Waffenbuch.* Frankfurt and Vienna, 1974.

Niox, General. *Le Musée de l'Armée.* Vol. I, Paris, 1917.

Norman, A. V. B., and D. Pottinger. *A History of War and Weapons, 449 to 1660.* New York, 1966.

Norman, V. *Arms and Armour.* London, 1964.

Payne-Gallwey, R. *The Crossbow: Mediaeval and Modern, Military and Sporting.* London, 1903.

Peterson, H. L. *Arms and Armour in Colonial America, 1526–1783.* Harrisburg, Pa., 1956.

Peterson, H. L., and R. Elman. *Les Armes célèbres.* Paris, 1972.

Post, P. *Das Zeughaus (Berlin).* Berlin, 1929.

Pranzo, F. M. *Armi bresciane della raccolta di Luigi Marzoli.* Palazzolo sull 'Oglio, 1943.

Quick, J. *Dictionary of Weapons and Military Terms.* New York, 1973.

Reid, W. *Arms through the Ages.* New York, 1976.

Reitzenstein, A. F. von. *Der Waffenschmied; vom Handwerk der Schwertschmiede Plattner und Büchsenmacher.* Munich, 1964.

Robert, L. *Catalogue des collections composants le Musée d'Artillerie en 1889.* Paris, 1889–90.

Rossi, F., and N. di Carpegna. *Armi antiche del Museo Civico Luigi Marzoli.* Milan, 1969.

Rybakow, B. A. *Der Moskauer Kremlin: Die Rüstkammer.* Prague, 1962.

Sacken, E. F. von. *Die vorzüglichsten Rüstungen und Waffen der k. k. Ambraser Sammlung Album.* Vienna, 1862.

Schneider, H. *Schweizer Waffenschmiede vom 15. bis 20. Jahrhundert.* Zurich, 1976.

Stocklein, H. *Meister des Eisenschnittes.* Esslingen, 1922.

Stone, G. C. *A Glossary of the Construction, Decoration and Use of Arms in All Countries and in All Times.* Portland, Me., 1934.

Thomas, B. *Die Waffensammlung des Schlossmuseums in Linz.* Linz, 1966.

———. *Gesammelte Schriften zur historischen Waffenkunde.* 2 vols. Graz, 1977.

Thomas, B., and O. Gamber. *Katalog der Liebrüstkammer.* Vienna, 1976.

Thomas, B., O. Gamber, and H. Schedelmann. *Arms and Armour of the Western World.* London, 1964.

Van Duyse, H. *Catalogue des Armes et Armures du Musée de la Porte de Hal.* Brussels, 1897.

Viollet-le-Duc, E. E. *Dictionnaire du mobilier français de l'époque carlovingienne à la Renaissance.* Paris, 1874.

Vita, C. de. *Gli Armaioli Romani.* Rome, 1974.

*Weapons. An International Encyclopedia from 5000 B.C. to 2000 A.D.* New York, 1980.

*Weapons and Warfare. The Illustrated Encyclopedia of the 20th Century.* 24 vols. New York, 1977–78.

Wegeli, R. *Inventar der Waffensammlung des Bernischen Historischen Museum in Bern.* Bern 1929–48.

Weiser, J. *Historische Waffen von der Sowjetunion übergeben.* (Ausstellung, Staatliches Museum, Schwerin, Mai-Juni, 1959.). Schwerin, 1959.

Whitelaw, C. C. *Scottish Arms Makers.* London, 1977.

Zygulski, Z., Jr. *Brón w Dawnej Polsce.* Warsaw, 1975.

# Armor and Edged Weapons


Ariès, C. *Armes Blanches Militaires Françaises.* Paris, 1966 to present.

Aroldi, A. M. *Armi e armature italiane fino al XVIII secolo.* Milan, 1961.

Ashdown, C. H. *British and Foreign Arms and Armour.* London, 1909.

Asselineau, A. *Armes et armures du Moyen Age et de la Renaissance.* Paris, 1864.

Aylward, J. D. *The small-sword in England.* London, 1960.

Beaumont, E. de. *Fleur des belles Epées.* Paris, 1885.

Behmer, E. *Das zweischneidige Schwert der Germanischen Völkerwanderungszeit.* Stockholm, 1939.

Blackmore, H. L. *The Armouries of the Tower of London.* London, 1976.

Blair, C. *European Armour: circa 1066 to circa 1700.* London, 1958.

———. *The Silvered Armour of Henry VIII in the Tower of London.* London, 1965.

———. *Three Presentation Swords in the Victoria and Albert Museum.* London, 1972.

Boccia, L. G., and E. T. Coelho. *Armi bianche italiane.* Milan, 1965.

Bosson, C. *Souvenirs de l'escalade au Musée d'Art et d'Histoire.* Geneva, 1952.

Bottet, M. *L'arme blanche de guerre française au XVIIIè siècle.* Paris, 1910.

———. *Monographie de l'arme blanche des armées françaises de terre et de mer, 1789–1870.* Paris, n.d.

Bruhn Hoffmeyer, A. *Middelalderens tveaeggede svaerd.* Copenhagen, 1954.

Calvert, A. F. *Spanish Arms and Armour.* London, 1907.

Carpegna, N. di. *Antiche armi dal Sec. IX al XVIII.* Rome, 1969.

Cassola, Guida P. *Le armi difensive dei micenei nelle figurazioni.* N.p., 1973.

Castle, E. *Schools and Masters of Fence.* London and New York, 1910; reprint, London, 1969.

Cimarelli, A. G. *Armi bianche.* Milan, 1969.

Claudelin, B. *Catalogue of the Collection of Arms and Armour at Hallwyl House, Stockholm.* Stockholm,1928.

Cosson, C. A. de. *Le Cabinet d'Armes de M. de Talleyrand-Périgord, Duc de Dino.* Paris, 1901.

Curtis, H. M. *2500 Years of European Helmets 800 B.C.–1700 A.D.* North Hollywood, Calif., 1978.

Dean, B. *Catalogue of European daggers.* The Metropolitan Museum of Art, New York, 1929.

Dean, B., and S. V. Grancsay. *Handbook of Arms and Armor.* New York, 1930.

Denkstein, V. "Pavises of the Bohemian Type," *Sborník Národního Muzea v. Praze.* Series A, Vol. XVI; 4–5 (1962), XVIII: 3–4 (1964); XIX: 1–5 (1965).

Dreger, E. H. M. *Waffensammlung Dreger.* Berlin, 1926.

Dufty, A. R. *European Armour in the Tower of London.* London, 1968.

———. *European Swords and Daggers in the Tower of London.* London, 1974.

Ellehauge, M. *The Spear Traced through Its Post-Roman Development.* Copenhagen, 1948.

ffoulkes, C. *European Arms and Armour in the University of Oxford.* Oxford, 1912.

ffoulkes, C., and E. C. Hopkinson. *Sword, Lance and Bayonet—A Record of the Arms of the British Army and Navy.* Cambridge, 1938.

Fillitz, H. *Katalog der Weltlichen und der Geistlichen Schatzkammer.* Vienna, 1961.

Fioroni, M. *Armi bianche del Museo Fioroni.* Legnago, 1965.

Florit y Arizcun, J. M., and F. J. Sanchez Canton. *Catálogo de las Armas del Instituto de Valencia de Don Juan.* Madrid, 1927.

Gamber, O. (ed.). *Glossarium Armorum: Arma Defensiva.* Graz, 1972.

Gilchrist, H. J. *A Catalogue of the Collection of Arms and Armour presented to the Cleveland Museum of Art.* Cleveland, 1924.

Giorgetti, G. *Armi bianche.* Milan, 1961.

Grancsay, S. V. *Sculpture in Arms and Armour. A Picture Book.*
The Metropolitan Museum of Art, New York, 1940.

———. *Loan Exhibition of Mediaeval and Renaissance Arms and Armor from the Metropolitan Museum of Art.* Los Angeles County Museum, Los Angeles, 1953.

———. *Catalogue of Armor. The John Woodman Higgins Armory.* Worcester, Mass. 1961.

Hayward, J. F. *Swords and Daggers.* Victoria and Albert Museum, London, 1951–1963.

Hencken, H. *The Earlier European Helmets.* Cambridge, Mass, 1971.

Hutton, A. *The Sword and the Centuries.* London, 1901.

Kelly, F. M., and R. Schwabe. *A Short History of Costume and Armour: chiefly in England: 1066–1800.* London, 1931.

Lacombe, P. *Les armes et les armures.* Paris, 1870.

Letošnikova, L. *The Armoury at Konopište Castle.* Prague, 1970.

Lorange, A. L. *Den Yngre Jernalders Svaerd . . .* Bergen, 1889.

Martin, P. *Armes et Armures de Charlemagne à Louis XVI.* Fribourg, 1967.

Martinez del Peral Forton, R. *Las Navajas.* N.p., 1974.

Marzetti, P. *Elmetti 1915–73.* Parma, 1973.

Meyrick, S. R. *A Critical Inquiry into Ancient Armour*. London, 1824.
Mallo, E. *Russian Military Swords, 1801–1917*. London, 1967.
Nickel, H. *Arms and Armour through the Ages*. London, 1969.
Norman, A. V. B. *Arms and Armour*. London, 1964.
———. *The Rapier and Small-sword 1460–1820*. London, Melbourne, and New York, 1980.
Oakeshott, R. E. *The Archaeology of Weapons*. London, 1960.
———. *The Sword in the Age of Chivalry*. London, 1964.
———. *European Weapons and Armour*. Guildford and London, 1980.
Panseri, C. *Ricerche metallografiche sopra una spada da guerra del XII secolo*. Milan, 1954.
Peterson, H. L. *Arms and Armor of the Pilgrims 1620–1692*. Plymouth, Mass., 1957.
———. *The American Sword 1775–1945*. Philadelphia, 1965.
———. *Daggers and Fighting Knives of the Western World from the Stone Age until 1900*. London, 1968.
Rathgen, B. *Das Geschütz im Mittelalter*. Berlin, 1928.
Rebuffo, L. *Armature italiane*. Turin, 1959.
Reitzenstein, A. von. *Der Waffenschmied; vom Handwerk der Schwertschmiede Plattner und Büchsenmacher*. Munich, 1964.
Robinson, H. R. *The Armour of Imperial Rome*. London, 1975.
Robson, B. *Swords of the British Army*. London, 1975.
Rossi, F. *Armature da parata*. N.p., 1972.
Rossi, Fil. *Mostra delle Armi antiche in Palazzo Vecchio*. Florence, 1938.
Sacken, E. F. von. *Die vorzüglichsten Rüstungen und Waffen der kk. Ambraser Sammlung*. Vienna, 1862.
Schneider, H. *Der Schweizerdolch*. Zurich, 1928.
———. *Schwerter und Degen*. Berne, 1957.
Schöbel, J. *Fine Arms and Armour, Treasures in the Dresden Collection*. New York, 1975.
Seifert, G. *Schwert, Degen, Säbel*. Hamburg, 1962.
Seitz, H. *Blankwaffen*. Brunswick (Germany), 1965.
Sercer, M. *Staro Oružie na Motki*. Zagreb, 1972.
Skelton, J. *Engraved Illustrations of Ancient Arms and Armour from the collection of Llewelyn Meyrick*. London, 1854 (Oxford, 1830).
Snodgrass, A. M. *Arms and Armour of the Greeks*. London, 1967
Tarassuk, L. "Some Notes on Parrying Daggers and Poniards." *Metropolitan Museum Journal*, Vol. 12, 1978.
Terenzi, M. *Considerazioni su di un tipo di pugnale detto stiletto da bombardiere*. Rome, 1962.
———. *Elmi del Trecento alla mostra di Poppi*. Rome, 1967.
Thimm, C. A. *A Complete Bibliography of Fencing and Duelling*. London and New York, 1896.
Thordeman, B. *Armour from the Battle of Wisby, 1361*. Stockholm, 1939.
Uhlemann, H. R. *Kostbare Blankwaffen aus dem Deutschen Klingenmuseum Solingen*. Düsseldorf, 1968.
Wagner, E. *Cut and Thrust Weapons*. London, 1967.
Wilkinson-Latham, R. J. *Pictorial History of Swords and Bayonnets, including Dirks and Daggers*. London, 1973.
Wise, A. *The History and Art of Personal Combat*. London, 1971.
Wise, T. *European Edged Weapons*. London, 1974.
Yadin, Y. *The Art of Warfare in Biblical Lands*. New York, Toronto, and London, 1963.
Zshille, R., and R. Forrer. *Die Pferdetrense in ihrer Formen-Entwicklung*. Berlin, 1893.
———. *Der Sporn in seiner Formen-Entwicklung*. Berlin, 1891–99.
———. *Die Steigbügel in ihrer Formen-Entwicklung*. Berlin, 1896.

# Firearms and Artillery


Alaba y Viamont, Don Diego de. *El Perfecto capitan.* Madrid, 1590.

Alberghetti, S. *Nova artilleria veneta.* Venice, 1703.

Allen, W. G. B. *Pistols, Rifles and Machine Guns.* London, 1964.

Alm, J. *Eldhandvapen.* Stockholm, 1933–34.

Angelucci, A. *Documenti inediti per la storia delle armi da fuoco italiane.* Turin, 1869–70; reprint, Graz, 1972.

Atkinson, J. A. *Duelling Pistols.* London, 1964.

Avalon, D. *Gunpowder and Firearms in the Mamluk Kingdom.* London, 1956.

Bailey, D. W. *British Military Longarms 1715–1815.* London, 1971.

Baker, E. *Remarks on Rifle Guns.* London, 1835.

Barnes, D. *The History of Winchester Firearms 1866–1980.* Tulsa, Okla., 1980.

Batchelor, J., and I. Hogg. *Rail Gun.* Poole (Dorset), 1973.

Baxter, D. R. *Superimposed Load Firearms 1360–1860.* Hong Kong, 1966.

Belford, J. N., and J. Dunlap. *The Mauser Self-loading Pistol.* Alhambra, 1969.

Belgrano, C. *Gli esplosivi.* Udine, 1974.

Belidor, B. F. de. *Le bombardier François.* Amsterdam, 1731.

Benassi, G. *Calibri, cariche e portate dei fucili da caccia.* Florence, 1961.

Bidwell, S. (ed.). *Brassey's Artillery of the World.* New York, 1979.

Biringuccio, V. *De la pirotechnia libri X.* Venice, 1540 (and later editions).

Blackmore, H. L. *British Military Firearms, 1650–1850.* London, 1961.

———. *Guns and Rifles of the World.* London, 1965.

———. *Royal Sporting Guns at Windsor.* London, 1968.

Blair, C. *Pistols of the World.* London, 1968.

Blanch, H. J. *A Century of Guns.* London, 1909.

Bonaparte, N. L., and I. Favè. *Etudes sur le passé et l'avenir de l'artillerie.* Paris, 1846–73.

Bonfadini, V. *La caccia dell'archibugio.* Bologna, 1672.

Bordino, S. M. *Struttura e governo del fucile di fanteria e del moschetto e pistola di cavalleria.* Turin, 1820.

Bossi, G. *Breve discorso delli Doppi Archibugi a Ruota.* Paris, 1629.

Bottet, M. *Monographie de l'Arme à feu portative des Armées françaises de terre et de mer de 1718 à nos jours.* Paris, n.d.

Boudriot, J. *Armes à feu françaises modèles reglementaires.* Paris, 1961–63.

Bravetta, E. *L'artiglieria e le sue meraviglie.* Milan, 1919.

Brownell, B. *Encyclopedia of Modern Firearms.* Montezuma, Iowa, 1977.

Brunet, J. B. *Histoire generale d'artillerie.* Paris, 1842.

Capobianco, A. *Corona e palma militare di arteglieria.* Venice, 1598.

Carey, A. M. *English, Irish, and Scottish Firearms Makers.* London and Edinburgh, 1954.

Cadiou, Y., and A. Richard. *Les armes à feu moderne.* Paris, 1975.

Carpegna, N. di. *Firearms in the Princes Odescalchi Collection in Rome.* Rome, 1975.

Chapel, C. E. *The Gun Collector's Handbook of Values.* 13th ed. New York, 1980.

Chastinet de Puysegur, J. F. de. *Art de la guerre.* Paris, 1749.

Chinn, G. M. *The Machine Gun.* Washington, D.C., 1951–54.

Cimarelli, A. *Quattro secoli di armi da fuoco.* Novara, 1972.

———. *Storia delle Armi delle due guerre mondiali.* Novara, n.d.

Cipolla, C. M. *Guns and Sails in the Early Phase of European Expansion 1400–1700.* London, 1965.

Colliado, L. *Platica Manual de Artilleria.* Milan, 1592.

Cominazzi, M. *Cenni sulla Fabbrica d'armi di Gardone Valtrompia.* Brescia, 1843.

Cottaz, M. *L'arme à feu portative française.* Paris, 1971.

Courally, F. *Les armes de chasse et leur tir.* Nancy, 1931.

Datig, F. *The Luger Pistol.* Alhambra, Calif., 1966.

Davis, T. L. *The Chemistry of Powder & Explosives.* New York and London, 1953.

*Deane's Manual of the History and Science of Fire-arms.* London, 1858.

Della Croce, F. *Teatro Militare.* Antwerp, 1617.

———. *L'essercitio della Cavalleria e d'altre materie.* Antwerp, 1617.

Dillin, J. G. W. *The Kentucky Rifle.* New York, 1959.

Dixon, N. *Georgian Pistols: The Art and Craft of the Flintlock Pistols 1715–1840.* London, 1971.

Dowell, W. C. *The Webley Story.* Leeds, 1962.

Drummond, J. (notes by J. Anderson). *Ancient Scottish Weapons.* Edinburgh, 1881.

Duchartre, P. L. *Histoire des Armes de Chasse.* Paris, 1955.

Dunlap, J. *American, British and Continental Pepperbox Firearms.* Palo Alto, Calif., 1967.

Eckardt, W., and O. Morawietz. *Die Handwaffen des Brandenburgisch-preussisch-deutschen Heeres 1640–1945.* Hamburg, 1957.

Edwards, W. B. *The Story of Colt's Revolver.* Harrisburg, Pa., 1953.

———. *Civil War Guns*. Harisburg, Pa., 1962.
Egg, E., et al. *Guns: An Illustrated History of Artillery*. Lausanne, 1971.
Ellis, J. *The Social History of the Machine Gun*. New York, 1975.
Essenwein, A. *Quellen zur Geschichte der Feuerwaffen*. Leipzig, 1872–77.
ffoulkes, C. *The Gun-Founders of England*. Cambridge, 1937.
Filippi, G. *Armi da fuoco*. Florence, 1975.
Fremantle, T. F. *The Book of the Rifle*. London, 1901.
Frost, H. G. *Blades and Barrels, Six Centuries of Combination Weapons*. El Paso, Tex., 1972.
Fuller, C. E. *Springfield Muzzleloading Shoulder Arms*. New York, 1930.
———. *The Whitney Firearms*. Huntington, W. Va., 1946.
———. *The Breech-loader in the Service 1816–1917*. New Milford, Conn., 1965.
Gaibi, A. *Le armi da fuoco portatili italiane: dalle origini al Risorgimento*. 2nd ed. Milan, 1963–68.
Gaier, C. *Four Centuries of Liège Gunmaking*. London, 1976.
Gelli, J. *Gli archibugiari milanesi. Industria, commerico, uso delle armi da fuoco in Lombardia*. Milan, 1905.
George, J. N., *English Pistols and Revolvers*. Onslow County, N.C., 1938.
———. *English Guns and Rifles*. Plantersville, S. C., 1947.
Giraud, A. *Dati sulle artiglierie della Regia Marina*. Genoa, 1901.
Gluckman, A. *United States Martial Pistols and Revolvers*. Buffalo, 1939.
———. *United States Muskets, Rifles and Carbines*. Buffalo, 1948.
Gooding, S. J. *The Canadian Gunsmiths 1608 to 1900*. Ontario, 1962.
Götz, H. D. *Die deutschen Militärgewehre und Maschinenpistolen 1871–1945*. Stuttgart, 1974.
Grancsay, S. V. *American Engraved Powder Horns*. New York, 1945.
———. *Master French Gunsmiths' Designs of the XVII–XIX Centuries*. New York, 1970.
Grandi, F. *Le armi e le artiglierie in servizio*. Turin, 1938.
Grant, J. J. *Single-shot Rifles*. New York, 1947.
———. *More Single-shot Rifles*. New York, 1959.
Greener, W. W. *The Science of Gunnery*. London, 1841.
———. *The Gun and Its Development*. London, 1910.
Gusler, W. B., and J. D. Lavin. *Decorated Firearms 1540–1870 from the Collection of Clay P. Bedford*. Williamsburg, Va., 1977.
Haas, F. de. *Bolt Action Rifles*. Northfield, Mass., 1971.
Hall, A. R. *Ballistics in the Seventeenth Century*. New York, 1969.
Hanson, C. E. *The Northwest Gun*. Lincoln, Neb., 1955.
Hatch, A. *Remington Arms in American History*. New York and Toronto, 1956.
Hatcher, J. *The Book of the Garand*. Highland Park, 1977.
Hayward, J. F. *European Firearms, Victoria and Albert Museum*. London, 1955–69.
———. *The Art of the Gunmaker*. London, 1962–63.
Heer, E. *Der Neue Støckel, Internationales Lexikon der Büchsenmacher, Feuerwaffenfabrikanten und Armbrustmacher*. 2 vols. Schwäbisch-Hall, 1978–79.
Hicks, J. E. *Ordnance Correspondence*. Mount Vernon, N.Y., 1940.
———. *U.S. Firearms 1776–1956*. Beverly Hills, Calif., 1957.
———. *U.S. Military Firearms*. La Canada–Flintridge, Calif., 1962.
———. *French Military Weapons: 1717 to 1938*. New Milford, Conn., 1964.
Hobart, F. W. A. *Pictorial History of the Machine Gun*. London, 1973.
———. *Jane's Infantry Weapons*. London, 1975.
Hoff, A. *Aeldre Dansk Bøssemageri Isaer I 1600-tallet*. Copenhagen, 1951.
———. *Feuerwaffen*. Brunswick (Germany), 1969.
———. *Airguns and Other Pneumatic Arms*. London, 1972.
———. *Dutch Firearms*. London, 1978.
Hogg, I. *The Guns: 1939–45*. New York, 1970.
———. *A History of Artillery*. London, 1974.
———. *The Complete Illustrated Encyclopedia of the World's Firearms*. New York, 1978.
———. *Deutsche Artilleriewaffen in Zweiten Weltkrieg*. Stuttgart, 1978.
Hogg, I., and L. F. Thurston. *British Artillery Weapons and Ammunition*. N.p., 1972.
Hogg, I. V., and J. Weeks. *Pistols of the World*. London, 1978.
Honeycutt, F. L., and Anthony (F. Patt). *Military Rifles of Japan*. Lake Park, Fla., 1977.
Hughes, B. P. *Firepower, Weapons Effectiveness on the Battlefield, 1630–1850*. London, 1974.
Jackson, H. J. (includes treatise by H. Whitelaw). *European Hand Firearms of the 16th, 17th, and 18th Centuries*. London, 1923.
Jinks, R. G. *History of Smith and Wesson*. North Hollywood, Calif., 1977.
Jones, H. E. *Luger Variations*. Los Angeles, 1967.
Kauffmann, H. J. *Early American Gunsmiths 1650–1850*. Harrisburg, Pa., 1952.
———. *The Pennsylvania-Kentucky Rifle*. Harrisburg, Pa., 1960.
Kenyon, C. *Lugers at Random*. Chicago, 1969.
Kindig, J., Jr. *Thoughts on the Kentucky Rifle in its Golden Age*. Wilmington, Del., 1960.
Kist, J. B., et al. *Dutch Muskets and Pistols*. London and York, Pa., 1974.
Korn, R. H. *Mauser-Gewehre und Mauser-Patente*. Berlin, 1908.
Lavin, J. D. *A History of Spanish Firearms*. London, 1965.
Le Blond, G. *A Treatise of Artillery*. London, 1746.
Lenk, T. *Flintlåset dess uppkomst och utveckling*. Stockholm, 1939.
Lewis, B. R. *Small Arms and Ammunition in the United States Service*. Washington, D.C., 1956.

Lindsay, M. K. *One Hundred Great Guns*. New York, 1967.
———. *The New England Gun: The First Two Hundred Years*. New Haven and New York, 1975.
Logan, H. C. *Underhammer Guns*. Harrisburg, Pa., 1960.
Lugs, J. *Handfeuerwaffen*. 4th ed. Berlin, 1973.
Lupi, G. *Grandi fucili da caccia*. Florence, 1972.
Madis, G. *The Winchester Book*. Dallas, 1961.
Mallet, A. M. *Les Travaux de Mars ou L'Art de la Guerre*. Paris, 1684.
Manganoni, C. *Caratteristiche di alcune armi da fuoco portatili*. Turin, 1930.
Marcianò, E., and M. Morin. *Dal Carcano al Fal*. Florence, 1974.
Marsden, E. W. *Greek and Roman Artillery: Technical Treatises*. Oxford, n.d.
Mathews, J. H. *Firearms Identification*. Springfield, Mass., 1973.
Mavrodin, V. *The Hermitage, Leningrad: Fine Arms from Tula*. Leningrad and New York, 1977.
Mazza, A. *Armi Esplosivi, Artiglierie*. Turin, 1929.
McLean, D. B. *Illustrated Arsenal of the Third Reich*. Wickenburg, Ariz., 1973.
Meyerson, A. *Stockholms Bössmakare*. Stockholm, 1936.
Miller, M. *The Collector's Illustrated Guide to Firearms*. London, 1978.
Montù, C. *Storia dell'artiglieria italiana*. Rome, 1935–53.
Moretti, T. *Trattato dell'Artiglieria*. Brescia, 1572 (Venice 1665).
Morin, M., and R. Held. *Beretta. The World's Oldest Industrial Dynasty*. Chiasso, 1980.
Müller, H. *Deutsche Bronzegeschützrohre, 1400–1750*. Berlin, 1968.
———. *Guns, Pistols, Revolvers*. New York, 1980.
Muller, J. *A Treatise of Artillery*. London, 1780.
Musgrave, D., and T. Nelson. *The World's Assault Rifles*. Washington, D.C., 1967.
Musgrave, O., and T. Smith. *German Machineguns*. Washington, D.C., 1971.
Myatt, F. *The Illustrated Encyclopedia of 19th Century Firearms*. London, 1979.
Neal, W. K. *Spanish Guns and Pistols*. London, 1955.
Negri, F. *Il fucile da caccia. Armi, munizioni, tiro*. Florence, 1961.
Nelson, T. B. *The World's Submachine Guns*. Edmond, Okla., 1978.
Noghera, A. *Armi da caccia, polveri, cartucce*. Milan, 1963.
Nonte, G. C. J. *Firearms Encyclopedia*. London, 1973.
Norton, R. *The Gunner, Shewing the Whole Practise of Artillerie*. London, 1628.
Nutter, W. E. *Manhattan Firearms*. Paris, 1958.
Olson, J. *The Famous Automatic Pistols of Europe*. Paramus, N.J., 1976.
———. *Mauser Bolt Rifles*. Montezuma, Iowa, 1976.
Otteson, S. *The Bolt Action*. New York, 1976.
Owen, J. I. H. (ed.). *Brassey's Infantry Weapons of the World 1950–1975*. New York, 1975.
Padfield, P. *Guns at Sea*. London, 1973.
Parson, J. E. *The First Winchester*. New York, 1952.
———. *Henry Deringer's Pocket Pistol*. New York, 1952.
———. *Smith and Wesson Revolvers*. New York, 1957.
Partington, J. R. *A History of Greek Fire and Gunpowder*. Cambridge,1960.
Pender, R. G. *Mauser Pocket Pistols 1910–1946*. Houston, 1971.
Perosino, S. *Armi da caccia*. Novara, 1967.
Peterson, H. L. *The Treasury of the Gun*. New York,1962.
———. *Encyclopedia of Firearms*. London and New York, 1964.
Peterson, H.L., and R. Elman. *The Great Guns*. New York, 1971.
Piobert, G. *Traité d'Artillerie*. Brussels, 1838.
Pollard, H. B. C. *A History of Firearms*. London, 1930.
Quarenghi, C. *Tecno-cronografia delle armi da fuoco italiane*. Naples, 1887.
Rathgen, B. *Das Aufkommen der Pulverwaffe*. Munich, 1925.
———. *Das Geschütz in Mittelalter*. Berlin, 1928.
Rensselaer, S. von. *American Firearms*. Watkins Glen, N.Y., 1947.
Reynolds, E. G. B. *The Lee-Enfield Rifle*. London, 1960.
Riling, R. *Guns and Shooting: A Selected Chronological Bibliography*. New York, 1951.
———. *The Powder Flask Book*. New Hope, Pa., 1953.
Ripley, W. *Artillery and Ammunition of the Civil War*. New York, 1970.
Roads, C. H. *The British Soldier's Firearms 1850–1864*. London, 1944.
*Robert Catalogue des Musées d'Artillerie*. Paris, 1889.
Rosa, J. G. *Colonel Colt, London*. London, 1976.
Rusticucci, L. *I fucili da guerra di tutti gli eserciti del mondo*. Campobasso, 1917.
Sawyer, C. W. *Firearms in American History*. Boston, 1910–20.
Schedelmann, H. *Die Wiener Büchsenmacher und Büchsenschäfter*. Berlin, 1944.
———. *Die grossen Büchsenmacher*. Munich, 1972.
Schmidt, R. *Die Handfeuerwaffen, ihre Entstehung und technisch-historische Entwicklung bis zur Gegenwart*. Basel, 1882.
Schmidtchen, V. *Bombarden, Befestigungen, Büchsenmeister*. Düsseldorf, 1978.
Schneider, H., et al. *Handfeuerwaffen System Vetterli*. Zurich, 1970.
Serven, J. E. *Colt Firearms 1836–1958*. Santa Ana, Calif., 1959.
Shumway, G. *Rifles of Colonial America*. York, Pa, 1980.
Smith, W. H. B. *Mannlicher Rifles and Pistols*. Harrisburg, Pa., 1947.
———. *Mauser Rifles and Pistols*. Harrisburg, Pa., 1950.
———. *Book of Rifles*. Harrisburg, Pa., 1960.
———. *Gas, Air and Spring Guns of the World*. Harrisburg, Pa., 1967.
———. *Book of Pistols and Revolvers*. Secaucus, N.J., 1979.
Smith, W. H. B., and E. Joseph. *Small Arms of the World*. London, 1973.

Smith, W. O. *The Sharps Rifle*. New York, 1943.
Stebbins, H. M. *Pistols, a Modern Encyclopedia*. Harrisburg, Pa., 1961.
Støckel, J. F. *Haandskydevaabens Bedommelse*. Copenhagen, 1938–43.
Stonehenge (J. H. Walsh). *The Shot-gun and Sporting Rifle*. London, 1859.
Surirey de Saint Rémy. *Memoires d'Artillerie*. Paris, 1745.
Tarassuk, L. *Russian Pistols in the Seventeenth Century*. London, 1968.
———. *Antique European and American Firearms at the Hermitage Museum*. Leningrad, 1972–73.
Tartaglia, N. *Quesiti et inventioni diverse*. Venice, 1551.
Taylerson, A. W. F. *Revolving Arms*. London, 1967.
Terenzi, M. *Catalogo della mostra delle armi da fuoco anghiaresi e dell'Appennino tosco-emiliano*. Sansepolcro, 1968.
———. *Gli Armaioli Anghiaresi nei Secoli XVII e XIX*. Rome, 1974.
———. *Michele Battista e il suo tempo*. Rome, 1978.
Thierbach, M. *Die geschichtliche Entwicklung der Handfeuerwaffen*. Dresden, 1886–87.
Thybourel, F., and J. Appier. *Recueil de plusieurs machines militaires et feux artificiels pour la guerrre de recréation*. Pont-à-Mosson, 1620.
Tout, T. F. *Firearms in England in the Fourteenth Century*. London, 1968.
Ufano, D. *Tratado de artilleria*. Frankfurt a/M, 1614.
Ugolini, L. *Il libro del cacciatore*. Florence, 1935.
Valturio, R. *De Re Militari*. Verona, 1472.
Venturi, G. B. *Dell'origine e dei primi progressi delle odierne artiglierie*. Reggio, 1815.
Venturoli, V. *Le armi da fuoco*. Florence, 1970.
Viterbo, S. *Fundidores de Artilharia*. Lisbon, 1901.
Wahl, P. *Carbine Handbook*. New York, 1969.
Wahl, P., and D. Toppel. *The Gatling Gun*. New York, 1965.
Walsh, J. H. *The Modern Sportsman's Gun and Rifle*. London, 1882–84.
Walter, J. *Luger*. London, 1977.
Wesley, L. *Air-guns and Air-pistols*. London, 1955.
Wilkinson, F. *Flintlock Guns and Rifles*. London, 1971.
———. *The World's Great Guns*. London, 1977.
Williamson, H. F. *Pepperbox Firearms*. New York, 1952.
———. *Winchester—The Gun That Won the West*. New York, 1952.
Wilson, R. K. *Textbook of Automatic Pistols*. London, 1975.
Wilson, R. L. *The Book of Colt Engraving*. Los Angeles, 1974.
———. *The Colt Heritage. The Official History of Colt Firearms from 1836 to the Present*. New York, 1979, London & Sidney, 1980.
Wilson, R. L., and R. Q. Sutherland. *The Book of Colt Firearms*. Kansas City, Mo., 1970.
Winant, L. *Pepperbox Firearms*. New York, 1952.
———. *Firearms Curiosa*. New York, 1955.
———. *Early Percussion Firearms*. New York, 1959.
———. *Small Arms of the World*. Harrisburg, Pa., 1978.
Zitz, D. *The Double Shotgun*. Tulsa, Okla., 1978.

# Oriental Weapons


Anderson, L. J. *Japanese Armour*. London, 1968.

Arai, Hakuseki. *The Armour Book in Honcho-Gunkiko*. London, 1964.

Boots, J. L. *Korean Weapons and Armour*. Seoul, 1934.

Buttin, C. *Les anneaux-disque préhistoriques et les tchakras de l'Inde*. N.p., 1903.

Clarke, C. P. *Arms and Armour at Sandringham*. London, 1910.

Crewdson, W. *Japanese Leather*. London, 1916.

Curey, M. C. *L'artillerie japonaise*. Paris, 1906.

Egerton (Wilbraham, Lord Egerton of Tatton). *A Description of Indian and Oriental Armour*. London, 1896, 1968.

Elgood, R. (ed.). *Islamic Arms and Armour*. London, 1979.

Fischer, W., and N. A. Zirngibl. *African Weapons*. Passau, 1978.

Garbutt, M. *Japanese Armour from the Inside*. London, 1913.

Gilbertson, E. *Geneology of the Miochin Family*. London, 1893.

Hendley, T. H. *Damascening on Steel or Iron, as Practised in India*. London, 1892.

Homma (Hiakuri). *Shoko-Gaishoku-Ichiran*. Tokyo, 1900.

Kawasaki, Chitora. *Military Costume of Old Japan*. Tokyo, 1893.

Kidder, J. E. *Japan*. London, 1959.

Kurihara, Nobuatsu. *Buke-Sode-Kagami*. Edo (Tokyo), 1843.

Laking, G. F. *The Wallace Collection. Catalogue of Oriental Arms and Armour*. London, 1914, 1964.

Leithe, F. E. *Japanese Hand Guns*. Alhambra, Calif., 1968.

Matsuoka, Asako. *The Sacred Treasures of Nara*. Tokyo, 1935.

Mayer, L. A. *Islamic Armourers and Their Works*. Geneva, 1962.

Moser-Charlottenfels, General H. *Collection H. Moser-Charlottenfels, Oriental Arms and Armour*. Leipzig, 1912.

Nickel, H. *Arms and Armor in Africa*. New York, 1971.

Ountai, Sadamasa. *Yoroi-Chakuyo no Shidae*. Edo (Tokyo), 1801.

Pant, G. N. *Studies in Indian Weapons and Warfare*. New Delhi, 1970.

Rawson, P. S. *The Indian Sword*. London, 1968.

Robinson, B. W. *Arms and Armour of Old Japan*. London, 1951.

———. *The Arts of the Japanese Sword*. London, 1961, 1971.

Robinson, H. R.. *A Short History of Japanese Armour*. London, 1965.

———. *Oriental Armour*. London, 1967.

———. *Japanese Arms and Armour*. London, 1969.

———. *Il museo Stibbert a Firenze*. Milan, n.d.

Sakakibara (Kozan). *The Manufacture of Armour and Helmets in 16th Century Japan*. London, 1963.

Sasama, Yoshihiko. *Nippon Katchu Zukan* (Catalogue of Japanese Armors and Helmets). Tokyo, 1964.

Stöcklein, H. *Orientalische Waffen aus der Residenz-Büchsenkammer in Etnographischen Museum München*. Munich, 1914–15.

Suenaga, Masao. *Nippon Jodai no Katchu*. Tokyo, 1934.

Vianello, G. *Armi e armature orientali*. Milan, 1966.

———. *Armi in oriente*. Milan, 1966.

Werner, E. T. C. *Chinese Weapons*. Shanghai, 1932.

Yamagami, Hachiro. *Japan's Ancient Armour*. Tokyo, 1910.

Yumoto, J. M. *The Samurai Sword*. Tokyo, 1958.

Zeller, R. and E. F. Rohrer. *Orientalische Sammlung Henri Moser-Charlottenfels*. Bern, 1955.